W9-ANJ-400

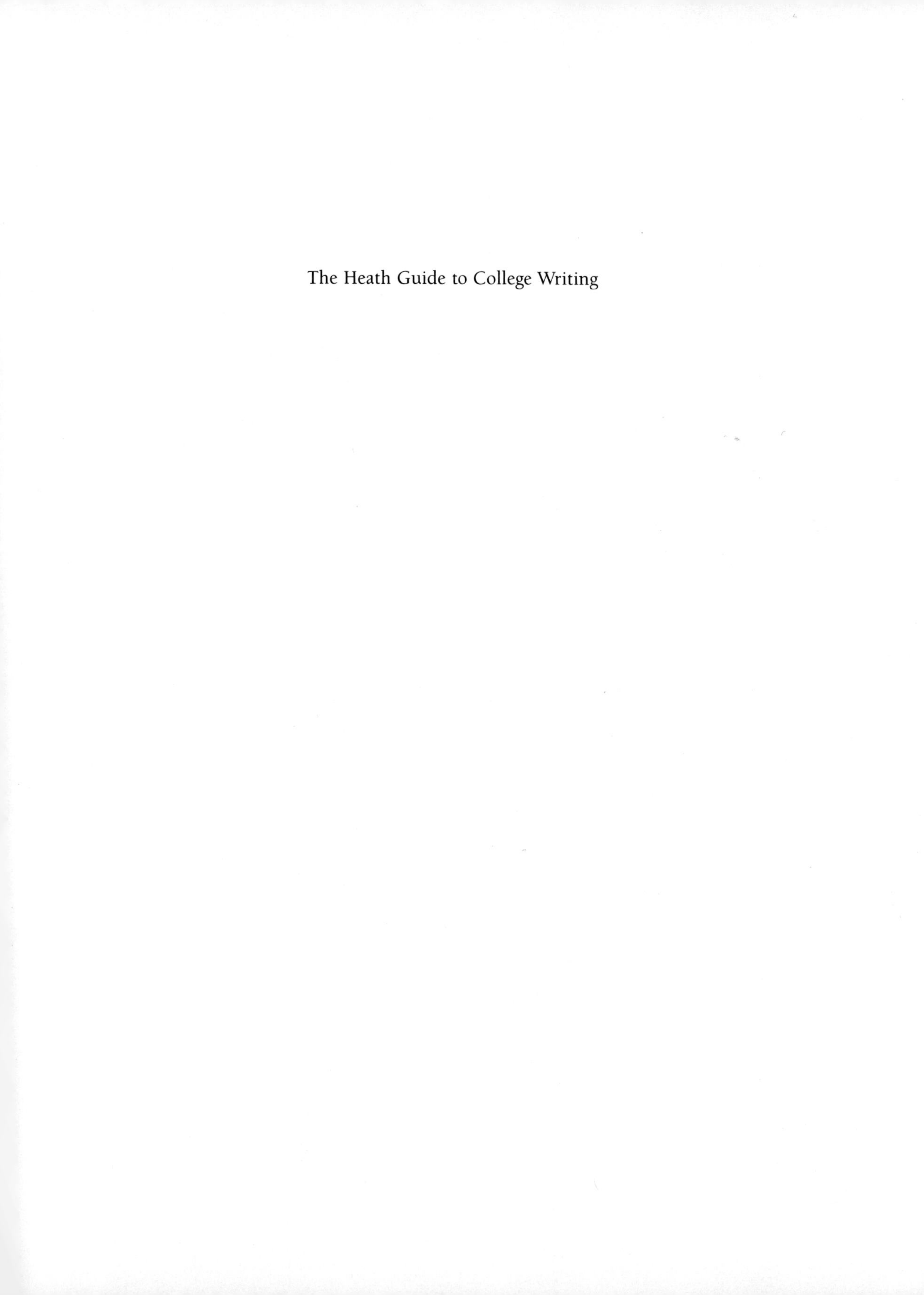

The Heath Guide to College Writing

The Heath Guide to College Writing

Annotated Teacher's Edition

Ralph F. Voss
University of Alabama

Michael L. Keene
University of Tennessee–Knoxville

D. C. Heath and Company
Lexington, Massachusetts Toronto

For our families,
and for Maxine Hairston

Address editorial correspondence to:

D. C. Heath
125 Spring Street
Lexington, MA 02173

For permission to use copyrighted material, grateful acknowledgment is made to the copyright holders listed on pages i–v, which are hereby considered an extension of this copyright page.

Published simultaneously in Canada.

Printed in the United States of America.

International Standard Book Number: 0-669-16785-1 (Instructor's Edition)
0-669-16779-7 (Student Edition)
0-669-16780-0 (Brief Edition)

Library of Congress Catalog Number: 91–71284

10 9 8 7 6 5 4 3 2 1

about the authors

Both of the authors are graduates of the University of Texas–Austin's rhetoric program. Together, they bring nearly fifty years of experience as both rhetoric teachers and textbook writers to *The Heath Guide to College Writing*.

Ralph F. Voss is Professor at the University of Alabama, where he teaches graduate courses in rhetoric/composition and American drama, and undergraduate writing. He is also Coordinator for Courses in Technical Writing, Advanced Composition, and second-semester Freshman English. Previously he has also served as Director of Freshman English, Graduate Teacher Trainer for Composition, Director of the Writing Center (at both the Universities of Alabama and Utah), and Mentor for First-Time Teachers of American Literature. He is the author of *Elements of Practical Writing* (Holt, 1985) and articles and reviews on composition theory and pedagogy in *College Composition and Communication, Teaching English in the Two-Year College, Journal of Advanced Composition*, and *The Writing Teacher.* He has also written *A Life of William Inge: The Strains of Triumph* (University Press of Kansas, 1989), biographical and critical articles in *The Dictionary of Literary Biography* and *Kansas Quarterly,* and reviews of scholarly works in American drama in *South Atlantic Review.*

Michael L. Keene is Associate Professor at the University of Tennessee–Knoxville (UTK), where he created and directs the program in technical communication and teaches in the graduate program in Rhetoric and Composition. He was also director of technical writing at the Tennessee Governor's School for the Sciences, a summer program for gifted and talented high school seniors, 1985–1989. Previously he taught Freshman English, Argumentation, and Technical Writing at Texas A&M University, where he helped create the Undergraduate Writing Specialization. He is the author of *Effective Professional Writing* (D. C. Heath, 1987) and the revised Eighth Edition of W. Paul Jones's *Writing Scientific Papers and Reports* (Wm. C. Brown, 1980). He has also published numerous articles on composition and technical communication in *Technical Communication, Journal of Advanced Composition, College English, CEA Critic, Teaching English in the Two-Year College,* and *ATAC Newsletter,* as well as chapters in collections published by Boynton/Cook, Heinemann; ATTW; MLA; NCTE; and Greenwood Press.

preface

The Heath Guide to College Writing brings together the best of the two most popular approaches to teaching writing, namely

- **The Product-Oriented Approach**, which focuses on teaching qualities of the written product, an approach that has long characterized teaching writing in North America; and
- **The Process-Oriented Approach**, which focuses on teaching the often-recursive steps the writer follows to complete the written product, an approach that has been gaining acceptance since the early 1970s. Bringing together the best of these two approaches, we aim to build bridges between *reading* (guiding students through reader response, close analysis, and critical thinking) and *writing* (giving students practice in observing the techniques of real writers at work—writing multiple drafts, collaborating, and revising critically).

The Heath Guide to College Writing is a full rhetoric intended for use in first- and second-semester composition courses at two- and four-year colleges and universities. It emphasizes processes of composing, the traditional rhetorical triangle (writer's voice, subject, and reading audience, all attuned to purpose), development of critical skills (writing, reading, thinking), and use of the modes (comparison, definition, description, etc.) for invention. *The Heath Guide* includes numerous sample readings, plus an extensive chapter on library research and a concise handbook for grammar (this last in the hardbound edition only). Because *The Heath Guide* incorporates writing-across-the-curriculum, chapters on writing essay test responses, reports, proposals, and preparing oral reports, and elements of business and technical communication, students using this book will develop not only as general writers but also as writers who can successfully meet the writing demands of other academic and career choices.

The distinctive structure of *The Heath Guide to College Writing* unites process and product approaches to writing and shows that reading and writing are two sides of the practice of critical thinking. Each of the eighteen chapters in Parts Two, Three, and Four begins with professional and student writing samples which students will analyze for key features, guided by questions that follow each sample. Once these key features are established, there follows a brief discussion of the writing purpose or technique the sample illustrates. Each chapter then leads students from responding to the reading samples, through writing and analyzing their own written responses, to producing more polished writing after reading a fully developed case study. Each case study follows a student through a typical assignment dealing with the kind of writing on which the chapter focuses,

Robert Scholes has observed that, "The writer is always reading and the reader is always writing" (*Textual Power,* p. 20). We agree. In the most basic way, neither writing nor reading would exist without the other. Also in the most basic way, the ability to do both proficiently has long been the hallmark of a well-educated person. Here's Scholes at greater length: "Reading and writing are complementary acts that remain unfinished until completed by their reciprocals. The last thing I do when I write a text is to read it, and the act that completes my response to a text I am reading is my written response to it. Moreover, my writing is unfinished until it is read by others as well, whose responses may become known to me, engendering new textualities" (*Textual Power,* pp. 20–21).

Although we believe the traditional "modes" have value as recognizable structures for patterning thought or developing lines of writing, we do not endorse them as models for whole written discourse. We do not, in other words, believe or tell students that, for example, comparison/contrast or definition is a self-sufficient pattern that can be followed to organize an entire essay.

Chapters on such special applications (¶ 2) are in Part Five. We recommend that you give them a cursory examination right away so that you can advise students about the help available there if they have such writing projects in other classes. After skimming those chapters, you may want to begin incorporating elements from them into this course right away.

When we refer to "kinds" of writing, we mean writing to express, writing to explain or inform, writing to analyze, and writing to persuade. That is, we refer to writing as characterized by the writer's primary purpose in writing, and not by other common features, such as letters, reports, synopses, or articles.

The occasional feature of alternative ways of reading a selection is our adaptation of Peter Elbow's "Doubting" and "Believing" games (see Elbow). Many of our selections involve viewpoints, attitudes, and interpretations that are at best debatable, and the truth may not be discoverable even with such exercises. Still, we believe these alternative ways of reading will help your students see the complexity of the key issues and the viability or validity of differing views.

zeroing in on a specific aspect of the writing process. Each chapter concludes with suggestions for individual and group writing activities.

Each chapter in Parts Two, Three, and Four also includes these features to reinforce and extend concepts:

- **Writers' Circle**, a group writing activity tied to one of the chapter's reading selections, to reinforce chapter concepts through collaborative learning,
- **Pre- and Postreading Worksheets** linked to a specific reading to reinforce students' application of critical reading skills, and
- **Bridges: Another Perspective**, a brief discussion of a single reading that encourages students to make connections with other readings throughout the book and to think critically about an issue the reading raises.

The Heath Guide to College Writing also seeks to show writing and reading as very human experiences that take place in a very real world. Each reading, for example, comes with a biographical sketch about its author, often explaining the context in which the author produced that particular work. Each part opens with a profile of a writer discussing his or her writing, and scattered throughout the text are brief, evocative comments writers have made about their experiences in the processes of writing.

We have tried to make the structure of *The Heath Guide* clear and easy to use. Because we believe people learn to write more effectively by *doing* reading and *doing* writing, we have tried to avoid solid pages of print that simply *talk about* writing. Instead, we ask students to *get involved in writing* frequently in each chapter.

To assist instructors using this book, we have provided *The Heath Guide to College Writing Starter Kit*, a nuts-and-bolts guide for the first-time teacher of freshman composition (from which more experienced teachers may also gain insights), available in both print and disk formats; *The Teacher's Resource Manual for The Heath Guide to College Writing*, with content tailored specifically to *The Heath Guide; The Heath Guide to College Writing Annotated Teacher's Edition*, with page-by-page tips for teaching the content of this book; and a set of overhead transparencies that illustrate key concepts from the text. All these aids are available from your D. C. Heath representative.

Acknowledgments

When a work of this length is finished there are always many good people whose encouragement, suggestions, and contributions are worthy of grateful acknowledgment. We couldn't have produced this book without these people, and we thank and salute them here.

Our own large Writers' Circle of colleagues has helped us prepare this book. Their constructive criticism helped make the book better; still, any faults it may have are our own. Gerald P. Mulderig of De Paul University and Eugenia Butler of the University of Georgia contributed greatly to the content and clarity of Part Six, "The Handbook: A User Manual for Writing" (in the hardbound edition). We thank them for their close readings of this section.

Many of our teaching colleagues have helped us by participating in focus groups and critiquing drafts of this book. For their assistance we thank Julia M. Allen, University of California–Irvine; Bruce C. Appleby, Southern Illinois University–Carbondale; Kathleen Bell, Old Dominion University; James Catano, Tulane University; Elizabeth Cooper, Lehman College (CUNY); Inge Fink, University of New Orleans; Michael Flanigan, University of Oklahoma; Adelaide H. Frazier, University of New Orleans; Sue Holbrook, Fordham University; Janice Kollitz, Riverside Community College; David M. Kvernes, Southern Illinois University at Carbondale; Bruce Leland, Western Illinois University; Elisabeth Leyson, Fullerton College; Ben McClelland, University of Mississippi; Susan Meisenhelder, California State University–San Bernardino; Elizabeth Metzger, University of South Florida; G. Douglas Meyers, University of Texas–El Paso; Don Perkins, University of Wisconsin–Milwaukee; Delma Porter, Texas A&M University; Louis H. Pratt, Florida A&M University; Elizabeth Rankin, University of North Dakota–Grand Forks; Duane H. Roen, University of Arizona; Marti Singer, Georgia State University; Karen Vaught-Alexander, University of Portland; Victor Villanueva, Northern Arizona University; Ed White, California State University–San Bernardino; Mary Ann Wilson, University of Southwestern Louisiana; and William F. Woods, Wichita State University.

The following students allowed us to use their papers and their names: Jane-Marie Gray, Chriss Hendrickson, Tom Lamb, Anne Odom, Kristy Porter, Page Powell, Arthur Raney, Sheryl Rollins, Susan Sheehy, Daniel Warner, and Kimberly Williams. Several other students allowed us to use their papers in whole or in part. We are grateful to and for all our students, without whom, *nada*.

Among associates we wish to thank for contributions of various kinds are Kate Adams, Chuck Anderson, Linda Bensel-Meyers, Joe Coppola, Laura Hunter, JoAnna Hutt, Claudia Johnson, Grace McEntee, James Raymond, Kathleen Turner, and Myron Tuman.

We are especially grateful for the professional savvy, guidance, and cooperation we have received from many people at D. C. Heath, especially Senior Acquisitions Editor Paul A. Smith, Developmental Editor Linda Bieze, Senior Production Editor Rosemary R. Jaffe, Senior Designer Henry Rachlin, and Senior Permissions Editor Margaret Roll.

As writers, we have the same feeling at the end of this long project that writers always have at the end of writing—we figure we got some things right and some things wrong. If you use this book and feel strongly about something in it, for good or for ill, drop us a line. Either way, we'd like to hear from you.

We're serious! Here's how to reach us:

Professor Michael L. Keene
Department of English
University of Tennessee
Knoxville, TN 37996–0430

Professor Ralph F. Voss
Department of English
University of Alabama
Tuscaloosa, AL 35487

Ralph F. Voss

Michael L. Keene

selected bibliography

The following titles have influenced our work in this book and helped form the philosophical basis for it. We recommend these to instructors wishing to increase their knowledge of composition theory and teaching.

Aristotle, *The Rhetoric of Aristotle.* Ed. and trans. Lane Cooper. New York: Appleton, 1960.

Bartholomae, David. "Inventing the University." *When a Writer Can't Write.* Ed. Mike Rose. New York and London: Guilford, 1985.

Bitzer, Lloyd F. "The Rhetorical Situation." *Philosophy and Rhetoric* 1 (1968): 1–14.

Booth, Wayne C. *The Rhetoric of Fiction.* 2nd ed. Chicago: U of Chicago P, 1983.

———. "The Rhetorical Stance." *CCC* 14 (1963): 139–45.

Britton, James, et al. *The Development of Writing Abilities 11–18.* London: Macmillan, 1975.

Bruffee, Kenneth. "The Brooklyn Plan: Attaining Intellectual Growth through Peer-Group Tutoring." *Liberal Education* 64 (1978): 447–69.

———. "Peer Tutoring and the Conversation of Mankind," in *Writing Centers: Theory and Administration.* Ed. Gary A. Olson. Urbana: NCTE, 1984.

Burke, Kenneth. *A Rhetoric of Motives.* Englewood Cliffs: Prentice, 1950.

Chomsky, Noam. *Reflections on Language.* New York: Pantheon, 1975.

Christenbury, Leila, and Patricia Kelly. *Questioning: A Path to Critical Thinking.* Urbana: NCTE, 1983.

Elbow, Peter. *Writing without Teachers.* New York: Oxford UP, 1973.

Fahnestock, Jeanne, and Marie Secor. "Teaching Argument: A Theory of Types." *CCC* 34 (1983): 20–30.

Flower, Linda. "Writer-Based Prose: A Cognitive Basis for Problems in Writing." *College English* 41 (1979): 19–37.

Flower, Linda S., and John R. Hayes. "A Cognitive Process Theory of Writing." *CCC* 32 (1981): 365–87.

Gage, John T. "An Adequate Epistemology for Composition: Classical and Modern Perspectives." *Essays on Classical Rhetoric and Modern Discourse.* Carbondale: Southern Illinois UP, 1984. 152–69.

Hairston, Maxine. *Contemporary Composition.* 4th ed. Boston: Houghton, 1986.

———. "On Not Being a Composition Slave." *Training the New Teacher of College Composition.* Ed. Charles W. Bridges. Urbana: NCTE, 1986. 117–24.

———. *Successful Writing.* 2nd ed. New York: Norton, 1986.

Harris, Muriel. *Teaching One-to-One: The Writing Conference.* Urbana: NCTE, 1986.

Hashimoto, Irvin Y. *Thirteen Weeks: A Guide to Teaching College Writing.* Portsmouth: Boynton/Cook, Heinemann, 1991.

Keene, Michael L. *Effective Professional Writing.* Lexington: Heath, 1987.

Kinneavy, James. *A Theory of Discourse.* Englewood Cliffs: Prentice, 1971. Rpt. New York: Norton, 1980.

Macrorie, Kenneth. *Uptaught*. Rochelle Park: Hayden, 1970.

———. *Telling Writing.* 4th ed. Portsmouth: Boynton/Cook, 1985.

Murray, Donald. *A Writer Teaches Writing.* 2nd ed. Boston: Houghton, 1985.

Rosenblatt, Louise M. *Literature as Exploration.* New York: Appleton, 1938. Rpt. New York: MLA, 1983.

Scholes, Robert. *Textual Power: Literary Theory and the Teaching of English.* New Haven: Yale UP, 1985.

Spear, Karen. *Sharing Writing: Peer Response Groups in English Classes.* Portsmouth: Boynton/Cook, 1988.

Stanford, Gene, and the NCTE Committee on Classroom Practices, eds. *How to Handle the Paper Load.* Urbana: NCTE, 1979.

Stern, Arthur A. "When Is a Paragraph?" *CCC* 27 (1976): 253–57.

Toulmin, Stephen E. *The Uses of Argument.* New York: Cambridge UP, 1964.

Trimble, John. *Writing with Style: Conversations on the Art of Writing.* Englewood Cliffs: Prentice, 1975.

Voss, Ralph F. *Elements of Practical Writing.* New York: Holt, 1985.

Weiss, Edmond H. *The Writing System for Engineers and Scientists.* Englewood Cliffs: Prentice, 1982.

brief contents

contents

part two Purposes for Writing 35

chapter 3 Critical Writing 43

chapter 4 Writing to Express: Emphasis on the Writer 55

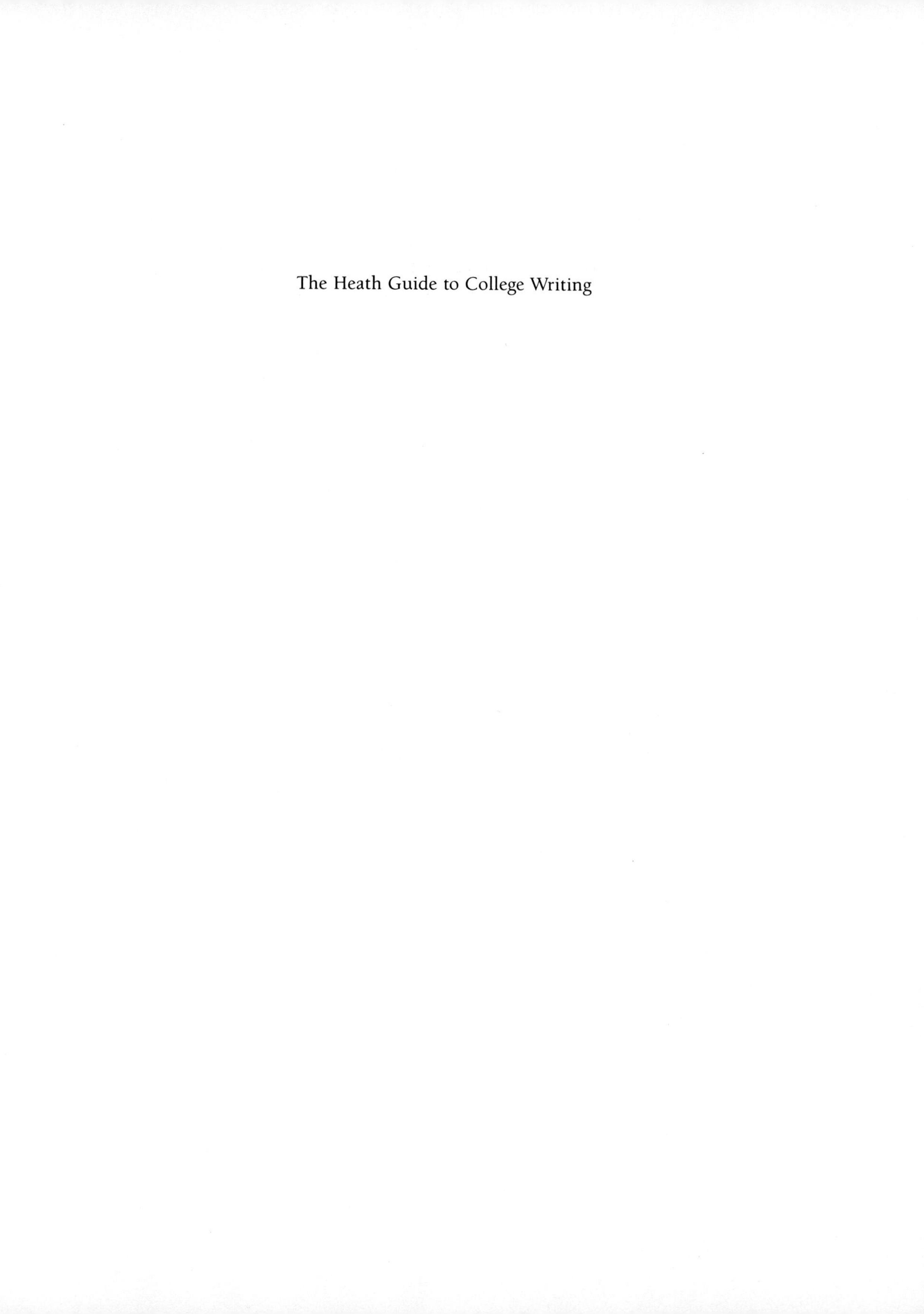

The Heath Guide to College Writing

part one On Writing

PROFILE ♦ OF ♦ A ♦ WRITER

Alicia Hallagan

Alicia was born in Kansas City, Missouri, in 1974 and is currently a freshman business management major at the university. She recently graduated from high school, where her overall grades were good and her marks in English, math, and social science were excellent. Her favorite course in high school was journalism, for which she completed one term as staff writer and ad seller and a second term as news editor and writer. Her best writing her senior year consisted of two projects, one a story for the school paper about a classmate who overcame a severe learning disability, the other a sociology class paper on capital punishment.

"I'm not the most eager writer in the world," Alicia

says. "It's always been hard work for me. But I discovered in high school that I'm more willing to work at writing if the subject is something that truly interests me." Asked what she thinks her greatest strength as a writer is, Alicia says, "Oh, organization. I usually have a much easier time getting a paper planned out than I do actually writing it. I can see how one thing ought to come before another thing—or how different parts of what I have to say relate to one another." Her greatest weakness, on the other hand, is "the mechanical stuff—spelling, punctuation, when to use *who* or *whom,* that sort of thing."

We believe it's important for your students to get to know one another as soon as possible. One good way to do this is the Name Game in chapter 2. Another good way is to have students do writer biographies—interviews of one another—using the Alicia Hallagan piece as an informal guideline, together with the following questions:

1. What is your name?
2. What is your major or intended major?
3. What was your favorite course in high school?
4. How would you describe yourself as a writer?
5. What is your greatest strength as a writer?
6. What is your greatest weakness as a writer?
7. What memories of writing experiences do you have?
8. Do you expect writing to be important to you in college? out of college?

You too should make an effort to get to know your students as soon as possible. Talk with them about their writing experiences—ask them the questions listed above if you don't have the students do interviews—and listen closely to their responses. Nontraditional students (older, foreign, part-time) may have different views on writing in particular and on school in general that might be interesting and valuable, not only to you but to the other students as well.

Writing used to be very confusing for Alicia. "I was confused because, for example, I couldn't understand why some of my teachers told me never to use *I* in a paper, while others told me it was perfectly all right. One teacher told me I could use contractions; then another told me contractions were strictly forbidden. Who was right? And grades! I thought the grades were purely the teacher's opinion, and not uniform at all."

So how did Alicia overcome some of this confusion? "I had a really good teacher in high school, just last year, who explained that *all* the point-of-view pronouns are perfectly good to use, depending upon the writing situation. The trick is deciding when it is appropriate to use *I* and when not. What was wrong was my being told *never* to use *I*. It's the same with contractions and other kinds of informal words." What about grading? "Well, it really is just the teacher's opinion," says Alicia, "but that's not really so bad if the teacher *explains* the reasons for a grade and *shows* you how to improve. Writing just isn't something you can grade like math, where one answer is right or wrong, period."

Asked how she thought writing might be important to her, Alicia says, "I'm majoring in business management and that requires not only the freshman-level writing classes in the English Department, but also the business writing classes in my field, which I'll be taking when I am a junior. My mom is an advertising CEO and she has told me many times that the best managers are people who can write effectively—reports, memos, letters, proposals, and so on. She told me that the most important ad campaign she ever did was successful because of the way she wrote the proposal for it. I'm sure that writing will be important to me during school, and even more important afterwards."

• • •

Many of you have some things in common with Alicia Hallagan: you're a freshman in college; you're probably a recent high school graduate; and you have probably been confused about what "good writing" is supposed to be. More likely than not, you too have what you consider writing strengths and weaknesses. And we are certain that writing will be important to you in the years to come—even though you might prefer otherwise.

This book is about building bridges in your writing experience: bridges between your reading and writing abilities, bridges between your present levels of writing skill and confidence and the higher levels you can reach, bridges between your past as a writer and the stronger, better future your life as a writer can hold. Some people want to believe the effort to build such bridges is unproductive; they tell themselves good writing ability is strictly a matter of talent, a talent they don't have, and thus they consider themselves excused from making any further effort to improve. That belief is a delusion, and a costly one, for improvement in writing is an almost-inevitable result of effort, the same kind of effort that is the key to success in virtually any undertaking—athletics, academics, professional life, or personal relationships.

You *can* build those bridges of improvement, and you *can* get positive results. We wrote this book to help you, and Alicia, and all those who are willing to make the effort to build their writing abilities. We're with you, because we've been there ourselves.

We recommend that you try to discern the attitude behind your students' efforts. There is a difference between a student doing poorly because of not knowing how to do better and a student doing poorly because of not generating the effort necessary to improve. Most freshmen will be sincere in their efforts—you'll be able to tell. For those trying hard, a patient approach and frequent conferences will help enormously. For those not trying hard but merely complaining, a gentle but firm statement of what you think is needed is entirely appropriate. See our Starter Kit for more advice on handling such matters. (Note that when we refer to our Starter Kit we mean both the "generic" guide for beginning teachers and the "text-specific" instructor's manual.)

chapter 1 Reasons for Writing: The Writing Process

Some students may be inclined to settle for that most basic of all reasons to write: they have to do the assignment. For such students, it might be productive in class discussion to push their analysis of the reason further: "OK, you're in a class, so you have to write for it, but *why* are you in the class?" (If the answer—likely in freshman English—is "Because it's a required class," push *that* reason further: "OK, why are you in school?") The idea here is to ascertain motives beyond the most immediate or obvious ones.

Often students haven't thought much about having to write outside of school situations; their experience tells them writing is something almost wholly connected to schoolwork. It may thus be useful to discuss nonschool writing, and a good way to begin is to ask students if they know people in the "outside world" who write routinely as part of their jobs—parents, relatives, friends. What do these people write? Why?

For an example of a professional writer who writes out of internal necessity, see the Madeleine L'Engle piece (on her fortieth birthday) in chapter 5.

Why write? No one writes without a *reason*—a motive, or motives, to write. For most student writers, the reason is automatic: they *have* to write. Teachers make writing assignments, and students have to write those assignments if they expect to pass the course. We know that, and we're pretty sure you know it too. In a larger perspective, the reasons of writers, even student writers, are often more complicated than that. A student writing a letter applying for a summer job has a reason a bit more complex than getting a good grade from a teacher. A student writing a "Statement of Educational Goals and Personal Career Objectives" section of a scholarship application also has a larger reason; so does a student completing a similar section on an application to law or medical school.

Outside the educational setting, many people who would not ordinarily call themselves writers find that they too must write for complex reasons. A business consultant finds she must write the results of her analysis and her recommendations for her client. A store manager finds he must not only write a projected budget for the next fiscal year but also add a written justification or explanation for that budget. An insurance agent must write a letter to a policyholder, informing her client as to how much of a claim is covered by the policy. There are, in fact, many occupations that require writing for several different reasons, even though not one of those occupations carries the job title "writer."

There are even more reasons to write. We write personal letters and notes to relatives and friends to let them know details of our lives and to keep channels of communication open. Some of us keep diaries or journals, not for others to read but for our own reflection or reference. There's something about writing things down that often helps us clarify and sort our thoughts—even if what we write is only a "to do" list for one day, or a grocery-shopping list.

Ironically, professional writers often write for the same reason students do: because they *have* to. For such writers, the need to write comes from complex inner reasons tied to their own creativity and their own ways of looking at and making sense of the world. For these professionals, their sense of themselves is as *writers;* they write as much for self-fulfillment as for a livelihood.

Four Reasons for Writing

Every writer of every kind, then, has some kind of *reason* or *reasons* for writing. In fact, it is because all writers have reasons for writing that some of the earliest writing advice put into textbooks used broad *reasons* for writing as ways to classify *types* of writing. Such classifications are always slippery things, not because of the reasons behind them but because of the frequent overlapping of those reasons. Nonetheless, we think it is useful to identify four major reasons that people write:

1. Writing to express
2. Writing to explain or inform
3. Writing to analyze
4. Writing to persuade

In other words, people write

- to express their feelings, attitudes, intuitions, thoughts, and philosophies (this can be done not only in a personal essay but also in poetry, fiction, and drama);
- to explain to readers or to inform readers about some person, place, thing, event, or procedure so as to convey that information for whatever use may be made of it;
- to analyze a person, place, thing, event, procedure, subject, or document so as to present an understanding of the relationship of its parts to a whole impression, assessment, or summary effect, or to show a fundamental grasp of its internal structure and pass along insights, formulations, or recommendations based on that analysis; and
- to persuade readers to understand and accept the writer's conclusions, opinions, viewpoints, recommended actions, or attitudes about a given subject.

In anyone's writing process, then, reasons are critical: your writing must have a purpose. But while a writer must have reasons, reasons alone will not produce effective writing. Writing is a process (or set of processes), a complex activity. Having reasons is just a start.

In identifying reasons for writing as a means of classifying types of writing, we are following the lead of several composition theorists, among them James Kinneavy and James Britton, though we follow neither's scheme strictly. Our approach has been influenced also by the eclectic and pragmatic teaching philosophy of Maxine Hairston. (For the full bibliographic information on relevant works by these and other authors cited in these notes, see the lists at the front of the text and in the Starter Kit.)

It is vitally important that you emphasize early and often to your students that these four primary reasons for writing are *not* mutually exclusive and *usually* overlap. This idea might be confusing to your students but is actually a mark of the complexity and richness of human communication. What's significant in our scheme and essential to your useful understanding of this book is that *one* of the four reasons will ordinarily be identifiable as primary in a given piece of writing.

"Writing is easy; all you do is sit staring at a blank sheet of paper until the drops of blood form on your forehead."

Gene Fowler

Your students have probably heard little if anything about writing as a *process.* Most likely, they still conceive of writing wholly as a *product,* something that must be as perfect as possible. It is therefore important to emphasize the idea of process early and often. Students should think about their own processes—how they go about getting the job done—and how they can improve. Especially early in a new term, it is far better for you and your students to be concerned about developing their own reliable, effective *processes* than to be worried about finished products.

It's a good idea to have your students prepare planning sheets for their writing assignments, writing out answers to each of the three questions we give as ways to "size up" the situation and then submitting these plans either with drafts or before beginning drafts. The exercise will be helpful, especially if you push students to write out plans that go beyond the obvious or the pro forma. For example, in answering question 1 some students simply write, "A student." That doesn't establish much. Insist that they describe the student's situation or attitude fully—for example, "A student who . . . [describe situation or attitude]." These planning sheets need not be exhaustive, but they should help clarify the writer's purpose, the reader's purpose, and the key choices writers must make.

Though thinking is indispensable to everyone's writing process, many experienced writers do quite a bit of their thinking without the aid of jotting things down, speaking into a tape recorder, freewriting, or other forms of what

The Process of Writing

Gene Fowler (in the quotation) presents a common—although exaggerated—view of how tough writing can be. It *isn't* easy, and there's no point pretending it is. But you don't really have to sweat blood: what you've got to do is *discover* and *engage* your own writing process.

Good writing is the result, the *product,* of an effective writing *process.* Though certain activities are common to everyone's writing process, each person develops an individual procedure (actually a sequence of procedures) for getting the job done. Thus, we can't describe a specific plan for you to follow. We can, however, identify some general sequential procedures that should give you a good idea of how to examine your own writing activities and develop your own effective process. As you proceed through the term and work with your teacher, your classmates, and this book, we hope your confidence and abilities as a versatile writer will grow.

Three Ways to Size up the Situation

Keeping your *reason* for writing in mind at all times, think about the following ingredients in your writing situation:

1. Who "are" you as a writer on this assignment? That is, what kind of person do you want to seem to be to your readers—expert? sincere? stuffy? angry? critical? If your purpose is to inform, you might want to sound confident and knowledgeable, your tone one of trustworthiness. If your purpose is to persuade, you might want to sound like the preceding but *urgently concerned* as well, personally convinced that you are urging the right course of action. Thinking about this question will help you begin to select the right tone of "voice" for your purpose and your audience.
2. Who are your readers on this assignment? What are their concerns and interests? What can you say that you know will be of special importance to them? How can you gain their attention and stand your best chance of achieving your purpose or reason for writing?
3. Given your reason for writing, the kind of readers you have, and the tone of voice you have chosen, what details—word choices, sentences, examples, facts, information—will most likely help you achieve your purpose or reason for writing? Which of these details are most appropriate for your writing task?

You won't be able to come up with a thorough list of answers to these questions while you're sizing up your writing situation, but that's all right. If you keep these considerations in mind throughout the time you are writing, you'll find they will help you make specific decisions about word choice, sentences, and content—and those are important decisions for any writer.

might be called physical thinking. Generally, less experienced writers need to complement their thinking with some kind of physical activity—note taking, freewriting, outlining, or the like. Encourage your students to think with their pens in their hands.

Four Kinds of Writing Process Activities

If you were to follow closely the activities of a successful professional writer doing some writing (a feasibility study or a business letter, for example), you might well be able to sort out these four kinds of activities:

1. Thinking
2. Drafting and reading
3. Revising and editing
4. Proofreading

Though these activities may be identified separately, they do not necessarily occur separately or always in the given sequence, because they can occur simultaneously (that is, thinking occurs during all activities; revising can occur during proofreading; and so on) and recursively (that is, while primarily engaged in revising something already written, a writer may find it necessary to draft an entirely new paragraph to insert).

Your conscious awareness of these activities in your own writing process should prove helpful to your improvement.

Students will not be familiar with the strategies we discuss here—class time in group invention activity will be well spent.

Freewriting. Freewriting involves writing nonstop, whatever comes into one's head, for a set period. Start with a five-minute period.

Brainstorming. This strategy takes several forms but generally involves conversation among students, with each jotting down ideas as they are mentioned. Start with a "toss-up" idea—bad movies, the best TV show, the greatest problem in our society today. . . .

Heuristic. Any list of probing questions can be used to analyze or explore a topic; see, for example, chapter 21's rubrics for analyzing prose fiction, drama, and poetry. Students can respond to such questions in group discussion.

Jotting. Jotting, doodling, scrawling—any sort of pen- or pencil-to-paper activity that gets ideas, phrases, diagrams, rough outlines, and the like on paper can serve as prompts to the writer's memory or further thought.

Thinking. Thinking—before, during, and even after writing activity—is vital to the overall experience of writing. All successful writers are successful thinkers; the finished product of their thinking is the writing itself, which, when it is read by its intended audience, then leads to even more thinking. Thought is expressed in language—words arranged a certain way for a certain meaning—and language provokes even more thought, which in turn provokes more language, and so on, endlessly.

Successful writers have developed many strategies to sharpen their thinking, particularly in the early stages of writing. Classical rhetoricians called such strategies invention, meaning roughly to "invent" subject matter. The term is apt, not only because of its meaning to create something new but also because it describes a process in which *discovery* is fundamental: important information or detail is discovered, one way or another, through some methodical procedure (such as library research, experimental research, brainstorming, systematic questioning, or freewriting). Some of these procedures involve putting words down on paper, but the thinking element still dominates. A student engaged in freewriting, for example, doesn't pause to read and contemplate what has been written down; the idea is to generate material that can be read *later.* Freewriting and some other invention techniques will be explained in detail elsewhere in this book.

Chapter 2 enlarges on the thinking stage of the writing process.

As a rule, the more students have on paper (regardless of what form it's in) when they begin the next stage (drafting and reading), the better.

The term *draft* can be slippery and vague. Be sure, therefore, that you clarify what you mean when *you* use the word. Ordinarily, no writing is called a draft until it is complete—that is, has a beginning, a developed middle, and an end and says all that was intended, even though it may yet need extensive revision (and even additions, based on new discoveries arrived at during writing or rereading that draft). "Drafting" is the activity of working on a "draft" in the sense defined here.

At first your students may be reluctant to work in groups, but the benefits drawn from consistent group work far outstrip the initial drawbacks. We think three to a group is ideal; each writer gets two viewpoints, and he or she can heed what seems most useful. Keep early group work purely supportive—discourage "red-pen editorial" attitudes. Responses should be at the level implied by these questions:

- Do you see what I mean in this writing? If not, how can I make it clearer?
- Can you think of more effective ways to say this?
- Are there spots where you had trouble reading? Where? How can these spots be improved?

For more discussion of the value of group work and practical suggestions for

As writers proceed in their thinking, many begin to eliminate some possibilities and add others—already a selecting and rejecting process that can be described as early planning, a kind of mental stocktaking that often takes the form of physical writing activity, such as listing or doodling, rough outlining, or sketching. Though other people might not be able to read and make sense out of such writing, the writer can, and is therefore about ready to move into the drafting/reading stage. Other writers near the end of the invention stage may be more sure of what they want to cover and in what order—thus they may make detailed outlines. Roughly at this stage of composing, most writers move into drafting and reading.

Drafting and Reading. Drafting is the physical writing activity of trying to put words on paper in some meaningful order. We include reading in this stage—though it is important in all subsequent stages as well—because most writers read what they draft and react to it as they write, often making changes or choosing alternative wordings as they proceed. Some writers who are drafting read less than others, but the proof that most drafts are read while being composed can be seen in a handwritten draft that has several markouts, crossovers, interpolations, and corrections. Drafting writers must make decisions: which example to use, which words will best express the point, whether or not a sentence is clear, and so on. Though no such decision may be final at this stage, it still must be made.

It is often during drafting that a writer discovers exactly how to organize the writing. The first paragraph written may eventually turn out to work better in the conclusion than in the introduction—but during drafting that doesn't matter, because the only time a piece of writing ought to have an orderly beginning, middle, and end is when it's *finished*, ready for its target readers. What is important at this stage is to *get it all written down*, reading and tinkering as you go, until it's complete. Then read it again, to see if it seems to fit together. Note that *thinking* remains crucial in this stage too.

Now it's time for the writer to share the draft with other readers. Classmates or friends (or, in the case of professional writers, prepublication reviewers) should read the drafts carefully and respond with criticisms and suggestions for improvement. Once these criticisms and suggestions are heard, the successful writer takes them into account and begins to write again, this time to *revise* so as to produce the best possible version.

Revising and Editing. The word *revision* means "reseeing," or "seeing again." A writer who is revising is literally "seeing again" and putting the results of that new sight to work in an improved paper. Revising can be massive, moderate, or minimal, depending on the results of the writer's earlier drafting efforts and the reactions of not only the writer but also others who have read the drafts. Whether or not the revision is extensive, it still involves *thought* and it still involves *drafting* and *reading*.

Once the revisions are made, the writer again shares the writing with other readers, as a way to see whether the revisions worked and as a final check that the substance, or content, of the writing is as it should be. This second round of responses is often called editing; for professional writers it is at this point that serious final corrections and adjustments in content are made before publication. For student writers this second round of responses should serve a similar purpose: after these changes, only such mechanical errors as spelling, punctuation, and usage should remain for the proofreading part of the process.

conducting group work, see Spear and Bruffee in the Bibliography. Both Spear and Bruffee have written extensively about group work.

For an excellent discussion of revising and how to approach it, see Murray.

Proofreading. Proofreading is polishing the final manuscript to make it as neat and presentable as possible. It is now that the writer should make sure that words are spelled correctly, that all subjects and predicates in all sentences agree in number, that all pronouns have clear referents, and so on. The standard printing conventions are brought to bear as criteria for the manuscript, which the writer wants to be as ready as possible for publication *as it is.*

Professional writers have proofreading help, and sometimes students may, too, depending on the teacher's policy. Most teachers want their students to become good proofreaders and therefore don't authorize "outside" proofing. In any case, student writers should work to become good proofreaders of their own work. After all, most teachers give their highest grades to papers that are excellent not only in content and organization but also in manuscript form. And all professional publishers seek to print work that is as flawless in matters of form as they can humanly make it.

The result of good proofreading is the equivalent of appropriate dress: just as you want to dress appropriately for a job interview or perhaps a celebratory event, so you want your writing to be appropriately "dressed" for its best possible appearance. What's important to remember—and a little sad—is that many student writers have long believed that proofreading correctness is the *most* important thing about their writing, and their worries about correctness have inhibited their growth as good writers. Too much concern about correctness in the early stages of the writing process can short-circuit the whole effort and reinforce negative stereotypes about writing.

Make sure your policy on outside help is clear, especially regarding proofreading. You should, as a general practice, probably discourage your students from having someone proofread their papers. (Among students, English majors are a favored resource for proofing papers—and they are notoriously, and mysteriously, none too good at it!) Rather, your students should work to improve their own proofreading skill. This would not rule out having someone read the paper and respond *generally* to it—its organization, clarity, effectiveness, and so on. Such responders could comment, "You have some spelling [punctuation, sentence structure, and so forth] problems," and let the *writer* look for them. The staff at most writing centers will respond in this way but not proofread the paper itself. See our Starter Kit for more advice on policy matters.

So What Can You Expect from This Book?

We've told you above what we think is the most important information at the heart of a writing course. For you to develop your abilities as a versatile writer is our uppermost goal, and we think if you first recognize your *reasons* for writing, next *size up your writing situation,* and then move systematically through your *writing process,* you'll produce effective and successful writing.

Each of the chapters in Parts Two, Three, and Four of this book shows you examples of effective, successful writing done by both students and professionals. Each of these chapters follows a typical student through a typical assignment, giving you an overview of that student's writing process in general and a detailed look at one specific part of the process (such as thinking, drafting and reading, or

Almost everyone has had a bad experience because of poor proofreading, and these experiences contribute to the fallacy that for writing to be any good at all it must be error-free. Few people are really sharp proofreaders, but everyone can *improve* as a proofreader. Lead a class discussion of the costliness of "proofreading consciousness": how obsession with errors can create needless grief and negative attitudes. You can share a "war story" with your students about a time when proofreading (or the lack of same) proved costly to you. Invite their "war stories," too.

revising). We reinforce, in other words, the dynamic principle of writing-as-process. We include material designed to help you sharpen your own critical reading and analytical abilities right along with your writing abilities. Here are the book's focal points in Parts Two, Three, and Four:

- Part Two focuses on reasons for writing, the reading audience, and the writer's "voice"—those components which in dynamic combination achieve the substance of any piece of writing.
- Part Three focuses on subjects—the primary material dealt with in writing.
- Part Four focuses on form—the particular organization that writing takes, that readers expect to see, and that writers themselves can use to learn more about their own subjects and purposes.

See our Starter Kit for suggested syllabi, various chapter combinations for possible course emphases, and other general "how to use this book" advice.

Part Five ("Special Applications") and Part Six ("The Handbook," which appears in the hardcover edition of this text) are designed to be used, as needed, in support of the chapters in Parts Two through Four. Part Five describes typical special applications of writing—by subject, field of study, and purpose. It should prove helpful for your writing in other courses and for other special purposes. Part Six is a user manual for writing, complete with a how-to section (a closer look at the processes of writing, cross-referenced to other chapters of this book), a grammar and sentence guide for writers, and a full treatment of twelve of the most common writing problems.

A Word About Word Processing

You should find out at the earliest opportunity what word processing facilities and programs are available for use at your school. What access will students have? What software programs work with those machines? Is word processing a part of the freshman program? As part of this discussion, let students know your policy on printers. We recommend accepting dot matrix print as long as it's done with a good ribbon. (Laser printing is nice but expensive. If you're having students turn in portfolios of their best work at the end of the term, however, laser printing at that stage gives a nice sheen to the finished product.)

The days of students scratching their papers out in blue books or of hammering them out on typewriters (and ripping out partially typed pages to start over after a big mistake) are fast disappearing—and good riddance! Growing numbers of students and colleges are using word processing to make student writing go faster and better:

- *Faster* because after the initial keyboarding of the first draft those original keystrokes need never be repeated, no matter how many revisions and later drafts you do.
- *Better* because the new technologies make doing multiple revisions so much easier. Ultimately, of course, the technology can't be any better than the student using it. But at least with word processing, your time and effort go directly into changes in the paper in front of you, and not into pounding (and repounding) the same old keys.

We have taken advantage of this technology to write this book—and we heartily recommend you learn to use such technology to your own advantage as well. (We'll have more to say about word processing later in the book, especially in chapter 28, "A Closer Look at the Processes of Writing," which, again, appears in the hardcover edition.)

And a Few Final Words

People come to freshman composition classes with lots of different expectations—some students want just to survive; others want to learn the things they need to know about writing to do well in college. It seems to us that the things a student can expect in freshman composition class are

- to write often, with feedback of some sort at every stage;
- to learn to read more critically, think more sharply, and incorporate those activities into better writing; and
- to come out of the course confident in having learned skills that will be important to success in other important college courses.

This book is designed to help you accomplish those goals.

Here we list only those general things we think a student can expect in freshman composition; you should clarify early in the term what *your* expectations are. The ideal time to do that is the first or second meeting, when you present your course description and policy statement regarding attendance, late papers, and so on.

Writers' Circle

Divide into groups of three students each to discuss and compare your individual writing experiences; each group should appoint a reporter to take notes. In the group discussion, each person in the group should respond to some or all of these questions:

1. What one word pops into your mind when you think about the act of writing?
2. We have all written assignments for school because we *had* to. Have you ever written something voluntarily? What? Why? Were there important differences between how you went about that voluntary writing assignment and how you go about mandatory assignments? Did those differences produce better writing?
3. What do you think is your strongest point as a writer? Where did that quality come from—did you learn it somewhere, or just find that you had it?
4. What do you think is your weakest point as a writer? Is it a matter of lack of knowledge, lack of ability, or lack of effort?
5. Reflect on your last writing assignment for a class; try to reconstruct the steps you took to complete the assignment. How would you describe your writing process? How could that process be improved?
6. What is the ideal situation for you in which to write? Do you need silence? background music? food and drink nearby? a certain kind of desk or lighting? Do you use a word processor? a typewriter? pen and paper? To what extent do you consciously control that environment when you write?

Now the group reporters should report to the class at large the general results of the group discussions, while the teacher makes notes on the board. What larger picture emerges of the class's writing, of the class as a group of writers? Do certain problems or experiences seem to be shared by significant numbers of the class members? To what extent do you think those problems or experiences will carry over into the writing class you're in now? What could be done to prevent a carryover of the negative experiences and to maximize a carryover of the positive ones?

WRITING ASSIGNMENT

The multiple exposure photograph of National Basketball Association star Alex English (page 5) shows him making a fundamental offensive move for a right-handed shooter in basketball. In general, the "fake-pivot-stride-shoot" move proceeds this way: English (with the ball) fakes a move to his left, then pivots quickly back to his right—turning the left side of his body toward the defense as he strides with his left leg—then plants his left foot and launches a hook shot with his right hand.

Basketball players practice this fundamental move every day, but every player does it differently. Although few reach Alex English's level of proficiency, most who practice this move long enough—however they have adapted it to their physical attributes and style of play—can make the move effectively.

Methodical practice in your own fundamental process of writing can yield similar results. This chapter has described a very sound *general* process of writing; as you practice it, you will undoubtedly find your own variations that help you make the process most effective for you. To begin, consider again the activities of (1) thinking, (2) drafting and reading, (3) revising and editing, and (4) proofreading. Then write a methodical description of how you usually handle each of these four basic activities when you write. (Feel free to draw upon the material you generated for activity number 5 in the Writers' Circle if your class did that particular activity.) Then, at the end of the term, you can look back on your descriptions and see how you have developed the "moves" that make up your writing process.

chapter 2 Getting Started

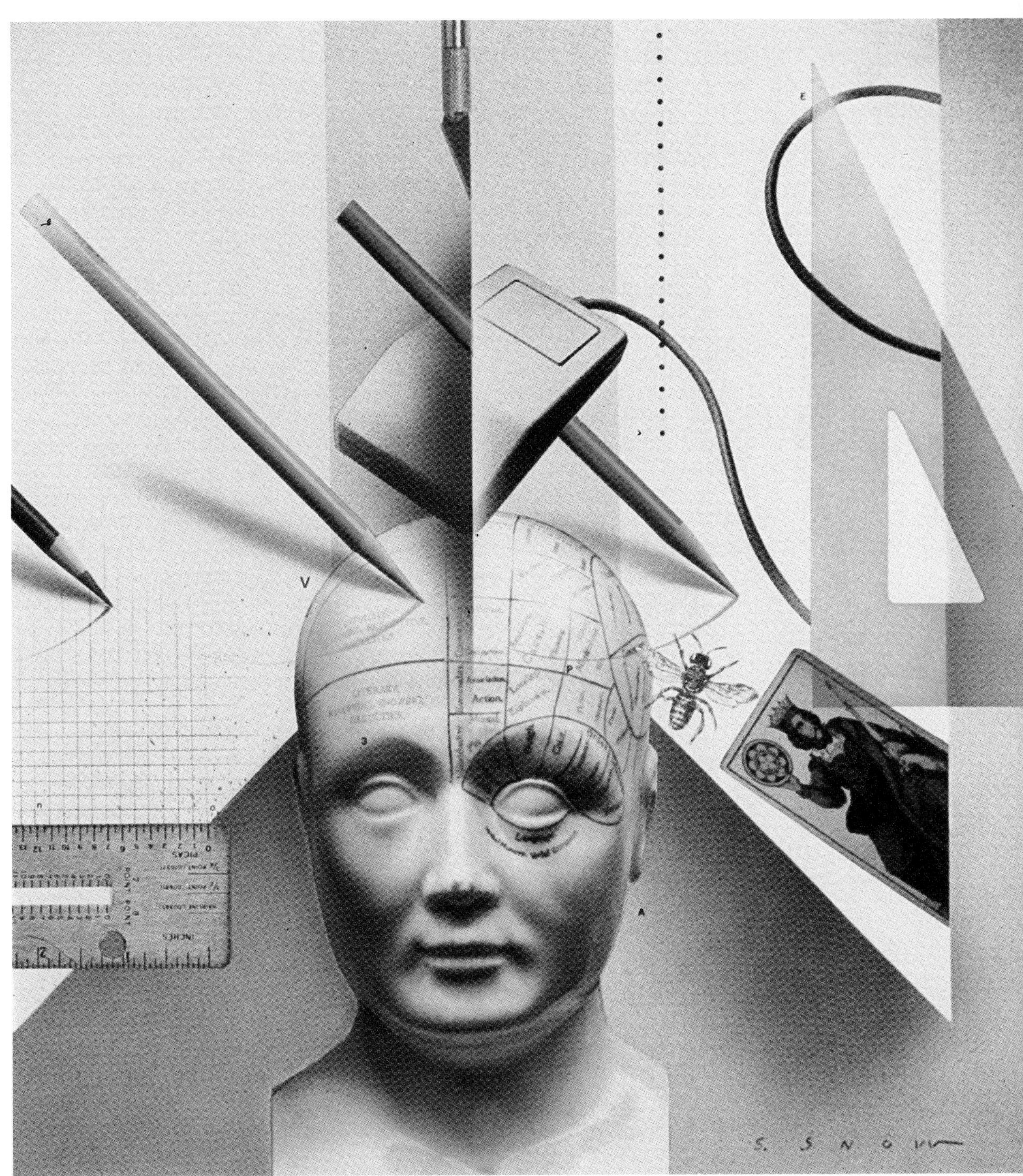

> "We are all apprentices in a craft where no one ever becomes a master."
>
> Ernest Hemingway

We would like to begin by assuming you have read our chapter 1. If you have not read that chapter, please turn to it and read it now. After you've read chapter 1, read only to "A Student Writer Writes: An Ideal Scenario" (page 22) of this chapter and do the writing assignment those first pages describe. (Then, for step 5 of that writing assignment, you will go on and finish the chapter.)

The first time we wrote this chapter we went into great detail explaining writing as a process, a purposeful activity that is simultaneously sequenced and repetitive. But most of our friends who read that first effort said that although they agreed with what we said, most of it seemed to them to be boring and unnecessary. We reread the chapter, reflecting on their remarks, and agreed with them. And so we saved from the original version what we thought was truly useful and blended it in with our chapter 1. Then we started writing a new second chapter (this one), trying to incorporate the useful suggestions made by our friends. Thus, we revised our first chapter *and* drafted a completely different second chapter, one we hope all our readers find clear and helpful, not boring and unnecessary.

Why are we telling you this? Because we feel it provides a good example of what we mean when we say writing is an activity that is both sequenced and repetitive. Perhaps if you see that your textbook authors had to draft, seek reader responses, and then revise, exactly as many student writers do, then we will make our point much better than with a long and detailed introductory chapter. That said, here's the rest of our new chapter.

In this chapter we're going to walk you through a good first writing assignment, one your teacher may well want you to go ahead and start on now. Then, in the second half of the chapter, we'll show you how one student wrote this assignment and how that paper turned out.

Starting Here and Now

The sooner you get your students writing, the better; this is less a course *about* writing than a course in which *students write.* We strongly recommend that you use the writing assignment that serves as the focus of this chapter (or use some other, comparable assignment) and thus establish early the routines that will best serve you and your students' purposes.

It's the beginning of the term and neither you nor your teacher knows exactly what to expect—except that you'll have to write in this course. You haven't read any essays or stories yet, just chapter 1, and so any first writing you do will probably need to be about some of your personal experience. Your teacher would like to have an early sample of your writing, not only to get a preliminary idea of how you write and to begin to get to know you better, but also to give you a preliminary idea of what the course will be like and how your teacher reacts to your writing. What we have here, then, is an introductory communication situation in which the principals (you, your classmates, and your teacher) are beginning to get to know one another.

Writers' Circle

The Name Game. We suggest that you first get to know the names of your classmates. Begin at the right or left of the room, with the first student giving his or her name. The next student must then name the first student and then add his or her own name. And so on, with the list of remembered names growing to the last student in the class and finishing with the teacher. (This doesn't have to be a game of memory challenge; write the names down if you wish—after all, it's a writing class!) Thus:

1. First student: "I'm Mary Kay Kennedy."
2. Second student: (Nodding his head toward Mary Kay); "Mary Kay Kennedy, I'm Dennis Bradford."
3. Third student: (Nodding to Mary Kay and Dennis) "Mary Kay Kennedy and Dennis Bradford, I'm Ramon Moreno."
4. Fourth student: (Nodding as above) "Mary Kay Kennedy, Dennis Bradford, and Ramon Moreno, I'm Mary Moore."

And so on around the room, ending with the teacher. Then, for the fun of it, see how the fortunate first few students—those who didn't have many names to keep track of, *your* class's Mary Kay, Dennis, Ramon, and Mary—do.

Once you have begun to know your classmates' names, we suggest you begin brainstorming ideas for a descriptive writing assignment that will not be "graded" in the usual sense. This assignment will be like the Name Game in that it is intended to be introductory—a writing assignment to get you started, to give you early experience in writing for this class and this teacher, and to give you a preview of the writing process activities we believe to be important to your continuing development as a writer.

The Name Game is a good tone setter, something that helps students see your classroom as their classroom too—a safe place where they can be at ease, or as much at ease as possible, while they approach their writing, a difficult subject for many of them. We are indebted to our friend James C. Raymond for the Name Game idea, but we recommend it only if your writing class has no more than about thirty students. (Of course, we firmly believe that writing classes should be small, much smaller than that. Fifteen students is ideal, but if you have twenty-one or twenty-two you can still manage things well. If you have thirty or more, you and your program administrator know you need to lobby your higher administration hard for a reduction.)

Why Descriptive Writing?

We're starting you out here with descriptive writing because description is a basic kind of expression. A fundamental way to communicate is to tell others what something looks, feels, smells, tastes, or sounds like. We learn descriptive techniques early in life and never stop developing and refining them. Often we combine our interest in description with narration—telling the story of how, why, where, and when something happened. The store of our personal experience is an excellent place from which to draw the raw material of a first paper, for we do not have to learn such material first in order to begin: we need look no further than the people, places, or events about which we already know.

When they think about description, many people think about adjectives, words which by their nature describe, point out, or in some other obvious way

This assignment supports your course's smooth beginning by quickly getting students writing and by walking them through a reasonable writing process, one emphasizing parts of composing that may be unfamiliar to them (but important). Descriptive writing is also one of the least intimidating sorts of writing, with roots in the expressive beginnings of language use.

affect the nouns they modify. Consider, for example, this brief passage, which has the adjectives italicized:

> On a *clear* day southwest of Limon, Colorado, on U.S. Highway 24, you can gaze off into the *blue* distance and see what appears to be a *low, hazy* line of *dim* clouds. Only with *gradual* awe do you realize that *those* "clouds" are in fact the *enormous Rocky* Mountains *towering* beyond Colorado Springs, still more than one hundred miles away.

To prompt discussion of how basic and vital descriptive language can be, try one or more of these suggestions:

- Bring examples of advertising to class and let students identify descriptive elements that "punch up" the ads' appeal.
- Find a passage of very dry prose that explains or describes a fairly clear idea or group of ideas. Have students rewrite it, enhancing the language to make it more descriptive and appealing.
- Bring a striking photograph or picture to class and have students write descriptions of it for readers who can't see it.

The adjectives in that passage help generate mental pictures for the reader; one can visualize the "clouds" on the horizon and then make the mental adjustment to realize that the "clouds" are in fact huge mountains.

But to consider using adjectives as the only way to describe is to limit severely our language's power to help us envision the people, places, or actions of which we speak. You can also get a good mental picture of the following action, which is described with very few adjectives. In fact, the italicized verbs convey most of the picture:

> Tied game, ten seconds *remain* on the clock. Visalia's guard *fires* a jumper; it *rims* off, and Lou *grabs* the rebound. Lou *heaves* it out to P.J., who *streaks* down the side and *looks* for someone to pass to. I *am tearing* down the middle of the court; we have no time-outs left. P.J. *lofts* a pass up toward the rim, and I *leap* to meet it. Time *freezes:* my left hand *meets* the ball and *shifts* it onto the fingertips of my right hand; I *push* the ball softly against the glass as I *soar* on under the goal and the ball *settles* into the net. The horn *sounds* as the crowd *explodes* in thunderous approval of our victory.

The above passage not only is quite descriptive but also is a *narrative*—the "story" at the end of an exciting basketball game. Our point here is that description is not merely a matter of adjective use and that good descriptive writing can be achieved in a number of ways already familiar to you.

Descriptive Writing About a Person, Place, or Event: Brainstorming for a First Writing Assignment

When we write, "more?" at the end of each list, get your students involved in adding to the list by writing their additions on the board. Try to become comfortable using whatever classroom aids are available to you—the chalkboard, an overhead projector, or other equipment—that will enhance class discussion and participation. A teacher who

Let's brainstorm for a while about some descriptive writing possibilities. We will give you the beginnings of lists. Every time we do that, you need to see if you can add details to these lists. Add them yourself, or ask your teacher to put them on the board.

Possibilities for Writing About a Person

- A favorite grandparent, aunt, uncle, or other relative.
- Your best friend, your best teacher, your best neighbor.
- Your worst enemy, your worst teacher, your worst neighbor.
- More?

You do not necessarily have to limit yourself to someone you know personally. Is there someone whom you have never met but whose life you have studied? Someone you admire, such as the following:

- An athlete.
- A political or business leader.
- A medical researcher.
- An inventor.
- More?

If so, consider the ways that writing about such a person might be *different* from writing about someone you know personally.

Potential Details About People

- Physical details: height, weight, amount and color of hair, facial features, other distinguishing physical features.
- Mannerisms: typical gestures and other kinds of "body language," sound of voice, typical remarks, habits.
- Preferences: kinds of food, clothing, entertainment, hobbies, attitudes.
- Achievements: education, profession, awards, designs, certifications.
- More?

Possibilities for Writing About a Place

- A secret hideaway, a vacation spot, a fishing hole.
- A special room, building, or corner of your campus.
- A neighborhood or other part of a city or town.
- A favorite hangout.
- A nonexistent "ideal" place you'd like to be.
- More?

You're not limited to a special or ideal place. You may prefer to describe a perfectly awful place:

- The worst place you've ever been.
- The most dangerous place you've ever been (or ever seen).
- The dirtiest (or cleanest) place you've ever seen (or been in)
- More?

Potential Details About Places

- Physical details: where it is, how big (or small) it is, how it is physically shaped, what is on the premises.
- How many people are (or are not) there, and what the local customs or activities are.

merely stands (or, worse, sits) in one place the whole period is missing opportunities to be more dynamic and interesting. Though your role is not that of entertainer, you shouldn't hesitate to be entertaining when opportunities arise.

Extra discussion questions:

How is writing about what you *already* know different from writing about what you have to *learn?*

How does writing about what you've had to learn feel different?

How does your writing process change between these two different writing tasks? For example, is one task more open to discovery along the way than the other?

Which are you better at?

To spark better brainstorming about people whom students do not know personally, bring in some entries from *Who's Who in America* for additional ideas. Look especially at the italicized "personal philosophies" at the ends of some entries.

If you've flipped through some of the readings in this book, you've seen several examples of "place" topics for writing. You may want to assign one or two of these, such as David Quammen's "Deserts" (chapter 12), Garrison Keillor's "Lake Wobegon" (chapter 9), or Joseph Conrad's "Along the African Coast" (chapter 10), to help students see some of the possibilities in this kind of writing.

- What things look like there (comparisons/contrasts).
- More?

Possibilities for Writing About Events

- A first experience, such as the following:

  First date.

  First time to drive the family car.

  First significant athletic (or dramatic, musical, or artistic) achievement.

  First move away from home (perhaps to go to college).

  More?
- A "big game."
- A special concert or performance (either as witness or as performer).
- A misunderstanding with humorous (or tragic) consequences.
- A major embarrassment (or triumph).
- More?

Potential Details About Events

- Who was involved. (What people participated? How were they affected?)
- What was involved. (What happened, and with what result?)
- Where this event occurred. (Is the location of the event significant in some way? How?)
- When it occurred. (Is the time or timing of the event significant in some way? How?)
- Why it occurred. (What caused the event or its effects?)
- More?

Doubtless you can add to these brainstorming lists; feel free to do so, for in such brainstorming lies a crucial part of your writing process: the ability to "invent," or generate material about which to write.

The Assignment: Descriptive Writing About a Person, Place, or Event

Once you have brainstormed possibilities for your first paper, select the particular person, place, or event about which you want to write. You may choose the subject about which you were able to generate the most information or material, or you may choose a subject about which you generated less information but are still the most interested. In either case, don't worry: you are likely to think of more to write once you get under way. "Invention" can take place at just about any time during the composing process. The important thing is to choose, and to get started.

For this assignment, consider that you are writing strictly as *yourself.* Your reasons for writing are not to argue a point or present a critique but to inform by

You may recognize the "journalist's questions" in these questions about events, that is, *who, what, where, when, why,* and *how.* Beginning journalists are taught as reporters to find answers to these questions in gathering information for writing a news story.

Regarding brainstorming, emphasize not so much the content of the lists as the brainstorming experience itself: this is what writing about things you have to *learn* about (rather than things you already know about) feels like. Many of your students may not be aware of having experience in thinking this way.

You may well want to monitor students' choices of subject for this assignment, either in individual conferences or by simply going around the room and asking each one.

In these papers, try to get a *personal* tone from your students. They need to feel that they "own" their writing, and starting with a personal tone invites that ownership.

Note that as your students work their way through the stages of this assignment, each step contains the directions for the next stage of the assignment. If you wish to assign other matters, you'll have to add those separately. We advise you not

describing. Your readers are your classmates. You hope too that you can also entertain them with your description and share some of your experience with them.

to give students much more than what this assignment calls for, as it is important for them to ease into the class.

Writers' Circle

Proceed as a class through the following steps in the next few days:

1. Select your topic for a descriptive paper—a person, place, or event—and prepare a complete, double-spaced first draft (use an outline if you wish). Bring this draft to the next class meeting.
2. At the next class meeting, divide into groups of three students each and read and respond to one another's drafts. For this first group session, talk among yourselves in response to the following questions and any other questions you wish to raise (the teacher will be available to consult with each group):
   a. Is the paper primarily descriptive? (Did you develop mental pictures as you read?)
   b. What do you think is the *best* description?
   c. What do you think is the *weakest* description?
   d. Could you read smoothly throughout, without confusion? In the spirit of helpful cooperation, note any spots where you had trouble understanding:
      (1) What was the writer trying to say?
      (2) What changes would make the writer's meaning clear?
   e. Does anything seem left out? If so, what?
   f. Do you think the paper fulfills the assignment? (Is the writer informing, entertaining, and sharing his or her experience via this description?)

   Take your drafts home and revise them in accordance with today's group discussions and suggestions. Bring the revised draft to the next class meeting.
3. At the next class, reassemble the original groups. Again read one another's drafts closely within each group, and talk among yourselves in response to the following questions about each draft:
   - What improvements do you see in comparison with the previous draft?
   - Do you see any sentences or groups of sentences that seem too short? Can some of these be combined into fewer, longer sentences?
   - Do you see any sentences that are so long you can't read smoothly through them without confusion? How can these sentences be fixed? Can they be shortened? broken into two sentences?
   - Do you see any sentences that contain needless repetition of information?

Get *involved* in this group work—move around the room, sitting in on each group's proceedings and helping to answer questions that arise. Try to help students become comfortable with the group and with you.

Stress that the quality of each group member's work reflects on the group as a whole: everyone needs to contribute.

You may want to have some (quiet) reading aloud go on here. Though it takes more time, some teachers find it much easier to get the groups to work well if the writer reads while other group members follow along on their own copies.

Remember: this early in the term, the *process* is more important than the product. Which aspect are your own comments and attitudes emphasizing? If you are a beginning teacher or are fairly new to teaching about process, it's easy to fall back on habits that may be OK for you but less helpful for your students.

- Do you see any sentences containing redundancies (internal repetitions, such as "fellow co-worker" or "blue in color")?
- Do you see any sentences containing unclear pronouns?
- Do you see any sentences containing confusing modifiers (for example, dangling modifiers, as in "Hanging from a tree I saw a monkey")?
- Do you see any sentence fragments that do not seem to work well as stylistic devices?
- Do you see any words that don't seem to fit well, that could be replaced with a more appropriate word or phrase?
- Can you read smoothly from one sentence to the next, and from one paragraph to the next, without having to go back, reread, or puzzle out connections? (Any spots still giving you trouble should be discussed: how can the problem be fixed?)

Slightly modified, the questions given in steps 1–4 of this assignment make a universal guide students can follow in working their papers through drafts, group responses, and the rest of their writing processes throughout the term.

4. Take your draft home and revise it again, in compliance with today's reactions and suggestions. Prepare the best, most error-free version you can, and then *proofread* it closely, using these three strategies:
   - Read the last sentence, then the next-to-last sentence, then the next-to-next-to-last sentence, and so on, back to the first sentence. Such reading shifts the focus to each sentence and you are more likely to spot errors.
   - Note each mark of punctuation you used; you should be able to give a reason for each one. Check chapter 30 (in the hardcover edition) or in another good handbook to find the answers to any punctuation questions you have.
   - Check the spelling or usage of any word about which you are uncertain. This is what dictionaries are for.

   If proofreading yields very many errors, recopy the paper carefully (if you hurry, you may make new errors). If you find just a few errors, make neat corrections in ink. Now you are ready to hand in your first paper at the next class meeting.

Mention how easy this recopying gets with word processors. (See also chapter 28—available in the hardcover edition of the text.)

Chapter 28 (in the text's hardcover edition) gives another look at how writing happens. You may want to assign parts of that chapter here, or perhaps just the section on "Myths, Mistakes, Traps, and Time Wasters."

5. Now read the rest of this chapter, which describes how a student handled the above assignment. As you read, keep a record of how your experience was the same as or different from his. When you bring your finished paper to class, be prepared to discuss your observations.

A Student Writer Writes: An Ideal Scenario

The Assignment

John Ross, a student in a first-semester freshman composition class at the largest university in his home state, was given a writing assignment on just the second day of class. "Read chapter 1 and to page 14 of chapter 2 in the textbook," said the teacher; "then write a descriptive paper about a person, place, or event. Make your paper about four or five double-spaced pages long, write it for your classmates as readers, and bring it to the next class." Many students groaned. They'd heard about "freshman English" at the university, and already they were getting a heavy dose. "Don't worry," said the teacher, in response to their chagrin. "What you bring to class will be just your first draft. I won't be grading it. Be sure you bring a complete paper, though—one you consider finished."

Ask your students what *they* heard about freshman composition—you might get some lively responses.

The teacher then started listing possible topics on the board:

- Person: a favorite grandparent or other relative, a friend, a teacher ("But not me," the teacher wrote), a neighbor
- Place: a secret hideout, a favorite vacation spot, a particular neighborhood in a city, a town, a hangout
- Event: a "big game," a concert, a first date or a first drive, moving away to college, an outstanding performance (given or seen)

We can't recommend that you allow your students to write any papers describing you or your class. Although you may think that your sense of humor and proportion are good and that you are capable of handling such things with aplomb, we'd bet you'd be wrong. Why invite possible discomfort when there's so much else to write about? (Anonymous feedback via early or midterm evaluation forms, on the other hand, can be very useful.)

The teacher then called on students to add suggestions in each category. The lists kept getting longer, and finally the teacher said that everyone seemed to have the general idea. The teacher then began talking about descriptive writing, asking students what they would expect to find when reading descriptive writing.

John and his classmates agreed that description is a basic kind of writing that might appear in a wide range of papers. As the teacher and the class discussed examples, John remembered that he had often written descriptively while at Randle County High School in his hometown, Alhambra. He had described the new band uniforms in an article in the *Clarion*, the school paper. And in English class he had once written a description of one week's summer camping in Montana's Glacier National Park. For a moment he thought perhaps he'd write about that camping experience again for this assignment, but then he realized doing so would make his paper too long. The paper had been more than ten typed pages long when he wrote it the first time, and his teacher then had said it needed cutting. No, that wouldn't do for this project.

Ask your students what kinds of things they wrote about in high school and how they felt about them. What can they bring with them from that experience to enrich this one?

When John left class he went to his dormitory room to read chapter 1 and the first fourteen pages of chapter 2 in his textbook. He knew it would be quiet back in the room, for his roommate was in a long lab class that afternoon. Chapter 1 dealt with stages of the writing process, and much of what was in chapter 2 echoed what the teacher had already said; however, there were more suggestions for writing and more emphasis on what good descriptive writing consists of.

When he finished the reading, John hauled out a legal pad and a black-ink ballpoint—his preferred writing tools. Allan, his roommate, had a personal computer with a word processing program and had offered to show John how to use it. That was fine, for later. Right now, John just wanted to jot down some ideas for his paper before Allan came back.

Ask your students how many of them own or use word processors. Encourage them to talk about their use of this technology so that others who may be apprehensive about using such equipment can begin to feel more comfortable with it.

At first John thought about a person he might want to write about. He was especially fond of his Granddad Dooley Ross, who had been a pitcher for the Oakland Athletics professional baseball team. Granddad Ross told many great stories about his playing days in the minor leagues. He also showed John how to pitch. Yet there was much, much more to Granddad Ross than baseball. He was very patient—John remembered when Granddad taught him how to drive a standard-transmission automobile in the vacant high school parking lot back in Alhambra. Over and over, John killed the engine or made the car buck, sputter, and jerk; he thought he'd never learn how to let out the clutch and accelerate smoothly. But Granddad stayed with him, kept him practicing, until driving a stick shift was a snap. Yes, Granddad Ross was a definite prospect for a descriptive paper about a person.

In the same vein, John wrote down the names of other people who might make good subjects. There were people who could be described not only physically but also in terms of personality and mannerisms. There were several people back in Alhambra who might make good subjects. John was, for example, especially fond of Grace Sykes, who operated the restaurant. But although such people were interesting to John, he couldn't be sure they would be interesting to others.

Small-town America has been richly represented in such writings as Larry McMurtry's *The Last Picture Show,* Harper Lee's *To Kill a Mockingbird,* Garrison Keillor's *Lake Wobegon Days,* and Olive Ann Burns's *Cold Sassy Tree.* You might want to bring in excerpts from such works to show how John Ross is "inventing" his details fruitfully. Keillor's excerpt appears in chapter 9.

Work with your city-bred students to list comparable places—the mall, the museum, the park, and so on. This way they too can see that writing about such community details is not limited to their more rural classmates.

John then started jotting down places he might write about. Automatically, almost before thinking about it, he wrote, "Alhambra." Sure, that was a real possibility. He looked over his notes from class and saw that the teacher had suggested a town or a particular neighborhood in a city. The word *city* seemed hardly appropriate for Alhambra; in fact, Alhambra didn't qualify too much as a *town.* But *neighborhood* seemed an excellent word to describe, or begin to describe, Alhambra. John could envision the main street, only recently resurfaced, with its one stoplight, which worked only some of the time. Until recently he had lived a block away from that main street his entire life. John jotted down some other ideas for "place" papers: Granddad Ross's farm, the swimming area at the lake, the Randle County High School baseball field (with the short left field because of the railroad tracks), and the museum at Randle City, the county seat.

By the time John was ready to jot down ideas for events—the time last year when he and three friends came to the university for a football weekend, the graduation events at Randle County High—Allan came into the dorm room, brimming with tales about his lab instructor. John decided it was time for a break. It had been a productive afternoon.

The Writing

The next day, John's freshman composition class didn't meet but his morning was filled with other classes. Luckily, he didn't have any upcoming exams and was able to finish the assigned reading for his other classes shortly after lunch. It was a nice day, but it was time to work on the descriptive paper if John intended to join Allan and others in the dorm to watch that night's World Series game.

John looked at his jottings about possible topics; Granddad Ross and Alhambra seemed to him the best options. Which one could he do a reasonably good job of finishing by game time? John decided that describing Granddad Ross would take more time because of his rich personality and varied background. There were just too many things he could say about Granddad, and choosing among them would be hard. Alhambra, on the other hand, could primarily be described physically: what it looks like, where things are. John knew he would be able to draw on plenty of details about Alhambra to fulfill the length requirement.

He began to list things he could tell about Alhambra:

1. How small it is
2. Where it is
3. How to get there
4. Main Street
5. Randle County High School (here, John realized he could describe even more: the building, the athletic fields, the tennis courts, and so on)

John looked back at his list. At "Main Street" he realized he could describe the homes and businesses on either side, and he could also mention the stoplight. He could also mention how the old Estevez mansion stood, a historical landmark at the north end of Main. The Estevez story could be told, in fact; it was how the town got its name. John also thought about Dennitt's General Store and the adjacent Chat 'n' Chew Café—the other two businesses in the village besides the Minute Market.

When you go over your students' papers with them, have them bring in their discarded ideas as well. These ideas serve as a nice double check on their process work and are a possible resource for revisions.

John knew there would be plenty of detail. The thing to do, he decided, was begin writing. After going down the hall to get a can of soda, he returned to the room, seated himself at his desk, tore his notes from his legal pad, grabbed a black-ink ballpoint, and wrote a title at the top of the fresh blank page of his legal pad: Alhambra. He then began a sentence: "Alhambra is a small town." He thought a moment. Then he wrote, "Alhambra is a very small town." Crossing out the first sentence, he then continued, "It is located in the center of the state." Then he paused again, realizing he had plenty of *details* he could use but no plan for *organizing* them. He returned to his list. When he saw item 4, "Main Street," again, he had an idea: why not describe the town from the south to the north end of Main Street? That would give him a logical organization. Thus, John began his first draft. He finished about two and a half hours later.

John Ross gets a can of soda before he writes. Ask your students what little rituals *they* usually perform before writing.

He then read back over the draft carefully and made a few changes, adding a bit of detail here and there, trying to make it as polished as he could. Following is part of what he had, with misspellings and other minor surface errors already corrected:

For how long do your students write in one sitting—thirty minutes? three hours? Ask each one how long his or her own most productive period of work lasts.

Alhambra

1 Alhambra is a very small town. It is in the center of the state on Highway 5, eleven miles north of the Highway 5 exit on Interstate 20. Alhambra got its name from a plantation owner in the last century. A Spanish man named Estevez built a mansion there that he called Alhambra, which was the name of a famous castle in Spain. The Estevez

family no longer lives in the area, but the mansion is still there where Main Street (Highway 5) turns east and leads to open country. It is owned and maintained by the Randle County Historical Society, and designated as a state historical landmark. Visitors can take a tour of the mansion, but not many do.

Main Street in Alhambra is three blocks long. From south to north, the first block has homes and one business, the Minute Market, which sits on the corner by the town's one stoplight. The Minute Market sells you-pump gas, oil, drinks, and groceries. The stoplight often doesn't work. You don't have to worry about the police, though, because there aren't any. The next block has the town's other two businesses on the left side, the Chat 'n' Chew Café and Dennitt's General Store, and more homes on the right side. The last block has Randle County High School on the right side, more homes on the left side, and the Alhambra mansion by the curve in the road. Just past the mansion, also on the left side, is an abandoned building that was once the town's full-service gas station. 2

John felt he had a good descriptive paper. He had enjoyed writing about the little town he grew up in, and he thought he had made the paper interesting enough for his classmates and his teacher. He watched the World Series game that night feeling pretty satisfied, even though his favored team lost. Bad pitching. Dooley Ross probably could have shown them a thing or two.

Back in Class

In class, the teacher divided the twenty-one students into seven groups of three each. In each group, each student was to read the other two students' drafts, and respond according to a checklist of items the teacher put up on the board. Among questions on the checklist were these:

Is the paper descriptive?

What are the strongest and weakest descriptions?

Could you read smoothly throughout?

Does anything seem left out? If so, what?

Et cetera (see the checklist in "Writers' Circle" or your teacher's checklist).

You may well want to come up with a customized peer-revision checklist for each assignment you give, adapted from steps 1–4 at the beginning of this chapter or from our Starter Kit.

John had to admit that some of those questions were tough. The other two students in his group, Eric and Bridget, both said that they liked John's paper and found it very descriptive but—to John's surprise—had had trouble clearly understanding several passages. "You say visitors can take a tour of the mansion," said

Bridget. "Who visits the town, anyway? Why would they visit? Is the mansion a tourist attraction?" Before John could answer, Eric said, "No, it can't be a tourist attraction, because John says very few people take the tour. If it was a tourist attraction, several people would come there to see it." John thought. In truth, the mansion was open for tours every day, all given by Mr. Sykes, the retired man who'd been the "tour guide" for years. But most days he didn't give any tours at all. There was a sign down by the interstate, but it was hard to tell whether it really attracted people. He could see that he might need to add some more about the mansion—or leave out the business of the tours.

Because there was a high school in Alhambra, Eric wanted to know if there was also a grade school. "Well, yes," said John. "It's in the block off Main Street, just down from the stoplight intersection. I went to school there too." John realized that if he was going to say he grew up in Alhambra and was a graduate of the schools there, it might not be enough just to describe Main Street. And besides, there were actually a few side streets branching off Main, one also having the town's only church.

Near the end of class, the teacher dissolved the groups and told everyone that the assignment now was to revise the drafts in light of the day's discussions. John had plenty he needed to work with and was grateful the teacher hadn't taken the drafts up for grading.

Ask students to describe the comments made in *their* groups—mostly negative? or mostly positive? Talk about examples of each kind and about how any group's members need to deal with one another in order for that group to work effectively.

More Writing

Later that day, back in his dorm room, John began revising. He clarified his points about the visitors to the mansion, and he accounted for both the grade school and the church, adding in each case useful detail, particularly about the church. Here is more of what he added or revised, again with minor surface errors already repaired:

1 The Chat 'n' Chew Café is owned and operated by Grace Sykes. Her father leads the rare tours at the mansion. Grace has had the café for many years and hasn't changed the menu very much. Recently, a man and a woman who were passing through stopped for lunch at the Chat 'n' Chew. When they were finished, the man tried to pay for the meal with a credit card. Grace told him she couldn't take the card. That she wouldn't know what to do with it. The man then tried to pay with a hundred-dollar bill. Grace couldn't take that either, because she couldn't make change for it. The man was getting a little angry. How did Grace expect him to pay? The man was amazed when Grace suggested a personal check. Grace didn't even care that the man was from out of state. After the man left, Grace told a regular customer that she figured anybody who tried to pay with a credit card and a hundred-dollar bill

> was probably good for a check. And if he wasn't, then Grace was out only a couple of hamburgers.
>
> 2
>
> Alhambra is that kind of little place. People are honest and expect other people to be honest too. Of course, being small has some disadvantages. Like everybody knowing everybody else and sometimes minding everybody else's business. At the local church, which is just a half-block off Main Street, the minister notes not only who is in attendance but who is not. He is likely to ask a present family member about a family member who is absent. When Travis Monroe bought a new car over in Randle City, half of Alhambra could tell you what he paid for it. The other half could tell you that the figure you heard was wrong.

John had added details and believed he had an even better draft of his paper. He was ready to take it back to class.

Some teachers like to have students turn in *all* their drafts with each assignment—with the first one on the bottom and the "final" one on the top. This practice means you have a lot of paper to shuffle, but it does let you see at least artifacts of your students' processes.

The Next Class

The teacher told the original seven groups to reassemble and to reread one another's drafts. This time the teacher put a new checklist of questions on the board, among them the following:

> Do you see any sentences or groups of sentences that seem too short? Can some of these be combined into fewer, longer sentences?
>
> Do you see any sentences that are so long you can't read smoothly through them without confusion? How can these sentences be fixed? Can they be shortened? Can they be broken into two sentences?
>
> Do you see any sentences that contain needless repetition of information?
>
> Et cetera (see checklist.)

This may be "pickier" than you want to get on a first assignment. There is a limit to how much you can productively ask students to focus on at any one time. Different teachers and different classes have different limits. Our advice is to soft-pedal these last steps in the early going.

Many of the students felt overwhelmed. There seemed to be so many things to look for, so many ways a writer could make a mistake. Again the teacher said not to worry, that the group members weren't looking so much for mistakes as for ways to help one another. The questions would be used over and over during the semester; gradually students would become more familiar with them and with what they referred to. Still, John was surprised that Bridget and Eric found so much to respond to in his draft.

Bridget, who hadn't said much about the introduction the first day, now noticed that the first two sentences could be smoothly combined. Thus,

> Alhambra is a very small town. It is in the center of the state on Highway 5, eleven miles north of the Highway 5 exit on Interstate 20.

became

> Alhambra is a very small town on Highway 5 in the center of the state, eleven miles north of the Highway 5 exit on Interstate 20.

Yes, John had to admit, that was a definite improvement. Bridget noted some other, similar combination possibilities, and soon Eric and John were noticing them too.

Eric really liked the story about Grace Sykes and the Chat 'n' Chew customer but wasn't sure the fragment about Grace's refusal of the credit card—"That she wouldn't know what to do with it"—worked very well. "It makes Grace sound like she doesn't even know what a credit card is," said Eric. "I agree," said Bridget, "and I'm not sure that the sentence just before it is clear either. Does it mean that Grace couldn't accept that particular credit card or that Grace doesn't accept *any* credit cards?"

John looked at the sentences:

> Grace told him she couldn't take the card. That she wouldn't know what to do with it.

He had to admit that a reader, at least initially, might think Grace didn't accept that certain kind of card, or, worse, that Grace had never seen a credit card. "I don't want to make Grace sound ignorant, because she's not," John said.

"That's right," said Eric. "You can tell that by the way she explained that she wasn't worried about the check. But what if you had them talking in that passage, you know, what do they call it—?"

"Dialogue," Bridget joined in. "That would make the whole passage better, I think." John didn't quite see what they meant. "Have Grace speak," Bridget explained. "She can say to the customer, 'I'm sorry, I don't take credit cards.' And when the man offers the big bill, Grace can say, 'I'm sorry, I can't make change for that either."' John now saw how he could revise the passage, and he agreed it would be better that way.

The session continued. Eric thought John's paragraph beginning "Alhambra is that kind of little place" shouldn't begin with that statement. He thought that statement and the one immediately after it ("People are honest and expect other people to be honest too") really belonged with the preceding paragraph, which tells the story of Grace Sykes and the café customer. John realized he was going to have to write the paper yet again to incorporate the improvements coming out of this exchange.

Near the end of class, the teacher again dissolved the groups and then distributed a mimeographed checklist of three strategies for proofreading. "Go write your papers again," said the teacher. "Revise them in accordance with what you discussed in your groups today, and write them very carefully. When you have finished, take a break; then come back to them with rested eyes and proofread them, following the proofreading strategies I'm giving you. After you've proofread

Trace your groups' effectiveness: are they becoming *more* productive as they get used to working together, or *less* so? If the answer is less, you need to intervene. Try shuffling group membership or meeting separately with each group, to get group members working together better.

Your students may think it's not OK to write dialogue—or to use the first person, contractions, the present tense, active voice, and so on. Better let them know . . . is it? Our own philosophy on such matters is liberal: we allow what seems *appropriate* for the kind of writing it is and the kind of readership it is for (see Trimble, especially chapter 9).

as carefully as you can, making any needed corrections neatly in ink, hand them in at the next class meeting."

Everyone seems to have his or her own favorite strategy for proofreading; why not teach your students yours? Then bring in a couple of pages of your own writing for students to proofread.

Yet More Writing

John looked at the checklist the teacher had given him. It advised him to read his paper backward—not word by word, which would be gibberish, but sentence by sentence. That method, the checklist explained, would force close focus on each individual sentence apart from its relationship to other sentences and would thus increase the likelihood that an error would be spotted. The list also advised John to give a reason for every mark of punctuation used in each sentence and to look up in his handbook any situations for which he was unsure of the reason or of whether or not punctuation of some kind was needed. In short, the need for a new revision and the need to apply the proofreading checklist meant more work for John. Though he had written quite a bit in high school and his teachers had been very helpful then, he had never before done much rewriting, and never before had classmates been quite so observant and helpful as Bridget and Eric.

The Upshot

John followed the procedure outlined by his teacher to the best of his ability and at the next class meeting handed in the descriptive paper about Alhambra. (He also resolved, as his roommate encouraged him to do, to learn how to use the word processor so that in the future all this revising and rewriting wouldn't be so time-consuming—or, rather, so that the time he spent on those activities could be devoted more to thinking and creating and less to black marks on pages.)

That day in class was spent discussing some of the questions students had about the items on the various checklists the teacher had used. It was time to start becoming more familiar with those checklists and why the questions they set forth had to be constantly asked. At the next class meeting, the teacher returned the papers, thoroughly marked, with questions and suggestions—and *grades.* All students were invited to come for a conference with the teacher; students with low grades were required to do so. Some students were already planning to revise their papers further. John was a little disappointed, not in his grade—which was good—but in some of the things the teacher had written: it seemed that plenty of things could still have been done to improve the paper. Nevertheless, he knew that all his work and the help of the teacher and his classmates had paid off; he never would have done as well otherwise.

You may want to withhold grades on your first assignment and to write only descriptive comments instead. But we urge you to *respond* to the writing your students do, whether or not you put a grade on this paper. Expect your students to *want* a grade; they're conditioned for it. In such cases, give them a *tentative* grade, based on the paper as it is *now*—not as it might be later—and try not to be discouraging in any way.

Here is John's paper, revised and polished yet again after it was graded.

Alhambra

Alhambra is a very small town on Highway 5 in the center of the 1
state, eleven miles north of the Highway 5 exit on Interstate 20. This
Randle County village was my home until very recently. It gets its name

from a plantation owner in the last century, a Spanish man named Estevez who built a mansion there that he called Alhambra, after a famous castle in his native land. The Estevez family no longer lives in the area, but the mansion is still there by the north end of Main Street, which curves in front of the mansion toward the east and the open countryside. The mansion is owned and maintained by the Randle County Historical Society and is designated as a state historical landmark. A retired man, Mr. Gene Sykes, is there each weekday to give tours to those who stop for one--but few people do, because not many venture north from the interstate to have a look, even though a sign down there invites them to and makes it clear that the tour is free.

2 Highway 5 is Main Street in Alhambra, and it is three blocks long. If you drive from the south to the north on Main, you'll see that the first block has homes on both sides, and one business, the Minute Market, rests on the right (east), at the first-block intersection. The Minute Market sells self-service gas, oil, cold drinks, snacks, and groceries. The village's only traffic light hangs above this first intersection. The light has become something of a local joke; half the time it doesn't work. It, like the unusually low twenty-five-mile-per-hour speed limit throughout town, was originally intended as a "fund-raiser" for the community; the local police officer, Reese McNabb, would catch speeders or those who ran the light and fine them. Now it doesn't matter much, because Reese moved to Charlotte better than two years ago and no replacement was hired. The serious crime rate of Alhambra hovers at zero.

3 The next block has the town's other two businesses on the left (west) side, the Chat 'n' Chew Café and Dennitt's General Store, and more homes on the right side. The Chat 'n' Chew is owned and operated by Grace Sykes, whose father leads the rare tours of the mansion. Grace has had the café for many years and hasn't changed the menu much. Recently, a man and a woman who were passing through stopped for lunch at the Chat 'n' Chew. When they were finished, the man tried to pay with a credit card. "I'm sorry sir, I don't take cards," said Grace.

4 "That's all right," the man responded. "I'll just pay cash." He then offered Grace a one-hundred-dollar bill. Grace just shrugged.

5 "I'm sorry, I can't make change for that either, and I don't know how I could get change for it." (The nearest bank is in Randle City, the county seat.)

The man got one of those what-kind-of-hick-joint-is-this looks on his face. "Just how can I pay you, then?" asked the exasperated customer. 6

"Well, can you write me a personal check?" asked Grace, to the utter amazement of the man and woman both, who were not only strangers but from out of state. The man wrote Grace a check and showed her numerous items of identification while thanking her over and over again. 7

After the couple left, a regular customer ventured the opinion that the check might not be any good. "Heck," said Grace, "I figure any man who tries to pay with a credit card and a hundred-dollar bill is probably going to be good for a personal check for $5.28. And if he isn't, well, it isn't costing me more than a couple of hamburgers." Alhambra is that kind of place--people like Grace Sykes are honest, and they expect other people to be honest too. Small towns have certain advantages. 8

Of course, there are some disadvantages too. The nearest bank, medical doctor, auto repair shop, and clothing store are all several miles away. What some consider neighborliness is really nosiness; in Alhambra everyone knows everyone else's business, and sometimes minds everyone else's business. At the local church, for example, which is just a half-block off Main Street and across the way from my parents' home, the minister notes not only who is in attendance but also who is not. He is likely to ask a present family member about a family member who is absent. When my cousin Travis Monroe bought a new car over in Randle City, half of Alhambra told me what he paid for it, and the other half told me that the figure I heard was wrong. 9

The last block on Alhambra's Main Street is lined by homes on the left side, ending with the mansion by the curve, and by Randle County High School on the right side. I am a graduate of both this high school and the elementary school that is one block off Main Street, behind the Chat 'n' Chew. I'm told that years ago Alhambra was in a battle with Randle City over which town would be the county seat. Randle City got the courthouse, and Alhambra got the county high school. After that, Randle City seemed to get almost everything else too. If the long-unoccupied mansion isn't enough proof of that, then the very last building on the left adds the finishing touches: abandoned now for nearly ten years, this was once the town's only full-service gas station. 10

Young people now come to Alhambra mostly in school buses. When the buses leave at the end of the school day, only a few youngsters, 11 including my little brother, remain to watch the athletes or the band practice. Later buses will take even the athletes and the band members away, and my brother and perhaps four or five others will walk to their nearby homes. But Alhambra isn't really all that isolated. Nearly every house has either a very high television antenna or a satellite dish. In a few minutes a car can take you to Interstate 20, and then in an hour or two the same car can take you to cities and universities that lie along that interstate. I doubt if I will ever live in Alhambra again. But it will always be home. And Grace Sykes will always take my check.

Remember that after you read these last pages of the chapter and turn in your own paper, your teacher will expect you to be ready to discuss how your experience of writing was similar to or different from John's.

After this assignment has been completed, spend some class time discussing your students' experience with this assignment compared with that of John Ross. What was similar? What was different? What did your students learn about their own writing processes?

WRITING ASSIGNMENT

Today there are many popular schemes that attempt to characterize how people think, feel, and behave. And most of these schemes have something to say about how this or that "type" of person handles creativity (a key element in chapter 2's subject, "Getting Started").

Consider the drawing on page 15. One popular scheme has it that there are "right-brained" and "left-brained" people. According to this idea, the right hemisphere of one's brain controls artistic ability and spatial perception, while the left controls speech, language, and calculation. Since everyone has one dominant side, we say that strong creative people are "right-brained," and strong computational people are "left-brained." Thus in this illustration, the ruler is on the left and the drawing instruments are on the right. This notion of "hemispherity" is often used to explain why one person excels, say, in artistic creation, while another's creativity is expressed, say, in computational fields.

Nearly all of the popular "hemispherity" articles ignore the many *millions* of connections between the brain's two sides, and the brain's several *layers,* and the *redundancy* of the brain's architecture (human brains seem able to do the same piece of thinking in many different brain sites). In that sense "hemispherity" is more true as a *metaphor* for a certain way people speak and act than as a physiological fact.

Other similar schemes abound today: Meyers-Briggs Type Indicator, Cognitive Styles, "male" and "female," and the Perry scheme, to name just a few. Chances are you have been "typed" by one of these schemes, and you may even account for some of your behavior by that typing.

We invite you to write up a description of your "type" of person, with particular attention to how such a "type" deals with creativity, especially the kind required for a writer who is "Getting Started." You may already know your "type" according to one or another of the schemes mentioned above (or some other, equally popular scheme). Or, with your teacher's permission, you may want to make up a "type."

part two Purposes for Writing

PROFILE ♦ OF ♦ A ♦ WRITER

Ursula K. Le Guin wrote the following selection, "Theodora," in 1985 as the introduction to the Yolla Bolla Press edition of *The Inland Whale.* Written by Theodora Kroeber (Le Guin's mother), *The Inland Whale* retells Native American stories.

Ursula K. Le Guin

Some people lead several lives all at once; my mother lived several lives one at a time. Her names reflect this serial complexity: Theodora Covel Kracaw Brown Kroeber Quinn. The last four are the names of men: Kracaw her father's name (and the source of her lifelong nickname Krakie), Brown, Kroeber, and Quinn her three husbands. Covel is a family name on her mother's side, used as a girl's middle name for several generations. Her first name came from a novel her mother liked, *Theodora Goes Wild.* She was Theo to some, Dora to none.

See our biographical sketch on Ursula K. Le Guin (page 121).

The Inland Whale is famous as the first collection of stories about Native American women.

PART OUTLINE

Ask students, "Why do you suppose Le Guin chooses to quote this biographical sketch of her mother?"

The (auto)biographical note about the author on the jacket of the first edition of *The Inland Whale* reads in part:

> Theodora Kroeber was born in Denver and spent her early years in the mining camp of Telluride, Colorado. She earned a B.A. in psychology and economics and an M.A. in clinical (then called "abnormal") psychology at the University of California. Offered a position in a boys' reformatory, she got married instead and had three sons and a daughter. When the children were grown and raising their own families, she began to write. Part of the background for her writing comes from Indians, rivers, and deserts encountered while accompanying her husband, A. L. Kroeber, the noted anthropologist, on professional journeys and field trips.

The bit about the boys' reformatory is a characteristically graceful piece of legerdemain: Theodora took her master's degree in 1920 and married Clifton Brown that same year; three years later, with two baby sons, she was widowed; in 1925 she met Alfred Kroeber; they married, and in 1926 and 1929 her other two children were born. Where the boys' reformatory comes in this crowded decade I can't quite figure out. Although she wrote two biographies notable for their exhaustive research and scrupulous selection of fact, Theodora's native gift was for the brilliant shortcut that reveals an emotional or dramatic truth, the event turned legend—not raw fact, but cooked fact, fact made savory and digestible. She was a great cook both of foods and of words.

Ask students, "What would a 'cooked fact' be? Why is that an apt way of describing?"

The Inland Whale was written in the late 1950s, when, as she says, her children were off having children, and she and Alfred were enjoying the freedom of his long emeritus career, during which he taught at Harvard and Columbia and was a resident of various think tanks—well-traveled, unhurried, productive years. Work, writing, was pretty much like breathing to Alfred Kroeber; he just quietly did it all the time. With time and energy now to spare, Theodora soon found her own breath. First she wrote a couple of essays with Alfred (interesting pre-computer attempts at counting word frequency in poetry), then some children's stories (often a woman's way into literature—threatening to no one, including herself). Then a first novel. And then this book.

Le Guin makes exceptionally creative and appropriate use of comparison imagery here: "the kind of distillation that makes fine liquors, the kind of pressure that makes diamonds." The implicit comparison is that Theodora's finished prose was like fine liquor or diamonds. Encourage students to discuss why those comparisons are so apt.

I don't know the genesis of the book, but would guess that separate stories, which she had tried retelling for their own sake and the work's sake, began to make a whole, a shape in her mind. Perhaps she set out to write a book of stories about women, but I think it more likely that the pattern became apparent and the connections imperative as she worked and reworked and re-reworked the material—for she was a hard writer, a merciless reviser. The coherence of the book and the clarity of her prose are the result of the kind of distillation that makes fine liquors, the kind of pressure that makes diamonds. She strove for a vivid simplicity, but she was never artless.

People ask if she told stories like these to her children. She read to us, but it is her aunt Betsy and my father whose storytelling I remember. Only a few times do I recall her making the "breakthrough into performance," as Dell Hymes calls it.

Once when she was eighty or so, six or eight kids and grandkids at table, John Quinn presiding, one of us asked her about her experiences as a child of nine on a visit to San Francisco when the great earthquake of 1906 struck. All the storytelling power of her books got unleashed, and none of us will forget that hour. But usually it was conversational give-and-take that she wanted and created among family and friends. And one sees her valuation of written narrative as "higher" or more "finished" than oral—the conventional and almost universal judgment of her time both in literature and anthropology—in her notes to *The Inland Whale.*

Still, it is very like her to have chosen from all the stories of the peoples of California nine stories about women, at a time when even in anthropology the acts of women were easy to dismiss as secondary, women being subsumed (oddly enough) in Man. From her mother Phebe and other strong women of her late-frontier Western childhood, Theodora had a firm heritage of female independence and self-respect. Her sense of female solidarity was delicate and strong. She made her daughter feel a lifelong welcome, giving me the conviction that I had done the right thing in being born a woman—a gift many woman-children are denied. But also she would say that she "liked men better than women"; her temperament inclined her to the conventional supporting roles of wife and mother; and she detested the direct opposition of a woman's will to a man's. She must have thought her loving empire was endangered by feminism, for her intolerance of what she called "women's lib" went beyond her general distrust of ideologies. But all the same, in her life as a writer, I think she was a true feminist.

Look for Native American women in White literature before 1960: if you find any at all, you generally find something called a "squaw." There are no squaws in *The Inland Whale*—only human beings. This is not freedom from racist stereotyping only, but also freedom from masculinist prejudice, and a deliberate search for the feminine. Theodora kept telling me to write about women, not men, years before I (the "women's libber") was able to do so. She did so herself from the start, not only because the feminists of her mother's generation had freed us both, but also because she was true to her being, her perceptions, her female humanity. In all her different lives she was entirely woman.

The book was written and published, and *Ishi* was begun, while Alfred was alive. After his death came her life as widow, soon famous in her own right for her great book *Ishi;* and then a new life, and new directions in writing, as Mrs. John Quinn. She never wrote till she was over fifty and she never stopped writing till she died at eighty-three. I wish she had started earlier: we might have had more books from her; her novels might have found a publisher; and she wouldn't have had to wait for validation and self-confidence till a time in life when most artists are at ease with their craft and are getting the recognition they deserve. I know she regretted having started writing so late. But not bitterly. She wasn't a regretter, or a blamer. She kept going on, out of an old life, into a new one. So I imagine she goes now.

Ishi is the moving story of the last member of a tribe of now-extinct California Indians.

"She never wrote till she was over fifty and she never stopped writing till she died at eighty-three"—have students state what this sentence tells them about writing.

• • •

The noted feminist and American writer Ursula K. Le Guin (see page 121) wrote the preceding biographical sketch of her mother primarily to serve as an introduction to an edition of *The Inland Whale,* one of the books her mother had written in her lifetime. The main purpose of "Theodora," then, was to inform readers about who the author of *The Inland Whale* was. Certainly, it serves that purpose very well.

But if you read closely, you can detect other, lesser but still-important purposes: Le Guin *expresses* her own love, respect, and admiration for her mother, along with a sense of gratitude for her mother's influence. She *analyzes* aspects of her mother's life and writing, finding evidence to indicate the conclusion that her mother "lived several lives one at a time" and that "in all her different lives she was entirely woman." She *persuades* us that Theodora Covel Kracaw Brown Kroeber Quinn was an altogether interesting and remarkable person who "in her life as a writer . . . was a true feminist."

Such overlapping of writing purposes is common, as we will see in this part of the book. But as we will also see, one particular purpose will usually be more important than the other purposes in a given piece of writing—just as the informing purpose is most important in "Theodora."

One reason we like this approach is that *purpose* drives people through instances of writing the way other methods of dividing up writing (such as by identifiable structures) do not. Any textbook makes artificial divisions in its subject matter, and ours is no different; however, we believe our way of dividing is *productive* because it is purpose-driven.

Notice that identifying writing by its purposes is not tied directly to identifiable structures in the writing, such as comparison/contrast, illustration, and definition, often called "the modes."

One popular way of dividing writing up into "kinds"—the way that makes the most sense to us—uses the main purpose of each piece of writing as the criterion for determining what "kind" of piece it is. Thus we talk about writing to express (in which the primary purpose emphasizes the writer's need or desire to communicate), writing to explain or inform (in which the primary purpose emphasizes the reader's need or desire to understand the communication), writing to analyze (in which the primary purpose emphasizes the inner workings or logic of the subject itself), or writing to persuade (in which the primary purpose emphasizes the writer's need or desire to affect the reader's belief or actions). This scheme makes sense to us for three reasons:

1. All writing has a purpose—a reason for being written.
2. All writing tasks begin with the writer's sense of purpose.
3. This set of reasons for writing seems not to have changed much in the past two thousand years.

Here's what these reasons mean to us:

All writing has a purpose. This statement may be one of those "self-evident" truths—whenever you write, you're trying to persuade, to get some information where it needs to go, to record a feeling or an experience, or to figure something out. About the only writing that may *seem* not to have some such guiding purpose is the kind exemplified by certain professionally written, ceremonial speeches—as when the speaker seems to talk for an hour but to have nothing at all to say. What could be the reason for that kind of language? People who study such things argue convincingly that the purpose is merely to establish the speaker's presence, as if to say (between the lines), "I'm here; I care enough about you and this occasion to be here; I'm communicating in person with you (although I really have nothing beyond that to say)." The purpose of that kind of language, then, is like a dial tone's: all it does is show that the potential for a message exists, although no message is currently being sent. If even the worst ceremonial speeches can be said to have purpose, then it is indeed true that all writing has a purpose.

Another way to put this: as a writer, until you have a *purpose* for your writing, you really don't have anything.

All writing tasks begin with the writer's sense of purpose. Sometimes that purpose is pretty simple, something like, "I want to satisfy this teacher's requirements for this assignment—to make an A if I can." Or, "I want to prove that recombinant DNA research on human chromosomes should never be permitted, period." Sometimes the reason for writing starts out pretty vaguely defined (novelist Henry Miller called it a feeling of a "fine, light tension") and needs to be worked out during the act of writing, something like, "Somewhere in the back of my mind is an explanation for why this biological [or chemical, mathematical, sociological] process works the way it does. Maybe if I just begin by writing about what I know and then start pushing the limits of that knowledge, I can work that explanation out on paper as I write." And sometimes that sense of purpose is pretty complex, something like, "I want to argue to the board of regents that the research facilities at our state colleges are in desperate need of upgrading, but I want to do so without making it look like the people in charge haven't been doing their jobs." But whether the purpose is simple or complex, fully formed at the start or something that evolves gradually, no one writes without a reason.

The reason might be fun (a letter, a note to a friend), money (a job application letter, a proposal), duty (something required by your boss that you think is silly to have to write out but you're going to do it anyway), or knowledge (something you're writing down to try to help you figure it out). Many times we are aware of that reason; sometimes we're not (as when you just start writing on a subject and don't realize until you're halfway through the first draft exactly what it is you really want to say); and sometimes our reason for writing changes and evolves during our writing (as when you set out to prove one thing and wind up surprising yourself by proving something quite different). We may not be fully aware of it while we're writing, but there's always a reason for writing.

We believe you should stress the writing-as-discovery aspect for your students. Writing-as-discovery means, in essence, that we don't always know exactly what we want to say until we write it down; that is, we discover what we mean by way of the writing experience itself. This doesn't mean we have no idea beforehand of what we want to say; rather, it means we don't get it right until we put it down, or we don't get quite the wording we want until we've done some of the writing or rewriting. The novelist E. M. Forster had this aspect in mind when he said, "How do I know what I think until I see what I say?"

This set of reasons for writing seems not to have changed much in the past two thousand years. As far as we can tell, the earliest people in the Western tradition who studied language identified essentially the same purposes we use to organize chapters 4–7. That is, this set of purposes isn't just unique to the United States, to the 1990s, or to freshman composition classes; there's something about this set of purposes that makes it keep coming up again and again.

In chapters 4–7 of *The Heath Guide to College Writing,* we discuss writing as being of four different kinds according to its *purpose*—writing to express, to explain or inform, to analyze, and to persuade. People write for all kinds of reasons, but it seems to us that these four reasons are the main ones. Obviously, each includes a number of varieties.

Expressive Writing: Emphasis on the Writer

People often write to capture their own feelings and emotions, to reflect (or help create) their innermost selves. Their writing may take the form of personal journals, diaries, poems, essays, letters, plays, novels, songs, or short stories. Many people do this kind of writing—not just great novelists or playwrights or poets but the person in the apartment next door or your best friend from high school. Beyond that, there's also a powerful expressive component to *any* well-written essay, to any well-done report. That element of expressive purpose is your own *personal investment* in what you write, present even though it may not show up in so many words in your writing. When you write about something you strongly feel or believe, you're writing with a powerful expressive component. That expressive purpose may be overshadowed by other purposes that are informative or persuasive, but it contributes an important element of investment and conviction that is essential to the final piece's quality.

Students like to think (or pretend) it's untrue that many people (besides professional writers) keep diaries or journals or write poems and stories. It's probably true that most people don't do so consistently—but also true that most people do such writing at some time in their lives.

The expressive element in writing often comes across as the writer's commitment, or belief, in what he or she is writing about. Stress to students that this element of caring is important, even if the writing isn't primarily expressive. No one wants to do writing that nobody will care about, and no one wants to read such writing, either.

Explanatory or Informative Writing: Emphasis on the Reader's Need to Know

The basis of most writing done on the job is writing to explain or inform so that the reader will clearly understand, because it is important that the reader know, in order to perform a task, understand a procedure, or account for an action or a result. How can you make this computer work? Why has production in the Santa Monica plant fallen below projections, and what can we do to increase it? How did the increasingly affluent middle class in France play a key role in the French Revolution? The writing done in response to all these questions is explanatory/informative writing. It answers these questions:

- What is this and why is it important to know?
- How does this work and can I make it work?
- Why is something this way and does it have to be this way?

Sometimes this mix between explanatory and informative writing appears as a kind of writing by itself, as in writing for record-keeping purposes—notes you keep in a laboratory journal, records people keep of meetings, and so on. More often explanatory/informative writing appears mixed with persuasive writing ("Here's why the machine doesn't work, and here's what we should do about it"), analytical writing ("Here's the cause of the problem"), or both ("Here's the cause of the problem; here's why the machine doesn't work; and here's what we should do about it").

This mixing of purposes in writing is a basic point. You may want to emphasize it by bringing in some examples or by noting examples in this book's chapter 5.

Analytical Writing: Emphasis on the Subject Itself

Writing done to analyze something is one of the toughest and most important kinds of writing today. Unlike explanatory/informative writing, which emphasizes *reader* understanding, analytical writing emphasizes *the subject itself,* although it usually does so for informative, expressive, or persuasive reasons. Why does this idea not fit the facts? How does this chemical interact with other chemicals to store light? What are the human motives that affect the committing of a crime? Which of three possible bridge designs is the best? What is the prevailing theme of this film or that novel? In each case, the writing is analytical writing. Analytical writing usually combines with other kinds, such as informative and persuasive; it seldom stands as a purpose by itself. But if the writing mostly focuses on the subject itself and seeks to answer the question, How? or Why? then it's analytical writing.

Again, you may want either to bring in examples for class presentation or to look briefly at the analytical writings in chapter 6.

Persuasive Writing: Emphasis on the Reader's Belief

When you're writing to convince someone, obviously it's persuasive writing. Some people would say that all writing is persuasive writing; certainly most pieces of writing do contain a strong persuasive element. Even in the most bare-bones set of directions on how to assemble a bicycle, for example, there's a key sense in which the writing has to persuade the reader that this really is the way to do it. In such a situation, the persuasive element may clearly be less important than the informative one, but the persuasion is there nonetheless. Other times, the persuasion is the main element, as in TV commercials, many political speeches, and editorials. Most of the papers people associate with English classes are persuasive papers—one way or another, the assignment is to introduce and state a thesis (that is, a main point you are trying to make), to use facts or arguments to support that thesis, and to explain its significance. It is not too much of an exaggeration to say that *all* language has a strong persuasive element. The important thing to remember is that writing that is primarily persuasive seeks to have an effect on the reader's beliefs or actions.

In the last paragraph on this page, we note again that the key is the way purpose *keeps the writing going.* While it's true (as Parts Three and Four show) that a certain subject or the commitment to a certain pattern can help keep a writer writing, we see purpose as fundamental; that's why we discuss it first.

A Note on "Kinds" of Writing

With the possible exception of expressive writing, each of these "kinds" of writing probably appears more commonly in combination with others than by itself. Thus, in the examples to come you will see pieces that, while focusing on one purpose or another, also contain strong elements of other purposes. Our point in devoting a separate chapter to each kind of writing is to help you get a better feel for the way each kind—whether alone or in combination—can contribute to your own writing. As you work through the following chapters, remember that each chapter is designed to help you answer these questions: "What do I say? What do I say next? and next? and next?" In chapters 4–7, the answers always come from looking back at the *reason* you are writing. (In Part Three of this book, the answer to "What do I say next?" comes from *what* you're writing about, and in Part Four the answer comes from the *pattern* you're using.)

These last lines explain our book's structure, which proceeds according to different ways of answering the critical student question, "How do I know what to say next?" The answer can come from a reconsideration of *purpose* (Part Two), *subject* (Part Three), and *pattern* (Part Four), often in combination. Continuous reconsideration of these factors is the way to keep students' writing processes engaged and productive.

chapter 3

Introduction to Critical Writing

> "There are books of which the backs and covers are by far the best parts."
>
> Charles Dickens

Compared with the writing you did in high school, writing in college has some different qualities you need to know about. For one thing, there's likely to be more writing in college. For another, there's likely to be a greater variety of kinds of writing. Finally, your writing in college needs to have an important critical quality that your writing in high school may have lacked. Let's tackle these one at a time.

Get your students involved in talking about the kinds of writing experiences they had in high school. Ask them if any of their college classes require writing and, if so, what kinds.

The Quantity of College Writing

College requires lots of writing. Certainly you can expect to write in your English classes—but also in political science, biology, geology, engineering, art history, sociology, history, and so on. Right now you're probably in a freshman composition class in which you have to write at least every other week, eight or ten or twelve papers a semester. That's probably what you expected. What you may not have expected is the history paper about the role of the emerging middle class in the French Revolution. Or the biology paper on mass extinctions. Or the geology paper on shale strata. Or the petition to the dean's office to be allowed to count toward graduation credit a statistics course instead of the second semester of a calculus course. Or the letters to people who might hire you as a summer intern. Or the report you have to write when you come back from your co-op position. The point is that you're going to find that more and more of your success will depend on writing—in all your classes, and after you graduate too—and this fact will make your writing both different and more important than it may have been before.

Some of your students may tell you they have *no* writing assignments in their other classes. That often happens in freshman experience. Don't be daunted. Ask them to check the junior- and senior-level required-course descriptions for their majors. There, they are highly likely to find courses requiring writing in substantial ways.

The Diversity of College Writing

Make a list of the courses your students are taking *besides* yours. Which courses require writing? Which offer interesting possibilities for writing subjects for English papers (even if no writing is required in that particular class)? Inquire whether these courses are taught by graduate assistants or full faculty members. Ask your students how the difference in those two kinds of teachers might affect how the students write in those courses.

Along with the changes you may have to get used to in the *amount* of writing you have to do in college, you will also see the *diversity* of it. The preceding section pointed out the number of different fields you can expect to write in. What can't be done in this short space is to explain the ways—the *inside* ways—that writing in all those various fields needs to be different. The interplay of different fields and different kinds of assignments—different purposes, and more—that all these courses require presents problems for you as a writer that you may not have seen before. Some assignments (such as lab reports) may be relatively straightforward and similar to things you have written before. Other kinds of assignments—problem-solving reports, critical essays, briefs, design papers, case studies, to name just a few—require you as a writer to do things you may well never have done before.

The Critical Quality of College Writing

The critical quality we're talking about here includes *at least* these three characteristics:

We find this notion of the *critical quality* of college writing the most elusive difference between high school and college writing, but also perhaps the most important difference. You can open up this topic for productive discussion by having your students bring in samples of their high school writing.

1. Compared with writing that asks you only to locate information and then simply report it, college writing expects you to locate and report the information *and* evaluate it. Writing that explicitly involves thinking at that level we call critical writing. As points 2 and 3 below explain, there's even more to it. And as the chapters corresponding to this one at the beginnings of Parts Three and Four will show, critical writing also involves critical reading and critical thinking.
2. In college writing you will be expected to make judgments—to make not only evaluations but also recommendations. You deal with more than "What is the best way for us to understand this problem [issue, event]?"; you deal as well with "What should we *do* about it?"
3. In the writing you do in college you'll be expected to be both more thorough and more precise. You'll need to have more than one piece of evidence, to use more than one source, to look at things more than one way. This frequently unspoken need to be more thorough shows up as writing that takes a more mature perspective on its subjects, writing that often takes a more balanced look. The need to paint with a finer brush—for example, to define terms very exactly—also contributes to this tone of maturity.

Tell your students about the writing that *you* do; share with them how many of these listed "critical quality" characteristics it has.

Rather than present more generalizations about the critical quality of college writing, let's look at a piece of writing, one done by professionals for a popular magazine, that seems to us to show this quality. This piece appeared in the *Atlantic Monthly,* a magazine aimed at reasonably well-educated readers, most of whom are middle class socially and economically. Such readers are likely to have young children in school. We've abbreviated the original somewhat in order to be able to highlight its critical qualities; our accompanying comments, shown between the paragraphs in small type, explain the gist of what we've left out.

Again—and always—it's a good idea to bring in samples of college-level writing that show these various critical characteristics.

Why Children Don't Like to Read

Bruno Bettelheim and Karen Zelan

Bruno Bettelheim (1903–90) was a psychologist, educator, and author, whose books include On Learning to Read *(with Karen Zelan, 1982),* Symbolic Wounds *(1954), and* A Good Enough Parent *(1987). Karen Zelan, his coauthor on this piece, was at the time an associate of Bettelheim's at the University of Chicago's Orthogenic School. She has since received a doctorate in educational psychology.*

What sort of family life influences on their reading and academic habits can your students recall? Approach this area with sensitivity; some students may not be eager to talk about their home environments in *any* connection—not just with respect to attitudes about reading, language development, and academic skills or values.

Is any evidence offered for the authors' claim that the teacher's presentation is "the most important influence"? Why are we inclined to accept that assertion?

This assertion that "the longer it takes . . . to advance from decoding to meaningful reading, the more likely . . . that his pleasure in books will evaporate" may be the principal point here. Do your students agree with it? Ask them to suggest ways one might recognize this "advance" from decoding to meaningful reading when it occurs.

"To enjoy literature and benefit from what it has to offer" is the authors' definition of *literate*. Yet there are other definitions, including simply "the ability to read and write." See what other operative definitions of *literate* you and the class can think of. Once you have several definitions, examine with the class what these definitions have in common and in what (possibly critical) ways they are different.

Here the authors make effective use of an example.

A child's attitude toward reading is of such importance that, more often than not, it determines his scholastic fate. Moreover, his experience in learning to read may decide how he will feel about learning in general, and even about himself as a person. 1

Notice how the authors start by stating the issue and giving a clear indication of the issue's importance.

Family life has a good deal to do with the development of a child's ability to understand, to use, and to enjoy language. It strongly influences his impression of the value of reading, and his confidence in his intelligence and academic abilities. But regardless of what the child brings from home to school, the most important influence on his ability to read once he is in class is how his teacher presents reading and literature. If the teacher can make reading interesting and enjoyable, then the exertions required to learn how will seem worthwhile. 2

See how the authors point out that other issues may be involved in learning to read but by the end of the second paragraph have gotten to what will become the key issue: the way reading is taught in schools. There's a thoroughness here that connects to the critical quality we're talking about.

A child takes great pleasure in becoming able to read some words. But the excitement fades when the texts the child must read force him to reread the same word endlessly. Word recognition—"decoding" is the term used by educational theorists—deteriorates into empty rote learning when it does not lead directly to the reading of meaningful content. The longer it takes the child to advance from decoding to meaningful reading, the more likely it becomes that his pleasure in books will evaporate. A child's ability to read depends unquestionably on his learning pertinent skills. But he will not be interested in learning basic reading skills if he thinks he is expected to master them for their own sake. That is why so much depends on what the teacher, the school, and the textbooks emphasize. From the very beginning, the child must be convinced that skills are only a means to achieve a goal, and that the only goal of importance is that he become literate—that is, come to enjoy literature and benefit from what it has to offer. 3

Here we get a restatement of the issues indicated by the title and the first paragraph—what the problem is and why it is important—but this time the lines are drawn much more precisely. From here, the authors go on to present their evidence. Now we need to give only the first lines of each paragraph to show you how many different *kinds* of evidence they use.

A child who is made to read, "Nan had a pad. Nan had a tan pad. Dad ran. Dad ran to the pad," and worse nonsense can have no idea that books are worth the effort of learning to read. . . . 4

5 Benjamin S. Bloom, professor of education at the University of Chicago, has found that who will do well in school and who will do poorly is largely determined by the end of the third grade. . . .

Here the authors make effective use of the testimony of authority. Argument from authority is one of Aristotle's classical topics, or proofs, to be used in bolstering persuasion.

6 That rote learning is the wrong way to teach reading was recognized more than seventy years ago. In the first important treatise on the teaching of reading published in this country, *The Psychology and Pedagogy of Reading* (1908), the author, Edmund Burke Huey, urged that drills be kept separate from the activity of reading. . . .

7 For many decades, textbooks have been used as the basis for reading instruction by the vast majority of elementary school teachers, and they are much worse today than the ones Huey objected to. . . .

The authors again make effective use of authoritative testimony and also give it the extra rhetorical force of a historical example. "We've known this to be true since way back in 1908," the authors therefore seem to say, "and so we ought to believe it by now." This historical appeal is akin to argument from precedent, another of Aristotle's classical topics.

Notice how these paragraphs use observable facts and published authorities to support the authors' point. The next paragraphs cite the number of words all children acquire *before* learning to read as proof that children learn words because they enjoy it, the decline in SAT test scores as proof that "regard for the written word" is declining, research in the teaching of reading as proof that reduction in number of words in texts has no demonstrated positive effect on learning to read, and the fact that book publishers cannot risk controversy—cannot risk anything but the most bland writing—in the face of the need for mass adoption of texts. The essay concludes with six paragraphs about elementary school readers in Switzerland, books the authors find to be more intellectually challenging and more entertaining than those used in our schools. Here is the final paragraph of the piece.

Having established a historical example by referring to Huey's 1908 book, the authors add punch to the gravity of the current situation by saying that today's textbooks are much worse than the ones Huey objected to in 1908. This is a rhetorical effect Aristotle called argument a fortiori ("all the stronger"), which works like this: "If you think the textbooks Huey objected to were bad, you should see how much worse they are now." The technique compares two things, the second thing being "all the stronger" by means of a transfer of value from the first to the second.

8 These primers, used in the German-speaking parts of Switzerland, have a special lesson to teach American educators and publishers. It has been argued that our primers have to employ unnaturally simple words because many minority children speak a different language at home: Spanish, Chinese, "black English," and so on. But the language that *all* children growing up in the German parts of Switzerland speak—a dialect called *Schweizer Deutsch,* or Swiss German—is very different from the High German they must speak and read in school. Although during the first few months of school the children are allowed to speak to the teacher in their dialect, from the start they learn to read only the High German in which their primers are published. For some reason, Swiss children do not find this enforced bilingualism such a handicap that they fail to become able readers. We believe that their lack of difficulty is explained to a great extent by the fact that they like what they are given to read.

Notice that in this last part of the article—about the last page and a half of the original—there's a clear recommendation implied: follow the Swiss example—use challenging, entertaining books.

Compare the last paragraph to L'Engle, "On Controlled Vocabularies" in chapter 7.

How would you characterize this last piece of evidence? It is, in classical terms, an argument by extended analogy: if it works in Switzerland in a comparable situation, why wouldn't it work here? Do your students find the analogy persuasive? Do they think the situations are truly comparable?

Questions for Writing and Discussion

Prepare short written answers to each of these questions. Be prepared to hand them in and/or discuss them in class, as your teacher directs.

1. What do you think Bettelheim and Zelan mean by the word *literature* in the last sentence of their third paragraph—only classics of fiction and poetry, such as *Moby-Dick* and "Dover Beach"? or printed material of wider variety?
2. What do the following words mean—*deteriorates, rote, pertinent* (¶ 3), *treatise* (¶ 6), *primers, bilingualism, handicap* (¶ 8)?
3. How well do you think Bettelheim and Zelan make their point? Do they convince you? Do you think they ignore any important evidence *against* their position?
4. Note that in referring to all students learning to read, the authors refer to the child in terms of "*his* scholastic fate," "*his* experience in learning," and how "*he* will feel about learning." What is this apparent male bias called? Do you think it is deliberate here? What is a good way to avoid it?

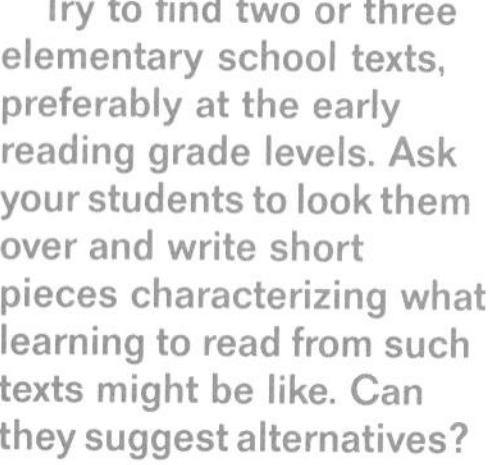

Try to find two or three elementary school texts, preferably at the early reading grade levels. Ask your students to look them over and write short pieces characterizing what learning to read from such texts might be like. Can they suggest alternatives?

Bridges: Another Perspective

In the reading above, Bettelheim and Zelan clearly believe that beginning reading instruction as widely practiced in American schools today is very poor, leading to increasing numbers of American citizens who neither enjoy reading nor read well. They point to German-speaking Switzerland as a model we should follow. Suppose you were an executive with a major American educational publishing company, a company that prints the country's leading reading instruction textbooks for elementary schools. How might you answer Bettelheim and Zelan's charges? Your job here is to defend your textbooks and the teachers who use them, but you know that simple denials—insisting that what Bettelheim and Zelan say isn't true—are not enough. What kinds of evidence would you need to have in order to counter or at least neutralize what they have to say?

Here we try to get students more involved with the reading by having them take a position against that of the authors. This is a variant of Elbow's "Doubting Game," which is based on the scientific method (doubting something is true until it can be proved so, or not so, conclusively). See the appendix to Elbow's *Writing without Teachers.*

Writers' Circle

Each member of the class should write down brief responses to each of these questions:

1. Did your mother, father, or some other family member read stories to you when you were little?
2. What is your first memory of learning to read at school?

3. Did you read out loud for your teacher and classmates in elementary school?
4. What is the best thing you've ever read?
5. What is the worst thing you've ever read?
6. Which best describes your own attitude about voluntary reading? (Circle one—and be honest!)
   a. Reading is a favorite pastime of mine and I do some voluntary reading just about every day.
   b. Ordinarily I don't read as a pastime. I will occasionally read something that someone recommends to me, or read a bit when there doesn't seem to be much else to do.
   c. I don't dislike reading, but I never seem to do it unless it's necessary.
   d. I don't like to read and do it only when I have to.
7. How would you rate yourself as a reader now?
   a. Excellent
   b. Good
   c. Average
   d. Below average
   e. Poor

After everyone has written down answers, go around the classroom, with each student reading his or her responses to the first five questions. The teacher or an appointed student can tally yes/no responses to questions 1 and 3 and can list responses to questions 4 and 5. Discuss the results. What picture of the class as readers emerges? (For the daring: using secret, uniform ballots, the class can poll its members on their responses to questions 6 and 7. The teacher or appointed student can tally the results. What conclusions can be drawn from the resulting data?)

You may want to build a writing assignment on this "Writers' Circle" activity, perhaps something about the role reading plays in a student's life and how that role changes from grade to grade right on into college.

PREREADING WORKSHEET

Before you read the following piece by William Raspberry, write brief responses to these questions:

1. Are you already a freshman in college or at a university?
2. Have you already declared an academic major?
   a. If so, what is it and why did you choose it?
   b. If not, why haven't you chosen a major?
   c. If not, what do you think you might major in?
   d. What do you want to do for a living after you graduate?
3. Based on the title of Raspberry's article, what do you expect him to say?

With these and all subsequent Prereading Worksheets in this book, we're working to help get your students involved in their reading. Our idea is to get them to call to mind attitudes, beliefs, values, and experiences relevant to the reading *before* they read, so that the reading experience itself might engage their fuller interaction with the text.

Majors Don't "Matter" That Much

William Raspberry

William Raspberry is a journalist, TV discussion panelist, and writer.

Soon to every fledgling student
Comes the moment to decide.
But since Angela's a freshman
My advice is:
Let it ride.

WASHINGTON—With apologies to James Russell Lowell, that is pretty much my counsel to my daughter, who is about to begin her first year in college. Soon enough, she'll have to face the sophomore necessity of choosing a major—whether or not she's decided on a career. In the meantime, I tell her, don't worry about it. 1

Ask your students how many of them think they'll stay with their majors throughout college.

A part of the reason for my advice is the memory of my own struggle to decide on a major. I eventually had four of them, none of them related to what was to become my career. 2

But the more important reason is my conclusion, regularly reinforced, that majors just don't matter that much. 3

The latest reinforcement is from John Willson, a history professor at Michigan's Hillsdale College, who, having heard once too often the question "But what do I do with a history major?" has decided to do what he can to put his students at ease. 4

"Every sophomore has a majoring frenzy," he wrote in a campus publication. "It is typical for sophomores to say, 'I want to be an anchorman. Therefore I will major in journalism. Where do I sign up?" They act like they have had a blow to the solar plexus when I say, a) Hillsdale has no major in journalism, and b) if we did, it would no more make you an anchorman than a major in English makes you an Englishman." 5

But rather than simply repeating what professionals already know, or urging colleges to dispense with the requirement for declaring a major, Willson has reduced his advice to a set of rules and principles. 6

The first, which college students often find incredible, is that aside from such vocational courses as engineering or computer science, any relationship between majors and careers is largely incidental. Physics majors are hardly more likely to become physicists than business majors to become entrepreneurs. The rule that derives from this principle: 7

> If you wanted your major to be practical, you should have gone to the General Motors Institute.

The second principle is that students (and colleges) should delay the necessity of choosing for as long as practicable. "Most students (and even more parents) have rather vague notions of what the subject of any given subject is. . . .Talk with your parents, but don't let parents, teachers, media experts, television evangelists or fraternity brothers pressure you into a majoring frenzy before you know what the major is all about." In short:

> All things being equal, it is best to know what you are talking about, which may even prevent majoring frenzies.

8 The third is a quote from the Rev. James T. Burtchaell (writing in "Notre Dame" magazine): "Pick your major on the pleasure principle, for what you most enjoy studying will draw your mind in the liveliest way to being educated."

9 The rule: People do not get educated by hitting themselves over the head with hammers.

10 It's good advice, and not only for students at small liberal-arts colleges. A few years ago, the University of Virginia published a booklet, "Life after Liberal Arts," based on a survey of 2,000 alumni of its college of arts and sciences.

11 The finding: 91 percent of the respondents not only believe that liberal arts prepared them for fulfilling careers but would not hesitate to recommend liberal-arts majors to students considering those same careers.

12 Those who responded to the survey included a biology major who later earned a master's of business administration and became a president of a bank, a psychology major who was a well-paid executive, and English majors whose careers embraced television sales, editorial production, systems analysis and law.

13 The "winning combination" derived from the Virginia survey: a liberal-arts foundation, complemented with career-related experience and personal initiative. Colleges aren't assembly lines that, after four years, automatically deposit students into lucrative careers. What is far likelier is a series of false starts followed by the discovery of a satisfying career. In the Virginia survey, for example, only 16 percent reported being happy with their first jobs.

14 Willson's advice, the results of the University of Virginia survey, and my advice to Angela come down to the same thing: Major in getting an education.

Ask your students who helped them select their majors (or intended majors).

Ask your students if they've ever had the kind of class in which they truly enjoyed studying and in which their minds were drawn "in the liveliest way to being educated." Was any such class in their major or intended major?

Several of your students may not believe Raspberry's assertion that "colleges aren't assembly lines that, after four years, automatically deposit students into lucrative careers." So much of our culture and their experience leads students to think exactly what Raspberry denies. Convincing your students that there's plenty to what Raspberry says would be a tough job, but we wouldn't blame you for trying. Writing Assignment 1 provides more guidance on this thorny issue.

POSTREADING WORKSHEET

Now that you have read the piece by Raspberry, write your responses to the following questions:

1. Why has Raspberry decided to tell his daughter not to worry about choosing an academic major?
2. What is a "majoring frenzy" (¶ 5)?

3. Restate here the three principles and the three corresponding rules that Professor John Willson has developed in advising Hillsdale College students suffering from "majoring frenzy."
4. What supports does Raspberry offer for his thesis that academic majors don't matter much?
5. How persuasive is Raspberry? Does he convince you? Why or why not? Look at your responses on the Prereading Worksheet. What reactions do you have now to your responses to question 2?

Questions for Writing and Discussion

Prepare short written answers to each of these questions. Be prepared to hand them in and/or discuss them in class, as your teacher directs.

1. Who was James Russell Lowell, and why does Raspberry begin "with apologies" to him?
2. Raspberry uses a hypothetical statement to present Professor Willson's first rule: "If you wanted your major to be practical, you should have gone to the General Motors Institute." What is the General Motors Institute? Does it exist? What do you know about it, even if you don't know anything else about it? How is that analogy similar to "If you can't stand the heat, stay out of the kitchen"?
3. What do the following words mean—*fledgling* (in poem), *counsel* (¶ 1), *solar plexus* (¶ 5), *entrepreneur* (¶ 7), *complemented, lucrative* (¶ 13)?
4. Raspberry uses hyperbole (overstatement) to present the third rule: "People do not get educated by hitting themselves over the head with hammers." Obviously, Raspberry is not being literal here. How would you state this principle literally, without hyperbole?

WRITING ASSIGNMENTS

1. Raspberry states: "Colleges aren't assembly lines that, after four years, automatically deposit students into lucrative careers." Yet many people believe that is exactly what colleges *ought* to be. What assumptions about education does Raspberry's view reveal? What assumptions about education does the "assembly line" view reveal? Which view do you consider most accurate and/or important? Write a brief essay explaining your view in relationship to Raspberry's.

Raspberry says colleges aren't four-year assembly lines depositing graduates into well-paying careers; others say that's exactly what colleges should be. Do your students think the issue is really that clear-cut? Why or why not?

2. "You can't judge a book by its cover" is a well-known expression indicating the need for a critical approach to what we read. We can think of other, similar expressions advocating a thoughtful, careful approach to the matters of life: (when buying a car) "Look at the engine under the shiny hood"; (when buying something that is packaged so that it is difficult to see) "Don't buy a

pig in a poke"; (when crossing a railroad track) "Stop, look, and listen." What other, similar expressions can you think of? Write an essay about sayings with which you are familiar. What wisdom do such sayings reflect?

3. The photograph at the beginning of this chapter (page 43) captures a courtroom scene from Stanley Kramer's 1960 film, *Inherit the Wind,* based on the stage play by Jerome Lawrence and Robert E. Lee. The story concerns the famous Scopes "Monkey Trial" in Dayton, Tennessee in 1926, when high school teacher John Scopes was found guilty of breaking a controversial state law against teaching evolutionary theory. The case pitted the argumentative abilities of well-known defense attorney Clarence Darrow against those of the well-known orator and frequent presidential candidate, William Jennings Bryan, who assisted the prosecution. The Darrow character, standing and pointing, was portrayed by Spencer Tracy. The Bryan character, seated in the foreground to the right, was played by Fredric March.

   The trial ultimately involved much more than a simple question of whether Scopes had violated the law (he did). Participants eloquently debated the nature of religious beliefs, what could constitute proof regarding such beliefs, the connections between science and faith, and the role of education in all such issues. The courtroom exchanges seemed to reinforce the folk wisdom that it's futile to argue about religion because argument (legal argument, anyway) depends upon a kind of logic that is bound by the realms of probability and proof, whereas religion depends upon faith—a willingness to believe without regard for strict proofs.

   Many debatable issues today involve both logic and emotion—whether drivers should be required to wear seat belts, whether states should sponsor lotteries, whether death penalties should be assessed for capital crimes, whether public funds should be spent on weapons or on social causes—the list goes on. Choose a complex, debatable issue, and write a "gut" opinion: how do *you* stand on the issue, and why do you believe as you do? As you write, try to be conscious of the *nature* of your support for your position; are you more influenced by facts, or feelings?

Notice that Raspberry uses specifics first, then leads up to generalizations. If your students do Writing Assignment 2, check their first drafts to see whether the students might not profit from doing the same. This specific-to-general structural pattern is often used in expository writing.

The critical quality of college writing that we have described here has many parts and can wear many faces, depending on the subject, the assignment, and the level of the course involved. The traits we've discussed—taking a mature perspective, going beyond locating and reporting information to include evaluating it, and applying your own judgment to the issue—cut across all subjects, assignments, and levels of courses. "Critical" in the sense we mean it here is not simple faultfinding; rather, it is sensible, seasoned, intelligent assessment and judgment: exactly what is expected of educated people. (If you want to see more of what goes into this quality we call critical writing, jump ahead to the discussion of critical reading in chapter 8 and the discussion of critical thinking in chapter 14. Meanwhile, in chapter 4 we will return to the primary reasons for writing.)

If you assign chapters 8 and 14 with this chapter, you can build your whole course around critical writing, reading, and thinking. That's a reasonable plan, and we provide a general syllabus following that arrangement in the Starter Kit. Our only problem with this arrangement is that it "front-end loads" the course with a good deal of theoretical abstraction, which can be difficult for students. We decided, in consultation with those who read drafts of our book and with others who frequently teach composition, that it is more manageable to introduce such a large body of theoretical abstraction incrementally. Our goal with the sequence of chapters presented in this textbook is to have students read and write (and think) early and often, and to bring in the necessary theory bit by bit along the way.

chapter 4 Writing to Express: Emphasis on the Writer

> "I had to write. I had no choice in the matter. It was not up to me to say I would stop, because I could not. It didn't matter how small or inadequate my talent."
>
> Madeleine L'Engle

> "It has always been my feeling that writing must come out of living, and the writer is no more than his personality endures in the crucible of his times. As a woman, I have come through the fires of hell because I am a black woman, because I am poor, because I live in America, and because I am determined to be both a creative artist and maintain my inner integrity and my instinctive need to be free."
>
> Margaret Walker

We think expressive writing is a good place to start. Many experienced writing teachers agree. (See, for example, Donald Murray's *A Writer Teaches Writing* and Kenneth Macrorie's *Telling Writing*.) We don't necessarily endorse everything either has to say, but both—especially Macrorie—understand the great value of expressive writing as a starting point for inexperienced writers.

Help your students think of other examples of how a writer's personal investment—his or her *feelings*, or deep fascination—add to the power of the writing. Note, for example, Carl Sagan's obvious love of his subject in "Science as a Way of Thinking" (chapter 5), Bob Greene's statements about his subjects (introduction to Part Three), or Peter Beidler's clear admiration for his teachers in "My Favorite Teachers" (chapter 9).

The most fundamental reason for writing may well be to express yourself: to let out something inside you or to explore your feelings about something by putting them into words. This kind of writing shows up all over our world. It's the essence of writing in the "creative" genres of fiction, poetry, and drama, but outside of literature courses, college classes often don't give it much credit. Many people see this kind of writing in poems and plays, songs and stories, and they often think, "Well, that's nice but it's not anything I'll ever do." What they don't see—or what they forget—are the notes, letters, diaries, and private journals that so many of us write. Those of us who don't write poems, plays, songs, or stories nonetheless pretty often wind up trying to put our own feelings and thoughts down on paper. Because of the way expressive writing responds to some of a person's deepest motives, and because it is the source of humanity's greatest creative writing, expressive writing is important.

Expressive writing is important for another reason too: nearly any *good* piece of writing has a significant expressive component. For example, consider a term paper on the role movies play in the way Americans in the 1990s feel about the war in Vietnam. The paper may successfully report facts about how the Vietnam War is reflected in movies, and it may successfully advance a thesis that attitudes about the war have changed, in part because of the effect of such movies. But if we want to understand the way the paper is written, if we want to ask what makes this writing work, we need to look more deeply into the paper. Thus it is ultimately more important that the writer have a personal fascination with the subject that fuels his or her imagination, a personal interest that adds a compelling edge to what is said.

Many good pieces of writing are primarily driven by the writer's personal commitment to the topic. And many bad pieces of writing have as the chief underlying cause of their badness the lack of an important expressive component.

When you read writing that seems dry and lifeless, when you read the kind of writing in which the writer seems to have written only because doing so was required, not because the writer had something worth saying, you're reading writing that is missing the expressive component. (Seeing such writing in a scholarly journal, one reader commented, "I can almost hear the drone of the word processor here.") The *worst* classroom writing—writing that no students would do unless they had to, that no students would read unless they were paid to—is often writing that lacks this expressive component as its basis.

How do you develop that crucial expressive component in all your writing? One good way is to work on expressive writing itself. As you read through the examples below, think about the places and times in your own life to which you might respond with this kind of writing. At the end of each piece of writing are questions we've designed for you to write answers to. We hope answering those questions will help open up for you key features of each piece.

Compare this with what William Raspberry says in chapter 3 about following the "pleasure principle" in choosing an academic major.

This is the second time we've stressed this point about lifeless, uncommitted, uninterested writing. It's important to care about what you're doing, no matter what it is. Though many students say they hate writing, usually what they mean is that they hate their memories of (a) working hard and still seeming to get poor grades for the effort or (b) having had picayune teachers, seemingly impossible to please. Some students believe it's impossible to be interested in *anything* they might write, because, at bottom, they're understandably not interested in repeating some of the "writing under duress" experiences that produced those negative memories.

PREREADING WORKSHEET

Before you read the following piece by Janet Sternburg, write brief responses to these questions:

1. Did you ever have a special room or place you retreated to when you were younger? If so, where was it and what role did it play in your imagination?
2. Looking back a few years, what memories do you have about a personal tradition you established—some fairly routine activity that held meaning for you and that you tried not to change? (It may be something as simple as always watching a particular TV show or always going to a movie on Friday nights—whatever it is, it was and remains important in your memory.)
3. When you were younger and used to imagine yourself as an adult, what roles, professions, or activities did you imagine yourself fulfilling as an adult?
4. What is the easiest and most satisfying way for you to express yourself now?

Notice that we're not trying to elicit perception of a common *structure* identifiable in expressive writing here (there isn't one, to our knowledge); rather, we're hoping that in reading these selections, students will perceive that they were all prompted by a common *purpose:* to express.

The Writer Herself: An Introduction

JANET STERNBURG

Janet Sternburg is a writer, editor, film producer, and director. Her book The Writer on Her Work *(1980) contains discussions of their writing processes by Anne Tyler, Joan Didion, Alice Walker, Susan Griffin, Toni Cade Bambara, Erica Jong, and Maxine Hong Kingston, among others. This selection begins Sternburg's introduction to the book.*

1 I'm drawn back to a room from my childhood—the back room of my aunt's apartment. When my parents and I visited, I used to vanish into that room. My means of escape was the typewriter, an old manual that sat on a desk in

Notice how quickly Sternburg establishes a setting. Can your students recall "means of escape" in similar situations?

Compare Sternburg's account of her aunt's writing ambitions with Ursula K. Le Guin's account of her mother's similar ambitions in "Theodora" (Part Two introduction).

Here Sternburg first mentions the door, which becomes a recurring and significant image in this selection.

Ask your students how they respond to this rather sudden turn of direction, of self-appraisal, Sternburg takes. How "severe" an "inquisition" is this, really, that she subjects herself to?

This self-constructed test is the *real* "inquisition."

Ask your students how Sternburg's remarks here about childhood attempts at self-definition compare with what Raspberry says about choice of a college major in chapter 3.

the back room. It belonged to my aunt, but she had long since left it for the adjoining room, the kitchen. She had once wanted to write, but as the eldest of a large and troubled first-generation American family, she had other claims on her energies as well as proscriptions to contend with: class, gender, and situation joined to make her feel unworthy of literature.

I now know that I inherited some of her proscriptions, but the back room 2
at age nine was a place of freedom. There I could perform that significant act: I could close the door. Certainly I felt peculiar on leaving the warm and buzzing room of conversation, with its charge of familial love and invasion. But it wasn't the living room I needed: it was the writing room, which now comes back to me with its metal table, its stack of white paper that did not diminish between my visits. I would try my hand at poems; I would also construct elaborate multiple-choice tests. "A child is an artist when, seeing a tree at dusk, she (a) climbs it (b) sketches it (c) goes home and describes it in her notebook." And another (possibly imagined) one: "A child is an artist when, visiting her relatives, she (a) goes down to the street to play (b) talks with her family and becomes a part of them (c) goes into the back room to write."

Oh my. Buried in those self-administered tests were the seeds of what, 3
years later, made me stop writing. Who could possibly respond correctly to so severe an inquisition? Nonetheless, that room was essential to me. I remember sitting at the desk and feeling my excitement start to build; soon I'd touch the typewriter keys, soon I'd be back in my own world. Although I felt strange and isolated, I was beginning to speak, through writing. And if I chose, I could throw out what I'd done that day; there was no obligation to show my words to anyone.

Looking back now, I feel sad at so constrained a sense of freedom, so 4
defensive a stance: retreat behind a closed door. Much later, when I returned to writing after many silent years, I believed that the central act was to open that door, to make writing into something which would not stand in opposition to others. I imagined a room at the heart of a house, and life in its variety flowing in and out. Later still I came to see that I continued to value separation and privacy. I began to realize that once again I'd constructed a test: the true writer either retreats and pays the price of isolation from the human stream or opens the door and pays the price of exposure to too many diverse currents. Now I've come to believe that there is no central act; instead there is a central struggle, ongoing, which is to retain control over the door—to shut it when necessary, open it at other times—and to retain the freedom to give up that control, and experiment with the room as porous. I've also come to believe that my harsh childhood testing was an attempt at self-definition—but one made in isolation, with no knowledge of living writers. In place of a more tempered view that acquaintance could have provided, I substituted the notion of a single criterion for an artist. Working women writers were beyond my ken; so too was the option to choose "all of the above."

POSTREADING WORKSHEET

Now that you have read the piece by Sternburg, write your responses to the following questions:

1. How does your experience as you responded on the Prereading Worksheet compare with Janet Sternburg's?
2. Do you agree with Sternburg that her childhood sense of freedom was constrained and defensive? Why or why not?
3. The central idea in Sternburg's conclusion is that it is an ongoing struggle to "retain control over the door"—the door being a metaphor for how she controls, via opening or closing, her writing life. If you needed to choose a metaphor to describe or represent your "other," or fantasy, life or career, what would that metaphor be, and why?
4. An advertising gimmick of the late 1980s implied that working women could "have it all"—husbands, families, careers, everything. Do you think that's what Sternburg is saying in her final sentence? Do you think such a thing—"having it all"—is possible?

Questions for Writing and Discussion

Prepare short written answers to each of these questions. Be prepared to hand them in and/or discuss them in class, as your teacher directs.

1. What does the expression "Oh my" do to the self-inflated image the writer has given herself in the first two paragraphs? What evidence later in the passage indicates she is aware of that image's destructive qualities?
2. What does the repeated image of opening and closing the door (for example, in ¶ 2 and ¶ 4) come to represent in this piece? What effect is this image likely to have on young readers? on older, adult readers?
3. Does the way the image of the door develops contribute to the sense of honesty you get from the passage? Or does it cause you to doubt the passage's honesty?
4. What does the writer suggest in the second paragraph, where she places "possibly imagined" in parentheses? What do those two words, coupled with the earlier "Oh my," tell you about the author's attitude toward her subject?
5. What do the following words mean—*proscriptions, familial* (¶ 2), *inquisition* (¶ 3), *constrained, ken* (¶ 4)?

We can see in the Janet Sternburg passage that she is primarily writing to express her feelings, to put into personal perspective the special memory she has. Although she also informs and analyzes, even persuades us that her feelings are strong, she is mostly *expressive* of those feelings. And whereas Janet Sternburg expresses her feelings and thoughts about a significant childhood experience, Benjamin Franklin, in the piece below, expresses a father's desire to communicate good advice to his son.

Some suggestions for brief writing assignments after the Sternburg piece:

1. Write a summary of Sternburg's development as a writer, tying it to (a) doors and (b) tests.
2. Compare Sternburg's initial feelings about writing with those of a child learning to read, as described by Bettelheim and Zelan in chapter 3.
3. In the two tests Sternburg poses we have instances of a person applying *one* criterion that is self-defined (in total ignorance of the reality of the situation), hence impossible to meet. Ask your students each to write about a similar situation in their lives—did they ever devise "tests" like this, equally ill-informed and -starred?

On "Character"

BENJAMIN FRANKLIN

Benjamin Franklin (1706–90) was a printer, patriot, scientist, and consummate writer, known primarily through the character he established in Poor Richard's Almanac. *His* Autobiography *was begun in 1771, left to lie for thirteen years, and completed in 1788. It shows not just his advice to his son but also his awareness of his role as a public figure. This passage depicts a pivotal time in Franklin's development, his brief flirtation with deism, the common eighteenth-century notion that saw God primarily as a clock maker—one who, having designed a perfectly machined universe, has withdrawn to be but a spectator of its proceedings.*

You're likely to need to add a bit of background on deism for your students' benefit. We suggest at least a dictionary definition or an encyclopedia summary. If time permits and/or interest seems high, sharing some of Voltaire's *Candide* might be enjoyable.

Before I enter upon my public appearance in business, it may be well to let you know the then state of my mind with regard to my principles and morals, that you may see how far those influenced the future events of my life. My parents had early given me religious impressions, and brought me through my childhood piously in the dissenting way. But I was scarce fifteen, when, after doubting by turns of several points, as I found them disputed in the different books I read, I began to doubt of Revelation itself. Some books against deism fell into my hands; they were said to be the substance of sermons preached at Boyle's lectures. It happened that they wrought an effect on me quite contrary to what was intended by them; for the arguments of the deists, which were quoted to be refuted, appeared to me much stronger than the refutations; in short, I soon became a thorough deist. My arguments perverted some others, particularly Collins and Ralph; but each of them having afterwards wronged me greatly without the least compunction, and recollecting Keith's conduct towards me (who was another freethinker), and my own towards Vernon and Miss Read, which at times gave me great trouble, I began to suspect that this doctrine, though it might be true, was not very useful. My London pamphlet, which had for its motto these lines of Dryden: 1

> Whatever is, is right. Though purblind Man
> Sees but a Part of the Chain, the nearest Link,
> His Eyes not carrying to the equal Beam,
> That poises all, above.

and from the attributes of God, his infinite wisdom, goodness, and power, concluded that nothing could possibly be wrong in the world, and that vice and virtue were empty distinctions, no such things existing, appeared now not so clever a performance as I once thought it; and I doubted whether some error had not insinuated itself unperceived into my argument, so as to infect all that followed, as is common in metaphysical reasonings.

You might want to bring in some of Franklin's resolutions from elsewhere in his *Autobiography*.

I grew convinced that *truth, sincerity* and *integrity* in dealings between man and man were of the utmost importance to the felicity of life; and I 2 formed written resolutions (which still remain in my journal book), to practice them ever while I lived. Revelation had indeed no weight with me as such; but I entertained an opinion that, though certain actions might not be bad *because* they were forbidden by it, or good *because* it commanded them, yet probably these actions might be forbidden *because* they were bad for us, or commanded *because* they were beneficial to us in their own natures, all the circumstances of things considered. And this persuasion, with the kind hand of Providence or some guardian angel, or accidental favorable circumstances and situations, or all together, preserved me through this dangerous time of youth, and the hazardous situations I was sometimes in among strangers, remote from the eye and advice of my father, without any *willful* gross immorality or injustice, that might have been expected from my want of religion. I say *willful,* because the instances I have mentioned had something of *necessity* in them, from my youth, inexperience, and the knavery of others. I had therefore a tolerable character to begin the world with; I valued it properly, and determined to preserve it.

Some of your students may themselves play the "Doubting Game" (see Elbow) concerning taking apart a piece of writing the way the questions below ask them to do. If so, ask students how they think Franklin would feel about such analysis. If students seem reluctant to pursue their challenge, let them hear this from Gore Vidal: "So what is the point to these desultory autopsies performed according to that little set of instructions at the end of each text? Have you seen one? What symbols to look for? What does the author mean by the word 'white'? I look at the notes appended to my own pieces in anthologies and know despair." In other words, if your students become more engaged in what our book has to say by playing the believing/doubting game with our own words (rather than those of the authors we include), it's fine with us.

Questions for Writing and Discussion

Prepare short written answers to each of these questions. Be prepared to hand them in and/or discuss them in class, as your teacher directs.

1. This famous passage is written in a language and style much more common during the eighteenth century than today. It is part of the *Autobiography* Franklin addressed to his son, wherein we see a father telling his son something important. Try to paraphrase Franklin's passage in modern language and style—you can use contemporary incidents and examples, so long as you still capture Franklin's chain of reasoning.
2. Although Franklin's eighteenth-century style may strike us today as a contrived and stuffy voice, he maintains the pose of a father speaking to his son. How does the fact that there is a fairly tight chain of reasoning in the passage affect Franklin's pose of this being a private communication between parent and child?
3. Part of what Franklin is saying is, in so many words, "When I was younger I had lots of wrong ideas about things, but I eventually became convinced that truth, sincerity, and integrity were the keys to life." How does his admitting he had been wrong in his earlier view of life affect your sense of the piece's honesty? That is, do you credit Franklin for admitting having made mistakes? Or do you fault him for using what seems in the end to have been a rather harmless philosophical flirtation with deism as a ploy to set himself up as now being nearly perfect?
4. What do the following words mean—*piously, deism, wrought, compunction, doctrine* (¶ 1)?

Note that Franklin's father seems to have played little or no role in Franklin's young life and development.

Additional items for discussion/writing after the Franklin piece:

1. Recall a time when you asked for advice and got a personal testimonial instead.
2. What did the word *tolerable* (¶ 2) mean in Franklin's time?
3. Write a short paper summarizing Franklin's development as reflected in this passage.

Bridges: Another Perspective

A strong trend in history writing is what is often called debunking—proving (or at least suggesting) that some long-held beliefs about a person or an event are in fact untrue or misleading. Some debunking is malicious, intended only to smear a good historical name and/or advance the career of the debunker; other debunking is honest and seeks only the truth in areas where legend is often preferred. How might a sharp-eyed and thoughtful debunker view Ben Franklin's above account to his son? Consider that although Franklin intended it for his son, it was published and exists today—suggesting, therefore, that Franklin had more motives than imparting wisdom to his son. Write a brief, skeptical critique of Franklin's tone and content.

One of the most common kinds of expressive writing occurs in individual diaries and journals, which are often private. Some such diaries and journals, however, have been published. Below is an excerpt from a diary.

The Laboratory of the Soul

Anaïs Nin

Anaïs Nin (1903–77) is perhaps best known for the six volumes of The Diary of Anaïs Nin. *Her other books include* The Glass Bell *and* Cities of the Interior. *The following diary entry is dated May 25, 1932.*

Help your students see how she establishes setting. Ask them what kind of person seems to go with this setting.

Ask your students what "experiments" or "discoveries" could be expected in a "laboratory of the soul"; if Hollywood made a movie about such experiments or discoveries, what would that movie be like? (Such a film *was* made, in part based on Nin's diary. Released amid some controversy as to language and subject matter, *Henry and June* premiered in 1990 without a rating.) Note the effect of Nin's invitation for us to "enter" her "laboratory."

Late at night. I am in Louveciennes. I am sitting by the fire in my bedroom. 1 The heavy curtains are drawn. The room feels heavy and deeply anchored in the earth. One can smell the odors of the wet trees, the wet grass outside. They are blown in by the wind through the chimney. The walls are a yard thick, thick enough to dig bookcases into them, beside the bed. The bed is wide and low.

Henry called my house a laboratory of the soul. 2

Enter this laboratory of the soul where every feeling will be X-rayed by 3 Dr. Allendy to expose the blocks, the twists, the deformations, the scars which interfere with the flow of life. Enter this laboratory of the soul where incidents are refracted into a diary, dissected to prove that every one of us carries a deforming mirror where he sees himself too small or too large, too fat or too thin, even Henry, who believes himself so free, blithe, and unscarred. Enter here where one discovers that destiny can be directed, that one does not need to remain in bondage to the first wax imprint made on childhood sensibilities. One need not be branded by the first pattern. Once the deforming mirror is smashed, there is a possibility of wholeness; there is a possibility of joy.

What might we call this "mirror"—ego? self-image? personality?

4 It is Dr. Allendy who does the dissecting and the explorative operations. I bring them home, and sift them to catch impurities, and errors in the diary. And then I tactfully, poetically, artistically, transmit what I have learned to Henry. By the time it reaches him it does not have a clinical odor, it is not expressed in the homely jargon of analysts. He balks at some of it, but when it is properly adorned, seasoned, dramatized, he is interested. So I tell Dr. Allendy all my life, and Henry tells me his.

Questions for Writing and Discussion

Prepare short written answers to each of these questions. Be prepared to hand them in and/or discuss them in class, as your teacher directs.

1. Sometimes expressive writing—because it's often done privately, for private purposes—is difficult for others to interpret. That doesn't mean it's any less worth doing for the writer, but it does make such writing hard to work with in a textbook. This famous passage introduces what becomes a theme in Nin's diaries, the "laboratory of the soul" metaphor. What do you suppose that comparison means to Nin in this passage?
2. The author compares her house to a "laboratory of the soul." What metaphor could you use to describe where you live? Flesh out the comparison with specific details, the way Nin does.
3. Do you have a "laboratory of the soul"? If so, where or what is it?
4. The "Henry" Nin refers to is her friend Henry Miller (1891–1980), the American expatriate writer. How does the nature of such writing as this—a diary—excuse Nin's failure to further identify "Henry"?
5. What is the effect of the details given in the first paragraph?
6. What is the effect of the repetition of "Enter" in the third paragraph?
7. What is Nin's attitude toward her subject—that is, what is her tone—in this passage? What features of this piece of writing support your claim about its tone?
8. What do the following words mean—*refracted, dissected* (¶ 3), *jargon, balks* (¶ 4)?

Additional questions after the Nin piece:

1. What kind of persona is this?
2. What is Nin's relationship with Henry?
3. What is the effect of Nin's statement near the conclusion when she offers the series of adverbs "tactfully, poetically, artistically" (¶ 4)?
4. Have you ever known someone who liked to listen to your troubles *too much?* If so, what did that feel like?

Anaïs Nin writes "The Laboratory of the Soul" intimately, mostly with herself and the sorting of her own thoughts foremost in her mind. Her self-expression is in fact a part of her therapy, something Dr. Allendy wants her to do. Even so, her sharing with her friend Henry gives her writing informational, analytical, and persuasive qualities. Now consider yet another kind of expressive writing.

Introduction to *One Day on Beetle Rock*

ROBERT MILLER

Sally Carrigher's classic One Day on Beetle Rock *(1943) follows the adventures of the animals—from their own point of view—around The Rock in Sequoia National Park on one 24-hour day. Here we have the introductory note, written by Robert C. Miller, who at the time was director of the California Academy of Sciences.*

Ask your students if they've ever read a "dangerous book." If so, what was it? Why was it considered "dangerous"?

Ask students, "How does the direction of this piece change in the third sentence? What effect does the accumulation of detail following the change and continuing to the end of the first paragraph have?"

Discuss with students whether any part of this piece strikes them as exaggerated or in some other way too elaborate. If so, try to find those passages which contribute to that sense.

This is a dangerous book, full of disturbing possibilities. Should it fall into the 1
hands of the young, it is extremely likely to make naturalists of them. Even a hardened adult must read it at his own risk—the risk of being seized with an overwhelming desire to hear the wind in the treetops; and to smell the incense of the forest; to watch a lizard sunning itself on a rock, to glimpse the lithe form of a weasel disappearing over a log, or to come briefly face to face on the trail with a startled buck; to hear the evening songs of birds, to see the bats come out at dusk, and to share with the creatures of the wilderness the adventures of the night.

He may even have to visit the particular place in Sequoia National Park 2
which is here so accurately, compellingly described, and to see with his own eyes its animal inhabitants leading their busy, interesting, self-sufficient lives.

These are stories of the adventures of animals, but with a difference—the 3
stories are of actual animals in an actual place, as the author has observed them. She has watched carefully and reported truthfully, always with sensitive understanding and a keen awareness of beauty. The tales are fiction, yes, but fiction closely parallel with fact. This is real natural history.

Questions for Writing and Discussion

Prepare short written answers to each of these questions. Be prepared to hand them in and/or discuss them in class, as your teacher directs.

1. In what ways does this passage meet the definition of expressive writing the same way the earlier examples did? What other kinds of purposes do you see being expressed here? Use paragraph numbers to cite specific examples.
2. How would you characterize the tone—the writer's attitude toward the subject—of this passage? In what ways is the tone expressive of the writer's feeling?
3. What is the effect of the details in the first paragraph? How does that effect fit (or fail to fit) with the point of the second paragraph?
4. A passage like this one—obviously designed to interest readers in the book—walks a thin line between being honest and being overdone. What parts of the passage do you find to be honest? Which ones seem overdone?
5. What is the meaning of the word *lithe* (¶ 1)?

Clearly Robert Miller, in introducing *One Day on Beetle Rock,* expresses his own love of nature, even though he is fulfilling the *form* of a book introduction. It is important to note that the forms of writing do not necessarily affect the basic purposes of writing we are discussing here. One can write expressively, for example, in several different forms: letters, diary entries, autobiographies, and so forth. Here, for example, is expressive writing in the form of a memoir, much like the earlier piece by Janet Sternburg.

Mountain Memories

Mary Travis, college writing student

1 We all have daydreams. One of my favorites is about a perfect world, a world where people and nature are one. One day last October I came closer to experiencing that world. Describing that hike in the mountains, I recall that day's visions--getting to the trailhead, finding myself alone on the climb, and realizing how much I hurt afterward.

What effect does Travis achieve by using "we" at the beginning?

What expectation about the rest of the piece does the first paragraph set up?

2 By the time we got to the trailhead, we had been bouncing over a jeep trail for nearly an hour. The first part of the four-mile trail was pretty easy. The fresh air, the pine and the maples everywhere around us, the stream rushing and gurgling below us, drew from me a sigh of relief. Further on we were briefly surrounded by a cloud of gnats; they hovered over one spot in the trail and we walked through them.

3 The steeper the slope became, the more aware I became of the physical nature around me: the huge rocks above on my left, the stream below on my right, the fallen trees in the lush forest (itself eventually to fall and to be replaced), and the strange silence of the mountain. Only the scuff and crunch of my boots on the graveled path broke the silence. As I trudged on, my attention increasingly focused only on the trail, steeper and more rocky, tortuous, inexorable. With each twist and turn I saw only more trail.

4 Soon enough, more by coincidence than by effort, I was at the front of my group. I was alone. Now, accustomed to the sound of only my own feet--maybe a little hypnotized by it--I became aware of the leaves on the trees rustling in the wind. With each turn my body became more weary, but my mind was more at rest. Physically, I hoped only to get to the top for a rest, then come back down to civilization. More and more I

Note that Travis uses narrative time-lapse sequence and movement from one location to another as ways to bolster the nature imagery in the third and fourth paragraphs, all while getting on with her story.

became aware of the physical nature of my own being--every bone, muscle, and sweaty inch. Mentally, the pain I was feeling became almost a kind of satisfaction--the hurt was a current that united me with the world around me, with the collage of brown, blue, green, and white. The less I thought, the more I just felt, the less the separation between me and the world around me. As I gave in to that merging, it seemed I was no longer tired at all--two legs churning toward some uncertain goal.

Later that day, on the ride home, I was in pain and I loved it. 5
Through that exertion I had become one with the mountain and the mountain one with me, and I knew that even though I was leaving the mountain, I would never be totally apart from it.

Questions for Writing and Discussion

Prepare short written answers to each of these questions. Be prepared to hand them in and/or discuss them in class, as your teacher directs.

1. To what extent is this passage directed at readers other than the author herself? Which words or lines in it mark it as one person writing to others? Which mark it as one person writing to herself?
2. How is the tone in this passage different from that in the preceding passage (Miller's)? How is it different from the tone in the first example (Sternburg's "The Writer Herself")?
3. *Imagery* is broadly defined as language that appeals to our five senses. Which of the five senses are appealed to most strongly in the imagery of this passage?
4. In what ways does the passage's ending bear out (or alter) the expectations established at the beginning, about a "perfect world, a world where people and nature are one"?
5. One of the odd things that happens when people do expressive writing in a classroom setting is that the writing often gets a moral tag at the end. That is, a strong temptation seems to be to end with, "And so I learned that crime doesn't pay," "And so I decided that my parents weren't so wrong after all," or some such line that takes the writing out of the realm of experience and into the realm of morality, ethics, and so on. Sometimes that works, and sometimes it doesn't. A key factor determining whether the moral tag works is its honesty (or lack of it); that is, does the last line really grow, inevitably and apparently necessarily, out of the experience, or is it just added on, perhaps to impress the teacher? Take and defend a position on whether or not the last line of this passage is honest.
6. What do the following words mean—*inexorable* (¶ 2), *collage* (¶ 4)?

Additional suggestions after the Travis piece:

1. State the effect on you as a reader of Travis's omission of a physical description of what things look like at the end of the trail.
2. Rewrite this piece in the "voice" of Anaïs Nin.

KEY POINTS TO REMEMBER: Writing to Express

What important qualities are shared by the sample pieces of writing you just read? Well, obviously, they're all examples of expressive writing. But what does that mean here? We want to draw your attention to three qualities in particular: honesty, a distinctive tone, and a high level of detail.

- Be honest.
- Maintain a distinctive tone.
- Provide plenty of details.

Be Honest

There's no reason not to be scrupulously, absolutely honest in this kind of writing, which emphasizes the writer. Because you're writing primarily to please yourself, why not enjoy this opportunity to be completely candid? It's that kind of concern to be honest with oneself which produces the type of revelation you see in the third paragraph of "The Writer Herself"—the sentences beginning with "Oh my" and ending with "Who could possibly respond correctly to so severe an inquisition?" In those sentences the writer (Janet Sternburg) sees how at that early point in her life she talked herself out of writing. The same kind of concern for honesty led Benjamin Franklin, in the second example, to point out that his adherence to "truth, sincerity and integrity" came not from direct concern for his earlier religious training but from his realization that "certain actions" were "forbidden because they were bad for us," and others were "commanded because they were beneficial to us in our own natures" (¶ 3).

Getting students to be honest in their writing is a good first step toward having them "own" their writing—that is, be fully in charge of what they say for their own purposes. As long as their writing is "false" in the sense we mean here (say, couched in pseudoacademic jargon), its success or failure—its quality—is not their responsibility but, rather, the responsibility of that phony persona or voice. For students to be honest in their writing is a first step toward claiming responsibility for it, which in turn is a necessary first step toward improvement.

Maintain a Distinctive Tone

The tone of expressive writing is often (but not always) a little different from that of other kinds of writing. (*Tone* when it's used in this sense names the author's attitude toward the subject and the audience.) In the examples at the beginning of this chapter that special tone shows up in a number of ways. In "The Writer Herself" it may be seen best in the third paragraph's "Now I've come to believe that there is no central act. . . ." That special quality is more apparent, although it has a slightly different sound, in "The Laboratory of the Soul," in the starkness of phrases like "Late at night" (¶ 1), "Henry called my house a laboratory of the soul" (¶ 2), and "So I tell Dr. Allendy all my life, and Henry tells me his" (¶ 4). A look at yet another facet of that special quality of tone comes from the start of "Introduction to *One Day on Beetle Rock*": "This is a dangerous book, full of disturbing possibilities" (¶ 1). And in "Mountain Memories" it shows up in the fourth paragraph: "the hurt was a current that united me with the world around me." From these examples we see that there is no one special tone to expressive writing but that such writing nearly always has a slightly unusual tone. Again, as with honesty, the highly personal tone may well occur because expressive writing is

Obviously, the word *tone* here relates closely to the idea of honesty.

If you are having your students keep journals, you will probably have plenty of examples of writing showing this elementary sincerity. Use such examples to share with the class only, however, with the permission of the writer.

first and foremost writing designed to satisfy the writer and, as such, has an elementary sincerity. One does not have to try to use someone else's ear to see if the piece sounds right—if expressive writing sounds right to the writer, then it *is* right.

Provide Plenty of Details

Some students may think that personal, expressive writing is abstract. Passages like Nin's show them otherwise.

One more characteristic all these pieces share is the use of plenty of details. In "Mountain Memories" the third paragraph in particular contains good use of specific details—a "steeper" slope, "huge rocks," "strange silence," "scuff and crunch," and a "rocky, tortuous, inexorable" trail. In the first paragraph of "Introduction to *One Day on Beetle Rock*" we are invited to "hear the wind in the treetops," to "smell the incense of the forest," and to "glimpse the lithe form of a weasel disappearing over a log." And in "The Laboratory of the Soul," in the first paragraph, the room is "heavy and deeply anchored in the earth"; there is the smell of "wet trees" and "wet grass"; there are thick walls and a bed that is "wide and low." Even though this kind of writing is not often written with other readers in mind—at least not originally—the amount of detail is fairly high. Perhaps the initial function of these details is to help the writer recapture the experience, hence the heavy use of imagery that appeals to sensory experience. The eventual function for other readers turns out to be much the same.

✓✓✓ **WORKSHEET: Writing to Express**

Try not to view this and other worksheets as mere recipes. The problem with such a view is that it seems to reduce writing to an activity for which cookbook recipes can be written, and writing is far more complicated than that. Our purpose here is a careful walk-through that avoids trivialization as much as possible.

Here's a procedure to follow when you're doing expressive writing. Remember the way we described the act of writing earlier—it has four parts (some people say it's one process with four subprocesses, others that it's four processes; both views, we feel, subdivide the act too much):

1. Thinking
2. Drafting and reading
3. Revising and editing
4. Proofreading

Now, the way writing actually happens for most people most of the time is not nearly so neatly divided up. Thus, don't be surprised if your experience of writing is not quite so orderly as the way it's laid out here. Because this is the first chapter dealing with writing for a reason, we're taking a brief look, below, at each of the processes of writing; later chapters will focus on specific processes in more detail.

Thinking

Expressive writing doesn't always start with an assignment—it's in the nature of expressive writing that often you do it for your own reasons. Perhaps you want to capture the way you felt last weekend when you went sailing for the first time, or when you attended your first college football game. Or maybe your teacher has asked you to write about a similar activity or occasion. Whatever the impetus for your writing, it's a good idea to think about the situation for a few minutes before you begin.

Usually one of the first steps in thinking about the situation is to *consider the reader*. But in expressive writing, when often you're writing primarily for yourself, that may not be so big a problem. (Of course, if you're doing this writing as part of a class assignment, you do need to think about your reader—is the reader your teacher, your classmates, or both?)

You also need to *size up the situation* in regard to this piece of writing. Are you on the inside looking out (using words that portray the world as seen through your own necessarily limited vision)? Or are you on the outside looking in (describing the world, including your own personal place in it, as though someone else were looking at the whole field of vision and commenting in a more detached way)? It may be that the more "internal" of these voices is the more common one in expressive writing, but in the abstract both voices are equally valid.

This idea is well handled in the Nin piece.

This idea is well handled in the Travis piece.

Another factor that becomes an issue in expressive writing is *control*. Are you writing as you think and feel (a sort of stream-of-consciousness approach)? Or are you writing on the basis of having already figured out the larger pattern of what you're writing about? Especially in expressive writing, you can't always sort all these things in advance, and in any kind of writing you will probably find you change your stance as the project evolves. But the more of these things you at least think about before you write (even if you later change your mind about them), the more you increase your chances of producing a piece of writing that pleases you and is done within a reasonable amount of time.

This idea of a larger pattern is well handled in the Franklin piece.

We don't want to make this part of the process seem too mentalistic. No one completely knows beforehand how the writing will turn out; nonetheless, it does seem true that the more forethought is given, the more likely the result will follow identifiably from that forethought.

While careful and detailed prior planning is usually necessary to produce effective persuasive and informative writing, good expressive writing may often result from a minimum of prior planning. The most important planning involves your choice of a subject—it needs to be something about which you feel strongly. And the more you know about that subject *and* your feelings toward it, the better your writing will be. Let's look at the two sides of that statement:

1. You need to know the subject you're writing about.
2. You need to know as much as you can about your own feelings toward it.

Note that few if any people *plan* a diary entry. Some writing purely "finds its own way" as it goes along.

The first of these is no different from the same requirement for any kind of writing—you'll find you write better when you're familiar with your topic. That really shouldn't be surprising. The second, knowing about your feelings, is essential in this kind of writing, for the real subject of expressive writing is not the sight, event, or occasion that triggered your feelings but your feelings themselves. Different people get in touch with their feelings in different ways, some by talking it out with others, and some by free-associating and freewriting until they see their own innermost selves more clearly through seeing them on the page.

The term *freewriting* refers to writing with a *minimum* regard for structure, purpose, audience, syntax, grammar, spelling, punctuation—all those things

Have your students do some freewriting in class. It's fun, and it focuses the class on writing while teaching students a new way (new to most of them, anyway) to start writing. At first, they might struggle against the idea of doing nothing but write, solidly, for a few minutes. Start with a short period—five minutes—and they'll be surprised at how "long" that is. But insist that they keep their pens moving, even if all that comes to mind is, "I can think of nothing" (tell them to write *that*, if that's what they think of). Eventually, they'll be more productive.

James Baldwin expressed the "discovery" potential of writing, the quality of never being certain of what he was going to say: "When you're writing, you're trying to find out something which you don't know. The whole language of writing for me is finding out what you don't want to know, what you don't want to find out. But something forces you to anyway." Young writers might not approach writing with his dread of what he might discover, and perhaps not with the compulsion he feels, but they may find more eloquence than they thought they had—if only they pursue it. See also the headnote to the Griffin piece in chapter 13.

Here's where peer reviewing of first drafts can truly help student writers see how *generative* writing can be; that is, writing can *generate* (create, make possible, suggest) more writing, better writing.

writers so easily worry about. What you want to do in freewriting is to write anything that comes into your mind on the subject, to write fast, to let the words go from your creative mind straight to the page, with a minimum of screening, monitoring, and restricting. Generally, the more you can do to re-create mentally the experience of what you're writing about, the better you will freewrite about it. You need to "put yourself back into that place," so to speak, and try once again to evoke the original feelings you seek to describe. Of course, much of what you generate will need to be rewritten completely or dropped altogether. But the idea is to come up with a wealth of material to use in subsequent parts of the writing process.

Suppose, for example, that you decide to write about the way you felt the first time you went to a funeral. To write well about it, you're going to have to work to recapture not only the details about the funeral itself but also the feelings you had at the time. And that means you have to re-envision that day: what it looked like, what the other people looked like, the music, the other sounds, the colors, the smells, what people said and did as the day wore on. In short, the more details you can recapture, the more you'll be able to do the same with your feelings. Freewriting about those details is one of the best ways to recapture them.

Learning about your feelings on the subject is more difficult than recalling physical details like sights and sounds. For many of us, our first attempts to put feelings down on paper are difficult and the results skimpy, no matter how much we've done to remember the physical setting. Often the only way to proceed is to hold those first few words up to scrutiny—why did you say *that?* What else is going on behind that statement? How did the setting contribute to that feeling? Why is this subject so moving to you? Asking these and many more questions of your first, possibly minimal attempts to write about your feelings will frequently help you go beyond those first attempts and dig more deeply into your true subject.

Once you feel that in your freewriting you've done as much as you can with the subject, that you've got down *all* (or what you believe now to be all) the details you can think of, you're ready to start drafting and reading.

Drafting and Reading

Students generally want to make their first drafts as nearly perfect as possible. That aim is understandable, but it can be reductive—very destructive—for it tends to cut off further development and improvement. We have deliberately slowed this phase of the process to try to counter this typical student attitude.

If you can manage doing so, the first part of this phase is to take a break—ideally, to let a night pass. Often your subconscious and the deeper parts of your memory will re-sort the material and allow you to add to it considerably if you will just let some time pass. At a minimum, you need to let a couple of hours pass so that you can look at what you have with fresh eyes. Then cull through the freewriting and ask questions of every line and every detail: "What else needs to go in here that I may have left out before?" "What other details need to be included to make this more evocative and expressive?" When you can think of no more to put in, you're ready to draft. You may want to begin with an outline, or you may want to simply begin writing; do whichever makes you more comfortable. As you begin to write, read your sentences for effect. Write and rewrite, adding layers and layers and layers until you're close to the content you want.

A certain amount of reshaping can go on now as well. At the very least, you can start separating out sentences—strings of words that start with capital letters, contain complete thoughts (with subjects and verbs), and end with periods. And you can start sorting paragraphs—marking where one idea or pattern of thought finishes and another begins. We know there is more to writing good sentences and structuring good paragraphs than that, but minimal structuring is enough for now.

By the end of this phase of writing, you should have a draft that someone else can read—at least for content. Your teacher may well encourage you to get other people's responses to this early draft, *not* for correcting grammar and spelling, but for doing the kind of review that answers such questions as, "Does this make sense to you?" Often other people will ask questions about your early drafts that will play useful roles in the writing's later development. And from other people's questions of your work (as well as from your questions of theirs) you can learn to become a much better *re*reader—hence a better reviser—of your work.

Suppose, for example, you're writing about being away from home for the first time, and your classmate who reads your first draft says something like, "What I see here is more description of the sights and sounds and smells of home than description of your own feelings. And when I do see mention of your own feelings, you hardly ever tell me how they're connected to the physical things you describe. Can you (a) do more about making your feelings explicit on the page and (b) tie those feelings more closely to the other details you include?" That's a valuable response! Don't be dismayed that your first draft wasn't "perfect"; in our experience, no one's ever is.

To avoid confusing this first draft for someone else to read with other "first drafts" that aren't ready for someone to read, we suggest you call this the *reading draft*. The word *draft* is used so much it can be confusing, and in fact a draft might be virtually any piece of writing not considered "finished" by the writer. We suggest this terminology:

- *Preliminary drafts:* all versions prior to the reading draft
- *Reading draft:* the first full draft intended to be read and responded to by someone else
- *Revision drafts:* all versions after the reading draft has been read and responded to

Drafting, in this scheme, refers to any writing activity during the production of any of the above kinds of drafts.

Revising and Editing

Once you've gotten to the point where you're showing the draft to others and they're getting the picture you want them to get, you've begun revising. That is, once you're comfortable that you have in fact included all the content you will need and that you've put it into a fairly readable structure, you can begin working to make it *good*. If you're doing the writing only for yourself—not for, say, a class assignment—you might stop here. Many people work over their own journal or diary entries until they have all the details that seem relevant, and then stop. Many others like writing for only their own consumption to be nevertheless as good as they can make it. And obviously, if you're writing for class you can't leave out revising, editing, and proofreading.

As we said before, the more feedback you can get from others on these early drafts, the better off you will be. You also want to try to achieve your own fresh look at the piece of writing. If thus far you've been writing only in longhand or working only on-line—on a computer screen, without a paper printout—a good way to get a fresh look at your work is to see it typed or printed out for the first time. Often these changes in physical appearance will themselves trigger your seeing the piece as if for the first time. Whatever you can do to see the piece not as its writer but as its reader will help you discern the changes you need to make to improve it.

You might get the erroneous impression from our endorsement of peer-group responses that we think all "feedback" a writer might receive from peers is good advice. Of course, that's not so: sometimes a writer will get useless or bad advice. *Our* advice to counter such instances is that the writer should trust his or her own instincts about the writing: if the writer doubts a piece of advice, he or she should respect that doubt. Maybe the advice seems not worth pursuing at all, or maybe it's worth getting a second (and third) opinion. The quality of advice can vary, but the writer's good judgment is always essential.

Serious revision—that is, using our suggested terminology, revision drafts—should not begin until the writer is certain that the *content* of the writing is established. We call this "commitment to content," and that commitment should be clear before the writing can be refined and polished.

Because this revising process begins with the *biggest* elements that need change and works its way down in waves to the *smallest* considerations for change, we call this a top-down process.

We teach revising very methodically, as a process—or series of processes—that involves going through a piece of writing several times, with a different focus each time. One way to explain this concept is as a series of waves. The first wave of revising concerns itself with the piece's largest elements—does it satisfy its purpose, does it have the right content, does its overall structure make sense? Middle waves of revising primarily concern the structure of individual paragraphs and individual sentences. And the last wave of revising looks at the smallest elements—your own problems as a writer concerning such things as spelling and commas. This process does not require that you rewrite the piece three, four, or five times but, rather, that you go over it that many times, with each going-over focusing on a different aspect of what you've written. (If you have the hardbound edition of this book, see the handbook section for a full description of this process.)

When a student reaches the proofreading stage, as a teacher you can begin to look for distinctions between that student's writing "know-how" and that student's writing "want-to." Although most people find the mechanics of tightening a manuscript dull, confusing, daunting, or otherwise undesirable, at this stage attention must be paid to exactly those things—and, with time and effort, improvement (even accomplishment) of these things is possible. But you've got to *want to* improve on these things, or it won't happen. Only the student's effort on such matters—with your patient assistance, of course—can convert "want-to" to "know-how."

Proofreading

The last thing you do—and obviously you do more of this when you're writing for a class (or, for example, for your boss)—is proofreading. All the concern for the niceties of grammar, spelling, syntax, and word choice that you deliberately eschewed during earlier writing stages can now be given close attention.

The handbook section of the hardbound version of this book contains a useful list of the most common problems and errors in freshman writing, trouble spots for you to look for in your piece. Based on your high school experience you probably already have a good idea of your own key problem areas in relationship to proofreading. Using a word processor with a good spellchecker truly can help, but ultimately there is no substitute for looking carefully at *each* word—even if that means resting the point of your pencil on the paper right under each word—to make sure that word (or comma or semicolon) is right.

The process of writing as adapted to expressive writing differs from the process for other kinds of writing mainly (a) at the beginning, in what it is you're trying to do, and (b) at the end, in how the amount of polishing you do depends on whether you're writing for yourself or for someone else. In terms of the final product, you need also to look at what you've written in terms of the qualities we discussed in the "Key Points to Remember" section of this chapter—its honesty, its tone, and its level of detail.

As you proceed with your students through the term, observe their ways of going about writing. How do they change from task to task? Do they adapt their processes differently for different tasks? More basic still, does their handling of the process aspect of writing grow—that is, do they become more confident, more sophisticated, from assignment to assignment?

SAMPLE WRITING ASSIGNMENT AND CASE STUDY CLOSE-UP

Sample Assignment. Write a short piece about an experience that is vivid in your mind. All you're trying to do here is to capture on paper the important qualities of the experience. Your first audience, then, is yourself. But because you will be sharing this paper with your teacher and your classmates, you'll want to make sure, during revising, that the paper also communicates to others besides yourself.

Here's the first draft of a paper written by a student whose teacher made the above assignment. (You've seen the final draft of this paper; it's the "Mountain Memories" piece you read earlier in this chapter.) First the teacher worked with the students to isolate what kinds of subjects might make for better writing in this class. Students sometimes find a subject (like the death of a close relative) too painful to share with classmates, and classmates sometimes find certain subjects (sexual experiences, embarrassing moments, and so on) too awkward to hear about. Subjects that work well for students are often those which have rich sensory stimuli associated with them. Subjects for expressive writing work well if students feel strongly about them. And, of course, subjects work better if the writers know a great deal about them.

You may want to monitor carefully students' choices of topics here—they need to choose subjects that can be comfortably shared with the rest of the class.

After group brainstorming of possible topics, the students went home to write first drafts. The draft you see here has been cleaned up slightly in terms of spelling and sentence structure; the content, however, is just as the original had it.

My Mountain Memories

[First Draft]

1 Everyone has daydreams and fantasies, hopes and aspirations. This is one of my favorites. It's about a perfect world in which man and nature are one and the same.

2 It was one day last October when I came close to that. I remember that day--first there was the ride into the mountains, finding the right roads once we left the highway, getting to the trailhead, starting up the trail, being alone on the climb, and then realizing how much I hurt afterward.

3 By the time we got to the trail, we'd been bouncing over a jeep trail for nearly an hour. The first part of the four-mile trail was pretty easy. We smelled the fresh air, looked at the pines and maples around us, heard the stream rushing and gurgling below us, and we all sighed with relief. As the day wore on we were briefly surrounded by a cloud of gnats; they hovered over one spot in the trail and we walked through them.

4 The slope became steeper, and I became more aware of the physical features Mother Nature had displayed all around me: the huge rocks, the stream, the trees in the forest, and the strange silence of the mountain. Only the scuff and crunch of my boots on the gravel broke the silence. As I trudged on, my attention increasingly focused only on the trail, steeper

> and more rocky, tortuous, inexorable. There seemed to be increasingly only me and the trail. With each twist and turn I saw only more trail.
>
> Soon enough, by coincidence, I found to my surprise that I was at the 5
> front of my group. I was alone. Accustomed to the sound of only my own feet, I became aware of the leaves on the trees rustling in the wind that had sprung up as I got closer to the peak. With each turn, my body became more weary. I hoped only to get to the top for a rest, then come back down to civilization. More and more I became aware of my own being--bone, muscle, and sweat. The pain I was feeling became satisfaction--the hurt somehow united me with the world around me, with the collage of brown, blue, green, and white. The less I thought, the more I felt, the less there was a separation between me and the world around me. As I gave in to that merging, it seemed I was no longer tired at all--a machine made of two legs driving toward some uncertain goal.
>
> On the ride home, I was in pain and I loved it. I had become one with 6
> the mountain and the mountain one with me, and I knew that even though I was leaving the mountain, I would never be totally apart from it.

Ask your students to compare this draft with the final version, read earlier. What changed?

After this draft was written, students in the class reviewed both it and a subsequent draft. The first draft had enough material in it that most of the other students' comments sought only extension or explanation of items already in the paper. When they read the subsequent draft, the students found little to suggest. You can compare the draft above with the final paper (see page 65) to see what changes were actually made.

WRITING ASSIGNMENTS

We're just brainstorming possibilities here, to get an array of ideas to start with.

1. What expressive writing could you generate in the following categories:
   a. The achievement I am most proud of
   b. The achievement I am least proud of
   c. The best learning experience [or family experience, vacation, and so on] I ever had
   d. When I first learned responsibility
   e. The time I learned what being outdoors is really all about
   f. Two very different people who are both close to me
   g. How book learning sometimes becomes real

2. If you, like Ben Franklin, were writing an autobiography for your child, what would you include? Write a fragment of such an autobiography, depicting yourself twenty-five years from now.
3. What contemporary issues do you feel strongly about—abortion, gun control, arms to Third World nations, capital punishment, nuclear power, acid rain, other issues? With your teacher's advice on your selection of a topic, write a short expressive piece that explains how you feel. (*Note:* You're not arguing in favor of your views; you're simply explaining them.)
4. Reread "The Writer Herself: An Introduction." Write a short expressive piece about how you feel when you're writing. Try to work in some consideration of the physical location(s) where that writing takes place.
5. Reread this chapter's selection from Franklin's *Autobiography.* Many people experience changes of heart of the sort Franklin describes in this passage. Write a short, expressive piece about a time you experienced a similar change in the way you understand life. Try to ground the piece not so much in what you did or didn't do in certain circumstances but in how your understanding of life evolved and changed.
6. The famous painting on page 55, *The Scream* (Edvard Munch, 1893), is a work that seeks primarily to express a mood or feeling rather than to depict a scene pictorially. There's no narrative to this painting, no detailed scenery to provide a plot, only a minimal human shape. We see just the painter's attempt to put feeling on canvas in the purest form possible. Scrutinize this picture, then write a few unified paragraphs on one of the following suggestions:
   a. How does this painting make *you* feel?
   b. How does this painting achieve its purpose of conveying mood or feeling? (Is its title appropriate? Why?)
   c. Make up a story to go with this picture, one that would either begin or end with this scene.

Focus on Critical Writing

7. Both the Franklin piece and the Nin piece at the beginning of this chapter are written as though for a limited audience (although those two audiences are very different). What are the two audiences for these pieces, and how does each audience affect the writing to which it's directed?
8. Write a brief paper in which you take another look at the expressive writing examples in this chapter. What, specifically, is the tone of each one? Use examples (more than the ones this chapter uses) to demonstrate each piece's tone. (Remember, tone is the author's attitude toward the subject or the reader.) What are the primary differences among the pieces' tones? Experiment with tone a little on your own—try, for example, doing Janet Sternburg's piece in Ben Franklin's tone, or try writing his piece as your own father (or mother) might write it to you. From all of these exercises, try to make a concrete generalization about the role of tone in expressive writing.

The last line of this suggestion makes the assignment tough for some students. Again, we recommend that anyone attempting this paper start with specifics and use them to lead into the generalization(s).

Writers' Circle

Write down an expressive image that appeals to each of the five senses: taste, touch, smell, sound, and sight. For example:

1. The bite of pizza hinted at licorice, certain proof that the cook had used anise as a seasoning.
2. David reached into the hole in the tree and immediately found a sticky, spongy mess that oozed through his fingers.
3. The stench from the feedlot overwhelmed the passersby.
4. Evelyn heard the hissing and buzzing in the grass at her feet, but she didn't see the rattlesnake until it struck.
5. The sun seemed to hover on the western horizon, a giant orange farewell to the lingering day.

Now go around the room, with each student reading his or her list of images. As each list is read, the other students should note their favorites in each of the five categories. After everyone has read, make a list of what the class considers the best three images in each category. Discuss why these images are effective.

You might want to put the best images on the board and then challenge your students to write brief compositions in which all the images are woven together.

chapter 5 Writing to Explain or Inform:
Emphasis on the Reader's Understanding

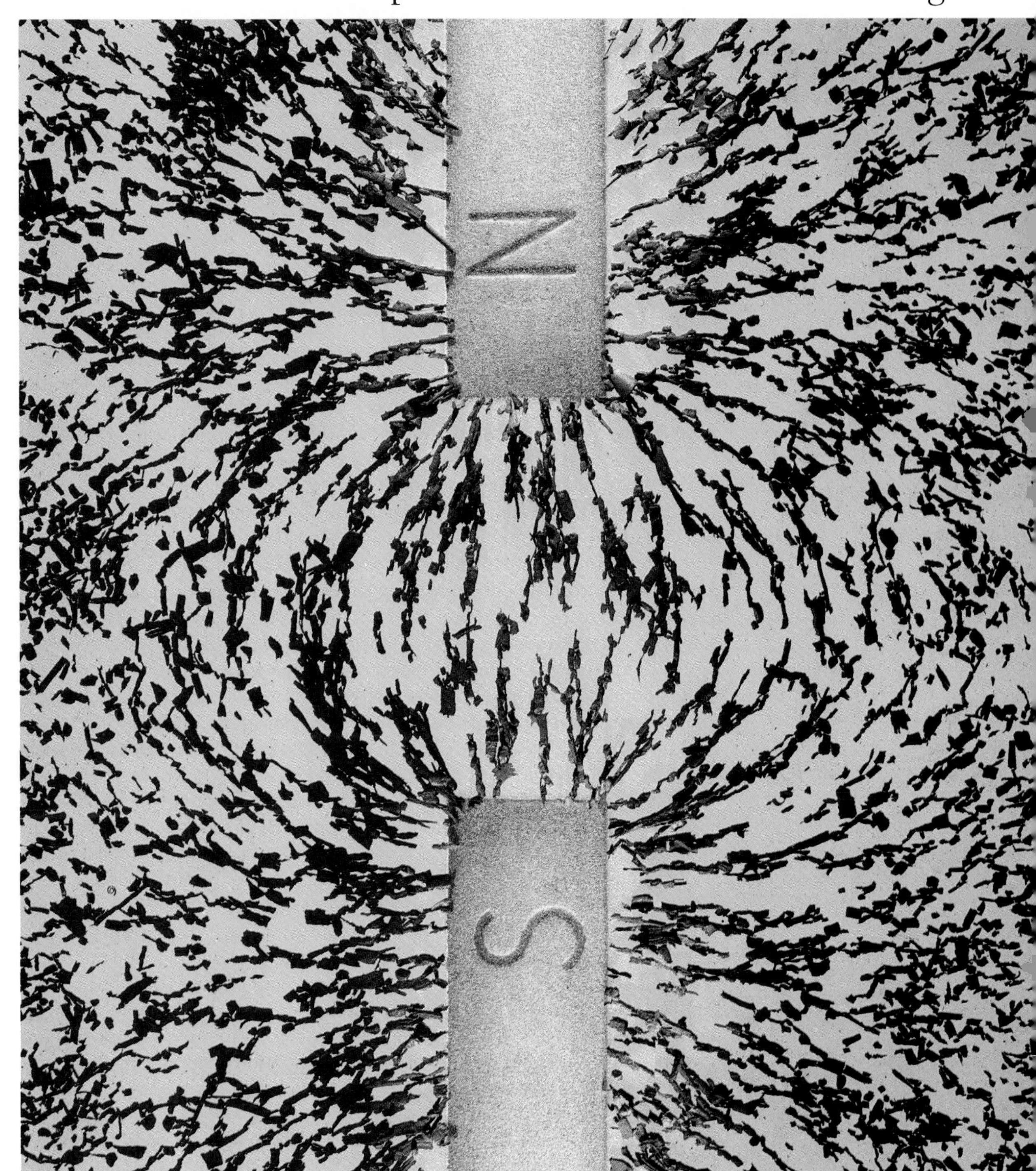

"Good writers are those who keep the language efficient. That is to say, keep it accurate, keep it clear."

Ezra Pound

"Of all the human tools invented, who would pick words to work with, the clumsiest for the job at hand? Shovels dig, wheels roll, levers lift, but words do not express."

Janet Burroway

Remember, our classification system is based not on form but on *purpose*, which we see as closely related to *function*—that is, the *reason*(s) the writer is writing and the objective he or she seeks to accomplish by way of that writing.

One of the most important kinds of writing for anyone to do—in college or out—is writing that explains or informs, emphasizing the reader's understanding as the primary communication goal. Whatever other reasons you have for writing, you're bound to be involved one way or another in explaining or informing. But explaining and informing come in myriad packages, as the examples that follow this brief introduction demonstrate. Writing to explain or inform could be something you use to show a teacher in any field that you *did* read the assignment and study your lecture notes; it could also be used to show that you've come to your own distinctive understanding of the material. Writing to explain or inform could come in the form of a description paper for your freshman English teacher, telling of your own background as a writer, or in the form of a description for botany class, telling how a particular kind of pinecone is aided by fire in releasing its seeds. Or writing to explain or inform could be part of a proposal you submit to request course credit for a summer co-op position. Obviously, then, the unifying element that allows us to talk about "writing to explain or inform" is not in that writing's structure or audience but in its purpose—in the writer's reason for writing and in the reader's reason for reading.

Many people who do lots of *expressive* writing—whether in the form of poetry for others to enjoy or in the form of a personal journal that only the writer sees—sincerely believe that expressive writing is an essential element of having a healthy emotional life. The phrase that comes up repeatedly is to "use the writing to help you get in touch with your feelings." Whether or not you yourself find doing expressive writing to be essential to your emotional life, you will certainly find explanatory/informative writing essential to your academic (and later your professional) life. Few students (and this book's authors feel that ideally there should be none) can graduate from any college or university without having to write in order to explain—to explain ideas, facts, or situations—and inform. And most professions today place even more communication requirements—reading, writing, speaking—on their members than they did when your parents were in school.

As a sidelight to the idea of writing to get in touch with one's feelings, you might point out that keeping a journal or diary is frequently an integral part of psychological therapy and counseling.

Here's another opportunity to poll your students on the writing requirements they face in their future professions.

In a sense, then, writing to explain or inform is nuts-and-bolts writing for students and professionals. And so it makes sense to take a nuts-and-bolts approach to getting better at doing it. In your effort to get better at it, you'll find that keeping a firm grip on the *reason* for the writing is the key. In this context, there are two sides of that reason to consider:

1. What's your purpose in writing this?
2. What's your reading audience's purpose in reading it?

After you answer these two questions, you must then make some hard decisions about how those two sides of the reason for doing this piece of writing need to shape the writing itself. We'll go into that activity—more a part of recognizing the reason for writing and sizing up the situation than of the physical process of writing—in more detail after showing you a few samples. But we need to make the point here: unless your writing to explain or inform is truly shaped by the *reason* for that writing—specifically, unless you let that reason help you decide what to leave in and what to leave out, as well as what structure to use—it won't be as good as it should be.

In writing to explain or inform, writers must unite their reasons for writing and their readers' reasons for reading. When the writing brings those reasons together successfully, the writing itself succeeds. To make this point more vividly, when you read the following passages try to envision the two sides of each negotiation: (a) what the writer wanted to accomplish and (b) what the reader wanted to see done.

Our first selection addresses a subject—writing college entrance essays—and an audience—students like you, just a few months ago—that we're sure you'll find of interest.

Each of us has published a technical writing textbook in which you can find elaboration of this theory of how purpose shapes the structure and content of writing to inform or explain.

This notion that meaning is negotiated between writer and reader is important. It doesn't mean literally that some sort of compromise meaning is discussed and agreed on between writer and reader; rather, it means that the actual meaning of what is on the page is arrived at by way of interaction between what the writer has intended to write and what the reader has intended to read.

Be Yourself When Writing College Essays

BOB LUNDEGAARD

Bob Lundegaard recently retired as a feature writer for the Minneapolis Star Tribune.

1 It's probably the most important essay a high school senior ever writes, and it's made all the more difficult by its open-endedness.

2 "Tell us something about yourself," suggests the college that the student is set on. "You may type or write by hand and attach additional sheets as necessary."

3 The student may have earned straight A's, creamed the college boards and had gobs of extra-curricular activities. Still, that personal essay can turn the palms sweaty and the stomach queasy. How can you put your best foot forward when you feel as though you have two left feet?

4 If that's your problem, the admissions directors at four colleges that require such essays from applicants have a word of advice: Relax.

Ask how many of your students wrote this kind of essay to gain entrance to either this or some other college. What approach did they take in their essays? Was it different from what Lundegaard advises?

Notice how the switch to "you" helps determine the tone of this piece—it's intended to be of interest to students.

This use of expert testimony is a typical persuasive technique. Aristotle called it argument from authority. Here it helps support Lundegaard's point.

Ask your students what general piece of advice this paragraph seems to boil down to.

Easy for them to say, right? But besides that obvious pointer, they have some specific guidelines for the would-be freshman. 5

"The best advice I can give anyone," said William Shain, dean of admissions at Macalester College in St. Paul, "is not to read any books on how to write college essays. It may lead you away from being yourself. There is no right answer to these essays, but the fun for us is that people suspect there might be. 6

"What we're seeking is something that will help us know you better. People tend to get too artificial about the application process, and the more they second-guess, the more they risk losing their individuality. When an essay reads like it's written by a 45-year-old attorney, that's counterproductive. When I was a high school teacher, I remember a student who wasn't an A student but was one of the wittiest, (most) offbeat, warmhearted students I knew. He wrote an essay for Yale that reflected this irreverence, but his parents told him he couldn't send something like that to Yale and helped him rewrite it, and it ended up sounding like the Treaty of Yalta. He was rejected by Yale, and I think that kid's strengths were shot down by too much interference." 7

Shain also emphasizes that "Essays that talk about feelings are better than those that talk about facts," a view echoed by James Reilly, dean of admissions at Ripon College in Ripon, Wisconsin. "The best recommendation I can give a student," Reilly said, "is to go beyond just sharing information and tell us why something is important. For example, students will write about their travel abroad and mention that everything was different there. Then they stop. They don't explain how those differences have changed them." 8

Reilly has another tip: "Don't send us your first draft. Read it and have a friend or teacher review it, not with the intention of rewriting but pointing out where things are vague." 9

Steve Syverson said, "We urge the students to be themselves." He is director of admissions at Lawrence College in Appleton, Wisconsin. "Some of the most impressive essays are not necessarily sophisticated in vocabulary but they communicate effectively," he said. "We want to hear something that's of interest to you. Don't treat it as a task you've been given. We're looking for two things: your ability to communicate and how you express your thoughts." 10

How important is the essay? Considerably, the admissions officers agree. "I'd say the essay has a truly major effect in about 5 percent of the cases," said Shain. "In another 15 to 20 percent, it's very important. The rest of the time, it serves to confirm what the rest of the file tells us, but it adds depth and texture so that you're not just computing numbers." 11

"It's very important to us," added Jon Nicholson, associate dean of admissions at Carleton College in Northfield, Minnesota. "Not so much for the content as for how the person expresses himself. The ability to write and 12 to write well is the single most important attribute of Carleton students. Poor organization, the lack of flow from one paragraph to the next—those are bad signs. The content comes in when we learn what makes that person different from anyone else. We're looking for people who've done interesting things and who express themselves well. In a college like ours where the great majority can handle the academic work, we're looking for things that will distinguish one student from another. We may find out more from an essay than a half-hour interview, and, since 75 percent of our students come from out of state, many don't even have that interview."

This clear statement of the importance of writing ability may surprise your students. Take comfort—now you have some support for what you've been saying!

13 Nicholson suggests, "Once you've chosen a topic, sit down and do a draft. Then put it away for three or four days. Don't even think about it. Then read it again and see if it makes sense. Does it say what you wanted to say? Does it say everything you wanted to say? Does it tell the admissions committee what you think they ought to know about you? Tell us what you're going to tell us, then tell us, then wrap it up and get out. Don't pad it and don't give us a lot of extraneous jargon. And exit gracefully."

14 Nicholson forwarded several essays from this year's freshman class that impressed the admissions office, but he added this caveat: "There's no one way to write an essay, no magic formula. The student who tries to figure out what will most impress the admissions committee or what's the 'right' way to do it will sacrifice both originality and spontaneity. These essays are good ones, but they shouldn't be used as models, but rather as examples."

Questions for Writing and Discussion

Prepare short written answers to each of these questions. Be ready to hand them in and/or discuss them in class, as your teacher directs.

1. Who do you suppose is the primary reading audience for this piece? How does what that audience wants or needs to know show up in the article? (It may be easier, in fact, for you to try to find places where you think that what the audience seeks does *not* show up.)
2. What kind of position on the subject does the writer take? That is, beyond the obvious (the writer is a newspaper reporter writing a column—doing the job), what is the writer's reason for doing *this* piece of writing? What is Lundegaard trying to accomplish?
3. Given the writer's and readers' reasons behind this article, what decisions do you think the writer would make about including each of the following pieces of information if he had access to them and room to add them?
   a. Statistics on what percentage of students who apply for college admission each year fail to get admitted
   b. Statistics on how standardized tests show that students' writing ability correlates closely with their college performance in all subject areas

c. Photographs of the people interviewed
d. A chart showing the average income of parents of students at each college whose personnel Lundegaard interviewed
e. Information on admissions standards from a large public and a small public institution (Lundegaard seems to have interviewed only officials of small private schools)

4. Notice how the grammatical point of view in the essay changes over the course of the first three paragraphs (from "the student" to "you"). How would you describe the effect of those changes?
5. How does the advice the author's four authorities give connect with the one word he uses, "Relax" (¶ 4)?
6. One real problem in writing to explain or inform is the issue of *authority*—why should the reader believe you on this topic? What is your authority to be saying these things? How does the writer of this piece deal with that problem?
7. If you were to write a similar piece advising college freshmen how to write papers for their English classes, how would you deal with the problem of authority?
8. What do the following words mean—*irreverence* (¶ 7), *extraneous* (¶ 13), *caveat, spontaneity* (¶ 14)?

Additional items after the Lundegaard piece:

1. **Ask your students how their response to what Lundegaard reports is different now from what it might have been when they were high school seniors.**
2. **Ask students to summarize what, according to this piece, good writing is. Is it significantly different from the descriptions we've been giving of good writing?**

Bob Lundegaard explains and informs regarding college entrance essays. His desire to inform is probably matched by his readers' desire to know. As you read the next piece, pay particular attention to being sensitive to the writer's reason for writing. More specifically, why would someone write something like this down? What's the writer's reason for writing it, and—based on evidence in the passage—how does she construe the reader's reason for reading it?

My Fortieth Birthday

MADELEINE L'ENGLE

This next selection is taken from the three-volume autobiographical series The Crosswicks Journal, *by Madeleine L'Engle, which details her family's life at their farm, Crosswicks. Madeleine L'Engle has written many books, including* A Wrinkle in Time. *In this selection she writes of her fortieth birthday, of a time before her career took off, when, as she says, "you could paper walls with my rejection slips." ("The Tower" is her study, over the garage, called by her children "the Ivory Tower.")*

On my birthday I was, as usual, out in the Tower working on a book. The children were in school. My husband was at work and would be getting the mail. He called, saying, "I'm sorry to have to tell you this on your birthday, but 1 you'd never trust me again if I kept it from you. [A publishing house] has rejected *The Lost Innocent.*"

2 This seemed an obvious sign from heaven. I should stop trying to write. All during the decade of my thirties (the world's fifties) I went through spasms of guilt because I spent so much time writing, because I wasn't like a good New England housewife and mother. When I scrubbed the kitchen floor, the family cheered. I couldn't make decent pie crust. I always managed to get something red in with the white laundry in the washing machine, so that everybody wore streaky pink underwear. And with all the hours I spent writing, I was still not pulling my own weight financially.

Ask your students if they've ever known anyone who felt guilty over spending what he or she thought was too much time writing.

3 So the rejection on the fortieth birthday seemed an unmistakable command: Stop this foolishness and learn to make cherry pie.

4 I covered the typewriter in a great gesture of renunciation. Then I walked around and around the room, bawling my head off. I was totally, unutterably miserable.

5 Suddenly I stopped, because I realized what my subconscious mind was doing while I was sobbing: my subconscious mind was busy working out a novel about failure.

L'Engle describes here a common experience: a moment in which a key decision—a life-affecting decision—is made. What "moments of decision" have your students had in their lives?

6 I uncovered the typewriter. In my journal I recorded this moment of decision, for that's what it was. I had to write. I had no choice in the matter. It was not up to me to say I would stop, because I could not. It didn't matter how small or inadequate my talent. If I never had another book published, and it was very clear to me that this was a real possibility, I still had to go on writing.

7 I'm glad I made this decision in the moment of failure. It's easy to say you're a writer when things are going well. When the decision is made in the abyss, then it is quite clear that it is not one's own decision at all.

Ask your students, "What is the logic of L'Engle's declaration here? What makes it convincing?"

8 In the moment of failure I knew that the idea of Madeleine, who had to write in order to be, was not image. . . .

9 During those difficult years I was very much aware that if I lost my ability to laugh, I wouldn't be able to write, either. If I started taking myself and my failure too seriously, then the writing would become something that was *mine,* that I could manipulate, that I could take personal credit—or discredit—for. When a book was rejected, I would allow myself twenty-four hours of private unhappiness. I'm sure I wasn't as successful in keeping my misery from the family as I tried to be, but I did try. Our house fronts on a dirt road—we didn't have the land with the brook, then—and I would go down the lane to do my weeping. I found that I could play games with the children during dinner (Buzz and Botticelli were our favorites), but I couldn't listen to Bach. But perhaps what was most helpful—and still is—is a white china laughing Buddha which sits on my desk in the Tower. He laughs at me, never with ridicule, but lovingly, tolerantly: you *are* taking yourself seriously, aren't you, Madeleine? What matters is the book itself. If it is as good a book as you can write at this moment in time, that is what counts. Success is pleasant; of course you want it; but it isn't what makes you write.

10 No, it's not. I found that out on the morning of my fortieth birthday.

Questions for Writing and Discussion

Prepare short written answers to each of these questions. Be prepared to hand them in and/or discuss them in class, as your teacher directs.

1. What's the relationship in this piece between writing to express and writing to explain? What in this passage makes you think that its author's reason for writing it is more to explain something to you than to sort something out for herself?
2. What could a reader hope to gain from reading this passage? How would that element change depending on whether the reader were (a) a fan of the author's or (b) someone who'd never heard of her?
3. What do you make of L'Engle's *voice* in this passage—the way her words sound, the kind of person she seems to be? How does that element compare with the voice in the preceding passage, about college entrance essays?
4. How does what L'Engle says in this passage compare with what is said about expressive writing in chapter 4?
5. According to L'Engle, what is it that makes her write?
6. What do the following words mean—*renunciation* (¶ 4), *abyss* (¶ 7), *laughing Buddha* (¶ 9)?

Additional items for the L'Engle piece:

1. Compare L'Engle's view of writing with Sternburg's. What are their differences and similarities?
2. Ask your students to tell their own stories about odd, symbolic things people do (or realize) on their birthdays.

Madeleine L'Engle informs us about a critically important discovery in her life as a writer. Her form is autobiographical. In the following piece, Carl Sagan informs us about the nature of science. His form is that of an article. As you read, pay special attention to the aspect of sizing up the reader. What type of reader do you think Sagan had in mind while writing? In particular, how well educated a reader do you think this piece is aimed at?

Science as a Way of Thinking

CARL SAGAN

Carl Sagan is a planetary astronomer, writer, editor, researcher, and lecturer. This selection is part of one of his books, Broca's Brain. *It introduces what is perhaps the central question of Sagan's book: can we* really *know the universe?*

Science is a way of thinking much more than it is a body of knowledge. Its goal is to find out how the world works, to seek what regularities there may be, to penetrate to the connections of things—from subnuclear particles, which may be the constituents of all matter, to living organisms, the human social community, and thence to the cosmos as a whole. Our intuition is by no means an infallible guide. Our perceptions may be distorted by training and prejudice or merely because of the limitations of our sense organs, which, of course, perceive directly but a small fraction of the phenomena of the 1 world. Even so straightforward a question as whether in the absence of friction a pound of lead falls faster than a gram of fluff was answered incorrectly by Aristotle and almost everyone else before the time of Galileo. Science is based on experiment, on a willingness to challenge old dogma, on an openness to see the universe as it really is. Accordingly, science sometimes requires courage—at the very least the courage to question the conventional wisdom.

2 Beyond this the main trick of science is to *really* think of something: the shape of clouds and their occasional sharp bottom edges at the same altitude everywhere in the sky; the formation of a dewdrop on a leaf; the origin of a name or a word—Shakespeare, say, or "philanthropic"; the reason for human social customs—the incest taboo, for example; how it is that a lens in sunlight can make paper burn; how a "walking stick" got to look so much like a twig; why the Moon seems to follow us as we walk; what prevents us from digging a hole down to the center of the Earth; what the definition is of "down" on a spherical Earth; how it is possible for the body to convert yesterday's lunch into today's muscle and sinew; or how far is up—does the universe go on forever, or if it does not, is there any meaning to the question of what lies on the other side? Some of these questions are pretty easy. Others, especially the last, are mysteries to which no one even today knows the answer. They are natural questions to ask. Every culture has posed such questions in one way or another. Almost always the proposed answers are in the nature of "Just So Stories," attempted explanations divorced from experiment, or even from careful comparative observations.

Call to students' attention how Sagan moves his essay along with such transitional markers as "Beyond this" and "But" at the beginnings of paragraphs.

3 But the scientific cast of mind examines the world critically as if many alternative worlds might exist, as if other things might be here which are not. Then we are forced to ask why what we see is present and not something else. Why are the Sun and the Moon and the planets spheres? Why not pyramids, or cubes, or dodecahedra? Why not irregular, jumbly shapes? Why so symmetrical, worlds? If you spend any time spinning hypotheses, checking to see whether they make sense, whether they conform to what else we know, thinking of tests you can pose to substantiate or deflate your hypotheses, you will find yourself doing science. And as you come to practice this habit of thought more and more you will get better and better at it. To penetrate into the heart of the thing—even a little thing, a blade of grass, as Walt Whitman said—is to experience a kind of exhilaration that, it may be, only human beings of all the beings on this planet can feel. We are an intelligent species and the use of our intelligence quite properly gives us pleasure. In this respect the brain is like a muscle. When we think well, we feel good. Understanding is a kind of ecstasy.

Ask students how this quotation can be seen as the heart of the piece: "If you spend any time spinning hypotheses, checking to see whether they make sense, whether they conform to what else we know, thinking of tests you can pose to substantiate or deflate your hypotheses, you will find yourself doing science."

Questions for Writing and Discussion

Prepare short written answers to each of these questions. Be ready to hand them in and/or discuss them in class, as your teacher directs.

1. How intelligent a reader does Sagan expect this passage to find? In your answer, cite evidence from the passage.
2. What is the point of this piece? Is it something about the nature of science, something about what it is to be a scientist, or something about the nature of understanding?
3. What is it in the third paragraph that contrasts with the means to knowledge as treated in the first paragraph (intuition or the evidence of the senses) and the means to knowledge as treated in the second paragraph (explanations that are like "Just So Stories")?
4. Sagan puts on one side of the issue intuition (¶ 1), perceptions (¶ 1), conventional wisdom (¶ 1), and "Just So Stories" (¶ 2). What does he put on the other side?
5. Both the second and the third paragraphs are built on accumulations of lists. Does this use slow down or speed up the reading of the paragraphs? How does this use of lists embedded in the text fit with the nature of writing to explain? What does it tell you about the kind of person Sagan wants us to think he is? What does it tell you about the kind of reader he envisions?
6. What specific facts does Sagan use in the essay? How much does one have to know about science to understand it?
7. What do the following words mean—*infallible, dogma* (¶ 1), *philanthropic* (¶ 2), *dodecahedra, exhilaration* (¶ 3)?

Additional items for the Sagan piece:

1. What are the three ways of thinking Sagan discusses?
2. What is Sagan's persona here?
3. If you were an aspiring scientist, how would you feel on learning that courage and thinking critically aren't enough?
4. How well does Sagan's enthusiastic, almost-mystical conclusion, (¶ 3) claiming that "understanding is a kind of ecstasy" fit with the rest of the piece? Has he built up to this kind of conclusion?

Bridges: Another Perspective

Carl Sagan has a popular and widespread image as a person who is a practicing scientist, one who believes deeply and enthusiastically in humankind's ability to use science in order to understand the universe. In Sagan's view, science is nothing less than an exciting search for the truth, for genuine knowledge that can be put to use for the good of all.

But the reality is that science is expensive, and science is only as good as the people who practice it. Much scientific research is funded by groups whose economic interests may lie in the suppression of the truth, the suppression of findings that could, if acted on, be disastrously costly for the funding groups. What if an utterly reliable scientific report, for example, informed a chemical waste management company that its current procedure of dumping chemical waste was dangerous, and the only safe methods of correcting the problem would cost so much that the company would have to close? Would there be pressure on the researcher to "find" the current methods safer?

Discuss the ethics of science. How can a balance be struck between the ideal and the real—or *should* such a balance be struck? Who should decide?

You should be able to find a wealth of material in newspapers and magazines regarding controversial issues on which science has a direct bearing—various kinds of waste dumping, depletion of the ozone layer, destruction of the rain forests, the greenhouse effect, and so on. Such material can be used to spur discussion as part of this Bridges exercise.

In this next example, the author, Robert M. Adams, has been talking about the history of England. As these two sections begin the year is 410, the last of the Roman legions has withdrawn, and a group called the Saxons is starting to make its presence felt. The two sections here describe, first, the Saxons, and second, that odd mixture of fact and fiction, King Arthur.

PREREADING WORKSHEET

Before you read the following piece by Robert M. Adams, write brief responses to these questions:

1. The excerpts are historical writing. What are your usual impressions about history as a subject and history as a kind of writing?
2. Have you heard of the Saxons before? If so, in what way?
3. Have you heard of King Arthur and the Knights of the Round Table? If so, what kinds of things have you heard?
4. Do you know where Denmark, Germany, Norway, the North Sea, England, Brittany, and Rome are? Where would you look for them on a globe?
5. What is a legend? How are legends built?

As you read these passages by Adams, look for ways he is working to make the subject matter easier and more interesting for the reader.

Saxon Wolves and Arthur the Briton

ROBERT M. ADAMS

Robert M. Adams is an editor of The Norton Anthology of Literature. The Land and Literature of England, *the source of this selection, is an extremely readable history; anyone who ever read a dull history book will appreciate Adams's writing ability. This selection describes some of the more interesting people in Britain during the time right after the last of the Roman legions left Britain (the fifth century* A.D.*).*

Saxon Wolves

1 Who were these Saxons, of whom we start to hear at the end of the fourth century? Like the Celts before them, they were a Germanic tribe from somewhere in the east, occupying, in the later stages of their wanderings, the middle part of that peninsula which today we call Denmark. Their neighbors in the province of Schleswig were called Angles or Angli, and the two tribes, mingling and intermarrying in the process, seem to have made common cause against tribal enemies in nearby Germany, like the Franks, Salii, and

Adams begins with a question he will subsequently answer—a technique often used as a simple organizational device to structure writing that explains or informs: [question] "Who were these Saxons? . . . [answer]

They were . . ." This device has kinship to what is known as the rhetorical question but is different in that the answer to a rhetorical question is always known and obvious; in fact, the answer is so well known that the usual result of asking the question is to cut off discussion, so as not to labor the obvious: "Are these barbecued ribs good, or what?"

Notice Adams's use of detail throughout the passage.

Do the Saxons sound a bit like groups of college students here?

Hermunduri, dwellers in the deep Thuringian forest. The part of Denmark where the Angles and Saxons settled is low and boggy; and from these bogs has been recovered a good deal of material from which we can get an idea of their civilization. They had the use of iron, from which they forged long swords and heavy battle-axes; and because they lived on the offshore islands as well as the mainland, they were quite at home on the water. Complete ships from a much later age survived in grave mounds and can now be seen in historical museums, like that at Oslo, Norway; and from them we can surmise what these early Saxon vessels were like. High in the prow and at the stern, they were low in the waist where rowers sat on benches; they were broad in the middle, pinching to a point at each end, so they were almost as easy to move backward as forward. When the wind was favorable, they could hoist a single square sail and skim over the water; to go against the wind, though by ever so little, the mariners had to down sail and row. For the vessels had little draft and hardly any keel; though this limited their sailing possibilities, it was advantageous in other ways: the ships could be rowed up shallow inlets and required practically no harbor facilities. And as each vessel could carry about four times as many warriors as it had oars (we may assume these early boats had not fewer than thirty oars), each ship was like a floating garrison.

The men who crossed the wild North Sea in cockleshells like this were 2
very tough customers indeed. Fighting was just about their only interest in life—fighting and getting enough loot to support them in glorious idleness till it was time to fight again. Their social organization emphasized the absolute importance of kinship and loyalty to the head of one's tribe; the most potent of all their gods was Ty or Tyr, the god of war. About the afterlife they did not think very much; probably most of them imagined it as a place where successful warriors got together, drank mead, and boasted of their prowess. In battle, their weapons were swords, spears, and heavy axes; they wore helmets and coats of mail (birnies), they carried shields. To begin with, they crossed the seas during the favorable summer season, caught the crops just as they were ripe for harvesting, and returned before winter; such a short campaigning season limited them to attacking settlements near the coast. About the middle of the fifth century a band of vagrant Saxons, or perhaps they were Jutes, led by warriors to whom later ages assigned, on doubtful authority, the names of Hengist and Horsa, came to England. They landed at Ebbsfleet on the Kent side of the Thames estuary, and were granted by King Vortigern a permanent home on the nearby island of Thanet. (It has not been an island since the channel silted up in the sixteenth century.) Vortigern wanted to use these dangerous acquaintances to fight off some troublesome Picts to the north. But the crafty barbarians said that without reinforcements they were unequal to so large a task; they would have to send home for more warriors. Vortigern took the bait. Angles, Saxons, and Jutes arrived in quantity, and before long they had defeated not only the Picts, but their host and his band of disorganized warriors, driving them back into the swamps and mountains of western England. This was a relatively easy job because the

Romans had set up their defenses against enemies coming from the west and north; the new invaders came from the south and east, and once ashore there was nothing to stop them. When they found themselves securely settled in the new land, they promptly acquired horses, which enabled them to make long, swift raids inland.

Arthur the Briton

3 A victim of the Saxons who hid away in remote Cornwall and southern Wales was a leader named Uther or Arthur. We know him as King Arthur, lord of the knights of the Table Round, the original of Tennyson's mournful gentleman in the *Idylls of the King.* What the historic Arthur was like is an agreeable if idle speculation; hardly anything can be seen through the mists of time except that he rallied the Welsh and Cornish outlaws, fought sundry battles, and was destroyed, perhaps by a traitorous friend or deceitful wife. Whether the tale of his exploits was carried directly to French Brittany by Britons fleeing the Saxon onslaught or ripened for centuries in Wales before crossing the channel has been much mooted. There can be little question that it germinated for a long time in darkness, getting confused here and there with sundry vegetation myths, solar legends, and fertility rites; it accumulated episodes and used up heroes. Over the centuries, it got heavily Christianized, and in Geoffrey of Monmouth's *History of the Kings of Britain* (early twelfth century), it swelled briefly to monstrous proportions. (Arthur not only becomes emperor of Britain, he carries his career of conquest abroad, and expands his sway as far as Rome.) Early or late, the saga crossed the channel to Brittany where professional minstrels picked it up, broke it into a number of short, interlaced narratives, and passed them along to Chretien de Troyes (late twelfth century), who made of them the substance of his poetic life work. Legendary materials based on the story of Arthur and his companions now became the common property of Europe; and, as different artists selected different parts of the story for use as diverting fable or pseudo-history, they naturally invented new characters or gave new coloring to old ones. Arthur himself was sometimes the boldest of all his knights, sometimes a sleepy old dotard, like Charlemagne in the other great cycle of romantic legends. The story of the Holy Grail, mixed with various Celtic fertility rituals and tales of pre-Christian heroes, was grafted onto the basic story of the Table Round. The story of Tristan and Iseult, once quite independent, also got built into the larger cycle of Arthur stories; the jointing was perfunctorily done, and you can still see that the story doesn't quite "belong" in Arthurian company. Other additions and changes were freely made as the tales went their rounds. In a word, the Arthur legend is a tiny grain of fifth-century fact around which have been deposited layer upon layer of other miscellaneous material from every kind of random source. We shall have more to say of it later, in connection with Sir Thomas Malory particularly; but as the Anglo-Saxon tide sweeps over Roman Britain, we have no business thinking of

You might bolster what students know about Arthur with references to the Holy Grail, the sword in the stone, Merlin, Camelot, and so on.

Other important works of world literature, among them *Iliad, Odyssey,* and *Gilgamesh,* have similar backgrounds.

Compare the effect of this "tiny grain" of fact with a similarly influential "grain" in Kim Chernin's "Kaahumanu and Eve" (see chapter 9).

Lancelot and Guinevere, Galahad and the Holy Grail. The Germanic horde is at the gate; they have driven off the cattle, torched the farmhouse, slaughtered the pig, raped the women, and are even now torturing the landlord—you can hear his choked screams—to find out where his money is hidden. For the old proprietors, it is lights out; whether the ragged, semistarved serf working his field in a lonely forest clearing recognized or regretted the Saxon invasion, we cannot know.

Ask students what effect Adams's narration in the last few lines achieves.

POSTREADING WORKSHEET

Now that you have read the piece by Adams, write your responses to the following questions:

1. Did reading Adams's piece alter your usual impressions about history as a subject and history as a kind of writing? If so, how?
2. How does Adams's account of the development and changes in the Arthurian legend compare with your earlier idea of how legends are built?
3. What do you think was the most interesting information in the "Saxon Wolves" excerpt? the least interesting part of that excerpt?
4. What do you think was the most interesting information in the "Arthur the Briton" excerpt? the least interesting part of that excerpt?
5. Extra credit:
   a. Locate all the named locations on an outline map of western Europe.
   b. Identify the following: Alfred Tennyson, Geoffrey of Monmouth, Sir Thomas Malory, the Holy Grail.
   c. Determine how many of your classmates are of Celtic origin and, within that classification, what different varieties are represented. Do any of these classmates still identify with their ancestors that many generations back? If so, in what ways?

Questions for Writing and Discussion

Prepare short written answers to each of these questions. Be ready to hand them in and/or discuss them in class, as your teacher directs.

1. What devices do you see the author of these passages using to heighten their sense of drama? (For example, consider the use of the opening question, in the first paragraph.) When you can sense an author working to make the subject matter more interesting, what does that tell you about how the author envisions the relationship between the author's reason for writing and the reader's reason for reading?
2. Judging from the evidence in these passages, does the author think his readers are more interested in ideas, or in individuals? in facts and figures, or

in actions? What do your answers to those questions tell you about the author's negotiation between his reasons for writing and our reasons for reading?

3. In what ways are your characteristics as a reader of this piece different from those of the readers the author probably had in mind originally?
4. How does the length of the paragraphs in this piece affect your responses to it? Do you see places where these long paragraphs could be broken up? Should they have been?
5. What do the following words mean—*surmise, garrison* (¶ 1), *cockleshells, prowess, mead, estuary* (¶ 2), *mooted, perfunctorily, dotard* (¶ 3)?
6. Do you think these passages tell you more than you want to know about the subject? Where do you want less? more?
7. How would you characterize the author's voice in these passages? Give specific examples from the passages.
8. Do you think the author could write an interesting history textbook? Why or why not?

So far in this chapter we have seen explanatory, informative writing in the form of a news feature, a personal memoir, an article on science, and a historical account. What follows is another common kind of informative writing: directions for performing a task.

How to Rig a Plastic Worm Texas-Style

Daniel Warner, college writing student

1 The best lure for bass is the plastic worm. More bass have been caught on a plastic worm than on any other lure. There are many ways to fish with a plastic worm, but the Texas-style rig is the most popular method with bass anglers because it is simple and productive. To produce a Texas-style rig you will need a plastic worm, a worm hook, and a bullet-shaped slip sinker. I use a 7½-inch Culprit worm, a 2/0 True Turn worm hook, and a ⅛-ounce slip sinker.

2 The bullet-shaped sinker makes it possible to fish through the thick weeds or branches without snagging the hook often in the tangled growth. The sinker also allows the rig to be cast a long way, then retrieved along the bottom. Another advantage of the slip sinker is that it doesn't "spook" a bass when it bites, because the bass feels only the

natural weight of the worm. If a bass bites a plastic worm and feels extra weight, it is likely to spit the worm out. Once you have your rod and reel, worm, hook, and sinker, you're ready to produce a Texas-style rig.

First, stick the end of the fishing line through the hole in the slip sinker and slide the sinker up the line. Be sure the narrow end of the sinker is pointed forward, as shown in figure 1. 3

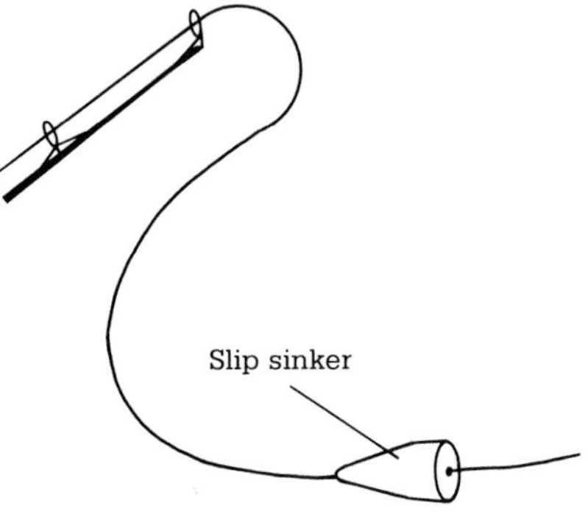

Figure 1

Next, tie the hook to the end of the line. I tie the hook on the line with what is called an Improved Clinch Knot. A diagram for tying an Improved Clinch Knot appears in the Appendix. 4

Now stick the point of the hook ½ to ¾ of an inch through the tip of the worm, and bring the point out the side of the worm as shown in figure 2. Continue to slide the worm up the hook until the tip of the worm reaches the eye of the hook, as shown in figure 3. 5

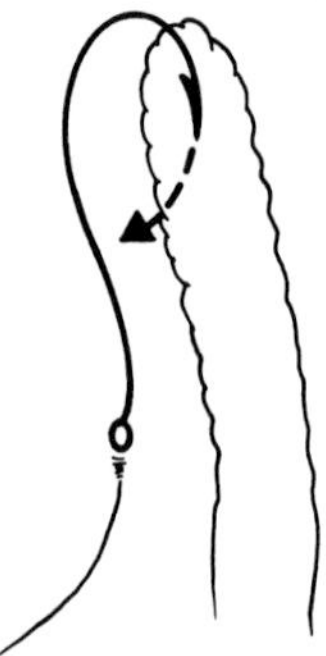

Figure 2

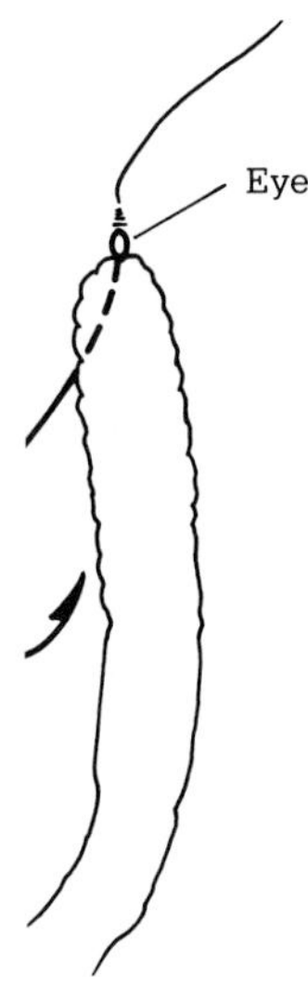

Figure 3

6 Finally, bury the point and barb of the hook just under the surface of the worm, as seen in figure 4. A good way to do this is to turn the hook so that the point and barb face the worm (as in figure 3) and then touch the hook's point against the worm to see where it should be stuck in. Be sure the worm is straight on the hook after the point and barb are buried, because a crooked worm can twist your line.

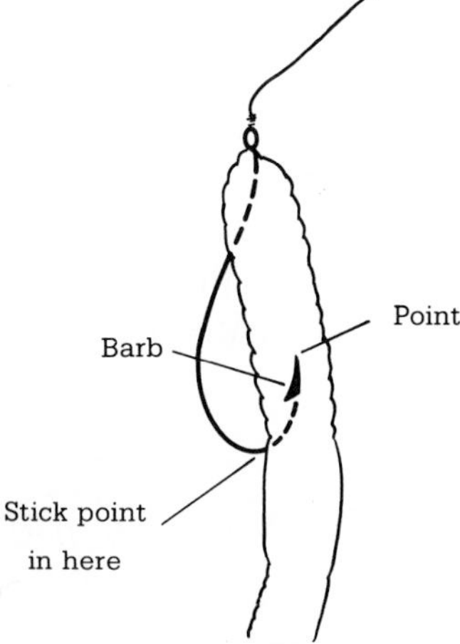

Figure 4

Now you have completed the Texas-style rig of the plastic worm. Your rig should look similar to the one shown in figure 5. If it does, gas up the bass boat, stock the cooler, and head for the lake. 7

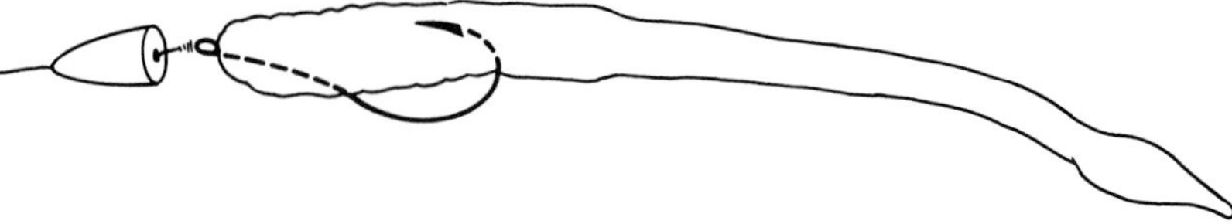

Figure 5

Appendix: Tying the Improved Clinch Knot

1. Pull about 6 inches of line through the eye of the hook and wrap the end around the standing part of the line five times.

2. Pass the end of the line through the small loop.

3. Pass the end of the line through the big loop and tighten the knot by pulling on the standing line and the end of the line.

4. Trim the excess line from the finished knot.

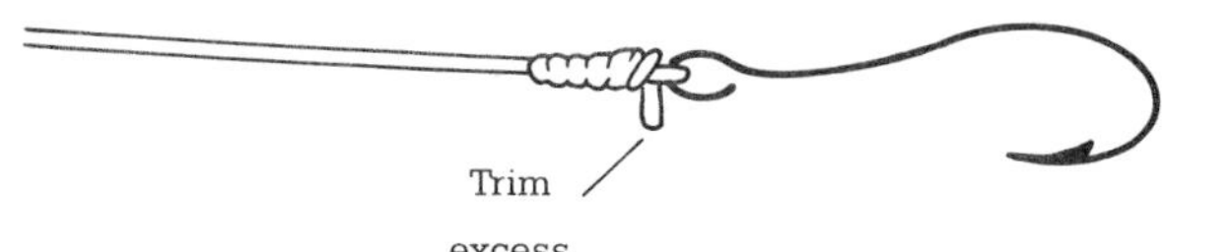

Questions for Writing and Discussion

Prepare short written answers to each of these questions. Be ready to hand them in and/or discuss them in class, as your teacher directs.

1. What kind of reader do you think this is aimed at—someone who has never been fishing, or someone who is already experienced at fishing? Why do you think that?
2. How does the author of this piece establish his own expertise on the subject? Is that expertise important?
3. How does the presence of drawings accompanying the text change your response to it? Why?

Additional items after the Warner piece:

1. How are this piece and Lundegaard's piece on writing essays for college entrance alike in the way the authors make assumptions about readers?
2. In the context of a piece like this, how much does the truth value of a statement like "more fish are caught with . . ." matter?

KEY POINTS TO REMEMBER: Writing to Explain or Inform

Because writing to explain or inform can occur in so many settings—from an English class in which you're explaining something about a poem to a government office in which you're explaining what a particular foreign aid plan involves—it's hard to generalize about the key points to keep in mind for this kind of writing. The infinite number of topics you could write about complicates the situation still further. In some ways, then, the key points for doing this kind of writing resemble key points for doing *any* kind of writing; the ones we list here are those we think especially important for writing to explain or inform, but they are also important for, say, writing to analyze—as you will see in the next chapter.

- Keep your *reason for writing* and your audience's *reason for reading* squarely in mind.
- *Adjust the content* of what you write to the reasons distinguishing that piece.
- Make your *reasoning* process explicit.
- Use a *structure* your reader can see.
- Don't let subject matter bog down *style and tone.*

Keep Your Reason for Writing and Your Audience's Reason for Reading Squarely in Mind

This kind of writing needs to be shaped from the inside by its purpose—usually, by some particular point needing to be made or idea needing to be explored. As part of recognizing the reasons for writing and sizing up the situation, it doesn't

Bringing in additional examples of writing in which the writer's and readers' purposes seem especially well met will reinforce this point effectively.

Remind your students that there is a danger in writing shaped totally by content. Doing such a draft is a good first-draft technique—"Just dump the content out on paper any way it comes out to see if you have enough to do this report with"—but that draft needs *lots* of revising, based on audience and purpose especially, before it's a finished piece.

hurt in this kind of writing to write down your reason for writing and what you construe to be your reader's reason for reading. How you construe those purposes may well change as you write—and as you revise—causing you to change the words you wrote down as your initial statement of purpose. That alteration in turn requires you to revise what you've already written to support more fully the purpose that evolved as you wrote the second half. That's just one of the ways this kind of writing needs to be driven by a sense of purpose.

You can see in this chapter's first selection the way purpose shapes an entire piece of writing to explain or inform. "Be Yourself When Writing College Essays" is a good example of an essay in which every line contributes to the development of one major point, here expressed by the title.

- The first paragraph ("It's probably the most important essay . . . ") establishes the importance of the topic and sets the problem ("it's made all the more difficult by its open-endedness").
- The second paragraph explains the open-endedness ("Tell us something about yourself"), and the third paragraph sharpens the problem to a fine point ("How can you put your best foot forward when you feel as though you have two left feet?").
- The remainder of the piece—another ten or so paragraphs—consists totally of statements by college admissions directors about how such admissions essays need to be written.

Adjust the Content of What You Write to the Reasons Distinguishing That Piece

If you wanted to explain how a tree turns sunlight into usable energy, how would you know when you had gone far enough? Earlier in your life you might have limited the scope of such a piece to what you know—write what you know, and then stop. But now you've got a college or university library to use, and with that much information just a short walk away the amount of data at your disposal can no longer be used by itself to establish the limits of your writing. So how do you decide how *deep* and how *long* to make the piece? The answer depends on the answers to three questions:

1. How much of the subject you're writing about are you *sure enough* of to be comfortable writing about it?
2. What kind of reader are you writing for?
3. What can you do to reach that reader most effectively?

Have your students look again at the Carl Sagan piece. See whether they can determine the level of knowledge of the audience based on internal evidence within the piece.

And many times, as in the third selection in this chapter (by Carl Sagan), although you may *know* a great deal more about your subject than you ultimately say, your goals in relationship to your audience—and the nature of that audience—may narrowly limit what you finally wind up doing.

In "Science as a Way of Thinking," Carl Sagan offers us a careful explanation of what scientific thinking is and what it is not. One might paraphrase the piece by saying that,

> According to Sagan, scientific thinking is *not* intuition, sense perceptions, conventional wisdom, or the kind of attempted explanations Sagan calls "Just So Stories." Scientific thinking *is* critical examination; it *is* questioning—the spinning of hypotheses; it *is* an attempt to "penetrate into the heart of the thing." And in that last sense, the understanding produced by scientific thinking is a kind of ecstasy.

Notable among other things in this essay is that Sagan does all this without mentioning much science—certainly the reader he is writing for is not expected to know any science. Thus the subject matter is not science but, rather, ways of thinking. Certainly Sagan knows much more about this subject than he says here—his knowledge is both deeper and broader—but his assumption that he's writing for an audience of nonscientists has apparently placed strict limits on how much and what kinds of his knowledge he can and cannot use here.

Make Your Reasoning Process Explicit

Often this kind of writing will show right on its surface the writer's process of thinking through a problem. It's as though the writer is saying to the reader, "Here's how I worked this out—follow me through this process and you can understand this problem [or issue, process, idea] as well as I do." A good example of this kind of structuring can be seen at the beginning of the piece by Madeleine L'Engle, "My Fortieth Birthday."

There are really two levels, two parts, to L'Engle's piece. One part (¶ 1–8) details a crisis in her inner life, when on her fortieth birthday the rejection of a book manuscript by a publisher causes her to think she's not really a writer after all. Through the first eight paragraphs of the piece she leads us through her thoughts and feelings as she rediscovers that she really is someone who simply has to write. The second part of the piece (¶ 9–10) then turns around and shows us her remembering not to take herself too seriously anyway. Throughout the selection we see inside her mind and heart; the points we come to understand are those we discover through watching her own discovery process at work.

Remember, this isn't rhetorical analysis for the sake of analysis; rather, it's for illustrating the point about how the writer needs to make his or her reasoning explicit, especially in writing to explain or inform.

The signposts along the path of L'Engle's thinking and feeling are easy to see in this selection: they're right there on the surface. Here's just a partial list:

"This seemed an obvious sign from heaven" (¶ 2).

"So the rejection . . . seemed an unmistakable command" (¶ 3).

"I realized what my subconscious mind was doing while I was sobbing" (¶ 5).

"In my journal I recorded this moment of decision" (¶ 6).

"I'm glad I made this decision in the moment of failure" (¶ 7).

"During those difficult years I was very much aware . . . " (¶ 9).

You may encounter doubt among your students as they read and/or discuss this material; they may ask, "Do people *really* write this way?" Yes, one way or another: they either *write* or *revise* this way (which amounts to the same thing, overall). Such signposts may not be planned, literally, but the writer will add them to make connections clear, to add the coherence needed for the reader. The point is that they may be added at any time during the writing process but are *always* there in the finished product of good writing.

Linda Flower is credited with making the useful distinction between "writer-based" prose (writing that is not ready, or intended, for readers other than the writer) and "reader-based" prose (logically, writing that *is* ready, or intended, for readers other than the writer). (See Flower, "Writer-Based Prose: A Cognitive Basis for Problems in Writing.") The distinction is useful, especially when we remember that virtually all writing begins as "writer-based" and then goes through the processes of revision that result in good "reader-based" prose. You can dramatize this difference (as we have tried to do at various places in this book) by showing students "writer-based" and "reader-based" versions of the same piece of writing.

No writing has to be stuffy and boring. What's critical is what the writer is willing to put into it. Notice, how Sagan *accepts* the challenge of writing about science so that it will be interesting. That acceptance goes a long way toward his success with the material.

Not only are we allowed to "hear" L'Engle's innermost thoughts; we also hear what her white china laughing Buddha has to say to her: "He laughs at me . . . you *are* taking yourself seriously" (¶ 9). With the aid of these signposts, the "inner" structure of L'Engle's writing is made outer.

Use a Structure Your Reader Can See

This point, for some pieces of writing, may take pretty much the same kind of form as the preceding point ("make your reasoning process explicit"). Or it may look totally different, as in the "Texas Rig" example earlier in the chapter. For instructions, as in "How to Rig . . . " the obvious sequence to use is the sequence of the process itself. Thus the piece begins with a statement of why the material is important ("The best lure for bass is . . . "; "More bass have been caught on . . . "). It then proceeds to list the materials needed to assemble a Texas-style rig, and to detail the steps to create the lure. The organization of the text is thus set according to what the reader needs to know next, and next, and next. This kind of *reader-based* structure—very apparent in the "Texas Rig" piece—characterizes much of the best writing to explain or inform.

Don't Let Subject Matter Bog down Style and Tone

Some people act as though this kind of writing—writing that often lacks either a strong argumentative edge or a powerful feeling behind it—must necessarily be stuffy sounding and boring. Or that while such writing may not necessarily *have* to be stuffy and boring, nothing's wrong if it is. Well, nothing could be further from the truth. This kind of writing, like any other kind of writing, can be as good as the author's time, talent, and determination can make it.

The selection titled "Saxon Wolves and Arthur the Briton" shows clearly how well written and interesting this kind of writing can be. One thing that makes these passages so interesting is the author's broad and deep knowledge of the subject, together with the ways that knowledge is reflected in his saturating the writing with facts and information. Literally every line adds new information, and few words are spent doing otherwise. Another thing that makes these passages so interesting is the way they're written.

The author, Robert Adams, uses so many ways to make the sentences interesting that it's impossible to list them all. Here's just a partial list:

Sentence 1 (¶ 1): question.

Sentence 2 (¶ 1): comparison.

Sentence 3 (¶ 1): nice parallelism in the verbs ("mingling and intermarrying") and a great, evocative phrase ("the deep Thuringian forest").

Sentences 4 and 5 (¶ 1): A change in sentence structure, rhythm, and length from those in the previous sentences, the change itself lasting long enough to set a new pattern. That is, sentence 3 is chopped up and involved, taking quite a while to get from beginning to end, whereas sentences 4 and 5 both

> have two very straightforward clauses: (a) in sentence 4, subject-verb-complement-semicolon-second clause and (b) in sentence 5, subject-verb-object-prepositional phrase-semicolon-long dependent clause ("because they lived . . . ")-short subject-verb-object.

A good indication of the complexity and variety of the style of this passage is that it takes so much longer to describe than it does to read. If you want to see a demonstration of real stylistic skill, look again at all the sentence-level variety in the last half of the third paragraph. Despite the fact that it's writing about history, this is not boring writing.

Ask your students each to bring in a piece of writing they consider boring. Choose the five to seven pieces *you* consider the most boring, and then divide the class into groups of three, assigning each group a selection to work on improving. Compare the improvements with the originals and discuss what specifically makes the improvements better.

✓✓✓ WORKSHEET: Writing to Explain or Inform

So what do you do when faced with a writing task that requires you to explain or inform? Remember the basic approach to writing we explained in chapter 1:

- Consider your motives: your reasons for writing.
- Think about what you're doing—what you're going to be writing about, who you're writing for, what details will help.
- Do your drafting, realizing that your priority in a first draft is to get the content down right. Then read over what you've written.
- Revise and edit systematically.
- Proofread carefully.

How does this process need to be customized for writing to explain or inform? Generally, getting the material down on paper is the easy part in this kind of writing. The parts that tend to get left behind—considering your purpose, your reader's purpose, and what kinds of revising need to go on in light of those factors—do so because the composing is fairly easy. So what you need to do is go ahead and get the content-based part of the writing done (obviously, that's vital), while remembering that the pre- and postcomposing phases are equally important, especially the role your purpose and your reader's purpose need to play.

As we said earlier, a good first draft of writing intended to explain or inform is usually strongly content-oriented—what computer fans call a "data dump": all information and no life. Good *reader-based* revising can make a good report out of a data dump. The problems come when someone turns in the data dump as a final version; even if it is grammatically sound and error-free, it's still deadly dull writing. All good writing always takes the readers and their needs and interests into account, and this is especially true of good explanatory/informative writing.

 SAMPLE WRITING ASSIGNMENT AND CASE STUDY CLOSE-UP

Here we're going to show you how one small feature of a student paper was controlled by considerations of audience. The student paper we'll be looking at is "How to Rig a Plastic Worm Texas-Style," which you read earlier in this chapter. The assignment, from a freshman English class at a large state university, asked the students to explain a process they were familiar with for an audience that did not know that process. One student, Daniel Warner, decided to write about how to construct a particular kind of fishing lure, called a Texas Rig.

What we'll examine here is the material currently in the Appendix: how to tie the Improved Clinch Knot. In an earlier draft of the paper, the material you read as an appendix, "Tying the Improved Clinch Knot," was part of the text itself. It looked like this:

> First, stick the end of the fishing line through the hole in the slip sinker and slide it up the line. Be sure the narrow end of the sinker is pointed forward, as shown in figure 1.
>
> Next, tie the hook to the end of the line. I tie the hook on the line with what is called an Improved Clinch Knot. The following instructions demonstrate how to tie that knot.
>
> 1. Pull about 6 inches of line through the eye of the hook and wrap the end around the standing part of the line five times.
>
>   **(Illustration)**
>
> 2. Pass the end of the line through the small loop.
>
>   **(Illustration)**
>
> 3. Pass the end of the line through the big loop and tighten the knot by pulling on the standing line and the end of the line.
>
>   **(Illustration)**
>
> 4. Trim the excess line from the finished knot.
>
>   **(Illustration)**
>
> Now stick the point of the hook ½ to ¾ of an inch through the tip of the worm, and bring the point out the side of the worm, as shown in figure 2. Continue to slide the worm up the hook until the tip of the worm reaches the eye of the hook, as shown in figure 3.
>
> **(Then the draft continues.)**

Again, it's reader-based (that is, audience-based) revising that turns a data dump into a good piece of explanatory writing.

The problem with this version of the paper is that the material on how to tie the knot is an unnecessary interruption in the paper, which is otherwise directed clearly toward how to fasten the worm on the hook. How to tie the knot needs to be there, but as an appendix, not as an interruption in the text. Thus when the author showed this draft to a classmate, he got the suggestion to put the knot-tying material in an appendix. The resulting version is what appears earlier in this chapter. The kind of revising that change shows—call it audience-based revising—is especially important when you're writing to explain or inform. Usually in that situation you know much more than you perhaps need to say, just as Daniel Warner obviously knows more about fishing than he can or should say here. The question then becomes how to decide what to include and what to exclude. The answer is to enter that negotiation between reader's purpose and writer's purpose described earlier in this chapter. In the case of "How to Rig a Plastic Worm Texas-Style," that meant moving the instructions on how to tie a clinch knot into the Appendix.

WRITING ASSIGNMENTS

1. Do the following in sequence:
   a. Take on the role of a high school English teacher trying to help her students do better at gaining admission to their choice of colleges—rewrite "Be Yourself When Writing College Essays" as a one-page handout for high school seniors.
   b. Now reflect on the decision making you did during task a. Write a short piece explaining how you decided what to leave in and what to leave out.
2. Take another look at Madeleine L'Engle's "My Fortieth Birthday." An alternative title for the piece might be "How I Learned I Really Am a Writer." Write an imitation of L'Engle's piece, titled "How I Learned I Really Am a ____________" (fill in the blank any way you want) or "How I Learned I Really Am Not a ____________." In your writing, make sure the process of reasoning that leads to your conclusion is clear to your audience.
3. Write a short explanation of one of the following phenomena (taken from Sagan's essay earlier in the chapter):
   a. The shape of clouds
   b. The shape of dewdrops
   c. The origin of a name or a word
   d. The reason for a human social custom
   e. Why the moon seems to follow us when we walk
   f. What prevents us from digging a hole down to the center of the earth
   g. The definition of *down* on a spherical earth
   h. How the body converts food into muscle
   i. How far is up (Does the universe go on forever?)

   You'll probably have to do a little library digging to write your essay; if so, be sure to credit your sources. Write the essay for your classmates, and try to make it as interesting as you can. Don't focus so much on telling everything you learn about the subject as on being clear and interesting.

Other "science phenomena" questions for which students might want to pursue written answers are these:

1. If rain falls so far and so fast, why doesn't it hurt us when it hits us?
2. Why do a penny and a silver dollar fall at the same rate of speed when they're dropped from a tall building?
3. Why does water swirl down a drain in a different direction south of the equator?

4. Pick any group of people from another time and another place—Columbus's crew, the Anasazi Indians, the early suffragists, the writers of the Declaration of Independence, the defenders of the Alamo—and write a short description in the style of Robert Adams's "Saxon Wolves and Arthur the Briton." Once again, write with an audience of college freshmen in mind. Try to imitate Adams's style, tone, and approach.
5. The picture at the beginning of this chapter (page 77) shows magnetism at work. With your class providing information as a group, help your teacher write a short paragraph on the board describing how and why magnetism does what it does. Then, with guidance from your teacher, go to your library and find a picture of some other natural phenomenon—the Northern Lights, a cell undergoing division, a volcano erupting—and write a short description of how and why that phenomenon does what it does. (You will need to be

scrupulous about informing your readers about the sources you used—title, author(s), publishers, date, page number(s), and so on.)

Focus on Critical Writing

6. The place you're probably most likely to see writing to explain or inform is in your college textbooks. Pick a short (one- or two-page) section from one of your textbooks and rewrite it for an audience one or two years behind you in knowledge of the subject. Provide your teacher with a copy of the original section and with an analysis of the decision making you did as part of rewriting the passage.
7. Both "Be Yourself When Writing College Essays" and "Saxon Wolves and Arthur the Briton" were originally written primarily for an audience of high school seniors. Write a short critical piece in which you compare and contrast these two authors' approaches. How does each author approach reaching that particular audience? Is it possible to make a decision in any meaningful way about which approach is better? Why or why not?

Writers' Circle

One of the most prolific authors of writing that explains and informs is Isaac Asimov, who has published more than four hundred books and numerous articles. Dividing into groups of three, go to the library and find a short piece by Asimov, make a copy of it, and then examine the piece to determine what kind of reader Asimov has written it for. Each group should collaboratively write a report of its findings regarding Asimov's audience, explaining why the group chose that audience based on evidence found in the writing itself. Attach the copy of the Asimov piece to the report and submit it. Possible audiences for consideration: expert, layperson, or science fiction fan.

chapter 6 Writing to Analyze: Emphasis on the Subject

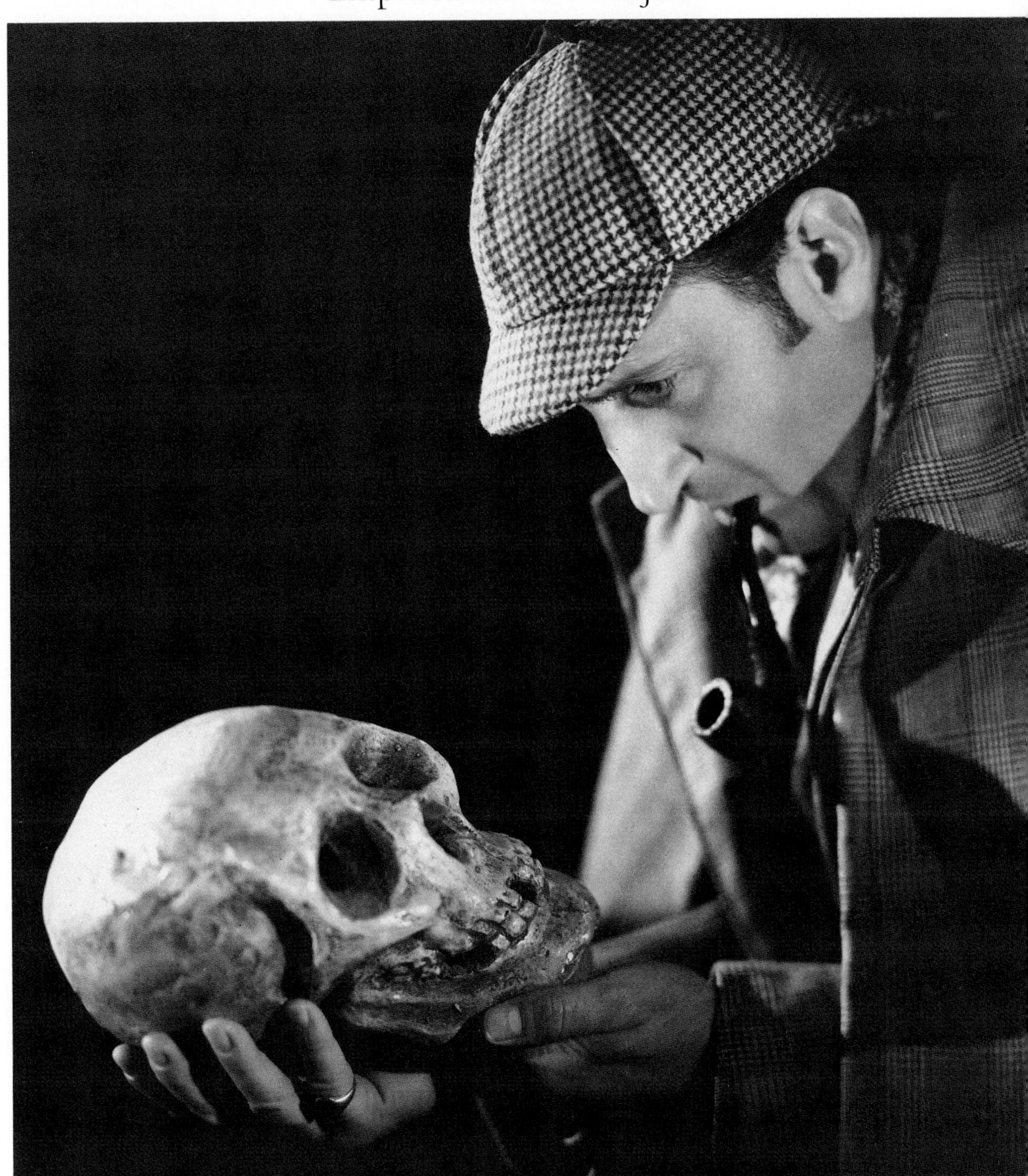

> "There are three rules for writing a novel. Unfortunately, no one knows what they are."
>
> Somerset Maugham

To analyze something is to separate it into its component parts—to take it apart, so to speak, and thus see how the parts fit together. Analytical writing is more interdependent on the other kinds of writing than they are on it because analysis is seldom done for its own sake; it usually complements other writing *purposes.* Analysis is always a mental activity, a *thinking* activity, even when it involves physical activities too, but it always puts its emphasis on the *subject itself.* Let's say that a couple buys a home in the country, and there is a water well in the backyard. The couple decides to have the well water analyzed to determine whether it is safe for drinking. The *physical* procedure of drawing a water sample and taking it to a laboratory, where a qualified technician submits it to standard tests (additional physical procedures), complements the *thinking* procedure of interpreting the test results. The emphasis, throughout all procedures, never strays far from the water itself—that is, whether it is or is not safe to drink.

After conducting the tests and interpreting the results, the technician writes a brief report: standard analysis shows that the well water is not safe for drinking; however, it can be used for irrigation. The report might also explain what treatment would be necessary to make the water potable, or it might state that there is no known way to make this particular water potable. Such analysis is logical and rather straightforward. That doesn't mean, however, that it necessarily leads to dull writing. Consider the role analysis plays in the following narrative, written some years ago, of medical detection in New York City. Though Berton Roueche's account of analytical detection is long, the emphasis on the subject never really changes: what happened to these men, and why?

Some of your students may notice that analysis is present in certain kinds of writing to inform or explain—for example, a set of directions for assembling an outdoor barbecue that separates the assembly process into its logical parts in order to explain how the whole process can be followed. Such writing analyzes the process, in other words. A key difference, however, is that explaining that process so that the reader can literally follow it in order to assemble the barbecue is the *purpose* of the writing. In the writing we are calling primarily analytical, the analysis *itself* is the purpose; the reader isn't going to try to reproduce the process.

Eleven Blue Men

BERTON ROUECHE

Science writer and reporter Berton Roueche has made a career of writing medical detective stories, including The Medical Detectives *(1980) and* The Medical Detectives II *(1984). This story is perhaps his most famous.*

Notice the first "guess" at what's happened.

At about eight o'clock on Monday morning, September 25, 1944, a ragged, aimless old man of eighty-two collapsed on the sidewalk on Dey Street, near the Hudson Terminal. Innumerable people must have noticed him, but he lay there alone for several minutes, dazed, doubled up with abdominal cramps, and in an agony of retching. Then a policeman came along. Until the policeman bent over the old man, he may have supposed that he had just a sick drunk on his hands; wanderers dropped by drink are common in that part of town in the early morning. It was not an opinion that he could have 1 held for long. The old man's nose, lips, ears, and fingers were sky-blue. The policeman went to a telephone and put in an ambulance call to Beekman-Downtown Hospital, half a dozen blocks away. The old man was carried into the emergency room there at eight-thirty. By that time, he was unconscious and the blueness had spread over a large part of his body. The examining physician attributed the old man's morbid color to cyanosis, a condition that usually results from an insufficient supply of oxygen in the blood, and also noted that he was diarrheic and in a severe state of shock. The course of treatment prescribed by the doctor was conventional. It included an instant gastric lavage, heart stimulants, bed rest, and oxygen therapy. Presently, the old man recovered an encouraging, if painful, consciousness and demanded, irascibly and in the name of God, to know what had happened to him. It was a question that, at the moment, nobody could answer with much confidence.

2 For the immediate record, the doctor made a free-hand diagnosis of carbon-monoxide poisoning—from what source, whether an automobile or a gas pipe, it was, of course, pointless even to guess. Then, because an isolated instance of gas poisoning is something of a rarity in a section of the city as crammed with human beings as downtown Manhattan, he and his colleagues in the emergency room braced themselves for at least a couple more victims. Their foresight was promptly and generously rewarded. A second man was rolled in at ten twenty-five. Forty minutes later, an ambulance drove up with three more men. At eleven-twenty, two others were brought in. An additional two arrived during the next fifteen minutes. Around noon, still another was admitted. All of these nine men were also elderly and dilapidated, all had been in misery for at least an hour, and all were rigid, cyanotic, and in a state of shock. The entire body of one, a bony, seventy-three year-old consumptive named John Mitchell, was blue. Five of the nine including Mitchell had been stricken in the Globe Hotel, a sunless, upstairs flophouse at 190 Park Row, and two in a similar place, called the Star Hotel, at 3 James Street. Another had been found slumped in the doorway of a condemned building on Park Row, not far from City Hall Park, by a policeman. The ninth had keeled over in front of the Eclipse Cafeteria, at 6 Chatham Square. At a quarter to seven that evening, one more aged blue man was brought in. He had been lying, too sick to ask for help, on his cot in a cubicle in the Lion Hotel, another flophouse, at 26 Bowery, since ten o'clock that morning. A clerk had finally looked in and seen him.

Notice the place that non-narrative lines (signposts) come in. You might have your students keep track of them.

3 By the time this last blue man arrived at the hospital, an investigation of the case by the Department of Health, to which all outbreaks of an epidemiological nature must be reported, had been under way for five hours. Its findings thus far had not been illuminating. The investigation was conducted by two men. One was the Health Department's chief epidemiologist, Dr. Morris Greenberg, . . . ; the other was Dr. Ottavio Pellitteri, a field epidemiologist. One day, when I was in Dr. Greenberg's office, he and Dr. Pellitteri told me about the case. Their recollection of it is, understandably, vivid. The derelicts were the victims of a type of poisoning so rare that only

ten previous outbreaks of it had been recorded in medical literature. Of these, two were in the United States and two in Germany; the others had been reported in France, England, Switzerland, Algeria, Australia, and India. Up to September 25, 1944, the largest number of people stricken in a single outbreak was four. That was in Algeria, in 1926.

The Beekman-Downtown Hospital telephoned a report of the occurrence to the Health Department just before noon. As is customary, copies of the report were sent to all the Department's administrative officers. "Mine was on my desk when I got back from lunch," Dr. Greenberg said to me. "It didn't sound like much. Nine persons believed to be suffering from carbon-monoxide poisoning had been admitted during the morning, and all of them said that they had eaten breakfast at the Eclipse Cafeteria, at 6 Chatham Square. Still, it was a job for us. I checked with the clerk who handles assignments and found that Pellitteri had gone out on it. That was all I wanted to know. If it amounted to anything, I knew he'd phone me before making a written report. That's an arrangement we have here. Well, a couple of hours later I got a call from him. My interest perked right up." 4

"I was at the hospital," Dr. Pellitteri told me, "and I'd talked to the staff and most of the men. There were ten of them by then, of course. They were sick as dogs, but only one was in really bad shape." 5

Notice the momentary switch into the present tense to give immediacy to Dr. Greenberg's words. Roueche is quoting Greenberg, whose exact words would naturally have been in the present tense when he spoke them in that situation. When Dr. Pellitteri resumes his narrative of events, however, he naturally uses the past tense because all those events occurred before he is telling about them.

"That was John Mitchell," Dr. Greenberg put in. "He died the next night. I understand his condition was hopeless from the start. The others, including the old boy who came in last, pulled through all right. Excuse me, Ottavio, but I just thought I'd get that out of the way. Go on." 6

Dr. Pellitteri nodded. "I wasn't at all convinced that it was gas poisoning," he continued. "The staff was beginning to doubt it, too. The symptoms weren't quite right. There didn't seem to be any of the headache and general dopiness that you get with gas. What really made me suspicious was this: Only two or three of the men had eaten breakfast in the cafeteria at the same time. They had straggled in all the way from seven o'clock to ten. That meant that the place would have had to be full of gas for at least three hours, which is preposterous. It also indicated that we ought to have had a lot more sick people than we did. Those Chatham Square eating places have a big turnover. Well to make sure, I checked with Bellevue, Gouverneur, St. Vincent's, and the other downtown hospitals. None of them had seen a trace of cyanosis. Then I talked to the sick men some more. I learned two interesting things. One was that they had all got sick right after eating. Within thirty minutes. The other was that all but one had eaten oatmeal, rolls, and coffee. He ate just oatmeal. When ten men eat the same thing in the same place on the same day and then all come down with the same illness . . . I told Greenberg that my hunch was food poisoning." 7

"I was willing to rule out gas," Dr. Greenberg said. A folder containing data on the case lay on the desk before him. He lifted the cover thoughtfully, then let it drop. "And I agreed that the oatmeal sounded pretty suspicious. That was as far as I was willing to go. Common, ordinary, everyday food 8 poisoning—I gathered that was what Pellitteri had in mind—wasn't a very satisfying answer. For one thing, cyanosis is hardly symptomatic of that. On the other hand, diarrhea and severe vomiting are, almost invariably. But they weren't in the clinical picture, I found, except in two or three of the cases. Moreover, the incubation periods—the time lapse between eating and illness—were extremely short. As you probably know, most food poisoning is caused by eating something that has been contaminated by bacteria. The usual offenders are the staphylococci—they're mostly responsible for boils and skin infections, and so on—and the salmonella. The latter are related to the typhoid organism. In a staphylococcus case, the first symptoms rarely develop in under two hours. But here we were with something that hit in thirty minutes or less. Why, one of the men had got only as far as the sidewalk in front of the cafeteria before he was knocked out. Another fact that Pellitteri had dug up struck me as very significant. All of the men told him that the illness had come on with extraordinary suddenness. One minute they were feeling fine, and the next minute they were practically helpless. That was another point against the ordinary food-poisoning theory. Its onset is never that fast. Well, that suddenness began to look like a lead. It led me to suspect that some drug might be to blame. A quick and sudden reaction is characteristic of a great many drugs. So is the combination of cyanosis and shock."

False leads are discussed fully, not papered over—another indicator of how thorough and exacting this kind of medical detection must be.

9 "None of the men were on dope," Dr. Pellitteri said. "I told Greenberg I was sure of that. Their pleasure was booze."

10 "That was O.K.," Dr. Greenberg said. "They could have got a toxic dose of some drug by accident. In the oatmeal, most likely. I couldn't help thinking that the oatmeal was relevant to our problem. At any rate, the drug idea was very persuasive."

11 "So was Greenberg," Dr. Pellitteri remarked with a smile. "Actually, it was the only explanation in sight that seemed to account for everything we knew about the clinical and environmental picture."

12 "All we had to do now was prove it," Dr. Greenberg went on mildly. "I asked Pellitteri to get a blood sample from each of the men before leaving the hospital for a look at the cafeteria. We agreed he would send the specimens to the city toxicologist, Dr. Alexander O. Gettler, for an overnight analysis. I wanted to know if the blood contained methemoglobin. Methemoglobin is a compound that's formed only when any one of several drugs enters the blood. Gettler's report would tell us if we were at least on the right track. That is, it would give us a yes-or-no answer on drugs. If the answer was yes, then we could go on from there to identify the particular drug. How we would go about that would depend on what Pellitteri was able to turn up at the cafeteria. In the meantime, there was nothing for me to do but wait for their reports. I'd theorized myself hoarse."

13 Dr. Pellitteri, having attended to his bloodletting with reasonable dispatch, reached the Eclipse Cafeteria at around five o'clock. "It was about what I'd expected," he told me. "Strictly a horse market, and dirtier than most. The sort of place where you can get a full meal for fifteen cents. There was a grind

house on one side, a cigar store on the other, and the 'El' overhead. Incidentally, the Eclipse went out of business a year or so after I was there, but that had nothing to do with us. It was just a coincidence. Well, the place looked deserted and the door was locked. I knocked, and a man came out of the back and let me in. He was one of our people, a health inspector for the Bureau of Food and Drugs, named Weinberg. His bureau had stepped into the case as a matter of routine, because of the reference to a restaurant in the notification report. I was glad to see him and to have his help. For one thing, he had put a temporary embargo on everything in the cafeteria. That's why it was closed up. His main job, though, was to check the place for violations of the sanitation code. He was finding plenty."

"Let me read you a few of Weinberg's findings," Dr. Greenberg said, extracting a paper from the folder on his desk. "None of them had any direct bearing on our problem, but I think they'll give you a good idea of what the Eclipse was like—what too many restaurants are like. This copy of his report lists fifteen specific violations. Here they are: 'Premises heavily infested with roaches. Fly infestation throughout premises. Floor defective in rear part of dining room. Kitchen walls and ceiling encrusted with grease and soot. Kitchen floor encrusted with dirt. Refuse under kitchen fixtures. Sterilizing facilities inadequate. Sink defective. Floor and walls at serving tables and coffee urns encrusted with dirt. Kitchen utensils encrusted with dirt and grease. Storage-cellar walls, ceiling, and floor encrusted with dirt. Floor and shelves in cellar covered with refuse and useless material. Cellar ceiling defective. Sewer pipe leaking. Open sewer line in cellar.' Well . . . " He gave me a squeamish smile and stuck the paper back in the folder. 14

Notice the wealth of detail, which provides a full setting for the problem-solving activity. It might be useful to stress here, if you haven't already done so, that Roueche is *reporting* true information; all his stories of medical detection are narratives of actual cases.

"I can see it now," Dr. Pellitteri said. "And smell it. Especially the kitchen, where I spent most of my time. Weinberg had the proprietor and the cook out there, and I talked to them while he prowled around. They were very cooperative. Naturally. They were scared to death. They knew nothing about gas in the place and there was no sign of any, so I went to work on the food. None of what had been prepared for breakfast that morning was left. That, of course, would have been too much to hope for. But I was able to get together some of the kind of stuff that had gone into the men's breakfast, so that we could make a chemical determination at the Department. What I took was ground coffee, sugar, a mixture of evaporated milk and water that passed for cream, some bakery rolls, a five-pound carton of dry oatmeal, and some salt. The salt had been used in preparing the oatmeal. That morning, like every morning, the cook told me, he had prepared six gallons of oatmeal, enough to serve around a hundred and twenty-five people. To make it, he used five pounds of dry cereal, four gallons of water—regular city water—and a handful of salt. That was his term—a handful. There was an open gallon can of salt standing on the stove. He said the handful he'd put in that morning's oatmeal had come from that. He refilled the can on the stove every morning from a big supply can. He pointed out the big can—it was up on a shelf—and as I was getting it down to take with me, I saw another can, just like it, nearby. 15

I took that one down, too. It was also full of salt, or, rather, something that looked like salt. The proprietor said it wasn't salt. He said it was saltpetre—sodium nitrate—that he used in corning beef and in making pastrami. Well, there isn't any harm in saltpetre; it doesn't even act as an anti-aphrodisiac, as a lot of people seem to think. But I wrapped it up with the other loot and took it along, just for fun. The fact is, I guess, everything in that damn place looked like poison."

16 After Dr. Pellitteri had deposited his loot with a Health Department chemist, Andrew J. Pensa, who promised to have a report ready by the following afternoon, he dined hurriedly at a restaurant in which he had confidence and returned to Chatham Square. There he spent the evening making the rounds of the lodging houses in the neighborhood. He had heard at Mr. Pensa's office that an eleventh blue man had been admitted to the hospital, and before going home he wanted to make sure that no other victims had been overlooked. By midnight, having covered all the likely places and having rechecked the downtown hospitals, he was satisfied. He repaired to his office and composed a formal progress report for Dr. Greenberg. Then he went home and to bed.

17 The next morning, Tuesday, Dr. Pellitteri dropped by the Eclipse, which was still closed but whose proprietor and staff he had told to return for questioning. Dr. Pellitteri had another talk with the proprietor and the cook. He also had a few inconclusive words with the rest of the cafeteria's employees—two dishwashers, a busboy, and a counterman. As he was leaving, the cook, who had apparently passed an uneasy night with his conscience, remarked that it was possible that he had absentmindedly refilled the salt can on the stove from the one that contained saltpetre. "That was interesting," Dr. Pellitteri told me, "even though such a possibility had already occurred to me, and even though I didn't know whether it was important or not. I assured him that he had nothing to worry about. We had been certain all along that nobody had deliberately poisoned the old men." From the Eclipse, Dr. Pellitteri went on to Dr. Greenberg's office, where Dr. Gettler's report was waiting.

18 "Gettler's test for methemoglobin was positive," Dr. Greenberg said. "It had to be a drug now. Well, so far so good. Then we heard from Pensa."

19 "Greenberg almost fell out of his chair when he read Pensa's report," Dr. Pellitteri observed cheerfully.

20 "That's an exaggeration," Dr. Greenberg said. "I'm not easily dumfounded. We're inured to the incredible around here. Why, a few years ago we had a case involving some numskull who stuck a fistful of potassium-thiocyanate crystals, a very nasty poison, in the coils of an office water cooler, just for a practical joke. However, I can't deny that Pensa rather taxed our credulity. What he had found was that the small salt can and the one that was supposed to be full of sodium nitrate both contained sodium *nitrite.* The other food samples, incidentally, were O.K."

21 "That also taxed my credulity," Dr. Pellitteri said.

"We're inured to the incredible around here," says Dr. Greenberg, but notice how *resistant* to belief both these doctors are. This is the "doubting stance" that rigorous scientific method requires, and what gives science its reputation as something precise and authoritative. A good scientist demands a lot of convincing, and neither doctor is willing to settle for any answer that doesn't explain *everything* about the case.

Dr. Greenberg smiled. "There's a great deal of difference between nitrate and nitrite," he continued. "Their only similarity, which is an unfortunate one, is that they both look and taste more or less like ordinary table salt. Sodium nitrite isn't the most powerful poison in the world, but a little of it will do a lot of harm. If you remember, I said before that this case was almost without precedent—only ten outbreaks like it on record. Ten is practically none. In fact, sodium-nitrite poisoning is so unusual that some of the standard texts on toxicology don't even mention it. So Pensa's report was pretty startling. But we accepted it, of course, without question or hesitation. Facts are facts. And we were glad to. It seemed to explain everything very nicely. What I've been saying about sodium-nitrite poisoning doesn't mean that sodium-nitrite itself is rare. Actually, it's fairly common. It's used in the manufacture of dyes and as a medical drug. We use it in treating certain heart conditions and for high blood pressure. But it also has another important use, one that made its presence at the Eclipse sound plausible. In recent years, and particularly during the war, sodium nitrite has been used as a substitute for sodium nitrate in preserving meat. The government permits it but stipulates that the finished meat must not contain more than one part of sodium nitrite per five thousand parts of meat. Cooking will safely destroy enough of that small quantity of the drug." Dr. Greenberg shrugged. "Well, Pellitteri had the cook pick up a handful of salt—the same amount, as nearly as possible, as went into the oatmeal—and then had taken this to his office and found that it weighed approximately a hundred grams. So we didn't have to think twice to realize that proportion of nitrite in that batch of cereal was considerably higher than one to five thousand. Roughly, it must have been around one to about eighty before cooking destroyed part of the nitrite. It certainly looked as though Gettler, Pensa, and the cafeteria cook between them had given us our answer. I called up Gettler and told him what Pensa had discovered and asked him to run a specific test for nitrites on his blood samples. He had, as a matter of course, held some blood back for later examination. His confirmation came through in a couple of hours. I went home that night feeling pretty good." 22

Dr. Greenberg's serenity was a fugitive one. He awoke on Wednesday morning troubled in mind. A question had occurred to him that he was unable to ignore. "Something like a hundred and twenty-five people ate oatmeal at the Eclipse that morning," he said to me, "but only eleven of them got sick. Why? The undeniable fact that those eleven old men were made sick by the ingestion of a toxic dose of sodium nitrite wasn't enough to rest on. I wanted to know exactly how much sodium nitrite each portion of that cooked oatmeal had contained. With Pensa's help again, I found out. We prepared a batch just like the one the cook had made on Monday. Then Pensa measured out six ounces, the size of the average portion served at the Eclipse, and analyzed it. It contained two and a half grains of sodium nitrite. That explained why the hundred and fourteen other people did not become ill. The toxic dose of sodium nitrite is three grains. But it didn't explain how each of our eleven old men had received an additional half grain. It seemed extremely unlikely that the extra touch of nitrite had been in the oatmeal 23 when it was served. It had to come in later. Then I began to get a glimmer. Some people sprinkle a little salt, instead of sugar, on hot cereal. Suppose, I thought, that the busboy, or whoever had the job of keeping the table salt shakers filled, had made the same mistake that the cook had. It seemed plausible. Pellitteri was out of the office—I've forgotten where—so I got Food and Drugs to step over to the Eclipse, which was still under embargo, and bring back the shakers for Pensa to work on. There were seventeen of them, all good-sized, one for each table. Sixteen contained either pure sodium chloride or just a few inconsequential traces of sodium nitrite mixed in with the real salt, but the other was point thirty-seven per cent nitrite. That one was enough. A spoonful of that salt contained a bit more than a half a grain."

24 "I went over to the hospital Thursday morning," Dr. Pellitteri said. "Greenberg wanted me to check the table-salt angle with the men. They could tie the case up neatly for us. I drew a blank. They'd been discharged the night before, and God only knew where they were."

25 "Naturally," Dr. Greenberg said, "it would have been nice to know for a fact that the old boys all sat at a certain table and that all of them put about a spoonful of salt from that particular shaker on their oatmeal, but it wasn't essential. I was morally certain that they had. There just wasn't any other explanation. There was one other question, however. Why did they use so *much* salt? For my own peace of mind, I wanted to know. All of a sudden, I remembered Pellitteri had said they were all heavy drinkers. Well, several recent clinical studies have demonstrated that there is usually a subnormal concentration of sodium chloride in the blood of alcoholics. Either they don't eat enough to get sufficient salt or they lose it more rapidly than other people do, or both. Whatever the reasons are, the conclusion was all I needed. Any animal, you know, whether a mouse or a man, tends to try to obtain a necessary substance that his body lacks. The final question had been answered."

Questions for Writing and Discussion

Prepare short written answers to each of these questions. Be prepared to hand them in and/or discuss them in class, as your teacher directs.

1. How does the opening paragraph hook the reader's interest?
2. Why does Roueche define terms like *cyanosis* (¶ 1) and *methemoglobin* (¶ 12) as soon as he uses them? What kind of reader does Roueche have in mind?
3. How does the repetition in this sentence reinforce the inevitability of Dr. Pellitteri's preliminary conclusion of food poisoning: "When ten men eat the same thing in the same place on the same day and then all come down with the same illness . . . I told Greenberg that my hunch was food poisoning" (¶ 7).
4. How does Dr. Greenberg show that he was even more deliberate and skeptical than Dr. Pellitteri?

5. How do Drs. Pellitteri and Greenberg show their belief in methodical, logical procedures for analyzing the cause of the "eleven blue men"? Consider these questions specifically:
   a. How and why did they eliminate gas as the cause?
   b. How did they narrow the cause to the food served for breakfast at the Eclipse Cafeteria?
   c. How did they pinpoint the cause as a drug in the food?
   d. How did they identify the drug?
   e. How did they determine why only 11 of the more than 125 diners received a toxic dose of the drug?
6. What do the following words mean—*lavage* (¶ 1), *irascibly* (¶ 1), *epidemiological* (¶ 3), *aphrodisiac* (¶ 15), *toxicology* (¶ 22), *plausible* (¶ 23)?
7. Sketch the relationship in the essay as it unfolds among evidence, preliminary hypotheses, more evidence, refined (or alternate) hypotheses, and so on. (You may find it easiest to literally draw a sketch of it.)

If some of your students really enjoy "Eleven Blue Men," recommend that they examine other books by Roueche. A student might want to do a report on the problem-solving process Roueche depicts in one (or more) of his accounts.

Although as a piece of writing, "Eleven Blue Men" depends on both mental analysis (the doctors' logical inferences and deductions based on the facts of the situation) and physical analysis (Drs. Gettler's and Pensa's laboratory tests of blood and food samples), its force as an interesting narrative also depends on Roueche's skill as a storyteller. Roueche tells the story of the medical detective work the doctors performed. He is obviously interested in entertaining as well as informing his readers. Analytical writing usually involves reporting in some way the results of analysis, keeping the subject of analysis itself always in focus. But the reporting is not always presented in the sort of first-person narrative form Roueche uses in "Eleven Blue Men"; nor is the purpose always to inform, as Roueche does, in an entertaining way.

Consider, for example, the following analytical piece about automobile safety features. Here the purpose is to analyze options and inform, but the tone is more serious than Roueche's, and justifiably so: one is much more likely to be involved in an automobile accident than in an incident of sodium nitrite poisoning.

PREREADING WORKSHEET

Before you read the following piece by Ed Henry, write brief responses to these questions.

1. Do you always wear a seat belt when you drive or when you are an automobile passenger?
2. What arguments have you heard, seen, or read for using seat belts? List them.
3. What arguments, if any, have you heard, seen, or read for *not* using seat belts? List them.
4. What arguments have you heard, seen, or read for using air bags? List them.
5. What arguments have you heard, seen, or read for *not* using or equipping cars with air bags? List them.

6. Whatever the newest models of cars are as you read this book, do you know whether all of them are equipped with either air bags or automatic seat belts? Do you know of a new car that isn't? If so, what is it?
7. Do you think the choice between seat belts and air bags is primarily a safety issue or primarily an automobile cost issue? Why?
8. Do you agree with states that have passed laws requiring the use of seat belts, or do you believe such use should be a matter of individual choice? Why or why not?

Air Bags vs. Seat Belts: Why You Should Care

Ed Henry

Ed Henry writes regularly for Changing Times. *The following article appeared in the March 1989 issue of the magazine.*

1 Next time you buy a car you could be faced with a choice between air bags and automatic seat belts. Does it make a difference which you choose? Yes it does, to both your safety and your pocketbook.

2 Under current federal regulations, 25% of all 1988 cars must be equipped with some kind of passive restraint—an air bag or automatic seat belt—to protect the front-seat passengers in a crash. Next fall the number will jump to 40%, and by 1990 every new car sold in the U.S. will be required to have automatic protection in the front seat. To encourage the installation of air bags, the National Highway Traffic Safety Administration (NHTSA) is permitting cars that are equipped with driver's-side air bags to have manual passenger belts until 1994, when all cars must have full front automatic protection. Only front-center seats are exempt from the federal regulation.

3 There are four main types of passive restraints. The first, a motorized shoulder belt that rides a track above the driver's and passenger's doors, moves into place when the door is closed. An accompanying lap belt must be hooked up manually. Such belts are standard equipment on some Chrysler, Ford, and Toyota cars.

4 A second type of passive belt—found on General Motors and Honda cars—is connected at three points, two of which are on the door and the other at your hip. The belt moves aside when the doors are opened and swings into place when they're closed. With this system you don't have to connect a lap belt by hand. As with all of the passive seat-belt systems there's an emergency release.

5 Another type, a two-point belt attached to the doors of some Chryslers, Peugeots and Volkswagens, also swings into place when the door is closed. The strap goes from a seat fastener at the hip, across the body and shoulder, to the door. There are no lap belts for Volkswagen's restraints. Instead, knee

Here again is the organizational direct-question, direct-answer technique, which sets up the entire piece: [question] "Does it make a difference which [air bag or seat belts] you choose?" [answer] "Yes it does. . . ."

The requirement that by 1988, 25 percent of all cars must be equipped with either an air bag or an automatic seat belt was changed to allow manufacturers more time to comply. You might have a student find out the current status of that requirement, or you might want to investigate and report it yourself.

bolsters on the dash and other padding help keep you in place during a crash.

The fourth option, the air bag, is designed to be used with a seat belt; an unbelted driver would move too much in a crash for the bag to be effective. Sensors in the front of a car react to a crash of about 12 miles per hour into a fixed object or 25 miles per hour or more into another car, deploying a bag that inflates from the hub of the steering wheel. Several Porsche models have passenger-side bags as well. 6

A few years ago most car companies opposed air bags. Only Mercedes-Benz bucked the trend, followed recently by Ford. Now others are rushing to join in. Air bags are being installed in Chrysler, General Motors and Japanese cars, with more to follow in the next few years. The air bag's trouble-free record—there have been no recent cases of accidental deployment—has quieted companies' fears of lawsuits. A federal credit for cars with air bags that allows makers extra time to plan for the 1994 deadline has sweetened the pot. 7

Safety Versus Cost

Ed Henry says, "There's no question that air bags are safer than automatic seat belts," as though he is completely convinced, but he offers no support for this claim. Are your students so uncritically convinced? If so, ask them why they believe Henry.

There's no question that air bags are safer than automatic seat belts when they're used with three-point lap and shoulder belts. Seat belts tend to stretch during a crash and provide limited protection against head and face injuries in high-speed crashes. 8

Government studies show that the combination of a three-point belt and an air bag reduces fatalities by as much as 55%. Those same studies demonstrate that air bags even without use of seat belts would save a significant number of lives. But they also show that the number of lives saved using automatic belts alone is hard to predict because people can choose not to use them. 9

Of equal importance is the kind of protection you get from air bags. "What the air bag offers that no belt system can is optimum protection for your face, head and brain in serious crashes," says Brian O'Neill, president of the Insurance Institute for Highway Safety. 10

Note that even if there's "no question" air bags are safer, there's still a problem: costs. This paragraph beginning with "But" signals the discussion of this problem.

But until their costs come down, air bags represent something of a mixed blessing to car buyers. Whether you purchase them as an option or as standard equipment, they add $500 to $1000 to the price of a car. (Production levels of more than a million a year by 1990 are expected to lower the price to an estimated $300 apiece.) If a bag is deployed in an accident, it can cost up to $2000 to restore the system to working condition. Says Earl Kautz, a ratings specialist for GEICO: "While the bag and components might cost $800, actual cost might be $1800 because of the labor involved." 11

Those costs aren't expected to affect your collision [insurance] rates appreciably. But you can expect better discounts for personal injury protection and possibly better rates for bodily injury protection. 12

The cost of medical payment coverage also drops as much as 40% for cars with passive restraints, depending on the insurer. GEICO and American Family Mutual offer 30% discounts for all passive restraints; Hartford Fire 13 offers 30% for full front passive-restraint protection and 20% for driver's-side-only protection. Allstate gives a 30% discount for full front air bags but none for automatic belts. Prudential gives 30% for air bags and 20% for automatic belts. Nationwide gives a 25% discount for driver's-side air bags, 40% for full front air bags and 10% for two automatic seat belts.

14 The discounts don't make much of a dent in the cost of the bag, however. A Cleveland family with a Ford Topaz that insures with GEICO, for example, would pay $16.50 for mandatory personal injury protection as part of an overall $641.30 liability, fire, theft, and comprehensive policy. With an air bag, the cost for medical coverage drops 30%, or $4.90. In another area, such as Baltimore, the same discount would be worth more because the personal injury protection rates are about seven times as expensive as in Cleveland.

15 Because the discounts aren't that significant, you spend much less in the long run on a car with automatic seat belts than you would on a car with an air bag. But you also give up a measure of safety. That's no easy choice.

POSTREADING WORKSHEET

Now that you have read the piece by Henry, write your responses to the following questions:

1. How has Henry's article affected your attitude about seat belts or air bags?
2. Have all the requirements mentioned by Henry in the second paragraph been met by car manufacturers, or have there been some adjustments in deadlines?
3. What sort of passive restraint do you think you prefer?
4. If you had to choose between seat belts and air bags, what would you choose?
5. Has Henry refuted any of the arguments you've heard, seen, or read, either for or against these restraints?

Questions for Writing and Discussion

Prepare short written answers to each of these questions. Be prepared to hand them in and/or discuss them in class, as your teacher directs.

1. How does the writer organize the summary of types of passive restraints?
2. How does the writer use statistical information? How does he use discount percentage "quotes" from different insurance companies?
3. How would you characterize each of the two parts the article is divided into?
4. Why is the choice of language in this sentence especially appropriate: "The discounts don't make much of a dent in the cost of the bag, however" (¶ 14).
5. Who are the primary readers for this piece? How do their interests and the things they need to know show up in the piece?
6. What seems to be the writer's primary purpose in analyzing the types of passive restraints?

Additional items after the Henry piece:

1. Henry discusses this problem in terms of our knowing we can be *x* times safer but it will cost us *y* times the money. That's purely an economic argument. Is this purely an economic issue? How do students feel about having in effect to make a calculation that trades increased safety for savings? Do they see this issue as parallel to the familiar "big car versus little car" debate: big cars are safer if you have a collision, but they burn much more gas; little cars are not safer if you have a collision, but they burn much less gas.
2. Interview car dealers and insurance agents, and write an investigative paper on the availability and cost of air bags on your two favorite cars.

Look back at the Sagan essay (chapter 5) for more on analytical thinking.

7. Compare the audiences the writers picture in the texts for "Eleven Blue Men" and "Air Bags vs. Seat Belts." What assumptions about the audience does the writer of each piece make? Keep careful track of the evidence you find for how each author has pictured his audience.
8. What do the following words mean—*passive* (¶ 2), *deploying* (¶ 6), *affect* (¶ 12), *comprehensive* (¶ 14)?

In the case of "Air Bags vs. Seat Belts," the analysis takes place first in the thought process of classifying passive restraint systems, comparing and contrasting their features, and then in the comparing and contrasting of insurance discount rates and the advantages and disadvantages of passive restraint systems in new automobiles. Ed Henry, without leaving his focus on the restraint systems, then reports the results of his analysis, adding his interpretation of what the analysis means to the new-car buyer. Whereas Berton Roueche has both entertainment and information as additional purposes in telling the story of analytical medical detection in "Eleven Blue Men," Ed Henry has information—the considered results of careful analysis of available passive restraint systems—as an additional purpose in "Air Bags vs. Seat Belts." But foremost is Henry's analysis of the equal systems and their costs, for he wants his readers to be able to make an intelligent consumer decision based on his analysis.

We have seen that analysis can be a habit of mind, as in the way Drs. Pellitteri and Greenberg approach their jobs as medical detectives, epidemiologists whose work is to identify and control communicable diseases before they can become epidemics. An analytical turn of mind is valuable to any student, because it inclines him or her to size up situations, gauge conditions, and explore options intelligently. "What is involved here?" is a common question in an analytical mind, as are such corollary questions as "What does this mean?" "Why is this happening?" "What is the best course of action and why?" "Of what does this consist?" and so on. Often what is needed are basic facts. Consider, for example, the following "Nutrition Information" printed on the side of a box of breakfast cereal:

Nutrition Information

Serving size: 1 oz. (28.4 g, about 1 cup)
Servings per package: 12

	Cereal	With ½ cup vitamins A & D skim milk
Calories	110	150*
Protein	6 g	10 g
Carbohydrate	20 g	26 g
Fat	0 g	0 g*
Cholesterol	0 mg	0 mg*

Sodium	230 mg	290 mg
Potassium	55 mg	260 mg

Percentage of U.S. recommended daily allowances (U.S. RDA)

Protein	10	20
Vitamin A	15	20
Vitamin C	25	25
Thiamin	35	40
Riboflavin	35	45
Niacin	35	35
Calcium	**	15
Iron	25	25
Vitamin D	10	25
Vitamin B_6	35	35
Folic Acid	25	25
Phosphorus	6	20
Magnesium	4	8
Zinc	25	30
Copper	6	8

*2% milk supplies an additional 20 calories, 2 g fat, and 10 mg cholesterol
**Contains less than 2% of the U.S. RDA of this nutrient.

Ingredients: rice, wheat gluten, sugar, defatted wheat germ, salt, corn syrup, whey, malt flavoring, calcium caseinate.

Vitamins and Minerals: Vitamin C (ascorbic acid), Niacinamide, Zinc (oxide), Iron, Vitamin B_6 (Pyridoxine hydrochloride), Vitamin B_2 (Riboflavin), Vitamin B_1 (Thiamin hydrochloride), Vitamin A (Palmitate), Folic acid, and Vitamin D.

To keep this cereal fresh, BHT has been added to the packaging.

Ask your students, "How is reading this from a book different from reading it from a cereal box over breakfast? How does the feeling of reading it in that setting compare with the feeling of reading it in this class? How do those different settings and different feelings affect your response to the information?"

Fascinating reading? Perhaps not. But imagine you are a person who must restrict sodium (salt) in your diet. The line of information telling you the amount of sodium in this cereal is therefore of interest—and importance—to you. And a great many people count calories—they'd like to know exactly how many calories they would consume in a serving of this cereal. Analysis of the product made the reporting of such information possible, and the table that reports the results never swerves from its emphasis on the cereal's ingredients.

In the case of an analysis-list of ingredients, interpretation of the information is up to the reader, for only the reader will know if some element of the information is significant. The primary purpose of whoever analyzed the cereal and wrote the list of ingredients was to analyze and inform; it is up to the reader to decide whether, for example, the number of calories rules out having a bowl of the cereal for breakfast.

Questions for Writing and Discussion

Prepare short written answers to each of these questions. Be prepared to hand them in and/or discuss them in class, as your teacher directs.

Ask students to brainstorm how else the information could be displayed.

1. What advantage does the cereal analyst/writer, the person who compiled the "Nutrition Information," derive from displaying the information as a table?
2. What advantage does the reader of the "Nutrition Information" derive from perceiving the information as a table?
3. What effect, both practical and legal, does the list's use of technical or scientific names have? For example, the list parenthetically gives a vitamin's equivalent name, as in "Vitamin B_6 (Pyridoxine hydrochloride)."

You can point out here that the writer's image, or persona, in this list is faceless and corporate: "Kellogg's provides this analysis of our cereal for your information." What other examples of this kind of faceless corporate writer can your students think of?

Naturally, since much of analysis involves a kind of sizing up of details, it is easy to see that analysis also involves *using* those details, or the interpretation of them, in writing. Like expressive and informative writing, analytical writing can appear in several forms; we have already seen it in a narrative (story), a magazine article on safety, and a table of breakfast cereal ingredients. Now we will see it as the basic kind of writing in a syndicated newsmagazine column.

Having done a rather thorough analysis of the infrastructure in this country, columnist George Will seeks to show, in the following piece, why that infrastructure is so important to him and to other Americans. As you read the piece, pay careful attention to the way the writer involves his audience in the analysis. What qualities in the audience is Will drawing on? How does the evidence he brings in support the claim he winds up making?

Listen to the Bridges

GEORGE F. WILL

George Will is an editor, political columnist, news commentator, and TV commentator. He is a Pulitzer prizewinner and the author of several books. This piece was written during the preconvention 1988 presidential campaign.

One of your students might want to write a report on the current status of the Williamsburg Bridge.

New York, New York, it's a wonderful town (songwriters are not under oath), the Bronx is up and the Battery's down. And so, almost, is the Williamsburg Bridge. That 85-year-old suspension span across the East River connects Manhattan with America, which may not be in the national interest, but nearly a quarter of a million people use it daily. Used it. Since last Tuesday 1 only pedestrians and bicyclists do. It is not quite collapsing—yet—but it is unsafe for vehicular traffic, and that is a considerable defect in a bridge.

2 The discovery last week of its corroded condition was serendipitous. The discovery occurred while the three surviving Democratic presidential candidates were careering around the Empire State promising to make America into a paradise and, in their spare time, pacify the Middle East. The mere crumbling of a bridge is too mundane a matter to arrest the attention of candidates who are bent on the betterment of all mankind. However, the sounds made by that tired old bridge (it was screeching and squealing ominously) should be listened to. It tells us more about our future than the candidates do. The nation has a huge bill coming due for the neglect of its infrastructure, meaning bridges, roads, airports, waterways, water and sewer systems—all things that make everything else possible.

3 This neglect, which reflects a weak ethic of common provision, may be a consequence of our individualism. Individually, Americans are exercising more and eating more sensibly to maintain their personal infrastructures while the nation's physical plant deteriorates. In the years dead ahead that physical plant is going to force itself upon our attention. It will be something to think about while we creep along in increasingly congested traffic, or wait for our delayed flights to take off at overburdened airports.

4 The *National Journal* reports that one out of four bridges is considered dangerous. More than 4,100 are closed. Every two days a bridge collapses. Sixty-five percent of the Interstate Highway System is in need of rehabilitation. The average age of the 184 locks on the inland waterway system is 40 years. The Army Corps of Engineers says 3,000 dams in populated areas are hazardous. Air traffic has doubled in the 14 years since the last new commercial airport (Dallas–Ft. Worth) opened. Los Angeles needs to spend $111 million more every year just repairing streets or 60 percent of them will be unusable by the end of the century. The Environmental Protection Agency says $108 billion will be needed between now and then just for construction of new sewage treatment plants.

5 OK, some of these numbers may involve overreaching and attention seizing and an appetite for pork. Still, there are many needs and not enough money. The cost of public-works investment is substantial, but so is the cost of underinvestment. Millions of worker-years are lost as congestion and detours sap economic efficiency. The cost of Los Angeles County congestion is estimated to be nearly half a million hours a day and half a billion dollars' worth of working time (and 72 million gallons of gas) a year. Unfortunately, blocking the road to a solution is a mountain—Mount Deficit.

6 The deficit is the numerical expression of a cultural tendency, the national tendency to live for the moment and beyond our means, consuming more than we produce and investing too little, heedless about the future. A government devoting 14 percent of its budget to pay interest on its debts—to rent money—has not enough money for the physical prerequisites of efficient and commodious living. Four federal trust funds—highway, transit,

Will is not the only writer in recent years to call attention to the plight of our national infrastructure. He's aware that others have pointed out the problem, and he's also aware that when many complain about the same thing, listeners begin to tune out what is said, thinking "Aw, it can't be that bad." Ask your students how Will works to make what he says striking, so that serious attention is more likely to be paid.

Will has a unique way of saying that Americans, as a people, don't care enough to keep public facilities up to safe standards: "This neglect, which reflects a weak ethic of common provision . . ." Ask your students what they think the phrase "ethic of common provision" means.

By "appetite for pork" Will means what is often called pork-barrel politics: the practice of legislators getting public money spent for projects in their home districts (dams, bridges, parks, and so on) whether or not those projects are needed. The "pork" is the money, the favor, the jobs, the economic benefits, and so forth, that such projects create for the legislator's district. Ask your students to share with the class any pork-barrel projects they know of in their communities.

aviation, and waterways—had a combined cash balance of about $24 billion at the end of 1987, all of it from user fees that can be spent only on infrastructure. But our leaders, ever imaginative at cooking the books to make the deficit seem smaller than it is, are hoarding the money. This is done so that deficit estimates will be smaller and the Gramm-Rudman knife will be easier to avoid.

Call to students' attention Will's use of historical fact and borrowing of historical prestige: he makes his case for internal improvements stronger by pointing out that no less a person than Abraham Lincoln once worked diligently for such improvements, and thus implies that such a cause is worthy not only now but always. Elsewhere, Will implies that had infrastructure been more carefully handled, one of the causes of the Civil War would have been avoided. He isn't so foolish as to suggest that, for example, the Civil War would never have occurred had John C. Calhoun gotten his bill passed, but that isn't Will's point either. Rhetorically, Will's analysis is more believable, more compelling, because he has used facts and figures from history.

"Internal Improvements": An earlier, more robust America had more energetic leaders regarding "internal improvements." On March 9, 1832, a candidate for the Illinois General Assembly distributed an open letter to the people of his county. The first plank in his platform was: "Time and experience have verified . . . the public utility of internal improvements," such as roads and navigable streams. Lincoln lost, but he soon won and authored a flurry of bills such as those pertaining to "a state road from the Wabash to the yellow banks of the Mississippi River" and "a canal upon the valley of the Sangamon River." 7

In 1808 Jefferson's Treasury secretary, Albert Gallatin, issued his "Report on Roads and Canals," a proposed network of projects, most of which were built over 60 years. It is unfortunate they were not built sooner. In 1816 John C. Calhoun, who eventually would sow seeds of secession, introduced a bill for internal improvements at federal expense. He warned that New York and other Northern states had public and private financial resources sufficient for such improvements, but that the South did not. Without federal help, the South would be consigned to inferiority, and "disunion" might result. President Madison, taking a crabbed view of federal power, vetoed the bill as unconstitutional. Denied federal help, the South's dependence on slavery grew, as did its sense of separateness. 8

Disunion is not a danger today. Decay is. That is a pity because public works are the sort of things government is good at. The Tennessee Valley Authority and the Interstate Highway System were not just good in themselves, they were good for the morale of government, which periodically needs some inspiriting successes. Alas, in election years we have this sort of dispiriting experience: 9

How effective do your students think this ending of Will's is?

You are driving warily down a street cratered with potholes deep enough to serve as silos for the MX missile. Your car radio is emitting the sounds of candidates promising to provide "meaningful jobs" and "a sense of community" in "model cities" in a disarmed world. And you are thinking (if thinking is possible as you jolt along, your radio chattering and radial tires disintegrating): Thanks a lot, but could we please start our trip to utopia on a well-paved street leading to a structurally sound bridge? 10

Questions for Writing and Discussion

Prepare short written answers to each of these questions. Be prepared to hand them in and/or discuss them in class, as your teacher directs.

1. How does Will use the 1988 presidential election as a kind of ironic background to his analysis of the country's infrastructure?
2. How does Will use humor to temper his critical tone?
3. How does Will use political history to help make his point?
4. How does he use statistical facts and figures?
5. How does he use figurative language—for example, "Mount Deficit," "the Gramm-Rudman knife," and "an appetite for pork"?
6. Which one sentence would you pinpoint as being Will's thesis sentence—the one sentence that best sums up his point?
7. What extra effect does he achieve by quoting "meaningful jobs," "sense of community," and "model cities" in the last paragraph?
8. What extraordinary use does Will give the term *infrastructure* in the third paragraph? Why is that use appropriate?
9. What do the following words mean—*serendipitous, careering, mundane* (¶ 2), *consigned* (¶ 8), *emitting, utopia* (¶ 10)?

In the Will example, analytical writing is done for important persuasive purposes, even though Will keeps his focus on the problems of the infrastructure. Will wants his readers to understand the full meaning of his statement "The nation has a huge bill coming due for the neglect of its infrastructure, meaning bridges, roads, airports, waterways, water and sewer systems—all things that make everything else possible." That statement (¶ 2) is the *result* of Will's analytical thinking on the subject, and he considers it something serious, even though he uses humor and wit in his article.

By now you can see that analytical writing is not so much analysis itself as the *result* of analysis. It has a strong resemblance to informative writing but emphasizes the subject being analyzed rather than the reader's understanding. As such, it can be used for auxiliary purposes of entertaining (Roueche), informing (Henry; "Nutrition Information"), and persuading (Will). It can also be used for a combination of purposes, as in chapter 21, where we see the analysis of a work of literature given both to inform and to persuade. And analysis can be a significant component of expressive writing, as in "Woman/Wilderness," the following example, from Ursula K. Le Guin's *Dancing at the Edge of the World.*

One mechanistic view of writing (which we don't share) promoted in many writing classes (and nowhere else on the globe) is that in good writing each paragraph has a "topic sentence" that is the key, point-making sentence of that paragraph and serves as a predictor of what follows in the paragraph. This rigid idea of a topic sentence is part of a larger pedagogical construct holding that a well-written essay consists of five paragraphs, the first presenting a "thesis sentence," which is the key, point-making sentence of the whole essay; the next consisting of three internal, developmental paragraphs; and the fifth forming a paragraph of conclusion (all paragraphs after the first having, of course, topic sentences). The particular idea that each paragraph has a topic sentence has been well exposed as a myth (see Stern).

Good writing *does* have focus, development, and coherence. And often a skillful writer—like George Will—will place within a paragraph a sentence or passage that serves not so much as a rigid topic sentence as a unifying, focusing *idea:* a centrality around which the rest of the paragraph's details gather. Discuss this issue of topic sentences with your students; with them, look over Will's essay paragraph by paragraph and search for the central *idea* (not topic sentence, although sometimes the idea will be expressed in a single sentence) in each. How does Will connect these ideas to make his complete essay?

Woman/Wilderness

URSULA K. LE GUIN

Ursula K. Le Guin is the author of a number of novels, short stories, children's books, and books of poetry and criticism. She is perhaps best known for her science fiction, including most notably The Left Hand of Darkness. *(See also "Profile of a Writer" at the beginning of Part Two.)*

Gary Snyder is an American poet whose work generally features the geography of the American West, especially the Pacific Northwest, and the cultures of the Native Americans and American beat poets.

Students may struggle to grasp the level of symbolic meaning Le Guin achieves in this piece. It may help to remind them that she is deliberately being *tendentious;* she *means* to get attention.

The great problem, as Le Guin views it, is that men don't see, don't know, the value of the female wilderness. In their drive to dominate, men are destroying the world, not really improving it. Le Guin's is ultimately an argument to save the world from the destructive excesses of men. Thus, it is both feminist and environmentalist. Students interested in pursuing the image back in time may want to look at Susan Griffin's book *Woman and Nature;* students interested in pursuing the image forward in time may want to look at Le Guin's "The Fisherwoman's Daughter," a longer essay.

Le Guin also wrote *The Word for World Is Forest,* in which she details just what the wilderness "says" in its "answer."

Notice the rhetorical effect Le Guin gets with this "The women are speaking" passage. It's a flourish, as though all the

In June of 1986, Gary Snyder invited me to come talk to his class in Wilderness at the University of California at Davis. I told him I would say a little about woman and wilderness and read some poetry, mostly from my book Always Coming Home. *What follows is what I said before getting into the reading. Highly tendentious, it was meant to, and did, provoke lively discussion.* 1

Civilized Man says: I am Self, I am Master, all the rest is Other—outside, below, underneath, subservient. I own, I use, I explore, I exploit, I control. What I do is what matters. What I want is what matter is for. I am that I am, and the rest is women and the wilderness, to be used as I see fit. 2

To this, Civilized Woman, in the voice of Susan Griffin, replies as follows: 3

> We say there is no way to see his dying as separate from her living, or what he had done to her, or what part of her he had used. We say if you change the course of this river you change the shape of the whole place. And we say that what she did then could not be separated from what she held sacred in herself, what she had felt when he did that to her, what we hold sacred to ourselves, what we feel we could not go on without, and we say if this river leaves this place, nothing will grow and the mountain will crumble away, and we say what he did to her could not be separated from the way that he looked at her, and what he felt was right to do to her, and what they do to us, we say, shapes how they see us. That once the trees are cut down, the water will wash the mountain away and the river be heavy with mud, and there will be a flood. And we say that what he did to her he did to all of us. And that one fact cannot be separated from another. And had he seen more clearly, we say, he might have predicted his own death. How if the trees grew on that hillside there would be no flood. And you cannot divert this river. We say look how the water flows from this place and returns as rainfall, everything returns, we say, and one thing follows another, there are limits, we say, on what can be done and everything moves. We are all a part of this motion, we say, and the way of the river is sacred, and this grove of trees is sacred, and we ourselves, we tell you, are sacred.[1] 4

What is happening here is that the wilderness is answering. This has never happened before. We who live at this time are hearing news that has never been heard before. A new thing is happening. 5

> Daughters, the women are speaking.
> They arrive
> over the wise distances
> on perfect feet.

The women are speaking: so says Linda Hogan of the Chickasaw people.[2] The women are speaking. Those who were identified as having nothing to say, as sweet silence or monkey-chatterers, those who were identified with Nature, which listens, as against Man, who speaks—those people are speaking. They speak for themselves and for the other people, the animals, the trees, the rivers, the rocks. And what they say is: We are sacred.

6 Listen: they do not say, "Nature is sacred." Because they distrust that word, Nature. Nature as not including humanity, Nature as what is not human, that Nature is a construct made by Man, not a real thing; just as most of what Man says and knows about women is mere myth and construct. Where I live as woman is to men a wilderness. But to me it is home.

7 The anthropologists Shirley and Edwin Ardener, talking about an African village culture, made a useful and interesting mental shape. They laid down two circles largely but not completely overlapping, so that the center of the figure is the tall oval of interlap, and on each side of it are facing crescents of nonoverlap. One of the two circles is the Dominant element of the culture, that is, Men. The other is the Muted element of the culture, that is, Women. As Elaine Showalter explains the figure, "All of male consciousness is within the circle of the Dominant structure and thus accessible to or structured by language." Both the crescent that belongs to men only and the crescent that belongs to women only, outside the shared, central, civilized area of overlap, may be called "the wilderness." The men's wilderness is real; it is where men can go hunting and exploring and having all-male adventures, away from the village, the shared center, and it is accessible to and structured by language. "In terms of cultural anthropology, women know what the male crescent is like, even if they have never seen it, because it becomes the subject of legend. . . . But men do not know what is in the wild,"[3] that is, the no-man's-land, the crescent that belongs to the Muted group, the silent group, the group within the culture that *is not spoken,* whose experience is not considered to be part of human experience, that is, the women.

8 Men live their whole lives within the Dominant area. When they go off hunting bears, they come back with bear stories, and these are listened to by all, they become the history or the mythology of that culture. So the men's "wilderness" becomes Nature, considered as the property of Man.

9 But the experience of women as women, their experience unshared with men, that experience is the wilderness or the wildness that is utterly other—that is in fact, to Man, unnatural. That is what civilization has left out, what culture excludes, what the Dominants call animal, bestial, primitive, undeveloped, unauthentic—what has not been spoken, and when spoken, has not been heard—what we are just beginning to find words for, our words not their words: the experience of women. For dominance-identified men and women both, that is true wildness. Their fear of it is ancient, profound, and violent. The misogyny that shapes every aspect of our civilization is the institutionalized form of male fear and hatred of what they have denied and therefore cannot know, cannot share: that wild country, the being of women.

10 All we can do is try to speak it, try to say it, try to save it. Look, we say, this land is where your mother lived and where your daughter will live. This is your sister's country. You lived there as a child, boy or girl, you lived there—have you forgotten? All children are wild. You lived in the wild country. Why are you afraid of it?

world's women were saying the same thing at the same time, and is thus an exaggeration made specifically for effect.

What Le Guin means by "Where I live as a woman" is deep inside, where both her consciousness and her subconsciousness reside and where her deepest instincts and feelings hold sway. It is that part of her spirit which is most fundamentally female, the place where her "female wilderness" abides, where the instincts for survival, procreation, and sustenance from the natural world lie.

It is a "place" men do not know and, therefore, as she will eventually conclude, fear.

Additional questions you might ask your students: Is women's experience totally not spoken? What would *spoken* experience for women be like, in the sense Le Guin means?

Compare Peter Steinhart's "Wildness and Weirdness" (see chapter 8).

What might Le Guin's "wild country, the being of women" be like?

Notes

1. Susan Griffin, *Woman and Nature* (New York: Harper & Row, Colophon Books, 1978) 186.

2. Linda Hogan, "The Women Speaking," in *That's What She Said: Contemporary Poetry and Fiction by Native American Women,* ed. Rayna Green (Bloomington: Indiana University Press, 1984) 172.

3. Elaine Showalter, "Feminist Criticism in the Wilderness," in *The New Feminist Criticism,* ed. Elaine Showalter (New York: Pantheon Books, 1985) 262. See also Shirley Ardener, ed., *Perceiving Women* (New York: Halsted Press, 1978).

Questions for Writing and Discussion

Prepare short written answers to each of these questions. Be prepared to hand them in and/or discuss them in class, as your teacher directs.

1. What effect does Le Guin achieve with her capitalizations of words not usually capitalized—"Civilized Man," "Civilized Woman," "Other," "Nature," and so on?
2. As we have pointed out, writing to analyze has closer automatic ties to writing to express, to explain, or to persuade than any of those kinds of writing have to it because analysis seldom stands alone as a purpose. In this piece, Le Guin analyzes the world by describing a diagram of culture, by citing several interpretive sources, and by equating part of women's experience with a true wilderness that men cannot know. Yet her purpose is not just that analysis; she analyzes also to persuade. What is she trying to persuade readers to believe?
3. What special effect does Le Guin achieve by using colons?
4. How does language—the ability to speak, the use of words to identify, label, and deal with things—relate to Le Guin's view of the world? Why does she use the term *muted* to label the "women's crescent" of the diagram? Why does she say the women are now *speaking*?
5. What important reservation does Le Guin hold about the word *nature,* and why?
6. What do the following words mean—*tendentious* (¶ 1), *subservient* (¶ 2), *bestial, misogyny* (¶ 9)?

If you're ready for a lively discussion, ask your students whether they agree or disagree with Le Guin's view. Have them tie their agreement or disagreement to their own, individual analysis of the situation.

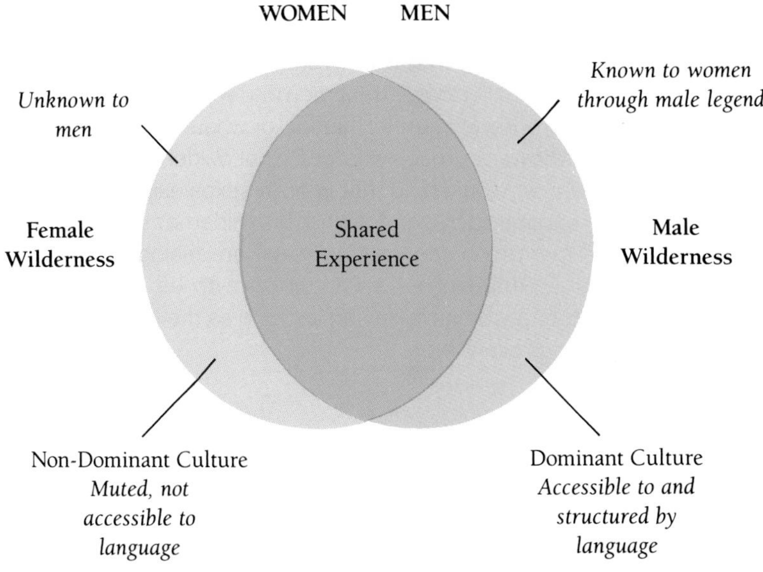

The Ardener/Showalter Diagram
(Referred to by Ursula K. Le Guin)

Bridges: Another Perspective

Ursula K. Le Guin analyzes the culture as being like two slightly overlapping circles of male and female experience. The male circle, which encompasses most of the female circle, represents dominant culture, known by both men and women and understood by the language of the culture, which is also male-dominated. The slight "crescent" of the male circle that is not also part of the women's circle is wilderness, but it is a male-fashioned wilderness, described by the language of machismo, and therefore understood, if only secondhand, by women. This "wilderness," however, is also seen by men as something to be mastered—ultimately tamed, controlled, subdued. That is a destructive impulse. Contrarily, the slight "crescent" of the female circle that is not part of the men's circle is wilderness wholly unsuspected (not to mention misunderstood) by men. Because women are dominated by men and the male-dominant language, this other crescent is muted—there has heretofore been no recognized, established language to express it. Yet this wilderness, which is primal, regenerative, life fomenting, and nurturing, is now gaining expression through women who are speaking for the first time, beginning to insist that men *not* destroy or master this particular wilderness, lest they destroy the planet and all life itself. In Le Guin's view, then, male language, experience, and attitude are destructive and must be curbed for the good of all.

A contrary view might hold that it is oversimplification and irrelevant to make wilderness a male/female issue—that men and women alike need to stop worrying about which is the better, gentler, kinder (or whatever) gender and take positive, realistic steps toward preservation of what wilderness we know we need to preserve. This view would hold that in both sexes exists an element of wilderness that is *not* separated by gender, and this wilderness is the instinct to survive and manage our resources. In this view, an analogy might be not overlapping circles of experience but an automobile to be driven: what difference whether a man or a woman is driving, as long as the trip is made safely and nothing happens to prevent more trips?

To accompany the Bridges exercise, you might have your students write papers expressing their own view of this situation. (Doing so could also produce lively group work, provided that the groups have both male and female members.)

KEY POINTS TO REMEMBER: Writing to Analyze

- Analysis is thought in action.
- Analysis may require tracing a process as well as causes.
- Analysis uses facts, statistics, and other gathered information.
- Analysis serves many purposes.

Analysis Is Thought in Action

All good analysis is the result of good *thought;* that is, some whole experience, item, concept, situation, or creation is systematically examined, separated methodically into its component parts, the better to understand how each of those parts functions or relates to the whole. The process may be as basic as an autopsy in a suspected murder case or as a thorough assessment of the symptoms of an automobile engine that doesn't run properly. It may be a careful process of logical elimination (of other possible causes, of false evidence), until one clear cause of a certain effect remains—as in Roueche's "Eleven Blue Men." It may painstakingly compare two or more products or options, so as to decide which is better or best, as in Ed Henry's "Air Bags vs. Seat Belts." Or it may simply break down a product into its component parts, as in "Nutrition Information." No matter what form it takes or for what purpose, analysis means careful and systematic thought, and writing to analyze means putting that systematic thought to work, usually along with expressive, informative, or persuasive purposes.

As always, outside examples will help strengthen instruction and understanding. Writing that analyzes news events or issues (from newspapers and news publications like *Time, Newsweek,* and *U.S. News and World Report*) often works well, as do reviews of popular films or books. Particular campus issues are also a reliable source for analysis. The idea with such examples is to note how *analysis* is involved, even if the overall purpose of the piece seems to be to inform, explain, express, or persuade.

Analysis May Require Tracing a Process as Well as Causes

Methodical procedure, as we have seen, is especially important in, say, the epidemiological work of the doctors in "Eleven Blue Men." The writer who compared air bags and seat belts went through a process of investigation, finding out as much as he could about each kind of passive restraint. Analyzing a process, then, is often the same as analyzing a cause; that is, it is finding out how a certain result came, or comes, into being. Hence, George Will analyzed the condition of the nation's infrastructure and could then conclude that, through a kind of process of neglect, that infrastructure is now in jeopardy.

Analysis Uses Facts, Statistics, and Other Gathered Information

You could say that analysis is a means of applying information—putting it to work to help derive more information. Note, for example, how George Will carefully marshals information from the *National Journal:*

> The *National Journal* reports that one out of four bridges is considered dangerous. More than 4,100 are closed. Every two days a bridge collapses. Sixty-five percent of the Interstate Highway System is in need of rehabilitation. The average age of the 184 locks on the inland waterway system is 40 years. The Army Corps of Engineers says 3,000 dams in populated areas are hazardous. . . . (¶ 4)

In Will's case, the sheer preponderance of this kind of information leads him inductively to an inescapable conclusion: the nation's infrastructure is in serious trouble. His logic is inductive in that he takes pieces of evidence and *adds* them together until they point to some general truth that can be stated: if *this* is true (that one out of four bridges is dangerous) and *this* is true (that more than 4,100 bridges are closed) and *this* is true (that every two days a bridge collapses), and so on, then *this larger thing* (that our nation's bridges by and large aren't safe) must also be true.

A writer like Will not only uses interesting evidence but also uses it in such a way as to make us appreciate his logic. Have a look at our discussion of Toulmin's persuasion pattern in the annotations to chapter 20 (see Toulmin).

Whereas Will goes from specific facts toward a generalization, Drs. Pellitteri and Greenberg in "Eleven Blue Men" go back and forth—evidence leads to a possible explanation, further evidence refutes it, still further evidence leads to another generalization, and so on. That is, they reach their early conclusion that they may have an epidemic on their hands (first one, then two, and eventually eleven "blue men" appear at the hospital); then they go the other way to eventually eliminate, say, gas as the cause of the poisoning. The logic that proceeds by a kind of addition (evidence + evidence + evidence leads to a generalization) we call *inductive.* The logic that proceeds by a kind of subtraction (if *this* generalization were the case, *that* would be happening, but it isn't) we call *deductive.* In "Eleven Blue Men," the doctors *know* the symptoms of gas poisoning and subtract from those symptoms the clinical fact that "there didn't seem to be any of the headache and general dopiness that you get with gas" (¶ 7). The doctors *know* that gas would have to be present in the Eclipse Cafeteria in a large enough concentration to poison the men through their normal breathing. But they subtract from that knowledge the fact that the men had eaten at different times over a span of three hours—meaning that the gas concentration would have had to be strong enough to poison people for three straight hours, "which is pre-

As kinds of reasoning processes, induction and deduction are fairly easy to trace and are types of reasoning your students can learn to employ without too much difficulty.

posterous," as Dr. Pellitteri says, because *everyone* at the cafeteria would have noticed such a powerful concentration, and in fact many more than eleven people would have become sick. Also through deduction, they conclude that a drug is involved, because they *know* (thanks to Dr. Gettler's laboratory analysis of the blood samples) that the presence of methemoglobin in the victims' blood rules out (subtracts) any other cause.

Analysis Serves Many Purposes

The results of analysis can appear in personal, expressive writing (Ursula K. Le Guin's "Woman/Wilderness"); writing that entertains and informs (Berton Roueche's "Eleven Blue Men"); writing that strictly informs (Ed Henry's "Air Bags vs. Seat Belts"); writing that persuades (George Will's "Listen to the Bridges"); and in fact just about any other kind of writing for any other kind of purpose. This idea should come as no surprise to you, since analysis is thought in action, and good thinking is always a part of good writing—an inescapable part of the process.

As a student, you can expect to use analysis many times in your career. You may need to analyze the causes of the Civil War in a history class or a sample's chemical components in the laboratory of a science class. For a literature class, you may be asked to analyze a novel's protagonist or a poem's theme. Later, in law or medical school, you may be required to analyze the precedents affecting an important legal decision or, like Drs. Pellitteri and Greenberg, the peculiar affliction of a patient. You may find yourself, like the student in the selection below, deeply concerned about a public health care issue that threatens the quality and availability of hospital patient care.

Ask your students to recall from their other classes instances in which they needed to employ analytical reasoning. You may come up with another good writing assignment as a result.

As you read the following passage, jot down for yourself (or mark in the text) (a) the places where the writer is moving from specific evidence toward a generalization and (b) the places where the movement flows in the opposite direction.

Medicaid and Medicare:

Friends or Foes of the Health Care Industry?

Page Powell, college writing student

Notice the use of "strangled" here—ask your students how appropriate that brutal image is to a paper describing the "treatment" of patients and small hospitals by the managers of Medicare and Medicaid.

Hospitals in America are being strangled by federal medical assistance programs that refuse to compensate them properly for the services they provide. Medicaid, which provides medical insurance for the poor, and Medicare, which covers the elderly, have substantially altered 1 their payment methods over the past several years. The current methods place restrictions on the amount of money the companies will pay hospitals for procedures performed on Medicaid and Medicare patients, regardless of the ever-increasing costs of such procedures. The result is a health care environment, especially in small communities, in which hospitals are forced to operate more like businesses, with profit making replacing patient caring as their primary goal. Two major consequences have resulted from this situation, and both are entirely unacceptable. The first is that many hospitals, again especially in small communities, are being forced to close their doors, depriving their communities of their only major health care facility. The second is that quality of care has deteriorated dramatically as hospitals in larger communities have had to try to provide the basic procedure at the most minimal cost possible, so as not to lose too much money on the procedure.

2 When hospitals in small communities close, the effect on the community can be devastating. Many jobs are lost, and doctors--what few there are--move away. The community suffers other severe economic repercussions because, for example, new businesses or light industries aren't likely to locate in a community where there is no hospital. No effect, however, is as harmful as is the loss, in such communities, of a place to receive quality health care. Citizens of these communities, many of whom are elderly, must often travel long distances to get medical treatment if their local hospital closes. Generally speaking, hospitals will stay open as long as they can break even or generate at least a small profit. But the Medicaid and Medicare payment systems, which cover a tremendous number of the patients cared for in small hospitals, are making it harder and harder for these hospitals to make money. The reason is mathematically simple: the medical procedures keep costing more and more, and the Medicaid and Medicare systems will pay a flat amount and not a penny more.

3 According to the 1989 annual report of the Federation of American Health Systems, Medicaid and Medicare account for nearly 50 percent of all hospital patient revenues. When these patients' bills are not fully paid, hospitals are forced to accept the losses. Thus hospitals often lose money on the very patients that provide the majority of their business. Large hospitals in cities can sometimes generate enough money from service to

other patients to cover their losses, but most of them lose money. And the large, public "nonprofit" hospitals are clearly operating as a civic, humanitarian service. As for the many small hospitals in small-town America--they are closing at an alarming rate.

Note how well Powell plays the humane idea of compassionate health care off against the bottom-line mentality of business managers of hospitals.

The second, more startling result of the profit demands being placed 4
on hospitals is a reduced standard of health care being provided to all patients. In an effort to cut costs, many hospitals are forced to discontinue or curtail vital patient services. This cutting occurs at all levels throughout the hospital: making fewer supplies last longer, raising the number of patients each on-duty nurse is responsible for, reducing assistance personnel to bare minimums, making former one-patient rooms into two-patient rooms, and on and on. New technologies are not taken advantage of, because they involve expensive equipment or procedures. Diagnostic lab work is reduced to barest necessity. All of these cost-cutting factors add up to one inevitable result: patients are receiving a lower standard of care than what they expect and deserve.

The health care industry is complicated, and surely no one factor can 5
be blamed completely for the financial problems now plaguing it. But the payment limits of Medicaid and Medicare have played far too large a part in the current dilemma. These systems were originally mandated out of a need to bring quality health care to all Americans in our land of advanced, best-in-the-world medical treatment. Yet they have been primarily responsible for driving many hospitals out of business and driving down the quality of care in the hospitals that manage to keep their doors open. These systems must be changed and brought into reality. Payment restrictions may be necessary, but they must just as necessarily be raised, and raised soon, to try to keep up with spiraling medical costs. If these changes are not made, the nation will have fewer and fewer hospitals to care for its patients, and there will be more and more needless suffering abroad in the land.

How authoritative is Powell's "voice" here?

Questions for Writing and Discussion

Prepare short written answers to each of these questions. Be prepared to hand them in and/or discuss them in class, as your teacher directs.

1. What readership might be most interested in this piece?
2. How does the writer signal the two main areas of his analysis in his first paragraph?

3. What does the writer analyze as the central cause of what he sees as a twofold problem in hospital health care?
4. How does he use an important statistic to bolster his analysis?
5. If you wanted to try to influence some change in current Medicaid and Medicare payments, where would you send a copy of this paper?
6. What qualities (values, beliefs, and so on) of the audience does the author rely on? How do those qualities figure in the piece's larger analytical/persuasive structure?

Additional items after the Powell piece:

1. What function is shared by the following words in the essay? *The result is, Two major consequences, The first is, The second is* (¶ 1), *the effect, No effect, however, Generally speaking, The reason is* (¶ 2), *According to* (¶ 3), *The second, more startling, one inevitable result* (¶ 4), *surely no one factor, But, Yet, These systems must be changed, If these changes are not made* (¶ 5).
2. What thematic similarities do you find between this piece by Powell and Will's "Listen to the Bridges"?
3. What are your personal experiences with American health care? with its costs?

✓✓✓ WORKSHEET: Writing to Analyze

What should *you* do when faced with an analysis writing project? First, and as always, remember your *reasons* for writing: are you going to inform your readers? inform *and* persuade them? entertain them? Clarify your goal. Then think about what else you're doing:

- What's your subject? What do you know about it already? What do you need to find out? How should you *analyze* your subject—that is, take it apart and study it? (Then *do* the analysis.)
- Who are your readers? What do they already know? What do they need to know? What is their interest in the subject?

Now begin your drafting—get the content down without worrying about correctness. Look over what you've written. In what places are you going from evidence to a generalization? In what places are you going the other way? Can your reader *easily* follow that movement? Have you involved your reader in the piece—by your choice of words, by playing on the reader's beliefs, and so forth? Get the input of a few helpful readers. Then revise and edit your writing systematically, getting that last version in shape. Finish by carefully proofreading the result.

CASE STUDY CLOSE-UP

The student who wrote "Medicaid and Medicare: Friends or Foes of the Health Care Industry?" was shocked when he heard that the hospital in his home town—the hospital his father and he had both been born in—was closing. At first he couldn't understand why; the town had actually grown over the years, and though it was by no means large, it wasn't suffering any real economic setbacks or population loss. In his way, he had a "case" on his hands, somewhat like Drs. Pellitteri and Greenberg in "Eleven Blue Men"—a puzzling effect for which he wanted to discover the cause. When his writing teacher assigned an analytical paper, she said, "Write about something you *care* about but also *wonder* about." This student chose the closing of small-town hospitals. An analysis of the situation was called for.

Have any of your students had a hometown hospital close?

In the early stages of working on his paper, the student thought about the problem. Where could he find information about the hospital's closing? He made

Notice that in this kind of research, talking directly with people involved is just as vital as, if not more vital than, digging information out of books and periodicals.

a note to talk with the hospital administrator as soon as possible. He also figured a chat with one of the doctors in his home town would be productive. After these two interviews, he knew exactly why the hospital was closing. All he needed to do was a bit of reading to discover just how widespread the problem was. Now much of his prewriting, his analysis, was over.

He had learned that the hospital closing in his home town was one of many similar closings throughout the country, all for the same basic reason: Medicaid and Medicare payments had a "cap," an upper limit, no matter what the necessary medical procedure was. Hospitals had to accept that cap as payment for the procedure, and if the patient wasn't personally able to pay the difference between the cap and the actual cost—as most patients, especially the elderly ones on a limited income, were not—then the hospital had to take the loss. Thus, most hospitals were losing money. Larger hospitals in cities, with more diverse patient care programs and incomes, could battle the losses more effectively, but small hospitals simply couldn't.

Notice that here we've emphasized the student's investigative, analytical process over the writing process, yet we by no means intend thereby to diminish the importance of the writing process. It's just that on projects like this, the research is critically important to the success of the writing.

Armed with this information as the results of his analysis, the student wrote the first draft of the paper. Then, after sharing the paper in a class workshop and getting the suggestions of two classmates (as well as those of his roommate at the fraternity house), he wrote another draft, clarifying and elaborating in spots where readers had questions or problems. The student then polished and proofread the paper, ultimately handing in the effective analytical paper you read on pages 128–30.

WRITING ASSIGNMENTS

1. Imagine you are a sportswriter. Witness and take notes on an important baseball (or football, tennis, and so on) game. Analyze the game with the goal of explaining how and why the winner won or the loser lost. Which plays were crucial? What events made the result? Let the results of your analysis dominate the piece. Your readers don't need to know about each play, each nuance—only those which truly matter in the result. Decide on your "voice"—how you will "sound" to readers—and decide on how you will organize the piece.
2. Analyze some aspect of your personality, your makeup. Let's say that you enjoy reading. Now push the analysis further: why is this so? Examine your past, reaching back into your memory. What factors, experiences, and so on can you identify that might have contributed to your current enjoyment of reading (or whatever aspect of your makeup you choose)?
3. Think of a complex situation in which you have been involved—a misunderstanding, a complicated arrangement—and analyze it. How did the misun-

derstanding occur, and with what results? What made the arrangement complicated? How was the situation resolved?

4. Recall some action-packed, perhaps dangerous situation in which you have been involved. Analyze it: of what did it consist?
5. Analysis is closely related to process—the step-by-step business of accomplishing a task. One of the more common forms of technical writing is the "process analysis," whereby the writer explains the steps of a particular procedure or how something operates. Think of a process you could analyze and explain. Here's a list of suggestions:
   a. How a rainbow is formed
   b. How a color-TV picture tube works
   c. How digital recording takes place
   d. How to break in a new baseball glove
   e. How to change the tire on an automobile
   f. How to jump-start an automobile
   g. How to develop black-and-white film
6. The photo on page 103 presents literary sleuth Sherlock Holmes (played by Basil Rathbone) in a classic "mystery-solving" pose. Remember a time when you had to solve a mystery or puzzle in a high school or college class, or in your personal life, and write a short paper describing the puzzle and how you went about solving it.

Focus on Critical Writing

When you add *evaluation* to analytical writing, you have critical writing as we discussed it in chapter 3. Here are some analytical writing assignments that couple analysis with evaluation:

7. Pick any two (or more) articles that involve recommendations for weight-loss diets. Analyze the diets in terms of which is more feasible for a typical, reasonably healthy college student living in a dorm at your university. Based on your analysis, recommend one of the diets. Make the reasons for your recommendation clear and explicit.
8. Billy, an incoming college freshman at your university, has unexpectedly been given five thousand dollars by his long-lost Aunt Ellen. The only condition is that he *must* spend the money on computer equipment to further his education. Billy wants you to help him choose what to buy. Make a detailed analysis of what he *could* buy—listing prices, noting availability, discussing ease of learning (he's never used a computer before), and so on. Recommend a system for him, in detail. Your report will have *two* audiences (other than your teacher): (a) Billy and (b) Darlene Young, the bank vice-president who must approve the wise expenditure of these funds. Billy knows nothing about computers; Darlene Young knows quite a bit.

Writers' Circle

Assume the following situation: the states of Eastern and Western Europe have banded together to declare themselves a nuclear-free self-defense zone and have invited all foreign powers to withdraw their forces from Europe; consequently, the United States finds itself with an extra ten billion dollars annually, money that had been spent maintaining troops in Europe. *How shall this money be spent?*

Divide into "economic advisory committees" of four students each and debate the expenditure of the money. Make majority and minority reports in each group, unless the group is unanimous. Each committee should then report to the class as a whole, with the teacher listing on the board the solutions and recommendations the class prefers. Next, each committee should elect a chair, and the committee chairs should draft a letter to a member of Congress or a U.S. senator, outlining the class's recommendations. When the letter is drafted, the rest of the class members should hear the draft and either suggest further revisions or approve it for actual sending to the legislator (along with an explanation of the class project).

chapter 7 Writing to Persuade: Emphasis on the Reader's Belief

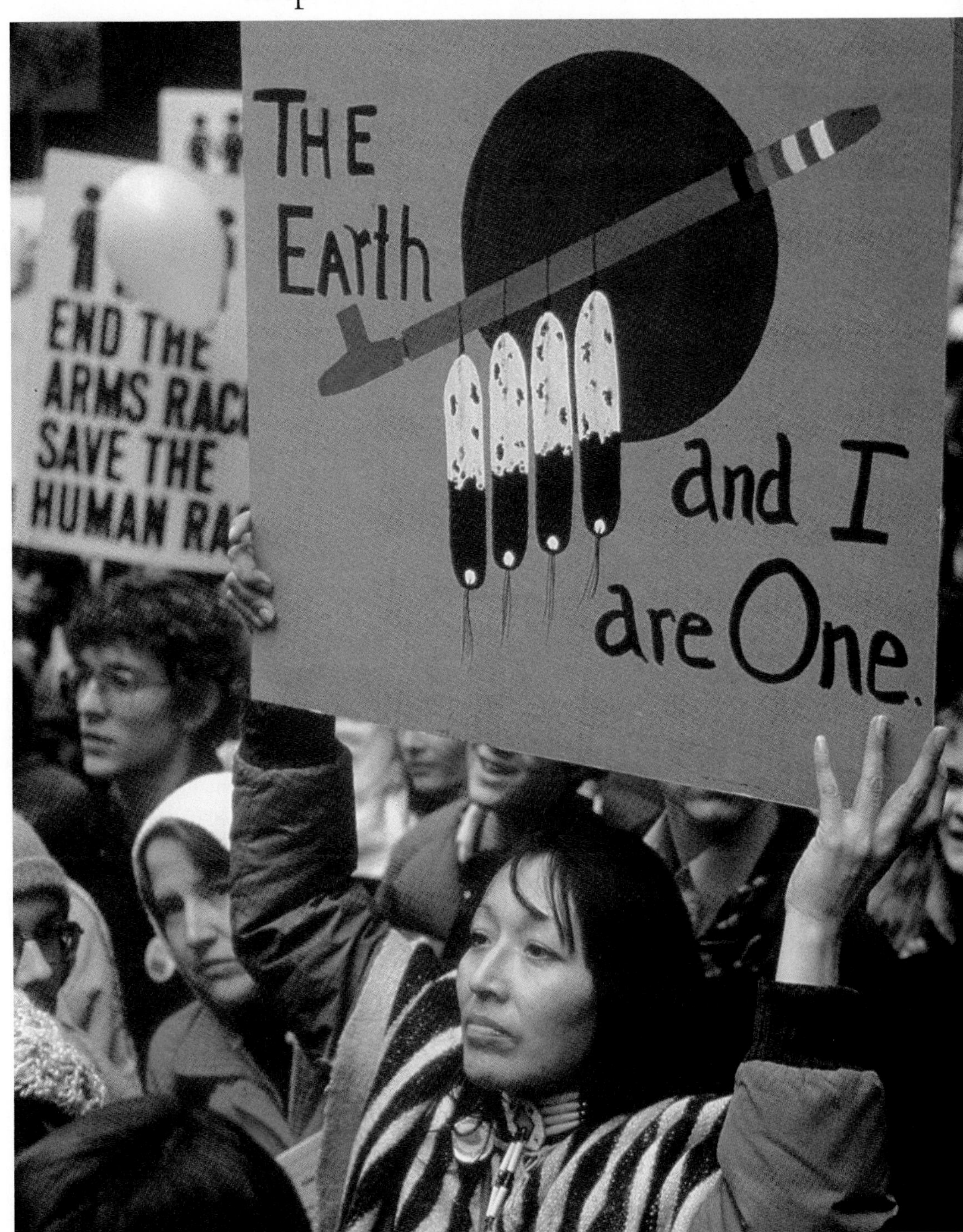

"What gets my interest is the sense that a writer is speaking honestly and fully of what he knows well."

Wendell Berry

"I told a woman who plays viola in a symphony orchestra how uncapturable music is, how I cannot think of organizing the music I hear, but only be its audience. But she said that writing is the most abstract form; the other forms have concomitant human sense organs; music has the ear, and painting the eye, sculpture the hands, and acting and dancing the voice and body. But writing, she said, does not have its organ. She began to cry; I'm not sure why."

Maxine Hong Kingston

One of the real challenges for any writer is writing to persuade. When you want to make a point convincingly, when you want someone to see things your way, when you want to change someone's mind, a piece of written persuasion can be the most effective communication tool there is. Not only is persuasive writing on its own an important reason for writing, but persuasion is an important element of most things people write—from essay exams to proposals, from job application letters to term papers. Mastering persuasive writing is crucial for every writer.

Writing to persuade may place more demands on you as a writer than any other reason for writing. Whole books take persuasive writing as their subject, and even so cannot cover it in full. Here we'd like to keep what we say about persuasion simple. In this chapter we want to make two key points about writing persuasively: when you're writing to persuade, you need to consider

1. what kind of point you want to make; and
2. the nature of your support for it.

You can find in the library countless books on persuasion; here we keep things *simple.* We suggest you let your students master this simple approach before assigning them the more complex matters treated in chapter 20.

(Later in the book—in chapter 20, "Argumentation"—we'll have more to say about argumentative patterns; in this chapter we're looking at persuasion as a purpose for writing.) And so as you read the following four sample pieces of writing, look especially for those two things:

- What is the point of this piece (the *claim* it is making)?
- What *support* is offered for that point?

Then, as the chapter progresses, we'll develop those ideas—and how to work with them in your own writing—in more detail.

Congressmen for Life: The Incumbency Scandal

ROWLAND EVANS AND ROBERT NOVAK

Rowland Evans and Robert Novak are authors, political columnists, and TV commentators. Their works include books on Presidents Johnson, Nixon, and Reagan. The following piece appeared in Reader's Digest *in 1989.*

1 If you were a member of the House of Representatives, you would be more likely to die in office than be defeated for re-election. In fact, in the last Congress, seven did die, six were unseated.

2 "There is less turnover in the House than in the Supreme Soviet," said former President Reagan after the 1988 elections, in which 99 percent of Congressional incumbents were re-elected.

3 The original intent of the Founding Fathers was for the House of Representatives to be a people's chamber. A two-year Congressional term, they believed, would assure a body closely attuned to changes in popular sentiment. And throughout the 19th century, about half of the House membership turned over in each election, either by defeat or by retirement. As recently as 1948, 21 percent of House members were defeated.

4 But today, membership has become a career undertaking. The average Congressman is 52 years old and has served nearly six two-year terms. Since 1966, every election but one (in the Watergate year of 1974) has produced a re-election rate over 90 percent. The House is already far less responsive than the Senate, where statewide election makes its members susceptible to significant swings in public opinion, as in 1980, when the Republicans assumed control, or 1986, when the Democrats regained it.

5 Warns David R. Mayhew, professor of government at Yale: the House is "becoming too impenetrable to be representative." *The Wall Street Journal* calls what was meant to be the people's chamber "The U.S. House of Lords."

6 What has gone wrong?

7 **Gerrymandering.** A key factor in incumbent power is the way Congressional districts have been gerrymandered, or carved into convoluted shapes to ensure one-party dominance. The term derives from Gov. Elbridge Gerry of Massachusetts, who in 1812 signed a bill remapping the state's districts into a salamander-like shape to assure his party's electoral success that year.

8 After every decennial census, Congressional districts are reapportioned and state legislatures redesign districts to reflect changing population. When both houses of a state legislature and the governor's office are controlled by the same party, gerrymandering is likely. The result is a reduction of genuinely competitive districts. (There are now only around 30 nationwide.)

9 Without question, the most brilliantly effective gerrymander in history was engineered in California, after the 1980 census, by the late Democratic Representative Phil Burton. Backed by a Democratic legislature and governor,

Let's play the role of skeptic intensely as this piece proceeds: does ¶ 1 have more of a *rational* or an *emotional* effect? What's the point of the comparison in ¶ 2?

What rhetorical force comes from claiming the "original intent of the Founding Fathers"? Is that force diminished by the inadvertent sexism of "Founding Fathers"?

What's the connection between "people's chamber . . . two-year Congressional term" and "turned over"? Does lack of turnover *necessarily* violate the idea of "people's chamber"?

What connection is implied in the fourth paragraph but is not necessarily a warranted, proven connection? (That lack of turnover in the House equals lack of responsiveness among members to their constituents—there simply is no proof that any such connection exists.)

Though it's impressive to quote a government professor from Yale, does the idea of the House being "impenetrable"—that is, hard for a new member to join—also mean that the House no longer *represents* its constituencies? (No—again there's no connection. Just because it's hard to get elected into the House and, once there, hard *not* to get reelected, it doesn't mean the congressperson isn't doing a good job of legislating for his or her district.)

Burton utilized computer technology to make a mockery of the state's district lines. In 1981 Democrats held a 22–21 House advantage. But in 1982, after the Golden State had gained two new House seats through reapportionment and Burton had completed his masterpiece, the Democratic margin soared to 28–17.

The effectiveness of Burton's gerrymandering was demonstrated in 1984: 10
Reagan carried his home state by landslide proportions and over half of California voters favored Republican candidates for Congress; yet, thanks to the new district lines, Republicans gained only one seat.

The 1990 census is expected to give California an extra five or six seats, 11
with population growth concentrated in Republican areas (as it had been in 1980). If California's 1990 election results in a Democratic governor and legislature, another gerrymander is likely. A similar situation could occur in Texas and Illinois, among other states.

PACs *are* controversial and have had effects not wholly beneficial to the electoral process. On the other hand, they were developed to halt even more abusive practices, when individuals gave *unlimited* amounts of money to candidates. Dismantling PACs isn't going to provide a simple corrective for the abuse of influence through campaign donations.

PC Power. Political action committees gained popularity when the 1974 12
campaign reform act imposed a $1000 limit on individual contributions. PACs have turned into heavy artillery for incumbents, favoring sitting House members over their challengers by an eight-to-one margin. Because there are more Democrats in the House and they control powerful committees, PACs favor Democrats over Republicans.

According to a study by Common Cause, a politically liberal citizens' 13
lobbying organization, Democratic House incumbents received an average $217,108 from PACs, versus $10,763 for their Republican challengers—a ratio of 20 to 1. (Republican House incumbents in 1988 received an average of $177,691, their Democratic challengers $49,469—a ratio of nearly four to one.)

Note that the Common Cause study proves only that incumbents of either party get more money than their challengers; it in no way reflects on the performance or integrity of those incumbents. The Evans-Novak attitude seems to be that if a House member is an incumbent, he or she is automatically a poor legislator.

PACs even give money to powerful Congressmen who run unopposed. 14
Last year Rep. John Dingell (D., Mich.), chairman of the Commerce Committee, got $459,242; Rep. Jack Brooks (D., Texas), chairman of the Judiciary Committee, got $276,262; Speaker of the House Jim Wright (D., Texas) collected $179,603.

Why should business heap money on unopposed Congressional barons? 15
"They're payoffs pure and simple," says campaign consultant Eddie Mahe.

A classic case of PAC power took place last year in Maryland's First 16
Congressional District, encompassing the conservative Eastern Shore. Rep. Roy Dyson (D., Md.) campaigned amid controversy over a top aide who threw himself out of a hotel window after the Washington *Post* reported he had made unusual demands on male staff members. Dyson himself had to publicly deny that he was a homosexual. Yet he received $403,647 in PAC funds, including a contribution from the PAC administered by the Unisys Corp., then under federal investigation for making improper Congressional campaign contributions. Dyson denied that his support for a Unisys shipboard radar system rejected by the Navy was influenced by his PAC contributions.

17 Dyson's Republican opponent—Wayne T. Gilchrest, a former teacher and part-time carpenter new to politics—received one $200 PAC contribution. Dyson won by one-half of one percent of the vote over his financially outmatched challenger.

18 **The Congressional Machine.** The House is served by some 11,000 staffers costing taxpayers $330 million a year. Each incumbent enjoys an average budget of $582,000 for staff and administrative expenses. No small part of that budget and staff is geared to keeping the Congressman in office.

19 "Every Congressional office and committee staff," writes Milton Gwirtzman, a liberal Democrat and former Senate aide, "has a cadre of assistants whose main incentive is to enhance their boss's public standing through bills, amendments, speeches, floor statements, newsletters, etc."

20 Case work—handling the many complaints and problems of constituents dealing with the federal bureaucracy—far eclipses a Representative's legislative duties. Voters who have trouble with Social Security, veterans benefits, taxation and federal regulation become indebted to their incumbent Congressman, which helps explain why a conservative district, for example, will return a liberal Representative to the House. "Congress never has a mandate," says David Hoppe, administrative assistant to Sen. Dan Coats (R., Ind.), "except to make sure the people who have Social Security checks coming get them."

Again, Evans and Novak write as though the employees of a congressional office only recently started bending their efforts toward getting their boss reelected. This has *always* been the first priority of a congressional staff; in fact, it is the priority of the staff of virtually every political office—federal, state, county, or municipal. If this long-standing practice is getting worse, that still doesn't mean necessarily that the officeholder is doing a poor job.

21 Another advantage incumbents have over challengers is the "franking privilege"—free mail. Direct mailings glorifying the Congressman are targeted by government computer to voters back home. In 1988, Congressmen sent out a staggering 548,437,000 pieces of mail.

You and your students (or their parents) probably get a fair amount of this congressional mail each year. How effective is it, really? Who reads it? (We admit we seldom do, but we do occasionally send a letter *to* our representatives!)

22 Television and radio feeds from the galleries on Capitol Hill are also beamed to stations in the home district, at government expense. Few challengers can afford a sustained media blitz to match this. Says Hedrick Smith in *The Power Game,* this "high-technology arsenal ensures all but a tiny handful of incumbents will survive any challenge."

23 Theoretically, House regulations prohibit franked mass mailings in the last two months of a campaign. To circumvent that rule, members last year delivered their bundles to the House Folding Room at the last possible minute so that voters would receive the propaganda as close to the election as possible.

24 A 58-million-letter backlog stretched out for more than a city block in corridors leading to the Folding Room. Temporary employees had to be retained at an additional cost to the taxpayer of over $500,000. Meanwhile, full-time employees were coerced into working 70-hour weeks to get out the members' election-year mail. The delay meant that some of the mail arrived just weeks before the election.

25 **The Good Life.** Although defenders of this year's proposed 51-percent pay increase claimed that Congressmen cannot live in expensive Washington on

"This year's proposed 51-percent pay increase" refers to 1989, when, in the face of strong public opposition, Congress

their existing pay, there is scant evidence that the level of compensation has driven any lawmaker back into private life.

voted against giving itself this raise. This recurring issue may be "heating up" in Washington again this very minute. At its core is this notion of "The Good Life": many people think what a legislator makes is *plenty* of money.

The $89,500 salary is deceptive. Fringe benefits, official and unofficial, can be substantial: junkets here and abroad; trips to vacation spots and other favors from lobbyists; use of office and committee staffers for personal duties; the opportunity to make off-the-cuff "speeches" to Washington lobbyists at $2000 a shot. There are also numerous business opportunities from supporters, often on generous terms. 26

Whether or not congresspersons are over- or underpaid is a lively question, but notice that it has nothing to do, again, with whether or not a congressperson is doing a good job. The question relates to low turnover only in the sense that, according to Evans and Novak, the pay is too good for a congressperson to want to leave office.

Thus another reason for the unprecedented lack of turnover in Congress is that so many House members live—and love—the good life. And the icing on their cake is their lavish, taxpayer-subsidized pension plan. A 62-year-old Congressman can start collecting after just five years in office. For those who have been around longer, the annual pension can exceed $80,000. 27

Today's Congressman is usually a Washington homeowner. Chances are he's in the social swim, and his children often attend private school there. He may not even maintain a home back in his district, just fly back and forth (at taxpayers' expense) to visit his constituency. 28

How could a lucrative pension plan (¶ 27) possibly cause a legislator to be unresponsive to his or her constituency?

Enjoyable though this life may be, it soured Thomas F. Hartnett, a South Carolina real-estate appraiser, who was elected to Congress as a Republican in 1980 and left after three terms. "A ruling class has emerged," he argues. "We no longer have government of, by and for the people but rather by professional legislators." 29

To combat the tendency toward lifelong incumbency, former Congressman Hartnett suggests a Constitutional limitation on House terms. "It is time we told our Representatives," he says, "that after a limited number of terms, we will give you a gold watch, a brass band, put you on a bus, send you home and let you live under the laws you passed while you were in Congress." 30

It is perhaps unrealistic to expect Congressmen to legislate themselves out of office. But there are other reforms that could make Congressional elections more competitive: 31

Is it realistic to think that gerrymandering can be stopped cold after all these years and all this practice by both parties?

Remembering that PACs were founded as part of a reform against the abuse by individuals of campaign contributions, some people could argue that these two suggestions contradict each other.

- At the state level, referenda can force strict guidelines for fairly remapping Congressional districts and avoiding gerrymandering.
- Congress can abolish the PACs, which grossly distort the electoral process, and remove the $1000 limit on individual contributions so that challengers can mount effective campaigns.
- In the interest of fundamental fairness, Congress should radically restrict election-year use of the franking privilege, and other high-tech, taxpayer-supplied political tools that are used to help members stay elected. It should also reduce the bloated office and committee staffs, which exist not for legislative but for re-election purposes.
- Finally, Congress should outlaw the honoraria that lobbyists and special interests shower on lawmakers, adding new restrictions on outside income from law practices and investments.

How would outlawing such honoraria help?

32 Cynics may say that Congress would never jeopardize a system that virtually guarantees their lifelong incumbency. But cynics also said that there was no way to stop the 51-percent pay raise for Congress.

An interesting point, but irrelevant.

33 Instead, a firestorm of grassroots opposition forced an 11th-hour roll-call vote in which both houses reluctantly bowed to public opinion and overwhelmingly rejected the pay grab. In the case of incumbency, too, an outraged citizenry can force its elected representatives to act, restoring democracy to the people's house.

The last-minute roll-call vote that defeated the 51 percent pay raise *could* be used as evidence that Congress *is* responsive to its constituents—regardless of "The Incumbency Scandal."

We have done a kind of counter-walk-through here, examining and weighing what Evans and Novak say in the way we think a good critical reader might. Your students should cultivate their critical reading abilities to develop a healthy skepticism about all they read, see, and hear in this world of advertising and propaganda. "Do you believe everything you read/see/hear?" is still a good question to ask. We're not out to make anyone's students cynics, but we *are* out to help them learn to distinguish between the bull and what the bull leaves behind.

Questions for Writing and Discussion

Prepare short written answers to each of these questions. Be prepared to hand them in and/or discuss them in class, as your teacher directs.

1. What is the point of this article?
2. What are the facts in this case?
3. What kind of connection do you see between the facts in this case and the point of the argument? Is it a weak connection, or a strong one?
4. What kind(s) of evidence does the piece offer? What other evidence might be brought into this argument to make it stronger?
5. What quality—or qualities—within the audience do the authors rely on to complete their persuasion?
6. What do the following words mean—*susceptible* (¶ 4), *decennial* (¶ 8), *incentive* (¶ 19)?
7. What nonsexist alternative do you suggest for the word *congressman*?

Evans and Novak provide strong support for reform in congressional elections. It is a public issue. Below, Anne Morrow Lindbergh writes persuasively about a more subtle matter, but something of concern to all women, even though the "today" Lindbergh refers to is 1955, the year the piece was first published.

Woman's Life Today

ANNE MORROW LINDBERGH

Anne Morrow Lindbergh is the author of a number of books, including North to the Orient *(1935),* The Steep Ascent *(1944), and* Spirit of St. Louis *(1953), about the famous flight of her husband, Charles, and* Gift from the Sea *(1955) from which the following piece is excerpted.*

1 Woman's life today is tending more and more toward the state William James describes so well in the German word, "Zerissenheit—torn-to-pieces-hood." She will be shattered into a thousand pieces. On the contrary, she must

This is a tough phrase. In your students' experience, what would "torn-to-pieces-hood" be like?

In your students' thinking, how or why might this experience be particular to women?

What do your students find strange about these examples?

Ask your students how this idea that "woman must be the pioneer in this turning inward" can be true.

Do your students think Lindbergh can possibly be correct here in saying that women, in competing with men, have neglected their "own inner springs"? Does that seem to be Lindbergh's main point?

Additional items:

1. One reader called Lindbergh's view "old-fashioned." Do you agree?
2. Compare Lindbergh's view with Le Guin's (chapter 6) and with Matthiessen's (chapter 9). Are they consistent?
3. Lindbergh had at least two experiences not all women could claim. First she married a national hero, Charles Augustus Lindbergh, whose nonstop, solo, transatlantic flight in 1927 is one of this century's greatest achievements. She lived largely in his shadow, despite her own talents. Second, her child was kidnapped and murdered in

consciously encourage those pursuits which oppose the centrifugal forces of today. Quiet time alone, contemplation, prayer, music, a centering line of thought or reading, of study or work. It can be physical or intellectual or artistic, any creative life proceeding from oneself. It need not be an enormous project or a great work. But it should be something of one's own. Arranging a bowl of flowers in the morning can give a sense of quiet in a crowded day—like writing a poem, or saying a prayer. What matters is that one be for a time inwardly attentive.

Solitude, says the moon shell. Center-down, say the Quaker saints. To the possession of the self the way is inward, says Plotinus. The cell of self-knowledge is the stall in which the pilgrim must be reborn, says St. Catherine of Siena. Voices from the past. In fact, these are pursuits and virtues of the past. But done in another way today because done consciously, aware, with eyes open. Not done as before, as part of the pattern of the time. Not done because everyone else is doing them; almost no one is doing them. Revolutionary, in fact, because almost every trend and pressure, every voice from the outside is against this new way of inward living. 2

Woman must be the pioneer in this turning inward for strength. In a sense she has always been the pioneer. Less able, until the last generation, to escape into outward activities, the very limitations of her life forced her to look inward. And from looking inward she gained an inner strength which man in his outward active life did not as often find. But in our recent efforts to emancipate ourselves, to prove ourselves the equal of man, we have, naturally enough perhaps, been drawn into competing with him in his outward activities, to the neglect of our own inner springs. Why have we been seduced into abandoning this timeless inner strength of woman for the temporal outer strength of man? This outer strength of man is essential to the pattern, but even here the reign of purely outer strength and purely outward solutions seems to be waning today. Men, too, are being forced to look inward—to find inner solutions as well as outer ones. Perhaps this change marks a new stage of maturity for modern extrovert, activist, materialistic Western man. Can it be that he is beginning to realize that the kingdom of heaven is within? 3

Questions for Writing and Discussion

Prepare short written answers to each of these questions. Be prepared to hand them in and/or discuss them in class, as your teacher directs.

1. What is the point of this article?
2. What are the facts in this case?
3. What kind of connection do you see between the facts in this case and the point of the argument? Is it a weak connection, or a strong one?
4. What kind(s) of evidence does the piece offer? What other evidence might be brought into this argument to make it stronger?

5. What quality—or qualities—within the audience does the author rely on to complete her persuasion?
6. What do the following words mean—*temporal, extrovert* (¶ 3)?
7. What effect does Lindbergh achieve with the series of inverted sentences that opens the second paragraph?

a highly publicized and controversial case. How might such experiences influence the attitudes she endorses in this piece?

Bridges: Another Perspective

Anne Morrow Lindbergh wrote of a "today" that was in fact 1955. She did not know at the time of the consciousness-raising about women that feminist writers of the 1960s, 1970s, and 1980s would contribute. Offer a 1990s perspective on Lindbergh's 1950s perspective: what does she say that is, or seems, no longer viable? What does she say that remains of value to women's lives? How might she express her thoughts on this subject in the "today" that you know?

Whereas Anne Morrow Lindbergh argues a subtle, philosophical point, Madeleine L'Engle takes on a less subtle, potentially volatile point. In this excerpt from her autobiographical series (see page 82), the award-winning author explains why authors of children's books shouldn't be required to use a specified (limited) vocabulary.

On Controlled Vocabularies

MADELEINE L'ENGLE

1 I have a profound conviction that it is most dangerous to tamper with the word. I've been asked why it's wrong to provide the author of a pleasure book, a non-textbook, with a controlled-vocabulary list. First of all, to give an author a list of words and tell him to write a book for children using no word that is not on the list strikes me as blasphemy. What would have happened to Beatrix Potter if she had written in the time of controlled vocabulary? Lettuce has a *soporific* effect on Peter Rabbit. "Come come, Beatrix, that word is beyond a child's vocabulary." "But it's the right word, it's the only possible word." "Nonsense. You can't use soporific because it's outside the child's reading capacity. You can say that lettuce made Peter feel sleepy."

2 I shudder.

3 To give a writer a controlled-vocabulary list is manipulating both writer and reader. It keeps the child within his present capacity, on the bland assumption that growth is even and orderly and rational, instead of some-

Note the force of the "I" in this piece. (And to think certain teachers—in some benighted attempt to "help" students write better, or out of some errant conviction that serious, college-level, and professional writers never use it—forbid their students from using the first person!)

Much of the force of L'Engle's use of the first person comes from her own authority: she clearly knows what she's talking about, and she's convinced she's right.

thing that happens in great unexpected leaps and bounds. It ties the author down and takes away his creative freedom, and completely ignores the fact that the good writer will always limit himself. The simplest word is almost always the right word. I am convinced that Beatrix Potter used "soporific" because it was, it really and truly was, the only right word for lettuce at that moment. One of my favorite authors, Anon, wrote, centuries ago:

> The written word
> Should be clean as bone,
> Clear as light,
> Firm as stone.
> Two words are not
> As good as one.

I should pay more attention to those lines than I do. The writer who listens to them will do his own limiting, but it will come from inside, it will come from a creative response and not from an arbitrary restriction, which is the structure that imprisons instead of the structure that liberates. 4

Point out to students that the last paragraph carries L'Engle's real argument. Note that she says essentially the same thing several different times, several different ways, and achieves the effect she wants: these limitations affect us critically in diverse ways, all of them detrimental, and we should be alarmed.

The more limited our language is, the more limited we are; the more limited the literature we give to our children, the more limited their capacity to respond, and therefore, in their turn, to create. The more our vocabulary is controlled, the less we will be able to think for ourselves. We do think in words, and the fewer words we know, the more restricted our thoughts. As our vocabulary expands, so does our power to think. Try to comprehend an abstract idea without words: we may be able to imagine a turkey dinner. But try something more complicated; try to ask questions, to look for meaning: without words we don't get very far. If we limit and distort language, we limit and distort personality. 5

Questions for Writing and Discussion

Prepare short written answers to each of these questions. Be prepared to hand them in and/or discuss them in class, as your teacher directs.

1. What is the point of this article?
2. What are the facts in this case?
3. What kind of connection do you see between the facts in this case and the point of the argument? Is it a weak connection, or a strong one?
4. What kind(s) of evidence does the piece offer? What other evidence might be brought into this argument to make it stronger?
5. What quality—or qualities—within the audience does the author rely on to complete her persuasion?
6. What do the following words mean—*blasphemy* (¶ 1), *bland* (¶ 3), *arbitrary* (¶ 4)?
7. Who is "Anon" (¶ 3)?

How does L'Engle's position about reading differ (if it does) from Bettelheim's and Zelan's (chapter 3)?

PREREADING WORKSHEET

Before you read the following piece by Sheryl Rollins, write brief responses to these questions:

1. When you hear the word *lawyer*, what image or images come to mind—
   a. male, or female?
   b. what race?
   c. shrewd? scheming?
   d. honest? dishonest?
   e. brilliant?

   Do any of those images change when you hear the word *attorney*?
2. Have you ever known—or known of—a lawyer who was a member of a minority group?
3. What stereotypes limit opportunities for women to become attorneys? for black women in particular?
4. What personality traits would you expect in an attorney?
5. Why do you suppose so few black women have become attorneys?

The Need for More Black Women Lawyers

Sheryl Rollins, college writing student

1 Today black women are making gains in many areas of employment. But recent statistics show that black women are highly underrepresented in the field of law. Because the law (including the legal profession) touches every area of human life, it's important that all segments of our society be represented within it. Thus increasing the representation of black women within the legal profession will enable them to make a valuable contribution not only to themselves but also to their society.

2 The lack of black women in the field of law has three primary causes: historical, sociological, and cultural. In 1910 there were only 798 black lawyers in the country. By 1940 there were 1,925--one for every 13,000 black people in the country. Only 64 were women. Today, while black people make up more than 25 percent of the national population, black lawyers represent less than 5 percent of the nation's lawyers. And women are a diminishingly small part of that 5 percent.

Notice how Rollins sets up her historical, social, and cultural examples in the second paragraph and then develops each in sequence, in the subsequent paragraphs. Yet she writes with such skill that the skeleton of the "five-paragraph model" isn't visible; besides, she develops other ideas in other paragraphs that make the essay much more complex, both in content and structure, than typical "five-paragraph" student efforts.

Part of the reason women are such a small part of this small percentage has to do with the historic admissions standards of law schools. Law schools in the United States have historically made it difficult for women, especially black women, to study law. Harlan Fiske Stone, legendary dean of Columbia's law school, once said that women would be admitted there over his dead body. Harvard did not admit women as students until 1950, or black women until the late 1960s. 3

Sociologically, men have long regarded women as frail, incompetent, and in need of protection. Black women, in particular, were regarded as frail, incompetent, and unworthy of protection. Thus women in general, and black women in particular, were regarded as temperamentally unsuited for the practice of law. Beyond that, our society's historic image of a successful man has been a person who is ambitious, upwardly striving, and--if necessary--capable of hostility or aggression. These norms are also, in many people's minds, those which characterize a successful lawyer. Historically, a successful woman is deferential, considerate, receptive, and emotional, which is not an image most of us would assign to a successful lawyer. 4

Culturally, many of the victims who come into courtrooms today are women, especially black women. Because courtrooms treat attorneys and clients differently, the preponderance of women victims has seemed to reinforce the logic of having a preponderance of male lawyers. And then there is the question of power--the law has been a white male domain for a long time. As late as 1960, when the Supreme Court stepped in, bar examinations in Tennessee, Georgia, Alabama, Louisiana, Florida, and Mississippi carried with them indications of the candidate's sex and race--and no blacks passed the bar. 5

Note that here Rollins takes an interesting turn, using the question-answer technique to frame what by now, after her historical, social, and cultural examples, is indeed a logical question: "Given these obstacles, why would any black woman want to practice law . . . ?" Having posed this obvious question, she proceeds with her answers, carefully marshaled in order (first, second, and so on).

Given these obstacles, why would any black woman want to practice law, and why should society care? First, practicing law offers tangible and intangible rewards for black women. The tangible rewards include the chance to make a decent living in terms of salary, to be a member of a profession that is widely respected. The intangible rewards include a chance to be of help to others: the blacks, the women, and the poor, who have somehow been lost in the legal loop of high-powered attorneys and astronomical fees. For anyone, but especially for a black woman, to be able to feel she is making a major contribution to the lives of others is an important reason for anyone to do anything. 6

7 The second reason for black women to practice law is that black women have something unique to contribute to society--their own unique experience as people, their own voice as citizens. Our society is based on the assumption that each of its members, all of its members, has something unique to contribute to the whole and should make that contribution. Without those unique experiences and those previously unheard voices that only black women can bring, the legal profession and society in general are impoverished.

What view of the individual's responsibility to society is involved here?

8 What can be done to increase the number of black women in the field of law? The answers can be found under the same set of headings as the causes. Institutions that have historically banned or discriminated against black women need to be opened up. If need be, those institutions need to recruit and offer career counseling for appropriate applicants, especially black women who seem to have potential. Black women in particular need to realize that the image their society has of what makes a successful woman is changing, that they can succeed independently of others' stereotypical images of what they should or shouldn't be if black women do not let themselves be dictated to by those stereotypes. Here, too, career counseling may be critical. Culturally, all kinds of biases in the workplace have been successfully challenged in the past twenty years; black women need to realize that the status of the law as an all-white, all-male domain is equally vulnerable. Such changes have already begun in some parts of the country and at some schools. Only when changes like these take place nationwide will black women begin to find their proper place in the legal profession.

Notice how Rollins begins her last paragraph with another question-answer device, one also serving as her transition into her conclusion.

POSTREADING WORKSHEET

Now that you have read the piece by Rollins, write your responses to the following questions:

1. What reasons does Rollins give for there being so few black women lawyers?
2. Is it still true that the law is a "white male domain" (¶ 5)?
3. How persuasive is Rollins? How do her different kinds of evidence—historical, sociological, cultural—bolster her argument?
4. How effectively does Rollins use statistics?
5. Has Rollins affected your viewpoint in any way? If so, how?

Questions for Writing and Discussion

Prepare short written answers to each of these questions. Be prepared to hand them in and/or discuss them in class, as your teacher directs.

1. What is the point of this article?
2. What are the facts in this case?
3. What kind of connection do you see between the facts in this case and the point of the argument? Is it a weak connection, or a strong one?
4. What kind(s) of evidence does the piece offer? What other evidence might be brought into this argument to make it stronger?
5. What quality—or qualities—within the audience does the author rely on to complete her persuasion?
6. What do the following words mean—*frail* (¶ 4), *preponderance* (¶ 5), *impoverished* (¶ 7), *stereotypical* (¶ 8)?

Ask your students to research the enrollment statistics (race and gender) of the law schools or other professional schools nearest you. How do those numbers square with what Rollins says? If similar numbers can be obtained for the past twenty years, what changes—if any—can be detected in enrollments? Can one conclude anything from these numbers?

KEY POINTS TO REMEMBER: Writing to Persuade

When writing primarily to persuade, keep in mind two key points:

- Consider the kind of point you're trying to make.
- Consider the nature of the claim's support.

Consider the Kind of Point You're Trying to Make

There may be as many different ways to persuade someone with words as there are issues to be persuaded about and people to be persuaded. Surprisingly, though, the issues addressed by written attempts at persuasion generally belong to one or more of just four types:

The technical term for this kind of rhetorical system is *stasis*.

1. Issues of *fact* (Did this happen or not?)
2. Issues of *interpretation* (Is this one of these or one of those?)
3. Issues of *value* (Is this good or bad?)
4. Issues of *policy* (What should be done about this?)

Many current topics of concern and debate—thus many pieces you might read or write—can be approached in any (or all) of these four ways. You'll do a better job of writing persuasively if you keep in mind what kind of issue—or, in this case, what type of development—you're dealing with. Here's an example of an issue developed all four ways.

Consider the ongoing argument about whether cigarettes cause serious health problems. This controversy can take any of the four forms:

An issue of fact. Bob says the statistics clearly demonstrate that people who regularly smoke cigarettes experience certain critical health problems (such as lung cancer) at a higher rate than nonsmokers do.

An issue of interpretation. Sue counters that the numbers don't resolve the issue of "cause"; that is, cigarettes may be *contributory* causes to ill health but are not so close to being *sole* causes (or even primary causes) as to warrant the kind of faith in those statistics that Bob suggests.

An issue of value. Anne responds that the real question revolves around what's really important in life: (a) living life the way each of us pleases (and if that involves some risks, well, so be it) or (b) living in a restrictive cage of rules and regulations "for our own good." "Isn't what's really important here that individuals be allowed to live their lives as they choose?" Anne asks.

An issue of policy. Tom, in an exasperated tone of voice, points out that the four of them can argue all night but that the question at hand is whether or not to put cigarette machines in the dormitory lobbies. "What should we do?" he asks.

You can parallel or follow this discussion with one or more issues of your own choosing—anything from campus parking to the national debt. You'll find that some issues naturally lend themselves more to one stasis than another; for example, finding the question of *value* behind the national debt takes some doing (although it *can* be found), whereas finding the questions of *fact, interpretation,* and *policy* behind that debt are all rather easy. (Too bad paying that debt is so hard.)

We've all been part of that kind of discussion. Often a person on one side of the issue makes an argument with one approach, and the opponent (or disagreeing reader) counters with a different approach. Spectators come away with the feeling that nothing has been resolved. What *was* the key issue there?

Despite what Tom says, in that discussion there were four key issues. Until the four students can decide which one they want to address, they'll go nowhere. They may decide that the issue of policy (that is, of yes or no to cigarette machines in the dorm lobbies) is the real one, for example, and that it can be decided only on the basis of the issue of fact (that is, the statistical linkage between smoking and health problems). The other issues, for these people, either are unresolvable or require so much strife to resolve that they decide not to tackle them.

You can see the same four types of issues reflected in the samples at the beginning of this chapter. The first piece, "Congressmen for Life," primarily treats an issue of *fact:* it is indeed the case that members of the U.S. House of Representatives get elected over and over again. Thus, most of the piece is devoted to making that point. To go on from there and make their point, the authors are relying on their readers' common sense (supported by the third paragraph's statements about the founders' original intent) that such a situation is fundamentally wrong. (That's an issue of *value.*) And then there's a brief nod to an issue of *policy* (¶ 30–36)—What can be done about this situation?—but the core of the persuasion concerns the issue of fact.

It's important that your students understand this system of stasis rhetoric. You may want to choose another reading and quiz them on which particular stasis each argument involves.

Once you see the kinds of issues that are at stake in "Congressmen for Life," then, what's the essay's point? Something like this: "Once elected, it's practically impossible for congress members to lose. Thus our congress members serve much longer terms than is good for the country. The situation needs to be changed, somehow."

Anne Morrow Lindbergh's "Woman's Life Today" makes a different kind of argument; here the issue at stake is not, What is the situation? but, What does the situation mean? That is, this piece primarily concerns *interpretation.* What is the meaning of women's lives? How are we to interpret this condition called "torn-to-pieces-hood" (¶ 1)? And what is the nature of this "inwardly attentive" time (¶ 1), this "new way of inward living" (¶ 2), this "turning inward" (¶ 3)? Well, explaining that nature is the point of the essay.

We're working toward an important point here: the distinction between what an author provides *for* the reader (whether facts, beliefs, or other matters) and what an author *assumes* the reader already knows or believes. Once we have that distinction clear, we can then talk about how skillful persuaders *use* that implicit assumption of knowledge. Evans and Novak, for example, make a key assumption about their readers to the effect that those readers will automatically think incumbency is equal to doing a poor job of representation. Lack of turnover in Congress, they further assume, is in itself bad. They do not bother trying to prove these assumptions; rather, they offer evidence proving that incumbents have significant advantages over their challengers. The authors prove those advantages, but they never prove that incumbency is bad and that incumbents are doing a poor job.

Notice that Lindbergh doesn't bother trying to *prove* that a situation of torn-to-pieces-hood exists. Again we see an author relying on a belief she is confident her audience shares in order to establish a key point in her persuasive plan. And she doesn't really debate whether the appropriate response should or should not be some kind of turning inward (to do so would be to switch to an issue of *policy*); rather, she addresses what that turning inward needs to *mean*.

What, then, is the essay's point? It's not that torn-to-pieces-hood exists—that's assumed to be something the readers freely grant the writer. Nor is the point that the response to torn-to-pieces-hood needs to be a turning inward—again Lindbergh assumes readers will grant that. Rather it is that this turning inward needs to have three qualities in particular—spending time that is inwardly attentive, finding a new way of inward living, and being the pioneer in these matters (not waiting for men to lead).

The third essay, "On Controlled Vocabularies," deals primarily with an issue of *value*. Is it a good idea for publishers of children's books to try to limit the vocabulary in those books? That's what this piece is about. There's no question that it happens—the author assumes her readers know that. There's no great discussion about what to do about it, either. The central question is whether controlled vocabularies are good or bad.

The fourth essay, on the need for black women lawyers, is an especially interesting example to look at this way because it uses all four approaches, in order. The first paragraph is really just an introduction, although it helps set the stage for the second, which deals with the issue of fact—does such a situation exist? The third through fifth paragraphs next carry the issue of fact into one of interpretation—the writer is doing more than showing the situation exists; she's starting to show some of what it means. The sixth and seventh paragraphs then discuss value—is this situation good or bad? And the eighth paragraph brings in policy—what should be done about this? (As you'll see later in this chapter, earlier drafts of this piece were not so neatly sorted out and thus not so effective.)

Consider the Nature of the Claim's Support

Once you know the point you want to make—the claim—you can start looking at how you're going to support that claim:

This is the beginning of our application of Toulmin's persuasive scheme (see Toulmin).

1. What support is there for this claim?
2. Is it the right *kind* of support?
3. Is it the right *amount* of support?
4. How *close* is the support to the claim?
   a. Are there *middle* steps between the support and the claim that are weak?

b. Are there *unstated assumptions* joining the support and the claim that need to be made explicit?

The Support for the Claim and the Right Kind of Support. People who are writing persuasive arguments can support their points in any of a number of ways—by statements of fact, by logic, by analysis, by emotional assertions, by history, by examples, or by analogy, to name just a few. For example, in "Congressmen for Life" the most direct support comes in the opening sentence, Reagan's quotation (¶ 2), the statistics on members of Congress (¶ 4), the result of gerrymandering (¶ 8), the results of the Common Cause study (¶ 12), the aspects of the congressional "machine" (¶ 17–23), and the description of fringe benefits (¶ 25). Most of that support comes in the form of numbers. The support in "Woman's Life Today," on the other hand, is of a quite different kind—some logic, some emotion, some poetry, and some examples. "On Controlled Vocabularies" uses logic, for the most part (with the exception of elements like the second paragraph, "I shudder"). A good example of its technique is the sentence "The more limited our language is, the more limited we are; the more limited the literature we give to our children, the more limited their capacity to respond, and therefore, in their turn, to create" (¶ 6). And in the final example, on black women lawyers, the support comes in a number of ways, especially those in which the *methodical* movement from one kind of argument to another, and then to another and yet another, has a cumulative effect.

In chapter 20 we'll address the point that certain kinds of claims (certain stases) will involve certain *kinds* of support. One supports a statement of fact differently from how one supports a statement of value, and so forth.

The Right Amount of Support and the Distance Between the Support and the Claim. When you're writing persuasively, it's not enough to make sure there *is* support; there also has to be enough of it. Only you (and your reader) can decide what is enough.

A difficult issue for many writers to handle concerns the distance between the support and the claim. That is, when the writer of "The Need for More Black Women Lawyers" cites numbers in her second paragraph, we need to ask ourselves whether those numbers exactly support the point she is trying to make. In this case, they don't quite do so. What we need are current numbers for the numbers of lawyers in the United States and what percentage of them are black women. That we don't get those numbers and that the numbers we do get aren't quite directly related to the point in question weaken the argument.

✓✓✓ WORKSHEET: Writing to Persuade

When you want to write something persuasive, your first task is to marshal your resources—to consider what kind of argument you want to make, what point you want to establish within that argument, and what evidence you have to use. But know that for most writers, those three things we just listed do not happen 1–2–3. When we write, sometimes we start by knowing we want to make a particular kind of argument. Sometimes we have a point to make but aren't sure how we're going to make it until we find some evidence. And sometimes we

As a process, writing is probably messier than any textbook can make it look. We admit that. But to *teach*, we have to systematize and rationalize writing. We worry, though, that making writing look so planned and orderly will frustrate students whose own experience proves less so. And we certainly don't want to blind students to the way writing *generates* new ideas and insights that may not have been part of the original plan. Bear with us, and try to get your students to bear with you, for we do believe that by working their way through the "mess" they will gain better results and become better writers in the long run.

change our mind about one or more of these elements midstream. Did you ever start to make one point in a paper, only to realize that the argument you just wrote really supported another point entirely, and so you had to go back and rewrite the beginning of the piece to make it look like that is what you were trying to do all along? Well, we do that too. And it's fine, as long as we realize the problem and make the change.

Once you've sorted out the kind of argument you want to make, the point you're trying to establish, and the evidence you want to use, you then need to start asking the questions listed on pages 150–51. Sometimes that may be a good way for you to move toward something like a sketch or outline of your paper. Other times you may want to use that list after you've already put together a fairly decent draft, as is done in the case study that follows.

Here's one final question to ask yourself as you're planning and completing a piece of persuasive writing: "Have I *earned the right* to assert this point?" Too many times, students (among others) approach persuasive writing mechanically, as though any piece that clearly states a thesis and then brings in three pieces of evidence (probably one per paragraph, we expect) to support it has done all it needs to do. But readers don't work like that, and neither do good writers. Readers want to feel that you, the writer, have *earned* the point you're trying to make, and the only way for you to achieve that very intangible quality in what you write is to make sure you feel it too. It's not enough just to connect a claim and some evidence in some fashion; to be fully effective, your persuasive writing must show a human being significantly engaged with a point that is worth making. Making a trivial point or making a point in a lackadaisical manner won't persuade anyone.

There is no way to *quantify* this; it's abstract, intangible, and vitally important.

CASE STUDY CLOSE-UP AND SAMPLE WRITING ASSIGNMENT

The techniques presented in this chapter are useful in many ways—while planning a paper, while revising it, and (as you will see in chapter 14) while doing critical reading. In this section we want to show you how one college student writer used these techniques for critical revising—that is, how she asked of her next-to-last draft questions about the kind of argument, the claim, the evidence, and how they were connected in order to turn the draft into a smoother, more effective piece of persuasion.

The assignment in this class was to write a piece of public persuasion on an issue of social justice. The audience for such a paper is not just the teacher and students but society at large. And the writer needs to be as persuasive as possible. Sheryl Rollins, whose final paper you saw earlier in this chapter, brought this next-to-last draft into her writing group (composed of her and three other students with whom she regularly worked) and asked this question: "I think this is already in pretty good shape; what can I do to make it better?" Here's that draft, with her friends' comments in the margin:

Why Aren't There More Black Women Lawyers?

1 Today black women are making gains in many areas of employment. But recent statistics show that black women are highly underrepresented in the field of law. Because the law and the legal profession touch every area of human life, it's important that all segments of our society be represented within it. Thus increasing the representation of black women within the legal profession will enable them to make a valuable contribution not only to themselves but also to their society.

Sheryl, I can't tell from this first paragraph what your main point is going to be—is it (a) that discrimination exists against black women who want to be lawyers, (b) that here are the reasons there aren't more black women lawyers, or (c) that both black women and the rest of society should be concerned about this? Any of the three would make a good persuasive paper, but can you do *all* of them in this one short piece?

2 The lack of black women in the field of law has three primary causes: history, sociological attitudes, and cultural bias. In 1910 there were only 798 black lawyers in the country. By 1940 there were 1,925--one for every 13,000 black people in the country. Only 64 were women. Today, while black people make up more than 25 percent of the national population, black lawyers represent less than 5 percent of the nation's lawyers. Part of the reason women are such a small part of this small percentage has to do with the historic admissions standards of law schools. Law schools in the United States have historically made it difficult for women, especially black women, to study law. Harlan Fiske Stone, legendary dean of Columbia's law school, once said that women would be admitted to there only over his dead body. One of the most eminent of the nation's law schools, Harvard, did not admit women as students until 1950, or black women until the late 1960s.

Now, in this second paragraph, we're talking about *causes*...

Should you start a new paragraph with "Part of the reason...? If you had maybe one more good piece of statistical evidence, this would make a good solid paragraph on its own.

3 The sociological and cultural reasons for the relative absence of black women from the legal profession have played just as big a part, although determining numbers to go with these reasons is impossible. Sociologically, men have long regarded women as frail, incompetent, and in need of protection. Black women, in particular, were regarded as frail, incompetent, and unworthy of protection. Thus women in general, and black women in particular, were regarded as temperamentally unsuited for the practice of law.

The first sentence in paragraph 3 is confusing. As big a part as what? The sentence also sounds like an apologetic afterthought.

4 Culturally, the reasons for the small number of black women lawyers have to do in part with the fact that many of the victims who come into courtrooms today are women, especially black women. Because courtrooms treat attorneys and clients differently, the preponderance of

The reason in the first two sentences isn't nearly as persuasive as the other two reasons in this paragraph—do you want to move it so it doesn't start the paragraph, or maybe drop it altogether?

women victims has seemed to reinforce the logic of a preponderance of male lawyers. Beyond that, our society's historic image of a successful man has been a person who is ambitious, upwardly striving, and--if necessary--capable of hostility or aggression. These norms are also, in many people's minds, those which characterize a successful lawyer. Historically, a successful woman is deferential, considerate, receptive, and emotional, which is not an image most of us would assign to a successful lawyer. Finally there is the question of power--the law has been a white male domain for a long time. As late as 1960, when the Supreme Court stepped in, bar examinations in Tennessee, Georgia, Alabama, Louisiana, Florida, and Mississippi carried with them indications of the candidate's sex and race--and no blacks passed the bar.

Given these obstacles, why would any black woman want to practice 5
law, and why should society care? There are two reasons. The first is that practicing law offers tangible and intangible rewards for black women. The tangible rewards include the chance to make a decent living in terms of salary. The intangible rewards include a chance to be of help to others: the blacks, the women, and the poor, who have somehow been lost in the legal loop of high-powered attorneys and astronomical fees. The second reason is that black women have something unique to contribute to society--their own unique experience as people, their own voice as citizens. Without those experiences and those voices, the legal profession and society in general are impoverished.

Sheryl, this will be a good paper if you turn it in as is. To make it better, I think you need to decide whether you want to make a point about the causes for this situation, the effects of it, or what needs to be done about it (something that really belongs in this kind of piece but that you leave out). That is, do you want to make a statement of fact (prove discrimination exists), interpretation (show what that means), value (show that it's harmful and wrong), or policy (show what to do about it)?

You know, if you really want to put some work into this, you could do all four kinds of statements—just about at one per paragraph. That would make a neat piece of persuasion!

That's a good idea. You could tighten up the wording a little by cutting out deadwood, pretty much throughout, and then add a little more on value and a new paragraph on policy and have a really neat paper.

As you can see by looking again at the finished piece earlier in this chapter, Rollins turned out to have a strong personal commitment to the subject and to doing this task well. She thus took the option that came up in the last comment. In this way, critical rereading and revising—based on the material presented in this chapter—were able to help one student turn an already-good paper into an excellent one. If you make similar use of that material, we think your writing will improve as well.

WRITING ASSIGNMENTS

1. How would you try to persuade Rowland Evans and Robert Novak that longer congressional incumbency is not bad but *good* for government (that is, turn their issue into one of value)? Write a piece of "counterpersuasion."

2. Anne Morrow Lindbergh first published her "Woman's Life Today" in 1955. Writing from your perspective now, what do you have to say about "Woman's Life Today"? Do you think the issue—*today*—is primarily one of fact? interpretation? value? or policy?
3. Consider again the photo on page 135, which shows people at a nuclear protest rally. Such rallies are, among other things, showcases for slogans. Many times such a slogan will catch on, persuading and driving people at a level out of all scale with its length or logic. With your classmates, brainstorm memories of slogans you have seen or heard. Use the resources of your university library, to add to your store of slogans by scanning recent newspapers or issues of weekly newsmagazines for photographs of other political rallies. Then write a short paper in which you speculate as convincingly as possible on how such slogans gain their hold on people, and on whether the existence and prevalence of such "persuasion" should tell us anything about how to write more convincing essays and reports.

Focus on Critical Writing

4. Read again, closely, George Will's essay "Listen to the Bridges," in chapter 6. Evaluate Will's persuasiveness. Is his argument based primarily on an issue of fact? interpretation? value? or policy? Point to the evidence in his essay that supports your judgment.
5. Put yourself in this situation: you have to write a speech for delivery at a Fourth of July celebration in your hometown. The audience is the local chamber of commerce, its members' families, and guests. What topic would you choose to speak about, and which of the four primary types of argument would you use? Defend your choices, based on that audience and that situation.

Writers' Circle

Poll the room: what are the issues of importance on your campus? Record the responses; when an issue is mentioned more than once, simply tally the response(s) beside that issue. After the poll, each student should select a listed issue and write to an appropriate administrator to make needed changes. Each student should marshal the most persuasive argument possible, and finish a draft of the paper before the next class meeting.

Bring the draft to class, divide into groups of three, and respond to one another's papers. Consider:

1. Is the issue clear and clearly stated?
2. Is a convincing argument made, using good support?
3. What other support could you add?
4. Is the appeal appropriate for the target audience?

Revise the piece after group editing and submit it to the appropriate administrator.

P R O F I L E ♦ O F ♦ A ♦ W R I T E R

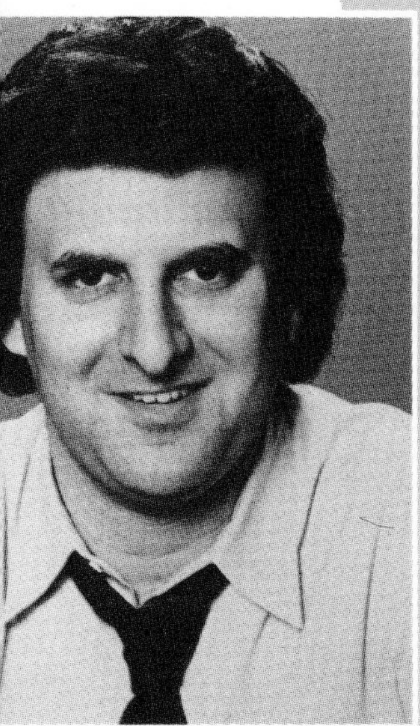

Bob Greene

Bob Greenė is a columnist, book author, and TV commentator. Born in Columbus, Ohio, in 1947, he received his bachelor's degree in journalism from Northwestern University in 1969 and began writing for the *Chicago Sun-Times.* He says he first knew he was to become a journalist in the seventh grade, when the Kuder Preference Test showed he was "supposed to be either a forest ranger or a journalist." He started working on the junior high school paper, the Bexley Junior High School *Beacon;* he was twelve years old.

His first break as a writer came that same year, when he and a friend were able to get an interview with the Ohio State basketball star Jerry Lucas, with whom even

PART OUTLINE

the local papers had been unable to get interviews. A bigger break came with a column Greene wrote the year after President Kennedy was assassinated, dealing with his feelings about the death; first a local magazine and then the local newspaper picked up the piece. Two of his columns are included in *The Heath Guide to College Writing:* "The Permanent Record" (chapter 13) and "The Man Who Wrote 'Louie Louie' " (chapter 12).

Greene became a syndicated columnist in 1976 and moved to the *Chicago Tribune* in 1978. Currently his columns are syndicated nationwide; he has published ten books; he appears regularly on ABC's "Nightline"; and he writes a column for *Esquire* ("American Beat"). He has also published columns and articles in the *New York Times, Harper's, Rolling Stone,* and *Newsweek.* Four of his books are compilations of columns: *We Didn't Have None of Them Fat Funky Angels on the Wall of Heartbreak Hotel and Other Reports from America* (1971), *Johnny Deadline, Reporter* (1976), *American Beat* (1983), and *Cheeseburgers* (1985). Two of his books describe his joining modern-day media circuses: (a) *Running: A Nixon-McGovern Campaign Journal* (1973), an account of the 1972 presidential campaign, and (b) *Billion Dollar Baby* (1974), an account of touring with the rock star Alice Cooper's band. And two of his books come from diaries of his own experiences: (a) *Be True to Your School: A Diary of 1964* (1987), a rewrite of his high school diary, and (b) *Good Morning, Merry Sunshine: A Father's Journal of His Child's First Year* (1984), a record of his first year (at age thirty-five) as a father.

When asked how he chooses the subjects he writes about, Greene has said, "If they interest me not as a 'journalist' but viscerally, as a person, then I'll write about them. That's why I don't take assignments from editors. Either you're enthusiastic about something or you're not, and I think about ninety percent of the success of what I do is due to the story selection. If a story is the first thing I would tell my best friend on the phone at the end of the day, then I know it's good to write a column about."

Greene's approach to his subjects is one that concentrates on specifics. Discussing the public's strong favorable response to *Good Morning, Merry Sunshine* and *Be True to Your School*—who, after all, would be interested in the diary of some seventeen-year-old growing up in a middle-size town in the Midwest?—Greene has observed, "What it teaches me is that, if you're very specific about what you write about, the universality will come through. In both of those cases the argument could have been made, who wants to read your diary? If you wrote a general book about the growing-up experience in high school in the sixties, I think it would be sort of boring. But by being very specific about one boy's life growing up in the middle of the country in the middle of the century, it was possible to capture the emotions. Other people's experiences may not have been the same as mine, but the emotions were the same. And I think the only way you can capture the emotions is to be very specific."

• • •

How much of what you have written in your school experience so far could stand the simple tests suggested by Greene:

- Is it the kind of subject that would be the first thing you'd tell your best friend about at the end of the day?
- Is it so specific that your readers will be able to see the universality behind it?

Take a quick look at the two Bob Greene pieces we've included in this textbook; based on what you've learned from this profile, can you see in them the secret to Bob Greene's success as a writer?

The Subjects for Writing: People, Places, Things, and Ideas

In Part Two of *The Heath Guide to College Writing* we explored the reasons (or motives) for writing—the "why" of writing. Part Three now focuses on the "raw material" of composing—the "what":

- What makes good writing?
- What makes writing possible?
- What makes writing worthwhile?
- What kinds of things are worth writing about?

Whatever the answers to those questions (and different people give different ones), the next important matter in writing (after the "why") is the "what"—having something to write about.

Part Three centers on the *subjects* for writing—people, places, things, facts, and ideas—most often encountered by college students.

Here in Part Three, the answer to "What do I write next, and next, and next?" is always found in the *subject* being written about: if you don't know what to say next, return to your subject for more ideas.

Each chapter begins with samples—written by both professionals and students—that represent different subjects for writing, and each sample's content comes primarily from the subject matter itself. We think you'll learn from each kind of example. Each chapter lists key points to remember when writing about these kinds of subjects, offers a worksheet for a sample student writing assignment, and develops one or more student writing samples from scratch through various aspects of the writing process to the final draft. In each chapter one part of that process is selected for a close-up, high-magnification look.

Before we begin our look at the subjects for writing, however, we want to introduce you to a second important component of a good student writer's preparation: critical reading. We introduced the first component, critical writing, at the beginning of Part Two of this book. You may want to review that

Ask students to list the last five (or ten) subjects they wrote about and give the lists to you. From those, put a mix of topics on the board and ask the class to discuss which ones look interesting on the surface (one of Greene's columns is about a woman in New Mexico who saw the face of Jesus on a tortilla) and which ones don't. Then go back through the "don't" list to see whether interesting ways to treat those subjects can be created with the help of the whole group brainstorming.

We could add "How does *what* you're writing about change the way(s) you go about writing?" The subject can influence the process. If, for example, a student wants to write about a Civil War battle and has read about it from only one source, part of his or her process will involve finding more source material. The writer's personal attitude toward a subject can also affect the way the writer presents it.

These lines are the practical key to how Parts Two, Three, and Four differ from one another.

Of course, content is also shaped by *purpose* (the point of Part Two) and *structure* (the point of Part Four). These are convenient distinctions for textbook organization and for teaching, but they are more real here than they are outside the classroom. We acknowledge the artificiality of most constructs created to analyze and explain something as complex as writing.

Some teachers will want to take a week or two out of the term to assign chapters 3, 8, and 14. That makes sense to us as an alternate organization *if* students are reading *and* writing all through that time. We think students don't learn much about writing *only* by reading about it; they have to practice the things they are reading about.

introduction (chapter 3) before reading this next chapter. Critical writing (chapter 3) and critical reading (chapter 8) are companions to the third component, critical thinking, which is discussed in chapter 14.

chapter 8 Critical Reading

"The greatest gift is the passion for reading. It is cheap, it consoles, it distracts, it excites, it gives you knowledge of the world and experience of a wide kind. It is a moral illumination."

Elizabeth Hardwick

"Reading is to the mind what exercise is to the body."

Richard Steele

This isn't just some abstract theory. Our orientation toward this view comes from our own experience: we both find that when we don't *read,* we don't write, and the *more* we read, the *more* we write. The two activities really do rely on and encourage each other. Moreover, one activity literally would not exist without the other.

The chapters in this book generally present writing as an activity that begins with reading. Much of any student's success in college—not just the writing—depends on careful, critical reading. This chapter presents a short account of the critical reading skills we believe will best support your success in college, both as a reader studying other subjects and as a reader preparing to write about what you've read.

Eight Questions for Critical Reading

Here's an overview of the questions to ask when you want to read critically (if you've worked through chapter 7, "Writing to Persuade," you'll recognize some of these questions):

Of course, determining "the reader" for a particular piece of writing can be a pretty sophisticated process nowadays. There's the reader the writer may have envisioned, the reader you or I construct from the text itself, the actual person reading the passage, and so on. If you want to get into all that with your students, we recommend you choose your examples carefully; the Ben Franklin piece (chapter 4) is a good place to start.

Again, we're following Toulmin's scheme here, fairly heavily modified. (See Toulmin.)

1. What kind of personality does the author's voice in the text project?
2. What kind of expertise does the author's voice reflect?
3. What is the overall tone of the piece?
4. What kind of picture of the reader does the text project?
5. What knowledge does the author assume the reader brings to the text?
6. What does the author assume the reader's attitude toward the subject to be?
7. What is the overall structure of the piece?
8. What are the important generalizations that are made in this piece?
   a. What *kind* of generalizations are they?
      (1) Are they statements of fact?
      (2) Are they logical statements (judgments)?
      (3) Are they emotional statements?
      (4) Or are they some other kind of statement?
   b. In what ways are those generalizations supported?
   c. How adequate is that support:
      (1) Is it the right kind of support?
      (2) Is it the right amount of support?

d. How close (tightly connected, adequate) is the support to the generalization:
   (1) Are there middle statements that join the support and the generalization that are weak (in other words, only partially or conditionally relevant)?
   (2) Are there unstated assumptions that join the support and the generalization that need to be made explicit?

Here is a short piece of persuasive writing, followed by a brief discussion of how it stands up to critical reading. As you read this short essay, make some notes to yourself about what you think the answers to the above questions are. Then after the essay, we'll give you our own answers.

Wildness and Weirdness

PETER STEINHART

Peter Steinhart is a contributing editor for Audubon, *writing a regular column, as well as features and essays. He lives in Palo Alto, California, and has recently published a book,* California's Wild Heritage, *with the Sierra Club. This selection appeared in* Audubon *in May 1980.*

1 A young man was struck by lightning while watching Old Faithful erupt. He remembers a terrific noise, and then everything became silent and he had the sensation of floating dreamily through the air. The bolt knocked him unconscious, burned his clothing, and neatly sliced off one of his motorcycle boots. The strangest part of his story was this: When he regained his senses, there was a man in a tractor cap standing over him asking, "What time's this here geyser gonna go off?"

2 The story suggests something I have suspected for a long time: Wildness is turning into weirdness. It is a change in the language of surprise, from the old beatnik-era phrase, "That's wild, man," to the more passive hippy-era phrase, "That's weird." The shift in diction indicates a change in the way many Americans view nature. Where once we sought to fit ourselves into the events of wild nature, we are increasingly becoming mere spectators and sensation-seekers.

3 I see hints of the change almost daily in the news. Not long ago, a man sleeping out under the stars in a campground near Los Angeles awoke with the sensation that something was breathing on him. He was a city man, steeped more in fear of burglars and madmen than in lore of the woods. He jumped to his feet and began blasting away at the night with the .357 Magnum he kept handy for just such alarms. The bear went off to bleed to death in a remote canyon, and the next morning, a thousand campers were evacuated lest the bear return in anger.

Ask students what kinds of attitudes a journal with a name like *Audubon* might have.

Do we need to point out that Steinhart begins with a striking opening? Are you shameless enough to pass on that pun?

Ask students whether this essay "works" for a reader who doesn't feel the incongruity in this question (¶ 1).

You might point out the unstated assumption here: that what one observer might disregard as only a casual change in slang could in fact be a sign of a significant change in society's values (¶ 2).

Do your students find Steinhart's statement—that he sees hints of this change almost daily—helps them understand his point? Helps prove his point? Why, you might ask them, does he begin his third paragraph this way?

You may have a student who sees nothing wrong with this. You can use that to advantage, as we did the quotation at the end of the first paragraph: someone who doesn't see that the problem here is not that the man fired at the bear but that the man felt he needed to keep a .357 Magnum with him in the park will quite possibly not get Steinhart's larger point. Does Steinhart worry anywhere in this essay about *that* reader? What does that tell us about Steinhart's readers as he envisions them?

What implicit value or belief on the part of the audience is required for the events in the fourth and fifth paragraphs to connect with the claim at the end of the second paragraph ("Where . . . sensation-seekers")? or the beginning of the eleventh paragraph ("The new activities . . . take its place")? To what extent is Steinhart (a) trying to take advantage of people who believe nature exists primarily for us to fit into, in order to prove a point and (b) trying to prove that very point? (To put this another way, Steinhart is saying that the wilderness isn't really *wild* anymore in its normal sense, because it is overrun with *people,* who naturally bring to it the attitudes and behaviors of people. Much modern human behavior is, alas, weird; hence, weirdness has encroached on the wilderness.)

As we were preparing this book, we learned that the 1990 figure for visitors at the Great Smoky Mountains National Park topped twelve million.

Do your students feel those earlier events we asked about actually support the claim(s) in the eighth paragraph better than the claims in the second or tenth paragraph?

Two hundred miles away in Death Valley, a man ignored barricades and warning signs to drive down a flash-flooded dirt road. Approaching a rain-filled gully, he sped up and tried to leap the chasm, Evel Knievel–style. The car came to rest with a bumper on each bank, badly damaged. The man sued the National Park Service, claiming it ought not to have operated such a dangerous gully. 4

In Yosemite National Park, six men were arrested for cliff-jumping off the rim of El Capitan, which rises 3,600 feet above the valley floor. "It's a great rush," explained one of the six. The same week, four people "bungee-jumped" the Golden Gate Bridge, leaping off the span on long elastic ropes that broke their falls and bounced them up and down like yo-yos over the water. 5

Increasingly, what we see going on in the wilds seems out of control. In the mountains of California, you hear little speculation these days about Bigfoot, and a lot about flying saucers. Instead of seeking some reassuring novelty within the abiding pattern of nature, the woodsmen seem intent upon the supranatural, on finding something that will make humanity seem irrelevant. 6

One reason is that it has become crowded in the wild. As civilization devours more and more landscape, we gather in greater densities in the remaining wild places. Nine million visit the Great Smoky Mountains National Park every year. Nearly three million visit Yosemite, most of them managing to find a toehold in the seven square miles of Yosemite Valley. Some 200,000 float down Pennsylvania's Youghiogheny River, and 100,000 down Idaho's Snake. In some areas, you may be turned away unless you make reservations. 7

Gone are the space and solitude we used to seek in these places. Fading are the traditional challenges we sought in wild nature, the mountains to climb, distances to walk, animals to contemplate, and solitude to enjoy, the tests that have allowed us to feel that our human nature is simple, individual, and personal. The things we do out there have less and less to do with nature. The wild is becoming citified. 8

Crowds aren't the only cause of the growing weirdness. There are more of us out there, but what we're doing there also is different. Ours is an age of action. We are caught between the blunders of the cold war and Vietnam and the triviality of the counterculture, between excesses of the mind and excesses of the heart. We mistrust both reason and feeling, and that leaves us stuck in the limbo of action. We are joggers, mountain climbers, tennis players, and off-road racers. Says Sandy Halladay of *Adventure Travel* magazine, "People work at an office job, and they want a little exertion. I hate to stress the risk part of it, but that may be one of the things that excites people about adventure travel." Adventurers repair to nature because it often is the only space available. 9

The wildlands always have been our theater of action, and traditionally have served America as a stage upon which the individual can take risks without endangering the rest of society. But, with the lack of solitude, the old 10 risks of hand to rock, eye to space, mind to night, imagination to animal form, the kinds of tests that tell of man's place in nature, are vanishing. Instead, we are inventing new risks. Look at the list of applicants for use permits in Yosemite: It includes hang-gliders, skydivers, roller skaters, snowmobilers, skiers, bicycle racers, marathon runners, balloonists, even high-wire walkers.

11 The new activities have little to do with the naturalness of the setting. They only have to do with the space and the accessibility of the place. And, as nature recedes in importance as a reason for visiting, citified risks and fantasies take its place. You see and hear a lot more guns in the wildland these days. Last year, a man in California's Emigrant Wilderness unloaded his pistol into the backside of a bear while other campers pleaded with him to stop. The same weekend, another man unloaded his gun into a fellow camper near Yosemite.

12 The challenges of the wild seem less and less personal and more and more societal. Old-timers say mournfully that years ago you could leave a $50 bill on a picnic table and come back a week later to find it still there. "Today," says one, "you can't turn your back on a trout fly. It's a jungle out there!" No wonder all those campers have begun packing guns into the woods. Not just deer rifles, but man-stoppers, big .357 Magnums, Dirty-Harry stuff. What moves the gun-toters is the realization that weirdness implies that we have no place in nature, that man is some kind of aberration to whom rules mean nothing. Nature is but a stage set, in which men act out urban dramas about greed, power, and survival. Animals and landscape cease to be entities in their own rights. There is nothing to judge men by except the actions of other men.

Ask students to name a time when things weren't this way.

13 We ought to resist this change. For real wildness implies that we can know the rules, predict the future, and exercise some control. Those are the things that give us a sense of consequence and make us feel good about being human. Those are the antidotes to the passivity and spectatorship that plague our public affairs and the irresolution that so often daunts our private lives. We need the personal challenge and reassurance of human competence that wildness makes possible. If we cannot somehow reassert the old quality of the experience over the quantity of the experience, reassert the thought and the feeling over the mere activity, we are likely to lose a great deal more than just birds and trees and solitude. We need all the wildness we can get.

Ask students to compare Steinhart's view of wildness with Le Guin's (chapter 6); you might find yourself in the middle of a lively discussion.

Vocabulary

What do the following words mean—*Bigfoot, supranatural* (¶ 6), *Vietnam, counterculture, repair* (in "repair to nature") (¶ 9), *societal, aberration* (¶ 12), *antidotes, irresolution, daunts* (¶ 13)?

Critical Reading Questions and Answers

Q: What kind of personality does the author's voice in the text project?

A: The personality projected by the author's voice is initially friendly and folksy

Make sure students notice how this discussion builds on specific examples. Steinhart uses his examples to deliver the rhetorical force of his essay: there are so many good examples, so well chosen, that his point about weirdness overtaking natural wilderness becomes very persuasive.

Ask students if they can characterize the way sensing the first personality's existence comes from a different kind of thinking on their part than does sensing the existence of the second personality.

The link between the two "personalities" in the piece is between humor (or a taste for the bizarre anecdote) and the serious point the anecdotes can be used to make. The second, serious personality grows logically from the anecdotes told by the first personality.

The connection among an author's language, that author's expertise, and our responses to a piece is important for any *writer* to grasp. Students can learn to be sensitive to that connection by critical reading. Critical reading draws together the reader's sense of the author and the author's language, the reader's acknowledgment or assessment of the author's expertise, and the reader's *own* reaction to the ideas and meanings in the material. In this way, critical reading is an act of creative interpretation, making meaning that can transcend the meaning(s) intended by the author. This additional, interpreted meaning can then generate more thought and more writing, thus perpetuating the process cyclically (and, potentially, infinitely).

It's one thing to identify an author's tone; it's another to know what to make of it. Students often struggle with the concept

and is set by the man in the tractor cap—"What time's this here geyser gonna go off?" (¶ 1). To the man in the cap, what's significant is the timing of Old Faithful's geyser, not the well-being of the lightning victim. The man's concern is misplaced, even illogical. Other phrases that stand out in this essay have the same sound: a man "jumped to his feet and began blasting away" (¶ 3); a man tried to leap a gully in his car "Evel Knievel–style" (¶ 4); the wild is "citified" (¶ 8); a man "unloaded his pistol into the backside of a bear" (¶ 11); and the guns are "Dirty Harry stuff" (¶ 12). This kind of humorous, folksy language makes the piece appropriate for an outdoors magazine (it was, after all, published in *Audubon*).

A second kind of language in the piece—and a second, more serious personality—shows up in the second paragraph, a couple of times in the middle paragraphs, and especially in the last paragraph. It's defined as much by the intellectual concepts the writer uses as by the words: in the second paragraph he sees "a change in the language of surprise"; in paragraph 6 he writes, "Instead of seeking some reassuring novelty within the abiding pattern of nature," followed by "The wildlands have always been our theater of action," (¶ 10) followed by the urgent, persuasive sound of the entire last paragraph. An interesting contrast exists between these two voices or personalities, the one folksy and the other seriously intellectual. Perhaps the point is that the two aren't mutually exclusive, or that the second can grow out of the first.

Q: What kind of expertise does the author's voice in the text project?

A: This issue of the contrast between the folksy and the intellectual voices sheds light on the author's expertise—at least as reflected by the sound of the passage. Could the same kinds of ideas—the "language of surprise," "novelty within the abiding pattern of nature," and so on—have as credibly been expressed by some kind of backwoods speaker who uses "this here" or "blasts away" into the "backside of a bear" with a .357 Magnum? A second insight into the author's expertise comes from the use of information from other sources. Even though this is a popular, not a scholarly, essay and so the sources for its information are not rigorously cited, still the author obviously reads widely, as seen by the events related in the first and third through fifth paragraphs, as well as the skillful use of the quotation in the ninth paragraph. That is, here we see a writer who not only knows what goes on in the field (or, more properly, the woods) and reads widely about other similar areas but also can draw fairly sophisticated observations based on those events.

Q: What is the overall tone of the piece?

A: In this piece, as in most, we judge the piece's tone (the author's attitude toward the subject and toward us) by the language the piece uses. The overall tone is set by the contrast between the folksiness of the examples and the sophistication of the occasional comments and the last paragraph. Just as the emerging "voice" is distinguished by humor and friendly concern, so we conclude that the writer wants to sound likable, knowledgeable, and finally very concerned about what's happening. As readers, faced with this kind of tone we are more likely to respond favorably to what is said.

Q: What kind of picture of the reader does the text project?

A: The reader here clearly is a person who has to be entertained before being convinced—thus all the half-funny stories and examples. And the concrete examples of the first twelve paragraphs perhaps soften the reader up for the argumentation of the last paragraph. We don't think, though, that the writer necessarily sees the reader as someone who needs hard convincing; rather, the writer sees the reader as someone who merely needs to have numerous specific examples before the big generalizations (the last paragraph) come in. But the writer clearly views the reader as someone who relates strongly to the outdoors and to the kinds of values the last paragraph assumes should be held near and dear: a sense of consequence, feeling good about being human, personal challenge, and so on.

of tone. Explaining that it is the writer's attitude toward the subject strikes them as elusive. You might try clarifying tone by asking students if one of their parents (or some other authority figure in their lives) ever said to them, "It's not what you said, it's the *way* you said it." Tone can be much more subtle than that, of course, and gaining sensitivity to it can take practice, but the ability to detect tone and understand how it is operating in a piece of writing is indispensable to critical reading.

Q: What knowledge does the author assume the reader brings to this?

A: The author apparently assumes the reader knows what "Old Faithful" is, what "beatnik-era" is, what a ".357 Magnum" is, who Evel Knievel is, what "Dirty-Harry stuff" is, etc.

Obviously, we intend our answer to the "picture of the reader" question to build on the questions we gave you in the marginal annotations of the essay itself.

Q: What does the author assume the reader's attitude toward the subject to be?

A: The author seems to assume a reader who will see the incongruity between the victim of a lightning strike lying on the ground and a person hovering over him asking, "What time does this here geyser go off?"—a reader who doesn't think it's necessarily the obvious thing to do to take a .357 Magnum along on a camping trip, etc.

Q: What is the overall structure of the piece?

A: There are really three specific statements (generalizations 1–3, below), a more general statement (generalization 4), and the final statement (generalization 5). Thus the structure of the piece goes from the particular to the general in a fairly systematic way, and the support for the generalizations proceeds accordingly from the particular to the general.

You might point out to your students that we're talking about the piece's *logical* (or argumentative) structure here; one could also talk about its narrative structure or its essay structure.

Q: What are the important generalizations made in the piece?

A: The important generalizations in this essay are as follows:

1. "Wildness is turning into weirdness" (¶ 2).
2. "The woodsmen seem intent upon the supranatural, on finding something that will make humanity seem irrelevant" (¶ 6).
3. "The challenges of the wild seem less and less personal and more and more societal" (¶ 12).
4. "We need all the wildness we can get" (¶ 13).
5. "We ought to resist this change" (¶ 13).

Generalizations 1–4 are actually support for generalization 5. Generalizations 1–4 are all supported with examples in the paragraphs immediately surrounding them. Generalization 5, then, has four supports, probably an adequate number, and each of them is supported with examples. Generalizations 1–3 are statements of fact, supported by other facts. Generalization 4 is a logical statement, although some may want to see it as an emotional assertion; how it is seen depends on whether one is convinced by the argument in that last paragraph. The kind of support for "We need all the wildness we can get"—on which "We ought to resist this claim" rests—lies more in the realm of reason and emotion, of values and feelings, than the support for the other generalizations in this piece do. That makes this last, most crucial part of the argument a little softer than the others. It's not that the evidence isn't close enough to the claim; rather, the evidence itself is debatable.

These make good in-class group activities, for either oral reporting or writing.

These kinds of critical reading skills can help you in college in a number of ways, from studying for tests to writing essays and reports. In terms of studying, these questions open up the passage so that you can see its key points and how those key points connect with the piece's main points. In terms of writing about the passage, if you want to critique the argument you can sing its praises for the way specific examples are used to support every claim right up to the last paragraph. If you want to ask whether the argument is really as well done as it might be, you can ask whether the two different tones really do successfully merge, or at least fit together.

In the chapters that follow, you will be given examples to read critically (as the skill is described above) and to write about critically (as described in chapter 3). In the meantime, here is a passage for you to work on.

PREREADING WORKSHEET

Before you read the following piece by Harriet Goldhor Lerner, write brief responses to these questions:

Be careful of students' feelings here; they may run deep. Be especially careful if you do this as an oral, in-class exercise.

1. Some people believe that in any relationship between a woman and a man, one of the two will naturally dominate. Do you agree or disagree, and why?
2. If you believe that one person, either the male or the female in a man-woman relationship, will naturally dominate, do you think that is automatically and necessarily a bad situation?
3. If you had to choose, which sex would you say dominates the most in male-female relationships—men or women? What makes you think so?
4. Do you agree or disagree with the saying "The art of marriage is the art of compromise"? Why or why not?

Now read this passage carefully.

De-Selfing

HARRIET GOLDHOR LERNER

Harriet Goldhor Lerner is a psychotherapist at the Menninger Foundation. The following selection is excerpted from The Dance of Anger *(1985).*

1 What is "de-selfing"? Obviously, we do not always get our way in a relationship or do everything that we would like to do. When two people live under the same roof, differences inevitably arise which require compromise, negotiation, and give and take. . . . The problem occurs when one person—often a wife—does more giving in and going along than is her share and does not have a sense of clarity about her decisions and control over her choices. De-selfing means that too much of one's self (including one's thoughts, wants, beliefs, and ambitions) is "negotiable" under pressures from the relationship. Even when the person doing the most compromising of self is not aware of it, de-selfing takes its inevitable toll. The partner who is doing the most sacrificing of self stores up the most repressed anger and is especially vulnerable to becoming depressed and developing other emotional problems. She (and in some cases he) may end up in a therapist's office, or even in a medical or psychiatric hospital, saying, "What is wrong with *me*?" rather than asking, "What is wrong with this relationship?" Or she may express her anger, but at inappropriate times, over petty issues, in a manner that may invite others simply to ignore her or to view her as irrational or sick.

Ask students what they think "sense of clarity" means here.

2 A form of de-selfing, common to women, is called "underfunctioning." The "underfunctioning-overfunctioning" pattern is a familiar one in couples. How does it work? Research in marital systems has demonstrated that when women and men pair up, and stay paired up, they are usually at the *same* level of "independence," or emotional maturity. *Like a seesaw, it is the underfunctioning of one individual that allows for the overfunctioning of the other.*

Ask students to come up with other images (figures of speech) that picture a seesaw kind of relationship. It doesn't have to be a human relationship; it can be any situation in which proper or smooth function depends on more than one working component.

3 A wife, for example, may become increasingly entrenched in the role of the weak, vulnerable, dependent, or otherwise dysfunctional partner. Her husband, to the same degree, may disown and deny these qualities in himself. He may begin to direct the bulk of his emotional energy toward reacting to his spouse's problems, rather than identifying and sharing his own. Underfunctioners and overfunctioners provoke and reinforce each other's behavior, so that the seesaw becomes increasingly hard to balance over time. The more the man avoids sharing his own weaknesses, neediness, and vulnerability, the more his woman may experience and express more than her share. The more the woman avoids showing her competence and strength, the more her man will have an inflated sense of his own. And if the underfunctioning partner starts looking better, the overfunctioning partner will start looking worse.

The Postreading exercise shows students the way in which readers having certain beliefs and attitudes before reading a piece may well come up with different analyses after reading it. Thus, don't try to resist the diversity of answers students may come up with here; try to get behind those answers, to find out why students A, B, and C came up with different readings. Doing so here is more important than achieving any kind of (largely mythical) "one true reading."

POSTREADING WORKSHEET

Now that you have read the piece by Lerner, write your responses to the eight critical reading questions on page 162. Add your response to this extra question:

9. Did reading "De-Selfing" change any of your responses given on the Prereading Worksheet?

Your teacher may want you to compare your answers with those of your classmates; be prepared to defend yours, because this passage frequently stimulates diverse responses from students.

Bridges: Another Perspective

Ask students how the passage's wording could be changed so as not to privilege either gender.

Lerner writes with the clear belief that most victims of what she calls de-selfing are women, particularly wives. Assume for our purposes here that she is wrong, that most sufferers from de-selfing are men, particularly husbands. In what ways would the passage be changed? Consider two levels of change: (a) superficial (surface changes, such as substituting *him* for *her,* and so on) and, more important, (b) substantive (changes in examples, lines of argument or reasoning, and basic content). Rewrite the excerpt to reflect such changes.

Writers' Circle

Divide into critical reading teams of three students each. Each team should then choose an appropriate selection that has been read and discussed during this term (see the list, below) and apply to that selection the eight questions for critical reading (page 162). Each team should discuss and evaluate the selection by the criteria outlined in the questions. After thorough rereading and discussion, each team should report to the class the results of its critical reading of the selection.

Or you can bring in a piece students haven't seen before and make this a written assignment.

1. Bruno Bettelheim and Karen Zelan, "Why Children Don't Like to Read" (chapter 3)
2. Ben Franklin, "On Character" (chapter 4)
3. Bob Lundegaard, "Be Yourself When Writing College Essays" (chapter 5)
4. Carl Sagan, "Science as a Way of Thinking" (chapter 5)
5. Ed Henry, "Air Bags vs. Seat Belts: Why You Should Care" (chapter 6)
6. George Will, "Listen to the Bridges" (chapter 6)
7. Ursula K. Le Guin, "Woman/Wilderness" (chapter 6)
8. Rowland Evans and Robert Novak, "Congressmen for Life: The Incumbency Scandal" (chapter 7)
9. Madeleine L'Engle, "On Controlled Vocabularies" (chapter 7)

WRITING ASSIGNMENT

The photo of the bikers at Mount Rushmore (page 161) reminds us of Steinhart's critical commentary and descriptions in "Wildness and Weirdness" because of the incongruity of the people and the setting. Recall a time when you saw people at odds with their surroundings—prom-goers changing a tire, uniformed football players shooting baskets, a kayak with an ice chest strapped to it. Describe what you saw and explain the way it made you feel.

chapter 9 Writing About People

Sinclair Lewis, America's first winner of the Nobel Prize in literature, was once the featured speaker at a gathering for aspiring young writers. He began with a question: "How many of you here are really serious about being writers?" Virtually every hand in the lecture hall went up. "Well, why the hell aren't you all home writing?" Lewis concluded, and took his seat.

One of the most interesting topics to write about is people. Each of us meets hundreds, eventually thousands, of people, and each person we meet has his or her own individuality—qualities that make that person unique and, often, remarkable. It's always a challenge to try to capture in words another person's essence—what it is that makes that person remarkable—in a way other readers will feel. This kind of challenge is met by all kinds of writers in all kinds of settings.

You might poll students to see how many different kinds of writing about people they can think of. Among their responses should be biography, news stories, personality features in popular magazines, writing on historical figures, and profiles. It might help to bring in examples.

Different Varieties of Writing About People

Often vivid word portraits of people come from the world of creative writing, something like the following excerpt, in which Toni Morrison introduces one of her most memorable characters. Notice how much you learn about what kind of person Eva Peace is, without ever being given much of a physical description; as you read, write a list of the things that actually *are* described:

Sula

TONI MORRISON

Toni Morrison is a native of Ohio. Her novels include Sula, The Bluest Eye, Song of Solomon *(winner of the 1978 National Book Critics Circle Award for Fiction), and* Beloved *(winner of the 1988 Pulitzer Prize in fiction).*

If any of your students have read *Sula,* they'll see how this quality of the house dooms Sula.

Sula Peace lived in a house of many rooms that had been built over a period of 1
five years to the specifications of its owner, who kept on adding things: more stairways—there were three sets to the second floor—more rooms, doors and stoops. There were rooms that had three doors, others that opened out on the porch only and were inaccessible from any other part of the house; others that you could get to only by going through somebody's bedroom. The creator and sovereign of this enormous house with the four sickle-pear trees in the front yard and the single elm in the back yard was Eva Peace, who sat in a wagon on the third floor directing the lives of her children, friends, strays, and a constant stream of boarders. Fewer than nine people in the town remembered when Eva had two legs, and her oldest child, Hannah, was not one of them. Unless Eva herself introduced the subject, no one ever spoke of

her disability; they pretended to ignore it, unless, in some mood of fancy, she began some fearful story about it—generally to entertain children. How the leg got up by itself one day and walked on off. How she hobbled after it but it ran too fast. Or how she had a corn on her toe and it just grew and grew and grew until her whole foot was a corn and then it traveled on up her leg and wouldn't stop growing until she put a red tag at the top but by that time it was already at her knee.

These humorous multiple views of what *might* have happened characterize much of Morrison's fiction.

2 Somebody said Eva stuck it under a train and made them pay off. Another said she sold it to a hospital for $10,000—at which Mr. Reed opened his eyes and asked, "Nigger gal legs goin' for $10,000 a *piece?*" as though he could understand $10,000 a *pair*—but for *one?*

3 Whatever the fate of her lost leg, the remaining one was magnificent. It was stockinged and shod at all times and in all weather. Once in a while she got a felt slipper for Christmas or her birthday, but they soon disappeared, for Eva always wore a black laced-up shoe that came well above her ankle. Nor did she wear overlong dresses to disguise the empty place on her left side. Her dresses were mid-calf so that her one glamorous leg was always in view as well as the long fall of space below her left thigh. One of her men friends had fashioned a kind of wheelchair for her: a rocking-chair top fitted into a large child's wagon. In this contraption she wheeled around the room, from bedside to dresser to the balcony that opened out the north side of her room or to the window that looked out on the back yard. The wagon was so low that children who spoke to her standing up were eye level with her, and adults, standing or sitting, had to look down at her. But they didn't know it. They all had the impression that they were looking up at her, up into the open distances of her eyes, up into the soft black of her nostrils and up at the crest of her chin.

Notice from the list you kept how many different ways we learn about Eva—through her house, the way people treat her, her history, her manner of dress, her chair, and the impression she gives people. Those different ways of describing someone are not the restricted property of creative writers—any writer can use them. Following is an excerpt from the same writer, Toni Morrison, being interviewed by Robert Stepto. Notice how much consistency exists between the way she accomplished describing a person and a place in her fiction (above) and the way she handles description during this interview. Once again, write a list of the different things that are actually described in this passage.

Place as a Character

Robert Stepto

This selection is excerpted from Robert Stepto's interview of Toni Morrison, called "Intimate Things in Place." Stepto has asked Morrison about the "sense of place" in her novels.

When I wrote *Sula* I was interested in making the town, the community, the neighborhood, as strong a character as I could, without actually making it "The Town, they," because the most extraordinary thing about any group, and particularly our group, is the fantastic variety of people and things and behavior and so on. But nevertheless there was a cohesiveness there in my mind and it was true in my life. And though I live in New York, I don't relate easily to very, very large cities, because I have never lived in a huge city except this one. My tendency is to focus on neighborhoods and communities. And the community, the black community—I don't like to use that term because it came to mean something much different in the sixties and seventies, as though we had to forge one—but it had seemed to me that it was always there, only we called it the "neighborhood." And there was this life-giving, very, very strong sustenance that people got from the neighborhood. One lives, really, not so much in your house as you do outside of it, within the "compounds," within the village, or whatever it is. And legal responsibilities, all the responsibilities that agencies now have, were the responsibilities of the neighborhood. So that people were taken care of, or locked up or whatever. If they were sick, other people took care of them; if they needed something to eat, other people took care of them; if they were old, other people took care of them; if they were mad, other people provided a small space for them, or related to their madness or tried to find out the limits of their madness. 1

Morrison also writes about the striking role of houses (and neighborhoods) in *Beloved.* You might want to (a) bring in that book and read such a passage or (b) refer interested students to it.

They also meddled in your lives a lot. They felt that you belonged to them. And every woman on the street could raise everybody's child, and tell you exactly what to do and you felt that connection with those people and they felt it with you. And when they punished us or hollered at us, it was, at the time, we thought, so inhibiting and so cruel, and it's only much later that you realize that they were interested in you. Interested in you—they cared about your behavior. And then I knew my mother as a Church woman, and a Club woman—and there was something special about when she said "Sister," and when all those other women said "Sister." They meant that in a very, very fundamental way. There were some interesting things going on inside people and they seemed to me the most extraordinary people in the world. But at the same time, there was this kind of circle around them—we lived within 23 blocks—which they could not break. 2

Ask students whether any of them have ever lived in such an environment; if they have, ask them to tell you what it was like. Compare Morrison's description of this "neighborhood" or "community" with John Ross's descriptions of Alhambra in chapter 2.

The reading and analysis are important. But remember, in this class the writing the students do is most important of all.

Compare the lists you kept as you read the two passages. Notice how many techniques these two passages have in common: the way people treat one another, feel about where they are, and so on. Writing about people does not have to be fiction to be good, or exotic to be creative. Here are several examples of writing about people for you to read carefully; as you read, see whether you can determine (a) how all the writers' approaches are the same and (b) how they're different. After each piece is a list of questions to help you focus on what we think are the key features of this kind of writing.

One of the approaches to writing about people that is always available to students is writing about teachers. Here is one example:

My Favorite Teachers

PETER BEIDLER

Peter G. Beidler is an educator and author. His books include Fig Tree John: An Indian in Fact and Fiction. *He says, "A teacher's task is not to convey knowledge, but to set up situations in which students cannot help but learn something."*

1 In college my favorite teacher was Wayne Booth, the man I had for freshman English. I went on to major in his field and to take four more courses with him. I remember nothing specific about the writing or literature in any of the courses he taught me, but I remember what he looked like, both with and without his beard. I remember how he smiled when he was amused—his was a soft smile, not a brittle one. I remember his quiet sparkle when he was helping us to trace out an idea. I remember how he cocked his head, looking with intense concentration at the classroom floor, when he was listening to someone try to express a thought. I remember the loving way he spoke of his wife Phyllis one day in class. I remember once when he told us freshmen about his own top three priorities in life. The most important thing, he said, was his family. I remember being disappointed because I had thought that we students must be the most important.

2 I do not remember what Wayne Booth taught me about Jane Austen's *Emma*. I remember, however, what he taught me about Wayne Booth.

Note here how Beidler concludes the Booth section with a brief, summative paragraph; then he uses a time transition (with the prepositional phrase "In graduate school") to move to the description of Severs. There's nothing tricky about this; it's just a good example of a good writer making sure his readers are with him as he moves from one part of his discussion to another.

3 In graduate school, my favorite teacher was Burke Severs, a totally different sort of man. Burke Severs was not a theatrical or demonstrative teacher. He sat, almost Buddha-like, at the head of the seminar table. He read from yellowed notes, many of them, I found out later, written at least two decades earlier. I do not, of course, remember what he read to us from his yellowed notes, but I remember and try to emulate what he stood for: a carefulness, a scholarly rigor, an attention to detail, an absolute precision in the use of language, a cautious but genuine sense of humor, a quiet self-deprecation, and especially, a loving reverence for the poetry of Geoffrey Chaucer.

4 Burke Severs did not teach me Chaucer. Chaucer I mostly taught myself by reading Chaucer and teaching Chaucer. Burke Severs taught me the loving reverence of Burke Severs. That was quite enough.

5 I do not think either Wayne Booth or Burke Severs ever realized it, but these two men taught themselves to me. They both, in different ways, provided me with models for my life, for my approach to students, for my approach to scholarly research, and for my feelings about the power that teachers can have when they reveal themselves to impressionable young seekers like me.

Questions for Writing and Discussion

Prepare short written answers to each of these questions. Be prepared to hand them in and/or discuss them in class, as your teacher directs.

1. People often use what seems to be a description of a person to make a point that is more important to the writer than the description of the person is. That is, the subject's significance overshadows the subject itself (or himself or herself). How does the author of this piece do that? How do you feel as a reader when the piece takes a different turn from what you might first have expected?
2. What point does this piece make about teachers? about academic subjects or courses of study? Would a student, after reading this piece, be better advised to choose a particular class solely because of the person who teaches it, or is the subject matter more important than the teacher?
3. Try rewriting the first or fifth paragraph from the third-person point of view. How does changing the point of view change the piece's effect?
4. How would you characterize the author's voice in this piece? How does the way his voice sounds help clue you in to his attitude about his subject?
5. What is the argument being offered in this piece—is it based on facts or on feelings? How does the argument's type of support affect your response to it?
6. What can you conclude about the kind of reader at which this argument aimed, based just on the information you already have? How did you reach that conclusion?

You might call students' attention to the textbook's other readings about mythical and historical figures, such as "Arthur the Briton" (chapter 5).

Maybe writing about teachers isn't your cup of tea. If you want to draw on a larger pool of possible subjects, one that lets you choose more colorful topics, you can write about mythical and historical characters. This next piece puts together portraits of (what some would conclude to be) two very different people. As you read, keep track of your response to the combination of the two.

Kaahumanu and Eve

KIM CHERNIN

Kim Chernin is a therapist and author in Berkeley, California. Her books include The Hungry Self, The Flame Bearers, *and* Reinventing Eve, *from which the following selection is excerpted.*

In my reading of her tale Eve becomes a heroine of disobedience, our culture's first compulsive eater. Eve broke a food taboo. By eating a food she was not supposed to eat she became responsible for the fall of man. But Eve, by eating the apple, also unstitched the authority of the ruler who had established the 1 taboo. When Eve fell, the terrifying power of the God worshipped through obedience to his diet fell with her. In this sense: Eve as rebel, the first woman to challenge the subjugation of woman in the patriarchal garden.

2 This reading of the Eden story is supported by an historic event. It, too, involves a food taboo, a woman who breaks it, the ending of a cultural order.

3 In this case, the forbidden food was a banana. The woman was the Hawaiian queen Kaahumanu, who consumed the fruit as a deliberate act of rebellion against the religious laws that subjugated women. In her time (1772–1832) women were not allowed to eat bananas, coconuts, pork, or baked dog. They could not eat with the men, or fish in salt water, or touch the nets men had laid out. A menstruating woman could not sleep in the same house as her husband. The penalty for breaking these rules was death.

4 Kaahumanu had been the favorite wife of King Kamehameha I. When he died she clothed herself in his feather cloak and lifted his spear. Then she persuaded his heir, Liholiho, to make her his vice-king. Outraged by the food taboos that maintained the suppression of women, Kaahumanu decided to get Liholiho to abolish them. Joining forces with Liholiho's mother, Kaahumanu set the stage for a revolt.

5 First, she ate the forbidden banana in the king's presence. Finally, she got the king to eat with women in the presence of the people.

6 "The people," writes the historian Maxine Mrantz, "though shocked, readily followed the king's example. It was as if . . . they had been waiting to destroy the kapu system. Led by the high priest, they set fire to idols. . . . Stone images were thrown into the sea. . . . Formal religion was a thing of the past in Hawaii."

7 This is the story of a cultural order brought down by the eating of a banana.

8 Eve, our rebel, has been forbidden two things in the Garden of Eden. One of them is knowledge. The other is food. She knows the risk involved but goes ahead anyway and consumes knowledge. Therefore, we ask: what kind of knowledge is this, associated with food, for which this first woman was compulsively hungering? Could it be knowledge of her capacity to become something far different than the Father God, creating her in his image, intended her to be? . . .

9 In other mythic traditions from the ancient world the apple tree in a garden belongs to a goddess. In Avalon, "apple-land," the Celtic queen of the dead was kept busy handing out apples to Irish kings, who ate them and became immortal. Idun, goddess of apple-land in Norse mythology, fed the gods her magic apples to keep them from dying. Gaea, the earth goddess of the Greeks, brought a tree bearing golden apples to the wedding of Hera and Zeus. The tree was planted in the garden of the Hesperides and guarded by Ladon, the watchful dragon. The magic apples may not have been for just anyone, but it certainly wasn't a sin to eat them. Growing from their sacred tree, stored with the power of the Mother Goddess, they offered resurrection and immortality to those who ate them.

If your students find this statement shocking, remind them that the traditional interpretation of the Adam and Eve story involves the loss of paradise through the eating of an apple.

Try letting your students interpret the American story of John Chapman ("Johnny Appleseed") this way.

We begin with an eating disorder, we end with a goddess. In the oldest tales it was she who created the universe, endowed it with laws, upheld nature, presided over the birth and dying of mortals. As mother and female she was more powerful than the male gods. The supreme presence in the universe, she was sculpted in stone, called by a thousand names; she appeared in stories and myths all over the earth, was known everywhere, always the same—a deity who embodies the possibilities of female self-development. 10

And so we reimagine Eve, eater of the apple, as she might behave in a mythic tradition that associates tree with goddess and symbolically invites the daughter to partake of the mother's flesh. Eve, who has been told that she was created from a disposable part of the male body, touches the divine fruit and discovers the Mother Goddess. Suddenly she realizes that she is not less than man, shaped as an afterthought according to his need for a subdued and dutiful helpmeet. She has been made in the image of the Divine Mother. She possesses the Mother's capacity for power, sovereignty, and self-assertion. Eve bites, she chews, she takes into herself that female creative power all mention of which has been left out of the genesis story, except for the obscure symbol of the fruit tree. This Eve, old and new at the same time, has eaten the apple of possibility. She knows what woman will become when one day she creates herself in the image of a goddess. 11

There were such women in Kaahumanu's time. Six feet tall, wide as possible, bare chested and magnificent. I love to think about the missionaries catching sight of them when they came to convert the Hawaiian people to Christianity. What did they think of Kaahumanu, who would swim over to visit them and stride proudly from the water, fully naked? Did they remember Eve, who had once been naked in the garden? Did they compare the radical nature of the two women? Sensing in both a subversive possibility in being female? We do not know whether a Hawaiian snake inspired Kaahumanu to eat the prohibited banana, or whether she was egged on by something restless and rebellious in herself. But I like to imagine that Kaahumanu, a huge and majestic woman, the ideal Hawaiian beauty, drew heavily upon the figure of Pele, the volcano goddess, whose fire was said to regenerate the soul. 12

We invite you and your students to reconsider this in light of Ursula Le Guin's "Women/Wildness" (chapter 6).

Questions for Writing and Discussion

Prepare short written answers to each of these questions. Be prepared to hand them in and/or discuss them in class, as your teacher directs.

1. How many different characters are described in this passage? List them, and tell which one's picture is the most vivid.
2. Do you feel it's the people or the events that are primary in this passage? Which event described herein is most vivid to you? Why?
3. What is the significance of Kaahumanu in this passage? of Eve? What's the point of putting the two in a single selection?

4. From this passage, what do you conclude about the author's personality? List specific words and phrases that lead you to this conclusion.
5. What attitude does the author show toward her subject? How do you know that?
6. What attitude does the author show toward her readers? How do you know that?
7. What do the following words mean—*subjugation, patriarchal* (¶ 1), *kapu system* (¶ 6), *sovereignty* (¶ 11), *prohibited, regenerate* (¶ 12)?

Bridges: Another Perspective

Kim Chernin provides an interesting speculation on the story of Eve's eating the forbidden fruit in the Bible's Book of Genesis. Chernin links Eve's story with that of the Hawaiian queen Kaahumanu, seeing both women as subverters of a patriarchal world that men dominate: forbidden by the ruling patriarchy to eat a certain fruit, both women eat the fruit anyway, and, in Chernin's words, "a cultural order" is "brought down." Both stories are ancient. In what ways does patriarchy still exist in our modern world? And in what ways do modern women subvert this patriarchy? Chernin, in describing Eve's actions, says, "Eve bites, she chews, she takes into herself that female creative power all mention of which has been left out of the genesis story." What similarities can you see between Chernin's description of this primal power and Ursula K. Le Guin's discussion of the "wilderness" part of female understanding in "Women/Wilderness" (chapter 6)?

What, in the opinions of your students, would Chernin make of Judith (who in one of the Apocryphal books of the Bible beheaded Holofernes)? Of Salome (who had John the Baptist beheaded)?

Of course, you can always invent your own characters and give them their own town—as in the famous example that follows.

PREREADING WORKSHEET

Before you read the following piece by Garrison Keillor, write brief responses to these questions:

1. When you envision a small town, what images come to mind?
2. What works of fiction, poetry, or drama have you read that feature small towns? What characteristics do those small towns have in common?
3. When someone tells about a small town, what *tone* (attitude toward the subject) do you expect when (a) the person is *from* that small town, born and raised there, or (b) the person is from a large city, born and raised there, and has spent just a brief time in the small town?

4. Have a look at John Ross's finished paper on Alhambra in chapter 2. What might it lead you to expect from the following piece by Keillor?
5. People talk about something called "small-town values"—what do you suppose this expression means?

While you read, keep track of how the people and the town fit together.

Before students read the "Lake Wobegon" passage, you might try bringing in a tape of Keillor doing a "Prairie Home Companion" monologue for them to listen to. (The tapes are widely available, and many National Public Radio stations still rerun the show at least weekly.) Alternatively, you could bring in a tape of the monologue section from Keillor's more recent show, "The American Radio Company of the Air." Play the Keillor tape for them; then ask them as they read "Lake Wobegon" to speculate on how the experience of reading differs from that of literally hearing the author's voice.

Lake Wobegon

GARRISON KEILLOR

Garrison Keillor is a writer and radio star, perhaps most famous for his show on National Public Radio, "A Prairie Home Companion." A native of Minnesota, he currently lives and works in New York City. The following selection is excerpted from Lake Wobegon Days.

It is a quiet town, where much of the day you could stand in the middle of Main Street and not be in anyone's way—not forever, but for as long as a person would want to stand in the middle of a street. It's a wide street; the early Yankee promoters thought they would need it wide to handle the crush of traffic. The double white stripe is for show, as are the two parking meters. Two was all they could afford. They meant to buy more meters with the revenue, but nobody puts nickels in them because parking nearby is free. Parking is diagonal. 1

Merchants call it "downtown"; other people say "up town," two words, as in "I'm going up town to get me some socks." 2

On Main between Elm and McKinley stand four two-story brick buildings on the north side, six on the south, and the Central Building, three stories, which has sandstone blocks with carved scallops above the third-floor windows. Buildings include the "Ingqvist Block," "Union Block," "Security Block," "Farmers Block," and "Oleson Block," their names carved in sandstone or granite tablets set in the fancy brickwork at the top. Latticed brickwork, brickwork meant to suggest battlements, and brick towers meant to look palatial. In 1889, they hung a man from a tower for stealing. He took it rather well. They were tired of him sneaking around lifting hardware off buggies, so they tied a rope to his belt and hoisted him up where they could keep an eye on him. 3

Out West they call these rubber-tire bellies "dunlops," as in "Mah belly done lopped over mah belt." The single-word name is also a pun, using the name of a commercially produced tire.

Most men wear their belts low here, there being so many outstanding bellies, some big enough to have names of their own and be formally introduced. Those men don't suck them in or hide them in loose shirts; they let them hang free, they pat them, they stroke them as they stand around and talk. How could a man be so vain as to ignore this old friend who's been with him at the great moments of his life? 4

5 The buildings are quite proud in their false fronts, trying to be everything that two stories can be and a little bit more. The first stories have newer fronts of aluminum and fake marble and stucco and fiberglass stonework, meant to make them modern. A child might have cut them off a cornflakes box and fastened them with two tabs, A and B, and added the ladies leaving the Chatterbox Cafe from their tuna sandwich lunch: three old ladies with wispy white hair, in sensible black shoes and long print dresses with the waist up under the bosom, and the fourth in a deep purple pants suit and purple pumps, wearing a jet-black wig. She too is seventy but looks like a thirty-four-year-old who led a very hard life. She is Carl Krebsbach's mother, Myrtle, who, they say, enjoys two pink Daiquiris every Friday night and between the first and second hums "Tiptoe Through the Tulips" and does a turn that won her First Prize in a Knights of Columbus talent show in 1936 at the Alhambra Ballroom. It burned to the ground in 1955. "Myrtle has a natural talent, you know," people have always told her, she says. "She had a chance to go on to Minneapolis." Perhaps she is still considering the offer.

Keillor loads his writing with these little unexpected toss-off lines, as in depicting a seventy-year-old woman who looks like a thirty-four-year-old who has led a hard life. What do your students think is the effect of such a line? Do they think Keillor intends us to admire that quality in her?

6 Her husband Florian pulls his '66 Chevy into a space between two pickups in front of the Clinic. To look at his car, you'd think it was 1966 now, not 1985; it's so new, especially the back seat, which looks as if nobody ever sat there unless they were gift-wrapped. He is coming to see Dr. DeHaven about stomach pains that he thinks could be cancer, which he believes he has a tendency toward. Still, though he may be dying, he takes a minute to get a clean rag out of the trunk, soak it with gasoline, lift the hood, and wipe off the engine. He says she turns cooler when she's clean, and it's better if you don't let the dirt get baked on. Nineteen years old, she has only 42,000 miles on her, as he will tell you if you admire how new she looks. "Got her in '66. Just 42,000 miles on her." It may be odd that a man should be so proud of having not gone far, but not so odd in this town. Under his Trojan Seed Corn cap pulled down tight on his head is the face of a boy, and when he talks his voice breaks, as if he hasn't talked enough to get over adolescence completely. He has lived here all his life, time hardly exists for him, and when he looks at this street and when he sees his wife, he sees them brand-new, like this car. Later, driving the four blocks home at about trolling speed, having forgotten the misery of a rectal examination, he will notice a slight arrhythmic imperfection when the car idles, which he will spend an hour happily correcting.

We think this is, finally, a fairly loving picture of Florian. He comes off as a nice person, and it is apparent in Keillor's tone that he feels warmly and well toward Florian. See whether your students get the same impression, and ask them what they think its source is.

POSTREADING WORKSHEET

Now that you have read the piece by Keillor, write your responses to the following questions:

1. Did any details or descriptions in Keillor's piece surprise you or seem contrary to the small-town images you expected? If so, what were they?
2. Generally speaking, the imagery associated with small towns is positive;

there is a tendency to consider small-town living healthy and worry-free. In your view, is this a true image, or a misleading stereotype? Why or why not?

3. Would you want to be a resident of Lake Wobegon? Why or why not?
4. Did any of the "small-town values" you listed earlier show up in Keillor's piece? If so, where?
5. Do you know anyone like Florian and Myrtle Krebsbach? If so, describe them—do they live in a small town? Today in America, is that character type restricted to small towns, or are such types present everywhere?

Questions for Writing and Discussion

Prepare short written answers to each of these questions. Be prepared to hand them in and/or discuss them in class, as your teacher directs.

1. What do the following words mean—*palatial* (¶ 3), *arrhythmic* (¶ 6)?
2. Notice how fine a level of detail Keillor uses: "diagonal parking," "a tuna salad lunch." What does this use of detail add to the description of people and place that the samples earlier in this chapter lack?
3. Here the descriptions of both place and people truly support each other. Explain how this relationship works in this passage. How are the buildings and the men alike? Myrtle Krebsbach and her husband's car? What do these correspondences add to the passage? What might the significance of those correspondences be?
4. How would you characterize the author's voice in this passage? What does that tell you about his attitude toward his subject?
5. What kinds of assumptions does Keillor make about his readers? How do you know that?

Of course, the most directly accessible source for writing about people is real people, real places, real lives. Here are two pieces from the same book describing the same people, one in general, the other via a specific example:

Men's Lives

PETER MATTHIESSEN

Peter Matthiessen is a naturalist, explorer, and writer. His writing includes short stories, novels (such as Far Tortuga*), and nonfiction books (*The Snow Leopard*, which won the National Book Award,* Under the Mountain Wall *and* Men's Lives*, from which the following piece is excerpted.).*

This book is witness to the lives of the commercial fishermen of the South Fork of Long Island. The inshore fisheries with which it will concern itself 1 fall into five divisions—netting, trapping, dragging, shellfishing, and setting pots. A full-time fisherman, or bayman, might participate in most of these activities in a single year. Those with large work boats of thirty-foot or better may devote themselves to dragging all year long, adapting their boats in certain seasons to lobstering, or setting cod trawls, or long-lining for tilefish, swordfish, tuna. Because a big boat with high fuel costs and overhead must be kept working, such men rarely fish inshore, and are not baymen. However, many baymen crew on draggers in the wintertime, and many draggermen return to the bay as they grow older.

2 Full-time baymen—there are scarcely one hundred left on the South Fork—must also be competent boatmen, net men, carpenters, and mechanics, and most could make good money at a trade, but they value independence over security, preferring to work on their own schedule, responsible only to their own families. Protective of their freedom to the point of stubbornness, wishing only to be left alone, they have never asked for and never received direct subsidies from town or county, state or federal government. Being self-employed, they receive none of the modern social supports such as unemployment insurance and sickness compensation, and because their income is uncertain and irregular, they can rarely obtain bank loans and mortgages. Yet every year they find themselves taxed harder for boats and trailers, trucks and gasoline, shellfish digging and fish shipping licenses, docking license, scallop opening license, permits to take certain species (shellfish, lobster, striped bass). Nearly a dozen taxes, permits, and licenses plague every bayman ready to engage in the various fisheries according to seasonal availability and market demand, as the inshore fisherman must do if he is to earn his living all year round. . . .

Note that in describing these baymen Matthiessen produces consecutive sentences that begin with participial phrases used as adjectives: "Protective . . . wishing . . ." and "Being . . ." The net effect is an accumulation of similarly styled sentences that affords rich description without seeming repetitious, because the sounds and types of adjectives differ.

Ted Lester

3 Ted Lester . . . was the most innovative fisherman, and the most ambitious; he sold frozen bait (bunker chum and squid) to the charter boats and bait shops and shipped fish to New York from his Montauk Seafood, a fish-packing and storage house that was used by the Posey haul-seine crews in an effort to hold back shipments of fish until the Fulton Fish Market would offer a fair price. Whether they liked it or not—for even among his brothers, he was controversial—Ted Lester was the spokesman for the fishermen, not only in their running battles with the market but in their defense against sport-fishing groups, which had renewed a long war of attrition against the commercial men in an effort to prohibit the netting of striped bass.

4 A quick stocky man with a stiff brush of hair that stood straight up from his forehead, giving him an expression of surprise, Theodore Roosevelt Lester (born in a rock-ribbed Republican county in 1908) was always in a rush and often shouting, for want of a better way to let off steam. I met him first on a wet May morning in the 4 a.m. darkness of his yard as he hurried to start up his ancient silver truck, a former weapons carrier of World War II. The truck's hood had rusted out and fallen by the wayside, and because it had rained hard

We assume most of your students will know that Theodore Roosevelt (1858–1919) was president of the United States, but they may not know when (from 1901 to 1909), or that he was a Republican—hence the reference to Ted Lester's being

born in a "rock-ribbed Republican county in 1908." Lester, in other words, was named for the man who was president at the time of Lester's birth. Theodore (or "Teddy") shouldn't be confused with his younger cousin Franklin Delano Roosevelt (1882–1945), the Democrat who was president from 1933 to 1945.

all night, the wiring was sodden. Ted Lester swore as he dumped gasoline on his engine and set it on fire.

The big silver truck, once the blaze was smothered, gave a shudder and 5
exploded into life. Seeing my thunderstruck expression, Ted winked and said, "There's a lot of shit built into them things, bub, and the more you kick out of 'em, the less is left in there to kick you back." Ted's language—and Bill's and Frank's, too—was actually a lot less rough than that of the younger fishermen, and if one of his daughters, who listened to blue speech all day as the seine crews came and went to the freezer under the house, said so much as "damn," Ted would chase her right across the yard, yelling in the same strong language that the girls were forbidden to use, "By the Jesus, Vinnie [or Gloria or Ruth Ann], I hear any more of them damn words . . . !"

Years before, chased in this manner by his father, Ted's son Stewart had 6
fallen in a woodpile, driving a hole through his cheek that survived as a permanent scar to the left of his mouth. The only son in a household of five daughters, nineteen-year-old Stewart was already contesting Ted's ideas on how things should be done. As strong, tough, and stubborn as four sons wrapped into one, he yelled back fiercely at his father until he went fishing on his own boat about five years later.

Questions for Writing and Discussion

Prepare short written answers to each of these questions. Be prepared to hand them in and/or discuss them in class, as your teacher directs.

1. How does the author's attitude toward his subject in the first part of the passage (¶ 1–2) compare with that in the second? Do they reinforce each other, or clash?
2. What does the content of the two parts do together that neither could do separately?
3. What does the truck incident tell you about Ted Lester? How does that compare with what you learn from the incident with his son Stewart? And how does all of that fit—or not fit—with the picture the first part of the passage paints of this kind of man?
4. Choose one paragraph and list all the descriptive words in it. Do they outnumber the other words? What kinds of words are the descriptive words—colors, textures, shapes, other qualities? Can you generalize about how those words fit in with the author's writing style—do they usually come early in the sentence, in clusters, in evenly distributed ways, and so on?
5. What do the following words mean—*subsidies* (¶ 2), *attrition* (¶ 3)?

"Character sketch" would be another good name for this, except that

Most of us have fond memories of special friends we had in our youth. Here is a memoir about youthful friendship, written by a student, Pete Stanton.

Old Friends Are Best

Pete Stanton, college writing student

1 We all have friends in high school whom we spent most of our time with, people who may continue to shape our lives for years to come. Let me tell you about a few of the people I knew back then. They're with me still, as real today as they were then.

2 My two best friends were "John-John" and "Fishface"; John-John got his name as a baby, and--courtesy of his baby face--even at age seventeen could not shake the name; Fishface was named for the goggle-eyed look his glasses gave him. When I went to football and basketball games, it was with them. When I went camping or hiking or fishing, it was with them. One or another of them was in every class I took from my sophomore year on. For nine months a year for three years, we saw one another almost every day.

3 Fishface's distinguishing characteristics were his pop-bottle-bottom glasses, his Marine colonel father, and his extreme intelligence. He was, to all intents and purposes, blind without his glasses, a real handicap in places like the swimming pool, or in our nonstop touch-football games in the street in front of his house. Dealing with his Marine colonel father was another part of being one of Fishface's friends. We were terrified of him, a quality that Fishface encouraged. I mean, a Marine colonel? Once the Colonel came home, we left. The last thing that really identified Fishface was his extreme intelligence: he was the smartest kid in the school--in math, in English, in science; on class tests, on reports, and on standardized tests. He played at least three musical instruments, and it seemed like he had read everything. These qualities (along with his glasses) gave him a kind of an egghead image that he at once enjoyed and fought against.

4 John-John seemed more like the all-American boy. A football player until his junior year when he hurt his knee, he had switched his allegiance to golf with unbounded devotion. A solid B student, he was also the only one of our group who had a steady girlfriend. In a way, his normalcy made Fishface's eccentricity tolerable. What really dis-

it carries with it the quality of reminiscence. Whether character sketch or reminiscence, such a piece makes a good writing project for students. They may also profit by comparing this one with Jane-Marie Gray's "Dollars to Doughnuts" (chapter 15).

Pete Stanton seems to think simple reference to "Marine colonel" is sufficient for his readers to understand why the boys were terrified of Fishface's father. Is it? Ask students what images they associate with the U.S. Marines, especially officers. Are those images consistent with the combination of fear and respect Stanton assumes?

tinguished John-John was his enthusiasm--for any kind of project, any kind of adventure--his ambition, and his love of golf. John-John probably never said no to anything. Want to see if we can stay up till dawn? Sure! Want to create a fictitious candidate for student council and put up outrageous campaign signs all around the school? Absolutely! Want to put out our own newspaper? No doubt about it! Maybe that same enthusiasm shaped his ambition--to be president of the United States. He wasn't shy about it. He figured he could do as good a job as anyone else--why shouldn't it be him? Where Fishface was kind of an egghead, John-John was a go-getter. The combination of the two--with my help as a go-between and resolver of quarrels--made quite a mix.

What the two of them saw in me I don't know--it might have been 5
that my parents let me take the car, and theirs didn't. That combination--the car, John-John's enthusiasm, and Fishface's problems with his egghead image--shaped one of the best adventures we had together. It began as one of those sitting-around-bored-in-your-senior-year-looking-for-something-to-do evenings. Fishface's father had seen us skateboarding out in the street and told us in no uncertain terms what a bad idea that was (especially where he could see us). So sundown found us at John-John's house, complaining that there was nothing to do we hadn't done already a hundred times. Our thoughts turned to the skateboards, to somewhere with lights where we could ride them, then to somewhere really adventurous to ride them. Then Fishface remembered it--the country club!

On a high hill outside town, the country club was off-limits to us. 6
None of our families were members; no one we knew belonged; we called the place "Snob Hill." That night we weren't interested in the club so much as the road to it--a road that wound two and a half times around the hill and only went to the club, a road that on a weekday night was likely to have little or no traffic. A road made for skateboarding! So I volunteered to drive the car behind John-John and Fishface, providing the only light they would have. It was in the character of Fishface to come up with an idea that good; it was in the enthusiasm of John-John to go for it; and it was in my basic chickenheartedness to volunteer to drive the car (and not to ride a skateboard downhill on a winding road in the middle of the night).

7 When we started, John-John and Fishface were side by side, slowly gaining speed down the hill, with me carefully driving behind them to light the way with the headlights. After the briefest of good starts, Fishface lost his balance and grabbed at John-John. John-John flailed his arms to regain his balance, accidentally knocked Fishface's glasses off, and fell off his skateboard. As I stopped the car to avoid John-John, Fishface--now minus his glasses--regained his balance and sped off down the hill. Unfortunately he no longer had my headlights--or any lights at all--to guide him. Since he no longer had his glasses, maybe that wouldn't have mattered. His scream as he flew down the hill was long and pitiful--fading into the night. John-John and I jumped back into the car and hustled down the hill, expecting to find a bruised and maybe bleeding Fishface off the side of the road somewhere. But he wasn't there. We found him instead at the bottom of the hill, after what must have been an incredible ride (which unfortunately no one saw). He had flown down the hill, across the road at the bottom--and straight into a mud puddle on the other side of the road. He wasn't bruised, or bleeding, but he sure was muddy.

8 I've had lots of adventures in my life since then, some of considerably greater proportions than the ride down Snob Hill, and I've had lots of good friends. But it's times like that with friends like Fishface and John-John that stay with me most vividly. After all kinds of people and all kinds of things happening, those friends and those adventures are still the best.

Questions for Writing and Discussion

Prepare short written answers to each of these questions. Be prepared to hand them in and/or discuss them in class, as your teacher directs.

1. How would the effect this piece has be weakened were the trip down "Snob Hill" not a part of it? Can a character sketch survive on its own, with no action in it? If your response is yes, bring an example to class; if your response is no, explain why.
2. What's the relative proportion in this piece between description of people based on physical details or attributes and description of people based on their actions?
3. Think about how this piece makes the point that people are important. What elements in the piece support this view? What specific comments? In your

judgment, how well are those comments in the piece justified by the incidents and scenes described in the piece *or* to what extent do the comments seem artificially tagged on?

KEY POINTS TO REMEMBER: Writing About People

Obviously, there are more ways to write about people than any one chapter (or any one book, for that matter) could explain. In the examples above, you saw a variety of approaches to writing about people. Here are the key points emerging from those examples—methods and guidelines the writers seem to share:

- Create a vivid portrait.
- Offer a detailed presentation of important incidents or scenes.
- Give a clear indication of the person's significance.

We offer these qualities not as a recipe list for writing—for if they *were* recipe ingredients, they would be too much alike to be easy to measure individually—but rather as qualities finished products share. One way to start understanding how these qualities get into the finished products is to recognize the qualities themselves.

Create a Vivid Portrait

Any profile or description of a person is built on the way the writer uses words to make that picture *vivid:* that is, to make the picture bright, crisp, and clear—not fuzzy, like an old black-and-white television picture. In the selections above, notice how many different ways the authors use words to make vivid pictures. The portrait of Eva Peace, from *Sula,* uses the description of her house to stand for something important about what kind of person she is, and the funny-but-grotesque description of her missing leg sets readers up for the surprise of "Whatever the fate of her lost leg, the remaining one was magnificent" (¶ 3). Here, as in "the story of a cultural order brought down by the eating of a banana" (¶ 7) from "Kaahumanu and Eve" and in the truck incident from *Men's Lives,* the central character is described indirectly, through the setting, through key incidents.

Of course, not just any incident will do; the event must be something that strikingly reveals the subject's character.

In other cases, the picture is painted more directly—for example, through the use of descriptive adjectives. Remember how the excerpt from *Sula* ends with "the open distances of her eyes," "the soft black of her nostrils," and "the crest of her chin" (¶ 3)? And in "My Favorite Teachers," Wayne Booth has a "soft smile," a "quiet sparkle," and "intense concentration" (¶ 1), and Burke Severs is "Buddha-like" (¶ 3). In "Lake Wobegon" we see "three old ladies" leaving the Chatterbox Cafe, "with wispy white hair, in sensible black shoes and long spring dresses with the waist up under the bosom, and the fourth in a deep purple pants suit and purple pumps, wearing a jet-black wig" (¶ 5). In each case the choice of a certain kind of word or of key incidents and surroundings adds to the vivid quality of the description.

Offer a Detailed Presentation of Important Incidents or Scenes

Another way descriptions of people can be made to work better is by including an appropriate level of detail. It's not always the case that the maximum number of details—or the most minute level of detail—is the best; the level of detail needs to be appropriate to what's going on in the rest of the piece. That is, while the excerpts from *Men's Lives* go into almost-microscopic levels of detail, that's no reason to say the piece is either more or less effective than, for example, "Kaahumana and Eve," which accomplishes its point through a different technique. The goal is to make sure the picture you paint is sufficient for its purposes, whether that means describing a setting, key incidents, a community, a group, an event, or a person's physical appearance.

Of course, the technique always associated with writing about people is the use of detail. In the passages above, the best example of the use of detail is perhaps in the excerpts from *Men's Lives.* The first excerpt (¶ 1–2) works almost totally by accumulating details. In fact, that's almost all the excerpt consists of; we have an accumulation of small items to paint a picture in three dimensions, a picture whose significance is not immediately apparent. Compare that with the way detail is used in the second excerpt, "Ted Lester" (¶ 3–6). In "Ted Lester" we see nearly as much detail, but it's in the service of describing "the most innovative fisherman," the "most ambitious" (¶ 3), the spokesman for the fishermen. And as the detail builds up, Ted Lester takes on an importance of his own. Think about the kind of man the episode with the truck shows him to be, and the kind of man the picture of his son Stewart shows him to be. The way detail is used in this excerpt should shed new light on its different use in the earlier excerpt. In both places, the point is understated—Ted Lester as "spokesman for the fisherman" in the second excerpt (¶ 3) and the book as "witness to the lives of the commercial fishermen" in the first excerpt (¶ 1)—but all the detail accumulated in each excerpt supports the excerpt's point.

Give a Clear Indication of the Person's Significance

What's the significance of Ted Lester? In "Lake Wobegon," what's the significance of Florian Krebsbach? In each piece, the person being described is significant in a different way, and the piece gets across that significance differently. Ted Lester stands as the archetype of his species, the twentieth-century version of the rugged Yankee individualist. The description of his species in the first excerpt from *Men's Lives* gives greater depth and more validity to the description of Ted Lester in the second excerpt. But the way the piece establishes Lester's significance is indirect. Florian Krebsbach's significance is shown even more indirectly. Like Ted Lester, Florian Krebsbach stands as an archetype of his species, the most representative of Lake Wobegon's cast of characters. Yet the reader has to be sensitive in order to do more than *feel* Florian's significance. Read more closely and you'll see that

By "archetype" we mean here something like "typical symbolic representation," rather than something of mythic proportions.

Florian and his car and his wife and the town are all part of the same piece; they all have the same characteristics. The significance of Florian Krebsbach, then, is that he's the human embodiment of everything the town and its people are. And in "Kaahumana and Eve" the larger significance of the people being described is broadly hinted at; we have two rebels (Eve and Kaahumana) and two goddesses (Idun and Gaea), and the passage wants us to ask what happens when we combine the rebel and the goddess.

There's no *one* way to give your reader a clear indication of a person's significance. If we look at the other samples in the chapter, we see still more ways to get that significance across. The point is not to establish one way or the other as the right way but to emphasize that your readers need—somehow—to be shown the person's significance.

✓✓✓ WORKSHEET: Writing About People

Here's a procedure to follow when you want to write about a person. You may have another way to do that, but here at least is one way that ought to work for you. In this chapter we're showing you a close-up of what we call the *invention process:* what goes on during your initial thinking about what to write about. The last section of this chapter then lets you examine and respond to what one student produced as a first draft, a second draft, and the finished paper.

First, Think

These prewriting questions can be presented to your students in any number of ways. Some teachers like to provide students with a list of questions for which the students must produce *written* answers before every assignment; others find that approach too mentalistic. Whatever your approach, we feel strongly that your student writers need to call this information to mind before they start writing.

As usual, the first thing to do is think: size up the situation. *What* are your reasons—*why* are you doing this piece of writing? *What* do you want to gain out of it? *Whom* are you writing for? And *whom* do you want to write about? These are the kinds of questions that people writing about anything need to answer before starting to write. Out of these, the most important choice is deciding whom you want to write about.

What kind of person is a good candidate to write about? As you can see from the earlier examples, the person doesn't have to be president of the United States or even a particularly stellar individual to be a good subject for writing about. The person does, however, have to be someone about whom you know enough to write about. Most important is to start with a wealth of detail to work from, for if you don't have the detail, you can't do the description. Of course, ideally some further detail will come to mind as you write, but you need to start with as much as you can. How do you do that? Again, by systematic thinking.

We use two different words for what may well be two different approaches to the same kind of thinking because our students are frequently strong in one and forget the other. That is, the student

Invention and Discovery. Two thinking processes are involved in finding the amount of detail you need to do a good piece of writing. For our purposes, we'll call them *invention* and *discovery.* Though they're quite a bit alike, there are some crucial differences. *Invention* is what you do when the material for your writing has to come mostly from inside your own head; *discovery* is what you do when you need to go to the library (or laboratory or field) to find the material to write about.

Discovery is also a good word for what happens when the words and ideas you have already written suggest new words and ideas you weren't aware of when you started writing. Because in freshman composition classes students who are writing about people are usually doing so from their own experience and from memory, we'll focus on invention here.

There are many ways to do invention—from organized group brainstorming sessions with classmates to sitting down and doodling notes on a blank pad. (Chapter 28, in the handbook section of the hardbound edition of this book, includes a fuller treatment of invention and discovery.) For an assignment that asks you to write about a person, it may be best to do a little free-associating. For example:

1. In the years you have been in school, who are the most notable teachers you have had? List them.
2. In the years you have been in school, who are the most interesting friends you have had? List them.
3. In the times you've spent outside of school activities—vacations, jobs, and so on—who are the most notable people you've met? List them.
4. Now from *each* list choose a person who has the most potential for your writing assignment (in other words the three people who generate the most memories and ideas). Write each name on a separate sheet of paper, give yourself a couple of minutes to think, and then write as fast as you can about the characteristics of each one. Note as many characteristics as you can. If you remember episodes, for example, just use one or two words to abbreviate them. Your aim is simply to see where the most—and best—material is; there's no need to develop any one item in great detail.

Generally when you're doing this kind of work, the faster you go, the better. Don't try to use your brain's deliberate, critical skills; strive instead to generate ideas for details as fast as you can, hoping to get into that frame of mind in which one idea automatically and easily leads to another, in which one memory triggers several more. Usually the faster you make your brain work, the more apt you are to get into this latter kind of thinking.

Once you've done the best you can listing the characteristics of the people you've chosen, you're ready to start narrowing down the lists. Looking at the three lists you made in step 4, give thought to which of those persons can be connected with some kind of significance the reader of your paper might be able to appreciate. That is, while there are probably people who mean a lot to you, people you can say a lot about, their significance may be difficult to convey to the reader of your paper; the person you want to select is someone you've got lots of detail on, someone whose significance you can easily explain to others.

To this point in your writing processes you've factored in (a) an initial appraisal of the situation, (b) an inventory of your own resources for material to write about, and (c) further consideration of the reader of your essay. These kinds of issues come up one way or another in any writing situation.

who runs out of information halfway through a term paper and is expert at going to the library to *discover* more is often the same student who, as soon as the writing of page one begins, shuts down whatever internal process of *invention* he or she has undertaken. Similarly, another student who is great on the internal process of *invention* will neglect to do any field, lab, or library work to let *discovery* support the writing. With two words, we can remind our students to do both—which gives their writing the kind of nourishment it needs.

In our experience, students will be reluctant to *write down* things in this brainstorming exercise; they see the point and often believe they can hold in their heads the ideas they come up with. But we think you should insist that they have pen or pencil in hand and really put things down as you go through this listing process. That writing not only preserves the list but also reinforces the process of writing itself.

Next, Organize

Now take the name on the list that has the most information under it, the one that has the kind of significance you can explain to someone else, and organize the details into their natural groups. You might have groups for physical descriptions, character traits, small events, and major events, for instance. You'll then be able to structure your paper from those groups.

Next, Write

Finally, you are ready to start writing. That process is explained in detail in other places in this book (see chapter 1, page 9, and, in the hardbound edition, chapter 28); what we've led you through here is a simple invention process. The point is that the more material you start with—and the better that material is—the better piece of writing you can finally come up with.

SAMPLE WRITING ASSIGNMENT AND CASE STUDY CLOSE-UP

Here's the first draft—a very fast first draft—of what Pete Stanton wrote when his teacher asked him to write about people from his past. Working through the invention process described above, Pete decided that the people about whom he knew the most were his two best friends from high school. He next determined that the best way to make his piece vivid and the significance of his friends clear was to tell the story of an adventure the three friends shared during their senior year. Following the draft are Pete's teacher's comments.

It Takes All Kinds

[First draft]

I guess we all have groups of people in high school whom we spend most of our time with. When high school ends, some of us walk away from those people and never look back. For others, those people continue to shape our lives for years to come. I'm in that second group, and I think that makes me one of the lucky ones. Let me tell you about a few of the people I knew back then. Although I haven't seen most of them in ten years or more, they're with me still, as real today as they were then. 1

Like most of the guys in my group of friends, although I spent lots of my time talking about girls, dates, and dating, looking back on it I never really seemed to have spent as much time actually on dates as I did talking about it. For whatever reason, there just isn't a girl I look back to 2 from those times as being very significant to me--or at least, not in the kind of way that my two best friends, "John-John" and "Fishface," were. When I went to football and basketball games, it was basically with them. When I went camping or hiking or fishing, it was with them. One or another of them was in every class I took from my sophomore year on. For nine months a year for three years, we saw each other just about every day.

3 Fishface was on the surface the more unusual of the two. His distinguishing characteristics were his pop-bottle-bottom glasses, his Marine colonel father, and his extreme intelligence. Each feature helped shape his personality greatly. He was, to all intents and purposes, blind without his glasses, which was a real handicap in places like the swimming pool, or in our pretty much nonstop touch-football games out in the street in front of his house. We always assumed that the "four-eyed" appearance was the reason he never dated. In the manner of sixteen-year-olds everywhere, we never looked below the surface far enough to realize he was just extremely shy around girls. I mean, he never was shy around us. His Marine colonel father was another part of being one of Fishface's friends. We never went to his house when his father might be home--we were terrified of him, a quality that Fishface encouraged. I mean, a Marine colonel? His mother tried to lure us there with Little Debbie cookies and Diet-Rite cola, but once the Colonel came home, we split. The last thing that really identified Fishface was his extreme intelligence: he was the smartest kid in the school--in math, in English, in science; on class tests, on reports, and on standardized tests. He played at least three musical instruments, and it seemed like he had read everything. This (along with his glasses) gave him a kind of an egghead image that he at once enjoyed and fought against.

4 John-John seemed in lots of ways like the all-American boy--a football player until his junior year when he hurt his knee, a solid B student, the only one of our group who had a steady girlfriend. In a way, his normalness made Fishface's eccentricity tolerable. What really distinguished John-John was his enthusiasm--for any kind of project, any kind of adventure--his ambition, and his love of golf. Where Fishface was kind of an egghead, John-John was a go-getter. The combination of the two--with my help as a go-between and resolver of quarrels--made quite a mix. John-John probably never said no to anything. Want to see if we

can stay up till dawn? Sure! Want to create a fictitious candidate for student council and put up outrageous campaign signs all around the school? Absolutely! Want to put out our own newspaper? No doubt about it! Maybe that same enthusiasm shaped his ambition--to be president of the United States. He wasn't shy about it. He figured he could do as good a job as anyone else--why shouldn't it be him? But the biggest thing that distinguished John-John was his love of golf. He was never available to us on Saturday or Sunday afternoons when the weather was good, because he was on the golf course. We could tell by his nonstop sunburn how he had spent his time.

I guess I was the mixer between Fishface and John-John. What the 5
two of them saw in me I don't know--it might have been that my parents let me take the car, and theirs didn't. It was the combination of the car, John-John's enthusiasm, and Fishface's problems with his egghead image that shaped one of the best adventures we had together. It began as one of those sitting-around-bored-in-your-senior-year-looking-for-something-new-to-do evenings. For some reason we all had skateboards with us, although they never had been a big part of our activities before. Fishface's father had come home and seen us skateboarding out in the street and told us in no uncertain terms what a bad idea that was, especially where he could see us. Sundown found us at John-John's house, complaining about how there was nothing to do we hadn't done already a hundred times. Our thoughts turned to the skateboards, to somewhere with lights where we could ride them, then to somewhere really adventurous to ride them. Then we remembered it--the country club!

On a high hill outside of town, the country club was off-limits to us. 6
None of our families were members; no one we knew belonged; we called the place "Snob Hill." That night we weren't interested in the club so much as the road to it--a road that wound two and a half times around the hill and only went to the club, a road that on a weekday night was likely to have little or no traffic. A road made for skateboarding! So I volunteered to drive the car behind John-John and Fishface, providing the only light they would have. It was in the character of Fishface to come up with an idea that good; it was in the enthusiasm of John-John to go for it; and it was in my basic chickenheartedness to volunteer to

drive the car (and not to ride a skateboard downhill on a winding road in the middle of the night). So when we started down the hill, John-John and Fishface were side by side, slowly gaining speed down the hill, with me driving behind them lighting the way with the headlights. We had the briefest of good starts; then Fishface lost his balance a little and grabbed at John-John. John-John flailed his arms to regain his balance, accidentally knocked Fishface's glasses off, and fell off his skateboard. As I stopped the car to avoid John-John, Fishface--now minus his glasses--regained his balance and sped off down the hill. Unfortunately, he no longer had my headlights--or any lights at all--to guide him. Since he no longer had his glasses on, maybe that wouldn't have mattered. Anyway, his scream as he flew down the hill was long and pitiful--kind of fading into the night. John-John and I jumped back into the car and hustled down the hill, expecting to find a bruised and maybe bleeding Fishface off the side of the road somewhere. But he wasn't there. We found him instead at the bottom of the hill, after what must have been an incredible ride (which, unfortunately, no one saw), having not just flown down the hill and across the road at the bottom--straight into a mud puddle on the other side of the road. He wasn't bruised, or bleeding, but he sure was muddy.

7 I've had lots of adventures in my life since then, some of considerably greater proportions than the ride down Snob Hill, and I've had lots of good friends. But times like that with friends like Fishface and John-John stay with me most vividly. After all kinds of people and all kinds of things happening, I still hold those friends and those adventures as the brightest and the best I've ever had.

How do you feel about Pete's first draft? Remember, what we're looking for from a first draft is to get the basic content and perhaps the basic structure right; the fine points of grammar and style come later, during revision. Do you think the piece took a long time to get to its point? Pete's teacher did; here are the teacher's comments:

> Pete, this is a good first draft. There is plenty of material in here for you to use in your next version, plenty of detail, and plenty of action, though I do think you could explain the names more. What I think you especially need to consider, though, is whether the piece doesn't kind of ramble. It goes on longer than maybe the topic justifies, at least it seemed that way to me. Ask yourself, "What's the one main

> purpose of this? What *one main point* do I want to get across?" Then strip away the parts that don't belong with that purpose. After you've done that, go back and see if you can tighten up the sentence structure a little, as well. OK?

Here is how the first two paragraphs of the next draft looked after Pete had sharpened his purpose but before he'd begun revising on the sentence level:

> [Second draft]
>
> I guess we all have groups of people in high school who we spend most of our time with. Those people continue to shape our lives for years to come. Let me tell you about a few of the people I knew back then. They're with me still, as real today as they were then. 1
>
> My two best friends were "John-John" and "Fishface." When I went to football and basketball games, it was basically with them. When I went camping or hiking or fishing, it was with them. One or another of them was in every class I took from my sophomore year on. For nine months a year for three years, we saw one another just about every day. 2

The final, revised essay appears earlier in this chapter.

WRITING ASSIGNMENTS

1. Try your hand at doing some short character sketches—say, one paragraph each—of friends you have at college. Try to develop each one a little differently—one through character traits, one through physical description, one through activities and events. Are you more comfortable with one mode or the other?
2. Sometimes individual people aren't as interesting to describe as groups are. Pick a group of people—it could be small, such as the people in your dorm, or large, such as the crowd at a football game—and describe them in three paragraphs: one for character traits, one for physical description, and one for actions or events. You may find that describing a group gives you more variety and more options as a writer. (You may, though, want to give thought to what describing a crowd does to finding some kind of significance for the description.)
3. Try writing an imitation of the excerpt from *Lake Wobegon* appearing earlier in this chapter. Experiment with making the people and the setting clearly part of the same fabric, the way Keillor does.

4. Turn again to the picture that opened this chapter (page 171), which shows a woman draped in a flag. Create a short biography or story about her.

Focus on Critical Reading

5. Carefully reread "My Favorite Teachers." Then write a brief piece that summarizes first the claims it makes and then the evidence offered in support of each. What is the larger, unstated claim the piece makes, the one that rests on the second, fourth, and fifth paragraphs? How sufficient are those paragraphs for supporting the claim?
6. Imagine that the piece "My Favorite Teachers" is shown to three different groups: college freshmen, their parents, and college teachers. Which group would respond most favorably? Which group would respond least favorably? Why?
7. Carefully reread "Kaahumanu and Eve," especially the tenth paragraph. What is the larger argument that makes sense out of bringing up Kaahumanu, Eve, Idùn, and Gaea in the same piece? Is it more than "these women are similar in the following ways"? How well do these varied examples support that larger argument's claim? What could further strengthen it?
8. Briefly summarize the argument of the first two paragraphs of the excerpts from *Men's Lives.* Is that claim which all the evidence supports explicit in the passage? On what values or attitudes on the part of the book's readers does the argument's success depend? What level of expertise does the author seem to have on this subject, and how does that level of expertise affect your response to the argument? Finally, how does the segment about Ted Lester fit into the earlier segment's general argument?
9. Analyze your response to "Kaahumanu and Eve." Do you find any of it shocking? Why or why not? Might the author, Kim Chernin, have intended to shock? What might be the point of doing so?

Writers' Circle

To practice brainstorming, an invention technique, divide into groups of three and have each group designate a secretary to record the impressions that come up. The idea is to create brief, descriptive details about each item in the following lists of people. After each group has brainstormed twenty to twenty-five minutes, have each secretary read each group's responses to each item.

Individuals

Someone named "Digbert Dweeb"

Someone called "The Dark Avenger"

An archaeology professor named "Dr. Musty"

Good brainstorming exercises abound. If your students need more practice with this part of the writing process, even a cursory search at the library will yield plenty of ideas. If students seem reluctant to believe this kind of thinking is worthwhile, we recommend you give them more practice in it.

An archaeology professor named Indiana Jones

A high school basketball coach

Groups

A motorcycle gang

An acting troupe

A rock band

A philharmonic orchestra

"Star Trek" fans

chapter 10 Writing About Places

"I admire Hemingway but I prefer what I know of Faulkner. *Light in August* is a marvelous book. The character of the little pregnant woman is unforgettable. As she walks from Alabama to Tennessee something of the immensity of the South of the United States, of its essence, is captured for us who have never been there."

Boris Pasternak

Sometime early in the semester we like to have our students write a piece describing their home town. It's not a flashy assignment, but it does produce good writing year in and year out, probably because most students know their home town well and do a lot of thinking about it during their first or second term in college.

Writing about a place lets you share with your readers some of the best experiences people can have. Everyone has access to places; everyone has a place that means a lot; and even the most ordinary place can be described so well that the words take on a life of their own. While it may at first seem to you that plenty of physical description ("tall green trees," "sparkling clear water") is essential to writing about places, in fact there are many ways to do it—and do it well, as the examples below show.

Varieties of Writing About Places

The first example, "Rainy Mountain," uses geographic and biological detail to make its description vivid. The second example, a famous passage from an even more famous novel, uses the rhythm and texture of its prose ("the empty immensity of earth, sky, and water") to put its readers in another place and another time. The third example, "Denver, a Mile High and Climbing," is public relations prose, doing its job with a mix of geography, colorful nouns and adjectives, and overstatement. The fourth example is a fanciful dialogue from Pyewacket, North Carolina, that shows us not only a place (and a region) but also an interesting moment between two people. The last example, "The Sitting Rock," is one student's response to an assignment asking for a description of a place that has special meaning. The variety of approaches to writing about places here should give you some indication of the many ways it can be accomplished.

Rainy Mountain

N. Scott Momaday

This short selection is from N. Scott Momaday's book, The Way to Rainy Mountain, *which follows the migration of his tribe (the Kiowa) from Montana to Oklahoma. Momaday won the 1969 Pulitzer Prize for another of his books,* The House Made of Dawn.

A single knoll rises out of the plain in Oklahoma, north and west of the Wichita Range. For my people, the Kiowas, it is an old landmark, and they gave it the name Rainy Mountain. The hardest weather in the world is there. Winter brings blizzards, hot tornadic winds arise in the spring, and in summer the prairie is an anvil's edge. The grass turns brittle and brown, and it 1 cracks beneath your feet. There are green belts along the rivers and creeks, linear groves of hickory and pecan, willow and witch hazel. At a distance in July or August the steaming foliage seems almost to writhe in fire. Great green-and-yellow grasshoppers are everywhere in the tall grass, popping up like corn to sting the flesh, and tortoises crawl about on the red earth, going nowhere in the plenty of time. Loneliness is an aspect of the land. All things in the plain are isolate; there is no confusion of objects in the eye, but *one* hill or *one* tree or *one* man. To look upon that landscape in the early morning, with the sun at your back, is to lose the sense of proportion. Your imagination comes to life, and this, you think, is where Creation was begun.

Questions for Writing and Discussion

Prepare short written answers to each of these questions. Be prepared to hand them in and/or discuss them in class, as your teacher directs.

1. What do the following words mean—*knoll, linear,* and *writhe?*
2. Notice the use of biology in the passage. How does that use add to the effect of the description?
3. What's the dominant impression this passage leaves you with? How is that impression produced?
4. Who are the Kiowa? What does that reference add to this passage?
5. How would you describe the voice of the writer in this passage? Is it stuffy, dry, sweet, personal, formal, factual, pretentious, or what?
6. What would you say is the point of this passage? Is there more to it than mere description? What kind of place are you left feeling this region is?

Similar pieces could be written about any distinctive physical feature of the country: the Grand Banks, the Outer Banks, the Okefenokee, the Gulf of Mexico, the Southwest Desert, Baja, Big Sur, the Olympic Peninsula, the Mississippi Basin, and so on. Depending on the location of your school and the areas students are from, any of these might well be worth pursuing as writing assignments.

While the piece above employs rich geographic and biological detail to convey the essence of place, the following passage from a novel uses topographical detail and sensory description to do the same.

Along the African Coast

JOSEPH CONRAD

Joseph Conrad (1857–1924) was a sailor and writer, perhaps best known for his novels Lord Jim, The Secret Sharer, *and* Heart of Darkness, *from which the following selection is taken.*

Ask students whether any of them have ever taken a long voyage by boat. While that experience is perhaps rare in our society today, if one of your students has done so and will describe the experience for your class, you have found someone who has truly seen "the empty immensity of earth, sky, and water."

1 Watching a coast as it slips by the ship is like thinking about an enigma. There it is before you—smiling, frowning, inviting, grand, mean, insipid, or savage, and always mute with an air of whispering. Come and find out. This one was almost featureless, as if still in the making, with an aspect of monotonous grimness. The edge of a colossal jungle, so dark green as to be

almost black, fringed with white surf, ran straight, like a ruled line, far, far away along a blue sea whose glitter was blurred by a creeping mist. The sun was fierce, the land seemed to glisten and drip with steam. Here and there greyish-whitish specks showed up clustered inside the white surf, with a flag flying above them perhaps—settlements some centuries old, and still no bigger than pin-heads on the untouched expanse of their background. . . .

Once, I remember, we came upon a man-of-war anchored off the coast. 2
There wasn't even a shed there, and she was shelling the bush. It appears the French had one of their wars going on thereabouts. Her ensign dropped limp like a rag; the muzzles of the long six-inch guns stuck out all over the low hull; the greasy, slimy swell swung her up lazily and let her down, swaying her thin masts. In the empty immensity of earth, sky, and water, there she was, incomprehensible, firing into a continent. Pop, would go one of the six-inch guns; a small flame would dart and vanish, a little white smoke would disappear, a tiny projectile would give a feeble screech—and nothing happened. Nothing could happen. There was a touch of insanity in the proceeding, a sense of lugubrious drollery in the sight; and it was not dissipated by somebody on board assuring me earnestly there was a camp of natives—he called them enemies!—hidden out of sight somewhere.

Questions for Writing and Discussion

Prepare short written answers to each of these questions. Be prepared to hand them in and/or discuss them in class, as your teacher directs.

1. Contrast the effects of the two paragraphs. What is the effect of the first paragraph, and how does it accomplish that effect? What is the effect of the second paragraph, and how does it accomplish that effect?
2. How do you feel about the use of "lugubrious drollery" in the second paragraph? Look the words up, and see if you can find acceptable contemporary alternatives. What are they?
3. What do the following words mean—*enigma, insipid* (¶ 1), *ensign, incomprehensible, projectile, dissipated* (¶ 2)?
4. How would you characterize the author's voice in this passage?
5. What would you say is the point of this passage? What kind of feeling are you left with about the landscape being described? Is there more going on than just description?

Bridges: Another Perspective

The selection by Conrad reminds us that there was a lengthy era of colonialism, when European countries—chiefly Spain, France, and England—spread their influence around the globe, claiming, exploiting, and politically controlling through far-superior military power many weaker peoples and lands. At one time or another, most of the continent of Africa was colonialized, as were significant parts of Asia (chiefly India) and America. This era supposedly ended in the first half of the twentieth century, after World Wars I (1914–18) and II (1939–45), won by the United States and its allies, who extended principles of self-determination and democratic government to lands that had previously been colonized and controlled.

Some, however, would argue that colonialism never ended, because world powers like the United States and the Soviet Union still exploit and control a great many weaker nations and peoples through a combination of economic and military measures. Colonialism, these people argue, merely changed its name to more subtle labels, such as North Atlantic Treaty Organization, Organization of American States, and Warsaw Pact, all groups of allied countries dominated by major world powers. The practices of colonialism, in this view, haven't changed—only the names and tactics of the colonizers have. Conrad's French ship shelling a few natives on the African coast in the 1800s, then, may not be so different from the U.S. campaign in Panama (1989) or the Soviet government's operations against Afghanistan (also in the 1980s), and against some of the Soviet provinces (in the 1990s).

In light of all of this, discuss colonialism then and now: what are the differences?

For another perspective on colonialism, invite students to read *The Nations Within*, by Vine Deloria, Jr., and Clifford M. Lytle.

Joseph Conrad's description of a place in some ways evokes typical images of primitive coastlines. Below, a public relations brochure evokes similarly typical images of a boomtown in the mountains of the American West.

Denver, a Mile High and Climbing

THE DENVER METRO CONVENTION AND VISITOR'S BUREAU (1987)

1 Located on high rolling plains just east of the Rocky Mountains, Denver was born in the great "Pike's Peak or Bust" gold rush of 1859. In its first few years, the city survived a flood, several major fires, Indian attacks and even raised an army that defeated an invading force of Confederates during the Civil War. With the discovery of more gold in the mountains, Denver became a boom town. Saloons, gambling halls and wagon trains lined the mud-filled streets, and almost every gunslinger, outlaw, lawman and desperado in the West made at least a visit to the Mile High City.

2 The turn of the century brought respectability, and the wealth of the mountains was poured into parks, fountains, statues, tree-lined streets and elaborate mansions. Denver became the most elegant city in a thousand-mile radius—the "Queen City of the Plains."

We remind you that this is promotional writing. If anyone in your class has been to Denver, ask that person whether Denver seemed still to be a small town. To us, it's a lovely city (especially on a clear day) but not at all a small town. Ask students what the role of such bending-of-the-facts is in promotional writing and whether the practice is more or less acceptable, depending on what kind of writing one is doing. Can there be degrees of honesty?

Today, that elegance can still be found in hundreds of restored Victorian buildings and homes, but at the same time, much of Denver looks like a model for the 21st century. From the futuristic symphony hall-in-the-round to the gleaming new mile-long 16th Street Mall, from the glass-enclosed Tabor Center to the many unusual towering skyscrapers, Denver is known for its modern architecture and design. The recent building boom has caused the city to nearly double in size, growing to a population of 1.8 million, making Denver the economic, cultural and transportation capital of the vast Rocky Mountain West. But at its heart, Denver has in many ways remained a small town. Quiet neighborhoods, beautiful tree-lined boulevards and over 200 parks and flower gardens make it easy to escape the hustle of the city and enjoy its relaxing and lovely location at the foot of the mountains. 3

A young, growing city with a young, highly educated populace, Denver has become a forerunner in the arts and is developing a growing reputation as a center for theatre, dance, and Western art. After dark, some 2,000 restaurants and nightspots give the city a nightlife reminiscent of the gold rush days. 4

With an ideal year-round climate, great location and interesting attractions, all in a clean, modern cultural city, Denver is truly a mile high and climbing. 5

Questions for Writing and Discussion

Prepare short written answers to each of these questions. Be prepared to hand them in and/or discuss them in class, as your teacher directs.

1. Many people would say that the writing in this passage lacks a certain quality that the passage before it has; that is, the writing in a Conrad novel is quite different from that in a promotional brochure. Based on comparing these two passages, can you identify those differences, giving examples?
2. What does the relative absence of challenging words suggest about the purpose, readership, and author's intentions in this passage about Denver?
3. Try your hand at writing a paragraph or two, in this same voice as the Denver piece, about your campus or hometown. Do it once as a parody of travel brochure writing, and another time "straight." How are the two kinds of writing different?

The American West indeed has the aura of a special place. Following is a piece about another distinctive and famous American place.

PREREADING WORKSHEET

Before you read the following piece by John Welter, write brief responses to these questions:

1. When you think of the American South, what images come to mind?

2. What, if anything, do you think is distinctive about southern U.S. speech? Is it different from your speech? If you yourself are from the south, how do you think the speech of those from other parts of the country differs from yours?
3. What states would you include in a list of states that belong in the Deep South?
4. What states would you classify as being in the South but not in the Deep South?
5. What images do you associate with these other regions:
   a. The Midwest
   b. New England
   c. Texas
   d. The Great Plains
   e. The Pacific Northwest
   f. California

Has His Southern-ness Gone with the Wind?

JOHN WELTER

John Welter is a reporter for the News and Observer *in Chapel Hill, North Carolina.*

1 At the Pyewacket Restaurant here in central North Carolina, where I'm always a suspicious alien from Kansas City, I was asking a native Southerner what the difference is between the Deep South and the rest of the South. "It's redundant to call me a 'native Southerner,'" she said. "You are either a Southerner, or you aren't. Judging from your accent, I'd say you're from Chicago."

2 "If you weren't judging from my accent, where would you say I was from?" I asked.

3 "I wouldn't know," she said.

4 "You're right. You don't know. I was in Chicago once, for two hours, but I don't think I got my accent there. I'm sorry if I did."

5 She smiled at me quizzically and said, "Where are you from?"

6 "I'm a Caucasian. I guess that means I'm from some mountains in Russia, but I think my parents lied on my birth certificate and said I was from Monahans, Texas."

7 The woman I was talking with was a friend of a friend, an associate professor of history at the nearby university in town, which I have started referring to as "that school." It's a very long name and I get tired of saying it.

8 "Then you're a Texan?" she asked.

9 "Not anymore. I gave it up."

10 "How can you give up being a Texan?"

11 "My parents moved. I had to go with them," I explained. "Do you know where we went next?"

12 She shook her head and said, "No. I wasn't with you."

13 "I'd have remembered if you were," I said. She has green eyes. I said, "Has anyone ever told you have green eyes?"

14 "A few people have mentioned it," she said, and returned to the subject of the Deep South as opposed to the rest of the South. She said the Deep South includes South Carolina, Georgia, Alabama, Mississippi and Louisiana.

15 "But not Antarctica, I take it?" I said.

16 "Antarctica is too far south," she said.

17 "That's what I've always thought. I think they should move it up to the Gulf of Mexico. It's just about the right size."

18 She ignored that, except to say that Antarctica was actually about twice the size of the Gulf of Mexico.

19 "Why you even mentioned Antarctica is beyond me," I said. "What I was hoping to find out, since you've lived in the South all your life, is if the Deep South is called Deep, what's the rest of the South called?"

20 She tilted her head with a kind of patient exasperation and said, "The rest of the South isn't called anything."

21 "That's not a very good name for it," I said. "I've lived in North Carolina four years and four months, and when my friends from Kansas City want to know what part of the South I live in, I write letters back to them saying, 'We don't have a name for it. Be quiet.' They assume that because the South is divided into two parts—the Deep South and the other part—that the other part has a name. At first, I wrote back and said this was the Shallow South."

22 Cindy grabbed my wrist lightly and said, "The Shallow South? Isn't that a little bit insulting?"

23 "Well if it is, I evidently don't mind it," I said. "What else would you call it? The unDeep South?"

24 "I don't call it anything, but you can," she said.

25 "Thank you," I said. "I hope you're not mad at me, are you?"

26 "Not now, but if I care to be later, I will," she said. She smiled at me handsomely. "So. Are you from Kansas City, then?" she asked.

27 "Four years and four months ago I was."

28 "Does that mean you aren't from Kansas City now?"

29 I didn't know. "I think once you've left a place, they won't let you be from there forever, will they? I've never thought about that before. Does it mean I'm a Southerner now?" I asked.

30 Cindy shook her head. "You can't be a Southerner unless you were born here. Rules is rules."

31 She has brown hair. "Has anyone ever told you have brown hair?" I asked.

32 "You have an awfully peculiar way of flirting," she said. "You must be from Texas."

33 "That's what my parents say."

Ask students if they've ever written dialogue as part of a paper for an English class. They won't have, we imagine. Encourage them, for this paper or some other, to use some dialogue, and ask them how they feel about doing so. Consider also the dialogue in "Uncivil Liberties" (chapter 12).

POSTREADING WORKSHEET

Now that you have read the piece by Welter, write your responses to the following questions:

1. What allusion (reference to previous historical event, character, or work of art) is in the title of this piece?
2. Why is the allusion in the title appropriate for the subject of Welter's selection?
3. Does the article's list of Deep South states match your own? If your list varies, which states are involved, and why do you think they were excluded (or included)?
4. Where are *you* from? Does your answer to this question reflect where you were born and spent most of your formative years, or merely where you lived last? What criteria should determine the answer to where a person is from?
5. When Cindy says, "Rules is rules" (¶ 30), do you think she is conscious of her error in subject-verb agreement? Why or why not?
6. What role does speech play in this article?

Questions for Writing and Discussion

Prepare short written answers to each of these questions. Be prepared to hand them in and/or discuss them in class, as your teacher directs.

1. This newspaper piece has short paragraphs and dialogue, techniques typical of newspaper writing. What does the abundance of dialogue give this piece that the earlier selections lack?
2. This piece starts out as a kind of a play on local-color descriptive writing. Actually, as the piece goes on, quite a different agenda is worked out. What is that agenda, and when do you start to suspect that portraying regional description is not the author's main interest?
3. If regional description is not what this piece is mostly about, what *is* it mostly about?
4. The convention for treating written dialogue generally requires it to be set off in separate paragraphs when there is intervening description. The convention also calls for a new paragraph each time the speaker changes. If this piece were told in retrospect, with much less dialogue, where would the paragraph changes most likely be?

Many of us have a hideaway, a retreat, some special place where we go to escape daily routines and shed our cares. On the following pages, a student writes about such a place.

The Sitting Rock

Jeannie Wilson, college writing student

Sometimes you can be in a place you've been countless times before, take a different turn, and find you don't know the place at all. That happened to me when I found "the sitting rock." Walking downstream instead of upstream one day, picking my way along the water's edge, I saw a place about hand-high in the rock face that looked like it was made for a person to sit in. I climbed up and found a perfect place to sit and watch the river. Sometime later, when I heard my parents calling me with concern in their voices, I learned what made the sitting rock special: time seems to stand still there, and (even better) when you're there no one can see you from above--no one knows you're there at all. 1

I was just fifteen when I first found the sitting rock. All through high school, it was my escape from the world around me. When I was sad I went there to feel sorry for myself. When I was happy I went there to remember how good I felt. Mostly, I just went there to be alone. 2

The river there isn't much, probably not more than thirty feet wide. The rock face runs several hundred feet along the river, and in most places you can't really climb it at all. When I first saw the sitting rock, it was hard to climb the eight or ten feet up to it. But once you know how, it's easy. Physically there's nothing much special about the rock besides its shape. But there's something about sitting on that rock, so solid and so private, combined with the smell and the sight and the sound of the water flowing by, that has never failed to have an effect on me. 3

I remember one day in particular, my senior year, when we were out of school for a teacher's meeting. My friends had all one way or another got involved in doing something else, and I wound up with the afternoon on my own. I had gone to the rock for no particular reason--just to sit and let the time go by. But while I was there it hit me how many years I had gone there, and how soon I would be leaving my hometown--and the rock I had found so special. About that time I saw a girl of about thirteen or fourteen picking her way along the river toward me. She was watching where she put her feet so closely that she didn't see me until the very last minute, when she looked up in surprise. "How did you get up there?" she asked, and without even thinking that I might be giving 4 up my secret place, I helped her up. We only talked for a couple of minutes before she headed back upstream, but somehow I knew she would be back. The sadness I had started to feel was gone, replaced by that nice feeling we get sometimes from sharing something special with someone who seems to appreciate it as much as we do.

5 Today, hundreds of miles from home and a half-year since my last visit to the rock, it makes me feel good to think of that other girl sitting there. I know the rock will be there whenever I go back, but it's nice to know someone else is there saving my place for me.

Questions for Writing and Discussion

Prepare short written answers to each of these questions. Be prepared to hand them in and/or discuss them in class, as your teacher directs.

1. Describe the use of time to shape the structure of this piece. How effective is that use? Can you think of other ways this piece might be organized?
2. One problem with this kind of writing is that it can easily become too sentimental. Does this piece come close to—or exceed—that line? If not, what kinds of details or events would, if included, have produced too much sentimentality in this piece?
3. This passage uses the grammatical first person ("I") liberally and naturally. What does that cause you to conclude about the "rule" never to use the first person?
4. How would you characterize the author's voice in this passage?
5. What would you say is the point of this passage? How does the author accomplish it?

KEY POINTS TO REMEMBER: Writing About Places

- Make the scene you describe vivid.
- Provide a detailed presentation of significant people and events.

Make the Scene You Describe Vivid

There are many ways to make a scene vivid; using colorful words or strong verbs are only two. For example, in "Rainy Mountain," much of the vividness comes from the use of specific details, usually biological: brittle grass; green groves of hickory and pecan; willow and witch hazel, grasshoppers; tall grass; and tortoises. In "Along the African Coast," the vividness comes from the two-word phrases: "monotonous grimness," "colossal jungle," "dark green," "white surf," and then "limp like a rag," "greasy, slimy swell," and so on. But in that piece another source of vividness comes from comparing the sights and sounds to

Take some time to apply this "vividness test" to the "Denver" and "Sitting Rock" pieces. You'll find more vivid description in those pieces than in the "Southern-ness" piece, which contains more emphasis on the dialogue and the interplay between its speakers. That, however, doesn't necessarily make "Southern-ness" less effective as a piece about place. Rather, it is the *significant people* (second key point), not the vivid scene, that carry off the sense of place.

human qualities: in the first paragraph, watching the coast is like "thinking about an enigma . . . always mute with an air of whispering . . . with an air of monotonous grimness"; in the second paragraph, the proceeding has "a touch of insanity" and "a sense of lugubrious drollery."

What additional techniques do you see in the other examples that help make the descriptions vivid and real?

Provide a Detailed Presentation of Significant People and Events

Whatever you're writing about, it needs to make a difference somehow. Make sure there is a clear indication of the place's significance. The third example—the description of Denver—makes itself significant in part by its tone, starting with the title—". . . a Mile High and Climbing." The accumulation of historic details in the first paragraph—floods, fires, Indians, armies, gold, saloons, wagon trains, gunslingers, outlaws, lawmen, and desperadoes—contributes to building in the reader a sense of the subject's importance (or would *grandeur* be a more appropriate word here?). In fact, most of the example could be said to be aimed at having the reader infer that Denver is not just nice but *important.*

The fourth example—"Has His Southern-ness Gone with the Wind?"—is a different kind of description of a place, one accomplished indirectly through the people's dialects and their attitudes as revealed in their dialogue. At the beginning of the piece—in the Pyewacket Restaurant in central North Carolina—you wonder whether this aspect is significant at all. But if you are sensitive to the progression that occurs within the encounter between the man and the woman—as they grow closer through the wordplay—you'll see that the significance is there, all right. It's just done indirectly, quite differently from how it's done in the "Denver" piece before it or the "Sitting Rock" piece after it.

Ask students to describe the tone of "Southern-ness" in the piece.

How do the first two sample passages ("Rainy Mountain" and "African Coast") show the description's significance? Is that significance of a different kind from what the next passages ("Denver," "Southern-ness," and "Sitting Rock") show?

✔✔✔ **WORKSHEET: Writing About Places**

Here's a procedure to follow when you want to write about a place. Though there are other ways to do that effectively, you'll find this way works for you if you give it a try.

By now you've noticed that there's a certain similarity about most of our worksheets, although each one is slightly different. That's our experience of writing—that it's always the same and always different, and that what you thought you had learned about writing last time (or last month, or last year) you have to learn all over again this time.

First, Think

Size up the situation you're in as a writer—especially your purpose *and your* audience. The fact that you're using this book probably means you're taking a freshman-level writing class; thus, some pretty clear-cut boundaries establish what you can and can't do with this piece of writing. Let's talk about *audience* first, since it's the easier of the two. The audience is probably your teacher; however, you need to find out whether the audience also includes your classmates or whether it perhaps is solely your classmates. Do you see what a difference the type of audience would make in your writing?

Once you know who your audience is, think about the *purpose* of this piece of writing. A few obvious things are still worth saying: you want to make a decent grade (if the piece is graded); you want to complete the assignment with a reasonable expenditure of time and energy; and you want to attend to all those other things that make you a student and this a school assignment. While those points are not profound, they're nevertheless worth keeping in mind. But *purpose* goes past those obvious things. Look back at the examples and think about the purpose of each description:

"Rainy Mountain"—The purpose here is to use a detailed and descriptive overview to give readers a sense of the place—really at this point just an informational purpose.

"Along the African Coast." The purpose here is to set a couple of tones: in the first paragraph, the words that name it more than any other are "Come and find out"; in the second, they're "nothing happened. Nothing could happen."

"Denver, a Mile High and Climbing." As we said before, the purpose here is twofold: (a) to make Denver look attractive and (b) to make Denver look important.

"Has His Southern-ness Gone with the Wind?" The point here is mostly entertainment, with a bit of an indirect story about friendly banter between a man and a woman thrown in.

"The Sitting Rock." Here the point is how a simple place can take on meaning beyond its merely physical presence—a straightforward message.

Obviously, there can be much more to writing about a place than just describing it. Think about these different kinds of purposes you've seen and about all the other kinds of purposes there are. What kind of purpose will be yours in this piece?

Once you've thought about your audience and purpose for this piece—once you've sized up the situation—you should have a better sense of where you stand in relationship to this writing task. The popular expression for this aspect is "locating yourself within the assignment"—perhaps best explained by saying that you have begun to find out where *you* are in all this. That realization is important. It's not always easy to attain, but once you've done so, everything else is simpler.

Next, Organize

Gather the materials you need to do the piece of writing you want. When you're writing about a place, there's really no substitute for going there to gather your impressions. Even better, go there and *write down* your impressions. (Does this

This point—that you can write about a place better if you go there with writing on your mind—is one of those basics about writing we addressed in a previous note. There are other corollaries: you write better about things you know more about, you write better about things you're more interested in, and so on. It might well be worth listing a couple of those basics on the board for your students and then asking them to add to the list. (No one is so smart or experienced as to be able to ignore basics like these, but sometimes we get so caught up in the knick-knacks that we miss the statuary.)

mean you can't write about places you've never seen? Basically, yes, it does.) Select the place you choose to write about carefully—it needs to be significant when you write it up. Sometimes that significance comes from an inherent quality of the place itself (if you're writing about, say, the Grand Canyon or Padre Island) or from something in your interaction with it (something you learned there, some insight you gained there, for example).

As you're gathering materials, you need to make a *plan* for your writing. For this kind of writing, you can generally get by with a pretty loose plan, something like "First I'll do this, then I'll do that, and then I'll close with this." You need only enough of a plan to get you through a first draft; more structure, if needed, can come later.

Next, Write

Write a fast *first draft of your piece.* Don't stop to anguish over whether this word or that word is better, or whether this detail is in exactly the right place. Try to get all the way through one draft—one that uses, if not all the material you have, then at least all the best of it—in one sitting. The key is to separate your creative mental processes from your critical ones. Write hard and fast until you have a draft of some kind finished. Worry later about making it good; the only looking back you should do at the minute you finish the first draft is to see that you have included in the piece all the *content* you intended to include.

Next, Revise

A nice word for getting your students to be happy with a draft, rather than trying to write finished copy in a first draft, is *satisficing.* A combination of *satisfy* and *suffice,* the term describes exactly the quality of knowing how much to expect from an experience and how much not to hope for. Or, as a friend of ours likes to say (she learned this while writing her dissertation), "How do you eat an elephant? One bite at a time."

Do an "80 percent fix" on your first draft. Doing an "80 percent fix" on a piece of writing means fixing the *big* problems, the obvious problems, the ones that are (usually) easiest and fastest to work on. Many students try to do all the levels of their revising simultaneously, and in our experience that simply makes revising too hard. A better tactic is to fix the big things first—to get the big picture into focus—before you start to fine-tune your writing. Thus, when we recommend the 80 percent fix, we mean that you can expend about 20 percent of the effort to fix 80 percent (the *big* 80 percent) of the problems of most drafts.

Here's a detailed look at the issues to consider during the process of the 80 percent fix:

1. Does the piece serve its purpose—does it get across the significance you wanted it to do? If not, add detail, delete detail, and move elements until it does.
2. Next, check your draft for overall structure. Does it have a nice flow, a clearly discernible beginning, middle, and end?
3. Look at the structure of each paragraph. Is each paragraph clearly organized around its own central point?

4. Also look at sentence structure. Can you find the subject and verb in each sentence? Do they fit together?
5. Try the passage out on a friend. Does the passage get a good reaction? Do any parts need more descriptive detail? Does the significance of the place come across?
6. In college classrooms, usually this kind of writing must succeed on two levels: the audience is composed of both your fellow students and your teacher. Try putting yourself in your teacher's place—is the passage successful from the teacher's perspective?

Each teacher will, of course, have a unique description of what constitutes an 80 percent fix. The significance of the phrase is to give you a clear way to specify to students a certain level of completion of a draft, a level that is a specified distance away from being a first draft, on the one hand, and a specified distance away from being a final draft, on the other.

Finally, Fine-Tune

Do as much fine-tuning as you have time for.

1. Check punctuation and spelling carefully.
2. Experiment with incorporating additional descriptive adjectives and colorful verbs.
3. Try varying some sentence structures—for example, put the subject and the verb of each sentence right next to each other. Do you like the sound of the sentences better that way?
4. Remember the key points to this kind of writing that were listed earlier—check your piece to see that it addresses those points.

CASE STUDY CLOSE-UP

The Assignment. Here's a typical writing assignment based on the fast first draft and revising:

> Write a description that captures for your reader the significance of a place you know well, one that means a lot to you. If you choose to describe a place you can't visit while working on the piece, choose a place you know so well you can close your eyes and see it in your mind's eye. Your goal is to get your reader to see the place and to see its significance for you. The audience for this piece is your classmates. The length should be 350 to 500 words. Do a fast first draft and an 80 percent fix; then pair with a classmate and review each other's drafts one-on-one in class before proceeding to the final copy.

One Student's Response. Jeannie Wilson is a seventeen-year-old college freshman from a small town. Though writing is not her favorite activity, there's a place back home she knows so well that she's sure if she can just get the place and her feelings about it down on paper, her piece will be well received. She calls her place "the rock"; we'll show you part of her fast first draft and the same part of her 80 percent fix.

The Sitting Rock

[Part of a fast first draft]

I was just fifteen when I first found the sitting rock. My family and I had been coming to the park ever since I can remember, just to picnic and enjoy being by the river. It's not much of a river really, more of a stream, but we call it a river around here. Anyway, I went walking downstream instead of upstream one day, and was picking my way along the water's edge, when I saw a place in the rock face, about hand-high, that looked like it was made for a person to sit in. It's a little hard to get up to the sitting place from where you're walking, but once you do it once, it's easy. And you can't get down there from the top of the rock face (about ten feet) at all. So I clambered up there, and sure enough it was a perfect place to sit and watch the river. It wasn't until sometime later, when I heard my parents calling me with a little touch of concern in their voice, that I learned the neatest thing about the rock: whenever I sat there, time seemed to stand still, and even better, when you're there, no one can see you from above--no one knows you're there at all. 1

All through high school "the sitting rock" was my escape from the world around me. . . . 2

In each chapter we're working to show your students the "messy work" involved in getting from one draft to the next. Sometimes students have trouble determining where each subsequent draft comes from; examples like this one (and the questions after it) will show, we hope, where those subsequent drafts come from.

When Jeannie started to do an 80 percent fix on her fast first draft, the thing that concerned her most was whether it took too long to get to a description of the rock; most of what she was looking for was the structure of this first paragraph—what to leave in and what to put off until later. Because Jeannie had done her first draft on a word processor, it was easy to read over a printout of that draft and then go back into the file and move (or delete) the parts that didn't seem to fit there. She wasn't planning to throw things away; rather, she wanted just to strip out the parts that didn't belong and save them, perhaps for reuse elsewhere. With that in mind, look now at the same part of her piece. (After it, we've given you a list of the parts she left out.)

The Sitting Rock

[Part of an 80 Percent Fix Draft]

Sometimes you can be somewhere you've been countless times before, take a different turn, and find you don't know the place at all. That happened to me when I found "the sitting rock." Walking 1 downstream instead of upstream one day, picking my way along the water's edge, I saw a place about hand-high in the rock face that looked made for a person to sit in. I climbed up, and sure enough it was a perfect place to sit and watch the river. Sometime later, when I heard my parents calling me with concern in their voices, I learned what made the sitting rock special: time seems to stand still there, and (even better) when you're there no one can see you from above--no one knows you're there at all.

2 All through high school "the sitting rock" was my escape from the world around me. . . .

Leftovers

I was just fifteen when I first found the sitting rock. My family and I had been coming to the park ever since I can remember, just to picnic and enjoy being by the river. It's not much of a river really, more of a stream, but we call it a river around here.

It's a little hard to get up to the sitting place from where you're walking, but once you do it once, it's easy. And you can't get down there from the top of the rock face (about ten feet) at all.

Questions

1. What else do you see going on in this 80 percent fix revision, besides the writer trying to get to the point faster?
2. Do you think the second draft is better than the first one? Why or why not? (If you want to review the final draft, it appears earlier in this chapter.)

WRITING ASSIGNMENTS

1. Do the same assignment Jeannie Wilson did, and see whether your writing has all the same strengths of hers without any of its weaknesses.
2. Write a "place" piece based primarily on physical description. See how well you can make your words match the picture in your mind.
3. Write a "place" piece based primarily on mood. Can you get a picture of the place and its significance across verbally without doing too much describing of the scenery?
4. We like to subtitle the photograph on page 199 "light and legend." Photographers like to capture places when the light is special—at sunrise or sunset, for example, or right after a rain storm. Writers, however, like to deal with fresh treatments of places of legend (such as Stonehenge). Thus in this

photograph we have the best of two worlds—a photographer's and a writer's. Parts of the United States present similar juxtapositions—sunrise at Cape Hatteras, on the east coast's Outer Banks; the morning light at Café du Monde, by the Mississippi River in New Orleans; sunset looking back onto New Mexico's Sangre de Cristo Mountains; taking off from San Francisco Airport at sundown and looking back at the city across the Golden Gate Bridge. Pick the best sunrise or sunset you've ever seen over a famous place and write as accurate a description of it as you can.

Focus on Critical Reading

One of the interesting things that have happened to writing in our lifetimes is the commonness with which a description of a place is combined with a sociopolitical motive—the "vanishing wilderness" essay (compare "Wilderness and Weirdness," chapter 8). Ask students to read the piece on acid rain (chapter 12) and to discuss in their writing groups how the addition of such a motive changes the nature of (a) descriptive writing and (b) our response to descriptive writing.

5. Today the distinction between "good literature" (Dickens, Hawthorne) and "popular literature" (Robert Ludlum, Ursula Le Guin) is less certain than ever. The readings at the beginning of this chapter represent diverse kinds of writing. Take another look at them and find a way to rank them in any order you choose, from "highbrow" to "lowbrow," from "writing for everybody" to "writing for English teachers," or any other reasonable scheme you choose. But explain the basis of your ordering, and use evidence from within each passage to justify that ordering.
6. What is the structure of "Rainy Mountain"? What effect on the passage does that structuring have?
7. Some people would claim that the Conrad passage, "Along the African Coast," makes a point. Do you agree? If so, what is that point? How is it made? What elements support it? How?
8. Can you detect an author's voice in "Denver, a Mile High and Climbing"? If so, how would you characterize that voice—that is, what kind of person would be saying (or writing) those words? How did you reach that conclusion?

Writers' Circle

Do any of the four suggested writing assignments and then divide into groups of two students each for two sequenced activities:

Of course, an 80 percent fix draft may not be the second one; it could be the sixth, depending on how long it takes a writer to feel that the rest of the paper is good enough to be ready for that level of fix.

1. Read each other's 80 percent fix draft and consider these questions:
   a. Is the place physically clear to the reader?
   b. Is the *specialness* of the place clear to the reader?
   c. Is more or less detail needed?
   d. Are any other suggestions in order?
2. Each group of two should report to the class about what they learned in responding to the questions in activity 1. What strengths and weaknesses in writing about a place are identified within the class as a whole?

Now, reflecting on changes suggested by the above sequence, write a final version for submission.

chapter 11 Writing About Things

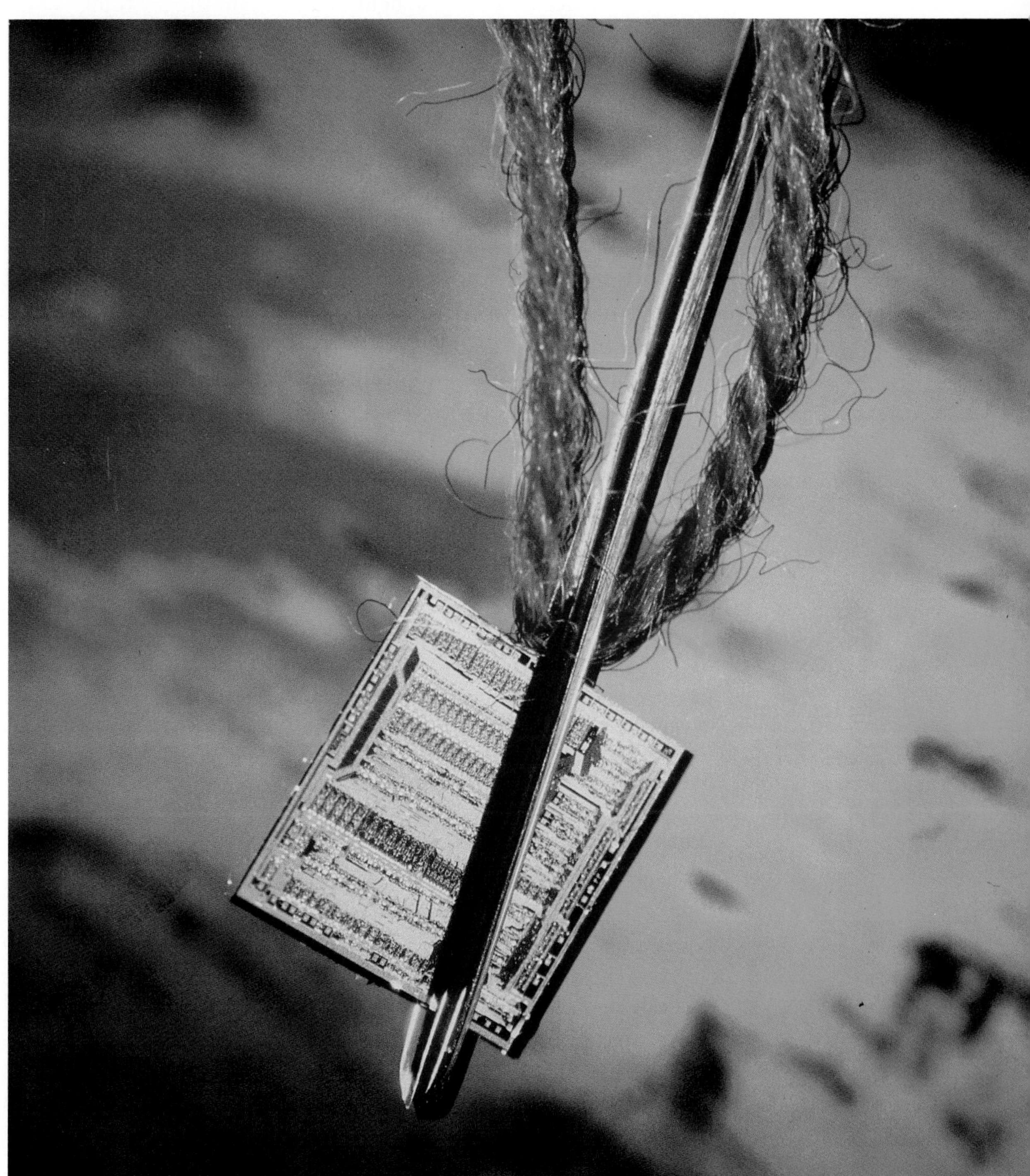

"The difference between the almost right word and the right word is really a large matter—'tis the difference between the lightning-bug and the lightning."

Mark Twain

"'Writing About *Things?*' some of our friends said when they saw the title of this chapter. '*Things?* Is that the best word you could come up with? *Things* can mean almost anything, so how can your chapter mean anything specific?' We pondered. What other word might fit our meaning? Writing About *Objects*'? No, that covers things like paintings, coffee cups, and power tools but not things like love, irony, and loyalty to the Red Sox. For similar reasons, 'Writing About *Abstractions*' won't work. Hmmm. 'Writing About *Items*'? No, irony isn't an item; neither is a board game. 'Writing About *Stuff*'? No, even we have standards."

Ralph and Mike

Writing about things is common, both in college and in the world of work. *Things,* of course, really *is* a vague term. It can apply to something concrete—a kite, a computer, a motorcycle—or to something abstract—cold weather, greed, talent. But whatever the "thing" in question is, the strongest influence on writing about it is the *reason* the writing is being done.

Purpose and Significance

We want to emphasize two points for you to keep in mind when writing about things:

1. *Why* am I writing this? What is my *purpose?* What do I hope to *accomplish?*
2. What is *distinctive* about the thing I'm writing about? What makes it important, *worth* writing about?

Once again, we recommend you begin a chapter by taking inventory of your students' prior experiences with this kind of writing: what kinds of things have they written about in the past?

For example, your biology teacher may ask you to dissect a frog and write a paper identifying its parts. In that case, your *purpose* is to show that you have completed the dissection and that you know each of the inner parts of the frog. You're writing to explain and inform, and your method will probably be process and analysis, thus conveying the results of the dissection. Or perhaps your agricultural engineering professor will ask you to write a paper explaining how a catfish-pond aerator keeps oxygen levels high in the pond. In that case, your paper's *purpose* is to explain not only how the aerator itself operates mechanically but also how its constant agitation of the water chemically keeps the oxygen level high.

Or the things you write about could be phenomena of nature, like storms, sunspots, tidal waves, earthquakes, or—as in the following piece, by the nineteenth-century American environmentalist John Muir—banners of snow caused by a windstorm in the Sierra Nevada Mountains:

Snow Banners

JOHN MUIR

John Muir (1838–1914), botanist, geologist, and naturalist, founded the Sierra Club and was instrumental in the establishment of Yosemite and Sequoia national parks. His books include The Story of My Boyhood and Youth, The Yosemite, Travels in Alaska, *and* The Mountains of California, *from which the following selection, describing an experience Muir had in 1873, is excerpted.*

You might want to review the last teaching note in chapter 10 in connection with this piece. We think one of the joys of reading this piece is its lack of a "and now all this is being destroyed by human beings" theme. Of course, Muir is describing something he saw in 1873, more than a century ago. It is doubtful that a current piece about the beauties of the Sierra Nevada could avoid noting how that environment is being threatened.

1 The most magnificent storm phenomenon I ever saw, surpassing in showy grandeur the most imposing effects of clouds, floods, or avalanches, was the peaks of the High Sierra, back of Yosemite Valley, decorated with snow-banners. . . . I have seen only one display of this kind that seemed in every way perfect. This was in the winter of 1873, when the snow-laden summits were swept by a wild "norther." I happened at the time to be wintering in Yosemite Valley, that sublime Sierra temple where every day one may see the grandest sights. Yet even here the wild gala-day of the north wind seemed surpassingly glorious. I was awakened in the morning by the rocking of my cabin and the beating of pine-burs on the roof. Detached torrents and avalanches from the main wind-flood overhead were rushing wildly down the narrow side cañons, and over the precipitous walls, with loud resounding roar, rousing the pines to enthusiastic action, and making the whole valley vibrate as though it were an instrument being played.

2 Indian Cañon, through which I climbed, was choked with snow that had been shot down in avalanches from the high cliffs on either side, rendering the ascent difficult; but inspired by the roaring storm, the tedious wallowing brought no fatigue, and in four hours I gained the top of a ridge above the valley, 8000 feet high. And there in bold relief, like a clear painting, appeared a most imposing scene. Innumerable peaks, black and sharp, rose grandly into the dark blue sky, their bases set in solid white, their sides streaked and splashed with snow, like ocean rocks with foam, and from every summit, all free and unconfused, was streaming a beautiful silky silvery banner, from half a mile to a mile in length, slender at the point of attachment, then widening gradually as it extended from the peak until it was about 1000 or 1500 feet in breadth, as near as I could estimate. . . .

Muir's spelling of *canyon* is the Spanish spelling, *cañon,* which is pronounced as if the *y* were present. Muir's spelling is doubtless traceable to the heavy Spanish influence in California place-names: Los Angeles ("The Angels"), San Francisco ("Saint Francis"), Chico ("young boy"), and so on.

Fancy yourself standing on this Yosemite ridge looking eastward. You notice a strange garish glitter in the air. The gale drives wildly overhead with a fierce, tempestuous roar, but its violence is not felt, for you are looking through a sheltered opening in the woods as through a window. There, in the immediate foreground of your picture, rises a majestic forest of Silver Fir blooming in eternal freshness, the foliage yellow-green, and the snow beneath the trees strewn with their beautiful plumes, plucked off by the wind. Beyond, and extending over all the middle ground, are somber swaths of pine, interrupted by huge swelling ridges and domes; and just beyond the dark forest you see the monarchs of the High Sierra waving their magnificent banners. They are twenty miles away, but you would not wish them nearer, for every feature is distinct, and the whole glorious show is seen in its right proportions. After this general view, mark how sharply the dark snowless ribs and buttresses and summits of the peaks are defined, excepting the portions veiled by the banners, and how delicately their sides are streaked with snow, where it has come to rest in narrow flutings and gorges. Mark, too, how grandly the banners wave as the wind is deflected against their sides, and how trimly each is attached to the very summit of its peak, like a streamer at a masthead; how smooth and silky they are in texture, and how finely their fading fringes are pencilled on the azure sky. See how dense and opaque they are at the point of attachment, and how filmy and translucent toward the end, so that the peaks back of them are seen dimly, as though you were looking through ground glass. Yet again observe how some of the longest, belonging to the loftiest summits, stream perfectly free all the way across intervening notches and passes from peak to peak, while others overlap and partly hide each other. And consider how keenly every particle of this wondrous cloth of snow is flashing out jets of light. These are the main features of the beautiful and terrible picture as seen from the forest window; and it would still be surpassingly glorious were the fore- and middle-grounds obliterated altogether, leaving only the black peaks, the white banners, and the blue sky. 3

Questions for Writing and Discussion

Prepare short written answers to each of these questions. Be prepared to hand them in and/or discuss them in class, as your teacher directs.

1. What do the following words mean—*precipitous* (¶ 1), *tempestuous, flutings, opaque,* and *translucent* (¶ 3)?
2. In describing the "snow banners," Muir relies heavily on detail forged with figurative language. In fact, "snow banners" is itself a metaphor. What other figures of speech in the passage caught your attention and enhanced your mental image of what Muir is describing?
3. For what reading audience do you suppose Muir was writing? In what ways is that audience now different? In what ways the same? How much of what you say about his audiences—then and now—comes from qualities within the text itself, and how much comes from other knowledge you may have?

You might review the Muir piece with students, this time underlining every descriptive word. More than many other writers, Muir builds his writing on

Muir is writing here about an impressive natural occurrence, a glorious thing. His purpose is to write vividly enough to enable his readers to share his sense of awe at what he has witnessed; he wants the thing he saw to be "seen" again through the imaginative eyes of his readers. He seeks, therefore, to inform and entertain through describing. In the following piece, however, in which Jack Rosenthal writes of the lowly penny, a common and decidedly unglorious thing, his purpose is the thing's abolition. Notice the contrast between what Muir is doing and what Rosenthal does—one writes to build up, the other to do away with. Note, as you read, how that *different* purpose shapes Rosenthal's writing.

adjectives and adverbs. Ask students what that practice adds to Muir's writing, or have the groups rewrite his piece without those descriptive words.

Dollar Wise, Penny Foolish

JACK ROSENTHAL

Jack Rosenthal is an editor and writer. He was principal author of the Kerner Commission Report on Urban Riots (1968) and in 1982 won the Pulitzer Prize in editorial writing.

1 There's something to value in a penny—a virtuous symbol of thrift, a poignant reminder of the way we were. But what's it *worth?* Not much.

2 Inflation has rendered pennies irrelevant to the price of things. They are reduced to being a nuisance for paying sales taxes, a gimmick for advertising 99-cent sales. Pennies have become so trifling that, to judge from the litter on New York sidewalks, only the penurious stoop to pick them up.

3 It's time to get rid of them, but don't hold your breath. The Treasury tried to do just that in the mid-1970's, but a newly elected Carter Administration scotched the idea. The public demand for pennies has declined in recent years, but the U.S. Mint still stamped out more than 10 billion in 1988—and somehow, somewhere, half of them vanished. Somebody out there must like them.

4 The only serious proposal to abolish the penny comes from Representatives Jim Kolbe and Morris Udall of Arizona, the principal source of American copper. No, they haven't forgotten who elected them. Their primary aim is a new dollar coin to be made mostly of copper. To that end, they've reintroduced a bill that had 65 co-sponsors last year but went nowhere; a subsection would order a study on phasing out pennies. (Since 1982, pennies have been mostly zinc with a copper coating; the proposed new dollar would be 80 percent copper, mixed or coated to look like gold.)

5 The bill is unnecessarily handicapped by a special-interest proviso that the new dollar use only American copper. Let the mint decide what to use and where to buy it. But Messrs. Kolbe and Udall are onto something. America's coinage and currency are out of date.

6 Official thinking on the dollar has been frozen by the Susan B. Anthony fiasco 10 years ago, another Carter misstep. The Anthony silver dollar bombed because it was too much like a quarter—same color, same ribbed

Examine with your students the feasibility of this plan to do away with pennies and make copper $1.00 coins. First, Rosenthal calls pennies "a nuisance for paying sales taxes." But if pennies were done away with, how would we pay sales taxes? How would we avoid *having* to raise (or lower, ho, ho, ho) such taxes to, say, 5¢ for the most minimal purchase—even one costing less than $1.00? The fact is that sales taxes (anywhere from 3¢ to 8¢ on each $1.00's worth of purchase) are widespread in the United States, making total purchase transactions involving pennies extremely common.

Second, if paper $1.00 bills were replaced by copper $1.00 coins, what kinds of inconveniences might ensue? Imagine, for example, the common situation in which change must be given in denominations of a dollar. Say that a 75¢ purchase is made with a $20.00 bill but the seller has nothing larger than ones in the till. If those "ones" are paper dollars, carrying that much change is a bit of a nuisance but is still feasible. Yet imagine what happens if those "ones" are large copper or silver coins.

Students can use some of these arguments in the "Bridges" exercise.

edge and virtually the same size. A new design need pose no difficulty. The greater problem is public resistance, which requires a broad plan that makes popular sense. The Kolbe-Udall bill asks the Treasury to study not just a phaseout of pennies but also 50-cent pieces, because they are cumbersome and not widely used.

Since 1980, nine countries have successfully introduced a high-denomination coin to replace paper currency—among them a British pound, a Dutch five-guilder piece and a Canadian dollar. To speed public acceptance, authorities have removed the paper equivalents from circulation, or allowed them to disappear with wear and tear. 7

It's estimated that retiring the penny and introducing a dollar coin to replace paper dollars would save the Government more than $100 million a year. This would delight shopkeepers, vending machine makers and public transit systems. And it would spare the public an increasingly senseless hassle with money whose time is past. 8

Questions for Writing and Discussion

Prepare short written answers to each of these questions. Be prepared to hand them in and/or discuss them in class, as your teacher directs.

1. What do the following words mean—*poignant* (¶ 1), *penurious* (¶ 2), *scotched* (¶ 3), *proviso* (¶ 5), *fiasco* (¶ 6)?
2. What kind of case does Rosenthal make against the penny—fact, interpretation, value, policy, or a combination (see chapter 7 to review those)? Give reasons for your judgment.
3. Examine Rosenthal's support for his argument that "America's coinage and currency are out of date" (¶ 5). How persuasive is he? Consider these additional questions:
   a. How do *you* use pennies?
   b. Would you pick up a penny lying on the ground? Why or why not?
4. How does Rosenthal use the metal analysis of coins to boost his argument?
5. At what readership does Rosenthal aim this piece? What evidence do you find that he seems to assume most of his readers will agree with him?

Bridges: Another Perspective

Imagine that you are on a debate team. In an upcoming debate, your opponent will present, in essence, Rosenthal's argument in favor of abolishing the penny. Your assignment is to counter his argument—to present the most effective argument you can for *keeping* the penny. Consult your classmates and friends: what ideas can they contribute in favor of pennies? Check the library: can you find any articles on the subject? Gather your argument and present it to the class.

Once you have a good list of pros and cons, you can work with your students to develop skeleton outlines of several different kinds of argumentative

While Muir writes of beautiful things for an aesthetic response from his readers and Rosenthal writes of common things for a reader response of practical action, columnist William Raspberry, in the following piece, writes about standardized tests—things that by themselves seem harmless enough but because of the way they are used create great controversy.

papers they might write on the topic. This topic is fun to play with, for students usually don't have to sidestep anyone's deeply held, strong feelings on it. (For many classes, however, that also makes the writing topic less than desirable.)

PREREADING WORKSHEET

Before you read the following piece by William Raspberry, write brief responses to these questions:

1. What standardized tests have you taken?
2. What effect(s) did those standardized tests have on you? Consider:
   a. Academic credit you received (or didn't receive) because of your test scores
   b. Courses you skipped (or didn't skip) because of your test scores
   c. Groups you joined (or didn't join) because of your test scores
   d. Jobs you got (or didn't get) because of your test scores
   e. Other effects
3. Do you think some standardized tests are better, more useful, or more meaningful than others? Why or why not?
4. What important standardized tests lie in your future? How do you know? How do you feel about them?

As we are editing this manuscript (in the spring of 1991), standardized tests seem still to be on the rise. At one of our universities, students have to take a test not only to get in but also when they leave! For the exit exam, students are told that their own graduation does not hinge on the results but that part of the school's budget appropriation from the state does. Ask your students if they've ever taken a test whose outcome made no difference to them and if so, how they did on it. Some of them may want to research the role of motivation in standardized test taking.

Standardized Tests Are Means, Not Ends

WILLIAM RASPBERRY *(See the headnote on page 50.)*

1 WASHINGTON—When it comes to standardized tests, there are two kinds of idiots: those who think the tests can measure nothing worth measuring and want them abolished, and those who think the tests can measure anything and want them enshrined.

2 The first category includes the researcher who, in the course of arguing against reliance on standardized tests as a "single criterion," told me a couple of weeks ago that flunking a general math test should not be accepted as evidence of unfitness to teach math.

3 The second surely must include the people who adopted Maryland's statewide writing proficiency test. Officials there, dismayed that almost half the 11th graders who have taken the test have failed it, are now looking at a $183,000 packet of changes in the testing program. The chances are it will be wasted money.

4 As a professional writer, it shouldn't be necessary to point out that I am not opposed to the teaching of writing skills, which I consider not just possible but vital. I have argued for years that children ought to be required to do far more writing than they now do: how-to writing, expository writing, descriptive writing, factual writing, argument, summary—all sorts of writing.

It's true William Raspberry is a professional writer, and a good, highly respected one. But here he produces a dangling modifier ("As a professional writer, it shouldn't be necessary . . . "), proving, we suppose, that even good professional writers and their editors make occasional mechanical errors that equally good professional proofreaders somehow miss. All that should be encouraging to some of your student writers.

5 I have threatened to organize sledgehammer-wielding posses to raid the schools for the salutary purpose of busting up those destroyers of writing: the ditto machines. The best way for children to learn writing, I have argued in my simpleminded way, is to let them write. The surest way to stunt whatever writing ability they may possess is to let them get by with filling in blanks on ditto sheets. ("Columbus' three ships were the (blank), the (blank), and the (blankety blank).")

6 But if teaching writing is vital, the standardized testing of writing is virtually impossible, like trying to devise standardized tests for painting, or singing, or public speaking.

7 Maryland, to its credit, didn't fall into the trap that ensnared some other school systems a few years back: the ludicrous attempt to test writing ability by penciling in the appropriate squares on machine-gradable answer sheets. Instead, it chose to rely on a panel of experts to assign numerical grades (based on necessarily subjective criteria) to writing samples. Still, they were embarrassed a few weeks back when newspapers published what seemed to be a quite decent sample written by an honor student who, nonetheless, flunked the test.

8 Teachers of writing can grade their pupils' writing ability against principles and techniques taught in class. But teachers—at least the good ones—understand that there are no absolute criteria, comparable to the correct answers in math and social studies. They know better than to put their faith in standardized measures of good writing.

9 What the combatants on both sides of the testing debates ought to recognize is that there are some things that standardized tests can measure (mathematical computation, facts, spelling, reading comprehension) and some things that are best measured by those who teach them (artistic expression, teaching technique, writing).

10 Some who oppose virtually all standardized testing really are opposed (it seems to me) to the unpalatable truths that such tests can reveal, including the fact that low-income and minority students tend to do less well on the tests than middle-class whites. Outlawing tests in an effort to mask these unpleasant facts makes about as much sense as outlawing thermometers and electrocardiograph machines to mask the fact that minorities tend to suffer poorer health.

11 But it's important to recognize that there are some things that standardized tests cannot do sufficiently well to make them worthwhile. Measuring writing skill is one of them.

Most large standardized tests now include "writing samples," usually twenty-minute drafts on a topic like "Fortune Favors the Brave." Discuss with students the ways in which that kind of setting, procedure, and topic violate much of what is presented in this book. Once students are confirmed in their opposition (and most if not all of them will be), ask them to come up with feasible alternatives—a reasonably inexpensive way, for example, to test a hundred thousand high school seniors each December in order to let their prospective colleges know something about their writing ability by January. (*Hint:* that "coming up with an alternative" isn't easy.)

POSTREADING WORKSHEET

Now that you have read the piece by Raspberry, write your responses to the following questions:

1. Do you agree, partly agree, or disagree with Raspberry on the subject of standardized tests? Which, and why?

2. Has Raspberry's argument in any way changed your mind about standardized tests? If so, in what way?
3. Many states have instituted minimum competency testing in basic subjects that must be passed before a student can graduate from high school. Do you have experience with such tests, or do you know anyone who does? Do those tests (as differentiated from SAT, ACT, and other college entrance tests) strike you as reasonable and fair?
4. How many attempts should a candidate be allowed to pass an important professional certifying exam, such as attorneys' state bar exams, accountants' CPA exams, or medical doctors' medical boards? What is the basis for your response?

An alternative writing assignment for standardized tests is that given on the LSAT, which runs something like this: "Judy Smith is an interior decorator with three years' experience working for a large design firm. She would like to start her own business, believing some of the major clients for her current firm would stay with her if she did; however, she lacks the capital to open a business. Meanwhile, she is renting an apartment and wishes she had a down payment to buy a home of her own. Her great-uncle leaves her ten thousand dollars in his will. Should she use the money to start a business or to put a down payment on a house?" Present this to your students (even better, find some old LSATs and use the actual topics) and ask them to discuss how or why this is or isn't a fairer test of writing ability than such a topic as "Fortune Favors the Brave." (See also pp. 309–11). The important issues for writers here are the ones we began our book with—purpose, setting, and so on.

Questions for Writing and Discussion

Prepare short written answers to each of these questions. Be prepared to hand them in and/or discuss them in class, as your teacher directs.

1. What do the following words mean—*subjective criteria* (¶ 7), *unpalatable* (¶ 10)?
2. Which sentence would you isolate as being the one carrying Raspberry's main idea? Why?
3. Raspberry writes about standardized tests in order to urge limitations on how they are used or interpreted. Is his argument therefore one of interpretation? or of policy? or value? What makes you think so? Does he use fact in any way?

Of course, a thing can also be a gadget—a tool, a pair of scissors, or perhaps something more complicated, like an electric can opener, an electronic typewriter, or a computer. Here is some writing about a thing—in this case, a computer mouse.

Logitech C7 Mouse

LOGITECH

Yes, we know this isn't an essay. But not all expository writing is essay writing. What makes "an essay" anyway, and what's the value of that distinction? If one were to fill in the missing verbs from the summary-style lines in this piece (for example, "Logitech C7 Mouse Driver—high performance implementation of industry standard mouse interface" would become "The Logitech C7 mouse driver provides users with high-performance implementa-

1 At **Logitech** we've spent years developing the most advanced mouse hardware and software. We provide the mouse for many of the industry's largest computer manufacturers, and have earned the reputation of the world's leading mouse experts. The **Logitech C7 Mouse** is part of our retail line of high quality mouse input devices.

Logitech C7 Mouse Features:

2
- Opto-Mechanical
- No Pad, No Power Supply Required

tion of our industry-standard mouse interface") and create paragraphing, would it be an essay? Ask your students to try it.

By the way, the classic meaning of the word *essay* derives from its use as a verb, meaning "to attempt" as in "I shall essay to solve the riddle." The word came to be associated with written *attempts* to persuade, explain, analyze, or express—in other words, the motives, purposes, or, as we have chosen to call them, *reasons* for writing.

- High Resolution (200 dots per inch)
- Programmable Baud Rate (up to 9600 bauds)
- High Quality Tactile Feedback Switches
- 3-Button Design

Logitech C7 Mouse Software:

- **Logitech C7 Mouse Driver**—high performance implementation of industry standard mouse interface. Fully compatible with all mouse-based applications. 3
- **Logimenu**—a programmable pop-up menu system for keyboard based applications. We provide menus for the most widely used applications. Use them as is, customize them, or create new ones for other applications. 4
- **Click**—a new concept in mouse software. **Click** resides in memory, detects which application you're using, and sets the mouse automatically to your predefined setting. Just add **Click** to your autoexec file and the **Logitech C7 Mouse** will be ready to go with each of your favorite applications. 5
- **Point and Click Shell** for Lotus 1–2–3™—no more jerky cursor movement, no more delays, no more beeping. Our software shell fully integrates the **Logitech C7 Mouse** into 1–2–3, and makes even experienced 1–2–3 users up to 30% more productive. 6
- **Point Editor**—the easy to use, mouse based text editor featuring multiple windows and color support. If you think a mouse was not meant for editing, **Point** will change your mind. 7

Questions for Writing and Discussion

Prepare short written answers to each of these questions. Be prepared to hand them in and/or discuss them in class, as your teacher directs.

1. How does the "chart" display style that categorizes the mouse features enhance understanding of its characteristics?
2. How does the writing in this selection work both for information and for advertising purposes?
3. What kind of computer-operating knowledge does the writer assume readers of this piece have? Consider the following words: *hardware, software, input devices* (¶ 1), *high resolution, baud rate* (¶ 2), *driver, interface* (¶ 3), *menu system* (¶ 4), *memory, autoexec* (¶ 5), and *cursor* (¶ 6).
4. If you didn't already know what this kind of mouse is or what it does, how helpful would this passage be? What does that tell you about its intended audience?

By now it's probably obvious that writing about things can be as diverse as other kinds of writing, and that the reasons for writing about things are as many and varied as a word like *things* implies. Informing, explaining, entertaining, persuading, analyzing, expressing, even selling—all these and more are reasons that can be turned to the service of writing about things. The following selection, written by a college student, informs and explains about a thing called a living will. As you read it, see if you hear echoes of one or more of the other pieces that begin this chapter, not so much in language and style as in the purpose(s) the author is trying to serve with her writing.

The Living Will

Kristy Porter, college writing student

1 You lie in a hospital bed. A respirator helps you breathe. A heart monitor keeps track of your heartbeat. You are unconscious. You are physically alive, but are you living? Some would say yes; some would say no. The most important question is, Do you think you are alive?

We can all envision situations in which this subject might be emotionally difficult for some students to deal with. We don't shy away from dealing with such subjects in our classes but, for that reason, are also careful not to approach such readings jokingly. There's nothing wrong with saying to your students, "This is a serious topic, and we'll treat it with sensitivity and tact." You can do that and still learn from how Kristy writes her paper.

2 Hundreds of people are in this position every day, but because they are incompetent they cannot make important decisions for themselves. The answer to this situation is a living will, a written statement to family and doctors stating wishes pertaining to medical care after one becomes incompetent. This legal document accomplishes two things. It gives the doctor immunity from liability for stopping medical treatment, and it requires that the doctor follow the directions of the will or give up the case (Robertson 97). Living wills are recognized in many states, but they are not always followed as they should be.

3 One problem with the living will is that the patient's family is not always aware of its existence. Copies of the living will should be given to family members as soon as the will is written. It should also be placed in medical records, and a person may want to carry a small card to note that he or she has a living will (Robertson 109). These things help to guarantee that the living will is carried out.

4 Another problem with the living will is that the family of the patient may attempt to override it. Several states have legislation to prevent this, but some do not. To ensure that the living will is carried out, the patient should obtain legal advice, follow state statutes in drawing up the will, and have at least two persons witness it. If a person revokes the will

without consent of the patient, he or she can be charged with a misdemeanor and/or sued by the patient's estate (Robertson 110-11).

Because some states recognize the living will while others do not, 5
there is some discrepancy as to how to execute these wills from state to state. Ideally, the wills should be carried out as they are written. They can be specific enough so that the patient's wishes are clear in any given situation. Physicians should be allowed to follow the directions of a living will in all states without the fear of legal reprisal.

Opponents of living wills argue that this refusal of medical 6
treatment is a form of suicide. Most laws governing the wills state that this is not suicide, because refusing medical treatment while one is competent would not be considered suicide (Robertson 108). These laws claim that a medically terminal patient has a right to live as well as a right to die, and that right should be granted.

Not only does a living will make a difficult time easier for the family, 7
but it also ensures that the wishes of the patient are carried out. If all states legalized this document, there would be no question as to what should be done when a patient is near death. Some people do not wish to be kept alive by machines, medicine, and so forth when they really are not living. Although patients may not be able to vocalize their wishes at the time, if they have had the motivation to make a living will, that will should be carried out.

Source

Robertson, John A. The Rights of the Critically Ill. Cambridge, Mass.: Ballinger, 1983.

Questions for Writing and Discussion

Prepare short written answers to each of these questions. Be prepared to hand them in and/or discuss them in class, as your teacher directs.

1. In what special sense does the writer use the word *incompetent* (¶ 2)?
2. What is the effect of beginning this piece with a series of short sentences addressed to the reader as an individual?
3. How does the writer organize the paper around the problems associated with living wills?

4. How does the writer document the information she paraphrases?
5. In your opinion, is the paper weakened by the fact that all its technical information on living wills seems to come from one source? In other words, has the writer, by consulting only one source, *earned* the voice she seems to use in her paper—the voice of one who is quite well informed on living wills?
6. From your perspective as a reader, do you think the paper fails to answer any important questions about living wills? If so, list some of those questions.
7. How would you recommend the writer proceed if she wanted to make the paper a better piece of writing—that is, if her teacher were to say to her, "This is good as far as it goes. Why don't you do a little bit more digging on the subject, take a few more pages, and see just how solid you can make it?" What specific points in the paper do you think might benefit from more detail? from more elaboration? What other points should the writer cover?

KEY POINTS TO REMEMBER: Writing About Things

When writing about things, keep the following in mind:

- Realize that your reason may be as important as the subject is.
- Use the right details to make your subject distinctive.
- Use appropriate levels of language and details.

Realize That Your Reason May Be as Important as the Subject Is

John Muir wished to share the awesome beauty of the snow banners. Only he had seen them, high in an isolated part of the Sierras, and he knew he had witnessed a beautiful thing that deserved telling about. Telling about the snow banners gives them a life, a memory, that we now read more than a hundred years later, and the communication over the years remains valuable long after the wind and the snow banners and Muir himself are gone. Jack Rosenthal writes about pennies, making it clear that he doesn't consider them important anymore; his point is that they're useless and obsolete. Clearly, William Raspberry thinks it's what the public wants to make of standardized tests—not so much the tests themselves—that needs attention. Kristy Porter emphasizes that the living will, to be any good, must be followed. And even a Logitech mouse is useless if its prospective owners don't know, or learn, what to do with it.

Use the Right Details to Make Your Subject Distinctive

Muir uses rich figurative language to emphasize the distinctiveness of the area and the snow banners:

> . . . that sublime Sierra temple where every day one may see the grandest sights.

You might want to remind students that "figurative language" is a broad phrase that includes various figures of speech. These examples from Muir, for instance, are (in order)

straight metaphor—"Sierra temple" (mountain = temple);

simile—valley vibrates *as though* it were "an instrument being played";
personification—"Cañon . . . choked" (canon = person); and
straight metaphor—"silky banner" (blowing snow = silk banner).

> . . . making the whole valley vibrate as though it were an instrument being played.
>
> . . . Indian Cañon . . . was choked with snow.
>
> . . . and from every summit, all free and unconfused, was streaming a beautiful silky banner.

Jack Rosenthal uses matter-of-fact information to enlighten anyone who may still think pennies are all copper: "Since 1982, pennies have been mostly zinc with a copper coating." William Raspberry uses humorous overstatement to launch his ultimately serious indictment of our mania for standardized tests: "When it comes to standardized tests, there are two kinds of idiots." And the makers of the Logitech mouse want users to know how compatible their product is with hardware manufactured by other companies; they don't hesitate to use computer jargon to ease their reader's concern: "Logitech C7 Mouse Driver—high performance implementation of industry standard mouse interface."

Use Appropriate Levels of Language and Detail

John Muir envisions an imaginative reader, someone capable of "seeing" what he so carefully describes. Jack Rosenthal seeks to convince most readers of the *New York Times* of the uselessness of the penny. Kristy Porter wishes to inform her classmates, other students in freshman English, and friends about living wills; she thus reduces specialized technical language, avoiding legalistic, dense detail in favor of explaining the "gist," or basic meaning, of living wills.

✓✓✓ **WORKSHEET: Writing About Things**

The key question here: what is different about the writing process when it's being done about a thing rather than a person or a situation?

Let's review the entire writing process as it can be applied in writing about things.

1. First, consider the thing you are writing about. What is it? Why are you writing about it? What is important about it? Who will be interested in reading about it and why? Jot down answers to those questions.
2. Next, consider the *details* you will need to fully treat the thing you've chosen. What characteristics are essential to convey? What details will give your readers the fullest, clearest picture or understanding of the thing? What details will already be clear to readers? What details will need explanation or elaboration?
3. Now write your first draft. Let its structure emerge from the details: what should your reader read first? What comes next? and next? How are you providing coherence—by physical relationships (the finger bones connect to the hand bones, which in turn connect to the small bones in the flexible wrist, and so on)? by narration in time ("We pulled off the road, parked on a level spot, and blocked the wheel opposite the flat tire. Then we opened the trunk and removed the jack")? or by some other method? No matter what order you draft things in, make sure your first full draft has a clear beginning, middle, and end before you share it with other readers.

4. Then share your draft with other readers. Ask for their reactions and suggestions, and discuss the draft with them.
5. Now revise the draft and edit out errors, repetitious or misfiring phrases, and the like. Polish the writing until you're ready to write the final draft. Then write that draft.

Ask students where in this process the 80 percent fix occurs. We think it's about here.

6. Next, carefully proofread the final draft. Remember, we recommend that you try reading your paper backward, from the end to the beginning, and doing so not word for word (which would be gibberish) but sentence by sentence; you'll thus concentrate more on individual sentences and be more likely to catch misspellings, omissions, and other errors. After following that process, focus next on *each* mark of punctuation—can you give a *reason* for that mark? To help answer questions, refer to the handbook section of this book (if you have the hardbound edition) or to a separate handbook. Make any necessary corrections, and make a copy of your paper.
7. Finally, hand in the original—and breathe a sigh of relief!

SAMPLE WRITING ASSIGNMENT AND CASE STUDY CLOSE-UP

The version of Kristy Porter's paper on the living will that you saw earlier in this chapter was actually her third full draft. Her second full draft was reviewed by one of her classmates and by her teacher. In this section we want to show you some of the comments that second draft got and the changes Kristy made, to give you a better idea of what one kind of *finishing* of a paper like this involves. Then we'll show you how Kristy herself found another kind of finishing process that enabled her to get more out of the work she put into writing the paper.

Once again, our plan is to show students the "messy work" that occurs in the process of any piece of writing. Our point isn't that this is exactly *the* right or archetypical kind of messy work; rather, we're trying to reach those students who think final drafts happen cleanly, smoothly, and immediately. Here's a nice figure for you to use: by the time the approximately twelve-hundred-page manuscript for this book was completed, we ran through more than five boxes of paper, each containing twenty-five hundred sheets!

Finishing Kristy's Paper: The Teacher's and a Classmate's Feedback on the Second Draft

Kristy's teacher commented on the last sentence in draft 2's first paragraph: "The most important question is, Do you think you are alive?" Feedback from her teacher helped Kristy realize that her meaning would be clearer—and the sentence more effective—if she underlined *you,* for "The most important question is, Do *you* think you are alive?"

Draft 2's second paragraph used the word *everyday.* The correct form here is the two-word version, *every day.*

In her documentation (the way she cited her source), Kristy had consistently put the period before the parentheses, as in ". . . or give up the case. (Robertson 97)" in her second paragraph. But her classmate pointed out that the documentation style the teacher had requested (Modern Language Association, or MLA, style) puts the sentence period *after* the parentheses.

In Kristy's third paragraph, draft 2 had originally begun, "One problem with the living will is that the family is not always aware of its existence." Adding the word *patient's* before *family* clarifies which family Kristy is talking about: "One problem with the living will is that the patient's family is not always aware of its existence." And the following sentence had originally read, "Copies of the living will should be given to family members." Adding "as soon the will is written" to the end of that sentence emphasizes the topic's timeliness.

Also in the third paragraph, draft 2 had read, ". . . a person may want to carry a small card to note that he has a living will." Changing the phrase to read "he or she" avoids the unnecessary sexist usage. And whereas the next sentence had read, "These things help to guarantee that it is carried out," Kristy, to avoid the unclear pronoun *it,* substituted "the living will."

Similarly, in the fifth paragraph Kristy replaced "Because some states recognize them while others do not" with "Because some states recognize the living will while others do not." And in the following sentence, draft 2 had read, "The wills should be carried out as they are written," a statement her teacher thought conveyed a tone of command that seemed to be ordering readers around. Putting the word *ideally* in front of that sentence softens and clarifies it.

Another sentence in the fifth paragraph had read, "Physicians should be allowed to follow the directions of a living will in all states without being charged with murder." To cover other lawsuit possibilities, besides those which might come from the death of the patient, Kristy broadened the phrase to "without the fear of legal reprisal."

Obviously, it's not the easiest thing in the world for your students to keep both the "before" and the "after" versions of Kristy's paper in mind while reading through these changes. You can reinforce the idea here if you bring in drafts of a student's paper (with permission, of course) and use an overhead projector to show the "before" version, the changes, and the "after" version.

In the sixth paragraph she had written, "These laws claim that an individual has a right to live . . . "; here her teacher and classmate both thought "an individual" was too general, and so Kristy changed it to "These laws claim that a medically terminal patient has a right to live . . . " And at the end of that sentence she had written, "and his rights should be granted." Again, to be more specific, she changed the wording to "and that right should be granted."

Finally, Kristy's last paragraph had concluded, "Although a patient may not be able to vocalize his wishes at the time, if he has had the motivation to make a living will, it should be carried out." To avoid the sexist usage ("his," "he"), she made the subject plural ("patients . . . their wishes . . . they"). And to clarify the pronoun reference for "it," she substituted "that will."

Another Kind of Finishing: For a Different Audience and Purpose

For that paper, Kristy got an A from her English teacher. She enjoyed the experience of writing the paper, and she found the subject interesting. She had originally heard about the subject in an ethics class she was taking in the philosophy department; the class had done a three-week unit on how advances in modern medical technology present ethical problems humanity has heretofore not had to face. Living wills are one kind of solution to an aspect of such problems. Because Kristy had to write a ten-page research paper for the ethics class, and because this topic interested her (and she had been successful with it), she asked her English teacher whether it would be all right to use her English paper as the beginning of the ethics paper. Her English teacher said that it probably would be but that Kristy must be sure to get her ethics teacher's permission, too. Kristy got permission, and then she faced a new problem:

What do you do with a piece of writing that you already know is good when you want to make it *better*? And how do you adapt a piece of writing originally written for one set of reasons and for one audience to a different set of reasons and a different audience?

We really like this idea because it conforms to our experience as writers and because we think any writer who has this experience learns something important from it. You have a piece you think is good enough for situation A, and maybe it is, but then someone comes along and wants you to make changes in it and to make it better for situation B. This is a good learning experience for any writer, at any level.

Kristy posed these writing questions to the small group of students in her English class with whom she regularly shared writing problems. Here is the gist of what they said to her (her teacher was involved in this too):

> Kristy, you know we all thought this was a good paper the last time we looked at it. That last wave of changes really fixed it up. But there was one thing that kind of bothered us that we never really did anything about. You use only one source for the whole paper. It leaves you coming off as some kind of "instant expert," talking in a voice you really haven't earned. Well, that probably goes with the territory of writing this kind of paper *at this length* for freshman English. But since you have more pages to work with for the ethics class, and since you're writing for an audience that knows more about the subject than we do (or than our freshman English teacher does), we think what you need to do is to dig deeper into the library on this subject, to find more facts and figures, concrete pieces of information of all kinds. You might even want to do an interview or two: with someone who has made a living will, or a lawyer, or a member of the clergy, or a doctor.

That sounded like a good plan to Kristy. Accordingly, she and her friends dove into a group brainstorming session, with copies of the paper in front of them, to help Kristy find *specific* places in the paper where she could do more with it. Here's her paper again, this time with the brainstorming comments also displayed in the margin:

1 You lie in a hospital bed. A respirator helps you breathe. A heart monitor keeps track of your heartbeat. You are unconscious. You are physically alive, but are you living? Some would say yes; some would say no. The most important question is, Do you think you are alive?

2 Hundreds of people are in this position every day, but because they are incompetent they cannot make important decisions for themselves. The answer to this situation is a living will, a written statement to family and doctors stating wishes pertaining to medical care after one becomes incompetent. This legal document accomplishes two things. It gives the doctor immunity from liability for stopping medical treatment, and it requires that the doctor follow the directions of the will or give up the case (Robertson 97). Living wills are recognized in many states, but they are not always followed as they should be.

Some real-life examples with people's names, etc., would drive this question home.

Can you find out exactly how many people are in this position on an average day? "Hundreds" fuzzes over a key point.

Incompetent how? Are there different ways? An extra sentence or two starting with, "They may be . . . , or maybe they are . . . , or maybe they are just . . . , but in each case they . . . ," could make this more solid.

How many states? Are there *notable* exceptions, places

> **where, because the wills are not recognized, there have been well-documented problems?**
>
> **Can you show us one of those cards and a living will? You can put them in an appendix and refer to them in the paper.**
>
> **Can you give us some examples of attempts to override wills?**
>
> **What states? How many states? See how "several" and "some" in this sentence weaken your right to pretend to be an authority on this?**
>
> **Are there examples of a person being charged or sued?**

3 One problem with the living will is that the patient's family is not always aware of its existence. Copies of the living will should be given to family members as soon as the will is written. It should also be placed in medical records, and a person may want to carry a small card to note that he or she has a living will (109). These things help to guarantee that the will is carried out.

4 Another problem with the living will is that the family of the patient may attempt to override it. Several states have legislation to prevent this, but some do not. To ensure that the living will is carried out, the patient should obtain legal advice, follow state statutes in drawing up the will, and have at least two persons witness it. If a person revokes the will without consent of the patient, that person can be charged with a misdemeanor and/or sued by the patient's estate (110-11).

> **Have there in fact been such reprisals? Tell us the story; don't just hint that there's a story there.**

5 Because some states recognize the living will while others do not, there is some discrepancy as to how to execute these wills from state to state. Ideally, the wills should be carried out as they are written. They can be specific enough so that the patient's wishes are clear in any given situation. Physicians should be allowed to follow the directions of a living will in all states without the fear of legal reprisal.

6 Opponents of living wills argue that this refusal of medical treatment is a form of suicide. Most laws governing the wills state that this is not suicide, because refusing medical treatment while one is competent would not be considered suicide (108). These laws claim that a medically terminal patient has a right to live as well as a right to die, and that right should be granted.

> **How does that make it easier for the family?**

7 Not only does a living will make a difficult time easier for the family, but it also ensures that the wishes of the patient are carried out. If all states legalized this document, there would be no question as to what should be done when a patient is near death. Some people do not wish to be kept alive by machines, medicine, and so forth when they really are not living. Although patients may not be able to vocalize their wishes at the time, if they have had the motivation to make a living will, that will should be carried out.

> **There must be plenty of magazine and newspaper articles about living wills. Why not check the *Readers' Guide to Periodical Literature* and the *New York Times Index* for some additional sources?**

Source

Robertson, John A. The Rights of the Critically Ill. Cambridge, Mass.: Ballinger, 1983.

After this productive work session, Kristy felt confident she had the feedback she needed to write a good paper for her ethics class. And that is exactly what she did.

WRITING ASSIGNMENTS

1. Write about your first bicycle, go-cart, or automobile. What details about it can you remember? What incidents and adventures? How did the thing itself play a role in your experience?
2. Write about your first conscious experience with an abstract thing—jealousy, anger, despair, joy, love, fear. How did it affect you? What did you learn from it?
3. Explain how some thing works: an air pump, an adjustable wrench, an amplifier, a compact disc player. Or do the same for the human heart or some other vital organ. Imagine a reader who knows very little about the thing you've chosen: how will you make your choice's function clear? Use illustrations if you like, but coordinate them with your writing.
4. Define some thing, explaining what it is and what its uses are: petroleum, calculators, VCRs, an index, a CB radio, a laser, fiber optics, napalm, aspartame, heavy water, light water.
5. Imagine you are a Red Cross instructor. Write a pamphlet explaining the Heimlich maneuver or cardiopulmonary resuscitation. Draw illustrations if you can. Your readers are students taking a safety class.
6. Consider again the photograph on page 217, showing a computer chip passing through the eye of a needle. To a child, the eye of a needle may seem an impossibly small thing. But, as the photograph shows, we know that size is relative, that one era's incredibly small object is another era's commonplace frame for something that is *really* small. Do a little library research and find out what is the smallest man-made object today, or the smallest natural object, or the smallest sound detectable, or the smallest sheep, the smallest airplane, or whatever. (You can *start* with *Ripley's*, but you'll need to know more about your topic than that.) Write a short paper describing what you've found. Be scrupulous about documenting your sources.

Focus on Critical Writing

7. Find the assembly instructions for a ten-speed bike, a bookcase or study desk, an outdoor barbecue grill, or some other thing requiring assembly. Critique the instructions: how thorough are they? how clear? Are illustrations well coordinated with text? For what age or maturity level are the instructions intended?
8. Select a vital issue involving technological advancements—things we have created that can enhance or destroy the quality of life, such as atomic power, genetic engineering, respirators, pacemakers, and organ transplants. Weigh the benefits and detriments of the invention. Is it ultimately a positive or negative thing?

9. What responses come to your mind at the mention of these things—telephone, chewing gum, candy, toothpaste, measles, mononucleosis, baseball, dentistry, fortune-telling, alcohol, beaches, rainbows? Choose any four and analyze your reactions. Why do you respond as you do?

Writers' Circle

Divide into groups of five, with each group appointing a recorder who will write down the group's findings. Each group should consider some small but common and useful item—something of such everyday value that we usually take it for granted. Name the item; then list what would or could happen did we not have it. To get things rolling, here is an example of possibilities:

Item	Without It
paper clip	1. Staples and staplers would be much more valuable.
	2. More pages of school papers would get lost.
	3. We couldn't make paper-clip chains.

After each group has at least five different items, each recorder should call out the listed items so that the teacher can write each new item on the board, tallying instances when the same item is named more than once. Then the recorder should read the lists of what would or could happen without the items, and the class as a whole can comment or add more instances to those lists. Which items are named the most? Which "result" does the class think is most inventive or humorous?

chapter 12 Writing About Facts

"The notion that writing about science and technology deals exclusively with facts is arbitrary and naive. Problems are not facts; conclusions are not facts; recommendations are not facts. Even when they are based on hard facts, the problems, conclusions, and recommendations must be put into a convincing case or a moving presentation. To be effective in their jobs, engineers and scientists must do much more than inform; they must explain, prove, evaluate, justify, defend, attack, choose, advocate, and refute. Facts alone can do none of these. Clear, well-argued reports and proposals can."

Edmond Weiss

Facts are proved—or provable—statements; they are not opinions, suppositions, theories, or hypotheses. Facts are unwaveringly *true:*

- There are 365 days in a calendar year (*fact*).
- The chemical sign for water is H_2O (*fact*).
- 2 + 2 = 4 (*fact*).
- On Friday, November 22, 1963, President John F. Kennedy was assassinated in Dallas, Texas (*fact*).

"Facts are stupid things," someone once said, and, in a way, that's right. A fact by itself cannot accomplish anything; someone must *use* it—*apply* it in some way so that it takes on meaning in a particular context. For example, two plus two is four. That is a fact, but it doesn't mean much by itself unless you are learning the most elementary kind of mathematics. Yet if you take the same basic arithmetic and apply it in a particular context—even a simple context—much more meaning is generated: "Bob and Elaine will be joining us for lunch," Jeff said to Paige, "so I'll need to set the table for four."

Facts might be called a kind of raw material for thought. Given facts, we think about what they might mean or not mean. A driver's education instructor, for example, tells a young man in her class, "Eighty-five percent of the accidents reported to insurance companies involve male drivers. What conclusions can you draw from that one fact?" The young man ponders a moment and then says, "Men are more careless drivers than women are." Another student, a young woman, says, "That's probably true, but it could also mean that there are more male drivers than female drivers." A third student, less interested in any debates about whether men or women make better drivers, chimes in, "What's really important about that fact is that it makes insurance rates for men drivers higher than for women drivers."

"You're *all* right," says the instructor. "Statistically speaking, men drive more miles in a year than women do. Whether they're by nature more careless than women hasn't been proved, but they definitely are 'on the road' more and therefore more at risk. And they have more accidents, by actual count. Insurance companies take all that into consideration when they set rates, and they *do* charge more to cover men than women." In such a scenario, one fact creates additional thought that has significant consequences.

Much of the richness or interest of facts comes from the thoughts they provoke. Take, for example, the last fact in the list above: "On Friday, November 22, 1963, President John F. Kennedy was assassinated in Dallas, Texas." That fact, sad and true as it is, has over the years spawned a great deal of thought regarding its significance, but most of that thought has not been *factual*. Rather, it has been speculative:

- Kennedy was shot by one man (*considered opinion, but not fact proved beyond doubt*).
- Kennedy was fired on from three different positions overlooking Dallas's Dealey Plaza (*carefully constructed theory but not proved*).
- Kennedy's death was Cuba's revenge for Kennedy-authorized attempts on Fidel Castro's life (*conspiracy theory, not proved*).

Fact is not concerned with what *may* be true. Fact must, by definition, *be* true.

It's fun to ask students at this point what facts they've been presented with in their classes during the past week. List the responses on the board; then review the list to see which ones are indeed facts. (Note that we even had some disagreement from our reviewers on the facts we list at the beginning of the chapter; there seems to be disagreement the world over concerning just what a fact is.)

Facts Can Be Used to Inform, Persuade, Analyze, and Express

The quality of factual truth is what makes writing about facts so important. Because facts are beyond question and utterly reliable, they are vital to several different kinds and purposes of writing.

- Facts *inform*: "At 6:15 P.M. a tornado descended on Pikeville, destroying five homes and damaging twenty more. No one was injured."
- Facts offer support for *persuading*: "The city council must authorize spraying of the Dunlap Addition immediately because conditions there are very swampy, ideal for mosquito hatches. We know that dangerous diseases—including malaria and encephalitis—are carried by mosquitoes. We can't afford to ignore the problem in the Dunlap Addition."
- Facts are often the basis for *analyzing*: "Because 85 percent of all automobile accidents reported to insurance companies involve men drivers, insurance companies charge more money to insure male drivers."
- Facts can even be the basis for *expressive* writing: "That Friday after lunch I saw Arvid Unruh walking down the hallway, shaking his head, his face flushed with rage. 'Kennedy's been shot. Just a little bit ago. He's dead, man.' He didn't pause to answer any questions, and the way he pushed on past me made me know in my guts that this was no joke. At the end of the hall, the television lounge, usually deserted that time of day, was full of quiet students, some weeping, some simply staring, all stunned as they watched and listened to CBS news anchor Walter Cronkite tell them the shattering fact that

Some of your more perceptive students will at this point recognize what we are showing here: that facts can be used in writing for all four of the major *reasons* for writing presented earlier and often in this book. Good!

President John Fitzgerald Kennedy was dead. I've never felt more dumbfounded, more helpless, more ineffectual in my life. One convulsive lunch hour suddenly made us all more vulnerable and fearful citizens of a suddenly much more uncertain world."

You might want to bring in another piece of writing and ask students to identify the facts it contains, with an eye toward analyzing how those facts are used.

Facts, then, are often integral to all kinds of writing for all kinds of purposes. Probably the most common use of facts in writing is in what is often called straight news reporting. One must only look at the well-known "journalist's questions" to see that they are all aimed at getting the facts of a story: *who, what, where, when, how* and *why.* Note the dominant emphasis on answering those journalistic questions in the following brief news story (in which the names have been changed):

Body of Youth Recovered

THE ASSOCIATED PRESS

GULF SHORES—Rescue workers located the body of a New Orleans teenager on the beach at Gulf Shores, one day after a sand bar where he was walking with friends washed out. 1

A police dispatcher said the body of Samuel Mabry, 15, was recovered on the beach Sunday. The body was found about 3 ½ miles from the area where he fell in the surf about 3:15 P.M. Saturday. 2

The boy and his 15 year-old sister, Dawn, were walking on the sandbar with other teens when the sand washed out from under them, said the victim's mother, Ila Mabry. A passer-by pulled the girl to safety, witnesses said. 3

Questions for Writing and Discussion

Prepare short written answers to each of these questions. Be prepared to hand them in and/or discuss them in class, as your teacher directs.

1. Which factual elements of the above brief news story are answers to the question *who?*
2. Which are answers to the question *what?*
3. Which to *when?*
4. Which to *how?*
5. Which to *where?*
6. Which to *why?*

The lack of emotion in the above story is intentional, not because the Associated Press writer is insensitive to the tragedy but because his or her job is, in this case, simply to report the facts. Thus, even the "why" question—which clearly has potential beyond the simple facts of the situation—is answered in only the most limited way; that is, the boy drowned because the sandbar suddenly washed away. The "how" question can be answered the same way. Emotional words are more appropriate in the kinds of *expressive* writing this death might prompt—eulogies, sympathy notes, commentaries on the inscrutable ways of nature. Those would be different reactions to the central fact and, in their way, just as appropriate as this news report.

Most news stories, even those often labeled analysis or commentary (that is, stories in which the writer has some freedom to interpret what the facts of the story might mean *beyond* the story itself), are still dominated by the facts.

Consider the following news story, published in *U.S. News and World Report,* after an air tragedy that occurred near Cerritos, California (a Los Angeles suburb), on August 31, 1986. The central fact is the crash itself. The story then draws on related facts to build the account. As you read, notice how often what the writers say *depends* on a fact—reporting that fact, explaining the significance of the fact, or speculating on what the fact might mean in terms of future air travel. Note the care taken to establish fact *sources.*

The issue of sources is part of how the "factness" of a fact is determined. Don't, therefore, let your students glide over it.

Too Many Planes, Too Little Sky

CLEMENS P. WORK, STEVE L. HAWKINS, and ELAINE CAREY

Clemens P. Work, Steve L. Hawkins, and Elaine Carey are staff writers for U.S. News and World Report. *This article appeared in 1986.*

Was it a 1-in-a-billion chance, or was it inevitable?

1 Safety experts say the August 31 midair crash of an Aeromexico jetliner and a single-engine Piper Cherokee over a Los Angeles suburb that killed at least 85 people was both extremely rare and as predictable as the law of gravity. And therein lies the nub of a growing concern: Do small airplanes belong near major commercial airports?

2 Private pilots have long argued that the skies belong to them as much as they do to such airlines as People Express and United, which would like to see more restrictions on small planes. But that's "like Greyhound asking to ban private automobiles because they lose money sitting through traffic jams," contends John Baker, president of the Aircraft Owners and Pilots Association (AOPA).

3 Private aviation's safety record has improved significantly over the past 25 years. The last fatal midair collision in the U.S. between a commercial jetliner and a private plane was almost eight years ago, when a PSA 727 rammed into a small Cessna on Sept. 25, 1978, on its approach to Lindbergh Field in San Diego, killing all 137 in the airplanes and 7 on the ground.

4 Still, at 8.56 accidents per 100,000 flying hours, general aviation's safety record is 30 times worse than that of commercial aircraft. Pilots of single-engine aircraft need as little as 35 hours of flight time. Commercial pilots

hired by major airlines last year had an average of 3,778 hours of flying time. But growing congestion—and more near-misses—in the air and on the ground at major airports, plus a creaky air-traffic-control system and obsolete ways to avoid other planes, are narrowing safety margins.

Nowhere in the U.S. are the problems of mixing small, private aircraft and commercial jets in the same airspace as bad as they are in Southern California. Within 90 miles of Los Angeles International Airport, there are 12 million people and 30 airports, including five where commercial operations have risen sharply in recent years. The 13 airports with control towers handled 3.7 million takeoffs and landings last year alone. 5

Skies over L.A. are particularly crowded. A recent count of planes on the radar scopes at the L.A. tower at a given moment showed 197 within a 45-mile radius. Recent tests by the Federal Aviation Administration in the L.A. basin showed an even higher peak density—13 aircraft within a 4-mile radius, only slightly below the FAA's predicted density for the year 2000. On weekends, complains Capt. Arnoldo Reyes Gomez of the Mexican Aviation Pilots Union, the problem gets worse. "There are too many people flying for sport, people who don't know the rules. We have to constantly be on the lookout," says Gomez. Statistics from the National Transportation Safety Board back him up: Almost 41 percent of accidents with small planes are on weekends, up from 36.6 percent in 1980. 6

The crowded conditions in the skies over major population centers prompted the FAA in the mid-1970s to curtail private-aircraft flights near major airports. The FAA carved out special zones between 1,000 and 7,000 feet over approach and departure areas at nine airports, including Los Angeles's. Called terminal-control areas (TCA's), they are shaped like an upside-down wedding cake and are as much as 25 miles across. No aircraft is permitted to enter unless the pilot obtains clearance from air controllers and the plane is equipped with a two-way radio and a transponder, an instrument that continuously signals an aircraft's position and altitude. 7

The flight restrictions were opposed by AOPA initially, but now "they are a fact of life," says spokesman Ed Pinto. He estimates that 75 percent of all private planes are equipped with transponders and half with the $2000 "altitude encoding" transponders required in the most restricted TCA's such as L.A. But complex airspaces with invisible boundaries can confuse any pilot. And, as the Aeromexico crash showed, TCA's cannot stop maverick, incapacitated or ill-equipped pilots from violating airspaces. The NTSB says the plane that hit the Aeromexico DC–9 did not have a transponder equipped to send altitude readings. Even if the controller had detected the Piper on his screen, he could only have given the Aeromexico pilot a routine advisory without warning him that the small plane was at his altitude, 6,500 feet, says NTSB member John Lauber. 8

The air-traffic-control system leaves little margin for error. If the restricted zone starts at 6,000 feet, private pilots can go up to 5,999 feet and not be in violation. In a crowded air basin such as L.A.'s or New York's, relying 9 on pilots to see and avoid aircraft "just doesn't hack it; it's just this side of the Wright Brothers," says Henry Duffy, president of the Air Line Pilots Association.

10 A large part of the responsibility for safety resides in the eyes and ears of the controllers. A number of experts insist there are not enough skilled controllers because the FAA has not yet recovered from the 1981 strike by 11,000 controllers and their subsequent firing by President Reagan. In the L.A. tower, which handles about 1,800 flights daily, there are five fewer controllers than before the strike. A third are not fully trained. The controller responsible for the sector where the L.A. crash took place was doing two jobs—monitoring traffic and "handing off" traffic to other controllers. Although traffic was light at the time, some experts question whether such a procedure could worsen safety problems in congested areas.

11 Drug use by controllers is another cause for concern. The FAA in August suspended three controllers at the Palmdale, Calif., regional center who had tested positive for cocaine and hashish. Palmdale was not implicated in the Cerritos crash, but on September 3 [1986], the FAA hired Compu-Chem Laboratories, a North Carolina firm, to test 24,000 employees annually.

12 More steps may be needed to reduce the volatile mix of private and commercial planes. Safety specialists believe that collision-avoidance systems on commercial planes to detect nearby aircraft and direct pilots to avoid them could be very useful. A traffic-alert-and-collision-avoidance system has been developed by Bendix Aerospace, but an evaluation of the system aboard a Piedmont B-727 has been delayed and may not start before 1987. The FAA and Piedmont have not been able to agree on pilot training.

13 AOPA backs the FAA's designating 244 "reliever airports" to take pressure off major hubs. The FAA also is pushing a back-to-basics education program. Requiring physicals for private pilots more often than biennially may be needed.

14 Nonetheless, pressure is mounting for stricter measures to keep private and commercial aircraft apart. Says Representative Guy Molinari (R–N.Y.): "We are reaching the point where strong steps must be taken. There's no such thing as the perfect system, but we have to reduce the opportunities for accidents."

You may want to invite students to glance over the readings at the beginning of the next chapter, so as to get even clearer the distinction between writing based on *facts* and writing based on *ideas*.

Questions for Writing and Discussion

Prepare short written answers to each of these questions. Be prepared to hand them in and/or discuss them in class, as your teacher directs.

1. The writers of this story are careful to state facts accurately. Notice, for example, their early statement that the August 31, 1986, Cerritos crash "killed at least 85 people." The "at least" is added wholly in the interest of accuracy; the article was written within a few days after the crash and published on September 15—only about two weeks after the crash. The sad

You might want to bring in today's issue of your local newspaper to compare its presentation of facts in an article or two. Though this is a negative exercise (a kind that involves faultfinding, which we don't usually recommend), your students could learn from it.

possibility was that the crash might yet claim more victims from among those injured; hence, the writers avoid a possible inaccuracy caused by a postpublication death by stating that the crash claimed "at least" eighty-five lives. There are other ways they might have achieved this accuracy: ". . . as of this writing has claimed 85 lives," ". . . by the end of last week had taken a toll of 85," and so on. Comb the article for similar instances in which the writers took special pains to be as accurate as possible.

2. How do the two questions, one at the beginning of the article, the other at the end of the second paragraph, help frame the focus of the article?
3. The writers often cite a source—an individual or an organization—and quote or paraphrase. An example occurs in the second paragraph, in which they paraphrase several safety experts, and in the third paragraph, in which they quote John Baker, president of the Aircraft Owners and Pilots Association (AOPA). Such citing and quoting add authority and persuasive force to their reporting. They also present "straight facts" frequently; for example, in the fourth and fifth paragraphs we learn about the last small-large plane collision and certain contrastive statistics about pilot training. Comb the article for other straight-fact statements. What is the net effect of so many facts presented as they are here?
4. This is the kind of news story often labeled news and analysis, but it is in no way an editorial or expression of opinion. The writers analyze the situation as they report it, and they conclude as best they can, offering no solution where none is immediately at hand. The effect is news-as-cautionary-tale: writing that both informs us and, to a lesser extent, tries to persuade us that a growing problem exists. To the extent that the piece is persuasive, which of the following types of persuasion (see chapter 7) does it seem to be, and why do you think so?
   a. Issues of fact (Did this happen or not?)
   b. Issues of interpretation (Is this one of these or one of those?)
   c. Issues of value (Is this good or bad?)
   d. Issues of policy (What should be done about this?)
5. What do all the acronyms (FAA, NTSB, AOPA, TCA, and so on) mean, and what overall effect do they lend to the article?
6. What does Henry Duffy, president of the Air Line Pilots Association, accomplish with his remark that relying on pilots to spot other aircraft in crowded areas like New York City is "just this side of the Wright Brothers" (¶ 9)?
7. What does *biennially* (¶ 13) mean? From what sport do the writers borrow the phrase "handing off" (¶ 10)?
8. This article was written some years ago for a weekly newsmagazine. Do you have any evidence or information that would update this story? Has the problem of congestion at major airports been solved? improved?

All the acronyms in this article can be confusing. You might take this opportunity to point out how acronyms are typically handled in writing: on *first* reference, the entire name (what the acronym stands for) is written out, followed by the acronym in parentheses. Subsequent references, then, use simply the acronym. For example: "J. Edgar Hoover was the first director of the Federal Bureau of Investigation (FBI), and he became famous in that job. No later FBI director has been as well known."

In the first example above, only a few facts related to the who-what-where-when-how-why nature of the news story are given. A wide variety of facts, including attributed quotations and paraphrases, statistics, and other who-what-where and so on kinds of information are given in the second example. In the first case the purpose is straight informational reporting *without* interpretive or persuasive purposes. In the second case the purpose is straight informational reporting *with* interpretive and persuasive aims. In the following example, the purpose is informational reporting with equal aims of informing (just what *are* the lyrics to "Louie Louie"?) and entertaining (humorous commentary on why that is, and long has been, such an important question in American popular culture). Whereas the previous pieces concern themselves with several facts, this article is primarily concerned with one central fact: establishing, once and for all, what the actual lyrics to "Louie Louie" are.

The Man Who Wrote "Louie Louie"

Bob Greene

Bob Greene writes for Esquire *and the* Chicago Tribune. *See his* Profile of a Writer *section at the beginning of Part Three.*

1 A woman with a son in high school wrote me a letter. She said that her son was studying the history of popular culture, and that the current class discussion was about the song "Louie Louie."

2 Her son had come home and told her that there had been an animated conversation in the class about the lyrics of "Louie Louie." Were the lyrics dirty or not? The teacher had played the song over and over, but no consensus had been reached.

3 The woman thought that I might be able to come up with the definitive answer to this historical quandary. Was "Louie Louie" a dirty song? My assistance would be greatly appreciated.

4 (Do you think George Will gets mail like this?)

Greene makes reference here to his well-known fellow writer George Will, whose work can also be found in these pages (see "Listen to the Bridges," chapter 6).

5 The "Louie Louie" argument, of course, has been going on for years. The song, as recorded by the Kingsmen, became a nationwide hit in the autumn of 1963. Almost immediately rumors started to circulate: the lyrics were dirty. Because the vocals were just about impossible to decipher, no one could be absolutely sure. Virtually every kid in America, though, knew that something was going on in that song. Among the lines reputed to be included on the record: *Every night at ten I lay her again. . . . She's the girl I've got to lay. . . . I tell her I'll never lay her again. . . .*

6 And now they are studying "Louie Louie" in high school classes. I thought it would be relatively simple to find the answer.

7 I was wrong. I had always assumed that the Kingsmen had written "Louie Louie." It turns out that they didn't.

8 I won't bore you with the details of how I found the man who did write "Louie Louie"; suffice it to say that I did find him, and his name is Richard

Students often want to think that facts are automatically and only about boring, stuffy subjects. As any good rock-and-roll history proves (or as this article proves), that isn't so.

Berry. He is fifty-three years old and lives in Los Angeles with his mother and the youngest of his six children, a nineteen-year-old daughter.

Berry said that he wrote "Louie Louie" in 1955. "I was performing with a Latin group in Anaheim," he said. "They were called the Rhythm Rockers. They were a full Latin band—twelve or thirteen pieces. 9

"I was back in the dressing room waiting to go on, and I heard the Rhythm Rockers playing an instrumental. I heard the congas and everything, and I thought that I could write a really interesting song to go with that kind of music. The title 'Louie Louie' just kind of fell out of the sky. I didn't have anything to write the words down on, so I took a piece of toilet paper and wrote the lyrics on the toilet paper. 10

"The whole idea was that Louie was the guy the singer was talking to—the singer wasn't Louie. It's like that song 'One for My Baby (and One More for the Road).' In that song, 'Joe' is the bartender. You know—'Set 'em up, Joe. . . .' Joe is the star, but the singer is not Joe. The same with 'Louie Louie.' The singer is a sailor, and he's talking to Louie. Louie could be a bartender, a streetcar driver, a barber . . . anybody." 11

Berry saw "Louie Louie" as a love song. He recorded it on a local label called Flip in 1956. "Actually, it was the B side of the record," he said. "The A side was 'You Are My Sunshine,' which of course I did not write. I sang 'You Are My Sunshine,' in a combination country/rhythm-and-blues style." 12

In 1957 Berry was getting tired of the music business—too much work, too little money. He wanted to get married, but he needed some cash. So he sold the rights to "Louie Louie" to a record-company owner. The price was $750. "Actually, the $750 was for the rights to 'Louie Louie' and four other songs," Berry said. "The deal was that I would sell the rights to five songs for the $750." 13

Six years passed. Then Berry started hearing people say that "Louie Louie" had been recorded by a rock group up in Oregon. 14

"Some of my black friends had heard it, and they said, 'These white guys recorded your song, and it's awful. They really messed it up.' I didn't care at the time. I thought it was kind of interesting that 'Louie Louie' had become a white kids' record, but I wasn't curious enough to go out and buy it. 15

"It wasn't until about eight months later that I heard the Kingsmen's version. It was . . . different. The Kingsmen sang it raggedy and real funky. If you listened to mine, mine was real smooth. But as to the Kingsmen's record, I didn't have any negative or positive feelings about it either way." 16

Berry was told that the Kingsmen had found a copy of "Louie Louie" in a record bin in the Portland area and had decided to perform it. Before long the rumors about the dirty lyrics began to circulate, and "Louie Louie" quickly moved toward the top of the record charts. 17

"No one really contacted me about it," Berry said. "I suppose when people saw the 'Richard Berry' writer's credit on the record label, they assumed that Richard Berry was one of the Kingsmen. I couldn't get too interested because I realized that I had made all the money I would ever make off 'Louie Louie' back in 1957 when I had sold the rights." 18

19 Finally, though, when he kept hearing the dirty-lyrics rumors, he got hold of a copy of the Kingsmen's record and played it.

20 "They were singing the same words exactly the way I wrote them," Berry said. "And they were not dirty lyrics. There was not one dirty word or suggestive phrase in that song."

21 This, of course, is the nugget of information that a nation has wondered about for a quarter of a century. I asked Berry if he would mind singing "Louie Louie" for me—very slowly, so I could write it all down. He said he would be more than happy to, just to set the record straight once and for all.

22 Here are the lyrics to "Louie Louie":

Louie Louie, me gotta go
Louie Louie, me gotta go

Fine little girl she waits for me
Me catch the ship for cross the sea
Me sail the ship all alone
Me never think me make it home

Louie Louie, me gotta go
Louie Louie, me gotta go

Three nights and days me sail the sea
Me think of girl constantly
On the ship I dream she there
I smell the rose in her hair

Louie Louie, me gotta go
Louie Louie, me gotta go

Me see Jamaica moon above
It won't be long, me see my love
I take her in my arms and then
Me tell her I never leave again

Louie Louie, me gotta go
Louie Louie, me gotta go

You might want to bring the Kingsmen's recording of "Louie Louie" to class and play it while your students look at the lyrics. The song, as you may know, continues to be played frequently on the radio, especially on "oldies but goodies" broadcasts.

23 In listening to the Kingsmen's "Louie Louie" after it was first released, Berry was absolutely convinced that the band had remained faithful to his lyrics. But no one wanted to believe it.

24 "A couple of radio stations banned the song," he said. "I even heard that the FBI wanted to get involved. It was ridiculous."

25 And something started to happen. "Louie Louie," because of the rumors, became more than a pop song. It became a cultural phenomenon.

26 "When the movie *Animal House* came out in 1978, 'Louie Louie' took on a whole new life," Berry said. "John Belushi and the guys who played his fraternity brothers sang it at that toga party in the movie, and all of a sudden at every university in the country kids were having toga parties and singing 'Louie Louie.' There is a whole generation of kids who probably think that 'Louie Louie' first appeared in *Animal House*."

Your students probably haven't heard of Julie London, whose long singing career was built on a soft, husky voice and slow love songs and blues songs (such as her best-known "Cry Me a River" in the late 1950s). "Louie Louie" was hardly a typical song for her—hence strength for Berry's point that just about everybody recorded the song. Rod McKuen is a sentimental poet who was popular in the late 1960s, and so his mention also strengthens Berry's point.

Berry said that more than four hundred versions of "Louie Louie" have been recorded; some music authorities place the figure closer to a thousand. "It's been sung by everybody from Julie London to Rod McKuen," he said. "I have been told that the Kingsmen have sold more than twelve million copies of their version over the years. And someone told me that there have been an estimated three hundred million copies of 'Louie Louie' sold worldwide by different artists. 27

"I never could understand the popularity of it. It was a song with three stupid guitar-chord changes in it. Every young musician I have ever met has told me that 'Louie Louie' was the first song that he ever learned. I can believe that; it's such an easy song to play. 28

"The marching band at my daughter's high school even plays it at half time of the football games." 29

It wasn't until twenty years after the Kingsmen's release of "Louie Louie" that Berry met one of the Kingsmen. 30

"I met the lead singer, Jack Ely, in 1983," Berry said. "I asked him why everyone thought it was a dirty song. He said that the Kingsmen had recorded it in this little fifty-dollar studio. The microphone was way up in the ceiling. So Ely's vocals couldn't be heard very clearly. When people couldn't understand the vocals, the rumors started. And then it snowballed." 31

Several years ago Berry received some legal help and was able to win back some of the rights to "Louie Louie." He is far from wealthy, but he says he is satisfied. 32

"Sometimes people will introduce me to their friends and say that I am the man who wrote 'Louie Louie,'" Berry said. "At first no one believes it. But then they start asking about the lyrics. When I explain to them that the words were clean, and I say, 'Yeah, the Kingsmen sang my straight lyrics,' they don't want to accept it. It takes away the mystery. They shake their heads and walk away disappointed." 33

I thanked Berry for his time and for the information, and I said that I had to bother him with one more detail. I told him that Esquire has a research department that fact-checks everything that goes into the magazine. So I asked if he could help me out with a seemingly minor question: Was there a comma in "Louie Louie"? 34

"A comma?" Berry said. 35

"Yeah," I said. "Is it 'Louie, Louie,' or is it 'Louie Louie'?" 36

"I don't know," Berry said. "I never thought about it." 37

"They're going to want to know, and they're going to drive you crazy until they find out," I said. "Could you look on the original song?" 38

Berry laughed. 39

"You must be kidding," he said. "That piece of toilet paper that I wrote 'Louie Louie' on fell apart many years ago." 40

That made sense. "Could you make a decision, then?" I said. 41

"Okay," Berry said. "'Louie Louie.' No comma." 42

Questions for Writing and Discussion

Prepare short written answers to each of these questions. Be prepared to hand them in and/or discuss them in class, as your teacher directs.

1. There is anticlimax in this article (primarily Greene's establishment that the song's lyrics aren't "dirty") and several ironies (unexpected twists in which the truth is not what is expected). What ironies do you find in what Bob Greene reports about Richard Berry and the song "Louie Louie"?

You may want to ask your students to compare Greene's techniques in this essay with his other essay, "The Permanent Record," in chapter 13.

2. What effect does Greene achieve by writing at the end of paragraph 6, "I thought it would be relatively simple to find the answer," and beginning paragraph 7 with, "I was wrong"?

Here you might point out other essays that have twists in them, such as Janet Sternburg's "The Writer Herself" (chapter 4).

3. Greene establishes in this article the central fact of what the song's lyrics are. What other, lesser fact does he establish about the song in his conclusion?
4. What do the following words mean—*quandary* (¶ 3), *decipher* (¶ 5), *suffice* (¶ 8)?
5. Part of Greene's technique as writer here is the idea of taking us, as readers, along on his quest for the facts in the case of "Louie Louie." As a result, we quickly warm to his friendly "voice," his light humor, and his ironic tone as he unearths the misunderstandings (the song isn't dirty, and it wasn't intended as a funky rock tune) and misjudgments (it wasn't intended as the "hit side" of the record). Imagine the essential discoveries he makes as they would be written in a straight who-what-where-when-how-why account. What would be lost? Would anything be gained? How does a difference in audience (readers of a magazine article versus those of a straight newspaper article) influence the way a writer presents facts?

Notice that this is the same technique used in several other pieces in this book, such as "Eleven Blue Men" (chapter 6).

We have now seen samples of professional writing that use facts to make a straight informational report, to make an informative report with a caution that something must be done, and to make an informative report that entertains us. Next we'll examine yet another way of writing about facts.

PREREADING WORKSHEET

Before you read the following piece by David Quammen, write brief responses to these questions:

1. Have you ever lived near or traveled through a desert? If so, what memories do you have of it?
2. If you were on a quiz show and were asked to name the chief reason a desert area exists, what would you reply?
3. What deserts in the world have you heard of? List them (don't worry about exact spelling).

4. Look up the word *desert* in your dictionary. What relationship do you see between the noun and verb uses?

If someone approached us with the question, "Should I use as a writing assignment, 'Write an essay about the cause of deserts'?" we might well answer no. Yet Quammen's essay proves we could be wrong, *if* the information is interesting and the writer finds a way to present it properly. Ask your students what quality they think raises Quammen's essay above the ordinary. Wouldn't *anybody* expect such a piece to be dull and pedestrian? So why isn't it?

The following selection, written by David Quammen, uses global facts of geography and weather to explain why the world has desert regions and why those regions tend to be in certain locations. Quammen's writing here is the result of careful *analysis* of the geographic and climatological facts he has gathered. Through careful, systematic, and logical study of these facts, he can draw conclusions that are in essence "new" facts, ones showing that various geographic and climatological causes unerringly create the effect of desert.

Deserts

DAVID QUAMMEN

David Quammen writes a regular column for Outside *magazine, and has published articles in numerous other journals. The following piece is excerpted from one of his books,* Natural Acts.

Three different geophysical factors combine, generally at least two in each case, to produce the world's various zones of drastic and permanent drought: (1) high pressure systems of air in the horse latitudes, (2) shadowing mountains, and (3) cool ocean currents. Together these three even cast a tidy pattern. 1

One of our readers thought this image ("like a fat woman in a hot red bikini") might offend someone; certainly that is not our intention. As we hope our selection of readings shows, we believe many of the voices in our global community should be heard. Another way to say that is this: the image is Quammen's, not ours.

Our planet wears its deserts like a fat woman in a hot red bikini. Don't take my word for it: Look at a globe. Spin the Earth and follow the Tropic of Cancer with your finger as it passes through, or very near, every great desert of the northern hemisphere: the Sahara, the Arabian, the Turkestan, the Dasht-i-Lut of Iran, the Thar of India, the Taklimakan, the Gobi, and back around to the coast of Baja. Now spin again and trace the Tropic of Capricorn, circling down there below the equator: through the Namib and the Kalahari in southwestern Africa, straight across to the big desert that constitutes central Australia, on around again to the Atacama-Peruvian and the Monte-Patagonian of South America. This arrangement is no coincidence. It's a result, first, of that high-pressure air in the horse latitudes. 2

The horse latitudes (traditionally so-called for tenuous and uninteresting reasons) encircle the Earth in two wide bands, one north of the equator and one south, respectively along the tropics of Cancer and Capricorn. The northern band spans roughly the area between latitudes 20° N and 35° N, and the counterpart covers a similar area of south latitudes. Between those two bands is the tropics, very hot and very wet, where most rainforest is located. That equatorial region is also the part of the terrestrial surface that—because of its distance from the poles of rotation—is moving with greatest velocity as 3 the Earth spins through space. (The equator rolls around at better than 1,000 mph, while a point near the North Pole travels much slower.) For climatological reasons only slightly more obscure than Thomistic metaphysics, this differential in surface velocity produces trade winds, variations in barometric pressure, and a consistent trend of rising air over the tropics. As the air rises it grows cooler, therefore releasing its moisture (as cooling air always does) in generous deluge upon those tropical rainforests. Now the same air systems are high and dry: high aloft in the atmosphere, and emptied of their water. In that condition they slide out to the horse latitudes, north and south some hundreds of miles, and then again descend. Coming down, they compact themselves into high pressure systems of surpassing dryness. And as the pressure of this falling air increases, so does its temperature. The consequence is extreme permanent aridity along those two latitudinal bands, and a first cause for all the world's major deserts.

4 The second cause is mountains—long ranges of mountains, sprawling out across the path of prevailing winds. These ranges block the movement of moist air, forcing it to ascend over them like a water-skier over a jump. In the process that air is cooled to the point where it releases its water. The mountains get deep snow on their peaks and the land to leeward gets what is left: almost nothing. Such a *rain shadow* of dryness may stretch for hundreds of miles downwind, depending on the height of the range. No accident, then, that the Sahara is bordered along its northwestern rim by the Atlas Mountains, that the Taklimakan stares up at the Himalayas, that the Patagonian Desert is overshadowed by the Andes.

5 Ocean currents out of the polar regions work much the same way, sweeping up along the windward coastlines of certain continents and putting a chill into the oncoming weather systems before those systems quite reach the land. Abruptly cooled, the air masses drop their water off the coast and arrive inland with little to offer. For instance, the Benguela Current, curling up from Antarctica to lap the southwestern edge of Africa, steals moisture that might otherwise reach the Namib. The Humboldt Current, running cold up the west coast of South America, keeps the Atacama similarly deprived. And the California Current, flowing down from Alaska along the Pacific coast as far south as Baja, does its share to promote all-season baseball in Arizona.

Quammen is a master of first lines of paragraphs. For people who worship topic sentences, he's a source of excellent examples.

6 Beyond all these causes of dryness, another important factor is wind, helping to shape desert not only through evaporation but also—and more drastically than in any other type of climatological zone—by way of erosion. Powerful winds blow almost constantly into and across any desert, with heavier cold air charging forward to fill the vacuum as hot light air rises away off the desert floor. Desert mountains tend to increase this gustiness, and in some cases to focus winds through canyons and passes for still more extreme effect. In the desert they call the wind *chubasco* if it's a fierce rotary hurricane of a thing, whirling up wet and mean out of the tropics and tearing into the hot southern drylands with velocities up to 100 mph, sometimes delivering

more than a year's average rainfall in just an afternoon. More innocent little whirlwinds, localized twisters and dust devils, are known as *tornillos*. The steadiest and driest wind goes by *sirocco*. Besides raking away moisture and making life tough for plants and animals, the wind works at dismantling mountains, grinding rock fragments into sand, piling the sand into dunes and moving them off like a herd of sheep. Uwe George has called desert wind "the greatest sandblasting machine on earth," and there is vivid evidence for that notion in any number of desert formations.

The winds and the flash floods are further abetted, in trashing the terrain, by huge fluctuations in surface temperature. A desert thermometer doesn't just go way up, but wildly up and down, by day and by night, because those clear skies and that lack of vegetation let nearly all the day's solar energy radiate back away after dark. Easy come, easy go: In the desert air there is no insulation to slow the transfer of heat. And the temperature of the land surface fluctuates even more radically than the air temperature—a dark stone heated to 175° F. in the afternoon may cool to 50° F. overnight. The result is a constant process of fragmentation: rocks splitting themselves into pieces, with a sound like a gunshot, as though from sheer exasperation. 7

Quammen is also a master of figurative language. We especially love this one: "rocks splitting themselves into pieces . . . from sheer exasperation." Do your students get it, though?

It is all so elaborately and neatly interconnected: The dryness of desert regions entails clear skies and a paucity of plants; which together entail fierce surface heat by day, bitter chill by night; which leads to rock fracture, crumbling mountains, and the eventual creation of sand. The thermal convection of air brings strong winds, which exacerbate in their turn the aridity and the erosion; also the irregularity of rainfall, acting upon soil not anchored by a continuous carpet of plants, creates the arroyos, the canyons, the badlands, the rugged bare mountains; wind and sand collaborate on the dunes and the sculpted rocks. Add to this a team of small thirst-proof mammals like the kangaroo rat, hardy birds like the poorwill, ingeniously appointed reptiles like the sidewinder, arthropods of all unspeakable and menacing variety—and what you have is a desert. A land of hardship, of durable living creatures but not many, of severe beauty, and in some ineffable way, of *cleanliness*. 8

POSTREADING WORKSHEET

Now that you've read the piece by Quammen, write your responses to the following questions:

1. How many of the globe's deserts that Quammen names have you heard of?
2. Look up the story of how the "horse latitudes" were named. Do you agree with Quammen that the name comes from "tenuous and uninteresting reasons" (¶ 3)?
3. Most people would never guess that ocean currents and mountain ranges play roles in the creation of deserts. How does Quammen explain those roles? Are they clear to you? How would you explain them to someone who hasn't read this piece?

We heard that the "horse latitudes" are so-called because once a sailing ship with a cargo including many horses became stranded in this area of the ocean notorious for long periods of calm. After many days

4. Judging from Quammen's detailed knowledge and tone, what would you say his attitude toward deserts is?
5. Has Quammen influenced your attitude toward deserts? If so, how?

without sufficient wind to sail on, the ship's rations, especially of water, became threatened. The horses were sacrificed to save water for the crew. That story may or may not be true (hence tenuous), but we don't agree with Quammen that it is uninteresting. The story inspired a song written and performed by the Doors ("Horse Latitudes," on the album *Strange Days,* 1968).

Questions for Writing and Discussion

Prepare short written answers to each of these questions. Be prepared to hand them in and/or discuss them in class, as your teacher directs.

1. How does Quammen set up the reader's expectations in the first paragraph, foreshadowing the presentation of the facts he has discovered?
2. Although Quammen is primarily concerned with explaining facts, he assists his explanation considerably with figurative language. Note, for example, "These ranges block the movement of moist air, forcing it to ascend over them like a water-skier over a jump" (¶ 4). What other similes or metaphors do you find in the piece?
3. As he relates the facts about how the world's deserts are formed, Quammen, like Bob Greene, uses the first person. But Quammen is more serious than Greene in his overall tone and attitude. Find the places where Quammen and Green sound almost alike in their "voices." Then contrast those with the places where the two writers sound different, where Quammen sounds more like a reporter. Which "sound" do you prefer? Why? Is one more appropriate than the other?
4. What do the following words mean—*geophysical* (¶ 1), *tenuous, terrestrial, Thomistic metaphysics* (¶ 3), *leeward* (¶ 4), *abetted* (¶ 7), *paucity, exacerbate, convection, arthropods, ineffable* (¶ 8)?

We have now seen facts used in essays intended primarily to inform ("Body of Youth Recovered"); to inform, analyze, and persuade ("Too Many Planes, Too Little Sky"); to inform and entertain ("The Man Who Wrote 'Louie Louie'"); and to analyze and inform ("Deserts"). Their common element being to inform, these pieces might give you the idea that all factual writing is informational, but that isn't true. In the following piece, Calvin Trillin takes one fact—that the Burger King on the Champs-Elysées in Paris does more business than any other Burger King in the world—and uses it as the basis for building a purely humorous, entertaining essay.

Uncivil Liberties

CALVIN TRILLIN

Calvin Trillin is a reporter, magazine writer, and book author. His books include Uncivil Liberties *(1982) and* If You Can't Say Something Nice *(1987).*

1 I heard about the Burger King in Paris first. It turns out that the Burger King on the Champs-Elysées in Paris does more business than any other Burger King in the entire world.

Trillin's tone reminds us of "Has His Southern-ness Gone with the Wind?" (chapter 10). Ask students what, beyond the obvious—the use of dialogue—the two pieces have in common. (We're thinking here of the witty repartee—though in Trillin's case we can't be too sure just how witty his wife intends to be—and the *trivial* nature of the conversation, which, without the humor, would make the piece hardly worth reading.)

"What do you make of that?" my wife said when I told her the news. 2

"What do you mean—what do I make of it?" 3

"Well, you're supposed to be a columnist," she said. "You're supposed to point out the significance, make the connections. That's what all the other columnists do. Does this say something about the inroads of American mass culture on European life? Does it say something about the New Europe? Is it a symbol of what's happening in the Western alliance? What does it all mean?" 4

"I don't know," I said. 5

"You don't know?" 6

"I haven't the foggiest," I said. 7

"But aren't you supposed to know this sort of thing?" 8

"I'd rather not say," I answered. 9

I really didn't know what it all meant. Making those connections was never easy for me, and it seemed to be getting harder every day. A couple of days before I learned about Burger King, someone had told me that in this country we spend $520,720 a minute on defense. "What does that mean to you?" he said. 10

"Well," I said, "that means that if you take the amount of money we spend annually on defense and divide it by the number of minutes in a year, you'd come out with $520,720." 11

He stared at me for a while. "Well, I knew that," he finally said, sounding a little put out. "But what does it mean? What's the significance?" 12

"Beats me," I said. 13

Then I heard on the radio that the Kentucky Fried Chicken outlet in Beijing does more business than any other Kentucky Fried Chicken outlet in the entire world. My wife was out of the room at the time. I didn't see any reason to tell her. I figured what she didn't know wouldn't hurt her. Also, she had no plans to go to Beijing anytime in the near future, and if she did I'm certain she would eat Chinese food rather than Kentucky Fried Chicken. So it wasn't as if I was withholding some information she'd find of practical use. 14

She found out anyway. Maybe she read it in the newspaper. Maybe somebody tipped her off. She has her ways. 15

"I guess you've heard the news," she said one night at dinner. 16

"News?" I said. "I've heard no news." That was almost true. The burden of trying to find some significance in the events of the day was beginning to take the pleasure out of watching the news on television. I was thinking of going over to *Wheel of Fortune.* 17

My wife told me that the Kentucky Fried Chicken outlet in Beijing does more business than any other Kentucky Fried Chicken outlet in the entire world. 18

"Well, I'll be darned," I said. "Is that right? Isn't that something?" I came close to saying, "Well, don't that beat all," because I couldn't think of anything else to say. 19

20 "First, Burger King in Paris, now Kentucky Fried Chicken in Beijing," she said. "There's a real parallel there. What do you think it means?"

21 "Search me," I said.

22 "You should probably come up with something," she said. "People are going to begin to wonder about you."

23 I was afraid she might be right. Even a beginning columnist is supposed to see some significance in a parallel. I couldn't just say, "Those Chinese sure do like their fried chicken." That's not enough to say about a parallel. Also, what if this sort of thing continued? If two is a parallel, more than two is a trend. I'd have to find some significance in a trend. There are standards.

24 I could imagine the news flashes coming from all over the globe. Pizza Hut announces that its number-one moneymaker is its outlet in downtown Stockholm. The Taco Bell in Budapest smashes the company's record for annual sales. In Montevideo, the local Domino's gives away free pizzas in celebration of beating out a Domino's in a Minneapolis shopping center as the most profitable outlet in the company. It's a trend!

25 I figure that I'd better make one last try. I say to my wife, "Do you realize that the Wendy's in Moscow may gross as much per year as we spend in almost a half-hour defending ourselves against the Russians?"

26 My wife says she hadn't realized that.

27 "What does this say about the influence of American mass culture on the Eastern bloc countries?" I say. "What does it say about the Western Alliance? What impact will it have on the cold war?"

28 "I don't know," my wife says.

29 "Exactly," I say.

Questions for Writing and Discussion

Prepare short written answers to each of these questions. Be prepared to hand them in and/or discuss them in class, as your teacher directs.

1. What seems to you to be the *point* of Trillin's essay?
2. How does Trillin use dialogue—conversation between him and his wife—for humorous effect? (Note that when writing dialogue with a minimum of unspoken written description between speeches, you should begin a new paragraph each time the speaker changes.)
3. In what ways does Trillin's piece satirize news columnists and commentators?
4. What effect does Trillin achieve by carefully repeating each word of his central "facts" (for example, in ¶ 14 and ¶ 18)?
5. The essential trick Trillin works on his wife is reversal: changing from the defensive to the offensive by initiating, rather than responding to, questions. How does his reversal help him make his point? How does it make for an effective conclusion?

Ask students to (a) return to the beginning of this chapter and review the different uses of facts and then (b) go back through the Trillin piece to see whether they can detect the nature of his use of each fact.

6. What does Trillin mean when he says, "I haven't the foggiest" (¶ 7)—foggiest *what?* How does he use the geometrical term *parallel* (¶s 20, 23)?

KEY POINTS TO REMEMBER: Writing About Facts

When writing about facts, keep the following points in mind:

- Facts are true.
- Facts find meaning in context.
- Facts can be used for any writing purpose.

Facts Are True

A fact is true, provable, beyond dispute; its value to both writer and reader is its truth. And because a fact is provable beyond question, it has complete reliability. You have often heard such expressions as "in fact," "as a matter of fact," and "the fact is"; such expressions reinforce the indisputable nature of facts by emphasizing that they are facts. Similarly, writers and speakers will often claim a desire to "set the record straight" by giving the facts in a particular case. They wish to use the unimpeachable nature of facts to present what they see as the truthful version of something. The reverence for "the record" is transferred from the reverence for truth—and, of course, facts are true and are therefore revered.

Anyone who has ever taught a technical writing course has already learned how important context is; look again at the Weiss quotation at the beginning of this chapter. When you ask someone, "Why is this written this way?" and the answer is "I just put down the facts," you need to make the point that facts *alone* usually don't mean much. We must *examine* facts in particular contexts to find their fuller meanings.

Facts Find Meaning in Context

Facts have little meaning by themselves and become significant only in particular contexts. Until facts are placed in a communicative context for some communicative purpose (that is, reason for writing), they generate little persuasive force. For example:

> In 1941, Ted Williams, the regular left fielder for baseball's Boston Red Sox, hit for a season average of .406. That is a fact. But the fact itself generates little significance unless the reader already knows quite a bit about professional baseball in America. The fact must be placed in a communicative context. To create that context for a reader unknowledgeable about baseball, we might note that

- professional, major league baseball in the United States is excellent, top-level baseball;
- any major league baseball player who plays regularly for a season and hits for a season average of more than .300 is considered to have had an outstanding season;
- a major league season batting average of .400 (four safe hits for every ten times at bat) is extremely rare; and
- no major league player has hit .400 for a full season since Ted Williams did so in 1941.

Although additional contextual and factual information could be supplied, the above information is sufficient to provide significance and communicative force to our original single fact. In this context it is immediately clear that only very rarely does a major league baseball player hit .400 or more for a season's average. With such contextual knowledge, even a non-baseball fan might be impressed with Williams's accomplishment.

Facts Can Be Used for Any Writing Purpose

Facts can be used for any of the four purposes for writing, and often for more than one of those purposes at the same time. Remembering that the four purposes for writing we have posited in this book are (a) to express, (b) to explain or inform, (c) to analyze, and (d) to persuade, we can see that facts can effectively be used for all these purposes. For example, we have seen facts used both to inform and to analyze:

- Eighty-five percent of all auto accidents reported to insurance companies involve male drivers (*informing*).
- That is why men pay more for auto insurance than women do (*analyzing*).
- A teenage boy, Samuel Mabry, drowned at Gulf Shores (*informing*).
- He fell in the surf when the sandbar he was walking on washed away (*analyzing*).

The article on the plane crash at the Los Angeles airport informs, analyzes, and persuades that something should be done. Bob Greene's article on the lyrics to "Louie Louie" informs and entertains. David Quammen analyzes the earth's geophysical features and also informs us as to the results of those features. Calvin Trillin reminds us in expressive writing that facts can be entertaining—and very nearly useless without a significant interpretative or communicative purpose. Consider the following student-written piece, which uses facts about acid rain primarily to inform but which also implicitly persuades, for it shows that not enough is being done about the problem.

Acid Rain

Theresa Moreno, college writing student

1 Paul Moreno, a landowner in upstate New York, recently tried to explain to his granddaughter from Idaho, Theresa, why she would not have any luck if she tried to fish in the large pond not far from his farmhouse. "The water has too much acid in it now, honey," he said, "and the fish all died. I'm sorry."

Theresa was on the verge of tears. It had been a long time since her last visit to her grandfather's farm, and one of her cherished memories of earlier visits was fishing with him at this pond, which was still clear, deep, and beautiful in spite of the acid. How could such a beautiful pond have become acid-polluted in such a wonderful place, where the sun was now shining brightly and the air smelled so clean and fresh? "It comes in the rain and snow," her grandfather explained. "The acid comes from the smoke, smog, and other pollution that goes up into the air from the smokestacks in the cities several miles north and west of here. It gets mixed up in the clouds somehow and then falls here as acid rain or snow. Eventually, the pond just got too much of that bad water mixed in with it." 2

Paul Moreno's farm pond is not the only essentially "dead" body of water in upstate New York. Nor is the problem limited to ponds, or even lakes, in New York State. Acid rain, which is a somewhat inaccurate term applied to acid that can be found in fog, smog, snow, hail, mist, or even dust, has been causing serious environmental damage for several years (Elsworth, 4). Gregory Wetstone and Armin Rosencranz, who have thoroughly studied its effects in both Europe and North America, report that acid rain has caused damage "to lakes, soils, forests and man-made materials"; moreover, they state that there is also "evidence of possible impacts on crops and human health" (28). Evidence of acid-rain damage in the United States includes not only dying or dead lakes and streams but also dying or dead foliage, most of it in areas downwind from industrial centers (Wetstone and Rosencranz, 28). It is surprising how far this airborne acid can travel; acid-rain damage to water and foliage in the United States stretches down the Appalachian Mountain chain all the way from New York to northern Georgia and Alabama. 3

There are two main components in acid rain: sulphur dioxide and nitrogen oxides. Sulphur dioxide, primarily a by-product of burning coal and oil, accounts for 70 percent of acid rain, and nitrogen oxides account for the other 30 percent (Elsworth, 6). Though auto exhaust or even the sulphurous flash of a kitchen match can contribute to acid rain, the primary problem comes from large, coal-burning industrial plants whose tall smokestacks are designed to release their smoke and smog into the upper air. According to Roy Gould, author of <u>Going Sour</u>, a study of acid 4 rain, some of these smokestacks "rival the Empire State Building in height." Gould also says:

> Nearly three quarters of the [sulphur dioxide] emitted east of the Mississippi River comes from power plants, and nearly half of that from just the forty largest coal-fired power plants. A single one of the largest coal-fired plants, such as the Muskingum plant in Ohio, annually emits as much [sulphur dioxide] as Mt. St. Helens' volcano--some 200,000 tons a year. (6-7)

5 Once in the upper air, the pollution travels incredible distances on the powerful wind currents. Steve Elsworth, author of Acid Rain, reports:

> Sulphur dioxide can stay in the air for up to four days and, if carried by a strong wind, can travel hundreds of miles in that time--sometimes well over a thousand. Depending on the wind currents, for example, pollution emitted over the UK [United Kingdom] can get to Scandinavia in two or three days. During this journey, the pollutants sometimes combine with water in the clouds to form dilute sulphuric and nitric acids . . . which then fall to the ground in rain, hail, snow or sleet. (9-10)

6 Given how long smokestack plants have been polluting the upper air, it is perhaps a miracle that Paul Moreno's farm pond sustained fish life as long as it did. The scale for measuring amounts of acidity and alkalinity is the pH (Paper-Hydrion) scale, on which descending pH numbers below 7 indicate logarithmically increasing acidity (the lower the pH number, the greater the acid content). Elsworth reports that aluminum is washed into lakes from acidified soil, where it joins with acid. "The combination of dissolved aluminum in water at a pH of around 5 is particularly lethal" to fish, says Elsworth, because it will "clog their gills with mucus, impede their respiratory systems, and lower the salt content of their blood" (26). Paul Moreno's pond water has a pH of 5.

7 Fish are far from acid rain's only living victims. Evidence has long existed that the smog (a word coined from combining smoke and fog) from burning fossil fuels is poisonous. Dramatic proof came in two infamous incidents when weather caused wind lulls that served to trap smog-laden air near the ground in Donora, Pennsylvania, and London,

England. The London incident is described by Fred Pearce in his book, also titled Acid Rain:

> On 5 December 1952, a trick of the winter weather clamped a lid over London. For five days, the pollution belching from London's chimneys was held fast. Smoke and gas filled the capital, which became pitch black at noon. When the smog lifted, it left the mortuaries full, with 4,000 dead. It was the worst disaster from pollution ever recorded anywhere in the world. (1)

Pearce says that the London incident also marks the beginning of our consciousness of acid rain, because the water drops in the London smog were found to be almost as acidic as water in an automobile battery (9).

Through the years, even more evidence of the dangers of acid-rain pollution has appeared. Acidification of water supplies in Sweden has adversely affected human health there (Elsworth, 49). Acid water, according to Pearce, can harm unborn babies "by giving them and their mothers lead." Pearce goes on to say that "if the lead does not kill the foetus, it may damage the development of the nervous system" (86). Michael R. Hoffman, an environmental engineer, has discovered that the fog in Los Angeles is often a hundred times more acidic than rain. The World Health Organization suspects a link between air pollution and cancer (Elsworth, 45). Clearly, smog is not the laughing matter that popular television talk-show host Johnny Carson often makes it out to be. 8

Of course, Carson, like any good comedian, knows that laughter is often the only alternative to tears. And tears did come to Theresa Moreno's eyes when she learned that nothing was being done to prevent acid rain that had destroyed life in her grandfather's farm pond. As of this writing, virtually no strong measures have been taken to curb the causes of acid rain. The industrial smokestacks still emit sulphur dioxide and nitrogen oxides into the upper air. The Environmental Protection Agency has taken some steps to curb auto exhaust in the United States, but auto exhaust causes very little of the acid rain that falls in the United States. 9

It seems as though everyone is aware of the problem, and for some time in the early 80s the United States and Canada talked seriously 10 about trying to stop acid rain, but the talks always dissolved into the larger stew of international politics and economic pressures. The bottom line by 1982 seemed to be that while Canada was generally willing to bear 50 percent of the massive cost of needed changes, the United States was not (McCormick, 148). There was no more substantial progress on solving the problem during the Reagan presidency, and the same is holding true during the Bush administration.

11 Meanwhile, acid rain continues to fall far from the smokestacks. A recent Associated Press story reported that the most decorative and distinctive blooming trees in the southern United States, the dogwoods, are now beginning to die because of acid rain (A.P., August 10, 1989). Who can blame Theresa for her tears?

Sources Cited

Associated Press. "Acid Rain Killing Dogwoods." Tuscaloosa News 10 Aug. 1989: 3A.

Elsworth, Steve. Acid Rain. London: Pluto, 1984.

Gould, Roy. Going Sour: Science and Politics of Acid Rain. Boston: Birkhauser, 1985.

McCormick, John. Acid Earth. London and Washington, D.C.: International Institute for Environment and Development, 1985.

Moreno, Paul. Personal interview. 14 Nov. 1989.

Pearce, Fred. Acid Rain. Harmondsworth: Penguin, 1987.

Wetstone, Gregory S., and Armin Rosencranz, assisted by Sarah Foster. Acid Rain in Europe and North America. Washington, D.C.: Environmental Law Institute, 1983.

Questions for Writing and Discussion

Prepare short written answers to each of these questions. Be prepared to hand them in and/or discuss them in class, as your teacher directs.

1. "Acid Rain" was written in response to an assignment calling for a research-based article about an environmental problem; the assignment specified that the article be appropriate for publication in a newspaper or an environmental magazine. How has the writer used research to present facts about acid rain? How effective is that use?

2. An important technique in presenting the results of research is *attribution*—letting your readers know the source of quotations and other kinds of information without their having to refer to footnotes or similar kinds of documentation. Note the attributions in this article. How many different ways are they done?
3. What is the "Empire State Building" (¶ 4)?
4. What do the following words mean—*mucus, lethal* (¶ 6), *adversely, foetus* (¶ 8)?

Bridges: Another Perspective

A key decision writers of articles make early in the writing process for a particular article is what *point of view* they will use. The first person ("I") is appropriate for some kinds of reportage and narration because it involves an immediacy, a kind of eyewitness perspective; however, it carries the danger that the writer will dominate the story, rather than the story taking precedence. In the case of "Acid Rain," the researcher-writer was Theresa Moreno herself. Because she did not want her personal distress about her grandfather's pond to detract from the larger problem of acid rain, she wrote the article in the third person, giving a point of view as if she were a reporter, not the Theresa Moreno mentioned in the article. Do you think that is an honest perspective for her to take? What if she had given the girl and the grandfather in the article fictitious names—would that have been more honest? Try rewriting part of the article in the first person, as if you were Theresa. What differences does that shift in perspective make? What issues of journalistic honesty and integrity do such changes raise? Are such distortions as name changing ever justified? If so, how and why?

✓✓✓ WORKSHEET: Writing About Facts

Here is a procedure you can follow when writing about facts. There doubtless are other ways, and you may vary from this procedure, but as a general guideline it should prove fruitful.

First, as always, *think* about the situation. What are your reasons for writing?

Second, do the research.

Third, put all your information and thinking together; then sort it out.

Fourth, keep drafting and reading as you go.

Fifth, share your draft with a reader.

Sixth, prepare your final draft, proofread it, and polish it.

Let's look at each of these steps more closely.

First, as always, think *about the situation. What are your reasons for writing? That is:*

- Why are you doing this piece of writing?
- What are you trying to accomplish?
- Whom are you writing for—that is, who is your reader?

This, of course, is a brief run-through of procedure for research-based writing. For a fuller, more detailed treatment, refer students to chapter 23, "Writing Research Papers."

Once you have determined the answers to those questions, focus your thinking on your *subject:* what are you writing about? Now is the time to get your facts straight about your subject:

- What fact or facts do you already know?
- What do you need to find out?
- Where and how will you find the needed new information?

Now jot down what you already know. Don't worry about organization at this point; just get what you know down, so that you won't forget it. As you write, add any other thoughts, points, or questions that pop into your mind. Then jot down a list of what you think you need to do to find out more. Consider this your research list—a plan for the discovery of more facts.

Second, do the research. Go to your library (see chapter 23, on doing library research) to look for the information you need, but don't ignore other research possibilities. Are there expert people you should interview—eyewitnesses, authors, researchers, and so on? Where might other useful information be found? (For example, a civil engineering student doing research on a dangerous road intersection can find the accident history of that particular intersection in the city's accident records at the police station.)

In terms of the distinction we made in chapter 9 between invention and discovery, we may well seem here to be unduly privileging discovery, the looking outside oneself for material, but we do not mean to do so. Both are critical means of generating material. Here we'd like to stress that invention can occur *after,* and consequent to, discovery.

Third, put all your information and thinking together; then sort it out. Now you're at the organizing stage. Thus, depending on your particular writing process you're probably ready to make an outline or to begin drafting the piece in the order that seems best suited to your purposes and readers.

Fourth, keep drafting and reading as you go. Do this until you have produced a readable, complete first draft.

Fifth, share your draft with a reader. A classmate, friend, or teacher (or all three) will do. And take into account their reactions and suggestions, as explained in other parts of this book.

Sixth, prepare your final draft, proofread it, and polish it. Now you're ready to share it with more readers.

SAMPLE WRITING ASSIGNMENT AND CASE STUDY CLOSE-UP

Theresa Moreno attended a small liberal arts college in the South. On her campus, teachers from different disciplines often collaborated on projects for their mutually enrolled students; thus, it was not extraordinary for Theresa's earth science and English professors to decide they would have their mutual students write about an environmental issue. Theresa had told her earth science professor about her trip the previous Thanksgiving to visit her grandfather on his farm near

Middleburgh, New York, and how disappointed she had been on learning that all the fish in his pond had died because of acid rain. Her earth science professor immediately suggested that acid rain would be a good subject for Theresa to write about, for it was a crucial environmental issue the class had not yet studied.

Theresa's English and earth science professors then established the requirements for the assignment:

1. The issue had to be environmentally important.
2. The paper had to be based on research using a minimum of three print sources (more sources, and other kinds of sources were nonetheless welcome). Documentation could follow either Modern Language Association (MLA) or American Psychological Association (APA) form, depending on the student's preference, but had to be consistently one or the other.
3. The paper had to be written as an informative article, appropriate for publication in a newspaper or environmentalist magazine.
4. Peer groups in the English class would be used for responses to drafts, and the English professor would also respond to a full draft before it would be submitted to the earth science professor.

Theresa decided she would use her grandfather, Paul Moreno, as a source, and at the library she found three books (print sources) on the subject of acid rain. She then went to work organizing her thoughts before examining the books, because she wanted to establish in her mind (a) what she already knew and (b) what she would need to find out. Here she made two lists, one of what she knew and the other of what she was reasonably sure she would need to find out (for instance, what exactly acid rain *is*). She then skimmed the books, keeping a sharp eye out for the kinds of information she needed and making notes whenever she found something she thought she might use. She decided to use MLA documentation form. When she was finished taking notes, she organized her information again, using a rough outline. Here is part of the first draft she shared with her peer group in English class:

A Beautiful Pond Destroyed

Last Thanksgiving I got my high school graduation present, a trip to my grandpa's farm near Middleburgh, New York. I hadn't been there since I was in the eighth grade, and I really looked forward to the visit because my grandpa's farm is really pretty and he has this wonderful pond where we went fishing on all my previous visits. Grandpa is a patient, nice man who tells funny stories while we fish. I wish I could have grown up around him, but that just wasn't possible. I was so disappointed to arrive at Grandpa's and learn that his pond, though still really pretty, had no fish in it. Acid rain had made it unable to support life. 1

2 Acid rain is really a poor name for acid in the atmosphere that can be just as easily found in snow, smog, fog, hail, mist, or even dust (Elsworth, 4). This acid forms from sulphur dioxide and nitrogen oxides that are major parts of the pollution that goes high up into the air from huge industrial smokestacks, some of which are as high as the Empire State Building (Gould, 6). Once up in the air, this acid can travel many miles--sometimes "well over a thousand"--then fall as rain or snow, doing damage to lakes, soils, forests, crops, and human beings (Wetstone and Rosencranz, 28). There are many of these smokestacks to the north and west of grandpa's place. They created the acid rain that eventually killed his fish.

3 Acid is measured on the pH (Paper-Hydrion) scale. Any number lower than a pH of 7 indicates acidity, and the lower the number the far greater the acid content in what's being measured. At ph5, acidic water in a pond will clog fish's gills with mucus, impede their respiratory systems, and lower the salt content of their blood. No wonder so many ponds and lakes in New York--not just grandpa's--no longer support fish life. . . .

Peer Review

Theresa's paper went on to conclude that little is being done about the problem of acid rain. When George, Ellen, and Yusuf read her draft in English class, they offered these responses:

George. Theresa, you do a good job of making this interesting, especially the personal angle of your granddad's pond being ruined. But there are places where it seems too personal, like when you talk about how nice your grandpa is. And it isn't until the end that we get some idea that the problem involves a lot more lakes and ponds than just your granddad's. I think you need more emphasis on acid rain and less on your grandpa's place. Maybe you could use your grandpa's place as a way of getting into the subject but not spending so much time on it after that.

I also wonder if that quotation you don't attribute—about how the acid might travel more than a thousand miles—is from your Wetstone and Rosencranz source or somewhere else. You have a list of things the acid rain affects after that—soil, forests, and so on—that comes from your Wetstone and Rosencranz source, so am I correct in assuming the quotation comes from that source, too?

You need to attribute that quotation some way, in any case.

Finally, you say that acid rain affects many other things besides fish life in ponds. You mention soil, forests, crops, even human beings. But you don't follow up with any more information about these other kinds of damage, and I think you should. For example, how does it threaten human beings?

One of the truly interesting and educational activities writing teachers engage in today is participating in—or just listening in on—students during peer conferences about their writing. The interaction among students in such situations can be fascinating. In sections like this, we try to give you and your students a vehicle for discussing not only writing but also what happens when people work together to make writing better. Another option you might want to explore is to have your students tape-record their peer conferences so that you can listen to the conferences later on, without being directly involved yourself. You may find that you learn something about teaching writing by listening in on people working on one another's writing.

Ellen. I agree with George that you need to talk about how more than fish life is affected. I also agree that the focus is too personal. Why not try using the third person? You can still put yourself into the story, but it isn't critical that it's *your* grandpa so much as it's critical that his pond's been destroyed by acid rain. You could start with "A girl recently visited her grandfather's farm in New York," something like that, and continue with her disappointment. It would still work like you want it to, without the unnecessary point that the girl is you.

I think you need to define *acid rain* a little better. You say it's made up of sulphur dioxide and nitrogen oxides and you say these come from big smokestacks, but what *causes* this particular kind of smoke? What's being burned? And *how* does all this pollution travel—wind?

Yusuf. I would like more explanation of the pH scale. You say the lower the pH number below 7, the higher the acid content. How much higher—by what increments? ten times? twenty times? Is pH 5, for example, ten or twenty or more times more acidic than pH 6 (assuming pH 7 is not acidic)? I would also like to know more about the threat to human life, not just fish life. And why don't you use more facts, more quotations, directly from your sources? I think that would add some punch.

Teacher Review

When Theresa's English teacher read the draft, she seconded most of what George, Ellen, and Yusuf had said. She suggested a more relevant title, "Acid Rain," and also urged Theresa to find a few more sources and use quotation more effectively. She recommended a third-person, "reporter" point of view and agreed that Theresa could begin her article with an account about her grandfather's pond, only this time quoting her grandfather and using him as a source. The teacher suggested giving more graphic examples of how far the wind could take the acid rain (for example, from Canada to Georgia) and definitely giving more examples of its threat to other forms of life besides fish.

When she presented the next draft to her earth science professor, he thought it was very good and had only one suggestion: that she add more to her conclusion about just how little is being done to solve the problem of acid rain. "Emphasize that it remains a serious environmental problem," he said. And so she did. And you read the final result earlier in this chapter.

WRITING ASSIGNMENTS

1. Imagine that, like Theresa, you are responsible for learning and reporting the essential facts about something in an informative article. How would you proceed? Here are some suggestions:

   a. A chemical spill has occurred at a nearby chemical plant. Your job is to find out what caused it, what is being done to clean it up, and what is being done to prevent its recurrence. You also need to find out about the chemical that was spilled. What is it? How dangerous is it? What are its effects? What does the public, especially those in the vicinity of the spill, need to know about it?

b. In geography you read about Mount Rushmore in South Dakota and saw an impressive photograph of it. You also learned about the ongoing project to sculpt, not far from Mount Rushmore, a monument to the Indian chief Sitting Bull. Your job is to find out all you can about the Sitting Bull sculpture. Whose idea was it? Who is doing it? How is it being paid for? How big will it be? You should also find out all you can about Sitting Bull. Who was he? Why is he important, worthy of this sculpture?

Your history classes provide these additional possibilities:

1) The Boston Tea Party
2) The Whisky Rebellion
3) The Dred Scott Decision
4) The *Brown* v. *Topeka Board of Education* Decision
5) The Lincoln Assassination
6) The Teapot Dome Scandal
7) The Wilderness Campaign
8) The Alamo
9) The Lewis and Clark Expedition
10) The Transcontinental Railroad

2. Take a central fact, such as the one reported earlier in this chapter—that 85 percent of all accidents reported to insurance companies in the United States involve male drivers—and use it as the crux of an argument either *for* higher insurance rates for male drivers or *against* such rates.

3. Take a different central fact—such as Calvin Trillin's fact about the Burger King on the Champs Elysées in Paris being the world's busiest Burger King—and write an expressive, entertaining piece, using the fact as a pivotal idea to which you often return.

4. Take a group of related facts and analyze them, reporting the logical conclusions you can draw from studying those facts. Here are some examples of facts:

If you want to come up with your own sets of facts, try looking in *American Demographics*.

a. Abdel Bakar started and played 30 minutes or more in all 22 of Kingsport High's basketball games last season.
b. He averaged 7 rebounds per game.
c. He averaged 18.2 points per game.
d. He averaged 6.8 assists per game.
e. He averaged 4.1 fouls per game.
f. He guarded the opposition's highest scorer 65 percent of the time he was on the floor.
g. He hit 92 percent of his free throws.

And, here are the *logical conclusions:*

a. Bakar is a reliable basketball player.

b. He is a good rebounder.
c. He is an excellent scorer.
d. He is a team player.
e. He plays outstanding, tenacious defense.
f. He is an excellent free-throw shooter. (Opposing teams won't want to foul him.)
g. He is an excellent, all-around basketball player.

Now imagine you are a food-service consultant, hired by the owners of the Crispy Chicken Restaurant to study their business and make recommendations. What logical conclusions can you draw from these facts?

a. The Crispy Chicken Restaurant at Fourth and Main is in the oldest part of the city's downtown area.
b. The Crispy Chicken has no parking lot; patrons must park on the surrounding streets.
c. The Crispy Chicken has a three-step entrance that makes it inaccessible to physically handicapped people.
d. The Crispy Chicken facade needs renovation.
e. The Crispy Chicken ownership hasn't changed in two generations. The owners take pride in the longevity of the business.
f. The Crispy Chicken Restaurant's prices are competitive.
g. The Crispy Chicken has a long-standing reputation for excellent food and service, and the owners take great pride in this too.
h. Recently, the Crispy Chicken Restaurant has been losing money as a business operation.
i. The owners of the Crispy Chicken Restaurant have the financial resources to make changes.
j. The Crispy Chicken has not run an ad in the paper or on the radio or television in years.

5. As the collage on page 237 shows, there are many known facts about the assassination of President John F. Kennedy. Despite this abundance of facts, some of the exact events of the day—especially concerning the person(s) behind the crime—remain the topic of debate. Look again at our definition of "fact" at the beginning of this chapter. How does the existence of *debated* facts—such as those surrounding the Kennedy assassination—call our definition into question? Write an improved definition of "fact," one that will help the writers in your class understand just what is meant when a certain piece of writing is said to be "based on fact." Use examples to illustrate and support your definition, drawing them from areas where the facts remain debatable. (Examples would be the Kennedy assassination, or the origin of the universe, or the role of humans in creating global warming.)

Focus on Critical Reading

6. Analyze yourself as a reader. What affects you most when you read—facts or theories? To what extent are your emotions involved when you are persuaded? Aristotle said we are persuaded in essentially three ways:

a. By pure logic (what he called *logos*), in which the facts dominate.
b. By emotion (what he called *pathos*), in which our feelings (never mind the facts) dominate.
c. By our estimation of the person or persons who are trying to persuade us (what he called *ethos*), in which our good or bad or indifferent opinion of the persuader dominates.

We offer more on Aristotle's *logos, pathos,* and *ethos* in chapter 20.

All three of these ways can be involved in whether or not we are persuaded about something. The important thing is to be *aware* of what is persuading us: are we looking at this logically? Or are we being affected by how we feel about this? Are we inclined to believe something because the person who told us is, in our view, honest, reliable, and trustworthy? (See chapter 20 for a fuller discussion of Aristotle's three appeals.)

Now look back over some of our readings in this chapter. Which of Aristotle's three appeals seems dominant to you in each one?

a. "Too Many Planes, Too Little Sky."
b. "The Man Who Wrote 'Louie Louie.'"
c. "Deserts."
d. "Uncivil Liberties."
e. "Acid Rain."

Writers' Circle

Divide into groups of five. Each member of each group is responsible for locating a reasonably detailed front-page newspaper story that will lend itself to analysis. Each student should examine the article to find answers to the "journalistic questions": *who, what, when, where, why,* and *how*? Then, each member should bring his or her article to class, where, working in the groups, students will find answers for each question in each article in the group. After discussion, each member will write a brief summary, answering each of the questions for his or her article; will attach the summary to the article; and will submit it. (*Note:* Sometimes *how* and *why* can be answered the same way.)

Or you may want to send different groups to different kinds of sources—a newspaper, *Science* magazine, *The State of Working America* (a book), the 1990 census, the statistics on the back of a cereal box, the box scores in a newspaper, and so forth.

chapter 13 Writing About Ideas

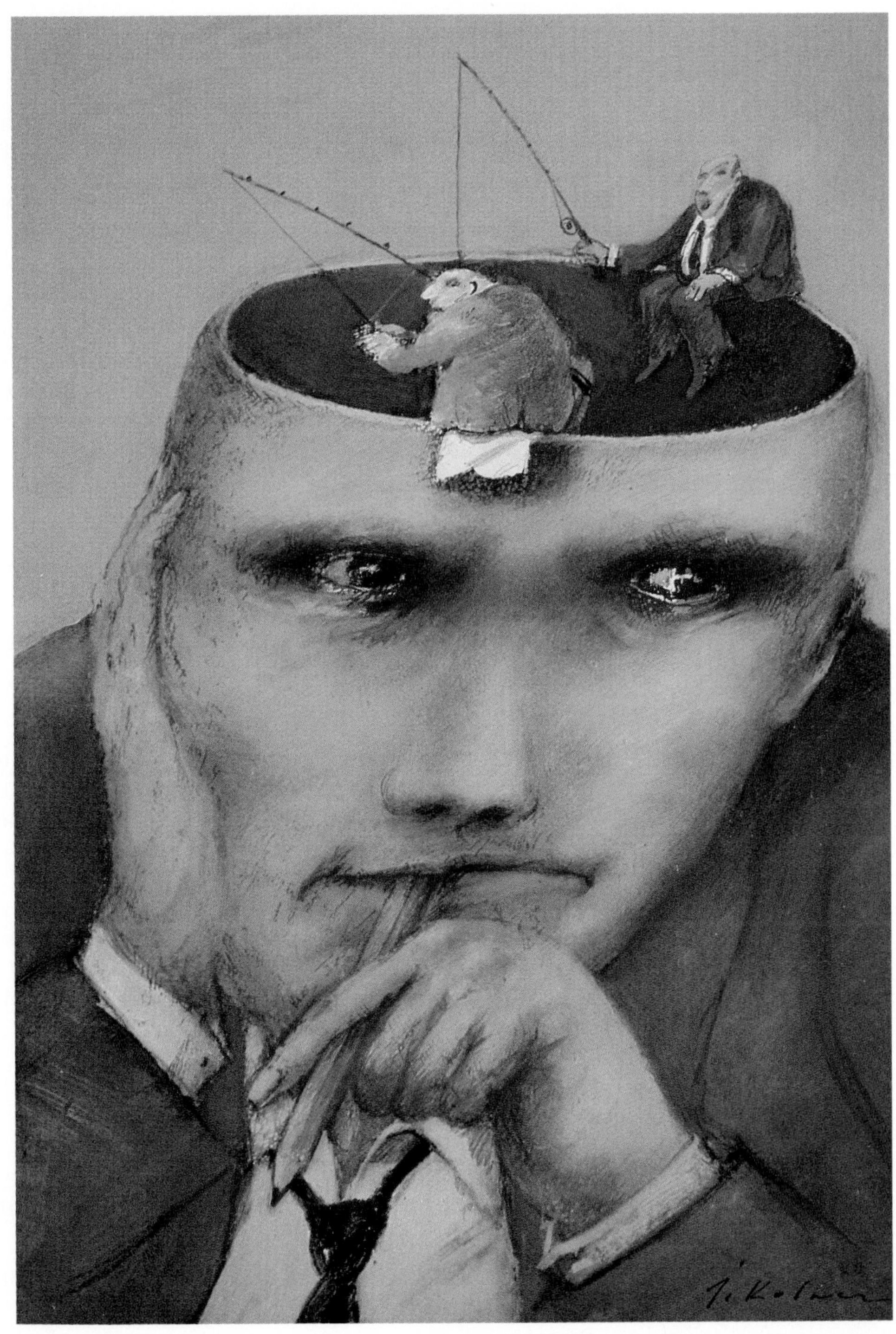

"I don't know anything about inspiration, because I don't know what inspiration is—I've heard about it, but I never saw it."

William Faulkner

"A writer must reflect and interpret his society, his world; he must also provide inspiration and guidance and challenge."

E. B. White

Once in a while when working with new writing teachers, we bump into a paper in which the teacher has responded extensively to the paper's grammar and mechanics but not at all to its ideas. That's a shame. No one in education at any level—and especially not those of us who teach writing—should ever abrogate responsibility for the students' thinking, thinking that is most accurately and directly reflected in the ideas (and not necessarily in the grammar and mechanics) their writing presents. Writing and thinking are inseparable; you can't teach one without teaching the other.

Reading and writing about ideas occupies much of college students' time. The two activities support each other in significant ways. Many times your ability to write about an idea depends directly on how well you've done your reading about it. And many times—for both you and your teacher—the most important aspect of the writing you do is the quality of the ideas it contains and the effectiveness with which they're presented.

Three Common Ways Ideas Are Presented

In the following brief selections we show you three common ways ideas are presented:

1. Direct presentation
2. Indirect presentation
3. Presentation through contrast

You need to be able to (a) recognize at least these three techniques in the things you read and (b) use these techniques in the things you write. Following are two pieces that present their ideas directly, two that present them indirectly, and two (from the same source) that present ideas through contrast.

These first two selections present the ideas they contain very directly—one humorously, the other seriously. As you read them, ask yourself whether you might be able to do the kinds of writing Bob Greene and Susan Griffin are doing. Both kinds are perfectly reasonable ways to present ideas, although they're quite different in execution.

The Permanent Record

Bob Greene

(*See his* Profile of a Writer *section at the beginning of Part Three.*)

There are thousands of theories about what's gone wrong with the world, but I think it comes down to one simple thing: The death of the Permanent Record. 1

2 You remember the Permanent Record. When you were in elementary school, junior high school, and high school, you were constantly being told that if you screwed up, news of that screw-up would be sent down to the principal's office, and would be placed in your Permanent Record.

3 Nothing more needed to be said. No one had ever seen a Permanent Record; that didn't matter. We knew they were there. We all imagined a steel filing cabinet, crammed full of Permanent Records—one for each kid in the school. I think we always assumed that when we graduated our Permanent Record was sent on to college with us, and then when we got out of college our Permanent Record was sent to our employer—probably with a duplicate copy sent to the U.S. Government.

4 I don't know if students are still threatened with the promise of unpleasant things included in their Permanent Record, but I doubt it. I have a terrible feeling that mine was the last generation to know what a Permanent Record was—and that not only has it disappeared from the schools of the land, but it has disappeared as a concept in society as a whole.

Ask your students whether they were ever threatened with "the permanent record" and, if so, under what circumstances. We do not, however, recommend that you push any who are reluctant to share. The issue can be sensitive.

5 There once was a time when people really stopped before they did something they knew was deceitful, immoral, or unethical—no matter how much fun it might sound. They didn't stop because they were such holy folks. They stopped because—no matter how old they were—they had a nagging fear that if they did it, it would end up on their Permanent Record.

6 At some point in the last few decades, I'm afraid, people wised up to something that amazed them: There is no Permanent Record. There probably never was.

7 They discovered that regardless of how badly you fouled up your life or the lives of others, there was nothing permanent about it on your record. You would always be forgiven, no matter what; no matter what you did, other people would shrug it off.

8 So pretty soon men and women—instead of fearing the Permanent Record—started laughing at the idea of the Permanent Record. The kinds of things that they used to be ashamed of—the kinds of things that they used to secretly cringe at when they thought about them—now became "interesting" aspects of their personalities.

9 If those "interesting" aspects were weird enough—if they were the kinds of things that would have really jazzed up the Permanent Record—the people sometimes wrote books confessing those things, and the books became best-sellers. And the people found out that other people—far from scorning them—would line up in the bookstores to get their autographs on the inside covers of the books.

10 The people started going on talk shows to discuss the things that, in decades past, would have been included in their Permanent Records. The talk-show hosts would say, "Thank you for being so honest with us; I'm sure the people in our audience can understand how much guts it must take for you to tell us these things." The Permanent Records were being opened up for the whole world to see—and the sky did not fall in.

11 If celebrities had dips in their careers, all they had to do to guarantee a

new injection of fame was to admit the worst things about themselves—the Permanent Record things—and the celebrity magazines would print those things, and the celebrities would be applauded for their candor and courage. And they would become even bigger celebrities.

As Americans began to realize that there was no Permanent Record, and probably never had been, they deduced for themselves that any kind of behavior was permissible. After all, it wasn't as if anyone was keeping track; all you would have to do—just like the men and women with best-sellers—was to say, "That was a real crazy period in my life." All would be forgiven; all would be erased from the Permanent Record, which, of course, was no longer permanent. 12

Greene's ideas about the "erasure" of the permanent record of celebrities who have battled drugs or other serious problems have been examined in a different but highly interesting light by the syndicated columnist Meg Greenfield. Greenfield has suggested that scare stories about the tragic deaths of various media heroes (athletes, rock stars, other performers) by drug abuse fail to scare (that is, deter) young emulators from engaging in similar self-destructive behaviors. Strangely, such tragic demise is just another part of the dead celebrity's appeal. You might want to discuss this idea—which is both a furthering and a contradiction of what Greene is saying.

And that is where we are today. Without really thinking about it, we have accepted the notion that no one is, indeed, keeping track. No one is even *allowed* to keep track. I doubt that you can scare a school kid today by telling him the principal is going to inscribe something on his Permanent Record; the kid would probably file a suit under the Freedom of Information Act, and gain possession of his Permanent Record by recess. Either that, or the kid would call up his Permanent Record on his computer terminal, and purge any information he didn't want to be there. 13

As for us adults—it has been so long since we have believed in the Permanent Record that the very mention of it today probably brings a nostalgic smile to our faces. We feel naive for ever having believed that a Permanent Record was really down there in the principal's office, anyway. 14

And who really knows if our smiles may freeze on some distant day—the day it is our turn to check out of this earthly world, and we are confronted with a heavenly presence greeting us at the gates of our new eternal home—a heavenly presence sitting there casually leafing through a dusty, battered volume of our Permanent Record as we come jauntily into view. 15

Questions for Writing and Discussion

Prepare short written answers to each of these questions. Be prepared to hand them in and/or discuss them in class, as your teacher directs.

1. How do you respond to Greene's evoking memories of the strict discipline of high school?
2. Once Greene establishes what he means by "the permanent record," he turns the argument into a familiar pattern of "things today aren't as good as they used to be" (compare ¶ 3 and ¶ 5). In doing this, is he lamenting the loss of the permanent record, or laughing at it?
3. In the last paragraph, when Greene suggests the possibility of a "heavenly" permanent record, do you feel he destroys the passage's humor by adding a moralistic tag?
4. Begging the question of whether there is indeed a heavenly permanent

record, do you believe in American society today there is indeed such a thing as a permanent record? If so, what is it, and how might it affect our lives?

5. What is the meaning of the following words—*candor* (¶ 11), *inscribe, purge* (¶ 13), *nostalgic* (¶ 14), *jauntily* (¶ 15)?

Thoughts on Writing:

A Diary

SUSAN GRIFFIN

Susan Griffin is a poet, teacher, and writer. Her books include Made from this Earth: An Anthology of Writings *(1983),* Pornography and Silence *(1981),* Unremembered Country *(1987), and* Women and Nature: The Roaring Inside Her *(1978). In an interview she said, "As a woman, I struggle to write from my life, to reflect all the difficulties, angers, joys of my existence in a culture that attempts to silence women, or that does not take our work, our words or our lives seriously. In this, I am a fortunate woman, to be published, to be read, to be supported, and I live within a cultural and social movement aiming toward the liberation of us all. And within and also beyond all this I experience the transformations of my soul through the holy, the ecstatic, the painfully born or joyously made* word. *I know now that never when I begin to write will I truly know what or how my vision will become." The following selection by Griffin is excerpted from Janet Sternburg's* The Writer on Her Work *(see p. 57).*

Women and Nature may have been the source for Le Guin's image in "Woman/Wildness" (chapter 6).

1 I come back to this problem of despair in writing, myself caught up in it today, feeling a dullness about all language. In the morning I am irritable. I feel as if my sleep had been disturbed, as if a dream were intruded upon, and I am not quite certain how to proceed. This is a profound disorientation. When I am not giving forth words, I am not certain any longer who I am. But it is not like the adolescent searching for an identity; no, this state of mind has an entirely different quality, because in it there is a feeling of loss, as if my old identity, which had worked so well, which seemed to be the whole structure of the universe, were now slipping away, and all my attempts to retrieve it seem graceless, or angry, or blaming. And the old voice of protection and order in me whispers like an Iago that I betray myself.

2 And now I remember the substance of a revelation about faith I had a few months ago. I was walking in the woods and became aware suddenly of a knowledge that enters me in that kind of silence, especially in the presence of an organic life that is not controlled by man. This is a knowledge of a deeply peaceful kinship with all that is alive, a state of mind that language struggles to render, and yet that, paradoxically, makes me want to sing. And at the same time I became aware that the whole impulse to science in western civilization must have been born of doubt. Indeed, all the great questions of science (what is the nature of matter, what is the origin of life, what is the cause of all

Ask students what they think Griffin means by "the feeling of presence," and whether and under what circumstances they have felt it.

This is what we mean by "invention" in what is probably its purest form. It is what is meant by the often-used phrase in the professional literature about writing and its instruction: "writing as discovery."

motion in the universe, what is light) all these began as religious questions, and remained essentially religious until the nineteenth century. So one doubts the feeling of presence, the feeling of unity with all beings, in oneself; one seeks instead a proof, "scientific," quantifiable. Sense data. So perhaps this accounts for the poetic quality of many scientific truths, and yet, also, the fact that the scientific method abolishes intuition (although indeed intuition has solved many "scientific" problems)....

Because each time I write, each time the authentic words break through, I am changed. The older order that I was collapses and dies. I lose control. I do not know exactly what words will appear on the page. I follow language. I follow the sound of the words, and I am surprised and transformed by what I record. 3

And so perhaps despair hides a refusal and perhaps in this refusal is that terror born of faithlessness, which keeps a guard over my thoughts, will not let dreams reach the surface of my mind. 4

When I had written the first draft of *Woman and Nature* the book had a disorganized quality. I had several small chapters, some a paragraph, some a few pages, and no final sequence for them. And so I put the little pieces all in a logical order, by topic, or chronology or whatever seemed most reasonable. But this order did not "work." It was like a well-built bench that had no grace, and so one did not want to sit on it. 5

So I began again putting the pieces together, but this time I simply followed the words intuitively, putting pieces next to one another where the transition seemed wonderful, and that was when the shape of the book began to seem beautiful to me. 6

Questions for Writing and Discussion

Prepare short written answers to each of these questions. Be prepared to hand them in and/or discuss them in class, as your teacher directs.

1. Can you paraphrase the idea that shapes this passage? What is that idea? What sentence in the passage comes closest to directly stating it? How do the passage's other major parts relate to it—are they logical support, personal background, examples, or what?
2. What is the sense of the comparison to Iago (¶ 1)?
3. Compare what Griffin says to what Carl Sagan says in chapter 5. Do they agree or disagree on the nature of science?
4. What does writing do for the author here? What sentences support your claim? Do you think that writing can have that function for you?
5. To whom is the author addressing this "diary"? Why?
6. What do the following words mean—*disorientation* (¶ 1), *paradoxically* (¶ 2), *chronology* (¶ 5)?

While both Bob Greene and Susan Griffin present the ideas in their passages directly—in each case there is a sentence (or sentences) appearing in the passage that says exactly what the piece is trying to get you to see or understand—these next two selections take an indirect approach. Though the selections present their ideas quite clearly, they do more with *suggestion* than with direct statement.

On Not Suppressing Rage

LINDA SCHIERSE LEONARD

Linda Leonard is in private practice as an analyst in San Francisco. She has written On the Way to the Wedding: Transforming the Love Relationship *and* The Wounded Woman *from which the following piece is excerpted. In the selection she uses the word* puella, *which is her term for a woman who is still fundamentally a small child inside.*

1 The fairy tale "The Frog Prince" shows what can happen when rage breaks into the open. . . . Quite often the wounded woman is afraid of the fire and energy raging within. But the analogy to the way one deals with a forest fire may be apt. There one "fights fire with fire." The forest fighters actually set a fire around the dangerous fire in order to limit it. In the same way, letting the rage out into the open with a burst of feeling can actually limit rage by releasing it. For rage can be an act of assertion that sets limits and establishes identity by saying, "I won't take any more of this!" Confronting the suppressed rage with rage is suggested by the Grimm Brothers' version of the fairy tale "The Frog Prince."

2 In that tale, a princess, whose golden ball has rolled away down into a well, has asked a frog to help retrieve her ball. The frog agrees to do so if the princess in return will feed and care for him and allow him in her bed. Once the princess has her ball back, she forgets about her promise. But while she is eating dinner with her father, there is a loud croak outside the door. Her father inquires who is there, and after he hears the frog's story, he tells his daughter she must keep her promise. The princess is repulsed by the frog, but takes him to her room and feeds him. To take him to bed with her is too repugnant, and so she leaves him on the floor. When the frog demands his due, the total fulfillment of the promise, she becomes enraged and throws him angrily against the wall, whereupon he is transformed into a prince, his original form before bewitchment.

Some of your students may here recall the old movie *Network*, in which a central character proclaims, "I'm mad as hell and I'm not going to take it anymore!" As we recall, the practice brought him no great healing or joy. Ask your students whether and under what circumstances they believe this kind of "letting it all out" is beneficial.

3 Here rage is the appropriate response. It releases the prince from his perverted frog form. This way may be especially appropriate for the puella who needs to confront rage. For in becoming enraged herself, she experiences the full force of her own strength and power, which previously she gave over to others. She also defies patriarchal authority. Throwing the frog back

against the wall is like throwing back projections that don't really fit; for example, throwing back a negative projection that women are passive and powerless. One frequent pitfall of the puella is that she accepts projections of powerlessness. But then the power she really has, the power of her feminine feeling and instinct, degenerates and often turns against herself. She is likely to be angry about her loss of power but, at the same time, afraid to show it. And so to avoid confrontation with self and others, she may veil her rage. But when the rage is veiled, its effective power is lost.

In "The Frog Prince" fairy tale, the princess takes responsibility for her 4
rage when she throws the frog against the wall. She pays attention to her feminine instincts and feelings and trusts them when she acts on her feeling of repulsion and disobeys her father's orders. When she first met the frog, she was a helpless little girl who let her golden ball roll away from her, as so many women lose access to the strong center of their feminine spirit. And as a helpless girl, she made a promise she didn't want to keep. How true this is of many women who exchange their independence for the promise of security and material well-being. . . . In "The Frog Prince" there is transformation because the princess finally takes responsibility for her feminine feelings and asserts them. In an act of rage, she redeems the frog and transforms him into a prince. When she asserts herself and throws the frog against the wall, he turns into her lover. So the possibility of intimate relationship happens along with the rage.

What do your students suppose to be the basis for Leonard's implying that this is something needed by women in particular? Where do men stand on this issue?

Women today need to do this not only in their personal lives but on the 5
cultural level as well. Many women in our time are angry because their feminine values have been put down. They need to assert themselves forcefully out of their own feminine experience, and this may take a few angry outbursts. Some of the cultural frogs (the projections and prejudices) need to be thrown against the wall. But ultimately this expression of rage needs to be not only forceful but formed and focused effectively as well. And this conscious awareness of one's energy and how one wants to use it may keep women from making those original false promises that keep them helpless. In learning to relate to their rage, they may raise the level of consciousness about the unresolved cultural rage which at its worst leads to war and persecution.

Questions for Writing and Discussion

Prepare short written answers to each of these questions. Be prepared to hand them in and/or discuss them in class, as your teacher directs.

1. Leonard says in the first paragraph that "rage can be an act of assertion that sets limits and establishes identity by saying, 'I won't take any more of this!'" In your experience, is that true? Can rage have this kind of healthful effect?
2. In Leonard's version, rage can transform both the person who becomes enraged and the person who is the recipient of it. Recall a time when you were the recipient of someone's rage—was it a transforming experience? Explain.

3. If you combine the statement quoted above in question 1 and the following passage, do you have *all* that the passage is really saying?

   For in becoming enraged herself, she experiences the full force of her own strength and power, which previously she gave over to others. She also defies patriarchal authority. Throwing the frog back against the wall is like throwing back projections that don't really fit; for example, throwing back a negative projection that women are passive and powerless. (¶ 3)

   Does the preceding passage *suggest* more than just this one idea? If so, what more does it *suggest?*

4. Do you feel that what Leonard says is true of men as well as women? Why or why not?
5. How well does the story of the frog prince fit Leonard's point? Do you think she tells the story to illustrate her point, or to prove it? What's the difference in the two techniques? How else could she illustrate her point? How else could she prove it?
6. What do the following words mean—*repugnant* (¶ 2), *patriarchal, negative, projection* (¶ 3)?

Bridges: Another Perspective

Linda Schierse Leonard urges against women's quiet suppression of their inner rage. Let some of it out, she seems to say; doing so is likely to do you more good than harm. Back in chapter 7, in "Women's Life Today," Anne Morrow Lindbergh urges what seems to be the opposite: a quiet turning inward, where self-knowledge can be found. Reread Lindbergh. Who's right? Are there ways in which both are right, or both wrong? Are they really saying opposite things, giving contradictory advice? Explain.

Ask students where they think Ted Lester, from the Matthiessen selection "Men's Lives" (chapter 9), would be on this issue. Does he need to let out his anger more?

PREREADING WORKSHEET

Before you read the following piece by William Least Heat-Moon, write brief responses to these questions:

1. What is your understanding of the meaning of the word *Cajun?* In what contexts have you previously encountered it?
2. What images come to mind when you think about Louisiana—particularly that area often called Bayou Country or Cajun Country, the regions west and south of Baton Rouge and New Orleans?
3. Have you heard of Henry Wadsworth Longfellow and his long narrative poem "Evangeline"? If so, what have you heard or read?

4. Whether you have knowledge of French or not, can you make a good guess at what these phrases mean—*Le Grande Dérangement, café noir, Petit Paris,* and *de l'Amérique?*
5. What is your understanding of the word *trinity?*

William Least Heat-Moon

William Least Heat-Moon is a writer and part-time teacher of writing at the University of Missouri's School of Journalism. In Blue Highways *(from which this excerpt is taken) the narrator, having lost both his job and his wife on the same day, decides to drive his van around the perimeter of the United States.*

By "Talk about your three-persons-in-one controversies," William Least Heat-Moon means no disrespect to the Christian belief in the Holy Trinity of Father, Son, and Holy Ghost. You might want to point out this aspect to students, some of whom may otherwise misunderstand the writer's intention.

Talk about your three-persons-in-one controversies. In St. Martinville a bronze statue of a seated young woman in wooden shoes, hands folded peacefully, head turned toward the Bayou Teche, commemorates—at one and the same time—Emmeline Labiche, Evangeline Bellefontaine, and Dolores Del Rio. The monument sits in the Poste de Attakapas Cemetery behind the great Catholic church of Saint Martin de Tours. After the bayou, the cemetery and church are the oldest things in town. The cruciform building, full of flickering candles, bloodied crucifixes, anguished representations of the Stages of the Cross, and plaster saints with maces and drawn swords, contains in one wing a twelve-foot-high replica of the Grotto of Lourdes. Although mass is now celebrated in English, the place, with its ancient torments, remains quite French in the old manner. 1

The bronze woman sits, literally, above the eighteenth-century grave of Emmeline Labiche, who, Cajuns say, wandered primitive America in search of her lover, Louis Arcenaux, whom she was separated from during the forced Acadian exodus (*Le Grand Dérangement*) out of British Nova Scotia. At the army outpost on the Teche, she finally found Louis—engaged to another. Emmeline, exhausted from her wanderings, went mad from the shock of his faithlessness and died shortly later. They buried her behind the church. That's history. 2

But the name on the statue above Emmeline's tombstone is Evangeline. Cajuns believe Longfellow patterned his wandering heroine on Emmeline, and probably he did, although the poet never visited Louisiana, relying instead on information furnished by Nathaniel Hawthorne and a St. Martinville lawyer once Longfellow's student at Harvard. To visualize the land, he went to Banvard's "Moving Diorama" of the Mississippi—a three-mile-long canvas painting of a boat-level view. Longfellow said the river came to him. He filled in with details from Darby's *Geographical Description of Louisiana* and his own imagination, changing the outcome so that in old age Evangeline 3 at last finds her love on his deathbed in a Philadelphia almshouse. That's the poetry.

4 Then there's Hollywood. The face on the statue, smooth and beautiful and untouched by madness or years of wandering the wilderness, is that of Dolores Del Rio, the Mexican-born actress who completed the trinity by playing Evangeline in the 1929 movie filmed nearby at Lake Catahoula. To thank the townspeople, the cast presented a statue of Evangeline-Emmeline that Miss Del Rio posed for. The actress, cynics said, saw a chance to have her beauty immortalized in something more durable than celluloid. If many citizens no longer know the name, they all know the face.

5 St. Martinville was pure Cajun bayou, distinctive and memorable in a tattered way. Wood and iron galleries were rickety, brick buildings eroded, corrugated metal roofs rusting. The church stood on the square, the courthouse down Main Street. On the upper side of the square that morning, Maurice Oubre's bakery turned out the last of the day's pastry, and on the west side at Thibodeaux's Cafe & Barbershop, Mr. Thibodeaux had been cutting hair since five A.M. Across the street, taverns got swept out, and the smell of last night's beer mixed with Thibodeaux's thick *café noir,* Oubre's croissants, and the damp air off the Teche.

6 In the *Petit Paris de l'Amérique* Museum gift shop next to the church, a powdery old lady asked the priest to bless a souvenir candle she'd just bought; he waved his hand over it and said, "May God bless this candle and all who use it, in the name of the Father, Son, and Holy Spirit." Above his head, on the Coke machine, a sign: SHOPLIFTING IS A CRIME AND SIN. GOD SEES ALL AND REMEMBERS!!! Sin was underlined three times.

POSTREADING WORKSHEET

Now that you have read the piece by Least Heat-Moon, write your responses to the following questions:

1. How does Least Heat-Moon adapt the word *trinity* from your understanding of its use to his own use?
2. How does his use of the trinity concept help to structure his piece?
3. *Cajun* is a dialect-influenced pronunciation of *Arcadian.* Least Heat-Moon refers to "the forced Arcadian exodus," when French settlers in British Nova Scotia (called Arcadia by the French) were forced to leave that area. Many migrated to southwestern Louisiana, where they came to be called Cajuns. These Cajuns became famous for their life-style—particularly music and cooking. How does this background match the contexts in which you have previously heard the word *Cajun?* How does this background relate to the images of Cajun Country that you listed earlier?
4. How did reading the terms *Le Grande Dérangement, café noir,* and *Petit Paris de l'Amérique* in context help you clarify the meanings of those words?

We make no great claims to proficiency in French, but in-context translations of these phrases would be, in order, "The Great Migration," "black coffee," and "Little Paris of [or in] America."

Questions for Writing and Discussion

Prepare short written answers to each of these questions. Be prepared to hand them in and/or discuss them in class, as your teacher directs.

1. How do you feel about the statue's triple nature? Does that quality in any way cheapen or lessen the statue's significance for you?
2. Least Heat-Moon shows how the statue brings together history, poetry, and Hollywood. What does that element have to do with (a) the fifth paragraph, which describes the town in the early morning, and (b) the fact that in the sign described in the last paragraph, *sin* is underlined three times?
3. Of the four passages you've read so far in this chapter, this one makes its point the most indirectly. What is its point, and how does what the passage *says* compare with what it *suggests?*
4. How would your response to this passage change had the progression of examples, rather than being history-poetry-Hollywood, been Hollywood-poetry-history?
5. What do the following words mean—*commemorates* (¶ 1), *exodus* (¶ 2), *almshouse, diorama* (¶ 3), *celluloid* (¶ 4)?

This question about the point of the selection is not meant to subject students to yet another experience in trying to guess some English teacher's idea of the one true meaning; rather, the question is designed to bring home to them strongly the idea that such passages may well have more—a lot more—going on in them than immediately meets the eye.

These next two passages, each from a single source, make their point(s) in more detail and more depth than the passages shown above. (They also take longer to do so.) Each passage makes its own point explicitly, but the two passages taken together make another point obliquely. We think these passages are typical of the kind of writing college students need to be able to read to prosper as students, and are also exemplary of a third common way ideas are presented: through contrast. Here are two matching passages from the authors of *Women's Ways of Knowing.* The first is their description of the development of human beings according to the Harvard psychologist William Perry; the second is their own description of human development.

One of our reviewers thought these passages too difficult for college freshmen. We hope that view is wrong.

Patterns of Human Development

MARY BELENKY, BLYTHE CLINCHY, NANCY GOLDBERGER, and JILL TARULE

Mary Field Belenky is on the faculty of the University of Vermont; Blythe McVicker Clinchy, Wellesley College; Nancy Rule Goldberger, the Fielding Institute in Santa Barbara; and Jill Mattuck Tarule, Lesley College Graduate School.

In his influential book *Forms of Intellectual and Ethical Development in the College Years* (1970), Perry describes how students' conceptions of the nature and origins of knowledge evolve and how their understanding of themselves as knowers changes over time. 1

2 While a few women were included in Perry's original study as subjects, only the interviews with men were used in illustrating and validating his scheme on intellectual and ethical development. Later, when Perry assessed the women's development with the aid of his map, the women were found to conform with the patterns that had been observed in the male data. While this strategy enabled the researchers to see what women might have in common with men, it was poorly designed to uncover those themes that might be more prominent among women. Our work focuses on what else women might have to say about the development of their minds and on alternative routes that are sketchy or missing in Perry's version.

Notice that the authors take on Perry not directly but obliquely. Later on, the high degree of their disagreement becomes much clearer.

3 In his book Perry depicts a passage through a sequence of epistemological perspectives that he calls *positions*. It is through these coherent interpretative frameworks that students give meaning to their educational experience. Perry traces a progression from an initial position that he calls *basic dualism*, where the student views the world in polarities of right/wrong, black/white, we/they, and good/bad. Here passive learners are dependent on authorities to hand down the truth, teaching them "right from wrong." Gradually the student becomes increasingly aware of the diversity of opinion and the multiple perspectives that others hold, and the dualistic faith in absolute authority and truth is shaken. Dualism gives way to *multiplicity* as the student comes to understand that authorities may not have the right answers, at least in some areas, such as the humanities, which seem to be more a matter of opinion and taste than fact. The student begins to grow beyond a dependency and trust in external authorities and carves out his own territory of personal freedom: "Everyone has a right to his own opinion and mine is as good as any other." As the student's personal opinion is challenged by a teacher's insistence on evidence and support for opinion, multiplicity yields to *relativism subordinate,* where an analytical, evaluative approach to knowledge is consciously and actively cultivated at least in the academic disciplines one is being tutored in, if not in the rest of one's life. It is only with the shift into full *relativism* that the student completely comprehends that truth is relative, that the meaning of an event depends on the context in which that event occurs and on the framework that the knower uses to understand that event, and that relativism pervades all aspects of life, not just the academic world. Only then is the student able to understand that knowledge is constructed, not given; contextual, not absolute; mutable, not fixed. It is within relativism that Perry believes the affirmation of personal identity and commitment evolves.

Ask students what the significance is of calling these perspectives *positions* rather than *stages.*

4 Since the introduction of the Perry scheme, educators and researchers have used it as a way of understanding intellectual development in young adults in academic settings and as a developmental framework to guide educational practice. The Perry scheme was very important as it stimulated our interest in modes of knowing and provided us with our first images of the paths women might take as they developed an understanding of their intellectual potential, as well as providing a description of the routes most often taken by men.

[Now the authors give their own description of human development.]

When we began our analysis by classifying the women's data using Perry's scheme, we found that the women's thinking did not fit so neatly into his categories. There were digressions of thought ("Do you want me to talk about what society says or what I think?"), twists and turns in perspectives, themes (for instance, the importance of firsthand experience and of gut reaction), and elaborations of points of view that we simply had not anticipated. It was our continued, and often heated, discussion of the disagreements first over our classifications and then over the classification system itself that led to some of the insights from which this book emerged. 5

Our work and classification system differs from Perry's in yet another way. In Perry's scheme, there is a clear sequential ordering of positions and, although he does not claim they represent an invariant developmental sequence since individuals can retreat or temporize, he does believe that each position is an advance over the last and that the ultimate end point in the move out of dualistic thought is what he calls "commitment within relativism." Harvard is clearly a pluralistic institution that promotes the development of relativistic thought. What we believe Perry heard in his interviews with men and captured so well in his developmental scheme is the way in which a relatively homogeneous group of people are socialized into and make sense of a system of values, standards, and objectives. The linear sequence in development stands out clearly when the context in which development occurs is held constant. 6

This is a key point; paraphrased, it means, "In the real world things are much more complicated."

When the context is allowed to vary, as it did in our study, because we included women of widely different ages, life circumstances, and backgrounds, universal developmental pathways are far less obvious. We describe in the book epistemological *perspectives* from which women know and view the world. We leave it to future work to determine whether these perspectives have any stagelike qualities. The question of why and when women shift from one mode of knowing to another, as many of our women evidently did at points in their lives, is an important, though difficult, one—and is not well addressed by our data, which, for the most part, are limited to single interviews with individuals. However, we draw on the retrospective accounts of the women about their life changes, as well as on some repeated interviews with the same woman over the course of several years, to speculate about different developmental sequences or trajectories. 7

Building on Perry's scheme, we grouped women's perspectives on knowing into five major epistemological categories: *silence,* a position in which women experience themselves as mindless and voiceless and subject to the whims of external authority; *received knowledge,* a perspective from which women conceive of themselves as capable of receiving, even reproducing, knowledge from the all-knowing external authorities but not capable of creating knowledge on their own; *subjective knowledge,* a perspective from which truth and knowledge are conceived of as personal, private, and subjectively known or intuited; *procedural knowledge,* a position in which women 8 are invested in learning and applying objective procedures for obtaining and communicating knowledge; and *constructed knowledge,* a position in which women view all knowledge as contextual, experience themselves as creators of knowledge, and value both subjective and objective strategies for knowing.

9 We recognize (1) that these five ways of knowing are not necessarily fixed, exhaustive, or universal categories, (2) that they are abstract or "pure" categories that cannot adequately capture the complexities and uniqueness of an individual woman's thought and life, (3) that similar categories can be found in men's thinking, and (4) that other people might organize their observations differently. Furthermore, the small number of women in our sample who fell into the position of silence makes these observations particularly tentative and underscores the need for continued efforts to understand the developmental consequences of severe violence and social isolation. Our intention is to share, not prove, our observations.

Ask students what it does for the author's position to have the purpose phrased this way. What does this phrasing require the author to do—or not do?

Questions for Writing and Discussion

Prepare short written answers to each of these questions. Be prepared to hand them in and/or discuss them in class, as your teacher directs.

1. Have you, in any of your other courses or other experience, run into a scheme like Perry's (or perhaps Perry's itself) being used to account for stages of knowledge or development? If so, describe it.
2. What do the following words mean—*epistemological, dualism, polarities, multiplicity, pervades, mutable, constructed, affirmation* (¶ 3), *digressions* (¶ 5), *invariant, temporize, pluralistic, relativistic, homogeneous* (¶ 6), *retrospective, trajectories* (¶ 7)?
3. How do you feel about the criticisms the authors make of Perry's scheme? Are the criticisms fair? How do you think Perry would respond to those criticisms?
4. Summarize in two lists the two sets of positions.
5. Do you see anything like those positions in your own life? If so, describe them—how do they match those the authors describe here (or match Perry's)?
6. What essential contrast emerges from reading both passages?

KEY POINTS TO REMEMBER: Writing About Ideas

When writing about ideas, keep the following points in mind:

- Plan the way you'll present your idea.
- Try direct presentation of the idea *or*
- Try indirect presentation of the idea *or*
- Present the idea through contrast.

Plan the Way You'll Present Your Idea

It's important to have a plan—a way to present ideas. You may want to use specific examples to get the idea across, to tell a story that illustrates the idea, to present its background in some detail, or to present it in contrast with some other, more familiar notion. However you choose to do so, the more strange your idea is to your reader or the more difficult your idea is, the more necessary your plan becomes. The point here is that although countless different plans and patterns are available to you for presenting ideas, you must have some kind of concrete plan.

Direct Presentation of the Idea

Direct presentation is a common way to present an idea. Consider, for example, the functions of the second and third paragraphs in Bob Greene's "The Permanent Record." The value of the background there is that it both defines what Greene is talking about and serves to center the reader on those characteristics of the permanent record which constitute the idea Greene wants to write about. Such "backgrounding," a sense that we're watching this idea develop over time, is typical of this piece; throughout the selection is a general movement of "the way things were then; the way they are now; the way they might be in the future (here the afterlife)," and we get to watch how Greene's idea unfolds through this easy-to-follow pattern.

The overall pattern in Susan Griffin's passage about writing is similar: the background for the idea she wants to create and communicate is given by a movement from the present (¶ 1), to a memory of the past (¶ 2), to two short paragraphs that directly state her idea (¶ 3–4), and finally to another memory that illustrates that idea (¶ 5–6). Thus, by the time she tells us straight out what it is she's talking about, we've been well prepared for it in terms of a description of her current status and the long example (¶ 2) from her past. This use of movement from past to present, of memories and specific examples that illustrate the idea being developed, is characteristic of the kind of patterning writers do when they're writing about ideas.

Indirect Presentation of the Idea

This is a second common method of presentation. A writer may use indirect presentation through telling a story or as in the Leonard passage about not suppressing rage, by borrowing someone else's story ("The Frog Prince") to illustrate the point. Of course, the story has to fit the point closely; you don't want to sidetrack readers into thinking, "But that really doesn't illustrate the point," or "I don't see the connection." Notice too how Leonard, at the end of her passage, turns from her indirect strategy of telling the Frog Prince story to her idea's application: "Women today need to do this . . . " (¶ 5).

An even more indirect way of presenting an idea is taken by William Least Heat-Moon in the "Three-in-One" passage from his book *Blue Highways.* He presents his reader with a specific, detailed, unusual situation that (he hopes) will be thought-provoking as well. By the end of the "Hollywood" paragraph (¶ 4), you may have been ready for him to draw a conclusion about the "meaning" of this three-in-one statue. But some writers don't lay it all out for you; instead, they invite *you* to see their idea. If readers are thus provoked to come to a conclusion, then the piece begins to be successful. Least Heat-Moon's final paragraph gives his readers one last hint about what he's thinking, but he's not going to come right out and tell us—to read this selection fully, we truly must think for ourselves.

Presentation of the Idea Through Contrast

Some writers follow a third common plan and tackle their ideas by contrasting them with someone else's. In the case of the two passages excerpted from *Women's Ways of Knowing*, the authors take Perry's model of "positions" of development—one with which they can assume many of their readers will be at least vaguely familiar—as a starting point for explaining their own. That is, they're explaining the *unknown* (their own model) in terms of the *known* (Perry's model). Notice in particular that when they begin to present their own model (¶ 5), they start by giving us information about how their model evolved at least partly from their experiences trying to use Perry's. And notice too that the selection ends with a paragraph suggesting the limitations and applications of their own model.

Once again, an unlimited number of ways are available for presenting ideas. We have discussed and illustrated only three of the most common ways here. The essential point to remember is that, because ideas are inherently abstract, you need to give specific consideration to how you're going to present the ideas you want to write about.

✓✓✓ WORKSHEET: Writing About Ideas

Here we're going to emphasize the *early* stages of writing a simple paper about an idea. Then, in the next section, you'll see more of how that paper subsequently developed. We'll thus be able to follow one student through most of her experience of writing this particular paper. Wendy Vermillion, our writer here, is a college freshman whose English class had been reading and discussing how such ideas as equality and liberty were fundamental to the writing of America's founders—even though those ideas were highly abstract and in fact difficult to explain clearly. This discussion led to a writing assignment in which students were asked to write about an abstract idea. Here were the options:

You can kick off this assignment by having students brainstorm a list of abstract ideas—for example, from their other classes.

1. Write about something you wish for, something that doesn't exist today but, if it did exist, would be perfect. An example might be a perfect computer, a perfect car, or a perfect book. The abstract idea here is *perfection:* what would it be like?
2. Write about an idea you've read of in one of your high school or college textbooks—such as civil rights, accountability, or laissez-faire. Compare the idea as you read of it with another version—your own—of the same idea.

3. Write about something you've seen that made you think in abstract terms about a philosophical idea, something like, for example, a nuclear power plant. Let the physical description be quite detailed, so much so that you *suggest* rather than *state* your idea.

As Wendy thought over the assignment that night, she made this list of possible topics:

- A perfect robot
- Thoreau's idea, from *Walden*, of "a simple life" and how that might (or might not) work today
- The first bad car wreck she ever saw, and what that made her think about her own life

The question then became one with two parts:

1. Which topic suggested to her more useful content right from the start? (Such a topic might make the paper easier to write.)
2. Which topic did she feel a larger *personal investment* in? (She remembered the chapter about expressive writing and its advice that unless writers have a powerful investment in their writing—whatever kind it is—the writing is unlikely to be good.)

Under those criteria, Wendy rejected the Thoreau topic, because once she got past the first line ("Thoreau's idea of a simple life as expressed in *Walden* can be usefully contrasted with such a life today because . . ."), she couldn't think of anything else to say that would be less than trite and boring; the piece sounded too much like something she was forced to write in high school. She also rejected the last topic—the car wreck—because, as she later explained to us, it was "just too icky."

The remaining topic, a perfect robot, seemed to have potential on two scores. First, Wendy's brainstormed list of things she might say looked pretty good. It had these items:

- Old, bad science fiction movies (Wendy's hobby) about robots—*The Day the Earth Stood Still, Robbie the Robot,* and their more recent sequels, such as *Star Wars*
- The build-it-yourself robots some electronics stores sell, and how well—or poorly—they might perform
- What a truly perfect robot might do

Second, Wendy did have some personal investment in this subject. One of her friends in high school had owned a robot from a local electronics store, and Wendy had helped her build a high school science fair project around that robot, the project having to do with designing a new "arm end" (we would call it a wrist) that would allow a greater range of motion and replaceable "hands." Though the project hadn't worked out that well, Wendy had gained considerable experience thinking about robots.

After deciding to write about the perfect robot, Wendy next went about making a rough plan for her paper. Despite years of advice from her previous English teachers, Wendy wasn't one for outlining English papers. She did, however, usually jot down a kind of a rough list of things she wanted to say. For the robot paper, the first part of her list looked something like this:

We don't mean to belittle outlining. We use it all the time, although more when we're revising than when we're planning. What we're showing, however, is that many good alternatives exist.

Introduction: old robot movies

What some robots are really like

What the ideal robot would be like—thinking, growing, and so on

When there might be such a thing

The plan, then, would be to use the examples of robots in movies and of mail-order robots to set up the idea of "Well, then, what would the perfect robot be like?"

Here's what Wendy's first draft looked like:

The Perfect Robot

Wendy Vermillion, college writing student

1 Anybody's list of the stars of <u>Star Wars</u> movies would have to include R2D2 and C3PO. So what's remarkable about that? Well, the remarkable part is that they're not people--or even Wookies. No, they're robots. Even more interesting, they're stars not because they're perfect but because they're not. One or the other of them seems to get dismembered in every movie, and neither excels in either common sense or courage. It's those qualities which make them, paradoxically, human; it's those qualities which make them interesting to us; and it is, in fact, those qualities which make them stars.

2 Is there such a thing as a perfect robot? If there is, it sure isn't the one my friend Mary owned. Whatever had possessed her parents to buy it for her out of some consumer electronics catalog I'll never know. What could it do? Go forward. Go back. Raise your right arm. Raise your left arm. Pretty impressive, eh? Oh, and by then it would need new batteries.

3 If there were a perfect robot, what would it be like? Imagine a machine able to wax the car, wash the dishes, and iron the clothes, not to mention the fact that it would also be able to entertain, learn, and perform several other jobs. What a time-saver a self-ambulatory robot would be. Who wouldn't want to sit back and relax while a robot did the house chores?

If I were to design my own robot it would need to do more than just the everyday house chores like making the beds and dusting the shelves. First of all, it would need to be intellectual. It would need to be able to reason, understand, and carry out other types of mental activity, such as helping me compute difficult math problems or proofreading my English papers for grammatical or spelling mistakes. Intellect would be the key quality of my personalized robot. 4

Although my computerized robot will not be able to physically grow, it will constantly grow mentally. It will be able to acquire knowledge, learn from experiences, and even ask questions when it is curious. It will apply this learned knowledge to solve problems, answer questions, and make decisions for itself and for others. 5

This robot will be activated by the sound of my voice and will be able to talk back to me as well as display its spoken words on its own computer screen. This way, I can simply dictate what I need it to do instead of using a keyboard. 6

Obviously, this is going to be a very valuable and prized robot, with so many qualities. To increase this value, my robot will be indestructible. There will be no way the information and abilities of my robot can be erased. It will be able only to expand its memory and knowledge and never forget or lose information unless I code it in to delete something. 7

Imagination is another quality that will be included in my robot. It will actually be able to "think" of ideas and able to analyze its own views. We, my robot and I, will be able to discuss or argue about issues because our views will be somewhat different. With this imagination it will be extremely creative. This will enable it to entertain with such games as checkers and ticktacktoe, or even design its own unique games. 8

My robot will be a masterpiece, able to perform almost any task with agile precision. It will be able to solve tough problems in a matter of seconds that would normally take human beings hours to complete. It will use its intelligence and agility to perform numerous tasks. My robot will be my maid, my business partner, my companion, and my own compact library rolled into one unique, dynamic, and complex machine. There is but one problem. How many decades until this ideal robot is actually built? 9

Do you think Wendy's plan worked? Did the use of robots from both movies and her own experience set up what she did later in the paper? Our own response is mixed—the two opening paragraphs present a good idea but don't really do enough to connect with the rest of the paper. And the rest of the paper is a little flat. Still, it's a good first draft, with plenty in it from which to build a solid paper. The next moves are the subject of the following section.

SAMPLE WRITING ASSIGNMENT AND CASE STUDY CLOSE-UP

Here are the comments Wendy's classmates made about the first draft you saw in the previous section. The paper was read by two other students:

Once again, we don't want to give the idea that all peer readers' comments are on the mark. We just don't see much point in showing things that aren't productive.

Reader 1. Wendy, this is a good start, but I don't understand how the first two paragraphs connect with the rest of the paper. If that's all you're going to do with them, why not just leave them out and start with "Is there such a thing as a perfect robot?" That point about why R2D2 and C3PO are popular is a good one. Can you use it in the later part of the paper somewhere?

Reader 2. I agree with what your first reader said, that you need to work some of what you set up in the first paragraphs into the body of the piece. Looking at the rest of the piece, it seems to take you lots of words to say what you say. Can you tighten up the sentence structure some too, pretty much throughout?

Here's the revision Wendy did that night. Notice that she addressed both sets of concerns, thus beefing up the first paragraph, dropping the second, and working on sentence-level revision for economy throughout. We'll show you both the original version and the revised version.

The Perfect Robot

[Original]

1 Anybody's list of the stars of Star Wars movies would have to include R2D2 and C3PO. So what's remarkable about that? Well, the remarkable part is that they're not people--or even Wookies. No, they're robots. Even more interesting, they're stars not because they're perfect but because they're not. One or the other of them seems to get dismembered in every movie, and neither excels in either common sense or courage. It's those qualities which make them, paradoxically, human; it's those qualities which make them interesting to us; and it is, in fact, those qualities which make them stars.

[Revised]

Any list of the Star Wars movie stars has to include R2D2 1
and C3PO. The remarkable part about that is they're not people, or even Wookies--they're robots. They have what must be a very unusual quality for stars: neither excels in either common sense or courage, and in fact one or the other of them seems to get dismembered in every movie. In fact, they're stars not because they're perfect but because they're not. Those failings and frailties are the qualities that make them human, and it's those same qualities that make them interesting to us. It is, in fact, those qualities that make them stars.

[Original]

Is there such a thing as a perfect robot? If there is, it sure isn't the 2
one my friend Mary owned. Whatever had possessed her parents to buy it for her out of some consumer electronics catalog I'll never know. What could it do? Go forward. Go back. Raise your right arm. Raise your left arm. Pretty impressive, eh? Oh, and by then it would need new batteries.

[Revised]

Could there ever be such a thing as a perfect robot? If there 2
were, what would it be like? And would we be interested in it, if it really was perfect?

[Original]

If there were a perfect robot, what would it be like? Imagine a 3
machine able to wax the car, wash the dishes, and iron the clothes, not to mention the fact that it would also be able to entertain, learn, and perform several other jobs. What a time-saver a self-ambulatory robot would be. Who wouldn't want to sit back and relax while a robot did the house chores?

[Revised]

3 Imagine a machine waxing the car, washing the dishes, and ironing the clothes, one that could also entertain, learn, and perform several other jobs. What a time-saver a robot that could walk, talk, and take care of the house would be. Who wouldn't want to sit back and relax while a robot does the house chores?

[Original]

4 If I were to design my own robot it would need to do more than just the everyday house chores like making the beds and dusting the shelves. First of all, it would need to be intellectual. It would need to be able to reason, understand, and carry out other types of mental activity, such as helping me compute difficult math problems or proofreading my English papers for grammatical or spelling mistakes. Intellect would be the key quality of my personalized robot.

[Revised]

4 My own perfect robot would need to do more than just the everyday house chores like making the beds and dusting the shelves. It would need to be able to reason, understand, and carry out other types of mental activity, especially to help me compute difficult math problems and proofread my English papers. Intellect would be the key quality of my personalized robot.

[Original]

5 Although my computerized robot will not be able to physically grow, it will constantly grow mentally. It will be able to acquire knowledge, learn from experiences, and even ask questions when it is curious. It will apply this learned knowledge to solve problems, answer questions, and make decisions for itself and for others.

[Revised]

My computerized robot will constantly be growing mentally. 5
It will be able to acquire knowledge, learn from experiences, and even ask questions when it is curious. It will apply this learned knowledge to solve problems, answer questions, and make decisions.

[Original]

This robot will be activated by the sound of my voice and will be 6
able to talk back to me as well as display its spoken words on its own computer screen. This way, I can simply dictate what I need it to do instead of using a keyboard.

[Revised]

This robot will be fully voice-responsive: able to speak, to 6
respond to spoken commands, to display its own words on its screen, and to take typed commands as well.

[Original]

Obviously, this is going to be a very valuable and prized robot, with 7
so many qualities. To increase this value, my robot will be indestructible. There will be no way the information and abilities of my robot can be erased. It will be able only to expand its memory and knowledge and never forget or lose information unless I code it in to delete something.

[Revised]

My robot and its memory will be indestructible. There will 7
be no way its information and abilities can be erased. It will never forget or lose information unless it is programmed to delete something.

[Original]

8 Imagination is another quality that will be included in my robot. It will actually be able to "think" of ideas and able to analyze its own views. We, my robot and I, will be able to discuss or argue about issues because our views will be somewhat different. With this imagination it will be extremely creative. This will enable it to entertain with such games as checkers and ticktacktoe, or even design its own unique games.

[Revised]

8 Imagination will be another quality of my robot. It will be able to think of ideas and analyze its own views. My robot and I will be able to discuss or argue about issues. This imagination will also make it extremely creative, so that it can not only entertain with such games as checkers and ticktacktoe but also design its own unique games.

[Original]

9 My robot will be a masterpiece, able to perform almost any task with agile precision. It will be able to solve tough problems in a matter of seconds that would normally take human beings hours to complete. It will use its intelligence and agility to perform numerous tasks. My robot will be my maid, my business partner, my companion, and my own compact library rolled into one unique, dynamic, and complex machine. There is but one problem. How many decades until this ideal robot is actually built?

[Revised]

9 My robot will be a masterpiece, able to perform almost any task with agile precision, to solve tough problems in a matter of seconds that would normally take human beings hours to

complete, to use its intelligence and agility to perform numerous tasks. My robot will be my maid, my business partner, my companion, and my own compact library rolled into one unique, dynamic, and complex machine. There is but one problem. How many decades until this ideal robot is actually built?

And when it is built, will its perfection keep me from liking 10
it, keep it from being my star? Well, what do you think?

WRITING ASSIGNMENTS

1. Write about how anger figures in your life. Where do you encounter it, what form(s) does it take, and how do you deal with it?
2. Pick one change you could make in the world by magic—*un*invent something. What would it be, and how would the world look without it?
3. Space exploration provides a range of new ideas. What should be humanity's position regarding space exploration—that is, where should we be ten, twenty, fifty, one hundred, five hundred years from now? How can we get there from where we are now?
4. Pick an idea that interests you from your reading and explain it in detail. Use plenty of examples.
5. The cartoon on page 271 presents the literal (and therefore, in this case, humorous) side of the expression, "fishing for ideas." Some people like to think that ideas can be made to happen through some kind of systematic mental (or physical and mental) process—be it meditation, formal logic, or some proscribed problem-solving pattern. Despite that line of argument, many of the best ideas have come to people accidentally—in the shower, during some other kind of hard work, or during sleep. We present you with two writing options based on this picture:
   a. When, where, how, do you get your best ideas? In particular, pick one of your best-ever ideas, and write about how it came to you.
   b. Do a little library research on an author, and write about where he or she thinks ideas (or creativity, in any sphere of human endeavor) come from. Be scrupulous about acknowledging your source(s).

Focus on Critical Writing

6. Take and defend a position on the subject discussed in the pair of readings entitled "Patterns of Human Development."
7. An argument often made about some countries and their people is that they're "not ready for democracy yet." Commonly given as reasons for that

view are such things as a poor, uneducated populace who cannot make informed voting decisions, a weak economy in need of close supervision and control, and a lack of technological expertise to develop raw materials. Attack or defend this notion. Are some countries and peoples "not ready for democracy yet"? How do they compare with the United States and its people in, say, the 1820s?

An alternative writing assignment is to have students write, individually, about an idea that shaped their lives. The more abstract the idea, the better.

Writers' Circle

Each member of the class should make a list of what he or she thinks are the three greatest ideas of all time. The lists should then be gathered, with the teacher reading the ideas from the lists and a student making a master list of ideas on the board (tallying any repeated ideas). In some cases, the class may need to decide whether differently worded ideas are the same idea (for example, "government by the people" and "democracy") or are different ideas. Then discuss the master list. Which ideas are the most abstract? the most concrete? What generalizations can be drawn about the class's values and interests?

part four Patterns for Writers

PROFILE ♦ OF ♦ A ♦ WRITER

Alice Walker

Alice Walker, a writer and former teacher currently residing in San Francisco, is perhaps best known for her Pulitzer Prize–winning book *The Color Purple* (1982), which was also made into a popular movie. A prolific writer, Walker has published novels (such as *The Third Life of Grange Copeland, Meridian,* and *The Temple of My Familiar*), short stories (collected in *You Can't Keep a Good Woman Down* and *In Love and Trouble*), poetry (including *Horses Make a Landscape Look More Beautiful*), and essays (most notably those collected in *In Search of Our Mothers' Gardens* and *Living by the Word*). While Walker's writing typically centers on the lives and difficulties of African-American women, many readers, regardless of race or

PART OUTLINE

gender, find in it a celebration of the best elements of the essential humanity we all share.

Asked about how heavily she revises her writing, Walker has said:

> It's been a totally different experience each time. In fact, *The Color Purple* was written originally almost entirely the way it appears in the book. . . . I think it had to do with the kind of solitude I wrote it in.
>
> I wrote *The Third Life of Grange Copeland* while living in Mississippi in the middle of incredible racial turmoil, and sometimes terror and silence and craziness. . . . It was a very different kind of writing. I was trying to capture something—then I *was* trying to capture something: partly the slipping away of a way of life. That was what I was trying to capture for myself, to remember a way of life that was changing and at the same time write this book which looks at, among other things, a lot of violence now in families and a lot of love in families and intergenerational relationships. It was very different. They're all very different.

In 1970 Walker had written, "My major advice to young black artists would be that they should shut themselves up somewhere away from all debates about who they are and what color they are and just turn out paintings and poems and stories and novels." Asked in 1988 whether she would revise that advice, she said:

> No, because in that it is assumed that the rest of the time they are right in the middle of life, of struggle, of everything else that's happening in the world. I know from my own experience that it's very hard to create something whole in the midst of a society in which everything is fragmented. You do have to get away and take those long walks and sit by the water and let your self come to you. One of the great dangers in a society that is so fragmented, so chaotic, is the loss of the self and the filling in of what would have been the self with TV. What you often have is a society full of people who are empty of themselves but full of television. This will never create art; this will only create more Big Macs to munch.

• • •

You can remind students how the structures and goals of Parts Two, Three, and Four work together. We think three elements (purpose, subject, and pattern) drive writing. Purpose is dominant, but there's seldom a situation when writers don't have to consider all three elements simultaneously.

We find that our students typically want to focus on imitation and repetition of

Part Four of *The Heath Guide to College Writing* focuses on *form,* the broad organizational patterns that writing often takes, the patterns that readers (consciously or unconsciously) expect to see, the patterns that writers themselves can use to learn more about their own subjects and purposes. Sometimes that form is dictated from *outside*—as when your boss asks you to write a report comparing two computer systems and recommending a choice; in such a case, the broad pattern of *comparison* is virtually inevitable. Sometimes that form comes from *inside*—as when you're writing a piece for class about the U.S. government's role in Central America. You may decide that making your point really depends on the *definition* of the term *nationalism,* or that you want to focus on the *narration* of the history of the issue without taking sides, or that you want to use *argumentation* to show that a certain policy should be followed in the future.

For students, the times when external factors dictate the form for a piece of writing are (comparatively) easy to handle: if someone says your lab report needs to contain a statement of purpose, list of materials, explanation of procedures, presentation of results, and conclusion, there's not (on the surface, anyway) a whole lot of worrying about form left for you to do. The times when the form of something you are required to write is *not* externally dictated are, however, more difficult to handle. It's in those cases, especially, that the more you know about common patterns of form, the better you can use them and creatively combine them to produce a successful piece of writing. And it's also true that as you become more aware of the role form plays in writing, you become a better reader as well.

form (probably as much because such things were emphasized to them previously as anything else); our emphasis, however, is on *discovery* of form, and on form as discovery.

We don't refer to our readings as "models": while we do want them understood as examples, we *don't* want them considered rigid patterns to be imitated or followed.

How Thought Shapes Form and Form Shapes Thought

In introducing a set of chapters like this, it's worth asking what these different forms—narration, description, definition, comparison, analysis, and argumentation—are for. Do we mean to suggest that ordinary people outside writing classrooms sit down on occasion and say to themselves, "Well, I think I'll write a piece of narration [or description, definition, and so on] today"? Hardly, although there are certainly plenty of times when people sit down and plan to write a piece of analysis or argumentation, and even times people sit down to write definitions—imagine a dormitory counselor who has to write the "official" definition of *excessively rowdy behavior* for the student handbook. The more common scenario is that a writer, whether in or out of school, *senses*—often during the act of composing—that the writing is developing toward a certain form. (Or perhaps we should say that ideally a writer would sense that developing tendency.) And that development may be at the level of the whole piece—three, ten, or a hundred pages—or at the level of an individual section, perhaps as short as a paragraph.

Many of you, and perhaps some students, will notice these forms as what countless other texts call the modes, or patterns (or methods) of development. They are familiar terms to any veteran teacher of expository writing. But we mean to use them here in different ways from how they are employed in such books, as we hope our explanation shows.

This business of (a) writing finding its own form, followed by (b) that evolving sense of form then shaping the writing, is both an important and a delicate idea:

- It's *important* because of the frequency with which writers must be sensitive to the form their writing *needs* to take (as opposed to times when someone dictates that form). That is, often writers have to know how much to be conscious of *following* a particular pattern and how much to *let the writing go* anywhere it seems to want to go.
- It's *delicate* because training writers to be sensitive to the *potential* for this or that form as their writing unfolds is difficult. Few writers *know* when that awareness of form happens; there certainly aren't many situations for which we ourselves, as people who do plenty of writing, can pinpoint that just *here* or just *there* we discovered the form we wanted to use.

We're always pleased when a student begins to develop this "sense" or "feel"—when a student says, "I started to write this as [one kind of paper], but it *feels* like it wants to be [another kind of paper]." That shows real development as a writer. We mean *intuition*, but we're reluctant to use that word in the text, for we don't want to risk mystifying the process. Experienced writers know when their intuition is operating and when to heed it, but beginners usually have to cultivate their receptivity to it.

Given the difficulty of teaching writers how to sense the way their thoughts (as well as their reasons for writing, their writing situations, and their audiences) shape the forms they use (and how those forms shape their thoughts), what can be done about form in writing classrooms?

We're being honest about this here; if you have any students still wedded to the "five-paragraph theme," maybe this will help you open them up to more interesting possibilities.

The approach we take in Part Four of this book is to teach you these forms as patterns—patterns to be used to come up with things to say, patterns to be used to come up with what to say *next*, and *next*, and *next*. That is, our use of these patterns is meant explicitly to be *inventional* and *shaping;* we are not interested in these forms being used like cookie-cutter molds by which you can stamp out look-alike pieces of your own experience. *If the only difference between your "movie paper" and the movie papers of the students around you is the nouns—you're writing about* Goodfellas, *the student on your right is writing about* Godfather III, *and the student on your left is writing about* Miller's Crossing, *and all the papers are the same except those names—you're* not *using these patterns (more specifically, the* idea *of these patterns) the way we intend.*

Another example you can use here might be situation comedies from television ("sitcoms"): many viewers feel that all sitcoms are the same.

This approach to patterns for writing based on using them to decide what to say *next*, and *next*, and *next* parallels our approaches in Parts Two and Three:

- In Part Two, the question "What do I say *next?*" found its answers in the *reasons* for writing: to express, to explain or inform, to analyze, and to persuade.
- In Part Three, the question's answers came from the *subjects* for writing: people, places, things, facts, and ideas.
- Here in Part Four, the answers to "What do I say *next*, and *next*, and *next?*" come from awareness of some of the patterns in writing: narration, description, definition, comparison, analysis, and argumentation.

An Important Note. Because you're in a writing classroom, by definition a learning situation, you have to expect that your teacher may well assign, for example, a "comparison paper." And by the time you have to write one of those, you'll have seen examples of that kind of writing. But don't expect *every* aspect of the examples you see in the chapter titled "Comparison" (chapter 18) to be comparison, for in each piece will be some description, some analysis, some argumentation—in other words, the usual mix of patterns—all within the larger form of a piece of writing that seems to us to be *generally* a comparison. Expect your own writing to be the same.

We've seen teachers assign papers in which students are to do *only* definition, or *only* comparison, and so on, and for the most part that produces pretty dreadful writing. What *might* make sense as a paragraph exercise, clearly only for teaching purposes, makes little or none as an essay.

Certainly your first draft(s) will not be all one form or all another form; if you write the way we do, the form of your writing is one of the messier aspects in early drafts. As you rework your early drafts, you should, if you're sensitive to this issue of form, be able to move toward a piece that has a more recognizable form, in this case comparison. But don't expect to do a "pure" comparison paper: no such document exists. Even if you were to strip away everything that *wasn't* comparison, you would still be left with some persuasion, some description, and so forth.

chapter 14 Critical Thinking

"An effect can become a cause, reinforcing the original cause and producing the same effect in an intensified form, and so on indefinitely. A man may take to drink because he feels himself to be a failure, and then fail all the more completely because he drinks. It is rather the same thing that is happening to the English language. It becomes ugly and inaccurate because our thoughts are foolish, but the slovenliness of our language makes it easier to have foolish thoughts. The point is that the process is reversible."

George Orwell

So far in these part-opening chapters we have talked about critical writing (chapter 3) and critical reading (chapter 8). There's still a key missing element: critical thinking. The three activities form a triangle:

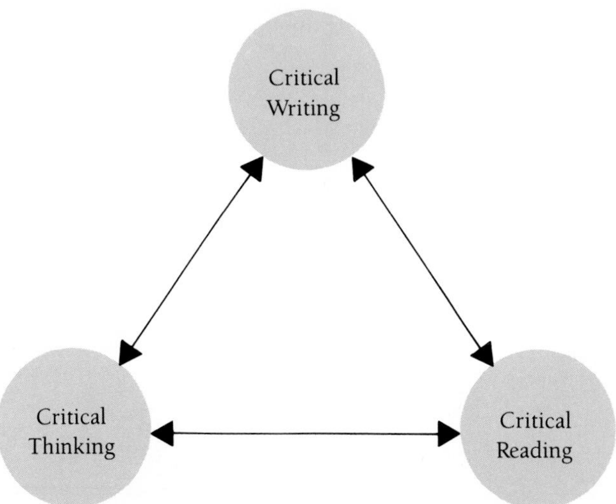

We are reminded again here of E. M. Forster's famous comment "How can I know what I think until I see what I say?"

As the triangular form suggests, the three activities are closely interrelated: you can't really do critical reading or critical writing without doing critical thinking. Critical reading and critical writing are the ideal activities to promote critical thinking. (Some people even say they're really three different ways of looking at the same activity.)

A more traditional rhetorician might ask, "What are the issues or questions at this point?" We're just translating that into language a little more familiar to students.

Key Components of Critical Thinking

1. First you need a way to pick out the key issue(s) or problem(s) within the material you're confronting, whether it's experimental data or a passage of literature.
2. Then you need a way of interpreting—or solving—those issues or problems.

3. Finally, you need a way to consider what you've done.

More specifically, critical thinking comprises three elements:

- Issue identification
- Problem solving
- Active reflection

None of these three is difficult at the level of brain surgery or rocket science; not a one involves anything you haven't done before. What we want to stress here is (a) the systematic combination of these activities and (b) the depth of each activity.

The three elements of critical thinking we identify as components certainly *are* key activities in both fields, however.

For early practice, you might ask students to trace these elements in "Eleven Blue Men," in chapter 6.

An Important Note (again). Here, as at other central points in this book, we are wary of seeming to be taking too much of a "cookbook" approach. If you don't put your own mental resources—your own creative and critical cogitation—into following these elements when you use them, they won't do you much good. We offer this presentation as a general guideline, not as a strict, paint-by-the-numbers pattern.

Issue Identification

The first part of critical thinking is to determine the key issue. Many times the things you read, the situations you examine, or the data you collect do not themselves tell you the key issue within them. But that doesn't mean it isn't there. We've already shown you, in chapter 8 ("Critical Reading") and chapter 7 ("Writing to Persuade"), two good ways to identify key issues in written material: (a) by asking what *kind* of argument is being made (fact, interpretation, value, or policy) and (b) by asking what *claim* is being made and how the evidence supports it.

Since our principal interest here is critical thinking as applied to what you read and what you write, we'll illustrate the two approaches to issue identification we've discussed so far. Consider this famous passage from Henry David Thoreau's *Walden:*

If you think through it first, you can also illustrate critical thinking with just about any other problem-solving process—from replacing a washer in a faucet to figuring out why the stainless-steel pipes used at critical places in oil refineries sometimes rust.

> Not long since, a strolling Indian went to sell baskets at the house of a well-known lawyer in my neighborhood. "Do you wish to buy any baskets?" he asked. "No, we do not want any," was the reply. "What!" exclaimed the Indian as he went out the gate, "do you mean to starve us?" Having seen his industrious white neighbors so well off,—that the lawyer had only to weave arguments, and by some magic wealth and standing followed, he had said to himself: I will go into business; I will weave baskets; it is a thing which I can do. Thinking that when he had made the baskets he would have done his part, and then it would be the white man's to buy them. He had not discovered that it was necessary for him to make it worth the other's while to buy them, or at least make him think that it was so, or to make something else which it would be worth his while to buy. I too had woven a kind of

> basket of a delicate texture, but I had not made it worth any one's while to buy them. Yet not the less, in my case, did I think it worth my while to weave them, and instead of studying how to make it worth men's while to buy my baskets, I studied rather how to avoid the necessity of selling them. The life which men praise and regard as successful is but one kind. Why should we exaggerate any one kind at the expense of the others?

There are certainly more ways to approach this passage than can be discussed here. Our point is to show that in approaching it one can fruitfully examine issues of fact, interpretation, value, and policy.

You might want to illustrate these following sets of questions (which are actually the questions central to stasis rhetoric—see chapters 7 and 20) by applying them to some ads at this point. Bring in an "image" ad, a "hard-sell" ad, and a political ad, for example.

Fact. Did this episode happen or not? Was there really already a story about an Indian, or did Thoreau make it up? Did Thoreau's decision making really follow this process? Does the episode exist to convince us of the truth of the last two sentences, or only to introduce the idea to us?

Interpretation. Is this passage fact or fiction, autobiography or parable? What is the "basket" Thoreau says he had woven? By what logic does Thoreau move from discussing baskets to discussing life—what's the sense of the comparison?

Value. What kind of judgment do we make of this passage? Not so much "Is it good or not?" in the sense of "Is this good writing?"—although that too is an interesting question at the level of "What makes it good [or not good]?"—but, rather, "Does this passage tell us something significant, or something trivial? something distinctly Thoreau's, or something commonplace?"

The Wilfrid Sheed piece about the Hamptons in chapter 16 is another good place to see the different kinds of issues weaving in and out of an essay.

Policy. Of course, there is the level of "How should this change our lives?"—an aspect Thoreau is particularly good at suggesting without stating outright. Beyond that are smaller questions of policy: "How does this change our developing sense of the book *Walden?*" "How does this change our sense of this chapter ('Economy')?" "What image does this give us of Thoreau's relationship with his contemporaries [or with us]?"

Once again we need to point out that there are many more ways to read this passage than those suggested by these four kinds of issues. For example, if you take what you decide to be the key issue in the passage and work it through the questions on the nature of the claim's support in chapter 7 and the questions for critical reading in chapter 8, you can dig at least two levels deeper into the passage. But even just looking at the passage in terms of these four kinds of issues and of how its evidence relates to certain claims is productive of a number of possible key issues.

Again, when you want to think critically, an essential first step is to decide what the critical issue is. Finding the issue is easier when you know it should be one of these types. And determining what constitutes adequate proof or an effective solution can be done only in light of a clear understanding of what kind of issue or problem you are facing. Of course, usually the hardest issues are the mixtures—for example, the issues involved in health hazards caused by cigarette smoking or the issues involved in literary interpretation.

Problem Solving

Another part of critical thinking is problem solving. Many times the "key issue" at hand is a *problem*—something is not as it should be, or there's an effect for which you don't know the cause. (The "Eleven Blue Men" piece in chapter 6, "Writing to Analyze," offers an excellent example of one problem-solving process.) How do you solve problems? Research suggests that you, like most people, approach problems in one of two ways: you solve the problem by either (a) seeing some similarity between it and another problem you've solved (solving the problem by analogy, that is, from the outside in), or (b) looking at its parts and puzzling out their relationships to one another (that is, from the inside out). In other words, you use either analogical or analytical thinking. The first kind (seeing similarities and differences) may or may not be teachable; the second (seeing parts and interrelationships) clearly is. Here are the steps in our version of this analytical component of critical thinking; notice how some of them correspond to dealing with certain kinds of issues (indicated in parentheses) and doing a certain kind of critical reading {indicated in braces}:

See also "The Long Habit" (chapter 18) for a different kind of problem solving.

1. Survey the territory.
2. Define the problem.

   (What kind of issue is it?)
3. Determine its boundaries.
4. Determine its components.

   (These boundaries and components will be of different types depending on the kind of issue posed by the problem.)
5. Identify possible solutions.
6. Test the solutions.

   {Treat each possible solution as a claim: does the available evidence support it, or can you predict—based on that evidence—the existence of other evidence that, if subsequently found, would tend to support the particular claim?}
7. Consult others.

   (Is this solution good?)
   {Part of the evidence that supports choosing one particular solution—one claim—is that informed others also support it.}
8. Choose a solution.

   (What should be done about this problem?)
9. Implement the solution.

If you want to see how a writer *portrays* an adaptation of this process, look at chapter 20's "The Untouchables."

For an example, let's return to the issue presented in chapter 7, on persuasion: the hazards of cigarette smoking. A group of students are trying to decide whether or not to allow cigarette machines in dormitory lobbies. Having determined that the issue of policy ("Do we or don't we?") will be decided by the issue of fact (people who smoke cigarettes have higher rates of lung cancer, heart disease, and so on), the group begins the problem-solving phase:

Many issues can be similarly approached: whether to limit congressional terms of office, whether to restrict gun ownership, how to determine under what conditions our country should intervene militarily in others, to name a few.

1. *Survey the territory.* Involved are five dorm lobbies, two with machines, a request from a third to put a machine in, and requests from some residents to take the other two out.
2. *Define the problem.* The problem is to come up with a practical, defensible, reasonable policy.
3. *Determine its boundaries.* The policy will apply to all dorms, whether or not they currently have machines.
4. *Determine its components.* The policy won't cover smoking in general (some residents wanted to declare all dorms no-smoking areas), just the machines.
5. *Identify possible solutions.* Possible solutions are to (a) ban all the machines, (b) allow all the machines, and (c) allow machines whenever two-thirds of any dorm's residents want them, banning them in individual dorms the same way.
6. *Test the solutions.* Solution c keeps the controversy going every year in every dorm, and solution b ignores the facts relevant to the issue; only solution a is, ultimately, reasonable.
7. *Consult others.* The head of university housing leans back in his chair, takes a deep puff from his pipe, and points out (a) that the solutions leave smokers no way out; (b) that smokers have an easy and attractive argument to use against this policy in the issue of value ("It's our right to smoke ourselves to an early grave if we want to"), a type of argument some college students in particular often find persuasive; and (c) that the value issue will bring students to rallies, demonstrations, and letter-writing campaigns, whereas the fact issue won't. He suggests always leaving an opponent a way out—but just making sure it's your way.
8. *Choose a solution.* The committee decides to ban all machines in the dorm lobbies but to leave one large machine in the lobby of the cafeteria all the dorms share—other vending machines are there as well, and the lobby is always open.
9. *Implement the solution.* The committee makes its recommendation to the head of university housing, who points out that the contract with the vending machine company won't expire until next August but promises the machines will be removed as requested then.

The same approach can be taken to writing about the *Walden* passage quoted earlier. Suppose you decide to look at Thoreau's use of such anecdotes, like the one about the Indian who wove baskets no one wanted. Thoreau uses such stories frequently in *Walden*—is there a pattern to how he does so? First you'd survey the territory, noting how many and what kinds of such stories *Walden* contains. Then you'd define the problem; here you'd need to reread each story, determine how Thoreau gets into and out of each, and then ascertain whether a repeated pattern exists and, if so, figure out how to interpret that pattern. To determine the boundaries you'd decide which parts of *Walden* to include as such stories and which to exclude. Next, you'd determine the components—not just of each story but also of how Thoreau gets into and out of them. To identify possible solutions in this context you would choose tentative patterns and, to test the solutions, would see which of the chosen patterns applied to most of the stories. In consulting others, you'd talk over with your teacher or classmates your "reading" of Thoreau's use of these stories. To choose a solution you'd decide which interpretation to base your paper on. And to implement that solution, you'd go ahead and write the paper.

We're being systematic here to make our point; obviously, this would make a fairly plodding piece of writing if it were written just as outlined here.

Active Reflection

The third component of critical thinking—active reflection—involves thinking about the issue or problem without doing so directly. Each of us has more brainpower than we can call up on command, and we can access that brainpower only indirectly—for example, by first fixing material in our minds so clearly and strongly that we can't forget it and then not thinking about it directly. One way you can begin this process is by mentioning the issue or problem, perhaps casually to a friend, but not getting immersed in it. Or you can begin by writing down the problem or issue, perhaps in a rough draft, and then not looking at it (except for an occasional quick glance) for a day or so. The trick is somehow to set your mind to the task and then ignore it (at least) overnight. Then see whether on the next day you've come up with a new perspective.

When you're using this approach to critical thinking while writing a paper, active reflection occurs each time you finish a draft (or a part thereof) and put the project down for a while, whether to sleep, attend class, or go for a swim. You can't help but "assign your subconscious" to think about what you're writing; our point here is merely that you need to listen to what your subconscious then has to tell you.

Active reflection is difficult to teach. It may help if you ask students whether they've ever had the experience of getting a good insight into a problem only *after* they've quit consciously worrying about it.

If you've not tried this technique, it probably sounds a little like those ads on late-night movie stations for the knives that slice tomatoes, skin bears, and overhaul semitrailer rigs—too much, too easy, there's got to be a gimmick somewhere. Let us assure you, though, that if you try this technique you'll begin to get results.

Trial Problems

Here are three brief situations on which you can try out your critical thinking skills. Each is followed by questions for you to answer on paper. Be prepared to hand in your answers or to discuss them in class.

You may want to have students write out their answers, 1–8, and so on, or you may want them to work the answers into essays.

The original of this is discussed interestingly in *Women's Ways of Knowing*, by Belenky and colleagues, in chapter 13.

Situation 1: Heinz and the Druggist. A man named Heinz has fallen on hard times. Now his wife is ill with a disease that causes intense pain and threatens her life. One drug exists that can lessen her pain and possibly save her life. Heinz has no way to pay for the drug. He goes to Jones, the druggist, and when Jones learns Heinz cannot pay for the drug, Jones will not give it to him. To save the life of his wife, Heinz is considering whether or not to steal the drug he cannot afford to buy. Should Heinz steal the drug?

1. What is the key issue here?
2. What kind of issue is it?
3. Have you ever heard of a similar problem? If so, how was it solved, and in what way(s) might that solution be modified so as to work here?
4. What are the key factors in this problem? What various solutions can you think of?
5. What should Heinz do?
6. Imagine you are the druggist. What do you think about the advice Heinz was just given in item 5?
7. Imagine you are Heinz's wife. What do you think about the advice Heinz was just given in item 5?
8. Imagine you are the judge hearing the case for felony theft brought against Heinz for stealing the drug. Heinz is claiming temporary insanity caused by seeing his wife suffer so much for so long. What are the key issues here?

This situation is modeled after the Law School Admission Test's typical writing prompts.

Situation 2: Christina Ng's Promotion. Christina Ng is a graduate of State University and holds a degree in hospital management. Currently, five years after receiving her degree, she is assistant administrator for County Hospital. It's a secure job, paying enough for Christina to pay the rent, make car payments, and afford a vacation, but not much more. At County Hospital are four other assistant administrators, and so Christina is unsure when or whether she will ever be promoted to administrator. Because her family lives nearby, she's reluctant to change hospitals, for that would mean changing towns. But she's tired of living in a rented apartment and tired of working where she doesn't feel she can get ahead. She would like to buy a house but can't afford one. She would like to manage the clinic office and business for a group of doctors, a situation in which she could be as much a partner as an employee; however, she would need at least twenty-five thousand dollars to buy her way into that kind of arrangement as a partner—otherwise she'd just be more hired help. Then one day Christina's aunt dies, leaving each of her nieces and nephews a sum that amounts to twenty-five thousand dollars after taxes. The money will enable Christina either to buy her way into a partnership with a group of young doctors who are just now setting up their own clinic or to make the down payment on a small house. If Christina buys in with the doctors and in a year or two they decide to disband the clinic and go their own ways, she is not certain to recoup her investment. If she buys the house, she faces still feeling frustrated and stuck in her hospital job. What should Christina do?

1. What is the key issue here?
2. What kind of issue is it?
3. Have you ever heard of a similar problem? If so, how was it solved, and how might that solution be modified so as to work here?
4. What are the key factors in this problem? What various solutions can you think of?
5. What should Christina do?
6. Imagine you are Christina's father, who wants only for her to have "a home of her own." What do you think about the advice she was just given in item 5?
7. Imagine you are Christina's best friend, who thinks Christina consistently sells herself short by refusing to take risks and believe in her own personal and professional competence. What do you think about the advice Christina was just given in item 5?
8. Imagine you are Christina's financial adviser, hearing Christina explain why she wants to do one or the other of these things, as opposed to investing the money in a diversified portfolio of high-yield, low-risk, nearly tax-free stocks, bonds, and other investment devices. What are the key issues here, and how can you use them to change her mind? What do you recommend she do?

If you use this as a writing assignment, track which students write directly to Christina and which write directly to you: do you think those two groups of students are doing fundamentally different kinds of problem solving?

Situation 3: An Educational Crisis. Following is a "real" piece of writing that will give you the opportunity to do some critical thinking, along with pre- and postreading comparisons. Read the piece carefully and critically; then write out answers to the questions after it.

PREREADING WORKSHEET

Before you read the following piece by Vivian Baylor, write brief responses to these questions:

1. What have you heard or read about the quality of science education in American high schools, compared with that in foreign high schools, particularly Japan, Taiwan, and Malaysia?
2. Do you believe the United States, compared with certain foreign nations, is at a disadvantage in technological innovation? Why or why not?
3. How many science courses did you take in high school? Did you enjoy those courses? Why or why not? Do you believe those courses were adequate for your educational goals and needs? Are you taking science courses in college? Why or why not?
4. How many math courses did you take in high school? Did you enjoy those courses? Why or why not? Do you believe those courses were adequate for your educational goals and needs? Are you taking math courses in college? Why or why not?
5. Do you plan to major in a scientific or mathematical field? Why or why not?

The Crisis in U.S. Science and Mathematics Education

VIVIAN BAYLOR

Vivian Baylor is a project manager at Oak Ridge National Laboratory (ORNL). (See her "Profile of a Writer" at the beginning of Part Five.) The ORNL Review, *in which this piece appeared, is a quarterly magazine that reports on science and technology at Oak Ridge National Laboratory.*

What is the crisis in mathematics and science education in the United States? 1
Why is the U.S. Department of Energy [DOE] (and Oak Ridge National Laboratory) so committed to helping solve it? The crisis is a matter of insufficient quantity and quality. Not enough U.S. students are pursuing degrees in science- and mathematics-related disciplines; as a result, a nationwide shortage of scientists and engineers is projected in an era when the United States is trying to lead the world in technology innovation. In addition, Americans interested in science and mathematics are prepared inadequately to compete with the next generation of foreign scientists, who seem to receive (and learn) much more by the time they graduate from high school than do U.S. youth.

DOE is concerned about the crisis because of manpower projections. 2
They indicate that the Department will be competing for a dwindling supply of well-trained, qualified U.S. scientists and engineers to perform energy-related research. ORNL has much the same concern; continuing to hire the best and brightest scientists and engineers may be increasingly difficult here as the pool of candidates decreases.

A 1985 report from the National Science Board of the National Science 3
Foundation (*Science Indicators: The 1985 Report,* National Science Board, 1985) provides considerable quantitative information describing the changing state of U.S. science and technology and science and mathematics education. From 1974 to 1983, the number of entering freshmen electing to major in science and engineering fell from 33.4% to 32%, although more of these freshmen in 1983 (37%) than in 1974 (30%) stated a desire to obtain master's degrees. The 1983 graduate school enrollment showed an increase of 18% over that in 1975; however, over the last decade, the number of bachelor's, master's, and doctoral degrees awarded in science and engineering disciplines has remained stable.

Meanwhile, the proportion of foreign Ph.D. candidates in all science and 4
engineering fields at U.S. universities has risen from 20% in 1972 to 26% in 1984, including increases from 14% in 1977 to 37% in 1984 in computer sciences and from 33% in 1972 to 56% in 1984 in engineering. Although an increasing number of these foreign doctoral students plan to stay in the United States (from 51% in 1972 to 60% in 1984), the long-term effects of

their employment on U.S. science and technology remain unclear. For example, concerns have been raised about the quality of undergraduate programs with a large proportion of foreign graduate teaching assistants and faculty members who cannot readily explain difficult concepts in English.

Is this concern reflecting an issue of fact or an issue of value?

5 Although the decreasing proportion of U.S. citizens in science and engineering is causing some concern, the precollege statistics show even more alarming trends that could adversely affect future U.S. college enrollments and manpower pools. Again, the quality of science and mathematics instruction and the quantity of recipients are concerns. The report states that "during a time when science and technology are playing an increasingly important role in the lives of all citizens, the average high school student knows comparatively less about these subjects" in 1982 than in 1970 based on achievement scores. Furthermore, the last time most high school students are exposed to science is in tenth grade. And, over the last three decades, the number of high school students enrolled in precollege science courses has dropped substantially from 54% to 44%.

6 Comparative studies show that American high school students "take substantially less coursework in science and mathematics than students in other highly developed countries such as Japan, West Germany, East Germany, and the Soviet Union." Another alarming figure shows that even the best U.S. students do not compare well with other nations' students; by the end of the 12th grade, for example, American students who had taken calculus equaled only the mean performance of mathematics students who were seniors in foreign high schools.

7 Although it is clear to many that a crisis exists, the causes and solutions are still being debated and are much too complex to address here. Meanwhile, ORNL is playing a role in trying to address some of these issues through an expanded university relations program. The program includes a number of new precollege activities aimed at enriching the curricula through both exposing teachers to new scientific research and exposing students to science at earlier ages. Our hope is that students will learn to enjoy and appreciate the stimulation of scientific investigation as they choose their career paths.

Or are there four different crises, one for each kind of issue?

1. What is the key issue here? (*Hint:* You may well find more than one. If you do, figure out their relationship[s]).
2. What kind of issue is it (or what kinds are they)?
3. Have you ever heard of a similar problem? If so, how was it solved? Can that solution be modified so as to work here?
4. What are the key factors in this problem? Are there various possible solutions? What are they?
5. What should our government do?
6. Imagine you are a student's mother who wants only that her child will have a rewarding career that pays top dollar. What do you think about the advice (the government's policy) just given in item 5?

7. Imagine you are a U.S. manufacturer of computer chips, foreseeing that competition against foreign manufacturers is only going to get harder in years to come, because their research and development departments get plenty of staffing from those natives of countries who are educated in our graduate schools, while you cannot find people with the right education anywhere. What do you think about the recommended government policy given in item 5?

Question 8 here is a particularly good source of classroom activities—group work, especially.

8. Imagine you are a student choosing between majoring in computer science (with a math minor) or engineering (with a business minor). The one will lead only to graduate school and, eventually, to a research job that may or may not be secure, either from the standpoint of its paying as much as that kind of education should be worth or from the standpoint of that kind of career being secure in a country where the entire computer business is increasingly dominated by foreign competition. (You don't want to postpone settling down and starting a family that long, and you don't want to risk never having a well-paying, secure career.)

   The other choice (engineering) will lead to a degree in four years that will immediately translate into a well-paying job and, with the business minor, a chance to open your own firm in just a few years, to be financially and professionally secure not too many years after graduation. (You don't want to sell your own intelligence short, however, and you are sensitive to the fact that our country obviously needs *more,* not less, people to go into fields that may not have such immediate or apparently certain rewards.) What are the key issues here? What will you do?

POSTREADING WORKSHEET

Now that you've read the piece by Baylor and worked your way through the critical thinking exercise that followed it, write your responses to these questions:

1. The author of "The Crisis in U.S. Science and Mathematics Education" clearly believes such a crisis exists. After reading the article and working through the critical thinking exercise, are you convinced such a crisis exists? Has your perspective changed from that you wrote about before reading the article? Why or why not?
2. In your own experience, what would you change about your science and math education so far, and why?
3. Do you believe that this "crisis" is overrated? Why or why not? Do you think that students in the United States *can* compete effectively in the global technology arena? If so, how?

Bridges: Another Perspective

The author of "The Crisis in U.S. Science and Mathematics Education" is worried that the United States lacks an edge over foreign countries in science and mathematics education. Because of this disadvantage, Baylor foresees continuing and significant losses of U.S. influence and prestige in the world technological marketplace. Lack of competitive science and math education, she argues, will make continued U.S. decline in all important matters inevitable.

But do U.S. power and influence depend *exclusively* on the quality and quantity of our nation's technology, which springs from its science and math education? Are there areas of significance in which the United States continues to be a world leader? How about government, philosophy, and the arts? How about medicine, nutrition, agriculture, food production? Do aspects of our educational program or general culture provide models for the rest of the world? Select an area of education or training in which you believe U.S. students are the best worldwide, or at least highly competitive, and present a counter-argument to Baylor's "The Crisis in U.S. Science and Mathematics Education."

Writers' Circle

Posit a broad curriculum division, as follows:

Science / Math	**Humanities**
Biology	Literature
Chemistry	Languages
Algebra	Drama
Calculus	Art
Physics	Music
Engineering	Journalism
Geometry	Entertainment
(And so on)	(And so on)

(Students can add to either list during discussion.)

Students in the class should first choose which of the two broad groups they see themselves fitting into most comfortably and then choose which subdivision they favor. Students with common subdivisions (all the physics students, all the art students, and so on) should meet together and write down what they believe an ideal high school curriculum *in their subject* should cover—the things they consider most basic. Each "curriculum" should be sequenced, as well as detailed as much as possible.

Next, each subgroup should appoint a secretary to put its ideal curriculum on the board. The class as a whole should then debate or discuss the "ideal curricula" of the subjects in each broad area.

Some students may want to use arguing for or against a particular curriculum as a writing assignment.

We have now covered all three parts of the important triangle of critical writing, reading, and thinking, and we encourage you to cultivate an awareness of all three as you proceed in your development as a writer. You'll find the three always central to your efforts and to any success you enjoy. Now we turn to the focus of Part Four: patterns for writers. In each of the subsequent chapters in this part we emphasize the patterns apparent in the readings as useful patterns for developing your own writing, depending, of course, on what you're writing about and whom you're writing for.

WRITING ASSIGNMENT

The photograph on page 303 was taken at the Hall of Mirrors in Glacier Park in Lucerne. The mirrors create a confounding visual maze that can be quite disorienting to a first-time visitor. For example, what looks like a hallway to the left of the person in the picture is only a reflection created by the pattern of the mirrors. The pattern of mirrors is laid out within an array of equilateral triangles marked on the floor. Some triangles have no mirrors, some have one, and some have two. Occasional pieces of Moorish furniture are strategically arranged in the maze. Usually, a person in the maze sees a jumble of images or one of the reflected hallways. It takes a calm, clear-headed person not to become disoriented in the maze.

After studying the photograph of the maze, read the quotation from George Orwell that begins this chapter on page 304. Write a brief paper in which you explore what the subject of the picture and the Orwell quotation have in common.

chapter 15 Narration

While speaking to a meeting of the Mystery Writers of America, author Mickey Spillane cautioned his audience not to look for anything deeply symbolic in the novels featuring his most famous character, Mike Hammer. "Mike drinks beer, not cognac," said Spillane, "because I can't spell cognac."

At its simplest and perhaps best level, *narration* means telling a story, even if it is a very short story, such as the one about Mickey Spillane, above. Sometimes the best stories are fact; sometimes they're fiction. And some of the best are such a good mix you can't tell *what* they are. The most familiar stories may be those told by travelers. From Chaucer's *The Canterbury Tales* to John Steinbeck's *Travels with Charley,* some of the greatest writers have exercised their art of storytelling within a travel setting. Our first example is from a contemporary storyteller, who relates one short episode from his driving trip around the perimeter of the United States.

We don't mean to imply that such travel narratives are necessarily simple, only that they are popular.

Roadhouse and Wilderness

WILLIAM LEAST HEAT-MOON

See page 280 for information on William Least Heat-Moon. In this selection from Blue Highways, *the narrator is entering the Adirondack Mountains.*

Some of your students may not know that the Adirondacks are mountains in northern New York State. You might ask your students at this point what they think a roadhouse is (we'll be asking them that soon too).

Notice the connections in mood and description between the people and the setting.

East of the village of Blue Mountain Lake, dominated by a bluish hump of the Adirondacks, the road descended to a small building—part house, part tavern—snugged against a wooded hill and surrounded by vaporous mountains. The mist glowed orange from a neon beer sign. The building, white clapboard trimmed in red with a silvery corrugated tin roof, was the Forest House Lodge. In fact, it wasn't a lodge, but something even better: an antique roadhouse. The roadhouse—institution and word—has nearly disappeared from America. 1

I ate a ham and cheese sandwich and drank Genesee Cream Ale. The pallid barmaid talked quietly to an old woman; when there would come a deep rumble of thunder, the women paused in conversation. There were no other sounds, no others about. The room was almost entirely of pine—immaculately scrubbed, hand-polished pine gleaming like lacquerware. Each table top, each wall, every stool and bench shone warmly in the soft incandescent light, and bottles of rum and brandy and whiskey glowed from within. It was as if the faded woman had given her life to buffing everything to a soft lustre and, in doing so, lost her own. Across from a photograph of an awakened hibernating bear hung an 1885 picture of the first Forest House Lodge when it was a stage stop. The present building, dating from the thirties, seemed to have absorbed the continuum of history. 2

3 Every so often a logging truck hissed wetly down the highway and rolled the mists before they settled in once more against the polished windows. I sat a long time in an event of no significance beyond simple joy. It lacked only the dimension of sharing.

4 A young man and woman came in carrying a tension as though an unexploded grenade had just dropped between them. He was a swelling of veins across the forehead and his speech a gnashing of teeth, but she was a light and airy woman, one who would move easily in loving. I was grateful for the company and forced a conversation about the Adirondacks that I ended up turning into an Izaak Walton League lecture.

Ask students what the Izaak Walton League is. (It's a conservation organization.)

5 The man said, "Wilderness! It's all a crock now. I rafted the Blue Nile in Ethiopia three years ago. After a couple of days, we got into country where the natives dressed like the old pictures you see—men almost naked, carrying spears. Women bare from the waist up. You know, darkest Africa. I was taking pictures when a girl wearing a necklace made out of the cap of a BIC pen held out her arm. She had a broken Timex on. She said, 'No *teek-teek*.' That almost ruined the trip. It's the same here—a bootprint on every square yard of Adirondacks."

Some of your better students may be able to pick out the narrator's own attitude toward this man right at this point.

6 "Wilderness doesn't mean untouched."

7 "Then it doesn't mean anything worth anything."

8 "If you knew a place that had never been walked over by civilized man, would you stay out of it?"

9 "I would. Of course I would."

10 "You wouldn't either," the woman said. "You'd walk every foot of it and brag about your experience and refuse to tell anyone else where it was."

11 "That's it," he said. "Get your coat."

If your students read the "Woman/Wilderness" essay earlier in the term (chapter 6), you can make some good connections to it here.

Make sure your students know that, for this couple, "Get your coat" is *not* a happy ending.

Questions for Writing and Discussion

Prepare short written answers to each of these questions. Be prepared to hand them in and/or discuss them in class, as your teacher directs.

1. Have you ever heard the word *roadhouse* used the way Least Heat-Moon does here? Have you ever been in one, or in a place like the one described here? What was it like—what were *your* impressions?
2. How does the description of the roadhouse (¶ 2–3) make you feel? What exactly in the description makes you feel that way?
3. What happens to the way the second and third paragraphs make you feel when you get to the sentence about the couple coming in carrying tension like a grenade?
4. Why would an author juxtapose two such moods as the one in the second and third paragraphs and the one following it?
5. What do the following words mean—*pallid, incandescent* (¶ 2)?

Narrative writing often begins in one kind of setting—such as a factual one—and moves into another—such as a fictional one. This kind of story-within-a-story may be familiar to you from Joseph Conrad's novel *The Heart of Darkness.* Here's a short sample of such a story (one that starts out, at least, as autobiography) by one of today's best storytellers:

White Tigers

Maxine Hong Kingston

Maxine Hong Kingston is a writer and former teacher. She is perhaps best known for her nonfiction book The Woman Warrior, *which won the general nonfiction award from the National Book Critics Circle (1976) and was named one of the top ten nonfiction works of its decade by* Time *magazine. Her other books include* China Men *and* Tripmaster Monkey. *In one interview she said, "Some of the things that happen to us in life seem to have no meaning, but when you write them down you find the meanings for them; or, as you translate life into words, you force a meaning. Meaning is intrinsic in words and sentences." The following selection is excerpted from her story "White Tigers."*

Do these opening lines run counter to your students' prevailing notions about the place of women in China?

When we Chinese girls listened to the adults talk-story, we learned that we failed if we grew up to be but wives or slaves. We could be heroines, swordswomen. Even if she had to rage across all China, a swordswoman got even with anybody who hurt her family. Perhaps women were once so dangerous that they had to have their feet bound. It was a woman who invented white crane boxing only two hundred years ago. She was already an expert pole fighter, daughter of a teacher trained at the Shao-lin temple, where there lived an order of fighting monks. She was combing her hair one morning when a white crane alighted outside her window. She teased it with her pole, which it pushed aside with a soft brush of its wing. Amazed, she dashed outside and tried to knock the crane off its perch. It snapped her pole in two. Recognizing the presence of great power, she asked the spirit of the white crane if it would teach her to fight. It answered with a cry that white crane boxers imitate today. Later the bird returned as an old man, and he guided her boxing for many years. Thus she gave the world a new martial art. 1

This was one of the tamer, more modern stories, mere introduction. My mother told others that followed swordswomen through woods and palaces for years. Night after night my mother would talk-story until we fell asleep. I couldn't tell where the stories left off and the dreams began, her voice the voice of the heroines in my sleep. And on Sundays, from noon to midnight, we went to the movies at the Confucius Church. We saw swordswomen jump over houses from a standstill; they didn't even need a running start. 2

Do your students think our cultural legends have any "woman warriors" or heroines? If so, what is their typical fate, in legend?

At last I saw that I too had been in the presence of great power, my mother talking-story. After I grew up, I heard the chant of Fa Mu Lan, the girl who took her father's place in battle. Instantly I remembered that as a child I 3 had followed my mother about the house, the two of us singing about how Fa Mu Lan fought gloriously and returned alive from war to settle in the village. I had forgotten this chant that was once mine, given me by my mother, who may not have known its power to remind. She said I would grow up a wife and a slave, but she taught me the song of the warrior woman, Fa Mu Lan. I would have to grow up a warrior woman.

Are any of the women in your class military veterans or in ROTC? If so, ask them what kinds of attitudes they meet from men concerning the status of "women warriors."

Questions for Writing and Discussion

Prepare short written answers to each of these questions. Be prepared to hand them in and/or discuss them in class, as your teacher directs.

1. What kind of status do you give the brief story of the "woman who invented white crane boxing" (¶ 1)? What is that story's function in this brief narration?
2. Why does Kingston say, "Perhaps women were once so dangerous that they had to have their feet bound" (¶ 1)? What does that have to do with the sense of this passage?
3. What is the parallel between (a) the white crane and the woman who invented white crane boxing and (b) Kingston's mother talking-story and Kingston?
4. What do the following words mean—*talk-story, heroines* (¶ 1)?

Bridges: Another Perspective

Maxine Hong Kingston, in the above excerpt from "White Tigers," writes of the Eastern cultural legends about women that her mother told to her. These legends are remarkable for their air of myth and supernaturality (for instance, the power, communication, and reincarnation of the white crane) and their emphasis on female, rather than male, heroic figures. Are there comparable legends in Western culture involving supernatural power, communication between creatures and human beings, and reincarnation? Given that Western legends tend to be male-dominated, are there any heroic female figures in Western culture? Finally, quite apart from Eastern or Western cultural differences, is Kingston saying anything about woman's power itself? Can women's ideas of their own power transcend culture?

Of course, not all narratives are nearly so colorful as Kingston's. Sometimes a writer just wants to tell how something happened, how two people acted, or what a situation was like. Even in such a case, the writing doesn't have to drag or be hard to follow—as the example below shows:

Elizabeth Cady Stanton and Susan Anthony

ELIZABETH GRIFFITH

Elizabeth Griffith is a writer, historian, and feminist activist. This selection is a description of the relationship between Elizabeth Cady Stanton and Susan Anthony, the two fast friends who began the women's movement in the United States.

Some students are confused by this—Griffith is quoting letters and so on as though they were dialogue.

As the two women grew older, more opinionated, and more secure, their relationship became more contentious. But they always came back together. As Stanton wrote to Anthony: "We have jogged along pretty well for forty years or more. Perhaps mid the wreck of thrones and the undoing of so many friendships, sects, parties and families, you and I deserve some credit for sticking together through all adverse winds with so few ripples on the surface." No matter how cruel or careless one was, she expected to be forgiven by the other. "We have said worse things to each other face to face than we have ever said about each other," Stanton admitted. "Nothing Susan could say or do could break my friendship with her and I know nothing could uproot her affection for me." 1

"The *History*" is a history of the women's movement, which Stanton and Anthony were writing.

Stanton and Anthony addressed the subject of their friendship in the *History.* Stanton referred to them as "two sticks of a drum . . . keeping up . . . the rub-a-dub of agitation." 2

These two "types" are fairly characteristic of writing teams, we find.

> In thought and sympathy we were one, and in the division of labor we exactly complemented each other. In writing we did better work together than either could alone. While she is slow and analytical in composition, I am rapid and synthetic. I am the better writer, she the better critic. She supplied the facts and statistics, I the philosophy and rhetoric, and together we have made arguments that have stood unshaken by the storms of thirty long years. . . . Our speeches may be considered the united product of two brains.

Refusing to acknowledge the fights and hurt feelings between them, Stanton continued:

> So entirely one are we that in all our associations, ever side by side on the same platform, not one feeling of jealousy or envy has ever shadowed our lives. We have indulged freely in criticism of each other when alone and hotly contended whenever we differed. . . . To the world we always seem to agree and uniformly reflect each other.

Help your students see the shift in tone here; invite them to speculate on its effect. The trick is that the author doesn't quite want us to wind up *believing* all those quotes.

The only accurate statement is that they always tried to agree in public. A slightly more objective source, presumably Theodore Tilton, noted: "Opposites though they be, each does not so much supplement the other's deficiencies as augment the other's eccentricities. Thus they often stimulate each other's aggressiveness and at the same time diminish each other's discretion."

3 The steadfast loyalty of Stanton and Anthony to each other became part of their mutual public image. People thought of them as a team long after they had ceased to cooperate closely. For most of their lives the friendship was genuine. But the assumption of automatic agreement between them by the public, the press, and their peers added stress to periods of disagreement and made their final years more difficult.

Theodore Tilton was editor of several newspapers that supported women's suffrage, and was a friend of both Stanton and Anthony.

Questions for Writing and Discussion

Prepare short written answers to each of these questions. Be prepared to hand them in and/or discuss them in class, as your teacher directs.

1. Is it the words of the author, Elizabeth Griffith, or those of Stanton and Anthony that primarily advance the movement of this passage?
2. Given the importance of the quoted words in this passage, what's the effect on you as a reader when the author says, "The only accurate statement is that they always tried to agree in public" (¶ 2)?
3. How is the author's comment "But the assumption of automatic agreement between them by the public, the press, and their peers added stress to periods of disagreement and made their final years more difficult" (¶ 3) different from the way you expect this passage to end up?
4. Though this is a narrative of the relationship between Stanton and Anthony over time, it is also highly descriptive and comparative. What elements of narration can you identify? What elements of description? What elements of comparison?
5. What do the following words mean—*contentious* (¶ 1), *the rub-a-dub of agitation, augment, eccentricity* (¶ 2)?

Some narratives, such as the story below, about a corporate takeover attempt, are straightforward accounts of events.

PREREADING WORKSHEET

Before you read the following piece by John Taylor, write brief responses to these questions:

1. What is your understanding of the phrase "corporate takeover"?
2. What kinds of images or ideas do you typically associate with the name Walt Disney?
3. What associations do you think of when these two "worlds" are juxtaposed:

Wall Street ⟷ Disneyland

4. How important do you think such Disney cartoon creations as Donald Duck, Mickey Mouse, Goofy, and Scrooge McDuck are to young Americans under age eleven or twelve?

The Battle for Disney Begins

JOHN TAYLOR

John Taylor, a professional writer and editor, is currently contributing editor to New York *magazine. Following is a scene from his book* Storming the Magic Kingdom, *as Wall Street corporate raiders—initially in the form of "financier Saul Steinberg, who had a reputation as the most feared corporate raider in the country"—begin their attempt to take over the Disney empire. As the passage opens, Donald Duck is celebrating his fiftieth anniversary.*

What effect is the author trying to produce with the juxtaposition here?

As the "irascible duck" was greeting crowds at Rockefeller Center in Manhattan—three blocks from Steinberg's office—the top executives of Walt Disney Productions were debating their response to Steinberg's offer. To accept it was unthinkable. Walt Disney Productions was not just another corporate entity, not just some holding company in a cyclical industry like natural gas or forestry that suffered from overcapacity and therefore needed to be rationalized by liquidation of its assets to achieve maximum value for the shareholders. Nor was Disney just another brand name—though it was, certainly, one of the most successful marketing stories of the twentieth century. The company's executives saw Disney as a force shaping the imaginative life of children around the world. It was woven into the very fabric of American culture. Indeed, its mission—and it did, they believed, have a mission as important as making money for its stockholders—was to celebrate and nurture American values. 1

The view given in this paragraph of what Disney productions mean to most Americans is perhaps more appropriate for Taylor's generation than for students'. Ask your students what images come to *their* minds when they think of Walt Disney Productions.

Thus, to Disney's executives, Steinberg's move was not merely an outrageous and ruthless profiteering tactic, it was somehow unpatriotic, almost anti-American—and they were not alone in this view. Expressing the popular reaction to the takeover attempt, Robert Knight, a staff member of the *Los Angeles Times,* wrote in an op-ed article in his paper that "while Steinberg and his ilk are making millions by threatening to tear down what took years to build, Disney and other creative institutions still are developing ideas, tangible products—and jobs. Steinberg apparently thought nothing of dissolving an American original, a monument to ingenuity and quality. His attitude is beyond cavalier. Breaking up Disney to cash in on its assets would be on the order of smashing a Tiffany vase to get at the penny that fell inside." Disney executives had actually heard from Jews voicing support for the company who expressed fears that Steinberg's actions would provoke an outburst of anti-Semitism, that the takeover battle might be regarded as an attempt by Jews to topple one of the temples of Protestant America. 2

3 Indeed, so pervasive were these feelings both inside and outside the organization that Disney's executives had always believed theirs was the one company a raider would never dare molest. And even after Steinberg made his offer, some of the elder members of the board argued that the company's unique position in American culture, the fact that millions of children loved its films and parks and characters, was protection enough. They thought that stockholders would support Disney because it *was* Disney—that, as children saved the life of Tinkerbell in *Peter Pan* by clapping, so Disney's shareholders would proclaim their faith in Disney and save it by refusing to sell Steinberg their stock.

4 Unfortunately, however, by 1984 small investors, the ones who might have been moved by such sentimental considerations, were not much of a force on Wall Street. A lot of Disney's stock was in the hands of institutional investors, who handled the portfolios of pension funds and insurance companies and banks, and who were obliged to seek the best short-term returns on their clients' money. Steinberg was prepared to buy the stock of Walt Disney Productions at a price more than $10 per share higher than the figure at which it had been trading before takeover speculation drove it up; the institutional investors were willing and even eager to sell.

5 To avoid being acquired, Disney's executives had to make the pilgrimage to Wall Street. There they discovered the tiny, incestuous world of takeover mercenaries: men, by and large, at a handful of investment banks, law firms, and public relations agencies, who were sometimes professional adversaries and at other times professional allies, depending on who retained them in any given battle. These men—together with the speculators, investors, and raiders who bought up the stock of a target company like Disney—knew each other and in a number of instances were even friends; they attended the same social functions, ate at the same expensive restaurants, belonged to the same exclusive clubs. In takeover battles they communicated with one another through an informal network of mutual acquaintances and back channels. Theirs was the consummate insiders' world, and their work constituted the ultimate insiders' game.

Note that Wall Street is described as yet another kind of fairyland.

In that our excerpt does not include the outcome of the Disney battle, your students may want to know that Disney did survive but was radically changed in the process by what it had to do to survive—with the result that the popular image described in Taylor's second paragraph is probably destined to fade away.

POSTREADING WORKSHEET

Now that you have read the piece by Taylor, write your responses to the following questions:

1. Did reading this selection in any way change your perception of what the phrase "corporate takeover" means? If so, how?
2. Did your response to the question about the importance of Disney cartoon creations (such as Donald Duck) to American young people find any support in the passage by Taylor?
3. Did Taylor's piece in any way affect how you view "corporate raiders," such as Saul Steinberg?

4. Do you agree with Disney executives who felt that Steinberg's takeover attempt was "somehow unpatriotic" (¶ 2)? Why or why not?

Questions for Writing and Discussion

Prepare short written answers to each of these questions. Be prepared to hand them in and/or discuss them in class, as your teacher directs.

1. What is the overall organizing principle of this passage? Give examples of where it shows up most clearly.
2. One of the characteristics of Taylor's writing here is frequent use of metaphoric language: Disney's business is "woven into the fabric of American culture" (¶ 1); breaking up Disney is like "smashing a Tiffany vase" (¶ 2); executives had to "make a pilgrimage" (¶ 5). Pick out as many of those instances of metaphoric language as you can in the passage; then try rewriting it without them.
3. What do the following words mean—*irascible, cyclical, entity* (¶ 1), *profiteering, op-ed article, ilk, cavalier* (¶ 2), *pervasive* (¶ 3), *portfolios, takeover speculation* (¶ 4), *mercenaries* (¶ 5)?

One of the most typical kinds of narration is the "story" we tell of our own experience—the things that we do, or that happen to us or to people we know, as we make our way through life. Our college years naturally provide us with many such narratives, like the one below.

Doughnuts to Dollars

Jane-Marie Gray, college writing student

I'd always heard good friends would do anything for each other. But I never really believed it until I met Lisa and Renée. We met in freshmen orientation at State University and lived on the same floor in Fulwiler Dorm. Lisa was from Chadom (population twelve hundred); Renée came from Key West; and I was from Statesville. But although we did not have much in common at first, we became immediate friends. As freshmen living together, we shared many special experiences that created lasting bonds of friendship. 1

One particular night Lisa and Renée went to the bars and I stayed home to study. It was midnight when Lisa and Renée burst into my room crying. After she calmed down, Lisa informed me that she had been issued a "Driving under the Influence" of alcohol (DUI) ticket. A police 2 officer had pulled her off the road and administered an intoxication test. She was taken to the courthouse, questioned, fingerprinted, and then issued a $300 DUI ticket. Lisa was hysterical. She did not have the money to pay the ticket, and her parents would never give it to her.

We certainly do not mean to encourage or condone student consumption of alcohol by including this student paper. Nor do we mean to encourage or condone acts of deception involving parents or others.

3 For a week, the three of us unsuccessfully discussed ways to accumulate money for Lisa. Then one night, while on our usual Krispy Kreme doughnut run, we noticed a sign advertising ideas for money-making organizational fund-raisers. Renée jokingly suggested we should ask about it as a method of raising the $300. Instantly Lisa was inquiring about the "Doughnuts to Dollars" program. The waitress explained how an organization can purchase doughnuts for $1 a dozen and sell them for $2. She also added that the doughnuts must be paid for in advance. Lisa furiously jotted down figures on a Krispy Kreme napkin: 200 dozen doughnuts at $2 a dozen would be $400 (a little more than she needed). Renée and I thought she was kidding, but she was not. Lisa was determined to earn the money for her DUI ticket by selling Krispy Kreme doughnuts.

4 Lisa's main problem was how to come up with the initial cash to place the order for the doughnuts. Lisa had only $50, and so I put in $50 and Renée covered the last $100. Renée and I asked Lisa what she planned to say if Krispy Kreme asked what organization she was from. Lisa told us that if they asked, she was going to tell them she was from the Geology Club. She said she would not be really specific which Geology Club, the university's or the local high school's. We made a list of potential selling areas: neighborhoods, businesses, and dorms. The next day, Lisa went to Krispy Kreme and made an order for 200 dozen doughnuts to be picked up at 8:00 A.M. the next morning.

At this point while they read, some students may think, "Another $100 and the fine is paid. So why not borrow the rest and skip the trouble with the doughnuts?" It's a good question, and we don't know the answer. But this way, at least, Jane-Marie has a good memory and narrative paper to share.

5 Renée and I agreed it was our duty as Lisa's friends to help her sell her doughnuts. Because I had the biggest car, I was appointed driver. That morning, I backed up my car to the loading gate behind Krispy Kreme, and we stacked doughnuts in my car for nearly thirty minutes. Then we pulled out of the parking lot and began our journey.

6 Lisa, who always had a flair with boys, suggested we start at the boys' dorm. Lisa was a great saleswoman; if the aroma from the doughnuts did not lure the boys, then Lisa's sweet southern voice and auburn-colored hair did. Renée and I stood behind Lisa listening to her convincing ploy to sell the doughnuts. She explained, in a very timid non-

Lisa voice, how she was out one night and got caught drinking and driving. Lisa told her customers that she wasn't really that drunk and she had no other way to pay the ticket. This sob story nailed a sale every time. Most boys agreed it could happen to them someday, and could sympathize with Lisa. Personally I was embarrassed to be seen pushing doughnuts at Pearson Hall, but because Lisa was my friend and because I had $50 invested in this venture, I did it anyway.

When we finished at the dorms, we had sold 60 boxes and earned $120. We continued to sell at other dormitories and were very successful. Lisa even went door to door at fraternity houses. While she was doing that, Renée and I decided we would sit in the car because we were afraid we would see someone we knew. By 4:00 P.M. we had sold 90 boxes and were left with only 50 more boxes. Renée and I were tired and ready to take a nap, but Lisa wanted to keep selling. Lisa asked me to drive my car around to the front of Fulwiler. Within minutes, Lisa returned with a luggage cart and proceeded to stack the remaining boxes on the cart. While Renée and I headed for our rooms, Lisa resumed selling. Later that night, Lisa came into my room with 25 remaining boxes and the $350 we had made. Renée, Lisa, and I ate some of the remaining doughnuts and gave the others away. We decided we would go out to dinner on the remaining $50, and Monday we would pay Lisa's ticket. 7

All of this happened four years ago, and all three of us have gone through some changes since then, but because of experiences like this, Lisa and Renée will always be special to me. It took Lisa a long time to scrape together the $150 she owed me and Renée, but she did it, even though we probably wouldn't have cared. I never knew Lisa to drink and drive again, either, and though she may have told other people a few more whoppers since our doughnut escapade, she has always been honest with her original two roomies. I don't know about Renée, but to this day I cannot drive past a Krispy Kreme, or eat doughnuts, without thinking of Lisa. 8

Questions for Writing and Discussion

Prepare short written answers to each of these questions. Be prepared to hand them in and/or discuss them in class, as your teacher directs.

1. How does this passage leave you feeling about Jane-Marie, Lisa, and Renée? What is it about the passage that produces that feeling?
2. Does the level of detail in the passage get in the way of the story, or does it let the narrative come through clearly?
3. What kind of reader is this passage targeted to? How do you know that?
4. The title of this piece is a play on words, based on a familiar saying. What is the saying, and what is its origin?

You and your students might want to talk about these students' honesty (or lack thereof). Are their various lapses minor, or major?

KEY POINTS TO REMEMBER: Writing Narration

Here are four key points to remember when you're writing narration:

- Keep the event/situation moving.
- Keep the sequence of the narrative clear.
- Make an appropriately detailed presentation.
- Give a clear indication of the event's significance.

Let's look at each of these in more detail.

Keep the Event/Situation Moving

Essential to the nature of narrative is that it keep moving. What constitutes "keeping moving," however, varies considerably from one piece of writing to the next; thus, just how you choose to accomplish this task in your own writing is largely an open question. You can get some idea of the possibilities, though, by reviewing the samples in this chapter. "Roadhouse and Wilderness" uses two methods to keep the story moving: In the first three paragraphs the movement comes from the description; in the remaining paragraphs the movement comes from the dialogue. The description in the first paragraph moves by stages from the broad scene ("East of the village of Blue Mountain Lake . . . ") to the specific ("an antique roadhouse"). The second paragraph moves in the reverse direction, from the specific ("I ate a ham and cheese sandwich"); through the description of the women, the tabletops, and the stools; to a picture of the whole building; to the building itself. The movement in the rest of the piece comes from the tense scene between the young man and woman, from the expectations the author creates and the contrary way those expectations are met: "It lacked only the dimension of sharing" (¶ 3), is met with a couple who comes in carrying tension like an "unexploded grenade" (¶ 4); "wilderness" (¶ 5) becomes a necklace made from a BIC pen cap; and the "dimension of sharing" we had been led to anticipate becomes an angry confrontation.

Indeed, movement is perhaps the distinctive characteristic of this kind of writing; a narrative that doesn't move toward its completion isn't a good narrative (or isn't a narrative at all).

The "White Tigers" passage uses different methods to keep the narrative moving. Here the primary mode is storytelling: the story of the girl who first learned white crane boxing, the story of Maxine Hong Kingston hearing about swordswomen from her mother, and the story of the author's realizing that her

This disjunction is difficult for students to see; you may want to review the selection to make sure students get this important point.

mother, too, was a "great power." "Elizabeth Cady Stanton and Susan Anthony" uses the quoted material—and the disjunction between what the quotations seem to be saying and what the author thinks is actually going on—to keep the narrative moving. And to keep its action going, "The Battle for Disney Begins" also uses the flow of events—and the Disney executives' gradual realization that, if they wished the fantasy world to survive, they would have to leave that world to do battle in the very different country of Wall Street.

Keep the Sequence of the Narrative Clear

You may want to choose another piece to have students identify similar words or groups of words. A good candidate would be chapter 16's "See the Hamptons," by Wilfrid Sheed.

While a narrative needs to keep moving, the sequence of events also has to be clear to readers. Only a small number of words may be needed to keep the sequence clear, as in "White Tigers," in which the sequence of the opening words of each paragraph controls the entire sequence: "When we Chinese girls listened to the adults . . . "; "This was one of the tamer, more modern stories . . . "; and "At last I saw that I too had been in the presence . . . " In "The Battle for Disney Begins" the cueing is similarly simple: "As the 'irascible duck' was greeting crowds . . . "; "Thus, to Disney's executives . . . "; "Indeed, so pervasive were these feelings . . . "; "Unfortunately, however, by 1984 . . . "; and "To avoid being acquired . . . "

This cueing is critical in readers' seeing the disjunction we spoke of in the piece about Elizabeth Cady Stanton and Susan B. Anthony.

In "Elizabeth Cady Stanton and Susan Anthony" both the sequence and the way it's signaled are more complex: the first paragraph says something about (what the author thinks to be) their real relationship, supported by quotations from Stanton. The second paragraph gives two longer quotations by Stanton, implying there had never been the slightest bit of difference between the two, followed by the author's own view and something of a counterquotation. The passage concludes with a still more complicated thought, the idea that the image of their closeness actually worked against Stanton and Anthony's being able to be as close as they might. In this passage the narrative movement is primarily one of ideas: idea A leads to idea B leads to idea C, and so on. The cueing that goes on to keep the sequence straight in the reader's mind is correspondingly more complex, buried in the sense of each paragraph and not so explicit as in the other passages.

Make an Appropriately Detailed Presentation

If you're ambitious, you can ask students to try this same kind of representation of levels of detail in chapter 16's "A Nation at Risk," by Ben Nelms.

Take a look at the level of detail in just the first two sentences of the first paragraph of "The Battle for Disney Begins":

> The irascible duck is greeting crowds at Rockefeller Center.
> Top executives of Disney productions are debating their response
>   to Steinberg's offer.
> Accepting it is unthinkable
>   because Disney Productions is not just another corporation,
>   not just some holding company
>   in a cyclical industry like natural gas

or forestry
that suffered from overcapacity
and therefore needed to be rationalized
by liquidation of its assets
to achieve maximum value for the shareholders.

When the level of detail is presented this way, it seems pretty high. But you're looking at the opening paragraph of an entire book, and as the book goes along each detail becomes important. Thus, for this passage, in this instance, the level of detail is appropriate. Compare that wealth of detail with the sparseness of detail in the first paragraph of "White Tigers"; for the story Maxine Hong Kingston is telling, the sparseness is also appropriate.

Give a Clear Indication of the Event's Significance

Whatever else you do, you need to ensure that your readers know *why* you're telling them what you're telling them. Some fortunate few writers are good enough to do straight narration and have us realize (between the lines) the event's significance. For the rest of us, however, generally we need to be a little more explicit. You can see both techniques in the first passage, "Roadhouse and Wilderness." The significance of the first section (¶ 1–3) is summed up in the two sentences "The present building, dating from the thirties, seemed to have absorbed the continuum of history" and "It lacked only the dimension of sharing."

We can clearly see the importance of cueing the reader as to the piece's significance in "Doughnuts to Dollars." Readers would feel cheated reading this piece were it not for the first and last paragraphs, which tell us what the experience means to the author—and to us. Narratives are always at least mildly interesting reading for most of us, but without a clear idea of where some level of human meaning comes in, they're not as good as they could be.

See whether your students can find the places where human meaning comes into the Joseph Conrad passage from *The Heart of Darkness,* "Along the African Coast," in chapter 10.

Narrative writing brings the power of storytelling to bear for a writer and can therefore be quite useful for accomplishing all the purposes for writing. As a writer, you'll find that you can often explain, persuade, analyze, or express much more effectively if you incorporate narration.

✓✓✓ WORKSHEET: Writing Narration

In this chapter we'll focus on two aspects of writing narration: the very early stages—what we call invention—and the finishing stages (the latter is discussed in the next section). When you have a writing task that requires narration—basically, telling a story—what's the best way to go about doing it?

To answer that question, we have to consider two possibilities: (a) the subject matter for your writing has already been dictated to you and (b) alternatively, you get to choose your own subject. It should be obvious that the way invention

You may want to remind students here of the inside/outside distinction from Part Four's introduction.

occurs differs, depending on which situation you're in. If the subject has already been dictated for you, you essentially must respond as directed, and so we won't say any more about that here. Instead, we'll look at the situation in which you are allowed to choose your topic. What kinds of things lend themselves to making good topics when you're writing narration? Here's just a partial list:

These kinds of "canned" lists are never as good as ones you and your students come up with—all we can do is give you a good place to start.

Experiences	Trips	Battles
Processes	Changes	Evolutions
Procedures	Special occasions	Revolutions
Activities	Games	Memories

Recall for students that the topic of how to choose things to write about comes up in the Bob Greene profile at the beginning of Part Three.

As we said, that's just a partial list. Our point is twofold: First, to stimulate you toward coming up with a good subject to write about and, second, to enable us to indicate what all those items have in common: someone (or something) is moving through time. That notion is the starting point for choosing a good topic for narration; if nothing is moving, you can't narrate.

The next two criteria are twins in importance but not identical in appearance:

- Write about something you *know* (or can easily find out) about.
- Write about something you *care* (or can get yourself to care) about.

Of course, these two criteria are key in selecting any topic for any piece of writing of any kind; however, in most classrooms they're not repeated often enough. Sometimes we all have to write about things we don't know enough about or don't care enough about. But when you have a *choice*, you might as well write about the ideal topic, one you have knowledge about and feelings for. Take a look at the list above to see what topics, under each category, you can come up with to write about, topics that also meet these two criteria.

Suppose you come up with a list like this:

Enrolling as a freshman
Being a free-lance housepainter
Learning windsurfing
Making divinity fudge
Combating the pollution of the Colorado River
Being a loyal friend
Living away from home

Which ones are you sufficiently interested in to write about? Which ones do you care enough about to write about? And if those questions don't fully sort out the situation, let's add one more question that should *always* be considered by the writer—which ones do you think will have the desired effect on your reader?

Once you have answered those questions, you should have narrowed down your list to the best selection for writing about through narration. In the following section, you'll see how one student developed a paper on the subject of how friends become friends.

SAMPLE WRITING ASSIGNMENT AND CASE STUDY CLOSE-UP

Here's a good second draft from a student writing on the subject of how friends become friends. Take a look at it and ask yourself what parts of it advance the narration and what parts get in the way. Remember, our main interest is the way the narrative pattern helps the writer decide what to say next, and next, and next. To begin with, let's talk about how the first two paragraphs developed, almost from scratch. Here are the original first few lines of text:

> Lisa, Renée, and I didn't come to college with much in common, but we soon became the best of friends. One night Lisa and Renée went to the bars and I stayed home to study. When they came back, Lisa was hysterical--she had been ticketed for DUI. Worse, she didn't have the money to pay the $300 fine.

What needs to be done to develop this initial idea further? Let's focus on two points in particular: (a) determining the level of detail and (b) letting the reader in on the event's significance. What questions about level of detail would you ask Jane-Marie Gray, the author of the piece, about this opening paragraph?

> Who are Lisa and Renée?
>
> Can you tell me more about when and where the three of you met?
>
> In what particular ways did the three of you not have much in common?

What question about the significance of the event would you ask?

> Why should I be interested in you and your friends?

As you read the following draft, notice how it responds to all the above questions. And if you compare this next-to-last draft with the final one, printed earlier in this chapter, you'll see more places where those two points account for important differences. You'll also notice how the other two key points we presented earlier (write about something you know about and care about) are reflected in the changes between the two drafts. In particular, you'll see that much "deadwood"—nonfunctional words and phrases—has been trimmed from the piece, especially from the first few paragraphs, to keep the action moving. Further, you'll see how changes have been made to keep the sequence of the action clear (for example, the sentence about planning potential places to sell the doughnuts was moved from paragraph 5 of this draft to paragraph 4 about planning the trip in the final version).

As you read this draft, then, think about how you would use the key points we listed earlier to improve it. Then you can take another look at the final version to see how right you were about the changes that needed to be made.

Doughnuts to Dollars

1 I've always heard that you would do anything for a good friend. But I never really believed this until I met Lisa and Renée. The three of us met as freshmen at orientation at State University and lived in Fulwiler Dorm on the same floor. On the surface, we did not have much in common: Lisa was from Chadom (population twelve hundred); Renée came from Key West; and I was from Statesville. Even though we did not have much in common at first, we became immediate friends. As freshmen living together, we shared many special experiences that created lasting bonds of friendship.

2 Renée, Lisa, and I enjoyed spending time together, but one particular night Lisa and Renée went to the bars and I stayed home to study. They had been gone a couple of hours, and it was midnight when Lisa and Renée burst into my room crying. I had difficulty understanding what they were saying. After she calmed down, Lisa informed me that she had been issued a ticket for "Driving under the Influence" of alcohol (DUI). She explained that a police officer pulled her off the road and administered an intoxication test. She also told me that she was taken to the courthouse, questioned, fingerprinted, and then issued a $300.00 DUI ticket. Lisa was hysterical; she did not have the money to pay the ticket and knew her parents would never give it to her.

3 For a week, the three of us discussed ways to accumulate money for Lisa. We could not come up with a solution. Then, a few days later, Lisa's prayers were answered. One night, while on our usual Krispy Kreme doughnut run, we noticed a sign advertising ideas for organizational fund-raisers. Renée jokingly made a comment about how we should ask about it as a method of raising the needed $300.00. But no sooner had she said it than Lisa was inquiring about the "Doughnuts to Dollars" program. The waitress explained how an organization could purchase doughnuts for $1.00 a dozen and sell them for $2.00. She also added that the doughnuts had to be paid for in advance of placing the order. Lisa furiously jotted down figures on a Krispy Kreme napkin. A few minutes later, she presented the calculations to Renée and me: 200 dozen doughnuts at $2.00 a dozen would be $400.00 (a little more than she needed). Of course, Renée and I thought she was kidding, but she was not. Lisa was determined to earn the money for her DUI ticket by selling Krispy Kreme doughnuts.

4 That evening Lisa plotted out everything; her main problem was how to come up with the initial cash to place the order for the doughnuts. Lisa had only $50.00, and so I put in $50.00 and Renée covered the last $100.00. Renée and I asked Lisa what she planned to say if they asked what organization she was from. Lisa told us that if they asked, she was going to tell them she was from the Geology Club. She said she would not be really specific which Geology Club, the university's or the local high school's. The next day, Lisa went to Krispy Kreme and made an order for 200 dozen doughnuts to be picked up at 8:00 A.M. the next morning.

5 Renée and I agreed that it was our duty, as Lisa's friends, to help her sell her doughnuts. Because I had the biggest car, I was appointed driver. That morning, I backed up my car to the loading gate behind Krispy Kreme. Renée, Lisa, and I stacked doughnuts in my car for nearly thirty minutes. The night before we'd made a list of potential selling areas--neighborhoods, businesses, and dorms; we pulled out of the parking lot and began our journey.

6 Lisa always had a flair with boys, and she suggested we start at the boys' dorm. Lisa was a great saleswoman; if the aroma from the doughnuts did not lure the boys, then Lisa's sweet southern voice and auburn-colored hair did. Renée and I stood behind Lisa, listening to her convincing ploy to sell the doughnuts. She explained, in a very timid, non-Lisa voice, how she was out one night and got caught drinking and driving. Lisa told her customers that she wasn't really <u>that</u> drunk and she had no other way to pay the ticket. This sob story nailed a sale every time. Most boys agreed it could happen to them someday, and could sympathize with Lisa. Personally I was embarrassed to be seen pushing doughnuts at Pearson Hall, but because Lisa was my friend and because I had $50.00 invested in this venture, I did it anyway.

7 When we finished at the dorms, we had sold 60 boxes and earned $120.00. We continued to sell at other dormitories and were very successful. Lisa even went door to door at fraternity houses. Renée and I decided we would sit in the car because we were afraid we would see someone we knew. By 4:00 P.M. we returned to our dorm, and we had sold 90 boxes and were left with only 50 more boxes remaining. Renée and I were tired and ready to take a nap, but Lisa wanted to keep selling. Lisa asked me to drive my car around to the front of Fulwiler. Within minutes, Lisa returned with a luggage cart and proceeded to stack the

remaining boxes on the cart. Lisa resumed selling while Renée and I headed for our rooms. Later that night, Lisa came into my room with 25 remaining boxes and the $350.00 we had made. Renée, Lisa, and I ate some of the remaining doughnuts and gave the others away. We decided that we would go out to dinner and then spend the remaining $50.00 and that Monday we would go and pay Lisa's ticket.

All this happened four years ago, but it seems just like yesterday. 8
Lisa and Renée were my first true friends in college and will always be special to me. To this day I cannot drive past Krispy Kreme or eat doughnuts and not think of Lisa, Renée, and my unforgettable freshman year.

WRITING ASSIGNMENTS

1. For another look at this personal experience narrative approach to writing, reread "Old Friends Are Best" in chapter 9. What are the basic similarities and differences between it and the version of "Doughnuts to Dollars" that appears earlier in this chapter?
2. Take another look at "How to Rig a Plastic Worm Texas-Style" in chapter 5. What are the basic similarities and differences between it and the version of "Doughnuts to Dollars" that appears earlier in this chapter?
3. Look again at the list on page 332 of this chapter. Choose a topic from that list and develop it into a paper that uses narration to make its point. Pay particular attention to the key points illustrated in this chapter.
4. From your own reading in other college classes, pick a short (about five hundred words) piece of narrative. Provide a copy for your teacher, and write an analysis of whether and how it does or doesn't meet the criteria presented in this chapter. Beyond that, in what way(s) is it good writing?
5. Examine the photograph (page 317) of the person contemplating the Bali Temple at Lake Beratan. In a brief paper, project your own thoughts and impressions into this picture, considering answers to some or all of the following questions:
   a. What is your overall impression of the picture?
   b. What do you think the person in the picture is doing, and why?
   c. What kind of culture do you think exists in the "world" of this picture, and what makes you think so?
   d. If you could enter the picture and take the boat in the foreground for a ride on the lake, where in the picture would you go, and why?

e. Though this picture obviously shows us another culture in another part of the world, what aspects of the picture seem to you to be universal—things that might be seen in any culture in any part of the world?

Focus on Critical Thinking

6. In the essay "Roadhouse and Wilderness," what is the key issue? What kind of issue is it? Does it shift from being one kind of issue to being another?
7. In "Elizabeth Cady Stanton and Susan Anthony," what is the key issue in the passage? How does your understanding of that issue change through the passage?
8. Reread the selection "Eleven Blue Men" in chapter 6. How is the problem-solving process depicted therein the same as or different from the one we depict in our introduction to Part Four? What is your own problem-solving process?
9. Reread the selection "Dollar Wise, Penny Foolish" in chapter 11. How does the author move the issue around to make his point?
10. Reread the selection "Standardized Tests Are Means, Not Ends" in chapter 11. How do the key issue's identity and type change during the piece? Does the author manipulate that changing to his advantage?

Writers' Circle

Divide into groups of three; then follow these directions:

Jane-Marie Gray's "Doughnuts to Dollars" narrative appears in early draft form near the end of this chapter (pages 334–36) and in final form earlier in this chapter (pages 326–28). In your groups, closely compare the two versions, looking for the following:

1. Important differences in the *money* calculations and in the handling of the money among the three friends
2. Important differences in attitudes toward drinking and driving
3. Important differences in attitudes toward *honesty* in dealing with others
4. Other important differences you see

Discuss in your groups *why* these changes were made, and compare these changes with what was found in the earlier "Case Study Close-up" comparison: did comparing the early draft and the final version yield more or less in the way of noticeable difference or improvement? Now poll each group for a brief report of differences found. How many groups found the same differences?

chapter 16 Description

"In almost all classes of composition, the unity of effect or impression is a point of greatest importance. . . . In the whole composition there should be no word written, of which the tendency, direct or indirect, is not to the one pre-established design."

Edgar Allan Poe

Descriptive writing is writing that has extraordinary appeal to our senses. In large part, our abilities to see, hear, touch, taste, and smell constitute our ability to experience. Impairment of any of our senses changes—and possibly impairs in turn—our ability to experience as well. Once we undergo experience, our memories record it and thus empower us to remember, enabling us, in our minds, to undergo the experience again as a function of our imaginations. Consider the following description:

The Tornado

Buddy Moss

It was a bright afternoon in late May, and I stood on our front porch with my mother and sister, staring at the western sky. There, against an implausible background of sunlight and blue sky, hanging like an elephant's trunk out of a small dark cloud, was the only tornado I have ever seen "for real" in my life. The trunk wobbled and spiraled, pumping up and down, but never quite touching the ground or disappearing into the cloud. We could tell by its movement across the horizon that it was not headed our way; rather, it seemed to be moving north-northeast, its whirling gray funnel seeming to expand and contract as though it were breathing. We were transfixed by this awesome proof of an overwhelming natural force; somewhere in our memories were news stories and photos of past disasters dealt by deathwinds such as this, but we were utterly powerless to do anything but marvel. 1

Suddenly the gray trunk dipped all the way to earth and instantly turned black. It must have sucked up a ton of topsoil and spit it up into the cloud. Near its base was a black blur, no doubt the whirl of whatever was so unfortunate as to be in its path. Then, just as suddenly, the spiral snaked all the way back up into the cloud, which then rolled and heaved in the heavens and spun apart, scattering streaks and wisps of leftover cloud all over the still-blue background of sky. The tornado was gone. We had watched it for perhaps ten minutes. 2

3 The next day a farmer north of town reported that the twister had touched down in his fields. A swath about 100 yards wide and a half-mile long had been carved out of his ripening wheat, and a stretch of fence and fence posts had been pulled up, rolled up, and deposited in his neighbor's pasture. No one was hurt; no buildings were damaged. Our tornado had been a small one, but photogenic because it came in such bright overall conditions. Another farmer who lived west of where the funnel tracked took such a good picture of it that some years later it was used on the cover of an issue of Scientific American.

The writer of "The Tornado" has re-created, from his memory, the striking visual appearance of a tornado, and he has done so primarily with description that invites our "mind's eye" to see the tornado for ourselves. We can engage our imaginations and vicariously stand on the porch with him and his mother and sister.

Ask students whether any of them have images they remember this vividly. If so, ask them to describe the images to the class.

The Role of Imagination

Imagination is a key concept here, for it derives from another word—*image*—which, in terms of language, means words that constitute an appeal to one or more of the senses. Thus, words like *bright* and *black* appeal to sight; words like *sour* and *sweet* appeal to taste; *shrill* and *bang* appeal to sound; *putrid* and *stench* appeal to smell; and *wet* and *slimy* appeal to touch. Depending on how they are used, other words may appeal to more than one sense; for example, *jagged* and *rough* can appeal to both sight and touch.

Ask students whether any other of their classes entail using their imaginations; if so, ask them to describe that use. If not, ask them whether they think using imagination *should* be a formal part of a college education.

Image has other applications as well, for in terms of the visual arts, such as painting and photography, it means any picture, whether re-created by skillful drawing or painting or recaptured through the process of photography. The tornado the writer describes above is re-created in his memory and in our own minds as we read; it is also "re-created" by the farmer's camera, an image so striking that it was later used on a magazine cover.

You might point out that something can be an "image" quite apart from whether it is or is not *representational.*

The Role of Descriptive Language

Given that one of the eight traditional parts of speech, the adjective, is defined as a word that describes or points out (for instance, *black* cloud or *that* cloud), it would be easy to surmise that descriptive writing is dominated by adjectives. But that's not so. Look again at the tornado passage above.

In the first paragraph, we indeed see several adjectives. The afternoon is *bright*. A *small dark* cloud presents a *whirling gray* funnel against an *implausible* background of *blue* sky. And so on. But note how many verbs also carry descriptive power: the tornado *wobbled* and *spiraled,* seeming to *expand* and *contract.* We learn in the second paragraph that it *dipped* to earth and *sucked* and *spit* dirt up into the cloud. Even nouns, used here as metaphors (implicit comparisons), are powerfully descriptive: because of the tornado's shape, it is called a *funnel.*

This notion that description uses *all* the resources of language, not just a superabundance of adjectives, is critical. Students will want to lean only on adjectives and adverbs—which doesn't work.

Because of its action, it is also called a *spiral*. A simile compares it directly to an elephant's *trunk*. Another simile compares the tornado's expanding and contracting "as though it were breathing," that is, as if it were a living thing. The writer names tornadoes *deathwinds*. We are told of a black *blur*. *Streaks* and *wisps* of cloud are all that remain after the tornado—in a verb born of noun and metaphor—*snaked* back up into the sky.

In the last paragraph the highly descriptive language continues, still not relying totally on adjectives. Another metaphoric noun provides yet another way to refer to the tornado: *twister*. Quite precisely we are told that a *swath* (noun) had been *carved* (verb) in a farmer's field and that a *stretch* (noun) of fence and posts had been *pulled up*, *rolled up*, and *deposited* (parallel verbs) nearby.

For more practice, you can lead your students in doing this analysis on "Putting a Brake on TV 'Sleeze'" in chapter 17.

Descriptive language prompts a strong appeal to our senses and, as such, can be very effective in a variety of purposes. Description is a powerful additive to the reasons you have for writing: you can often explain, persuade, analyze, or express to a greater degree if you write descriptively.

If any of your students have seen the film version of *Shane*, they can bring another perspective to this discussion. (The film is available on videocassette.)

The following passage forms the beginning of a classic American western novel, *Shane*, by Jack Schaefer. Here the narrator seeks to describe and thereby express what the experience of seeing Shane for the first time was like. The passage is full of hints as to the heroic deeds Shane would soon perform. If you have seen the excellent film version of this novel (starring Alan Ladd, Van Heflin, Jean Arthur, Brandon De Wilde, and Jack Palance, directed by George Stevens, Paramount, 1953), you may recall the opening scenes, as young Joey (played by De Wilde) observes the approaching stranger on horseback.

Shane

JACK SCHAEFER

Jack Schaefer (1907–1991) was a reporter, editor, and writer of novels and short stories. His books include Shane, The Plainsmen, *and* Monte Walsh. Shane *and* Monte Walsh *have been made into Hollywood movies.*

Ask students whether they can visualize this scene two different ways: (a) through the eyes of a camera, watching the boy (the narrator) who is watching the mysterious stranger ride into the valley, and (b) through the eyes of the boy himself. Which way works better for different students? Why?

He rode into our valley in the summer of '89 [1889]. I was a kid then, barely topping the backboard of father's old chuck-wagon. I was on the upper rail of our small corral, soaking in the late afternoon sun, when I saw him far down the road where it swung into the valley from the open plain beyond. 1

In that clear Wyoming air I could see him plainly, though he was still several miles away. There seemed nothing remarkable about him, just another stray horseman riding up the road toward the cluster of frame buildings that was our town. Then I saw a pair of cowhands, loping past him, stop and stare after him with a curious intentness. 2

He came steadily on, straight through the town without slackening pace, until he reached the fork a half-mile below our place. One branch turned left across the river ford and on to Luke Fletcher's big spread. The other bore ahead along the right bank where we homesteaders had pegged our claims in 3 a row up the valley. He hesitated briefly, studying the choice, and moved again steadily on our side.

4 As he came near, what impressed me first was his clothes. He wore dark trousers of some serge material tucked into tall boots and held at the waist by a wide belt, both of a soft black leather tooled in intricate design. A coat of the same dark material as the trousers was neatly folded and strapped to his saddle-roll. His shirt was finespun linen, rich brown in color. The handkerchief knotted loosely around his throat was black silk. His hat was not the familiar Stetson, not the familiar gray or muddy tan. It was a plain black, soft in texture, unlike any hat I had ever seen, with a creased crown and a wide curling brim swept down in front to shield the face.

This paragraph is loaded with great description; notice the high level of detail. (In fact, some readers may think the description here is overdone—hence text question 6 after the passage.)

5 All trace of newness was long gone from these things. The dust of distance was beaten into them. They were worn and stained and several neat patches showed on the shirt. Yet a kind of magnificence remained and with it a hint of men and manners alien to my limited boy's experience.

6 Then I forgot the clothes in the impact of the man himself. He was not much above medium height, almost slight in build. He would have looked frail alongside father's square, solid bulk. But even I could read the endurance in the lines of that dark figure and the quiet power in its effortless, unthinking adjustment to every movement of the tired horse.

Point out to students that purely through the description we get a real feel for Shane's character, a kind of weary magnificence.

7 He was clean-shaven and his face was lean and hard and burned from high forehead to firm, tapering chin. His eyes seemed hooded in the shadow of the hat's brim. He came closer, and I could see that this was because the brows were drawn in a frown of fixed and habitual alertness. Beneath them the eyes were endlessly searching from side to side and forward, checking off every item in view, missing nothing. As I noticed this, a sudden chill, I could not have told why, struck through me there in the warm and open sun.

8 He rode easily, relaxed in the saddle, leaning his weight lazily in the stirrups. Yet even in this easiness was a suggestion of tension. It was the easiness of a coiled spring, of a trap set.

9 He drew rein not twenty feet from me. His glance hit me, dismissed me, flicked over our place. This was not much, if you were thinking in terms of size and scope. But what there was was good. You could trust father for that. The corral, big enough for about thirty head if you crowded them in, was railed right to true sunk posts. The pasture behind, taking in nearly half of our claim, was fenced tight. The barn was small, but it was solid, and we were raising a loft at one end for the alfalfa growing green in the north forty. We had a fair-sized field in potatoes that year and father was trying a new corn he had sent all the way to Washington for and they were showing properly in weedless rows.

10 Behind the house mother's kitchen garden was a brave sight. The house itself was three rooms—two really, the big kitchen where we spent most of our time indoors and the bedroom beside it. My little lean-to room was added back of the kitchen. Father was planning, when he could get around to it, to build mother the parlor she wanted.

11 We had wooden floors and a nice porch across the front. The house was painted too, white with green trim, rare thing in all that region, to remind her,

Your students may not realize how significant it was to have wooden floors on the frontier; it was a real sign of aspiration.

mother said when she made father do it, of her native New England. Even rarer, the roof was shingled. I knew what that meant. I had helped father split those shingles. Few places so spruce and well worked could be found so deep in the Territory in those days.

Call students' attention to the way this paragraph narrows down the focus, bit by bit.

The stranger took it all in, sitting there easily in the saddle. I saw his eyes 12
slow on the flowers mother had planted by the porch steps, then come to rest on our shiny new pump and the trough beside it. They shifted back to me, and again, without knowing why, I felt that sudden chill. But his voice was gentle and he spoke like a man schooled to patience.

"I'd appreciate a chance at the pump for myself and the horse." 13

I was trying to frame a reply and choking on it, when I realized that he 14
was not speaking to me but past me. Father had come up behind me and was leaning against the gate to the corral.

Questions for Writing and Discussion

Prepare short written answers to each of these questions. Be prepared to hand them in and/or discuss them in class, as your teacher directs.

1. Comb each paragraph for adjectives (words or groups of words that describe or point out; they modify nouns and pronouns). For example, in the first paragraph, *barely topping the backboard* is an adjective phrase (group of words) describing the speaker. *Old* modifies the noun *chuck-wagon. Upper* modifies *rail; small* modifies *corral; late* and *afternoon* both modify *sun;* and so on. How many adjectives can you find? How do they help you form a mental picture of Shane as he rides in?
2. Now comb each paragraph for descriptive words or phrases that are *not* adjectives. For example, in the first paragraph, what effect does Schaefer achieve with the verb *soaking? swung?* In the second paragraph, what image do you get from Schaefer's description of "cowhands" *loping?* Elsewhere, Schaefer's narrator describes Shane's glance as it *hit* the boy, *dismissed* him, and then *flicked* over the homestead. These suggest much stronger actions than are actually taking place, yet are still appropriate. Why?
3. *Shane* is the story of a gunfighter who knows the old "Wild West" has largely passed by 1889 and who no longer seeks the kind of trouble he once welcomed. Yet as he stays to work awhile with the narrator's father, it becomes apparent that a "range war" is in progress between Fletcher, owner of the "big spread" referred to in the third paragraph, and the homesteaders who had "pegged . . . claims in a row up the valley." Shane is inevitably caught up in this war on the side of the homesteaders, and eventually vanquishes Fletcher and his hired gunmen. How is this plot foreshadowed in Schaefer's simple description, in the third paragraph, of Shane's approach?
4. The fourth paragraph elaborately describes Shane's clothing (you probably found more adjectives in this paragraph than in any other). The clothes, in essence, are *different* from those the narrator is most familiar with. How does

that fact also serve to indicate something special about Shane? What other descriptions in subsequent paragraphs augur that Shane is someone with whom to be reckoned? How do you explain the apparent contradiction in "Yet even in this easiness there was a suggestion of tension. It was the easiness of a coiled spring, of a trap set"?

5. This passage tells us quite a bit not only about what to expect from Shane but also about the boy's father, mother, and the boy himself. How do the descriptions of "place" and the house provide a key to the kind of people Shane has just ridden up to?
6. One person who read this passage remarked that the description in this passage is "a bit overdone." Do you agree? Why or why not?

The Role of Figurative Language

You can use description to explore ideas or experience and thus help make decisions about what you will write. We have seen the "journalistic questions" used to help develop material for informative writing of various kinds—who, what, where, when, how, and why?—and, in conjunction with the senses, a similar questioning technique can help develop material:

- What does something *look* like (*sight*)?
- What does something *taste* like (*taste*)?
- What does something *sound* like (*hearing*)?
- What does something *smell* like (*smell*)?
- What does something *feel* like (*touch*)?

To provide more practice, ask students to trace the way answers to these questions shape the content of the selection from *All I Really Need to Know I Learned in Kindergarten*, in chapter 18.

The repeated word *like* is important, for it encourages the creation of similes—explicit comparisons that are a less sophisticated kind of metaphor. The imagination is thus engaged as we attempt to make an apt comparison that will explain the unfamiliar in terms of the familiar:

The tornado (an unfamiliar thing) *looks* like a funnel (a familiar thing).

The frozen yogurt (unfamiliar) *tastes* like ice cream (familiar).

The tornado *sounds* like a freight train.

This new lotion *smells* like lilacs.

Nick's unshaved chin *feels* like sandpaper.

Once similes are created, they can be shortened into metaphors, in which the comparison is implicit rather than explicit:

The road looked like a ribbon of moonlight.

becomes

"The road was a ribbon of moonlight."
(from "The Highwayman," by Alfred Noyes)

Readers know that the road isn't literally a ribbon; they understand that the writer is being descriptive with imaginative language.

Language that deliberately uses simile, metaphor, or some similar device is known as *figurative language* (see chapter 18, "Comparison"). Figurative language, as you might expect, is primarily used by poets, but it would be a mistake to think that only poetry uses figurative language to advantage. In fact, all language for all purposes—written or spoken—can be figurative. Human beings are language-making creatures, and as human experience and knowledge grow, figurative language plays a vital role in giving names to that experience and knowledge.

We have already seen how one writer described a tornado as, in a simile, "hanging like an elephant's trunk." In the next sentence, the simile is converted to a metaphor: "The trunk wobbled and spiraled." A much more sophisticated use of metaphor occurs at the beginning of "Shane" when our narrator tells us he was "soaking in the late afternoon sun." Literally, he couldn't be soaking in sunlight; the verb derives from a metaphor that compares the sunlight to water.

It's fun to join with your class in looking at the literal roots of today's slang. What do you and your students think the real origins of these phrases are?

Don't have a cow, man!

Chill!

Head-bangers!

See how many more of such expressions your students can list and how many of these you and the class can explain.

In the same paragraph, the narrator tells us the road "swung" into the valley from the open plain, as though the road were a conscious being who could make a choice to go (or "swing") into the valley or not. Such metaphors are common; they are called, more specifically, *personification:* human qualities are given to nonliving things. Thus, when the narrator refers to his mother's kitchen garden as a "brave" sight, he isn't saying that the garden is literally brave—for a garden can be literally neither brave nor cowardly—but that to him (and to Shane) the flourishing garden in the otherwise-rough territory shows the bravery, persistence, and hard work of the family who is growing it.

Figurative language is so much a part of our communication that we often use it without any consciousness of it. When the narrator in "Shane" refers to "the fork a half-mile below our place," he of course doesn't mean that an eating utensil lies below his home; rather, he means that the road divides ("forks"), creating a choice for the traveler, who must then go one way or the other. Likewise, we refer to a sphere attached to a spaceship as a "pod" and never think of the garden peas from which the usage originally came. When we speak of the "hands" on a clock, we don't think of the human limbs that inspired the original comparison.

In the following informative piece about the Hamptons on New York's Long Island, note how naturally the author, Wilfrid Sheed, employs figurative language to help him describe.

See the Hamptons in Autumn, When the Coast Is Clear

Wilfrid Sheed

Wilfrid Sheed is a critic, columnist, reviewer, and author of articles, books of fiction (including Max Jamison*), and books of nonfiction (including* Muhammad Ali: A Portrait in Words and Photographs *and* The Kennedy Legacy: A Generation Later*). Commenting on having written both fiction and nonfiction, Sheed told the* New York Times Book

Review, *"Fiction is more rewarding, even if it dumps you out of a flying door into a mudbath. But whatever the word on that, one's nonfiction gains tremendously from having known the pressure, just as a political commentator would gain from running for office. Whatever you can still do when you can't be fastidious is your essence."*

1 Even in high season, nobody would mistake this place for a vacation resort. Although once a year, from Memorial Day through August, the East End of the South Fork of Long Island (to give it its full title) is obliged to operate under the flashy stage name of the Hamptons, it refuses even then to wear makeup. There are no boardwalks or Ferris wheels or cotton-candy stands to mislead the pleasure-mad. In fact, as many a small child has complained, there is absolutely nothing to do out here.

The personification introduced by "it refuses even then to wear makeup" is an important use of figurative language throughout this piece, for it presents the location as though it were an independent-minded person, a person who merely tolerates (but does not indulge) the necessary tourism so vital to its economy.

2 Except, of course, look, which is what we residents do all year round. The South Fork might best be compared to an English stately home that allows the public in for a few months every year in order to pay for its lonely, gorgeous winters. By October, just about everybody has pulled out and we have the whole joint to ourselves for the best, or at least the best-looking, months of the year.

3 Apart from the stray dog-owner draped in wool, the beaches will have returned by then to the primal emptiness that is their optimum condition. (All beaches look better empty, but ours look infinitely better, as the dunes form and re-form themselves with a kind of mad artistry.) Our architecture also comes into its own in the subtler light of autumn, and without anybody standing in front of it; and there are, if that be possible, even fewer tourist attractions to blotch the view. The restaurants, except for a few hardy perennials, have folded their menus one by one and gone home, taking with them the last vagrants who still need something to do.

4 With the coast thus clear, you are reminded starkly that the first settlers came out here in the mid-17th century not to sunbathe but to survive. The fishermen and farmers who have been going about their business unobtrusively all summer seem somehow more central to life in the fall and winter: they are what the South Fork is all about in a way that this year's crop of tourists will never be. And although the tourists might currently bring in more cash than fish or potatoes, times can change, and the old Fork is built to last. Indeed, with the great houses abandoned and parking once more a possibility, you can picture the South Fork returning overnight to its old self and resuming its old ways, with the Tourist Era all but forgotten.

Here, as in the title, Sheed employs a shrewd double meaning: "the coast is clear" has long been a figurative way of saying that nothing should interfere with what one wants to do, and usually it has nothing to do with an actual coast. Here, however, there *is* a coast; further, it is "clear" of tourists and other distractions. Thus, Sheed uses the expression in its figurative and literal meanings simultaneously.

5 And in the meantime, what besides beaches do the tourists come for anyway, but to rent houses designed for fishermen in order to gaze out over fields tilled by potato farmers? Nothing worth looking at out here was ever built with tourists in mind, and the politics of winter (if you want to know what we do out here) consists largely of keeping it that way, against the unlovely thrusts of developers who believe that a priceless landscape becomes somehow more so if you build all over it.

6 To an extent, our second notable wave of settlers in the South Fork might be seen as a roundabout tribute to the first. The pioneers of abstract

expressionism such as Jackson Pollock and Willem de Kooning, who bloomed here after World War II, came in homage not only to the scenery, though that would have been enough, but to the villages themselves with their unself-consciously perfect shops and churches and water mills, built by the locals for their own pleasure and nobody else's.

As for nature, the word around here is water. You can't live in the neighborhood without bumping into it every five minutes or so, and if you fly over, you will observe how it tends to keep sneaking up on the Montauk Highway, even occasionally elbowing its way between the houses in the form of ponds, inlets and our last line of defense, the Shinnecock Canal. It floats sternly between us and the outside world to remind the summer people that if ever they get completely out of hand, we know what to do: open the dikes and let the water reclaim us. 7

Secure in the knowledge of our watery escape hatch, we have always decided, up to now, to spare them for another year while we sit back to enjoy just one more autumn, and winter, and spring. After that, we'll see. 8

Questions for Writing and Discussion

Prepare short written answers to each of these questions. Be prepared to hand them in and/or discuss them in class, as your teacher directs.

1. In the first paragraph, the East End of the South Fork of Long Island is personified, as though it were a stage actor "obliged" to used the "stage name" of the Hamptons. How does Sheed then immediately extend the metaphor?
2. Why is "cotton candy" (¶ 1) a metaphor?
3. What elaborate comparison does Sheed draw in the second paragraph?
4. How does Sheed personify the sand dunes in the third paragraph? In the same paragraph, how does he personify the restaurants?
5. Explain how the following figures of speech operate as descriptions:
   a. "sunbathe" (¶ 4)
   b. "crop of tourists" (¶ 4)
   c. "you can picture the South Fork returning overnight to its old self and resuming its old ways" (¶ 4)
   d. "unlovely thrusts" (¶ 5)
   e. "wave of settlers" (¶ 6)
6. What comparison is implicit in Sheed's description of "pioneers of abstract expressionism . . . who bloomed here" (¶ 6)?
7. What other descriptive figures of speech can you find?
8. What do the following words mean—*primal, optimum, infinitely, subtler, perennials* (which is also a metaphor) (¶ 3), *unobtrusively* (¶ 4), *homage* (¶ 6)?

Description as a Key to Analysis

Clearly, Wilfrid Sheed seeks to describe the Hamptons in ways that make a reader understand both the beauty and the utility of the place. His admiration for and pride in the Hamptons are evident in his tone of praise and reverence for the area, coupled with his mild disdain for the seasonal tourists who now contribute so much money—and nothing else of value—to the place.

But if description can expressively recapture an exciting moment in life, as in "The Tornado" or "Shane," or if it can be used to explain the charms of a geographic area, as in Sheed's piece about the Hamptons, it can also be used as a powerful assist to analysis, as in the following article, by Pete Hamill, about a community up the Hudson River from New York City.

Notice that, as we saw in the preceding chapter, there is in the Sheed piece an element of difference between the surface of the words—what they seem to be saying—and what the words actually say: for example, in the idea of the seasonal tourists who contribute so much money but nothing else.

PREREADING WORKSHEET

Before you read the following piece by Pete Hamill, write brief responses to these questions:

1. What thoughts come to your mind when you read this description:

   Newburgh, New York, has a population of 25,000 people and lies by the beautifully winding Hudson River 60 miles upstream from New York City. This 280-year-old river town has streets lined with splendid Victorian and Greek Revival mansions and ancient oak and maple trees. There are spectacular views of the river at the foot of Storm King Mountain.

2. What sociological phenomenon do you think is described by the phrase "white flight"?
3. Are unemployment, inadequate housing, violent crime, drugs, and political corruption problems limited to big cities? Why do (or don't) you think so?
4. Briefly describe the kind of piece you expect to read when you see a title like "Our Town."

Our Town

PETE HAMILL

Pete Hamill is a reporter, editor, columnist, and author of articles and novels (including Flesh and Blood, A Killing for Christ, Dirty Laundry, *and* The Guns of Heaven*). This selection appeared in* Esquire *in 1989.*

1 The woman came around the corner into Lander Street and you could see right away that she was in trouble. She was big and brown and solid, but she

kept looking behind her, down toward Broadway. Then came the man, thin as a razor, walking quickly along the wall of Woolworth's. It was a few minutes after three in the afternoon.

"Yo!" the man shouted. "Yo, Coreema, you stop, hear?" 2

Coreema didn't stop. She glanced across the street at clumps of silent 3 women and children sitting on wooden stoops, then back at the man. She moved faster and so did he, and she was starting to run when he caught her. He spun her around and smashed a fist into her face. She wobbled and he hit her again, and she went down.

"Bitch!" he screamed, kicking her in the sides and the chest. "Bitch!" 4

Her face was a bloody smear, and she rolled and put her hands up to her 5 eyes and he kicked her again. Her large body shuddered and went very still. The man was through with her. He looked around him for the first time: at the women and children, at four teenagers on the far corner, at me. He took a knife from his pocket, flicked open the blade, said nothing, and hurried back to Broadway. When he turned the corner, a large woman heaved her bulk off one of the wooden stoops and started across the street to help Coreema. She squinted at me and whispered hoarsely, "You better get the fuck out of here, man."

This wasn't Times Square. This was the east end of Newburgh, New York 6 (population: 25,000), sixty miles up the lovely Hudson River from the biggest, meanest city in America. Nevertheless, I decided to follow her advice. Even on a sun-drowned afternoon, that particular street in that particular town can be scary. And these days in America, alas, Newburgh is not unique. There must be a thousand lost towns like it around the country, wasted by time and indifference, and I never get used to seeing them. Poverty, dilapidated housing, drugs, casual violence: they're supposed to be exclusive to life in big cities.

But Newburgh, a 280-year-old river town, is far from the mayhem and 7 nihilism of New York. Ancient oaks and maples line some of its streets. George Washington really did sleep here at the end of the Revolution. Geography alone should make the town immune to our urban contagions. It doesn't.

Some of your students may not understand why Hamill says, "George Washington really did sleep here." We don't know the origin of the "George Washington slept here" cliché—perhaps it was an oft-used advertising gimmick for inns during the early days of the Republic—but you may need to explain that (at least at one time) "George Washington slept here" was used as a way of indicating that a particular place was of good reputation, sort of "If it's good enough for George Washington, it's good enough for me."

I first saw Newburgh as a young man in the 1950s, when it was a pleasant, 8 dull, middle-class town with a wide main street called Broadway that seemed shaped by an odd collaboration between Edward Hopper and Norman Rockwell. I passed through every few years, usually on my way somewhere else. On each trip, the town seemed shabbier, but compared with the dissolution of the big cities, it never struck me as sinister. Then, over the last year, I started noticing items out of Newburgh in the newspapers: stories of drug busts, assaults, occasional murders. From a distance, the town seemed to be getting deeper into trouble, and I wondered why.

To a visitor from the big city, the latest version of Newburgh felt oddly 9 familiar. Two days after I saw the woman named Coreema kicked into a shambling pile, a man named Richard D. Woods Jr. pulled his car up in front of his house on Carson Avenue. He yelled something at one of the eight children of a man named Julio Estela, with whom he'd been feuding for a year. Estela came out of his house across the street carrying a .22-caliber Ruger carbine. He fired six shots and one of them hit Woods in the chest and killed him. When Woods's brother, Noel, arrived at the scene, he said: "That was definitely the wrong move."

10 Newburgh is full of people who are always making the wrong move. Usually this is done in anonymity. But occasionally the town does become part of the public imagination, as it did during the media hysteria over the Tawana Brawley case. Ms. Brawley claimed to have been held prisoner by six white men for four days; investigators later learned that on one of those days she was attending a party thrown by a crack dealer at 163 Lander Street. When a grand jury decided that Brawley was just a little girl who told a big lie, Newburgh faded again. The life of casual violence and steady drugs went on.

11 On ordinary weekends, the emergency room of St. Luke's Hospital takes in dozens of the beaten, the stabbed, and the shot. Sometimes the doctors and nurses only have to clerk the corpses. Typical was poor Romance Maise Brock, who arrived with two screwdrivers jammed into her chest and an electrical cord wrapped around her neck; her half brother told the police he had to chill her because she was going to tell them he was using cocaine.

12 But murder is usually only a melodramatic highlight in places like Lander Street; life is more often about surviving a soul-grinding routine of assaults and robberies. Many go unreported. "What's the point?" one black woman said to me. "Police don't do nothin' anyway." The police try, but there are only seventy-two cops on the city's payroll; sometimes as few as six are patrolling its streets. And since 1986, when crack conquered the east end, the lives of the poor have become infinitely more dangerous. "Crackerjacks don't care who gets hurt," one older man told me, "long as they get their crack." Even the dead aren't safe; a few months ago, someone stole the antique wrought-iron gates off the entrance to the town's cemetery.

13 One afternoon I drove around Newburgh with Tim McGlone, then covering the mayhem beat for the *Newburgh-Beacon Evening News*. It was clear that crack had found an ideal market in Newburgh. Like so many other hurt places around the country, the town needed better housing, schools, jobs—all the usual "liberal" remedies so glibly sneered at in the age of Reagan. It got drugs instead. "See that little deli?" McGlone said. "It's been busted four times, selling crack." He pointed out three more tiny stores as we moved along pothole-ridden streets. "They sell it like it was Wonder Bread," McGlone said, showing me a place that had been raided so many times the locals called it Stop 'n' Cop.

14 The context for all this is sadly familiar. There are several thousand welfare clients in this small city, many of them living in the eight-story Bourne Apartments overlooking the Hudson (or in the Imperial Motel or the Hotel Washington). Others are jammed into the Hotel Newburgh on Broadway, where too many children spend most of their days eating junk food,

watching television, and learning other things. "They all be doin' drugs an' fightin' an' stabbin'," a seven-year-old boy named Rondo told me, standing alone in front of the hotel. "At night, it's bad here. . . ."

If welfare and crack are the present tense of this old, small city, it is almost impossible to ignore its long, often booming past. The section called Balmville at the edge of the city evokes the nineteenth century, when rivers were the nation's highways and Newburgh was a whaling town, a town of shipfitters and boatbuilders, men who shipped food and ice to the growing maw of New York City. The splendid Victorian and Greek Revival mansions they erected are still here, complete with spectacular views of the river winding south into the gorge at the foot of Storm King Mountain. The world they made seemed built to last forever. It didn't. 15

"Newburgh was a nice, solid town," said a barber named Sam Martino, who now lives twelve miles away in Wallkill. "Then everything changed. Just like that." 16

Newburgh was wasted by a number of forces, including racism. In the 1950s, blacks and Puerto Ricans came to work on the nearby apple farms as migrant workers; many stayed on to work in the mills of Newburgh, and whites slowly began to leave. This "white flight" was not unique to Newburgh—in the 60s and 70s it happened all over the United States. It was just more blatant here. "They see a black face," a man named Errol said, "and they run." 17

Two enormous shopping centers opened on the outskirts of town and devastated the shops along Broadway. The passenger railroad stopped running on the west bank of the Hudson. Urban renewal projects were begun in the 1960s and never completed; black leaders charged racism was the motive, the process a crude form of "urban removal." Then, in 1969, Stewart Air Force Base was ordered closed, ending nine hundred civilian jobs, removing 2,500 servicemen and $30 million from the local economy. The tax base eroded and so did Newburgh's physical plant. By 1981 the federal government had listed Newburgh as number one on the list of the nation's distressed urban areas. 18

There were other problems: Neanderthal politics; racial disturbances in the late '60s and early '70s; corruption in the police department. Cynicism flourished. The drug trade began to establish itself. By 1987, the only house on Lander Street with a backyard swimming pool belonged to a crack dealer named Randy "D Day" Davis. 19

These days, the political air in Newburgh still has a ripe odor. Consider the delicious case of Wilbert Sanchez. In 1987 he ran in the Republican primary for mayor, and on paper he was a great candidate: a thirty-seven-year-old Vietnam veteran, always impeccably dressed, the head of a Hispanic community group called FUENTE. He was vocal about education, immigration, and employment issues, and helped raise money for the homeless. A Republican who talked like a Democrat. Perfect. He was also very critical of the police, claiming that they weren't doing enough to combat the spread of 20 crack and cocaine. He ran hard in the Republican primary and lost by only seventy-eight votes.

21 Then, not long after the election, he was indicted by the feds. They charged him with—*of course!*—conspiring to distribute cocaine. The trial was brief. Even his stepdaughter testified against him. He was convicted in May.

22 The saddest thing about the mood in Newburgh these days is that a revival of sorts was actually under way for a few years. New people were coming in, buying old Victorians and restoring them to past glory. Key Bank built its corporate headquarters at the foot of Broadway. Some new factories opened for business. An old red-brick factory building was converted into a condominium called The Foundry. There were familiar complaints that gentrification was going to dislodge the poor. But the city briefly experienced a new emotion: hope.

23 Then came crack.

24 Now there are FOR SALE signs everywhere. And the problems never go away. They are the same problems eating at the hearts of many American cities, and you have to wonder: If a town the size of Newburgh can't be saved, how can any of the country's injured cities? One little scene last spring suggested to me that perhaps it is already too late.

25 A group called the Newburgh Drug/Alcohol Task Force had announced a project called "One Street at a Time." They would go into the crack-ravaged streets of the east end, backed by the police, and drive out the dealers by moral persuasion. And for one evening, the present mayor, a former mayor, CORE* chairman Roy Innis, and a number of locals marched into Lander Street. Dealers faded into the dusk. Coffee and doughnuts were served. Kids chanted, "No more drugs! No more drugs!"

26 The cops stayed around. So did most of the middle-class marchers. And then just before dark another group arrived, young and tough and black, with the cold, blank eyes of their generation. They turned from South Street into Lander, and they were chanting, too. "We want drugs!" they shouted. "We want drugs! We want drugs!"

POSTREADING WORKSHEET

Now that you have read the piece by Hamill, write your responses to the following questions:

1. How does the effect that Hamill's piece had on you compare with the thoughts that came to your mind when you read the description of Newburgh in the Prereading Worksheet?
2. How did your experience of reading "Our Town" differ from what you expected based on the title of the piece?

*CORE—acronym for Congress for Racial Equality, a civil rights group.

3. What is your view of Newburgh now? How does it compare with your view of your own hometown?
4. How does Hamill's piece demonstrate the seriousness of the problems drug abuse has brought to our society?

Questions for Writing and Discussion

Prepare short written answers for each of these questions. Be prepared to hand them in and/or discuss them in class, as your teacher directs.

In noting these anecdotes, you might point out to students that an anecdote is a brief *story* and that *narration* (chapter 15) is another word for *story.* Thus we see that though Hamill is using description powerfully, he is also using narration—more evidence that these patterns in Part Four, like the reasons for writing in Part Two, can and do overlap.

1. Hamill begins this powerful analysis with an anecdote (the assault on Coreema) and ends it with another anecdote (the anti- and prodrug marchers). How do these anecdotes do more than frame the analysis of Newburgh's problems? How do they indicate Hamill's thesis—the main point of his article? What *is* Hamill's thesis?
2. What simile do you find in the first paragraph? Why is this particular simile appropriate for the situation Hamill is describing?
3. Often Hamill achieves vivid mental pictures with such language as "a large woman heaved her bulk off one of the wooden stoops" (¶ 5). Find other passages that evoke similar vivid mental pictures.
4. What comparison does Hamill imply with this extended metaphor: "Geography alone should make the town immune to our urban contagions" (¶ 7)? What effect does he achieve by following that sentence with the curt "It doesn't"?
5. What does Hamill mean by "George Washington really did sleep here"? Who were Edward Hopper and Norman Rockwell?
6. Discuss the comparisons implicit in the following:
   a. "clerk the corpses" (¶ 11)
   b. "just a little girl who told a big lie" (¶ 10)
   c. "he had to chill her" (¶ 11)
   d. "Crackerjacks" (¶ 12)
   e. "They sell it like it was Wonder Bread" (¶ 13)
   f. "junk food" (¶ 14)
   g. "white flight" (¶ 17)
   h. "the political air in Newburgh still has a ripe odor" (¶ 20)
   i. "soul-grinding" (¶ 12)
7. Hamill is a master of the stylistic reversal, whereby one sentence "sets up" a possibility or alternative and the next sentence (usually very brief) completely undercuts that possibility or alternative, leaving a bleak resonance. One example is cited in question 4 above ("Geography alone should make the town immune to our urban contagions. It doesn't"). Can you find similar stylistic reversals in this piece?
8. Hamill also uses sentence fragments for stylistic effect. An example is his description of mayoral candidate Wilbert Sanchez: "A Republican who talked

like a Democrat. Perfect" (¶ 20). Can you find similarly effective uses of fragments?

9. What effect do Hamill's descriptions of bodily injuries have on the reader?
10. What do the following words mean—*mayhem, nihilism* (¶ 7), *dissolution* (¶ 8), *hysteria* (¶ 10), *glibly* (¶ 13), *blatant* (¶ 17), *impeccably* (¶ 20)?
11. Hamill uses as the title of his article the same title used by playwright Thornton Wilder for one of America's most enduringly popular plays. Read Wilder's play or a synopsis thereof. How is Hamill's use of the title ironic relative to Wilder's play?

Description as a Key to Persuasion

It is clear from Hamill's article that description can be highly effective in presenting writing that is primarily for analytical purposes. Hamill presents a grim analysis of the problems of Newburgh, and his vivid descriptive language makes the analysis memorable. His title is not only ironic relative to the idealized *Our Town* of Thornton Wilder; it is also intended to show clearly whose problem Newburgh is: *ours.* Moreover, Hamill is not very optimistic about our chances of making things better. Powerful description has long been used in the service of social criticism—we can find it in the great written documents of our mostly European heritage, in our nation's Declaration of Independence, in the remarkable Civil War speeches of Abraham Lincoln, in such classic novels as John Steinbeck's *The Grapes of Wrath,* and so on.

In the following editorial, Ben Nelms, editor of *English Journal,* a journal for English teachers, also uses description for analysis; however, his primary purpose is persuasion: convinced that political use of our language is increasingly dishonest, Nelms urges English teachers—and by extension, you, their students—to do something about it.

A Nation at Risk

BEN F. NELMS

Ben F. Nelms is an English professor at the University of Florida.

We've added the notes that appear at the end of this essay.

1 This editorial is being written on November 9, the day after the 1988 presidential election. Our morning newspaper features a photograph of a prominent local Republican, who has just been elected to a minor public office, making an obscene gesture at the television set on which he is watching Michael Dukakis'[1] concession speech. It is a particularly graceless act in a moment of victory, but it somehow seems an appropriate symbol of what Ted Koppel[2] characterized as the "squalor" of the campaign.

This is a good place to raise the notion of *ethos*, the author's persuasive character that a reader can sense through the text. The author's good reputation, or character, helps make his or her argument persuasive. We discuss Aristotle's three types of rhetorical appeal (*ethos*, *pathos*, and *logos*) in chapters 7 and 20.

As an English teacher and an editor, I worry about this campaign, not only because of the issues involved but even more because of what it shows about our national use of language and communication technology. 2

This morning I reread George Orwell's[3] "Politics and the English Language" for the first time in several years. I admit that when I first read this years ago, I thought Orwell was a bit of an alarmist, somewhat fastidious in his own use of the language. I wish I could think so now. I wish that his maxims did not seem so apt: 3

> In our time it is broadly true that political writing is bad writing.
>
> In our time, political speech and writing are largely the defence [British spelling] of the indefensible.
>
> The great enemy of clear language is insincerity.
>
> Political language—and with variations this is true of all political parties . . . —is designed to make lies sound truthful and murder respectable, and to give an appearance of solidity to pure wind.

We have been told for ten years now by politicians and media commentators that America is a nation at risk and teachers are at fault. This morning I am convinced that America is indeed a nation at risk, but it is the politicians and the media who are at fault. This presidential campaign is evidence enough. Political cynicism, media manipulation, linguistic obfuscation, and voter apathy feed on one another, each growing fat gorging on the excesses of the others. The "P-R" mentality among what are called political handlers exploits television's insatiable appetite for sound bites, and the "show-biz" mentality among television news departments provides recipes for staged, gimmicky, photogenic non-events—"fast food" for a busy electorate. But, alas, voter apathy is also voter gullibility: we like sound bites, we make up our minds on the basis of thirty-second commercials, we prefer capsule news, we avoid long speeches and debates, position papers, and print analyses. 4

America is a nation at risk, and has been before. In the *English Journal* for September 1952, Lou LaBrant wrote reflecting her memory of recent history and anticipating the excesses of McCarthyism[4] just then beginning ("New Bottles for New Wine," 41: 341–47). She said, 5

> Remember that man's progress depends upon the acceptance of communication, upon the ability of one to transfer to another what he has seen and thought and believed. But today we have the big lie. Hitler[5] dared to sponsor it: "If I say to you enough times what you know is not true, you will cease to know what is true, you will be confused, unable to think." A recently reported research study discovers that even those who angrily reject a big lie, who know it is not true when first they hear it, at the end of six months have not only remembered a considerable part of it but have lost their original rebuttal. . . . The big lie is abroad in our own land, condoned by those who might be expected to defend honor and truth. "Something comes

> from it," defenders say; "it gets attention." Something does come from it, something much more than attention, than a dribble of the truth: what comes from it is a breaking-down of man's most basically human invention, language. This is a threat to us as human beings, a denial of our greatest accomplishment, faith in the word of man. Without it no society can hold together, no progress toward right be possible. Are our students aware of the heritage they must defend? Here is something much more than a choice between he and him, between I and me; here is a choice between man and brute, between civilization and savagery. (346)

6 America is a nation at risk, but I fear, after all, that teachers are partly at fault. Just as "educated" Germans in the 1920s and 1930s believed the Big Lie, students educated in our English classes passively accept the little lies perpetrated upon them every-day by advertisers, media con-artists, political handlers—and, yes, educationists. English teachers, intent on pronoun references, five-paragraph essays, and the plot/character/setting syndrome, have strained at the gnat and swallowed the camel. On this same dismal morning, I have read Miss Fidditch's[6] responses to a questionnaire on eleventh grade, college-bound English. Asked to identify the major goals of the course, she lists but four: (1) ability to analyze plot, character, setting, and theme; (2) knowledge of literary terminology, such as "protagonist," "flashback," "deus ex machina"; (3) ability to write a well-organized five-paragraph essay; and (4) development of a college-prep vocabulary. Where is the excitement of ideas? the exploration of values? the struggle toward clarity? the shock of recognition?

7 English as envisioned by Miss Fidditch will not produce students who seek out challenging reading material and read it carefully. English as envisioned by Miss Fidditch will not encourage students to inform themselves on controversial issues and to articulate their views, to use the written word to effect change in their environment. English as envisioned by Miss Fidditch will not produce a generation of self-confident writers and speakers who temper idealism with pragmatism and the impulse toward personal aggrandizement with altruism.

8 English as envisioned by Miss Fidditch will produce only clones of Miss Fidditch: "good students" whose fussy smugness masks their insecurity, passive students who feel more comfortable receiving and repeating verbal formulas than participating actively in critical dialogue. Moreover, English as envisioned by Miss Fidditch does not take with some students, and they feel alienated and may turn apathetic or hostile or go underground.

9 But Miss Fidditch and her ilk need not feel threatened by the politicians. Politicians may, in fact, feel quite comfortable with an electorate which raises no troublesome questions and, hence, with a national cadre of teachers who confine themselves to nouns and verbs, titles and authors, five-paragraph essays and efferent reading, recall of verbal formulas rather than analysis of

By the time you are using this book, another presidential election may well have passed. If so, ask students to talk about whether these descriptions match that one as well.

ideas. A sociologist friend of ours writes that the CIA [Central Intelligence Agency] treats Joseph Goebbels'[7] "big lie" as "the best thing to come out of World War II." He continues, "They employ [these techniques] regularly in attempts to destabilize 'unfriendly' governments." He insists that the presidential campaign of 1988 "brings back the stench of Germany in 1933–45. Should their tactics succeed, it may well spell a difficult time for the continuation of democracy in America. . . . The ghost of Goebbels stalk[ed] this election campaign." Maybe he exaggerates. Maybe not.

Author James Michener, writing in the *Miami News,* also detected tactics that "Joseph Goebbels found useful in destroying the German Republic in the 1930s"; namely, the Big Lie, the appropriation of emotional symbols such as the flag and the Pledge of Allegiance, the use of litmus tests of patriotism and loyalty, and the callous use of racist innuendo in the case of Willy Horton.[8] He blames not only "these shadowy men who served Bush so well and their nation so poorly," but also the Dukakis team for "the supine way" they allowed themselves to be maligned. He worries that the success of the "ugly strategies" in this campaign "flashed signals that this was the kind of electioneering we should expect during the next three national campaigns of this century." 10

What can English teachers do to assure that this year's tenth graders—all of whom will be eligible to vote in 1992—will not succumb to gullibility, exploitation, and political naivete? How can we prepare our students to be critical without pushing them toward cynicism? How can we engender skepticism and at the same time nurture idealism? Those are questions that we hope you will address. . . . For starters, we suggest that you join with history and civics and psychology teachers to deconstruct the "texts" of the 1988 presidential campaign: the commercials, the newscasts, the speeches, the newspaper analyses and editorials, the cartoons, the slogans, the position papers, the interviews, and the "debates." Examine the artifacts: the good, the bad, and the ugly. Talk about them; write about them. Respond. Responsible citizenship requires active response—informed, thoughtful, concerned response. These are the basics to which we must return if the schools are to fulfill their role in achieving the Jeffersonian ideal of making democracy safe for the world. 11

Notes to the Text

1. *Michael Dukakis:* Democratic party candidate for president in 1988; governor of Massachusetts.
2. *Ted Koppel:* news reporter/commentator, American Broadcasting Company.
3. *George Orwell:* pen name for Eric Blair, British author and philosopher of language. He wrote the essay Nelms quotes from, "Politics and the English Language," in 1946, shortly after the end of World War II. In 1949 he published the famous futuristic political novel *1984*.

4. *McCarthyism:* a practice named for U.S. Senator Joseph McCarthy, who embodied powerful anti-Communist sentiment in this country in the early 1950s; McCarthyism refers to the excesses of this sentiment as practiced by the senator, excesses that included baseless innuendos and accusations, as well as wholesale character assassination. McCarthyism embraced the "big lie" in the service of anticommunism and blind patriotism.
5. *Hitler:* Adolf Hitler, the chancellor of Germany from 1933 to 1945 who led the German people into barbaric ideology, total war, and utter defeat. His name has become synonymous with evil.
6. *"Miss Fidditch":* a fictional stereotype of an English teacher (male or female) who dwells on trivial aspects of language and learning.
7. *Joseph Goebbels:* Hitler's minister of propaganda in Germany. Goebbels used the media to distort and lie, and thereby to manipulate the populace. He knew how to put Hitler's idea of the big lie into effect.
8. *Willy Horton:* a black man convicted of violent crime and held prisoner in Massachusetts. He was granted a weekend furlough by the state of Massachusetts and committed another violent crime. The George Bush campaign for president in 1988 used frequent references to Horton to suggest that Dukakis was in some way directly responsible for Horton's furlough and was therefore not well qualified to be president. That Horton was black carried an unstated but strong appeal to racism among voters.

Questions for Writing and Discussion

Prepare short written answers to each of these questions. Be prepared to hand them in and/or discuss them in class, as your teacher directs.

1. Explain how figurative language aids description and meaning in the following examples:
   a. sound bites (¶ 4)
   b. capsule news (¶ 4)
   c. Miss Fidditch (¶ 6)
   d. litmus tests (¶ 10)
2. Explain how figurative language operates both descriptively and meaningfully in the following quotations:
   a. "recipes for staged, gimmicky, photogenic non-events" (¶ 4)
   b. "fast food" (¶ 4)
   c. "The Big Lie" (¶ 6)
   d. "strained at the gnat and swallowed the camel" (¶ 6)
   e. "go underground" (¶ 8)
   f. "unfriendly governments" (¶ 9)
   g. "the stench of Germany in 1933–45" (¶ 9)
   h. "the ghost of Goebbels stalked this election campaign" (¶ 9)

3. Nelms's primary purpose in writing this editorial is to persuade teachers to (a) recognize the relevance of Orwell's remarks in the politics of today and (b) take responsible action. As editor of the journal, Nelms suggests that English teachers write about this issue and submit their manuscripts for future publication in the journal. What other actions does he suggest? What actions could *you* take as a student who most likely will be eligible to vote in the next presidential election?
4. Nelms does something editors don't ordinarily like to do: he includes a lengthy quotation, from a 1952 article by Lou LaBrant. Why do you suppose Nelms makes an exception to standard practice in this case? What persuasive effect does he achieve by quoting from an article almost a half-century old?
5. What do the following words mean—*squalor* (¶ 1), *fastidious, maxims* (¶ 3), *cynicism, linguistic obfuscation, insatiable, electorate* (¶ 4), *rebuttal, condoned* (¶ 5), *clones, apathetic* (¶ 8), *cadre, destabilize* (¶ 9), *innuendo, supine, maligned* (¶ 10), *succumb, skepticism* (¶ 11)?
6. Why do you suppose Nelms puts the word *debates* (¶ 11) in quotation marks when he refers to the televised debates of the presidential candidates?

Bridges: Another Perspective

Ben F. Nelms writes a scathing critique of political use of language in America during the 1988 presidential campaign. He paints a generally bleak picture of candidates, voters, and language educators in America and warns that America, in its political uses of language today, has too much in common with 1930s Germany, wherein the world witnessed the rise of totalitarianism under Hitler and the tragedy of World War II. Imagine you have been asked to write a response to Nelms's critique—to present a refutation, an effective disagreement with him. How would you proceed? What would you say, and what support would you use?

We have now seen that descriptive writing, like all other kinds of writing discussed in Part Four of this book, can be used for all the major purposes of writing: to express, to explain or inform, to analyze, and to persuade. We have seen that good descriptive writing is always more than just a grouping of adjectives; useful as they are, adjectives can't carry the whole weight of human imagination, any more than other parts of speech can. What is needed is a unified effort, a combination of words in sentence structures that engage the reader's mind in active, participatory imagination. Beyond our own sensory experience, language is the means which we also see, hear, feel, touch, taste, and smell. It is as necessary to our clear communication as our voices, or our pens and tablets, typewriters, or word processors.

Don't let your students lose track of the role of metaphor too.

KEY POINTS TO REMEMBER: Writing Description

Here are some points to remember when writing description.

- Descriptive writing isn't necessarily dominated by adjectives.
- Descriptive writing appeals primarily to our senses via our imagination.
- Descriptive writing reaches the senses via figurative language.
- Description can easily be overdone.

Descriptive Writing Isn't Necessarily Dominated by Adjectives

Without question, adjectives describe:

> "She was a *long, cool* woman in a *black* dress."
> (song lyrics by the Hollies)

Our ability to describe would be severely impaired without them. The important thing to remember, though, is that other words and other combinations of words can also be descriptive:

> Bobby Lee *sashayed* up to Verna (verb).
> The battle plan was *like the letter V*, with the French forces beginning at each tip and converging toward the intersection (simile).
> Bennington met his *waterloo* in the chess match with Daly (noun as metaphor for total defeat, an allusion to European history: Napoleon's career-ending defeat in the Battle of Waterloo).

Descriptive Writing Appeals Primarily to Our Senses via Our Imagination

Our minds hold the ability to re-create images—sights, sounds, smells, tastes, and feelings—and this ability is prompted when we compose or read descriptive writing. That's why so much descriptive writing strikes us as visual, aural, or in some other way sensory.

> In the jungle a lion *roared*.
> The door opened to reveal a *blinding light*.
> The milk was hopelessly *sour*.
> The cloth was *coarse*, roughly spun but durable.
> The *acrid* pall hung over the mine's entrance.

Descriptive Writing Reaches the Senses via Figurative Language

Asking ourselves how something sounds, smells, tastes, feels, or looks can take us a long way toward generating ideas for descriptive writing:

> Coach Warren sounds like he's got a ton of gravel in his throat when he talks.

Invite your students to imagine more of these.

Barb's chemistry experiment smells like rotten eggs.

The taste of this coffee mixture reminds me of bitter almonds.

Running into their defensive tackle was like running into a brick wall.

His hair looks like he was frightened by a ghost.

The world of figurative language can be colorful indeed:

Have your students imagine more of these, too.

Dellinger let out a belch that trembled the tabernacle.

Melissa is as nervous as a long-tailed cat in a room full of rocking chairs.

I decided that Yardley had no more sense than a medium-size grape and therefore vigorously ignored him for the balance of his life.

In the West the sun quietly slid below the coverlet of the horizon, and our world entered the deep dreams of night.

The hawk soared upward against the sky and then hurtled downward, an arrow straight toward its mark of the defenseless field mouse.

Sam Spade approached San Francisco as Caesar approached Gaul: he came, he saw, he conquered.

Description Can Easily Be Overdone

Some of the examples immediately above are a bit too colorful. You can sense the writers straining—believe us, we did—in some of the cases. Any writing that calls attention to itself as writing is probably writing that should be reconsidered and revised. We're not saying that if you become aware that a piece of writing is exceptionally good you should automatically hold it suspect; rather, we're saying that if your reading is more affected by the *way* the writing is done than by *what* it is saying, then in all likelihood that writing is overdone and should probably be recast. This is especially true of writing that strains so hard to be descriptive that about all that shows is the strain:

This is a good passage to have your students imitate, even if some of the imitations are actually parodies.

> Last summer I saw the towering, rocky, majestic mountains of western Wyoming. They were so magnificent and high that they took my breath away. I couldn't believe my eyes. The peaks were snowcapped, and some of them were even above the clouds. We drove up a canyon by a bubbling, babbling brook and saw many cute, cuddly forest creatures. A good time was had by all.

That is poor description, plagued by clichés. Mountains have been described as majestic too many times for the adjective to evoke a vivid mental picture anymore. Likewise with snowcapped peaks, babbling brooks, and cuddly creatures.

Have students look at chapter 19's "Ain't Nobody's Business but My Own" for an extreme of this kind of "piling on."

Descriptive writing, to be good, should strain neither the writer nor the reader. There's no need to pile on adjectives when one good one will do. Neither should such writing seem effortless; lazy writers who use such clichés as "They took my breath away" and "I couldn't believe my eyes" are making no effort to produce fresh, engaging descriptions for their readers.

Balance is the key. Try to describe with accuracy; make your description true to your experience. Try also to describe with originality; describe your subject in a new way, one you haven't seen or heard before.

✓✓✓ WORKSHEET: Writing Description

In this chapter our worksheet concentrates on the early stages of the process of writing description—not because the other stages aren't important; they always are. Yet we want to emphasize how thinking descriptively can be important to "invention"—the generation of material to write about—and to drafting. The other recursive stages of writing (revising, polishing) remain important and are emphasized in worksheets in other chapters.

Brainstorming

Brainstorming descriptive writing can take many forms. Let's say that your teacher has asked you to describe a favorite place of yours and that one such place is your grandparents' farm. You might close your eyes and imagine the farm as it appears when you approach it on the road: you see the house, the large front yard, the barn several yards away in back of the house, and the granary near the barn. You see the big cottonwood trees that shade the house, and the smaller hackberries that line the front driveway. Now list the items in the scene:

We don't mean these to be "rhetorical" exercises; your students will learn more about the brainstorming aspect of writing if you lead them in doing either this or your own brainstorming exercise.

The house
The yard
The barn
The granary
The trees
The driveway

Next, beside each item on the list, add additional descriptive detail. The house, for example: how large is it—one or two stories? What kind of roof does it have—pitched, flat, or some combination? What color is the house? How many windows does it have, and of what kind? Does it have a porch? a porch swing? lightning rods? a chimney? shutters? You get the idea. Repeat such additional detailing for every item on the list. Soon you'll have more than enough detail to describe the farm.

But that might not be all you want to do. You might want to make it clear to readers why the farm means so much to you. Start again with your list: what events in the house are strong and dear in your memory? What rooms, items of furniture, or other features of the house are special to you—and why? What about the yard? What events have happened over the years in that yard that constitute important memories? the barn? the granary? And so on.

Description affords countless ways to invent. As noted earlier, you can employ the "sensory questions": how does it taste (feel, smell, look, sound)?

Again, we don't mean these to be "rhetorical"; you should work through these with your students.

Or you can create similes:

Going to Grandpa's farm is like ___________ .
Waterskiing is like ___________ .
Calculus is like ___________ .
Dining at *Le Grande Fromage* is like ___________ .
Cheering for the Chicago Cubs is like ___________ .

Or metaphors:

Calculus is *a major headache.*
That new car is *a lemon.*
This computer software is a ___________ .
My pal Bruno is a ___________ .

Drafting with a Controlling Metaphor

Sometimes a metaphor or simile will give you an organizational basis or theme that you can use for an entire piece of writing. Let's say you're writing about a new car you bought, and you've described it metaphorically as a lemon—a poor car, a bad buy. You can write about all the things that have convinced you the car is a lemon:

Other similar topics might be "I know my roommate's a creep because . . . ," "I know my college career's important because . . . " and "I know I'm destined for a career in ______ because . . . "

> I know my car's a lemon because the day I bought it I couldn't get the key out of the ignition. I should have paid attention to that warning signal. I finally got the key out, but two days later the tape player ate my favorite Run-DMC tape. I'd just cleared the carnage out of the tape player when I noticed that the left front speaker wasn't working. It took two trips back to the dealer to get the tape and stereo problems solved. All this was just before I hit the lemon bonanza—the forward gear went out of the transmission. Of course, it was under warranty, but I ask you, What kind of new car shells its transmission at 620 miles? (Think of a popular citrus fruit, my friend.) At 1,200 miles the power brakes failed. I considered driving it down to the dealership anyway, and just stopping it by running it into the wall of their showroom. Instead, I called them and told them to come and tow it—and keep it.

Remember, whatever descriptions you come up with should be clear, vivid, and evocative not only in your mind but also in the mind of your reader. Apply this inventory to your first draft:

1. Do the details re-create the pictures I had in my mind when I wrote?
2. Have I accurately and originally captured the sensory experiences I sought to share? Is my description true to my experience? Have I described my experience in a new way?

3. Are my descriptions appropriate, balanced nicely with the primary reason (persuading, informing or explaining, expressing, or analyzing) I had for writing?

If you can answer yes to your inventory questions, you should be able to proceed with drafting until you are ready to share a full draft with other readers. Then you can proceed through the revision and polishing stages.

SAMPLE WRITING ASSIGNMENT AND CASE STUDY CLOSE-UP

Tom's composition teacher assigned a descriptive paper on the Monday before Thanksgiving. "I don't want you to miss out on any turkey or good times," she said, "but I do want you to come back after vacation with a first draft of your descriptive paper. Here are possible topic areas: a memorable event, a memorable person, a personal fantasy, and a favorite place. You can choose other areas if you clear them with me before you leave for the holiday."

Tom had long had a fantasy that at last was beginning to come true—he had just joined a rock band and was excited about having earned his first income as a musician. But he didn't see how he could project this new experience into fantasy any longer—or at any rate he didn't want to spin some totally fanciful yarn about becoming rich and famous. Puzzled, he went to see his teacher before he left for the holiday.

"You seem to want to write about your music fantasy but not about your music reality," his teacher said, "and right now it's hard for you to separate the two." Tom agreed that might be the problem. "Why don't you look into your past—what sort of fantasies about having a *future* music career did you have then?" Tom hadn't thought about that. He remembered that his earliest dreams of making music had begun in the fourth grade, with his friend Kyle. They'd had a great time, pretending to play and sing along with records. "That sounds productive," his teacher encouraged him. "Why don't you write about some of your 'performances' with your friend?" Thus armed with a topic he considered workable, Tom left campus for Thanksgiving. A draft workshop was scheduled on the students' return after the holiday.

As we've emphasized elsewhere, we're not saying our presentations of conversations between student writers and their teachers (or among student writers in groups) are verbatim accounts of actual conversations. But we *are* saying that these are the *sorts* of conversations that need to take place for teachers (or for peer-group work) to be truly effective in contributing to a student's writing process. And we can verify that in our own experience as writers we have had, and continue to have, conversations like this with our teachers, colleagues, editors, students, and others who help us improve our writing for publication.

Following Tom as He Drafts "Rock-and-Roll Fantasy"

When Tom got some quiet time to do a bit of work over the vacation, he reminisced about how he and Kyle would "perform." They'd go into Kyle's den, which contained an up-to-date stereo system, a few track lights, and a pool table. They'd fix the lights to shine right on the pool table, which became their "stage." Although neither one of them played guitar, they'd take pool cue sticks and pretend to be "playing" them while music blared on the stereo. They'd stand on the pool table—something Kyle's father would surely have forbidden, had he known—and they'd "play" their cues while lip-synchronizing with the vocalists on record. Tom saw all this again in his mind's eye, and he also "heard" their

Ask students whether they think this activity is *invention* or *discovery*. (You may need to remind them of the basic distinction: *discovery* is deliberate searching, such as library research, for usable details; *invention* is brainstorming, taking mental inventories, inspiration, and other *thinking* strategies for generating usable details.)

favorite album again. He began to draft. He made some changes, rearranged some parts, and finally put together the following draft to take back to campus.

Rock-and-Roll Fantasy

Tom Lamb, college writing student

"Ladies and gentlemen, the family den is proud to now present, in their ninth consecutive appearance, Tom and Kyle." That's where it all began; it's my earliest memory of wanting to be a rock-and-roll player, and it is still my most prevalent. 1

My best friend, Kyle, lived two houses down from me; he moved in just before our fourth-grade year, and moved away shortly following it. His house was different from anyone else's that I knew, because his parents were much younger than any of my other friends'. His house had a pool table, cablevision, and, most important, a real component stereo. This was amazing to me, because the only stereos I'd ever seen were the old cabinet systems that everybody's parents had got just after they married. 2

Kyle's new and improved den altered the rest of my life, causing a fire in my soul that nothing has ever matched. We would enter his house every day after school, making sure his folks weren't home, before beginning our ritual. We'd rush to change the mild-mannered den into a concert stage. First we aimed the track lights so they hit just in front of, and on, the pool table. Then to the pool rack to choose our instruments. Kyle always took the shortest stick, so he played lead and I always went directly for the longest stick so I could be the bass player. At the time I really didn't know what a bass player was, but I had seen one on TV once and it was bigger than a regular guitar, so it was for me. Next we chose our music. We usually preferred Aerosmith's album <u>Toys in the Attic</u>. We chose it because it was the most rock-and-roll we owned. We turned it all the way up. 3

We were now ready to start our performance, so the lights went out and the record player started. As the first few notes came from the speakers, there was a flash of lights and in came Kyle and me with our finely tuned instruments. Not a single note was ever missed, even 4 though we were continuously jumping on and off the pool table. Our show was well worth the price of admission. At the age of ten I had already mastered the Chuck Berry "duckwalk" and I had also perfected playing behind my back. Kyle preferred jumping off the pool table, falling to his knees, and playing with his teeth. We knew every beat of every song on that record, so mistakes were rare and our movements were timed perfectly. We took turns doing the vocals for the songs (funny how our voices sounded exactly alike), and an old radio antenna served as our microphone. Most of our stage show had been learned by watching the bands on "American Bandstand" every Saturday.

5 Our stage show went on for an entire year, at least three shows a week. Then about a week into summer, Kyle moved. I kept in touch for a while, but ten-year-olds aren't awfully good at that. With Kyle gone, so was the show; none of my other friends could ever understand how important each step in the process was.

6 So I tucked my little dream away, left only with the hope that I would someday try again.

Back in class after vacation, Tom shared his draft with Vince and Barbara. Vince wanted to know who was "talking" in the quoted matter at the beginning: "Is this supposed to be like an auditorium announcer or someone like that? And if it is, it's not clear when you say, 'That's where it all began' where *that* is." Tom saw he needed to clarify this aspect.

We hope these conversations we report help to "model" for your students the ways in which people in writing/revising groups talk with one another.

Barbara asked what he meant by saying that the Aerosmith album was "the most rock-and-roll we owned": "Do you mean that there were more rock-and-roll songs on that album than on other albums you had, or that the songs on this particular album were better than other rock songs you had, or what?"

"Both, really," Tom said; "the album had more rock than most other albums in our collections, and had more favorite songs on this one album than on other albums."

"I see," said Barbara. "Then I think you should reword that passage. And something else: in the fourth paragraph you say 'the lights went out and the record player started'; then you say 'there was a flash of lights'—as if those things operated by themselves. Surely one of you was at the light switch or the record player or something."

"Yeah," Tom said. "Kyle set the stereo, and I hit the lights; then we both grabbed our cue sticks for our big entrance. I can fix that."

Other suggestions from Vince and Barbara included Tom's doing some mechanical tidying up; Vince noticed that some words were misspelled; Barbara suggested that "most prevalent" didn't seem to fit the idea of a memory. Tom

When you think the time is right, you need to talk about the fact that not all peer comments are productive, that each writer has to take responsibility for sifting what teachers, coaches, tutors, and peers say and for choosing what to act on and what to ignore. In the passage here with Tom, Vince, and Barbara, the comments are scattered; it's up to Tom to figure out how to use their comments to improve his writing.

revised according to his classmates' suggestions and handed in the paper, which came back with a few additional errors noted and a remark that the ending seemed weak. "You did 'someday try again,'" wrote Tom's teacher. "I think you could bring in your present musical interest as part of your conclusion." Tom's grade wasn't bad, but later that term he selected this paper as one he wanted to revise even more to include in his course portfolio. He made some changes, including the teacher's suggested addition to his conclusion. This is the final, polished version he resubmitted:

Rock and Roll Fantasy

Standing beside the already-spinning stereo turntable, my friend Kyle cupped his hands over his mouth and spoke in as low, yet powerful, a voice as he could: "Ladies and Gentlemen, welcome to the Family Den Arena . . . TOM AND KYLE!" On the other side of the den, I hit the track lights trained on the pool table on and off twice in rapid succession; then, grabbing my long pool cue, I hit the lights a last time to leave them on as I leaped toward the pool table to the opening riffs of Aerosmith's <u>Toys in the Attic</u>. After his announcement, Kyle had dropped the stereo arm onto the right spot on the record, grabbed his short pool cue, and matched my leap for the pool table, coming from the other direction. The pool table, the den, indeed the whole basement--and probably most of the upstairs--then shook as we strutted, "sang," and "played," the idols of imagined thousands seated somewhere nearby our pool-table "stage" who were having as good a time as we. That's where my earliest memory of wanting to be a rock-and-roll player began--in Kyle's basement den, when Kyle and I were best buddies in the fourth grade. 1

Kyle lived two houses down from me, having moved in just before our fourth-grade year. His parents were younger than most of my other friends' parents and his house was consequently different in important ways--especially the den, where there was a pool table, cablevision, and, most amazing of all, a real component stereo system. The only other stereos I'd ever seen were those old cabinet systems that everybody's parents got shortly after they were married. This was truly a new and improved den. 2

That den changed my life, starting a fire in my soul that nothing since has matched. Our afternoon music-playing fantasies began when we would enter Kyle's house every day after school, making sure his folks 3 weren't home to see (and hear) the raucous fun we were up to. If, as was usually the case, we had the house to ourselves, we wasted no time turning the den into a concert arena, with the pool table as our stage. First we'd aim the track lights so they shone just in front of, and on, the pool table. Then we'd draw our "instruments"--pool cues--from the rack. Kyle always chose the shortest stick, the better to play "lead guitar" with. I selected the longest stick, so as to play "bass guitar." I didn't really know what a bass player was at the time, other than having seen one or two on television, where I noticed that the bass was a larger guitar than the others--which is why I took the longest cue. Now we were ready to turn on the stereo component system and choose our music. We usually preferred the Aerosmith album because almost all the songs were real rockers, and we liked all the songs on it. After Kyle placed the record on the turntable, we were ready to begin the show.

4 I'd turn out the lights; Kyle would make his announcement; I would wag the lights on and off and on, grab my cue, and make my leap with Kyle at the first earsplitting notes. Not a single note was ever missed, even though we were continuously jumping on and off the pool table. We put on a dynamite show. I was only ten, but I had mastered Chuck Berry's "duckwalk," and I could play behind my back. Kyle liked to jump off the pool table, fall to his knees, and play with his teeth. We knew every beat of every song on that record, so our movements were precision-timed with only rare mistakes. We took turns doing vocals on the songs (funny how our voices sounded exactly alike!), using an old radio antenna as our microphone. Most of what we did we learned by watching groups perform on "American Bandstand" every Saturday. We were a gas.

5 Our stage show went on for an entire year, at least three shows a week. Then, about a week into the summer vacation, Kyle moved. I kept in touch for a while, but ten-year-olds aren't awfully good at that. With Kyle gone, so was the show. None of my other friends could ever understand how important each step in the process was. Looking back on it now, I guess they might have thought I was a little nuts. So I tucked my fantasy away, left only with the hope that I would someday try again.

6 This year I finally brought the fantasy back to life. After years of guitar lessons and solo singing with the radio, I joined a band. Now I get paid to do some of the same things I only pretended to do in the confines

of Kyle's den. It's funny, though: I never did learn to play the bass, and I can't come close to playing a real guitar behind my back. But I can "duckwalk" when I'm cutting up, and I can jump and hit a clean note at the same time. And I still know every word and every beat in every Aerosmith song on Toys in the Attic.

WRITING ASSIGNMENTS

Following are some suggestions for planning and writing a descriptive paper. Choose one, or follow other suggestions from your teacher.

1. Brainstorm some of the most intense visual moments of your life—times when what you saw stamped itself indelibly in your mind and memory. List those moments. Here, for example, is a partial of list ours:
   a. Looking down, down, down into the Royal Gorge of the Arkansas River near Canon City, Colorado: far below, a ribbon of rushing water with a miniature train track and train beside it.
   b. Standing on the observation deck of the Empire State Building in Manhattan, New York City: to the southeast, the East River, Brooklyn Bridge, and Brooklyn, then the hazy sprawl of Long Island behind; to the southwest, the twin towers of the World Trade Center (no King Kong, alas, either there—as in the more recent version—or here, as in the original film), the Statue of Liberty out in the bay, the mouth of the Hudson, Staten Island. (There are more directions, and more to see there, but you get the idea.)
   c. The face of my father the day my mother died.
   d. Dean Brown's turnaround jump shot that danced in the net and fell through as the buzzer sounded and Lyons beat Ellinwood by one point.

Study *your* list: which topics have the best potential to develop into descriptive papers? Choose the most promising one for a descriptive paper.

2. Repeat the process in question 1 for other sensory experiences: the most memorable taste, smell, feeling, sound.
3. Review the descriptive-paper process described in chapter 2, for a paper describing a person, place, or event. Apply those suggestions here too.
4. How might you use description for *informative* or *explanatory* purposes? For example:
   a. How an adobe house is built.
   b. How to add, divide, multiply, and subtract common fractions by hand (without a calculator).
   c. How to make watermelon-rind pickles.
   d. How a radio works.
   e. How the human heart works.

f. How scoring is done in football.
g. How to develop black-and-white film.

5. How might you use description for *persuasive* purposes? For example:
   a. To convince school officials that yours should be a pedestrians' campus.
   b. To convince legislators that eighteen-year-olds should be able to drink alcohol legally.
   c. To convince the owner of a local radio station to discontinue a certain program.
   d. To convince your city engineer that a certain intersection is dangerous.
   e. To convince your congressperson to oppose Political Action Committees (PACs).
   f. To argue the opposite view for any of the above.
6. How might you use descriptive writing for *analytical* purposes? For example:
   a. To examine the symbols in John Steinbeck's short story "The Chrysanthemums."
   b. To examine the causes of Acquired Immune Deficiency Syndrome (AIDS).
   c. To examine the results of a general election.
   d. To examine the results of a laboratory experiment.
   e. To examine the good or bad (or both) points about a book, a film, a restaurant, a service, and so on.
7. How might you use descriptive writing for *expressive* purposes? For instance:
   a. To express feelings about an unforgettable person, place, thing, or event.
   b. To express your feelings about some experience.
   c. To express what some intense sensory experience was like.
   d. To express your creation of a story, poem, or play.
8. The picture of the tornado on page 339 was taken in Kansas in the kind of "bright afternoon sunlight" described in the tornado piece at the beginning of this chapter. In a brief paper, project yourself into this picture. Imagine that you are standing at a safe distance, watching this tornado as it moves across the horizon. Describe what you see and feel. Have you ever actually seen a spectacle of nature like this tornado (or an eclipse, an erupting volcano, a hurricane, a flood, and so on)? Describe what you saw and felt on *that* occasion.

Focus on Critical Thinking

9. Read George Orwell's "Politics and the English Language," then reread Ben Nelms's "A Nation at Risk." In your library, browse through several news publications for August, September, October, and early November 1988 (the *New York Times, Time,* and *Newsweek* should be sufficient). How accurate are Orwell's "maxims"? How justified is Nelms's concern? You can find a copy of Orwell's essay in your library, too; it has been printed in many sources.

Orwell's essay is widely available; you might want to put it on reserve in the library for students to read. It is without doubt one of the most important brief essays ever written on the need for clear and honest writing in a democratic society.

10. Vivid description has the power to work on our emotions. It can be highly inflammatory and consequently very persuasive. Aristotle included the appeal to emotions (*pathos*) among the three major ways of persuading people (along with logic, or *logos*, and the ethics of the speaker or writer, *ethos*). How does description create emotional appeal in "Our Town," by Pete Hamill? in "A Nation at Risk," by Ben Nelms? What uses do Hamill and Nelms make of logic and ethics? Cite passages in each essay that primarily appeal to emotions, to logic, and to your sense of the sincerity and goodwill of the writer.
11. Tom Lamb's "Rock-and-Roll Fantasy" is primarily expressive writing, undertaken to entertain us with his descriptive memories. But do you detect any informative purpose as well?

Writers' Circle

Stage 1. Divide into "figurative language teams" of three writers each. Each group should then collaborate in the creation of *one of each* of the following categories of figurative language:

1. Simile
2. Metaphor

Each instance of figurative language must be used in a sentence or group of sentences. Though each team may come up with more than one good entry in each category, each team must decide which sentence or groups of sentences it will enter in each category and then turn over all leftover ones to the teacher.

Stage 2. The teacher should then read to the entire class each team's entries in each of the categories, inviting comment and response. Then the teacher should turn each team's entries over to a reasonably qualified, impartial judge (a faculty committee, the editor of the school's creative writing magazine, other faculty members, and so on). Have the judge pick first-, second-, and third-place winners in each category; then announce the winners (and read those entries again) in class.

Stage 3. The teacher should read the leftover entries to the class, again inviting comment and response.

chapter 17 Definition

"The American novel is a story in which two people want each other from the beginning but don't get each other until the end of the book. The French novel is a story in which two people get together right at the beginning but from then until the end of the book they don't want each other anymore. The Russian novel is a story in which two people don't want each other or get each other—and brood about it for 800 pages."

Erich Maria Remarque (a German), author of *All Quiet on the Western Front*

When most of us think about definition, the first thing that comes to mind is a dictionary—a compendium of words that tells us, among other things, what meanings a word has, what part (or parts) of speech the word is, and what uses the word has been given. A dictionary, in its broadest sense, is just an alphabetical list of words people have used, together with the words' meanings when people have used them.

You can make this more concrete by bringing in an *OED* or other dictionary that makes use of etymology to aid in definition.

If you were to study dictionaries over a long period, you would note that some words fall from frequent use—some disappearing altogether—while other, newer words come into use. That occurs because our language is "alive"; as things change in our lives, often we need new words to describe or refer to those changes. Similarly, when changes make older words obsolete, those words eventually disappear. All the compilers of a good dictionary can hope to do is keep a fairly thorough and current list. Thus, though dictionaries can't really stabilize language and keep it from changing, they can help standardize its usage and increase our chances of clear communication. When we can agree on what words mean, we can communicate much more effectively. That's why most people—not just Scrabble players—accept dictionary definitions as authoritative.

Definition as a Mental Process

In a broader though related sense, definition goes well beyond the word-usage descriptions given in a dictionary. The urge to define is powerful, for it is an urge to *understand* something in a fundamental way. It is likewise an urge to *clarify*, to *explain* the essence of some idea, experience, or object. Definition, in this broader sense, involves most of our thought processes—our ability to analyze, to categorize, to explain.

Even the simplest kinds of definition engage such processes. For example, consider this definition of a screwdriver:

> A screwdriver is a hand tool that fits the head of a screw and is then turned clockwise to tighten the screw securely.

This dual process of classification and differentiation is also worthwhile to trace in chapter 18's "Antipsychotic Drugs."

Notice that classification and differentiation are going on simultaneously as mental processes here. First the screwdriver is placed in a larger classification of objects called hand tools. But then we get details that differentiate it from other kinds of hand tools, such as hammers or pliers: it fits the head of a screw. The user turns it clockwise to tighten the screw. Understanding of what a screwdriver is—the essence, if you will, of screwdrivers—is achieved through this process of classifying and differentiating. In this case, differentiation is achieved through explaining function. Many things in our world can be defined in the above manner: fuel injectors, typewriters, lawn mowers, forks, tape cassettes, software, and so on.

Definition as a Key to Pinning down Abstractions

But definition applies to more than just things. The urge to define, to clarify and understand, extends to abstractions, ideas that are much more difficult to pin down in neat categories and differentiations. For example, how would you define *love?* How would you define *art?* Such definitions usually force our imaginations and experience to work in tandem in order to *suggest* definitions, provide clarification by way of analogy, or show comparison of some other sort. Some definitions, in other words, can be achieved only by example or by lengthy differentiations drawn from experience rather than from the essence of something. That is why, for instance, the U.S. Supreme Court has so often struggled to define, by way of separate rulings, what "discrimination" in our society is. Or to define what our founders meant by forbidding "cruel and unusual punishment."

In fact, some of our most spirited sociological debates have concerned what abstract words or concepts mean. Following, for example, is an excerpt from Paul Theroux's *Sunrise with Seamonsters,* regarding what the concept of manhood means.

You can further involve your students in learning about defining if you bring in a list of "mystery words and phrases" for them to try to find definitions of. Here are three good ones to start with: (a) "technological condors" (condors that can survive in the wild only with all the resources of high technology supporting them), (b) "stress homeostasis" (the idea that human beings, as individuals or groups, not only can come to tolerate a certain level of stress but also may, when something reduces that level, seek to bring the level back up), and (c) "preselling the high concept" (what a producer does when selling the idea for a movie to a financial backer, explaining the movie's idea in twenty-five extremely well chosen words).

"Being a Man"

PAUL THEROUX

Paul Theroux is a teacher and writer, author of articles and books of fiction (including Jungle Lovers, Saint Jack, *and* The Mosquito Coast*) and nonfiction (including* The Great Railway Bazaar, The Old Patagonian Express, The Imperial Way *and* Sunrise with Seamonsters, *from which the following is excerpted.*

1 There is a pathetic sentence in the chapter "Fetishism" in Dr. Norman Cameron's book *Personality Development and Psychopathology.* It goes, "Fetishists are nearly always men; and their commonest fetish is a woman's shoe." I cannot read that sentence without thinking that it is just one more awful thing about being a man—and perhaps it is an important thing to know about us.

2 I have always disliked being a man. The whole idea of manhood in America is pitiful, in my opinion. This version of masculinity is a little like

Ask students to notice in particular this odd opening; whereas most essays begin by going forward, this one begins by backing up. What do students think the purpose/effect of that is? How might their reading of it change after you've gone over the whole essay together?

having to wear an ill-fitting coat for one's entire life (by contrast, I imagine femininity to be an oppressive sense of nakedness). Even the expression "Be a man!" strikes me as insulting and abusive. It means: Be stupid, be unfeeling, obedient, soldierly, and stop thinking. And yet it is part of every man's life. It is a hideous and crippling lie; it not only insists on difference and connives at superiority, it is also by its very nature destructive—emotionally damaging and socially harmful.

The youth who is subverted, as most are, into believing in the masculine 3 ideal is effectively separated from women and he spends the rest of his life finding women a riddle and a nuisance. Of course, there is a female version of this male affliction. It begins with mothers encouraging little girls to say (to other adults) "Do you like my new dress?" In a sense, little girls are traditionally urged to please adults with a kind of coquettishness, while boys are enjoined to behave like monkeys towards each other. The nine-year-old coquette proceeds to become womanish in a subtle power game in which she learns to be sexually indispensable, socially decorative and always alert to a man's sense of inadequacy.

Ask students how they feel about this idea of a "natural friendship" between men and women.

Femininity—being lady-like—implies needing a man as witness and 4 seducer; but masculinity celebrates the exclusive company of men. That is why it is so grotesque; and that is also why there is no manliness without inadequacy—because it denies the natural friendship of women.

Questions for Writing and Discussion

Prepare short written answers to each of these questions. Be prepared to hand them in and/or discuss them in class, as your teacher directs.

1. Theroux "defines" *manhood* and *masculinity* through a series of examples, or illustrations, of what he means when he pronounces the "idea of manhood" as "pitiful" (¶ 2). What are these examples? Expand on each of them—what do you think he means by each? Do you agree, partly agree, or disagree with him?
2. Elsewhere in the piece Theroux refers to "the terrible ambition of manliness"? What do you think he means by that?
3. Theroux defines *femininity* much the same way he defines *masculinity*. What examples/illustrations does he use to define femininity? Again, what do you think he means by each, and to what extent do you agree with him?
4. Theroux makes vivid use of description. What simile do you find in the second paragraph? What personification?
5. What figurative language do you find in the third paragraph?
6. What do the following words mean—*pathetic, fetish* (¶ 1), *connives* (¶ 2), *subverted, affliction, coquette* (¶ 3), *grotesque* (¶ 4)?
7. What do you think Theroux means by saying women become "socially decorative" (¶ 3)?

Bridges: Another Perspective

Paul Theroux makes a case that is not often made: that fulfilling the stereotyped role of an ideal male, particularly as defined in American society, is difficult and painful, even destructive. He goes on to note that the stereotyped role of an ideal female as defined in American society is just as bad. How might a dedicated and thoughtful feminist respond to Theroux's ideas? To what extent is the issue especially American in nature? To what extent is it sexual, regardless of geography?

Clearly Theroux, for all his conviction, must finally rely on comparisons, approximations, examples, and rather vague indictments to convey the reasoning behind his definitions of masculinity and femininity in our culture. This isn't to say Theroux is a poor thinker or a sloppy definer; rather, it is to recognize that some things just can't be easily defined. Their essences, their meanings, are slippery, elusive, almost defiant. Given their nature, they could not be otherwise. Witness, for example, the ongoing difficulty in our culture of clarifying, once and for all, what pornography is.

Following is an article from *Time* magazine in which Richard Zoglin reports that, paradoxically, many people recognize that "sleaze" on television must be minimized—even though they also realize the near impossibility of defining just what sleaze is.

Putting a Brake on TV "Sleaze"

RICHARD ZOGLIN, WITH MARY CRONIN and NAUSHAD S. MEHTA

Richard Zoglin is an associate editor for Time *magazine.*

1 TV's sin-and-sex parade marches on. Highlights on last week's tabloid shows ranged from a story on "the undercover Romeo," a drug informant who allegedly lured innocent women into dope deals, to an ogling visit to a topless coffee shop. Can't something be done, critics and concerned viewers cry, about such tasteless shows? Now a campaign against TV sleaze appears to be gathering steam. But the cure may be worse than the disease.

Notice how the last line of this first paragraph signals the essay's eventual change in direction.

2 The issue leaped to the fore two weeks ago, when a Michigan housewife, Terry Rakolta, became an instant celebrity for her successful letter-writing campaign against the bawdy Fox network sitcom *Married . . . With Children.* Responding to her complaints, several major advertisers, including Kimberly-Clark and Procter & Gamble, said they would no longer run ads on

Some students may want to research, as the topic of an eventual paper, the current status of this issue vis-à-vis "Married . . . with Children."

the show because of its "offensive" content. The sitcom—Fox's highest-rated show—is in no mortal danger: ad time is sold out for the season, Fox officials say, and only one company, Tambrands, actually canceled a scheduled commercial because of Rakolta's complaints.

Her one-woman ground swell, however, has exposed a growing skittishness among advertisers. While many are "tonnage" buyers, willing to place their commercials anywhere, others carefully select shows in order to avoid being associated with questionable material. With the proliferation of so-called trash TV, the number of troublesome programs has multiplied. Among them are such tabloid shows as *A Current Affair, Inside Edition* and *The Reporters;* sensational talk programs like *The Morton Downey Jr. Show* and *Geraldo;* and occasional over-the-edge network offerings like Geraldo Rivera's NBC special last fall on Satanism. 3

Ask students what they consider "trash" and why.

Most of these shows do quite well in the ratings. But as the *Married... With Children* flap demonstrated, ratings are not everything, even along Madison Avenue. "What *Married... With Children* has done is make everybody take a sharper look at standards," says Betsy Frank, a senior vice president of Saatchi & Saatchi advertising. NBC, under attack for its low-road programming, is re-creating the position of vice president of program standards and policy, eliminated last year for budgetary reasons. The network is also setting up meetings with ad executives to explain its policy for screening out offensive material. 4

In 1990 it was "Uncle Buck" that wreaked havoc. What is it in the year you're using this book? Or (we admit we think it's unlikely) has the issue been solved?

In a TV marketplace that seems to be operating with fewer and fewer restraints, it is ironic that advertisers have become the new guardians of quality. The trouble is: Whose definition of quality? Campaigns against "tasteless" shows usually come from the most conservative elements of American society. One pressure group, Christian Leaders for Responsible TV, is making plans to monitor TV programming this spring and to organize a boycott of major sponsors of "anti-Christian" shows. Rakolta's objections to *Married... With Children* managed to miss totally the show's satirical point. This sitcom family—male-chauvinist husband, unliberated wife, sluttish teenage daughter—is being lampooned by exaggeration. The same sort of complaints—just as misguided—were launched against the bigoted Archie Bunker in the early 1970s. 5

One does not have to like *Married... With Children* or TV's tabloid shows to be disturbed by campaigns to drive them from the air. Advertiser boycotts, if successful, do not make TV better, only blander. They also reveal a remarkable lack of faith in the ability of viewers to lodge the ultimate protest: turning off the set. 6

You might provoke a lively discussion by asking which side(s) your students are on in this issue.

Questions for Writing and Discussion

Prepare short written answers to each of these questions. Be prepared to hand them in and/or discuss them in class, as your teacher directs.

1. What one sentence in Zoglin's article seems to sum up best what is most problematic about TV "sleaze"?

2. Zoglin's is a "news and commentary" article. What parts of it would you say are strictly news? strictly commentary?
3. Consider the following descriptive words and phrases. How effective is each?
   a. "TV's sex-and-sin parade marches on." (¶ 1)
   b. "Now a campaign against TV sleaze appears to be gathering steam. But the cure may be worse than the disease." (¶ 1)
   c. "The sitcom . . . is in no mortal danger." (¶ 2)
   d. "one-woman ground swell" (¶ 3)
   e. "so-called trash TV" (¶ 3)
   f. "over-the-edge network offerings" (¶ 3)
   g. "screening out offensive material" (¶ 4)
4. How would *you* define sleaze?
5. What do the following words mean—*ogling* (¶ 1), *bawdy* (¶ 2), *proliferation* (¶ 3), *satirical* (¶ 5), *boycott* (¶ 6)?
6. Which of the TV shows or personalities mentioned in the story have you watched? Would you agree that they are "sleaze"? some of them? all of them? Are some of these shows or personalities no longer on television?

Some of your students may be surprised to learn which side Zoglin is on; students often expect writers to take the obvious position—here the "down with smut" argument is what they expect.

You might want to explain each of these briefly before you discuss their effectiveness.

You might want to bring in a TV schedule and make a list of daytime shows and nighttime shows for students to divide into some kind of "TV taxonomy."

Definition as an Aid to Invention

Zoglin's article makes it clear that many kinds of definition are problematical. In a way, that is why definition can be so inventive—it can challenge our imaginations to come up with suitable illustrations or examples to make our definitions meaningful, especially if the terms we are trying to define are abstract:

Intelligence: When you spot the flaw in your boss's reasoning.

Wisdom: When you refrain from pointing it out.

In those two related examples, James Dent (of the Charleston, West Virginia, *Gazette*) used imaginative illustration to define, with considerable humor, two abstract terms.

You have probably seen and heard other abstractions defined in similar ways. A greeting card some years ago showed Snoopy, the lovable dog in Charles Schulz's "Peanuts" comic strip. "Happiness Is a Warm Puppy," it proclaimed. In a satiric and ironic song of the late 1960s, the Beatles said, "Happiness is a warm gun." A popular romantic film and novel, *Love Story,* written by Erich Segal, stated, "Love means never having to say you're sorry." Another popular song, "Me and Bobby McGee," by Kris Kristofferson, held, "*Freedom*'s just another word for nothing left to lose." In these and countless other instances, an apt definition is reached through what at first appears to be an illogical comparison or illustration. But on reflection, we see that these "definitions" carry useful meanings.

It's fun to see how many different "Happiness is . . ." sayings you and your students can come up with. Similar enjoyment usually results from "Love is . . . ," "Gross is . . . ," and "You know you're ______ when ______."

In our modern world, *stress* has come to be recognized as an abstract but important medical term, one taken quite seriously. The nature and causes of stress are complex, however, and pinpointing a precise definition of the term can thus be difficult. This imprecision has led to numerous articles in popular magazines, such as the following, by Randi Londer.

Stressed Out: What Puts the Pressure on Families?

Randi Londer

Randi Londer is a New York–based free-lance writer who specializes in health and medical writing.

Notice that the introduction begins with examples that are both specific and general; ask students what effect that has. The second paragraph cites authority, and the third explains a process associated with the thing being defined.

Johnny feels saddened by the death of his beloved hamster. Mom is concerned about Grandpa's health. Dad worries that his job may be phased out. When one family member feels stress, *everyone's* emotions get stirred up. Even pleasant events—a wedding or a birth, for example—put stress on the whole family. 1

To help you rate your family's stress level—so you can *do* something about it—we recruited Arthur Bodin, Ph.D., president of the family psychology division of the American Psychological Association, to tell us about some common areas of family stress and to help interpret the following quiz, which is designed so that each family member—including the children—can take it separately. (Participation is, of course, voluntary.) The quiz has four parts; simply answer the sections that apply to you. For example, a grandparent would respond to numbers 1 to 17 ("For Each Family Member") and 38 to 41 ("For Each Grandparent"). 2

Dr. Bodin points out that most families will show evidence of stress on at least several items. However, the more times you find yourself responding "moderate" or "high"—particularly if you're uncomfortable about your ability to *cope* with these stresses—the more important it may be to discuss your concerns with someone, perhaps family or friends. You might also consider consulting a mental health professional: a psychologist, psychiatrist, clinical social worker, marriage or family counselor. 3

Test Yourselves

As you go down the list, rate the stress level—*none (n), low (1), moderate (m), or high (h)*—you feel *today* as a result of these crises, concerns, and changes in your family's life. (If an event listed did not occur, or if it did occur but does not bother you, write *n*—meaning no stress—next to the appropriate number.) It's important to remember that it doesn't matter whether or not the event affected you directly. In some cases, you may feel stress over an event that occurred in the past or one that is *about* to happen in the family, such as an impending divorce or change of job. Or perhaps you just worry that such an event *could* take place. After completing the quiz, count the number of times you answered "moderate" or "high." Then [look below] for Dr. Bodin's comments and some steps you can take that will prove useful in lowering your family's stress level. 4

For Each Family Member

5 1. A loved one has died.
2. Our family has gone through a divorce.
3. An important relationship has broken up.
4. We have had financial problems.
5. A family member has had legal problems.
6. Our family seems to argue a lot.
7. Our family doesn't communicate very well.
8. We disagree over how much time we should spend together.
9. We have moved to a new home.
10. We have had, or will soon have, a wedding.
11. We are expecting or have had a baby.
12. Someone in our family has had a difficult or unwanted pregnancy.
13. I'm worried about a family member who has been ill or hospitalized.
14. A family member has been the victim of a crime, accident or disaster.
15. A loved one is acting in a self-destructive way (e.g., drugs or alcohol abuse).
16. A loved one has hinted about, threatened or attempted suicide.
17. One family member has abused another.

For Each Parent

6 18. There are problems with in-laws.
19. A child has run away.
20. A child has moved away from home.
21. There is worry about a child's schooling (homework, grades, behavior).
22. There is worry about a child's chores or social life (choice of friends, use of car, helping at home).
23. My mate and I disagree about our child's discipline.
24. There is worry about a child's development.
25. My mate and I have problems expressing or receiving affection.
26. There are job difficulties (boredom, burnout)
27. There is a job transition (being fired, quitting, retiring, new career).

For Each Child

7 28. My parents argue a lot.
29. My parents seem unhappy.

Of course, many of your students will want to rate themselves on this list. You should therefore be careful about joking about it; the odds are that you'll have at least one or two students who will not rate well and to whom nothing about the article and its content can be seen as humorous.

30. I worry about my parents' health.
31. I'm afraid of a parent, sibling, or grandparent.
32. I fight with my parents over my school attendance, grades, homework.
33. My parents and I disagree about my chores or social life (friends, car, curfew, helping at home).
34. My pet died.
35. I am disappointed that I didn't get into a certain club or group.
36. I go to a new school.
37. We moved to a new neighborhood.

For Each Grandparent

38. I don't see my children or grandchildren as much as I'd like to. 8
39. I disagree with my children over how they are raising my grandchildren.
40. I'm worried about my health.
41. I'm afraid I will become a burden to my children.

Stress-coping Strategies

According to Dr. Bodin, people who don't learn how to cope with stressful life events may find the strain interfering not only with their family life, but with their job and relationships with friends as well. Here are some suggestions from Dr. Bodin that may be helpful for coping with the stresses and strains in your life: 9

Whenever possible, try to space out life changes. If you are about to have a baby, for example, you might try to postpone moving to a new home. But, says Dr. Bodin, don't place even more pressure on yourself by attempting to get rid of *all* stress. "Stress is a natural, normal—and inevitable—part of life." 10

Communicate, communicate! "It's essential to establish a climate of love and acceptance so that no one is afraid to express his or her feelings because they fear someone else in the family will disapprove or be judgmental," says Dr. Bodin. In order to avoid falling into such hurtful patterns, it's important to recognize that when you interrupt another person or speak to her without making any eye contact or even ignore her when she tries to talk to you, you are—in effect—telling that person: "You're not very important to me." 11

It's O.K. to disagree, but it's not O.K. to be disagreeable. If your opinion differs from that of another family member, instead of saying, "That's ridiculous!" you could say, "I never looked at it that way." Or: "That's an interesting point, but what still puzzles me is . . . " 12

13 **Avoid pressuring, begging, or wheedling.** If someone in the family is having a problem but prefers not to talk about it, Dr. Bodin suggests that you might tell that person, "I'm here and I want to listen if you feel like talking with me."

14 However, Dr. Bodin warns parents that sometimes children will try to extract a promise—in advance—that you "won't be mad at me if I tell you something." One way to avoid that trap: Say to the child, "Since I don't know what it is, I will try to control what I say, but I may not be able to control my feelings."

15 **Use good timing and plain old common sense.** If grandma has just been diagnosed with a serious disease, Mom might want to wait until *after* her son takes his college exams to tell him the bad news.

16 **Stay alert to signs of stress in your children.** Children are especially sensitive to family stress and can become very upset by arguments or the tension they perceive between their parents. And it's not uncommon for youngsters to express these feelings through play in which, for instance, two dolls hit or scream at each other. Take the opportunity to draw out your child's feelings by saying something like, "Those dollies seem really mad at each other." You could point out that although dolls—like Mommy and Daddy—may have arguments, they can still love each other.

Questions for Writing and Discussion

Prepare short written answers to each of these questions. Be prepared to hand them in and/or discuss them in class, as your teacher directs.

1. Based on what you have read in this article, how would you define *stress?* How would you define *family stress?*
2. How does Londer establish credibility for Dr. Bodin, his test, and his advice?
3. Who would be most likely to read and heed this article?
4. The article doesn't so much define stress as it tries to establish what might be called levels of stress. How does the test aid this goal?

This kind of "test" article is common; you might ask students to find another one and examine how it accomplishes definition.

Stress can take many forms and remains a complex health problem for human beings, a problem difficult to assess and difficult to deal with. Some other kinds of human frailty, however, can be more clearly defined. The world of medicine knows of many diseases and illnesses and often defines them by causes, symptoms, or other results of the sickness. Diagnoses, in fact, are generally based on definitions derived from medical history and symptoms. Here, for example, is a student paper defining and explaining multiple sclerosis (MS).

Notice how this definition piece starts right out with the core of its definition, whereas the earlier examples started more indirectly.

Multiple Sclerosis: The Misunderstood Disease

Susan Sheehy, college writing student

Multiple sclerosis, also known as MS, is a chronic neurological disorder whose onset usually occurs in adults between twenty and forty. It is the most common of all diseases affecting the central nervous system. This disabling disease is often characterized by spells of relapse and remission. The degree of severity, symptoms, psychological impact, and family acceptance often varies with each individual. What causes MS is unknown, although evidence indicates the possibility that a virus is the source. Unfortunately, there is no cure. 1

MS is brought on by lesions on the central nervous system. The central nervous system is made up of nerve bundles found in the brain and spinal cord. Each nerve has three parts: a cell body, dendrites, and the axon, which is the part affected by MS. The axon's main function is to transmit messages to and from the brain. Axons are usually covered with a fatty insulation, myelin, that helps the nerves transmit messages more rapidly. People with MS have axons that have somehow lost this coating of myelin, and lesions of varying size and location form as a result. The conduct of messages to and from the brain is delayed in axons that have these demyelinated lesions. Symptoms, however, are never quite the same for any two people. This variation of symptoms, along with the unknown cause or causes, makes diagnosis of MS very difficult. 2

The primary criterion for diagnosing MS is the occurrence of at least two neurological malfunctions (attacks) a month or more apart. A neurological attack is any clear instance of the brain's not "receiving" a message, resulting in a temporary malfunction. The occurrence of two clearly separate attacks eliminates the possibility of other diseases mimicking MS symptoms; only MS is likely to take so long between instances. Once two such distant attacks have occurred, the patient should be examined by a neurologist. The neurologist will perform a number of tests to try to determine the sites of the lesions causing the attacks. 3

One test removes fluid from the spine to obtain the banding pattern of the patient's spine. The specialist will label the bands as normal or abnormal. Another test, called evoked potentials, can determine the rate 4 of nerve transmission in the spinal cord. Finally, a computed tomography (CT) scan can take pictures of tissue layers in the brain to check for possible lesions. These test results and patient's symptoms are essential factors in the neurologist's decision either to confirm or to reject a diagnosis of MS. But the symptoms, as noted before, can be very tricky.

5 The central nervous system relays, interprets, and controls reactions in every part of our body. Because of the system's vast area, a lesion has many possible sites of infection. Fortunately, sometimes the symptoms a patient contracts can reveal the location of the lesion fairly accurately. For example, if an MS patient suffers from visual loss in one eye, the physician knows that the lesion is on the optic nerve. Other symptoms experienced by MS patients are much less easy to pinpoint, for they include motor defects resulting in spastic movements, bladder and bowel disturbances, sensory defects such as partial or intermittent paralysis, and, in more serious cases, mood swings. And the most notable symptom experienced by all MS patients is fatigue--something even the healthy are vulnerable to.

6 The kinds of symptoms just mentioned, and a diagnosis of MS, can have a traumatic effect on the emotional stability of an MS patient. Though depression is common, the biggest obstacle for an MS patient to overcome is the feeling of being "abnormal." Stress becomes a villain, forcing MS patients to reexamine their life goals, jobs, and relationships. Because most MS patients are diagnosed in the prime of life, career goals and family plans must often be changed. Marriages and other important relationships (employers, friends, professional associates) can be strained. Spouses of MS patients may feel they cannot handle the burden of caring for their husband's or wife's special needs. Fatigue and other physical disorders may make it impossible for the patient to continue working at all. The negative emotions that an MS patient feels can sometimes be improved with the help of a good listener. Moral support--even if it is professional counseling--can be vitally important.

7 MS can also have an impact on the patient's family. Members might feel anxiety, guilt, and anger toward the patient and his or her illness. The family should receive counseling as well as the patient in such cases. A reevaluation of the situation is important; family members must face the fact that the patient's condition may worsen, requiring additional attention and care. Family (and friends as well) should

understand that MS does not affect the brain and does not result in mental illness. The lesions cause physical, not mental, abnormalities. Each family member may have to make adjustments in personal schedules and relationships to include the MS patient. This daily commitment requires love and dedication, but its result makes the MS patient's life more bearable.

MS is the most common neurological disease known to science, yet it is still widely misunderstood because of its various symptoms and lack of known cause or cure. It can claim the life of its victim in one day or thirty years. It can almost seem to "go away," then come back worse than ever. It can bring out the worst, and, with some understanding and sacrifice, the best in us. And we can retain hope that one day we will know more about its causes, so that we may also one day find its cure. 8

Questions for Writing and Discussion

Prepare short written answers to each of these questions. Be prepared to hand them in and/or discuss them in class, as your teacher directs.

1. Sheehy moves from an extended definition of MS to a discussion of its impact on patients and their families. How does she manage a definition of this disease when there is no known cause and no known cure?
2. Often Sheehy uses specific medical or physiological terms, such as *dendrites* and *axon,* without offering definitions for them. Yet we understand them broadly in the context of her discussion, for our understanding depends not on precise definitions of these terms but on a grasp of their function. What other instances of contextual definition can you find?
3. What do the following words mean—*lesion* (¶ 2), *criterion, neurological, mimicking* (¶ 3), *spastic* (¶ 5)?
4. In what ways is the elusive quality of diagnosing MS similar to the elusive quality of defining an abstraction like anger?

Definition: Connotation and Denotation

It must be clear by now that some kinds of definition are fairly uncomplicated, as in defining a screwdriver, an internal combustion engine, or a fountain pen—things that can quickly be categorized and differentiated by way of describing their appearance, purpose, or function. It must also be clear that other kinds of definition are more difficult; anything abstract, such as an idea, concept, or complicated illness, can almost defy precise definition. It's the tough definitions that challenge us and that force us, through our language and logic, to try to understand and, to the extent we can, control our world.

Of course it's also the tough definitions that are often the most important ones: *liberty, duty, honor,* and so on.

As noted earlier, our language is a living thing, constantly undergoing changes. New technology gives us new words (*byte, fax,* and *scanner,* for example, and, from a slightly earlier time but still within the lifetimes of your authors, *astronaut*). Historical changes make some words change along with them too; since the resignation of President Richard M. Nixon in 1974, for instance, *Watergate* has come to mean far more than the name of a Washington, D.C., office complex—it is the noun symbolically associated with the political scandal that ended Nixon's presidency. In fact, a "new" suffix, *-gate,* has attached itself to several lesser political scandals since Watergate: Irangate, Contragate, and so on.

Other words become associated with something they originally did not mean, causing them to take on new shades of meaning called *connotations.* Connotation refers not to the precise, "dictionary" definition of a word but, rather, to the associations, whether positive or negative, that cluster around the word as a result of some action or event that served to help change the way the word is perceived.

In 1938, for example, the British prime minister Neville Chamberlain, seeking to negotiate with the German dictator Adolf Hitler and avoid war, met with Hitler in Munich. Hitler was demanding that a part of Czechoslovakia inhabited by mostly German-speaking people become a part of Germany. This demand was but the most recent in a series of moves Hitler had made, aimed at strengthening Germany's position in Europe despite the terms of the treaty that ended World War I. Chamberlain, in seeking to avoid war at almost any cost, emerged from Munich having in effect given Hitler what Hitler wanted in exchange for vague assurances that there would be no more warlike demands. This settlement was called appeasement, and Chamberlain declared that it guaranteed "peace in our time." About a year later, Hitler ignored his Munich assurances and ordered the invasion of Poland, thus beginning World War II. *Appeasement,* never before a word that had a negative connotation, suddenly became a spiteful word, a word associated with foolish judgment. It has remained so to this day: no politician would ever emerge from a negotiating session with representatives of another country and claim to have "appeased" them.

You can make this point real in group work by bringing in, say, *U.S. News and World Report, Time,* and *Newsweek*—one magazine per group—and asking each group to find five similar words and work out their definition from the context each is in. Then the groups can report their findings to the class.

Similarly, the word *depression* is no longer used to refer to present or future economic conditions in the United States. Why? Because the Great Depression of the 1930s was so profound, and so stamped the consciousness and memory of the people, that economists will use another, similar word so as to avoid unduly upsetting the public. (*Recession* is much more likely to be used, and usually with the adjective *mild* before it, so that any alarm will be minimized.)

Besides *recession,* there's also *inflation, stagnation,* and *stagflation.*

You can see that a word's connotation can often be more significant than its *denotation.* Compare these words that are similar in meaning but different in connotation:

thin / skinny

short / stubby

house / home

portly / fat

As the following lengthy piece by Pete Hamill shows, some of our most interesting and vital writing comes from attempts to define concepts that for one reason or another are difficult to define.

PREREADING WORKSHEET

Before you read the following piece by Pete Hamill, write brief responses to these questions:

1. How would you define *ethics*?
2. How would you define *conscience*?
3. How would you define *integrity*?
4. How would you define *morality*?
5. Do you believe there is always a distinct difference between right and wrong? Why or why not?
6. Do you believe there is widespread lack of ethics in America? Why or why not?

Ethics in the 80s: Is There No Longer Right or Wrong?

PETE HAMILL

See page 349 for information on Pete Hamill. This piece appeared in Cosmopolitan *in 1988.*

Once again, we've added the notes that appear at the end of this essay.

There they were, pirouetting across the public stage, all the smarmy figures of the 1980s. Ivan Boesky,[1] one of the most powerful doges in the world of Big Money, grinning his mirthless grin all the way to his prison cell. Oliver North,[2] telling America that a good patriot lies to Congress, destroys evidence, and sneers at the laws of the land. Dennis Levine, the prince of insider trading, singing to the prosecutors with the sincerity of a Pavarotti,[3] trying to save his hide by betraying his friends. Gary Hart,[4] destroying his career and the illusions of his followers with his icy contempt for the rules. 1

Others seem not even to have heard of those rules. And this should not surprise us. We are in the last years of the Awful Eighties, and the loss of respect for ethical conduct seems general. 2

The evidence of the decline and fall of practically everybody lies around us. On an almost weekly basis, we watched the Feds cart away handcuffed Wall Street yuppies. We saw Jimmy Swaggart[5] sob on TV about his sins, instantly making himself the only contender to challenge Jackie Mason[6] for the comedy championship of the decade; then we collapsed in ribald mirth when the good preacher was forced to choose between penance and cash flow 3 and opted for the ratings. It seems that in any contest between God and Mammon, Mammon wins, at least on points.

Some of your students may not know what "winning on points" means. The expression comes from the sport of boxing, wherein judges score "points" for each fighter according to some agreed-on system of scoring. With this system, a winner can be determined if there is no knockout.

4 Swaggart's hilarious confession followed (and topped) the spectacular performance of that quintessential religious couple, the Bakkers,[7] who managed to turn God into a character out of the tabloids. Who could not cherish the public sobbing of Jim and Tammy, their dealing and angling, their clothes and makeup, their jammed press conferences, their invincible hypocrisy? In the end, of course, they couldn't pray away the lurid image of that infamous Florida motel room. But on their way to obscurity, they did leave us with another extraordinary public icon: poor Jessica Hahn. She first gladly accepted her hush money and then went public for a price. Within weeks, she was bobbing her nose and lifting her boobs and applying for permanent citizenship in the sad nation of celebrity. Twenty-five years after the feminist revolt, we were served up Donna Rice, Fawn Hall,[8] and Jessica Hahn. Greetings from Bimbodelphia.

5 Meanwhile, the Governor of Arizona was impeached and thrown out of office for misusing state funds and impeding the investigation of an alleged death threat. Larry Speakes [former White House press secretary] was forced to resign his flack's job at Merrill Lynch after telling the world that he made up quotes for Ronald Reagan. A major defense-contract scandal involving top Pentagon officials made headlines. All over the country, corrupt local politicians were being hauled to the hoosegow for taking bribes, peddling drugs, or otherwise engaging in acts of criminal malfeasance. And during this time, as if to underline the prevailing moral squalor, the Attorney General of the United States [Ed Meese]—the most eminent law-enforcement official in the land—was spending most of his working hours in grand juries that were examining his own questionable personal affairs . . . a mess that—despite his denials—many experts believe prompted his resignation.

Notice that this paragraph omits mention of anything good; ask students about the effect of that omission.

6 On the most primitive level, this has been grand entertainment. It is virtually impossible to observe hypocrisy exposed or the mighty humbled without bursting into a good healthy horselaugh. But on a more profound level, it is clear that we have been witnessing something deeper and darker in American life.

Notice that this paragraph is a turning point in the essay.

7 Certainly, contempt for the most elemental ethical behavior seems to be more widespread than it has been in many years. Ordinary citizens brag about cheating on their income taxes or fixing traffic tickets. Public servants charged with enforcing safety or health regulations routinely use their offices for self-enrichment, as if they were bureaucrats in a banana republic. Journalists have been caught taking loans from people they are covering, manufacturing stories and quotes, or plagiarizing the work of others. More than a few clerks in government agencies have sold military secrets to the highest bidders. In many businesses, lying is routine. Cheating is rewarded. And after the indictments are drawn, the latest accused felon protests with some justice, "Everybody's doing it."

8 All of us are not, of course, but all of us pay the price. When health inspectors take bribes, we risk disease, even death. When a cop looks the

other way, the crack dealer is free to spread his poison. When politicians are caught gorging at the public trough, the entire system that chose them is made suspect. The failure to abide by ethical rules corrupts the entire society. I've spent many years living in or visiting Mexico and have witnessed the growing cynicism that permeates that country. Corruption has poisoned the air of Mexico City, made the justice system a joke, impaired Mexican agriculture, made drug smuggling a way of life in some northern states. And I've seen that corruption also affects the corrupted; a bureaucrat who takes a bribe (even when "everybody's doing it") suffers a loss of pride. He has a secret he cannot tell his children. He acquires a shadow life that leaves him always vulnerable to exposure. The society itself begins to rot; citizens lose faith; daily life loses all semblance of security. That has happened on a wide scale in Mexico and many other countries; it is happening now in the United States to a degree not previously seen in this country.

Here, finally, the essay gets to the core subject: definition.

For more than three thousand years, men and women have tried to construct codes of human behavior. This has been no easy task. The word *ethics* is derived from the Greek *ethos,* meaning "character," and the dictionary defines ethics as "the study of standards of conduct and moral judgment." But most humans would agree that study without practice is not enough. In our time, we have learned painfully that there is often an immense gap between theory and practice, promise and reality. We have all witnessed so much hypocrisy that when we hear the word *moral,* many of us back up a few feet, expecting the worst. Too often, moralizing has been the only genuine competitor with patriotism for the claim to be the last refuge of scoundrels. It is no wonder that Ernest Hemingway once remarked, "I know only that what is moral is what you feel good after and what is immoral is what you feel bad after." 9

Hemingway's remark was typically more complicated than it appears. For one thing, it assumes the existence of a conscience, without which human beings can feel nothing about their transgressions and betrayals; it is certainly not a formula based on mere appetite and its satisfaction. Hemingway's generation was shaped by the mindless slaughter of the First World War. In the aftermath of that horrendous war, all the old moral assumptions lay dead; empires were destroyed, authority was eroded, and Hemingway and many others tried to shape a moral code that would allow men and women to be good without God. In the tail end of this squalid century, many human beings are still struggling with that problem. 10

But obviously, this is not the first century in which people have struggled to bring sense to the world in which they live. Even a cursory reading of the great thinkers shows that concern for behavior has been at the heart of the matter since the earliest days of civilization. Plato and Socrates discussed in their separate ways the problem of imposing some form of ethical order on the chaos of the world. Aristotle's great book on ethics was written three centuries before Christ, and much of it remains valid today. The religions derived from the teachings of Moses, Jesus, Confucius, Mohammed, and Buddha were all concerned with shaping codes for decent human conduct, 11 and more secular philosophers, from Marcus Aurelius to Albert Camus, have offered other routes to the same basic goal.

12 When stripped of their mysticism, convoluted language, poetry, these theories are generally a form of common sense. Some thinkers favored reason and enlightened self-interest as the means of persuading people to behave themselves; a few preached universal love; others created notions of a prosecutorial God standing guard over the entrance to an eternal afterlife filled with reward or punishment, good or bad karma.

13 Alas, none have succeeded in any complete way. There seems to be no end to the human capacity for folly, brutality, and what used to be called sin. And all attempts at constructing utopia on this poor earth have led either to the pyre or the gulag. The pattern is familiar: A brilliant human being constructs a theory for the salvation of the human race; the theory is embraced by many followers, often with joy; after a few generations, the code of conduct is transformed into dogma, enforced with violence, the engine of the creed driven by fanatics. The argument soon is transformed from "How should we live?" to "How should *you* die?" In the endless conflict over belief, literally millions have died.

14 But for all the wearying failures, it is safe to say that most of what we think of when we use the word *civilization* has come from an ethical approach to life. I don't mean that Beethoven or Michelangelo were by definition good men or that Jane Austen or Virginia Woolf were candidates for sainthood. Artists are as capable of cruelty, stupidity, and treachery as many other human beings. But in their separate ways (and with the usual exceptions), the superior men and women of an epoch always transcend their own time by adhering to at least one basic principle: They do the very best work of which they are capable. They have no responsibility to preach or to judge, but by the example of their work, they move society out of its entropy. In our time, dominated as it is by every manner of charlatan, hustler, and faker, I think doing good work is a moral choice.

15 Indeed, at the core of all good work is a sense of right and wrong, a feeling of belonging in a society and endorsing its ethical values or standing up in a lonely way to rebel against them. In the end, when fad and fashion have shifted and passed, when journalism has become the raw material for history, the ethics of an era determine its value.

16 Most of us do not require a detailed analysis of ethics or an agonized history of its triumphs and failures to understand what the word means. Most of us know. And common sense is our great instructor. We admire people who are brave, generous, honorable, faithful, just, temperate, truthful, and loving. In short, we admire those who behave the *right* way more often than the *wrong* way; that is, we are more comfortable with people who behave ethically. Most human beings in my experience make distinctions this way, without blind adherence to orthodox dogma.

17 We simply don't need the advice of archbishops or sages to know that we are better off shunning the company of cowards, misers, cheats, bullies, drunks, liars, and haters. We say of such people that they are Bad News. They

can almost never be our friends, because the trust and candor at the heart of friendship are beyond them. And in spite of the frequency of certain fatal attractions, most of us try not to live with them or marry them.

Again, common sense is the basic guide. Obviously, we can live more easily with a human being who tells the truth than one whose life is a collage of fictions, large and small. Obviously, nobody enjoys life with a drunk or a junkie, except other drunks and junkies. Obviously, we don't easily love or admire ill-tempered human beings, bullies, men or women who are mean to the core or who run at the first sign of trouble. We can pity such people. We can offer them help. We can understand them. Only saints can love them, and I have never met a saint. The abstract definitions of the philosophy tracts are useful to those who are interested in refining the meaning of human life. But we don't really need them. We *know* what we mean when we say that someone is a "good" man or a "good" woman. 18

We admire "good" human beings precisely because we know how difficult it is to behave decently. It is easier to be a coward than to be brave. It is easier to take shortcuts than to put in the long hard hours that result in the making of something of value. It is easier to buy insider information to make a quick score on a sure thing than it is to risk everything on an educated gamble. It is easier to bully the weak than to offer a helping hand. It is easier to drown yourself in whining self-pity, blaming the world for its indifference, than to face your personal follies and weaknesses with lucidity and detachment. Living a full, decent life is a difficult proposition, and somehow, many Americans have become convinced that life should be easy. It is not. 19

It is important here to state clearly that not a single human being in my experience has lived a flawless life. I certainly haven't. The people I love and admire have not. But for the "good" people I know, acts of moral stupidity and blindness are aberrations. These men and women are good more often than they are bad; most of the time, they follow the rules. Heroes are all good or all bad only in the false world of melodrama; even Hitler, the archvillain of the twentieth century, was said to love dogs and children. But if you do good things often enough, you are a good person; if you are consistently corrupt or evil, faithless or cowardly, you get the reputation you deserve. 20

Here's another turning point, from definition per se to applications—what we can and can't do, based on the way things are.

That is why we can't stand in haughty judgment of Gary Hart, Ivan Boesky, Dennis Levine, and the other players of the Awful Eighties without also facing ourselves. All of these people have done good things; their lives are not yet complete, and we don't know what they will do in the future. Thousands have done far worse. For the moment, they stand only as public symbols of a broader private malaise. 21

Also, in our personal lives, we often can't take the scrutiny we inflict on those who live more publicly. In a healthy society, an ethical code can't be limited to the world of business or politics. It is part of everyday life or it is nothing. Every marriage, for example, is based on a simple *ethical* contract made between a man and a woman. Such a union can bring immense joy to its partners but not without effort and kindness and creativity of the most 22 fundamental kind. But we have all learned that in the modern world, it is easier to break a vow than to adhere to one. Every marriage has its hazards, its surrenders of self, its compromises and irritations. The decent man or woman welcomes these challenges.

23 But it's unlikely that any marriage can thrive if its partners don't have an ethical understanding, that is, a fundamental agreement about what is right and what is wrong. Most of those "open" marriages of the 1960s turned out to be, as far as I can tell, disastrous experiments, pathetic attempts to overthrow in one generation the accumulated traditions and understandings of centuries. They reduced marriage to an arrangement about food and shelter; they attacked the "exclusivity" of the institution; they elevated selfishness to a virtue. A few of my friends were involved in such unions; when they ended, they reported that by sleeping with everyone, they were sleeping with no one; jealousy could only be eased by blunting feeling to the point of numbness; they discovered that there was as much pathos in having everything as in having nothing.

24 The problem is *not* promiscuity. In my experience, men and women who have had wide sexual experience before marriage make the best husbands and wives. But some husbands do take mistresses; wives take lovers. The moral problem revolves around the nature of the contract. In many marriages, alas, sexual desire eventually wanes while love goes on, even deepens. It was much easier to promise lifelong sexual fidelity to a partner when human beings usually died at forty; today, in the United States, we live into our late seventies and beyond. If the partners can handle limited extramarital arrangements with candor, the marriage usually survives; if they require a tissue of lies and deceptions, it withers and dies. But marriage combined with full-out promiscuity does not seem possible. And the moral problem of infidelity is deepened in the age of AIDS; no husband or wife has the right to put a partner at such terrible risk for the pleasure of the moment.

25 It is probably no accident that the ethical malaise of the eighties has followed the personal confusions of the past several decades. If a man feels no need to be true to his own wife, why should he be true to the rules of an abstraction like society?

26 The ethical problem in the United States is made more complicated by the tenets of our own popular culture. Americans have often made heroes of Western outlaws, big-city gangsters, and a variety of killers, bad boys, and picaresque rogues. I'm sure that more Americans have admired Jesse James than Henry James. Hollywood has made more movies about Al Capone than about Albert Einstein. Our Constitution promises liberty; some confuse this with license. We extol the virtues of the individual. This often degenerates into a self-absorbed philosophy that boils down to "Pull up the gangplank, I'm aboard."

27 At the same time, most Americans have learned to despise hypocrisy. When we see in our leaders a drastic difference between what is said and what is done, we often turn upon them. Europeans often sneer at this as an

example of American character, probably because we are a nation that had a written constitution before we had a history; we are constantly measuring the words of that extraordinary contract against the deeds of those we elect to enforce it. Citizens from countries with longer histories and deeper cynicism are frequently amused by such moral seriousness. Recent United States history helps explain the moral swamp of the 1980s, although it sometimes baffles those foreigners. Frenchmen were astounded when Americans drove Richard Nixon from office for violating the contract; Italians were appalled; the British gasped. But for most Americans, the hypocrisy of Nixon had finally become too clear. The system worked for a few hours and then was sullied when Nixon was granted the sort of pardon that would never be granted to an ordinary citizen. It is no accident that Nixon's tarnished reputation began a slow revival in the Awful Eighties.

We can never accurately measure the effect of the moral dramas of the American sixties and early seventies upon the ethos of the eighties. But surely they must have had some effect. A nation cannot go through such turbulence without an aftermath of *some* kind. For most Americans, Vietnam started out as a war and was transformed into a moral struggle. Vietnam's bastard son, Watergate, was a moral problem from the beginning. Both played into a context that included a revolt of the young against all authority. Once again, this was basically a battle over ethical standards. If leaders abused their authority by waging an immoral war or supporting the institutions of racism, then *all* authority must be suspect. 28

So there was a long sustained assault on the authority of the university, the institution of marriage, the taboos about sex and drugs and dirty words. In a way, rock and roll was part of the campaign; it attacked the sentimental pieties that were perceived as a mask for society's sexual hypocrisy, and the lies at the core of mindless patriotism. It was no accident that rock and rollers adopted the outlaw style while proclaiming their own idealistic purity or that they also championed an all-out hedonism. The young citizens of Woodstock nation donned the uniforms of rebellion, and for a while, as the civil-rights struggle turned into violent revolt and the white young formed their guitar armies, the republic itself seemed to totter. It didn't. The war ended. The cities cooled down. Nixon departed. The young grew older. And Ronald Reagan came to power on a broad promise to lead a counterrevolution. 29

That brought us to where we are today. It is a cliché to say that the sixties hippie, with his slogans about love and revolution, was to become the insider trader of the eighties. But clichés always contain a certain amount of truth. In the Reagan Era, when greed was praised as an engine of society, many middle-aged Americans were embarrassed by the idealism of their younger selves. They entered the time of *The Big Chill*.[9] Some realized how spoiled they had been, talking of revolution while waiting for an allowance from Dad. Others were chastened by events in Vietnam and Cambodia and Poland. They were not the first human beings to turn from the chaos of the world to tend private gardens. 30

31 As the Reagan Era went on, however, we noticed something peculiar. The children of the 1960s had toppled many of the old moral assumptions. But no new ones had replaced them. For all the mumbo jumbo of New Age philosophies, a *moral* philosophy never did emerge. To be sure, there was no going back in some areas; feminist gains could not be repealed nor could the enormous triumphs in civil rights. But Reagan's people, most of whom had been formed by the 1950s, merely called for a return to the old hypocrisy. They succeeded for a long time until, in the Iran-Contra mess, that hypocrisy caught up to them. And increasingly, citizens began to notice what was termed the Sleaze Factor.[10]

32 Now we are moving into the last decade of a brutal century, and ethical questions are becoming even more complicated. What are the ethical implications of genetic engineering? What are the ethical consequences of increasing dependence upon the computer and thinking machines? What is good for the planet's environment and the ecology of our own nation? What are the rules for AIDS victims? Why are so many educated people going to prison? Why are scientists faking data to propel their own careers? Why do so many lawyers break the law? What is to become of the fractured American family? What is *right?* What, after all, is *wrong?*

33 There are no easy answers to any of those questions, but there are signs everywhere that many Americans are giving them serious thought. More and more universities are insisting that courses in ethics become mandatory for all students. Some are exploring the Japanese system of teaching moral philosophy from grade school. This might fill a hole in the American education structure caused by the Constitutional separation of church and state. Newspapers increasingly feature op-ed pieces that discuss ethical issues with the intensity usually reserved for military affairs.

34 Although experience has taught me to be skeptical about all abstractions, I am also enough of an optimist to believe that human beings generally learn from their mistakes. As we enter the 1990s, I would like to believe that as individuals and as a people, we will step back and try to understand the dreadful story of the century. That is, we will talk about what is good and what is bad. And from that great sustained discussion, we will evolve a shared public philosophy of conduct that honors decency, justice, tolerance, and candor. And we will practice it in our private lives with the same rigor that we will demand from our public men and women. We can call this ethics or we can call it common sense. But such a code of conduct must replace the present narcissistic anarchy. If it doesn't, then all of us—the nation and the human race—are almost certainly doomed.

As students are finishing this essay, ask them whether they think the ethics of the 1990s are looking any different from those of the 1980s. If so, how? If not, why not?

Notes to the Text

1. *Ivan Boesky:* Wall Street trader convicted of inside trading in a highly publicized case. Dennis Levine, mentioned later, gave testimony in return for a lighter penalty.

2. *Oliver North:* a member of President Ronald Reagan's White House staff who was found chiefly responsible in what came to be called the Iran-Contra scandal, a complicated, illegal, covert operation that supplied arms to terrorists. President Reagan claimed no knowledge of the operation.
3. *Pavarotti:* Luciano Pavarotti, a famous opera tenor.
4. *Gary Hart:* a onetime senator from Colorado who was a strong contender for the 1988 Democratic nomination for president until his affair with the model Donna Rice (mentioned below) was discovered and publicized.
5. *Jimmy Swaggart:* a popular television evangelist who confessed to having liaisons with a prostitute, thereafter suffering a decline, but not total loss, of popularity.
6. *Jackie Mason:* a stand-up comedian whose one-man show, *The World According to Me,* was a great Broadway success in the 1980s, revitalizing his career.
7. *The Bakkers:* television evangelists Jim Bakker and his wife, Tammy, whose prosperous broadcast and theme-park operations suffered a severe setback when a former secretary in their employ, Jessica Hahn (mentioned below), accused Jim Bakker and one of his aides of forcing her to have sexual relations with them in a Florida motel.
8. *Fawn Hall:* the attractive secretary to Oliver North who became well known during her brief testimony at the public hearings on the Iran-Contra scandal.
9. *The Big Chill:* a popular film of the 1980s that portrays a group of adult friends reunited several years after their highly idealistic college days. Their lives have become compromised and comfortable despite their former convictions against such compromise and comfort.
10. *Sleaze Factor:* a phrase used in many media sources to refer to the presence of corruption (both actual and merely suspected) in public institutions during the 1980s.

POSTREADING WORKSHEET

Now that you have read the piece by Hamill, write your responses to the following questions:

1. Did Hamill convince you that a serious erosion of ethics in this country got under way in the 1980s?
2. Did anything in Hamill's article affect the definitions you earlier wrote of *ethics, conscience, integrity,* or *morality?* If so, what? And why?
3. In his seventh paragraph, Hamill lists a wide range of corrupt practices that he sees as common and that many people would consider minor, such as

cheating on income taxes, fixing parking tickets, and bribing inspectors. Do you consider any of these practices minor? excusable? Why or why not?

4. Hamill's article appeared near the end of the 1980s. Do you think that, so far, the 1990s have been a better decade in terms of ethics?

Questions for Writing and Discussion

Prepare short written answers to each of these questions. Be prepared to hand them in and/or discuss them in class, as your teacher directs.

1. Hamill's is a carefully organized essay, beginning with a broad, detailed, and partially entertaining indictment of modern American corruptions and then pivoting into a more serious, general indictment of human ethical behavior now and in the past. Which is the first "pivot" paragraph?
2. Later, Hamill pivots again, this time moving to a more personal, individual focus, discussing how we as individuals behave and can examine our behavior. Which is this second "pivot" paragraph? This long essay in fact has several pivots, or transitions, as Hamill develops his argument, which ultimately turns on his elaborated definitions of the concepts of right, wrong, and ethics. Can you locate these additional pivots? If you were plotting a summary of the essay, how would you describe its overall structure and its individual sections between pivots?
3. Hamill tries to define the notion of good with a series of examples drawn from common sense. How effective is his definition technique here? How does he circle back to common sense as a kind of synonym for ethics?
4. Hamill's indictment of the sad state of ethics in our world is almost overwhelming, yet he argues that individual change can lead to collective change and warns that if we do not "talk about what is good and what is bad" then we and our world are "almost certainly doomed" (¶ 34). How persuasive is his argument?
5. How do these uses of figurative, descriptive language enhance the effectiveness of what Hamill says?

   a. "pirouetting" (¶ 1)
   b. "the prince of insider trading" (¶ 1)
   c. "singing to the prosecutors with the sincerity of a Pavarotti" (¶ 1)
   d. "Within weeks she was bobbing her nose and lifting her boobs and applying for permanent citizenship in the sad nation of celebrity." (¶ 4)
   e. "Greetings from Bimbodelphia." (¶ 4)
   f. "as if they were bureaucrats in a banana republic" (¶ 7)
   g. "And all attempts at constructing utopia on this poor earth have led either to the pyre or the gulag." (¶ 13)
   h. "violence, the engine of the creed driven by fanatics" (¶ 13)

   What other examples of figurative, descriptive language can you find?

You might ask students to compare the presence of figurative language in this piece with its relative absence in "Antipsychotic Drugs" in the next chapter (18).

6. Hamill makes frequent use of allusion, a reference to a historical person, event, or item that carries with it associated meanings; for instance, "Woodstock nation" (¶ 29) refers to the Woodstock music festival of August 1969, when thousands of young people gathered in a pasture in upstate New York to hear several days of music. Despite the overwhelming crowds, the presence of abundant drugs and alcohol, and the primitive conditions, no serious incident occurred. Other such uses are Hamill's references to Watergate (¶ 28), *The Big Chill* (¶ 30), Al Capone (¶ 26), Ernest Hemingway (¶ 9), Buddha (¶ 11), and Albert Camus (¶ 11). Track these allusions. Who or what is involved? How do they add to Hamill's essay?
7. What do the following words mean—*smarmy, doges* (¶ 1), *ribald, Mammon* (¶ 3), *quintessential, tabloids, icon* (¶ 4), *flack, hoosegow, malfeasance, squalor* (¶ 5), *permeates* (¶ 8), *cursory* (¶ 11), *karma* (¶ 12), *pyre, gulag* (¶ 13), *entropy, charlatan* (¶ 14), *orthodox, dogma* (¶ 16), *candor* (¶ 17), *malaise* (¶ 21), *chastened* (¶ 30), *narcissistic* (¶ 34)?

KEY POINTS TO REMEMBER: Writing Definitions

Here are some points to remember when writing definitions.

- The simplest definitions are of concrete things.
- The hardest definitions are of abstract things.
- Definitions can be used for all purposes in writing.
- Connotations of words can alter your meaning.

Let's examine each of these points a bit more closely.

The Simplest Definitions Are of Concrete Things

The essence of these concrete things can be defined by classification and description of form and/or function. Recall our definition earlier of a screwdriver:

> A screwdriver is a hand tool that fits the head of a screw and is then turned clockwise to tighten the screw securely.

The classification clarifies that a screwdriver is a hand tool—an instrument for performing some mechanical task (tool) that is also small enough to be carried and used with the hands. Then the definition proceeds by describing a screwdriver's function. We could easily describe its form as well before describing its function:

> It has a relatively short shaft of varying lengths, with a handle on one end and a flattened and beveled shaft end. It is this flattened and beveled end which fits the head of a screw.

Such definitions are highly useful, and this kind of defining is most common to technical and legal writing.

What must be avoided in this and all other kinds of defining is the *circular definition*—a definition in which the term being defined appears in the definition, therefore defining nothing clearly; the attempt to define in this case leads readers in a "circle," bringing them back to where they started, with the original term still undefined:

A screwdriver is a driver of screws.

Without the descriptions of classification, form, and function, the term means little or nothing.

Remember that defining involves showing understanding of something in a fundamental way—giving its essence, its nature. When you must write precise definitions of terms, always ask yourself, "What is the *essence* of the term?" When your subject is something concrete, like a screwdriver, classify it and describe its form and function. When it is something abstract but still precise, like a legal or historical term (*felony, laissez-faire*), you'll need to get at the essence by analogy, that is, by providing an example that implicitly or explicitly involves a comparison:

At this point, it's traditional to have your students practice defining. Be sure not to overdo it—we're interested in the ability to define as part of the things a writer needs to be able to do in the context of larger writing tasks, and we're skeptical about the usefulness of too many raw-definition exercises in that regard.

felony: a serious crime, such as murder, grand theft, or kidnapping, that carries a serious penalty.

The comparison implicit in the above definition is to crime that is not considered so serious—crime usually called a misdemeanor—such as a traffic violation or petty theft. A circular and therefore nearly useless definition of *felony* would be "a crime committed by a felon."

The Hardest Definitions Are of Abstract Things

These definitions are the most challenging and meaningful because their essence is elusive and must be suggested by relevant examples or illustrations, where the definition is made by analogy. Abstractions can be categorized—for example, *love* is an emotion—but in such cases the larger category, emotion, is also abstract. Likewise, functional descriptions of abstractions are generally inadequate, because the abstractions can't be said to have a specific function, a physical or definite activity. Such definitions thus usually require an example, an illustration, or a listing of similar words. The noun *love,* for example, is defined as follows in an old dictionary we have near our desk:

love: **1 a.**: affection based on admiration or benevolence **b.**: an assurance of love **2 a.**: warm attachment, enthusiasm or devotion [as in love of the sea] **b.**: the object of such attachment or devotion **3 a.**: unselfish concern that freely accepts another in loyalty and seeks his good: (1): the fatherly concern of God for man (2): brotherly concern for others **b.**: man's adoration of God **4 a**: the attraction based on sexual desire : the affection and tenderness felt by lovers **b**: a god or personification of love **c**: an amorous episode : love affair **d**: the sexual embrace : copulation **5**: a beloved person : darling **6**: a score of zero in tennis

(*Webster's Seventh New Collegiate Dictionary*, Springfield, Massachusetts: G. & C. Merriam Company, 1967, 501.)

Our point here is not to show the obvious complexity of the noun (we won't even bother showing you the listings after the verb usage); rather, it is to show how even professional definers of words must use illustrations and examples, often of *other* abstractions, when they define abstractions.

Their difficult nature makes defining abstractions challenging. Yet we have seen how in, for example, Pete Hamill's essay "Ethics in the 80's" the attempt to define, to clarify, to understand important abstractions in our lives can make for provocative, exciting, informative, and persuasive writing. Paul Theroux reminds us how difficult it truly is to understand—and in many cases to accept—our notions about the meaning of *masculine* and *feminine.* Richard Zoglin makes us aware that *sleaze* is much easier for individuals to recognize than to define. Randi Londer assumes we all have a pretty good idea of what *stress* means, and offers us both a test to determine how serious our stress may be and advice on how to cope with the stress we have. Susan Sheehy defines through careful description just what multiple sclerosis is and what it means to one MS patient and her family.

All these writers work to convey the *essence* of their meanings, and that is what any good writing of definition does.

Definitions Can Be Used for All Purposes in Writing

Definitions can express, persuade, analyze, or inform. Although there is always overlap (for example, Hamill analyzes almost as much as he persuades), it is clear from our readings here that, as always, the *reasons* for writing are served by the various *kinds* of writing—not the other way around:

Theroux writes primarily to *express.*

Zoglin writes primarily to *inform.*

Londer writes primarily to *inform.*

Sheehy writes primarily to *inform.*

Hamill writes primarily to *persuade.*

Kilpatrick (later in this section) writes primarily to *analyze.*

Connotations of Words Can Alter Your Meaning

In 1905, Willa Cather published a short story, "Paul's Case," about a young man who is ill-suited to his life of near-poverty and who dreams of finer things. Cather presents Paul as frail and as obsessed with art, music, and the airs of the rich and irresponsible. At a couple of points Cather uses the word *gay* to describe Paul's perceptions, and at another point she describes him as burning "like a faggot in a teapot." In 1905, the use of *gay* to mean or suggest homosexuality was not widespread; neither was *faggot* commonly recognized as a slang term for a homosexual male. Whereas *faggot* meant, strictly, a stick of firewood, *gay*'s primary definition was accomplished through synonyms: happy, high-spirited, of good cheer. It is almost certain that Cather did not mean to characterize Paul as openly homosexual. Yet many students today, reading this story, think otherwise because of the present-day connotations of *gay* and *faggot.* We are not saying that Cather didn't perhaps know the homosexual connotations of *gay.* But we *are* saying there's a good chance that back in 1905 Cather didn't intend to explain "Paul's Case" as complicated by homosexuality. Our point is that connotations—and therefore denotations—change over time, and any writer (or reader) must therefore be careful in their use. Still, no use of language is connotation-free. Nor *should* it be. Poets, playwrights, people in love, baseball announcers—all of us depend on the powers of connotation to help our words color our lives. The point in *your* writing is to be aware of the connotations involved.

A final caution about definition before we turn to our worksheet. In English are many words that sound but are not spelled alike and that have significantly different meanings. Such words we call *homophones.* The following short essay, by James Kilpatrick, reminds us of how tricky it can be to keep such words straight.

Homophones Haunt Careless Writers

JAMES KILPATRICK

James Kilpatrick is a reporter, editor, and columnist. His books include The Sovereign States, The Smut Peddlers, *and (with Eugene J. McCarthy)* A Political Bestiary.

1 No gremlins in English prose composition are more mischievous, or more treacherous, than the sound-alike words known as homophones. They cause incessant grief.

2 There was the resort hotel in Sedona, Ariz., that ran an advertisement aimed at prospective guests: "Skip the usual hare-raising routine!" The ad recalled a feature story several years ago in the Terre Haute (Ind.) *Tribune-Star,* in which a leading citizen (he had twice been nominated for the "Noble Prize") was quoted on downtown revitalization. His committee had participated in remodeling the Deming Center, "and we came within a hare's breath of doing the same thing with the Terre Haute House." A hare-raising business might be a nice backyard enterprise, assuming one could ignore the hares' breath, but come now! Let us try hair-raising and hair's breadth.

Note how Kilpatrick uses examples as the primary means of accomplishing his definition.

3 In March the Rochester (N.Y.) *Democrat and Chronicle* reported the difficulties encountered by a chamber music group in getting some music from England. The music finally was acquired, but only "after much adieu

with publishers." Perhaps the ensemble could try the madrigal that begins, "Ado, ado, kind friends, ado, yes, ado."

A couple of years ago the *Miami Herald* reported the trial of former Labor Secretary Raymond Donovan. After a nine-month trial, the jury deliberated only nine hours before returning a verdict of acquittal. The judge complimented the jurors and offered to exempt them from jury duty for the next four years. His offer was greeted with cries of "Here, here!" What, what? 4

We had to look at this twice, too; it should be "Hear, hear."

One Sunday in April, the *Seattle Times* carried a classified ad for old French furniture, including one item that might be hard to sell. This was a "guilt mirror." At about the same time the Owensboro (Ky.) *Messenger-Inquirer* carried an ad for "guilt frames." Well, as the Donovan jury demonstrated, gilt is sometimes hard to find. 5

The foregoing homophones are oddballs. It might be more useful, if less fun, to comment on the reliable gremlins that turn up all the time. At the head of the list is affect/effect. In Roanoke, Va., a schoolteacher was cited for having a "positive affect" on community relations. In New York in late May, George Steinbrenner said the Yankees are so bad that the team "is effecting his digestive system." In the comic strip "Archie," a teacher asked her pupils how modern technology had "effected" their lives. And so on. 6

Let us get straight on these tormentors. To affect something is to influence it; to effect something is to bring it about. The Yankees were affecting Steinbrenner's digestive system, which perhaps was only titsy for tatsy, and technology was affecting students' lives. Only in psychiatry is "affect" a noun. The teacher had a positive effect. 7

Grisly/grizzly. It's difficult to understand how this pair could cause such trouble, but behold: Mike Royko of the *Chicago Tribune* took a cold look in June at the "grizzly scenes" in Tienanmen Square. A sportswriter for the Spartanburg (S.C.) *Herald-Journal* spared his readers the "grizzly details" of a loss. In a book catalog, a publisher advertised a "grizzly collection" of fairy tales by Grimm. It's grisly, dears. Grisly! *The Barnhart Dictionary of Etymology* traces it to the Old English *grislic,* meaning *horrible,* with companion roots in Dutch and German. A grizzly nightmare would be hard to bear. 8

Almost every week brings a citation of someone "pouring" over books or records; the word is "poring." Many writers have trouble with heal and heel. Contestants tow a line instead of toe it. Bells are peeled and potatoes are pealed, which is just exactly backward. And the frustrating thing is that word-processing software won't detect the little devils. 9

Questions for Writing and Discussion

Prepare short written answers to each of these questions. Be prepared to hand them in and/or discuss them in class, as your teacher directs.

1. Although Kilpatrick doesn't define a single word in this essay, he makes it

clear he knows what the homophones he discusses mean. How does he do that?

2. Most people don't think these homophones are all that troublesome. That makes Kilpatrick's assertion that they are "gremlins" (¶ 1) seem appropriate. Yet elsewhere he uses overstatement to indicate how widespread the problem truly is. One example is his remark that homophones are "treacherous" and "cause incessant grief" (¶ 1). Some notion of their prevalence is hinted at in the article when he indirectly points out the difference between *hare/hair, breath/breadth, adieu/ado,* and other pesky soundalikes. What other sound-alikes do you find in the essay?
3. A *pun* is a linguistic trick, a use of a word or phrase in an unexpected way—for example, Kilpatrick's reference to a "Noble" (instead of Nobel) prize (¶ 2), and his remark that "a grizzly nightmare would be hard to bear" (¶ 8). What other puns or verbal tricks can you find?
4. What do the following words mean—*madrigal, adieu* (¶ 3), *poring, pealed* (¶ 9)?

✓✓✓ WORKSHEET: Writing Definitions

First it is vital to invent, to brainstorm, your topic. How could you express the essence of the subject?

Is What You Are Defining Abstract or Concrete?

One way to begin is with a fundamental question: is what you are defining *abstract* or *concrete?* That is, is it an idea or concept, like anger or laissez-faire, or is it an object or other tangible thing, like a computer or a bicycle? If it is concrete, then you are likely to be successful by considering its physical features and how it functions:

- What size is it?
- What is its shape, weight, length, width, and so on?
- What other distinguishing physical features does it have?
- How does it work?
- What does it do, or what do *you* do to make it work?

You may want to give your students the option of including a picture as well.

If what you are defining is abstract, then you are more likely to be successful by considering *examples*—illustrations, similes, metaphors, or anything else that helps, by explicit or implicit comparison, to convey the essence of what you're defining:

- What are some examples of what you are defining?
- What is the subject of your definition *like?*

- What does it do, or how does it work? (For example, how is the principle of eminent domain applied in our culture?

Invention Processes and Definition

As always when you brainstorm, write down what you're thinking—try to get your thoughts in written words, however rough, that you can bring to bear later. Once you've jotted down your brainstormed ideas, *organize* them into what seems to be the most logical and coherent sequence. If doing so helps, make an outline. Then draft.

When you have a readable first draft, proceed through the rest of the process as you normally would, being careful to get feedback and suggestions from other readers before you revise and polish. Remember, even getting a graded paper back from your teacher isn't necessarily the end of that piece of writing: you may be able to revise it further, either for a higher grade or for eventual use in another context. It is arbitrary to say that any writing is "finished" before it is published—and even then, authors sometimes revise previously published material for subsequent editions.

SAMPLE WRITING ASSIGNMENT AND CASE-STUDY CLOSE-UP

Mohammad Kaffir was assigned a definition paper in his English class. Though it could be on any subject of interest to him, it had to define something abstract, something challenging, and he was permitted to use one or more sources for information (although this was not a regular research-paper assignment). As a communications major hoping to break into television as a weather forecaster, Mohammad decided to write about hurricanes, following a conversation in his dormitory, when Mohammad had told his roommate that he wanted to be a weather forecaster. "I'll let people know the things about the weather they really need to know," said Mohammad, "like when a hurricane is coming."

"Aw, you won't even know what a hurricane is," kidded his roommate. "You'll know more about hairstyles and products to make your teeth shine."

"That's not so!" Mohammad protested. "I'm really going to know about my job and not be just another pretty face." The banter had continued in that vein, but Mohammad realized that he had set a worthwhile challenge for himself: he really did want to know about his work. He wanted to be a knowledgeable weather reporter—not just someone with flawless hair and flashing teeth who reads weather information from a TelePrompTer. Thus, when the writing assignment came up he was reminded of his roommate's remark. He knew that a hurricane is a big storm, with powerful winds, rains, and great destructive capability, yet he didn't *really* know what a hurricane is—what causes it, what makes it different from other storms, and so on. He decided to define a hurricane.

One of the things we want to show here is how a good topic comes about.

Mohammad began by going to the library, where he found a book called *1001 Questions Answered about the Weather,* by Frank H. Forrester. Intrigued by the book's title, Mohammad located his questions about hurricanes and found what he considered enough information. Following is a second draft that he brought to class for a draft workshop.

What Is a Hurricane?

Mohammad Kaffir, college writing student

1 If you lived in the Pacific Ocean area and a hurricane approached, you would say that you had to prepare for a typhoon. In other parts of the world, with the same kind of storm approaching, you might say, depending on just where you were, that you had to prepare for a baguio, a cordonzos, a cyclone, or a willy-willy. All are the same kind of storm--begun in the tropical parts of an ocean as a "depression," with a drop in barometric pressure, and grown to a large circle covering many square miles. The circle turns counterclockwise around a calm inner "eye" that is formed by the centrifugal force of the winds, which suck ocean water up into the clouds of the storm, thus "feeding" the storm for more rain and yet more wind. At any given point in the outer part of the circle, the wind seems to be blowing straight, in one direction. But actually it is blowing in a circular pattern, causing rain, lightning, and, if the storm has come ashore, considerable damage.

2 Hurricanes come in different sizes and with different levels of wind and rain intensity. Residents in the United States are especially at risk on the Atlantic and Gulf of Mexico coasts, where hurricanes formed in the tropical Atlantic often find their way to shore. Hurricane landfall brings heavy rain and high winds, which make beach areas dangerous because of wind damage and a high wave, called the storm surge, that engulfs the area and causes immediate flooding. Later the rainfall adds to the flooding, and so a considerable toll is therefore taken on buildings and other beachfront construction.

3 The storm then moves inland and gradually loses strength as it "blows out" its wind power and drops its rain. It creates atmospheric conditions that can cause tornadoes as it moves over land, and sometimes leaves a trail of trouble hundreds of miles inland. Whether you are in the path of a hurricane (simply what this kind of storm is

called when it comes from the Atlantic Ocean) or a typhoon (the preferred Pacific Ocean term), or any of the other colorful names for this kind of storm, you would be wise to tie things down and take a holiday somewhere inland.

Source

Frank H. Forrester. 1001 Questions Answered about the Weather. New York: Dodd, 1957.

Ask students whether they agree with Paula and/ or Amy's observations.

In class, Mohammad heard several criticisms and suggestions from classmates Paula and Amy, whose remarks are digested here for illustrative purposes:

Paula. Paula liked Mohammad's general definitions and explanations, especially that hurricanes have different names in different parts of the world. But she felt Mohammad needed more specific information about the characteristics of hurricanes. For example, she pointed out that some tropical storms are called tropical depressions and are not called hurricanes until reaching a certain size. What criteria, Paula wondered, determine when a storm is classed as a hurricane? And what kinds of precautions should be taken?

Amy. Amy echoed Paula's sentiments and added a few questions of her own. She wanted to know, for instance, whether hurricanes were more likely to occur at certain times of the year than at others, for she had heard the phrase "hurricane season" before. And what does a drop in barometric pressure really mean, she wondered. An example or two—information about actual hurricanes—would, she felt, be a good idea. (Mohammad knew this suggestion would entail finding and using more sources, but he decided Amy was right.)

Mohammad went back to work. At the library he found more source material and made new notes. He then revised his paper to address the concerns voiced by Paula and Amy. Here is the result:

What Is a Hurricane?

A hurricane is a storm, a destructive force of nature that generally occurs between the months of June and November in the Atlantic Coast and Gulf of Mexico areas. Called by such other names as typhoon, willy-willy, baguio, cyclone, and cardonzos in other parts of the world, all hurricanes begin in the tropical ocean as low-level disturbances that are characterized by a drop in barometric pressure and a counterclockwise wind motion that begins to pump condensed heated moisture and seawater centrifugally. The wind motion tends to increase, causing the 1 tropical depression to "fan out" over a wider sea area, constantly growing until, once winds hit 74 miles per hour or higher, the "tropical depression" is reclassified as a hurricane.

2 Generally speaking, hurricanes have these characteristics in common:

1. They usually develop between June and November, as noted.
2. They carry powerful winds of at least 74 miles per hour (often much higher), moving counterclockwise around the calm center, or "eye," of the hurricane.
3. Barometric pressure within the hurricane drops almost constantly until it reaches its lowest point in the calm "eye."
4. Hurricanes travel at about 12 miles per hour.
5. They have an average life of about 9.5 days.
6. Their movements are not easily predicted; they don't move in straight lines, for example.
7. They're usually shaped like a circle, with one tail extending from the top, and another spiraling down to the bottom, the top tail pointing northeast and the bottom pointing southwest.

3 The word hurricane comes from Hunraken, which is the Carib Indians' name for their god of stormy weather. Given the powerful destructive capability of hurricanes, it is not surprising that the Indians named it after one of their most potent gods.

4 In modern times, hurricanes can be monitored quite closely from the time of their inception in tropical waters to their last gasps hundreds of miles after landfall. This monitoring is done by the U.S. Weather Service, which names each hurricane each year shortly after it forms, and then carefully tracks its movements, using reconnaissance flights in and around the storm. (The names are chosen alphabetically each season, alternating male and female names--Alan, Betty, Carl, Denise, and so on.) The time of most critical interest is when the hurricane is nearing full force and moving toward land. Wind force, amounts of rain, and possible landfall times and places can be predicted--though not with high accuracy, because of the storm's ability to shift directions and vary its own acceleration.

One thing is certain: landfall can be deadly. First there's the wind, bringing a wall of water known as the storm surge that then smacks down much of what lies in its path. Wind rips debris loose and sends it hurtling through the air with lethal velocity. Flooding is instant and massive, abetted by the torrential rains of 6 to 12 inches that quickly follow the storm surge. Atmospheric conditions become ideal for the formation of numerous tornadoes, enormously destructive and intense local windstorms that also spin counterclockwise. Areas that experience the "eye" passing overhead are doubly troubled, for the first surge is followed by the brief calm of the eye, and then is followed by a second surge, in which the wind is blowing in an opposite direction--but just as hard as the first time. 5

In the past thirty or so years, the United States has experienced many hurricanes, but one in particular was especially destructive. In August 1969, Hurricane Camille began as a tropical wave off the west coast of Africa and moved west toward the Gulf of Mexico, where it intensified. By its landfall near Bay St. Louis, Mississippi, near midnight of August 17, 1969, a reconnaissance flight recorded its winds at about 200 miles per hour. Its eye had a diameter of 12 miles, and its storm surge at Pass Christian, Mississippi, was measured at 22.6 feet above sea level. Destruction was massive, and 262 deaths were eventually the result. Gulf Coast residents will long remember Camille. 6

Certain precautions should be taken when a hurricane threatens landfall near you: 7

1. Houses and other buildings should have storm shutters, or, at least, windows on windward sides should be boarded up.
2. Lay in a generous supply of safe drinking water, canned food, and other necessities, including a first-aid kit.
3. Have plenty of emergency-lighting devices: lanterns, flashlights (and batteries), candles, and so on.
4. Store all yard furniture, trash cans--anything loose--in a building to keep the wind from turning such items into deadly projectiles.
5. A battery-operated radio is essential.
6. Stay inside.

7. If officials predict that the storm will be especially powerful and recommend evacuation, evacuate!

Hurricanes are potential disasters the moment they form. Always try to do what you can to minimize that potential's chance to affect your home or your life.

Works Consulted

Frank H. Forrester. 1001 Questions Answered about the Weather. New York: Dodd, 1957.

James A. Ruffner. The Weather Almanac. Detroit: Gale, 1974.

United States. Army Mobile Engineer District. Hurricane Camille, 17-18 August 1969, After-Action Report. Mobile: U.S. Army Engineering District, 1969.

You might want to inform your students that such a listing is considered an "acknowledgment of general indebtedness."

WRITING ASSIGNMENTS

1. Have another look at Paul Theroux's "Being a Man" selection. Do you agree, disagree, or partly agree with Theroux? Write your own personalized definition of masculinity or femininity.
2. There are always two broad kinds of definitions: (a) those which are collectively recognized in the culture—such as dictionary definitions—and (b) those which are peculiar to us, linked to our own experience with whatever it is we are defining. Unless we have no personal experience with the particular term, both kinds of definition apply in every case. The same is true of connotations. For example, the word *grandfather* has collective connotations of someone kindly, older, gentle, loving, patient, and so forth. But *grandfather* also has particular personal connotations for each of us, for it makes us think of our *own* grandfather or grandfathers. Write your personal connotations about these or other terms:
   a. High school
   b. A big brother (sister)
   c. The experience of learning to drive
   d. A teacher
   e. A close friend
3. Formulate your own definition of *sleaze* and apply it to television, films, or some other vehicle for public entertainment.
4. How would you define the word *stress*? What do you find stressful?
5. How would you define a particular fantasy you have?

6. Write an essay on the homophones that give you the most trouble. How can you keep them straight?
7. Doing whatever research you find necessary, write a definition paper on one of the following items, seeking to inform your reader:
   a. Exercise bulimia
   b. Anorexia nervosa
   c. Laissez-faire
   d. Acupuncture
   e. The Monroe Doctrine
   f. Heavy-metal music
   g. Four-wheel drive
8. The photograph of the katydid on the leaf on page 373 dramatizes the phenomenon of natural camouflage. The katydid very nearly blends in with the leaf and the rest of the background, an effect that helps conceal the katydid in the same way that a deer's color and markings help it blend into the scenery in wooded areas, and a water moccasin's dark skin often makes it indistinguishable from branches in the water. As a distorter between appearance and reality, natural camouflage can be both beneficial and hazardous, depending upon point of view. The same may be said of artificial camouflage, such as the different uniforms soldiers wear when they are fighting in the jungle as opposed to those they wear for desert combat.

   In a paper explain the paradox of how all camouflage can be both beneficial and hazardous. Use the examples given, and others that you can think of.

Focus on Critical Thinking

9. What do you think Hamill means by the terms *ethics, right,* and *wrong* in his essay? What do *you* mean by those terms?
10. What is the thesis of Kilpatrick's essay on homophones?
11. What is Londer's thesis in "Stressed Out: What Puts the Pressure on Families"?
12. Compare Hamill's essay "Ethics in the 80s" in this chapter with his essay "Our Town" in chapter 16. Consider as points for comparison:
    a. The thesis of each piece: in what ways are they similar?
    b. Hamill's tone in each piece: in what ways are they similar?
    c. Hamill's style: in what ways are they alike? different?
    d. Your response—which piece do you prefer and why?

Writers' Circle

Divide into teams of three students each. Each team should then discuss the differences between the following pairs of homophones and other frequently confused word pairs and agree on what each word means *without* using a dictionary. Next, each team in turn should explain the difference between the words in a pair of homophones. A scorekeeper can keep track of which team gets the most right. The team with the highest score wins.

As an extra credit assignment, write out the differences between the words in each pair, this time using a dictionary when necessary.

1. sole / soul
2. plain / plane
3. for / fore
4. compliment / complement
5. phase / faze
6. break / brake
7. credibility / credulity
8. site / cite
9. jeans / genes
10. bale / bail
11. allude / elude
12. illusion / allusion
13. essay / assay
14. sale / sail
15. discrete / discreet
16. its / it's
17. their / there
18. principle / principal
19. except / accept
20. male / mail
21. accede / exceed
22. precede / proceed
23. loose / lose
24. loath / loathe
25. insure / ensure
26. advice / advise
27. council / counsel
28. coarse / course
29. device / devise
30. illicit / elicit
31. imminent / eminent
32. stationary / stationery
33. waive / wave
34. your / you're
35. formerly / formally
36. farther / further
37. imply / infer
38. moral / morale
39. to / too
40. sighs / size
41. incite / insight
42. doe / dough
43. tail / tale
44. know / no
45. rain / reign
46. sine / sign
47. higher / hire
48. hale / hail
49. mote / moat
50. mite / might

chapter 18 Comparison

"The only thing more difficult than being a writer is being a happily published one."

James Charleton and Lisbeth Mark

Comparison is one of the chief tools all writers use. It takes many forms, one of which is the refusal to compare, as in the following:

You might bring in copies of other of Shakespeare's sonnets (or poems by other poets) to look at additional examples of comparison. Choose your favorites, and have some fun teaching something different—we think rhetorical analysis of poetry is always worthwhile.

My mistress' eyes are nothing like the sun;
Coral is far more red than her lips' red;
If snow be white, why then her breasts are dun;
If hairs be wires, black wires grow on her head.
I have seen roses damask'd, red and white,
But no such roses see I in her cheeks;
And in some perfumes is there more delight
Than in the breath that from my mistress reeks.
I love to hear her speak, yet well I know
That music hath a far more pleasing sound.
I grant I never saw a goddess go;
My mistress, when she walks, treads on the ground.
　　And yet, by heaven, I think my love as rare
　　As any she belied with false compare.

Shakespeare's sonnet 130 provides a good illustration of what can be done with comparisons. No tool is more essential to a writer's craft. Sometimes the comparisons writers use are direct and strictly utilitarian, as when a new-products guide for shoppers compares two compact disc players or two new cars. Other times the comparisons writers use are, like Shakespeare's, more creative, more suggestive, and more artistic.

Figurative Versus Literal Comparisons

Each of us has used the old-war-horse assignment that asks students to write according to this pattern; we no longer see much use in it beyond paragraph practice or some similar, very limited exercise.

The kind of comparison that, for example, places two products side by side is *literal;* the kind that places, say, a person's eyes in comparison to the sun is *metaphoric.* The literal comparison isn't a real challenge for writers: A and B have five characteristics in common, and so you compare A1 with B1, A2 with B2, and so on. Then you write a paragraph on features A has that B doesn't, and a paragraph on features B has that A doesn't. Comparisons that are more metaphoric, however, require more work from writers and offer more rewards to readers. That is, using metaphor, one can always *suggest* more than any *literal* user of language can say. (In fact, it can be persuasively argued that the fundamental nature of language is essentially metaphoric and that what we would call strictly literal language is an aberration.)

What does Shakespeare gain by saying his mistress's eyes are nothing like the sun—why not say simply that they're like stars? For one thing, Shakespeare is working within a tradition that has pretty well worked over the use of direct comparisons (see, for example, Shakespeare's other sonnet "Shall I Compare Thee to a Summer's Day?"), a tradition that has also valued the kind of novelty or freshness that turning the obvious back on itself produces (here, suggesting a comparison by refusing to compare). While each new subject in the poem's first twelve lines is a traditional one for this kind of poem—eyes, lips, breasts, hair, cheeks, and so on—what Shakespeare does with the comparison is novel. That tension between a review of the standard topics and the novelty with which they're treated carries the poem into the last two lines:

We worry that we're saying too much about the poem; that's one reason we invited you to bring in other poetry for students to do their own "readings" of.

> And yet, by heaven, I think my love as rare
> As any she belied with false compare.

Those two lines say a lot:

- The speaker thinks his love is rare.
- When she's compared with other women, all the traditional favorable comparisons (between them and the sun, coral, snow, roses, and so on) are proved false.

That it takes so many more words of prose to paraphrase what Shakespeare is saying than the poem itself takes testifies to the power of the metaphoric comparisons he uses.

Although we do mean to call attention to the economy of words metaphor allows, that's not our major point. We believe students need to learn how using more figurative language can make them better, more effective writers.

The right comparison can shape a whole piece of writing, as it does in David Quammen's essay "Deserts," (chapter 12). The comparison he uses follows:

> Three different geophysical factors combine, generally at least two in each case, to produce the world's various zones of drastic and permanent drought: (1) high pressure systems of air in the horse latitudes, (2) shadowing mountains, and (3) cool ocean currents. Together these three even cast a tidy pattern.
>
> Our planet wears its deserts like a fat woman in a hot red bikini. Don't take my word for it: Look at a globe. Spin the Earth and follow the Tropic of Cancer with your finger as it passes through, or very near, every great desert of the northern hemisphere: the Sahara, the Arabian, the Turkestan, the Dasht-i-Lut of Iran, the Thar of India, the Taklimakan, the Gobi, and back around to the coast of Baja. Now spin again and trace the Tropic of Capricorn, circling down there below the equator: through the Namib and the Kalahari in southwestern Africa, straight across to the big desert that constitutes central Australia, on around again to the Atacama-Peruvian and the Monte-Patagonian of South America. This arrangement is no coincidence. . . .

You'll have a better sense of how you can use comparisons in your own writing after you've read critically the way some other authors use them. First, let's look at a straightforward, literal comparison.

PREREADING WORKSHEET

Before you read the following piece by Susan Sheehan, write brief responses to these questions:

1. Clear your mind—try to get a "blank." Now think of this one word: *drugs*. Write down what comes to mind immediately when you think of that word.

2. What medical complaint(s) do you associate with patients for whom Miltown, Librium, or Valium is prescribed?
3. If your physician told you she needed to prescribe one of two drugs for you, either of which would solve your problem with no negative side effects, and gave *you* the choice, would you choose a drug she described as a *neuroleptic* or one she described as an *antipsychotic?* Why would you choose as you did?
4. Clear your mind again, trying to get a "blank." This time, write down what immediately comes to mind when you think of the phrase "mental health."

Antipsychotic Drugs

SUSAN SHEEHAN

Susan Sheehan is a writer of articles and books of nonfiction. She won the Pulitzer Prize and the American Book Award nomination for Is There No Place on Earth for Me? *(Her other books include* A Welfare Mother *and* A Prison and a Prisoner.*) Following is a chapter opening from* Is There No Place on Earth for Me? *This book gives a detailed history of a year in the life of a woman struggling with schizophrenia; this selection discusses some of the drugs used in treating schizophrenics.*

Ask students whether they can find *any* metaphors in this piece. We think they'll be hard-pressed to find any usage that is clearly a metaphor.

When Thorazine, Stelazine, Mellaril, Compazine, and Trilafon—all of them members of a group of drugs called the phenothiazines—were first used in the United States, in the 1950s, they were called tranquilizers. Later, as Miltown and, still later, Librium and Valium came to be widely employed and generally referred to as tranquilizers, psychiatrists began to distinguish between these two distinctive groups of drugs by calling the former major tranquilizers and the latter minor tranquilizers. They soon regretted this nomenclature by comparison, because it gave the false impression that these drugs were of the same type, with one group simply stronger than the other. The minor tranquilizers are completely ineffective in treating the symptoms of psychosis, and are all potentially addictive. What the minor tranquilizers have in common with the major tranquilizers is that both have anti-anxiety effects; the minor tranquilizers are now more accurately called anti-anxiety drugs. The major tranquilizers—which are not addictive—were eventually renamed antipsychotic drugs, not only in an attempt to differentiate them from the minor tranquilizers but also to clear up a common misconception that they worked by making people groggy and easily manageable. Unlike the barbiturates that were used in mental hospitals for decades, these drugs don't work by putting people to sleep or dulling their senses. They work by reducing the hallucinations, the delusions, and the thinking disorders characteristic of the psychotic phase of schizophrenia and other psychoses, without putting psychotic patients to sleep. More recently, many psycho-pharmacologists have preferred to call these drugs neuroleptics, for they are 1 all capable of producing certain neurological side effects. In addition, some neuroleptics were found to be useful in other branches of medicine. Compazine, for example, is useful for treating nausea and vomiting, and a parent is more likely to give it to a normal child if it is called a neuroleptic than if it is called an antipsychotic. Twenty neuroleptics are currently in use in the United States; many others are used in other parts of the world.

2 For some years after Thorazine and the other neuroleptics were introduced, it was not known how they worked. In the last few years, psychopharmacologists have achieved a better understanding of this. There are hundreds of billions of cells in the brain called neurons, which interconnect. The connecting points between neurons are called synapses. At most synapses, a chemical known as a neurotransmitter is released at the end of one neuron, travels a minute distance to the next neuron, and influences that neuron to transmit the impulse. About a score of different neurotransmitters are known today, and a large number are probably yet to be discovered. The neurotransmitter that has been most implicated in schizophrenia is dopamine. During the psychotic phase of schizophrenia, there seems to be an excess of dopamine transmission in the neurons in specific areas of the brain. All the neuroleptics are known to block the dopamine receptors so that the dopamine released at the end of one neuron cannot get to the receptor site of the next neuron.

Notice the simple ordering of these three paragraphs: (a) a general introduction, (b) an account of how these drugs work, and (c) an explanation of how doctors select which drug to use, with special attention to Thorazine.

3 More than ninety percent of all schizophrenic patients undergoing their first psychotic episode will respond to any one of the twenty neuroleptics if the proper dose is given for the proper length of time. One neuroleptic is thus normally no more effective than another in ridding a patient of delusions, despite claims of drug companies to the contrary. The drugs do, however, have different side effects. The reason that a knowledgeable doctor usually prescribes one neuroleptic rather than another for a patient with no prior history of treatment is that he is familiar with a drug or knows that it has a particular spectrum of side effects. Thorazine is one of the neuroleptics that have a strong sedative side effect. A number of specialists in psychopharmacology have gone so far as to call it "obsolete" and have ceased to use it clinically, because it has numerous undesirable side effects, including the oversedation. The sedative property is the characteristic that makes it especially popular in understaffed state hospitals, where attendants find heavily sedated patients easier to control.

POSTREADING WORKSHEET

Now that you have read the piece by Sheehan, write your responses to the following questions:

1. Was what you wrote down in response to the word *drugs* negative (*drug abuse, addiction, crime, crack,* and so on) or positive (*healing, recovery, lifesaving,* and so on)? Why do you think you responded as you did? Did reading Sheehan's piece alter that response in any way? If so, how and why?

2. When you wrote down the medical complaint(s) you associate with patients for whom Miltown, Librium, or Valium is prescribed, was your response positive, negative, or neutral? Why do you think so?
3. Did you choose your drug as Sheehan might have predicted you would? Why or why not?
4. Was what you wrote down in response to the phrase "mental health" negative (*insanity, paranoia, derangement,* and so on) or positive (*sane, normal behavior, soundness,* and so on)? Why do you think you responded as you did? Did reading Sheehan's piece alter that response in any way? If so, how and why?

Questions for Writing and Discussion

Prepare short written answers to each of these questions. Be prepared to hand them in and/or discuss them in class, as your teacher directs.

1. The passage compares two groups of drugs, once called "major" and "minor" tranquilizers. What are the bases of that comparison?
2. What parts of the comparison in this passage are built on discussing what something is *not?* on what something *is?*
3. How are the second and third paragraphs related to each other—what qualities of the drugs are being compared?
4. In the last few lines of the passage, how are the reasons some attendants *use* Thorazine compared with the reasons some specialists *don't?*
5. Although this passage has a number of literal comparisons, as questions 1–4 above have helped you to realize, it is notably lacking in metaphoric comparisons. Choose one of the literal comparisons and replace it with a metaphoric one, rewriting that part of the passage appropriately. For example, can you think of two things that have the same kind of relationship as the major and minor tranquilizers as described in the first paragraph? If you wanted to use that comparison to clarify the paragraph, how would you have to rewrite it?
6. What do the following words mean—*nomenclature, schizophrenia, psychosis* (¶ 1), *neurons* (¶ 2)?
7. On a first reading, one might say that the passage betrays no hint of an attitude held by the author toward the subject—the passage seems merely factual, the author neutral. Take a second, closer look at the passage to see whether there might be a hint of something more going on in terms of Sheehan's attitude.
8. In American society today, people's attitude is increasingly one of looking critically—and often negatively—at any kind of drug use that isn't essential for medicinal purposes. What are your feelings about the reliance on drugs in our society? Interview a health care professional—such as a doctor, nurse, technician, or athletic trainer—about his or her feelings about the over-reliance on drugs. Compare those views with your own.

Throughout Sheehan's book is an unexpressed sense of shock and dismay, as though one can hear the author saying (under her breath) such things as "Can the world really be this cold? Can people really suffer this much?" or, in this passage, "Can it really be that drug companies claim their drug is more effective when it isn't? Can it really be that a drug with strongly sedative side effects is chosen over drugs with no such side effects because attendants want their patients heavily sedated?" Sheehan always lets her readers draw their own conclusions, but her attitude sometimes comes through in her very lack of editorializing.

If you want to be audacious, invite your class to divide into groups and work on rewriting one of Shakespeare's sonnets, using no comparisons at all. Then the class can listen as the rewrites are read aloud.

Whether you see more literal or more figurative comparison depends on what you read. Science textbooks, for example, will offer more literal comparisons, like the one above by Susan Sheehan. More figurative comparisons will be found in philosophical writing (and in potboilers). You shouldn't be surprised to learn that figurative comparisons are more interesting to read; we think you'll also find they're more interesting to write.

The Dance of Relationships

ANNE MORROW LINDBERGH

See page 141 for information on Anne Morrow Lindbergh. The following is taken from her book Gift from the Sea.

1 A good relationship has a pattern like a dance and is built on some of the same rules. The partners do not need to hold on tightly, because they move confidently in the same pattern, intricate but gay and swift and free, like a country dance of Mozart's. To touch heavily would be to arrest the pattern and freeze the movement, to check the endlessly changing beauty of its unfolding. There is no place here for the possessive clutch, the clinging arm, the heavy hand; only the barest touch in passing. Now arm in arm, now face to face, now back to back—it does not matter which. Because they know they are partners moving to the same rhythm, creating a pattern together, and being invisibly nourished by it.

Ask students what kind of dance they think this is describing. Is it literal as well as figurative? Why might they think both?

2 The joy of such a pattern is not only the joy of creation or the joy of participation, it is also the joy of living in the moment. Lightness of touch and living in the moment are intertwined. One cannot dance well unless one is completely in time with the music, not leaning back to the last step or pressing forward to the next one, but poised directly on the present step as it comes. Perfect poise on the beat is what gives good dancing its sense of ease, of timelessness, of the eternal. It is what Blake was speaking of when he wrote:

> He who bends to himself a joy
> Doth the winged life destroy;
> But he who kisses the joy as it flies
> Lives in Eternity's sunrise.

The dancers who are perfectly in time never destroy "the winged life" in each other or in themselves.

3 But how does one learn this technique of the dance? Why is it so difficult? What makes us hesitate and stumble? It is fear, I think, that makes one cling nostalgically to the last moment or clutch greedily toward the next. Fear destroys "the winged life." But how to exorcise it? It can only be

If this gets too mystical for some of your students, ask them to rewrite this paragraph so that it is literal.

exorcised by its opposite, love. When the heart is flooded with love there is no room in it for fear, for doubt, for hesitation. And it is this lack of fear that makes for the dance. When each partner loves so completely that he has forgotten to ask himself whether or not he is loved in return; when he only knows that he loves and is moving to its music—then, and then only, are two people able to dance perfectly in tune to the same rhythm.

Questions for Writing and Discussion

Prepare short written answers to each of these questions. Be prepared to hand them in and/or discuss them in class, as your teacher directs.

1. To help you see how this comparison works, copy and fill out the following grid. The first column is the categories for the shared qualities of a good relationship and a dance; the second is how that quality is manifested in a dance; and the third is how it is manifested in a good relationship. We've filled in the first line to show how this works; you should extend the three columns as needed.

This same kind of exercise can be worked out by your writing groups in reference to the next reading, "The Long Habit."

Quality	A Dance	A Good Relationship
Pattern	Partners move together	Partners move together
[other similar qualities of pattern?]	__________	__________
	__________	__________
	__________	__________
Touch	__________	__________
__________	__________	__________
__________	__________	__________
__________	__________	__________

2. Do you find this passage persuasive? Or is that the purpose of the comparison? Why do you suppose Lindbergh uses this comparison? How does having this kind of extended metaphoric comparison change your reaction to the passage compared with that to, say, Sheehan's passage earlier in this chapter?
3. If a good relationship is like a dance, what is a bad relationship like? Write a paragraph that fleshes out your comparison.
4. In the lines by the poet William Blake, a comparison is made between what and what?
5. Anne Morrow Lindbergh is, of course, not the first person to compare relationships between people to a dance. Does it bother you that her comparison is not brand-new? One of the reasons a metaphoric comparison like this repeatedly comes up is that it is so *productive:* that is, the more you think about it, the more ways you can apply it. In how many other ways can you successfully and easily compare a relationship to a dance?

6. Lindbergh concludes her first paragraph with a deliberate sentence fragment. What makes that fragment stylistically effective and therefore appropriate?
7. What do the following words mean—*intertwined* (¶ 2), *exorcise* (¶ 3)?

The use of metaphoric comparisons is not always so obvious as in the preceding passage. The following selection is permeated with comparisons—comparisons literal, metaphoric, and every shading in between. As you read through it, keep track of the comparisons.

If seeing how many ways students can compare a relationship to a dance seems to go well, you can continue the work by varying the sides of the comparison: if a good relationship is like a dance, what, then, is a bad relationship like? Or, given different kinds of dances (a polka, a square dance, a waltz), describe first the dance and then what kind of relationship would match it.

The Long Habit

LEWIS THOMAS

Lewis Thomas is a medical doctor (a specialist in pathology), professor, author, and columnist. His books include The Lives of a Cell, *from which this piece is excerpted, and* Night Thoughts on Listening to Mahler's Ninth Symphony.

1 We continue to share with our remotest ancestors the most tangled and evasive attitudes about death, despite the great distance we have come in understanding some of the profound aspects of biology. We have as much distaste for talking about personal death as for thinking about it; it is an indelicacy, like talking in mixed company about venereal disease or abortion in the old days. Death on a grand scale does not bother us in the same special way: we can sit around a dinner table and discuss war, involving 60 million volatilized human deaths, as though we were talking about bad weather; we can watch abrupt bloody death every day, in color, on films and television, without blinking back a tear. It is when the numbers of dead are very small, and very close, that we begin to think in scurrying circles. At the very center of the problem is the naked cold deadness of one's own self, the only reality in nature of which we can have absolute certainty, and it is unmentionable, unthinkable. We may be even less willing to face the issue at first hand than our predecessors because of a secret new hope that maybe it will go away. We like to think, hiding the thought, that with all the marvelous ways in which we seem now to lead nature around by the nose, perhaps we can avoid the central problem if we just become, next year, say, a bit smarter.

2 "The long habit of living," said Thomas Browne, "indisposeth us to dying." These days, the habit has become an addiction: we are hooked on living; the tenacity of its grip on us, and ours on it, grows in intensity. We cannot think of giving it up, even when living loses its zest—even when we have lost the zest for zest.

Your students may well resist the notion that being "hooked on" something positive, like living, could possibly be bad. One anti-drug campaign even invites us to get "hooked on life." What kind of existence is it that esteems being hooked on *nothing?*

3 We have come a long way in our technologic capacity to put death off, and it is imaginable that we might learn to stall it for even longer periods, perhaps matching the life-spans of the Abkhasian Russians, who are said to go on, springily, for a century and a half. If we can rid ourselves of some of our

chronic, degenerative diseases, and cancer, strokes, and coronaries, we might go on and on. It sounds attractive and reasonable, but it is no certainty. If we became free of disease, we would make a much better run of it for the last decade or so, but might still terminate on about the same schedule as now. We may be like the genetically different lines of mice, or like Hayflick's different tissue-culture lines, programmed to die after a predetermined number of days, clocked by their genomes. If this is the way it is, some of us will continue to wear out and come unhinged in the sixth decade, and some much later, depending on genetic timetables.

If we ever do achieve freedom from most of today's diseases, or even complete freedom from disease, we will perhaps terminate by drying out and blowing away on a light breeze, but we will still die. 4

Most of my friends do not like this way of looking at it. They prefer to take it for granted that we only die because we get sick, with one lethal ailment or another, and if we did not have our diseases we might go on indefinitely. Even biologists choose to think this about themselves, despite the evidences of the absolute inevitability of death that surround their professional lives. Everything dies, all around, trees, plankton, lichens, mice, whales, flies, mitochondria. In the simplest creatures it is sometimes difficult to see it as death, since the strands of replicating DNA they leave behind are more conspicuously the living parts of themselves than with us (not that it is fundamentally any different, but it seems so). Flies do not develop a ward round of diseases that carry them off, one by one. They simply age, and die, like flies. 5

We hanker to go on, even in the face of plain evidence that long, long lives are not necessarily pleasurable in the kind of society we have arranged thus far. We will be lucky if we can postpone the search for new technologies for a while, until we have discovered some satisfactory things to do with the extra time. Something will surely have to be found to take the place of sitting on the porch re-examining one's watch. 6

Notice Thomas bringing in once again the terminology of addiction, here using "withdrawal" both to evoke the painful-but-eventually-beneficial process of withdrawal from drug addiction and to talk about withdrawing from life. Work with your students to develop their sense of how, in the context of this essay, Thomas can call withdrawal a sickness.

Perhaps we would not be so anxious to prolong life if we did not detest so much the sickness of withdrawal. It is astonishing how little information we have about this universal process, with all the other dazzling advances in biology. It is almost as though we wanted not to know about it. Even if we could imagine the act of death in isolation, without any preliminary stage of being struck down by disease, we would be fearful of it. 7

There are signs that medicine may be taking a new interest in the process, partly from curiosity, partly from an embarrassed realization that we have not been handling this aspect of disease with as much skill as physicians once displayed, back in the days before they became convinced that disease was their solitary and sometimes defeatable enemy. It used to be the hardest and most important of all the services of a good doctor to be on hand at the time of death and to provide comfort, usually in the home. Now it is done in hospitals, in secrecy (one of the reasons for the increased fear of death these days may be that so many people are totally unfamiliar with it; they never 8 actually see it happen in real life). Some of our technology permits us to deny its existence, and we maintain flickers of life for long stretches in one community of cells or another, as though we were keeping a flag flying. Death is not a sudden-all-at-once affair; cells go down in sequence, one by one. You can, if you like, recover great numbers of them many hours after the lights have gone out, and grow them out in cultures. It takes hours, even days, before the irreversible word finally gets around to all the provinces.

9 We may be about to rediscover that dying is not such a bad thing to do after all. Sir William Osler took this view: he disapproved of people who spoke of the agony of death, maintaining that there was no such thing.

10 In a nineteenth-century memoir on an expedition in Africa, there is a story by David Livingston about his own experience of near-death. He was caught by a lion, crushed across the chest in the animal's great jaws, and saved in the instant by a lucky shot from a friend. Later, he remembered the episode in clear detail. He was so amazed by the extraordinary sense of peace, calm, and total painlessness associated with being killed that he constructed a theory that all creatures are provided with a protective physiologic mechanism, switched on at the verge of death, carrying them through in a haze of tranquillity.

11 I have seen agony in death only once, in a patient with rabies; he remained acutely aware of every stage in the process of his own disintegration over a twenty-four-hour period, right up to his final moment. It was as though, in the special neuropathology of rabies, the switch had been prevented from turning.

12 We will be having new opportunities to learn more about the physiology of death at first hand, from the increasing numbers of cardiac patients who have been through the whole process and then back again. Judging from what has been found out thus far, from the first generation of people resuscitated from cardiac standstill (already termed the Lazarus syndrome), Osler seems to have been right. Those who remember parts or all of their episodes do not recall any fear, or anguish. Several people who remained conscious throughout, while appearing to have been quite dead, could only describe a remarkable sensation of detachment. One man underwent coronary occlusion with cessation of the heart and dropped, for all practical purposes dead, in front of a hospital; within a few minutes his heart had been restarted by electrodes and he breathed his way back into life. According to his account, the strangest thing was that there were so many people around him, moving so urgently, handling his body with such excitement, while all his awareness was of quietude.

13 In a recent study of the reaction to dying in patients with obstructive disease of the lungs, it was concluded that the process was considerably more shattering for the professional observers than the observed. Most of the patients appeared to be preparing themselves with equanimity for death, as though intuitively familiar with the business. One elderly woman reported that the only painful and distressing part of the process was in being

interrupted; on several occasions she was provided with conventional therapeutic measures to maintain oxygenation or restore fluids and electrolytes, and each time she found the experience of coming back harrowing; she deeply resented the interference with her dying.

I find myself surprised by the thought that dying is an all-right thing to do, but perhaps it should not surprise. It is, after all, the most ancient and fundamental of biologic functions, with its mechanisms worked out with the same attention to detail, the same provision for the advantage of the organism, the same abundance of genetic information for guidance through the stages, that we have long since become accustomed to finding in all the crucial acts of living. 14

Very well. But even so, if the transformation is a coordinated, integrated physiologic process in its initial, local stages, there is still that permanent vanishing of consciousness to be accounted for. Are we to be stuck forever with this problem? Where on earth does it go? Is it simply stopped dead in its tracks, lost in humus, wasted? Considering the tendency of nature to find uses for complex and intricate mechanisms, this seems to me unnatural. I prefer to think of it as somehow separated off at the filaments of its attachment, and then drawn like an easy breath back into the membrane of its origin, a fresh memory for a biospherical nervous system, but I have no data on the matter. 15

Ask students whether they feel this last bit of the essay, about the aunts who have "received Communications," strikes them as a legitimate and logical conclusion for the essay, or whether it seems to trivialize the piece. Then ask, "How would *you* end an essay on the inevitability of dying?"

This is for another science, another day. It may turn out, as some scientists suggest, that we are forever precluded from investigating consciousness by a sort of indeterminacy principle that stipulates that the very act of looking will make it twitch and blur out of sight. If this is true, we will never learn. I envy some of my friends who are convinced about telepathy; oddly enough, it is my European scientist acquaintances who believe it most freely and take it most lightly. All their aunts have received Communications, and there they sit, with proof of the motility of consciousness at their fingertips, and the making of a new science. It is discouraging to have had the wrong aunts, and never the ghost of a message. 16

Questions for Writing and Discussion

Prepare short written answers to each of these questions. Be prepared to hand them in and/or discuss them in class, as your teacher directs.

1. What do the following words mean—*volatilized, predecessors* (¶ 1), *indisposeth* (¶ 2), *technologic, genomes* (¶ 3), *mitochondria, a ward round of diseases* (¶ 5), *physiologic* (¶ 10), *neuropathology* (¶ 11), *occlusion, quietude* (¶ 12), *indeterminacy principle, Communications, motility* (¶ 16)?
2. List the comparisons you found in this passage. Of the many comparisons herein, which do you think is the core comparison, the one underlying all the others?
3. Besides the comparisons, does the passage contain other major structural devices? If so, what are they?

4. This essay was written several years ago; what do you suppose Thomas would say today on the subject (¶ 6) of whether we have found anything useful to do with the extra years of life science has given us?
5. What is the effect of Thomas's use of "hanker to" (¶ 6)?
6. What do you think of Thomas's suggestion that we might be biologically predetermined to be able to accept our own deaths when the time comes, that in effect, when the time comes we cannot help but know what to do (¶ 14)? Can you put into words how that idea makes you feel?
7. How does the fourteenth paragraph mark a turning point in the essay's structure? How does the author's approach in the last two paragraphs compare with his approach in all others till the fourteenth?

Bridges: Another Perspective

Lewis Thomas provides a discussion about death that does not fit the most common ways we think or talk about death. (In fact, we usually avoid thinking or talking about death, as Thomas points out.) But death is just as much a part of life as birth. In keeping with this chapter's focus on comparison, we can frame a question probably asked by each member of each generation but thus far never truly answered: *What is death like?* Using Thomas's piece as your springboard, dive into this question, with such ancillary questions as these:

How do different people view death?

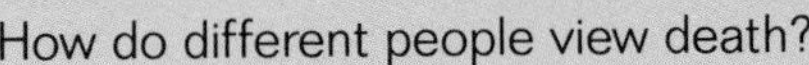

Why do we fear death?

Is death ever a good thing?

What do *you* think happens to consciousness when someone dies?

Thomas says he is surprised by the idea that dying might be "an all-right thing to do" (¶ 14). How do you feel about that idea?

KEY POINTS TO REMEMBER: Writing Comparisons

Whether you're writing a literal or a metaphoric comparison, here are a few commonsense guidelines to follow:

- Be orderly.
- Be thorough.
- Use the comparison to enrich your writing.

Be Orderly

The three points brought up here are good things for peer editors to check for when responding to one another's drafts.

Let the comparison be *orderly* enough that it makes the material easier, not harder, for the reader to follow. With any kind of comparison, you are immediately writing not just about two subjects but about three: the third is the relationship between the two, which is part of the point of using comparison. If the comparison is at all elaborate but lacks orderliness, you risk creating a word structure so unwieldy that your attempt to add benefit will instead add liability—your piece will be harder, not easier, to understand.

Be Thorough

If the comparison is literal, let its *thoroughness* give the writing depth; if the comparison is metaphoric, let its *suggestiveness* give the passage depth. Again, here in Part Four of our book we encourage you to make mainly *inventive* use of particular patterns for writers. That is, you can use your awareness of the existence of a particular pattern to help answer the question all writers face repeatedly: "What do I say next, and next, and next?" If your comparison is literal, be thorough in your comparing—not just subject 1 compared with subject 2, but also subject 1, characteristic A, compared with subject 2, characteristic A, and so on. If your comparison is metaphoric, let the metaphor range where it will so as to produce as full, creative, and inventive a comparison as possible.

This last point may be the toughest criterion of all: whether the comparison slowly unfolds before the reader or brings the reader a sudden insight, its most meaningful role is its role for the reader, not the writer.

Use the Comparison to Enrich Your Writing

Whichever kind of comparison you use, make sure the comparison makes the writing *richer*. Beyond making what you write easier to follow, whatever kind of comparison you use needs also to make the writing more rewarding for the reader.

Comparison, like all other patterns discussed in this part of the book, can be used in writing for all the purposes heretofore identified: informing/explaining, persuading, analyzing, and expressing. It draws its most basic strength from our natural tendency to compare—to see how one thing is like or unlike another. Because human nature seeks to compare, comparing can be a powerful and valuable pattern for writers.

✓✓✓ WORKSHEETS: Writing Comparisons

There are two different ways to approach writing comparisons—literal and metaphoric—so we've divided this worksheet presentation into two corresponding subsections. We do so even though writing is writing, no matter how you do it, and even though there isn't nearly so much difference in the two approaches as such division might seem to suggest.

When we say "writing literal comparisons," note that we are among those who are fairly well convinced that *all* language (including writing) is fundamentally metaphoric. Or, as Noam Chomsky said, "Normal human language use is always creative."

Writing Literal Comparisons

The situations in which you'll most often use a literal comparison—school assignments; scientific, technical, or business writing—are also those which usually reward being systematic and orderly.

Invention via Listing. A good way to start writing a literal comparison is to make a chart that lays out the important characteristics of the two (or more) things being compared. We're not going to call this chart an outline; although considerable evidence indicates that all successful writers begin with some kind of structural plan, outlines are only one of many such plans. What we're urging you to do is create, on paper, some kind of graphic representation of the material—in particular, the compared traits—you're planning to write about. Suppose, for example, you were to compare the Phil Collins albums *Face Value* and *No Jacket Required* with the Chicago albums *Chicago 16* and *Chicago 17*. A simple, two-column list would suffice in providing the inventional core for your writing:

You might try mapping this same comparison on the board.

Phil Collins	Chicago
Album shows confusion resulting from a broken relationship	Album shows confusion resulting from a broken relationship
Focus is on humility of honest self-expression	Focus is on flawless, near-perfect performances
Album begins with deserted lover jeering, "In the air tonight"	Album begins with deserted lover jeering, "What you're missing"
Remainder of album traces sequence from depression to beginning of new relationship	Remainder of album traces sequence from depression to beginning of new relationship
Album features a wide variety of instrumentation	Album features many vocalists and styles
Album succeeds in evoking strong feelings in listeners	Album succeeds in evoking strong feelings in listeners

Once you've made a visual presentation like this for your own use, it's a relatively straightforward task to write a good first draft of the paper. You can also ask yourself, even before you start writing, whether (a) you have enough solid details and points of comparison and (b) the comparison itself makes sense as the graphic helps you visualize it. Looking at the two-column list above, you may well feel that the comparison seems mechanical, that it needs more specific detail on both sides, and that its *point*—the shaping purpose of the whole piece of writing—needs to be developed more fully and made more explicit. (That's how the students who review this list in our classes usually feel.)

Actually, one student called this potential paper "dull as dirt." But really, no topic or pattern is inherently dull. What this topic needs is someone to write about it who cares greatly about it. What we've called elsewhere the *expressive* component—a strong human investment in the task at hand—is the way good writing starts.

Writing Metaphoric Comparisons

Here again our focus is on the *inventional* value of metaphoric comparisons, for when you find the *right* comparison, it can pull you all the way through the piece of writing you're doing, from start to finish.

Inventional Value of a Fresh Comparison. It helps if the comparison you use is reasonably fresh—not so overworked that anyone reading it moans, "Oh, no, she's not trotting that old horse around the track again, is she?"—but it doesn't have to be brand-new. Here are three comparisons to evaluate:

Have your students brainstorm more possibilities here.

- Graduating is like coming to a crossroads.
- Monoclonal antibodies work like magic bullets.
- Trying to figure out the microstructure of atomic nuclei by smashing them in particle accelerators is like trying to figure out how the inside of a car's engine works by smashing the car into a brick wall at thousands of miles an hour.

What do you think about the first one? To us, it's so hackneyed that people moan and groan when it starts—probably not a good one on which to base a whole paper. The second is one we've heard a few times before—popular in magazines like *Time* and *Newsweek*—but not so overused that we can't stand to see a good new treatment of it; still, to write that comparison requires detailed knowledge of what monoclonal antibodies are and how they work. The third comparison is probably the freshest of the three, suggestive and interesting, but anyone who wants to use it as the basis of a piece of writing had better have a thorough knowledge of particle physics—here the faint of heart need not apply.

When one of our students used the "magic bullets" comparison, here are the initial points of comparison he came up with:

Monoclonal Antibodies	**Magic Bullets**
Highly specific for tumor antigens	Hit only—and always—what they're aimed at
Seek a specific substance found only in cancer cells	Seek only a specific target
Not only find the substance but also draw more antibodies to it	Hit the target and draw more bullets to it
Are difficult to create and are expensive	Are difficult to create and are expensive
If come apart during use, results could be dangerous	May have hidden drawbacks

Of course, the writer of this paper has an advantage: since no one knows exactly what a "magic bullet" would be or how it would work, the comparison can be fudged a little on that side as needed. Looking at the list above, you might notice another problem with this plan—little specificity is involved on either side, which aspect may not matter much when it comes to talking about magic bullets but will certainly need to be present for the discussion of monoclonal antibodies to be successful.

You can drive the inventional point home if you also do sketch outlines of a couple of the other comparisons your students brainstormed.

We've focused here on the inventional use of comparisons because we think it's important—one of the best ways you can build quality into your writing from the very start. A good comparison—the right comparison—will go a long way toward seeing you through to a good piece of writing. Such comparisons are often called extended metaphors or extended analogies when they serve as a pattern for all, or a significant part, of a piece of writing; an example is Anne Morrow Lindbergh's "The Dance of Relationships."

There is also a *discovery* use of comparisons, what we earlier called analogical problem solving: "If this [thing that I don't know about] were *like* that [thing I do know about], then the following would be true." Thus scientists test one member of a family of viruses to see whether it behaves similarly to the way other members of the same family do, and teachers work with one student in ways they've found successful with other, possibly similar students.

 **CASE STUDY CLOSE-UP**

Let's look at the middle draft of the paper Ricardo Estevez produced on the subject of monoclonal antibodies, using the comparison to magic bullets. Ricardo is a college freshman who is also a twenty-three-year-old army veteran. In the army he was trained as a medical laboratory technician, and he's now planning to major in biochemistry, based on an interest in that field his army training encouraged; Ricardo thus knows a little more about the subject than some people might. He's writing the paper for Ms. Artivera, an English department graduate student who's teaching his freshman English class; nevertheless, another important audience is his classmates. Ricardo therefore wants enough technical information to satisfy his teacher but also enough use of the metaphoric comparison to keep the paper interesting to his classmates.

It's *critical* that students *know* whether they're writing for you, writing for their classmates, or writing primarily for you and secondarily for their classmates, or writing primarily for their classmates and secondarily for you. We all preach that writers need to know their audiences, but we sometimes forget to give it the emphasis it requires.

Magic Bullets: Fact or Fiction?

Ricardo Estevez, college writing student

1 Imagine your favorite Saturday morning cartoon show--"Mutant Teenage Ninja Ghostbusters Rock Band in the Twenty-first Century." What do you suppose Muffy and Jack, the two heroes, would use to send those twenty-first-century ghosts, goblins, and miscellaneous beasties back to the proto-world that they got here from? What could be better than magic bullets?

If there were such a thing as magic bullets, how would they work? Well, they would hit only what they were aimed at and would hit always what they were aimed at. There would be something in the bullet that would cause it to seek the specific target it was made to hit, and nothing else. Some quality in the bullet that seeks out a matching quality only possessed by the target. Not only that, but once one magic bullet finds its target, it draws other bullets to the same target. 2

Of course, there would have to be some drawbacks, or there would be no story. These bullets would be extremely difficult to create, and very expensive. And they may have hidden drawbacks in some circumstances--circumstances not very well defined or understood. They might hurt the people they're supposed to help. 3

Sounds pretty farfetched, doesn't it? The stuff of Saturday-morning cartoon shows, and the twenty-first century, but nothing to do with our lives today? Well, in medicine today, especially in the detection and treatment of cancer, magic bullets are a reality. 4

What are these medical magic bullets? Their real name is "monoclonal antibodies." Antibodies are the body's natural defense against disease--they locate harmful agents within the body, fasten onto them, and signal other components of the body's defense to come help destroy the harmful agents. The problem with using antibodies to fight cancer is that only a few of the body's natural antibodies might destroy cancer cells, and that the ones that do tend to change into substances that destroy noncancerous cells as well when they are mass-produced in the lab. Today's genetic engineering techniques, however, can produce hybridized antibodies in which every cell is identical to every other cell. Not only are they all the same, but these "monoclonal" cells can be engineered to be specific to one type of cancer cell, and they can be mass-produced. These cells are drawn to a protein that appears only on the surface of cancer cells (a "marker" protein), and when they find it, they bind onto it. 5

By themselves these monoclonal antibodies help destroy cancer cells by triggering some of the body's natural defenses. But by themselves they seem to work mostly as "magic cancer markers" rather than "magic cancer destroyers." The most effective monoclonal antibodies are the ones that have been combined chemically with other substances that are 6 highly effective in destroying cancer cells but that are not usually used in cancer treatment, because they destroy other important body cells as well. Because the magic bullet only and always reaches its very specific target, it can be coupled with substances (radioactive elements, poisons) that will destroy anything they hit. That combination, called the "modified monoclonal antibody," constitutes the true magic bullet.

7 Sound too good to be true? Well, there are some disadvantages and problems. For one, the whole treatment is still experimental. For another, anyone who wants to use this magic bullet had better make very sure that the substance it's designed to locate and destroy occurs only on cancer cells, because the magic bullet is very thorough about finding that substance and destroying it. For another, there seems to be some risk that the most effective monoclonal antibodies--those modified by being joined to really deadly substances--can, under conditions not very well understood, come unjoined from those deadly substances, leaving really harmful poisons loose in the body. And finally, the technology by which these magic bullets are produced is very delicate and very expensive, making the bullets, even in laboratory settings, rare items indeed. But if those problems can be solved, doctors all over the world will have another, extremely effective weapon to use in their war against cancer.

Notice how frequently Ricardo begins paragraphs with direct questions or uses direct questions within paragraphs. Ask students how they feel about that technique. What does it tell them about this writer's relationship with his audience?

When Ricardo and his classmates brought copies of these middle-level drafts to class, the teacher asked them to break up into their writing groups and to give her each group's best draft, together with a list created by the group of the qualities that caused them to select it as the best. Ricardo's was the one selected by his group. Take a couple of minutes now to reread his draft and jot down a list of the things you find *good* about it.

Again, this is not "rhetorical"; we really do mean for you to have your students do this, and for you to look at (or listen to) and comment on their responses.

The qualities Ricardo's group found to like about his draft started with his use of the metaphor of magic bullets: though Ricardo was hardly the first person to use that comparison, his classmates found the comparison especially productive—it worked well in the piece. His classmates also liked the opening; compared with the other papers they read, his had lots of imagination and a little more life in it. Finally, they liked the transitions he used between paragraphs. (In fact, adding those transitions was the biggest change Ricardo made between the first draft and this one. His high school English teacher had been emphatic about using them, and for once, on this assignment, he had time to pay specific attention to following her advice.) Have another look at Ricardo's draft and pick out those transitions.

Check your students on this point; let them actually tell you the transitions.

Critical Thinking

One of the best-selling nonfiction books of this decade is a collection of essays called *All I Really Need to Know I Learned in Kindergarten,* by Robert Fulghum, a Unitarian minister from Seattle. The piece that gave the collection its name was originally a graduation speech the author gave at a grade school. People who have read it usually remember it for the list of "things I learned." But they usually don't remember that the whole thing starts with a very simple but very creative comparison. (Notice that it's *not* the "crossroads" speech.) Read the passage we've printed for you here, enjoy it, and then use your critical reading skills (see chapter 8) and critical thinking skills (see chapter 14) to answer the questions that follow.

All I Really Need to Know I Learned in Kindergarten

ROBERT FULGHUM

Each spring, for many years, I have set myself the task of writing a personal statement of belief: a Credo. When I was younger, the statement ran for many pages, trying to cover every base, with no loose ends. It sounded like a Supreme Court brief, as if words could resolve all conflicts about the meaning of existence. 1

The Credo has grown shorter in recent years—sometimes cynical, sometimes comical, sometimes bland—but I keep working at it. Recently I set out to get the statement of personal belief down to one page in simple terms, fully understanding the naive idealism that implied. 2

The inspiration for brevity came to me at a gasoline station. I managed to fill an old car's tank with super-deluxe high-octane go-juice. My old hoopy couldn't handle it and got the willies—kept sputtering out at intersections and belching going downhill. I understood. My mind and spirit get like that from time to time. Too much high-content information, and *I* get the existential willies—keep sputtering out at intersections where life choices must be made and I either know too much or not enough. The examined life is no picnic. 3

One could create an ugly but descriptive metaphor and call this existential gridlock.

You might point out to students that in saying "The examined life is no picnic," Fulghum is not only making a comparison by saying what something is *not*—an interesting twist on the usual pattern—but also making a comment on a famous quotation from Plato: "The life which is unexamined is not worth living." Plato meant that everyone should be reflective; "examining" one's life is paying attention to what one does, thinks, says, and so on, to see if one might

I realized then that I already know most of what's necessary to live a meaningful life—that it isn't all that complicated. *I know it.* And have known it for a long, long time. Living it—well, that's another matter, yes? Here's my Credo: 4

All I really need to know about how to live and what to do and how to be I learned in kindergarten. Wisdom was not at the top of the graduate-school mountain, but there in the sandpile at Sunday school. These are the things I learned: 5

Share everything.
Play fair.
Don't hit people.
Put things back where you found them.

Clean up your own mess.
Don't take things that aren't yours.
Say you're sorry when you hurt somebody.
Wash your hands before you eat.
Flush.
Warm cookies and cold milk are good for you.
Live a balanced life—learn some and think some and draw and paint and sing and dance and play and work every day some.
Take a nap every afternoon.
When you go out into the world, watch out for traffic, hold hands, and stick together.
Be aware of wonder. Remember the little seed in the Styrofoam cup: The roots go down and the plant goes up and nobody really knows how or why, but we are all like that.
Goldfish and hamsters and white mice and even the little seed in the Styrofoam cup—they all die. So do we.
And then remember the Dick-and-Jane books and the first word you learned—the biggest word of all—LOOK.

somehow better one's life. Fulghum is saying that such reflectiveness is not always a good thing, because it's a lot of trouble.

6 Everything you need to know is in there somewhere. The Golden Rule and love and basic sanitation. Ecology and politics and equality and sane living.

7 Take any one of those items and extrapolate it into sophisticated adult terms and apply it to your family life or your work or your government or your world, and it holds true and clear and firm. Think what a better world it would be if we all—the whole world—had cookies and milk about three o'clock every afternoon and then lay down with our blankets for a nap. Or if all governments had as a basic policy to always put things back where they found them and to clean up their own mess.

8 And it is still true, no matter how old you are—when you go out into the world, it is best to hold hands and stick together.

Questions for Writing and Discussion

Prepare short written answers to each of these questions. Be prepared to hand them in and/or discuss them in class, as your teacher directs.

1. The third and fourth paragraphs present the core comparison that—if you buy it—sets up the entire rest of the piece. Lay out that comparison in detail.
2. Is the comparison in the third and fourth paragraphs truly sound—are people and old cars really alike in important ways?
3. Does the real-world likeness or difference between people and old cars have anything to do with this piece's effectiveness? That is, does this key metaphor need to be a true comparison, or only an imaginative, creative one?
4. Does another, less obvious comparison underlie the rest of the passage? If so, what is it?

Could it be the author is suggesting that in important ways we're all children? We certainly hope so.

5. Review your answers to the preceding questions. Choose one answer and add to it an account of the thinking process you used to discover the answer.

WRITING ASSIGNMENTS

1. Today's news reports are filled with descriptive phrases that might make good comparisons to begin papers with, especially if you don't have to tie yourself to what those phrases *really* mean—"star wars," "brilliant pebbles," "Long Bombs," "Hail Mary passes," "Smart Bombs," and so on. Pick three such phrases out of today's paper and write a paragraph using a fictitious definition of each phrase as the basis for a comparison.
2. Write a paper about six hundred or seven hundred words long that uses as its basis a metaphoric comparison. Try to be creative in what you say and how you say it.
3. Each part of the country and each group of people tend to have their own favorite, "folksy" ways of expressing comparison: a graduate student in agriculture says he has got his statistical analyses to turn out so well that they are "finer than frog hair"; a summer in Oklahoma is "so dry the catfish have fleas." Collect five such expressions from a group you belong to or know well and then write a paper about how those expressions characterize that group.
4. Do an analysis of the social scene at one of your campus's local hangouts (we know the research for this will be tough). Compare the physical layout there to a stage, the people to actors and actresses, and the activity to a theatrical production (whether farce, tragedy, musical comedy, or another form is up to you). Who are the major characters? the bit players? What's the plot? Where's the audience? And so on.
5. Sporting events are often referred to as "microcosms of life today," "another chapter in the eternal struggle between . . . ," or "mythic confrontations." Find an article that describes a recent sporting event you witnessed and that uses such a phrase. Explore the meaning of the phrase in reference to that event; flesh out the comparison. When you expand both sides of the comparison, how well does it hold up? Write a paper that describes the results of your analysis.

Another good writing assignment might be "All I Really Need to Know I Learned in ______"; each student fills in the blank differently (possible ideas: summer camp, high school, drama club, spring training two-a-days, Y-Teens).

6. Using gray-painted automobiles, Jim Reinders, a geologist, created "Carhenge" (see page 413) on his Nebraska farm. Compare the "Carhenge" photo with the photograph of Stonehenge on page 199. Clearly, the "Carhenge" photo is intended as a reaction to, or commentary upon, Stonehenge. A similar effect is achieved when one sees a comic version of a famous picture (for example, a "Mona Lisa" with a mustache, or a "Leaning Tower of Pisa" that has fallen down). In a brief paper, compare and contrast the "Carhenge" and Stonehenge pictures. Is the humor worthwhile? Is there respect for the original, even though the second picture is a send-up? What other "reaction to" pictures of famous originals have you seen? Which do you like (or dislike) best, and why?

Focus on Critical Thinking

7. Return to the Shakespeare sonnet at the beginning of this chapter. Work out exactly what all the comparisons (including the refusals to compare) mean in that sonnet. What do the results of your investigation suggest to you is the main issue involved in the poem?
8. The passage by Susan Sheehan on antipsychotic drugs suggests, in its last sentence (page 416), a particular problem. Define that problem in more detail, and explore whether there are any good solutions to it. (You may need to get to know your school library better to answer this question.)
9. Take a look at the dancing typical on your college campus. If relationships were like that kind of dancing, what would the relationships be? Can a primarily social activity be accurately taken as usefully similar to or indicative of anything as personal as a relationship between two people? What if relationships were compared not to different kinds of dances but to different kinds of sports, such as football, golf, or bowling?
10. Compare Pete Hamill's "Ethics in the 80s" (chapter 18) with Anne Morrow Lindbergh's "The Dance of Relationships" or with Robert Fulghum's "All I Really Need to Know I Learned in Kindergarten." In what ways do the two authors see the world similarly? differently? Are they even looking at the same world? Is one right and the other wrong? Can they both be right? Take your own position on the subject and defend it against theirs.
11. Examine one complete issue of the local (not your college's) newspaper from the town where your school is located. What attitudes toward old age, dying, and death do you see in it? Compare those attitudes with the ones in the issue of your school's paper for the same day. What does the comparison reveal?

Beyond that, what if relationships between people were epitomized by sports? For example, professional baseball is supposedly "America's game"; what does that tell us about relationships in America (which here really means the United States)? Canada's game is ice hockey; what does that tell us about relationships in Canada? What about a country whose distinctive sport is Ping-Pong? fencing? bowling? gymnastics? crew (rowing)?

Writers' Circle

Divide into groups of three students each. Each group should then collaborate to write a detailed paragraph that uses an extended metaphor (or analogy) as its basic comparative pattern. The tone can be humorous, serious, or somewhere in between ("Life is the pits," "My blind date was an animal," "Chemistry lab is anxiety city," "Society will die of its addictions," "My last paper was a national disaster," and so on). The paragraph can serve any primary purpose—to explain/inform, persuade, analyze, or express. Each member of each composing group must contribute at least one sentence.

After each group has composed its paragraph, each should appoint a reader to read its paragraph to the rest of the class; one at a time, all readers should then read the paragraphs to the class.

Discussion. What similarities are noticeable among the paragraphs, in addition to the obvious extended-comparison pattern? Which paragraph is most detailed? most effective? most entertaining?

chapter 19 Analysis

"Some of the things that happen to us in life seem to have no meaning, but when you write them down you find the meanings for them; or, as you translate life into words, you force a meaning. Meaning is intrinsic in words and sentences."

Maxine Hong Kingston

We have seen in chapter 6, "Writing to Analyze," that analysis is one of the primary reasons for writing. Analysis is critical, evaluative thought put into action, and analytical writing is largely writing that reports the results of such thought. Analysis is valuable to any writer because it involves sizing up situations, gauging conditions, and exploring options intelligently—it's *thoughtful,* and as we have said repeatedly in this book, *thought* is a key initial and ongoing part of any writer's composing process.

In this chapter we focus on analysis as an inventive *pattern* for writing; in chapter 6 we focus on analysis as a primary *purpose* for writing.

Analysis as a Pattern for Invention

While analysis is a powerful *purpose* for writing, the use of analytical *patterns* is also an important tool for writers. Because analytical patterns allow—even encourage—the writer to probe a subject for its constituent information, analytical patterns are highly *inventive* for writers. Consider, for example, a writer who asks these questions of a topic:

Cite a few common examples here. If your car won't start, there's a certain set of questions you ask in that situation to try to analyze the problem for a solution—is there enough gasoline, is the battery operating properly, and so on. If your printer won't print, likewise; if the lights in the apartment go out, the same; and so on.

- What does this subject consist of?
- What is involved here?
- How is this put together?
- What does this mean?
- Why does this happen?
- What should be done?
- Why is one response better than another?

And so on. Seeking answers to such questions (an analytical thought process) will almost certainly generate useful material for a writer. A familiar example of this kind of process is the "journalist's questions" for generating a story: who, what, where, when, why, and how?

External Analysis

Similar probing questions can be asked about virtually anything you read:

Rubric for Analytical Reading

1. What's the point (thesis) of this?
2. What support or evidence is there for this thesis?
3. What other, lesser points are made?

4. What support or evidence is there for those lesser points?
5. How *good* is this evidence?
   a. Is it appropriate for its purpose?
   b. Is it fact or is it opinion?
   c. Is it clear?
6. What kind of person does the writer seem to be? How does the writer "sound" on paper?
   a. Expert?
   b. Honest?
   c. Concerned?
   d. Sincere?
   e. Witty?
   f. Joking?
   g. Serious?
7. What is the primary appeal of the writing based on?
   a. Calm, orderly logic (*logos*)?
   b. Emotions (*pathos*)?
   c. The good character of the writer as revealed/created in the text (*ethos*)?

   And what makes you think so? Can you find evidence of all three kinds of appeal?

Ethos isn't so much what the writer brings to a text as what the reader perceives a writer (actually, the image of the writer the text creates) to have. In writing, more so than in speaking, *ethos* is created, not imported.

8. What assumptions does the writer make about his or her audience?
9. What is the structure of the writing?
   a. How does the organization help (or hinder) the effectiveness of the writing?
   b. How does the writer make ideas and development cohere (that is, proceed clearly and logically)?
10. What is the style of the writing?
    a. What kinds of figurative language does the writer use to make the writing clearer, more vigorous, more effective?
    b. Does the writer vary sentence structure and length to keep the reader's interest?
    c. How does the writer's vocabulary—especially the connotations—help convey attitude and meaning?

These questions are universal and can therefore be applied to almost any kind of writing, be it expressive, analytical, informative, or persuasive. They constitute a kind of *external* analysis, or analysis from *outside* the piece of writing itself.

Internal Analysis

Notice that, from a writer's viewpoint, both "external analysis" and "internal analysis" are more closely related to *discovery* as we have defined it than to *invention,* because both external analysis and internal analysis involve systematic steps or actions to be taken in order to discover details. They don't involve brainstorming or inspiration in any major way.

You may want to bring in other examples here.

There is, however, another, equally vital and useful approach to analysis: analysis based on the nature of the material itself. Such *internal* analysis seeks to find the naturally significant characteristics within the material, situation, or problem at hand, those characteristics which mark it, define its nature, and make it distinctive. Such analysis derives from an assessment of the individual case:

1. What is this situation?
2. What is here, available for use within the context of this situation?
3. What is unique to this particular situation?

Let's say that the answers to those three questions are as follows:

1. I need to tighten the nuts on my bicycle wheel. To do this properly, I need two ¼-inch open-end wrenches.
2. I don't have two ¼-inch open-end wrenches. I have one such wrench and a pair of channel grips. I can improvise with the channel grips.
3. Both nuts must be tightened on either end of the axle, and to ensure proper function they must be tightened to approximately equal points on the threaded axle.

The thought process analyzes not only the situation but also what is needed to solve the problem.

Similarly, you can analyze a task before attempting it in order to determine the best way to accomplish the task. How, for example, does an airplane mechanic know which tools to take along on a job? Most likely she envisions *doing* the job, step by step, and notes which tools are needed for each step. Or say that a doctor sees a patient who exhibits certain symptoms the doctor knows are consistent with a particular illness. How does the doctor know which lab tests to order? He calls for the particular tests that he trusts to confirm or deny the diagnostic hunch he already has. How does a scientist know which lab equipment will be needed to perform a particular experiment? And finally, how does a writer know which pattern or patterns to use to develop a topic? The answer often lies within the topic itself.

Let's say that a writer wants to explain to her readers how dangerous a chemical dump site is to a nearby water supply. Her purpose is twofold, as is her primary readership: (a) she wants to warn the people who live near the site as to the potential hazard, and to persuade them to take preventive action, and (b) she wants to warn everyone—all her readers, regardless of where they live or where their water comes from—about the dangers of this kind of chemical dumping, and to persuade them that they should also take preventive action in this and similar cases. How can she accomplish her goals?

Notice that our writer is *beginning* with *discovery;* what might she come up with were she to consciously do some *invention* first?

One way would be to look at the dumping problem that is the focus of her writing. The questions she first applies are those of the journalist:

- What is being dumped?
- Who is doing the dumping?

- Where is it being dumped?
- Why is it being dumped?
- When is it being dumped?
- How is it being dumped?

Although answers to these questions are certainly important to her writing, those answers don't reveal the urgency or danger of the situation. For that, she must probe from *within* the answer to the question of what is being dumped: *what* is the chemical? *What* are its properties? *What* can it do to the water supply, and *what* in turn can it do to people who use the contaminated water? This line of questioning, or analysis, will prove highly productive.

What other *external* patterns can your students think of that might be brought to bear on this subject?

Let's say she learns that several studies have shown this particular chemical to be a cause of cancer, of deformities in children, of sight and hearing loss, and of other serious afflictions. She finds case after documented case of such results where water has been contaminated this way. She begins to see that an excellent and highly effective way to present her analysis and persuade her readers would be to begin with a partial list of victims. Her article begins like this:

> Not No, but *Hell No!*
>
> David and Martha Steinle moved into Eden Estates in January 1985. Their son, Mark, was born with no arms on January 12, 1987.
>
> Lewis and Lena Thompson moved into Eden Estates in 1979. Both died of cancer within a month of each other in 1989.
>
> Stella Collins bought a new home in Eden Estates in 1976. In 1982 her eyes and ears began to fail her. By 1985 she was blind and needed a powerful hearing aid. By 1988 she was told she had cancer.
>
> Beth Sparma was two when she and her parents moved into Eden Estates in 1985. Little Beth died of cancer two days short of her fifth birthday.
>
> Obviously, all these people have in common their residence in Eden Estates. Less obvious but infinitely more significant is what else they have in common: last year the Steinles, Stella Collins, Beth Sparma's parents, and all their neighbors learned that their water supply at Eden Estates is hopelessly contaminated with chemical waste by-products. Now traces of the same chemical have been found in the much-larger water supply for the town of Haskell.
>
> Haskell Chemical Company, the town's largest employer, has been dumping the waste in a supposedly "safe" place. The company plans to look elsewhere for a new dump site but meanwhile has asked Haskell residents for a referendum on closing the plant until a new site is found. The company wants to know if the people of Haskell would approve of the plant's staying open—with the present dump site continuing in use—until a new site is found. Haskell residents, and all others faced with decisions like this, should make their answer clear and unmistakable: can you keep polluting our water until you find a safer place to pollute? Not no, but *hell no!*

Analytical Patterns

How would the paper have been different had she chosen to begin with an emotional appeal based on "Earth is the only home we have"? How would it have been different had she begun with a discussion of the NIMBY ("Not in My Back Yard") syndrome—everyone wants the benefits of all these sophisticated products, but no one wants to deal with the resultant waste?

In the excerpt above, the writer found a developmental "hook" in the list of illustrations in the first four paragraphs. The sheer weight of the tragic results of the Eden Estates pollution makes the Haskell request—involving a potentially much wider pollution—outrageous. In this case, the nature of the subject itself and the nature of the writer's purpose combined to suggest a developmental pattern based on the accumulation of evidence. Such accumulation, which in chapter 6 we called a logic of addition, is *inductive.* That is, things "add up" to a conclusion that is logically based on the accumulation of evidence.

Inductive and Deductive Patterns

There's more on induction in chapter 20.

One of the most important investigative methods is the "scientific" method, in which careful observation and the adding up of the details of observation lead to logical conclusions. The above writer assembled her knowledge inductively: this + this + this = that. Induction is a common analytical thought process. And so is its opposite but equally productive process, called *deduction.*

If *induction* involves a kind of logical addition, *deduction* involves a kind of logical subtraction. Instead of adding possibilities to reach a clear conclusion, deduction involves subtracting possibilities. Deduction doesn't seek to add similar evidence to accumulate; rather, it seeks to eliminate so that a logical conclusion remains *because* of the process of elimination. Recall how the epidemiologists in "Eleven Blue Men" (chapter 6) eliminated possible causes of the men's illnesses until only one logical conclusion remained: sodium nitrite poisoning interacting with alcohol. Likewise, consider the following syllogism:

1. All residents of Eden Estates are at risk from chemically polluted water.
2. The Luis Aparicio family resides in Eden Estates.
3. Therefore, the Luis Aparicio family is at risk from chemically polluted water.

Once you include the Aparicio family among those who reside in Eden Estates, you eliminate (or subtract) the possibility that they are not at risk. The third statement is an inevitable conclusion if the first two statements are true.

Many kinds of writing employ inductive and deductive analytical thinking. Such thinking is similar to, and often underpins, the lines of thinking and persuasion we discussed in chapter 7 and will briefly review at the start of chapter 20.

Four Types of Claims

Different kinds of claims (of fact, interpretation, value, or policy) need different kinds of warrants. A claim of fact is often a matter of definition, which needs for its warrant perhaps an authority. A claim of interpretation might rely on consensus of experts for its warrant. A claim of

Claims come in four types:

1. Claims of *fact* (something did or did not happen; something is or is not true)
2. Claims of *interpretation* (how to classify something as this or that)
3. Claims of *value* (something is good or bad)
4. Claims of *policy* (what should be done)

All claims need to be supported by evidence—data gleaned from observation, the use of authority, or the use of further argument. Moreover, all claims need to have warrants—lines of reasoning that connect the evidence with the claim—in order to add veracity and rhetorical force to the claim. Different types of claims require different types of warrants.

Being aware of how to employ induction, deduction, claims, and warrants is not only an important consideration for readers but also a key way for writers to analyze their own subjects—to get at the *internal* characteristics that might suggest logical ways to present what they have to say. Getting to the point where analysis of a topic can suggest ways to write about that topic is a kind of art, or knack—a productive sort of knowledge that becomes a way of doing things, one that opens up a variety of possibilities. As we shall presently see, those possibilities are almost unlimited. A subject can be presented from a different attitude or perspective; from an inductive accumulation of evidence, illustrations, or instances; from a free-associative "flow" of thoughts; from a historical perspective (such as then/now or recollection); from a full analysis of the given situation—even from a deliberately illogical kind of "logic" or antilogic. The knack of seeing such possibilities doesn't come easily, but once it does come it pays lasting dividends.

This knack of seeing the internal structure—of a topic, a situation, or any kind of writing task—is one way successful writers attack the problem of writing. It's a knack, all right—it comes easier to some than to others—but we can all get better at it by observing carefully how others do it and then practicing it ourselves.

value might need the warrant of an appeal to ethics. And a claim of policy might need a warrant built out of demonstrations of the impossibility of any other course of action.

We're discussing a seasoned writer's versatility here, a knack for sensing and pursuing possibilities within a writing task. This ability is akin to what the classical rhetorical theorist Aristotle called *tekne*. For lack of a better term, we'll call it productive knowledge.

See Art Buchwald's "Why We Need Our AK-47's," below, for an example of a logical antilogic structure.

We'll leave it to Michael Polanyi and others to determine whether, finally, "seeing" the internal structure of a topic actually means seeing something mostly inside oneself. We like the notion that we bring from within ourselves some structure to the topics we write about and find some other structure within the act of writing—but this isn't the place to argue such points.

We've brought up the "rhetorical situation" in our teaching notes to chapters 3, 6, and 8; that's what we're talking about here too.

KEY POINTS TO REMEMBER: Writing Analysis

Because the "right" method of analysis always depends on some particular combination of the subject, the situation, and the available materials, there are obviously more methods of analysis, each perfectly fine, than anyone could list, much less provide examples of or discuss. What we've chosen to do here, then, is present a small number of readings that illustrate typical patterns of analysis writers use successfully. After each example, we'll briefly discuss the author's inventional and shaping use of analysis and then refer you to other examples of the same pattern.

Analysis via Different Ways of Looking at Things

If we were to write instructions for doing a piece of writing with the analytical pattern of different ways of looking at things, they might read something like this:

> Pick a subject or a phenomenon that interests you or that you think is important and trace as many different ways of looking at it as you can. Then write an essay documenting the major different ways of looking at the subject and making a decision about which is best (or more likely to win out over the others).

Yet when you look at that paragraph apart from specific examples, its instructions seem woefully vague. And so let's illustrate them, first via the following piece of professional writing, "Madison Avenue's Blind Spot."

PREREADING WORKSHEET

Before you read the following piece by Eva Pomice, write your responses to these questions:

1. Think of recent TV or radio commercials that depict senior citizens. Would you say those commercials portray the elderly in a positive or negative way? Why did you respond as you did?
2. What connotations or mental images do you associate with the following terms: *the elderly, the aged, golden years, senior citizens, grandma/grandpa?* Are they different from one another? If so, how?
3. At what age would you say most people should be considered "old" or "elderly"? Why do you think so?
4. Think of people you know whom you consider old or elderly. What characteristics *besides* their age cause you to regard them that way?

Here's another selection that begins with examples. Your students may be too young to remember the Clara Peller commercial for the Wendy's hamburger chain. She portrayed a feisty senior citizen who, on receiving a burger at a competing chain, raised the top of the bun to stare at a tiny hamburger patty. "Where's the beef?" she loudly demanded. Another commercial featured Peller driving rather recklessly but purposefully from a competing chain's drive-through window to Wendy's drive-through after repeating her "Where's the beef?" question on receiving her order at the first window.

Here's the thesis (¶ 3). We don't have any problem with Pomice taking three paragraphs to get to it; do your students? What does this location of thesis imply about the classic "five-paragraph essay" form?

Madison Avenue's Blind Spot

EVA POMICE

Eva Pomice is a staff writer for U.S. News and World Report, *in which this selection appeared in 1988.*

Stuck on Youth, Advertisers Are Missing a Golden Market.

Remember Clara Peller? The crusty grandmother's outraged cry of "Where's the beef?" raised Wendy's sales in the famous 1984 promotion. But the ad itself also raised hackles among Peller's contemporaries. The elderly figure recklessly speeding from one burger drive-in to the next insulted senior citizens by portraying them as crotchety and ridiculous and as bad drivers. 1

The Peller ads weren't alone. In fact, in a recent survey by advertising agency Ogilvy & Mather, 40 percent of the over-65-year-old respondents agreed that Madison Avenue usually presents older people as unattractive and incompetent. "Advertising shows young people at their best and most beautiful," says Treesa Drury, advertising-standards director for *Modern Maturity* magazine. "But it shows older people at their worst." 2

Catering to a society fixated on youth, Madison Avenue has long neglected older Americans. Most advertisers see seniors as frugal, stubborn and closed-minded. Advertisers have compounded the problem, many industry critics charge, by showing older people as sickly and silly, rather than portraying them in the positive light in which many seniors see themselves. 3

4 None of these negative images seem warranted. Seniors as a group have money and aren't afraid to spend it. "People 50 and older have survived orthodontia and house payments and are more than willing to reward themselves," says Richard Balkite, Donnelley Marketing's director of senior marketing. People over 50 earn 42 percent of all total after-tax income and control half the nation's discretionary-spending power. A Donnelley study shows that mature consumers are much more interested in trying new brands and products than marketers had previously assumed.

In terms of traditional rhetoric, this paragraph is a preemptive strike on the other side's case (a refutation).

Old Images

5 Despite such golden buying power, many ads still invoke stale and offensive stereotypes of seniors. A recent Subaru spot features its own feckless grandmother sneaking away from her rocker to take a spin around the block in Dad's new rocket. An ad for Denny's shows two frumpy old sisters; one of them is too hard of hearing to get the name of the restaurant right. Other commercials play too much on the fears and embarrassments of growing older. In an insurance ad, Danny Thomas pats the hand of an infirm senior citizen in a hospital bed and warns viewers not to wait "until it's too late." Says Leonard Hansen, chairman of Senior World Publications, "Few marketers communicate to older adults as successful humans who have accomplished a great deal in their lives."

6 One explanation for such failings may be the relative youth of Madison Avenue's marketers and copywriters. Critics claim that they have failed to recognize the gap between a person's chronological age and the psychological age, typically 15 years less. "People do not grow old; their bodies betray them," says Jay Jasper, creative director at Ogilvy & Mather. "If you want to sell something to a man over 50, you don't put him in a cardigan, because cardigans are what grandpas wear." Direct references to age also doom many product pitches. A now legendary blunder was Johnson & Johnson's 1983 introduction of Affinity, a shampoo for "older" hair. Analyst James Gollub of SRI International recommends against "age typing" phrases such as golden oldies and golden years.

Action and Romance

7 Advertisers fear that an old-age image is the *coup de grâce* for mass-market products. Marketers could avoid that pitfall by using older actors in family and social settings, suggests David Ward, planning director at Ogilvy & Mather. Cereal makers like General Mills and Quaker Oats have included people over 50 in a crop of recent ads. Ralph Lauren pictures elegant older American women as part of a family dynasty. Marketers have been most successful with seniors, however, when they have touted the financial and personal freedom that comes with growing older, and stressed romance and glamour. McDonald's, for example, made a hit with the over-65 set with a romantic spot showing an old man bold enough to sit next to a comely older

woman. An American Airlines print ad for its Senior Savers Club shows an attractive couple with windblown hair in a powerboat.

Notice the ending that waffles on the major issue, an ending characteristic of contemporary journalistic prose. Do your students think use of such endings is bad?

To some analysts, such ads presage real recognition by Madison Avenue of America's fastest-growing age group. But skeptics doubt whether an industry hooked so long on the elixir of youth can overcome its preconceptions, even to capture so golden a market. 8

POSTREADING WORKSHEET

Now that you have read the piece by Pomice, write your responses to the following questions:

1. Have you seen or heard any recent commercials that portray older people in a positive light that has nothing to do with their being grandparents? If so, briefly describe that portrayal. Does it fit anything Pomice says about the positive portrayal of older people?
2. What effect did reading Pomice's piece have on you? Did you discover anything about your own attitudes toward older people? If so, what? If not, why do you think you did not?
3. Pomice's article describes the media image of older people in the mid-1980s and suggests that the world of advertising is beginning to realize how vital (and lucrative) the market among older people is. Do you see any signs *now* that the world of advertising has become more aware of this "golden" market and has improved its attitude toward older consumers in the years since Pomice wrote?
4. If you were an ad writer, what would you emphasize about older consumers to improve their image and boost the market among older consumers for your client?

Questions for Writing and Discussion

Prepare short written answers to each of these questions. Be prepared to hand them in or discuss them in class, as your teacher directs:

1. How many different words for "old age" do you find in this piece? List them.
2. How many different views of older people do you find in this piece? List them.
3. Watch one hour of network prime-time television (we know this is a tough assignment) and keep a list of all the images of people over fifty you see. How many of those images are positive? negative? What kinds of shows had which kinds of ads? What kinds of products did the ads endorse?

You may need a third category here—"ambiguous." Those will be the interesting ones to discuss!

4. If you could go back in time to watch when the writer first got an idea for this piece, what do you suppose that first "germ of invention" was? Alternatively, if the piece was assigned by an editor, what do you suppose put the idea for the piece in the editor's mind?

5. What do the following words mean—*hackles* (¶ 1), *frugal* (¶ 3), *orthodontia* (¶ 4), *feckless* (¶ 5), *cardigan* (¶ 6), *coup de grâce* (¶ 7), *skeptics, elixir* (¶ 8)?
6. Pomice gets great mileage out of the "golden" pun in this piece—that "golden" can mean older as well as lucrative. Do you think she overdoes it?

Let's consider a few more examples of pieces of writing done with the analytical pattern we call "different ways of looking at things." Suppose you were to write a piece about anger, and about the different ways "pop psychology" encourages people to view it. Some typical advice from pop psychology is "Always let it out," meaning it's better to ventilate anger than to suppress it. Other popular advice directly counters that dictim, maintaining it's better to be calm, to be the peacemaker, and to work things out without getting angry. In your writing you could lay out each view and illustrate each with a situation, before coming up with your own idea. What would that idea be? Well, one way would be to get angry at all the advice we get nowadays, to let your anger show in the writing, and to let *that* be your final comment on the subject. That way, you would ridicule the whole pop psychology and advice-book business with a final paragraph like the one below, which shows how one writer humorously decided to deal with her anger about columns and advice books that give contradictory advice about how to deal with anger:

Compare chapter 13's "On Not Suppressing Rage."

Ain't Nobody's Business but My Own

MARCELLE CLEMENTS

Marcelle Clements has written articles for Rolling Stone, Vanity Fair, Esquire, New York Woman, Village Voice, *and* Cosmopolitan. *Some of those articles have been collected into the book* The Dog Is Us and Other Observations.

1 I know what I'm going to do to console myself. I'm going to eat more red meat, that's for sure. Mmmmmm. Nice juicy hamburgers. Not broiled—fried. With cheese. And bacon. And french fries. For dessert, nothing but chocolate mousse will do. With whipped cream. From a can. And I think I'll drink more. Bourbon, that's for me. Bourbon and Coke, and I don't mean Diet. Followed by several cups of nice strong *coffee.* No, make that double espressos. And over dinner, I intend to *worry about what other people think of me.* And to be *as stressed as possible.* And if any morons dare to tell me I have a problem with authority, I think I'll just become snide, sarcastic, and *negative.* Oh, hell, maybe I'll slap them. Then perhaps I'll just go and have some *sex.* In a relationship that includes absolutely no commitment. In which there is unconditionally *no* chance of growth. And *zero* mutual respect. With a sailor. And when I come home at night (*late* at night, before getting *insufficient* sleep on a *soft* mattress, without giving a single thought to brushing, flossing, or skin care), I think I'll just have a nice, hot, nutritious bowl of crushed Valiums. Then maybe I'll calm down.

A good short writing assignment here is to bring in a recent, simple self-help article (something with a title like "Lose Weight Fast" or "Amazing New Invention Doubles Gas Mileage") and let your writing groups work up short parodies. Then ask them how invention and discovery, internal and external analytical patterns, helped the writing they did. Did they plan first, or just dive into the writing?

While truly inventional writing often does not know where it's going until it gets there, all writers need to leave their minds open to invention, no matter what kind of writing they're doing. When this writer, Marcelle Clements, started cataloging different attitudes toward anger, she may well not have known she would wind up writing a send-up of the whole pop-psychology and advice-column movement. But that's where the analytical pattern took her, and as the above paragraph shows, it turned out to be a good piece of writing.

Analysis via Facts, Figures, and Numbers

Just as common as the piece that proceeds via different ways of looking at something is the piece that proceeds by an accumulation of facts, figures, or examples. The result is like a mosaic or a collage, wherein one gets a truer view of the "big picture" by looking simultaneously at a collection of smaller—but significant or representative—pieces put together creatively. Here's an excellent example. As you read it, think about an answer to these questions: what was it that got this writer started on this piece of writing? What gave it its beginning and initial shape?

These points come up in the profiles of Bob Greene (Part Three's introduction) and Alice Walker (Part Four's introduction).

The High Cost of Being an Actress

GEOFFREY T. GRODE

Haircuts, Agents, Wardrobe, Head Shots—Take a Look at the Real *Price You'd Have to Pay to Break into Show Business!*

It's certainly no news that it's hard to break into acting and build and sustain a career. But few people pay much attention to just how *expensive* it is to do these things. To see how expenses vary with different levels of success, I asked four actresses, ranging from beginner to superstar, to detail the costs involved in developing, maintaining, and promoting their careers. 1

How would this piece's tone have been changed had this paragraph (and the corresponding ones later in the piece) instead been summarized in a table? Had you found it that way, what would it have told you about the audience the writer envisioned for the piece?

Lauren Shpall, twenty-two, is a graduate of UCLA's theater-arts program. Recently, she returned to Los Angeles after studying for a year at the London Theatre School. Shpall, who is at the "beginning, beginning stages" of her career, has so far earned less than $1,000 as an actress. Her estimated expenses for the current year are: photos and photo postcards, $210; stamps and envelopes, $70; résumé, $50; voice and acting classes, $600; Shing Yi, $600; flute lessons, $480; therapy, $1,000; gym, $80; business-travel expenses, $500; auditions, $200; hair, eyebrows, facials, and makeup, $360; clothing, $250; books, $150; telephone calls, $600; portfolio and Filofax, $115; theater events, $200; subscriptions, $95. Total: $6,160. 2

To make ends meet, Shpall works three part-time jobs. But with an estimated annual income of only $10,000, Shpall's anticipated expenses amount to over 60 percent of her expected gross income. As she readily admits, she wouldn't be able to pursue her acting career if not for the fact that 3 she lives (and eats) at home with her parents, who also pay for her car insurance and gas.

4 Even though Shpall's expenses seem high in relation to her income, she claims that she skimps almost everywhere. For example, she hired the cheapest photographer and can't afford an "appropriate wardrobe." Right now, she and some friends are trying to raise money to mount a production so she can be seen by agents and casting directors.

5 Rebecca Brooks, a blue-eyed blond in her thirties, moved to Los Angeles from New York two years ago. For the past twelve years, Brooks has earned most of her income as an actress, appearing in off-Broadway theater, TV episodes, features, and commercials. Occasionally, she has supplemented her income with temp work and catering jobs. Brooks's estimated expenses for this year are: nails, $600; trade papers, $250; gym, $500; union dues, $600; voice lessons, $2,100; pictures and résumés, $600; answering service, $170; gas, $800; car insurance, $2,000; telephone, $400; therapy, $2,400; *Players Directory and Guide,* $90; hair, $1,000; clothing, $5,000; agent, 10 percent of gross. Total, with agent's fees: $18,000.

6 Considering that during her career, Brooks's annual earnings have ranged between $15,000 and $30,000—making her expenses more than 50 percent of her gross—it's hardly surprising when she says that "surviving has been a struggle." Like Shpall, Brooks has had to cut corners to make ends meet. She can't afford a publicist or a personal trainer, and she spends far less on clothes, pictures, and voice lessons than she would like to.

7 After years of struggle, Brooks decided to give up acting. She locked herself in her bedroom for a weekend, cried for three straight days, and prayed for a "sign from above" to tell her what to do with the rest of her life. The following Monday, she got an acting job and decided to remain an actress. But the struggle—financial and emotional—continues. "I feel like I have a lot to offer but no opportunity to show it." Yet she has no regrets about "choosing a course of life that's given me the most pleasure."

8 Not surprisingly, expenses skyrocket as actresses become more successful. Caren Kaye, who modestly describes herself as a "recognizable commodity," has starred in five TV series (including *Blansky's Beauties* and *It's Your Move*), two feature films (*My Tutor* and the upcoming *Teen Witch*), and numerous TV episodes. Although raising two children has limited her work in the past few years, Kaye has averaged approximately $100,000 a year for the last decade, sometimes falling below that figure, sometimes making substantially more. Kaye's estimated expenses for the year are: agent, 10 percent of gross; manager, 10 percent of gross; business manager, 5 percent of gross; telephone, $1,200; personal, $1,280; therapy, $3,900; Players Academy, $45; union dues, $1,000; hair, $1,800; tooth cleaning and bonding, $2,070; facials, $600; full-time nanny, $8,400; clothing, $20,000; business entertaining, $4,800; photos, $1,000; manicures, $360; public relations, $14,400; acting classes, $3,120; lawyer, $1,000. Total: approximately $65,000 plus 25 percent of gross.

9 Although Kaye's expenses seem extraordinary, her high income also allows her options not available to less successful actresses. For example, she

has personally incorporated herself, a situation that provides certain tax advantages but requires a minimum annual income of $90,000. And some things that seem like dubious expenses—such as a full-time nanny—may be absolutely essential to maintaining a career. Even though Kaye says she enjoys being an active parent, she adds, "I must have someone available at a moment's notice to care for my children when I work." To balance the "narcissism" in her life, Kaye spends twelve hours a week counseling teen runaways and is also pursuing a Ph.D. in social work.

Predictably, superstar actresses have super-duper expenses. Fifteen-year-old Alyssa Milano, who plays Tony Danza's daughter, Samantha, on *Who's the Boss,* is one of the most successful teen actresses in the world. Success, however, does not come cheap. Alyssa's expenses are: agent, 10 percent of gross; business manager, 5 percent of gross; manager, Milano's mother, Lin, 15 percent of gross; phone, $2,700; private trainer, $15,600; *Players Directory,* $45; union dues, $1,425; orthodontist, $3,000; oral hygiene, $350; clothing (Milano's regular wardrobe), $12,000; business entertaining, $2,400; professional photos, $6,000; manicures and pedicures, $1,040; school (private tutor), $3,600; fan mail, $25,000; bodyguard, $26,000; personal assistant, $12,500; wardrobe (special occasions such as the Emmys), $5,000; new BMW convertible, $40,000, upon sixteenth birthday; insurance, gas, and car expenses, $6,000. Total: 35 percent of gross plus $174,660. 10

How do your students feel about including a $40,000 convertible as an expense that is necessary to "developing, maintaining, and promoting" one's career?

With Milano's off-the-top expenses of approximately $175,000 (35 percent of $500,000) added to her almost identical itemized expenses, her total expenses for the year come to a staggering $350,000. Fortunately, her income (which includes poster sales, a workout video, and Japanese endorsements) is $500,000 a year. A law covering child actors stipulates that 30 percent of that amount be set aside in a special account, which Milano will have access to on her eighteenth birthday. 11

Meanwhile, for a teenager with an income of a half million dollars a year, Alyssa receives a modest allowance of $25 a week. She professes to be perfectly happy with her life, leaving her career planning to her mother-manager and allowing her parents to indulge her on occasion (Los Angeles Kings season tickets, for example). Unfair as it may seem, Milano has achieved her mind-boggling success without ever taking an acting lesson. 12

Ironically, while one frequently hears actresses complaining about the emotional toll of their profession, the financial toll—which, as we have seen, is considerable at all levels of success—is rarely mentioned. It's a cost of doing business that is borne without apparent bitterness. 13

Notice how straightforward this piece is in its approach. The author has the right figures on four different things and lays them right out in front of us.

Questions for Writing and Discussion

Prepare short written answers to each of these questions. Be prepared to hand them in or discuss them in class, as your teacher directs.

1. For each paragraph tally up how many sentences are accumulation of detail and how many are interpretation and comment by the writer. Do you feel the relationship is somehow disproportionate here?
2. Do you feel that any of the details were irrelevant? If so, which ones? Were any misplaced (such as the BMW)? Does it seem odd to you that the writer didn't comment on such things?
3. Did the ending seem abrupt to you? How else might this piece have ended?
4. What do you suppose was the "inventional germ" for this piece? Does it seem likely to you that the author was walking down the street one day and suddenly had the thought, "I'll do a piece on the high cost of being an actress"? What seems to you to be a more likely beginning scenario?
5. What do the following words mean—*Shing Yi* (¶ 2), *commodity* (¶ 8), *narcissism* (¶ 9), *pedicure* (¶ 10), *borne* (¶ 13)?

Bridges: Another Perspective

Geoffrey Grode shows us a little-considered aspect of careers in entertainment—the expenses involved in maintaining such careers at differing levels of success. What seems clear is that the more successful one is in that career, the more—*far* more—money one both makes and spends for career maintenance.

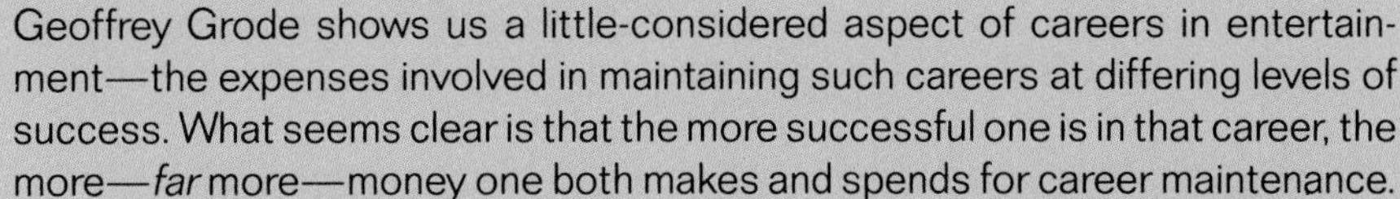

What Grode *doesn't* examine is what might be called the sociological, psychological, or philosophical costs of a culture that rewards big-name entertainers (movie, television, and music stars; professional athletes in football, baseball, and basketball) with monetary fortunes and public admiration far beyond what it pays in money and respect to people in such truly admirable careers as teaching, nursing, counseling, and other helping professions. What are the costs—monetary, psychological, emotional—of *these* careers?

Analysis via Association

In writing as in other parts of life, sometimes one thing just seems to lead to another. There's a game people who remember song lyrics play that works like that—I sing a song that ends with a certain word, and then you have to sing one that starts with that word, and so on. Like that game, a piece of writing sometimes takes on a life of its own, moving from one point to the next mostly because wherever point A ended is where B starts. The pattern may not be logical, chronological, or any other "-ical," but the piece often works out to be fresh and original. Here's an excellent example of analysis via association:

Not all students will follow this piece's associational structure the first time through it; you might want to work through it with them.

Rea refers here to the 1988 presidential campaign of George Bush.

Sociology 101 in a Shoe Box

DAN REA

Dan Rea is a television news reporter in Boston, Massachusetts.

Baseball Cards Taught Me How to Read, Do Math, Learn Geography and Understand Life.

Hardly a month passes these days without some newspaper article or television report on the "bull market" in old baseball cards. There are some who suggest that no single investment from the 1950s has resulted in a better financial return than a baseball-card collection. Those Topps and Bowmans are now more valuable than some stocks and bonds. Such stories prompt every young collector from the '50s to review his player portfolio in high hopes of finding a Mantle in mint condition. Yet the quick cash to be made in today's boom market does not necessarily measure the real worth of that cache of old baseball cards. 1

Way back in the days of Sputnik and Dwight Eisenhower, baseball cards taught me how to read. They were infinitely more interesting than any silly stories about Dick, Jane and Spot. Better yet, flip those cards over and those columns of statistics of at-bats, hits and runs batted in gave arithmetic purpose. What better way to teach an 8-year-old to multiply and divide than to introduce him or her to the magical calculation of an earned-run average? 2

For just five pennies, throw in a tour of America—pre–New Frontier. No geography book ever held my interest longer than those old cards; they introduced me to the far regions of all 48 states, the hometowns of my heroes. Decades later, my work as a television reporter has taken me to more than 30 states to cover news stories. When the Vatican appointed a new archbishop of Boston, I found myself in Springfield, Mo., the bishop's previous diocese. There, with complete confidence, I was able to surprise my cameraman with an extemporaneous explanation of the Sherm Lollar (a great White Sox catcher from the '50s) Bowling Alley. 3

This fall, the end of a long day following the Bush campaign found me on the road from South Bend, Ind., to Kalamazoo, Mich. In the middle of that stretch of road, at 65 miles an hour, a small oasis: a sign pointed to Paw Paw, Mich. My crew soon learned the name of the town's most famous resident, Charlie (Paw Paw) Maxwell, a left-handed, power-hitting Detroit Tiger of summers long past. 4

No collector of baseball cards in the 1950s could long ignore that players with strong ethnic names like Kluszewski, Malzone and Skowron probably came from a Northern city, while any player with initials for a first name was almost assuredly from below the Mason-Dixon line. Sociology 101 with a stick of bubble gum tossed in. 5

6 From the lengthening perspective of a quarter century, there are even more valuable lessons to be gleaned from those old cards. For virtually all the players, the game between the lines is now over. But as the box scores of life came in, not all those fortunate young men were treated alike. Fate cruelly deserted the young Chicago Cubs infielder, Ken Hubbs, who died in an off-season plane crash. His death introduced mortality to any serious young baseball-card collector at a time of genuine innocence—long before Vietnam. Later, much later, few deaths of world figures rivaled the loss of Roberto Clemente as far as I was concerned. A New Year's Eve airplane disaster in the early '70s deprived the world of the Pittsburgh Pirates Hall of Famer. Clemente surrendered his life and his career at the height of his talent, helping to transport much-needed supplies to earthquake victims in Managua, Nicaragua.

7 As the years passed, so did the immortals. Roger Maris, for me the Babe Ruth of my generation, stroked more home runs in one single season than any other player in history. Yet Maris was never able to remotely rival his epic season of 1961. He won world championships in both leagues, retired early and passed away much too soon. Every year now the sports pages carry the obituaries of great players like Elston Howard, Ken Boyer, Jerry Adair, Dick Farrell and Norm Casy—young men of the '50s and '60s who will never lose their youth. Meanwhile, others lost their innocence. More than a few of my heroes ended up on the wrong side of the law. Perhaps best known is Denny McLain, the Cy Young Award winner of 1968 who last year pleaded guilty to racketeering and cocaine possession, thus proving that the blessings of youth do not necessarily last a lifetime.

Rea refers to the Cy Young Award, named for the major league pitcher who won more games in his career than any other pitcher has. Each season, a Cy Young Award is given to the pitcher considered the best that year in each of the two major leagues of professional baseball.

Young Hero

8 For the athlete, life is often a cruel irony. The greatest triumphs come too easily and too early, leaving him in later life with a frustrating inability to repeat past achievements. Still, some of my baseball-card heroes took their lives far beyond the days of summer. Congressman Jim Bunning of Kentucky threw no-hitters in both the American and National leagues, and former congressman Wilmer (Vinegar Bend) Mizell of North Carolina wears a Pittsburgh Pirates ring from their world championship of 1960. Former Washington Senators outfielder Chuck Hinton now practices his craft as a baseball coach at Howard University. And a few like Vern Law, Marty Keough, Dick Ellsworth and Gus Bell have the unimaginable thrill of watching their own sons 30 years later follow their footsteps down big-league base paths.

9 I have held onto my baseball-card collection for a quarter of a century, even though that collection was complete by my early teens. Those cards accompanied me through my boyhood while taking me to a world far beyond my imagination. Baseball games on the back-porch radio at night assumed an additional dimension with a stack of baseball cards nearby for easy reference.

A leisurely perusal of those old cards would lead me through the lives of players, time and again showing me that nothing—in life or baseball—is accomplished without hard work and, sometimes, great disappointment.

Those lessons from so long ago now sitting in a shoe box are still relevant today. And those lessons convince me that any catalog price these old baseball cards might attract will never fully measure their genuine value. 10

Seller beware: childhood memories and lifelong lessons have no price tag. 11

Questions for Writing and Discussion

Prepare short written answers to each of these questions. Be prepared to hand them in or discuss them in class, as your teacher directs.

1. How is it the author gets from paragraph 3 to paragraph 4? 4 to 5? 5 to 6? 6 to 7? 7 to 8?
2. If associational logic ties paragraphs 3 through 8 together, what, then, can be said about 1 and 2, 9–11?
3. What connects the frame (¶ 1–2, 9–11) with the narrative (¶ 3–8)? Do you feel that connection needs to be strengthened?
4. There's a sense in which paragraph 10 is hackneyed, a term referring to a pattern of speech used so often that it's almost counterproductive to use it again. How else might the essay have concluded? Would the essay be better without its present ending?
5. What do the following words mean—*bull market, cache* (¶ 1), *extemporaneous* (¶ 3), *oasis* (¶ 4), *gleaned* (¶ 6), *perusal* (¶ 9)?

When it works, an essay whose sections are joined by association is especially effective because its parts seem to connect naturally, to "flow." That structure can also be an effective comic device, especially in cases of dialogue between two people, as in "Has His Southern-ness Gone with the Wind?" from chapter 10.

Analysis via "Then and Now" Snapshots

This comparison can also be between the way things are and the way we want them to be.

Another popular technique for writers wanting to analyze a situation is to pair a picture of the way things are now with one of how things used to be. All of us have our personal and family snapshot albums, whether mental or physical, and so looking at things in this kind of "before versus after" pattern is a comfortable way for any piece of writing to proceed. The writing may take a particular historical incident as its grounding (the first plane flight, the first Jewish homesteaders in the Oklahoma Panhandle, and so on) and juxtapose that with where things are now. Or the writing may look at the way things are now and compare that information with the way things used to be. Both techniques are common analytical schemes based on comparison, and nothing is inherently wrong (and a great deal is inherently right) with both. For example, imagine a young black girl in 1960 starting to notice that all the faces in the soap operas on her mother's new TV set are white. And then the first black face she sees on the screen is that of

Martin Luther King—being arrested for leading a civil rights protest in Alabama. What would that mean to her today?

The Civil Rights Movement: What Good Was It?

ALICE WALKER

Alice Walker is well known for her fiction, poetry, and essays that deal with the lives of African-American women. See her "Profile of a Writer" on page 299. This piece was written in the winter of 1966–67 when the momentum of the Civil Rights Movement seemed to Walker to have stalled.

1 Someone said recently to an old black lady from Mississippi, whose legs had been badly mangled by local police who arrested her for "disturbing the peace," that the Civil Rights Movement was dead, and asked, since it was dead, what she thought about it. The old lady replied, hobbling out of his presence on her cane, that the Civil Rights Movement was like herself, "if it's dead, it shore ain't ready to lay down!"

2 This old lady is a legendary freedom fighter in her small town in the Delta. She has been severely mistreated for insisting on her rights as an American citizen. She has been beaten for singing Movement songs, placed in solitary confinement in prisons for talking about freedom, and placed on bread and water for praying aloud to God for her jailers' deliverance. For such a woman the Civil Rights Movement will never be over as long as her skin is black. It also will never be over for twenty million others with the same "affliction," for whom the Movement can never "lay down," no matter how it is killed by the press and made dead and buried by the white American public. As long as one black American survives, the struggle for equality with other Americans must also survive. This is a debt we owe to those blameless hostages we leave to the future, our children.

3 Still, white liberals and deserting Civil Rights sponsors are quick to justify their disaffection from the Movement by claiming that it is all over. "And since it is over," they will ask, "would someone kindly tell me what has been gained by it?" They then list statistics supposedly showing how much more advanced segregation is now than ten years ago—in schools, housing, jobs. They point to a gain in conservative politicians during the last few years. They speak of ghetto riots and of the survey that shows that most policemen are admittedly too anti-Negro to do their jobs in ghetto areas fairly and effectively. They speak of every area that has been touched by the Civil Rights Movement as somehow or other going to pieces.

4 They rarely talk, however, about human attitudes among Negroes that have undergone terrific changes just during the past seven to ten years (not to mention all those years when there was a Movement and only the Negroes

knew about it). They seldom speak of changes in personal lives because of the influence of people in the Movement. They see general failure and few, if any, individual gains.

They do not understand what it is that keeps the Movement from "laying down" and Negroes from reverting to their former *silent* second-class status. They have apparently never stopped to wonder why it is always the white man—on his radio and in his newspaper and on his television—who says that the Movement is dead. If a Negro were audacious enough to make such a claim, his fellows might hanker to see him shot. The Movement is dead to the white man because it no longer interests him. And it no longer interests him because he can afford to be uninterested: he does not have to live by it, with it, or for it, as Negroes must. He can take a rest from the news of beatings, killings, and arrests that reach him from North and South—if his skin is white. Negroes cannot now and will never be able to take a rest from the injustices that plague them, for they—not the white man—are the target. 5

Perhaps it is naīve to be thankful that the Movement "saved" a large number of individuals and gave them something to live for, even if it did not provide them with everything they wanted. (Materially, it provided them with precious little that they wanted.) When a movement awakens people to the possibilities of life, it seems unfair to frustrate them by then denying what they had thought was offered. But what was offered? What was promised? What was it all about? What good did it do? Would it have been better, as some have suggested, to leave the Negro people as they were, unawakened, unallied with one another, unhopeful about what to expect for their children in some future world? 6

I do not think so. If knowledge of my condition is all the freedom I get from a "freedom movement," it is better than unawareness, forgottenness, and hopelessness, the existence that is like the existence of a beast. Man only truly lives by knowing; otherwise he simply performs, copying the daily habits of others, but conceiving nothing of his creative possibilities as a man, and accepting someone else's superiority and his own misery. 7

When we are children, growing up in our parents' care, we await the spark from the outside world. Sometimes our parents provide it—if we are lucky—sometimes it comes from another source far from home. We sit, paralyzed, surrounded by our anxiety and dread, hoping we will not have to grow up into the narrow world and ways we see about us. We are hungry for a life that turns us on; we yearn for a knowledge of living that will save us from our innocuous lives that resemble death. We look for signs in every strange event; we search for heroes in every unknown face. 8

It was just six years ago that I began to be alive. I had, of course, been living before—for I am now twenty-three—but I did not really know it. And I did not know it because nobody told me that I—a pensive, yearning, typical high-school senior, but Negro—existed in the minds of others as I existed in my own. Until that time my mind was locked apart from the outer contours and complexion of my body as if it and the body were strangers. The mind 9 possessed both thought and spirit—I wanted to be an author or a scientist—which the color of the body denied. I had never seen myself and existed as a statistic exists, or as a phantom. In the white world I walked, less real to them than a shadow; and being young and well hidden among the slums, among people who also did not exist—either in books or in films or in the government of their own lives—I waited to be called to life. And, by a miracle, I was called.

10 There was a commotion in our house that night in 1960. We had managed to buy our first television set. It was battered and overpriced, but my mother had gotten used to watching the afternoon soap operas at the house where she worked as maid, and nothing could satisfy her on days when she did not work but a continuation of her "stories." So she pinched pennies and bought a set.

11 I remained listless throughout her "stories," tales of pregnancy, abortion, hypocrisy, infidelity, and alcoholism. All these men and women were white and lived in houses with servants, long staircases that they floated down, patios where liquor was served four times a day to "relax" them. But my mother, with her swollen feet eased out of her shoes, her heavy body relaxed in our only comfortable chair, watched each movement of the smartly coiffed women, heard each word, pounced upon each innuendo and inflection, and for the duration of these "stories" she saw herself as one of them. She placed herself in every scene she saw, with her braided hair turned blond, her two hundred pounds compressed into a sleek size-seven dress, her rough dark skin smooth and *white.* Her husband became "dark and handsome," talented, witty, urbane, charming. And when she turned to look at my father sitting near her in his sweat shirt with his smelly feet raised on the bed to "air," there was always a tragic look of surprise on her face. Then she would sigh and go out to the kitchen looking lost and unsure of herself. My mother, a truly great woman who raised eight children of her own and half a dozen of the neighbors' without a single complaint, was convinced that she did not exist compared to "them." She subordinated her soul to theirs and became a faithful and timid supporter of the "Beautiful White People." Once she asked me, in a moment of vicarious pride and despair, if I didn't think that "they" were "jest naturally smarter, prettier, better." My mother asked this: a woman who never got rid of any of her children, never cheated on my father, was never a hypocrite if she could help it, and never even tasted liquor. She could not even bring herself to blame "them" for making her believe what they wanted her to believe: that if she did not look like them, think like them, be sophisticated and corrupt-for-comfort's-sake like them, she was a nobody. Black was not a color on my mother; it was a shield that made her invisible.

12 Of course, the people who wrote the soap-opera scripts always made the Negro maids in them steadfast, trusty, and wise in a home-remedial sort of way; but my mother, a maid for nearly forty years, never once identified herself with the scarcely glimpsed black servant's face beneath the ruffled cap. Like everyone else, in her daydreams at least, she thought she was free.

Notice how this piece discusses a turning-point event in the author's life. You may want to invite your students to compare it with a similar "self-recognition" piece, Madeleine L'Engle's "My Fortieth Birthday" (chapter 5).

Six years ago [in 1960], after half-heartedly watching my mother's soap operas and wondering whether there wasn't something more to be asked of life, the Civil Rights Movement came into my life. Like a good omen for the future, the face of Dr. Martin Luther King, Jr., was the first black face I saw on our new television screen. And, as in a fairy tale, my soul was stirred by the meaning for me of his mission—at the time he was being rather ignominiously dumped into a police van for having led a protest march in Alabama—and I fell in love with the sober and determined face of the Movement. The singing of "We Shall Overcome"—that song betrayed by nonbelievers in it—rang for the first time in my ears. The influence that my mother's soap operas might have had on me became impossible. The life of Dr. King, seeming bigger and more miraculous than the man himself, because of all he had done and suffered, offered a pattern of strength and sincerity I felt I could trust. He had suffered much because of his simple belief in nonviolence, love, and brotherhood. Perhaps the majority of men could not be reached through these beliefs, but because Dr. King kept trying to reach them in spite of danger to himself and his family, I saw in him the hero for whom I had waited so long. 13

What Dr. King promised was not a ranch-style house and an acre of manicured lawn for every black man, but jail and finally freedom. He did not promise two cars for every family, but the courage one day for all families everywhere to walk without shame and unafraid on their own feet. He did not say that one day it will be us chasing prospective buyers out of our prosperous well-kept neighborhoods, or in other ways exhibiting our snobbery and ignorance as all other ethnic groups before us have done; what he said was that we had a right to live anywhere in this country we chose, and a right to a meaningful well-paying job to provide us with the upkeep of our homes. He did not say we had to become carbon copies of the white American middle class; but he did say we had the right to become whatever we wanted to become. 14

Because of the Movement, because of an awakened faith in the newness and imagination of the human spirit, because of "black and white together"—for the first time in our history in some human relationship on and off TV—because of the beatings, the arrests, the hell of battle during the past years, I have fought harder for my life and for a chance to be myself, to be something more than a shadow or a number, than I had ever done before in my life. Before, there had seemed to be no real reason for struggling beyond the effort for daily bread. Now there was a chance at that other that Jesus meant when He said we could not live by bread alone. 15

Here Walker employs the "before and after" view.

I have fought and kicked and fasted and prayed and cursed and cried myself to the point of existing. It has been like being born again, literally. Just "knowing" has meant everything to me. Knowing has pushed me out into the world, into college, into places, into people. 16

Part of what existence means to me is knowing the difference between what I am now and what I was then. It is being capable of looking after myself intellectually as well as financially. It is being able to tell when I am being wronged and by whom. It means being awake to protect myself and the ones I 17 love. It means being a part of the world community, and being *alert* to which part it is that I have joined, and knowing how to change to another part if that part does not suit me. To know is to exist: to exist is to be involved, to move about, to see the world with my own eyes. This, at least, the Movement has given me.

18 The hippies and other nihilists would have me believe that it is all the same whether the people in Mississippi have a movement behind them or not. Once they have their rights, they say, they will run all over themselves trying to be just like everybody else. They will be well fed, complacent about things of the spirit, emotionless, and without that marvelous humanity and "soul" that the Movement has seen them practice time and time again. "What has the Movement done," they ask, "with the few people it has supposedly helped?" "Got them white-collar jobs, moved them into standardized ranch houses in white neighborhoods, given them nondescript gray flannel suits?" "What are these people now?" they ask. And then they answer themselves, "Nothings!"

19 I would find this reasoning—which I have heard many, many times from hippies and nonhippies alike—amusing if I did not also consider it serious. For I think it is a delusion, a cop-out, an excuse to disassociate themselves from a world in which they feel too little has been changed or gained. The real question, however, it appears to me, is not whether poor people will adopt the middle-class mentality once they are well fed; rather, it is whether they will ever be well fed enough to be able to choose whatever mentality they think will suit them. The lack of a movement did not keep my mother from *wishing* herself bourgeois in her daydreams.

20 There is widespread starvation in Mississippi. In my own state of Georgia there are more hungry families than [ex-governor] Lester Maddox would like to admit—or even see fed. I went to school with children who ate red dirt. The Movement has prodded and pushed some liberal senators into pressuring the government for food so that the hungry may eat. Food stamps that were two dollars and out of the reach of many families not long ago have been reduced to fifty cents. The price is still out of the reach of some families, and the government, it seems to a lot of people, could spare enough free food to feed its own people. It angers people in the Movement that it does not; they point to the billions in wheat we send free each year to countries abroad. Their government's slowness while people are hungry, its unwillingness to believe that there are Americans starving, its stingy cutting of the price of food stamps, make many Civil Rights workers throw up their hands in disgust. But they do not give up. They do not withdraw into the world of psychedelia. They apply what pressure they can to make the government give away food to hungry people. They do not plan so far ahead in their disillusionment with society that they can see these starving families buying identical ranch-style houses and sending their snobbish children to Bryn Mawr and Yale. They take first things first and try to get them fed.

21 They do not consider it their business, in any case, to say what kind of life the people they help must lead. How one lives is, after all, one of the rights left to the individual—when and if he has opportunity to choose. It is not the

prerogative of the middle class to determine what is worthy of aspiration. There is also every possibility that the middle-class people of tomorrow will turn out ever so much better than those of today. I even know some middle-class people of today who are not *all* bad.

I think there are so few Negro hippies because middle-class Negroes, although well fed, are not careless. They are required by the treacherous world they live in to be clearly aware of whoever or whatever might be trying to do them in. They are middle class in money and position, but they cannot afford to be middle class in complacency. They distrust the hippie movement because they know that it can do nothing for Negroes as a group but "love" them, which is what all paternalists claim to do. And since the only way Negroes can survive (which they cannot do, unfortunately, on love alone) is with the support of the group, they are wisely wary and stay away. 22

A white writer tried recently to explain that the reason for the relatively few Negro hippies is that Negroes have built up a "super-cool" that cracks under LSD and makes them have a "bad trip." What this writer doesn't guess at is that Negroes are needing drugs less than ever these days for any kind of trip. While the hippies are "tripping," Negroes are going after power, which is so much more important to their survival and their children's survival than LSD and pot. 23

Everyone would be surprised if the Israelis ignored the Arabs and took up "tripping" and pot smoking. In this country we are the Israelis. Everybody who can do so would like to forget this, of course. But for us to forget it for a minute would be fatal. "We Shall Overcome" is just a song to most Americans, *but we must do it.* Or die. 24

What good was the Civil Rights Movement? If it had just given this country Dr. King, a leader of conscience, for once in our lifetime, it would have been enough. If it had just taken black eyes off white television stories, it would have been enough. If it had fed one starving child, it would have been enough. 25

If the Civil Rights Movement is "dead," and if it gave us nothing else, it gave us each other forever. It gave some of us bread, some of us shelter, some of us knowledge and pride, all of us comfort. It gave us our children, our husbands, our brothers, our fathers, as men reborn and with a purpose for living. It broke the pattern of black servitude in this country. It shattered the phony "promise" of white soap operas that sucked away so many pitiful lives. It gave us history and men far greater than Presidents. It gave us heroes, selfless men of courage and strength, for our little boys and girls to follow. It gave us hope for tomorrow. It called us to life. 26

Because we live, it can never die. 27

Questions for Writing and Discussion

Prepare short written answers to each of these questions. Be prepared to hand them in or discuss them in class, as your teacher directs.

1. In this essay, what is the "then"? the "now"? What connects the two?
2. What does Walker mean by "that song betrayed by nonbelievers in it" (¶ 13)?
3. Recall an important experience from your own childhood and outline a similar essay on the "then versus now" pattern.
4. Take a current situation—the environment, network television, the role of big-time college athletics, the Civil Rights Movement, anything that interests you—and compare it with the way things were five or ten years ago. What moral can you legitimately draw from the comparison?
5. What do the following words mean—*disaffection* (¶ 3), *innocuous* (¶ 8), *vicarious* (¶ 11), *ignominiously* (¶ 13), *manicured* (¶ 14), *nihilists* (¶ 18), *paternalists* (¶ 22)?

One student who was assigned question 4 above decided to compare cartoon shows on television from today with those from a decade or so ago. Here's his brainstormed list of things to talk about:

Then	Now
Fred Flintstone	Mumrah the Ever-living
Wile E. Coyote	Skeletor
Scooby Doo	Hordak
Elmer Fudd	Teenage Mutant Ninja Turtles
SuperFriends	Transformers
Batman and Robin	Bravestar

What do you suppose the point of his analytical comparison turned out to be? Was it that yesterday's cartoons were trite and simpleminded? Or was it that today's cartoons are leading children to violence and the occult? Which way would you go with this? (The finished essay appears later in this chapter.)

Analysis via Key or Typical Features

Often the elements of an analysis are things you are more or less expected to know. In your high school English class you may have been expected to analyze a poem, and your teacher probably wanted you to include specific things in your analysis. Similarly, if an investigator from the government General Accounting Office believes a product costs too much—hammers that cost $150, for example—her analysis will look at a standard set of things, doubtless including what a good hammer sells for at retail in a hardware store. And if a writer were analyzing a movie, what things would you expect to come up? The directing, the script, the lead actors' performances, the cinematography, and how the script does or does not reach something like "the human spirit," right? Consider, for example, the following review of *The Untouchables*:

Of course, the trick lies in knowing the key features. In most cases, they will be the obvious things one would expect to be concerned about, the things naturally important in the situation.

Other choices that have obvious key features students might be asked to name include choosing a car, ordering a meal in a strange restaurant, selecting a movie to invite a friend to watch with you, and evaluating a college.

The point here is to get students involved in thinking about what kinds of things they *expect* to find covered in a movie review.

If available time and equipment can be worked out, you might bring the videocassette of this film to class for viewing as a complement to reading Schickel's review. (*Note:* Because the film is rated R and depicts considerable violence, you should preview it [and all other films you might be considering for classroom use].)

In the American Grain: The Untouchables

RICHARD SCHICKEL

Richard Schickel is a reporter, editor, columnist, and writer of books of nonfiction (including The World of Carnegie Hall, Movies, The Disney Version, *and* The Men Who Made the Movies), *books of fiction (including* Another I, Another You), *and television scripts. His review of the movie,* The Untouchables, *appeared in* Time *in 1987.*

"So much violence," murmurs Eliot Ness (Kevin Costner) as he cleans out his desk at the end of *The Untouchables.* 1

A truer, sadder sigh has never escaped from a movie sound track. He has, after prodigies of bloodshed and the loss of precious friends and values, fulfilled the classic destiny of a movie hero. Garbed in a mysterious, often near comical purity, he has arrived in a profoundly corrupted community and, by imposing his eerie conscientiousness on it, awakened its conscience. Now the city is at peace, in part because Ness has taken upon himself some of its wickedness. Or, as he puts it, "I have become what I beheld, and I am content that I have done right." 2

The Untouchables is not a realistic recreation of Chicago during Prohibition. Nor is it a typical effort from Brian De Palma [director of *The Untouchables*], who has often put his awesome technique and his admirable sense of film history to trashy (*Dressed to Kill*) or trivial (*Wise Guys*) ends. Instead, it goes to that place that all films aspiring to greatness must attain: the country of myth, where all the figures must be larger and more vivid than life. 3

We might therefore join De Palma and Screenwriter David Mamet in a prayer that their epic work—a masterpiece of idiomatic American moviemaking as well as a plangent commentary on its traditions—will be spared from the literalists, complaining both that the gore is too real and that the characters are not real enough. Protect them as well from the wrath of the traditionalists who resist the intrusion of originality on their passion for the endless restatement of stale generic conventions. Deliver them instead to the audience that will be galvanized, as the filmmakers were, by the chance to reimagine all the clichés of crime fiction. 4

Begin with Al Capone, from whom all factual and fictional descendants have learned some of the elements of style. But skip all that gangster-as-tragic-hero stuff. In Robert De Niro's grandly scaled performance he is demonically expansive, our first thug celebrity. And a man who in his secret life, the life his romanticizing fans did not want to hear about, illustrates a lecture on teamwork by taking a Ruthian clout at a traitorous underling's skull with a baseball bat. What he evokes, finally, is pure horror (and maybe some black humor) but—and the film is rigorous on this point—no sympathy. 5

6 Ness is even more radically redefined. [David] Mamet [author of the screenplay] says he sees him as a lone town tamer of Western legend. De Palma has evoked the name of John Ford to suggest the classic qualities he was aiming for. And Costner has something of the grave beauty Gary Cooper used to bring to these roles.

7 But he is something more than the Western hero transplanted to the city's wilderness. He is not a detached solitary; he is a family man, pleased when his wife tucks a love note into his brown-bag lunch, careful to include both an Eskimo and a butterfly kiss in his little daughter's good-night ritual. Nor is he a man who has educated himself along the trail; instead, he proudly asserts his learning through the punctilious formalities of his manner and diction. Indeed, he is a man whose survival (and killer) instincts are in dire need of on-the-job training and support.

8 That is where his untouchable (read incorruptible) "posse" comes in. Moral fiber might be enough to carry the day against frontier bandits. But in urbanized America, where crime is mechanized, industrialized and partially subsidized by government, it needs a modest organization to back its play: the nerveless trigger finger of George Stone (Andy Garcia), like Capone, Italian; the accounting genius of wimpy-looking, stouthearted Oscar Wallace (Charles Martin Smith); and above all, the mentoring heart and long memory of the Irish cop, Jimmy Malone (Sean Connery). He is a weary, steady man, very clearly seen by an actor whose every gesture is wryly informed by the humorous, and uncynical knowledge of a lifetime.

9 What is true of Connery's work applies to the whole movie. Mamet's elegantly efficient script does not waste a word, and De Palma does not waste a shot. The result is a densely layered work moving with confident, compulsive energy. One sequence is set in Chicago's Union Station, where Ness and Stone must take a key witness from the Mob's protective custody. Into their stakeout blunders a mother maneuvering a baby carriage up a staircase. What delirious conflict between Ness the lawman and Ness the family man, as he tries to protect the infant and simultaneously conduct a shootout. What wild comedy in this conflict between duty and humanity. And De Palma ices the cake by shooting the scene as a parody of Eisenstein's Odessa Steps sequence from *Potemkin.*

10 Such riches abound in this film, but it is as parable, not parody, that it grips us. The Untouchables all begin as archetypes of American goodness. And they do triumph over evil; they send Capone to prison. But the cost is death or loss of innocence, for it is only by adapting crime's methods that they can defeat it.

11 This is, perhaps, the implicit lesson of almost all action films. But most of them have permitted their heroes to reclaim their honor at the end. The good guys are allowed to think their fall from purity and motive was a temporary aberration. There is no such escape for Eliot Ness. Despite its driving pace, style and wit, this film's pervasive mood is a strange and haunting sadness. *The Untouchables* is, of all things, touching.

Questions for Writing and Discussion

Prepare short written answers to each of these questions. Be prepared to hand them in or discuss them in class, as your teacher directs.

1. Besides those listed before the essay, what other standard parts of a movie review does Schickel include here? Does he leave any important ones out?
2. Do you think using a fairly common set of topics to cover in his review helps or hurts Schickel's analysis? Why or why not?
3. If you were to write a review of a course you had taken, what would be the standard set of topics to cover?
4. If you were to write an analysis of the likely victor in a sporting contest (choose one—football, tennis, volleyball, and so on), what would be the standard set of topics to cover?
5. What do the following words mean—*prodigies* (¶ 2), *aspiring* (¶ 3), *idiomatic, plangent, galvanized* (¶ 4), *evoke* (¶ 5), *punctilious* (¶ 7), *parable, parody, archetype* (¶ 10), *aberration* (¶ 11)?

Would the set of topics for a tennis match be different for men and women? for men's and women's basketball? for a novel written by a woman and a novel written by a man?

Suppose you were to do an article about the rising costs of college education. What things would most college student readers expect to see in it? How would that list of topics differ were it drawn up with the students' parents in mind? Here's the list of topics on that subject one writer used in *Reader's Digest;* what would you add to the list?

Again, we think you should have your students *do* this.

Changes in tuition costs, 1981–1989

Negative effects on students' families

Increasing numbers of taxpayers' dollars going to federal aid to higher education

Availability of government money letting schools be fiscally irresponsible

Absence of price competition

Administrative costs going up much faster than instructional costs

Student services costs going up

Tuition increases having no discernible beneficial effect on quality of education

Question whether value of college education may have actually gone *down*—in effect, less education for more dollars

John Hood, "Must College Cost So Much?" *Reader's Digest* April 1989: 108.

What other obvious factors might need to be addressed to prepare an analysis of this—or any—product that seems to be delivering less quality for more money? When you think about writing this way, you're reaching a good understanding of the inventional role of analytical patterns in writing. (If you want to see how another writer did a thorough analysis of rising educational costs, see "The Untouchables"—not a film review this time—at the beginning of the next chapter.)

A little group work with *Consumer Reports* can really drive this point home.

Analysis via Parody of Analysis

We can't leave this topic without pointing out another use of analysis—humor, in which the analysis proceeds by parodying a typical analytical pattern. *Parody* is writing that imitates the recognizable style or content of another type or piece of writing for humorous and satiric purposes. For example, if you've read many movie reviews, you may start to feel that the phrases and structures therein are so overworked that a well-crafted review like Schickel's of *The Untouchables* almost sounds like a parody of itself. A good writer—say, a Mark Twain or an Art Buchwald—can take a typical analytical pattern—say, logic—and create a hilarious send-up of it—in this case, a very logical illogic.

A continuing debate in the United States concerns the desirability of banning "assault weapons"—guns like the AK-47, that seem uniquely suited for shooting people, and not for much else. When President Bush announced he would ban "assault weapons" via Presidential Order in order to support the "War on Drugs" (then being led by federal anti-drug "czar" William Bennett), the anti-gun lobby rejoiced. Later qualifications and loopholes made the ban not nearly so much of a victory as that lobby had expected. As usual, Art Buchwald offers a definitive view of the subject.

Why We Need Our AK-47s

ART BUCHWALD

Art Buchwald is a syndicated columnist and essayist. Books include Art Buchwald's Paris, Don't Forget to Write, I Chose Capitol Punishment, *and* You Can Fool All of the People All of the Time. *Once, when attacked by a presidential press secretary for writing "unadulterated rot," Buchwald replied, "I have been known to write adulterated rot, but never unadulterated rot."*

1 The debate on who should own guns and who shouldn't is not going to go away tomorrow. It's becoming very emotional, and George Bush would like us all to calm down and not throw the baby out with the AK-47.

2 The thing we must do is look at both sides of the argument and then make our decision whether banning guns is a plus or a minus for the country.

3 I am prepared to make my argument for guns, and leave it to some bleeding heart liberal to give the other side.

4 Here is why you should bite the bullet.

5 The main source of food in this country is provided by hunters. If you took their guns away, the people of America would starve.

6 By disarming you would be threatening the great sport of target shooting; Japan would win all the medals at the next Olympics.

7 The environment would become endangered if people were not permitted to shoot empty Coca-Cola cans off brick walls.

Instead of taking away anybody's right to bear arms, it would make a lot more sense to issue everyone in the country a good bulletproof vest. 8

Law-abiding gun owners should not be punished just because policemen are being shot in the streets. 9

If you make someone in a gun store wait two weeks for a weapon, he may lose interest and spend the money on groceries instead. 10

Take a gun away from an honest citizen, he becomes impotent. 11

Gun owners who are heavily armed feel very threatened by all the hysteria on guns. If stirred up, they might use their weapons to make their point. 12

If we demand all semiautomatic weapons be banned, there would be no way of keeping grapes out of the United States. 13

The economic havoc caused by our inability to buy assault weapons could cause the worst recession in 60 years. 14

The boom in the sale of assault weapons at the present time is the only thing that will make up for the losses of the savings and loan industry in the United States. 15

If we do anything to stop the sale of weapons, the Russians will read it as a sign of weakness and land troops on Kennebunkport, Me. 16

If William Bennett does anything to cut back on gun sales in the United States, President Bush will be stripped of his lifetime membership in the NRA. 17

If you want to stop people in families from being accidentally killed by guns, build more jails. 18

If Congress wants to get tough about guns, let members get campaign money from the anti-Constitution rats on the other side. 19

The greatest challenge to a sportsman is to shoot a deer before she shoots you. 20

Questions for Writing and Discussion

Prepare short written answers to each of these questions. Be prepared to hand them in or discuss them in class, as your teacher directs.

1. Each of Buchwald's paragraphs—each one-liner—uses essentially the same technique. Describe it.
2. Why is this piece funny?
3. Find another Buchwald column in a recent newspaper and examine it for use of similar techniques.
4. Select an issue you're tired of hearing people argue/preach about and, using it for a topic, write an imitation of this Buchwald column.

Maybe it's an indication of how strong some of these standard analytical patterns are that they are so easy to parody. You can find another example of the same kind of satiric send-up of logic in *Adventures of Huckleberry Finn,* in the scene in which Huck tries to explain to his friend Jim why the French people do not talk the same way he and Jim do. Huck's analogies, such as cats talking cats' language but not cows' language, fall in ruins when Jim asks, "Is a Frenchman a man?" Huck replies yes. Then Jim closes his "illogical" point: "*Well*, den! Dad blame it, why doan' he *talk* like a man?"

The "right" method for analysis always depends on the subject being analyzed, the situation at hand, and the available materials. The preceding examples have shown you some of the more important typical ways writers use analytical patterns to shape what they're writing from the inside out. In the next section, you will follow a student like yourself, working on a similar assignment.

CASE STUDY CLOSE-UP

Assigned to do a paper drawing a moral or advancing a persuasive point, Arthur Raney, who had loved watching television cartoons in his youth and who had recently been watching them again as part of a psychology class project, decided to do an analytical comparison of cartoons "then" (that is, in his youth) and now. He first brainstormed the list of cartoon characters you saw earlier (page 461) and then expanded his list by jotting down typical details he had observed about each character, noting the differences he perceived between the "then" and "now" character groupings.

As he jotted, he began to notice that the older cartoon characters have a certain harmless-seeming unreality about them—they are very human, even though they may have distorted bodies, as with Fred Flintstone's disproportionately large head. They suffer exaggerated speech impediments, as with Elmer Fudd or Daffy Duck. Or they have to rely on ingenuity, as Batman does, rather than superhuman strength or speed to apprehend evildoers. In other words, although they are unreal they do have realistic limitations because of their humanlike dimensions. Moreover, distinctions between good and evil are always clear in their world. In the old cartoons no doubt is left, and even the evildoers often turn out to be harmless, as in the case of the hapless Wile E. Coyote, destined never to dine on the Roadrunner-"hero."

On the other hand, Arthur noticed that modern cartoon characters lack these human qualities—all are mystical, otherworldly, even occult. They are horrid mutants or inhuman creations, drawing on dark powers that tend to blur distinctions between good and evil, right and wrong. The persuasive moral point Arthur's paper was required to make began to suggest itself strongly as his jotting continued: it seemed clear that modern cartoons are not really wholesome and healthy for young people to view. The same is true of the products modeled after these modern characters and heavily advertised while the cartoons are being televised.

Arthur at first organized his material in large "then" and "now" groupings, but before doing his first full draft he decided to stagger the "then" and "now" comparisons a bit more, the better to emphasize the contrasts. His first draft nonetheless began with quite a bit of detail about the old cartoons. His classmates, however, suggested that he instead begin with a vivid anecdotal description of a particularly revolting modern cartoon character and then move into his argument that such fare isn't as good as the old cartoons. A couple of readers of his first draft also pointed out that Arthur's strongly implied cause-effect relationship between modern cartoons and youthful drug abuse, disrespect for authority, interest in the occult, and so on was not proved in his essay. They questioned whether changed cartoons could be blamed for such a pervasive problem in our society, and they suggested Arthur "tone down" his claim in this regard. Following this good advice, Arthur produced the following essay.

What About Some Real Cartoons?

Arthur Raney, college writing student

The frail body of a bandaged man rises from his resting place, the crypt. He cries, "Ancient Spirits of Evil, transform this decayed form to Mumrah the Ever-living." He groans and screams. His appearance changes from that of a mummified being to a seven-foot-tall muscular creature donned in hideous apparel. Two snakes are intertwined and blazoned on his chest and head. As the zombielike being turns to show his full transformation, his eyes, and the eyes of the stuffed creatures of evil on the pyramid wall, glow with a burning red. 1

No, this is not a scene from the latest Stephen King flick or Freddy Kreuger's latest escapade. This is a semifictitious but representative scene from a popular afternoon children's cartoon, "Thundercats." Yes, this is definitely a far cry from the 1970s' after-school television fare for youngsters. Then the roughest thing going was Fred Flintstone slamming his foot in a door, or Wile E. Coyote becoming an accordion after a perilous fall. These days, children are exploited and negatively influenced by the animated shows that cover the airways on weekday afternoons and Saturday morning. 2

Characters of old like Scooby Doo, the SuperFriends (let me emphasize Friends in that word), and Bugs Bunny have been replaced with Mumrah, the Ever-living Force of Evil; Skeletor; and Hordak, with his Evil Horde. We often wonder why so many children of today seem to have very little respect for authority, seem to be more interested in the occult, and seem to be overall behavior problems, and at least a partial 3 answer may lie in the cartoons they are exposed to. The subjects being presented on these once-educational and -entertaining shows can lead children away from general respect for authority and morality and into revolt and the black world of mysticism.

4 Most of the main characters in popular television cartoons of today are no longer human beings or personified animals, as were Scooby Doo, Yogi Bear, and Elmer Fudd. Now most of the characters are variations of human beings and animals caused by supernatural forces, or totally new beings created in the mind of a cartoonist. Teenage Mutant Ninja Turtles, Transformers, and Lion-o all fall into this category and are all very popular today.

5 This trend has led children away from a pseudorealistic look at animation to an unnatural, sometimes-mystical view of the shows. Where the SuperFriends had powers caused by birth (Superman coming from another planet) or ingenuity (Batman and Robin with their Utility Belts), Bravestar now summons his powers from the mystical side of nature and the animal kingdom, and He-Man is strengthened by the "powers of Greyskull." Children receive a severely warped sense of reality and see no visible role models in these shows. They look at these cartoon characters as heroes but then look in the "real world" and find nothing remotely like them.

6 Shows today also deal very pointedly with the occult, satanism, and demonology. Mumrah, from "Thundercats"; Hordak, from the show "She-rah"; He-Man; and Bravestar all call on spiritual forces to strengthen them and empower them. "Ghostbusters" is filled with every sort of spook, specter, and demon. "Dungeon and Dragons," a cartoon of a couple of years ago, very openly suggested demonic notions, beginning with the horned Venger, the program's evil overlord, riding a black mare. Seven-headed dragons, sorcery, and pentagrams (a common satanic symbol) filled this Saturday-morning show. Even the lovable Smurfs had demonic characters: Asriel the Cat, who bore the same name as one of Satan's angels; and his master, Gargamel, who performed his magic spells on a pentagram.

7 It is true that some of the older cartoons have also been deemed questionable in the eyes of some. The "Bugs Bunny Show" was once edited to cut out the violent actions toward the coyote, Daffy Duck, and other characters. The old show "Isis" dealt with an Egyptian nature

goddess who was married to Osiris, the god of the dead. But these shows did not focus on these negative aspects. They were secondary to the positive plot of the show. Sure, the coyote's falling and smashing himself is a big part of the show, but so is the Roadrunner's always getting away.

Today, the cartoons focus on the supernatural and mystical side of the plot. The climax comes when Venger appears on the screen with a red background and light shining off his ivory horn. It comes when Bravestar summons the spirits to give him the "speed of the puma." The focus of the show is on this bizarre, unnatural act or scene, not on the action itself. 8

Not only are children receiving some rather negative and nonproductive images from the cartoons themselves, but the advertisers are exploiting them also. A bill was just recently vetoed by President Reagan that would have regulated the amount of commercial advertisement during children's television shows. [This essay was written in late 1988.] It is a fact that children are extremely impressionable, and advertisers use this fact to their advantage. Often dolls and board games that are representative of a certain show or character will be advertised during that program. This leads the young viewer to a heightened sense of desire for the object. Also, the subject of repetitiveness and persistence of the commercials have raised questions in the minds of critics. Is it right or fair to the child viewer to fill the advertising time slots with such pointed appeals for purchasing? Are the media being responsible servants to the public? 9

Cartoons are, and will remain to be, a very important part of the upbringing of children. We hold in our hands a powerful means of shaping the future. We can allow the same type of shows to continue, and thus reap the too-frequent results of such a decision: drug abuse in schools even on the elementary level; continued disrespect for authority; heightened interest in the occult; overly aggressive children. Or we can take a stand and force producers to create wholesome, educational, yet entertaining shows for our children to enjoy. We need to trade in "Thundercats" and "Dungeon and Dragons" for reruns of "Hong Kong Phooey" and "Spiderman." We need to show our kids that we care, and give them some *real* cartoons. 10

WRITING ASSIGNMENTS

1. In this chapter Arthur Raney analyzes old and new television characters in a paper that criticizes the new characters and suggests they are negatively affecting the children who watch them. In chapter 17 Richard Zoglin urges us to "put a brake on television sleaze." Television indeed seems a fertile field for analysis. Analyze some aspect of television programming for yourself and write the results of your analysis. Here are some possibilities:
   a. What is the image of older citizens as reflected in television situation comedies ("sitcoms")?
   b. What is the image of the family as reflected in sitcoms?
   c. What is the quality of talk on television talk shows?
   d. Is there a difference in the quality of talk between daytime and nighttime talk shows?
   e. What difference do you perceive in or among the following:
      (1) National network evening (5:00 or 6:00 P.M.) newscasts.
      (2) Local-station nighttime (10:00 or 11:00 P.M.) newscasts.
      (3) "News networks" that feature constant news.
      (4) Various music-video channels.

2. Analyze a full-color "photo spread" advertisement in a "slick" magazine, such as *Esquire.* What appeals (*ethos, logos, pathos*) do you spot? What assumption does the advertiser make about the audience? How does the advertiser use logic and/or language?

3. Recall a galvanizing moment in your own life, similar to that of Alice Walker's seeing Martin Luther King on TV, and analyze the importance of that moment in your own life.

4. Rent a film for your VCR (or see one at a local theater if you do not have access to a VCR). "Read" the film closely, analyzing it as you might a book for which you have to write a review. Then write a review of the film, taking care to assess its success (or lack of same) in such areas as these:
   a. Acting.
   b. Script/story (dialogue, plot, pace, setting, theme).
   c. Photography.
   d. Direction.
   e. Music.
   f. Visual or special effects.

This would work well if you and your class watch the same movie together on the VCR or attend the same screening at a theater. (Remember, however, that all films should be previewed, and you need to find ways to make productive the time spent viewing any films.)

5. The American folk musician and humorist Woody Guthrie is rumored to have said, when recalling the hard times of the Great Depression, "I ate twice a week, whether I was hungry or not." On another occasion, referring to the care he took with his money, he said, "I never spend my money foolish, unless I'm by myself or with somebody." Such remarks cause us to do a double take: they seem logical, for they are cast in sentence structures often used for

serious, logical statements. But their logic also betrays them as humorous, because, in the first case, (a) eating only twice a week is *not* enough to sustain a healthy person and (b) during the hard times of the depression, for some people hunger was such a constant, and unsolvable problem that it didn't matter that they were hungry—they weren't getting anything to eat anyway. In the second case, Guthrie is actually saying the opposite of what he seems to mean, for we are always either alone or with other people; hence, he always spends his money foolishly.

Flights of humorous illogic are manifest in Art Buchwald's "Why We Need Our AK-47s." Explore other writers who use similar wit in entertaining us—Lewis Grizzard, for example, Erma Bombeck, or Roy Blount, Jr. Analyze these works for the use of humor to address an otherwise-serious problem.

6. Consider the drawing, *Relativity,* by M. C. Escher on page 437. Write a brief paper in which you explore these questions.
   a. What do you think Escher is trying to express in the drawing, and why do you think so?
   b. How or why is the title of the drawing appropriate?
   c. What generalizations or claims might you make about the attitudes, thoughts, or philosophy of this artist?
   d. What thoughts or attitudes does the picture evoke in *you?*

Focus on Critical Thinking

7. We've seen that analysis can be used for all writing purposes: expressive, informative, persuasive, and analytical. Look back through the preceding chapters in this section. In an excerpt by Elizabeth Griffith, for example, we have a narration about the lives of Elizabeth Cady Stanton and Susan B. Anthony. Though the gist of the passage is narrative, intended to inform, what elements of analysis do you also detect? What elements of comparison (chapter 18)? How do those lines of development contribute to the purpose of informing?
8. In the context of the entire novel by Jack Schaefer, the passage from *Shane* in chapter 16 can be analyzed as a symbolic scene, forecasting the events of the novel's plot. If you're familiar with the whole story, develop that symbolic analysis.
9. *Tone* is defined as the writer's apparent attitude toward his or her subject and/or audience. Analyze the tone in the following selections:
   a. Wilfred Sheed, "See the Hamptons in Autumn, When the Coast Is Clear" (chapter 16).
   b. Pete Hamill, "Our Town" (chapter 16), and "Ethics in the 80s" (chapter 17).
   c. Ben F. Nelms, "A Nation at Risk" (chapter 16).
   d. Paul Theroux, "On Being a Man" (chapter 17).

10. Analyze Dr. Arthur Bodin's "Stress Test" in chapter 17. Based on the content and kinds of questions in each section, what can you conclude about stress and its causes?
11. How does Pete Hamill align morality with "common sense" in "Ethics in the 80s" (chapter 17)?
12. Refer to the rubric for analytical reading given on pages 438–39 at the very beginning of this chapter. Apply each of the ten questions of that rubric to "The Long Habit," by Lewis Thomas, in chapter 18.
13. Apply the rubric for analytical reading to Robert Fulghum's "All I Really Need to Know I Learned In Kindergarten" (chapter 18).

Writers' Circle

Divide into teams of three or four students each. Each team should first choose a profession from the list below and then investigate the following aspects of each profession:

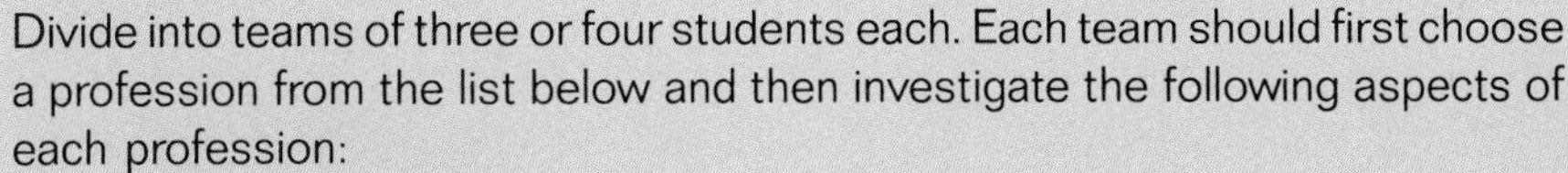

How training takes place
How long training lasts (including apprenticeships)
What full, official (licensed) status requires
What training, overall, costs
What entry-level, full professionals earn

After investigating via library research, interviews, and so forth, each team should collaborate on writing a report of its findings. Then, when each team's report is complete, all reports should be shared with the class in two ways:

1. Oral report, read by a person appointed by the team
2. Written report, to be combined with all other reports into a career-guide project for all interested students

The Professions

Medical doctors—general practice	Plumbers
Medical doctors—specialists	Carpenters
Attorneys-at-law	Bricklayers
Elementary or secondary teachers	Auto mechanics
University professors	Welders
Air-traffic controllers	Dentists
Medical assistants	Computer technicians

chapter 20 Argumentation

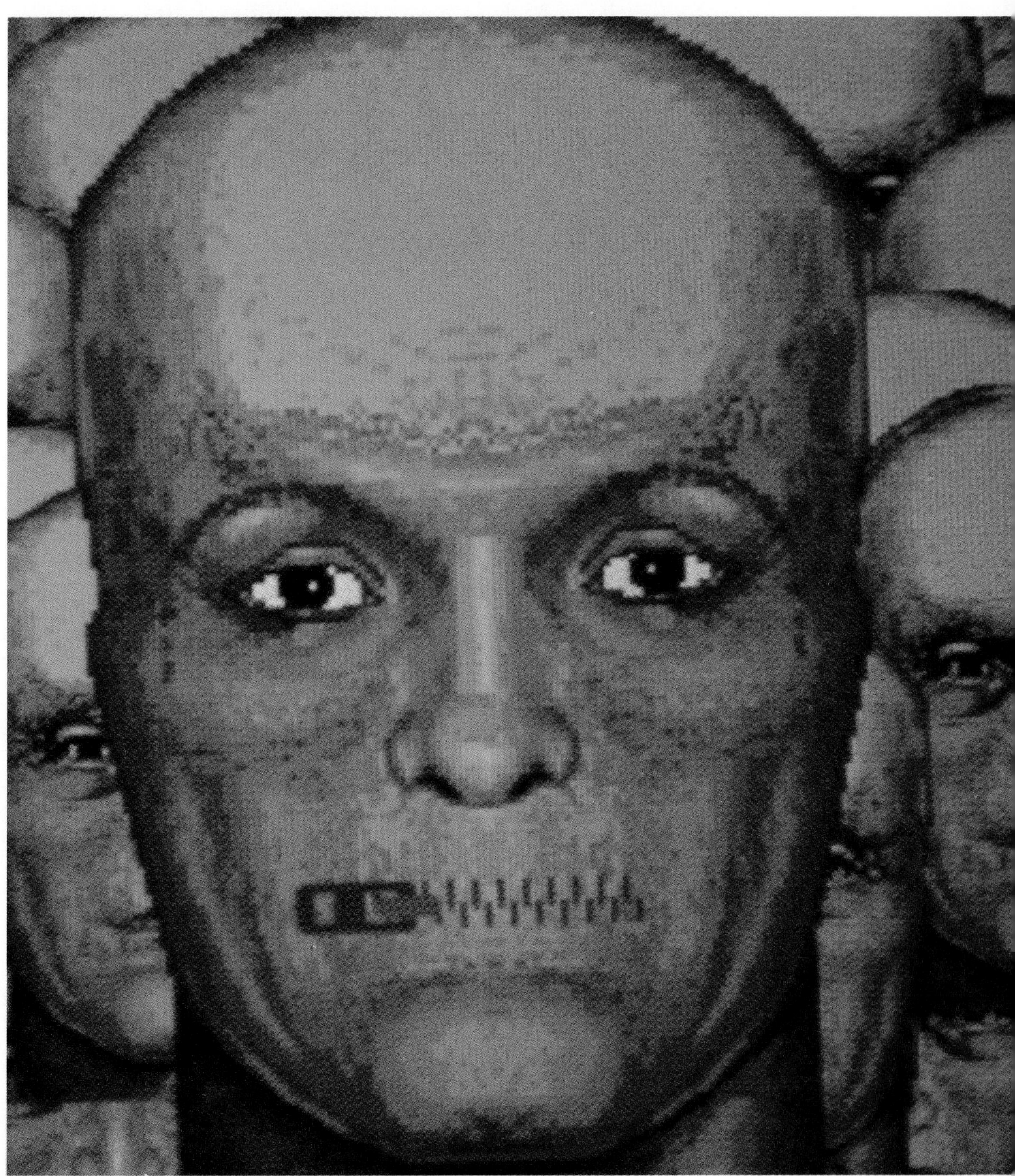

"Argumentation is the art of influencing others, through the medium of reasoned discourse, to believe or act as we wish them to believe or act."

J. M. O'Neill, C. Laycock, and R. L. Scale, ***Argumentation and Debate***

"Writing argumentative essays tests and enlarges important mental abilities—developing and organizing ideas, evaluating evidence, observing logical consistency, expressing ourselves clearly and economically—that we need to exercise all our lives in our various social roles, whether or not we continue to write after college."

Annette T. Rottenberg, ***Elements of Argument***

This chapter builds on material presented in several places earlier in this book:

- Chapter 3 (on critical writing)
- Chapter 7 (on persuasion as a purpose)
- Chapter 8 (on critical reading)
- Chapter 14 (on critical thinking)

The chapter begins with a brief review of that material, but if for some reason you've not already carefully read one or more of those sections, you should page back in the book and do so now.

A Brief Review of Critical Thinking

You might want to use some ads or an article to review the material in this section. One good choice would be the "Ethics in the 80s" piece from chapter 17.

What we're doing here is adapting and combining stasis theory and the Toulmin persuasion model (see Toulmin).

Early on in this book (chapter 3, to be exact), we talked about the *critical* quality of college writing—the frequent need in college (and in professional life) not just to report information but also to evaluate it and use the information to make judgments. As you move further into your college experience and into your eventual profession, those evaluations and judgments need to be more and more precise, more and more clearly based on specific evidence, and more and more persuasively presented. And in chapter 7 we talked about persuasion as a *purpose* for writing. There we focused on determining the *claim* a piece of writing makes and the *support* offered for that claim. Claims generally are of four types: *fact* (Did something happen or not? Is or is not something true?), *interpretation* (Is it one of these or one of those?), *value* (Is it good or bad?), and *policy* (What should be done?). Once you know what kind of claim is being made, what the claim itself is, and what the support for that claim is, you can ask whether the support is the *right* kind and whether it is *close* enough to the claim to support it (a) adequately and/or (b) persuasively. In chapter 8, on critical reading, we added the question of whether there were middle steps or unstated assumptions that join the support and the claim, *warrants* that need to be beefed up or made explicit to make the argument more persuasive. And chapter 14, on critical thinking, added the important element of making a careful decision about just what *key issue* is under discussion.

Stasis theory shapes the Toulmin model in two important ways: (a) the kind of warrant an argument needs will vary according to the argument's stasis, and (b) students can find an argument's principal claim more easily if they are aware of the argument's stasis.

Elsewhere we have also discussed the three primary bases of argumentative appeal as described by Aristotle: *logos*, in which the appeal is couched primarily in the logic of the argument; *pathos*, in which the appeal is couched primarily in the emotions the subject may elicit from the audience; and *ethos*, in which the appeal is couched primarily in the audience's perception of the good character of the person making the argument. These appeals certainly may overlap, and often do, but one will usually dominate.

- *Logos* generally takes the form of a calm, reasoned presentation in which claims and support are given straightforwardly. When *logos* dominates the argument, the person making the argument is usually confident that the logic itself is the argument's most forceful aspect.
- *Pathos* seldom takes the form of a calm or reasoned presentation, because the presenter wishes to use the emotions inherent in the subject to help persuade the audience. Although in this kind of appeal reasons are less important than feelings, that doesn't necessarily make such appeals less important or less valuable than logical appeals. Some of our most vital issues—euthanasia, abortion, capital punishment—have strong emotional characteristics.
- *Ethos* is an appeal that turns almost exclusively on the audience's perception of the good character of the presenter. Though logic or emotion may also be a part of the argument, the most persuasive force comes from the way the audience perceives the reputation of the presenter. If the audience knows the presenter, the line of thinking *ethos* exploits goes something like this: "Carstairs is a good person; therefore, what Carstairs wants me to think (or do) must also be good." If the audience doesn't know the presenter, the argument goes this way: "Carstairs seems like a good person in the things she is saying here; therefore, what Carstairs wants me to think (or do) must also be good."

None of these appeals is inherently better than the others, and all three are vulnerable to abuse. What is important to you, as a writer and reader, is to be aware of these appeals and how they operate so that you can recognize them in the arguments made by others and use them in the arguments you make yourself. They will help you, along with your understanding of the elements of claims, evidence, and warrants, to be a more critical and effective interpreter and maker of argument.

This Chapter's Goal: Writing Effective Arguments

Our goal in this chapter is to show you how to put the preceding elements together as structures that accomplish effective arguments—words put together in particular patterns for the express purpose of changing someone else's mind, of moving someone to a specific line of action. Whereas chapter 7 approached the *purpose* of persuasion, this chapter presents the *patterns* of persuasion, what we call elements of argumentation. As the preceding discussion indicates, most of what we present here you have probably seen before in different contexts. With the addition of just a few new elements, you will have everything you need to write effective arguments.

Where in your life as a college student do you see arguments—explicit, overt attempts to change someone's mind, to urge someone to action? Here's one example.

The Legend of "Dirty" Potato Chips™

CHICKASAW CHIPS, INC.

Note the "turn" on an archetypal opening—a play on a flag-waving appeal to nostalgia and patriotism: "good ol' American mass production ingenuity."

Note in this paragraph the appeal to our growing distrust of technology.

In paragraph 3 we're invited to believe "the problem" is a simple one.

In paragraph 4 they're appealing to our liking for things handmade. This is largely an emotional appeal, like the nostalgic patriotism appealed to in paragraph 1, harkening back to a time when things were made by hand, with the implication that these things were then made more carefully, with a loving expertise that ensured high quality.

In the last paragraph, we're invited to become "true believers." Note the slight "snob" appeal here also: if you are "a true potato chip lover" you'll buy these chips. (Others, with less love of chips, can settle for lesser chips.) The appeals to nostalgia and patriotism, to our reverence for handmade things, and to our sense of

Once upon a time, all potato chips tasted good. Very good. They were very crisp. And they tasted like real potatoes. Then, good ol' American mass production ingenuity took over. Bags of potato chips had to be produced by the millions. Every day. And that was a very sticky problem. 1

Because when you slice a potato, you know, the juice makes the slices stick together. Well, that was a real bugaboo for potato chip makers who had to cook 'em by the millions. If the slices stuck together you couldn't send them down a lickity-split production line. So, the potato chip making geniuses solved the problem. "We'll wash off those juices," one said, "and then they won't stick together." 2

Problem is, when you wash off the juices two things happen. Both bad. You lose a whole lot of the crispness. And you wash off that natural potato flavor. 3

So, now you know our secret. We don't wash off the natural potato juices. It means we have to hand-cook our chips one batch at a time. Stirring them so they don't stick together. 4

Are they really "dirty?" No. We just said that because we don't wash off the juices. And it makes it easy to remember the name of the good one. We promise we don't drop any of them on the floor. 5

And if you show the wisdom of a true potato chip lover you'll tuck this bag on the top of your shopping cart. And you'll never again eat one of those other, squeaky clean chips that taste like . . . well, they don't taste like much of anything. 6

[Signed]

Frank and Richard
The "Dirty" Potato Chips Brothers

Questions to Ask About Audience, Writer, and Purpose

This simple but effective piece of advertising does a good job of making its point by playing on the potential customer's qualities. If you jot down answers to the following questions so that you can talk about them in class, you'll dig deeper into how this passage—and any good piece of argument—accomplishes its goal:

1. What can you judge about the audience for this piece just by what goes on in it? Do you think the appeal is primarily logical, ethical, or emotional? Why?
2. What values or attitudes on the audience's part do the authors make use of as part of the argument?
   a. What quality of the audience would cause the piece to start with "Once upon a time"? What does starting that way say to readers about what is to follow?
   b. What attitude on the part of customers is being appealed to by the line "good ol' American mass production ingenuity" (¶ 1)? Are readers meant to take that phrase at face value, as straightforward praise, or is there something in the *tone* of the piece—the writers' implied attitude toward the subject—that causes you to suspect the writers' attitude might be just the opposite of what the surface of the words seems to be saying? How do you suppose the writers think customers feel about things "produced by the millions" (¶ 1)?
3. What attitude on the writers' part do you infer from the phrase "potato chip making geniuses" (¶ 2)?
4. How do the third and fourth paragraphs succeed in creating an "us versus them" situation, with potato-chip buyers and Frank and Richard ("The 'Dirty' Potato Chips Brothers") on one side and all other potato-chip makers on the other? What goes on later in the passage to reinforce and validate that choosing of sides?

As these questions point out, you can't have effective argumentation without full consideration of *audience,* whether that be readers or listeners. Arguments are effective only if they move audiences. You can't really ask whether this piece of evidence adequately supports—much less convincingly establishes—a claim without including the people involved.

exclusivity (that is, snob appeal) are different kinds of emotional (*pathos*) appeals. In fact, most of the appeals in this ad are primarily emotional. That is, they turn more on feelings than on logic (*logos*) or the ethical appeal of the writer (*ethos*). Still, you can see the three appeals overlapping here somewhat; there's a certain logic that if something is carefully done by hand it will be of high quality, and by signing the ad "Frank and Richard, the 'Dirty' Potato Chip Brothers," the chip makers make an ethical (*ethos*) pitch, trying to create an image of honest, hardworking, "regular" fellows.

We see pictured in the preceding text an audience that has the qualities of humor, distrust of technology, yearning for simplicity, liking for things handmade, and desire to be among the "true believers." Such an audience could see virtue in chips facetiously called "dirty" to emphasize the (supposedly) flavor-saving (but painstaking) way they are made.

Questions to Ask About Claims and Types of Argument

Once you've considered the audience, then you can look in more detail at the claims involved:

5. Arguments usually have several claims, some major and some minor. List the various claims you find in this piece, and note which ones depend on other claims.

6. Go back to your list of claims, and indicate which ones are claims of fact, which are of interpretation, which are of value, and which are of policy.
7. What is the major (the biggest) claim of the passage, and what specific evidence is offered in support of it?
8. As you go back through the argument, pencil in light brackets ([ ]) in the margin those places in which the authors are reporting information, evaluating information, or using the information to make judgments. Does a consistent relationship exist between which kind of statement is being made and whether it's a claim? In other words, are the claims mostly concerning *evaluations* of information, *judgments* based on information, or *reports* of information? Or are the claims spread pretty evenly among all three kinds of statements?
9. Choose one of the subarguments to analyze in detail—what is the claim, how is it supported, and is the support sufficient, of the right kind, and close enough to the claim?

We're working on the idea here that it's much more effective to base your persuasion on a quality the audience already has than to ask them to formulate a new belief. Thus, if one were to have to argue in favor of gun control to an audience of gun lovers, it would be wiser to base one's argument on tying one's claim to some quality the gun lovers already have and hold dear (perhaps the desire for personal freedom) than to try to create some new quality (maybe the desire for a gun-free society) in them. And so one builds an argument that works as hard as possible to tie gun control to the preservation and advancement of personal freedom; the minor claim, that personal freedom is something to be desired, needs only to be alluded to, not argued for. Thus qualities of audience are built into arguments.

Advertising is certainly one of the realms in which all of us are most often exposed to—some would say victimized by—argumentation. Whether we like it or not, we are bombarded daily with advertisements that, at their most successful, adroitly combine sound, logical structures (such as those discussed in chapter 7) with an acute awareness of the attitudes and preferences of the target audience. Effective argumentation—changing people's minds, moving them to action—has always been a matter of tailoring the substance of the argument to fit the particular audience for which it is intended.

Advertising's attempts to change people's behavior are usually brief, and apart from whatever effect advertising's countless repetitions have, its lasting effect on people is still debated. Where else do you see people using written words openly and explicitly to change your mind or urge you to action? And what kinds of topics do they discuss? Our focus in this chapter is on a particular kind of argument, not short snippets but long, detailed pieces—those you might find in newspaper investigative or editorial reporting or in magazines. (What you probably see in your college newspapers is really a subset of this kind of argumentation.) In these next two pieces, from the magazines *Forbes* and the *Atlantic Monthly,* you'll see fully developed examples of the kinds of issues that, at least on our college campuses, usually attract this kind of argumentation: (a) the rising costs of attending college and (b) U.S. defense policy.

We'd like you to read each of these selections carefully, and then we'll ask you to answer essentially the same set of questions we asked about "The Legend of 'Dirty' Potato Chips." To answer those questions you'll probably need to reread the passages, doing so even more critically. Remember our focus—how does *audience* figure in the argument?

The Untouchables

PETER BRIMELOW

Peter Brimelow is a senior editor at Forbes, *a columnist for the London* Times, *and a contributing editor for* Influence *magazine.*

1 *Efficiency and cost-cutting are demanded of unions and industry. Even government is under pressure to deliver value for the dollar. Why then does higher education get away with delivering a deteriorating product at ever rising prices?*

2 Most of America's famous colleges were first founded to train clergymen, and though higher education now trains far more technicians than theologians, it still retains a religious mystique. Educators preach, and parents and politicians faithfully accept, the gospel that education is morally good and more education is morally better. When *Forbes* asked "Are We Spending Too Much On Education?" (Dec. 29, 1986), many were genuinely outraged that such a crass economic question be posed at all.

3 Of course, there is a moral value to education that cannot be expressed in dollars and cents. But education nevertheless has to be paid for in dollars and cents. Particularly higher education—in recent years the cost of college has far outstripped inflation. And public disquiet at the results has been rising just as fast. One symptom: the surprise success this summer of Professor Allan Bloom's philosophical blast at modern universities, *The Closing of the American Mind,* on the *New York Times* bestseller list since May.

4 The malaise of higher education can be traced to its economic structure. Or as Adam Smith, himself a respected academician, wrote in 1776: "The discipline of colleges and universities is in general contrived, not for the benefit of the students, but for the interest, or more properly speaking, for the ease of the masters."

5 If true then, truer today.

6 Thanksgiving, and the kids are home from college. Over the turkey, maybe you'll want to catch up with the latest on the haute culture front. Why is Bloom's critical book such a runaway success? Why did art critic Hilton Kramer say recently that there's "less serious work being done in the humanistic studies than at any time in my life" and speak of "a lost generation of scholars" as a result of academic pettifogging and pervasive politicization in the academies?

7 As we spend more on higher education, it seems we get less.

8 According to the American Council on Education, in 1986–1987 public college students paid an average of $5,579 for tuition, room, board and incidentals; private college students paid $11,113. Since 1980, overall college charges have been rising at twice the inflation rate (see chart). And the ACE

In paragraph 1 Brimelow establishes the notion that higher education is something we want to believe is above reproach.

In paragraph 2 Brimelow gets in a preemptive strike—on the one hand conceding that education has a high moral value, on the other asserting that its finances must be governed by a "bottom line," or cost-effective, rigor. Thus he has "separated the issue"—split the question of *value* from the question of *policy.* In other words, for effectiveness of his argument he has split the issue into separate stases, value and policy, the better to argue in the realm of policy.

Paragraph 4 uses a rhetorical trope called argument *a fortiori,* which roughly means "all the stronger." It works as a hypothetical device that borrows an established value and transfers that value to something new—for example, "You know how good our milk is, and now you can try our new ice cream, too." The trope doesn't have to work in a positive direction—"If you think last week's exam was hard, wait till you take *this* week's exam." Brimelow's variant is similarly straightforward: if Smith was right about colleges in 1776, his sentiments are even more to the point now.

Brimelow uses apparent contradiction for excellent rhetorical effect in such one-liners as "As we spend *more* on higher education, it seems we get *less*" (emphasis added).

Charge fiercely, Harvard

Adjusted for inflation, college charges (left) lagged stagnant family income through 1980, then shot past it as times improved. But student enrollments have been flat since 1980. In effect, then, colleges kept revenues rising by substituting price for volume. (Public college charges are lower in part thanks to taxpayer subsidies and a shift to cheaper two-year schools!) Real expenditures per student, always ahead of inflation, leapt since 1980 (center). Charges at Ivy League schools and Stanford (right) are in a class by themselves.

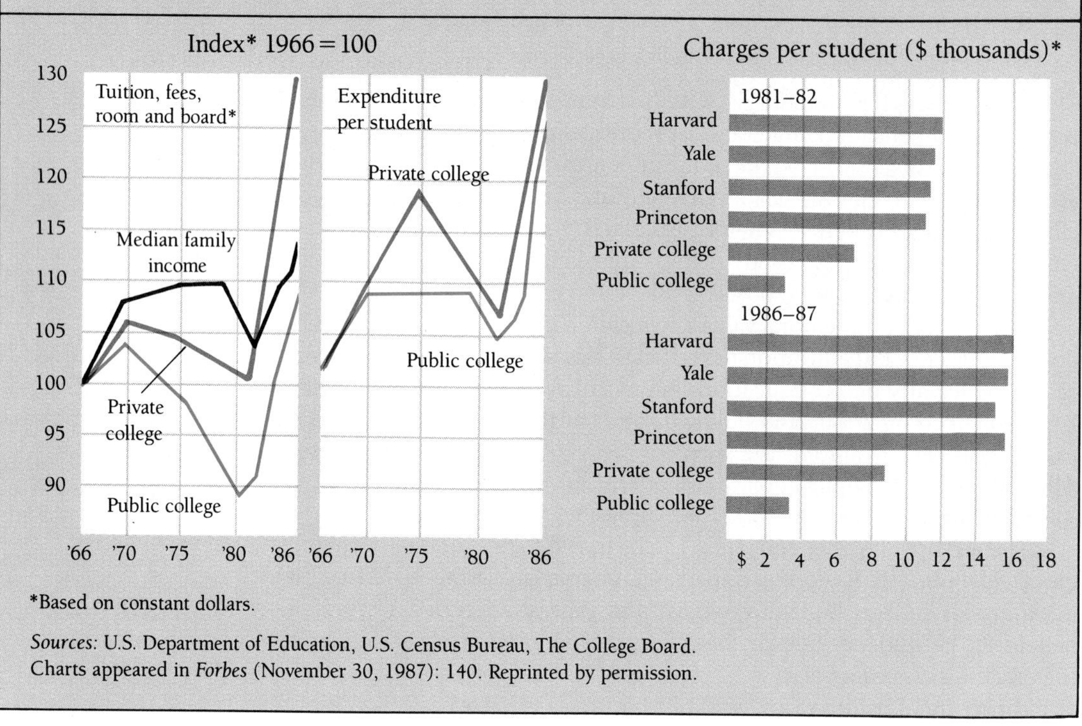

*Based on constant dollars.

Sources: U.S. Department of Education, U.S. Census Bureau, The College Board. Charts appeared in *Forbes* (November 30, 1987): 140. Reprinted by permission.

The author is building on something we all feel: that when we spend more dollars we should receive better products or services.

sees no relief in sight: It predicts college charges will continue to outpace inflation by as much as 30% for the rest of the decade.

We know why medical costs are rising faster than inflation—people are demanding and getting better health care. But why college costs? Are we really getting better college training? 9

In 1950 total expenditure on colleges and universities amounted to less than 1% of the gross national product. Since then it has increased to 2.7% of GNP in 1986, or about $100 billion. In the process, colleges and universities are edging aside the elementary and secondary school sectors—their combined share of educational expenditure has fallen from 69% to 61% over the same period. 10

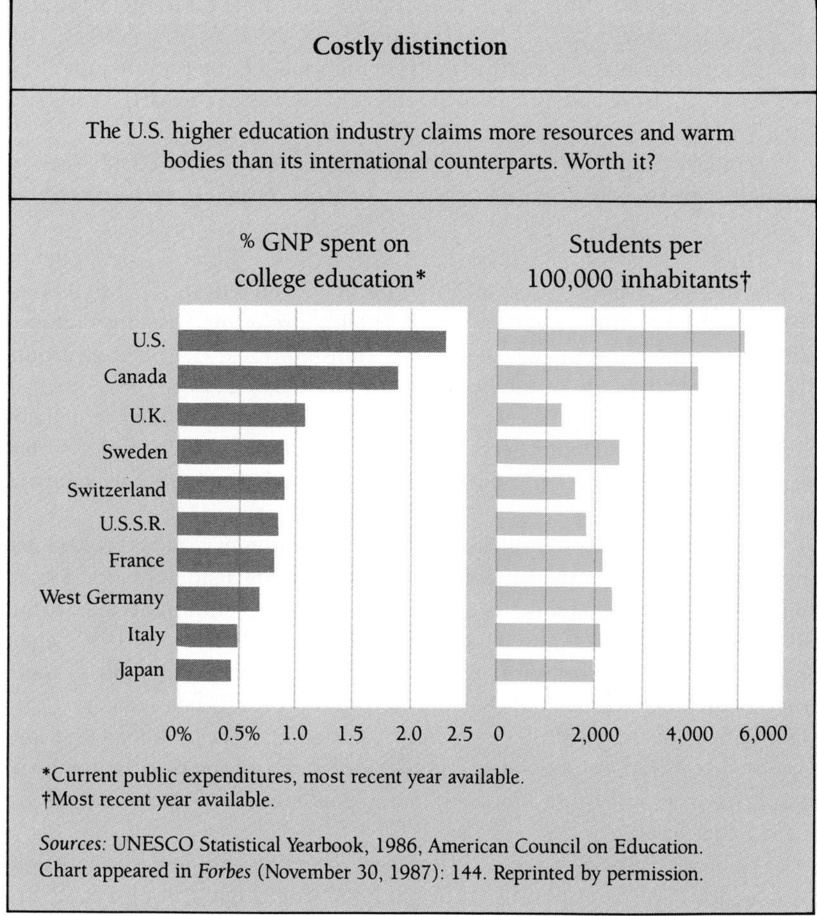

Sources: UNESCO Statistical Yearbook, 1986, American Council on Education. Chart appeared in *Forbes* (November 30, 1987): 144. Reprinted by permission.

11 This impressive growth by the U.S. higher education industry is out of all proportion to what is happening in other advanced countries. Japan and West Germany spend only 0.4% and 0.6% of their respective GNPs on college education (see chart)—and an excellent case can be made that Japan and Germany have better-educated citizenries than the U.S. does.

12 The growth in our spending on higher education has occurred even though its traditional market has contracted sharply in recent years. The number of 18-to-24-year-olds in the population is declining, from 30.4 million in 1980 to an estimated 25.8 million in 1990. But total enrollment in higher education is holding steady at about 12.4 million, and the number of institutions involved has actually increased, to an alltime high of 3,340 in 1985–86.

13 The higher education industry has been able to maintain its volume partly by reaching further down into its traditional market. In recent years

The author is building on something else we all feel: that growth should bring improvement.

Note how Brimelow uses statistics in paragraph 12 and elsewhere. Statistics can be highly persuasive, even though it is well known that numbers are also highly manipulable. Any argument that depends primarily on statistics is making a logical appeal—but also needs to be closely examined and evaluated. Brimelow uses numbers effectively here; of that there is no doubt.

some 62% of graduating high school seniors have gone on to higher education, compared with 52.5% 20 years earlier and less than 40% before 1950. Since more students are graduating from high school, the proportion of the age group entering college is now double what it was in the early 1950s and nearly four times what it was in the early 1930s.

Similarly, higher education is retaining its traditional clients longer. 14
Higher degrees now comprise about a quarter of all degrees granted, as opposed to less than a fifth in 1960 and less than a tenth in 1920.

Higher education has also been energetically pursuing new clients. 15
These include women (up from 41% of total enrollment in 1970 to 53% in 1985) and minorities (up from 8.8% to 14.1%, excluding Hispanics). Above all, higher education has discovered the "nontraditional" 25-plus age group. These supplied 27.8% of total enrollment in 1970, 41.1% in 1985.

"They won't rest until you and I are both back in school," Department of 16
Education Deputy Under Secretary Bruce M. Carnes (Ph.D.) told a *Forbes* reporter (M.B.A.), referring only half-jokingly to his former colleagues in academe.

Your students may—and should—detect Brimelow's implicit assumption that people with higher IQ scores are (somehow) better people. He not only accepts IQ scores as meaningful (many people *don't* accept IQ scores as indicative of real intelligence—or anything else), but also assumes his readers do, too. Note that once this assumption is accepted, it is easy to accept Brimelow's "logic" that those colleges which serve people with "lower" IQs must necessarily be inferior to those colleges which serve only people with "higher" IQs. How do your students feel about IQ distinctions? Do your students agree or disagree with Brimelow? Why or why not?

Unfortunately, much of the result is less impressive. Stockbrokers are 17
required to inquire into "suitability" before peddling a stock to a customer. But apparently "suitability" is an adjustable notion. The higher education industry's voracity has caused it to eat through the IQ barrier. "In 1952, when I wrote my Ph.D. dissertation on education as an industry, I was able to argue that a student required an IQ of 110 in order to benefit from college," says Fordham University's Professor Ernest van den Haag, a psychoanalyst and sociologist. "That implies a maximum of about 25% of the population. I still think it's true, but quite obviously many students in college today are far below that level."

To broaden their markets, colleges are accepting students who formerly 18
would not have been permitted to graduate from high school. People are being graduated with IQs below 110, according to Berkeley educational psychologist Arthur R. Jensen. That means they haven't the innate ability to acquire the degree of knowledge and skills formerly associated with a bachelor's degree. The higher education industry has frequently coped with this phenomenon, claims Jensen, by lowering its standards. "There are colleges for every level of ability. There are colleges where the average IQ is below 100."

Suitability? Department of Education figures show that 87% of colleges 19
offered remedial instruction in 1985; 63% reported an increase in remedial instruction since 1978; 33% had established permanent remedial departments or divisions.

And although it has been little reported, there has been a 20-year decline 20
in average scores on Graduate Record Examinations (GREs) and professional school admission tests taken by candidates for higher degrees (see chart). This decline strikingly parallels the prolonged slippage in the Scholastic Aptitude Test (SAT) results obtained by high school seniors contemplating

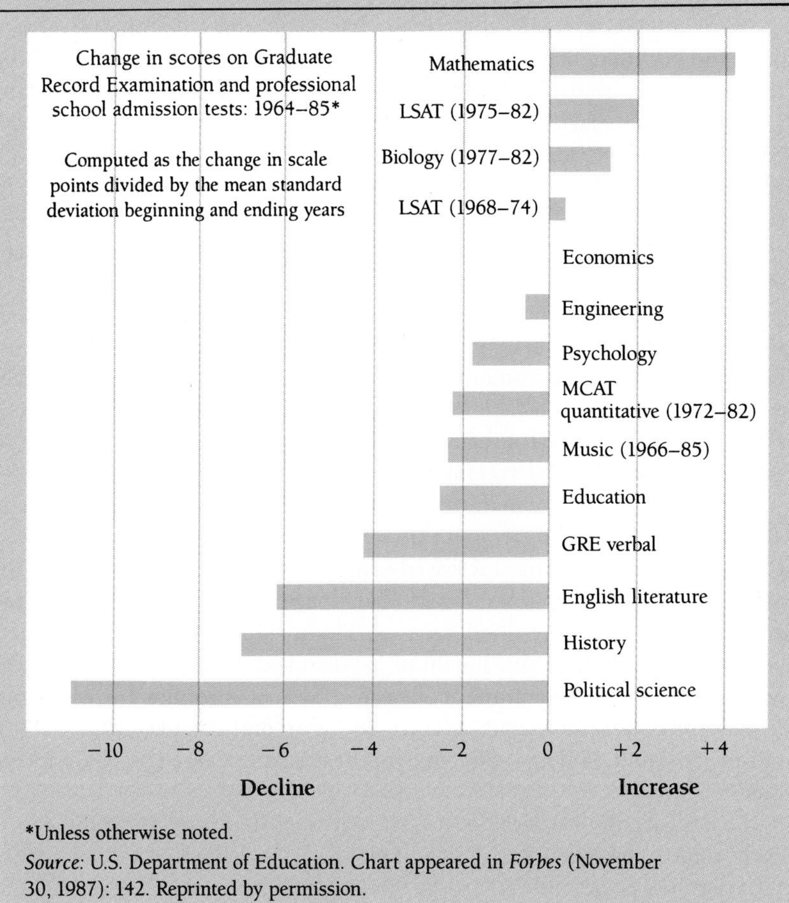

college. It can only be the result of the lower average quality of students, or of a deteriorating higher education system—or both.

21 Not coincidentally, the value of a bachelor's degree has been falling. The difference between the median annual incomes of college graduates and high school graduates over 25 was only $9,690 in 1986. The bottom line is that people are spending $25,000 to $75,000 to buy a piece of parchment that could be a marginal proposition, considering the opportunity cost of the funds and the time spent out of the work force.

Do your students believe there is an "Ivy cartel" of colleges? Discuss this issue. Are there "brand-name" degrees and, if so, from where? How do your students feel about this?

Point out to students the subtle way Brimelow classifies and thereby evaluates statements. Education that promotes democratic values or makes people "better people" is in the area of qualitative *assertion*—something stated but not necessarily proved, or provable, because it is subjective; it can't be objectively quantified. Such arguments, to Brimelow, are not as persuasive as arguments based on quantifiable proof (that is, statistics again, or anything that can somehow be reduced to numbers). You should point out to students that Brimelow has a bias shared by many people: that *quantifiable* proofs for arguments are better than *qualitative* proofs, because numbers are seen as more objective, more "scientific."

Some readers question whether the statistics in paragraph 26 really prove the author's point. (Yes, statistics again! Brimelow is fond of them.)

Students with lower IQs but possessing patience and a bankroll will eventually graduate, particularly from mediocre colleges. But their degrees are universally regarded in academia as simply not comparable with those from the top 50 to 100 schools, where there is competition to enter. The accreditation agencies that are supposed to keep colleges up to par have been no help: They focus largely on input measures such as the number of Ph.D.s on staff, not on ensuring a comparable level of education. 22

Thus the triumph of egalitarianism has been achieved at the expense of the standards that make a college degree worthwhile. In making college education easily available, the educational industry has debased the product. The main beneficiaries: the established colleges, the "Ivy cartel," whose brand-name protection is sought by clients with increasing desperation. What has been sold as an antidote to elitism has become, in fact, a spur to elitism. 23

Not surprisingly, this has enabled the folks who run the elite schools to push their prices up faster than those at the ordinary schools. 24

Educators traditionally wave aside all such criticisms with airy talk of an education's intangible benefits to society—or, if they are economists, of "externalities" such as promoting democratic values or making you "a nicer person" that are unreflected in individuals' incomes. This is an assertion rather than an argument. It cannot be quantitatively assessed. But it has to outweigh some powerful arguments that can be objectively assessed. 25

Whatever the higher education industry is doing to its clients, it is unquestionably spending more to do it. Inflation-adjusted expenditure per student since 1959–60 has increased some 37% for public colleges, 91% for private schools [see right section of chart, page 482]. This is despite three important cost-reducing developments: The increased proportion of part-time students, 30.5% of enrollment in 1966 and 42.2% in 1985; the expanding role of two-year "commuter colleges," 17.7% of enrollment in 1963 and 37% in 1985; and the heavier reliance on cheap part-time faculty, 21.9% of staff in 1970 and 37% in 1986. None of these savings were passed on to the consumer. 26

Overall faculty salaries are not the cause of increased expenditures. A recent study by economic consultant Eva C. Galambos shows these "instructional expenditures" proportionately stable since the mid-1970s and actually down substantially from pre–World War II levels. Plant and maintenance expenditures are also flat. 27

The big increases? They have been in administrative cost categories—from 16.2% in 1929 to 29.7% in 1985. Indeed, Galambos understates the total amount of paper-pushing (or floppy-disk flapdoodling) going on in colleges. She factors out costs attributable to administering research and other school activities. Including these, administrative costs in 1985–86 amounted to 62% of instruction, up from 48.7% in 1974–75. Galambos also does not estimate administration costs buried in the instructional budget itself. According to another source, this amounts to perhaps a third or more. 28

29 The escalation in college costs is occurring because it enables the people who run colleges to extract profits from an ostensibly nonprofit system and redistribute them as they wish. Of course, they claim to have only the highest of motives.

Notice that we're this deep into the piece when the author finally states his thesis.

30 "Our policy is total Robin Hood," Eamon M. Kelly, president of Tulane University ($15,950 a year, up 10% from 1986) told the *New York Times* in May. "We put our tuition up as high as possible and then put most of the extra money into financial aid."

31 Who could argue with spending money to keep worthy students in college? Most schools in effect offer discounts to selected students—from poor families, from minorities or with outstanding athletic abilities. But the overall college budget pays for these scholarships (most of which actually go straight back to the college itself), and this means higher fees for students from relatively affluent middle-class families. (A couple earning, say, $50,000 a year is no longer affluent if it must keep one or two kids in college at $10,000 to $15,000 each.)

32 Moreover, just as with the combination of high marginal income tax rates, loopholes and transfer payments, this policy can mean money is being taken from one pocket and put back into the other by administrators who have a vested interest in running a complex financial aid system.

33 Harvard, which says two-thirds of its undergraduate students receive some form of financial aid, gave nearly $20 million in grants and scholarships in 1986—meaning an extra $20 million burden on the relatively affluent parents.

34 Of course, Harvard could have simply reduced tuition across the board, by more than $3,000. Education Department officials say that many colleges could reduce charges by a quarter to a half if they charged flat-rate fees. Parents would no doubt be pleased—they are increasingly being forced to turn to consultants for help in filling out financial aid forms. But pleasing parents is not a higher education priority.

35 Raising fees is also a way to put the arm on the taxpayer. Federal subsidies to college students, currently running at $14.5 billion, are unchanged in real terms since 1981 despite constant caterwauling to the contrary. Washington's shift to "need-based" programs in the late 1970s effectively allowed higher educators to tap federal funds simply by raising their fees, sparking the present cost conflagration. Federal funds, however, have also brought costly federal regulation.

36 College costs are also kept unnaturally high by what can only be called featherbedding on a scale that few private businesses could tolerate, often in the form of noncash benefits. Many faculty members do extraordinarily little teaching. Former Vanderbilt Professor Chester E. Finn Jr., now Assistant Secretary for Education, estimated in 1984 that the "average professor at the average college" works at most 22 ½ hours a week in term time—"and that's still fewer than thirty weeks a year." He thought that only one in ten did any useful research. If those figures are correct, a college professor earning a

relatively low $35,000 a year is making about $50 an hour for his actual time—not, of course, counting his generous fringe benefits.

Another noncash emolument is tenure. Ostensibly a guarantee of academic freedom, this peculiar phenomenon has proved compatible with the creation of impressive ideological monoliths. Recent notorious cases: The University of Colorado's College of Arts and Science in Boulder has reportedly hired no registered Republicans (that's not conservatives—*Republicans*) for the last ten years. At Stanford University, faculty opposition succeeded in driving away the proposed Reagan Presidential Library—of 167 professors in the economics, English, history and political science departments, only 11 were registered Republicans. 37

From an economic standpoint, however, tenure is essentially a cartelizing device in the face of a glut of Ph.D.s Basically, tenured insiders have been able to hog resources at the expense of nontenured outsiders—the new academic proletariat of so-called gypsy scholars, forced to work on short-term contracts. 38

We can't set the clock back. But if the American people really think a college diploma should be every young person's right, there are still sensible ways of reining in the cost of higher education. Mark Gelber of the Washington-based College-University Resource Institute believes that charges could be reduced by as much as 25% if colleges could be persuaded to "unbundle" the package of services they currently offer. Students would be able to buy a no-frills education alone if they wished, without having to pay for athletics, health insurance and other peripheral services that colleges acquired thoughtlessly in the expansionary 1960s. 39

Ask students to speculate what this "unbundling" would sacrifice about college life.

Unbundling is an attractive concept. Higher education is a concatenation of cross-subsidies, with undergraduates (and their parents) supporting graduate study, pure research and other activities. And unbundling could have wider applications. One is implicit in one of Allan Bloom's throwaway lines: "If the focus is careers, there is hardly one specialty, outside the hardest of the natural sciences, which requires more than two years of preparatory training prior to graduate studies. The rest is just wasted time. . . ." In short, does college really need to be a four-year affair? 40

Perhaps the whole idea of the resident campus and multiyear academic degree courses is just a freak hangover from a patrician age, destined to go the way of the Grand Tour, the debutante's ball and compulsory Latin and Greek. Quaint but hardly useful, let alone necessary. 41

Perhaps the future lies with night school, with specific courses, with faster access to professional training and with on-the-job learning—a 1985 Carnegie Foundation report estimated that corporations were already spending an astonishing $40 billion to $100 billion to train perhaps 8 million people, and had even quietly set up 18 degree-granting institutions. 42

Why should such proposals sound sacrilegious at a time when efficiency is increasingly demanded of industry, when labor unions are forced to give up 43 longstanding privileges and when industry is under pressure to slim down and shape up? Why is higher education alone exempt from giving a dollar's worth of product for a dollar?

44 In 1209 the University of Oxford went on strike when the town authorities executed two scholars who had murdered a woman. Sacrilege! So outraged was the Pope at this application of ordinary standards to university folk that he later ordered the town to do penance by annually distributing 42 shillings barefoot to "poor scholars" and holding a St. Nicholas Day feast for them, and by freezing rents for ten years.

45 The American higher education guilds can't quite do that. But they do have the same power to rise above the public interest by wrapping themselves in holy garments.

Sometimes seeing the argumentative structure of a piece this long can be difficult if you try to do so all at once. For that reason, before we ask you about its large-scale structure, we're going to ask you some smaller questions:

You may want to have student groups write answers to these questions.

Questions Based on Critical Reading

1. What values in the audience does the headnote to the piece (¶ 1) play on or evoke?
2. How do the first five paragraphs of the piece succeed in linking education's "religious mystique" to its economic structure?
3. How does paragraph 7 set the structure for most of the rest of the essay? What quality in the audience makes the claims in this paragraph—if they are proved true—effective?
4. What specific claim do paragraphs 8–10 support?
5. What claim do paragraphs 11–16 support? What is its relationship to the claim in question 4 above?
6. What is the connection between paragraphs 18 and 13–16?
7. What claim do paragraphs 17–23 support?
8. How do paragraphs 23–25 connect with the Adam Smith quotation (¶ 4)?
9. How does paragraph 26 constitute an important summation of the argument so far and a transition to an especially audience-derived issue? Why not use these figures earlier, in paragraph 10, for example? What quality in the audience does the last line of paragraph 26 evoke?
10. How does paragraph 28 connect with the Adam Smith quotation?
11. Where does the essay begin moving toward a conclusion?
12 What earlier parts of the essay does paragraph 43 echo and reinforce? What value on the reader's part does its effect depend on?

13. One good test of whether the author's argument has been successful is whether the reader sees the final anecdote (¶ 45) as fitting and appropriate or as irrelevant. Which is it for you, and why?

Questions for Writing and Discussion

Once you've seen the essay's structure on a smaller scale, you can do a better job answering these larger questions:

1. What can you judge about the audience for this piece just by what goes on in it?
2. What values or attitudes on the audience's part does the author make use of as part of his argument?
3. What is the major (the biggest) claim of the passage, and what specific evidence is offered in support of it?
4. Any argument this long is bound to have several claims, some major and some minor. What various claims do you find in this piece? Which ones depend on other claims?
5. Go back to your list of claims. Which ones are claims of fact? Which of interpretation? Which of value? Which of policy?
6. As you go back through the argument, pencil in light brackets ([ ]) in the margin those places in which the author is reporting information, evaluating information, or using the information to make judgments. Does a consistent relationship exist between which kind of statement is being made and whether it's a claim?
7. Choose one of the subarguments to analyze in detail—what is the claim, how is it supported, and is the support sufficient, of the right kind, and close enough to the claim?
8. Which of Aristotle's 3 appeals—*logos, pathos,* or *ethos*—do you think dominates this essay? Why? In what ways do you think your status in life (that of a student) shapes your answer to that question? How might your answer to the question change if you were a faculty member in a college? an administrator?
9. What do the following words mean—*pettifogging, pervasive* (¶ 6), *GNP* (¶ 10), *egalitarianism* (¶ 23), *affluent* (¶ 33), *featherbedding* (¶ 36), *ostensibly, emolument* (¶ 37), *concatenation* (¶ 40), *quaint* (¶ 41), *sacrilegious* (¶ 43), *penance* (¶ 44)?

Bridges: Another Perspective

Peter Brimelow raises strong arguments against American higher education as it now operates (although his article appeared in 1987, little has changed in the costs of higher education since then). Among questions he raises are these, which you should ponder and discuss:

1. Does college really *need* to be a four-year affair?
2. Is the "whole idea of the resident campus and multiyear academic degree courses . . . just a freak hangover from a patrician age" (¶ 41)?
3. Is a college education today truly important for the person's intangible benefits—cultural understandings, better citizenship, general erudition—or is it important primarily as training for a successful career?
4. Implicitly, one question Brimelow raises for you as a college student is, "What are *you* going to college for?" (Frame your answer in the context created by question 3 above.)

Of course, in making the first long sample argument in this chapter one about rising costs of higher education, we too are drawing on a quality we know our readers all have—the desire to get the most out of what they spend on their educations (or to get the best education for the least money). In that sense, most or maybe all of the people in your class will feel the same way about the above argument. Sometimes it's easier to see how different arguments rely on qualities in their readers (and because people are different, the arguments move different readers different ways) when the argument is on a subject that not all the readers agree about. Thus, as you read this next example and answer the questions that precede and follow it, take note of where, how, and why your responses to the argument are the same as or different from those of your classmates.

PREREADING WORKSHEET

Before you read the following piece by Colonel Harry G. Summers, Jr., write brief responses to these questions:

1. What do you understand is meant by the phrase "cold war"?
2. Do you believe that U.S. nuclear weapons and the threat that the United States will, if necessary, use those weapons prevent the outbreak of a war with an adversary? Briefly, why or why not?
3. Have you given much thought to the military role the U.S. plays in the world? Why or why not?
4. Do you think modern nuclear weapons make traditional forces (army, navy, and so on) unnecessary or obsolete in the event of an all-out war?
5. Based on what you have read and heard over the years, do you consider a total nuclear war possible? Why or why not?

Can students tell whether they are the kind of audience this piece is aimed at? As they read, ask them to make notes on how they seem to be, or not to be, the kind of reader for whom this piece is intended. Ask them to track exactly what words or phrases in the piece trigger those realizations.

Of course, in the time since this piece was published there have been even more changes in the political climate. Yet as of this writing (fall 1990), no one seems to have a clear idea of what the geopolitical climate of the next century is going to be like.

A Bankrupt Military Strategy

COLONEL HARRY G. SUMMERS, JR.

Colonel Harry G. Summers, Jr., is a career army officer, strategic analyst, and military correspondent. His many articles and books include On Strategy: A Critical Analysis of the Vietnam War *and* Sound Military Decisions. *This piece was published in June 1989, six months before the collapse of the Berlin Wall.*

Our Military Assets Can No Longer Cover Our Foreign-Policy Liabilities

Ten years ago, on assignment to the Army General Staff's War Plans Directorate, I sat in on a briefing by a navy planner on the strategic rationale for the U.S. Navy. Slide after slide portrayed the Soviet naval threat to U.S. interests around the world, and there followed slide after slide depicting how the U.S. Navy was countering the threat. When he finished, the planner, an admiral, asked my boss, an army major general, what he thought of the presentation. 1

"Very interesting," the general said. "But what you've just said is that if the Soviet navy sank tomorrow, we could do away with the U.S. Navy." 2

The admiral laughed. "You don't understand," he said. "If the Soviet navy sank tomorrow, I'd get me a new set of slides." 3

The slide makers in the bowels of the Pentagon should be working overtime. Although the Soviet navy is still afloat, most of the other post–Second World War rationales upon which our military force structure was built either have sunk or are listing badly in the water, swamped by a sea change wrought not only by time and technology but also by a new dynamism in international politics. These erstwhile dreadnoughts include the pivotal role once played by nuclear weapons, the short-war scenarios derived from such nuclear dependence, and the strategies that call for the forward basing of troops which we have clung to since the signing of the North Atlantic Treaty, forty years ago. 4

Strategic Forces

For many years nuclear weapons were such an important part of our national military strategy that they virtually defined the word *strategic,* which classically had meant the use or threatened use of military means to achieve the political ends of the state. At the beginning of the nuclear age, in a brilliant semantic maneuver, the nuclear theorists hijacked the word and misappropriated it to advance their conviction that nuclear bombs were "strategic" weapons capable by themselves of achieving the political goals and objectives of the United States. As a result, for many years *strategic* almost automatically meant the use of nuclear means, as in the phrases *strategic forces, strategic weapons,* and *Strategic Air Command.* 5

6 Indeed, at one time nuclear weapons were synonymous with strategy itself. In 1953, for budgetary more than for military reasons, the Eisenhower Administration adopted the strategy of "massive retaliation," whereby our national defenses relied almost entirely on nuclear forces. This "maximum deterrent at a bearable cost," as John Foster Dulles called it, had enormous, long-lasting consequences.

7 For one thing, the conventional (that is, non-nuclear) forces of the navy, air force, and especially the army and Marines were all but deprived of their *raison d'être.* As the historian Russell Weigley has noted, "A national military policy and strategy relying upon massive nuclear retaliation for nearly all the uses of force left the Army uncertain of its place in the policy and strategy, uncertain that civilians recognized a need even for the Army's existence and uncertain therefore of the service's whole future."

8 The reaction was twofold. First, all the services tried to break the Strategic Air Command's monopoly by acquiring nuclear weaponry of their own. "Tactical" nuclear weapons (artillery shells, small bombs, rockets, and missiles intended for short-range battlefield use) proliferated, as the army, the navy, and the air force's Tactical Air Command scrambled to get a piece of the nuclear, and budgetary, action.

9 This nuclear armament forced the second reaction. Instead of allowing strategy to define the armament necessary to carry it out successfully, the process was turned on its head to the point that the nuclear armament now defined the strategy. The result, under the Kennedy Administration, was the doctrine of "flexible response," ostensibly the strategy under which we are operating today. While moving away from the almost total reliance on nuclear weaponry called for by massive retaliation, flexible response still rested on a foundation of nuclear weapons.

10 But though a nuclear-based strategy like flexible response may have made at least some sense while the United States enjoyed an enormous nuclear advantage and could credibly threaten "escalation dominance"—that is, raising a crisis to a level at which the adversary could not respond—it made little sense once the Soviet Union achieved nuclear parity.

11 A decade ago the army staff was presented with a conundrum that came to be known as Darling's dilemma. The War Plans Directorate had a policy of allowing select staff officers to present controversial issues to the most senior planners. A Lieutenant Colonel Dean Darling challenged them to imagine that they were the Joint Chiefs of Staff and that he was the President of the United States.

12 "The Soviets have just launched a major cross-border attack on Western Europe," he said. "CINCEUR [Commander in Chief, European command] has just asked me for the authority to use tactical nuclear weapons to slow their advance. I'm quite prepared to approve his request, and the only thing I need from you is an assurance that the Soviets will not respond with a strategic nuclear attack on the American homeland. Now, I know from our Second World War experience that we can lose the whole continent of Europe and survive as a nation. But you've told me that a strategic nuclear

exchange would kill as much as three quarters of the American people. I know that you can't give me a one-hundred-percent assurance. So I'll go with fifty percent or better."

Summers is also adept at the language of apparent contradiction for rhetorical effect: *deafening silence.* Such striking phrases or single-word combinations (for instance, *bittersweet*) are called oxymorons.

There was a deafening silence in the room. None of the planners was willing to give the assurance that Darling sought. The dilemma upon which the army was impaled was clear. 13

"We have built our strategy in Europe," Colonel Darling concluded, "on nuclear weapons systems that we will refuse to use when the time comes to use them. Not only that—by relying on this nuclear facade, we have undermined the war-fighting abilities of our conventional forces as well." 14

While admitting the validity of Darling's remarks, the army planners did not want to acknowledge what they portended. Neither did anyone else—particularly our NATO allies, who were not prepared to pay the cost in conventional forces that acknowledging the bankruptcy of flexible response would entail. 15

In paragraph 16 Summers refers to the final days of the U.S. withdrawal from the Vietnam War. Saigon was the capital of South Vietnam, the nation the United States was trying to help in its resistance to Communist-controlled North Vietnam, whose capital was Hanoi. The United States failed, despite increasing involvement through five U.S. presidencies (Eisenhower, Republican, 1953–61; Kennedy, Democrat, 1961–63; Johnson, Democrat, 1963–69; Nixon, Republican, 1969–74; and Ford, Republican, 1974–77).

But not only are the war-fighting aspects of nuclear weaponry bankrupt; so is their deterrent value. In April of 1975, a week before the fall of Saigon, I was in Hanoi negotiating the terms of the withdrawal of the U.S. embassy personnel. Crowing about the impending North Vietnamese victory, my NVA counterpart said, "This just goes to show you can't stamp out a revolutionary idea with force." 16

"That's nonsense and you know it," I replied. "Almost eight hundred years ago Genghis Khan stamped out the *jihad* [holy war] declared against him in Central Asia by killing ten million or so Muslims, and you know full well that with our nuclear arsenal we always had the means to destroy you totally." 17

"We knew that," he replied. "We also knew you'd never do it." 18

Note that Summers here makes use of the argument a fortiori trope, discussed earlier in these notes.

If strategic nuclear weapons could not deter a small non-nuclear nation like North Vietnam (or North Korea twenty-five years earlier, for that matter), it should be obvious that their ability to deter the adventurism of a major nuclear-armed opponent is questionable indeed. Yet that point has evidently not sunk in. 19

President James Earl (Jimmy) Carter, a Democrat, succeeded Gerald Ford as president after defeating Ford in the 1976 election.

Shortly after President Carter announced his Carter Doctrine to protect the Middle East from Soviet aggression, the scenario was seriously advanced that if the Soviets invaded Iran, we'd send in the 82d Airborne Division as a show of force, and if they didn't back off then, we'd be forced to use tactical nuclear weapons. 20

What was missing from the scenario was the dispiriting recognition that the Soviets have as many tactical nuclear weapons as we do, if not more; if we breached the nuclear threshold, they'd surely respond in kind. Who then would be more vulnerable to nuclear fire—Soviet units advancing through mountain passes, or U.S. lodgments on the coast? You don't have to be a nuclear-weapons expert to figure that out. And you don't have to be a strategic expert to see the fallacy in such nuclear-based strategies. 21

The Short-War Theory

22 The reliance on nuclear weapons for our war-fighting strategies was bad enough, but even worse were the false assumptions that these weapons spawned. Most pernicious was the so-called short-war theory—the assumption that any major future war would inevitably go nuclear and would therefore be concluded in a matter of hours or at most days. Until the past few years most global war-fighting scenarios were played out within a ninety-day period; those units that could not reach the battlefield within that time were, for all practical purposes, considered useless.

23 The short-war theory helped to reinforce several trends in military planning. Particularly hard hit were America's reserve forces, which supposedly no longer had a role to play on the battlefield. The draft, which was abolished because of domestic and fiscal pressures, received an additional blow, because according to the short-war scenario, the shooting would be over before draftees could be conscripted, trained, and deployed. Dismissed as well were our manpower and industrial mobilization capabilities, which had proved to be decisive in two world wars. No need for them in a short war.

24 The navy and the air force did not have major objections to this theory. It enhanced the role of the navy's submarine-launched ballistic-missile force and the air force's Strategic Air Command, with its nuclear bombers and intercontinental ballistic missiles. And, since the conventional navy and air force consisted primarily of active-duty units and ready-reserve forces that could meet the ninety-day test, their manpower was not threatened either.

25 It was left to the army to lead the fight against the short-war theory, not so much out of self-interest (although that was certainly involved) as because the army was convinced that the theory would lead to disaster on the battlefield. In the mid-1970s the perception among officers on his staff was that John Vessey, then a brigadier general (later the chairman of the Joint Chiefs of Staff), was passed over for promotion for continuing to ask, What happens on the ninety-first day? But the lack of promotion did not stop him. He persisted until a full-scale examination of America's mobilization capability was ordered. The results were shocking. As it then stood, on the ninety-first day we'd either lose the war or be forced to resort to nuclear weapons, for our mobilization procedures were virtually nonexistent. A reconsideration of the short-war theory was clearly needed.

26 Another aspect of the theory which particularly bothered the army was that it cut the military off from the American people. This was deliberate. Short-war theorists argued that in modern war there would be no time to follow constitutional procedures and involve Congress (and thereby the people) in the decision-making process.

27 The Vietnam War was a case in point. Instead of calling for a constitutionally mandated declaration of war by Congress (in Alexander Hamilton's felicitous words, "the representatives of the people, periodically elected"),

President Johnson used his authority as Commander in Chief to order the military into action. Not wishing to pay the political price involved, he deliberately refused to mobilize the reserve forces or to take his case to the American people. The American people soon made it known that they had some say in the matter. As General Fred C. Weyand, America's last commander in Vietnam, observed, "The American army really is a people's army in the sense that it belongs to the American people, who take a jealous and proprietary interest in its involvement. . . . The army, therefore, cannot be committed lightly."

A quiet subtext in this piece is the number of times it offhandedly states that a certain strategic or policy position that was ostensibly taken for one reason was in fact taken for quite another reason (not the least of which was the self-interest of branches of the military and their leaders). Ask students to find and list those instances; what kind of picture of U.S. policy-making does that compilation create?

Partly with that thought in mind, and seeking to avoid a repetition of the Vietnam fiasco, General Creighton Abrams, then the army chief of staff, set out in 1973 to debunk the short-war theory and to create an army that could not be committed to sustained combat without the approval of the American people. The resulting "total army" concept created an army whose active-duty divisions were "rounded out" with brigades from the National Guard. It would take specific congressional approval to commit such forces to sustained combat—approval that, as experience has shown, would not be forthcoming unless members of Congress were assured of the support of their constituents. For obvious reasons, Abrams did not trumpet the rationale behind the total army; instead, he allowed the belief to spread that manpower and budgetary considerations impelled the change, although these were in fact secondary. 28

John F. Lehman, Jr., was appointed secretary of the navy by President Ronald W. Reagan, a Republican who defeated the incumbent Democratic president, Jimmy Carter, in the election of 1980. Reagan was reelected in 1984 and was serving as president at the time this article was written. Thus Summers is discussing U.S. military policy over the course of several years and several different administrations, from the end of World War II (when the president was Harry S Truman, Democrat) until the Reagan presidency.

In the 1980s the army found a most unexpected ally in its battle against the short-war theory: Secretary of the Navy John F. Lehman, Jr. The fundamental purpose of his maritime strategy and 600-ship navy was to gain control of the seas and allow the construction of a "sea bridge" to Europe which would enable the mobilization capability of the United States to be brought to bear. His strategy was based on two assumptions: any future conflict would be prolonged, and any future conflict would be fought, as far as possible, by conventional—non-nuclear—means. 29

Forward Basing

Among the several reasons the maritime strategy was controversial was that its non-nuclear provisions challenged the assumptions undergirding America's forward-basing strategy. Originally, U.S. forces were maintained in Europe to validate guarantees by the United States that it would use nuclear weapons to turn back Soviet aggression. The scenario called for a "come as you are" war that would be concluded within ninety days by the use, if need be, of nuclear weapons. Although the time limit has been extended, the threatened first use of nuclear weapons to stop a Warsaw Pact attack is still the crux of NATO strategy. 30

But for a long time this scenario has made no military sense. Over the past decade the horns of Darling's dilemma have continued to grow as Soviet nuclear parity, and in some cases outright nuclear superiority, have spread inexorably from the strategic to the operational to the tactical level. Because of a refusal, primarily for budgetary reasons, to face this change in the 31 correlation of forces, NATO strategy has degenerated to the point where the message it is sending is not "You attack me and I'll destroy you" but instead the pathetic "You attack me and I'll commit nuclear suicide!"

32 U.S. forward-based forces now find themselves in the worst of all worlds. They lack sufficient conventional combat power to stand alone; the NATO allies, still officially relying on U.S. nuclear guarantees that have long since lost their validity, also lack sufficient conventional combat power; and the nuclear forces upon which both once depended have become paper tigers. The nuclear foundation upon which our post–Second World War strategy was erected is fast crumbling away. It is only a matter of time before tactical nuclear weapons are withdrawn from Europe. Like intermediate nuclear weapons, they have long since lost their battlefield utility.

33 This strips the underpinnings from the nuclear-based short-war scenarios and the whole U.S. forward-basing strategy. The reason the United States built its strategy on nuclear forces to begin with, as John Foster Dulles made clear, was that they were much cheaper than conventional forces. And the reason NATO welcomed U.S. forward-deployed forces in Europe was that they served as a trip wire to those U.S. nuclear forces.

34 As long as the nuclear-based strategy was credible, both the United States and its NATO allies could avoid spending the huge sums that a conventional-based strategy would have entailed. But as the perceived value of the nuclear deterrent declines in the face of the intermediate-nuclear-forces agreement and Soviet *glasnost* and *perestroika,* so does tolerance for the forward basing of American troops, which are increasingly seen as an irritant, even by our staunchest allies. Other allies, like Greece, have turned into parasites. What began as an exercise in collective security and coalition defense has degenerated to the point where we are paying ransom for the "privilege" of protecting our "friends" from external aggression. Common sense tells us that it may be time to come home.

Some of your students may want to research and report on the *current* status of "forward basing" of U.S. troops.

35 The most obvious step would be to scrap our nuclear-based short-war scenarios and our forward basing in favor of long-war scenarios that rely on conventional arms. But that would be a major undertaking. To meet our present worldwide commitments with conventional forces alone might take something in the vicinity of a sixfold increase in ground-force divisions and a corresponding increase in defense spending.

36 The projections vary widely, because they depend on different scenarios, but according to some of them, it would take up to 200 divisions to meet all of America's worldwide military commitments simultaneously. The gap between those commitments and the army and Marine Corps's present thirty-two active and reserve divisions is evidence that as it now stands our conventional-force military strategy is almost literally bankrupt, for our foreign-policy liabilities far exceed our operational military assets.

37 It is not that we have too few military forces; it is that we have too many jobs for them to do. Through a multiplicity of mutual-defense treaties and agreements, the United States has given solemn pledges to nations around the world that we will protect them from external aggression. But these pledges can no longer be credibly covered by nuclear means, and the U.S.

Some of your students may not remember that the State Department is the civilian side of U.S. military leadership, responsible for formulating and enforcing U.S. foreign policy. It is nominally headed by the president, but its chief operating officer is a cabinet official, the secretary of state. (Ultimate military authority rests with the president, as commander in chief of the armed forces, but the Constitution holds that only Congress can authorize war.)

defense budget, already seen as excessive, is not about to be expanded to close the present conventional-force gap.

What is to be done? Like any bankrupt, we need to reexamine both our assets and our liabilities. Our foreign-policy goals and objectives must be brought back into balance with the military means available for their attainment, enhancement, and protection. 38

It's not only time the Pentagon got a new set of slides. It's time the State Department got a new set as well. 39

POSTREADING WORKSHEET

Now that you've read the piece by Summers, write your responses to the following questions:

1. Colonel Summers published this article before the considerable "warming" of the cold war signaled by such events as the tearing down of the Berlin Wall, the subsequent reunification of Germany, the agitation for an end to Soviet hegemony in Eastern Europe, and the several reforms of the Soviet president Gorbachev (who won the Nobel Peace Prize in 1990). How might these events affect what Colonel Summers said?
2. Did Colonel Summers's arguments change any of your perceptions regarding the deterrent power of U.S. forces? of U.S. nuclear weaponry? of traditional forces? of the possibility of nuclear war? If so, in what ways?
3. Given what Summers says, together with events since Summers wrote the piece, do you think the United States should keep forces in Europe? Why or why not?
4. What is your understanding of the terms *glasnost* and *perestroika* (¶ 34)?

Questions for Writing and Discussion

Prepare short written answers to each of these questions. Be prepared to hand them in and/or discuss them in class, as your teacher directs.

1. What can you judge about the audience for this piece just by what goes on in it? How does the author want, for example, the admiral's comment (¶ 3) to affect his readers? What does the last sentence in paragraph 4 do for the reader?
2. What values or attitudes on the audience's part does the author make use of as part of his argument? Look especially, for example, at "Darling's Dilemma" (¶ 11–15): How did Colonel Darling's presentation play on (both depend on and help reveal) the army staff members' attitudes? What would you, in their shoes, have said?
3. What is the major (the biggest) claim of the essay, and what specific evidence is offered in support of it?
4. Any argument this long is bound to have several claims, some major and some minor. List the various claims you find in this piece, and draw a diagram

that shows which ones depend on which ones. How do the three major sections ("Strategic Forces," "The Short-War Theory," and "Forward Basing") relate to the piece's larger structure?

5. Go back to your list of claims, and indicate which ones are claims of fact? Which of definition? Which of value? Which of policy?
6. As you go back through the argument, pencil in light brackets [ ] in the margin those places in which the author is reporting information, evaluating information, or using the information to make judgments. Which of these places occur in paragraph 31?
7. Choose one of the subarguments (one of the three sections listed in question 4 above) to analyze in detail—what is the claim, how is it supported, and is the support sufficient, of the right kind, and close enough to the claim?
8. Do you think Colonel Summers is using primarily an ethical, logical, or emotional appeal? Why?
9. What do the following words mean—*listing, dreadnoughts* (¶ 4), *semantic maneuver* (¶ 5), *retaliation* (¶ 6), *raison d'être* (¶ 7), *proliferated* (¶ 8), *parity* (¶ 10), *impaled* (¶ 13), *facade* (¶ 14), *portended* (¶ 15), *jihad* (¶ 17), *dispiriting, fallacy* (¶ 21), *pernicious* (¶ 22), *conscripted, deployed* (¶ 23), *felicitous, proprietary* (¶ 27), *constituents* (¶ 28), *inexorably, degenerated* (¶ 31)?

THE KEY POINT TO REMEMBER: Writing Effective Arguments

We've gone to some lengths at the beginning of this last chapter in Part Four to make sure you are comfortable with principal structural elements of effective arguments. Understanding those elements—claims, evidence, kinds of arguments, kinds of appeals, and so on—is essential to *understanding* how arguments work.

But when it comes to *writing* successful arguments, there's no easy formula. All the various elements presented earlier in this book and reviewed in this chapter's opening pages are important. But *including the reader in the argument* may be the most important element of all. That aspect—what we call here *the reader's share*—is at once the most important and the least tangible. It has three components, and they range from the very general to the very specific:

> In general, be aware of the possibility (and beyond that the desirability) of your reader's investment in your argument.
>
> More specifically, try to build your reader's key qualities into the structure of your argument.
>
> In particular, some quality in the reader—an attitude, a belief, etc.—needs to become the necessary link (a warrant) between key evidence in your argument and the claim.

Notice that these elements do not appear here as a 1–2–3 list ("first do this, then do that"); rather they build on each other: if you are aware of the possibility and the desirability of giving your reader a "stake" in your argument, then you can look for ways to build your reader's key qualities into the structure of your argument. And the classical way to do that is to let a key quality that already exists in your reader—an attitude, a belief, the knowledge of a body of facts, etc.—become one of the necessary links (perhaps *the* necessary link) in your argument. Because these three components of writing successful arguments are really all part of the same thing, we will discuss them together in the following section. Just as any good piece of writing requires an investment on the writer's part (the expressive element discussed in Chapter Four), so any effective piece of argumentation will give the reader a share in it.

The Reader's Share. You've already seen some examples of how this concept works in writing done by professionals. For example, in the "Dirty Potato Chips" passage it's readers' potential hostility toward mass-produced products (something like "If it's mass produced, it must lack quality") that connects the unorthodox manufacturing process of "dirty" potato chips with claims to quality. In "The Untouchables," the *reader's share* is, among other things, the willingness to believe that education no longer merits that "religious mystique" it has traditionally been accorded, that it's therefore time to demand a dollar's worth of educational gain from every education dollar spent. This feeling is made more acute by the argument against educational administrators, which itself plays upon Americans' innate distrust of bureaucrats and bureaucracies. And one of the central parts of the reader's share in "A Bankrupt Military Strategy" is our susceptibility to historical arguments, especially when they're offered by someone whose credentials and testimony *seem* so valid. Did the scenario actually happen exactly as the author tells it? It's a measure of his success at playing on our credulity that we tend not to ask that question. Rather than lecture you about the reader's share some more, let's take a look at how one student wrestled with it.

CASE STUDY CLOSE-UP

Here's a set of theses from students' argumentation papers. As you inspect the list, can you determine which qualities of the reader each might incorporate?

- We need to clean up the oceans.
- The United States should do away with the electoral college in presidential elections.
- We need to clamp down on corruption in college athletics.
- People should avoid fad diets.
- Swimsuit competitions in women's beauty pageants are demeaning and unnecessary.
- Liberal arts educations are better than purely scientific ones.

Obviously, each argument would need to draw on different qualities of the reader in different ways. Let's look in more detail at how *revision* of one of those arguments, "SOS: Save Our Seas," enabled the author to write a more effective piece by building the reader into it even more.

Here's a good, middle-level draft by Chriss Hendrickson, a freshman at State University. Although the essay got a good grade in this form, Chriss wanted to use it for her portfolio (a set of papers that get extra revision and play a large role in her final grade in the course). Accordingly, she asked the teacher how she could make it better. Here's the draft Chriss gave her teacher, along with the teacher's comments on how to improve it.

SOS: Save Our Seas

Chriss Hendrickson, college writing student

1 "The very survival of the human species depends upon the maintenance of an ocean clean and alive, spreading all around the world. The ocean is our planet's life belt" (Toufexis 44). Marine explorer Jacques-Yves Cousteau said these words some years ago, and the very significance of them holds true today in an even stronger sense. We are polluting the ocean at an alarming rate, and the consequences might prove to be irreversible. We must take action now in order to try to save the earth's greatest supplier of food, recreation, and animal life.

2 For thousands of years, the ocean has been a source of unlimited industry for human beings. In the United States alone, commercial fishing is a $3.1 billion industry (Toufexis 48). But in the past few years, many fishermen have seen a drop in income of almost 50 percent, owing to decreased numbers of fish, shellfish, and crabs. These valuable ocean creatures are being killed by poisonous chemicals that are being dumped into coastal waters (Toufexis 48). These chemicals are deposited into the ocean by large corporations that make everything from plastic garbage bags to nuclear power (Asmus and Johnson 9). Because of the limited area on land to put the excess wastes from manufacturing these products, the ocean is used as a massive dump site, receiving and retaining millions of gallons of garbage and harmful chemicals each year (Asmus and Johnson 9). The fish that are able to survive these pollutants are often contaminated, and there is a rising incidence of illnesses among people consuming these fish, including hepatitis A, cholera, and gastroenteritis (Toufexis 48).

3 Besides being a source of industry, the ocean has always been a place for human recreation. But lately, going swimming in the ocean is about as healthy as going swimming in your local sewage plant. Last

year, from New Jersey to Long Island the beaches were filled with garbage that had floated in from the dumping site used by New York, miles off the coast. Since 1986, ten million tons of sewage have been released into the water, and the results are beaches filled with plastic tampon applicators, crack vials, needles and syringes, stained bandages, prescription bottles, and dozens of vials of blood. Six of these vials tested positive for antibodies to the AIDS virus (Toufexis 44). Today, going to the beach is a hazardous and life-threatening pastime.

The problems with oceanic pollution also affect the thousands of species of fish and mammals that use the ocean as a permanent home for reproducing and food gathering. Last year off the coast of Texas, 307 tons of litter were collected by volunteers, two-thirds of which was plastic, including 31,733 bags, 30,295 bottles, and 15,631 six-pack yokes. These nonbiodegradable plastics kill and maim more than two million seabirds and a hundred thousand marine animals every year. "Sea turtles choke on plastic bags they mistake for jellyfish, and sea lions are ensnared when they playfully poke their noses into plastic nets and rings. Unable to open their jaws, some sea lions simply starve to death" (Toufexis 47). 4

But what can be done about these life-threatening situations to both human beings and animals? There are many agencies set up to deal with these problems, but often the jurisdiction of these agencies, both state and federal, are conflicting and confusing, and usually very little is accomplished. For example, in North Carolina a state agency and the federal Food and Drug Administration regulate the harvesting of shellfish. A third agency, the state's health department, takes surveys and samples of the shellfish and water. Another state agency is responsible for setting the guidelines for opening and closing the shellfish beds. With so many agencies, communication and cooperation are often hard to find (Toufexis 49). The answer seems to lie within the various waterfront communities and with increased awareness and activity of all their citizens. 5

Many communities are getting involved by "forbidding retail food establishments to use plastic grocery bags, food containers, and wrappers" (Toufexis 50). Sixteen states have passed laws requiring that the plastic yokes that hold beer and soda be biodegradable. Also, stiff fines and even prison sentences are being used in order to deter would-be polluters (Toufexis 50). 6

7 With an increase in awareness of citizens in all countries and through better organization of state and federal agencies, we might be able to reverse the damage that has already been done. And hopefully return the ocean to a state of harmony that humans and animals can live with. As Jacques Cousteau said, "The very survival of the human species depends upon" this harmony.

Works Cited

Asmus, Peter, and Richard Johnson. "A Sea of Troubles." Greenpeace March-April 1988: 6-10.

Toufexis, Anastasia. "The Dirty Seas." Time 1 Aug. 1988: 44-50.

Chriss's Teacher's Comments

After reading the draft, Chriss's teacher made these comments.

> Chriss, "SOS: Save Our Seas" is a reasonably well written piece in the draft I just read. The claim is clear, the structure is solid, the evidence seems to fit the claim nicely, the grammar is generally sound. So how could it be made better? Well, it seems a little *heartless*, a little lacking in human feeling, a little lacking in something essential that might make it really convincing. After all, the point it is making, here in the 1990s, is one no one would really resist.
>
> What this draft is lacking is a sense that it is written *to* somebody and *from* somebody. That is, it is characteristic of much writing done in freshman composition classes in that it seems to come from nowhere and anywhere and to be headed nowhere and everywhere. Sure, it's good, but it's not really as convincing as it could be. The problem, Chriss, is finding a way to build *audience* into it.

Chriss's Response

As Chriss and her teacher considered how to improve the essay, they came up with several ideas for ways to build the readers' thoughts and feelings into Chriss's argument. Which of these ideas do you think would work best—which would you choose? And can you think of other ways to build the audience into this piece?

Have your students do this kind of audience analysis and adaptation.

1. Open the essay with a personal experience [as does the "Acid Rain" essay in chapter 12]:
   a. "John Doe was walking barefoot on his favorite beach when . . ." [but would it be acceptable to invent this, Chriss wondered?].

b. "The year is 2020 and your grown child wants to honeymoon at the beach, but . . ."

2. Shift to using "you" throughout.

3. Add a paragraph somewhere to heighten those feelings of environmental responsibility which the reader already has (mention that from space our planet is mostly ocean blue, use the phrase "big blue marble," use the fact that we evolved from the oceans, state that oceans are three-fifths of the globe, and so forth).

Chriss and her teacher briefly evaluated each tactic. Each would put quite a different stamp on the piece's structure. The first—(opening with a personal experience)—would have been good had Chriss indeed had some personal experience of this problem, or had she been willing to return to the literature on the subject and dig out someone else's personal experience. Chriss asked her teacher whether it would be acceptable just to invent one, and the teacher said no. That led to the next option (item b) under this tactic, a hypothetical future occurrence ("The year is 2020 . . ."). This option seemed more workable, but Chriss thought it weaker than she preferred: "too make-believe" was how she dismissed it.

The second tactic, a shift to "you" throughout, would have the advantage of giving some teeth to the fourth sentence's "we," and of putting the reader's share in the entire piece. Chriss tried rewriting two paragraphs with that tactic:

> "The very survival of the human species depends upon the maintenance of an ocean clean and alive, spreading all around the world. The ocean is our planet's life belt" (Toufexis 44). Marine explorer Jacques-Yves Cousteau said these words some years ago, and the very significance of them holds true today for each of us in an even stronger sense. You and I are polluting the ocean at an alarming rate, and the consequences might prove to be irreversible. Each of us must take action now in order to try to save the earth's greatest supplier of food, recreation, and animal life.
>
> For thousands of years, the ocean has been a source of unlimited industry for human beings. In the United States alone, commercial fishing is a $3.1 billion industry (Toufexis 48). But in the past few years, many fishermen have seen a drop in income of almost 50 percent, owing to decreased numbers of fish, shellfish, and crabs. These valuable ocean creatures are being killed by poisonous chemicals you and I dump into coastal waters (Toufexis 48). These chemicals are deposited into the ocean by large corporations that make everything from plastic garbage bags to nuclear power (Asmus and Johnson 9). Because of the limited

> area on land to put the excess wastes from manufacturing these products, the ocean is used as a massive dump site, receiving and retaining millions of gallons of garbage and harmful chemicals each year (Asmus and Johnson 9). The fish that are able to survive these pollutants are often contaminated, and there is a rising incidence of illnesses among people consuming these fish, including hepatitis A, cholera, and gastroenteritis (Toufexis 48).

To Chriss and her teacher, the result was "too preachy"; moreover, the "you and I" emphasis was undercut by the fact that "large corporations" are the actual dumpers, for the most part. As Chriss said, "It's too easy to get an effect by just pointing a finger over and over. On environmental issues especially, nowadays lots of people just turn off anyone who does that 'you . . . you . . . you' business." Her teacher's explanation was along the same lines, though perhaps a little deeper: "The problem is a writer—any writer—has to *earn* the right to use that 'you.'" Starting this essay out with the "you" pronoun is a problem because the essay hasn't yet earned the right to use it.

At this point Chriss and her teacher looked back at the essay's overall structure to see whether it would accommodate the addition of a new paragraph and, if so, where. They liked this option because they felt the new paragraph wouldn't really have to *create* new thoughts and feelings in the reader, just make the reader more aware of thoughts and feelings he or she already had. The structure of the essay now was basically as follows:

Here's that point about building in the reader again.

> A one-paragraph introduction, ending with a forecast of the next three topics
>
> Those three topics
>
> A shift to "what can be done" (¶ 5)
>
> A conclusion that suggests the benefits of taking action and reiterates the urgency of the problem

Where in this structure would be the best place to put in the kind of "reader's share" paragraph we're talking about?

It seemed to both Chriss and her teacher that the obvious place was between the fourth and fifth paragraphs. This placement would enable Chriss to "bring it all back home" to the reader right *after* presenting the evidence established the problem and right *before* suggesting solutions. Here's an early draft of the new paragraph, followed by the finished essay as it went into Chriss's portfolio:

> "Cleaning up the environment is fine," you may say, "but what does this have to do with me? I don't work for a large corporation that dumps its waste. I don't live in New York or New Jersey, and I recycle my plastic trash and aluminum cans." The problem is that ocean pollution is not limited to certain beaches or certain states, and because of that it can't be stopped effectively by any one person or any group of people (say, the

citizens of New York City) stopping their polluting. The only solution is for us all to act, collectively. Maybe as a child you had a great vacation at the beach, or maybe your parents honeymooned there. Imagine what your children and their children will have lost if the oceans and the beaches wind up as dumps that cover three-fifths of the globe. Is that what you want your children to live with?

As you can see, Chriss tends to overdo it in her early drafts. As she says, "I like to start out by writing down just about everything that comes to mind, not screening out anything. Then I go back later on and make it good." Here, now, is the portfolio draft of her essay, complete with the revised version of the new paragraph:

SOS: Save Our Seas

"The very survival of the human species depends upon the maintenance of an ocean clean and alive, spreading all around the world. The ocean is our planet's life belt" (Toufexis 44). Marine explorer Jacques-Yves Cousteau said these words some years ago, and they hold true today in an even stronger sense. We are polluting the ocean at an alarming rate, and the consequences might prove to be irreversible. We must take action now to try to save the earth's greatest supplier of food, recreation, and animal life. 1

For thousands of years, the ocean has been a source of unlimited industry for human beings. In the United States alone, commercial fishing is a $3.1 billion industry (Toufexis 48). But in the past few years, many fishermen have seen a drop in income of almost 50 percent, owing to decreased numbers of fish, shellfish, and crabs. These valuable ocean creatures are being killed by poisonous chemicals that are being dumped into coastal waters (Toufexis 48). These chemicals are deposited into the ocean by large corporations that make everything from plastic garbage bags to nuclear power (Asmus and Johnson 9). Because of the limited area on land to put the excess wastes from manufacturing these products, the ocean is used as a massive dump site, receiving and retaining millions of gallons of garbage and harmful chemicals each year (Asmus and Johnson 9). The fish that are able to survive these pollutants are often contaminated, and there is a rising incidence of illness among people consuming these fish, including hepatitis A, cholera, and gastroenteritis (Toufexis 48). 2

3 Besides being a source of industry, the ocean has always been a place for human recreation. But lately, going swimming in the ocean is about as healthy as going swimming in your local sewage plant. Last year, from New Jersey to Long Island the beaches were filled with garbage that had floated in from the dumping site used by New York, miles off the coast. Since 1986, ten million tons of sewage have been released into the water, and the results are beaches filled with plastic tampon applicators, crack vials, needles and syringes, stained bandages, prescription bottles, and dozens of vials of blood. Six of these vials tested positive for antibodies to the AIDS virus (Toufexis 44). Today, going to the beach is a hazardous and life-threatening pastime.

4 The problems with oceanic pollution also affect the thousands of species of fish and mammals that use the ocean as a permanent home for reproducing and food gathering. Last year off the coast of Texas, 307 tons of litter were collected by volunteers, two-thirds of which was plastic, including 31,733 bags, 30,295 bottles, and 15,631 six-pack yokes. These nonbiodegradable plastics kill and maim more than two million seabirds and a hundred thousand marine animals every year. According to Anastasia Toufexis, "Sea turtles choke on plastic bags they mistake for jellyfish, and sea lions are ensnared when they playfully poke their noses into plastic nets and rings. Unable to open their jaws, some sea lions simply starve to death" (47).

5 "Cleaning up the ocean environment is fine," you may say, "but what does this have to do with me? I don't work for a large corporation that dumps waste. I don't live in New York or New Jersey, and I recycle my plastic trash and aluminum cans." But because ocean pollution is not limited to certain beaches or certain states, it can't be stopped by any one person or even any one group of people (such as the citizens of New York City) stopping their polluting. We all need to act, collectively. Imagine what your children and their children will have lost if the oceans and the beaches--the world's greatest natural resources--wind up as the world's greatest dumps.

6 What can be done about these life-threatening situations to both human beings and animals? There are many agencies set up to deal with these problems, but often the jurisdictions of these agencies, both state and federal, are conflicting and confusing, and usually very little is accomplished. For example, in North Carolina a state agency and the federal Food and Drug Administration regulate the harvesting of

shellfish. A third agency, the state's health department, takes surveys and samples of the shellfish and water. Another state agency is responsible for setting the guidelines for opening and closing the shellfish beds. With so many agencies, communication and cooperation are often hard to find (Toufexis 49). The answer seems to lie within the various waterfront communities and with increased awareness and activity of all their citizens.

Anastasia Toufexis informs us that many communities are getting involved by "forbidding retail food establishments to use plastic grocery bags, food containers, and wrappers" (50). Sixteen states have passed laws requiring that the yokes that hold beer and soda be biodegradable. Also stiff fines and even prison sentences are being used in order to deter would-be polluters (Toufexis 50). 7

With an increase in awareness of citizens in all countries and through better organization of state and federal agencies, we might be able to reverse the damage that has already been done and hopefully return the ocean to a state of harmony in which people and animals can live peacefully together. As Jacques Cousteau said, "The very survival of the human species depends upon" this harmony. 8

Works Cited

Asmus, Peter, and Richard Johnson. "A Sea of Troubles." Greenpeace March-April 1988: 6-10.

Toufexis, Anastasia. "The Dirty Seas." Time 1 Aug. 1988: 44-50.

Questions to Answer When You're Writing Arguments

If you jot down answers to these questions as you're preparing to write an argument, we think you'll find you write a more effective argument.

1. What are the key characteristics of your audience (attitudes, beliefs) that you want to build into the structure of your argument?
2. What place in the structure of your argument do your audience's attitudes and beliefs have?
3. You might also want to take another look at the questions in the worksheet in chapter 7; we've summarized it for you here:
   a. What kind of argument do you want to make?
   b. What point (claim) do you want to establish within that argument?

c. What evidence do you have to use? What support is there for this claim?
   (1) Is it the right *kind* of support?
   (2) Is it the right *amount* of support?
   (3) How *close* is the support to the claim:
      (a) Are any *middle* steps between the support and the claim weak?
      (b) Do any *unstated assumptions* that join the support and the claim need to be made explicit?

4. Here's one final question "Have you earned the *right* to assert this point to this reader? Many times writers approach persuasive writing mechanically, as though any piece that clearly states a thesis and then brings in three pieces of evidence to support it has done all it needs to do. But, as we said in chapter 7, readers want to feel that you've *earned* the point you're trying to make and that you've taken their own thoughts and feelings into account in the argument. It's not enough just to connect a claim and some evidence somehow; to be fully effective, your argumentative writing must show a human being significantly engaged with a point that is worth making to another specific, real human being. Making a trivial point or making a point in a lackadaisical manner won't persuade anyone.

WRITING ASSIGNMENTS

1. In an essay of 750–1,000 words, take a position on an issue of local concern and argue convincingly in its favor.
2. In an essay of 750–1,000 words, take a position on an issue of national or global concern and argue convincingly in support of it.
3. Bring in an example of (a) a well-written argument and (b) a poorly written argument, and then do a written analysis and critique of the two pieces.
4. Antonio M. Rosario's *Man with Mouth Zipped Shut* on page 475 can be seen to illustrate at least three visions writers might have, all of them negative:

   a. A world in which writers *want* to "speak" or "talk," but *can't,* their mouths (pens, typewriters, word processors) being "zippered" or otherwise rendered nonfunctional. (Think about those writers who have said that they write, in effect, because they *have* to—they have no choice; it is their very nature. Now think about the various ways such writers might be "zippered"—censorship, for example.)
   b. A world in which writers *can* "speak" or "talk," but their audiences or readers, for whatever reason, *can't respond.* The writer never knows whether his or her message is having any effect.
   c. A world in which writers are heard, but the audience or readers are so hostile (perhaps angry) that they *choose* to "zip" their lips and make no response, thus leaving the writer aware only that his or her message is not welcome.

In a brief paper, elaborate on one, two, or all three of these negative visions. Which do you think would be the worst for the writer? For the audience? For society in general?

Focus on Critical Thinking

5. Working with your writing group, do an extended analysis and critique of the argument presented in "Bankrupt Military Strategy." Make both an oral and a written presentation of the results of your analysis.
6. Analyze a historical document—such as the Gettysburg Address or the Declaration of Independence—for its argumentative strategy. In particular, try to determine what qualities of the audience for each document the writing builds into its argument.
7. Reread the essay "Eleven Blue Men" (chapter 6). In what ways can persuasion and argumentation be said to be shaping the way that incident is written up?

Writers' Circle

Divide into teams of three students each. Each team member should then comb newspapers, magazines, fliers, and the like for an especially effective advertisement that combines pictures and text. The ad each member chooses should have at least one of these characteristics:

1. Strong emotional appeal (*pathos*)
2. Strong ethical appeal (*ethos*)
3. Strong logical appeal (*logos*)

Each team should then (a) meet to analyze each of the three ads brought in by its members and then (b) collaborate on writing a brief analysis of the ad's characteristics, based on such considerations as these:

How the ad takes its audience into account

How the ad's picture adds to its effectiveness

How the ad's text uses language to strengthen its claim(s) and support

Finally, each team should then present its ads and reports to the class as a whole, followed by a classwide discussion of the ads and a classwide vote of the three best ads overall.

part five Special Applications

PROFILE ♦ OF ♦ A ♦ WRITER

Vivian Baylor

Vivian Baylor, author of "The Crisis in U.S. Science and Mathematics Education" (chapter 14), is an engineer and project manager at Oak Ridge National Laboratory (ORNL). She describes herself as "a child of the sixties" and, laughing, as "a high school nerd." She entered Virginia Polytechnic Institute (now Virginia Tech), as a math major. In her freshman year (1969–70), like many of her generation, she "got politicized," and changed her major to political science. After graduation, in 1972, she returned to school to seek a second Bachelor's degree, this time as an English major.

Q: So how did you end up as an engineer?

A: Not too long after that I got married, and my

PART OUTLINE

husband was an engineer. We came down to Tennessee, and the opportunities available to me with an English degree were limited. I could have gotten a job editing, that was clear, but I really didn't want to do that. And so I said what the heck, I'll go back to school again. . . . Before I graduated from UT [University of Tennessee] with my BS in engineering, I ended up getting a job at ORNL as a summer student, and I ended up writing several reports that were published. That was rather unprecedented for a summer student, and they decided that maybe I was a keeper, so they kept me on a part-time basis while I finished my degree and then offered me regular employment when I finished.

Q: What kinds of writing did you do in your engineering classes?

A: In the engineering classes themselves there was almost no writing. They really just don't stress that at all. In engineering itself, if you're actually doing lab work, obviously it [not having training in writing] doesn't match at all, because it's incumbent upon you to communicate the results of your experimentation. In fact, the Laboratory is very similar to a university environment, in that it is almost a publish or perish situation. You are in fact evaluated on the number and quality of your publications. After you actually move away from engineering into engineering management, into engineering administration, writing is even more important, for proposals and also for the communication of ideas.

Q: What kinds of things do you write; can you characterize them generically?

A: The kinds of things that I write now are mainly to get money, or to describe the program that we're managing. For example, people will send rough drafts of proposals to me, and obviously it's their baby, and they're responsible for the meat of it, but then I put it in real "English" for them, and try to communicate that idea to the sponsor. So first of all I may rewrite the proposal itself, and second of all what I do is abstract that proposal and maybe turn it into a one-page concept description and use that as a marketing tool. . . . What I'm trying to do is to give them [clients] a piece of paper they can have in their hands that they can refer to later, and there's no task descriptions or anything: You have a problem, we have a solution, this is how much it's going to cost, this is what it looks like. You have to be very succinct and get your message across.

If you haven't already done so, this is the time to poll your students about their writing in other classes. Specifically, how much and what kinds of writing did they do, and in what classes, in high school? How much and what kinds of writing do they do in their classes in their current year in college? How much and what kinds of writing do they anticipate doing in future classes for the remainder of their college careers? And how much and what kinds of writing do they anticipate doing once they're out of college? Whether or not students' answers conform to your own values about how much writing students *should* be doing, you need to teach this next part of the book with your eyes wide open to the reality of your students' lives as writers beyond your classroom.

Q: What sense do you have of the audience for this writing?

A: The audience is mostly bureaucrats with a former technical background. What we try to do is gear it toward the lay person who has a smattering of a scientific background, who has enough intelligence to understand what you're getting at, but doesn't know all of the nuts and bolts about, say, quantum physics. You would be surprised about how large that audience is. Almost all of the government people we deal with are of that audience.

Q: Do you feel that the need for engineers and scientists to be better communicators will continue to increase?

A: Oh I think it has to. It concerns me . . . people are afraid of what they don't understand. Science and engineering and mathematics are just getting more and more complex; they're not getting any simpler at all. People need to have some understanding of what scientists and mathematicians and engineers are doing, in order that they can allay their fears and understand and appreciate that there's good work being done, work that will make their lives better. If scientists and engineers can't communicate what they're doing on a lay level, then I think we're in trouble. I'm really concerned about that. That's the whole situation with nuclear energy, for example, people equate nuclear weapons with nuclear power plants. A simple mistake like that has never been rectified.

• • •

Up to this point in *The Heath Guide to College Writing*, we have focused on the writing process, reasons for writing, subjects for writing, and inventional/developmental patterns for writing. Important as they are, those discussions are generic, representative of principles that fit myriad kinds of writing situations you may encounter.

Now we are going to narrow our focus to fit the particular *kinds* of writing students—and professionals—often have to do. This part of the book addresses the reality of your curriculum: at some point in your college career, you most likely will have to do *each* of the specific kinds of writing tasks we cover in the chapters in this section:

Essays About Literature. No matter what your major, you will probably have to take at least one or two courses in the study of literature. Most likely, those courses will require you to write analytically or critically about works of fiction, drama, or poetry. The most typical kind of analytical paper on literature usually involves analysis of *theme*—that is, discussion about the main idea or group of ideas you think the work of literature communicates. Ordinarily, the key to theme will be *characterization* or *symbolic language*. In chapter 21 we cover this fundamental approach to literary analysis. Our examples are (a) for prose fiction, the John Steinbeck short story "The Chrysanthemums" and a student paper about it; (b) for drama, William Inge's "A Social Event" and a student paper about it; and (c) for poetry, Robert Frost's "Stopping by Woods on a Snowy Evening" and a student paper about it.

Of course, most people in English departments have their own approaches to the study of literature. For our admittedly basic approach here, we are assuming that close critical reading is essential to all such approaches.

Essay Tests. In college, essay tests are given in a wide variety of courses. Most essay tests make it your responsibility to *recall, analyze, evaluate,* and *synthesize* information. That is, you will need to remember and recite information, but you may also need to assess the information's significance. Additionally, you may well be expected to determine particular logical relationships (such as cause and effect) within the information. The key to success on essay examinations is combining knowledge, preparation, and good writing skills. We're unable to offer much help with the knowledge part of the equation, but we do cover—in chapter 22—how best to prepare for the writing component of essay examinations, in terms of recall, analysis, evaluation, and synthesis. In particular, we show you in detail one way to take advantage of the fact that *writing* is at the heart of all such tests. We also look at how one student prepared for, wrote, and learned from an essay test in an environmental ethics class.

The fairly tight sequence to chapters 21–23 allows you to treat them almost as a block, especially if you're teaching a strongly literature-based course.

Research Papers. Beginning with freshman composition, you can expect to take many courses that will require you to prepare a paper based on the results of research. In fact, knowing how to *find* information about a subject—any subject—is one of the hallmarks of a college-educated person, and knowing how to *assemble* and *present* that information in a properly documented research paper is another such hallmark.

Nowadays you can do that kind of search two ways: by hand or by computer. Depending on where you are and what you're working on, you'll find you need to know both methods. Certainly computers have increased the efficiency of retrieving information (as well as of storing it). And so in chapter 23 we explain how you can use computers to aid your search for information on a given subject. We also explain how you can search for—and find—information without the aid of computers. Once you know both ways to look for information, you will greatly appreciate the time computers can save researchers. And you will know how, in a pinch, you could *still* find information even if you had no access to computer technology.

After helping you learn to find information, we next discuss various ways that information can be put to use, including proper procedures for quotation, paraphrase, and documentation. Thus the entire research process, leading to the research paper, is the subject of chapter 23. The chapter closes with a case study concerning one student's research and writing of his research paper "Steroid Abuse in Football: A Dead Man's Hand."

The similarly strong sequence to chapters 24–26 allows the three to be taught as a block.

Reports. A research paper is one kind of report; that is, in most reports, information has been found and/or created and then passed on to readers, with appropriate documentation. There are many other kinds of reports, however: reports that give not only information but also suggestions regarding the use of that information (user manuals), reports that inform readers on the progress being made on a certain project (on construction of a new roadway, building, or sports facility, for instance); reports on books, plays, films, and products. In fact, excepting only the letter, the report is the most common kind of writing found in the everyday world of business and industry—a world many of you will join beyond the college doors. In chapter 24 we cover common strategies for writing reports.

Success at report writing begins with a detailed sizing up of the situation—in terms of needs, goals, audiences, sources, and stases—and, after completion of a content-based first draft, proceeds with consideration of those elements as pointers for revision. A student report on corporate accounting is included to illustrate those points.

We like to teach proposal writing in just about every writing class we have. In a technical communication oriented curriculum, the proposal becomes a feasibility study for the major report. The same application can be

Proposals. A common kind of writing in business and industry is the proposal. In its simplest form, a proposal is a *request;* it asks for permission, approval, or support. One typical kind of proposal is the grant proposal, usually a request for funding. Here a grantor or granting agency specifies what the grant amount will be and what requirements the grant proposals must meet; those seeking this grant will prepare their proposals in accordance with the specifications given by the grantor. Other kinds of proposals include bids on publicly advertised jobs, budget requests, and in-house suggestions for improvements in production, sales, or other aspects of the business. Writing an effective proposal invites you to present certain facts, interpret those facts, persuade your readers, and recommend a course of action. Proposals are therefore a practical exercise in rhetoric: if ineffectively written, they will not be persuasive and thus will not be approved. In chapter 25 we present our strategies for preparing the kinds of proposals undergraduates usually write. In this chapter we look at the writing of a proposal for (a) an independent-study course, (b) an internship, and (c) a grant, thereby providing practical examples of how writers can use the idea of stasis (chapter 7) in helpful ways.

made in a literature-oriented curriculum—the proposal "sets up" the major (library) report. In both cases, the proposal offers a wonderful, practical exercise in rhetoric: however much of a pose of "objectivity" it may bear, it must also be fully persuasive. It needs to convince the reader (in these applications, the teacher, and possibly other classmates) that the proposed project is worth doing, is worth supporting, is feasible, and satisfies the goals of the task that was assigned.

Letters, Especially Job Applications. By far the most common kind of writing in daily business is the letter. Letters are written for many reasons: to inform; to clarify; to request or order; to implement procedures; to transmit major reports, proposals, or statements of policies; to thank; to persuade; to initiate relationships; to keep relationships viable—just about any reason you can think of for human communication. In chapter 26, in addition to discussing letter strategies and forms, we also devote special attention to that most important kind of letter virtually everyone writes at some time or other: the letter applying for a job. Chapter 26's coverage of letters includes letters as requests for information, as complaints, and as job applications, as well as the key principles underlying all such letters.

Oral Presentations. Innumerable surveys of business and industry leaders in America have asked what these men and women view as the most valuable skills people entering their professions must have. Invariably, an (if not *the*) essential skill cited is communication, and, just as invariably, these surveys break communication down into two broad categories: writing and speaking.

Being able to stand before a group and make a presentation is undoubtedly a valuable skill; think of the kinds of situations in which this skill is required of professionals:

- Making a proposal to a board of directors or some other group holding decision-making power
- Presenting a recommended plan for the consideration of company employees or clients
- Introducing a new product or service to potential customers
- Making a formal announcement of company policy or position for public information
- Making favorable public relations impressions for one's business

Many other situations call for oral presentations, and most of them entail careful planning—including writing—beforehand. In chapter 27 we present strategies and principles for writing and giving the kinds of presentations students often have to do: introductions, research reports, meetings, and poster displays.

We particularly admire writing programs that stress speaking as well. No definition of literacy that omits the ability to speak clearly and persuasively adequately represents the human condition. Your students do not need to make formal speeches to satisfy this requirement, but they do need to hear their own voices aloud in front of their peers—in small-group work, in whole-class presentations, and, if it seems wise to you, perhaps in more formal settings. Public speaking is, after all, the basis of rhetoric, and its current viability is undeniable.

Of course, you are the one who will in most cases make this choice for your students. While your own curricular demands and professional values will undoubtedly shape that decision, you need to make it with students' own backgrounds and current and future needs squarely in mind.

And so, keeping in mind the advice we have given you in the first four parts of this book—advice we believe will stand you in good stead no matter what you have to write—we recommend you approach this part of the book on an as-needed basis. If you need to write about literature, see chapter 21; if you need to prepare for an essay test, see chapter 22; and so on. We think these chapters will prove just as helpful as all those which precede them.

chapter 21 Writing Critical Essays About Literature

"I write at [age] 83 for the same reasons that impelled me to write at 43: I was born with a passionate desire to communicate, to organize experience, to tell tales that dramatize the adventures which listeners might have had. The job of a storyteller is to tell stories, and I have concentrated on that obligation."

James Michener

"No entertainment is so cheap as reading, nor any pleasure so lasting."

Lady Mary Wortley Montagu

You may want to contrast our definition of literature with other definitions—for example those which emphasize literature less as reflecting and more as creating an image of life. (See also our first teaching note in chapter 27.)

Traditionally, *literature* means writing in the three genres usually called "creative": prose fiction, drama, and poetry. Such a definition is admittedly narrow, for a reader can see and appreciate the writer's creativity in other kinds of writing—personal essays, arguments, editorials, in fact every kind of writing we have already seen in this book. But the body of fiction, drama, and poetry you are likely to study during your college years is often considered humanity's highest level of writing, for it draws on the most intensely felt creativity of the writer and on the keenest sensibilities and understandings of the reader. Such literature is sometimes referred to as a mirror of life the way various people perceive and experience it, and it usually appeals to traces of universal human experience in all of us. While not always *literally* true, such writing is generally *truthful*—that is, it is a believable representation of human experience in its wide range of possibilities.

Because of its appeal to our human sensibilities, reading literature is usually considered an important part of our education. While no single story, novel, play, or poem is *indispensable* to one's education, knowing that these forms of expression exist and recognizing why they exist are notable parts of what it means to be a human being. This literature is evidence of our species' active imagination, our storytelling ability (and our love of stories), our appreciation of powerful and beautiful language—evidence, that is, of our desire to create and to discover meaning, whether as writers or as readers.

People may disagree as to what in *particular* we should all read and profit by, but there's little disagreement that we should all *read.* At the risk of committing some form of heresy, we think that while it is probably better to have read Herman Melville's *Moby-Dick* than Peter Benchley's *Jaws,* it is also better to have read *Jaws* than no novel at all. Perhaps best is to have read both novels, for each tells us something about the pride, struggle, and pain of dealing with natural forces beyond our control—and entertains us into the bargain.

Of course, literature speaks much more eloquently for itself than we can for it, and our purpose is not to make an argument for the value of reading literature. Rather, inasmuch as you, in your collegiate studies, will be taking courses in which you will be expected not only to read literature but to analyze it critically and write the results of your critical analysis, our purpose in this chapter is to provide guidance in how to do such analysis and critical writing.

As usual, we think a good way to begin a new chapter is with an inventory. Ask your students to list what books they have read in the past year *other* than those required of them by schooling. Compile the list and circulate it. Then have students analyze the list, group the works under each of the four stases (fact, interpretation, value, policy), and report their findings to the class. What conclusions can students draw about themselves as "volunteer" readers?

Reading Literature: What's the Point?

The main reason to read literature is to enjoy it. Much good literature appeals to our love of *narrations*—stories—and repays our attention by catching us up in a good tale of adventure, love, conflict, or regret. Often we identify with the characters we read about, or at least see some aspect of our own lives in their stories. Or if we don't identify with the characters, we sympathize with their situations or vicariously share their experience (as the writer creates it for us) in some other way. Sometimes a short story, novel, play, or poem will not leave us with a dominant impression, but ordinarily it will—and that impression is often some central point, some main idea the work communicates to us. It is often this point, generally called *theme,* that teachers want students to discuss or write about.

Introduction to Theme

We are aware that our approach to literature in this chapter is chiefly rhetorical. We consider our approach appropriate because it is basic: it offers a fundamental way for students to interpret literature. We also like to emphasize *theme* because it is a rhetorical aspect of literature. Our approach shows our debt to Wayne Booth's *The Rhetoric of Fiction*, 2nd ed.

Once you have read a work of literature, whether prose fiction, drama, or poetry, a legitimate reaction is to ask, "What's the point?" What is the short story, novel, play, or poem communicating to you as a reader? Sometimes the answer will be fairly easy to discern. In Aesop's familiar fable about the hare and the tortoise, we readily grasp that the hare's bragging, confident attitude leads him to carelessness that winds up embarrassing him by costing him the race with the much slower tortoise. The point of Aesop's fable about the hare and the tortoise is that just because a hare is faster than a tortoise, the hare won't necessarily always win a race between the two; other factors—attitude, industry, dedication—can enter into the contest. And, of course, a *fable* is a story with a deliberate *point,* a "lesson" intended to be understood by the reader. The larger lesson of Aesop's fable is that (a) attitude, industry, and dedication might often make up for other inadequacies in life—for people as well as tortoises—and (b) overconfidence can lead to carelessness and costliness—for people as well as hares.

Similarly, the tragedy of William Shakespeare's *Romeo and Juliet* (and of *West Side Story*) is caused by the foolish and unreasonable antagonism between the two lovers' families; even a novice reader can understand that at least one point of the play is that Romeo and Juliet's parents and family, in failing to allow and appreciate the genuine love of the young couple, bring death to them both. A reader who decides that *Romeo and Juliet* shows how tragic and costly foolish antagonism can be has perhaps oversimplified the play but has not grossly misread or misunderstood it.

It will help this discussion come to life for your students if you bring in a short and fairly simple poem for them to read and discuss here in terms of its theme. We suggest a poem like Emily Dickinson's "There Is No Frigate like a Book" or Robert Frost's "The Road Not Taken."

Joyce Kilmer's famous poem about trees—"I think that I shall never see / A poem as lovely as a tree . . . "—is quite clearly a tribute to the everyday beauty of a tree, something most people take for granted and give little thought to. "Trees" intends to open our eyes to the trees we see daily and give little thought to; it is a celebration of a commonplace that suddenly makes trees seem anything but common. As Kilmer concludes, "Poems are made by fools like me / But only God can make a tree."

We don't mean to reduce the reading of literature to a search for an obvious point; far too much literature is far too subtle for that. Indeed, several great works of literature do not present an obvious point. Instead, one must read closely, analytically, and imaginatively to discern a point or points in such works. And many modern literary theorists argue that in this nuclear world of ours, traditional meanings, or *themes,* break down and no longer mean much—if they ever did. Certainly many modern works of literature do not present obvious points, though one could argue that their lack of a point *is* the point. Reading literature, finally, has always been a richer experience than reading sermons or lessons.

What we *do* mean is that reading literature will usually repay our attention in a number of ways—appreciation, beauty, excitement, enjoyment, vicarious experience, maybe puzzlement—and that one still-important way is the communication of a point or points—*themes*—that give a certain unity and purpose to a work of literature.

Prose Fiction: Characteristics

Of course, we mean *lie* here in a positive sense: a lie told with good intentions.

Prose fiction is a deliberate and elaborate lie, or series of such lies, written in prose (which is the kind of writing you're reading now, not poetry). Fiction usually involves narrative—that is, storytelling—and therefore exhibits characteristics that can be isolated and considered separately. Among those characteristics are plot, characterization, conflict, point of view, and rich language.

Plot

Plot is a sequence of events, things happening in a sequence of time or cause and effect: *first* this happens, *next* this occurs, *then* this, and so on. Plot is primarily *what* happens and *when;* occasionally it involves *why* things happen. The plot line of a conventional love story is (a) man and woman meet; (b) they fall in love; (c) they experience some complication in their relationship; (d) they overcome this complication; and (e) they marry and things look like they'll always be happy.

Characterization

Characterization is the "human interest" element; that is, characterization provides the *people* of the story. Typically, there will be a main character with whom we identify or about whom we care the most. Often there will be a central opposing character (not necessarily a villain, but someone who is definitely at odds with the main character). Most stories also have supporting characters, much as a film (another kind of storytelling) might. Major characters can often be classified as *flat* or *round*, a *flat* character being a one-dimensional personality who serves some functional purpose in the narrative but in whom we have little interest; and a *round* character being much more fully described and more central to the narrative—a more believable person because we know more about his or her personality. Characters can also be classified as *static* or *developing*: a *static* character is one who undergoes no essential change in his or her basic personality or attitude throughout the course of the story; a *developing* character, by contrast, experiences some substantial change in personal outlook or philosophy—a key internal change, where one's true nature lies. Often the purpose of a story is to show how the main character undergoes a fundamental change in outlook. Minor characters can be *foils*—used to draw out qualities in major characters—or *stock*—stereotyped roles (for instance, the strong, silent sheriff; the innocent and helpless young person). What can make characters memorable and important to us is their *conflict*.

The terms *flat, round, static,* and *developing* come from E. M. Forster's *Aspects of the Novel.*

Try illustrating the terminology in this paragraph via characters in your students' favorite television shows.

Conflict

Conflict creates the story, generating plot and bringing characterization into focus through actions. Conflict presents the problems to be resolved. The concept of conflict is present in the root *agon*, which means "struggle"; typically, the main character in a story is called the *protagonist* because the reader is "for"—that is, *pro*—this character. *Protagonist* is overall a more serviceable term than *hero*, for *hero* by definition requires a character to be admirable, a true "good person" who may or may not be very believable. A protagonist needs only to be central; whether or not he or she is all that admirable may be unimportant to the story. The person or problem creating the opposition for the protagonist is called the *antagonist*, because the reader is "against"—that is, *anti*—this person or problem. Without conflict, there's little story. Conflict usually takes three forms, all of which can be present in a given story:

1. Person versus person: a direct, often physical conflict between two or more persons, usually the protagonist and the antagonist
2. Person versus environment: conflict between a person (again, usually the protagonist) and the surroundings, often a storm, the sea, or a war
3. Person versus self: psychological conflict between a person (yes, usually the protagonist) and his or her own nature, psyche, attitude, conscience, and so on

Of course, these also establish three different ways to "read" any story: *Romeo and Juliet* could conceivably be read in any or all of these three ways.

Point of View

Point of view is the vantage point from which a story is told. The author assumes the "voice" of a narrator (or storyteller), who may be located either *outside* or *inside* the story itself. Point of view is a technical consideration of great importance, because it can become a key part of the reader's understanding of the story. Basically, a story can be told from four points of view:

Our discussion of point of view covers most possibilities, but we don't intend (or pretend) to go into experimental or unique points of view that some authors may develop.

Third Person Omniscient. An omniscient narrator is all-seeing; that is, he or she is located outside the story and tells not only what happens but also what selected characters are thinking. *Omniscient* means "all-seeing," and the truly omniscient narrator sees and knows all in ways no actual human being could. The omniscient narrator tells everything in the third person (*he, she, it*), moving from character to character, scene to scene, mind to mind, in whatever way suits how the story is to be told. Note that in the following brief example the narrator is *not* a part of the story and can thus observe and report not only scenes and what characters say but also what the characters *think:*

> Margo reclined on her favorite sofa. She did not like Jane but knew she would have to deal with her. Sighing, she regarded Jane as the latter crossed the carpet and sat on the love seat. "What will you do now, dear?" Margo asked, trying to sound as though she cared.
>
> "I don't know," said Jane, trying to keep her own tone as civil as possible; after all, it wasn't her dead husband Tom's fault that his sister Margo was such a selfish, conniving soul. "I'll be all right," Jane concluded, not only to Margo but to herself and to her image of Tom in the Beyond Somewhere, worrying because he left her so suddenly, so tragically.

In the above scene, the narrator not only knows what each woman is thinking and saying but also creates a bit of distance for his or her own perspective, implying that Jane needs to try to convince *herself* that she'll be all right much more than she needs to convince Margo. This third-person-omniscient point of view is powerful and allows the narrator virtually unlimited options.

Nearly all the features discussed in this chapter can be profitably exemplified in readings earlier in this book. For example, compare Anaïs Nin's "The Laboratory of the Soul" (chapter 4) with Madeleine L'Engle's "My Fortieth Birthday" (chapter 5) in terms of their uses of point of view.

Third Person Limited. This point of view is similar to third person omniscient except that the author deliberately *limits* what he or she can "see," usually to one character. In this kind of storytelling, there may be many characters but we are allowed to know what only one of them is thinking or feeling; anything else we know because the third-person narrator *tells* us or because the other characters *speak.* Notice the difference in the above story when it is told again by an outside narrator but this time with its point of view limited to what only Jane can think and feel:

> "What will you do now, dear?" asked Margo, who was seated on the sofa. Jane, who had crossed the carpet, settled into the love seat.
>
> "I don't know," she replied, trying to keep her intense dislike of Margo from coming through in her voice. Margo was Jane's dead husband Tom's selfish and conniving sister, but this was no time to focus on that; Tom had suddenly died and Jane had a future to worry about. "I'll be all right," Jane said, as much to herself as to Margo, and as much to try to convince Tom, whom she imagined worrying out there in the Beyond Somewhere.

In this version of the scene, only Jane's inner thoughts are shared; we have to take Jane's view of what Margo is like (the narrator seems to agree, however, with

Jane on the subject of Margo). Again, the narrator enjoys a bit of distance that allows the hint that Jane is struggling to convince herself. Such a point of view could show Jane as hopelessly self-deceived, if the author so chose.

First Person. A first-person narrator, unlike a third-person narrator, is usually *inside* the story—a character, or participant. As the pronoun suggests, this narrator tells the story of which he or she is a part and uses "I" and "we" freely. The first person is a creative point of view, for it permits the author to create a narrator who is also a character and then, because of the limitations of the point of view, add ironic perceptions that the *reader* can detect when the narrator is seemingly unaware. Imagine that our scene above features a first-person narrative by Jane, who is a little-educated woman who happened to have been married to a wealthy aristocrat named Tom. Tom's sister Margo has always been appalled that Jane was her sister-in-law. Jane, though not socially polished, is aware of Margo's attitude but doesn't care. She tells a friend about the scene:

William Least Heat-Moon's "Roadhouse and Wilderness" (chapter 15) is a good example of the first-person point of view.

> Yeah, Margo sits on the couch like, you know, she owns it—which she don't, it's *mine,* like everything else Tom left me—and says, "What will you do now, dear?" Just like she cares, you see? Well I don't know what I'm gonna do, but you can bet I won't tell that selfish and connivin' so-and-so I'm worried about it. "I don't know," I tell her, "but I'll be all right." I just hope I will, and I hope Tom, wherever he is, won't be troubled.

The first person is a very rich point of view. Mark Twain, in *The Adventures of Huckleberry Finn,* probably exploited it better than any other American writer. So often in that novel Huck says something that is truer or funnier than he realizes, because the *reader* can perceive some truth that is beyond what Huck himself can understand.

Dramatic. The dramatic point of view comes from, as might be expected, the genre of drama. At a play, all the audience knows is what it sees and hears. The set and the actions of the players constitute what is seen; the dialogue spoken by the actors constitutes most of what is heard. The dramatic point of view in prose fiction, then, involves minimal description and speech. The narrator is much like a video recorder, presenting only what is visually and aurally recorded. Descriptions are basic and without judgment or embellishment, and we "hear" only what the characters *say,* not what they're *thinking.* There is no interpretation, as is possible in the other points of view, except for what can be *inferred* by the thoughtful reader. Our scene again:

John Welter's "Has His Southern-ness Gone with the Wind?" (chapter 10) is a good example of the dramatic point of view.

> Margo sat on the sofa. Jane crossed the carpet and sat on the love seat.
> "What will you do now, dear?" asked Margo.
> "I don't know," Jane replied. Then, after a brief pause, she added, "I'll be all right."

As you can tell, the objective, dramatic point of view makes it difficult for the narrator to add detail that might be important to the story. In the above scene, the *attitudes* of the two women, so central to understanding the scene fully, are not discernible. Yet a skillful writer can often use minimal dialogue and description in revealing ways. The American novelist and short story writer Ernest Hemingway has long been famous for his frequent use of a terse but evocative dramatic point of view.

Rich Language

William Least Heat-Moon's "Three-in-One" (chapter 13) is a good example of rich language being employed for thematic purposes.

By "rich language" we mean the word choices, the *diction* a writer chooses in telling a story. Some rich language is a matter of thematic texture; that is, the language is significant and contributes to the story's point or meanings. *Symbolism* is an example of such rich language. In the story that follows, John Steinbeck's "The Chrysanthemums," the chrysanthemums are symbolic—that is, they have a literal function in the story (they are flowers that the protagonist, Elisa Allen, can grow very well), but they also have an important *symbolic* function: as flowers that Elisa can grow so well, they represent her special gift of a "green thumb" (or "planter's hands," as she calls this gift). They also represent her other special gifts: she is a beautiful woman with much talent and much love to share. As beautiful things, the chrysanthemums symbolize, finally, Elisa herself. And Steinbeck's rich use of the chrysanthemums—his repeated references to them at key points in the story—make them unmistakably important. By the story's end, the reader can see that the symbolism of the chrysanthemums carries a vital part of the story's overall meaning.

But symbolism isn't the only way authors use rich language to help convey their stories. Imagery—language that appeals to our various senses—is also at work in good prose fiction (and also, as we shall see, in drama and poetry). Imagery is a broad concept, best limited here to a few quick examples. Consider:

Some of your students might benefit from reviewing the material on figurative language in chapter 16, "Description."

"The moon was a ghostly galleon." (Alfred Noyes). This is a metaphor (implied comparison) that appeals to our sense of sight.

"Splash! Woof! Crash! Snore, Slurp, Screech, Bang!" These are examples of onomatopoeia, in which the word when spoken mimics the sound it describes. The appeal is to our sense of sound.

"His jaw felt like sandpaper." This is a simile (explicit comparison) that appeals to our sense of touch.

"The margarita was salty but satisfying." The adjective here, *salty,* implies a comparison with the taste of salt and thus appeals to our sense of taste.

"Being downwind of Barnabus was like being downwind of something not long enough dead." The simile here appeals to our sense of smell.

Imagery generally involves comparisons, language that engages our imaginations so that we can vicariously experience, through our *imagined* senses, what the author describes. And imagery is just one aspect of the use of rich language. Rich language also includes the writer's style—the particular way each writer arranges words in sentences so as to keep us interested even when we might pause to note a particularly well-turned phrase or way of saying something.

This discussion of plot, characterization, conflict, point of view, and rich language has furnished just a brief rundown of typical characteristics of prose fiction. The rundown hasn't been comprehensive; we've left out some characteristics, such as *setting*, that we'll discuss later. Nevertheless, the characteristics just presented are the major ones that ideally combine into a unified work, each characteristic helping to present the theme or themes the work conveys.

Now let's look at these characteristics working in concert in an excellent short story by a great American writer.

The Chrysanthemums

John Steinbeck

John Steinbeck (1902–68) won the Pulitzer Prize for his novel The Grapes of Wrath, *the New York Drama Critics Circle Award for his play* Of Mice and Men, *and, in 1962, the Nobel Prize in literature. His other novels include* Tortilla Flat, The Red Pony, *and* Cannery Row; *his nonfiction includes* Travels with Charley *and* Sea of Cortez. *As a writer Steinbeck had a clear vision of America and the virtues of the American dream, as well as of the threat materialism posed to those virtues.*

1 The high grey-flannel fog of winter closed off the Salinas Valley from the sky and from all the rest of the world. On every side it sat like a lid on the mountains and made of the great valley a closed pot. On the broad, level land floor the gang plows bit deep and left the black earth shining like metal where the shares had cut. On the foothill ranches across the Salinas River, the yellow stubble fields seemed to be bathed in pale cold sunshine, but there was no sunshine in the valley now in December. The thick willow scrub along the river flamed with sharp and positive yellow leaves.

Like many good writers, Steinbeck begins with a description of the setting. His technique here is almost like a zoom lens—beginning in broad focus, then gradually zooming in on the ranch and, finally, Elisa. Compare this with the opening of *Shane*, excerpted in chapter 16.

2 It was a time of quiet and of waiting. The air was cold and tender. A light wind blew up from the southwest so that the farmers were mildly hopeful of a good rain before long; but fog and rain do not go together.

3 Across the river, on Henry Allen's foothill ranch there was little work to be done, for the hay was cut and stored and the orchards were plowed up to receive the rain deeply when it should come. The cattle on the higher slopes were becoming shaggy and rough-coated.

4 Elisa Allen, working in her flower garden, looked down across the yard and saw Henry, her husband, talking to two men in business suits. The three of them stood by the tractor shed, each man with one foot on the side of the little Fordson.* They smoked cigarettes and studied the machines as they talked.

5 Elisa watched them for a moment and then went back to her work. She was thirty-five. Her face was lean and strong and her eyes were as clear as water. Her figure looked blocked and heavy in her gardening costume, a man's

*A Fordson is a small tractor made by Ford Motor Company.

black hat pulled low down over her eyes, clodhopper shoes, a figured print dress almost completely covered by a big corduroy apron with four big pockets to hold the snips, the trowel and scratcher, the seeds and the knife she worked with. She wore heavy leather gloves to protect her hands while she worked.

This is the first mention of the chrysanthemums, which will become the central symbol in the story.

She was cutting down the old year's chrysanthemum stalks with a pair of short and powerful scissors. She looked down toward the men by the tractor shed now and then. Her face was eager and mature and handsome; even her work with the scissors was over-eager, over-powerful. The chrysanthemum stems seemed too small and easy for her energy. 6

She brushed a cloud of hair out of her eyes with the back of her glove, and left a smudge of earth on the cheek in doing it. Behind her stood the neat white farm house with red geraniums close-banked around it as high as the windows. It was a hard-swept looking little house, with hard-polished windows, and a clean mud-mat on the front steps. 7

Elisa cast another glance toward the tractor shed. The strangers were getting into their Ford coupe. She took off a glove and put her strong fingers down into the forest of new green chrysanthemum sprouts that were growing around the old roots. She spread the leaves and looked down among the close-growing stems. No aphids were there, no sowbugs or snails or cutworms. Her terrier fingers destroyed such pests before they could get started. 8

Second mention of chrysanthemums. Note Elisa's "terrier fingers" keep the chrysanthemums free from pests. This implicit comparison of Elisa's care to the fierce determination of a dog is a tip-off to her pride in her chrysanthemums.

Elisa started at the sound of her husband's voice. He had come near quietly, and he leaned over the wire fence that protected her flower garden from cattle and dogs and chickens. 9

"At it again," he said. "You've got a strong new crop coming." 10

Elisa straightened her back and pulled on the gardening glove again. "Yes. They'll be strong this coming year." In her tone and on her face there was a little smugness. 11

"You've got a gift with things," Henry observed. "Some of those yellow chrysanthemums you had this year were ten inches across. I wish you'd work out in the orchard and raise some apples that big." 12

Note that though Henry is joking about having Elisa help out in the orchard, *she* isn't. The moment she lets him know seriously that she thinks she could help, he dismisses the idea with "Well, it sure works with flowers."

Her eyes sharpened. "Maybe I could do it, too. I've got a gift with things, all right. My mother had it. She could stick anything in the ground and make it grow. She said it was having planter's hands that knew how to do it." 13

"Well, it sure works with flowers," he said. 14

"Henry, who were those men you were talking to?" 15

"Why, sure, that's what I came to tell you. They were from the Western Meat Company. I sold those thirty head of three-year-old steers. Got nearly my own price, too." 16

"Good," she said. "Good for you." 17

"And I thought," he continued, "I thought how it's Saturday afternoon, and we might go to Salinas for dinner at a restaurant, and then to a picture show—to celebrate, you see." 18

"Good," she repeated. "Oh, yes. That will be good." 19

Henry put on his joking tone. "There's fights tonight. How'd you like to go to the fights?" 20

21 "Oh, no," she said breathlessly. "No, I wouldn't like fights."

22 "Just fooling, Elisa. We'll go to a movie. Let's see. It's two now. I'm going to take Scotty and bring down those steers from the hill. It'll take us maybe two hours. We'll go in town about five and have dinner at the Cominos Hotel. Like that?"

23 "Of course I'll like it. It's good to eat away from home."

24 "All right, then. I'll go get up a couple of horses."

25 She said, "I'll have plenty of time to transplant some of these sets, I guess."

26 She heard her husband calling Scotty down by the barn. And a little later she saw the two men ride up the pale yellow hillside in search of the steers.

27 There was a little square sandy bed kept for rooting the chrysanthemums. With her trowel she turned the soil over and over, and smoothed it and patted it firm. Then she dug ten parallel trenches to receive the sets. Back at the chrysanthemum bed she pulled out the little crisp shoots, trimmed off the leaves of each one with her scissors and laid it on a small orderly pile.

Again, note the great order and care Elisa takes with her chrysanthemums. Elsewhere are suggestions that she is orderly and careful about everything.

28 A squeak of wheels and plod of hoofs came from the road. Elisa looked up. The country road ran along the dense bank of willows and cottonwoods that bordered the river, and up this road came a curious vehicle, curiously drawn. It was an old spring-wagon, with a round canvas top on it like the cover of a prairie schooner. It was drawn by an old bay horse and a little grey-and-white burro. A big stubble-bearded man sat between the cover flaps and drove the crawling team. Underneath the wagon, between the hind wheels, a lean and rangy mongrel dog walked sedately. Words were painted on the canvas in clumsy, crooked letters. "Pots, pans, knives, sisors, lawn mores. Fixed." Two rows of articles and the triumphantly definitive "Fixed" below. The black paint had run down in little sharp points beneath each letter.

The disheveled state of the tinker and his wagon are in sharp contrast to the order in Elisa's world.

29 Elisa, squatting on the ground, watched to see the crazy, loose-jointed wagon pass by. But it didn't pass. It turned into the farm road in front of her house, crooked old wheels skirling and squeaking. The rangy dog darted from between the wheels and ran ahead. Instantly the two ranch shepherds flew out at him. Then all three stopped, and with stiff and quivering tails, with taut straight legs, with ambassadorial dignity, they slowly circled, sniffing daintily. The caravan pulled up to Elisa's wire fence and stopped. Now the newcomer dog, feeling outnumbered, lowered his tail and retired under the wagon with raised hackles and bared teeth.

30 The man on the wagon seat called out. "That's a bad dog in a fight when he gets started."

31 Elisa laughed. "I see he is. How soon does he generally get started?"

32 The man caught up her laughter and echoed it heartily. "Sometimes not for weeks and weeks," he said. He climbed stiffly down, over the wheel. The horse and the donkey drooped like unwatered flowers.

33 Elisa saw that he was a very big man. Although his hair and beard were greying, he did not look old. His worn black suit was wrinkled and spotted with grease. The laughter had disappeared from his face and eyes the moment

Although his appearance is not of the sort one would expect Elisa to find attractive, this detail lets us know that Elisa somehow finds the stranger interesting. He's different, someone from beyond her narrow and orderly existence. His loose, seemingly careless life-style strikes her as somehow free and, by contrast to her own life-style, desirable.

his laughing voice ceased. His eyes were dark and they were full of the brooding that gets in the eyes of teamsters and of sailors. The calloused hands he rested on the wire fence were cracked, and every crack was a black line. He took off his battered hat.

"I'm off my general road, ma'am," he said. "Does this dirt road cut over 34
across the river to the Los Angeles highway?"

Elisa stood up and shoved the thick scissors in her apron pocket. "Well, 35
yes, it does, but it winds around and then fords the river. I don't think your team could pull through the sand."

He replied with some asperity, "It might surprise you what them beasts 36
can pull through."

"When they get started?" she asked. 37

He smiled for a second. "Yes, when they get started." 38

"Well," said Elisa, "I think you'll save time if you go back to the Salinas 39
road and pick up the highway there."

He drew a big finger down the chicken wire and made it sing. "I ain't in 40
any hurry, ma'am. I go from Seattle to San Diego and back every year. Takes all my time. About six months each way. I aim to follow nice weather."

Although it's a small gesture, Elisa's taking off her gloves is a precursor of her later discarding the clothes she usually wears in her ordinary role.

Elisa took off her gloves and stuffed them in the apron pocket with the 41
scissors. She touched the under edge of her man's hat, searching for fugitive hairs. "That sounds like a nice kind of a way to live," she said.

He leaned confidentially over the fence. "Maybe you noticed the writing 42
on my wagon. I mend pots and sharpen knives and scissors. You got any of them things to do?"

"Oh, no," she said quickly. "Nothing like that." Her eyes hardened with 43
resistance.

"Scissors is the worst thing," he explained. "Most people just ruin 44
scissors trying to sharpen 'em, but I know how. I got a special tool. It's a little bobbit kind of thing, and patented. But it sure does the trick."

"No. My scissors are all sharp." 45

"All right, then. Take a pot," he continued earnestly, "a bent pot, or a pot 46
with a hole. I can make it like new so you don't have to buy no new ones. That's a saving for you."

"No," she said shortly. "I tell you I have nothing like that for you to do." 47

His face fell to an exaggerated sadness. His voice took on a whining 48
undertone. "I ain't had a thing to do today. Maybe I won't have no supper tonight. You see I'm off my regular road. I know folks on the highway clear from Seattle to San Diego. They save their things for me to sharpen up because they know I do it so good and save them money."

Elisa is no easy "sell," and the stranger is about defeated, until he sees the chrysanthemums.

"I'm sorry," Elisa said irritably. "I haven't anything for you to do." 49

His eyes left her face and fell to searching the ground. They roamed about 50
until they came to the chrysanthemum bed where she had been working. "What's them plants, ma'am?"

In this one brief paragraph, Steinbeck reveals the means of Elisa's vulnerability: her chrysanthemums.

The irritation and resistance melted from Elisa's face. "Oh, those are chrysanthemums, giant whites and yellows. I raise them every year, bigger than anybody around here."

52 "Kind of a long-stemmed flower? Looks like a quick puff of colored smoke?" he asked.

53 "That's it. What a nice way to describe them."

54 "They smell kind of nasty till you get used to them," he said.

55 "It's a good bitter smell," she retorted, "not nasty at all."

56 He changed his tone quickly. "I like the smell myself."

57 "I had ten-inch blooms this year," she said.

58 The man leaned farther over the fence. "Look. I know a lady down the road a piece, has got the nicest garden you ever seen. Got nearly every kind of flower but no chrysanthemums. Last time I was mending a copper-bottom washtub for her (that's a hard job but I do it good), she said to me, 'If you ever run acrost some nice chrysanthemums I wish you'd try to get me a few seeds.' That's what she told me."

59 Elisa's eyes grew alert and eager. "She couldn't have known much about chrysanthemums. You can raise them from seed, but it's much easier to root the little sprouts you see there."

60 "Oh," he said. "I s'pose I can't take none to her, then."

61 "Why yes you can," Elisa cried. "I can put some in damp sand, and you can carry them right along with you. They'll take root in the pot if you keep them damp. And then she can transplant them."

62 "She'd sure like to have some, ma'am. You say they're nice ones?"

63 "Beautiful," she said. "Oh, beautiful." Her eyes shone. She tore off the battered hat and shook out her dark pretty hair. "I'll put them in a flower pot, and you can take them right with you. Come into the yard."

Note that Elisa's feminine beauty emerges even more as she warms to the subject of her chrysanthemums.

64 While the man came through the picket gate Elisa ran excitedly along the geranium-bordered path to the back of the house. And she returned carrying a big red flower pot. Then she picked up the little pile of shoots she had prepared. With her strong fingers she pressed them into the sand and tamped around them with her knuckles. The man stood over her. "I'll tell you what to do," she said. "You remember so you can tell the lady."

65 "Yes. I'll try to remember."

66 "Well, look. These will take root in about a month. Then she must set them out, about a foot apart in good rich earth like this, see?" She lifted a handful of dark soil for him to look at. "They'll grow fast and tall. Now remember this. In July tell her to cut them down, about eight inches from the ground."

67 "Before they bloom?" he asked.

68 "Yes, before they bloom." Her face was tight with eagerness. "They'll grow right up again. About the last of September the buds will start."

69 She stopped and seemed perplexed. "It's the budding that takes the most care," she said hesitantly. "I don't know how to tell you." She looked deep into his eyes searchingly. Her mouth opened a little, and she seemed to be listening. "I'll try to tell you," she said. "Did you ever hear of planting hands?"

70 "Can't say I have, ma'am."

71 "Well, I can only tell you what it feels like. It's when you're picking off the buds you don't want. Everything goes right down into your fingertips. You

watch your fingers work. They do it themselves. You can feel how it is. They pick and pick the buds. They never make a mistake. They're with the plant. Do you see? Your fingers and the plant. You can feel that, right up your arm. They know. They never make a mistake. You can feel it. When you're like that you can't do anything wrong. Do you see that? Can you understand that?"

She was kneeling on the ground looking up at him. Her breast swelled 72
passionately.

The man's eyes narrowed. He looked away self-consciously. "Maybe I 73
know," he said. "Sometimes in the night, in the wagon there—"

For a brief moment, it's hard to tell if the subject is (a) still the care of chrysanthemums or (b) Elisa's great longing for more meaning and fulfillment in her life.

Elisa's voice grew husky. She broke in on him. "I've never lived as you do, 74
but I know what you mean. When the night is dark—why, the stars are sharp-pointed, and there's quiet. Why, you rise up and up! Every pointed star gets driven into your body. It's like that. Hot and sharp and—lovely."

Kneeling there, her hand went out toward his legs in the greasy black 75
trousers. Her hesitant fingers almost touched the cloth. Then her hand dropped to the ground. She crouched low like a fawning dog.

He said, "It's nice, just like you say. Only when you don't have no dinner, it 76
ain't."

She stood up then, very straight, and her face was ashamed. She held the 77
flower pot out to him and placed it gently in his arms. "Here. Put it in your wagon, on the seat, where you can watch it. Maybe I can find something for you to do."

The stranger has "won"—but for Elisa it was no contest after he brought up the chrysanthemums.

At the back of the house she dug in the can pile and found two old and 78
battered aluminum saucepans. She carried them back and gave them to him. "Here, maybe you can fix these."

His manner changed. He became professional. "Good as new I can fix 79
them." At the back of his wagon he set a little anvil, and out of an oily tool box dug a small machine hammer. Elisa came through the gate to watch him while he pounded out the dents in the kettles. His mouth grew sure and knowing. At a difficult part of the work he sucked his under-lip.

"You sleep right here in the wagon?" Elisa asked. 80

"Right in the wagon, ma'am. Rain or shine. I'm dry as a cow in there." 81

"It must be nice," she said. "It must be very nice. I wish women could do 82
such things."

"It ain't the right kind of a life for a woman." 83

"Her upper lip raised a little, showing her teeth. "How do you know? 84
How can you tell?" she said.

"I don't know ma'am," he protested. "Of course I don't know. Now there's 85
your kettles, done. You don't have to buy no new ones."

"How much?" 86

"Oh, fifty cents'll do. I keep my prices down and my work good. That's 87
why I have all them satisfied customers up and down the highway."

Note the defiant pride and self-assurance in Elisa's tone here.

Elisa brought him a fifty-cent piece from the house and dropped it in his 88
hand. "You might be surprised to have a rival some time. I can sharpen scissors, too. And I can beat the dents out of little pots. I could show you what a woman might do."

He put his hammer back in the oily box and shoved the little anvil out of 89 sight. "It would be a lonely life for a woman, ma'am, and a scarey life, too, with animals creeping under the wagon all night." He climbed over the single-tree, steadying himself with a hand on the burro's white rump. He settled himself on the seat, picked up the lines. "Thank you kindly, ma'am," he said. "I'll do like you told me; I'll go back and catch the Salinas road."

90 "Mind," she called, "if you're long in getting there, keep the sand damp."

91 "Sand, ma'am? . . . Sand? Oh, sure. You mean round the chrysanthemums. Sure I will." He clucked his tongue. The beasts leaned luxuriously into their collars. The mongrel dog took his place between the back wheels. The wagon turned and crawled out the entrance road and back the way it had come, along the river.

The tinker has already forgotten the chrysanthemums.

92 Elisa stood in front of her wire fence watching the slow progress of the caravan. Her shoulders were straight, her head thrown back, her eyes half-closed, so that the scene came vaguely into them. Her lips moved silently, forming the words "Good-bye—good-bye." Then she whispered, "That's a bright direction. There's a glowing there." The sound of her whisper startled her. She shook herself free and looked about to see whether anyone had been listening. Only the dogs had heard. They lifted their heads toward her from their sleeping in the dust, and then stretched out their chins and settled asleep again. Elisa turned and ran hurriedly into the house.

This passage will stand in sharp contrast to the story's conclusion.

93 In the kitchen she reached behind the stove and felt the water tank. It was full of hot water from the noonday cooking. In the bathroom she tore off her soiled clothes and flung them into the corner. And then she scrubbed herself with a little block of pumice, legs and thighs, loins and chest and arms, until her skin was scratched and red. When she had dried herself she stood in front of a mirror in her bedroom and looked at her body. She tightened her stomach and threw out her chest. She turned and looked over her shoulder at her back.

94 After a while she began to dress, slowly. She put on her newest underclothing and her nicest stockings and the dress which was the symbol of her prettiness. She worked carefully on her hair, pencilled her eyebrows and rouged her lips.

This scene brings out all Elisa's previously hidden femininity and her previously subdued sense of it.

95 Before she was finished she heard the little thunder of hoofs and the shouts of Henry and his helper as they drove the red steers into the corral. She heard the gate bang shut and set herself for Henry's arrival.

96 His step sounded on the porch. He entered the house calling "Elisa, where are you?"

97 "In my room, dressing. I'm not ready. There's hot water for your bath. Hurry up. It's getting late."

98 When she heard him splashing in the tub, Elisa laid his dark suit on the bed, and shirt and socks and tie beside it. She stood his polished shoes on the floor beside the bed. Then she went to the porch and sat primly and stiffly down. She looked toward the river road where the willow-line was still yellow with frosted leaves so that under the high grey fog they seemed a thin band of sunshine. This was the only color in the grey afternoon. She sat unmoving for a long time. Her eyes blinked rarely.

99 Henry came banging out of the door, shoving his tie inside his vest as he

came. Elisa stiffened and her face grew tight. Henry stopped short and looked at her. "Why—why, Elisa. You look so nice!"

"Nice? You think I look nice? What do you mean by 'nice'?" 100

Henry blundered on. "I don't know. I mean you look different, strong and 101
happy."

Henry sees the difference in Elisa, but he's too dull-minded and self-absorbed to handle it well.

"I am strong? Yes, strong. What do you mean 'strong'?" 102

He looked bewildered. "You're playing some kind of game," he said 103
helplessly. "It's a kind of a play. You look strong enough to break a calf over your knee, happy enough to eat it like a watermelon."

For a second she lost her rigidity. "Henry! Don't talk like that. You didn't 104
know what you said." She grew complete again. "I'm strong," she boasted. "I never knew before how strong."

Henry looked down toward the tractor shed, and when he brought his 105
eyes back to her, they were his own again. "I'll get out the car. You can put on your coat while I'm starting."

Elisa went into the house. She heard him drive to the gate and idle down 106
his motor, and then she took a long time to put on her hat. She pulled it here and pressed it there. When Henry turned the motor off she slipped into her coat and went out.

The little roadster bounced along on the dirt road by the river, raising the 107
birds and driving the rabbits into the brush. Two cranes flapped heavily over the willow-line and dropped into the river-bed.

Even a novice reader is likely to understand how the stranger's discarding of the chrysanthemums is a symbolic rejection of and utter emotional disaster for Elisa.

Far ahead on the road Elisa saw a dark speck. She knew. 108

She tried not to look as they passed it, but her eyes would not obey. She 109
whispered to herself sadly. "He might have thrown them off the road. That wouldn't have been much trouble, not very much. But he kept the pot," she explained. "He had to keep the pot. That's why he couldn't get them off the road."

The roadster turned a bend and she saw the caravan ahead. She swung 110
full around toward her husband so she could not see the little covered wagon and the mismatched team as the car passed them.

In a moment it was over. The thing was done. She did not look back. She 111
said loudly, to be heard above the motor, "it will be good, tonight, a good dinner."

"Now you're changed again," Henry complained. He took one hand from 112
the wheel and patted her knee. "I ought to take you in to dinner oftener. It would be good for both of us. We get so heavy out on the ranch."

"Henry," she asked, "could we have wine at dinner?" 113

"Sure we could. Say! That will be fine." 114

She was silent for a little while; then she said, "Henry, at those prize 115
fights, do the men hurt each other very much?"

"Sometimes a little, not often. Why?" 116

"Well, I've read how they break noses, and blood runs down their chests. 117
I've read how the fighting gloves get heavy and soggy with blood."

He looked around at her. "What's the matter, Elisa? I didn't know you 118
read things like that." He brought the car to a stop, then turned to the right over the Salinas River bridge.

119 "Do any women ever go to the fights?" she asked.

120 "Oh, sure, some. What's the matter, Elisa? Do you want to go? I don't think you'd like it, but I'll take you if you really want to go."

121 She relaxed limply in the seat. "Oh, no. No. I don't want to go. I'm sure I don't." Her face was turned away from him. "It will be enough if we can have wine. It will be plenty." She turned up her coat collar so he could not see that she was crying weakly—like an old woman.

It's beyond Henry's comprehension to entertain even the possibility that Elisa might enjoy the idea of a hurt man.

Early in the story, the narrator tells us Elisa is only thirty-five. Now, however, she cries "like an old woman."

Questions for Critical Analysis

These questions are *analytical;* that is, they force you to focus on individual parts, or features, of the story. They are therefore fundamental both to *critical thinking* about the story and to *writing* about the story. Because you will need to be comfortable with the terms presented in these questions in order to follow the rest of this chapter, you should answer and discuss them all.

1. *Setting.* Setting refers to *when* and *where* a story takes place. It includes consideration of the physical surroundings of the story and can therefore be a significant factor in the story. What details about setting do you find in "The Chrysanthemums"? In what ways does the setting contribute to the story? Consider the following:
   a. Details indicating the time period of the story—not only the time of day but general time, such as the season and the era. For example, Henry and Elisa go to town in a car, but the traveling tinker still uses a wagon drawn by animals. That information suggests the early twentieth century, a time, too, when women's roles were quite stereotyped and limited.
   b. Details about the valley and the fog, the lack of sunshine, the isolation of the ranch, and so forth.

Ask students to flip back to Pete Hamill's "Our Town" (chapter 16) and describe its setting.

2. *Plot.* What *happens* in this story? How much action is there? Briefly state the line of development. Is this story a rough-and-tumble thriller? Or is the development more subtle? Which scenes would you call most important, and why?

Ask students to flip back to Linda Schierse Leonard's "On Not Suppressing Rage" (chapter 13) and describe its plot. (We are using *plot* here in a broad sense that allows it to be applied to nonfiction—that is, what happens, when, and why. Similarly, below we will ask you to have your students examine other works of nonfiction using the "tools" of literary analysis. Our purpose is not to blur the distinctive characteristics of fiction; rather, we mean to show certain universalities in writing.

3. *Characterization.* How many characters are there? Who are they, and how important are they? Consider the following:
   a. The men talking with Henry at the beginning of the story.
   b. Scotty.
   c. Henry.
      (1) What is Henry's attitude about women doing substantial farm or ranch work? How do you know?
      (2) How does Henry regard Elisa? How do you know?
      (3) Is Henry a static or developing character? flat or round?
   d. The traveling tinker.
      (1) What is the tinker's main motive in coming to the house?
      (2) How does he manage to get on Elisa's "good side"?

(3) How sincere is he about the chrysanthemums?
(4) Is he flat or round? static or developing?
(5) Is he a foil for Elisa? If so, how?
(6) How does Elisa regard him? How do you know?
(7) How does he regard Elisa? How do you know?

e. Elisa.
 (1) How do you know Elisa is the protagonist?
 (2) Who or what would you say is the antagonist(s) in this story?
 (3) What kinds of conflict does Elisa have:
  (a) Person versus person?
  (b) Person versus environment?
  (c) Person versus self?
  Can you give examples of each kind of conflict?
 (4) Is Elisa flat or round? static or developing? Consider these related questions:
  (a) What kind of housekeeper is Elisa?
  (b) How does Elisa dress at different times in the story? What affects her choice of dress?
  (c) What are Elisa's work habits?
  (d) What does Elisa take pride in?
  (e) How would you describe Elisa physically—what does she look like?
  (f) Do Henry and Elisa have any children?
  (g) Is Elisa a happy, satisfied person?
  (h) How would you trace Elisa's spirits throughout the story—how do they rise and fall?

Ask students to flip back to Garrison Keillor's "Lake Wobegon" (chapter 9) and describe its characterization.

4. *Point of view.* Which point of view does Steinbeck's narrator use? What advantage does Steinbeck exploit by using this point of view? How would the story differ if given from, say, Henry's point of view? from the tinker's? What if the point of view were in the first person—whose narration would be best then?

Ask students to flip back to chapter 13 and compare the point of view in Susan Griffin's "Thoughts on Writing: A Diary" with that in Belenky, Clinchy, Goldberger, and Tarule's "Patterns of Development."

5. *Language.* How do we know the chrysanthemums are symbols? What do they symbolize? Consider images in passages that contribute to the sense of the story. Here are a few; how do these images represent not only what they actually say but also what is going on in the story?

 a. "The high grey-flannel fog of winter closed off the Salinas Valley from the sky and from all the rest of the world. On every side it sat like a lid on the mountains and made of the great valley a closed pot." (¶ 1)

 b. "She looked toward the men by the tractor shed now and then. Her face was eager and mature and handsome; even her work with the scissors was over-eager, over-powerful. The chrysanthemum stems seemed too small and easy for her energy." (¶ 6)

 c. "'I wish you'd work out in the orchard and raise some apples that big.'

"Her eyes sharpened. 'Maybe I could do it, too. I've a gift with things, all right. . . .'

"'Well, it sure works with flowers,' he said." (¶ 12–14)

d. "'What's them plants, ma'am?'

"The irritation and resistance melted from Elisa's face. 'Oh, those are chrysanthemums . . . I raise them every year, bigger than anybody around here.'

"'Kind of a long-stemmed flower? Looks like a quick puff of colored smoke?'

"'That's it. What a nice way to describe them.'" (¶ 50–53)

e. "'Beautiful,' she said. 'Oh, beautiful.' Her eyes shone. She tore off the battered hat and shook out her dark pretty hair." (¶ 63)

f. "She was kneeling on the ground looking up at him. Her breast swelled passionately. . . .

"Elisa's voice grew husky. She broke in on him. 'I've never lived as you do, but I know what you mean. When the night is dark—why, the stars are sharp-pointed, and there's quiet. Why, you rise up and up! Every pointed star gets driven into your body. It's like that. Hot and sharp and—lovely.'

"Kneeling there, her hand went out toward his legs in the greasy black trousers. Her hesitant fingers almost touched the cloth. Then her hand dropped to the ground. She crouched low like a fawning dog." (¶ 72–75)

g. "She stood up then, very straight, and her face was ashamed. She held the flower pot out to him and placed it gently in his arms. 'Here. Put it in your wagon, on the seat, where you can watch it.'" (¶ 77)

h. "'It must be nice,' she said. 'It must be very nice. I wish women could do such things.'

"'It ain't the right kind of life for a woman.'

"Her upper lip raised a little, showing her teeth. 'How do you know? How can you tell?' she said." (¶ 82–84)

Ask students to flip back to Maxine Hong Kingston's "White Tigers" (chapter 15) and discuss the role of language in it.

6. There are other scenes, other exchanges of dialogue or descriptions of action that convey considerable meaning in this story. For example:

   a. Elisa's scrubbing and examining herself in the mirror, and her dressing for the evening with Henry. What importance does this scene have in terms of Elisa's self-perception after the encounter with the tinker?

   b. Although sex is not uppermost in Elisa's mind during the scene in which she describes the "pointed stars" and although it is *probably* not uppermost in the tinker's mind (we can't know, because Steinbeck's narrator never tells us what anyone except Elisa is thinking), the scene is nonetheless sexually charged. Why is that? In what ways does the language of such passages ("Oh, beautiful"; "Hot and sharp and—lovely") and the descriptions of actions ("She tore off the battered hat and shook out her dark pretty hair") show us the conflict and turmoil within Elisa?

Actions—like language or dialogue or conflict—reveal character and theme. Ask students to look back at chapter 15's "The Battle for Disney Begins" and "Doughnuts to Dollars" and to discuss and compare the way action in each piece reveals character and helps establish theme.

c. One of the most symbolic actions in this story is the tinker's dumping of the chrysanthemum shoots in the road and keeping only the pot. Explore this action: what does it *mean*, especially to Elisa, when she sees the rejected shoots? What connection does it have to her self-perception at the end of the story?

7. If you were assigned to make a statement of the point—the main idea, or theme—of this story in a sentence or two, what would that statement be? (Try for a general statement that *accounts* for the various details, or considerations, of the story without contradicting or ignoring any of those considerations.)

Writing About "The Chrysanthemums"

A class reading of "The Chrysanthemums" should generate a good deal of discussion by exploring answers to the questions above. Writing assignments that might be typical as a follow-up to studying Steinbeck's story are as follows:

You may want to assign these questions, one per group, to students, asking each group to produce a statement of *theme* based on its question. After all the statements have been heard, lead a discussion of how the question(s) one asks helps determine the theme one finds.

1. Analyze Elisa Allen's character. (To a lesser extent, it might be interesting to analyze the character of the tinker or of Henry.)
2. Formulate a statement of theme and support that statement with appropriate details from the story.
3. Analyze how the setting (both time and place) contributes to the story's effect.
4. Analyze how Steinbeck's language reinforces the story's meaning.
5. Analyze the different kinds of conflict Elisa Allen experiences: how do these conflicts contribute to the story?

Such topics turn primarily on an analytical understanding of how certain elements of literature, when considered separately, advance the work's meaning. But there are other angles of thoughtful approach. Also good topics are these:

For help with this analysis, students can refer to Harriet Goldhor Lerner's "De-Selfing" (chapter 8) and Anne Morrow Lindbergh's "The Dance of Relationships" (chapter 18).

Some would say that Linda Schierse Leonard's "On Not Suppressing Rage" (chapter 13) sheds much light on Elisa's condition.

6. Analyze the marriage of Elisa and Henry. What's wrong with it? right with it? If you were a counselor, how would you advise Elisa? Henry? both persons?
7. Analyze the series of scenes involving Elisa and the tinker: what is going on? How does each character affect the other?
8. In what ways is Elisa a captive of her ranch wife's role as she perceives it? Why wouldn't Elisa consider counseling, divorce, or some sort of rebellion? (Alternatively, why *should* she consider such alternatives?)
9. Agree or disagree with the following statements, basing your judgments on details from the story:
   a. Elisa is a weak person who lets others manipulate her.
   b. The tinker is a devious person who cares only about himself.
   c. Henry is a cruel husband.
   d. The theme of "The Chrysanthemums" is that loneliness and frustration can lead a person to making poor choices that only worsen the loneliness and frustration.

e. The theme of the "The Chrysanthemums" is that people can get trapped in their own self-concepts and, though they may try, cannot escape them. (*Note:* It is possible to have more than one "correct" statement of theme for the same work; in fact, a really good story, play, or poem may convey several truths that, though usually related, could be reasonably supported from the work. What's important is not to formulate a statement of theme that is contradicted by elements of the work.)

f. The theme of "The Chrysanthemums" is that some marriages lack communication, making it possible for a couple to live together for a long time without really knowing and understanding each other.

g. The theme of "The Chrysanthemums" is that some people have great reserves of talent, ability, and desire for which they must find outlets; everyone needs to feel needed and appreciated.

A Student Writes About "The Chrysanthemums"

In her second-semester freshman English class, Kimberly Williams read "The Chrysanthemums." The class members got into some spirited discussions as they went over the questions above. The teacher had assigned a paper in which students were to provide a statement of theme and analyze either the symbolism or a major character. "Don't worry about any overlapping at first," said the teacher; "worry about *understanding* the story's characters and situations. The rest will take care of itself."

Class Discussion. "I think Elisa's a wimp," said Paul. "She just lets Henry keep her in her place, and she's a pushover for the tinker when he brings up her precious chrysanthemums."

Here, as in other, similar discussions we present in this book, we are not saying that student discussions went exactly like this; this is not a transcript. But this *is* the way many such discussions proceed.

"That's not quite fair," replied Kimberly. "This story is taking place probably back in the 1920s or even a little earlier. Nobody heard of assertiveness training then. More people expected women to be housewives, secondary to their husbands in almost every way. Elisa is bearing a pretty heavy burden to just be called a wimp and dismissed."

"Kim's right," put in Blair. "A big part of Elisa's conflict is with her overall environment, not just with herself. She's living in times when her role is limited and she isn't even aware she has any choices. The whole society, not just Henry, expects her to grow those chrysanthemums and stay out of the orchard. They probably expect her to have babies, too—though for some reason she hasn't. One thing's sure: she's expected to be a good housekeeper, and she is. She's doing the best she can with the assignment life has given her."

Notice that Blair sees the conflict mostly as person versus society.

"If that's true, and I guess it is, then it's still pretty sad," said Paul. "I wish she'd just bust out and tell Henry she's going down to Los Angeles and will be back in a week or so. And what's this business when she's talking about the stars piercing her body? That all sounds a little like she's making a pass at the tinker. Is she that desperate for love and attention?"

Paul sees the conflict mostly as person versus person.

"Absolutely!" exclaimed Kimberly. "Only she doesn't even realize how desperate she is. She isn't aware that she's being sexy or suggestive in that scene. It's

Kimberly sees the conflict mostly as person versus self.

just all that neglect and frustration coming out under the disguise of talking about her chrysanthemums and how good she is at growing them."

The discussion continued, spirited and thoughtful, until the class period ended.

You can "externalize" this process for students via putting on the board the notes Kimberly *might* take were she to write down each step in her thinking.

Thinking. Kimberly, back at the dorm, reread the story. She noted many passages that revealed something about Elisa and her situation. And she made a list of characteristics about Elisa.

Kimberly decided that surely Elisa is a *round* character, quite complex in her personality and outlook. Kimberly also decided that Elisa is a *developing* character, because she undergoes fundamental internal changes—all to the worse—in the course of the story. In fact, Elisa's spirits begin on an even keel, heighten to a dramatic awakening of self-esteem, and then plunge to an all-time low at the end of the story. Described early in the story as a mature-but-still-young woman with great subtle reserves of beauty, Elisa at the end is reduced to crying "like an old woman," even though the story's events take place over only a few hours.

The chrysanthemums, Kimberly noted, are the key, in terms of detail, to the heart of the story. They symbolize everything that is both good and weak about Elisa. It is ironic that such a source of strength and pride should also be the means of Elisa's vulnerability, yet many people's weaknesses, Kimberly knew, also stem from their sources of pride. We all have blind spots, weak points, in whatever armor we think we have protected ourselves with.

Kimberly decided to make a few preliminary statements of theme, keying them to the chrysanthemums, to see whether she could come up with a general statement that would cover the story's essentials. After reviewing many of the statements that had been made in class (most of which are given above), she eventually settled on the notion of the vulnerability inherent in something deeply loved (like Elisa's chrysanthemums) and the risks involved in showing that vulnerability.

Drafting. Kimberly began her draft with a statement of what she considered to be the theme of the story:

> John Steinbeck's "The Chrysanthemums" shows that people are vulnerable through the things they love best and are most proud of, and that there is a risk in letting others know about that vulnerability.

She decided the sentence was too abrupt a beginning. She wanted something less businesslike, a bit more indirect. She remembered her mother saying that one of the greatest gifts anyone can ever give is one's self—one's time, one's care, and, if necessary, one's love. Surely, Elisa's chrysanthemums, the product of her great gift of "planter's hands," were extensions, or representatives, of her *self.* Kimberly tried again:

> We give the most we can give when we give freely of ourselves. In John Steinbeck's "The Chrysanthemums," the protagonist, Elisa Allen, learns that such giving can also leave one vulnerable to great pain.

Kimberly liked that much better. She continued drafting.

In this first draft, Kimberly wanted to develop that central idea of Elisa's vulnerability and pain, following from the giving of her chrysanthemum shoots to the unworthy tinker. Kimberly didn't want to ignore the unhappy, unfulfilling circumstances of Elisa's marriage, but she considered that aspect a necessary part of Elisa's vulnerability, something that leaves Elisa even more exposed to the pain that comes at the end of the story.

First Full Draft of Kimberly's Paper. Here is the draft Kimberly took to class for a draft workshop.

Symbol and Theme in "The Chrysanthemums"

Kimberly Williams, college writing student

1 We give the most we can give when we give freely of ourselves. In John Steinbeck's short story "The Chrysanthemums," the protagonist, Elisa Allen, learns that such giving can also leave one vulnerable to great pain. In the story, the chrysanthemums that Elisa grows so well symbolize her talent, love, and femininity--her best qualities. Superficially, when Elisa gives the traveling tinker her chrysanthemum buds, she is giving something she has cared for and nurtured, something she takes pride in. Symbolically, she is therefore giving the tinker a part of herself.

Notice that Kimberly brings this opening line in from her own background experience. It's something she *imports*, not something she directly derives from her experience of analyzing the story.

2 Elisa gives the tinker the chrysanthemum buds in order to allay her feelings of frustration and to revive her femininity, which she feels she has lost through her age and her environment. After she gives the buds to the tinker, a change in Elisa is apparent: "She put on her newest under-clothing and her nicest stockings and the dress which was the symbol of her prettiness." She is given a new hope for her femininity, a new sparkle in her relationship with her husband. And so the act of giving the flower buds is most important to Elisa because she is giving a part of herself.

Because she is giving what she loves most, she is very vulnerable. When Elisa prepares the buds for the tinker, she expresses hidden sexual qualities that normally are not apparent: "Her voice grew husky . . . her breast swelled passionately." She becomes vulnerable to the tinker by displaying these characteristics. She is openly relating to him, something she does not even accomplish with her husband. The only way in which the tinker can convince Elisa to let him do work is by recognizing her love for the flowers: "'What's them plants, ma'am?' . . . The irritation and resistance melted from Elisa's face." Here, Elisa is also vulnerable to the tinker. Later, when she finds the buds dumped on the side of the road, she realizes that it was not worth physically giving him the buds and, more important, mentally giving him this precious part of herself. 3

Through the symbolic flowers and the theme of "The Chrysanthemums," Steinbeck recognizes the importance as well as the risk of giving of one's self. Although Elisa takes the risk of giving the buds and renewing her lost femininity and sexuality, she is painfully disappointed and saddened to find her attempt at giving fruitless. 4

Notice that no one wants to entertain the notion that he might have thrown the flowers into the middle of the road *deliberately;* ask students what that assumption would do to the rest of their reading of the story. Notice also that his dumping the flowers in the middle of the road causes readers from that point to reinterpret the story totally.

Revising Based on Peer Comments. "I like this," said Paul after reading Kimberly's draft in the workshop. "But I think you need to fix some small details. For one thing, the chrysanthemums aren't *buds;* they're *shoots* that she's carefully trimmed. And the tinker doesn't toss the shoots beside the road—he's too insensitive for that, too eager to hang onto the pot they came in. He tossed them right *in* the road. He didn't care who saw them."

Blair too liked the draft. "But I don't think you make nearly enough out of the fact that Elisa is frustrated," she said. "And you make it sound like Elisa is *aware* of her own suppressed femininity, but I don't think she really *knows* that—it's not like she's deliberately primping when she feels for—what did he call them?—"fugitive hairs" under her cap. And she's not *thinking* about impressing the tinker sexually when she takes her hat off and shakes down her hair. The narrator tells us her hair is beautiful but never tells us that Elisa thinks it is, too."

"That's right," responded Kim. I need to avoid any suggestion that Elisa is trying to be seductive."

"You know, I think she's worse off at the end of the story than she is at the beginning," said Paul. "I think you ought to mention that, somehow—that her vulnerability, as you put it, has really been costly."

"And it's been so costly because she is so frustrated," chimed in Blair. "She's frustrated on many levels, not just sexual. For example, she really *wants* to contribute more substantially to the ranching and farming operations, but Henry just can't conceive of that—it's not like he's mean; it's just that he would probably feel threatened by such ability in a woman."

"That's another little thing," said Paul, "but you ought to go ahead and give her husband's name. Henry's not really a villain here; he's an important part of her life. And *he* doesn't understand things any better than she does."

Revised Student Paper. Back at the dorm again, Kimberly set about revising her paper. She knew she had the essence of her paper as she wanted it, but she wished to develop Elisa's frustration more and to add increased emphasis to how events in the story change Elisa's situation for the worse. What follows is Kimberly's finished, proofread version.

Symbolism and Theme in "The Chrysanthemums"

1 The philosopher and poet Kahlil Gibran noted, "You give but little when you give of your possessions. It is when you give of yourself that you truly give." Gibran's observation is applicable to the actions of Elisa Allen, protagonist of John Steinbeck's short story "The Chrysanthemums." Unfortunately, in giving so freely of herself in this story, Elisa learns that there are also great vulnerability and risk in such giving, and that deep and abiding pain can be the result.

2 Elisa Allen grows bigger and better chrysanthemums than anyone else in central California's Salinas Valley. Blessed with what she calls "planter's hands," Elisa is confident she could bring her growing talents to bear on her husband Henry's cash crops, such as apples. But Henry is not eager to have a wife whose economic impact is so obvious; the story is set in the early twentieth century, when women's roles were much more limited in society, and well before two-income marriages became virtual necessities. Elisa's chrysanthemums symbolize not only her talent but also her love and her femininity. They represent her very best qualities. Thus, when in an important action in the story Elisa gives a traveling tinker some new chrysanthemum shoots to take with him out of the valley, we see not only that she is giving something she has cared for and nurtured, something she takes pride in, but also that she is giving something of her innermost self.

3 Without fully realizing her motives, Elisa gives the tinker the shoots in order to allay her deep frustrations, which come from many sources. For one thing, she feels trapped in her ranch wife's role, which severely limits her opportunities for self-expression and meaningful contributions to the ranching and farming enterprise. Henry jokes that he wishes Elisa

would use her "planter's hands" to help him grow apples, but when she shows she's willing to accept that challenge ("Maybe I could do it, too," she tells him), he cuts the discussion short ("Well, it sure works with flowers") to make it clear where he thinks Elisa's talents and efforts belong. And so Elisa's talents and best efforts are to be reserved only for housekeeping--she keeps the house terrifically clean--and flower gardening. She can be proud of growing the best chrysanthemums around (something that doesn't compete with what Henry does), but not the best apples; moreover, celebrations are to mark *Henry's* successes, such as selling cattle at nearly his own price, and not any of Elisa's.

4 Elisa is also frustrated because there is little or no delight left in her life. She and Henry are childless for reasons never explained or hinted at in the story, but in their time and in their society, being childless might well be a matter of deep concern for both of them. In any case, they have clearly been married for several years and, though they are outwardly prosperous and stable, Elisa seems to desire more excitement or adventure. She imagines that the tinker's life of traveling up and down the Pacific rim and sleeping in the wagon would be "a nice kind of a way to live" just because the sheer freedom of movement and lack of specific responsibility strike her as exhilarating. Though Elisa is from a background and generation of women who would probably not seriously consider counseling or divorce, and though it is a time when marriage was, for whatever reasons, a more durable institution, she nonetheless seems to have a vague sexual yearning. This yearning is based not so much on Henry's neglect of her as on their life-style on the isolated ranch, where on the day of the story the fog "sits like a lid on the mountains and made of the great valley a closed pot." Only thirty-five years old and still beautiful, Elisa needs more demonstration of Henry's love than she's getting. Her self-image is poor; she muffles her femininity in her "gardening costume," which makes her actually attractive figure look "blocked and heavy."

5 Into such frustrated vulnerability creaks the wagon of the traveling tinker. The tinker is at first an intruder on Elisa's turf; he has no skill of which she has need. But his long practice at wheedling what he wants out of potential customers causes his straw-grabbing conversation to discover the chrysanthemums, the symbol of Elisa's strength and

vulnerability--"What's them plants, ma'am?" As Steinbeck's narrator, whose vision is limited to Elisa's consciousness, reports: "The irritation and resistance melted from Elisa's face." Suddenly, Elisa is blind to the tinker's motives. Suddenly, she is vibrantly alive to what she wrongly thinks is his interest in her chrysanthemums and his willingness to transport this symbol of her talents and beauties out of the valley, to some other place, where she can at least make some contribution, some giving of herself.

6 Unconsciously, Elisa shares with the tinker not only her chrysanthemums but also her own reawakening and beautiful self: "Her eyes shone. She tore off the battered hat and shook out her dark pretty hair." Her attempts to explain how her "planting hands" feel when they are cutting the shoots baffle her ability to express, and, looking "deep into his eyes searchingly," she gives a description that hints at a sexual union between her fingers and the plants, all while she is "kneeling on the ground looking up at him," while her "breast swelled passionately." When the by-now self-conscious tinker tries to respond, she interrupts him with a husky-voiced remark about sharp-pointed stars being driven--"Hot and sharp and--lovely"--into her body, and she reaches out and almost touches his trousers. The tinker, by now embarrassed, manages to explode her reverie of awakening and get some make-do work into the bargain, but his function as a foil for Elisa's awakening--her blooming--is complete.

7 After the tinker leaves with her chrysanthemums, her pot, and her fifty cents, Elisa shows a new self-awareness and a new self-confidence as she prepares for her evening with Henry. The encounter with the tinker has given her life "a bright direction." She had given the tinker the chrysanthemum shoots in the pot almost as though she had given him her child: "Here. Put it in your wagon, on the seat, where you can watch it." Something wholly of herself, of her own, was going out to spread her beauty and talent, to share them with the world. She showers and cleans herself vigorously and takes new stock of her naked body in the mirror. She dresses in her finest, most feminine things and takes special care in applying her makeup. She feels strong, radiant, confident--and even the rather dull, well-meaning-but-ignorant Henry notices, though his attempt to compliment her comes out clumsily.

Unfortunately, Steinbeck does not end his story with the newly awakened Elisa going to town to explore some new horizon--a romantic dinner, and then maybe even the fights--with Henry. Rather, he presents the scene where Elisa spies the rejected chrysanthemum shoots--her shoots--lying in the road. The tinker has callously tossed them aside. Only Elisa and the reader know the full extent of this rejection, and why Elisa has turned her collar so that Henry cannot see her "crying weakly--like an old woman." How different this story would be were it not for this scene--as dramatic a use of a symbol as a reader is likely to find anywhere in prose fiction. 8

Note that Kimberly's paper doesn't account for the boxing queries at the end of the story, or for the blood imagery (Henry's comment that Elisa could break a calf in two and eat it, the bloodied boxers, and the wine—symbolic blood—being enough for her).

In giving truly of herself, Elisa Allen, a round, developing character, initially finds a brief flicker of less frustration and new life in herself. Sadly, such giving eventually leaves her vulnerable to a deep pain that will not soon depart. She sees herself again trapped in the valley, trapped in her life, with even less hope for changes that might mean a salvation of her depressed spirit. 9

Questions for Writing and Discussion

Prepare short written answers to each of these questions. Be prepared to hand them in and/or discuss them in class, as your teacher directs.

1. How has Kimberly used some elements of *plot summary*—usually to be avoided when writing about literature—to present support for what she sees as the unifying theme of "The Chrysanthemums"?
2. How has Kimberly woven in direct quotations from the story? Note how such quotations are handled: smoothly integrated both with sentences and with the flow of ideas in the paper. Now look again: how has Kimberly used punctuation in relation to the opening and closing quotation marks? How has she handled quotations within quotations?
3. Do you think Kimberly has accounted for the most important details of the story? Explain how her view of theme does or does not ignore any central part of the story.

WRITING ASSIGNMENTS

1. Choose one of the agree/disagree statements of theme listed in question 9 on page 536 and write a paper proving or disproving it, using—*as always*—evidence from the story itself.

2. Imagine that you are Elisa's best friend, a woman who has known her for years. Elisa has told you this story. What would you say to her? How would you respond in trying to help your friend?
3. Imagine that you are Henry. Despite Elisa's efforts to hide behind her collar, you see her crying. You have also seen the chrysanthemum shoots in the middle of the road, though you have no idea how they got there or where they came from. How would you go about trying to get Elisa to explain her tears?
4. The photograph on page 517 is from Franco Zeffirelli's 1990 film of William Shakespeare's famous play, *Hamlet.* Hamlet, played by actor Mel Gibson, contemplates the skull of Yorick, a man he once knew well, "a fellow of infinite jest, of most excellent fancy." (*Hamlet,* V, 1) The scene is important in the context of the play, but its essence can be distilled as Hamlet's realization, in seeing what remains of poor Yorick, of his own mortality and what the actions he is soon to take might bring upon him. Study the scene in Shakespeare's play, then study the photograph, noting especially the emotion in Gibson's face and eyes. How do Hamlet's feelings come through in this scene? What details of the scene in the play and the photograph convey Hamlet's thoughts and fears?

A Rubric for Analyzing Prose Fiction

Whenever you read a short story or novel, apply these questions to the experience to generate more understanding and help pinpoint the kinds of details you might use in class discussion or in writing about what you've read. This is a universal rubric, a kind of "adjustable tool," and so certain questions may not be relevant to a particular work or may not yield productive information. But if you apply them systematically, you should generate *some* answers that will prove useful.

1. Setting
   a. *When* does this take place: what century? decade? What do you know about that general time in history? Is this factor relevant in understanding some aspect of the story?
   b. When does this take place: what specific year or years? What do you know about this specific time? Is this factor relevant in understanding some aspect of the story?
   c. When does this take place: what season of the year? month or months? What do you know about this specific season? Is this factor relevant?
   d. When does this take place: What day? time of day? What do you know about this specific time? Is this factor relevant?
   e. *Where* does this take place: what country? state or province? What do you know about this general place? Is this factor relevant?
   f. Where does this take place: what is the "lay of the land" (the terrain, the town, the city, and so on) like? Is the *physical* element of this location (river, beach, busy city, crowded building, outer space, and so on) a relevant factor?

g. Where does this take place: what is the atmosphere? That is, what is the overall environment like, mentally as well as physically? Does the atmosphere affect the characters' feelings, attitudes, or actions?

h. Is any aspect of the setting symbolic; that is, does it have significant meaning beyond its function as setting?

2. Plot

a. What do you, as a reader, learn in the *exposition* (the introductory part, in which you meet key characters, learn the main situation and conflicts, and get whatever background information you need for understanding the situations)?

b. What happens to *complicate* matters? That is, what occurs, or what action is taken, that launches the story and starts the conflicts building—what is the development of the problem or problems?

c. What is the *climax* of the work? (The term *climax* refers to the dramatic high point of the plot—an action or scene so important that, once it occurs, nothing will ever be the same within the confines of the work.)

d. How does the work move toward *resolution*—the solving of the problems, the tying up of loose ends, and so on? What has happened to whom, and why?

3. Character

a. Who is the main character (protagonist)? How do you know? Is the character flat or round? static or developing? What kinds of conflicts does the character have:
(1) Person versus person?
(2) Person versus self?
(3) Person versus environment?
How are these conflicts important? What are the *motives* of the character? Why does he or she do the things he or she does?

b. Who are the other characters? List them in order of importance: does your list contain an antagonistic character? If so, who? Why? What "types" are these characters:
(1) Flat?
(2) Round?
(3) Static?
(4) Developing?
(5) Foils?
(6) Stock?
What are their *motives*?

c. Are any of the characters symbolic; that is, do they represent not only themselves but some important meaning?

4. Point of view

a. Who is telling the story:
(1) An omniscient third-person narrator outside the story?

(2) A third-person narrator outside the story, limited to the consciousness of one or two characters only?
(3) A first-person narrator who is not a character in the story?
(4) A first-person narrator who is a character in the story?
(5) A third-person narrator who reports only basic details and conversation and has no insight or entrée into the thoughts of characters?

b. Does the point of view allow the reader any ironic distance? That is, do you, as a reader, know more about what is going on than your first-person narrator does? Or can you tell that the third-person narrator is reporting that a character is deluding himself or herself? In other words, can you trust that what your narrator is telling you is absolutely true? Is it possible that your narrator is wrong and is unaware of it (but that the author wants *you* to know this)?

A strong example of this kind of ironic distance is Art Buchwald's "Why We Need Our AK-47's" in chapter 19. In important ways it's that ironic distance—what the reader knows that the writer's persona doesn't seem to—that makes the piece funny.

c. Does the point of view *add* to the story's meaning or depth? If so, how or why?

5. Language
   a. Are there any symbols? If so, what are they, where do they appear, and how do they function as symbols?
   b. Are there any figures of speech—images, metaphors, wordplay—that add pleasure and/or meaning?
   c. Is *irony* operating at any level? Irony always involves *discrepancy*—something doesn't quite fit—and takes three common forms:
   (1) *Situational irony* occurs when the discrepancy lies in the situation itself. Something is expected (they will live happily ever after; the butler did it), but something *else* happens (they go their separate ways; the heroine did it). Or the situation calls for an expected response (a fire fighter aims a water hose at a fire), but something unexpected happens instead (the fire fighter, secretly an arsonist, aims a gasoline hose). (In the play that follows—William Inge's *A Social Event*—it is a situational irony that the vain Hollywood couple's black maid has an invitation to an event to which the couple has *not* been invited.)
   (2) *Verbal irony* occurs when the discrepancy lies between what is said and what is meant. Usually the exact opposite, or a near-opposite, is what is meant: an eager softball player looks out the window and sees that it's raining. "Oh, great!" she says, meaning exactly the opposite. Verbal irony is often delivered with *sarcasm*, which is a matter of tone, and is *not* always ironic. Many people confuse sarcasm with irony, but they are two different things.

An example of verbal irony comes later in this chapter, with the Wilfrid Owen poem "Dulce et Decorum Est."

   (3) *Dramatic irony* occurs when the discrepancy lies between what a character says and knows and what the readers (or the members of the audience at a play) know. For example, in the beginning of Sophocles's classic tragedy *Oedipus the King*, Oedipus, the protagonist, does not know what the audience already knows: that he has unwittingly killed his father and married his mother. The audience

already knows Oedipus is the cause of the terrible plague of sickness devastating the city of Thebes. Thus it is dramatic irony when Oedipus says to the people of Thebes: "Yes, I know / that you are sick. And yet, though you are sick, / there is not one of you so sick as I." (*Oedipus the King,* translated by Thomas Gould)

d. *Tone* is the writer's attitude toward the subject. Tone is a matter of how the speaker or narrator *sounds* to us as readers. Is the tone sympathetic? critical? noncommittal? nasty? sweet? phony? How does the person telling the story sound to us? What kind of personality or attitude is coming through? One key to tone is word *connotations,* the suggestions or hinted meanings that can cluster around a word or an expression, coloring its image and meaning positively (a *slender* person) or negatively (a *skinny* person). What word choices show tone?

Ask your students to flip back to the excerpt from Toni Morrison's *Sula* in chapter 9, and discuss the connotations of the language in that selection.

Ask your students to compare the style in Robert Adams's "Saxon Wolves and Arthur the Briton" (chapter 5) with the style in Kim Chernin's "Kaahumanu and Eve" (chapter 9).

e. *Style* is an elusive term, meaning, among other things, how the writing is done—whether it contains long, hard-to-follow sentences or tough vocabulary items; whether instead it contains short, terse sentences that seem to under- rather than overstate details; whether the flow of information is smooth or difficult; and the like. Finally, one of the most important and honest responses to style is to decide whether or not you like it—much as whether or not you like the way someone dresses or carries himself or herself. It is never amiss to think about your personal reactions to the *way* a work of literature is written. Do you like the story's point but not the way it's told? The difference is probably style. What do you *like* about the writer's style? What do you *dislike* about it? And, as always, *why?* Be able to give examples.

The above rubric should prove helpful to you when you must write analytical or critical essays about fiction. It would also prove useful in writing fiction reviews—assessments for other readers of the value or enjoyment of reading a given work of fiction.

Another Genre: Drama

Drama is similar to prose fiction in that it too is literally untrue—and usually involves a story about people. It therefore includes plot, characterization, conflict, and imaginative use of language.

Seeing a Play Versus Reading a Play

The drama audience's point of view can, of course, be varied by the staging—for example, whether the proscenium arch constitutes a "fourth wall" through which we view the play or whether there is a thrust stage; whether the theater is in

The great difference between drama and prose fiction is that drama is primarily written to be *performed* before an audience. As such, its printed form is the playwright's guide for performance, complete with stage descriptions, directions, cues, and suggestions for how the play should be presented. The only possible point of view in the theater is that of the audience: its members must see the set and the actions of the players, hear their speeches, and infer all meanings from this limited perspective. Audience members do not have immediate access to the play's script, which contains the playwright's stage directions and other remarks.

When you read a play, you have a great advantage that a theater audience does not have, because you can read those parts which a theater audience cannot know about. You can reread parts that surprise or puzzle you. You can dramatize the play in your mind, and soon the experience is somewhat similar to reading fiction. You can pause between acts or even between lines of dialogue; you can put the play down to answer the phone, let the cat out, or any other activity that might interrupt other kinds of reading. The physical limitations and the practical conventions of theater make playwriting significantly different from fiction or poetry writing (although many plays, notably those of William Shakespeare, are in poetry), but the appreciation and evaluation of a play can be quite similar to those of a short story or novel.

Following is a one-act play by the American playwright William Inge. Note that the stage directions are italicized, along with all cues and suggestions that Mr. Inge provided for the actors and director who will be following the script in order to prepare it for performance.

the round or whether we are seeing "street" theater. In all variations, however, the audience is limited to seeing and hearing only what the performers do and say in the particular setting.

A Social Event

WILLIAM INGE

William Inge (1913–73) was an important American playwright and screenwriter whose best-known plays are Picnic *(for which he won a Pulitzer Prize) and* Bus Stop*. His screenplay* Splendor in the Grass *won an Academy Award.*

The scene is the bedroom in the home of a young Hollywood couple, RANDY BROOKS *and* CAROLE MASON*, who have been married only a short time and whose careers are still in the promising stage. It is late morning and both* RANDY *and* CAROLE *are still asleep, but* RANDY *soon comes awake, reaches for a cigarette, lights it, and rubs his forehead discouragedly. Something profound is troubling him. He gets out of bed, slips a robe on and paces the floor discouragedly. Finally, he presses the buzzer on the house phone and speaks to the cook.*

RANDY *[Into the house phone]* Muriel? We're getting up now. Bring up the usual breakfast.

[He hangs up and goes into the bathroom to wash. Now CAROLE *wakes up. She too lights a cigarette and looks troubled. Then she calls to* RANDY*.]*

CAROLE I hardly slept a wink all night, just thinking about it.

RANDY *[From bathroom]* There's nothing to do but face the fact that we're not invited.

CAROLE Oh, there's *got* to be a way. There's *got* to be.

RANDY *[Entering]* But, honey, the services start at noon. It's now ten-thirty.

CAROLE Everyone in the business will be there.

Note that Inge expects readers of the play to infer certain things from his descriptions of the setting—Hollywood—and the young couple "whose careers are still in the promising stage." At a performance, members of the audience would have to wait until dialogue begins before they could infer anything, yet Inge's readers already know that the Hollywood setting probably means that the couple are aspiring performers. Moreover, Hollywood's reputation as a glittery filmmaking center where appearances mean almost everything makes readers suspect that the nature of Hollywood society will be important in the play.

RANDY After all, honey, there's no reason to feel slighted. We're both pretty new in pictures. It's not as though we were old-timers who had worked with Scotty.

CAROLE Sandra and Don never worked with Scotty, either. Neither did Debby and Chris, or Anne and Mark.

RANDY I know, honey, we've been through all this before.

CAROLE And I may never have worked with Scotty, but I did meet him once, and he danced with me at a party. He was very nice to me, too, and said some very complimentary things. I met his wife, too. *[An afterthought]* I didn't much like her.

RANDY Maybe I better call Mike again.

[He picks up the telephone and dials]

CAROLE What good can an agent do? We're not looking for jobs.

RANDY He may have found some way of getting us invited.

CAROLE I bet.

RANDY *[Into the telephone]* Mike Foster, please. Randy Brooks calling.

CAROLE All the invitations are coming from Scotty's wife. Tell Mike you think there's been an oversight. Maybe he could call her and remind her that you've been referred to in all the columns as "the young Scotty Woodrow," and that Scotty's always been your idol and . . .

RANDY *[Into the telephone]* Mike? Randy. Look, Mike, Carole and I still haven't been invited, and I can't help wondering if there's been an oversight of some kind. After all, Carole was a great friend of Scotty's and she feels pretty hurt that she's been overlooked . . . I never knew him but everyone knows how much I've always admired him. In an interview just last week, I said "Scotty Woodrow is still the greatest." Now, I didn't *have* to say that . . . If you ask me, it showed a lot of humility on my part to say a thing like that when, after all, I've got a career of my own to consider . . . Well look, try to do *something,* Mike. Carole and I both should be seen there . . . O.K., Mike, call us as soon as you find out.

With just a few speeches between Carole and Randy, Inge handles the necessary exposition (introductory details) for us to see what the problem is; he also gives us an early dose of the shallow values of the ambitious couple.

[He hangs up]

CAROLE He couldn't get us an invitation to Disneyland.

RANDY He said just Scotty's closest friends are being invited.

CAROLE Oh yes! Half the people going, I bet, have never met him.

RANDY Well! What are we going to do?

CAROLE Sandra had an entire new outfit made. Perfectly stunning. And she had the dress made so that she can have the sleeves taken out later and wear it to cocktails and supper parties. After all, black is a very smart color now.

RANDY Did you tell Sandra and Don we weren't invited?

CAROLE Of course not. I lied and said we were going. Now, if we don't get an invitation, I'll have to lie again and say we came down with food poisoning, or something.

RANDY How did Anne and Mark get invited?

CAROLE Mark played Scotty's son in a picture once.

RANDY When? I don't remember.

CAROLE A long time ago, before either of us came on the scene.

RANDY *[Thinks a moment]* That means Mark's a little older than he admits.

CAROLE I don't know. The part was very young, practically an infant.

RANDY Just the same, I'll bet Mark's thirty.

CAROLE Damn! What am I going to tell Sandra? She invited us to come to her house afterwards and I accepted.

RANDY *[A little shocked]* She's not giving a party!

CAROLE No. She just invited some friends to come in afterwards to have a few drinks and talk about what a great guy Scotty was, and everything. She said she thought we'd all feel terribly depressed. After all, Scotty Woodrow was practically a landmark, or something. Think of it. He's been a star for forty years.

RANDY Yes. He was really great. It makes me very humble to think of a guy like Scotty.

CAROLE They say flowers came from the President, and from Queen Elizabeth, and . . .

RANDY The guest list is going to be published in every paper in the country.

CAROLE You know, we *could* crash.

RANDY No, honey.

CAROLE Who'd know the difference?

RANDY How would we feel afterwards, when we had to shake hands with Mrs. Woodrow?

CAROLE She's probably forgotten whether she invited us or not.

RANDY Honey, I'm *not* going to crash. That's all. I'm *not.*

CAROLE Everyone would just take it for granted we'd been invited. I mean, we're both just as prominent as Sandra and Don, or any of the others. If you ask me, it'd be a lot better to crash than not to be seen at . . . Well, you can't call it a social *affair* exactly, but it's a social *event.* Anyway, *everyone* will be there. *Everyone.*

RANDY It could be some of the others are lying about their invitations, too. You realize that, don't you?

CAROLE *[Considers this]* I wonder . . . Well, anyway, they're all going. I *think* they got invitations.

RANDY I don't know why the studio couldn't have managed it for us with a little pull. They should realize it's in the best interests of my career to be seen there, and my career means as much to them as it does to me.

CAROLE Same here. Oh, I just don't know how I can face Sandra and Anne and all the others, and make them believe that we really did have food poisoning.

RANDY You know, we could give ourselves food poisoning. Just a light case. A little rotten meat would do it. Then we'd call the doctor and . . .

CAROLE *[Horrified]* No! I'm not going to make myself sick.

Despite the pressing problem, Randy can't help speculating about Mark's age. Age is crucial in this society; even more crucial is whether or not one's age *shows.*

In this speech, Carole presents the true heart of the matter: neither character cares about the deceased; what's important is being seen at his funeral and hence being perceived as socially significant in Hollywood—a sign concomitant with career success.

RANDY Just a slight case so you could tell them with a straight face . . . *[A soft tap comes at the door]* Come in. *[MURIEL, the maid, enters with a tray]* Hi, Muriel!

MURIEL Good morning!

CAROLE Hi, Muriel. Put it here on the coffee table. *[MURIEL does as she is told]*

MURIEL Miss Carole, I hope you remember I told you I'd be gone this morning.

CAROLE Oh, yes, I'd forgotten. What time will you be back, Muriel?

MURIEL Oh, I'll be back in time to fix dinner.

RANDY Is this your day off, Muriel?

Here is classic situational irony: the socially lowly maid has an invitation to the "social event" that Carole and Randy so desperately want to attend.

MURIEL No, Mr. Randy. I'm going to Mr. Woodrow's funeral. *[There is a slight air of superiority about her now.* RANDY *and* CAROLE *look at her with sudden surprise]*

RANDY Oh . . . is that right?

MURIEL And after the funeral, Mrs. Woodrow has asked me to join the family at her home.

CAROLE Muriel, you didn't tell me!

RANDY Uh . . . were you a friend of Scotty's, Muriel?

MURIEL My mother worked for him when he was starting out in the business. I was born in Mr. Woodrow's beach house, before he bought that big house up in the canyon. *[She has thus established herself as near-royalty to RANDY and CAROLE]*

RANDY *[Amazed]* Really?

MURIEL Oh, yes. Mr. Woodrow was very good to me when I was a child. Mama worked for him until she died. I could have stayed on, but after Mr. Woodrow got married the last time, *she* hired a lot of French servants I didn't get on with, at all. But they went right on sending me Christmas cards every year.

RANDY Uh . . . Muriel, do you have a ride to the funeral?

MURIEL No, Mr. Brooks. Mrs. Woodrow's secretary said I could bring my family, but now that Vincent has left me and taken the car, I guess I'll have to take a taxi.

RANDY Gee . . . that's too bad.

CAROLE *[Thinking]* Yes. Isn't it?

MURIEL *[Starts for the door]* Well, I have to be getting ready now. I got a new black dress to wear. All the big names in Hollywood will be there. I want to look my best.

RANDY *[Holding her]* Uh . . . Muriel, you don't want to go to the services all alone!

MURIEL Oh, I don't mind.

CAROLE Look, Muriel, why don't we all go together? I mean . . . Well, of course, Randy and I are invited, too, but we'd be glad to go along with you . . . as your family, you know. Well, after all, you're one of us, Muriel.

MURIEL *[Appears to examine the idea]* All of us go together, huh?

CAROLE Of course.

RANDY I'll drive us there in the Cadillac.

MURIEL *[This idea appeals to her]* Oh . . . that'd be nice.

CAROLE And then after the funeral, we'll take you to the house.

MURIEL *[Without sarcasm]* I see.

RANDY And you won't have to worry about coming back to fix dinner.

CAROLE Of course not.

MURIEL Well, it suits me. I didn't want to have to call a taxi. If you folks wanna come along, fine and dandy. You'll have to pardon me now. I have to get into my new black dress.

RANDY We'll meet you downstairs in fifteen minutes, Muriel. *[MURIEL exits. CAROLE and RANDY both jump into action, getting their clothes out of their respective closets.]*

CAROLE I told you we'd find a way.

RANDY Yah. *[Taking a suit from closet]* Say, this suit could stand a pressing. Do I have to wear black?

CAROLE Of course, honey. After all, it's a very solemn occasion.

RANDY Well, O.K.

CAROLE I'll have to call Sandra.

[She picks up the telephone and dials]

RANDY It's going to look all right, isn't it? I mean, our going with Muriel. After all, she's our cook.

CAROLE Of course. You don't worry about things like that at a funeral. *[Into the telephone]* Sandra? Carole. Darling, I'm awfully sorry but Randy and I won't be able to come to your house after the funeral . . . Well, you see, we have a duty to Muriel, our cook. She's the daughter of Scotty's old housekeeper . . . Yes, Scotty practically raised her. And we feel that we should take her with us, and then, of course, we'll have to go to the home afterwards. Just family and a few of his very closest friends. We can't get out of it . . . You'll forgive us, won't you, darling? . . . Oh, it's all going to be terribly sad.

RANDY *[To himself, while dressing]* I guess it'll look all right. After all, funerals are very democratic affairs.

Curtain

Questions for Critical Analysis

1. Why is Randy's remark at the close of the play—that funerals are "very democratic affairs"—ironic?
2. *Satire* is literature that pokes fun at people and the ways they think and behave, usually in order to provide a kind of constructive criticism—to point out flaws and excesses that can, with conscientious effort, be corrected. Yet not all satire, particularly in modern times, has such a benevolent purpose. How is Inge's play satiric of (a) young, excessively or obsessively career-minded people; (b) the celebrity world of Hollywood; and (c) shallow values?
3. What is the greatest irony in this play?
4. As characters, are Carole and Randy flat or round? static or dynamic?

5. What are Carole's and Randy's *motives?*
6. How would you state the theme of this short play?
7. Serious drama is usually classified as tragedy or comedy, though more modern types of drama often mix elements of both. Is there anything truly tragic about this little play? How is humor present, and in what service?

You could apply the rubric on pages 545–48 to this and other plays. For example, the time setting is the present, and what's most significant about setting is the place: Hollywood, where careers and attitudes like Carole's and Randy's are common. Their motives are those of self-centered young careerists in one of the vainest places in the world—they want to be *seen,* to advance their careers any way they can. They're round but static characters: they don't even reflect on the irony of how they manage their "invitations"; they're too busy celebrating getting to go, and rubbing it in to their so-called friends. In short, they're just as shallow and phony at the end of the play as they are at the beginning. Other applications of the rubric can be made, allowing for the difference between genres.

Sometimes stories are made up of people changing in a critical moment; at other times stories are made up of people coming to a critical moment and *not* changing. *A Social Event* represents the latter category.

CASE STUDY CLOSE-UP

Following is a paper a student wrote after studying *A Social Event.*

William Inge's A Social Event: A Hollywood Satire

Pat Reeves, college writing student

William Inge's A Social Event is a one-act play that satirizes the shallowness, conceit, and deceit of young Hollywood actors whose obsession with their careers overrides all other concerns. It occurs in the present, after the death of longtime Hollywood acting legend Scotty Woodrow. The principal characters, Randy Brooks and Carole Mason, are recently married and both bent on furthering their careers. They both know that visibility—being seen at all important Hollywood occasions—is vital to their success, and they are desperate for invitations to Woodrow's funeral, even though they've heard that only the actor's closest friends have been invited. Certain they are being excluded from what Carole says they can't call "a social affair exactly, but . . . a social event," they call their agent to plead with him somehow to get them an invitation. As they await the none-too-promising prospect that their agent might wangle an invitation, they show, through their conversation, just how shallow, conceited, and deceitful they are. 1

2 Neither is capable of thoughts more shrewd than the venture that others like them may be lying when they claim to have been invited:

> RANDY It could be that some of the others are lying about their invitations, too. you realize that, don't you?
> CAROLE *[Considers this]* I wonder . . . Well, anyway, they're all going. I *think* they got invitations.

That's about as brilliant as they get—until they spy their chance to worm their way to the funeral with, of all people, their maid. Already they've lied to friends who claim to have been invited, solely to avoid the embarrassment of truth, and so Carole must ponder the need to lie again: "Now, if we don't get an invitation, I'll have to lie again and say we came down with food poisoning, or something." Another mark of their shallow values occurs when Randy seriously suggests deliberately giving themselves food poisoning in order to validate their "excuse" for not being at Woodrow's services. Neither is intelligent enough (let alone humble enough) to appreciate the irony of needing their maid's invitation to get what they want. It doesn't occur to either of them that they are, in effect, groveling. In such a superficial world, there's no room for anything deeply genuine.

3 Like many obsessed young actors, both are extraordinarily conceited. Trying to persuade their agent to get them an invitation somehow, Randy says, "In an interview just last week, I said, 'Scotty Woodrow is still the greatest.' Now, I didn't *have* to say that." He goes on to say, "If you ask me, it showed a lot of humility on my part to say a thing like that." Carole is no better; she admits (only to Randy) that she met Scotty just once, but "he danced with me," she says, "and said some very complimentary things." It's clear that Woodrow meant little to either of them; it's being seen at his funeral, to advance their credentials as a Hollywood couple who *matter,* that means everything. Neither really knows more about Scotty Woodrow than the average film fan; they're so full of concern for themselves that their idea of respect for Woodrow is to "have a few drinks and talk about what a great guy Scotty was, and everything." Their talk, as Inge presents it, is as conceited as it is shallow.

4 Finally, they are also deceitful. The lies to their friends about having invitations are only a part of the routine falsehoods they first create and then embrace. After Carole has told him she met Woodrow only once, Randy says to the agent on the phone: "After all, Carole was a great

friend of Scotty's and she feels pretty hurt that she's been overlooked." They routinely spin lies to each other, with a numbing casualness that both seem to expect. "It makes me very humble to think of a guy like Scotty," Randy says to Carole—to whom he doesn't have to lie—but perhaps they think it's important to stay in practice. Carole is certainly Randy's peer in phoniness; consider the way she curries Muriel, the maid who holds the all-important real invitation: "Well, of course, Randy and I are invited, too, but we'd be glad to go along with you . . . as your family, you know. Well, after all, you're one of us, Muriel." Uh-huh. Carole's telephoned "regrets" to her friend Sandra at the close of the play ring just as false.

In this short play William Inge has skewered with considerable 5
humor the attitudes, behavior, and language of unconscionably ambitious young actors and actresses in Hollywood. Showing Carole and Randy as shallow, conceited, and deceitful, Inge's satire makes us see, hear, think—and laugh.

Different Types of Papers on Prose Fiction and Drama

If you want to dramatize these options, you can assign each group to do a skeleton of an essay on one of these types and have the skeletons presented in class.

Following are common kinds of papers teachers assign on prose fiction and drama.

1. Character analysis (flat, round, static, developing, motives, conflicts, and so on)
2. Thematic analysis (how plot, conflict, character, point of view, language, and so on contribute to a central, unified meaning, insight, or understanding)
3. Scene analysis (close explanation of how a particular scene is central to the meaning or development of the story)
4. Point-of-view analysis (how the point of view used adds depth of meaning, irony, or some other important consideration to the story)
5. Language analysis (how symbolism or allegory, imagery, irony, connotation, or other considerations of language add texture and meaning to the work)

Poetry: Characteristics

And, of course, Wordsworth himself revised extensively.

Poetry is virtually undefinable. Although the British poet William Wordsworth once defined poetry as "the spontaneous overflow of powerful emotions," he was giving a highly romantic, almost-mystical spin to his meaning. One could hardly, for example, admire the carefully crafted couplets of Wordsworth's predecessor Alexander Pope and still think poetry is *spontaneous*—it had to take Pope considerable time and effort to make such impressive rhymes in such rigid forms. The fact is that poetry comes in many forms, on many subjects, and requires only that its language be *intense*, charged in some way so as to make it extraordinary. In this sense, even some passages of prose can be very poetic.

Consider, for example, this excerpt from "Neighbour Rosicky," a short story by the Pulitzer Prize–winning American writer Willa Cather (1873–1947). Cather is describing New York City's Manhattan as her protagonist, Anton Rosicky, sees it on a deserted Fourth of July afternoon:

> The lower part of New York was empty. Wall Street, Liberty Street, Broadway, all empty. So much stone and asphalt with nothing going on, so many empty windows. The emptiness was intense, like the stillness in a great factory when the machinery stops and the belts and bands cease running. It was too great a change, it took all the strength out of one. Those blank buildings, without the stream of life pouring through them, were like empty jails. It struck young Rosicky that this was the trouble with big cities; they built you in from the earth itself, cemented you away from any contact with the ground. You lived in an unnatural world, like the fish in an aquarium, who were probably much more comfortable than they ever were in the sea.

While we would not argue that the above passage *is* a poem, we would point out the charged, special language—so descriptive as to engage the reader's imaginative eye and ear. First are the visual images of emptiness. Next are the visual images given by metaphor (for instance, "the stream of life pouring through" buildings) and simile ("like empty jails"). Then are the appeals to sound, first through the echoing of the word *empty* and variant forms of that same word. Even the stillness, paradoxically, has sound that reinforces the idea of emptiness, effected through another simile: "like the stillness in a great factory when the machinery stops." Cather's third-person narrator isn't presenting us with a poem, but we are reading language that is highly poetic.

With a word processor it's easy to present the same passage to your students in two different ways—once as a poem (with each line or phrase centered on the page) and once as prose—in order to dramatize the elusiveness of this distinction.

Of course, many people prefer poetry that has precise rhymes and predictable rhythms. Such poetry, often called lyric poetry, has been enjoyed for centuries. Here is a lyric poem familiar to many American readers:

Stopping by Woods on a Snowy Evening

ROBERT FROST

Robert Frost (1874–1963) won the Pulitzer Prize four times (1924, 1931, 1937, 1943). His books of poetry include New Hampshire, A Further Range, A Witness True, The Gift Outright, In the Clearing, *and* Collected Poems.

Whose woods these are I think I know.
His house is in the village though;
He will not see me stopping here
To watch his woods fill up with snow.

My little horse must think it queer
To stop without a farmhouse near
Between the woods and frozen lake
The darkest evening of the year.

He gives his harness bells a shake
To ask if there is some mistake.
The only other sound's the sweep
Of easy wind and downy flake.

The woods are lovely, dark and deep,
But I have promises to keep,
And miles to go before I sleep,
And miles to go before I sleep.

In this familiar poem, the rhyme scheme is pleasantly precise, and so is the rhythm, which is iambic (an accented syllable following an unaccented syllable) tetrameter (four accented syllables per line). The poem is often considered a tribute to winter beauty, with a hint of darker meanings (see the student paper later in this chapter).

Not all poems, however, are on beautiful subjects. In fact, poetry can be written about any subject known to human beings—even death and destruction. Here is a vivid poem, "Dulce et Decorum Est," written during World War I by a soldier who died shortly after writing it. The title comes from the Roman poet Horace, who wrote, "*Dulce et decorum est pro patria mori*," which means "It is sweet and fitting to die for one's country." This poem, like much modern poetry, is in free verse, which follows no set rhyme or metric pattern.

Dulce et Decorum Est

WILFRID OWEN

Wilfrid Owen (1893–1918) was killed in battle in World War I while leading his troops across the Sambre Canal in France, one week before the armistice was signed.

You may need to review the World War I setting (trench warfare, first use of tanks, first use of chemical weapons, massive slaughter, and so on) for your students to help them grasp some of Owen's details. Of special importance is that war's use of mustard gas, which plays a key role in the poem.

Bent double, like old beggars under sacks,
Knock-kneed, coughing like hags, we cursed through sludge,
Till on the haunting flares we turned our backs,
And towards our distant rest began to trudge.
Men marched asleep. Many had lost their boots,
But limped on, blood-shod. All went lame, all blind;
Drunk with fatigue, deaf even to the hoots
Of gas-shells dropping softly behind.

Gas! Gas! Quick, boys!—An ecstasy of fumbling,
Fitting the clumsy helmets just in time,

But someone still was yelling out and stumbling
And floundering like a man in fire or lime.—
Dim through the misty panes and thick green light,
As under a green sea, I saw him drowning.

In all my dreams before my helpless sight
He plunges at me, guttering, choking, drowning.

If in some smothering dreams, you too could pace
Behind the wagon that we flung him in,
And watch the white eyes writhing in his face,
His hanging face, like a devil's sick of sin;
If you could hear, at every jolt, the blood
Come gargling from the froth-corrupted lungs,
Bitter as the cud
Of vile, incurable sores on innocent tongues.—
My friend, you would not tell with such high zest
To children ardent for some desperate glory,
The old Lie: *Dulce et decorum est*
Pro patria mori.

Even though there is no set rhyme scheme, Owen's poem is still highly poetic. We realize here that poetry is very much an aural experience, for despite the lack of rhyme, this poem was still meant to be *heard,* to be read aloud, as though the soldier were speaking to us all and sharing his deep pain and poignant memories. Poetic language need not rhyme, need not be in precise meters. It requires only strength and power of expression, through vivid and evocative diction.

Owen's poem provides much for our eyes—"like old beggars under sacks," "blood-shod," "Dim through the misty panes and thick green light / As under a green sea, I saw him drowning," "the white eyes writhing in his face," and more. He offers appeals to our ears—"coughing like hags," "the hoots / Of gas-shells dropping softly behind," "guttering, choking," "the blood / Come gargling," and more. Indeed, he appeals to all our senses as he marshals details of war in order to blast the old patriotic myth advanced by Horace. Owen's poem tells us that poetry is not always just for beauty but sometimes for powerful rhetorical purposes. Here the message is that although war may be necessary, it isn't sweet or becoming or glorious—it's gruesome and deadly and awful.

A Rubric for Analyzing Poetry

Analysis of poetry can make some use of the rubric given earlier for prose fiction and drama but is sufficiently different to necessitate its own rubric. As with the rubric for prose fiction and drama, this rubric contains questions that may not generate useful information on a given poem. But if you apply the rubric thoughtfully and thoroughly, you should be able to analyze poems in at least a rudimentary way.

1. Voice
   a. Who is speaking in the poem? Is the speaker telling experience in the first person ("I")? If so, consider the following:
      (1) Who is this person?
      (2) What kind of person does the speaker seem to be?
      (3) Why is this person sharing these impressions or thoughts?
      (4) What sort of tone comes through?
      (5) Is the speaker telling a story (narrative) that could be (but isn't) told in regular prose form?
      (6) Is the speaker a major or a minor character in the narrative?
   b. Is the speaker telling experience in the third person ("he," "she," "it," "they," and so on)? If so, consider the following:
      (1) Is the speaker telling a story in poetry, a narrative of events that could be (but isn't) presented in regular prose narration?
      (2) Is the speaker not telling a story but simply giving an observation or a series of observations?
      (3) What sort of tone comes through?
2. Theme
   a. What do you think the point, or main idea, of the poem is? What makes you think so? Try to find your evidence, as always, from *within the poem* itself.
   b. What ideas related to theme can you also discern? How do these ideas relate to theme? How do they add to (or subtract from) the poem's meaning?
   c. What is this poem about?
3. Language
   a. What kinds of imagery—appeals to senses of taste, touch, smell, sight, and sound—do you find? How do these enhance the poem's overall impression or meaning?
   b. What particular poetic devices do you find operating here? Consider:
      (1) Do you discern any apparent prevailing meter (that is, rhythm)?
      (2) Do you discern any apparent prevailing rhyme pattern?
      (3) Do you find literary devices, such as the following:
         (a) *Personification* ("The face of the clock")?
         (b) *Metaphor* ("The moon was a blood-red ball in the night sky)?
         (c) *Simile* ("My love's like a red, red rose")?
         (d) *Submerged metaphor* ("Her face melted" [face = wax image, candle, or anything else meltable])?
      (4) Are there any sound devices, in addition to rhythm or meter, such as the following:
         (a) *Alliteration* ("Dull, dull, deadly dull / The doctor drones along")?
         (b) *Assonance* (repeated vowel sounds: "The rushes cried 'arise! arise!'")?

(c) *Onomatopoeia* ("Bang! Slap! Ding dong!")?
(d) *Internal rhyme* ("Ah, distinctly I remember it was in the bleak December; / And each separate dying ember wrought its ghost upon the floor")?

c. What *connotations* or other particularly apt word choices does the poet use?

d. Are any patterns discernible besides rhyme scheme? Is there a reason for the lines being arranged the way they are?

4. Appreciation
   a. Do you like the poem? Why or why not?
   b. What other poems have you read on the same subject?
   c. Do you think this poem is more effective or less effective than any of those other poems?
   d. Are there any stories or plays this poem reminds you of? If so which ones, and why?
   e. If you could speak to the poet, what would you say?

CASE STUDY CLOSE-UP

Typical of papers on poetry are *explications*—papers explaining what the poem is about, or what it means, based on evidence taken from within the poem itself or from what is known about both poem and poet. Here is an explication paper done by one of our students, Anne Odom, on Frost's "Stopping by Woods on a Snowy Evening":

Winter Interlude or Suicidal Deliberation?

Anne Odom, college writing student

1 Robert Frost is one of the most well known and loved American poets of this century. His poem "Stopping by Woods on a Snowy Evening" is one with which most high school and college students are familiar. The most common interpretation of this poem paints a picturesque winter scene of forest, snow, quiet beauty--and little else.

2 Another interpretation, however, points to a winter forest scene that is not merely picturesque. Getting beyond the simpler, "scenic" reading of the poem, one may note that certain words and phrases set a tone not of cheerfulness and lightness but of uncertainty and somber thoughts. A stanza-by-stanza examination of the poem best serves to reveal this less cheerful interpretation.

3 In the first stanza, the speaker has stopped in a forest to watch the snow fall. The speaker is aware that others might wonder, "What is this person doing here?" We learn that the owner of the woods lives in the village and is not around to catch trespassers--if trespassers are a matter of concern--but the notion that something is out of the ordinary is reinforced by the speaker's observation that "he [the owner] will not see me stopping here." Perhaps the speaker simply wants to watch the snow as it falls quietly in the forest, but, if so, why mention that he will not be seen, as if he prefers privacy?

4 The second stanza reinforces the idea of being in the wrong place at the wrong time. There are no farmhouses near the woods, and the horse doesn't understand why the rider has stopped. The lake is frozen. It is already evening, and it will only get darker, and soon. All logic argues against stopping. "The darkest evening of the year" could literally refer to the winter solstice, December 21, which is the day with the fewest hours of sunlight each year. But it could also refer to the speaker's mental state: a mood of dark reflection, perhaps even depression. Depression in human beings occurs most frequently during the winter months, especially as a holiday approaches (which would also be the case on December 21). Whether "the darkest evening" refers to a specific day or a mental state, it is clearly not routine for the speaker to be out in the snowy evening right before darkness falls, and it is also not routine to be stopping where he is and under the conditions that exist.

5 The third stanza continues the mood of uncertainty. The horse is ready to return to the comfort of the barn and seems to think "there is some mistake." The cold, dark forest is not where the horse would choose to be. Surely the horse senses that stopping here is extraordinary, and since the only other sound besides the horse's harness bells is "the sweep / Of easy wind and downy flake," it is again clear that the speaker and the horse are isolated. The forest doesn't seem to hold another living creature.

6 Could something be causing the speaker such mental anguish that stopping here and contemplating the scene is a reaction to it? Could these quiet woods filling with snow beckon the speaker simply to stay and let the gradual cold and snow also cover him, until all care is forgotten and frozen like the lake? Certainly, the word clues so far can

support such a view: "will not see me," "queer," "darkest evening," "frozen," "some mistake," and "without a farmhouse near." All these focus on the coldness and isolation the speaker must be feeling. At this point the possibility that the speaker is simply enjoying a winter interlude from the care and bustle of the world now seems much more remote.

7 The final stanza offers nothing that works against this more somber interpretation. It begins with an odd combination of descriptive terms. "Dark and deep" is paired with "lovely." While "lovely" has a light tone with no connotation of dreariness, "dark and deep" alliteratively connotes a feeling of foreboding, even a sinister feeling. Thus there is a contrast of tone as if there were a struggle within the mind of the speaker. The "promises to keep" could refer to obligations the speaker has. These could include a promise to help a neighbor with some task, or perhaps an obligation to a spouse or child. There could even be a business commitment that demands the speaker's attention. Whatever the reason, this line about keeping promises indicates that stopping here has not solved anything. The spell of the wondrous solitude and seductive quiet of the forest has been broken.

8 The last two lines of the poem are alike. This repetition forces the reader to think about "miles to go before I sleep." Some readers may think that the first line literally refers to the distance the speaker must yet travel before he will be home for his night's rest. In that view, the second line then metaphorically refers to the length of time the speaker must yet live, discharging the responsibility of his promises, until he dies ("sleep") and is relieved of his cares. But it is also possible to view both lines as giving the metaphoric view: the speaker simply has too much life yet to live to be thinking of just quietly "ending it all." Repeating the line reinforces the truth and conviction of the speaker's conclusion. He repeats it as he stirs, and nudges the horse into movement.

9 Finally, it would seem that Frost's poem reflects both a winter interlude <u>and</u> a suicidal deliberation: just as winter itself often symbolizes the end of the annual life cycle, this particular winter scene symbolizes a contemplation of death, brought on by the sheer beauty of a quiet wood filling with snow and then rejected as premature. Thus, though the dark images and tone are present in the poem, its overall

impression is optimistic: the speaker may be depressed, may be enduring rough times, but after this quiet interlude is ready to face life again.

Questions for Writing and Discussion

Prepare short written answers to each of these questions. Be prepared to hand them in and/or discuss them in class, as your teacher directs.

We hope most of your students see the "five-paragraph theme" formula at work in the student paper on *A Social Event*.

1. Note that Odom structured, or developed, her paper on a stanza-by-stanza analysis. How does that contrast with the structure apparent in the student essay on Inge's *A Social Event* (pages 549–53)? (What familiar structure can you discern in the *Social Event* paper?)
2. How has Odom used quotation to help prove her points? Is her use effective?
3. Note that when you are quoting fewer than four complete lines of poetry, the words are placed in quotation marks within your regular text, with slash marks (/) indicating where one line of the poem ends and another begins. How should you display four or more full lines of poetry?
4. What uses of the above rubric do you find Odom making?

Four or more lines should be set on the page as they are in the poem.

This chapter is far from comprehensive. Indeed, whole books have been written on the subject of writing about literature. We hope this chapter has nonetheless proved helpful, and we'd like to close with just a few hints to help you as you write about literature:

1. Always write about literature (or film, painting, music, or any other work of art) in the *present tense*. This is sometimes called the historic present. For example:
   a. Though painted long ago, da Vinci's *Mona Lisa* is still smiling.
   b. In Margaret Mitchell's novel of the Old South, *Gone with the Wind*, Rhett Butler still leaves Scarlett O'Hara at the end, just as he does [not *did*] in the film.
   c. Although William Faulkner is dead, his literature remains alive, as do the characters and events within it.
2. Generally avoid simply summarizing plot. Your teacher has read the story; there's no need to retell it. Rather, select only those incidents or events which help you make *your* point. In other words, be in control of your own paper and what you want to say. If you let plot dominate, you'll have let the story, play, or poem dictate the organization of your paper—probably to your regret.
3. Don't be reluctant to *discuss* literature. Get involved in class discussion or in dorm-room arguments about the assignment. Hear the ideas of others.
4. Don't be afraid to form an opinion so long as you can either back it up in presenting it yourself or find reasonable support for it within the work.

Much more on this "plot summary" problem appears in the next chapter.

Writers' Circle

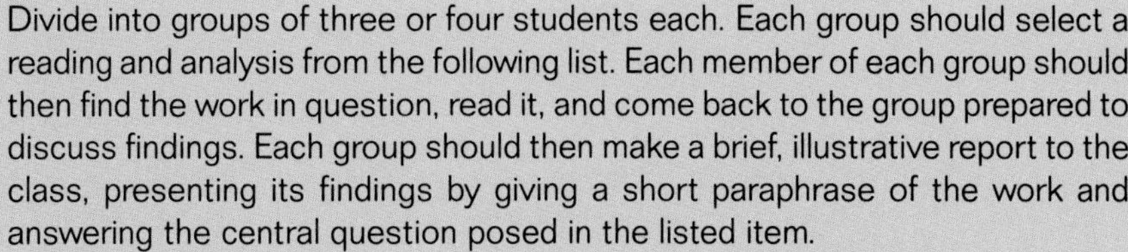

Divide into groups of three or four students each. Each group should select a reading and analysis from the following list. Each member of each group should then find the work in question, read it, and come back to the group prepared to discuss findings. Each group should then make a brief, illustrative report to the class, presenting its findings by giving a short paraphrase of the work and answering the central question posed in the listed item.

Choices

1. How does symbolism help convey thematic meaning in Katherine Anne Porter's short story "Flowering Judas"?
2. How does point of view help convey thematic meaning in Katherine Anne Porter's short story "The Jilting of Granny Weatherall"?
3. How does the character of Phoenix Jackson help convey thematic meaning in Eudora Welty's short story "A Worn Path"?
4. How do the metaphors in Sylvia Plath's poem "Metaphors" help convey the thematic meaning of the poem?
5. How do tone and appeals to the reader's sense of sound help convey thematic meaning in Gwendolyn Brooks's poem "We Real Cool"?
6. How do words and images related to formal worship help convey thematic meaning in Emily Dickinson's poem "Some Keep the Sabbath Going to Church"?
7. How does dialogue reveal character and theme in Susan Glaspell's one-act play *Trifles?*

chapter 22 Writing Essay Tests

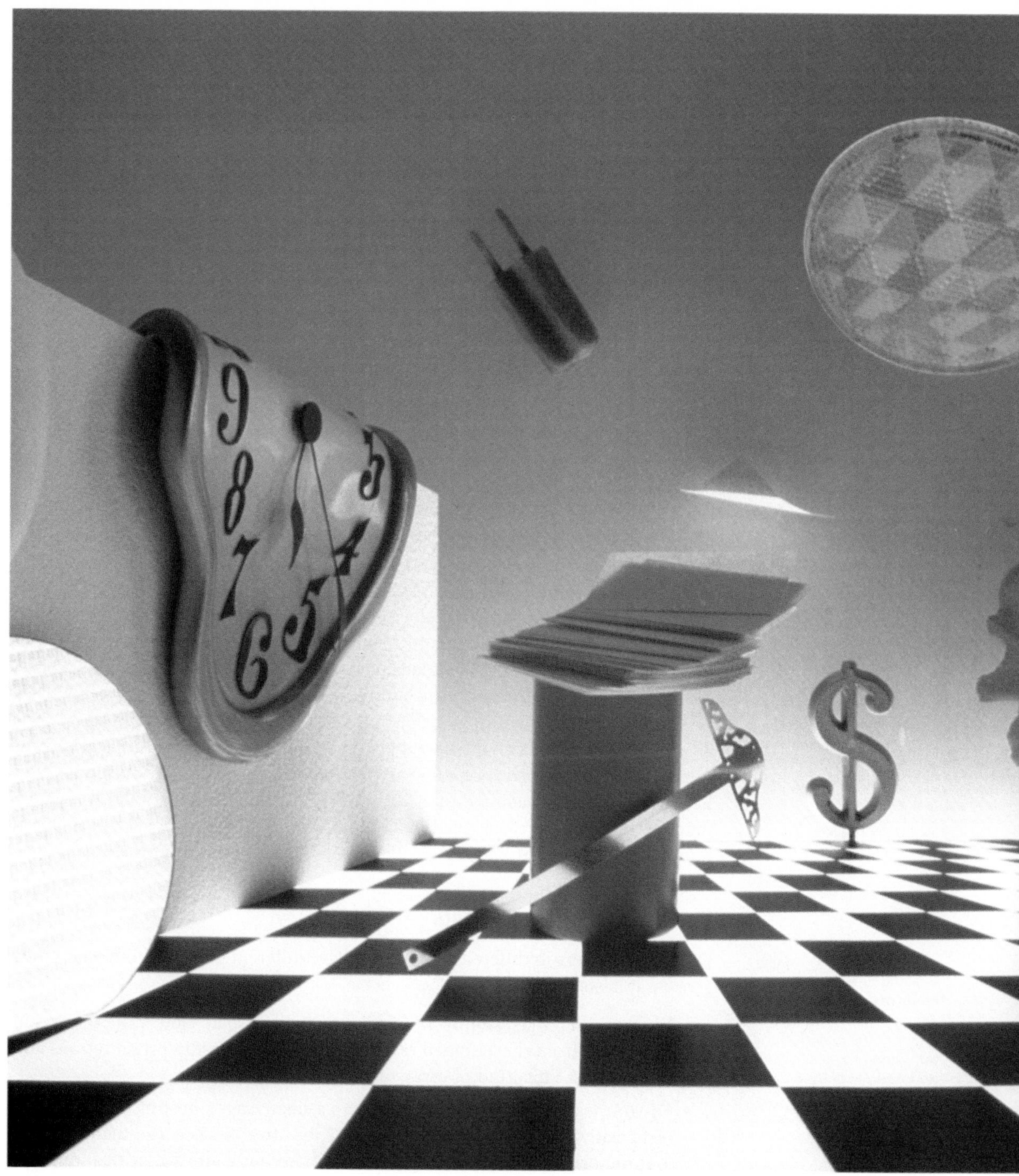

"Grasp the subject; the words will follow."
Cato the Elder

If you haven't taken an inventory with your students about their backgrounds, current academic situation, and anticipated future vis-à-vis taking essay tests, you should do so now.

Whatever subject you're studying—literature, history, biology, or human ecology—your college experience is almost certain to present you with an essay test. These tests may be short (twenty minutes seems to be the minimum) or long (graduate students taking Ph.D. preliminary exams are often asked to complete several three-hour written exams). Essay tests may be open-book, closed-book, or even a combination of the two: some professors will give you the essay question (or a short list of possible essay questions) during the class meeting before the exam so that you can mentally prepare yourself to write on those subjects, but you must then do your actual writing without the assistance of notes, books, and so forth.

Study Skills Versus Writing Skills

A number of activities can help you do well on essay tests in any subject—reading the appropriate textual material early and often, reading it *critically* (chapter 8), keeping your mind plugged in during classroom discussions (even if you don't participate orally), reviewing your class notes the evening after each class meeting, perhaps doing a little extra reading, forming study groups with your classmates, and so on. But those activities—called generically *study skills*—are not the focus of this chapter. Instead, we focus here on how you can use your *writing ability* to help you do well on essay tests.

We don't want to imply that excellent writing skills can cover ignorance of subject matter. But skill as writers can certainly allow your students to make the most of what subject knowledge they *do* have, and that can be especially important in situations in which such knowledge is not all it ideally should be.

This chapter explains and demonstrates one way to do well when you're writing essay tests; we think that by trying it out, you'll find it works well for you. Obviously, there are plenty of situations in which you'll need to adapt this advice. Moreover, if you totally ignore the study-skills part of your classes, there will be profound limitations on how well your essay tests turn out regardless of your writing ability. In this chapter we'll also let you follow a student in an environmental ethics class as she prepares for a test, writes her answer, and then talks over her essay with her teacher. Moreover, we'll give you the opportunity to write a practice test and get your classmates' and your teacher's feedback on it. First, however, let's survey the territory of essay tests themselves a bit further.

Four Kinds of Essay Tests

A good vehicle for discussing these different kinds of questions and answers is the final student paper in the previous chapter, Anne Odom's "Winter Interlude or Suicidal Deliberation?"

Different teachers in different disciplines have different goals in mind when they give essay tests:

- Your teacher may simply be asking you to display how much you can remember from the assigned reading and from classroom presentations and discussions. This kind of essay test asks you to *recall*.
- Or your teacher may be looking only in a small way for testing your memory (especially if you've already taken an "objective" test on the material) but looking principally for testing your ability to put your own critical mind to

work on the material within the assigned reading: how do you make sense of what you read, does it persuade you (and, if so, how), are there internal inconsistencies within it, and so on. This kind of essay test asks you to *analyze.*

- Or your teacher may be looking for what you can make of the material—"Show me your own thinking," your teacher may say. This kind of essay test asks you to *evaluate.* (You may need to analyze in order to evaluate, but on this kind of essay test your evaluation and its support are more important than the analysis.)
- Or your teacher may be asking you to put several different elements together—say, two or more sets of facts, or two or more pieces of reading—and explain what they add up to. This kind of essay test asks you to *synthesize.*

To do well on essay tests, you need to be able to identify which of these skills the test you are taking seems to be looking for, and you need to know how to *recall, analyze, evaluate,* and *synthesize* information: to remember and recite information, to determine particular logical relationships (such as cause and effect) within that information, to assess the significance of the information, and to put things you've already learned together with new material. (For many teachers and for many tests, often these four activities are not clearly sorted, and in fact they usually overlap.) Each activity invites a slightly different kind of test preparation and a slightly different approach to writing. In the following four sections we'll mention those particulars (of preparation and of writing) under each kind of test; then later in the chapter we'll discuss preparation and writing techniques in more detail.

You might point out to students that anticipating the kind of essay test the teacher expects them to write changes drastically depending on whether the test is open- or closed-book. Most teachers we know on the college level place little emphasis on recall when the test is open-book, and too few students appreciate that fact fully and realize its implications for the essays they write (that is, that the teacher is looking for answers that make greater use of analysis, evaluation, and synthesis).

To Recall

At a minimum, any closed-book essay test will ask you to recall information from your reading and from class discussions. Three points need to be made about this "recall" component:

1. *Deciding how much detailed information to recall is crucial.* Some situations require you to remember only broad outlines of reading material; others require quite a bit of detail. Read the exam closely and then see if you can answer this question: Is the exam designed to test (a) whether you've read and studied the material *or* (b) whether you've thought about it? Sometimes, the first option involves much more detail than the second. If you can figure out (perhaps by asking the teacher) how the test's purpose balances the two options, you may do better on the exam.
2. *Using your capacity for memory appropriately is vital.* Too many variables occur in testing situations for us to be able to tell you *how much* to rely on your memory. But we do know that you will need to use your memory and will need to have some idea of what your capacity for memory is. We can, at

least, sort out some of the most important variables for you regarding memory:

a. *Just how much detail can you remember?* Undoubtedly, how much detail you are *able* to recall will have significant bearing on how much you have at your command for the exam. To do the best job possible on the test, you need to be able to recite this material—to your roommate, to a friend, to yourself in the shower, and so on. The more times you do that, from memory, the better you'll do on this component of the exam. Memory is a flexible ability, capable of getting better the more you use it. Don't overtax your memory on any one exam, but do push it a bit more each time.

One of our favorite professors used to say, "Your brain is a muscle—the more you use it, the more it can do; the less you use it, the more you lose it." While physiologically that isn't quite true, the comparison has enough points of evocative similarity to be worth considering.

b. *What should you add to the memory component of your answer?* It's our sense, based on a combined fifty or so years of college experience, that the majority of teachers want students to do *more* than just rote memorization and recitation. A safe way for students to produce more is to bring in material from the class discussions, particularly material that has dominated one or more of those discussions. Such additions do not need to be precisely remembered; rather, you are presenting the general sense of the discussion and adding your own observations (which you may not have shared at the time of the class discussion).

Suppose, for example, an in-class discussion of "The Chrysanthemums" (from the previous chapter) had brought up consideration of just what Elisa's questions about the boxing matches at the end of the story—and her responses to Henry's answers—might suggest about what was going on inside her at that time. The teacher had brought up the *possibility* that Elisa was, because of her anger, seriously considering going to see men beat on each other. Such a point can be something a student can profitably add to the memory component of her answer (assuming, of course, that it's consistent with the rest of her reading).

3. *Determining a structure for your essay answer is important.* If you can identify the fundamental structure of the material you're to be tested on, write your test using that structure. That is, if the material has a historical or chronological structure, write it down that way; if its structure is logical, write it down that way. Using the structure of the test information for your essay answer helps you remember the information.

To Analyze

Suppose that when you're taking an essay test, your teacher asks you to go beyond summarizing the material so as to *analyze* key relationships within it. Generally such relationships are those which may not have been spelled out in the material itself (though they may well have been mentioned in class). That is, this kind of test suggests by its wording that, within whatever material the test covers, there are relationships the text itself may only have hinted at. Can you figure out those more or less hidden relationships, describe them on paper, and work out how they affect the material you've committed to memory? In that sense, this kind of test asks for *analysis*—of what you've read, heard, and been able to determine on your own. The point of such a test might be paraphrased as "Is there anything *else* important going on in this material that isn't being made explicit in it?"

We're tempted to say that this is the point of most essay tests on literature in English classes. Whether or not that's true, keep in mind that teachers in other fields may well have other, very different expectations.

Using the patterns for critical reading and critical thinking presented earlier in chapters 8 and 14 is your best guide in preparing for this kind of test. Certainly if class discussion has suggested the existence of noteworthy but unstated relationships in the material the test is to cover, you should prepare yourself mentally for writing an essay that requires you to identify and discuss those relationships.

Suppose, for example, you've been reading Nathaniel Hawthorne's short stories—"Young Goodman Brown," "The Artist of the Beautiful," "The Minister's Black Veil," and the like. Your professor might ask you to summarize three stories and discuss the role of guilt in each. *If* you've anticipated that this kind of question might come up, you can handle the important analytical component of it (that is, how guilt is important in each story). Such a discussion would strengthen your essay answer above and beyond a simple summary of the stories.

Or say that your history class has been surveying the antislavery movement in the United States during the nineteenth century and you've memorized only the important chronology (names, dates, and so on); you could thus be a little thrown by a question that asks you to analyze the role of territorial expansion in the antislavery debate through the century. But if you've read the material critically and thought about it carefully, you are more likely to see the crucial link between the slavery debate and the question of whether or not slavery should be allowed in the new territories.

If you are working by yourself, you may have limited possibilities for this "What if the professor asks us to . . . ?" preparation. Many students find that group study sessions are useful for this "what if" test preparation, both for anticipating what kinds of analytical questions may be asked and for preparing skeleton answers to those questions.

Ask students to share their group study experiences, good and bad, with the rest of the class. When someone had a good experience, ask for details about the arrangements that seemed to make it work well. When someone had a bad experience, ask for comments about why it went badly.

Many times students who are writing answers to such test questions will accidentally fall into summarizing the text's material *first*—perhaps as a way of jogging their brain to produce the analytical part of the essay. A much better plan is to (a) start your answer by tackling at least a forecast of the analytical component head-on and (b) then proceed to summarize the material after that strong first paragraph, connecting pieces of the material back to the analytical question along the way.

The paragraph-length San Francisco earthquake example (page 572) does this—if one assumes that "lessons learned" was *not* a topic mentioned in class. Or see the later example that begins with "Discuss the evolution of perspective in Renaissance painting," or see what went wrong with the essay Cindy Black writes (later in this chapter) in response to the Barry Lopez piece.

To Evaluate

What should you do when the test question says, "Evaluate A in terms of B"? The question is asking for another kind of analysis—not one seeking hidden relationships within the text but one giving you a piece of (usually) new information in light of which you will evaluate the material in the lectures and/or the text. The approaches here are similar to those discussed above under "To Analyze."

For example, if the material you're being tested on discusses the decisions a family must make about how to care for aging relatives and one of the class discussions has been a presentation of opposing views not reflected in the text, you may well want to take time during your test preparation to consider how you'd answer a question requiring that you both summarize the text's key points *and* argue the pros and cons of each (even though those pros and cons came up only in classroom discussion and weren't in the text itself).

Notice here that the extra element is provided not by the student's analysis but by some other source (here, class discussion).

Or perhaps in an engineering class you're preparing for an exam covering the unit on designing structures that are particularly resistant to earthquakes and your professor took one class meeting to discuss how lessons learned from the 1989 San Francisco earthquake might change some of what was in that unit. As part of your test preparation, it may well be a good idea to work out your answer to a question that asks you to analyze the unit's presentation of how to increase a structure's earthquake resistance based on the lessons learned from the San Francisco quake. A good answer to the earthquake question would *not* begin by summarizing the text. Rather, it would begin something like this (remember, this is *in-class* writing; don't expect too much polish):

> The four lessons learned from the San Francisco earthquake shed new light on the material presented in unit 3 of our structures textbook. In particular, the lesson about the role of the kind of soil the building is on makes that a much more important element in the design engineering process than our book suggests. Similarly, the question of whether such structures as double-decker highways can be safely built at all in earthquake-prone regions makes much of the textbook's discussion of the need to strengthen such highways almost irrelevant.

The essay would then summarize the unit's main points, or at least the ones relevant to the four lessons learned from the San Francisco quake. When the summary got to the points mentioned in the first paragraph, much more would need to be said.

To Synthesize or to Showcase

So far we have discussed questions that range from the most "closed" through increasingly "open" forms: from recall exams, in which the entire answer usually lies explicitly within the lectures and the reading material, through analytical and evaluative exams, in which you may have to do a considerable amount of "reading between the lines" to discern the more or less hidden relationships within textual material or between textual and lecture material in order to be able to write a good response. Some teachers like to ask the most open kind of question of all, the "synthetic" (or "showcase") question. Suppose, for example, your art history question reads something like this: "Choose *one* painter from this period and discuss that painter's best-known works in detail—what they were, what influences they showed, and what their role in shaping later art has been." In a way, this kind of question asks, "Pick something you know really well and dazzle me—show me just how well you can do." In that sense it's a *showcase* question. Or it might be seen to ask, "Show me what you can put together on your own out of this material," and in that sense it's *synthetic*.

You may need to remind students that *synthetic* is not always a negative term (suggesting something not genuine). We mean it here in a positive sense: bringing information together to create a new, better whole, an answer that *synthesizes.*

It's important that you realize the affinity this kind of question has with evaluative and analytical questions: *in none of these three cases will mere recitation or summary suffice.* This "synthetic" or "showcase" kind of question also requires material that goes beyond what is explicit in the lectures or text, but in this case the teacher has left it to you to decide on the focus of that analytical material. That is, you may choose to answer by saying, "The painter ____________ 's works exemplify the best and the worst of Renaissance art in England. In their

___________ they are among the best, and in their ___________ they are among the worst." Your essay would then go on to summarize the painter's works, tying them to these two points (that you yourself have selected) when and where doing so is appropriate.

This kind of question can be the easiest to answer *if* you've anticipated the possibility of its being asked. But answering it can be difficult if you've studied material in *depth* (a few points very closely) but not much in *breadth* (several points, none of them quite so closely). Obviously, the premium here is on anticipating such a question. Some teachers always include one such question; others never do. There's a sense in which this kind of question can be as difficult for teachers to grade as it is for students to write, because it asks not for a single "right" answer but, rather, for any number of different answers that may be varying degrees of good. Obviously, this kind of question repays extensive recall work. Whatever you decide to write about, the more sheer facts you can remember, the better. Equally obviously, you've got to have something of your own, some judgment or higher-level claim (that is, analysis and evaluation) that you can tie all that recall summary to.

When you're writing an answer to a synthetic or showcase question, you can choose either (a) to begin with summary and bring up larger issues as appropriate or (b) to start out (as with the analytical or evaluative questions) with at least a forecast of what larger issues give meaning to the summary. The important point is to make sure, once again, that you get beyond summary—somewhere, somehow.

How to Prepare for Essay Tests

Here we'll go into more detail about certain techniques for preparing for essay tests, techniques specifically tailored to the idea that *writing* is at the heart of all such tests; these are the techniques that other books, more subject specialized, may not cover. Though in the previous sections we've anticipated most of these techniques, here we'll discuss them on their own.

We've already talked about the kinds of study skills needed to prepare for essay tests (see page 568) and certainly are not the first to give you such advice. Let's now return to two key points: (a) how much and what to remember and (b) what to add over and above what the material itself offers—with specific attention to how you *write* your essay test.

How Much and What to Remember

Obviously, how best to prepare for any test depends on the course, the teacher, and the kind of test you anticipate. Probably the best advice along those lines is to know the textual material so well that you can substantially re-create it from memory. This technique requires remembering the structure of the chapter, often reflected in terms of the pattern of headings and subheadings. You may even need to memorize the core of that structure. Then you need to know the material well enough to be able to play back in your mind what goes on under each of those headings.

For example, suppose you're being tested on chapter 3 of your art history textbook, the chapter titled "The Renaissance Comes to England." At the very least you need to be able to explain that chapter's connections with those just before and after it, the gist of the material that chapter covers, the chapter's main parts (such as "Music," "Painting," and "Theater"), and the coverage in each part. That is, you will *always* need to be able to summarize the reading at some level. But do you need to know the names of specific composers, painters, and dramatists; the names and dates of their principal works; and what other Renaissance works of art they were influenced by? Do you need to be able to describe in detail only one key work by each artist, or three such works?

In trying to find the best answer to such questions, look again at two key variables to consider:

1. *Just how much detail can you remember?* Memory works best when it's used *hierarchically.* Thus, by asking your mind to remember the material *only* one level at a time, you can usually work your way pretty deep into the material. Thus, you would remember *first* that the chapter you are being tested on is one of a sequence of four chapters in unit 1 of the book (name them); then, that the name of the chapter is ________ ; that the chapter explains ________ ; and that the chapter has three parts, ________ , ________ , and ________ . You can recall that part 1, ________ , covers the years ________ ; that three key painters discussed here are ________ , ________ , and ________ ; that the first painter, ________ , lived from ________ to ________ and spent most of his time in the city of ________ ; and that his most important paintings are ________ , ________ , ________ , and ________ .

    The accompanying figure graphically illustrates the hierarchical nature of memory; an engineer would call this a "right-branching tree structure." How *deep* into that tree (how far to the right) can *your* memory take you, keeping in mind that you'll need to be able to work your way through the whole chapter this way? Would you have stopped with "three key painters are," or can you make your brain work well enough to remember more, so that you can go on with "his most important paintings are ________ , ________ , ________ , and ________ ; the first of these, ________ , depicts ________ ; in this painting, his use of ________ shows the influence of ________ ; [and so on]"?

    Doing your memory work hierarchically will help you be able to remember more than you otherwise might. As we said earlier, to do the best job possible on the test, you need to be able to recite this material—to your roommate, to a friend, to yourself, and so on. The more times you do that, from memory, the better you'll do on this component of the exam.

    One of the problems with this practice-recitation approach is that it's easy to fool yourself. Another problem is that many people find they have to

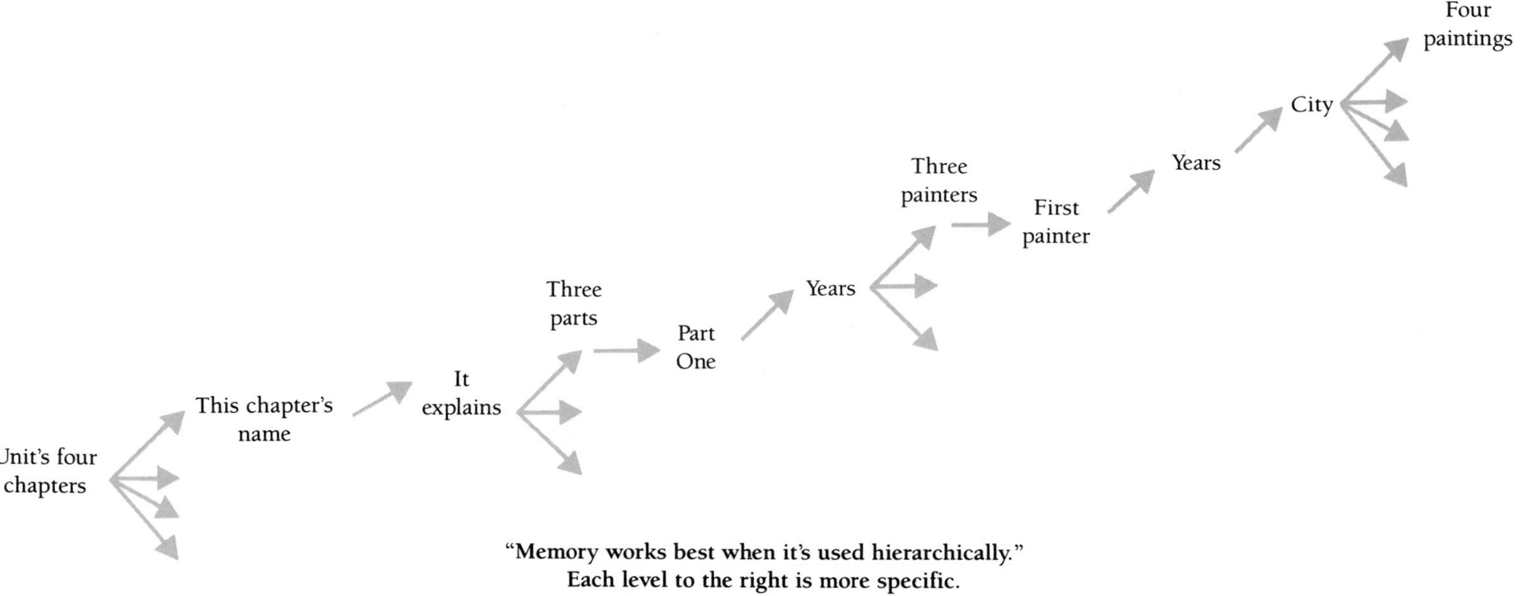

"Memory works best when it's used hierarchically." Each level to the right is more specific.

We've taken a long time to lead up to this point—that practice in *writing down* anticipated answers in important situations makes the actual writing go better—because we want it to be persuasive enough to change the way your students prepare for essay exams. It's a crucial technique, and too few students take advantage of it.

do numerous repetitions before the material becomes something they truly know. Finally, *saying* something is inevitably different from *writing* it. The way to solve all these problems—and the best way to practice knowing that information from memory—is to *practice writing it down.* (Long before anyone wrote anything into a computer's memory, human beings were writing vast amounts of information into their own memories.) If you can anticipate big chunks of the material the test will cover, why not practice writing the test a few times? There's no better way to see for yourself how much or how little of the material you actually have in your memory, and no better way to "write" that material more firmly into your own memory.

Yes, prewriting tests is tedious. Yes, it's work. Most important, yes, it does pay big dividends.

2. *What should you add to the memory component of your answer?* Sometimes a student writes an essay exam that rigorously but *only* summarizes the reading. That's what some teachers want, but most teachers want more. What could you add to that rigorous summary? How about some material from class discussions, material that isn't directly in the textbook but that shaped one or more substantial pieces of classroom discussion? Wouldn't your essay inevitably be a better piece of writing if you added to it something like, "As we discussed in class, there were also important influences on these painters that had little to do with the Renaissance in art but had more to do with closely associated political events. In particular, the court of . . . " What you're doing here is adding to your essay something beyond rote memory of the text, something that, because it's basically your notes from a class discussion, you're certain does not put you at great risk. Thus, whereas the first variable to consider when deciding how much detail to commit to memory concerns just how much detail your memory can hold, the second variable concerns what and how much *you* want to add to your memory-work part of the essay.

   Options for what you can add beyond what's in the text itself include material from class discussions, material from other reading you've done on your own, and material you've figured out for yourself.

Should you choose to go beyond bringing in material presented in class—which is really still memory work—you're into the next component of writing good essay tests: analyzing and evaluating the material, a component that involves figuring out on your own some aspect of the material. (If this sounds like a more challenging kind of intellectual exercise than simple recall, you're right—it is.)

Figuring It out on Your Own

To prepare for writing a more analytical or evaluative kind of exam, you need to do a good job of *critical reading,* as described in chapter 8. While you probably cannot anticipate the particular angle on the reading material your teacher will ask you to take on the test, you can certainly improve your chances of doing well on the exam by reading the material as critically as possible. Why? Because the better you *understand* the material, the better you'll do on any test of your understanding—which is what this kind of essay test is. For your convenience, here again are the questions we stress to our students for critical reading. (We've reordered them here to serve these purposes a little better.)

1. What is the overall structure of the piece?
2. What are the important generalizations that are made in the piece?
   a. What kind of generalizations are they?
      (1) Are they statements of fact?
      (2) Are they logical claims (judgments)?
      (3) Are they emotional assertions?
      (4) Are they some other kind of judgment?
3. How are those generalizations supported?
   a. What *facts* support those generalizations?
   b. What *arguments* support those generalizations?
   c. What *other kinds* of support are there in the piece?
4. How adequate is the support for the claims:
   a. Is it the right kind of support?
   b. Is it the right amount of support?
5. How close is the support to the claim:
   a. Are there middle steps between the support and the claim that are weak? If so, what are they?
   b. Are there unstated assumptions that join the support and the claim that need to be made explicit? If so, what are they?
6. What kind of personality does the author's voice in the text project?
7. What kind of expertise does the author's voice reflect?
8. What is the overall tone of the piece?
9. What kind of picture of the reader does the text project?
10. What knowledge does the author assume the reader brings to the text?
11. What does the author assume the reader's attitude toward the subject to be?
12. What appeal seems dominant in the piece: logical, ethical, or emotional?

You would do well here to choose one of this book's earlier pieces that students have read, perhaps chapter 14's "The Crisis in U.S. Science and Mathematics Education"; bring in an overhead projector with a transparency of the essay and a marking pen; and "walk" your students through the process of annotating the piece according to these questions. If your students are reluctant to mark in their texts, you can ask them to bring in photocopies of the piece (it's short).

Perhaps the author's tone in places isn't quite matter-of-fact; maybe some irony is involved. That could indicate a place where you could open up the text a bit. Or perhaps the text makes three key points, but one of them has only a tenth of the support of the other two. Or maybe two of the three key points are supported with facts, while one is supported mostly with argument. What are the *issues* involved in the material as it is presented? In each case, you need to be reading the material carefully enough to *feel* that little anomaly, to probe it, and to ask many questions about it.

What we're talking about here is, of course, beyond memory work; we're talking about *understanding*. If you haven't tried to understand the material (if you've focused only on memorizing it) before the test and your teacher asks you the kind of question that requires understanding, you're in trouble.

How to Write Essay Tests

To summarize our presentation so far, preparing for the writing part of an essay test involves deciding what kind of skills you think the test will require; figuring out how much you yourself are going to try to learn; reading the material critically to look for hidden relationships, paying particular attention to the material's structure; and prewriting the exam. All these activities need to be part of your preparation for the exam. Now let's look at the actual writing of the essay.

Suppose that as part of the art history class we've been discussing you go to the library and carefully study a book of a hundred paintings from the English Renaissance. Then the exam's question says, "Discuss the evolution of perspective in . . . " Some students might be thrown, for "perspective" never comes up in the textbook as a major issue; it receives only occasional mention as one of the aspects of English paintings that changed during the Renaissance. The only students who will do well on such a test are those who go beyond *remembering* the material to attempt to *understand* it. In this case, understanding what *perspective* means and knowing instances of how it was affected or changed during the Renaissance are vital to a successful answer.

Notice that in terms of the first part of this chapter, this test asks students to *analyze*, despite that the teacher says, "Discuss." Every teacher we know uses a fairly imprecise vocabulary for such things, frequently making little distinction in the way the test question or prompt is written. Students need to be aware of this factor and make their own decisions about what the teacher is actually looking for.

Or suppose you've read a chapter in your history textbook about the role of the emerging middle class in the French Revolution and the test question instead asks you about the role of the large, baronial estate holders in the revolution. How can you have prepared to write on that subject? Only by thinking about how the rise of the middle class could affect the upper classes—something implicit, but not explicit, in the reading. In other words, you need to have worked hard to understand the material on your own—through critical reading, critical thinking, or perhaps working through the material with classmates in study groups.

However you come to that understanding, how do you write an essay exam that reflects it? Suppose the essay question you're responding to says not "Summarize the effects of the Renaissance on artists in England" but "Summarize the effects of the Renaissance on artists in England with particular attention to the way political winds within the court helped shape the careers and works of key artists in the period." At this point, you're being asked a question not only of *fact* but also of *analysis*. Another way to phrase the question is, "What do you make of what you've read in the textbook in light of the class discussion we had about court politics in England?"

Keep in mind that you probably *do* still need to *summarize* the textual material. In fact, one of the ways students go wrong on essay exams that ask this kind of question is to dive right into analysis without making sure they also demonstrate that they recall the material. The *easiest* way to write this kind of exam response is first to summarize the material and then to do your analysis. That approach works *if* you're positive you'll have time to get to the last section, in which you'll do the analysis that truly answers the essay question. If there is *any* chance you won't have enough time to do that analysis, you'd better take a different tack.

Once again, the proportions of recall versus analysis change drastically depending on whether the exam is open- or closed-book.

A *safer* approach to writing this kind of essay is to summarize your analytical points first. That is, if you have three or four points you want to make in general about how political developments in the court helped shape the art of the day, make them briefly in your opening paragraph(s). Then, as you write your next paragraphs, reciting what you remember about each painter and so on from the text, you'll have that foundation of evaluation to come back to and to build on. (But do remember to get back to the analytical points.)

Probably the *worst* way to handle this kind of assignment is to try to do the analysis and the summary at the same time. If you had time to plan your essay carefully, write it, and rewrite it, you might be able to pull that off. But under the pressure of a timed, in-class essay exam, attempting to produce the kind of complicated structure that would make this plan work is more than many students can accomplish. What typically happens when a student tries to do factual summary and analysis simultaneously on an essay exam is that the first few topics (here, maybe painters 1, 2, and 3) get fully developed but then time starts to run out and things get pretty chaotic. Nothing—neither summary nor analysis—gets done thoroughly.

We can make the same point another way: when the question asks you to compare one piece of given material (say, an issue that dominated class discussion one day) with another piece of given material (say, from the textbook), it's best to put *first* what you think is most important from the comparison. Although you can develop that material more as you go through the recitation part of your essay, it's best to begin with it because that's obviously an important part of what the teacher was looking for when he or she wrote the question. Cindy Black's essay exam, included later in this chapter, shows this technique.

Perhaps the biggest difference between this and the other kinds of tests is the way you write it. The pattern to use is more like the recall pattern than the analysis or evaluation pattern. Nevertheless, you still need to avoid doing pure recitation; whatever significant generalizations you have discovered or learned during your study need to be brought in, but here you bring them in as they naturally come up, not deliberately at the beginning.

So much for the general structure of your essay. Here are a few additional test-taking tips, many of them frequently covered in study-skills courses, that will help you in the writing of essay tests as well:

Underline Key Words in the Question. Teachers will tell you that it's a frequent error made by students to *forget to answer* a key part of the question. To avoid this error, underline the question's key points. For example, the question used earlier in this chapter, with its most important points underlined, would look like this: "Summarize the effects of the Renaissance on artists in England with particular attention to the way political winds within the court helped shape the careers and works of key artists in the period."

Outline Your Answer. Here's your chance to take the advice we've given you in this chapter. What should the basic structure of the answer to the question above look like? Do you want to make your first statements about (a) the effects of the Renaissance on artists in England, (b) political winds within the court, or (c) the interaction of items a and b? We believe it's best to have an introductory paragraph that makes it clear you intend to look at the interaction of items a and b in your answer, perhaps even giving a brief summary of those political winds, however you choose to proceed from there. You might then want to single out three artists to discuss, artists whose works you know you can relate to political activity within the court. Accordingly, your brief outline (and all you really have time for in this setting is a brief outline) might look like this:

1. [Forecast of structure] How movements in the court affected artists A, B, and C
2. Court and ____________ (artist A)
3. Court and ____________ (artist B)
4. Court and ____________ (artist C)

Alternatively, you might summarize the movements in the court as item 2, especially if you would otherwise have to trace pretty much the same territory in 2–4 above. Thus you might have a "scratch outline" that looks like this:

1. [Forecast of structure] How movements in the court affected artists A, B, and C
2. Summary of movements in the court
3. Court and ____________ (artist A)
4. Court and ____________ (artist B)
5. Court and ____________ (artist C)

Budget Your Time. Essay tests generally cover an hour or less. How many good points can you make in that time? To some extent, that depends on how well you know the material and on whether you have to spend much time stopping and thinking about it. For us, taking essay tests draws more on what we *already* know than on what we can *figure out at the time.* If, then, you spend the whole hour writing, how many key points can you cover—maybe five? In other words, the five-part outline above is all you *can* do, and even doing that much is going to require keeping a close eye on the clock. Look at it this way—to do a five-part essay in the fifty minutes most college "hours" amount to requires doing one part of the answer every ten minutes and not stopping. The only way you can do that is by budgeting your time rigorously.

Cover the Basics. If you do what you've got outlined to do, will you have satisfied the question? Go back to underlining the key points in the question—will the answer you write deal with those key points? Again, this question requests discussion of key artists in relationship to the court; whatever else you do, you must show that you know that material.

Add Something of Your Own. You may be resourceful enough to bring in information from additional reading you've done or from your learnings in another course so as to enrich your answer. Doing so is a fine idea so long as you don't sacrifice covering the basics and so long as you're sure the additional information is accurate and relevant. In terms of the question we've been discussing here, such information might concern how the court in Renaissance England had one kind of effect on artists, whereas later courts had different ones.

Remember that the Quality of Your Communication Counts—Can the Reader Follow What You Say? You can't afford to be incoherent, even though it's an in-class essay you're writing. Such essays have a particular emphasis on larger-scale structural elements; therefore, make sure that your short introduction clearly lays out what you're going to do, that your paragraphing reflects the essay's structure, and that your sentences don't get so long that you yourself lose track of where they're going.

How to Improve on Your Next Test

One of the ways any student can get better grades is to study his or her past performance on tests in order to improve it on future ones. We're talking here about something beyond "I need to study more" (which, of course, is also a valid response); we're talking about looking at how you *wrote* your previous essay test as a way of perhaps improving on the next one. In this, there are two specific techniques we recommend for improving on your next essay exam:

1. *Review your performance yourself, right after the exam.* Did you feel like you had budgeted your writing time wisely? Or did you run out of time before you had used half of what you intended to say? Did you manage to fulfill the structure you set out to do, or did you have to skip over some key points? Were you able to fall into some of the patterns of answers you had prewritten before the exam, or did you feel you were writing things for the first time? Depending on how you answer these questions, you may want to change your procedure on subsequent exams.
2. *Review your performance with the teacher.* Once you get your exam back, make an appointment to review with your teacher the *way* the exam is written. Questions about "Why did I get this grade?" or "How is this answer wrong?" are different from questions about "How could I have changed the *writing* in this test so as to get a better grade?"

If you give your students a practice exam as part of this chapter, ask each to write a short paragraph evaluating his or her performance immediately on finishing the exam. Students can keep those evaluations and bring them in the day you hand back their exams with your own evaluation. An interesting class meeting ensues when students compare their own evaluations and yours!

a. Does the teacher feel that you focused appropriately on the material the question sought, or that you misunderstood what was being asked?

b. Does the teacher feel that you tried to cover too much and thus were too superficial, or that you were too narrow?

c. Most important, did you understand what kind of question the teacher was asking—was it a question looking for recall, analysis, evaluation, or synthesis? If you can improve how well you understand what *kind* of test the teacher is giving, you'll nearly always improve your performance.

SAMPLE WRITING ASSIGNMENT AND CASE STUDY CLOSE-UP

Here we want to follow one typical student as she prepares for an essay exam, take a look at the exam she wrote, and look in on her conference with her teacher after the graded exam has been returned to her. Our student, Cindy Black, is a second-semester freshman in Environmental Ethics 101, her first elective course in college. The teacher has been talking about the complicated motives of the different groups of people (or "constituencies") who want to exercise some voice in how the wilderness lands in the United States are used. Hunters, lumber companies, environmentalists, native Americans, the Bureau of Land Management, farmers, ranchers, and so on—all seem to have different notions of proper wilderness management. Because all have different motives driving them, even when they *do* advocate the same course of action it's often for divergent reasons. The teacher assigns Cindy's class to read the following essay, "Gone Back into the Earth," by Barry Lopez, and to be prepared on returning to class to write a twenty-minute essay on it, a closed-book exam. The purpose of the test, he says, is to emphasize to the class the value of close, critical reading and to test students' ability to remember what they've read. Here's the essay; as you read it, envision what you would do to study for an essay test over it.

Gone Back into the Earth

BARRY LOPEZ

Barry Lopez won the National Book Award in nonfiction for Arctic Dreams. *He also has written* Of Wolves and Men, Winter Count *(fiction), and* Crossing Open Ground *(essays, from which this selection is taken). He says, "A writer has a certain handful of questions. . . . Mine seem to be the issues of tolerance and dignity. You can't sit down and write directly about those things, but if they are on your mind and if you're a writer, they're going to come out in one form or another. The form I feel most comfortable with, where I do a lot of reading and aimless thinking, is in natural history."*

For an essay on the same subject that differs, at least superficially, you might look at the selection from John McPhee's *Encounters with the Archdruid* that is printed in *The John McPhee Reader.*

I am up to my waist in a basin of cool, acid-clear water, at the head of a box canyon some 600 feet above the Colorado River. I place my outstretched hands flat against a terminal wall of dark limestone which rises more than a 1 hundred feet above me, and down which a sheet of water falls—the thin creek in whose pooled waters I now stand. The water splits at my fingertips into wild threads; higher up, a warm canyon wind lifts water off the limestone in a fine spray; these droplets intercept and shatter sunlight. Down, down another four waterfalls and fern-shrouded pools below, the water spills into an eddy of the Colorado River, in the shadow of a huge boulder. Our boat is tied there.

2 This lush crease in the surface of the earth is a cleft in the precipitous desert walls of Arizona's Grand Canyon. Its smooth outcrops of purple-tinged travertine stone, its heavy air rolled in the languid perfume of columbine, struck by the sharp notes of a water ouzel, the trill of a disturbed black phoebe—all this has a name: Elves Chasm.

3 A few feet to my right, a preacher from Maryland is staring straight up at a blue sky, straining to see what flowers those are that nod at the top of the falls. To my left a freelance automobile mechanic from Colorado sits with an impish smile by helleborine orchids. Behind, another man, a builder and sometime record producer from New York, who comes as often as he can to camp and hike in the Southwest, stands immobile at the pool's edge.

4 Sprawled shirtless on a rock is our boatman. He has led twelve or fifteen of us on the climb up from the river. The Colorado entrances him. He has a well-honed sense of the ridiculous, brought on, one believes, by so much time in the extreme remove of this canyon.

5 In our descent we meet others in our group who stopped climbing at one of the lower pools. At the second to the last waterfall, a young woman with short hair and dazzling blue eyes walks with me back into the canyon's narrowing V. We wade into a still pool, swim a few strokes to its head, climb over a boulder, swim across a second pool and then stand together, giddy, in the press of limestone, beneath the deafening cascade—filled with euphoria.

6 One at a time we bolt and glide, fishlike, back across the pool, grounding in fine white gravel. We wade the second pool and continue our descent, stopping to marvel at the strategy of a barrel cactus and at the pale shading of color in the ledges to which we cling. We share few words. We know hardly anything of each other. We share the country.

7 The group of us who have made this morning climb are in the middle of a ten-day trip down the Colorado River. Each day we are upended, if not by some element of the landscape itself then by what the landscape does, visibly, to each of us. It has snapped us like fresh-laundered sheets.

8 After lunch, we reboard three large rubber rafts and enter the Colorado's quick, high flow. The river has not been this high or fast since Glen Canyon Dam—135 miles above Elves Chasm, 17 miles above our starting point at Lee's Ferry—was closed in 1963. Jumping out ahead of us, with its single oarsman and three passengers, is our fourth craft, a twelve-foot rubber boat, like a water strider with a steel frame. In Sockdolager Rapid the day before, one of its welds burst and the steel pieces were bent apart. (Sockdolager: a nineteenth-century colloquialism for knockout punch.)

Some of your students may well have had "group wilderness adventure" experiences of their own. If so, you might ask them to share those experiences with the class.

Such groups as ours, the members all but unknown to each other on the first day, almost always grow close, solicitous of each other, during their time together. They develop a humor that informs similar journeys everywhere, a humor founded in tomfoolery, in punning, in a continuous parody of the life-in-civilization all have so recently (and gleefully) left. Such humor depends on context, on an accretion of small, shared events; it seems silly to those who are not there. It is not, of course. Any more than that moment of fumbling awe one feels on seeing the Brahma schist at the dead bottom of the canyon's Inner Gorge. Your fingertips graze the 1.9-billion-old stone as the boat drifts slowly past. 9

With the loss of self-consciousness, the landscape opens. 10

There are forty-one of us, counting a crew of six. An actor from Florida, now living in Los Angeles. A medical student and his wife. A supervisor from Virginia's Department of Motor Vehicles. A health-store owner from Chicago. An editor from New York and his young son. 11

That kind of diversity seems normal in groups that seek such vacations—to trek in the Himalaya, to dive in the Sea of Cortez, to go birding in the Arctic. We are together for two reasons: to run the Colorado River, and to participate with jazz musician Paul Winter, who initiated the trip, in a music workshop. 12

Winter is an innovator and a listener. He had thought for years about coming to the Grand Canyon, about creating music here in response to this particular landscape—collared lizards and prickly pear cactus, Anasazi Indian ruins and stifling heat. But most especially he wanted music evoked by the river and the walls that flew up from its banks—Coconino sandstone on top of Hermit shale on top of the Supai formations, stone exposed to sunlight, a bloom of photons that lifted colors—saffron and ochre, apricot, madder orange, pearl and gray green, copper reds, umber and terra-cotta browns—and left them floating in the air. 13

Paul Winter's music is widely available. If you play some of it for your class, students will have a richer perspective on this aspect of Lopez's essay.

Winter was searching for a reintegration of music, landscape and people. For resonance. Three or four times during the trip he would find it for sustained periods: drifting on a quiet stretch of water below Bass Rapids with oboist Nancy Rumbel and cellist David Darling; in a natural amphitheater high in the Muav limestone of Matkatameba Canyon; on the night of a full June moon with euphonium player Larry Roark in Blacktail Canyon. 14

Winter's energy and passion, and the strains of solo and ensemble music, were sewn into the trip like prevailing winds, like the canyon wren's clear, whistled, descending notes, his glissando—seemingly present, close by or at a distance, whenever someone stopped to listen. 15

But we came and went, too, like the swallows and swifts that flicked over the water ahead of the boats, intent on private thoughts. 16

On the second day of the trip we stopped at Redwall Cavern, an undercut recess that spans a beach of fine sand, perhaps 500 feet wide by 150 feet deep. Winter intends to record here, but the sand absorbs too much sound. 17

Unfazed, the others toss a Frisbee, practice Tai-chi, jog, meditate, play recorders, and read novels.

18 No other animal but the human would bring to bear so many activities, from so many different cultures and levels of society, with so much energy, so suddenly in a new place. And no other animal, the individuals so entirely unknown to each other, would chance together something so unknown as this river journey. In this frenetic activity and difference seems a suggestion of human evolution and genuine adventure. We are not the first down this river, but in the sloshing of human hands at the water's edge, the swanlike notes of an oboe, the occasional hugs among those most afraid of the rapids, there *is* exploration.

19 Each day we see or hear something that astounds us. The thousand-year-old remains of an Anasazi footbridge, hanging in twilight shadow high in the canyon wall above Harding Rapid. Deer Creek Falls, where we stand knee-deep in turquoise water encircled by a rainbow. Havasu Canyon, wild with grapevines, cottonwoods and velvet ash, speckled dace and mule deer, wild grasses and crimson monkey flowers. Each evening we enjoy a vespers: cicadas and crickets, mourning doves, vermilion flycatchers. And the wind, for which chimes are hung in a salt cedar. These notes leap above the splash and rattle, the grinding of water and the roar of rapids.

20 The narrow, damp, hidden worlds of the side canyons, with their scattered shards of Indian pottery and ghost imprints of 40-million-year-old nautiloids, open onto the larger world of the Colorado River itself; but nothing conveys to us how far into the earth's surface we have come. Occasionally we glimpse the South Rim, four or five thousand feet above. From the rims the canyon seems oceanic; at the surface of the river the feeling is intimate. To someone up there with binoculars we seem utterly remote down here. It is this known dimension of distance and time and the perplexing question posed by the canyon itself—What is consequential? (in one's life, in the life of human beings, in the life of a planet)—that reverberate constantly, and make the human inclination to judge (another person, another kind of thought) seem so eerie.

21 Two kinds of time pass here: sitting at the edge of a sun-warmed pool watching blue dragonflies and black tadpoles. And the rapids: down the glassy-smooth tongue into a yawning trench, climb a ten-foot wall of standing water and fall into boiling, ferocious hydraulics, sucking whirlpools, drowned voices, stopped hearts. Rapids can fold and shatter boats and take lives if the boatman enters at the wrong point or at the wrong angle.

22 Some rapids, like one called Hermit, seem more dangerous than they are and give us great roller-coaster rides. Others—Hance, Crystal, Upset—seem less spectacular, but are technically difficult. At Crystal, our boat screeches and twists against its frame. Its nose crumples like cardboard in the trough; our boatman makes the critical move to the right with split-second timing and we are over a standing wave and into the haystacks of white water, safely into the tail waves. The boatman's eyes cease to blaze.

The first few rapids—Badger Creek and Soap Creek—do not overwhelm us. When we hit the Inner Gorge—Granite Falls, Unkar Rapid, Horn Creek Rapid—some grip the boat, rigid and silent. (On the ninth day, when we are about to run perhaps the most formidable rapid, Lava Falls, the one among us who has had the greatest fear is calm, almost serene. In the last days, it is hard to overestimate what the river and the music and the unvoiced concern for each other have washed out.) 23

There are threats to this separate world of the Inner Gorge. Down inside it one struggles to maintain a sense of what they are, how they impinge. 24

In 1963, Glen Canyon Dam cut off the canyon's natural flow of water. Spring runoffs of more than two hundred thousand cubic feet per second ceased to roar through the gorge, clearing the main channel of rock and stones washed down from the side canyons. Fed now from the bottom of Lake Powell backed up behind the dam, the river is no longer a warm, silt-laden habitat for Colorado squawfish, razorback sucker and several kinds of chub, but a cold, clear habitat for trout. With no annual scouring and a subsequent deposition of fresh sand, the beaches show the evidence of continuous human use: they are eroding. The postflood eddies where squawfish bred have disappeared. Tamarisk (salt cedar) and camel thorn, both exotic plants formerly washed out with the spring floods, have gained an apparently permanent foothold. At the old high-water mark, catclaw acacia, mesquite and Apache plume are no longer watered and are dying out. 25

On the rim, far removed above, such evidence of human tampering seems, and perhaps is, pernicious. From the river, another change is more wrenching. It floods the system with a kind of panic that in other animals induces nausea and the sudden evacuation of the bowels: it is the descent of helicopters. Their sudden arrival in the canyon evokes not jeers but staring. The violence is brutal, an intrusion as criminal and as random as rape. When the helicopter departs, its rotor-wind walloping against the stone walls, I want to wash the sound off my skin. 26

The canyon finally absorbs the intrusion. I focus quietly each day on the stone, the breathing of time locked up here, back to the Proterozoic, before there were seashells. Look up to wisps of high cirrus overhead, the hint of a mare's tail sky. Close my eyes: tappet of water against the boat, sound of an Anasazi's six-hole flute. And I watch the bank for beaver tracks, for any movement. 27

The canyon seems like a grandfather. 28

One evening, Winter and perhaps half the group carry instruments and recording gear back into Blacktail Canyon to a spot sound engineer Mickey Houlihan says is good for recording. 29

Winter likes to quote from Thoreau: "The woods would be very silent if no birds sang except those that sing best." The remark seems not only to underscore the ephemeral nature of human evolution but the necessity in evaluating any phenomenon—a canyon, a life, a song—of providing for change. 30

31 After several improvisations dominated by a cappella voice and percussion, Winter asks Larry Roark to try something on the euphonium; he and Rumbel and Darling will then come up around him. Roark is silent. Moonlight glows on the canyon's lips. There is the sound of gurgling water. After a word of encouragement, feeling shrouded in anonymous darkness like the rest of us, Larry puts his mouth to the horn.

32 For a while he is alone. God knows what visions of waterfalls or wrens, of boats in the rapids, of Bach or Mozart, are in his head, in his fingers, to send forth notes. The whine of the soprano sax finds him. And the flutter of the oboe. And the rumbling of the choral cello. The exchange lasts perhaps twenty minutes. Furious and sweet, anxious, rolling, delicate and raw. The last six or eight hanging notes are Larry's. Then there is a long silence. Winter finally says, "My God."

33 I feel, sitting in the wet dark in bathing suit and sneakers and T-shirt, that my fingers have brushed one of life's deep, coursing threads. Like so much else in the canyon, it is left alone. Speak, even notice it, and it would disappear.

34 I had come to the canyon with expectations. I had wanted to see snowy egrets flying against the black schist at dusk; I saw blue-winged teal against the deep green waters at dawn. I had wanted to hear thunder rolling in the thousand-foot depths; I heard Winter's soprano sax resonating in Matkatameba Canyon, with the guttural caws of four ravens which circled above him. I had wanted to watch rattlesnakes; I saw in an abandoned copper mine, in the beam of my flashlight, a wall of copper sulphate that looked like a wall of turquoise. I rose each morning at dawn and washed in the cold river. I went to sleep each night listening to the cicadas, the pencil-ticking sound of some other insect, the soughing of river waves in tamarisk roots, and watching bats plunge and turn, looking like leaves blown around against the sky. What any of us had come to see or do fell away. We found ourselves at each turn with what we had not imagined.

35 The last evening it rained. We had left the canyon and been carried far out onto Lake Mead by the river's current. But we stood staring backward, at the point where the canyon had so obviously and abruptly ended.

36 A thought that stayed with me was that I had entered a private place in the earth. I had seen exposed nearly its oldest part. I had lost my sense of urgency, rekindled a sense of what people were, clambering to gain access to high waterfalls where we washed our hair together; and a sense of our endless struggle as a species to understand time and to estimate the consequences of our acts.

37 It rained the last evening. But before it did, Nancy Rumbel moved to the highest point on Scorpion Island in Lake Mead and played her oboe before a storm we could see hanging over Nevada. Sterling Smyth, who would return to programming computers in twenty-four hours, created a twelve-string imitation of the canyon wren, a long guitar solo. David Darling, revealed suddenly stark, again and then again, against a white-lightning sky, bowed furious homage to the now overhanging cumulonimbus.

In the morning we touched the far shore of Lake Mead, boarded a bus 38
and headed for the Las Vegas airport. We were still wrapped in the journey, as though it were a Navajo blanket. We departed on various planes and arrived home in various cities and towns and at some point the world entered again and the hardest thing, the translation of what we had touched, began.

I sat in the airport in San Francisco, waiting for a connecting flight to 39
Oregon, dwelling on one image. At the mouth of Nankoweap Canyon, the river makes a broad turn, and it is possible to see high in the orange rock what seem to be four small windows. They are entrances to granaries, built by the Anasazi who dwelled in the canyon a thousand years ago. This was provision against famine, to ensure the people would survive.

I do not know, really, how we will survive without places like the Inner 40
Gorge of the Grand Canyon to visit. Once in a lifetime, even, is enough. To feel the stripping down, an ebb of the press of conventional time, a radical change of proportion, an unspoken respect for others that elicits keen emotional pleasure, a quick, intimate pounding of the heart.

Some parts of the trip will emerge one day on an album. Others will be 41
found in a gesture of friendship to some stranger in an airport, in a letter of outrage to a planner of dams, in a note of gratitude to nameless faces in the Park Service, in wondering at the relatives of the ubiquitous wren, in the belief, passed on in whatever fashion—a photograph, a chord, a sketch—that nature can heal.

The living of life, any life, involves great and private pain, much of which 42
we share with no one. In such places as the Inner Gorge the pain trails away from us. It is not so quiet there or so removed that you can hear yourself think, that you would even wish to; that comes later. You can hear your heart beat. That comes first.

How to Study for an Essay Test on This Piece

Consider these questions:

1. *How much of the piece's factual presentation would you want to remember?*
   a. What's the author's name?
   b. What kind of trip is it, for how long, and where does it go?
   c. Who is on the trip with the author?
   d. What key incidents occur along the way?
2. *But would this kind of factual study of the piece be enough?* Aren't there important aspects of it—perhaps the *most* important aspects of it—that are not, strictly speaking, reflected in its facts?

   For example, would it be worth listing the motives that brought each of the travelers to the journey? All different kinds of people are on the trip, for all different kinds of reasons. Which reasons get featured most prominently?

   How would you *know* (or be able to make a guess) that *motives,* not *fact,* are what this essay (and presumably any test on it) is about? One way would be by observing that the teacher has been emphasizing the various motives of the wilderness's many constituencies. Another way would be by reading critically—notice the sparseness of actual description of events compared with the richness of description of motives, and notice how the piece ends, with a long consideration of what the author himself gained from the experience.

3. *What could you do to prepare for an essay test on this piece that goes beyond looking at the piece itself?* You could go over your notes for the class meetings immediately prior to the test (which might alert you to the concern for motives). Or you could do a little independent research about the author, Barry Lopez, who turns out to have won a book award for *Of Wolves and Men* and who has also written several other books of nonfiction, including *Arctic Dreams.* If you found *Crossing Open Ground,* the collection of essays this one came from, you would learn that although Lopez frequently publishes in *Harper's* magazine, this essay originally appeared in *Notre Dame Magazine.* If you wanted to, you could find a copy of that magazine and make your own decisions about the kind of audience it reaches.

Cindy Black Takes the Exam

Cindy's preparation for the exam included the steps listed in items 1 and 2 above, but not those in item 3. (Like many students, Cindy usually confines her test preparation to materials at hand. If such preparation requires seizing the initiative and going to the library, she won't—unless she's really desperate for a grade—usually do it.) Here's the question she received, together with her essay in response to it. (Remember, this was an in-class, closed-book essay; don't expect grammatical perfection.)

Environmental Ethics 101
Spring 1992
Essay Test 1

Read the following question carefully and write a twenty-minute essay in response to it. Be careful that your essay addresses the question fully. Try to make your writing clear and correct.

In class for the past few meetings we've looked at the different motives people have in their concern for how wilderness and open spaces are used. Barry Lopez's essay "Gone Back into the Earth" offers us a look at a group of people with a variety of motives for taking a wilderness trip. List as many of those motives as you can remember, and consider whether and how they perhaps relate to the author's own motives for taking the trip. How convincing is Lopez's presentation of his own motives?

Here's Cindy's essay. As you read it over, see whether you can identify in it any of the aforementioned strategies for writing essay tests. Also think about whether use of a different strategy would have given Cindy a different, perhaps better answer.

> Barry Lopez's essay "Gone Back into the Earth" presents a number of motives for people going on a wilderness trip. Probably first and foremost is the famous musician Paul Winter. Winter and his friends have gone down the Grand Canyon on a ten-day trip in order to make music at sites on the way. From the music they make will come a recording to bring the same release and enjoyment they find to a new world of listeners. Above all, Winter seeks a "reintegration" of music, people, and landscape. One of the places this happens best is in a place called Blacktail Canyon.
>
> The others on the trip include a preacher from Maryland, a computer programmer, a mechanic, an editor, an actor, a medical student, a builder, and others. All have their own motives for going down the canyon. Of course, the thing that unites all of them is the simple goal of running the river. Beyond that they seek the joy of discovery of new sights and sound, new feelings, and new friends. They also seek a loss of self-consciousness that comes from being among and touching the nearly two-billion-year-old rocks around them. Their loss of self-consciousness opens the landscape up to them.
>
> The author of the essay, Barry Lopez, has his own reasons for going down the river. They include all the same motives as the others, plus to lose his sense of urgency and to regain his sense of who people are. More important, he regains the ability to hear his heart beat, to rid himself of the pain we all face just from being alive.

Feedback from Cindy's Teacher

Cindy was fairly pleased with the essay she had written. Although she had run out of time at the end, forcing her to hurry through the last section, she felt she had used most of what she had memorized about the essay. Here are her teacher's comments:

> Cindy, this is a good essay. I especially like the amount of specific detail you remembered. I wish you had paid a little bit more attention to Lopez's own motives, though. Grade: B.

Cindy wasn't too happy with a B on the test; after all, nothing was marked as being *wrong*. She thus went to see her teacher and asked him what he saw wrong in the essay that led to the B. He said, "Let's rephrase your question—suppose you ask me, 'What could I do to make it *better*?'" Along those lines, he suggested they look at the test question again (see page 589).

The teacher asked Cindy to underline in the essay question those words to which she thought her answer was responding. Here's the question with those words underlined.

> In class for the past few meetings we've looked at the different motives people have in their concern for how wilderness and open spaces are used. Barry Lopez's essay "Gone Back into the Earth" offers us a look at a group of people with a variety of motives for taking a wilderness trip. List as many of those motives as you can remember, and consider whether and how they perhaps relate to the author's own motives for taking the trip. How convincing is Lopez's presentation of his own motives?

At that point Cindy began shaking her head up and down, remarking, "I think I understand what you're saying."

Do *you* see what happened?

The problem with Cindy's essay—and keep in mind that it's a good one, just not as good as it *could* be—is that it slights the most important part of the question, that part which asks how the various motives relate to Lopez's and how convincing Lopez's own presentation is. Cindy's teacher had—as teachers often do—asked several questions, all leading to one final question whose answer needed to sum up all the others. Had Cindy not run out of time in her last paragraph, perhaps she would have developed the subject of Lopez's own motives more fully. But given her interpretation of the test, it's doubtful she would ever have got around to trying to relate Lopez's motives to the others', or to examining how convincing his own motives seem to be.

How could Cindy have approached this exam differently? She could have read the question more thoughtfully, made a more accurate assessment of the teacher's view of the heart of the question, and thus *started* her essay with a presentation of Lopez's motives as he states them in the essay, not just in paragraph 42 but in paragraphs 40–41 as well. She might then have gone on to connect the way Lopez's motives are gradually revealed piecemeal at various spots in the essay (¶ 7, 20, 23, 26, 34) before the end (where he articulates them more fully) as she connected them to the motives of the others.

You might build a skeleton outline of this improved version of Cindy's essay on the chalkboard to help students visualize the changes.

What else could Cindy have done? Well, had she gone to the library and looked up other books by Lopez, she would have seen that the landscape and wilderness's therapeutic effects on human beings are a constant theme of his—which would have been a nice point to bring into this in-class essay. And had she found the particular book *this* essay was taken from, she would have seen that several of the pieces in it are concerned with human pain, loss, and healing—which also would have been a good point to bring up.

Writers' Circle

With your classmates, select another reading from one of the other chapters in this book, a reading you want to study further. Working in groups of three or four, come up with your own study questions. Record them. Then come up with an essay test (one test per group) about the piece. Turn the questions and tests in to your teacher, who will discuss them with you as a class. Then let your teacher select one of the essay exams to give you for practice. Afterward, take a look with the class at several of the exam papers to see whether by studying them you can improve your own performance on future exams.

WRITING ASSIGNMENTS

1. Interview two of your current teachers (*not* the one teaching this class) about their "philosophy" of essay tests. In general, which kind(s) do they like to give? What factors control their choice(s) of which kind(s) to use? Write up the results of your interview, and include a short piece on how those results agree or disagree with what this chapter says.
2. Refer to the passage from *Patterns of Human Development* (chapter 13). How would you go about preparing for a twenty-minute essay test over that short selection? What are the key points in it you would need to remember? What is the structure of the passage? What kinds of analytical or evaluative questions would you anticipate being asked about it?
3. Your teacher will select a piece you haven't seen before and will lead you through discussing the piece, formulating appropriate questions for an essay test on it, discussing those questions, and then selecting one of them for a practice essay test.
4. Consider the photo on page 567. Does the world look like this when you're taking a timed essay test? Papers are stacked up, and numerous; the clock itself is warped, inadequate; the whole world seems to consist of those papers and that clock, and the only escape seems to be in the further warping or disappearance of the clock—meaning that the time will expire before the papers are done.

   Write a brief paper responding to this picture with your own experience in taking timed essay exams. In your experience, how accurate is this mental-image description of taking these timed exams? To the extent that it is accurate, why do you think it is? To the extent that it is not accurate, what in your experience makes it inaccurate? Were you able to try some of the techniques given in this chapter for preparation and performance on essay exams? How effective were they?

We have included a number of wilderness essays in this book. You may want to build an out-of-class writing assignment calling for comparison of them—"Woman/Wilderness" (chapter 6), "Mountain Memories" (chapter 4), "Wildness and Weirdness" (chapter 8), "Snow Banners" (chapter 11), and "Roadhouse and Wilderness" (chapter 15).

chapter 23 Writing Research Papers

"Writing teaches us our mysteries."
Marie de L'Incarnation

As usual, we recommend taking an inventory of your class at the beginning of the chapter, to determine how much and in what ways your students have experience with (or need for) the material in it. What experience with research papers have they already had? Which current classes require a research project? What classes requiring research papers will students take in the future?

Most university libraries have tours designed to familiarize new students with the library facilities; we strongly recommend that your students take advantage of any such tour available. Better yet, contact your library to see if you can arrange for a class tour in place of a regular class meeting; then you can take the tour with students. We recommend that you schedule such a tour *after* a few initial class meetings in which you cover the rudiments of library research and explore tentative research topics.

Ask students whether any of them have learned, in previous research projects, anything that was (a) strikingly new to them or (b) new to the person who made the assignment. If so, ask such students to share the experience.

Of course, this is not a complete list of the ways new knowledge comes about; ask your students to help you come up with a fuller list.

In all likelihood, you will have to write at least one research paper in your freshman composition class. Chances are you wrote at least one research paper in high school, and so the procedure isn't *completely* new to you.

Even so, research papers at the college level are generally more challenging than those assigned at earlier levels, in part because the libraries on most college campuses have far more extensive holdings than hometown public or high school libraries do, thereby allowing a much wider range of research topics and information sources. In certain academic areas, particularly the sciences, where new knowledge is constantly being discovered, college libraries often have much more extensive and up-to-date information than is found in smaller public libraries. And in academic areas like history, where the basic factual knowledge has remained more stable, college libraries are apt to hold comparatively more sources exploring varying interpretations of the factual knowledge, reminding us that what we "know" is always open to new understandings and meanings.

As a relatively new college student, you should familiarize yourself with your library: where it is (and, if appropriate, where its branches are), how it is organized for student use, what its hours of operation are, what its procedures for use are, and so on. Your library is a depository of *retrievable* information; as a student writer you may often need to retrieve and use some of that information—typically in a formal paper. The information skills you develop can last a lifetime and be of enormous benefit to you even after your formal education is complete. This chapter will introduce you to the processes of doing library research and writing research papers.

Research as Discovery and Synthesis of Learning

Above all else, research is about discovery: finding things out. The research process is a systematic way to learn new things, and the research-paper writing process is a systematic way to evaluate what you've learned, to synthesize it with what you already know, and to present that synthesis in the form of a report showing what you have discovered and why it is significant.

Aside from information reported to us as we watch television or listen to the radio, new knowledge can also come from a variety of activities:

- *Reading* information that is new to us
- *Interviewing* knowledgeable people who can give us information that is new to us
- *Conducting certain experiments or following certain procedures* that give us results constituting information new to us

Reading is probably the most common *active* way to seek new knowledge. We read books, newspapers, magazines, and other print sources primarily to find things out, and when we intensely focus such reading on a particular subject, we indeed begin to learn much more about that subject. Often what we read is a report based on the *writer's* reading—or perhaps based not just on the writer's reading but also on the writer's interviewing of a person or on the writer's conducting of a test, experiment, or other procedure.

For example, later in this chapter we will see how one student, Collin Walker, did research on steroid use among football players. Most of his research came from his reading, but we will notice that many of the sources he read reported the results of *interviews* with football players who had taken steroids; in addition, some of Collin's sources reported the results of *drug tests* conducted by independent researchers. In other words, even research that is primarily conducted by reading print sources can draw on the nonprint information-gathering skills of those who produced the print sources, so long as those sources are accurate and reliable.

No one kind of information gathering is inherently better than another; what's important is to use the appropriate method for the kind of research you are doing. If you rely on print sources, make sure they are (a) accurate and (b) do not present opinions as facts. Ensure that when opinion is given, it is clearly presented as such, no matter how expert it is. Try to use *only* reliable sources. An advertisement for an automobile, for example, no matter how impressive it may be in seeming to "report" on performance, is not as reliable as an independently researched, written, and published article assessing the same vehicle's performance.

If you rely on interviews, make sure the people you interview know what they are talking about. A doctor's remarks about the dangers of a disease are more authoritative than those of a school teacher whose third cousin had the disease. If you rely on experiments, procedures, tests, and the like, make sure you follow the proper steps to ensure that the resultant information is accurate. Sample A must be unmistakably identified as sample A throughout all testing; any mix-up confusing sample A with sample B makes all results erroneous.

Rigorous insistence on authoritative and accurate information is indispensable if research is to be meaningful and worthwhile. Never settle for less.

Primary and Secondary Sources

In research there are essentially two kinds of sources, primary and secondary. A *primary* source is an original source, what might be called firsthand information. A *secondary* source is at least once removed from the original; it is a commentary on the original, an interpretation of the original, or a synthesis of the original with other, similar originals and thus might be called secondhand information. If, for example, you are studying the Vietnam War speeches of President Lyndon Johnson, the speeches themselves are primary sources, as would be Johnson's own memoirs about the speeches; secondary sources would be the contemporary analyses and commentaries of network newscasters and newspaper columnists, as well as the remarks and judgments of Johnson biographers. Or if you are studying the novels of William Faulkner, the novels themselves are primary sources; the interpretations of various critics and literary scholars are secondary sources. If

One of the interesting things that happen to teachers who assign research papers is an implied commitment on the teacher's part to whatever kind of research those papers take; you should consider that when you are approving your students' topics. While no one kind of research is inherently better than another, some kinds *are* easier to carry out in the context of a freshman composition class, while other kinds are better left to other forums.

We don't think you should compromise on this point. Authoritative, accurate, *partial* information is better than questionable, inaccurate, *complete* information. Source reliability is sometimes a difficult concept for young learners, especially in a world where outlandish "newspapers" featuring gossip and fabrication are sold alongside serious, responsible newspapers, and where television "news" is often thinly veiled advertisement or relatively unimportant (but entertaining) fluff.

The more examples you can give to your students of the distinction between primary and secondary information (especially examples drawn from students' own work), the better.

Of course, there are also kinds of research that occupy gray areas between primary and secondary research. One such area is reflected in the current debates in various fields over the reports of participant-observers in ethnographic research: if these reports are objective, then the research is primary; if the reports are filtered through the perceptions of the observer, then the research is secondary. It really depends on who wins the argument over interpretation. (In case you're wondering, we don't think it's possible for such a reporter to be wholly objective, and we therefore consider such sources secondary—but very compelling nonetheless.)

We firmly believe that the best papers come from a mix of primary and secondary research, although what constitutes the best mix obviously varies from topic to topic.

We're aware that some teachers prefer to discuss library sources before discussing nonlibrary sources, and that's their choice. We discuss less obvious sources here because we want to emphasize to students that they "do research" even at times when they don't think of themselves as being so engaged.

One of the differences between how professionals do research and how students do research is the *variety* of resources professionals use and the way they tend to start their research the instant they conceive of a writing project.

you are studying the effects of steroids on football players, as our student writer Collin Walker did, an interview with a player who formerly used steroids is a primary source; an article in *Sports Illustrated* about a player who formerly used steroids is a secondary source.

In more rigidly scientific or empirical research, primary sources would include results of experiments you conducted, other data compiled from experiments or from other forms of systematic information gathering (such as questionnaires or a series of laboratory tests), client case studies or histories, and the like. Secondary sources would be the published reports of others doing similar kinds of methodological research, background studies, and support data derived from other research.

Primary sources are not inherently better than secondary sources. The distinction is useful and significant; after all, without primary sources there would be no secondary sources. What's important, however, is what can be learned from *both*. For example, ex-President Nixon's memoirs about the Watergate scandal differ considerably from more neutral accounts by historians. In such a discrepancy lies room for your own discovery and interpretation. Or you might, for example, not appreciate the first section of Faulkner's novel *The Sound and the Fury* (primary source) until you later read the views of a commentator (secondary source) who explains that in this section Faulkner tries to imitate in stream-of-consciousness style the thoughts of an idiot. *That,* you realize, explains the erratic sentences that seem to jump about in time and meaning. In such a case, the combination of primary and secondary sources enhances your knowledge significantly.

When you conduct research, usually you should try to find the most important primary *and* secondary sources. Only in that way will you be sure to find the authoritative and accurate information that worthwhile and meaningful research requires.

Nonlibrary Sources of Information

Day-to-day living supplies us with *some* of the information we might find useful in a research project. You might, for example, hear from a friend about a new book that proves to be extremely helpful in your investigation. You might see a news special on television about your subject. Your eye might catch a bulletin-board poster telling you that an expert on your subject is going to speak at a certain time and place. Often we don't think of such occurrences as research, but why not? Just as you are "writing" a paper the moment you begin to *think* about it—even if you haven't put a single word on paper—so are you doing "research" the moment you discover something in your daily life that bears on your topic.

Direct, Firsthand Investigation

There are other, more systematic ways to discover information outside of a library, such as *direct, firsthand investigation.* Let's say that you want to find out what kind of computers a local shop most frequently repairs. Obviously, particular brands or models that spend the most time in repair shops might well be computers worth avoiding. Or let's say you work for the traffic engineering department in a city and want to find out how many accidents have occurred in recent years at a particular intersection. At the police department you examine the accident reports on file and find out not only how many accidents have occurred there but what the most frequent causes were. Such information might be vital to a decision by your department to authorize a traffic light or some other change at that intersection.

You may gather (rightly) from this that we like practical topics for student research papers.

The Interview

A common type of nonlibrary research is the *interview.* If you find a cooperative informant—say, a witness to a storm or an expert on bicycle repair—you can get information you and others might find useful. Interviews, whether conducted in person or by telephone, should be properly planned so as not to seem disrespectful of the informant's time. Questions should be planned in advance. Permission to use any kind of recording equipment should also be requested in advance. In cases of recorded field research (collecting folklore, interviewing witnesses, and the like) it might be necessary to try to make the informant as relaxed and unmindful of the recording as possible. The more at ease and "natural" the informant feels, the more likely the information will be useful. If you've ever watched a television program like "60 Minutes," you know that effective interviewing demands considerable skill and, often, considerable diplomacy. As a method of research, it's potentially far too complicated for elaborate treatment here.

When our students say they're planning to do interviews, we like to arrange a prior office visit to go over some ground rules with them ("Plan your questions, make sure you have *prior* permission to tape, interview at the *informant's* convenience," and so forth).

It's important to remember that interviewing has shortcomings as a research technique. For one thing, an interview is often only as good as the interviewer's skill or the informant's reliability, and both of those can be suspect. If you don't ask the right questions the right way, you might not get useful (or honest) answers. If the informant has some purpose unknown to you, the interview might prove unsatisfactory. Common sense, however, will go a long way in determining the quality of interview information. Among key considerations are these:

- *Is the informant an expert on the subject?* It's reasonable to expect that the famous tennis star Steffi Graf can tell you something authoritative about tennis. But if she's telling you how to tune your car engine, she's not as authoritative on that subject as your auto mechanic.
- *If the informant is speaking as a firsthand witness to events or conversations, is there any reason to think the informant might* not *be candid?* Informants might for some reason wish to "color" the facts, or present only a partly true picture—a very human tendency among informants. Many researchers (biographers, for example) do not consider an informant's information reliable unless it is repeated by a second informant who has no link to the first. This "second-source confirmation" method in regard to critical information is also a fundamental procedure of investigative journalists.

When our students do interviews, we like them to add a phrase to their bibliographic entry for that item to explain the subject's expertise (if that information is not explicit in the text).

Students may not appreciate that (a) many people in our society already feel overinterviewed and overpolled and (b) not all people are reliable sources in interview situations.

It *is* possible to write a paper from this kind of research, but one must strictly limit conclusions that generalize about all (or a significant part) of the population from such a small sample.

The point is to make students aware of when they're talking about *instances* and when they're talking about *generalizations. Instances* are still individual in nature and relatively isolated; they may or may not be representative of the experiences of a larger group. *Generalizations* are collective in nature and thus, to be accurate or useful, must represent the experiences of a larger group.

Your students may have trouble seeing the point here, for we're often inundated with language that *pretends* to be so reliable or "scientific" that we miss the subtle omissions or distortions that make all the difference. As another illustration, let's say that (a) at a major state university with twenty-five thousand students, a surveyor asks ten students in a tavern if they drink alcohol and (b) nine of the ten students reply yes, they drink alcohol (hardly a surprising number, since the setting is a tavern). The

Survey Questionnaires

Another common type of nonlibrary research is formulating and administering a *survey questionnaire.* Such questionnaires should be carefully planned; in fact, proper survey techniques are so important (and so variable) that comprehensive discussion here, as for interviewing, is not possible. Suffice it to say that questionnaires vary from single-question polling (such as political surveys asking which candidate a person plans to vote for or whether or not a person favors certain legislation) to elaborate, multipage response sheets (such as market research trying to determine whether or not a particular product or service might be profitable). Many of the social and behavioral sciences rely on such nonlibrary research approaches as interviewing (case studies, for example) and surveying (asking a representative sample of college freshmen whether or not they have had sexual experience, for instance).

Just as there are some important cautions regarding interview sources, so too are there significant cautions with survey information:

- *Is the sample of persons surveyed large enough to draw a useful or statistically significant conclusion?* Suppose a university has a freshman class of 5,000. A surveyor asking 10 students if they have had sexual experience has not asked enough students to draw *any* conclusion. (If 5 of the 10 said yes, it would be dangerous folly to make any sort of statement like "Fifty percent of the freshmen at the university have had sexual experience," or "Fully half of the 5,000 freshmen at the university have had sexual experience.") The larger the sample, the more reliable the conclusions that might be drawn. If 500 of the students (10 percent of the class) were surveyed and 250 said yes, then a more reliable—but still-guarded—generalization could be drawn: for example, "Half the 500 freshman students surveyed at the university said they have had sexual experience." (Note that the statement carefully limits the group to *those students who were surveyed.* It would still be a mistake to conclude, on the basis of this sample, "Half the freshmen at the university have had sex.")

  Whether it's accidental or incidental, deception with numbers and statistics is all too easy; in fact, it's just as easy as deception with language. Look closely at this statement: "Half the freshman students surveyed at the university have had sexual experience." That statement is true even if only 10 students were surveyed and 5 said they have had sexual experience. No survey polling only 10 of 5,000 students could be statistically reliable, but the statement deceives because it makes no claim to statistical accuracy—it merely states that half the students surveyed have had sexual experience. It *implies* that a much larger sample was taken and that therefore a very high number of students have had sexual experience. It's easy to see how such a statement could be used to mislead.
- *Is each question in the questionnaire carefully worded so that only the desired possible responses can result?* The problem here could be that the question is flawed, making the responses unreliable. If, for example, the intent of a

question is to learn whether or not a person has a college degree, the question, "Have you been to college?" is too imprecise to elicit the desired information, for a respondent may have attended college without getting a degree. "Do you have a college degree?" would elicit the desired response. Similarly, complex questions calling for a yes-or-no response may put off respondents, who realize that, with some questions, *any* response seems to show them in a bad light. For example, "Do you believe you have improved your driving?" cannot be answered yes or no without seeming to admit either to a past as a poor driver or to a continuing present as a poor driver. Pitfalls like this require that survey questionnaires be carefully formulated.

Library Sources of Information

Searching for information in even a small library can be complicated for a student who has never tried systematic library research. Perhaps the most important beginning advice to any such student is to remember that *librarians are employed to help you*. Librarians know the library in ways even highly experienced researchers do not. So don't be afraid or embarrassed to ask for help; a polite request is ordinarily all that's needed. As you become more familiar with library research you will eventually need less help; nonetheless, it takes time to learn how to do anything, and in the meanwhile you can often save much time and frustration by *asking*. The following discussion explains a basic approach to information retrieval in libraries.

Deciding on a Topic

Before you go to the library, you should already have a very general topic, or subject, in which you are sufficiently interested to do research. This subject may be one of your own choice or one suggested by your teacher or a friend; it doesn't so much matter *where* your subject comes from as that you have one as a place to begin. We urge you to choose something of genuine interest to you so that your level of inquisitive energy can remain high while you work.

Once you know what your subject is, you need to write it down, along with any other term you can think of that is either a synonym (a word meaning roughly the same thing) or closely related. Think of as many synonyms and related terms as you can, because when you go to the library to begin searching, these terms will help you narrow your topic. A common problem of beginning researchers is choosing a topic far too broad for the usual length and coverage requirements teachers specify for a freshman writing class. Most teachers of college freshmen writers want to see that their students know how to do research and how to write properly documented reports of their research. Those goals can usually be met by students who write on narrow topics for about eight to twelve double-spaced, typewritten pages. It makes sense, then, to choose a topic that interests you; then *keep narrowing it*.

statistical sample is far too small to allow any sort of conclusion about the entire student body at the university; moreover, the fact that the sample is taken at a tavern makes the sample wholly unrepresentative—possibly thousands of the university's students wouldn't even walk into a tavern. But if the surveyor is sloppy or unscrupulous, he or she could make a statement that is entirely true but *very misleading* to, say, the parents of a prospective student at this university: "Nine out of ten students I surveyed at the university drink alcohol." To parents worried about the social atmosphere of the school their son or daughter attends, that statement can be far too influential. From the surface of that statement, such parents might infer that 90 percent of the students at the university are drinkers—and yet no such meaning is ever claimed.

The primary difference between students who do well on research papers and those who don't turns out to be the student's level of interest in the project. *Any* amount of time you spend on that aspect of topic selection, therefore, is not wasted.

Many times the best papers are those which explore the intersection of two—or even three—topics: that is, a paper not just about drugs, but about the intersection of the two topics, drugs and athletics. Or the paper might treat the intersection of drugs, athletics, and punishment/treatment of proven offenders (how does "banned for life" in a professional sport translate into a one-year ban?).

Narrowing Your Topic

Suppose, for example, that your topic is drugs. You can be sure that you're going to need to *narrow* it: what *kind* of drugs? Think of the possibilities: legal drugs (in which case you will probably find information about drugs that can be purchased without prescriptions)? medicinal drugs (in which case you will probably find information about both prescription and nonprescription drugs that are used for medical purposes)? generic drugs (in which case you will probably find information about non-brand-name prescription drugs or common nonprescription drugs, such as aspirin)? The possibilities continue: natural drugs? synthetic drugs? addictive drugs? You may well discover, as did our student writer Collin Walker, that even a specific drug type commonly heard about—steroids—must be even more specifically identified (as we shall see, Collin had to search for information for his research paper under *anabolic* steroids). Our point is this: make your list of terms, and don't worry about how long it gets—most likely, the longer your list is, the better start you'll get when you begin your library research. And library research is one of those processes in which getting a good start is critically important.

Library Holdings

Most American library holdings are identified and stored according to systems based on subject headings (names for the kind of information the book or other holding contains) identified by the Library of Congress in Washington, D.C. These subject headings are printed in a book entitled *The Library of Congress Subject Headings,* which you will usually find near the card catalog (in smaller, older libraries) or near computer-search terminals (in larger, newer libraries). Know where *The Library of Congress Subject Headings* is in your library; it is the source to use if your list of terms fails to get you properly started.

Ask your students today, in class, to tell you where *The Library of Congress Subject Headings* book is. If they don't know, tell them there will be a one-question test about its location during the next class meeting.

Early in the research process you need to discover whether or not your library has computerized access to its holdings. If it has, you should proceed to a terminal and follow the instructions given there for beginning your search on the keyboard. By following printed information either beside the terminal or on the screen (or in both places), you'll be able to call up screens telling you the basic information you need for deciding whether you want to go and get a particular source. Libraries differ in the types of computer terminals available to students and the methods of storing and retrieving search information; therefore, it would be impractical for us to explain a particular operation here, beyond offering the most general advice.

For us, the biggest difference between searching by hand and searching by computer is the time the computer printer saves us over the time copying information by hand takes (that, and the computer printer's accuracy).

However your library's computers work, you'll eventually be given the opportunity to tell the computer what you want to look for. Generally, you'll be able to choose among three kinds of searching strategies (these strategies also work in libraries not equipped with computers, so take special note):

1. *Title search.* If you happen to know the title of a book on your subject, you can enter the title, beginning with the first word (you may have to ignore *a, an,* and *the* when they fall at the beginning of a title—for instance, *Rise and Fall of*

the Roman Empire, The). The resultant screen will tell you whether your library has that particular book and, most important, what its call number is. It will also tell you who wrote it, whether it's currently checked out, and other, general information about its form and content. The call number will enable you to find the book on the library shelves or request it from a librarian if your library's shelves aren't open for student searching.

If the computer doesn't tell whether or not a source is checked out, students should jot down the titles and call numbers so that after using the computer they can go to the circulation desk and ask the attendant which sources are available for checking out.

2. *Author search.* If you know the name of someone who has written a book (or books) on your subject, you can enter the author's last name, followed by first name and any initials the author may use (such as Brady, Matthew H.). The resultant screen will tell you whether your library has the book(s) by this author and will again supply the key information you need for retrieval.
3. *Subject search.* Finally, you may not know any titles or authors relevant to your subject but instead may have only your list of subject headings. Here is where your hard work of brainstorming subject headings and subheadings should pay off. The computer will direct you to enter a subject heading and will flash additional information to help you narrow the subject field until you reach a range specific enough for the computer to list titles and call numbers of relevant works or provide cross-references to other, closely related subject headings. If you exhaust your list, you can consult *The Library of Congress Subject Headings* to look for additional subject headings you may not have thought of earlier.

   With certain computerized systems, you can instruct the computer to do some searching for you; for example, you might ask the computer to scan the library holdings, looking for subjects that intersect in either titles or subject descriptions. As we will see later in the chapter, Collin Walker, for example, asked the computer to scan for sources that tied two subject headings: anabolic steroids and football. The result was a helpful list of relevant sources, complete with retrieval information. In systems in which you cannot direct such a search yourself, often you can ask a librarian to conduct the search for you. Again, it's important to remember to *ask for help* if you need it. (*Note:* Subject searches are the least specific searches you can do. This limitation can be (a) good when you're just trying to find anything on a subject or (b) bad when you're looking for a specific source and, because you don't use the precisely correct subject term, the computer doesn't give it to you. Subject terms are notoriously slippery.)

As mentioned above, once you have called up the appropriate screen, you can get the most crucial information about a source you want to examine: the *call number.* With this number you can find out where in your library you can locate that source. Most large libraries display charts, or "locator lists," in conspicuous places (by the computer terminals or the card catalog and by the elevators or stairways) to tell you which floors hold which kinds of sources. All you have to do is match the call number with a locator list to learn where you can find the source.

It's a good idea to give students practice on this in class; give them locator lists and then, as you give each book's call number, have them tell you where various books can be found.

Most libraries use one of two systems for call numbers: Library of Congress or Dewey Decimal. Neither is especially complicated, and once you know how each works you should be able to find your sources fairly quickly.

Library of Congress System

Library of Congress call numbers begin with a short line of capital letters that indicate very general subject areas. Each letter in this line represents an increasing level of particularization. For example, *Q* indicates the general subject area of science; the *A* within *QA* indicates the more specific subject of mathematics within the general area of science; and *QB* indicates the subject of astronomy within the general area of science. Similarly, *J* indicates the general area of political science; *JX,* the more specific area of political science known as international law. *A* indicates general works, such as reference books and encyclopedias. And so on.

The second line of a Library of Congress call number consists of a number (usually three digits) that will be of special use in locating the particular shelf on which you will find the book.

The third line of a Library of Congress call number is a short line that begins with a capital letter, usually the last-name initial of the author, followed by a single- or double-digit number that generally indicates either which copy of a book this particular book is (when multiple copies of the same book are held by the library) or which book by a given author this particular book is (when the library holds several different books by the same author). Thus, the following Library of Congress call number reflects subject matter, library location, and author:

QB 312 R1	Ross, Herbert T., Galaxies to Explore. [An astronomy textbook of which the library has one copy, shelved in the QB section, on the shelf labeled QB 300-350.]

Serendipity suggests the experienced researcher will scan a few books up and down the shelf from the target book, just in case there's another, equally valuable source there. Because of the way subject-based indexing works, the possibility of such a source being not far from the target is pretty good.

Say you want to find in your library the Herbert T. Ross book listed above. Once you have the call number your next step is to identify, by consulting a locator list or chart, where your library shelves its QB (astronomy) books. Let's say the chart tells you that all books with a "Q" Library of Congress call number are on the second floor. You then go to the second floor, where, typically, you find many shelves of books. Each shelf has a prominent label and a range of numbers. You find the shelf labeled "QB" that indicates the range of numbers including the ones in your call number's second row (in this case, 312). You then comb that shelf, looking at the call numbers on the spines of the books, until you find QB/312/R1 on a spine. Now, you've found your book. Pull it off the shelf and examine it. If you decide to check it out, go through the library's checkout procedure. If, however, you decide not to check it out, *follow your library's instructions.* Most libraries will *not* want you to reshelve the book; a misshelved book can be extremely difficult to find. Rather, you will probably find a sign telling you to place the book on a special empty shelf nearby (most likely, part of the same large rack of shelves from which you removed the book). A librarian will later properly reshelve the book.

Dewey Decimal System

The Dewey Decimal system for library call numbers essentially works just like the Library of Congress system. The main difference is that whereas the Library of Congress system uses a combination of key letters and numbers, the Dewey system uses only key numbers.

Dewey Decimal call numbers begin with a short top line that consists of a range of hundreds. A top-line number falling between 000 and 099, for example, indicates that the book is a general reference work or encyclopedia. A number between 100 and 199 indicates that the book falls in the general area of philosophy; works listed between 200 and 299 indicate the general area of religion; and so on. As with the Library of Congress system's first line, increasing particularity of subject is indicated by increasing particularity within the general numerical category. For example, in the Dewey system the 500–599 range is the range for the pure sciences ("Q" in the Library of Congress system). Ranges of 10 *within* this range indicate particular subcategories of pure science—for example, 510 = mathematics, 520 = astronomy and allied sciences, 530 = physics, 540 = chemistry and allied sciences, and so on. Thus, in a Dewey Decimal call number, the above astronomy text by Herbert T. Ross, *Galaxies to Explore,* might be as follows:

523
312
R1

With this call number you would search the stacks exactly as you would with a Library of Congress call number, except that you'd need to find where the "500" books are stored.

Information Searching Without a Computer

The information about a source that you can call up on a computer screen in some libraries is essentially the information that, in less technically equipped libraries, you will find in either the card catalog (for books) or the serials or periodicals lists (for magazines, journals, and newspapers). What follows is a discussion of how to use the card catalog and periodicals listings in libraries that are not yet computerized.

Card Catalog. The card catalog is a bank of small drawers holding standard-size cards that describe the library's book holdings. The catalog is centrally located in most libraries and contains alphabetically arranged cards of three types: (a) author, (b) title, and (c) subject. *Author cards* bear on their top line the last, then first, then middle names or initials of the book's author. *Title cards* bear on their first line the title of the book (starting with the first major word—never *a,*

If your library puts different kinds of cards in different sets of drawers, be sure to stress to your students that they not look up the wrong kind of item in the wrong kind of drawer.

an, or *the*). *Subject cards* bear on their first line the Library of Congress subject heading. Many libraries mix all the cards together; some separate author and title cards from subject cards.

If you know the author's name but not the book name, you can find the book under the author's alphabetized last name—for instance, *Ross,* Herbert T. In the drawer holding "R" cards, you should search until you find "Ross, Herbert T." You will then find, among any other books the library holds by Herbert T. Ross, *Galaxies to Explore.* The card will give you considerable information about this book—the call number, the publisher, the number of pages, whether or not there is a bibliography, whether or not there are illustrations, what other subjects the book is listed under, a brief synopsis of what the book is about, and more. You can then proceed, with the call number, to find the book.

If, however, you know only the title of the book—*Galaxies to Explore*—and not the author's name, you can look in the drawer holding "G" cards until you find the title. That card tells you the same information the author card does.

If you are searching only with subject headings, you need to look in the drawer that alphabetizes the subject heading under which you are searching. In the case of the Ross book, the subject is astronomy—American. The drawer holding "A" cards is where you should begin your alphabetic search. Specific subject cards are slightly harder to find, but eventually you will find a subject card for the same book, Herbert T. Ross's *Galaxies to Explore,* and this card too will give you the same information as the author and title cards contain. You can thus find specific books in the library by beginning with an author, title, or subject search in the card catalog.

Infotrac is one popular computerized index; if your library has computerized periodicals searching, you should check which computerized indexes your library has and call them to students' attention.

Periodicals Searching. The term *periodicals* refers to any publication that comes out periodically—magazines, journals, newspapers. If your library does not have a computerized method for periodicals searching, go to your library's reference shelves and find the appropriate periodicals indexes. These indexes are cumulative listings of articles, arranged by subject and author, that have appeared in the periodicals covered by a given index. Such indexes are usually bound in volumes by year, with the most recent supplements also shelved with the yearly volumes. Because indexes exist for popular magazines, specialty journals, and major newspapers, you should be sure to use the appropriate index for your subject. If you're uncertain which index to use, ask a reference librarian for help or consult Eugene P. Sheehy's *Guide to Reference Books,* which can usually be found near the place your library shelves its indexes. Among commonly used indexes are these:

The Readers' Guide to Periodical Literature

The New York Times Index

Science Citation Index

Social Sciences Index

Business Periodicals Index

Applied Science and Technology Index

Biological and Agricultural Index

Education Index

You'll need to learn how to use an index efficiently. Though they vary somewhat in their layout and method, most indexes provide front matter that explains how to interpret each entry. They also contain a list of abbreviations—for example, of the various periodicals they index, as well as abbreviations indicating particular features of an article. At first you'll need to refer frequently to an index's front matter to know what is being described in the index entries. Among typical index entries are these:

Frankly, whenever we have to use a new index, we just ask a librarian to explain it to us.

Name or subject

Author(s) of article

Title of article

Name of periodical

Date of periodical

Volume of periodical

Page numbers of the article

Cross-references to related articles or cross-listings

(See the sample page from *The Readers' Guide to Periodical Literature,* on page 606.)

Some indexes also provide a brief abstract of the article.

Once you have written down the basic information on an article (author, title of article, name and date of periodical, page numbers), you can proceed to your library's periodicals list or serials catalog to determine whether your library holds the particular article you seek.

It's a good idea to point out to students that if they can choose between an index with abstracts and one without, they should prefer the former: using abstracts, a researcher can narrow down a preliminary list of thirty citations to ten in about a third of the time it would take to look up each item.

Let's say you are looking for an article entitled "What Exactly *Is* Astronomy?" by Herbert T. Ross; the article appeared in the July 1990 issue of *Scientific American.* Your first step is to look in the periodicals list or serials catalog (which will be alphabetized) to see whether your library subscribes to and holds past issues of *Scientific American.* The listing or card informs you that your library does in fact receive *Scientific American.* It also tells you that the library holds each issue of that magazine from the January 1959 issue until the present. In addition, the listing tells you which volumes are bound and shelved, which are available on microfilm, and—again, most important—what the call number is. As with books, the call number will direct you to the part of the library where you can find the particular issue of the periodical you are seeking.

This procedure works essentially the same for all periodicals, whether they are weekly magazines, daily newspapers, monthly magazines, or quarterly journals. And if at any time your search is stymied, *ask for help.*

Reference Area. Your college library will have a useful area or room designated for shelving and use of reference works. Here you'll find the periodicals indexes

Sample Index Page from *The Readers' Guide to Periodical Literature*

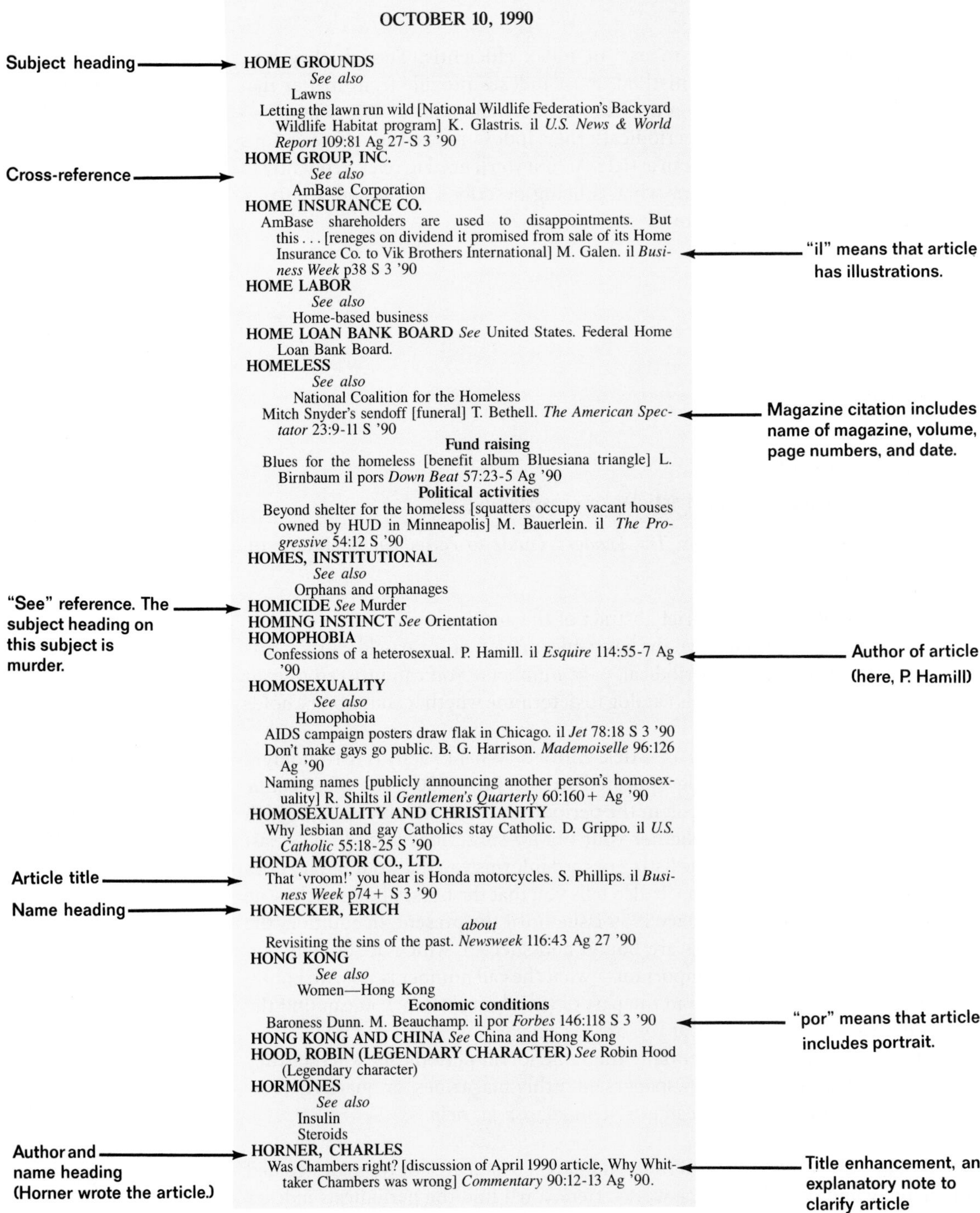

OCTOBER 10, 1990

HOME GROUNDS
See also
Lawns
Letting the lawn run wild [National Wildlife Federation's Backyard Wildlife Habitat program] K. Glastris. il *U.S. News & World Report* 109:81 Ag 27-S 3 '90
HOME GROUP, INC.
See also
AmBase Corporation
HOME INSURANCE CO.
AmBase shareholders are used to disappointments. But this . . . [reneges on dividend it promised from sale of its Home Insurance Co. to Vik Brothers International] M. Galen. il *Business Week* p38 S 3 '90
HOME LABOR
See also
Home-based business
HOME LOAN BANK BOARD *See* United States. Federal Home Loan Bank Board.
HOMELESS
See also
National Coalition for the Homeless
Mitch Snyder's sendoff [funeral] T. Bethell. *The American Spectator* 23:9-11 S '90
Fund raising
Blues for the homeless [benefit album Bluesiana triangle] L. Birnbaum il pors *Down Beat* 57:23-5 Ag '90
Political activities
Beyond shelter for the homeless [squatters occupy vacant houses owned by HUD in Minneapolis] M. Bauerlein. il *The Progressive* 54:12 S '90
HOMES, INSTITUTIONAL
See also
Orphans and orphanages
HOMICIDE *See* Murder
HOMING INSTINCT *See* Orientation
HOMOPHOBIA
Confessions of a heterosexual. P. Hamill. il *Esquire* 114:55-7 Ag '90
HOMOSEXUALITY
See also
Homophobia
AIDS campaign posters draw flak in Chicago. il *Jet* 78:18 S 3 '90
Don't make gays go public. B. G. Harrison. *Mademoiselle* 96:126 Ag '90
Naming names [publicly announcing another person's homosexuality] R. Shilts il *Gentlemen's Quarterly* 60:160+ Ag '90
HOMOSEXUALITY AND CHRISTIANITY
Why lesbian and gay Catholics stay Catholic. D. Grippo. il *U.S. Catholic* 55:18-25 S '90
HONDA MOTOR CO., LTD.
That 'vroom!' you hear is Honda motorcycles. S. Phillips. il *Business Week* p74+ S 3 '90
HONECKER, ERICH
about
Revisiting the sins of the past. *Newsweek* 116:43 Ag 27 '90
HONG KONG
See also
Women—Hong Kong
Economic conditions
Baroness Dunn. M. Beauchamp. il por *Forbes* 146:118 S 3 '90
HONG KONG AND CHINA *See* China and Hong Kong
HOOD, ROBIN (LEGENDARY CHARACTER) *See* Robin Hood (Legendary character)
HORMONES
See also
Insulin
Steroids
HORNER, CHARLES
Was Chambers right? [discussion of April 1990 article, Why Whittaker Chambers was wrong] *Commentary* 90:12-13 Ag '90.

Source: The Readers' Guide to Periodical Literature, 1990 (New York: H. W. Wilson, 1990) 57.

you need for researching information published in magazines and newspapers, as well as many other helpful materials, including dictionaries, encyclopedias, atlases, gazetteers, abstracts, and specialized biographical sources. Following are typical sources your library's reference area may hold:

We start all our searches here, in the reference area, looking up the basics on our topic in encyclopedias and/or specialized dictionaries. We also stay alert to (a) the possible existence of other relevant reference books listed in Sheehy's *Guide to Reference Books* and (b) the names of relevant periodicals in that field as listed in Ulrich's *International Periodicals Directory*.

General Encyclopedias

Encyclopedia Americana

Encyclopedia Britannica

Biographical Articles About Deceased Persons

Dictionary of American Biography (for the United States)

Dictionary of National Biography (for Great Britain)

Biographical Articles About Living Persons

Contemporary Authors

Current Biography

Who's Who in America

International Who's Who

Specialized Dictionaries and Encyclopedias

Encyclopedia of Art

Oxford Companion to Art

Cambridge Encyclopedia of Astronomy

Encyclopedia of the Biological Sciences

Encyclopedia of Chemistry

Encyclopedia of Computer Science

Encyclopedia of Dance and Ballet

Encyclopedia of Earth Sciences

Encyclopedia of Economics

Encyclopedia of Education

International Encyclopedia of Film

Dictionary of American History

Encyclopedia of World History

Black's Law Dictionary

Oxford Companions to Literature (several, divided by nations and/or literary periods)

Universal Encyclopedia of Mathematics

Stein and Day International Medical Encyclopedia

Oxford Companion to Music

Encyclopedia of Philosophy

Encyclopedia of Physics

Encyclopedia of Psychology

Encyclopedia of Religion and Ethics

Harper Encyclopedia of Science

Dictionary of Social Sciences

Articles in these special reference works will usually provide basic information—a good starting point for your research—and a bibliography. For the most up-to-date information on a subject, however, you should refer to articles in recent periodicals or journals.

Government Publications. The largest single publisher in America is the U.S. government. Often, a government publication will provide the most recent, most up-to-date information you could possibly find on a subject. Although not every library holds government publications, most college libraries either hold some or provide a means whereby you can locate and borrow a particular government source. The best course of action when seeking government publications is to obtain assistance from a librarian, especially the Government Documents Librarian—if your library is large enough to have such a person. In any case, there are special indexes to government publications, among them these:

Laurence F. Schmeckebier and Roy B. Eastin, *Government Publications and Their Use.*

Joe Morehead, *Introduction to United States Public Documents.*

U.S. Superintendent of Documents, *Monthly Catalog of United States Government Publications.* (Each December issue indexes the full year by author, title, and subject.)

National Technical Information Service, *Government Reports Announcement and Index.* (Biweekly.)

The route from any of these indexes to the source usually involves requesting the source from the Government Documents Librarian.

The above is only a general guide to systematically searching for information in your library. The best way to become truly familiar with library research is to *do* it, and that's always much easier to say than to do. But don't be faint of heart: the library and its holdings are there for you to discover, and if you follow the above advice *and* remember that it is always appropriate to ask a librarian for help, you should eventually be able to find not just what you're looking for but also much more information you might want to use or at least be glad to know about.

Using and Documenting Information

When you are writing a research paper, finding information is only a preliminary activity, something that still fits into that stage of the writing process which some teachers call *invention* or *discovery* but we call *thinking.* Even if you take elaborate notes while you're finding information, you aren't really *drafting* yet, because at this stage you can't be sure exactly how—or even if—you're going to use a particular piece of information you've found. And that's as it should be, because when you are doing the initial research that will eventually result in a paper, it is too early to be drafting. First you need time to make sure your research is complete or nearly so, and then you need time to think about how you might use that research and in what order.

We don't think it's worth arguing over whether a particular activity is really invention or really discovery. But we do think the distinction between *finding* and *inventing* is useful for student writers; *all* such activity comes under the heading of *thinking* in our conception of the writing process.

Regardless of how you might later use the information you are finding, you should undertake certain procedures *while* you are discovering the information, procedures that, if properly handled, will save you much trouble later on. Different people have different ways of accomplishing what we are about to describe, and you should develop your own way that works best for you. What's important is to *have* a system, one you're fully in control of, so that when you actually use some information you won't be lacking anything you need for proper use and documentation. A good system for handling information should include an *invariable* way of identifying sources, of taking notes, of distinguishing between quoted and paraphrased material, and of recording necessary specific information, such as page numbers.

Identifying Sources

When you are examining a print source, such as a book or an article in a magazine or newspaper, you should record all pertinent bibliographic information for documentation the moment you realize you might *use* information from this source. The best way to do this is to write down, on a blank three-by-five or five-by-eight card or on a separate sheet of paper, the full bibliographic information according to the particular system of documentation you are supposed to use for your research paper. Several varying research documentation systems are in use today, one for nearly every academic or professional field. Among these are the Modern Language Association's (MLA) *Handbook for Writers of Research Papers,* the American Psychological Association's (APA) *Publication Manual of the American Psychological Association,* and *The Chicago Manual of Style. Note:* It's *essential* that you find out what documentation system your instructor wants you to use. Our examples will be from the MLA system.

Let's say that you've found a source on your topic. You begin to scan the source and find some specific information you think you are likely to use in your paper.

Stop!

Get your card or blank sheet of paper and write the *full* bibliographic information about the source at the top of your card or page. If you're using the MLA system, following are a few typical citations you can use as models. Note that these citations are alphabetized, as your finished Works Cited list should be.

It's in this kind of situation that the speed and accuracy of an on-line catalog's computer printout really help.

- **Book by One Author**

Adeler, Thomas L. In a New York Minute. New York: Harper, 1990.

- **Book by Two Authors**

  Bennett, Julia, and Dawn A. Kelley. Wildlife in the Carolinas. Raleigh: Research Triangle, 1991.

  [Note that only the first author's name is inverted for alphabetizing.]

- **Anthology or Collection Edited by One Person**

  Coleman, Cecil D., ed. Essays on Baseball: Perspectives on the Great American Pastime. New York: Harcourt, 1990.

- **Book by a Corporate Author**

  Detroit Commission on the Renaissance. Toward the Future. Detroit: Wolverine, 1989.

If the source you are reading is a magazine, journal article, or newspaper, following are typical citations for these:

- **One-Author Article in a Weekly or Biweekly Magazine**

  Early, Tony. "Carolina on His Mind." Newsweek 4 Oct. 1990: 26.

  [Note that the article title is quoted and the name of the magazine is underlined, that is, italicized. Page number(s) come after the colon.]

- **One-Author Article in a Journal with Continuous Pagination Throughout All Issues Within the Volume**

  Fahey, Marlyne. "Let's Stop the Confusion about Apostrophes." Writing Teacher 5 (1989): 152-57.

  [Note that the volume number follows the name of the journal; then the year is given in parentheses. Next comes a colon and then the pages covered by the article. In such journals, the first issue of the year begins with page 1. If that first issue ends with page 149, the *next* issue in the volume begins with page 150, and so on, until the volume is completed—usually with the last issue of that year.]

- **One-Author Story in a Daily Newspaper**

  Gregory, Tina. "When All Else Fails." Philadelphia Inquirer 2 Apr. 1990: C12.

  [Note that the section of the paper ("C") is given as part of the pagination if the paper is divided into sections.]

- **Anonymous Newspaper Articles**

  "Harm's Way." Denver Post 17 January 1991: E6.

  [Note that alphabetizing in this case begins with first word—excluding *a, an,* and *the*—of the title. Proceed the same way with unsigned magazine articles.]

More examples will be given later, but the above sampling will suffice to get you started. As we said, write down such information *as soon as* you are fairly sure you will be taking notes from a source. You need to write down the information thoroughly only once; if you take additional notes from the same source, you can identify that source by using an abbreviated title, a number you've given *this* (and no other) source, or some other reliable means of identification.

Taking Notes

"Why take notes in the age of copy machines?" you may ask. It seems so much easier just to make a machine copy of any page of any source from which you think you might take quoted or paraphrased information. It is true that note taking is much more trouble than machine copying; however, note taking is a highly valuable skill, one you should develop fully, because in some research situations it's impossible, for one reason or another, to make machine copies. For example, some libraries hold material that has special restrictions, including that no machine copies may be made. In such situations, a researcher given access to these materials must comply with the library's regulations. Doing so usually means that the researcher can only *read* the material and take pencil notes on separate pieces of paper or cards.

Sometimes you might learn something pertinent to your research when you're unprepared for it—when even immediate note taking, let alone machine copying, is impossible. When such learning occurs, you need to make a note of it as soon as you can afterward; that way, you'll be able to preserve as much as you can of what you've learned, so that you will know not only the information but when and from what source you learned it. This "unexpected knowledge" situation often occurs during conversations, and the surest way to make use of it is to learn to make notes as soon as possible afterward.

There are other arguments for note taking as well. For one thing, taking careful notes by hand gets your mind actively involved in sorting out, organizing, and synthesizing your research at an early stage—and the earlier you begin that process, the better. For another, few students can afford the expense of massive copying on machines (the copy cost per page at this writing is five cents). Moreover, the copy machine does not take down the essential bibliographic source information for you; thus, even if you machine-copy everything, you must still make notes fully identifying your sources, page numbers, and so on. Therefore, the advice that follows on how to take notes can and should prove beneficial to you at some point in your research.

It's especially important that writers engage their minds with the material as early as possible in the writing process, thus note taking by hand.

Take One Note per Card or Page. After you have written down *all* the necessary bibliographic information at the top of your first note card or note page, write just *one* note on that card or page. If, after you've finished that first note, you find information for a second note from the same source, put the new note on a *new* card or page but be careful to identify on the card or page the *particular* source the note comes from. For example, if your first note comes from the aforementioned source by Tony Early ("Carolina on His Mind") and you have the full bibliographic information on that first note card, the second note from that same source can be simply identified as "Early." Take the second, third, and however many additional "Early" notes you wish, using a new card or page for each note, and giving *the appropriate page number(s)* for the information each note represents.

Stress to students that being systematic and particular about even the smallest research details at this stage will pay huge dividends in later times of possible panic. One of us neglected to put the page number on a note card during initial dissertation research, and that missing page number eventually necessitated a frantic trip back to the library to find the source and page number only hours before the finished, typed dissertation was to be defended, signed, and delivered to the graduate dean's office.

Examples

NOTE 1 **Short Paraphrase and Short Quotation Combined**

> Early, Tony. "Carolina on His Mind." Newsweek 4 Oct. 1990: 26.
>
> Early says that "North Carolina has produced some great fiction writers in this century." Though authorities disagree as to which of these writers is the greatest, every authority mentions Thomas Wolfe prominently. [26]

NOTE 2 **Long Quotation**

> Early, 26
>
> "To any discerning reader, [Thomas] Wolfe's Eugene Gant of Look Homeward, Angel and George Webber of You Can't Go Home Again are clearly the same person, and that person is, just as clearly, Wolfe himself. Similarly, the small Appalachian hometown of both Gant and Webber is Wolfe's Asheville, North Carolina." [26]

Don't Confuse Quoted and Paraphrased Material. When you take notes, be absolutely sure you do not confuse *quoted material* with *paraphrased material.* Remember, quotation means you have put down the words *exactly* as they are in your source. In your note, put all quoted material in *double quotation marks* (") and remember that you must have quotation marks at the beginning *and* end of the quoted material; quotation marks *always* come in pairs—opening *and* closing. In note 1 above, only those words enclosed in quotation marks are the words exactly as they appear in the Early source. The rest is *paraphrase*—which means that the note writer has put the information in his or her *own* words. In note 2 above, the entire note is quoted.

Here are some other things to remember about quoted material:

- Try to avoid inserting any of your own explanatory words into quoted material. If you must insert such words, though, do so in *brackets.* Look at note 2 above. The note writer had to insert [Thomas] in brackets in order to identify clearly the novelist under discussion.
- Try to avoid leaving out words of any material you are quoting. If, however, you must omit one or more words, indicate such omission with an *ellipsis* (three spaced periods, four when the quoted sentence ends with the ellipsis). Following is note 2 above, this time reflecting ellipses:

NOTE 2

> Early, 26.
>
> "To any discerning reader, [Thomas] Wolfe's Eugene Gant of Look Homeward, Angel and George Webber of You Can't Go Home Again are clearly the same person, and that person is . . . Wolfe himself. Similarly, the small Appalachian hometown of both Gant and Webber is Wolfe's Asheville, North Carolina."

- When you are quoting, whether you are inserting words, omitting words, or presenting the words exactly as they are in the source, you must *blend* the quoted matter smoothly into your own writing. In note 1 above, for example, you can see that the note writer took a direct quotation—"North Carolina has produced some great fiction writers in this century"—and blended it smoothly and grammatically into the note's first sentence. The second sentence, which contains no direct quotation, nevertheless fits well with the first sentence. The reader has no problem clearly following the meaning of the note. And when such notes are used in a finished and polished paper, the blending should still be smooth and grammatical. Typically, you should use a colon before a quotation that you are formally introducing; otherwise, use a comma or no punctuation at all when the quotation serves smoothly as a part of the sentence. Note our handling of these matters in the various examples that follow.

Remember, When You Are Taking Notes, Always Place Quoted Material in Quotation Marks. Otherwise, put the information in your *own* words (paraphrase). Do *not* make a poor paraphrase, changing only minor things. Except for certain words for which there are no substitutes (such as *a, an, the,* and most conjunctions and prepositions), a good paraphrase does not imitate the language of the original; nor does it imitate the sentence structure of the original. (For related guidance, see the section entitled "Plagiphrasing" below.)

Remember, Each Note You Take Should Clearly Indicate Which Source and What Page(s) of That Source It Comes From. Nothing is more frustrating than to find that you forgot to put this most basic information on a note that you are going to use. The remedy, too often, is a hurried trip back to the library.

Using Information from Sources

Many students find *sketching* a more useful early stage structural representation than outlining; both are quite acceptable to us. A student who starts with a sketch and then in some later stage transfers it into an outline is doing a very respectable job, it seems to us.

Once your research is complete, you are ready to begin organizing what you've learned. If you write out an outline or sketch showing the general developmental pattern you think your paper should follow, you've begun the *drafting* stage of your writing process. If you don't write any plan down yet—if you're just thinking about what you've learned, letting it "incubate" for a while—then you're still in the *thinking* stage. Whichever stage you're in, you are definitely beginning to *organize* what you have learned, and you therefore need to be aware of the following guidelines for using specific information that you've discovered.

What to Document. The word *documentation* refers to citing the source of your information (whether it is a long or a short quotation or is a long or a short paraphrase). Essentially, you'll be trying to write your entire paper from memory and in your own words. There is no need to document specific information that is generally known—such as that Christopher Columbus is widely credited with being the "discoverer" of America. But at certain points you will need to report specific information that is not widely known, such as

a statistical figure (or figures);

a paraphrased fact (or facts); or

a short or a long quotation (when the original words are far more effective than any paraphrase you could create).

Such specific borrowings *require* documentation. Most contemporary documentation systems, including the MLA, call for in-text parenthetical documentation.

In-text Parenthetical Documentation. In-text parenthetical documentation depends on an alphabetized list of sources that you use in your paper. This list, which should give correct bibliographic information according to the form prescribed by the system your teacher wants you to use, will appear at the end of your paper. You don't have to make this list before you draft your paper, for you can simply make it after the draft is complete and you know exactly which sources you used. What is important is to include this list in proper form at the end of your finished paper, for all your in-text documentation will refer to it.

In-text parenthetical documentation should pinpoint the exact page or pages of the source you used. Such documentation should be brief, so that the parenthetical information does not interfere with the smooth reading of the paper. Ordinarily, giving in parentheses the author's last name and the page number will suffice. Here, for example, is how a paraphrase of note 1 above might appear, properly documented, in a double-spaced paper:

> The state of North Carolina has produced a great many outstanding writers of fiction, and there is little agreement as to who the most important of these writers is. Virtually every authority, however, mentions Thomas Wolfe as being among the greatest (Early 26).

Note that the period ending the sentence comes *after* the parenthetical documentation. A reader who wanted to check the reference could turn to the Works Cited list at the end of the paper, find there the full publication information for the Early article, and then go find the Early article in a library and read it.

All quotations should be *attributed;* that is, the source should be named in setting up the quotation. Because the source is already named, all that needs to be placed in the parenthetical documentation is the page number(s) from which the quotation comes. Here, for example, is how a short direct quotation from note 2 might be incorporated into a paper. Because the quotation blends smoothly with the sentence leading into it, no punctuation is needed before the quotation:

Because attribution is so important in use of source material, we strongly emphasize it in this chapter on research papers. Additional material on proper quotation procedure can be found in chapter 30 of the hardbound edition of this book.

> Many authorities have noted the prevalence of autobiography in the fiction--particularly the early work--of several American writers. Critic Tony Early, for example, has said of novelist Thomas Wolfe that "Wolfe's Eugene Gant of Look Homework, Angel and George Webber of You Can't Go Home Again are clearly the same person, and that person . . . is Wolfe himself" (26).

Note that in this case the parenthetical documentation comes *after* the closing quotation mark and *before* the period ending the sentence. Because the author of the source, Tony Early, is already mentioned, his name need not be repeated in the documentation.

The same sort of brief parenthetical documentation can be used when a *long* quotation is presented after attribution. Here, for example, is how note 2 might be incorporated as a long quotation (more than four complete lines of quoted material) in a paper:

> Autobiography seems to be a staple in the work of many American writers, regardless of genre. The exuberant "I" in Walt Whitman's poems is always the poet himself; Tom Wingfield in Tennessee Williams's first play, The Glass Menagerie, is unmistakably the

playwright himself; and, as critic Tony Early has noted of novelist Thomas Wolfe:

> To any discerning reader, Wolfe's Eugene Gant of Look Homeward, Angel and George Webber of You Can't Go Home Again are clearly the same person; and that person is, just as clearly, Wolfe himself. Similarly, the small Appalachian hometown of both Gant and Webber is Wolfe's Asheville, North Carolina. (26)

The citation here is "(26)" and not "(Early 26)" because Early's name is given right before the quotation.

Note here that long quotations are *not* placed in quotation marks. Their uniform indentation (usually ten spaces from the margin) is the signal to the reader that the material is quoted. Long quotations should employ quotation marks only when the quoted material already contains quotation marks, as in spoken dialogue. In those cases, the quotation marks signal the source's exact speech, not the source's exact writing.

Though author and page number are the most common way to handle parenthetical documentation, there are other ways to provide more complex documentation in parentheses. Here are a few:

(Allen and Brubaker 25-28)

[This documents a paraphrase of information taken from three pages of a source by two authors.]

(Carlyle, "Violence" 24)

[This documents an article by an author who has more than one work included in the Works Cited list. The author's name here means that the author is not mentioned in the text prior to the documentation. If he were, the documentation would be simply ("Violence" 24). "Violence" is a shortened version of the full title, "Violence in the Movies," given to identify *which* Carlyle source is being documented. Shortened titles are important in cases like this to save space and keep the parenthetical information brief.]

(Carlyle, "Yet More" 42-43)

[This documents another Carlyle source used in the same paper. The paraphrased material begins on page 42 and concludes on page 43 of the source. The full title of the source is "Yet More Movie Mayhem."]

(MacAlester 31; Reed and Zollner 44-45)

[This documents related information that comes from two different sources.]

("Prime Time" 62)

[This documents an anonymous magazine article. Because there is no author's name, a shortened version of the full title, "Prime Time Talk

Show Hosts," is given to identify the source, which is not named in the text prior to the documentation. If it had been mentioned, the documentation would be simply (62).]

These models will not cover every possible documentation situation that may arise in your paper. In such cases, consult either the handbook or the style guide for the system that your teacher requires or consult directly with your teacher. Note also the way documentation is handled in the student research paper by Collin Walker, later in this chapter, and in other student research–based papers in this textbook (such as Theresa Moreno's paper on Acid Rain in chapter 12).

Plagiphrasing

"Plagiphrasing" is what Dr. Kathleen Turner, a friend of ours, calls a student's serious—but failed—attempt to avoid plagiarism by changing just a few words from the original source. It occurs frequently when beginning writers are still a bit foggy on how to paraphrase a source well. For review, let's note the following:

Plagiarism is deliberately copying someone else's written or spoken words and presenting them without acknowledgment of the source, as if they were your own words. Plagiarism is dishonest at best, and a serious academic offense. When it occurs outside the school setting, it is punishable under copyright laws.

Paraphrasing is taking someone else's words and ideas and rephrasing them almost exclusively in your own words. A good paraphrase presents the essence of what someone else has written or said, but in no way does it present the wording—or even the same sentence structure and organization—contained in the original. Paraphrases must still be properly acknowledged by attribution and/or accurate documentation.

Often, beginning writers who are not yet experienced in research techniques lack the confidence to produce a good paraphrase or summary of what someone else has written or said. Knowing they cannot copy the original without plagiarizing, such students change a few of the words and present what amounts to a bad paraphrase—a plagiphrase—of the original, and then document it. The documentation shows that such students are not trying to be dishonest. But they must still learn how to paraphrase well to avoid being inadvertent plagiarists.

This is a good time to review with students your school's policy on plagiarism.

An Example of Plagiphrasing. Here is how a student of ours recently began a research paper on the 1989 Exxon *Valdez* oil-tanker spill:

> The Exxon Valdez oil tanker went aground at 12:04 A.M. on a drizzly Good Friday, March 24, 1989. Its hull was torn open in eight places, sending eleven million gallons of crude oil into ocean waves that broke as high as two feet on the surface (Adler 59). A contingency plan mandated by law requires the Alyeska Pipeline Service Company, located in Valdez, to respond to a spill within five

hours. The response took up to twelve hours (Marshall 244). Nearly all the tanker's oil was released during those critical hours.

That's interesting, and it is well written. It is also a plagiphrase from the two different sources:

Adler, Jerry. "Alaska after Exxon." Newsweek 18 Sept. 1989: 50-64.

Marshall, Eliot. "Valdez: The Predicted Oil Spill." Science 7 Apr. 1989: 20+.

[*Note:* The + sign in the Marshall citation means that the article begins on page 20 and is continued farther back in the issue, on an additional page or pages.] First, let's see what Adler actually wrote on *Newsweek*'s page 59. We quote:

> The Exxon *Valdez* went aground in the middle of a drizzly night in March. Its hull was ripped open in eight places, sending oil surging into the water in waves that broke as high as two feet on the surface (59).

Here's what Eliot Marshall wrote on page 244 of *Science:*

> A contingency plan mandated by law requires the Alyeska Pipeline Service Company, whose terminal is at Valdez, to respond to a spill within 5 hours. The response took 10 to 12 hours. . . . Nearly all the oil was released in the first 12 hours. . . . (244).

Here is the student's paragraph again, this time with the duplicated words, phrases, and clauses in all capitals:

THE EXXON VALDEZ oil tanker WENT AGROUND at 12:04 A.M. on a DRIZZLY Good Friday, March 24, 1989. ITS HULL WAS torn OPEN IN EIGHT PLACES, SENDING eleven million gallons of crude oil into ocean WAVES THAT BROKE AS HIGH AS TWO FEET ON THE SURFACE (Adler 59). A CONTINGENCY PLAN MANDATED BY LAW REQUIRES THE ALYESKA PIPELINE SERVICE COMPANY, located in VALDEZ, TO RESPOND TO A SPILL WITHIN FIVE HOURS. THE RESPONSE TOOK up to TWELVE HOURS (Marshall 244).

Even if you grant that the student could hardly have come up with substitutes for words like *Valdez, hours,* and *Alyeska Pipeline Service Company,* you must also grant that there are many other ways to say the weather was drizzly, the tanker had eight fractures, and so on. Trying to put these passages into her own words, this student unintentionally paraphrased badly—plagiphrased. Our point is that although it takes time, effort, *and* resourcefulness to come up with a good paraphrase, anything less than a good paraphrase may disappoint your readers (including your teacher) and thus may also disappoint you.

What *is* a good way to paraphrase the Adler and Marshall information? Here's one possibility:

> Exxon's tanker Valdez foundered in light rain and two-foot waves on March 24, 1989. Some eleven million gallons of crude oil then escaped through eight tears in the ship's hull (Adler 59). By law, Alyeska Pipeline Service Company of nearby Valdez is supposed to respond to such spills within five hours, but virtually all of the tanker's oil had leaked by the time a response was actually made, nearly twelve hours after the accident (Marshall 244).

Always do your best to use your sources fairly and accurately. Eventually you will find it easier to do so, and the ultimate beneficiaries will be your readers and—while you're still a student, anyway—your grades.

A Student Writes a Research Paper

Collin Walker, a freshman at his state university, was assigned a research paper in his composition class after being given an introduction to the research process and to the use of the library on his campus. The teacher said that students could choose general topics of their own interest but that the papers had to (a) reflect what the students learned in their research and (b) document that research properly.

Collin, a longtime sports fan who had played high school football, had recently read an article about the use of steroids among bodybuilders, and decided he would do his research paper on athletes' steroid abuse. In class, the teacher asked each student what he or she was planning to do. When Collin said he planned to do research on the abuse of steroids among athletes, the teacher asked, "What kind of steroids? Which athletes?" The questions were unexpected, and Collin had to admit he hadn't thought about the possibility of different kinds of steroids and different kinds of athletes. "You'll need to narrow it down," said the teacher, "but the basic idea sounds good."

Collin remembered that fairly recently an Olympic runner had been disqualified for using steroids, but this runner had taken the steroids to build his endurance, not to add muscle mass and strength, the way the bodybuilders had done. Different athletes, different goals, and even different steroids had to be taken into account; Collin could see what his teacher meant by the need to narrow his topic down. He decided he needed to go to the library as soon as possible. Within a week he had to submit a specific topic and a "working source list" of at least five sources from his library.

When Collin arrived at the library, he went straight to the computer terminals for his library's book holdings; a couple of weeks earlier, during an orientation, he had been shown how these terminals operate. He started up the system and, using the term *steroids,* initiated what the computer called a "subject search." The result was a barrage of related subject headings, many of them directing him to be more specific. "Narrow it down," Collin muttered, as he tapped the keys and tried to think of ways to do just that. He then remembered that the article he had originally read had been about bodybuilders who abused steroids. He decided he would search now by concentrating on steroid *abuse*, and he initiated a search for sources that reflected both "abuse" and "steroids." This approach was much more productive. He got a much more manageable list of specific sources, and he noticed that a particular kind of steroid—anabolic—was often mentioned in the list. He wrote down the authors, titles, and call numbers of some of the more promising looking books.

Collin then moved to the group of computers that would give him access to the library's computerized magazine and journal index. Some of the bodybuilders, he remembered, were football players as well—a group of athletes that interested him more than bodybuilders in general. Collin thus ran subject searches for "steroids—anabolic" and "steroids—football" and was pleased to see many listed articles, including the one he had read originally. This new search had eliminated material about the kinds of steroids that were irrelevant to his interest. Now Collin had plenty of sources for a working source list for a paper about anabolic steroid abuse among football players. He checked the library's serials catalog to see which of the indexed articles his library held and to get the call numbers for those magazines and journals.

Because his library had not yet computerized access to its newspaper holdings, Collin had to search for newspaper articles "the old-fashioned way." Realizing that he already had more sources than he was likely to need, he elected to check only *The New York Times Index* for the preceding five years. He reasoned that such an important newspaper would contain the most pertinent articles over that period of time, and he knew that his library held daily issues of the *New York Times* on microfilm; hence, if the index entry looked promising, Collin could be assured that his library held the issue he'd want to look at. Checking the *Times* index yielded several more potentially useful articles. Collin was now satisfied that he had a good working list of sources. He could meet the next stage of his assignment, which was to submit to the teacher a statement of his now-narrowed-down topic, along with a working list of sources—complete with call numbers.

As you can see, we recommend at least three "checkpoints" for your students to meet with you while writing their research reports. These checkpoints usually involve a short office conference with you, although some teachers prefer to accomplish this monitoring via group work. This is the first checkpoint.

His teacher was pleased but noted on Collin's source list that further narrowing might be in order. "Consider the different levels of football—professional, college, high school, even children's leagues," his teacher wrote. "Are steroids being abused at all levels?" Collin had meanwhile read one of the magazine articles he'd found, about a professional player who'd used steroids before they were discovered to be harmful. He decided he'd concentrate on abuse among professional players.

Such surprise is characteristic of the discovery stage.

But as Collin began to read more, he was surprised to learn that steroid abuse was indeed going on at just about every level of play his teacher had cited. Professional, collegiate, and even high school players were using steroids to build their bodies and strength, even when some of these players were aware of the risks. It seemed sad to Collin that such young players were being caught up in the dangerous business of seeking a competitive edge through risking not just their general health but their lives as well. One article he read about a high school football player who died from steroid abuse convinced Collin that his focus should be on abuse not just in the pros but throughout the sport. In fact, he decided that his emphasis should be precisely on how shocking it is that the abuse occurs at virtually every level of competition.

Collin began taking notes on anabolic steroid abuse wherever organized football is played in the United States. At the next checkpoint, he had easily prepared enough notes from different sources to show his teacher that his research was under way and making progress. He outlined a rough plan for his paper:

This is the second checkpoint.

- An introduction explaining what anabolic steroids are and why football players use them, despite their dangers, at three different levels of play: professional, collegiate, and high school
- A section on steroid abuse among professional players
- A section on steroid abuse among collegiate players
- A section on steroid abuse among high school players
- A conclusion refocusing the issue and urging reform

His teacher approved the plan, and Collin began to draft.

While he drafted, Collin let Michael, his roommate, and Maria, a friend from class, read what he was writing. "I think you need to interview someone yourself," said Maria. "Do you think you could find somebody who used to play high school football and took steroids for a while?" Michael was even more enthusiastic about the idea of an interview. "Find somebody on the university team who's using steroids now," he suggested. "Guarantee you won't tell his name. Tell him you just want to know his impressions." But Collin's dad vetoed that idea the next weekend, when Collin called home. "Too dangerous," his father said. "From what I hear about players who abuse those steroids, they can be pretty hostile. I don't want you to get hurt seeming to meddle in somebody else's problem."

After Collin read an article about the behavior of a college football player who had abused steroids (an article he wound up using extensively in his paper), Collin decided his father was right: to approach a powerful stranger about this sensitive subject *would* be risky. Fortunately, one evening in the dorm recreation room Collin met a resident who, on learning the subject of Collin's research paper, casually mentioned his own use of steroids during his high school football–playing days:

> I used them for a while. I gained weight and strength, but I also got depressed a lot and did things I usually wouldn't do—grumpy, grouchy, destructive things. My folks noticed right away, and so did most of my friends. I quit using them, and later, when I began to hear about what was happening to other people, I was glad I had quit. Taking steroids is gambling, plain and simple, with your life. Your game improves, but your life gets worse—lots worse. It's like Wild Bill Hickock, holding aces and eights at that poker table in Deadwood—he had a good hand for the game, but his back was exposed, and that wound up costing him his life.

The resident said Collin could quote him in the paper but asked to be kept anonymous. The interview proved very useful in Collin's paper; what's more, the gambling analogy gave him an idea that strengthened the paper's development.

As he returned to drafting his paper, Collin sorted his notes. His book sources had mostly provided highly technical, medical information about steroids. He knew he needed a section in which he defined anabolic steroids generally, explaining what they are and what they are used for. But most important, he'd found an abundance of written information about players who had suffered from their abuse of steroids. Now it was time to select the best examples and get the draft put together for an upcoming draft workshop in class.

This is the third checkpoint.

One week later, Collin took a draft of his paper to class for the workshop. There he got constructive suggestions that helped him to make his examples clearer and his organization tighter. Specifically, he narrowed his examples to three detailed cases, one at each level of play. After ironing out a few questions about documentation, he was ready to put together his final version, which follows.

Collin Walker

Professor Smith

English 101

5 December 1992

Steroid Abuse in Football: A Dead Man's Hand

"Taking steroids is gambling, plain and simple, with your life." That's what the college freshman said, matter-of-factly, as he sipped a soft drink in the dormitory's recreation room. The conversation had been about using anabolic steroids to enhance strength and aggressive play among high school football players. The freshman had used steroids when he was a high school player but had quit when he found out what a serious risk he was taking. "Your game improves, but your life gets worse--lots worse," he continued. "It's like Wild Bill Hickock, holding aces and eights at that poker table in Deadwood--he had a good hand for the game, but his back was exposed, and that wound up costing him his life" (Anonymous interview, 3 November 1992). 1

This freshman isn't the only ex-football player to decide that the combination of anabolic steroids and football isn't a winning hand, but he is one of the luckier ones because he quit long before serious damage was done. Increasingly, the media are full of stories about players who 2 are much less fortunate. The high-pressure, succeed-at-any-cost world of competitive football, even at the amateur high school level, has caused too many players to make bad decisions in their frantic effort to get an edge.

3 In the case of anabolic steroid abuse, the edge comes from the drug's effects on both the body's strength and the mind's psychological attitude. Players who use steroids generally get bigger, stronger, and--at least in strict terms of on-field performance--better. As William N. Taylor, author of Hormonal Manipulation, says:

> Anabolic steroids do in fact enhance the performance and alter the appearance, size, and psychological makeup of the athletes who use them. And the use of anabolic steroids may be serving as an impetus for the hormonal manipulation of future athletes in many ways. (8)

In other words, better players through drug use. The ultimate cost for such better players, however, can and often does come tragically high. This "downside," though, is seldom on a young football player's mind when he first seeks to improve his game.

4 If the player is a professional, he may believe his only chance to make the team is to abuse steroids. His livelihood is involved. People have known for a long time that professional football players have abused and still abuse steroids, but what is becoming more apparent and even more shocking is that steroid abuse is climbing down the football ladder. More and more college players and even high school players are now abusing anabolic steroids to enhance their football-playing performances. A recent survey conducted by Charles Yesalis, a professor of health at Pennsylvania State University, showed that 6.6 percent of all high school seniors take steroids. Food and Drug Administration Commissioner Frank Young, moreover, estimates that 10 percent of all high school students take them (Noden and Telander 75). What all these people do not seem to understand is that steroid abuse is a losing hand. They should hear about the cases of the professional player Steve Courson, the collegiate player Tommy Chaikin, and the high school player Benji Ramirez.

We are intentionally using "he" to refer to football players. We recognize that there have occasionally been female players in the tackle version of the game, but under the circumstances use of "he or she" here seems unnecessarily solicitous. If the paper dealt with track and field, for example, the gender of pronouns would be more of a problem.

5 Steve Courson was a player for the Pittsburgh Steelers of the National Football League (NFL). Only the best players make it to the pinnacle of playing professionally in the NFL. How to maintain that

pinnacle is a constant challenge to all NFL players. Courson took steroids to remain competitive in the NFL. Because there was no antisteroid policy in the NFL at the time, in May 1985 Courson spoke to a reporter from *Sports Illustrated* about his steroid use. In the resulting article, "Getting Physical--and Chemical," he was quoted as saying, "Right now, there's an X factor. You don't know what it is, but you're reaping the benefits" (Lieber 54).

According to an unsigned article in the same magazine four years 6
later, however, one of the "benefits" Courson seems to have "reaped" is a seriously damaged heart. In this later article, Courson's physician, Dr. Richard Rosenbloom, says, "Steve's heart is stretched and dilated. It is flabby and doesn't pump as a normal heart should." Rosenbloom is not sure whether steroid use definitely caused Courson's heart damage. In fact, he suspects a virus, not steroids. But he cannot rule out the possibility that steroids caused the problem, which can be corrected, if at all, only by a heart transplant. Rosenbloom points out that heavy steroid use usually leads to a thickening of the walls of the heart. This is the opposite of what has happened to Courson's heart. Still, concludes Rosenbloom, "We don't know that Steve's condition is not the result of heavy anabolic steroid use" ("X Factor" 34). And that uncertainty is why steroid use is like poker: it is a gamble one takes. Chances are that had Steve Courson known in 1985 what steroids might do to him, he wouldn't have taken that gamble.

A college player, Tommy Chaikin, took the same risk. Chaikin, a 7
football standout at the University of South Carolina, abused steroids to such an extent that his personality was affected and he became suicidal. He saw his life pass before him one traumatic night, and he narrowly escaped taking his own life. He had gone to South Carolina dreaming of a great career playing college and possibly professional football, only to lose his health and, at times, his sanity.

Chaikin had taken steroids in order to compete with his teammates, 8
most of whom were also on steroids. Before he took steroids, he simply got tired of getting knocked around in practice by his bigger, quicker friends. He knew that taking steroids would give him greater strength and weight, and would also increase, as William N. Taylor describes it, his "tendency toward 'explosive,' aggressive behavior" (Taylor 18).

Chaikin expected steroids to improve his football performance. They did. But they also gave him a heart murmur, high blood pressure, severe anxiety attacks, sleepless nights, and a near-heart attack.

9 Eventually, one night Chaikin found himself staring down the barrel of a .357 Magnum pistol, ready to end it all. His body and self-esteem had been torn down by steroids--the opposite of what he had originally intended. To others, it might have seemed that Chaikin had all he wanted: size, strength, looks, and a starting position on the South Carolina football team. And yet he was ready to end his life, to get out of what he later called a "living hell" (Chaikin and Telander 102).

10 Tommy Chaikin didn't pull the trigger. His father knocked on the dorm-room door before Chaikin could do so, and thus by chance Chaikin's suicide was avoided and he eventually began his long road toward recovery. What would have happened if Chaikin's father had not unexpectedly arrived? Things had started out fine for Chaikin, who at first seemed to be gambling with a good hand. But it very nearly became a dead man's hand. Now he has added his voice to those cautioning everyone--not just athletes--against using steroids.

11 From the professional players, down through the college players, and even down to the high school players, it seems as though no one is exempt from the temptation to gamble with steroids. Benji Ramirez, once a senior at Ashtabula High School in Ohio, is a tragic example of what can happen if a player risks his life by abusing steroids and loses.

12 Ramirez had taken steroids not only for football, but, as M. Noden and R. Telander report, also to give him a big body to "get girls" (72). He didn't seem to be unhealthy; as a matter of fact, he seemed "strong and fit" (Noden and Telander 70). But during a football practice he collapsed and died from an apparent heart attack. How does a seventeen-year-old die from a heart attack? The practice was not strenuous. There was no apparent good reason for his death. Gradually, however, it came to be known that Ramirez was a heavy abuser of steroids. In fact, his nickname at school was "'Roids" (Noden and Telander 76).

13 Benji Ramirez, like Tommy Chaikin, seemed to have it all. He was being considered for a football scholarship at Youngstown State University and was popular around school. "He was a really nice guy," says Aaron Morris, one of Ramirez's closest friends. "I don't think Benji had

any enemies. He was really low key. He didn't even like rock and roll" (Noden and Telander 70). That doesn't sound like someone who would use steroids, but it shows just how tempting the risk can be if the imagined results are attractive enough.

Gambling with anabolic steroids, like other forms of gambling, can be an addiction. The steroid addiction is so strong that once one starts to use steroids, it is next to impossible to stop. Tommy Chaikin knew steroids were wrecking his body; he just didn't do anything about it because he *looked* healthy, and he was getting plenty of playing time in the football games. Benji Ramirez, too, must have known something was wrong. In fact, he complained frequently to his mother about not feeling well. He probably had no idea that the steroids were making him sick, because few young people have been fully educated about the dangers of steroids. If they've learned anything, it is often only what they would consider the good effects of steroids. 14

Those "good" effects are as follows: 15

> increased skeletal muscle mass, increased organ mass, increased hemoglobin concentration, increased red blood cell mass, control of the distribution of body fat, increased calcium in the bones, increased total nitrogen retention, increased retention of several electrolytes, and increased protein synthesis. (Taylor 9)

That would probably sound good to any tempted young gambler. But M. Noden and R. Telander explain some of the harsher possible side effects: "liver and kidney disorders, temporary acne and balding, hypertension [high blood pressure], decreased sperm count, aggressive behavior, depression and irritability" (72). As a former high school football player and steroid user said of his steroid use: "I gained weight and strength, but I also got depressed a lot and did things I usually wouldn't do--grumpy, grouchy, destructive things" (Anonymous interview, 3 November 1992).

It's a shame that our society puts so much pressure on individual athletes to succeed. This pressure is so great, according to Alvin Sanoff of U. S. News and World Report, that "for that extra measure of strength and muscle many young athletes run the risk of damaging their health" (64). No game is worth that. It is ironic that one of the reasons sports developed was to help keep athletes physically fit, and now steroid 16 abuse is helping to undermine the purpose of participating in athletics. Steve Courson, Tommy Chaikin, and Benji Ramirez are just three players of the many who have lost. Sadly, there will be others who will lose in the poker game all athletes enter when they abuse anabolic steroids.

Works Cited

Anonymous. Personal interview [with former steroid abuser]. 3 November 1992.

Chaikin, Tommy, and Rick Telander. "The Nightmare of Steroids." Sports Illustrated 24 Oct. 1988: 82-88+.

Lieber, Jill. "Getting Physical--and Chemical." Sports Illustrated 13 May 1985: 38-42+.

Noden, M., and Rick Telander. "Death of an Athlete." Sports Illustrated 20 Feb. 1989: 68-72+.

Sanoff, Alvin P. "Drug Problem in Athletics: It's Not Only the Pros." U.S. News and World Report 17 Oct. 1983: 64+.

Taylor, William N. Hormonal Manipulation: A New Era of Monstrous Athletes. Jefferson: McFarland, 1985.

"Was the X Factor a Factor?" Sports Illustrated 3 April 1989: 34.

We are aware that Collin Walker's paper relies heavily on articles appearing in one particular magazine. In fact, his teacher rightly cautioned him about overreliance on different articles in one magazine. We think you should point out this overreliance and second the teacher's caution. That noted, however, we selected Collin's paper to include here because he demonstrates good overall sense of his subject, good organization, good integration of material learned through his research, and proper documentation of that research.

Collin Walker's paper is primarily a report of research and thus more informative than analytical, expressive, or persuasive. Its cautions about steroid abuse do give it a persuasive slant, however. If you want your students to see more analytical and persuasive student papers based on research, refer them to Theresa Moreno's paper "Acid Rain" (chapter 12) or Sheryl Rollins's "The Need for More Black Women Lawyers" (chapter 7).

General Guidelines for Preparing the Works Cited List

Each alphabetized entry has three main components: author, title, and publication information. Each component should be followed by a period and two spaces.

- **Book, Single Author**

  Allenby, Jack. Four Seasons in New England. New York: Knopf, 1991.

When additional components of information are required, continue to use the period-and-two-spaces means of separating those components.

- **Short Story in an Edited Anthology**

  Bennett, Jason. "Minute by Minute." Modern American Fiction. Ed. Jasper Johnson. 3rd ed. New York: Dutton, 1989. 234-45.

Some additional models follow:

- **Anonymous Book**

  Dictionary of Ballet. Lexington: Heath, 1990.

- **Anthologized Poem**

Lowell, Amy. "Patterns." A Treasury of Verse. Ed. Louis Junkin. San Francisco: City Lights, 1988. 34.

- **Article by Two Authors Appearing in a Learned Journal with Continuous Pagination Throughout the Volume**

Gregorian, Victor, and Marvin Mitchel. "Discourse Theory and the Politics of Instruction." University English Studies 3 (1991): 133-51.

- **Introduction to a Book (When the Book Is Written by Someone Else)**

Hallam, Nestor. Introduction. In a New York Minute. By Thomas L. Adeler. New York: Bantam, 1992. iii-ix.

- **Translation**

Ignacio, Valdes Arturo. Ladron. Trans. Susan Skidmore. Dallas: Mesquite, 1989.

- **Republished Book (First Date Is Original Date of Publication)**

Inge, William. Picnic. 1953. Lawrence: UP of Kansas, 1991.

- **Signed Article in a Multivolume Reference Book Edited by Several People**

Jefferson, Boggs. "American Theatre during the Depression." Encyclopedia of American Drama. Ed. Travis Kerbow, et al. 3 vols. New York: Thespian, 1988.

- **Pamphlet**

Law-Making in Washington: From Bill to Law. Chicago: Myers Educational Publications, 1989.

- **Article in a Scholarly Journal that Pages Issues Separately**

Nabors, Thomas. "Prairie Architecture." Nebraska Horizon 12 (1987): 45-50.

- **Article in a Monthly Magazine**

Oglethorpe, Presley. "Southern California and the Great Debate over Water." Ecology Today Aug. 1990: 22+.

(For magazines issued more frequently, see the Newsweek and Sports Illustrated citations earlier in this chapter.)

- **Daily Newspaper Article, Edition Specified**

Parsons, Alan. "Surviving the Tax Menace." New York Times 15 Apr. 1991, natl. ed.: 18.

Writers' Circle

Although we give a list of possible topics at the end of this "Writers' Circle," we want to stress that the best topics are the ones you help your students come up with. Whenever we give such lists, they are meant to be indicative, not restrictive.

Divide into teams consisting of three investigative reporters each. Each team should then (a) choose a subject for research from the list below and (b) divide the research into tasks so that no researcher is likely to duplicate the efforts of another. For example, one reporter on the team could investigate books; another, newspapers; and the third, magazines and journals. The object is for each researcher to find, examine, and take informative notes from at least two different sources on the subject.

After each researcher has completed those tasks, each group should then meet and combine its information into a brief, documented report for the rest of the class.

Subject Choices

The Watergate scandal (1972–74)

The *Roe* v. *Wade* Supreme Court decision (1972)

The *Brown* v. *Topeka Board of Education* Supreme Court decision (1954)

The first moon landing (1969)

The Iranian hostage crisis (1979–80)

The Normandy invasion (June 6, 1944)

The Kennedy versus Nixon presidential campaign (1960)

The Selma-to-Montgomery civil rights march (1965)

The Kaliningrad Oblast

The San Francisco earthquake (1989)

WRITING ASSIGNMENTS

1. It's instructive to know the sizes of the various libraries you use. Write a report comparing your high school library, your hometown library, and your college library, being sure to credit your sources properly. How big is each in number of square feet, size of holdings, and number of periodicals? Digging a little deeper, name what classification system each uses, explain to what extent and in what ways access to the collection is computerized, and tell whether (and under what conditions) outsiders are allowed access to the materials. If you can, report the approximate budget for each library. Include any other information you deem relevant. From all that, draw (and support) a conclusion about the appropriateness of each collection for its users.
2. Survey other university libraries in your state and compare them (on points such as those in question 1 above) with your own. Can you draw conclusions about the quality of those universities from those data? Write the results in the form of a short report. Be sure to document your sources.

3. Choose one national or world news event that had an effect on your life when you were in high school. Using your library's resources, collect data about that event to put into a short, factual report. Be sure to credit your sources. Include in your report some explanation of how and why this event affected your life. In particular, how does the event continue to influence you? Do you see it the same way now as you did then?
4. Choose a popular rock-and-roll band from the 1970s or 1980s and write a report naming its original members and, to the extent you can, documenting where they are now. Be sure to credit your sources.
5. With advice from your teacher, interview a faculty or staff member at your university who has published a book or patented an invention. Inquire especially about the creative process involved in the work. Write the results of your interview in the form of a short report on creativity, making sure to distinguish between primary and secondary sources.
6. Research your library's important reference tools for your college major (if you don't have a major yet, choose a field you may major in). In particular, what are the periodical indexes for that major? List and briefly describe them. Which ones seem most accessible? most useful? most complete? Write the results in the form of a short report entitled "Reference Tools at ____________ Library for ____________ Majors."
7. With your teacher's advice as to topic, length, format, and so on, write a library research report, paying careful attention to all the points covered in this chapter. Remember that the *best* reports include a mix of primary and secondary information. As you write your report, keep a journal (in a format your teacher specifies) describing each time period you work on the report; you need dated, timed entries for each activity period. Also, save all your research notes, note cards, photocopies, rough drafts, and so on—anything you put on paper in connection with this project—for possible review by your teacher. Expect to be asked to submit your journal at regular intervals for your teacher to review.
8. The photograph on page 593 depicts a typical "stack" of bookshelves in a university library (here, Harvard's Widner Library). In spite of modern research aids such as computerized searches and on-line data bases, one time-tested method of discovery remains browsing shelves like these: once you find a section with several books on your general subject, you might just find most of what you need. The photo reminds us that all libraries are, in essence, places where sources are collected and made available for learners. This is true regardless of the size or age of the library.

   In a brief paper, reminisce about your library experiences: what is the earliest library you used? Was it your parents' collection of books or magazines? What is the public library in your home town like? What about the libraries in your schools? How did going to and using those libraries make you feel? Are your memories of libraries mostly good, bad, or neutral? When you use your university library now, do you feel industrious, like a serious discoverer on the prowl? Or do you feel intimidated by its size and (apparent) mysteries?

chapter 24 Writing Reports

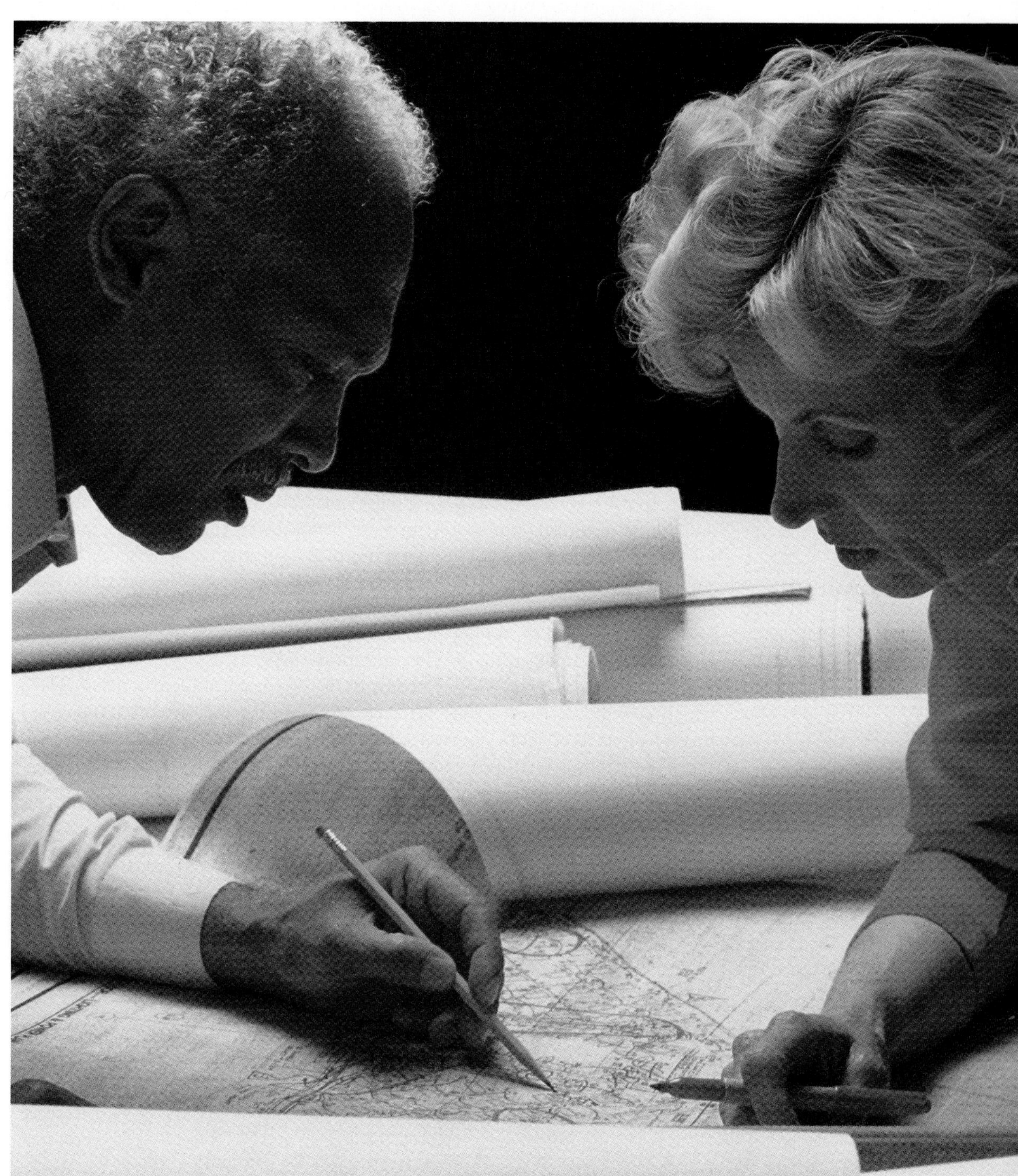

"A whole is that which has beginning, middle, and end."

Aristotle

We know people write more letters than reports. But we believe reports are more important in the career sense students are usually most concerned about. They're certainly more substantial!

After completing freshman composition, many college students find that report writing is their central writing activity as students. It is also the central writing activity of American business, industry, and government.

Five Key Questions for Report Writers

We believe that finding good answers to five key questions lies at the heart of writing a good report:

1. What is the *need* for this report?
2. What is the *goal* of this report?
3. What is the *audience* for this report?
4. What is the *source* of this report's information?
5. What is the primary issue, or *stasis*, of this report?

It's a truism by now that writing has both static and dynamic elements—that is, both product- and process-driven qualities. We wish it were also a truism, also as widely known and frequently discussed, that the essence of good writing (or of a good writing class) is the successful integration of the two.

The better job you do of answering these questions about each report you write, and the more you let your writing process be *affected* by those answers, the better job you will do writing *any* kind of report, in any setting. We believe this because we believe that all good writing reflects the writer's *reasons* for writing (as we show in Part Two of this book), the writer's *knowledge* of the subject (the result of critical reading and thinking), and the writer's assessment of the *audience*—all of which are subsumed in the five key questions above.

Please stress that this is a *review* draft; it was not handed in as finished work. We open with a review draft here so as to show your students, at length and in depth, the road to successful integration of process and product discussed in the preceding annotation. Here this road involves answering the "five key questions for report writers" and applying those answers to the review draft.

This chapter opens with a "review draft" of a brief, student-written report, which we will discuss in terms of the five questions listed above. We'll then dwell further on each of those questions, along with describing ways that answers to those questions can fit into your writing process. Finally, we'll follow a student through her own report-writing process. (The next chapter looks at a particular type of persuasive report—proposals—in detail.)

Draft of a Student Report

First we would like you to read this draft of a student's report. As you read it, jot down your ideas for how it could be made better in a subsequent revision. Later in this chapter we'll talk about how we think the points made in the chapter could be used to revise the draft. Don't be surprised or disappointed if you find this draft dull, that's intentional.

One of the things we've learned from research and experience is that once a student declares "closure" on a writing project—for example, when a teacher puts a grade on it—there's not much hope the student will learn anything more

Elements of a Master Budget

[Review Draft—Not for Grading]

Jewella Sadeghi, college writing student

1 Like most people, corporations use budgets to plan and control their expenses. This report explains the five components of a corporation's master budget. In addition to learning more about how corporations work, from reading this paper you may pick up some good hints for handling your own personal budget.

2 A corporation's master budget has five main parts:

1. Sales Budget
2. Production Budget
3. Manufacturing Cost Budget
4. Purchases Budget
5. Selling and Administrative Expense Budget

In addition to these parts, the master budget includes forecasted financial statements based on the results of the above estimates.

1. Sales Budget

3 Predicted sales are based on several items, such as last month's sales, industry growth rate, and the company's share of the market. Each corporation also adapts the forecast to fit its own needs, and so no standardized method for predicting sales is available. The prediction is usually based on judgment and stated in both dollar sales and unit sales.

2. Production Budget

4 The production budget shows how many units of product have to be produced in the budgeted time period (which can be a week, a month, a quarter, or a year) to meet projected sales and inventory requirements. This budget has two subparts: the finished-goods requirement and the production requirement.

Finished-Goods Requirement

5 The finished-goods requirement is the number of units of finished goods that must be available during the budgeted time period to meet sales and inventory requirements. The number of unit sales for that time period (desired sales) is added to the number of completed units that need to be in inventory at the end of the period (desired ending inventory).

from that task unless the *teacher* insists on it. Thus, the longer students continue to work on a piece, one draft after another, without declaring such closure, the better in terms of their learning. Through detailed, thoughtful revision of *adequate* drafts like the one shown here, we teach students how to keep working until *they* are satisfied with their writing.

Production Requirement

The production requirement is the number of units that must be 6
produced to meet sales and inventory requirements. The number of units on hand at the beginning of the period (beginning inventory) is subtracted from the finished-goods requirement.

3. Manufacturing Cost Budget

The manufacturing cost budget shows the costs incurred to produce 7
the number of units calculated in the production requirement. Two types of costs make up the manufacturing cost budget: variable costs and fixed costs.

Variable Costs

Variable costs are applied on a basis of cost per unit produced. 8
Variable costs would include any cost that changes depending on how many units are produced. For example, labor costs are variable costs; if no product is produced, there is no labor cost.

Fixed Costs

Fixed costs are those which remain the same each time period 9
regardless of the number of units produced. The rent paid on the building is a fixed cost.

4. Purchases Budget

The purchases budget lays out the number of units of raw materials 10
that need to be purchased in order to meet production and inventory requirements. While the production budget is based on sales forecasts and is presented in units of finished product, the purchases budget is based on production requirements and is presented in units of raw materials. Two figures are necessary for preparation of this budget: the raw-materials requirement and the purchases requirement.

Raw-Materials Requirement

The raw materials requirement is the total units of raw materials 11 required to meet production and inventory requirements. It equals the sum of the raw materials required for production and the desired ending inventory of raw materials. The raw materials required for production comes from the number of units required for production in the budgeted time period times the raw materials required per unit. The desired ending inventory of raw materials for the budgeted time period is how much raw material is needed on hand at the beginning of the next time period. Most firms want to have a certain percentage--maybe 30 percent--of the next time period's raw materials on hand at the beginning of that time period. That much raw materials will have to be added to the raw materials required for the time period's production.

Purchases Requirements

12 The purchases requirement is the units of raw materials that must be purchased in order to meet production and inventory requirements. The purchases requirement equals the raw-materials requirement minus the beginning inventory of raw materials (raw materials available at the beginning of the budgeted time period).

5. Selling and Administrative Expense Budget

13 This budget enables the firm to estimate its expenses of selling goods and of conducting administrative work. This budget also has two parts: fixed costs and variable costs. Fixed costs are the same for each time period; variable costs change per units <u>sold</u>. Added together, they equal the selling and administrative expense budget.

Conclusion: The Income Statement

14 With the other five parts of the master budget worked out, the firm can prepare an estimated income statement, which predicts the net income (total revenues minus total expenses) for the firm. This statement typically includes total revenue (number of units sold times the price per unit), total expenses (manufacturing costs and selling and administrative costs), and the estimated taxes. At this point the firm can begin to plan ahead to control costs and maximize profits.

Selected Bibliography

General information on this subject was obtained from these sources:

Batty, J. Management Accountancy. London: MacDonald and Evans, 1975.

Morse, Wayne J. Cost Accounting: Processing, Evaluating, and Using Cost Data. Reading: Addison-Wesley, 1981.

Shillinglaw, Gordon. Managerial Cost Accounting. Homewood: Richard D. Irwin, 1982.

Answering the Five Key Questions

First let's look again at those five questions you need to answer before you start writing your report. We'll use the above report as an example.

First Question: What Is the Need *for This Report?*

By "need" here we mean whatever it was that *motivated* the report—its reason(s) for existence: was it mandated by the Environmental Protection Agency, assigned by a professor, written in response to a request for proposals, or what?

We *intend* these needs to seem weak—they are!

Can you tell by reading it what the *need* for the sample report was? Different reports in different settings come about because of different kinds of needs. Until you as the writer have a clear idea of the *need* for the report, you'll be unable to make sound decisions about what to include and exclude, what tone to use, and a number of other critical issues.

For example, the sample report was written in response to several different needs:

- A student needed a paper to turn in.
- The paper had to be on a topic pertaining to her planned major (accounting).
- The student wanted to write on a topic that challenged neither her knowledge nor her writing ability; she felt this arrangement would maximize her chance for a good grade.

Compare that situation with the one faced by, say, a research scientist writing a quarterly progress report on his or her work, a report that goes to the funding source—perhaps the National Science Foundation (NSF)—and also to the researcher's own division head. The NSF's need for that kind of report is to justify continued funding by showing that work is progressing in an orderly, responsible fashion. The division head's need is similar but is probably less critical. Thus the NSF report writer makes several "safe" decisions: there's no *need* to go out on a limb with anything; there's no *strong* persuasive advantage to be gained of the sort that would justify risks. In many ways, that kind of report is really just "for the record," and this difference in the report's need affects everything about how it is written.

Or compare those two report-writing situations with that of a report written by a congressional investigating committee, such as the one that investigated the 1986 explosion of the *Challenger* space shuttle. Do you see how much more *pressing* the need for this third kind of report is, how the *need* for this investigative report—both to account for the disaster and to recommend effective measures to prevent a recurrence—dominates all other concerns?

Sometimes the biggest problem with a student report is that it fails to respond to any need. That is, the teacher who assigns "ten pages on any subject" or the student who takes the attitude "I just have to turn in ten pages—somehow—of anything" will probably wind up with a poorly done report. The problem is that the report doesn't respond to any sense of need that might energize its writer. The sample report at the beginning of this chapter has a good portion of that "ten pages—somehow" attitude contributing to its dryness; most people reading it get a feeling there's little need behind the report. The point is that the *best* written reports are often those driven by the *strongest* need—either a need the writer feels from the start or a need discovered during writing, but a compelling need nonetheless.

This need "just to turn something in" is the need that characterizes too much student writing. Anything you can do to get your students beyond this kind and level of need is probably worth doing.

Once again, topic selection (actually, topic invention and discovery) is critical. To the extent that curricular or other academic requirements permit, students should *always* write about something that sparks their interest, something that makes the "need" real and important to them. (We are not, however, among those who believe that *anything* students want to write about for their schoolwork is automatically appropriate.)

How Does the Need Affect the Writing Process? Need has early, strong effects on the writing process. Most of us do a reasonable job of assessing the need for our writing projects, and we do that assessment unconsciously. Problems arise when writers do not accurately assess the need for a report—for example, you may have known a student who thought she was writing a "just turn in ten pages" kind of report and then discovered she was actually working on something that counted as 45 percent of her course grade. (Would the writer of the sample report at the beginning of this chapter want a large portion of her grade to ride on it? We doubt it.)

Similar problems occur in the opposite direction when a professional puts fifty hours into a writing job that needed to be done at a level of quality more commensurate with a ten-hour job. Because need affects this vital issue of how much time and energy you budget for your writing task, your best course of action is to assess the report's need early on: try to write a brief paragraph describing the need. If you have any uncertainty about the accuracy of what you write in that paragraph or if you find the paragraph short on specifics, meet with the person who has assigned the writing task (your teacher or your boss) and go over the paragraph together.

Getting your students to articulate need fully is important. In the invention and discovery they do while coming up with that articulation, they will bring to their minds the full consciousness of need that is likely to propel their writing forward successfully.

Second Question: What Is the Goal of This Report?

If the *need* for the report can be said to push the report forward from its very beginnings, then the report's *goal* pulls it toward completion. Perhaps the goal is to secure continued funding, to prevent further disasters, to demonstrate that the strength of Hemingway's prose style comes from his use of particular words. Or perhaps your goal in a report is to show your professor you really do understand "amortization of goodwill" or even to persuade your professor and your classmates to see the current political scene as you do. Each different goal, and each different kind of goal, has its own way of affecting the report.

For example, Jewella Sadeghi, the writer of the sample report above, had the following three goals:

Again, we don't mean to be denigrating our writer; these really are the honest goals students often have.

1. To get a good grade
2. To write a report without having to go to the library (thus using textbooks in her possession)
3. To finish the assignment in a short time with a minimum of effort

Can you see what those goals do for the report? What if one goal was "To show my classmates how corporate master budgets can teach them something about how to do their own personal budgets"? Wouldn't a more personal, more focused goal have made a considerably different (and better) report?

We're recalling here the ideas we brought out in chapter 4, on writing to express.

Compare that situation with the goal of, say, the final report from a group of engineering students in a senior design class who expect their report to accomplish these three things:

1. To impress their professor with their thinking and writing abilities
2. To present in a persuasive and professional manner their idea for the design and construction of a car that is capable of setting a world record for land speed
3. To be nominated, on the basis of their work's quality, to enter the national design competition, for which only the best engineering students at each university are eligible

Those goals, each of them high and demanding in its own way, place a number of requirements on the report writers, their writing processes, and the final characteristics of their report. Among other things, their writing needs to be fully *persuasive* on at least two levels: (a) persuading their professor of their intelligence and ability and (b) persuading classmates, the professor, and contest judges that their design is the best.

On the other hand, many student-written reports (and quite a few professional ones) have less ambitious goals. For example, a student in an entry-level philosophy class, assigned to write a report on Heidegger's philosophy of being, may well want to restrict herself to these three goals:

1. To be clear
2. To not pretend to understand material she doesn't in fact understand
3. To finish a good, middle-level draft of the report in time to take advantage of her teacher's offer to go over drafts with students who might be worried about how well they've handled the admittedly difficult subject matter

Once again we're being honest here; there's a goal *range* that students generally have to find their own place in for every assignment. This range covers goals from "Do I just rehash class and text material?" to "Do I try to say something new?"

This student doesn't feel it's as though she were supposed to be making her own addition to the world of philosophy; she wants only to show to her professor that she has figured out this difficult topic for herself and is capable of presenting it clearly. Thus, this draft's basic goal is more to inform than persuade.

In contrast, a student writing a report summarizing her activities during a summer technical communication internship in a hospital's publications office may have as her goal to impress her technical communication teacher with the range of activities she performed and to demonstrate by the way the report itself is done how much she has learned. Thus, within a report that is primarily written to record there can still be a powerful persuasive element.

How Do Goals Affect the Writing Process? Oddly enough, many students begin writing without a clear idea of their goals for the project at hand. One of the best warm-up activities for writing is to write down your goals for your project and to do so in as much detail as you can. When you find yourself later on, during your writing time, staring at a blank screen or looking at pages and pages of printout and shaking your head, thinking, "This piece wanders all over the place and never really reaches its point," then you can get out your goals statement and use it to pull you back onto a productive course. That is, if you know—even in general terms—where you're trying to get to, you'll have a much better idea of what the next step, and the next and the next, need to look like. Similarly, if you haven't articulated (and we mean writing down) your goals for a report, how will you gauge whether you've been successful in your writing?

As with articulating need fully, articulating goals fully is a real help to the writing process, at any level.

The longer the piece one is writing, the more important this full and early articulation is.

Third Question: What Is the Audience *for This Report?*

Identifying the audience for your report is one of the most fundamental things you can do to make your report's writing better. Reports can have all different kinds of audiences, from the public to experts. It's critical that you know just how much *knowledge* about and *interest* in your subject your audience has.

For example, what can you guess about the audience for the sample report on "Elements of a Master Budget" that began this chapter? Is the reader someone who is interested, who *wants* to read the report? How much curiosity does the report give the reader credit for? How much personality? Does the report assume a reader who has the option of *not* reading it? What could the report do to portray a more human, curious audience? How would the report's writing change if the person making the assignment said something like this: "If your paper doesn't *hook* me in the first two paragraphs, I won't read it—I'll just return it to you for audience-based revision"?

For another example of the importance of audience analysis, consider an agricultural marketing representative sent to Japan by the tomato growers' association to investigate why Japan doesn't import any tomatoes from the United States and to determine whether something can be done to open up that market. What can we assume about the audience for his report at the end of his trip? Will that audience tolerate boring writing? Will it need technical details of tomato growing to be explained? How about technical details of Japan's internal economy?

For a final example, consider a student writing a report on some aspect of human genome research for a scientist who last year was nominated for a Nobel Prize for her research on human genetics. How will that audience's qualities affect the writing of the student's report? Now consider the same student writing basically the same material for a biology graduate assistant who has no particular claim to fame on the subject. How will that audience shape the way the report is

Actually, *identifying* is an ambiguous term. It's good to identify your audience; it's much better to get to *know* your audience.

We find it useful to have our students practice reconstructing audiences from published pieces we bring to class. Interesting discussions then follow from comparing that version of the audience with the one that, say, the author may have had in mind while writing (and to the one that is actually reading the piece now—a class of freshman composition students).

As you may have guessed, we enjoy working with audience analysis and adaptation, *especially* when they're tied to particular instances of writing.

written? And now consider the two reports, one for the Nobel Prize nominee, the other for the graduate assistant—see how the audience changes the report? The same report, done for two different audiences, isn't really the same report at all. It's the *audience* (and the writer's awareness of it) that makes the difference. (And what if the report were to be written for an English department graduate assistant?)

One good exercise is to have your students, perhaps working in groups, rewrite for different audiences selected pieces from our collection here.

How Does the Audience Affect the Writing Process? It's good to know *about* your audience; it's even better to know your audience *directly.* Certainly there's a benefit to focusing on your audience's identity early in any writing process. In fact, sometimes a writer who is "blocking" on a task can get the words going again by switching from a distant, abstract, vaguely defined audience to a nearby, tangible, well-known one. For example, students often have trouble with their *first* piece of writing for each new professor; these writers can help themselves out of those troubles by picturing—for the purposes of finishing an early draft—an audience much closer and better known, such as a roommate, friend, or spouse. The question, "How would I write this if I were writing it for my roommate?" will often get things going again. (Of course, a later step of revision will have to be devoted to adjusting the draft to a different audience.)

Some students seem to think that getting to know their teacher better is unethical at worst and unseemly at best; you may need to explain that the purpose we mean here is to gain a sense of what the teacher is looking for in the student's writing and overall academic performance—a perfectly legitimate aim for any serious student. Experienced teachers usually have little trouble handling relationships with students and can put students at ease during conferences. (If you're not an experienced teacher, we suggest you read our discussion of this aspect of teaching in our Starter Kit.)

An even better trick, however, is to get to know the *real* audience better. If you're writing for a new professor, make an office appointment to discuss the project prior to writing; the sense you gain of the person you'll be writing for can pay big dividends when you start writing. And if you can get that professor to review a draft of the report later on and give you direct feedback on it, you'll be using your knowledge of the audience to an even greater advantage.

Fourth Question: What Is the Source of This Report's Information?

Most reports have one or both of two basic sources for their content:

1. The report can be primarily made up of something its writer has seen, read, or done; that is, its source is *external.*
2. The report can be primarily made up of the author's own thoughts (and perhaps feelings); that is, its source is *internal.*

Some writers seem to work more easily with external sources, and some with internal (as we distinguish between the two here). But most important is recognizing *which* type of source seems dominant in the particular piece of writing one is doing, and allowing the report to develop naturally from that recognition.

Of course, many reports have both internal and external sources. Now, we don't want to offend the philosophically minded among our readers, who could rightly argue that the distinction between what is *internal* and what is *external* is a slippery line indeed, one that has been debated for thousands of years. We're not pretending to have resolved that debate. But we do think we can make a useful and practical distinction between *external* and *internal* sources that will help you if you have to write a report based on both kinds of sources.

To illustrate our distinction between external and internal sources, we present the following generic outline for many scientific reports. Consider each of these four as a specific part of the written report:

1. Purpose
2. Procedure

3. Results
4. Discussion

Many science students who use this outline find that it is easier to write parts 2 and 3 than to write parts 1 and 4. Why? Because the material for parts 2 and 3 comes from things the student writer *did*, following established forms—that is, from an external source. Material for parts 1 and 4, however, must come from things the student writer *thinks*—that is, matters of interpretation and assessment whose source is internal. It's almost always easier to respond to the need to write reports that have external sources because such things as procedures and specifications are usually predetermined. On the other hand, reports (or sections thereof) that come from internal sources necessarily involve more reflection and creativity on the writer's part.

Another, equally common structure, is

Introduction (internal, mostly)
Materials (external)
Method (external)
Results (external)
Discussion (internal)

English majors may be a notable exception (if not the complete opposite) to these generalizations.

How Does Source Figure into the Writing Process? How can you use the distinction between internal and external sources in order to make your writing better? One way is in your choice of subjects to write about. If you're more comfortable writing about things that are outside you—external sources—choose a topic susceptible to that approach. If you're the opposite, choose a more internal kind of topic. In terms of the kind of generic science report outlined above, student writers often have difficulty doing the report at all if they start with part 1; usually they're better off writing parts 2 and 3—the meat of the report, after all—before they tackle 1 and 4. Then they can let parts 1 and 4 grow out of 2 and 3.

Another way to use the distinction between primarily internal sources and primarily external sources is to realize that the best writing contains something of both. Part of what's wrong with the report draft at the beginning of this chapter is that there's nothing *internal to the author* in it. In its absence of a person speaking to us, as in its absence of a person hearing it, the report is so sterile that it's neither interesting nor enjoyable to read. How could it be made better? Well, how could a student writer put something of her own thoughts and feelings into it? What if it began something like this:

> All beginning business students have the same fear: at some point they're going to be asked to look at this incredibly complicated page (or, more likely, pages) of numbers--called a budget--and be expected to make sense out of it. That's how I felt too, when I first saw a solid page of numbers littered with phrases like "unit sales," "finished-goods requirements," and "selling and administrative costs." But with a little knowledge and careful reading, anyone can make sense of a budget. And that's what this paper is about: I'll take you, step by step, through the same process I followed when I learned how to...

The rest of the paper would then build the understanding of a budget as seen through the eyes of a beginning business student who herself is just starting to understand it.

Compare chapter 4. The expressive motive, or reason, for writing is often considered the least important, but its tie to the writer's personal interests and concerns gives it an emotional dimension that often makes the writing much more lively, vital, and effective than it otherwise might be. Why? Because the expressive reason is the most *internal* of the four main reasons for writing that we posit in this book (to express, to inform/explain, to analyze, and to persuade).

See how the writer's act of wrapping all that external material in a web of internal material can work to make the report as a whole more readable?

Fifth Question: What Is the Primary Issue, or Stasis, of This Report?

As we explained in chapter 7, there are basically four kinds of issues or arguments writers can write about:

1. *Fact.* What is the case? For example, a description of current research, based on library findings, about microbes that "eat" oil spills.
2. *Interpretation.* What does the case mean? For example, a reading of the play *Waiting for Godot* from the perspective of a person from a Third World nation.
3. *Policy.* Given the case, what should be done? For example, an explanation of how U.S. foreign policy should change in light of the apparent disintegration of the Iron Curtain.
4. *Value.* What is the worth of the case? For example, an argument that in a world of diminishing natural resources, Brazilian rain forests are too valuable a resource to allow occasionally shortsighted regional leaders to continue to permit the destruction of these forests.

Compare the treatment of stases in chapter 25 (proposals).

You can make your writing task easier and your writing come out better if you realize that each of these four divisions, called *stases* (each one is a different *stasis*), requires a different approach.

For example, how does the report writer get the reader to take the meaning of the report seriously? To consider this issue, let's look at each of the reports listed in the four examples above to learn how each writer needs to go about establishing the report's points as something to be taken seriously.

1. *An issue of fact (What is the case?).* For example, a student writing a description of current research about microbes that "eat" oil spills faces a relatively simple task in establishing his report as serious. He needs to present a survey of the current research, *and* the survey needs to be documented fully and carefully. Documentation is especially important in this stasis; though there are other ways to establish the factuality of what the report says, full documentation is the best method. What would happen were the student writing this paper to use only a general credit of sources, as did the writer of the report at the beginning of this chapter? Do you see how that would undermine the report's seriousness?
2. *An issue of interpretation (What does the case mean?).* For example, a student who is producing a reading of the play *Waiting for Godot* from the perspective of a person from a Third World nation could rely on citing authorities (as does the writer in item 1 above); however, making an argument about meaning requires much more (as is presented in chapter 17 on definition). The report will require, among other things, careful definitions (for example, of the term *surrealism*), probably an expressive element (the writer must seem to care about the subject), and quite probably some argumentation ("If *this,* then *this,* and so *that*").

Of course, two or more stases often work together, thus complicating the rhetorical situation, but one of the stases will dominate, causing other stases to fill subordinate, supportive roles.

3. *An issue of policy (Given the case, what should be done?).* Issues of interpretation require arguments about what something *means;* issues of policy require arguments about what should be *done.* Again, to make an argument about what needs to be done is quite different from making an argument about what is the case. The student writing an explanation of how U.S. foreign policy should change in light of the apparent disintegration of the Iron Curtain must certainly present facts and interpret meaning but must also address the element of what should be done. Somehow, the writer must produce a sense that an action has to be taken, that the current situation needs to be changed. Doing so might involve, for example, making a persuasive case that the current situation is less than desirable, showing that a change is indeed possible, and connecting the desired change with a better state of affairs that (presumably) will result from it.
4. *An issue of value (What is the worth of the case?).* Here the student making an argument about the destruction of Brazilian rain forests must deal carefully with facts, with interpretations, and with policy, all in a context of *worth.* How do human beings establish worth in conversation among themselves? We can appeal to common sets of values (religions, systems of government); we can appeal to moral, ethical, or philosophical yardsticks (the greatest good for the greatest number, the maximum development of each individual, and so on); or we can appeal to logic (if *this,* then *that,* and so on). But the differences between arguments of value and other kinds of arguments are many and important, and arguments of value (like those of policy), cannot be handled merely by a bare accumulation of sources.

What it takes to urge someone to action depends, initially, on whether (a) the decision to take *some* kind of action has already been made or (b) the decision of whether or not to take action is still open. Such a distinction actually involves a difference in stases. If taking action has already been decided on, then the dominant stasis is the issue of policy (that is, what action should be taken). If acting or not acting is still the question, then the dominant stasis is also undecided; it could prove to be primarily an issue of fact, interpretation, or value, depending on the overall situation, and therefore no action is yet possible.

Notice that the appeal to common sets of values or to moral, ethical, or philosophical yardsticks is in some ways more of an appeal to something preexisting in the audience, whereas the appeal to logic is an appeal to something that—as today's society would have it—needs to be created anew on each occasion.

How Does the Stasis Affect the Writing Process? The sooner you realize what the primary stasis of your report (or of the section in question) is, the more you can direct your writing appropriately. That is, the idea of stasis affects, as is shown above, the *kind* of proof you need to be using. But you can profitably use stasis for much more than that *if* you use it to help you visualize the entire communication situation: what do you have to do to convince someone about a factual issue? about an interpretation? about a policy? about values? In each case, more is at stake than just the kind of proof involved: an appropriate tone, an appropriate stance the writer takes toward the subject, an appropriate way the audience is or isn't allowed to figure into the piece of writing.

CASE STUDY CLOSE-UP

The student-written report that began this chapter is characteristic of what students often produce in drafts of reports: there's some good content there, but it's such a bare-bones approach to the subject that it's hard to imagine *anyone* reading it of his or her own free will, or, having read it, responding to it positively. Fortunately, that particular report was submitted in draft form to give the student the opportunity to "get it right." At present, the report is at the level of "I have the content that I want down on paper; now all I have to do is make it good." That's an excellent time to get a review, either by a peer (in the classroom situation, one of

In our view, this kind of "content" draft, having all the anticipated material in it but lacking many of the requisite finishing touches, properly needs peer (student) review *first.*

your classmates) or by someone above you in the organization (in the classroom, that means the teacher).

What we want to do here is show you how the five key issues this chapter has raised concerning report writing—need, goal, audience, source, and issue (or stasis)—can be used as guides for *revision* of such a content-oriented draft. First we would like you to reread the report draft at the beginning of this chapter with the following five questions in mind, as well as your own notes (or recollections) of how you responded to the report the first time you read it:

1. What is the *need* for this report?
2. What is the *goal* of this report?
3. What is the *audience* for this report?
4. What is the *source* of this report's information?
5. What is the primary issue, or *stasis*, of this report?

Jewella Sadeghi's Report-Revision Conference

Here's a description of the main points the teacher covered when discussing the draft with Jewella. At the end of this section is a summary of "Points for Revising" that Jewella took into consideration; that summary is followed by the report as it was actually revised.

Here, more than in any other case studies we've offered, we're conscious of painting a picture that is much more orderly and methodical than real life usually is. Obviously, we're doing so for pedagogical purposes that we think justify whatever slight distortion our portrayal involves.

Revising According to a Report's Need. To assess the report's *need*, the teacher asked Jewella to look behind the report draft itself to the assignment that stimulated it. Here's the way the teacher wrote the assignment (in a freshman-level writing class that encourages students to write about topics in their expected majors):

> Write a three- to five-page report on a basic topic of some importance in your major. What you want to do in this report is to explain that topic, from the point of view of a student in the field, to students from other fields.

Considering that assignment and the draft you've read, what can you determine about how the need for the report can contribute to its productive revision? The teacher asked Jewella to list honestly the needs she wanted her report draft to meet. Here's what Jewella wrote:

- I needed a paper to turn in.
- The paper had to be on a topic pertaining to my planned major (accounting).
- I wanted to write on a topic that doesn't challenge either my knowledge or my writing ability. I felt this would maximize my chance for a good grade.

The draft on pages 632–36 addresses those needs, but it falls short of several other important needs—for example, the reader's needs. Jewella then thought about her reader's needs and, with some difficulty, produced this list:

- To have a report written according to the assignment's specifications
- To have a report that was easy to read
- To have a report that was sufficiently interesting so as not to make the reading painful

The teacher talked over this list with Jewella and reviewed the basics of classroom situations with her: how many teachers—on any level—are satisfied with students who do just enough to get by? In a classroom situation, one of the teacher's needs is always "to see how well my students can do," and one of any wise student's needs must then be "to show that I'm learning new things, doing the best I can." Jewella saw that the current draft of her report does not address this set of needs; there's no sign of the writer stretching in any way to reach or to please her reader.

Revising According to a Report's Goals. A report's goals are closely allied to its needs; sometimes the needs and goals are in a one-to-one matching relationship, and sometimes they're practically indistinguishable. In the case of this report, its goals (as initially listed by Jewella) were these:

1. To get a good grade
2. To write a report without having to go to the library (thus using textbooks in my possession)
3. To finish the assignment in a short time with a minimum of effort

The teacher talked with Jewella along the lines suggested earlier in this chapter: wouldn't some kind of more personal, more focused goal have made a considerably different (and better) report? And aren't these goals so exclusively *writer-motivated* that they seem to assume the report's *reader* doesn't exist? (Here we're seeing the same thing we saw under "Revising According to a Report's Need.") How could the reader's goals be added to the report—for example, by stating a goal that included at least some mention of the reader? What if a goal of "To show my classmates how corporate master budgets can teach them something about how to do their own personal budgets" were added? What if "To show my teacher something interesting about accounting" were added? Isn't it right at the heart of what's wrong with this current draft that the *reader's* share of the report's needs and goals is unattended to?

Revising According to a Report's Audience. Jewella saw that nothing about this draft of the report suggests anything positive about its intended audience. Here are some of the questions we've already asked about the report's audience; Jewella's teacher asked them again about the draft:

- Is this draft written for someone who is already interested in the subject?
- How much curiosity does the report give the reader credit for? How much humanity?

- Does the report assume a reader who has the option of not reading it?
- What could the report do to portray a more human, curious audience?
- How would the report's writing change if the person making the assignment said something like this: "If your paper doesn't *hook* me in the first two paragraphs, I won't read it—I'll just return it to you for audience-based revision"?

In fact, the teacher had already tried to get *audience* to be a large part of the report-writing process by specifying in the initial assignment an audience of "students in other fields." But Jewella knew her draft seems written by a dull person for dull readers—and she knew that was what neither she nor the teacher wanted. The biggest thing that could be done to introduce *audience* into the report, the teacher told her, would be to make the report more clearly something *from* a person and *to* a person—in this case, from a student and to students.

Revising According to a Report's Source. Once again, here are the possibilities for reports' sources:

1. The report can be *external*—primarily made up of something its writer has seen, read, or done.
2. The report can be primarily *internal*—made up of the author's own thoughts (and maybe feelings).
3. The report may have both internal and external sources.

Jewella's current draft uses only one kind of source, her reading in the field of accounting. It doesn't go very deeply into that source, being mostly a survey of material presented in basic accounting textbooks. It could be improved, then, both by going deeper into the external source(s) it draws upon and by using the internal source (personal knowledge) to enrich its content. The teacher told Jewella that the lack of personal knowledge is striking in this report, a point that parallels earlier insights about the report as well.

Revising According to a Report's Stasis. Jewella and her teacher reviewed the various stases:

- Fact (What is the case?)
- Interpretation (What does the case mean?)
- Policy (Given the case, what should be done?)
- Value (What is the worth of the case?)

Jewella saw that this draft addresses only the first stasis, fact, and does that only superficially. The teacher noted the importance of *documentation* in the stasis of fact, and how relatively little this draft does with documentation. A general acknowledgment of sources, especially if those sources are mostly or entirely basic textbooks, does not especially contribute to establishing the report's seriousness; indeed, this bibliography contributes to the reader's sense of the report's superficiality. The teacher asked Jewella how she could take better advantage of the report's stasis in terms of documentation. Jewella decided to find a specific source for one specific budget, to include that specific budget in the report, and to document it in the bibliography.

Points for Revising

At the end of their conference, Jewella and her teacher decided to settle on these points as targets for Jewella's revision activities that would produce the report's next draft:

- To include the reader's needs in the revision by trying to make the report interesting to read
- To include the reader's goals by putting something in the report for the reader, some benefit for the reader to come from reading the report
- To include the audience by changing the point of view (addressing "you" throughout the report and correspondingly using "I" if the need arose)
- To explore the use of internal sources
- To go deeper into the "fact" stasis by including a specific budget taken from a specific company, to document that, and to consider entering other stases as well

Here's the revised report:

We think there are still many ways to improve this report. Invite your students to join you in finding them.

Elements of a Master Budget

1 If you're like most college freshmen, you're living away from home for the first time. And you are probably managing your own finances for the first time as well. If that's your situation, you may find you can learn something of value by looking at the way companies make their budgets. Like most people, corporations use budgets to plan and control their expenses.

2 This report will show you the five components of a corporation's master budget. The example that will be used throughout is based on a real corporation's budget (simplified a little for clarity). This paper will also give you some good hints for handling your own personal budget.

3 A corporation's master budget has five main parts:

1. Sales Budget
2. Production Budget

3. Manufacturing Cost Budget
4. Purchase Budget
5. Selling and Administrative Expense Budget

In addition to these parts, the master budget includes forecasted financial statements (such as a net income statement) based on the results of the above estimates.

1. Sales Budget

Sales are the major source of income for most companies. The sales 4
budget is a prediction of sales for a specified time period. A company's predicted sales are based on several items, such as last month's sales, industry growth rate, and the company's share of the market. Each corporation also adapts the forecast to fit its own needs, and so no standardized method for predicting sales is available. The prediction is usually based on judgment and stated in both dollar sales and unit sales.

Here's how the Bioremediation Technology Associates (BTA) sales 5
budget for February 1991 looks:

Table 1 BTA Sales Budget for February 1991

	January	February	March
Unit sales	1,000	1,200	1,300
Dollar sales ($150/oz.)	$150,000	$180,000	$195,000

For students, the major source of income is usually a part-time job, 6
with possible help from loans, parents, and savings. Again, setting up a monthly budget requires estimating this income. No two people will do that the same way. Obviously, for an individual's budget this prediction will be stated in dollars.

Table 2 Individual Budget for February 1991

	January	February	March
Income			
Jiffy-Trip	$ 250	$200	$250
Loan	$1000	---	---

2. Production Budget

7 A company's production budget shows how many units of product have to be produced in the budgeted time period (which can be a week, a month, a quarter, or a year) to meet projected sales and inventory requirements. This budget has two subparts: the finished-goods requirement and the production requirement.

Finished-Goods Requirement

8 The finished-goods requirement is the number of units of finished goods that must be available during the budgeted time period to meet sales and inventory requirements. The number of unit sales for that time period (desired sales) is added to the number of completed units that need to be in inventory at the end of the period (desired ending inventory).

Production Requirement

9 The production requirement is the number of units that must be produced to meet sales and inventory requirements. The number of units on hand at the beginning of the period (beginning inventory) is subtracted from the finished-goods requirement.

10 Students don't really have anything like a production budget, which perhaps tells us something about why some people think students have a fairly easy existence.

Here's how BTA's production budget looks: 11

Table 3 BTA Production Requirements for February 1991

	January
Unit sales (from table 1)	1,000
Desired ending inventory	500
Finished-goods requirements	1,500
Beginning inventory (end of Dec.)	400
Production requirements	1,100
	February
Unit sales	1,200
Desired ending inventory	500
Finished-goods requirements	1,700
Beginning inventory (end of Jan.)	500
Production requirements	1,200

3. Manufacturing Cost Budget

The manufacturing cost budget shows the costs incurred to produce 12
the number of units calculated in the production requirement. Two types of costs make up the manufacturing cost budget: variable costs and fixed costs.

For students there are analogous budget factors. Students have 13
to pay for being students, and they too have both variable costs and fixed costs. In this part of the student budget we will only include items

that are musts (in other words, costs that are not optional).

Variable Costs

14 Variable costs are applied on a basis of cost per unit produced. Variable costs would include any cost that changes depending on how many units are produced. For example, labor costs are variable costs; if no product is produced, there is no labor cost.

15 For students, important variable costs include books, car repairs, medical expenses, and parking and library fines.

Fixed Costs

16 Fixed costs are those which remain the same each time period regardless of the number of units produced. The rent paid on the building is a fixed cost.

17 Here's how BTA's manufacturing cost budget looks:

Table 4 BTA Manufacturing Costs

Variable costs (1,100 oz. @ $30)	$33,000
Fixed costs (per month)	$50,000
Total manufacturing costs	$83,000

18 Students also have fixed costs. Usually the big ones are tuition, food, and rent. Here's how a sample student's costs budget might look:

Table 5 Student Costs Budget

Variable costs	
Books	$100
Car repairs	$35
Medical expenses	$35
Fines	$15
Total variable costs	$185

Fixed Costs	
Tuition	$200
Food	$150
Rent	$150
	____
Total fixed costs	$500

4. Purchases Budget

The purchases budget lays out the number of units of raw materials 19
that need to be purchased to meet production and inventory requirements. While the production budget is based on sales forecasts and is presented in units of finished product, the purchases budget is based on production requirements and is presented in units of raw materials. Two figures are necessary for preparation of this budget: the raw-materials requirement and the purchases requirement.

Students, too, occasionally make purchases. Typical purchases 20
include clothing and entertainment.

Raw-Materials Requirement

The raw-materials requirement is the total units of raw materials 21
required to meet production and inventory requirements. It equals the sum of the raw materials required for production and the desired ending inventory of raw materials. The raw materials required for production comes from the number of units required for production in the budgeted time period times the raw materials required per unit. The desired ending inventory of raw materials for the budgeted time period is how much raw material is needed on hand at the beginning of the next time period. Most firms want to have a certain percentage--maybe 30 percent--of the next time period's raw materials on hand at the beginning of that time period. That much raw materials will have to be added to the raw materials required for the time period's production.

Purchases Requirements

The purchases requirement is the units of raw materials that must 22 be purchased in order to meet production and inventory requirements. The purchases requirement equals the raw materials requirement minus the beginning inventory of raw materials (raw materials available at the beginning of the budgeted time period).

23 Here's a sample corporate purchases budget, followed by a sample student purchases budget.

Table 6 BTA Purchases Budget

	January
Production requirements	1,100
Raw material required for production (1,100 × 10)	11,000
Ending inventory (1,200 × 10 × 30%)	4,000
Raw-materials requirements	15,000
Beginning inventory (Dec. ending inventory)	4,000
Purchase requirements	11,000

Table 7 Student Purchases Budget

Clothing	$25
Entertainment	$50
Total	$75

5. Selling and Administrative Expense Budget

24 This budget enables BTA to estimate its expenses of selling goods

and of administrative work. This budget also has two parts: fixed costs and variable costs. Fixed costs are the same for each time period; variable costs change per units sold. Added together, they equal the selling and administrative expense budget.

Table 8 BTA Selling and Administrative Expenses

	January
Variable costs (1,000 [Table 1] × $5) ($5 cost per unit)	$5,000
Fixed costs (per month)	$5,000
Total costs	$10,000

Until they prepare for graduation and the job search, students have 25
no parallel to this budget. Once they begin searching for a postgraduation job, they do. Here's a sample of what a budget for that might look like:

Table 9 Postgraduation Budget

New suit	$250
Résumés	$20
Cards	$15
Letters	$30
Telephone	$30
Total	$345

Conclusion: The Income Statement

With the other five parts of the master budget worked out, BTA can 26
prepare an estimated income statement, which predicts the net income

(total revenues minus total expenses) for the firm. This statement typically includes total revenue (number of units sold times the price per unit), total expenses (manufacturing costs and selling and administrative costs), and the estimated taxes. At this point the firm can begin to plan ahead to control costs and maximize profits.

Table 10 BTA Income Statement

Total revenue	
Sales	$150,000
Total expenses	
Manufacturing costs	
Variable costs	$33,000
Fixed costs	$50,000
Selling and administrative	
Variable costs	$5,000
Fixed costs	$5,000
Income before tax	$57,000
Tax (38% tax rate)	$21,660
Net income	$35,340

27 Similarly, once a student has worked out all of these pieces, a comprehensive budget (for a week, a month, or a year) can be made. Here's what one student's comprehensive budget looks like:

Table 11 Student Comprehensive Budget

Income	
Jiffy-Trip	$250
Loan	$1000
Variable costs	
Books	$100

Car repairs	$35
Medical expenses	$35
Fines	$15
Fixed costs	
Tuition	$200
Food	$150
Rent	$150
Purchases	
Clothing	$25
Entertainment	$50
Job-hunting costs	
New suit	$250
Résumés	$20
Cards	$15
Letters	$30
Telephone	$30
Total income	$1250
Total expenditures	$1105
Total (cash on hand at end of month)	$145

From this budget, our student can learn that some of her costs will 28
have to be controlled in subsequent months, and that her income may have to be increased. Otherwise she won't be able to finish the school year.

Bibliography

Annual Budget, 1991. Bioremediation Technology Associates, Thomas Printers, 1991. Quoted by permission.

Other Sources

General information on this subject was obtained from these sources:

Batty, J. Management Accountancy. London: MacDonald and Evans, 1975.

Morse, Wayne J. Cost Accounting: Processing, Evaluating, and Using Cost Data. Reading: Addison-Wesley, 1981.

Shillinglaw, Gordon. Managerial Cost Accounting. Homewood: Richard D. Irwin, 1982.

Writers' Circle 1

In groups of three, investigate one of the food items listed below (or a food item of your own choosing). Each group should first find out all it can about the food item and then write a brief collaborative report for the class, describing the item in detail, listing its ingredients, telling any important or unusual aspects of its preparation, and explaining its nutritional or health benefits (or lack of such benefits).

Coq au vin	Fried pork rinds
Beef Wellington	Taco chips
Welsh rarebit	Veal *cordon bleu*
Sushi	Sorbet
Vienna sausage	Reuben sandwich
Pickled pig's feet	Fried tofu

Writers' Circle 2

In groups of three, choose a nearby state and, working from census and other available statistical data in the library, produce a short report on population trends and projections (covering perhaps the past one hundred and next twenty years). Each group should choose its own goal(s) for the report and write the report group members feel best exemplifies those goals. After the reports have been read to the class, those goals should be discussed with the class.

WRITING ASSIGNMENTS

1. Write a short (about five-page) report on a subject of some importance in your major. Target as your audience your classmates.
2. Do enough reading in your major to discover some new change (invention of a new piece of technology, change in regulatory laws, and so on) that will soon affect the whole field. Write a report describing that change and its

effects. Target as your audience other students like yourself, people planning to major in that field.

3. Write a report on a new book. Find a book that was published within the past year, and write a report summarizing the book, its sales, any reviews it has received, biographical facts about the author, how it compares with similar books, and so on. Target as your audience local public library patrons who are thinking about whether to check the book out.
4. The picture on page 631 shows two colleagues as they pore over a report that they have jointly written. The picture captures the spirit of the kind of collaborative writing that frequently takes place in business and industry. For a brief report project, team up with a classmate and brainstorm a product or service and an ad campaign for that product or service. Imagine that you and your teammate must impress your boss, the president of the ad company you both work for, with the report for the ad campaign. Include in your ad campaign ideas for television, radio, and magazine/newspaper advertising. Consider slogans, pictorials, gimmicks (free samples, trial offers, and the like).

   Some suggested products:

   stain or spot remover
   pet food
   pet toys
   an action film (or a love story film, a comedy, and so on)
   a soft drink

   Some suggested services:

   a typing service
   a laundry
   a car wash
   a clinic
   a gas station
   a carpenter

chapter 25 Writing Proposals

"Sir, no man but a blockhead ever wrote except for money."

Samuel Johnson

This chapter is closely linked to chapter 24, particularly in terms of the theoretical underpinnings of report writing. We treat proposals in a separate chapter because they are an important aspect of the careers many students will pursue.

Proposals are a special variety of report, one that always needs to be primarily persuasive, whatever else it might be. Basically a proposal is a *persuasive request,* and in that sense it shares important characteristics with other kinds of persuasive writing (see chapter 7) and with other kinds of written requests (see chapter 26).

There are various kinds of proposals, or situations that require proposals:

- Proposals requesting funding
- Proposals requesting research approval
- Proposals for exceptions to rules
- Proposals for changes in procedures
- Proposals for courses of action or study
- Proposals for theses, term papers, dissertations, articles, and books

Proposals can be subdivided a number of other ways. Sometimes proposals are *competitive* (a certain amount of money is available, and not all, perhaps even very few, of the proposals submitted will be funded), and sometimes proposals are *pro forma* (merely the putting down on paper of a deal that has already been arranged, as when your academic adviser tells you, "Take what we just discussed about substituting COBOL for a foreign language, write it in the form of a proposal, and I'm sure the dean will grant it"). Sometimes proposals are *solicited* (an official announcement has gone out requesting them), and sometimes they're *unsolicited* (someone has a good idea for a project and uses a proposal to put it forward). Most important for our purposes are the kinds of proposals *students* typically write, which in many respects resemble those typically written by *professionals* in business, industry, and government; however, although both kinds of proposals share similar principles, the two do have somewhat different parts.

Typical Student Proposals

Throughout this chapter we'll be dealing specifically with three kinds of proposals students commonly write:

Another obvious possibility is to ask students to write proposals seeking approval from you for their major research or report topics.

1. A proposal for an independent-study class
2. A proposal for an internship
3. A proposal for a grant

Notice that although each of these is a proposal written by a student, three distinct audiences are involved: For the first, a faculty member in an administrative position (often the director of undergraduate studies or a department head); for the second, someone from outside the university community (a businessperson, someone from management); and for the third, a person from a funding agency. We shall see as the chapter proceeds how these different audiences affect the three kinds of proposals.

As you can tell from these three proposals, we're still working with the significance of audience, as we developed it in chapter 24.

The Structure of Student Proposals

Proposal writing allows you to use all your skills as a writer. Because it is writing that everyone expects will be persuasive, the only limit on what you can do in a proposal is a very practical one: whatever you do, it should be calculated toward maximum effect. If you feel convinced that the best way to get your proposal approved (or funded) is to make a strong factual argument, that's what you should do. If you feel some other kind of approach is better, then *that's* what you should do.

Of course, "whatever you do" needs to be bounded by the concerns of ethical conduct. We are in no way suggesting that with proposal writing (or anything else) the ends always justify the means. Distortion, misrepresentation, dishonesty, and deception are never appropriate.

In our experience, most student proposals contain parts that perform the following four functions, although the parts are never given exactly these names:

1. Describe the problem
2. Explain its negative effects
3. Propose the solution
4. Explain its positive effects

This same pattern can be used to write a short, persuasive summary of *any* longer problem-solving report.

These parts match up nicely with the four basic stases (chapters 7 and 24):

1. Describe the problem: what are the *facts* (stasis of fact)?
2. Explain its negative effects: what do the facts *mean* (stasis of interpretation)?
3. Propose the solution: what should be *done* (stasis of policy)?
4. Explain the solution's positive effects: what is the solution's *worth* (stasis of value)?

Although other large-scale considerations enter into successful proposal writing, and although certain kinds of proposals contain other parts, this quality of using all four stases, one per large-scale section, underlies the basic structure of nearly all proposal writing. Thus everything we've said so far in this book about writing under the different stases (see, for example, chapters 7, 20, and 24) applies directly to proposal writing. This use of all four stases contributes strongly to the effectiveness of proposals because of the range of human concerns it addresses: each stasis reaches into a different area of human experience (knowledge, feelings, values, and so on), and each involves a different kind of proof. Accordingly, we will discuss here proposals that have the four basic parts listed above.

Some proposals are much more one-dimensional than this; we don't think they are as well written.

What Is the Case? The Problem

Any good proposal must first give the reader a sense that something needs to be done. This factor, called by rhetoricians "exigency," is crucial. Proposals that don't

Normally a fair translation of *exigency* is *need,* but we've used *need* in chapter 24 in a more narrow sense, meaning the specific reason for the writing of the report or proposal (for example, a supervisor has requested it). As we understand the term *exigency,* it refers to the *entire* situation from which the document arises, from authorization for the document (such as a request for proposals, or what we call "need" in chapter 24) to the real-life circumstances (such as the existence of a hazardous waste site) that themselves brought about the request for proposals.

The trick is to define the problem in just the right way.

establish exigency get responses like "If it ain't broke, don't fix it" or "I don't see any need to depart from standard operating procedures in this one instance." Although the section of your proposal that really drives home the need is the next section (negative effects), *that* section's force depends on what you set up in *this* section, which defines the problem. Let's look at how this section might appear in three sample student proposals:

A Proposal for an Independent-Study Class
"Problem" Section

As an undergraduate major in political science, I read the current U.S. policy literature regularly. One of the most important recent ideas in that literature is "endism," the idea that with the apparent crumbling of the Iron Curtain we have reached what Fukuyama calls "the end of history"--a new stage in human political evolution. Yet there are no classes in State College's political science curriculum on this important subject. Thus, this proposal requests approval of an independent-study class in "Endism."

A Proposal for an Internship
"Problem" Section

State College's minor in technical communication provides students with a good textbook knowledge of the field; however, getting a good job after graduation also requires having some real-world experience along the way. In order to acquire such real-world experience, I am requesting three hours' course credit for an internship in technical communication to be carried out this summer (June 1-August 15) at the National Laboratory's Publications Division.

A Proposal for a Grant
"Problem" Section

While Appalachian folk art has been extensively collected, documented, and studied, one traditional Appalachian musical instrument, the dobro, is largely misunderstood and forgotten. In order to contribute toward saving the dobro and its music from extinction, I am requesting $500 from the State Folklife Federation to finance the taping and transcription of original dobro music to be collected at the Eastboro Folk Music Festival this summer.

Do you see how each of these paragraphs, in stating the problem to be solved, sets up the following section, on negative effects of the problem? Now, you might think this is enough for an opening section, that you can go right into the "Negative Effects" section. Recall, however, our earlier discussion (chapter 24) on the stasis of fact and on what it takes to get someone to take such a presentation seriously. In most situations, successful presentation of facts requires support, usually in the form of documentation. Thus each of these openings will require support of some kind. That support might look like this (for your convenience we're repeating the first paragraph of each proposal; the support is in the *second* paragraph of each):

You might discuss with students some alternatives to documentation as support for claims of fact: how could one support this claim—that the apparent fall of the Iron Curtain is an important subject well worth study—with logic? with an appeal to the audience's values and beliefs? with an ethical appeal? with other kinds of appeals?

A Proposal for an Independent-Study Class

1 As an undergraduate major in political science, I read the current U.S. policy literature regularly. One of the most important recent ideas in that literature is "Endism," the idea that with the apparent crumbling of the Iron Curtain we have reached what Fukuyama calls "the end of history"--a new stage in human political evolution. Yet there are no classes in State College's political science curriculum on this important subject. Thus, this proposal requests approval of an Independent-Study class in "Endism."

2 Journals from The National Interest (Francis Fukuyama, "The End of History?" Summer 1989) to Reader's Digest (Fred Barnes, "Communism's Incredible Collapse," March 1990) have published important articles on the effects that the crumbling of the Berlin Wall and of the Iron Curtain will have on the shape of the future. Many important concepts are behind this discussion of "Endism" that has become current worldwide. Because this concept is so recent (most writers date it from August 1989), State College's established political science curriculum cannot pay more than passing attention to it. The only course that deals substantively with events more recent than 1978, Political Science 484: Contemporary Issues, this semester devoted only two weeks to a

segment called "After the Berlin Wall--Then What?" According to Professor Smith, who teaches that course, "Endism" will get at most only two weeks' worth of attention in future sections of 484. Thus, the only way to study "Endism" in detail on the undergraduate level is through the kind of independent-study class proposed here.

A Proposal for an Internship

State College's minor in technical communication provides students with a good textbook knowledge of the field; however, getting a good job after graduation also requires having some real-world experience along the way. In order to acquire such real-world experience, I am requesting three hours' course credit for an internship in technical communication to be carried out this summer (June 1-August 15) at the National Laboratory's Publications Division. 1

A survey of thirty-two different ads for technical writers and editors that appeared in the Collegetown Times from February 1, 1991, to February 28, 1991, reveals that all the ads requested at least some experience. The minimum amount of experience was one to three years (sixteen ads), followed by three to five years (eight ads) and five years or more (eight ads). Thus, for a new graduate to have any chance in this job market, having at least some experience is a necessity. I feel sure I will gain the necessary experience via the internship proposed here. 2

A Proposal for a Grant

While Appalachian folk art has been extensively collected, documented, and studied, one traditional Appalachian musical instrument, the dobro, is largely misunderstood and forgotten. In order to contribute toward saving the dobro and its music from extinction, I am requesting $500 from the State Folklife Federation to finance the taping and transcription of original dobro music to be collected at the Eastboro Folk Music Festival this summer. 1

Our Appalachian history is important to save because it contains unique customs, ideas, and worldviews; certainly the music of the region has 2 already played a significant role in establishing our identity around the nation and the world. Yet much of the most purely Appalachian music has never been recorded, and some of the most purely Appalachian instruments are now seldom seen outside museums. Dobro music has never been more than something played in small family gatherings in the hollows, and the dobro itself has never found much favor outside amateur ranks. Thus David Lennox, music critic and historian, recently said in Folk Music News (February 16, 1990: 42), "Of all the folk instruments of Appalachia, the dobro is the least understood and its music the most in need of collecting."

Notice that the support in the first example (the "Endism" proposal) is made up entirely of documentation. In the second example a survey (performed by the student?) adds the dimension of documentation, and in the third example an appeal to existing values and one authority add the "factual punch" that helps make the proposal's exigency persuasive.

You can see how the second paragraph in each case adds persuasive strength to the statement of the problem. Which of the three new paragraphs do you think is the strongest—the one doing the best job of substantiating the claims made in the first paragraph? How could the weakest of the three be made stronger?

What Does It Mean? Negative Effects

Because establishing need (exigency) is so important in proposal writing, proposals usually devote a separate section to it. The length of that section depends largely on the proposal's topic: in some cases the negative effects (the bad things that will happen if the proposal isn't granted) are so obvious they don't need to be stated; in other cases they're relatively obscure and need more explicit attention. What this section needs to do is *interpret* the meaning of the facts laid out earlier in the proposal. And because the argument is based on interpretation, the premium in this section is on definition and on making readers feel that the interpretation being offered is not just yours but is one *any* reasonable person would arrive at once fully aware of the facts.

In terms of the three sample proposals being developed in this chapter—a proposal for an independent-study class, for an internship, and for a grant—how might you go about writing this section? One approach would be to describe the negative things that will happen to you if the application isn't granted. But it's a hard task to "universalize"—to make others feel the force of—the bad things that will happen if you don't get the independent-study class, internship, or grant. As the writer, what you'd be saying in effect is, "Here's what this grant's not being accepted means to *me*." And just as it's hard to get others to "sign on" to our own problems, so too is it difficult to get people to accept interpretations that are (apparently) centered on our own experience.

Here we're distinctly counter to chapter 24's general advice to personalize one's report writing; in this instance, the writing needs to be impersonal in order to make the proposal seem less egocentric.

When you're writing the "Negative Effects" section of your proposal, it's better to take a broader view: rather than looking at the negative things that will happen if *you* don't get to study Endism, look at what will happen if *Endism* isn't studied; rather than looking at what will happen if *you* don't get an internship, look at what will happen if *internships* aren't given; rather than looking at what will happen if *you* don't get a grant to study dobro music, look at what will happen if *dobro music* isn't studied. With such an approach, you're already taking the kind of long—or "universalized"—view that's necessary to get others to agree with what you say.

A Proposal for an Independent-Study Class (continued)
"Negative Effects" Section

As the central issue of debate today within political science "policy" circles, "Endism" is a vital area of study. Beyond that, the issues that are key to the philosophy of "Endism"--the alleged demise of Marxism, the success of "liberal mercantilism" worldwide, the apparent anomaly of China--are perhaps the chief issues that will shape world history as we enter the twenty-first century. The importance of studying these issues lies in every student's need to be a fully aware, intelligent participant in society. The university's role in producing such students will thus be fulfilled particularly well by approving this request for independent study.

One reviewer thought these last few lines were overblown, reflecting rather grandiose notions of individual and institutional educational commitment. In our experience with proposals, however—which is considerable—there are indeed places to make this kind of admittedly broad, idealistic pitch, so long as it's made briefly and in reasonable proportion to the rest of the document. Ask your students how they feel about the matter.

Notice how this section doesn't talk about what will happen to this student if the request isn't granted; rather, the section discusses how granting the request will demonstrate that the university is fulfilling its responsibility especially well. That's the trick in doing this section: to interpret the negative effects of allowing the status quo to continue in terms of human universals, not in terms of one's own limited experience.

What Should Be Done? The Solution

Obviously, this third section is the most important part of the proposal. Depending on the situation you're in, your writing of this section may need to be much more detailed than that of the previous sections. Here are some of the things that might come up in this section:

Notice that all this material comes from external sources.

- Exactly what (step by step) needs to be done
- Why *this* course of action (as opposed to another course of action) should be followed
- How you will do it
- What your budget will be
- What your timetable will be
- What qualifications you have for doing it

- How you will deal with obvious problems
- How you will meet reporting requirements

Your choice of which of these elements to include is important, and particular proposals may well require other minor sections not mentioned here. The choice should be made based on the situation in which you're placing the proposal. For example, in the case of the student applying for an independent-study class in Endism, including a budget doesn't make much sense; a timetable, on the other hand, does—as does a reading list. By contrast, including a budget *is* essential in any proposal asking for money, as in the case of the student seeking to study Appalachian dobro playing. For the student applying to a company for an internship, making a persuasive presentation of his or her qualifications is vital; discussing why that course of action is preferable to other ones probably isn't.

Let's look at the continuation of the "Endism" proposal that we presented earlier.

Emphasize to students that in the absence of specific, formal guidelines provided to proposal writers, they must be the ones who take responsibility for making decisions about what sections each proposal needs or does not need; no one else can give the definitive answer as to what the proposal needs to be fully persuasive. Just as important, when specific guidelines *are* given it is the proposal writer's responsibility to ensure that all guidelines are properly followed.

A Proposal for an Independent-Study Class (continued)

"Solutions" Section

1 Professor Arthur Smith, who teaches the political science department's contemporary issues course, has agreed to direct this independent study. We will meet once a week for approximately one hour per session to discuss reading that I will pursue independently. The reading will be based on the following books:

Aron, Raymond. War and Industrial Society. London: Oxford UP, 1958.

Burns, Weston, ed. Alternatives to Nuclear Deterrence. Boulder: Westview, 1989.

Dahrendorf, Ralf. Essays in the Theory of Society. Stanford: Stanford UP, 1968.

Kennedy, Paul. The Rise and Fall of the Great Powers. New York: Random, 1987.

Kojeve, Alexander. Introduction to the Reading of Hegel. Ed. Allan Bloom. Trans. James Nichols. New York: Basic, 1969.

Mueller, John. Retreat from Doomsday: The Obsolence of Major War. New York: Basic, 1989.

Nye, Joseph S., Jr. American Power: Past and Future. New York: Basic, 1990.

> We will thus be discussing one book every two weeks, and this list will be supplemented by relevant current articles as the need arises.
>
> I will write three short reports as part of this independent study. The 2
> first (due at the end of week 5) will cover the background of Endism. The second (due at the end of week 10) will review the current theoretical understanding of Endism. The third (due during final exams) will review how the very latest events in world politics continue to force theorists to refine their ideas.
>
> If this proposal is approved, the independent study will take place 3
> during spring semester 1992. As a senior in political science with a 4.0 grade point average in my major and a 3.4 grade point average overall, I am confident I can successfully complete the independent study in the time allotted.

Because this section of the proposal is working in the stasis of policy, we know that demonstrating both the need for action and the feasibility of action is important. Fortunately, need has already been addressed in earlier sections. This section addresses feasibility by showing that the appropriate professor has already approved the plan, that there is already a detailed schedule, that the student is already aware of exactly what needs to be done (in the form of a detailed reading list and the papers to be written), and that the student has the kind of credentials that make successful completion of the project likely.

Your students will have an opportunity at the end of the chapter to flesh out the other proposals. If you don't plan to use that learning experience for them then, use it now.

Of course, in a different kind of proposal the "solution" section might look quite different, as might the way the feasibility of the proposed course of action is demonstrated. The important underlying issue—demonstrating feasibility—nonetheless remains.

What Will Result? Positive Effects

The last section of most student proposals makes one final argument for granting the proposal, this one based on what the solution is worth (a stasis of value). In some ways this section is like that on negative effects, in that as a writer you want to emphasize that your idea or plan goes beyond your own benefit and clearly appeals to values and interests of the proposal's readers. While it's all right in this section to point out (briefly) the way in which the proposal's being granted will benefit you, it's more important (and deserves more attention) to point out how the proposal's being granted will accomplish the goals and satisfy the values of the proposal's audience. And though it's possible, in a longer proposal, to create new values in your audience (addressing a need the audience has not hitherto felt, arguing convincingly that such a need is consistent with existing ones), in the kinds of short student proposals discussed here you're largely confined to appealing to the values your audience already has.

More on the analysis of audience appears in chapters 7 and 20.

In terms of the student proposal for the independent-study class in Endism, what kinds of goals or values would the people to whom the proposal is addressed have? How could the writer connect the granting of the proposal to the achievement of those goals? Obviously, any university's mission includes educating the people, and any academic department's mission includes preparing its students as well as it can. In particular, a political science department is always going to have one eye on the current political scene and is bound to respond positively to students who are interested in studying that scene. Because these values or goals already exist strongly within the person(s) who will be reading this report, it doesn't take much to bring up these values emphatically enough so as to give the proposal a strong finish:

A Proposal for an Independent-Study Class (continued)

"Positive Effects" Section

As a senior in political science, I feel it's in my own best interest for me to have the most complete education possible. Because of my particular interest in current affairs, my education would be lacking without specific attention to the "Endism" movement. Following the successful completion of this independent study, I will be well prepared to represent State College's political science department and State College itself, wherever my future takes me. Whether I choose to enter law school or graduate school in political science, putting this last finishing touch on my education will benefit both me and the college.

Notice that this ending to the proposal puts the emphasis equally on what approving the project will do for (a) the writer and (b) the reader (what business communication people call "reader benefits"). Again, the pitch is rather idealistic, but it should help the student because it's hard to argue *against* a proposal that promises to make both the student and the institution look good.

Notice that this final paragraph appeals specifically to the audience's goals as we've already described them. Again, in a proposal this short there's neither time nor space to create new values in the reader; it's best to focus instead on plugging your goals into the existing values of your audience.

Writing Student Proposals

Students usually write proposals in response to a need they already feel or a problem they already have some understanding of; thus, it's frequently easy for a student to write a first draft of a proposal addressing such a situation. Often a student writing a proposal has seen a problem and devised a solution even before commencing to write the proposal; hence, "writing" becomes more a matter of revising, taking material that is already on paper and putting it into a structure more like that of a typical proposal.

Planning

Even though you may already have a couple of paragraphs of your proposal jotted down in scratch form, to turn those into a good working first draft we recommend you write answers to these questions:

- What are the facts?
- What do those facts mean?
- What should be done?
- What is the solution's worth?

By writing answers to these questions you're giving yourself at least the skeleton of an outline for your proposal. You're also treating whatever you're writing about in a specific way—to use an awful piece of jargon, we can say you are *problematizing* the situation. The problem/solution structure is basic to all human endeavors and thus provides a convenient framework for your proposal.

There's something about the experience of frequently writing proposals—"grantsmanship"—that encourages jargon. Thus our use of *universalize* and *problematize* here. (But at least we don't *historicize* while we try to *personalize.*)

Discovering Context

Before proceeding further than this fast first draft, you should do, we suggest, a little more skull work. Do you remember our saying earlier that you make the important decisions about how your proposal should be written based on knowledge of its *context?* Well, this is the time to find out about that context. The questions you need to answer now are the ones whose answers will guide you through the expansion and revision of your first draft into an effective, finished document. Specifically, you need answers to these questions:

- Who is the audience for this proposal?
- How much does the audience know about this subject?
- What important goals or values of the audience are relevant to this problem?
- What kind of facts/documentation might be available to support your description of the problem?
- Are there other kinds of support you can offer for your analysis of the problem, for the rightness of your solution, or for your claim to be able to carry out the solution?
- What kinds of negative outcomes of allowing the status quo to continue can you mention that might move your reader to see the need for action the way you do?
- When you describe your solution—the proposed plan of action—what details about it are significant—its timing? its feasibility? its budget? other elements?
- What kinds of evidence can you bring in to show the feasibility of your solution?
- What goals or values in your audience can you appeal to in support of your solution?

Other chapters of this book set forth more examples of audience-based revising than we can count. This list of questions is another expansion of the same idea.

You can brainstorm some of the answers to these questions; other answers will take more time for thought. But those answers will give you the material for filling out the draft you composed earlier, and they will also help you answer other questions that arise as you write.

Finishing

Because proposals *always* ask something of someone—often doing so in a very competitive situation—and because your own ability and expertise are directly on the line in every proposal you write, the level of *finish* you apply to your proposal is especially important. Of course, that quality is important in every piece of graded work you do, but proposal writing has in many contexts become an area requiring the utmost care on the part of the writer to make sure that every *i* is dotted and every *t* crossed.

It's best to treat any proposal you write as a document of a more professional quality than most of the other writing you do as a student. Perhaps you've written a term paper this way before; if you haven't, now is the time to learn. Here are what seem to us the *minimum* "finish" characteristics of any proposal:

- The proposal has a cover.
- The proposal has a title page.
- The proposal is done in letter-quality type.
- The proposal's margins are one and a half inches all around.
- The proposal is completely free of mechanical and grammatical errors.
- If other mechanical restrictions (such as format) have been placed on the proposal, they must be complied with to the letter.

You may wish to make up a "Request for Proposals" form to which your students will respond in fashioning their proposals. Look at *Commerce Business Daily* for different kinds of proposal specifications.

The worst thing you can do as a proposal writer is to submit a document that is sloppily prepared, carelessly constructed, or poorly thought out. Because whatever else you are selling in the proposal you are first of all selling yourself, the *appearance* has to be impeccable: every proposal you write needs to be wearing a business suit.

Writers' Circle

In professional life, proposals are often written by teams. In order for you to get some valuable practice writing proposals (and working in teams), we'd like you to divide up into small groups (of, say, three or four students each) and revise and complete the proposal for an internship and the proposal for a grant on pages 664–65. If you need more factual information to finish one, you can invent what you need, so long as what you invent is plausible. As you work to complete your proposal, don't just grind through the parts spelled out in this chapter. Ask yourself at each stage, "Is there something additional I can do to make this a better proposal?" When you submit the finished proposals to your teacher, expect the best one(s) to be singled out for praise.

Have a competition and *reject* any proposal that doesn't adhere to the requirements you've provided. (We believe students should realize that there are situations in which someone who has specified, say, one-and-a-half inch margins all around will simply reject a document with one-inch margins.)

WRITING ASSIGNMENTS

1. Write a proposal to your dean requesting the waiver of the math requirement.
2. Write a proposal to a business requesting a summer internship.
3. Write a proposal to the State Endowment for the Arts requesting $500 to study some aspect of regional folk music in your area.
4. Working with the other students in your writing group, write a proposal to create *A Guide to Freshman Composition: The Student's Perspective*, to be written by students, desktop-published in your college's computer laboratory, and sold at a copying service at nominal cost. The audience will be (a) your current teacher, (b) your college's director of freshman composition, and (c) the manager of the local copying service.

This multiple and complex audience is characteristic of proposal audiences.

5. Consider the photo on page 659. Today much of the research conducted in colleges and universities concerns the environment. *Waste disposal and management* deals with everything from household to industrial trash. *Hazardous materials processing* deals with everything from low-level toxic materials, such as hospital trash, to spent fuel rods from nuclear power plants. *Environmental toxicology* examines the role possible "toxins" (poisons) play in the environment. ("Poisons" is construed to include anything placed into the environment, such as agricultural fertilizer, that might *eventually* harm another living thing.) And, *bioremediation* deals with repairing environmental damage via biological means (for example, creating a microbe to "eat" the oil in an oil spill, rather than mopping up the oil with sponges).

   Funding for most of this research is acquired through competitively evaluated proposals, and the conduct of the research requires a team effort that places a premium on efficient management skills. Thus today's environmental scientist, whether in agriculture, biology, chemistry, or human ecology, must be a *good scientist* (of course), an *entrepreneur* (to see and pursue funding opportunities), a *writer and editor* (to develop successful proposals), and a *manager* (to lead the research team and handle the funds responsibly).

   In fact, the picture developed here applies to *most* fields of science. Your task, then, is to find someone involved in science (at least a graduate student, preferably a doctoral candidate, perhaps even a professor, definitely someone already involved in funded research) and interview that person regarding (1) how necessary the skills just described are, and (2) how well or poorly that person's educational background provided basic training in the skills. Use the results of the interview to prepare a short oral report, and present it to your class.

If you want to make this into a written assignment, refer your students to the Vivian Baylor interview on pages 511–13.

chapter 26 Writing Letters, Especially Job Applications

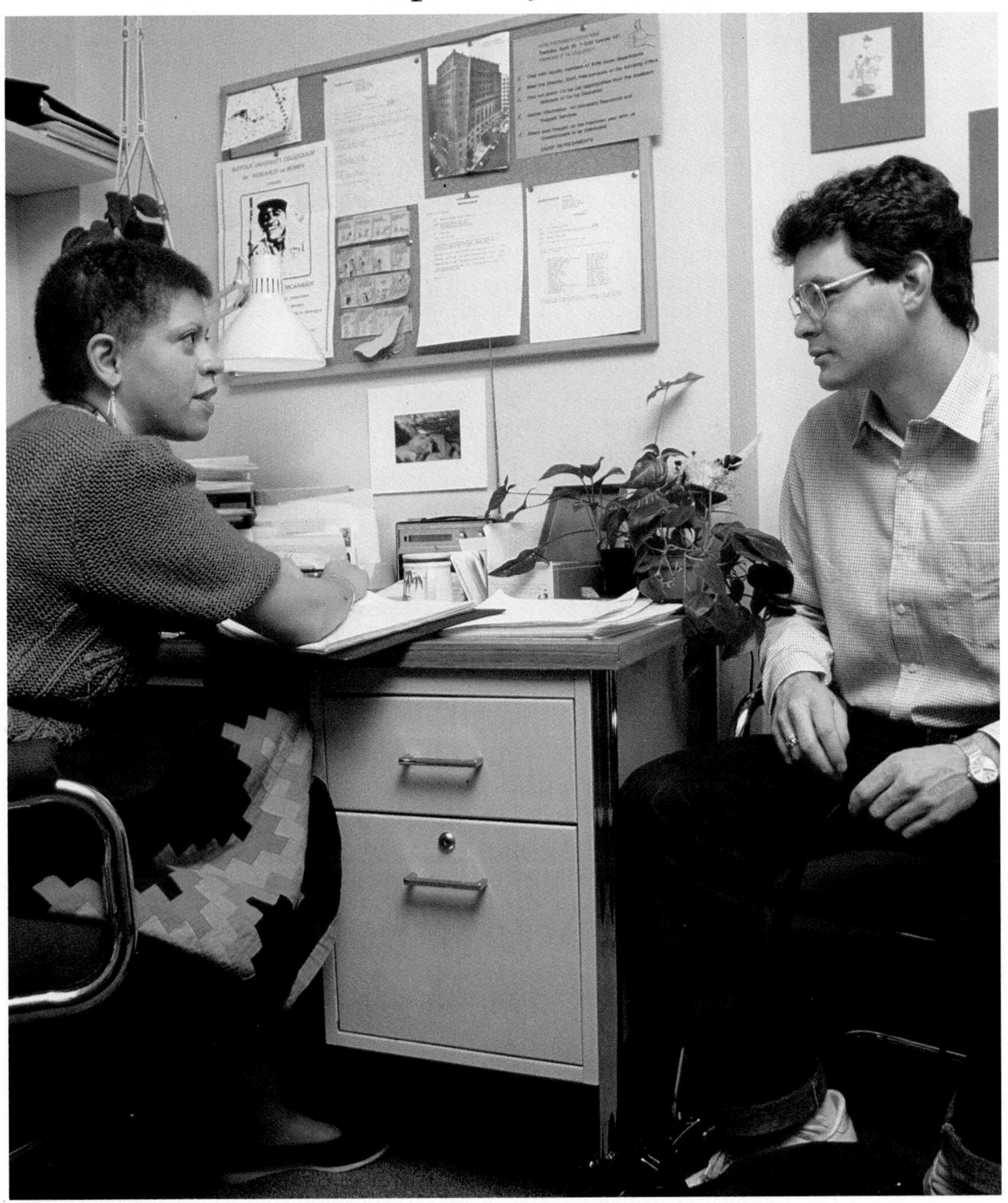

"The desire to write grows with writing."
Erasmus

The Role of Writing in a High-Tech Age

In an age when even income tax returns can be sent via electronic media from your own computer straight to the IRS without ever being on paper, you may be tempted to think that letter writing isn't an important part of a college graduate's writing skills. A little reflection on the facts shows that this tempting thought is incorrect.

Most professional jobs are sought (and their terms confirmed) by letter. Much professional correspondence—offers to sell, sales orders, cost adjustments, requests for information, travel plans, and so on—still relies on letters, even if initial contact has been made by telephone. A letter allows the writer to bring up a *detailed* sequence of facts in *exactly* the order the writer desires and to present a situation to a reader in such a way that the reader can take as much time to respond as he or she wants. And letters leave a "paper trail": a record of *what* communication happened and *when.* That paper trail is always valuable in business and is often valuable in private life as well.

The importance of a paper trail is sometimes difficult for younger students to grasp; if you have students who have been in the work force full-time, you might get their help in bringing home this point.

As a student, you may have already had the experience of wishing you had created and maintained a paper trail:

- Did you pay a utility deposit when you moved into your apartment, and can you get it back when you move out? If you sent it with a letter and kept a copy, you probably can.
- Did you agree to pay a certain price for a service, such as home remodeling, and then find the final price considerably higher? A paper trail (including a letter of agreement from you to the contractor) specifying the agreed-on price can help resolve that situation in your favor.
- Were you told by the registrar that a certain course would count a certain way, only to find out later that it wouldn't? Again, what you needed to have made and kept was an official letter to that effect—a paper trail.

The opening line of this kind of "letter of agreement" often is "I just want to review the terms of . . . that we discussed . . . "

These are only a few typical situations in which students can benefit from the kind of paper trail good letters create. Obviously, there are even more such situations found by professionals, home owners, and parents.

Certainly you will use the telephone, direct person-to-person contacts, electronic mail, and so on a great deal in your life. But letters are important too; they remain one of the primary ways we show ourselves to others with words. Thus it's worth taking time to get better at writing letters—especially job applications.

Of course, we can't here attempt to list all the possible kinds of letters that might be written. But what we will do in this chapter is talk briefly about alternate *forms* for letters, look briefly at simple *types* of letters, and then complicate the picture a bit by examining several of the important *principles* involved in letters (and how use of those principles allows you to write complicated letters that are still clear and effective).

Forms for Letters

To do well at letter writing you don't really need to know a lot about all the different forms there are. Figure 1 shows what we think is the easiest one. This is a

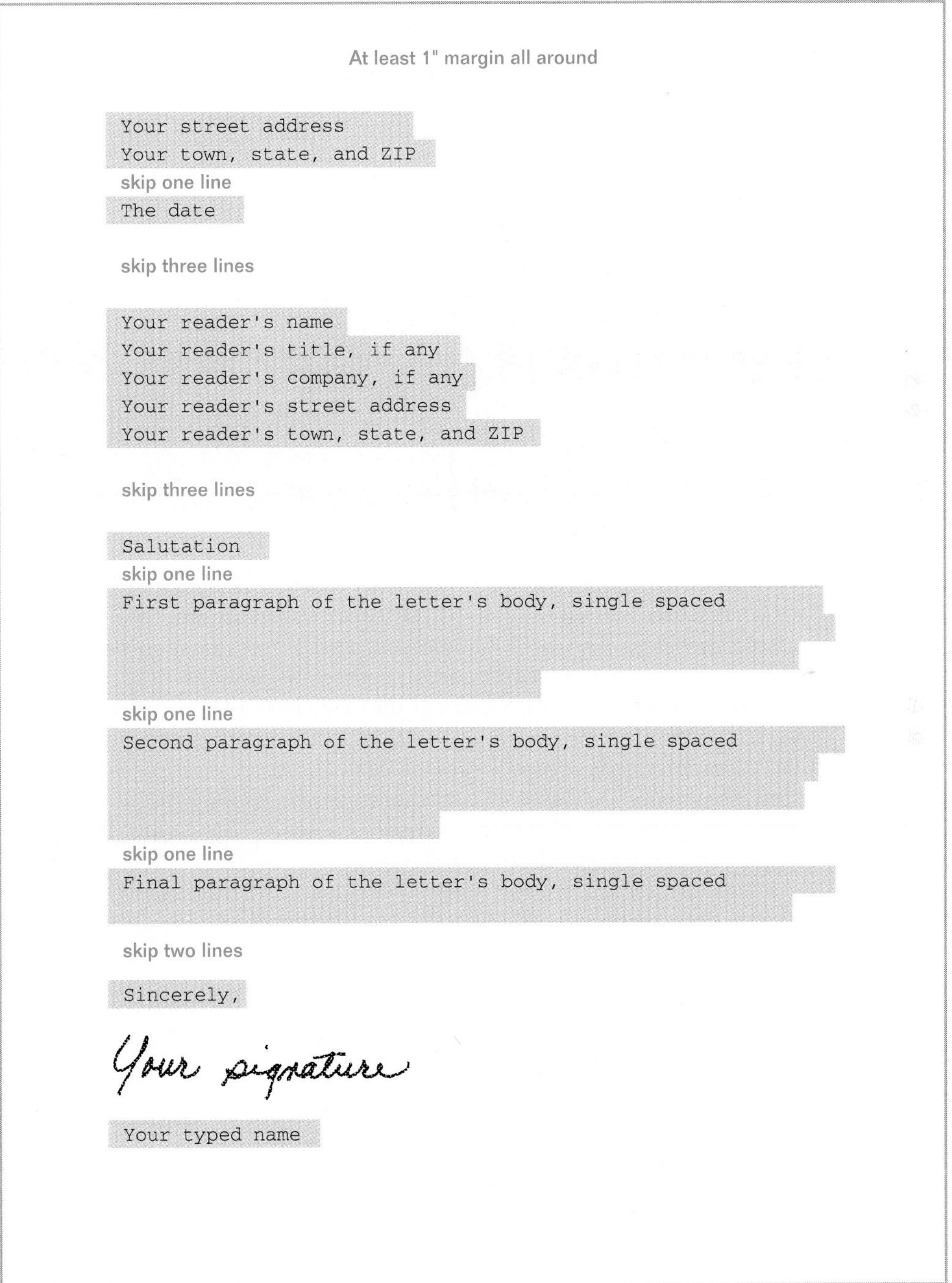

At least 1" margin all around

Your street address
Your town, state, and ZIP
skip one line
The date

skip three lines

Your reader's name
Your reader's title, if any
Your reader's company, if any
Your reader's street address
Your reader's town, state, and ZIP

skip three lines

Salutation
skip one line
First paragraph of the letter's body, single spaced

skip one line
Second paragraph of the letter's body, single spaced

skip one line
Final paragraph of the letter's body, single spaced

skip two lines

Sincerely,

Your signature

Your typed name

Figure 1 A Basic Business Letter Form

really basic letter form, and it's all you really need to know. *Everything* starts at the left margin; no tricky spacing is necessary. Each element (the inside heading, the individual paragraphs of the body, and so on) is single-spaced, and double-spacing separates the elements. (Blank lines in the form are noted for you in the figure.)

These letters are characteristically short. Should you need a second page, it has a particular first line, shown in figure 2.

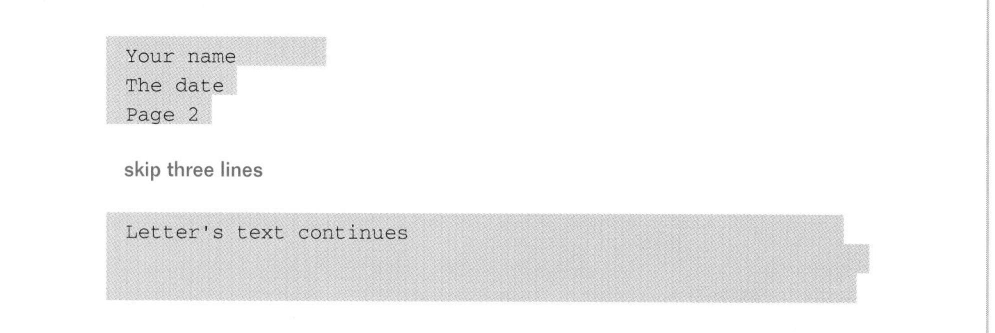

Figure 2 Basic Business Letter Form: How to Begin Second and Following Pages
This continues the preceding form.

There's really only one major alternate form you need to know about, that shown in figure 3 on page 677. It's a little fancier and a little more traditional (and a little harder to keyboard). Should you need a "continuation page" in this alternate form, its top is also shown, in figure 4 on page 678.

Here you may need briefly to discuss the sensitive issue of pronoun gender with students (that is, why "Dear Sir" may not be an appropriate salutation). More on sexism in language appears in chapter 30 of the hardbound edition of this text.

Sometimes you just can't find out the name or gender of the person you're writing to. Your first alternative is to substitute the appropriate *title*, in which case the salutation line becomes "Dear Personnel Manager:" or "Dear Service Manager." Sometimes you can't even come up with a title for the letter's recipient—in which case you can substitute a *purpose* line for the salutation: "PURPOSE: Request for refund on defective product."

Although there are many other letter forms that are acceptable, you really need to use only one of these two. The rest, frankly, is window dressing.

Types of Letters

As a private person (as opposed to being the representative of a corporation), you are most likely to write three kinds of letters (other than letters to friends):

1. The request for information
2. The letter of complaint
3. The letter of application

At least 1" margin all around

Your street address
Your town, state, and ZIP
skip one line
The date

skip three lines

Your reader's name
Your reader's title, if any
Your reader's company, if any
Your reader's street address
Your reader's town, state, and ZIP

skip three lines

Salutation
skip one line
First paragraph of the letter's body, single spaced

skip one line
Second paragraph of the letter's body, single spaced

skip one line
Final paragraph of the letter's body, single spaced

skip two lines

Sincerely,

Your signature

Your typed name

Figure 3 An Alternate Business Letter Form

Your name	Page 2	The date

skip three lines

Letter's text continues

Figure 4 Alternate Business Letter Form: How to Begin Second and Following Pages
This continues the preceding form.

These three kinds of letters have some important things in common. Each is, in its own way, a letter of request. That is, in each case you are asking someone for something.

The *request for information* is usually written as an inquiry about a product or services. This may be your way of asking about exchange programs at different colleges, about new accessories for your personal computer, or about services available at a beach resort. In all those cases, the letter is simple and routine, and it should get a simple and routine answer.

One step up in degree of difficulty is the *letter of complaint*, specifically one about a service or a product. It may strike you as odd that this kind of letter has a strong affiliation with other letters of request, but there's a logic to it. The kind of letter of complaint we're talking about is one in which in the first paragraph or two you lay out the facts of the unhappy situation and then, in the next (sometimes the final) paragraph, request a particular action (such as a price adjustment or a refund) as compensation. Although we've all at one time or another written letters of complaint that don't have this final section, there really isn't much point to such letters (other than getting something off our chest). If you're going to take the time to write a letter of complaint, it makes much more sense to include a request for an adjustment of the situation. *That's* the kind of letter of complaint we're talking about.

We take a pragmatic view here. What's the use of taking the trouble to write a letter if you're not going to try to obtain some kind of redress of your grievances?

The third type of letter, the *letter of application,* is also related to the first two types. Whether you're applying for a scholarship, a summer job, an internship, admission to an academic program, or a full-time professional position, this kind of letter of request can be very important to you. In this chapter we'll look in detail at a job application letter, perhaps the most significant example of this kind of letter. We'll also look at a simple résumé.

The Request for Information

Frequently it's easier to make a request for information by telephone, rather than by letter. There's no denying that telephoning can save time and trouble. But long-distance telephoning is more expensive than sending a letter, and once the conversation is over no written record of it remains. Other than the difference in costs, the biggest advantage of using a *letter* as a request for information is to get the written record and level of detail the letter and its response provide.

In most cases you're writing a letter requesting information to someone who is in a position to expect such a letter—you're writing to request information about a product from a manufacturer, a service from an agency or a company, or a program from an educational institution. In each case, the person you're writing to views that kind of request as part of a day's work and can be expected routinely to respond to your letter. This makes your task as a letter writer fairly simple. Mostly, your concern should be to get the right information in the letter—the right kind of detail, the right level of detail—so as to ensure that your respondent sends you back the information you want and not the wrong information.

Here's what the body of one such letter might look like:

Jane Smith

Manager, Acme Beach Resort

Acme, Washington 98597

Dear Ms. Smith:

Last year my wife and I drove by your resort on our way from Vancouver to Portland, and we were both struck by the view of the ocean from there. We would like to plan our next vacation to include a stay at your resort.

Will you please send us information concerning your resort, including a schedule of room fees? In particular, we are interested in whether you have off-season rates and whether your rates for rooms by the week differ from those for rooms by the night.

Thank you,

Remind your students that even though we *show* letters double-spaced here, the form they should follow is single-spaced as on pages 675–77.

Now, why would someone send a letter with that request, when a phone call would do? The answer is simple: there's no need to spend the cost of a phone call, for there's no urgency to the request, and the person writing the letter wants a written record of the response (in this case, room fees and services). Notice also in this letter the level of detail—the specific information about off-season rates and rooms by the week.

The written record, or paper trail, is of primary importance with this kind of letter. That means you need to keep a copy of *both* your initial letter *and* the response; if you don't do this record keeping, there's not much point in using this kind of letter.

Here's that paper trail again.

Let's look at one more example of a simple letter requesting information. Here a student requests information about a summer internship program:

> Dr. Susan Jones, Director
>
> San Francisco Center for Internships
>
> 1106 Market Street
>
> San Francisco, California 95955
>
> Dear Dr. Jones:
>
> My adviser, Professor Mary Gomez of the State College history department, has told me that each summer your organization makes available a small number of internships for undergraduates to work in San Francisco city agencies. I am an undergraduate history major at State College, planning to get a B.A. in history and then an M.A. in public administration, and I am looking for a summer working and learning opportunity in a large city government such as San Francisco's.
>
> Will you please send me whatever information you have on summer internships working in San Francisco city government? The questions I need answered are the obvious ones--how to apply, whether course credit is available, whether any pay is involved, whether housing is available, and so forth. It's especially important to me to learn whether course credit is available, because I would like to have whatever internship I do show on my transcript.
>
> Thank you for sending me this information.
>
> Sincerely,

Again, there's no great complexity to such a letter. It's worth noting that this one contains something a little different about its opening: it uses what letter specialists call a "contact" phrase—a few words to tell the reader what prompted the request. Here it's "My adviser, Professor Mary Gomez of the State College history department, has told me that. . . . " In fact, we saw the same kind of thing in the earlier letter. Can you spot it? It's the line, "Last year my wife and I drove by your resort on our way from Vancouver to Portland, and we were both struck by the view of the ocean from there." The purpose of using this kind of line is to add to the specificity of the request; something in how you came to be asking for this information may help the letter's recipient give exactly the information you need.

The Letter of Complaint

A letter of complaint involves a more complicated kind of request than a letter asking for information. As noted earlier, our focus here is not on the kind of letter in which you say, "I'm unhappy about this product [or service]"; rather, our focus is on the kind of letter in which you also ask for an adjustment or a remedy to the situation. Such a letter asks for more than information; it asks for action, and thus needs to be more carefully written. But the idea behind it is the same. To be successful you need to explain what motivates the situation, being sure to use an appropriate level of detail and being *precise* about what you're requesting.

Here's an example. Suppose you pay your cable television bill on time as usual and, to your surprise, soon receive a notice stating that your payment is now ten days late. A twenty dollar service charge has been added to the bill, and unless the company receives your payment in full by the twentieth of the month your service will be cut off and the account turned over to a collection agency (which action automatically increases the bill another fifty dollars). You have the canceled check showing the bill was paid on time; now you need to get the cable company to see things your way and correct the problem. Because you want a written record of the situation, you decide to use a letter rather than a phone call. Here's what the letter might look like:

Complaints Department
ZAP Cable Company
Collegetown, Nevada 45981

SUBJECT: Adjustment to bill #456-789

On March 31 of this year I paid my cable bill in full as usual. Please note the enclosed copy of my canceled check. On April 12 I received a letter from your company claiming that the bill had not been paid, that I now owed an additional twenty dollars, and that unless I paid within five days my account would be turned over to a collection agency and my service would be terminated.

> As my canceled check shows, I paid the bill on time. Therefore I would appreciate your removing the additional charges from my account and sending me a letter confirming that you have done so.
>
> We all make mistakes, and I trust you will correct this one promptly.
>
> Sincerely,

We anticipate some debate about including this "mistakes" line. Is it a good idea, in your students' minds? Or is it perhaps a bit of a sneer?

Notice there's no pettiness or vindictiveness in this kind of letter. You're taking the position that you're the wronged party, that certain facts (of which you have proof) accurately describe the situation, and that a particular course of action will remedy it. You're detailed and to the point, not harsh, but very straightforward. In the letter above, only the very last line ("We all make mistakes") offers any softening, but it just sets up the straightest line of all ("and I trust you will correct this one promptly").

Most businesses and individuals are aware that they sometimes make mistakes, and they are receptive to having their mistakes pointed out and quite willing to correct them. By not being abusive in your letter you make it easier for them to give you what you want. On the other hand, if you take a *confrontational* stance you make it easier for them to be confrontational as well.

Let's next look at a somewhat more challenging situation: say that on a recent visit to a city you stayed at the Acme Plaza Hotel and, while there, made six long-distance, collect calls. When you went to pay the bill, you were unhappy to note that an extra forty-two dollars had been added onto it above the cost of the room. The desk clerk explained that the hotel added an extra seven dollars per call "connect fee," that the fee was hotel policy, that notice of the fee was printed on the phone card in the room, and that you could appeal to the manager, who would not be available for several hours. In order to meet your plane flight, you grudgingly paid the bill. But now you're home, you're still angry, and you want at least *some* of your forty-two dollars back. What might your letter look like in this situation?

> General Manager
> Acme Plaza Hotel
> Capitol City, Anystate 12345
>
> Dear General Manager:
>
> I am writing to request an adjustment on the bill I was charged when I stayed at your hotel from March 15 to March 17 of this year. As the attached bill shows, included in the total was forty-two dollars of

"connect fees" on six collect calls I made during my stay. I feel that these charges are unfair, and I'm asking you to refund that sum.

When I asked the desk clerk about the charges at the checkout in the morning, she said that they were clearly posted in each room and that if I wanted to discuss them further I would have to wait to see the manager, who would not be available until much later. Because I had a noon plane to catch, I grudgingly paid the bill.

I have two problems with this: (a) The "connect fee" was nowhere posted in the room, and certainly not on the phone. Maybe it is posted on other phones in other rooms, but it wasn't on mine. If it had been, I would not have made six calls. (b) I think it's unfair to put guests who have a problem with their bill in a situation in which they must wait three or four hours to discuss adjusting their bill. How many of your guests can interrupt their trip long enough to do that?

One last problem: I think charging a seven-dollar "connect fee" is ridiculous on the face of it. Some states have already taken action to ban such fees--which supports my position that they're unjust.

For the reasons listed above, I'm asking that you refund the forty-two dollars I paid under protest at checkout. Thank you for giving your prompt attention to this matter.

Sincerely,

This letter too has the same characteristics as the letters shown earlier in this chapter. It addresses a more difficult problem and, frankly, has a smaller chance of success than the preceding complaint letter. More frankly still, it's about all the person in that situation could do at the time.

Do you think the letter would be successful? We rate its chances at no more than fifty-fifty. Can you think of a way to change its writing so as to improve its chances? Suppose the request were turned down; what other steps could the letter writer take then?

We would like to say we have a magic formula for writing complaint letters that achieve 100 percent success. We don't; no one does.

In fact, in our experience, refunds from hotels in situations like the "connect fee" phone charges are rare. More common is a discount coupon or coupons on subsequent nights' stays at the same hotel (when, probably, we'd use the pay phone in the lobby).

The Letter of Application

The most important kind of letter of request, and the one you need to be most careful about writing, is the job application letter. The phrase "job application letter" encompasses various kinds of letters whose writing is closely related, among them applications for internships, law school, medical school, and scholarships. Once again, this letter has significant affinities with the other kinds of letters of request discussed above.

Job application letters share with other letters of request the need for a contact phrase, the need for an appropriate level of detail, and the need to be specific in the request section. In the job application letters you write, using the right kind and amount of detail is especially important in the section describing your qualifications for the position you're applying for.

This parallels sections in other letters where the right kind and amount of detail are important.

Because we assume that you're using this book in a freshman course, we figure it's unlikely that you're going to be writing letters looking for full-time professional employment at this time in your life. Accordingly, the sample letters we'll show you here are for the kinds of positions our experience shows us students like you write letters for. Consider this situation: Larry Kramer, a freshman at State University, seeks a summer internship in a public information office. He's trying to decide whether a career in writing, editing, and publications is right for him and, if so, whether he would be better off majoring in journalism or in the English department's writing concentration. Because one of his professors has told him that a local hospital often employs summer interns in its public information office, Larry has decided to apply there. Here's his letter; see whether you can identify its components.

Bettye Jorgensen
Director, Public Information Office
Southwest Regional Hospital
Collegetown, Anystate 12345

Dear Ms. Jorgensen:

Professor Anne Prosser of the State College English department has informed me that your office often employs summer interns who are college students. If you are planning to sponsor such internships this summer, I would like to apply for one. I am a freshman at State College and am considering a career in some aspect of writing, editing, and publishing.

My experience working with publications started in high school, with two years on our student newspaper. On that paper, I wrote stories, edited stories, and did some page layout on the computer. This year at State College I took two semesters of freshman composition, making an

A in the first and currently having an A average going into the midterm in the second. We write something every week, read and help revise one another's writing, and take turns as proofreader in our four-person writing groups.

I can send you letters of reference from my high school newspaper adviser, my freshman composition teacher, and a former employer, as well as writing samples, if you wish. I am available for an interview anytime at your convenience.

Sincerely,

Can you tell from reading Larry Kramer's letter what the background is for his request and how (briefly) explaining the nature of that background helps the letter's recipient know how to respond? Can you tell exactly what it is in the writer's background that might help motivate the recipient to grant the request? And can you tell exactly what the writer wants the reader to do? If you answer yes to all these questions, then the letter is doing the things it needs to do. Of course, that doesn't guarantee it will be successful—ultimately, whether or not Larry gets the summer internship depends on much, much more than the letter. But Larry can at least be confident he's made the best possible presentation of his credentials.

We suggest you and your students pick out these instances in the letter.

Let's look at another example, this one an application for an engineering co-op position. (Co-op positions allow students to alternate working one semester and going to school the next.) Willadean Johnson, a sophomore in chemical engineering, is looking for a co-op position with a company that specializes in environmental engineering. She's writing to Research BioTechnics, a company specializing in the prevention, emergency management, and treatment of petroleum-related pollution.

J. R. Pinelli
Personnel Manager
Research BioTechnics
Capitol City, Anystate 12345

Dear Mr. Pinelli:

The Engineering Co-op Office at State College recently posted your notice advertising co-op positions for environmental-minded engineering students. I am a sophomore chemical engineering major at State College, and I would like to apply for one of your co-op positions. My career goal following graduation is to find professional employment as an engineer with a firm that is heavily involved with environmental work.

As part of my major, I have taken a number of general required courses (calculus, biology, freshman composition) and three engineering courses: fundamentals of engineering, basic structures, and basic statics. Last summer I worked as a volunteer for EarthWatch, documenting sources of pollution along the Crystal River, and I helped with the chemical analysis of samples we took along the river. That experience, together with the pleasure I take from the analytical work my courses have given me, convinced me that a career in environmental work is the right choice for me.

I will be in Capitol City during the week of March 21-28, State College's spring break. May I call you the week before that to arrange an appointment? I look forward to learning more about the work of Research BioTechnics.

Sincerely,

This time, we suggest your students pick out these elements without your help.

Can you find in this letter the same basic elements that were in the last one? If you can, then the letter is doing what it needs to do to make the best possible presentation of Willadean's qualifications.

Even though the fundamental approach to writing job application letters presented here is sound, you cannot do your own *best* letter just by imitating these. There's a certain value in imitation—for training or for a way of producing a fast first draft that later gets thoughtfully customized. But the only way you can truly make the strongest possible letter is to couple your awareness of this general approach to writing letters with a good familiarity of the important principles in writing *any* letter. The next section of this chapter thus offers a short presentation of the key principles in letters today; for examples we'll use parts of the letters you've already seen in this chapter.

Principles for Letters

One of the chief natural divisions among business letters is based on whether the recipient has asked for, expects, or somehow anticipates the letter. If you're writing to someone who in this sense expects the letter, your letter is called *solicited;* the opposite is *unsolicited.* If you're writing a letter responding to someone else's letter to you, your letter, obviously, is solicited. If you're writing to someone who is in a position where letters are regularly received from strangers (such as the mail-order department of a catalog store or the personnel manager of a firm advertising a job opening), your letter is also solicited (whereas if you send a letter to the personnel manager and the firm is *not* currently looking for employees, the letter is unsolicited.)

Solicited Versus Unsolicited Letters

Part of the function of the first paragraph of your letter is to help your reader understand (metaphorically speaking) "where this letter is coming from." In the application letter, the first paragraph specifies that application is being made, noting where the job advertisement to which the letter responds was seen. It then goes on to state the applicant's primary qualification for the job. This primary qualification is what "connects" the applicant to the job; it needs to be the best card you have in your hand. In the letter of complaint, the first paragraph explains the background of the problem, again letting the reader know immediately why the letter is being written. And in the letter of request, the first paragraph once again sets the stage for the writer's request, with the request itself, of course, making the letter's purpose clear. In each case, the first paragraph is reinforcing the fact that the letter is solicited, that its writer has good reason for writing *this* letter to *this* recipient.

What's the point in distinguishing between solicited and unsolicited letters? Well, most people respond to unsolicited mail with at least a slight negative reaction, a kind of "Who is this person and why am I being bothered with this?" tendency that may be enough to produce a negative response to your otherwise-quite-normal request. On the other hand, solicited mail at least has a chance to make its own way. The point? That you want your mail to be solicited, if at all possible. Because each of these letters, in its own way, gives the recipient a chance to say yes or no, you must try to maximize your chances for a yes answer. If you *must* send an unsolicited letter, that first paragraph (the one explaining the motivation for the letter) becomes even more important. But whether a letter is solicited or unsolicited, by the end of that first paragraph you want your reader to see things your way.

Remember the role of the "contact" phrases in the earlier letters.

Positive Versus Negative Messages

Another key principle behind business letters is the distinction between *positive messages* and *negative messages.* Positive messages consist of statements your reader wants to hear; negative messages are things your reader doesn't want to hear. It's a basic distinction, and so without belaboring it, we'll present here a few paragraphs similar to those in the earlier letters, rewritten to include negative messages. Can you spot the negative messages? Can you tell how these (probably accidental) negative messages hurt the request's chances?

Negative messages, by their nature, are hard to write gracefully. Certainly, any *needless* negative message should be avoided; there's no point in making a bad situation worse. Tact is always appropriate.

Dear Ms. Smith:

Will you please send us information concerning your resort, including a schedule of room fees? In particular, we are interested in whether you have off-season rates and whether your rates for rooms by the week differ from those for rooms by the night. And we do need to know what your policy on pets is; we have three large German shepherds that must stay in our room with us.

Mrs. Jones,

I am looking for a summer working and learning opportunity in a large city government such as San Francisco's.

Not only are the things the writer needs to know not listed in parallel form; they also include careless repetition. The last line is too pushy for this kind of letter.

Please send me information on summer internships working in San Francisco city government. Also I need to know how to apply, if course credit is available, if there is any pay involved, what about housing, and whether course credit is available.

Please send the information as soon as possible.

Even though this salutation may be true, it's still an insult. If you were the recipient, would you read on?

Dear Incompetents:

On April 12 I received a letter from your company claiming that my bill had not been paid. I paid the bill on time.

The tone of harsh, condemning criticism here will probably gain the writer no compensation beyond the satisfaction of having vented anger.

What a stupid mistake! That's about what I'd expect from a company that provides the kind of service yours does.

Try to get it together, OK?

Unless you *know* you are writing to a man, "Dear Sir" is a risky salutation; it could become a negative if the recipient is a woman. If you don't know the recipient's gender, it's usually better to address that person by title (for instance, "Dear Manager").

Dear Sir:

I am a sophomore philosophy major looking for a co-op position in environmental engineering.

Last summer I worked as a volunteer for Greenpeace, but I quit because they took too passive an approach to dealing with the industrial billionaires and their wage-slaves who are responsible for the destruction of our world.

This barrage of extreme ideology makes the *writer* sound like a risk.

I will call you next week to arrange an appointment. I look forward to telling you more about my background.

Sincerely,

In terms of figuring out why these letters will not get favorable responses, they're obviously pushovers. If you want to go deeper into letter writing, you might bring in samples whose problems are subtler.

Always keep in mind two points about positive and negative messages. First, avoid unnecessary negative messages. Second, if you must send a negative message, make sure you explain its motivation. One way to explain the motivation for a negative message looks like this: "*For the reasons listed above*, I'm asking that you refund . . ." Another way might be, "Although your credentials are excellent and your interview was impressive, we had only one fellowship to grant and the strong competition forced us to choose another candidate."

Action Closing

The last principle we'll highlight concerns the need to end the letter with a clear statement of what you expect the reader to do in response. This statement, called an *action closing*, keeps the letter's recipient from being left wondering what to do next. Here are the action closings from some of the letters in this chapter:

> Will you please send us information concerning your resort, including a schedule of room fees? In particular, we are interested in whether you have off-season rates and whether your rates for rooms by the week differ from those for rooms by the night.

> Will you please send me whatever information you have on summer internships working in San Francisco city government? The questions I need answered are the obvious ones--how to apply, whether course credit is available, whether any pay is involved, whether housing is available, and so forth. It's especially important to me to learn whether course credit is available, because I would like to have whatever internship I do show on my transcript.

> I will be in Capitol City during the week of March 21-28, State College's spring break. May I call you the week before that to arrange an appointment? I look forward to learning more about the work of Research BioTechnics.

If you are always careful to end your letters with a clear statement of exactly what you expect (or hope) the reader's next step to be, you'll find that your letters will be much more successful.

Composing Processes and Business Letters

Writing a one-page letter doesn't require much elaboration here in terms of the process you use to produce it. Of course, you must give some thought to the features discussed earlier in this chapter, but it doesn't take too many drafts and too many revisions to make a workable letter.

We don't intend to suggest that coming up with the right content in these letters is all that hard; letters provide an excellent opportunity for students to focus sharply on trying to produce a perfect finished product, or at least one that is error-free in terms of grammar, spelling, and mechanics.

What makes this kind of writing a bit different from some of the other writing you've done is the need for the finished product to be *carefully* polished—on the levels of grammatical correctness, physical appearance on the page, attention to the level of word choice you use, and so forth. Once again, because each of these letters—and especially the job application letter—is asking something of someone, you want to have your best appearance showing in the letter. This means that you need to be sure to look up anything related to the production of a polished letter that you aren't *certain* about, whether it is the spelling of a word, the punctuation of a sentence, or the exact way a company prints its name (Is it *Biotechnics* or *BioTechnics?*). If you have any doubts after you've looked up the troublesome features, ask someone (such as your writing teacher) to review the draft for you. And when it comes to job application letters, you might as well plan from the start to get someone else to check the letter for you and to do so carefully. As anyone in business knows, some letters are just too important *not* to have someone else check for all kinds of mistakes, errors in tact as well as errors in grammar. And *proofreading* is crucial.

It's *BioTechnics.*

Proofreading Steps

There's plenty to learn about what constitutes an effective process of proofreading. When you have a lot on the line with a letter, we recommend you follow these five steps:

Notice that steps 1 and 2 are not at all the same activity.

1. *Get a fresh look at the document.* Never rely on proofreading done the same day the document is finished. The best thing to do is to "sleep on it"—whatever time on Thursday you finish writing, do your proofreading on Friday. Otherwise, your brain has a tendency to see what you *want* to be there, not what is *really* there.
2. *Get a look at a fresh document.* If you've been handwriting your letter, proofread it after it has the different appearance typing gives it. If you've been word-processing it and trying to proofread it on the screen, print out a fresh copy for your final proofreading. If you've been proofreading hard copy all the time, switch your printer to a different type style for the last proofreading before the final copy.

The purpose here is once again to find a way to prevent your brain from fooling you by showing you what you *want* to be there instead of what is *really* there. In this, one of the best techniques is to change the typographic appearance of the piece.

3. *Proofread one word (or punctuation mark) at a time.* You may need to use an index card to slide along the page in front of your eyes, revealing each word, mark, or line only as you need it. This technique helps you focus your attention on each solitary feature and keeps you from hurrying.
4. *Read the piece back to front.* Students often laugh when we first mention this technique because it sounds so odd—but it really works. Starting at the end of the document, put your pencil under each word or punctuation mark—last to first—one at a time. As your pencil rests at each point, ask yourself "Is this right?" Again, the purpose is to get yourself to look carefully at each individual word or mark and not as part of a phrase, clause, or sentence. Obviously, you'll miss some things this way, such as subject-verb agreement, but for things like spelling errors and typos the technique is excellent.
5. *Ask someone else to proofread the piece as well.* In this you need someone who has not only a good grasp of grammar, spelling, and so on but also a good understanding of how important the letter is to you. If your helper glances at the page for five or six seconds; says, "Looks good enough to me"; and then hands it back, you need to find someone else.

This advice goes for peer editing too.

Nothing detracts from a business letter, especially a job application letter, like a sloppy job of finishing. And effective proofreading counters just that problem, thus applying a final, high-gloss finish to your good work and making the outside look as good as the inside. Doing the task well takes focused energy and only a little time; the investment is worth it.

And Be Sure to Include a Résumé

It wouldn't make sense to discuss writing job application letters without including at least a simple, one-page résumé. Several of the same considerations apply—being careful to have the right amount of detail in the right places, avoiding needless negative messages, and making sure there are no typographic, spelling, or mechanical errors. With those principles operating underneath, the surface of your résumé needs to include at minimum these elements:

Your name, address, and phone number

Your level (full-time, part-time) and date(s) of availability

Your education

Your work experience

Your computer ability

The availability of reference letters

That's as much as (and maybe more than) you'll have room for on one page. Here's what such a résumé might look like:

> JACK SMITH
>
> 5515 College Lane
> College Town, Anystate 12345
> (555) 555-5555
>
> Availability:
> Full-time, May 15
> Part-time, immediately
>
> EDUCATION
>
> State College, completing sophomore year, architecture major; grade point average, 3.2/4.0
> Graduation expected, May 1994
> Capitol City High School diploma, May 1990
>
> Important College Course Work
>
> Graphic Design
> Freshman Composition
> Programming in COBOL
> Calculus
> Small-Group Communication
> Introduction to Landscape Design
> Botany
> Art History
>
> WORK EXPERIENCE
>
> General carpentry, summers 1988-90. AAA Builders, Capitol City.
>
> Landscape maintenance, summers 1986-87. Thompson GreenLawns, Capitol City.
>
> COMPUTER ABILITY
>
> Proficient with Apple and Mac II
> Experienced with IBM
> Proficient with Word, WordPerfect, MacDraw, and MacPaint
>
> REFERENCES
>
> [If you have room, give names, addresses, and phone numbers of three to five persons; otherwise write "Available upon request."]

Writers' Circle

Divide into groups of three, each student in the group producing *one* of the letters called for in the situations listed below. After one student in a group has drafted the letter, the other two students in the group should critique the draft to see how well it complies with the principles for effective letters as set forth in this chapter. After the critiquing, each student in each group should then revise and polish the letter, making it as effective and flawless as possible.

Next, each group should exchange its letters with those of another group and then discuss and evaluate the other group's letters. After this discussion and evaluation, the groups should report the results of those proceedings to one another.

The Situations

1. Write to Pat Janeway, director of the Montana Mountain Camp, Route 6, Butte, Montana 32181, requesting full information for your child to attend that camp next summer. You need to know about all costs (transportation, food, lodging, activities), about the camp's dates, about what the camp recommends your child bring, about medical facilities, and so on.
2. Write to the manager of the Mall Cinema in your town (make up the address if need be) about noise levels the past three times you attended films at that theater: at each showing, children ran in the aisles and paid scant attention to the film, some patrons talked loudly during the film, and—worst of all—the last time you were there you complained about these conditions to the people at the concession stand but nothing was done.
3. Write to Angel Moreno, the director of personnel (make up a company name and address to fit your major), to apply for an advertised summer job related to your academic major; you saw this job advertised on a bulletin board on campus. Write the letter as though you're enclosing a résumé (though we aren't asking you to prepare one to complete this assignment). Show how your academic work and experience so far make you a good candidate for the job.

WRITING ASSIGNMENTS

1. The photo on page 673 of the university student with his faculty advisor reminds us that school days don't last forever (they only seem to!) and that it pays to look ahead to things we might do when formal schooling is not part of our lives.

   A good exercise is to project yourself as an incipient graduate—someone about to receive his or her degree. Check the job listings in newspapers, and at the campus placement office, or comb the journals in your anticipated field of study, and look for advertisements of jobs *for which you will be qualified when you graduate.* Note closely all details of the ad: what are the minimum educational requirements? The minimum experience requirements? Who or what company is the prospective employer? What is the salary range? Where is the job? Imagine yourself as a graduating senior: how will you "stack up" against these job requirements and details? If you think you'd be a good candidate for the job, compose a letter of application as if you were *really* applying for that job. Compose a résumé as well, projecting what claims you think you will be able to make for yourself when you are about to graduate. Attach the résumé to the letter, making them as neat and well-done as you possibly can.

Then take the ad, your letter, and your résumé to your faculty advisor. Get his or her opinion of how effective the letter is for the job advertised. *Repeat* this exercise each year until you are ready to do it for an actual job. And good luck!

2. Here's a fictional story of one student's adventures while seeking a summer internship. At several points in the process, our student, Susan, needs to write letters to solve problems. As directed by your teacher, write those letters to turn in. Most of the facts you'll require are provided here; should you need to invent additional ones, try to make them consistent with the existing characters and story line.

As our story begins, Susan Dressler, a freshman at State College, is talking with her accounting professor about trying to find a summer job that will give her useful professional experience and provide some income. Her professor, Jack Salizar, mentions that a bank in Capitol City, Acme Trust, hires summer accounting interns, and he suggests that she write to their personnel manager, Elizabeth White, to request an internship. As their discussion progresses, Susan decides to mention her career goal (accounting, and eventually a CPA), her grade of A in Beginning Accounting during her first freshman semester, her work as the accountant for three school clubs in high school, and her willingness to provide letters of recommendation from (a) the sponsors of those high school clubs, (b) her accounting professor, and (c) her adviser (Jack Salizar).

Professor Salizar also recommends that Susan enclose a résumé with her letter, listing her address while attending school, her date of high school graduation, her availability, her computer experience, and her (volunteer) work experience.

- Assignment 1—write the letter.
- Assignment 2—write the résumé.

A week later, Susan is thrilled to get a letter from Elizabeth White, inviting her to come to Capitol City on Friday, April 13, for an interview at 10:00 A.M. Susan accepts the invitation and prepares to go to Capitol City. She tells her parents, who offer to pay (a) her gas expenses (Capitol City is two hundred miles away) and, so that she can be fresh for the interview, (b) motel expenses for a stay in Capitol City the night before the interview. Susan gets her best (and only) "superwoman business suit" dry-cleaned, has her car tuned by a friend, makes a reservation at the Gold Card Inn in Capitol City (located only three blocks from Acme Trust), and eagerly awaits the coming of April 12, when she will leave for her interview.

Driving toward Capitol City on April 12, Susan's car's "engine overheat" light begins to flicker. Fifty miles from town she stops at a service station, where she learns her fan belt is slipping, is about to break, and needs to be replaced. The station operator tells her he doesn't have the right one in stock but can get one "directly." Time passes. At 7:30 P.M. Susan is on the road again, mildly peeved but determined to be positive—and also $50 poorer. She arrives at the Gold Card Inn to learn her room is gone, rented to a conventioneer in town for an insurance convention. She maintains that her reservation was guaranteed; the motel maintains that it wasn't. Susan doesn't have a piece of paper to prove it was. After considerable discussion at the desk, she uses the pay phone in the lobby of the posh motel to start trying to find a place to stay. No luck: there's a convention in town (as if she didn't know). An hour on the phone later, she arranges to take a room fifty miles away (in the same town where she had her car repaired four hours earlier), one at not nearly so nice a place, and one costing twice as much.

At 11:00 P.M. Susan is in her room, unpacking and telling herself "Tomorrow will be fine" at which point she discovers her suit is decorated with mysterious white blotches that somehow have been added by the dry-cleaning company. Sponging off the blotches doesn't work. In despair, Susan tries to phone her roommate to bring her roommate's superwoman suit. No answer. Susan wearily climbs back into her car, at midnight, to drive back to State College, abandoning her $120 room. At 2:00 A.M. she wakes her roommate, borrows her suit, sets her alarm for 5:00 A.M., and collapses on her bed. Very early the next morning she climbs back in her car, drives back to Capitol City, arrives at the bank at 9:45, enters Elizabeth White's office at 10:00 A.M., and is really doing a pretty good job of appearing "bright, hardworking, and ambitious"—until about fifteen minutes into the interview. At that time she opens the portfolio she's brought with her to get out her letters of recommendation to show Ms. White, and the reservation slip from the Gold Card Inn—clearly stamped LATE ARRIVAL GUARANTEED—falls out. Ms. White is surprised when this composed, nattily dressed young lady starts laughing hysterically in the middle of the interview.

After a while, things settle down, explanations are made, there are some laughs, and the interview proceeds. Ms. White ends it with, "Thank you for coming—I really admire your perseverance. We need to talk with some other candidates, but you will hear from us one way or the other by May 1. Have a safe, calm trip back."

That evening Susan and her roommate are talking through just how Susan is going to explain to her parents that she'll be asking them to pay $35 for gas, $50 for car repairs, and $120 for a room she didn't use—more than $200, all for a forty-five-minute interview only two hundred miles away. Susan, as she thinks about her treatment by the Gold Card Inn and how much of those expenses she incurred because of its mistake, decides to write a letter asking the Gold Card Inn to pay half the gas and half the $120 room rent (the difference in the price between the rate where she stayed and the Gold Card's rate).

- Assignment 3—write the letter.

(By the way, Susan got the internship. Ms. White said, in part, "Though you weren't really the most qualified applicant in terms of college course work, your resourcefulness and determination are important qualities that we really like.")

chapter 27 Preparing and Making Oral Presentations

"The picture's pretty bleak, gentlemen. ... The world's climates are changing, the mammals are taking over, and we all have a brain about the size of a walnut."

"Learning without thought is labor lost;
thought without learning is perilous."
Confucius

"In every work regard the writer's End,
Since none can compass more than they intend."
Alexander Pope

At both the beginning and the end of this paragraph, we stress *both* that which is found and that which is made, paralleling our earlier discussion of discovery and invention.

As we've seen so far in this book, there are many ways writing can help you both reflect and create new ways of perceiving yourself. The ability to present yourself in words, however, takes many forms today. Making oral presentations—from short, impromptu "talks" to long, planned "speeches"—is another important way to use words both to show who you are and to help you become who you want to be.

Typical Oral Presentations

Oral presentations take varied forms—short and long, formal and informal, impromptu and planned. If you think you're going to be making very many long, formal, planned presentations, either in college or in professional life, you probably need to take a speech course. What we cover in this chapter are short, informal, and *relatively* unplanned presentations. "Short" means speeches lasting maybe three to ten minutes; "informal" means you're not standing up on a stage "reciting"; and "unplanned" means your presentation is made from notes, not from a fully developed script.

We find having students do this kind of short speech works well in our writing classes. More formal speeches often take more class time than we can usually afford.

Our primary concern here centers on the kinds of oral presentations you'll encounter in classroom situations, although this kind of presentation is also common in professional life. Our students tell us that their classes and activities require them to do these kinds of presentations:

- Introductions
- Research reports
- Meetings
- Poster display presentations

These match well with the most common kinds of talks professionals do: introductions (of oneself, one's product, one's service), research reports (of the nature of a problem, of a competitor's product, of a plan for change), meetings (to work out a plan for change, to analyze a situation, to review progress), and poster display presentations (at professional or trade meetings).

Following are brief descriptions of each type of presentation as it occurs in the life of a student.

Introductions

In many classes, the professor asks students to stand and introduce themselves. This kind of short presentation also occurs frequently in professional life. Who you are, where you're from, what brought you here, what your goals and hobbies are—these are the areas typically covered. While the impression you leave is important in any kind of oral presentation, in this kind it's the *whole* point.

As chapter 1's introductory class activity suggests, we recommend doing this kind of exercise.

Research Reports

Students in all disciplines do research, and in class they're often asked to make at least a brief oral presentation of the results. This presentation frequently coincides with the time the *written* version is handed in. Two general approaches characterize this kind of presentation: (a) walking quickly through the whole process (typically in the form of introduction, materials, methods, results, and discussion) and (b) focusing only on what you've learned (for example, introduction, results, and discussion). In the absence of specific guidelines from your teacher, the most practical way for you to decide which approach to use is to size up the particular situation. In college it may be only your grade that rides on the effectiveness of such a presentation; in professional life, it can be much more.

We recommend that your students report orally on their research projects in your class.

Meetings

When you work in a small group, especially in a meeting-room setting, you are also presenting yourself. Meetings take two forms, each requiring different roles from you: (a) *directed* meetings, in which one person is calling all the shots, and (b) *shared* meetings, in which the entire group has the responsibility equally. Whether or not you're in charge of the meeting, you need to recognize which kind of meeting you're in and to select and adjust your role accordingly.

This is paralleled in most composition classes by class work versus group work.

Poster Display Presentations

The newest of these common forms of oral presentations, poster display presentations, consists of the speaker standing by a small number of posters that depict the speaker's material or research. Once again, there is frequently an earlier, written report you can work from. Although the speaker may have rehearsed a few short comments to go with each poster and although handouts describing the work in more detail may be available, no "captive" audience is assumed, and the audience most often comprises persons who pass by the exhibit, look at the posters, and may or may not ask questions about the work the posters describe. This new forum, an interesting combination of the "speech" and one-to-one conversation (complete with visuals), can be a powerful medium of communication if properly accomplished.

Principles of Oral Presentations

In each kind of presentation, the key principles are the same:

These principles provide in a nutshell a good review of much of what, earlier in the book, we've said about writing. Not surprisingly, oral presentations are an excellent medium in which to learn rhetoric.

- Adjust what you say:
  Reinforce the structure.
  Simplify the content.
- Prepare yourself properly:
  Do your homework.
  Practice.
- Deliver your talk effectively:
  Adjust your presentation to what people remember.
  Use appropriate technology.

In the following sections we'll briefly discuss each of these principles and its application for each kind of presentation. Although entire books have been written about each type of presentation, here we will first deal with the basics that cut across all modes and then present a few specific examples to illustrate those principles.

Adjust What You Say

We're assuming that you already have a report or paper ready to use and that you now need to make the content adjustments necessary to fashion an oral presentation from them. What kinds of adjustments should you make, and on what basis?

The *basis* of your adjustments is easy to name, for it's the same as that governing your decisions about any piece of communication, be it written or spoken: you need to find a balance among what you want to say, the people you want to say it to, the forum you must say it in, and the way you want to say it. In earlier chapters, specifically chapters 5, 20, and 24, we've covered those points with respect to *writing;* here we'll cover them with respect to *speaking,* in particular the need to (a) reinforce the structure and (b) simplify the content.

Reinforce the Structure. One of the changes required by speaking instead of writing is that in speaking the structure must be reinforced. Because *listeners* cannot look back over the past text to refresh their memory (or jump ahead to see where the text is going), a person who wants to be an effective *speaker* must take on the responsibility of *reinforcing the structure* of his or her material. Depending on where you're speaking and what you're speaking of, you can reinforce the structure of your talk in various ways. In a classroom setting, it may be as simple as putting a three-, four-, or five-item outline on the board, or making separate mini-outlines out of construction paper for each step of your talk. In a professional setting, the structural reinforcement may be quite different, perhaps incorporating color overhead transparencies with pictures and inset outlines, or utilizing a film or video. The principle, however, is the same. In the case of a meeting, such reinforcement might be a blueprint of the troublesome design, a calendar to hold the focus of the group, or another outline.

Simplify the Content. Just as listeners have less ability to grasp structure than readers do, so too do listeners have a harder time sorting out the less important details from the key points. Thus another obligation speakers bear that writers do not (not, at least, to so great an extent) requires speakers to *simplify the content* of their presentations. It's hard to generalize about what that means in different kinds of presentations, but here's a good rule of thumb. Suppose you're making an oral presentation, seven minutes long, reporting on a research project you did for your freshman composition class. How many key points can you make? Three, maybe four. How much support can you offer for each key point? Three, maybe four facts or details for each. Not only is that all there is time for; that's also all your listeners have any hope of remembering.

Let's look at this idea of simplifying the content from another perspective. Suppose you've been asked to make four posters, 22 by 28 inches apiece, describing the results of your research. Each is to be balanced fifty-fifty between words and pictures. How much *detail* can you present that way? How many small parts of the larger pictures on the posters can you usefully label? How much detail can the text on the posters convey? Once again, the answer is, "Much less than you might initially imagine." A good rule for detail on visuals is the "magic number seven, plus-or-minus two." That is, people will be able easily to see and absorb no more than nine (seven plus two) parts to any visual—your drawing, photo, or sketch can have that many parts, and that's it. Similarly, each poster's verbal aspect can have five, maybe seven, maybe nine points; that's it.

Your students will resist accepting this point; their presentations will prove its truth. It's typical to over-prepare, typical to try to "cram" material into a tight time limitation. Practice and experience are the correctives.

We didn't draw this "magic number seven, plus-or-minus two" idea out of our hats; it's traceable to memory research conducted primarily by George Miller, and it is, among other matters, the reason local telephone numbers don't exceed seven digits. (Note that when more digits are required, as for long-distance direct dialing, the numbers are "chunked" with hyphens into groups of three or four, as in 617–555–1212. This "chunking" principle also comes from memory research.

Prepare Yourself Properly

One of our friends, a nationally known film scholar, says fondly, "I used to have this fantasy when I was in school that once I finally graduated I'd never have to do homework again. How wrong I was." Any professional still has homework to do, and that's especially true before any kind of presentation or meeting. And part of that homework is practicing, going over the material until you're sure you know it, if not cold, then at least with help from your notes. In this section we'll look at what form preparing yourself properly—doing your homework and practicing—takes in the reality of two students' lives; we'll see one student getting ready to do a short presentation in an environmental biology class and another preparing for a student government meeting.

This same point came up in preparing for essay tests (chapter 22).

Do Your Homework. Ann Jones is in an honors environmental biology class in which she and some classmates have been comparing studies of species diversity in streams in a nearby park with similar studies done by students during each of the past five years. (The diversity of species in a stream is one indicator of the stream's water quality; a healthy stream has a highly diverse population. As the water quality diminishes, the diversity does likewise.) Ann's job is to make an oral

To us, too many people who write about making oral presentations stress various tricks of delivery and (at least by omission) gloss over the hard work that has to be done in the weeks and days before the delivery occurs. Some people can pull off those delivery tricks well and some not so well, but anyone can do an excellent job of preparation.

presentation of the preliminary results of her group's study. She is thus concerned about a variety of issues: her own queasiness at standing up in front of people, whether she will "get through it OK," the visual aids she wants to use (those aids being prepared by another member of her group), and especially the possible responses by her classmates and her teacher.

Ann goes over these concerns in a meeting with her teacher the week before the presentation. To deal with her queasiness at making oral presentations, he recommends practicing in front of friends. To deal with her worries over visual aids, he recommends she explain her worries to the group member who's doing the visuals and offer to help (or to get him extra help from other group members) if he's feeling pushed. "Ask him, 'Will these absolutely, unfailingly be ready the day *before*, so I can practice with them?' If he hesitates on the answer, he needs more help, and you can get it for him," advises Ann's teacher. To deal both with whether she can "get through it OK" and with possible responses, her teacher recommends that Ann make sure she knows the material—backward, forward, sideways, and inside out: not memorize but *know* it. That means going over it again and again, and understanding it. In the case of these tests, it means fully understanding their background, how they were done, what problems were encountered, what their results were, how those results compare with the results of other (similar) tests, and what (tentative) conclusions can be drawn. Ann's teacher recommends that in the week before her presentation, she go over and over these points, both in her head and in front of any friends she can get to listen. That activity, what he calls "doing her homework," will give her the inner confidence she needs to do a good job.

Bill Mooney has a different challenge. He and four other students constitute a task force designated by the campus student government to recommend a solution to an important, campuswide policy question: should cigarette machines be allowed anywhere on campus? No student was placed in charge of the task force; the idea is that if these five students cannot agree among themselves on a course of action, there's no chance of getting enough agreement by the student body at large to implement it. And so Bill, who's a little concerned about whether that committee-by-consensus approach is the right one in this instance, decides to take individual action by doing some homework on the subject. As he considers the subject—possible banning of cigarette machines on campus—he decides there are three key issues:

One of the problems with nondirected meetings like the ones Bill Mooney and the other students will have is that sometimes, because no one has been designated as being responsible for the meeting, no one takes the responsibility of making it work. That's why Bill's actions are so important here.

1. Is smoking a problem among State University's students?
2. Is such a ban legal?
3. What will be the costs and benefits of such a ban?

To answer these questions, Bill has to do some research that takes the form of legwork—going to the campus health center to interview a doctor about frequency of smoking on campus (and possible health effects), visiting the university attorney's office to interview an assistant attorney about whether such a ban is legal, and stopping by the Office of Student Services (the office through which such vending machine leases are handled) for information on how much those vending machine leases profit the university and whether the loss of revenues will matter. Armed with answers to these questions, Bill feels he can go to the meeting confident that at least *something* will be accomplished.

Practice. Just as the "do your homework" component of these two presentations is quite different, so is the "practice" segment. In Ann's case, practicing is just another phase of doing her homework. The more she practices her presentation—and the more questions she answers about it, the more different ways her preliminary audiences force her to look at it—the more confidence she will have in herself, and the better job she will do before the class. In Bill's case, it's hard to practice for that kind of meeting. About the most he can do is to ensure that he does indeed know the things he knows, that he has his facts and figures sorted out and written down in such a way as to have ready access to them when he needs them. To accomplish that goal, he decides to make a "fact sheet" for each of the three issues he investigated: in each case, he has one fact sheet that summarizes the essential points of the case. He figures he can spread those three sheets out in front of him and speak in detail to whichever of those issues comes up at any time during the meeting. Thus, for Bill Mooney, "practicing" consists of getting his materials together, making sure he himself has ready access to them.

Deliver Your Talk Effectively

However well you adjust what you say and prepare yourself for your oral presentation, the ultimate test of the process is your delivery. If you go into an oral presentation or a small-group interaction with your material wonderfully adjusted and magnificently prepared but then get so flustered that you're incoherent, you haven't gained much. Obviously, it's important not to get flustered, but we can't offer much help in that area other than what we've already said about being well prepared and practicing your delivery. What we want to focus on is two key points, the need to (a) adjust your presentation to what people remember and (b) use appropriate technology for your presentation.

Adjust Your Presentation to What People Remember. What do people remember from an introduction speech? from an oral research report? from a small-group interaction? and from a poster display presentation? If you can successfully figure out how those memories are different in each situation, you can turn that information to your advantage.

Here we're working with audience analysis and adaptation again.

Introduction Speeches. We've already talked about what people remember from an introduction speech—they remember what kind of person you seemed to be. And while that is true to some extent for any kind of presentation, it's so true for introduction speeches that it's worth your time to adjust your entire presentation to take advantage of that characteristic. What would that mean in terms of an introduction speech? Do you emphasize *facts,* or values? Do you emphasize *history*, or anecdotes? Do you emphasize *plans*, or dreams? If you don't have time to emphasize both items in each pair, you may want to make sure that you give at least some attention to one, two, or three of the latter items in each pair. Why? Because those items—values, anecdotes, and dreams—say *more* about who you are, what kind of person you are, than facts, history, and plans do. Of course, ideally you should cover both kinds of things, but if you get limited by time, don't totally omit the more personal items—as we see too many of our students do. An "introduction speech" with no values, anecdotes, or dreams is a poor introduction.

Research Reports. Let's look next at oral presentation of research reports. Assuming a standard written format, something like "introduction-materials-methods-results-discussion," and too little time to do all that, how much and what kinds of things will people remember? Well, first the point needs to be made that people once again will remember what kind of person you seemed to be, probably more than they'll remember what you said. But considering only the things you said, what kinds of things will people remember? Probably what you say *first* and *last*. Accordingly, what should you put in those slots? If you have ten minutes, how should you spend the first two minutes and the last two minutes? Once you know those are the most important times, you can plan for them better. In the first two minutes, you need to (a) make sure people understand what prompted this research and (b) lead into the purpose of the research. Two simple points—don't try to do more in those two minutes: develop those, reinforce those, but make them clearly, and give them the time they deserve. Especially at the beginning you need to be methodical enough and to move slowly enough for your audience to follow you; in an oral presentation, if you lose the audience in the first two minutes, you're sunk.

Most people addressing others in any setting need to slow *way* down. This applies from people in church reading Scripture aloud to presidents reading brief prepared statements.

What should you do in the last two minutes? How much attention should you give to results and to discussion, and should you end on the often-ambiguous note of discussion? The answers to those questions depend on how much discussion you intend to do. But don't end with the discussion if there's a chance you may have got so far away from the *results* that your listeners have forgotten them—and remember, listeners' memories are fleeting at best and practically nonexistent at worst. It's a good idea to end with a brief summary, taking perhaps one minute to repeat the results and one key point from the discussion. *That's* what you want to leave your listeners with.

A good model of this type of concluding summary, or recap, is the BBC morning news carried by most National Public Radio stations.

Meetings. What do people remember from meetings, and how can you adjust your meeting behavior accordingly? That depends on which kind of meeting you're involved with (directed versus shared) and what your role in it has been (leader or member). Basically, though, what people remember is, first, whether the meeting accomplished what it was supposed to do in a reasonably efficient manner and, second, whether your role in it was as a person who was prepared for the meeting, was articulate in stating thoughts, and was group-oriented in terms of making possible compromises. Generally, the best way you can contribute to the accomplishment of the first goal is by actively pursuing the second. It's not, ultimately, within your control to ensure that each meeting you are a part of reaches its goal; it is, however, within your control to make your own contribution as helpful as possible.

We've already discussed proper preparation for meetings. Being articulate about your own thoughts is also largely a matter of prior preparation—you can become articulate by practicing your articulation. Meet one-to-one with as many other members of the committee as you can prior to the meeting, going over the relevant facts and issues again and again. (Besides helping you become comfortable with and adept at articulating your positions, this interchange with other committee members is an excellent and creative rehearsal for the larger meeting.) If you can't meet with enough committee members to become reasonably articulate on the major foreseeable points, try writing out your position. Then tear that up and write it out again. And again. Soon you will have "grooved" your articulation so as to make being clear much easier in the meeting itself.

Being reasonable in terms of making compromises is a tough thing to learn. In our experience it comes from understanding the *real* reasons behind your own positions and beliefs (*real* in the sense that you look deeper than "It's my position because it's right") and from spending your time before and during the meeting working hard to understand the real reasons behind others' beliefs. A good indicator of whether you're approaching the meeting from the standpoint of being willing to make reasonable compromises is how much time you spend in the meeting *making statements* (not, generally, a compromise attitude) versus *asking questions* (trying to understand other people's positions and their reasons, which *is* a compromise position). Generally, the more you are asking questions to clarify other people's positions and reasons, the more of a compromiser you're going to be.

Poster Display Presentations. Poster display presentations open up a whole new area for taking advantage of what people remember. However good any of us may or may not be at remembering words or ideas, most human beings are excellent at remembering visual images, especially if the images are clear and striking. A poster whose visual component is too cluttered or is too faint to see clearly is hard to remember. By contrast, a poster whose visual component has strong lines and a simple appearance can be memorable—and can be made more memorable still by adding one or two extra colors, by adding a handout, and by having the presenter stand next to the poster and give a clear and simple explanation of what the presentation is about. Poster display presentations invite you to find a striking image to leave in your listener-viewer's mind—a rare chance you shouldn't pass up.

Your students' experiences with group work may well already have illustrated this distinction between making statements and asking questions in meetings. Our advice here may make it seem that being a compromiser is *always* better than refusing to compromise. We're not saying that. Rather, we're saying that it's generally better to seek compromise based on mutual understanding for as long as compromise seems possible. There are, however, times when everyone's position in a meeting is clear and there's simply nothing to be gained from further discussion. If all parties have made every effort to understand and have exhausted possibilities for compromise on the point, a vote or some other sort of ruling to allow business to move forward is in order.

By contacting your colleagues in agriculture, science, or engineering, you can probably find a faculty member or graduate student who will do a poster presentation for your class. Graduate students in those disciplines often look for venues in which to practice their presentations.

Use Appropriate Technology. The last area we want to stress in terms of delivering your talk effectively is the use of *appropriate technology,* with the emphasis on *appropriate.* Such use might range from deciding to use no technology at all for an informal, classroom introduction speech, to deciding to use an overhead projector and five transparencies to deliver a research report, to deciding to use a flip chart during a meeting, to deciding how much of which color to use in a poster display. We can't tell you in each instance, even in each *type* of instance, what the appropriate technology consists of. We can, however, offer a few general thoughts on technology and oral presentations.

We're aware that we're striking a negative note here, a kind of technological Murphy's Law (that is, that if something can go wrong with your presentation equipment, it will). But remember, we're discussing student presentations, not those done by the chief executive officer of a major multinational conglomerate (who can, after all, blame somebody else if things don't work, and fire that unlucky person).

Our general guideline is this: the more complicated the technology you use, the greater the chance that something will go wrong. We recall with a shudder a presentation on "Hypertext," given in a large, darkened auditorium before 150 professionals, wherein the speaker was using a high-technology device that enabled him to project images directly from the computer, through an overhead projector, onto a screen on the stage. Because the speaker had to sit in the orchestra-pit location, which is where the computer and overhead projector were situated, no one ever saw his face, although through a lapel microphone we heard his voice (as well as his tie rustling). If only the computer had worked right, we could have seen the visuals in order—except that we couldn't see them at all, because they were light blue lines on dark blue backgrounds. The moral? The fancier your technology, the more chance for trouble. You do need to use technology, but you need to use the lowest appropriate level. That way, you can maximize your gains and minimize your risks.

What, then, might be "appropriate technology" for an introduction speech? Probably nothing—just you.

What might be appropriate technology for presenting the results of a research report in a classroom setting? Though that's hard to generalize about, certainly the audience needs at minimum to have access to a simple outline of your presentation, either via handouts or on the board. Beyond that, you might want to use construction-paper posters resting in the chalk trays, putting them up one after another, or perhaps overhead transparencies if you have access to an overhead projector (OHP). Technology at that level is relatively foolproof, if you use stiff-enough construction paper and if you don't wind up with a grounded (three-pronged) plug on the OHP trying to go into an ungrounded (two-hole) socket.

Appropriate technology for a meeting might well be a handout in the form of a fact sheet summing up the data on the problem you're attacking. Or it might be a wallboard or a flip chart used to keep track of key points discussed or agreed on during the meeting; slides of, say, the newly proposed waste dump site, used to keep the meeting focused on the issue; or a tape recorder (or someone taking good notes) to keep track of what transpires during the meeting.

Appropriate technology for a poster display presentation depends even more than the other kinds of presentations on the setting. In any environment outside the classroom, you probably need to consult a publications professional (graphic artist, designer, editor, public relations expert) for assistance. Within a classroom setting, you should at *minimum* make sure the lettering on your posters looks professionally done (no freehand lettering, please), either by attaching computer-generated sheets or by using stencils or a lettering kit. Make sure the poster can be read from ten feet away. At *minimum* the artwork must be clear, strongly drawn, and not cluttered by too much detail. (We'll show you examples of posters later in this chapter.) If you're using charts, graphs, or diagrams, you can produce a nearly professional looking product with a straightedge and a felt-tip marker, especially if you first trace the lines with a pencil. If you're using photographs, you can make sure they're large enough and clear enough to be seen without strain from ten feet away. And if you're using drawings—well, unless you're a good artist, perhaps you need to get a friend to help you there too.

TWO CASE STUDY CLOSE-UPS

Consider again the student research report from chapter 23, "Steroid Abuse in Football: A Dead Man's Hand." Let's follow its author, Collin Walker, as he prepares to present it in two different ways, to two different audiences: (a) as a seven-minute oral presentation for his freshman composition class and (b) as a three-poster presentation for the Campus Issues Committee's exhibit on the dangers of substance abuse. To refresh your memory, go back to chapter 23 and read Collin's paper. As you take another look at it, put yourself in Collin's shoes—how would you approach this as an oral presentation? as a poster display presentation?

Many other pieces in this book could be used for conversion to oral presentation. See, for example, Daniel Warner's explanation of "How to Rig a Plastic Worm, Texas-Style" in chapter 5; David Quammen's factual account about "Deserts" in chapter 12; or Randi Londer's "Stressed Out: What Puts the Pressure on Families?" in chapter 17.

An Oral Report

To present this paper as an oral report, Collin has chosen to work on the factual side of the issue, not on the character side. His choice was between (a) doing three character sketches (of Steve Courson, Tommy Chaikin, and Benji Ramirez) to show the harmful effects of steroid abuse and (b) presenting simply the facts. Collin was worried that his classmates might find the character sketch approach a little too melodramatic, and he didn't want to come across as a fanatical antidrug alarmist; thus, he has decided just to stick to presenting the facts. He plans to use the examples, all right, but only as a small part of his presentation. He's decided to "talk" his presentation based on six note cards; he won't be reading the cards but will just have them with him for reminders and moral support. Here are his cards:

Card 1
[Introduction]

(1)

High-pressure, competitive football has caused too many players to make bad decisions to get an edge.

Motto: better players through drug use?

Card 2

(2)

Anabolic steroids enhance the performance and alter appearance, size and psychological makeup.

"Good" effects: increases in skeletal muscle mass, organ mass, hemoglobin concentration, red blood cell mass, calcium in bones, total nitrogen retention, retention of electrolytes, and protein synthesis.

Card 3

(3)

Anabolic steroids are an addiction.

Bad effects: "liver and kidney disorders, temporary acne and balding, hypertension [high blood pressure], decreased sperm count, aggressive behavior, depression and irritability."

Quote: "I gained weight and strength, but I also got depressed a lot and did things I usually wouldn't do--grumpy, grouchy, destructive things."

Card 4

(4)

Professional football players have abused and still abuse steroids.

College players and even high school players now abuse anabolic steriods.

Some 6.6 percent of all high school seniors take steroids.

The FDA estimates that 10 percent of all high school students take steroids.

Card 5

(5)

Three examples:

Professional, Steve Courson—seriously damaged heart.

College, Tommy Chaikin—became suicidal.

High school, Benji Ramirez—at football practice, collapsed and died from apparent heart attack.

Card 6
[Conclusion]

(6)

Sports developed to help keep athletes physically fit; now steroid abuse undermines that very purpose.

Many have suffered; there will be others.

A Poster Display Presentation

Although he has chosen the relatively conservative "factual" approach for his oral presentation in freshman composition class, downplaying the more dramatic aspects of his three examples, for his poster display for the Campus Issues Committee Collin has decided to try for a more dramatic effect, building his three posters around profiles of each of the three athletes whose cases he documented.

The *preliminary* layout sketches of Collin's three posters are on page 710. Collin's roommate, Buddy, who is a photography buff, is going to help him out by taking pictures of the players from Collin's magazine sources and blowing them up to fit into Collin's posters. Page 710 shows Collin's *design* for the posters.

Between 10:00 A.M. and 12:00 noon and between 1:30 and 3:30 P.M. on Tuesday, Collin will be standing by his posters, along with twenty-five or thirty other students standing by similar posters, along the main corridor through the Student Center, as part of the Campus Issues Committee's "Say No to Drugs Day." Collin will be prepared to talk about his research with any students who come by, and he will have copies of his research paper available for people who want further information on steroid abuse. If he has time, he'll also make up a one-page fact sheet to hand out, listing just the facts (the hard data and the sources) from his paper. He figures he can hand those out liberally, whereas handing out copies of his entire report to everyone who came by could be expensive.

STEROID ABUSE: Example 1

Name:
Position:
Diagnosis:
Result:
Disposition:

[Blow-up photo goes here]

STEROID ABUSE: Example 2

Name:
Position:
Diagnosis:
Result:
Disposition:

[Blow-up photo goes here]

STEROID ABUSE: Example 3

Name:
Position:
Diagnosis:
Result:
Disposition:

[Blow-up photo goes here]

Collin Walker's Poster Designs

Writers' Circle

Divide into groups of three students each. Each group should then plan an oral presentation to the class about some important campus issue, such as student parking, tuition increases, student health care, hazing at social group initiations, or crime on campus. Each group should consider how its members would research the issue and how they would organize and present a seven-minute report at a meeting with the college's president, deans, and other key administrative figures. After this planning, each group should proceed with its research and prepare and practice its presentation. At a time designated by the teacher, each group will present its report to the class (at the teacher's discretion, some students in the class may be designated to "role-play" administrators).

PRACTICE ASSIGNMENTS

1. Select a reading from an earlier chapter in this book and design an oral presentation of it. Then design a poster display presentation of it.
2. Write a journal entry recording a meeting you attended and analyzing how the meeting worked and the different roles each person played.
3. Revise Collin Walker's note cards for a three-minute (rather than seven-minute) speech.
4. Prepare Collin's fact sheet.
5. If you're doing a research paper for this course, prepare and deliver a seven-minute presentation on it for your class.
6. If you're doing a research paper for this course, prepare a poster display presentation on it for your class.
7. Read a recent issue of the *Journal of the American Medical Association*, the *New England Journal of Medicine*, or *American Demographics* and choose one article that interests you. As your teacher directs, prepare and present either an oral report or a poster display presentation on the article's substance.
8. The cartoon on page 697 affords a humorous view of how a "negative message" speech might be given—straightforward, with no punches pulled. The hindsight that we enjoy from studies like biology and archaeology tells us that the speaker in the cartoon is right—he and his audience of dinosaurs are doomed. Underneath this humor, however, lies a more serious matter: what *is* the "best" way to deliver bad news, or is there a "best" way?

   In a brief paper, recall some of the "bad" or negative messages you've heard in your life: how were they given? How did you receive them? What would you change, and why?

part six

The Handbook: A User Manual for Writing

Writers today can choose among many handbooks. Each gives you much more than just the basics of grammar; consequently, some are more than nine hundred pages long. As you become more and more a member of a particular community of writers, as you settle into being an engineering or political science major, as you move into professional life as a lawyer or a teacher, you will find that one or two of those encyclopedic books will be paramount in support of the writing you do.

What, then, can we hope to do, in these three closing chapters, that can't be done *better* by those fuller presentations?

PART OUTLINE

Well, have you ever tried to *use* one of the major handbooks for college writers? When those books are examined from the viewpoint of a typical freshman writing student, they suffer from two problems:

1. Because they (rightly enough, for their purposes) must include everything, their contents are huge and their organization encyclopedic. Do you want to find out how to solve or avoid any one of the twelve most common problems facing writers like you? In such books, that information is usually buried amid a mass of things you will *never* worry about. Moreover, because so many things should be included, each item tends to get the same amount of attention, whether the item is something you as a writer face ten times a day or once in a lifetime, whether it's something important (from your standpoint) or trivial. Do you want to find out how to *write* a good sentence (as opposed to how to fix a bad one or how to correct grammar errors)? Even though these books may well have something on your point of interest, it may indeed be so buried among all the other information that you'll never find it.
2. Most such handbooks—because of their sheer bulk—also have to be encyclopedic in the way they make information available to you. The assumption is that, for anything you want to know about, you'll look it up in their alphabetic or numerical system. That's great if you happen to know the right name (or number) for what you need to look up. It's also great if you aren't also interested in reading about closely related items at the same time. For example, suppose you do happen to find "How to Write a Good Sentence" in one of these books. Can you go straight from there to "How to Write a Good Paragraph"? Or does that involve a whole new search? (We've put "How to Do It Right" in a separate chapter from "How It Looks When It's Wrong.") Or suppose you're trying to decide whether to use a comma or a semicolon in a particular place. Wouldn't it be nice if the people who put the handbook together had anticipated that question? Most handbooks force you to find one place in the book and read "all about commas"; then turn to another place in the book and read "all about semicolons"; and *then* try to figure out how the two sets of rules correspond to each other. Wouldn't it be better if in addition to a set of rules for commas and a set of rules for semicolons, those books also contained a troubleshooting section that included an entry called "Comma or Semicolon?" to show you an example of exactly that situation and the right way to deal with it?

A college freshman, struggling with how to avoid sentence fragments, does not especially need a long explanation about how to do "where" lists or about the difference between an em dash and an en dash. And that college freshman may well want the information on sentence fragments to be side by side with information on other common mistakes—including how to avoid, recognize, and fix them.

Thus, what we do in this final part of *The Heath Guide to College Writing* is present you not so much with a complete handbook for everything everyone ever wanted to know about English grammar (that's been done before, anyway) as with a *user manual for freshman writers.* It has three parts:

1. *Chapter 28,* "A Closer Look at the Processes of Writing," provides a thorough review of planning, drafting, revising, and finishing, seen from step 1 through the end, generatively, with cross-references to substantive discussions in other chapters. This chapter answers the question, "How to . . . ?"
2. *Chapter 29,* "A Grammar and Sentence Guide for Writers," presents key features of the system of written English, focusing on the elements and processes essential to *coherent* sentence structure and concluding with a few basic sentence stylistics. This chapter answers the question, "What is . . . ?"
3. *Chapter 30,* "The Dirty Dozen: Twelve Common Manuscript Problems Writers Face," tells how to recognize and troubleshoot problems with sentence forms, sentence logic, agreement, modifier placement, shifts, imprecise diction, word and thought flab, punctuation confusion, quotation procedure, faulty comparison, spelling, and sexism. This chapter answers the question, "What if . . . ?"

We have tried to make our presentation simple to use, sorting out the material by explaining how someone should use it. We avoid repetition by using extensive cross-references, and we achieve brevity by focusing on features our experience shows us college freshmen have trouble with or need to know about. We leave completeness to encyclopedic reference grammars, several of which we will recommend that you consult as "advanced user manuals" when you are ready for them. We hope you find this to be the most *usable* grammar handbook you've seen; that's why we called it "A User Manual for Writing."

After our critique of full-blown handbooks, you might be surprised that we *can* recommend some for you or for your students' reference. For those who write frequently and who want more coverage than we can offer in these last chapters, one of these "advanced user manuals" in its most recent edition would be a good desktop reference:

- Mulderig and Elsbree, *The Heath Handbook*
- Hairston and Ruskiewicz, *The Scott, Foresman Handbook for Writers*
- Hodges and Whitten, *The Harbrace College Handbook*
- Aaron and Fowler, *The Little, Brown Handbook*
- Crews, *The Random House Handbook*

chapter 28 A Closer Look at the Processes of Writing

"Writing and rewriting are a constant search for what it is one is saying."

John Updike

"A writer is not so much someone who has something to say as he is someone who has found a process that will bring about new things he would not have thought of if he had not started to say them."

William Stafford

In this book's first twenty-seven chapters, we've shown through use of examples many of the different activities writers engage in and the important ways those activities change depending on the particular writing task the writer is facing. In this first chapter of Part Six (the handbook), our aim is to cover in one place many of the different features we've explained elsewhere and to elaborate on a few things we haven't covered thoroughly.

For those of you who have read all or most of the first twenty-seven chapters, we don't want to imply that so far you've seen twenty-seven pieces of the puzzle and now we're going to show you "the big picture." Writing is much too varied and complex an activity for that, and our book (or any book) cannot possibly be long enough or smart enough to show you everything there is to know about writing (in fact, we're still learning about writing ourselves). Rather, our purpose here is to show you three particular features of writing:

Many theorists and scholars of the writing process have emphasized the "recursive" and nonlinear characteristics of that process. It would be a mistake to conceive of the process as a series of discrete steps, even though for convenience it has often been described that way. Writers can invent while they revise, polish while they draft, revise while still brainstorming—there simply are no clear boundaries. We elaborate on this point much more in Part One and on pages H-6 and H-15–H-16 of this chapter. Once again, our goal in *this* chapter is to show how the process *flows;* that element of flow is every bit as important as what goes on in any step, stage, or wave.

1. A comprehensive overview of the processes of writing from start to finish, cross-referenced to important aspects and examples presented in other chapters. (This overview can serve either as a *re*view, if you're reading this chapter toward the end of the term, or as a *pre*view, if you happen to be reading this chapter first.)
2. A unified sense of the continuous *flow* of any act of writing, via a close look at how those writing processes *connect.* (Writing processes don't stack one on top of the other, or even dovetail into one another; they flow, slosh back and forth, and generally mix in all kinds of ways.)
3. A sense that although writing, as with any other human activity, sometimes has problems, those problems are identifiable and, if not totally avoidable, then at least fixable. Any writer can be more effective if given access to a little process-oriented information on troubleshooting. The problems we discuss at the end of this chapter are those which occur so often—to all writers, including us—that it's well worth giving you answers to this question: what do you do when your writing processes break down?

A Review of the Processes of Writing

Writing comprises two major parts: (a) sizing up the situation and (b) doing the writing. Obviously, if you don't go ahead and do the writing, no amount of sizing up will do you much good. But leaping into writing without doing some preliminary analytical work can be self-defeating too. It's like painting a wall without scraping it first. Or trying to make a sailboat go without sails. So let's take a close look at those two major parts of writing, with specific attention to how they develop in the kinds of writing situations presented in this book's other chapters.

Sizing up the Situation

"Sizing up the situation" includes determining three main things: who you are, who your readers are, and what your reasons are for writing. Let's examine in detail some of those aspects of sizing up the situation:

These "three main things," of course, are also the primary components of any rhetorical situation: speaker/writer's persona, audience, and subject/purpose.

- You need to think about your purpose for writing—are you writing to *express* (chapter 4), to *explain* or *inform* (chapter 5), to *analyze* (chapter 6), or to *persuade* (chapter 7)?
- If you're new to writing in college, you may also want to give careful thought to how such writing involves certain qualities that other kinds of writing do not. In particular, college writing demands a *critical* quality (chapter 3), which typically requires informing, evaluating, and recommending; it also needs to be both more thorough and more precise. Chapter 6 offers many examples of writing with this critical quality and also illustrates how one student's thought process improved that quality in his writing.
- Sizing up the situation may also entail figuring out how your purposes as a writer need to mesh with those of your reader (chapter 5), an activity that will help you determine how to customize your own typical writing process to match each particular writing situation, including essay tests (chapter 22).
- Sizing up the situation may also involve paying attention to the nature of your subject—are you writing about people (chapter 9), places (chapter 10), things (chapter 11), facts (chapter 12), or ideas (chapter 13)? While we don't pretend that these exhaust all possible topics for writing, discussion of these commonplace topics allows us to show that the writing's element of significance needs to change in interesting ways as the nature of the topic changes.
- Another aspect of sizing up the situation involves thinking about the kind of issue you're writing about—is it an issue of fact, value, interpretation, or policy (chapter 7 and chapter 14)? Chapters 24 and 25 develop this concept of "kind of issue" (or *stasis*) in detail with respect to reports and proposals, using the idea both as an outlining aid and as an aid to revising. Or are you writing about prose fiction, drama, or poetry (chapter 21)?
- Finally, what kind of audience are you writing for and how do that audience's important qualities need to be factored into your writing (chapters 17 and 24)?

When you regard what we describe as sizing up the situation in this way, it appears that we're asking you to do a great deal of work. At this point you may want to ask, "Do *real* writers work like that?" Well, we're not sure that *real* writers is a useful distinction: you've done a fair bit of writing or you wouldn't be in college at all; thus, you're as *real* a writer as anyone. Do *you* work like that? Our students do plenty of writing, and so they're real writers and, yes, *they* work like that; in fact, the more they work like that, the better their writing is. The authors of this book also do plenty of writing, and you'd better believe we work like that! How much proof do you need? *Anyone* who writes is a real writer, and the more writing that person does (and the better that person does it), the more attention the writer pays to sizing up the situation.

Additional items could be added to the list of elements essential to sizing up the situation. Obviously, you need to marshal your resources—are you going to compose in longhand, at a typewriter, or on a word processor? Are you going to work alone on this project, or with a group? How, when, and to what extent are you going to involve your teacher (or whoever assigned you the writing task) in the planning, drafting, and revising of this piece of writing?

Doing the Writing

As we explain in chapter 1, doing the writing has four main parts: thinking, drafting and reading, revising and editing, and proofreading. Actually, it's hard to find a good word to name those parts: *subprocesses, processes, stages, phases*—each is a little misleading. One useful way to explain them is in terms of *waves*, a word we'll use later in this chapter to suggest that there's no clear-cut dividing line among them, that they're all truly a part of the same whole, and that they manage to overlap one another almost as much as they manage to follow one another. (See also the next major section of this chapter, "How Writing's Processes Connect.") For now we'll just call them "activities."

Thinking

Of course, it's hard to tell where and when your "sizing up the situation" stops and your "thinking" starts, and there's little point in trying to fuss over the distinction. Broadly speaking, when you take pencil in hand and start putting any kinds of words or marks on paper, you've moved into the "thinking" activity. Let's put it another way: large parts of sizing up the situation are, if not unconscious, then somewhat undirected; by contrast, "thinking," as used here, is a fairly conscious, directed process. Take a look, for example, in chapter 13 at what went through student Wendy Vermillion's mind as she prepared to do some writing for her freshman composition class; at what Cindy Black did in preparing for an essay test (chapter 22); or at the section in chapter 25 on "problematizing" a proposal situation.

Various things come under this "thinking" heading: invention, discovery, freewriting, brainstorming, listing (chapter 18), sketching, use of rubrics (chapter 21), group work, and especially reading. Many of these things could be broadly grouped under the heading of *brainstorming activities* (chapters 15–18). Some of what you write in college will come from what you know, and are able to learn, about yourself in this kind of thinking (chapter 4). Much of the material you write in college will come from your reading, which is one reason so much of this book's content is tied to *critical reading* (chapters 8 and 21–22). Another sizable component of your writing comes from *critical thinking* (Part Four's introduction and chapters 7 and 21–22 especially), from being consciously aware of your audience's nature (as in chapter 26), and from letting your audience in on your thinking process (chapter 5).

Drafting and Reading

Once you begin putting words together into sentences and sentences together into paragraphs, you're doing what we call drafting. You may not have considered that reading is an important part of that process, but research shows that writers read as an integral part of their writing process. They read while they write, in the short pauses during their writing, after they write, and before they resume writing.

The part of writing we call drafting—literally putting words down on paper—is the hardest part to generalize about (see, for example, the presentation in chapter 4). Some people do it slowly, some fast; some people like to write in total silence and away from distractions, whereas others like to have lots going on while they write. One of this book's authors, Ralph, likes (demands?) quiet while he writes; the other, Mike, likes things going on (right now, National Public Radio news is on the radio and the TV picture is set on CNN). Some people use pencil, others ballpoint; some white lined paper, others yellow legal pads; some use typewriters, others word processors (and some fight for Macs, others for IBM). Whatever works best for you is probably fine for your freshman year, but we want to make a strong pitch for you to switch to using a word processor (chapter 1).

Writing with Word Processors. Contradictory evidence abounds regarding the effects of word processors on your writing. Ultimately, your route to becoming a better writer isn't really affected directly by the technology you use; nevertheless, using a word processor has several advantages over other forms of drafting:

- Word processing lets you revise more quickly and easily, thus *inviting* you to do more revising (a key to good writing).
- Word processing lets you use many interesting features that other writers can't—"idea generators," outlining tools, spellcheckers, style and readability checkers (not as good as their claims, but interesting nonetheless). The most important, of course, is spellcheckers: they won't catch everything, but they do make it easier to find the few problems they miss.
- Word processing allows you to turn in a truly good looking finished product. There's no hassle with correction fluid, cutting and pasting, and the like.

(And when your teacher asks, "How would you like to take one more run at this; just make the few changes I've noted in the margins, and then resubmit it?" you can smile and say, "Sure, it's all on disk; if you're still going to be here in a half-hour, I'll make those changes and bring the new version right back.")

Speed of Writing. Another important element in your writing is the speed at which you compose. To some extent, your speed will vary depending on the kind of writing you're doing—if you are writing about something you know about or are writing from facts right in front of you, it may be easy to compose quickly. By contrast, if you are doing expressive writing or a tough analytical piece requiring you to stop and think after every sentence, you'll be more likely to draft more slowly. Apart from those considerations, however, we want to encourage you to compose *quickly;* convincing evidence shows that if you can get yourself to just let the words flow (committing yourself to careful revision later on), your writing will generally go much more easily (chapter 9). After all, the more you expect your writing to be perfect after only one draft, the harder you make it to write. And in college there are some people who manage to make writing so difficult that they don't do it at all. You're much better off using this book and your writing classes to gain confidence in your ability as a *reviser*—and not expecting your first drafts to come out so well.

The idea of getting things on paper as quickly as possible and relying on extensive revision/rewriting to improve the text is generally resisted by students, especially those for whom writing is painful, something they want to get over with as soon as possible. You'll need to work hard to convince most of your students that first drafts *aren't* final versions, even for (especially for!) professional writers. Put simply, many students don't want to work that hard at writing. And just as simply, if they want to get better at writing, they're going to have to work that hard.

Another key element of your drafting is the time of day you do your writing. Do you write when your brain is fresh and your body relaxed, or do you write when your brain is weary and your body tense? Only you know when these times occur for you in your daily schedule. If you write when you're weary or tense, you shouldn't be surprised if writing comes hard for you. Writing uses more of your brain than almost any other activity does; you'll find you do it best when your brain is fresh. Try doing your writing when you feel fresh and rested, and see if that helps.

Reading and Rereading What You've Written. One last point about drafting brings back the subject of reading. Are you conscious of how much you read and reread what you've already written as a preparation for writing further? When you begin writing again after taking a break, do you start by rereading what you've already written? When you get stumped in the middle of a paper or a paragraph, do you help break the logjam by rereading what you've already written? Perhaps you can pick up the thread of your thinking or can locate where you went off the track. And as you reread what you just wrote, are you careful to stay sensitive to the form that's trying to emerge in the writing itself, a form that may be quite different from the form you originally planned to use (chapter 14)? Doing more critical reading (chapter 8) and more rereading will probably help your writing.

Revising and Editing

All kinds of factors come into play when you're revising and editing. Revising is the process (actually, another whole set of processes) that takes you from your first draft to a final draft. Editing takes you from that final draft to a copy that is almost ready to turn in. In particular, revising needs to be done with careful attention to the role your audience plays in your writing's success (chapters 2, 7, 9–10, 15, 20, and 24). Chapter 5 shows in detail how one student writer used considerations provided by his audience to make a major improvement in the final draft of his paper.

Because revising is such an important part of writing, we discuss it often in chapters 1–27. For the same reason, we think revising is worth an additional, systematic treatment here. In particular, we want to suggest two procedures for you to use when you're revising something you've written: (a) a systematic procedure for revising (what we call "top-down" revising) and (b) a systematic procedure for getting others to review your work (the "revise-review-revise-review-revise" cycle). Chapter 7 shows how one student used review comments from her peers to revise her paper, "Why Aren't There More Black Women Lawyers?"

Top-down Revising. What constitutes an ideal revising process? Well, first you need to know when to start revising. Of course, revising actually goes on all the time—writers always loop back and change a word here, move a line there, as they compose. (Remember, though, that if you're doing so much of this *interim* revising that your writing is slowing down, you're probably doing too much.) But if you seek to pinpoint a certain time when you can say, "*Here* is when I begin revising," we think that time comes when you're *committed* to a certain body of *content;* that is, when you look at a draft and say to yourself, "All the material I can think of right now that I might want to use is here on these pages in front of me," you've begun revising. Naturally, there is always more material to be added, material that your revising will trigger in your mind, but you begin revising at the time of an initial commitment to content. (We'll assume, for the purposes of this discussion, that you're using a word processor for your writing.)

The first step in top-down revising is to print out a copy of your writing and look at it for its largest, most abstract qualities:

- Does what you've written fulfill the purpose you set out to fulfill?
- Does it cover the required material?
- Does it successfully address your targeted audience? (See especially chapter 20.)
- Does it present you the way you want to appear in this situation?
- Does the overall structure make sense? (See, for example, Pete Stanton's first draft and revising in chapter 9 or Arthur Raney's revising in chapter 16).

Until you're comfortable with your answers to these questions, there's little point in doing any fine-tuning. (Notice also chapter 24's presentation of large-scale issues as considerations for revising.) Make whatever changes in the disk file are needed to successfully answer those questions (compare the "80 percent fix" in chapter 10), and print out a fresh copy.

The second step in top-down revising is to look at the next-most-important elements of the piece you've written: the structure of individual paragraphs and the way each paragraph leads (or does not lead) into or links (or does not link) with the others. Does your paragraph have a clear pattern, one any reader will sense? Usually in freshman composition, that means the paragraph needs to begin with a *topic sentence*—one sentence that holds the rest of the paragraph together. (In this paragraph, for example, it's the first sentence.) Make whatever changes in the soft (disk) copy you need to in order to strengthen your paragraph structure; then print out a fresh hard copy.

The third step in top-down revising is to look at your sentence structure. Are the sentences clear? Do they use active verbs? (See chapter 30 for more on this aspect.) Check your sentence structures, make whatever changes are necessary in your disk file, and print out another draft.

The last level of top-down revising is really the same as editing: check for the smallest elements of all, from how the title of your piece of writing is put on the page (and what page it's put on) to spelling errors and problems with such things as "it's" versus "its." (We'll have more to say about these elements in the next two chapters.)

You need not rewrite each piece four times in this ideal vision of the revising process, but you probably will need to print out four different versions before the final one. Thus, to get one very good three-page paper finished for your freshman composition class you need to print out about fifteen pages. We don't think that's excessive. We do think, however, that you should use a letter-quality printer only for the last copy; dot matrix is fine for the rest. Learning a consistent, thorough revision procedure is one of the biggest steps you can take to becoming a better writer, in any setting.

The Revise-Review-Revise-Review-Revise Cycle. At the same time as you're working through your own top-down revising process, you can help your writing by learning to avail yourself of other people's responses to what you've written (as Kristy does in chapter 11). You can also profit by other people's responses before you start writing, as Tom Lamb does in chapter 16. Moreover, getting an early start at learning such a procedure will help prepare you for the reality of professional life, where even in the rare instances when a company document has a single author, virtually no piece of writing ever goes outside the company without someone else reading over it first.

It takes awhile for students to get comfortable reading and responding to one another's writing, but peer reviews add a significant and rewarding dimension to your class's development. Group work is increasingly important as students mature as writers. If you want to learn more about group work, see Bruffee, "The Brooklyn Plan: Attaining Intellectual Growth through Peer-Group Tutoring," and "Peer Tutoring and the Conversation of Mankind." See also Karen Spear's *Sharing Writing*.

We recommend that you build at least two *external* loops of review into your revision cycle. (Doing so is easy in conjunction with top-down revising; you can circulate the same drafts you're printing out as part of that process.) At least one of those external loops needs to be for review by a peer. For student writers, peer review means review by another student (or students), as chapters 12 and 17 show; for, say, professional engineers, peer review means review by another engineer (or engineers) at the same level in the firm. You must be sure your reviewer gives what you've written a thorough going-over; someone who looks over the piece in thirty seconds and says, "Looks fine to me," is not a helpful reviewer. If your teacher has offered no particular guidelines for that review, you need to provide some of your own—for example, from one or more of the steps described above under the section "Top-down Revising." Once you get your peer reviewer's comments, you need to think about them in conjunction with your piece of writing. While you never need to slavishly follow every reviewer's suggestions, you do need to (a) ask yourself what it was about that particular part of your writing that set the reviewer's alarm bells off and (b) try, if necessary, to find your own way to deal with the problem.

At a later point in the processes of writing you should consider getting a second review, one that is also *external*, from someone above you in the organization (in a classroom setting, this usually means your teacher, but it may mean going to one of the tutors in your college's writing center). Here you must be more careful about trying to steer this level of review, but you can still suggest areas to focus on. Again, when you get the reviewer's comments, consider each suggested change thoughtfully. (An interesting example of this situation is presented in chapter 20, with Chriss Hendrickson's paper, as well as in chapter 22, when Cindy Black considers how her essay test could be improved.)

Editing. Once you've done top-down revising and gone through the review-revise cycle, you're ready to begin editing (which is approximately the same as the last stage of top-down revising). Editing is the process by which you produce the almost-final copy of your piece of writing. How much and what kind of editing you do depend largely on your own situation as to that particular piece of writing (chapter 26). Although this kind of editing varies somewhat from that which professional editors do, there are useful parallels nonetheless. We therefore invite you to consider two concepts from the *profession* of editing: (a) levels of editing and (b) types of editing.

Levels of editing. Before an editor accepts a piece of writing to edit, he or she will typically be certain to reach an agreement with the author on what level of editing is required. These levels may be indicated in a simple scheme like this:

- *A light edit.* Do you want me *simply* to clean up the obvious spelling and grammatical problems and to make sure the document meets the standards for manuscript preparation (spacing, margins, cover page, and so on) specified for it?
- *A medium edit.* In addition to what's included in a light edit, do you want me to look at the sentence structure, paragraph structure, and overall structure, and perhaps do a little restructuring or an occasional rewrite of a line, as well as look at the piece's internal logic and indicate whether I think the piece will be successful in terms of the audience and purpose you specify for it?
- *A heavy edit.* In addition to the elements of a medium edit and a light edit, do you want me to feel free to rewrite or reorganize anything for which I see a better way of handling the matter?

Because editors typically charge not only by the number of hours they work on a project but also by the level of difficulty of the writing and the editing, it's important for editors and authors to have the same understanding of which editing level is involved in a particular project. Similarly, when you begin editing a piece you've written it's important for you to have an idea in your own mind of what your level of commitment to the document is. Frankly, there are times when the light edit's "quick fix" is about all a person has the time or energy to do; moreover, there are times when, believe it or not, a light edit is all the writer *needs* to do. And there are other times—as with major reports that count toward 35 percent of your grade or as with job application letters—when you really do need to commit to a maximum edit. Thus, before you start editing you need to ask yourself, "How important is the final quality of this piece?" Only after you've decided what level of edit you need to be using can you edit intelligently and effectively.

Types of editing. Professional editors engage in a wide range of activities:

- *Screening* is the main component of a light edit—checking for errors in spelling, subject-verb agreement, and pronoun reference and agreement; dangling modifiers; and sentence fragments.
- *Mechanical style editing* ensures that such features of the document as capitalization, use of sources, abbreviations, use of visuals, and use of acronyms conforms with a specified standard (in freshman composition classes, this standard is often the Modern Language Association [MLA] style, the American Psychological Association [APA] style, or perhaps the Council of Biological Editors [CBE] style).
- *Language editing* looks at spelling, grammar, punctuation, usage, parallelism, verb tense, syntax, and style.
- *Substantive editing* examines the content of the document to ensure that it does indeed make sense, that it has all the parts it needs, that the parts are in the right order, and that—in the editor's estimation—the document's specified reader(s) will understand it.

When you look at your own writing or at someone else's, it's good to have in mind not only the level of edit that is appropriate but also the type or types of edit appropriate to the situation.

Proofreading

Proofreading is truly the last stage of writing. Once you firmly believe you have everything perfect in your piece of writing, you're ready to proofread. There are many ways to proofread; probably the most effective one is that described in chapter 26—you turn to the last page of the document and read the whole thing one word and punctuation mark at a time, from back to front. If it's hard to discipline yourself to do that, try using a very sharp pencil while you do it: put the pencil point lightly on the paper under each word or mark, one at a time. In this way, if you miss anything, either you didn't know it was an error (in which case you should look up that feature in chapter 29 or 30) or you didn't look at it (in which case you won't find a light pencil mark under it). There really isn't any other alternative.

Not knowing or understanding a particular mechanical or grammatical feature is one kind of problem with one kind of solution; failing to concentrate sufficiently is a very different kind of problem with a very different kind of solution. This proofreading technique forces you to acknowledge responsibility for your errors—if you really don't understand a feature and you make an error with it, this technique prevents you from fooling yourself into believing "I know that's wrong; I just must have missed it when I was proofreading." If there's a pencil mark under the error, you didn't "just miss it"; it was something you didn't know.

How Writing's Processes Connect

Earlier we said there are myriad ways to explain the various activities writers engage in—a process, several processes, subprocesses, phases, stages, and so forth. Each of these terms has some right things about it and some wrong things about it. We like to use the term *waves.* Sizing up the situation happens in waves. Thinking, drafting, reading, revising, editing—all happen in waves, and the whole *flow* that produces a piece of writing is one big pattern of waves. At times you can do certain things to predict, produce, or control a wave, or at least change its direction; at other times that wave is going to roll on no matter what you do, and so it's wise to go with it, to ride on it and enjoy it.

This comparison has several interesting implications for writers. Specifically, the way the different activities of writing connect may change from one writing task to the next and from writer to writer, just as a pattern of waves may change from day to day or from beach to beach. If you've been assigned to write something that is only one page long, such as a response to a short story you read in English class or a description of a piece of architecture on campus, you may well think about the assignment for a couple of minutes, jot down a few notes, and then dash through the page rather quickly. Then you may well mark up that page a bit before preparing a new version to turn in. For many students today, this kind of writing starts as longhand, gets marked up with a colored pen, and then gets keyboarded, proofread, and turned in. That's certainly less complicated than much of what we've talked about in this book, and entails only three or four little waves making up the one big one; hence, in this case, worrying very much over where and when one wave stops and another wave starts is probably pointless.

On the other hand, if—perhaps for a management class—you're working on a financial analysis of a corporation from the viewpoint of a potential investor, you're looking at a thirty-page report, and it would be wise to be considerably more systematic about it. Here you probably want to separate the different writing activities, even breaking each into smaller pieces. You may even want to make each of your report's several sections an independent act of writing, carrying one or another section through to near-completion before doing much more than the research for the next. Or you may want to assemble your materials and your structural plan and, in one long day of writing, produce a draft that is admittedly *very* rough (things are left out; grammar and mechanics are shaky) but nevertheless goes all the way through the piece, from beginning to end.

Different techniques fit different writers and different tasks at different times. If you get stymied or "blocked," you may well want to circumnavigate that block and work on another wave or another part of the piece—waves do that sometimes. Or you may want to use one of the techniques presented in this book, such as getting feedback from a classmate, friend, or teacher, to smash your way through the block—waves do that sometimes too.

Waves also intersect in interesting ways and patterns and can reinforce one another as they go. Writers can thus profit from working with other writers, especially as long as they're all headed in basically the same direction. That leads us into our next section, on troubleshooting.

Troubleshooting Your Writing Processes

What do you do when your waves of writing just don't flow? Well, many times you simply keep on writing. Not all writing flows; not even all *good* writing flows. The notion that writing *has* to flow is one of a number of mistaken and harmful assumptions our students often bring to our writing classes. Here's a list of others:

Myths, Mistakes, Traps, and Time Wasters

> "If I start to write and nothing comes out, I should stop and wait till writing 'feels' right. You can't force inspiration."

Not much of the writing that makes the world go around is based on inspiration; it's based on hard work. Size up the situation, gather your materials, and start putting your information down on paper. If the first draft is extremely rough and extremely sketchy, that's all right. You've found a place to start. Or, as an old friend of ours who is a prolific and well-known short story writer says, "You don't *wait* for inspiration; you *write* for inspiration."

> "There's nothing I can do if I just can't get started writing. I just keep trying to write that catchy first sentence, ripping the page out of the typewriter and starting over again. Writing is a mystical process that can't be hedged, helped, or hurried."

This complaint is really a variant of the first, and it's equally wrong. There are plenty of things you can do to *force* your writing to go better, to make getting started easier. For example, each of this book's first twenty chapters offers another way to help you decide "What do I say next, and next, and next?" You might also want to forget the destructive notion that your first sentence has to be catchy, or even good. All your first sentence needs to do is to get you to the second one. Let that be enough pressure to put on it while you're composing it; later on, after you've finished an entire first draft, you can worry about making it *good*.

> "Writing is an essentially *solitary* activity. You're better off not showing your writing to anyone until after it's finished; otherwise you might somehow kill your inspiration."

Depending totally on inspiration is destructive and erroneous. Between the two of us we know many creative writers—poets, fiction writers, and playwrights—and they all, at one time or another in their creative process, share their writing with other people. As we've shown throughout this book, working as part of a writing group, getting feedback from a friend or a teacher, is a normal and often essential process of anyone's writing activity.

> "I don't need to start writing till I finish all my research. Once I have all the notes and materials gathered together, then I can do all the writing in a day or two."

This one is one of the biggest mistakes a student—or any writer, for that matter—can make, especially on a project of considerable size. *Nothing* written the night before it was due is ever really good enough. You would be amazed at the number of intelligent, mature research scientists, people with years of college and professional experience behind them, who fall into this trap. Two qualities of writing contribute to making this "first all the research, then all the writing" plan such a mistake:

1. Writing is always a *discovery* process. You may think you have assembled everything necessary to write your paper, but as you write you *inevitably* discover other things you need. By then it may be 11:00 on the night before your report is due, and the library is closed. Consequently, you do an awkward job of writing around the holes in your report, holes tnat have become apparent only *as* you've been writing. If only you had started writing sooner . . .
2. Writing is always a *maturational* process. That is, like seeds that have to spend the winter underground before they will sprout, writing needs time to grow. Once in a while, especially if you're doing a short piece of writing from which you expect little, you can force some quick growth. But if you want to do something of significant size, say, three or more pages, you need to allow the writing time to mature. On any writing task, the sooner you *start* writing, the better the writing can be, because it has had the time it needs to grow, to mature.

WRITING ASSIGNMENTS

1. Interview three persons for whom writing is an important part of life. These persons could be faculty members, staff at your school, friends who are professionals whose jobs involve writing, the person who writes the newsletter for the local zoo, a graduate student writing a dissertation or thesis, or someone who works for a newspaper—but *not* other students in freshman composition (unless the person fits one of those former categories). Ask particularly about the person's writing processes—how are they the same as or different from what we've portrayed here? Write up the results for your classmates to read.

2. Read other information about how writers (of all kinds) write; your teacher can steer you to some helpful sources. Write up the results for your classmates to read.
3. Keep a journal of your own practices as a writer. How do those practices vary from subject to subject, assignment to assignment, reader to reader? Write up the results for your classmates to read.
4. Try a simple "talking-writing" exercise. (This exercise requires a small tape recorder; if you don't have access to one, arrange to borrow one.) Record your observations as you take a walk (through a park, a museum, an art gallery, or the like). Verbalize as much as you can about what you see and feel. When you get home, use that *oral* draft as your first draft, and write a simple descriptive piece about the experience. (We're not looking for great writing here.) When you finish the piece, write three or four paragraphs (*this* is the point of the exercise) about how that approach to writing felt better, worse, easier, harder, or otherwise different from your normal practice. What limitations does the technique have? What other kinds of experimentation with your writing process does the "talking-writing" experience suggest?
5. The story goes that Ernest Hemingway (page H-5) revised the ending to his novel, *A Farewell to Arms,* thirty-nine times. In Hemingway's case, agonizing over revisions produced great writing. Obviously, that isn't always what happens. Write a paper about your *failures* as a writer, analyzing their causes and/or common factors. In particular, were those failures in the process you used, the motivation you possessed, or the knowledge you had?

chapter 29 A Grammar and Sentence Guide for Writers

> "Sentences are not different enough to hold the attention unless they are dramatic. No ingenuity of varying structure will do. All that can save them is the speaking tone of voice somehow entangled in the words and fastened to the page for the ear of the imagination."
>
> Robert Frost

As an interesting exercise, you might poll students before they read this chapter: what do they think of when they hear the word *grammar?* To what do they think *grammar* refers? We expect you'll get the kind of varied, negative picture we describe here.

Some people consider *grammar* to mean a kind of general correctness in their use of the English language. Such a view is doubtless fostered by experience in English courses throughout school, courses in which students often spend a great deal of time and effort studying how to avoid errors of usage or how to correct punctuation. In fact, *grammar* is often the term students apply to anything they study in English class that isn't literature. No wonder the term causes confusion. And not surprisingly, usually the term is also viewed negatively. Though in this chapter we may not be able to change a negative view of grammar, we do hope at least to clear things up a bit.

- First, our view of grammar here is limited to the idea of *coherent sentence structure.* That is, grammar is understanding how words can be combined to create clear, understandable *sentences.*
- Second, because our grammar is sentence-based, we are concerned with correctness only insofar as it is a matter of sentence structure, or form. *Other* kinds of correctness—spelling, most marks of punctuation, capitalization, and the like—we treat elsewhere, as matters of manuscript preparation, revision, editing, or proofreading.
- Third, because grammaticality is an important aspect of understanding the meaning and structure of sentences, we also treat it as it relates to certain basic sentence styles. Thus, to begin our review of grammar for writers here, we begin with the sentence.

What Is a Sentence?

A sentence is a group of words consisting of at least one *subject,* at least one *predicate verb,* and at least one *complete thought.* Sentence subjects are, exclusively, nouns or pronouns or their equivalents. Subjects are what the sentence generally is about. The subject is italicized in the following sentences:

noun subject	The *meadowlark* flies over the prairie.
pronoun subject	*It* is the official state bird of Kansas.
noun phrase	In the picture *the soldier on the right* is my father.
noun clause	*What I saw* surprised me.

Subjects by themselves cannot be sentences, because nothing is said *about* such subjects—they are not shown in an action or condition, and no statement is made. Notice that nothing is really said *about* the above subjects when we present them in isolation:

> meadowlark
>
> It
>
> the soldier on the right
>
> What I saw

What's needed is a *predicate*, or finite, *verb* to present the subject in an action or state of being, to complete a statement *about* the subject:

action verb	The meadowlark *flies* over the prairie.
state-of-being verb	It *is* the official state bird of Kansas.

Predicate verbs are like engines for sentences. Without them, subjects (and sentences) won't "go." All verbs convey action in the past, present, or future time (*went*, *go*, *will go*) or state-of-being in the past, present, or future time (that is, some form of *to be*—*was*, *were*, *am*, *are*, *will be*, and so on).

Some sentences are completely grammatical when they consist only of one noun and one verb, because although they have only two words, they also present a single, *complete thought*, or statement:

> Birds [subject] fly [predicating verb].
>
> People work.
>
> Rain falls.

Adding modifiers makes the sentence longer and more complex but doesn't change the basic "subject + predicate = complete thought" components:

> The soaring *birds fly* south for the winter.
>
> These dedicated *people work* long, hard hours.
>
> Cold, wet, and invigorating, the *rain falls* on the thirsty soil.

Thus we see that the basic written English sentence must have at least one of *each* of three different, but related, components:

- A *subject* (noun, pronoun, or equivalent)
- A *predicate verb* (verb that completes an action or state-of-being statement about the subject)
- A *complete thought* (a finished and logical remark or statement is made)

Some groups of words in written English are not sentences, because they lack one or more of these three essential components:

> The smoke rising above the cabins on a lazy October morning.

The above group of words has a subject, the noun *smoke*. But it has no *predicate verb*, and thus no thought is completed about the smoke; consequently, the group of words is what is called a "fragment" of a sentence. "What is *rising?*" you may ask. Here, *rising* is a descriptive word, an *adjective* (see "The Eight Parts of Speech" and "Verbals," below), that describes the smoke but doesn't tell us anything conclusive *about* the smoke. Compare:

> The *smoke is rising* above the cabins on a lazy October morning.

In this second version, *is rising* is a predicate verb that truly completes a thought—in this case, an action: the smoke *is rising.* In this version, *rising* is part of the verb, not an adjective that simply describes the smoke.

That *rising* can be used in more than one way in a sentence demonstrates an important principle of our sentence grammar: *the way a word is used in a sentence determines what part of speech it is.* This principle also applies to phrases and clauses, which are explained below. The following group of words has no subject:

> Ran a mile before breakfast.

Here there is a predicate verb (*ran*), but no thought is completed, because among other things we don't know *who* ran the mile. Thus, because we have no subject, we have another sentence fragment. Supplying a subject in this case creates a legitimate sentence:

> Bob ran a mile before breakfast.

And in the following group of words, there is both a subject and a predicate verb, but no thought is completed:

> When I am driving my car.

I is a subject, a pronoun, and *am driving* is a perfectly good predicate verb. In fact, were it not for the opening word, *when,* the group of words would be a grammatical sentence: I am driving my car. But *when* creates a mystery of sorts—a mystery of time or even attitude. "What about when you're driving your car?" we're entitled to ask, and until we get that mystery solved, we do not have a sentence. Compare:

> When I am driving my car, I have a tendency to speed.

In the above version, the subject, predicate verb, and complete thought all belong to the second clause: *I have a tendency to speed.* The first clause, *When I am driving my car,* could go either before or after the other clause; either way, it adds important meaning, or modifies, the second clause. But it cannot be a sentence by itself, because it doesn't complete a thought. *When I am driving my car* has a subject (*I*) and a predicate verb (*am driving*), but the presence of *when* raises more questions than it answers.

Remember: If the group of words doesn't have *at least one* subject, *at least one* predicate verb, and *at least one* complete thought, it *isn't* a sentence.

We stress "at least one" because sentences may have more than one of all three components. Here are examples:

> *Bea* and *Elaine* drove to Colorado last week. (Compound subject: Bea *and* Elaine.)

They *told* stories and *sang* songs about traveling. (Compound predicate verb: told *and* sang. Note that *They*, the subject, is a pronoun referring to Bea and Elaine.)

They arrived in Denver on Monday, and *they left for home the following Friday*. (Two complete thoughts—two grammatical sentences, in fact—joined by the coordinating conjunction *and*. Note that in a case like this you also have more than one subject and more than one predicate verb, although you don't have compound subjects or verbs.)

Exercise

In the following groups of words, find the subject and the predicate verb. Which groups are fragments? Why?

1. Trapped in a restaurant where he couldn't even read the menu, unable even to claim his French was "rusty."
2. Melanie, the only person in this office who can get the computer mess straightened out, and Carl, the only person in this office who knows where Melanie is.
3. Dogs barking, cats meowing, parakeets chattering, all merchandise making noise as though a sudden calamity has visited the pet store.
4. The Missouri River rises in Montana and meanders its way eastward and southward across the plains states until it joins the Mississippi at St. Louis.
5. To order chicken gumbo when you know you don't like chicken.
6. In 1952, the year Dwight Eisenhower was elected president, the war in Korea had been raging for over two years.
7. If you think you have problems, and if you think your car is the first one in history to blow a head gasket.
8. The function of a diesel engine, often wrongly thought to operate like a gasoline engine, to which it bears a superficial resemblance.
9. Though the United States has fifty states, only four intersect perfectly at one point: New Mexico, Arizona, Colorado, and Utah.
10. Denise and Marjorie, the co-captains of this year's volleyball team; Sam and Julian, the co-captains of this year's soccer team.

Because we're sure you can answer these and following exercises yourself, as a general rule we won't supply answers for exercises in the handbook section of our book. Answers are given here to the first few exercises as a kind of "warming up," to get things rolling.

1. Fragment, because there's no subject.
2. Subjects: Melanie and Carl. Fragment; no predicate verb.
3. Fragment, because there's no complete thought, even though we have several descriptive phrases and a dependent (subordinate) clause.
4. Subject: Missouri River. Predicate verbs: rises, meanders. This is a sentence.
5. Fragment, because there's no complete thought.
6. Subject: war. Predicate verb: had been raging. A sentence.
7. Fragment; no complete thought.
8. Fragment; no complete thought.
9. Subject: four. Predicate verb: intersect. A sentence.
10. Fragment; no predicate verb.

Phrases and Clauses

Important to understanding our grammar of the sentence is understanding the difference between phrases and clauses. Many people, if they use these terms at all, use them interchangeably because *both* terms mean "a group of words." Yet the difference, though simple, is significant:

- A *phrase* is a group of words.
- A *clause* is a group of words *having a subject and a predicate verb*.

The italicized parts of the following sentences are *phrases:*

> The man *walking down the street* is my uncle Sidney.
>
> There's no more water *to drink.*
>
> They struggled their way *to the top of the mountain.*
>
> The main idea *of this project* is *to win public support.*
>
> Corned beef *prepared with cabbage* makes a good dinner *for guests with hearty appetites.*
>
> *Muttering to himself,* Paul mowed the lawn *before noon.*

Note that although these phrases contribute much toward the meaning of each sentence, none of them contains both a subject and a predicate verb—no phrase does. Although numerous kinds of phrases can be used in different ways in sentences, their versatility need not concern us at this point.

Now look at the italicized parts of the following sentences, demonstrating *clauses:*

> The baseball player *who hits many home runs* is always greatly admired.
>
> *Because it stood unbroken for thirty-four years,* Babe Ruth's record of sixty home runs in 1927 was considered unbreakable.
>
> Roger Maris, *the player who broke Babe Ruth's home run record in 1961,* was often hampered by the extreme publicity *that he received.*
>
> *Until his sixty-first homer cleared the right-field fence in Yankee Stadium,* Maris was hounded by reporters.
>
> The fact *that he had finally passed the "magic number" of sixty home runs* proved *that no record is unbreakable* and *that human achievement can be inspiring*

Note that although all the italicized clauses above contain subjects and predicate verbs, none are complete sentences because, in isolation, none completes a thought. Here are three examples:

> Until his sixty-first homer cleared the right-field fence in Yankee Stadium
>
> that no record is unbreakable
>
> that human achievement can be inspiring

By themselves, those clauses are fragments of sentences. But look closely again at the sentences displayed above, ignoring for the moment the italicized clauses. The parts that remain are also clauses—because they have subjects and predicate verbs—but most of them are also complete sentences; that is, they are what are often called *independent,* or main, *clauses:*

> The woman was the winner of the prize.
>
> I will have to vote against it.
>
> Roger Maris was often hampered by the extreme publicity.
>
> Maris was hounded by reporters.

Our point is that there are *two* kinds of clauses, and knowing the difference is also important to understanding our sentence grammar:

- *independent*, or main, *clauses* are groups of words that have subjects and predicate verbs and can stand alone as complete grammatical sentences.
- *dependent*, or subordinate, *clauses* are groups of words that have subjects and predicate verbs but *cannot* stand alone as complete grammatical sentences, because they do not express a complete thought. They must be attached in some way (usually as a modifier) to an independent clause. Otherwise, they are sentence fragments.

The Eight Parts of Speech

Depending on how they're used in a sentence, nearly all words, phrases, and clauses in written English can be classified as one of the eight parts of speech:

1. Nouns
2. Pronouns
3. Verbs
4. Adjectives
5. Adverbs
6. Prepositions
7. Conjunctions
8. Interjections

Because these parts of speech are best understood in terms of how they function in relation to sentences, that is how we intend to discuss them here. The parts of speech function in relationship to sentences in the following ways:

- As *subjects, objects,* or *predicate nominatives* (nouns, pronouns, noun phrases, noun clauses)
- As *predicate verbs* (verbs, verb phrases)
- As *modifiers* (adjectives, adjective phrases, adjective clauses; adverbs, adverb phrases, adverb clauses; prepositions, prepositional phrases)
- As *connectors* (conjunctions)
- As *isolated expressions* (interjections)

It is in this order that we will discuss them.

Parts of Speech as Subjects, Objects, or Predicate Nominatives in Sentences

We have already seen that nouns and pronouns can function in sentences as subjects:

> *Yellowstone Park* is in Wyoming.
>
> *It* is one of America's most beautiful national parks.

- Because they can function as subjects, *nouns* can be defined as the names of persons, places, things, or ideas.
- *Pronouns* can be defined as words that substitute for, or take the place of, nouns that are previously referred to, or are already understood by the reader (for example, *I, who, whom, anyone, whoever*).

Thus pronouns are references to already-mentioned or -known persons, places, things, or ideas. Pronouns allow us to avoid tiresome repetitions but demand that we carefully align each pronoun with its *referent*, or antecedent, so that no confusion arises as to what noun the pronoun substitutes for. In the second example above, the subject pronoun *it* refers to the proper noun *Yellowstone Park*, which is the subject of the first sentence.

Nouns and pronouns can also be used as *objects* in sentences. An *object*, in such cases, is a *direct object*, an *indirect object*, or the *object of a preposition*. Note, though, that when used as an object, a noun or pronoun cannot be the subject of a sentence.

Direct Objects. When a predicate verb is *transitive*, it conveys the action from the subject through the verb to the noun or pronoun that is serving as the direct object. Here are examples of sentences in which transitive predicate verbs convey such action to an object:

> The girl *flew* the *kite*. (*Flew* is the transitive verb; *kite* is the noun used as a direct object.)
>
> The boy *lost it* when the wind came up. (*Lost* is the transitive verb; *it* is the pronoun used as the direct object, referring to the kite.)

Indirect Objects. Similar to direct objects, indirect objects require transitive verbs that convey action to an indirect object as well as to a direct object:

> You give *Fred* that key right away!

In the above sentence, *key* is the direct object (you give that *key*) and *Fred* is the indirect object, a proper noun. (Proper nouns are the names of *particular* persons, places, things, or ideas; for example, Fred, Cadillac, Toledo, Marxism.) You can tell when an indirect object is at work in your sentence by inserting *to* or *for* before the first object and seeing whether it fits: You give *to* Fred that key right away!; Millie made *for* Sara a mince pie. Father gave *to* me my allowance.

Objects of Prepositions. Prepositions are words that have virtually no meaning by themselves; they're primarily used to be the lead word in phrases that in turn modify parts of the sentence. Common prepositions are *to, toward, at, beyond, by, along, over, up, around, into*—virtually any word you could put in the following sentence blank:

> The rabbit ran ____________ the woodpile.

Note that these phrases, called prepositional phrases, consist of three parts: (a) the preposition itself, (b) the object of the preposition, and (c) any modifiers of the object. Thus, in the italicized prepositional phrase

> Bob liked watching television *in the spacious living room*

in is the preposition, *room* is the object of the preposition, and *the*, *spacious*, and *living* are all adjectives modifying the noun *room*.

Predicate Nominatives. Finally, nouns and pronouns can be used as predicate nominatives. In such cases, the noun or pronoun appears in the sentence *after* a state-of-being, or *linking*, predicate verb and renames or elaborates the subject in some way. In the following sentences, the predicate nominatives are italicized:

> Rod is the *president* of the organization. (Common noun, not capitalized, used to rename or explain something about the subject. Note that the verb is a form of *to be*, as many linking verbs are. Linking verbs are never transitive; they cannot be followed by an indirect or direct object—only by a predicate nominative (or a predicate adjective, as we will see below).
>
> The president of the organization is *Rod*. (Proper noun, used to rename or explain something about the subject. Note again the linking verb.)
>
> It is *she* who will guide you to the next level. (Nominative-case pronoun—explained below—used to rename the subject pronoun, *it*. Again, the verb is a linking verb.)

Noun Phrases and Clauses. Noun phrases and noun clauses may also be used as subjects, objects, or predicate nominatives. A *noun phrase* is merely a group of words that functions in the same way a single noun or pronoun can within a sentence. In the following sentences, the noun phrases are italicized:

> *The tall boy* [subject] is my cousin Hector.
>
> Wilma gave *the yellow sweater* [direct object] to Bernice.
>
> The gift was *a yellow sweater* [predicate nominative].
>
> *Your giving me your coat* [subject] was a kind gesture.
>
> *To trust your instincts* [subject] is a wise choice.

As we will see below, a noun phrase is actually a noun form with its various modifiers.

Similarly, a *noun clause* is a group of words with a subject and predicate verb that functions in the same way a single noun or pronoun can within a sentence. In the following sentences, the noun clauses are italicized:

> *What you told me* [subject] is our secret.

I forgot *what Bernice said* [direct object].

The sadness is *what I regret* [predicate nominative].

Noun clauses are also noun forms with their various modifiers, with the important difference being that they also have verbs.

Pronoun Case

Pronouns have different forms, or cases, that must be used depending on their function in a sentence. Essentially, there are three pronoun cases: nominative, objective, and possessive.

Nominative Case. This case is the form the pronoun takes when it is used either as a sentence subject or as a predicate nominative. The case form also covers whether a pronoun is singular, plural, masculine, or feminine. For example:

Nominative Case

Singular: *I, he, she, it*

Plural: *we, they*

Singular subject	*I* hope this solution works.
Singular masculine predicate nominative	David is *he* who leads the group.
Plural subject	*We* will determine the winners.
Plural predicate nominative	It is *they* who must apologize.

Objective Case. This case is the form the pronoun takes when it is used as a direct or indirect object or as the object of a preposition. The case form also covers whether a pronoun is singular, plural, masculine, or feminine. For example:

Objective Case

Singular: *me, you, him, her, it*

Plural: *us, them, you* (*you* as a group)

Singular direct object	The batter hit *it.*
Singular indirect object	Julie gave *me* the car keys.
Singular object of preposition	We can't reach our goal today; but we can make progress toward *it.*
Plural direct object	The child's antics drove *them* crazy.
Plural indirect object	Paula gave *us* the instructions.

What is important to remember about pronoun case in relation to our sentence grammar is that the appropriate case to use depends on how you are using the pronoun within the sentence.

Possessive Case. This third pronoun case is not critical to our sentence grammar. The special pronoun forms that indicate possession do so by their very definition and therefore require no apostrophe to designate possession. The possessive case also covers whether a pronoun is singular, plural, masculine, or feminine:

> **Possessive Case**
>
> Singular: *his, her, hers, your, yours, its*
>
> Plural: *our, ours, their, theirs, your, yours*

Exercises

A. Identify the italicized part of each sentence below as one of the following: subject noun, noun as object of transitive verb, noun as object of preposition, noun as predicate nominative.

1. *Women* have contributed much more to the history of American culture than some people realize.
2. Susan B. Anthony was *one* of the earliest advocates for women's right to vote.
3. In 1984, Geraldine Ferraro was the first woman to make a major-party run for the *vice-presidency* of the United States.
4. Amelia Earhart flew her *plane* into the history of aviation when she tried to fly around the world.

Answers to A

1. subject noun
2. predicate nominative
3. object of preposition
4. direct object

B. Identify the italicized part of each sentence below as one of the following: subject pronoun, pronoun as object of transitive verb, pronoun as indirect object of transitive verb, pronoun as object of a preposition.

1. Marla and Elaine played two sets of tennis, and Elaine won *them* both.
2. *They* played tennis in the early morning before work.
3. I've got to give *them* credit for playing so early.
4. I brought a thermos of coffee for *them* after their match.

Answers to B

1. pronoun as object of transitive verb
2. subject pronoun
3. pronoun as indirect object of transitive verb
4. pronoun as object of preposition

C. Identify the italicized part of each sentence below as a noun phrase or noun clause.

1. *What is special* about an NCAA College Division I basketball championship is that it must be won in actual competition—not in a poll.
2. *The Bruins of UCLA* have won ten championships, more than any other team in Division I.
3. Kentucky and Indiana have won the title four times, and *a few schools,* including San Francisco, Cincinnati, Louisville, Kansas, North Carolina State, and North Carolina, have won the title twice.
4. The overwhelming fact is *that most schools have never won the title.*

Answers to C

1. noun clause
2. noun phrase
3. noun phrase
4. noun clause

D. In the blank, write an appropriate pronoun case form.

1. Give ____________ credit.

Answers to D: Of course, different correct answers are possible on most of these, so long as the appropriate pronoun case is used; the answer to item 5, however, must be *whom.*

2. The dog ate ____________ supper slowly.
3. ____________ is the person I told you about.
4. ____________ cannot possibly win the bowling tournament.
5. To ____________ do you wish to speak?
6. The problem is not ours; it is ____________ .

E. Which of the following clauses in brackets is dependent (or subordinate), and which is independent (or main)? How do you know?

Answers to E

1. independent
2. dependent
3. independent
4. dependent

1. Perched atop a craggy Colorado mountain peak, [the lone eagle surveyed the swollen river below].
2. [Because an enormous volume of water was coursing through the Royal Gorge], officials worried about disastrous flooding downstream.
3. A few miles to the east, [nervous citizens began to sandbag the Arkansas River] while it rose.
4. The flood threatened [because a record amount of winter snow in the higher altitudes had melted rapidly].

Parts of Speech as Predicate Verbs in Sentences

We have seen how the first two parts of speech, nouns and pronouns, are used in sentences. We turn our attention now to verbs, which are the most vital single element in a sentence. First, a bit about the nature of verbs.

- *Verbs indicate action or state of being.* All verbs are action words with the exception of those verbs which are a form of *to be* or which indicate a condition (for example, *seem*).
- *Through their many forms, verbs indicate time (present, past, future, and variations of these).* You may remember conjugating verbs either in English or in a foreign language. Such conjugating arranges the forms of the verb in several ways, including arrangement according to time (sometimes called *tense*). For example:

  I *walk* (simple present time)
  I *walked* (simple past)
  I *am walking* (present progressive)
  I *have walked* (present perfect)
  I *will walk* (simple future)
  I *will have walked* (future perfect)
  I *had walked* (past perfect)
  And so on

  The chief point to remember about verb time or tense is that you should use it *consistently* when you write, and not switch from one prevailing tense to another. If you begin writing something using the present tense, you should generally maintain that tense consistently throughout, unless the particular situation calls for a variation. (See chapter 30, pages H-69–H-70).

- *Verbs are transitive, intransitive, or linking* As we have seen, a *transitive* verb takes a direct or indirect object, or both:

    Beverly *fed* the dog. (transitive verb, *fed;* direct object, *dog*)

    Beverly *gave* me the dog. (transitive verb, *gave;* indirect object, *me;* direct object, *dog*)

    Beverly *runs* daily. (intransitive verb, *runs;* no object)

    Beverly *is* a dog-lover. (linking verb, *is;* predicate nominative, *dog-lover*)

    Beverly *is* sentimental. (linking verb, *is;* predicate adjective, *sentimental*)

    Beverly *is raising* a stray dog. (transitive verb, *is raising;* direct object, *dog*—note that some forms of *to be* are not linking verbs but are sometimes called helping verbs)

As you can see, verbs are powerful parts of speech because they indicate not only action or state of being—and thus energize our thoughts into sentences—but also *when* these actions or states of being take place.

In fact, verbs are the only parts of speech that could, in one word, convey an entire sentence:

> Jump!

In the above example, *you* is the "understood" subject of the sentence, and the (intransitive) predicate verb is *jump.* Together, the understood subject and the verb constitute a complete thought. Only a verb could carry that much power and meaning by itself. Of course, verbs are not usually used as one-word sentences.

Verbs can include the various auxiliaries, or helpers, that mark a verb's tense, as in these examples (the helpers are italicized with their verbs):

> By tomorrow I *will have dieted* for a month. (future perfect tense)
>
> I *had* already *gone* to the pharmacy by 8:00 A.M. (past perfect tense)
>
> Charlene *has accomplished* many objectives. (present perfect tense)

Verbs consisting of more than one word are, of course, *verb phrases.* Technically, a verb phrase is any predicate verb along with all its helpers. Thus the following italicized passages are verb phrases that constitute the grammatical predicates of the sentences.

> Andy Warhol *has made* high art out of a soup can.
>
> Some people *will argue,* however, that a soup can is not art.
>
> According to my textbook, twentieth-century art *has been defined* as a matter of perspective.
>
> The textbook *did not say* whose perspective prevails.

According to this same book, Warhol *is making* a statement.

What *is* he *saying?*

This discussion has skimmed only the surface of verbs, a subject that can be very complex. Our purpose here, however, is simply to show the role verbs play as a part of speech that contributes vitally to the formation of sentences.

Parts of Speech as Modifiers in Sentences

The fourth (adjectives), fifth (adverbs), and sixth (prepositions) parts of speech are the modifiers. *Modify* means, in this sense, "to change." Modifiers act on the basic nouns, pronouns, and verbs of a sentence to provide richness of detail, precision, or some other change that affects the sentence's communication in important ways.

Adjectives. Adjectives can be single words, phrases, or even dependent (subordinate) clauses. In all cases, adjectives modify *nouns or pronouns.* In so doing, they may describe, point out, compare, limit, or perform some other specific function on the particular noun or pronoun they modify. Note in the following examples that adjectives can appear before or after the word they modify:

Preston drove a *hard* bargain. (single adjective modifying *bargain*)

It was *an old hickory* handle, *worn* from use. (several single adjectives, all modifying *handle;* note that *hickory* can also be a noun, as in "a handle made of *hickory*")

Sun Yat-sen was a *Chinese* leader. (single proper adjective, modifying *leader;* again, placement determines part of speech—*Chinese* can also be a proper noun)

Lena is the *tallest* daughter in the *Colby* family. (superlative comparative adjective, modifying *daughter; Colby* is a proper adjective, modifying *family*)

This horse is the one I want to buy. (single adjective pointing out—modifying—which *horse* is desired)

Julia is my *third* daughter. (single adjective, modifying *daughter*)

Adjectives can also appear in sentences *after* linking verbs, in which case they become *predicate adjectives,* or adjectives that modify the subject of the sentence:

At seven feet, two inches, Robert is *gigantic.*

Of the three Colby daughters, Lena is the *tallest.*

The articles—*a, an,* and *the*—are always classed as adjectives.

Exercise

Underline the adjectives in the following sentences. What nouns or pronouns do they modify?

1. Belinda Casey is an impressive athlete.
2. Short and slow, Belinda nonetheless amazes her basketball coach.
3. An honors student who deeply loves the game, Belinda is the team captain.
4. Several older girls are taller and faster, but none of them hustles like Belinda.
5. The tireless Belinda plays enthusiastic defense.

Most of the single-word comparison forms in English are adjectives. Commonly such adjectives are classed three ways: basic, comparative, and superlative. Some require regular formulaic suffixes to show these comparisons (for example, *-er, -est*); others are irregular; and still others require auxiliary words to effect the comparison. Here are a few examples of regularly formed comparatives:

Basic	**Comparative**	**Superlative**
large	larger	largest
high	higher	highest
green	greener	greenest
thin	thinner	thinnest
sad	sadder	saddest

Here are a few irregular comparatives:

bad	worse	worst
good	better	best
much	more	most

And here are a few requiring auxiliaries, such as *more, most, less,* and *least:*

peaceful	more peaceful	most peaceful
hostile	more hostile	most hostile
hostile	less hostile	least hostile
reactionary	more reactionary	most reactionary
doubtful	less doubtful	least doubtful

Adjectives can also be phrases. Remember, a phrase is simply a group of words. There are many kinds of phrases—participial, gerund, infinitive, prepositional and more—and many are used in sentences as modifiers. The italicized phrases in the following sentences are *adjective phrases:*

Broken beyond repair, the watch has been put away in a drawer. (past participial phrase, modifying *watch*)

The player *scoring the most points* will win the match. (present participial phrase, modifying *player*)

I have no money *to spend.* (infinitive phrase, modifying *money*)

Half *of these oranges* are spoiled. (prepositional phrase, modifying *half*)

A man *with his talent* should pursue a career *in music.* (prepositional phrases, modifying *man* and *career*)

Dependent (subordinate) clauses can also be used as adjectives. The italicized clauses in the following sentences are *adjective clauses:*

The player *who scores the most points* will win the match. (adjective clause, modifying *player*)

Dennis Simpson is the player *who scored the most points.* (relative adjective clause, modifying *Dennis Simpson*)

The fact *that he lost control of the war in Vietnam* persuaded President Lyndon B. Johnson not to seek reelection in 1968. (adjective clause, modifying *fact*)

It was Johnson's decision *that set the stage for the political return of Richard M. Nixon.* (adjective clause, modifying *decision*)

Adjective phrases/ clauses exercise answers

1. "that was dropped on Hiroshima, Japan"—clause—modifies *bomb;* "that are available today"—clause—modifies *bombs.*
2. "dropped in August 1945"—phrase—modifies *bomb.*
3. "who made the decision to use the bomb"—clause—modifies *president.*
4. "that left their powerful stamp on the first fifty years of this century"—clause—modifies *world wars.*
5. "Winning in both of these wars"—phrase—modifies *the United States;* "one of the earth's most powerful nations"—phrase—modifies *the United States.*

Exercise

Find the adjective phrases and clauses in the following sentences. What do they modify?

1. The bomb that was dropped on Hiroshima, Japan, to end World War II was very small compared with the bombs that are available today.
2. That bomb, dropped in August 1945, began the nuclear age.
3. The president who made the decision to use the bomb was Harry Truman.
4. There were two world wars that left their powerful stamp on the first fifty years of this century.
5. Winning in both of these wars, the United States became one of the earth's most powerful nations.

Adverbs. Like adjectives, adverbs can be single words, phrases, or dependent (subordinate) clauses. Also like adjectives, they modify, but instead of modifying nouns and pronouns, as adjectives do, adverbs modify *verbs, adjectives, or other adverbs.* By their nature, adverbs tell how, when, where, why, or how much. In some cases, they also offer comparison (for instance, Monroe worked *harder* than Billy).

In understanding modifiers, it is important to remember our principle of sentence usage: *the way a word is used in a sentence often determines what part of speech it is.* Consider the word *daily* in these two sentences:

Travis liked to read his *daily* paper.

Travis bought a paper *daily.*

In the first sentence, *daily* modifies the noun *paper.* That makes it an adjective. In the second sentence, *daily* modifies the verb *bought.* That makes it an adverb.

The italicized words in the following sentences are *adverbs:*

"We played *badly,*" said the coach. (modifies the verb *played*)

"On offense, we used *very* bad judgment." (modifies the adjective *bad*)

Terrell *slowly* climbed *down.* (both modify the verb *climbed*)

Crying *quite passionately,* Julie persuaded her mother to give permission. (*passionately* modifies the adjective *crying; quite* modifies the adverb *passionately*)

Adverbs can be phrases. The underlined phrases in the following sentences are all *adverbial phrases:*

To walk your dog in Manhattan, you must carry and use a "scooper," or you may be fined. (infinitive phrase used as an adverb to modify the verbs *must carry* and *use*)

Chadwick climbed *to the top* of the tree. (prepositional phrase used as an adverb to modify the verb *climbed;* note that the second prepositional phrase is an adjective because it modifies the noun *top*)

We returned *from the lake without any fish.* (both are prepositional phrases used as adverbs modifying the verb *returned*)

To overcome fatigue, you should carry vitamins. (infinitive phrase used as an adverb to modify the verb *carry*)

Likewise, adverbs can be dependent (subordinate) clauses. The italicized clauses in the following sentences are all *adverbial clauses:*

When you are walking your dog in Manhattan, carry and use a "scooper," or you may be fined. (adverbial clause modifying the verbs *carry* and *use*)

You must pay your taxes *because it is the law.* (adverbial clause modifying the verb *must pay*)

The time to excel is now, *while the boss is watching.* (adverbial clause modifying the adverb *now*)

Because the response was poor, Dr. Johnson tried the technique again. (adverbial clause modifying the verb *tried*)

Exercise

Identify the single adverbs, adverb phrases, and adverb clauses in the following sentences. What do they modify?

1. In old Dodge City, the stagecoach arrived weekly.
2. When the railroad came to Dodge City, prosperity came too, because the trains made Dodge a center for receiving and shipping cattle.
3. After driving cattle up from Texas through the Indian territory, most cowboys were eager to celebrate when they arrived in Dodge City with their herds.
4. Gamblers, swindlers, and cutthroats quickly flocked to Dodge City, where they profited from the free-spending, celebrating cowboys.

5. Soon it became obvious that a brave marshal and deputies were needed in Dodge.

Prepositions. Prepositions by themselves are of little use. Nothing of consequence is communicated by such words as these:

to	toward	after
from	above	below
up	down	around

As we noted earlier, a preposition's real use is as the lead word in a *prepositional phrase*—a group of words consisting of a preposition, the object of the preposition, and all modifiers of the object:

Preposition	*Modifier(s)*	*Object*
to	the	lighthouse
from	the madding	crowd
toward	a better	understanding
at	the very	least
under	a paper	moon

As we have also noted, prepositional phrases are modifiers—that is, they are used in sentences as adjectives or adverbs.

Consider how the italicized prepositional phrases in the following sentences are used:

> Many critics consider the guitar work *in "Layla" by Derek and the Dominoes* excellent. (adjectives)
>
> Janis Joplin, the blues singer, came *from Port Arthur, Texas.* (adverb)
>
> *From Maine to California,* young Americans *in 1956* enjoyed "Heartbreak Hotel" *by a talented newcomer* named Elvis Presley. (adverb, adverb, and adjective)
>
> The "British invasion" *of rock-and-roll music* began *with the Beatles,* who hailed *from Liverpool.* (adjective, adverb, adverb)

Remember that the object of a preposition will always be a *noun or pronoun;* it will never be the subject of a sentence. Prepositional phrases will always be used as adjectives or adverbs.

Parts of Speech as Connectors in Sentences

Conjunctions—the seventh part of speech—are somewhat like prepositions in that they are of little use by themselves. They become important because of their *function,* which is to connect words, phrases, and clauses, making it possible for writers to create longer, more complex sentences.

The most common kinds of conjunctions are the *coordinating conjunctions: and, or, nor, but, for, yet,* and *so.* It's important to note that although these conjunctions are primarily functional, they each have separate meanings, or applications, that govern their use; they cannot be used interchangeably. At their simplest level of usage, conjunctions connect single words: ham *and* eggs, rich *or* poor, poor *but* happy. They also connect phrases: trying to be happy *and* trying to be rich, winning the election *but* losing the voters' respect, played fast *or* played slow.

Coordinating conjunctions, however, play a key role in the creation of longer, more complex sentences. They can function, for example, to join two independent (main) clauses:

> Harriett practiced diligently, *and* she became an outstanding guitarist.
>
> I can understand some of these mathematical principles, *but* logarithms baffle me.

We'll take a closer look at this use of coordinating conjunctions below, when we discuss compound sentences and stylistic coordination.

Another important type of conjunction is the *subordinating conjunction,* used to connect dependent (subordinate) clauses to independent (main) clauses, thereby creating a complex sentence in which the dependent clause is of lesser importance than the independent clause. Among subordinating conjunctions are the ones in this list:

Nature of Conjunction	Conjunction
time	after, before, since, while, when, until
cause	because, since
condition	if, in case, whether, unless
admission	although, even though, though
manner	as if, as though
purpose	so that, in order to
comparison or result	than, as, as if, as . . . as, so . . . that, such . . . that

Note again that usage determines part of speech; *after,* for example, is often a preposition, as is *before.* But when they are used as subordinating conjunctions, they are not prepositions:

> David and I discussed the budget *after* we ate lunch.
>
> I never discuss money *before* I eat.

Above, *after* and *before* are subordinating conjunctions that both begin and connect dependent clauses. The dependent clauses connect with and "depend on" the independent (main) clauses in each sentence, and in both sentences the dependent clauses are adverbs that modify the predicate verbs *discussed* and *discuss.*

We will treat subordinating conjunctions more fully below, when we discuss complex sentences and stylistic subordination. Meanwhile, note the italicized subordinating conjunctions in the following sentences:

> The pilot Amelia Earhart has been missing *since* her plane disappeared many years ago.
>
> Women in aviation admire Amelia Earhart *because* she was every bit as dedicated and brave as Charles Lindbergh.
>
> It is sad *that* Earhart's plane disappeared *while* she and her navigator were trying to fly across the Pacific Ocean.
>
> On the eve of the twenty-first century, we should remember and honor pioneers like Lindbergh and Earhart *as much as* we can.
>
> Aviation would not be so important in our lives today *if* they had not met their challenges back in the 1920s and 1930s.

Other, less important kinds of connectors occur in written English, among them the *correlative conjunction,* which is a specialized kind of coordinating conjunction that pairs conjunctions in fairly rigid sentence patterns. Frequently used correlative conjunctions are these:

> not only . . . but also
> either . . . or
> neither . . . nor
> both . . . and

And they are used in the following kinds of sentence patterns:

> Glenda *not only* wrote the song *but also* recorded it.
>
> *Either* Theresa *or* Dawn is going to be promoted.
>
> Davidson has *neither* the talent *nor* the will to handle the job.
>
> Marcia Chase is *both* the editor *and* the publisher of the magazine.

Another kind of connector brings together independent clauses with what are sometimes called *conjunctive adverbs* and *transitional phrases.* These are words like *however, moreover, therefore, nonetheless,* and *rather* and short phrases like *in fact* and *on the contrary.* Such connectors typically join independent (main) clauses, and are preceded by a semicolon (so as to avoid a comma splice; see chapter 30) and followed by a comma:

> In 1938 Adolf Hitler promised the rest of Europe he would make no more territorial demands; *however,* in 1939 he ordered the German invasion of Poland, thereby igniting World War II.
>
> Prior to the Polish invasion, Hitler promised Russia that Germany would not push on past Poland into Russia; *moreover,* he asserted that Germany had no quarrel with Russia.

Hitler had lied to the Western Allies at Munich in 1938; *therefore,* the Russians weren't very surprised when Hitler ordered the invasion of Russia in 1941.

The Germans very nearly defeated Russia; *in fact,* they came within a few miles of Moscow—but they never took it.

We will discuss this kind of conjunction in more detail when we discuss stylistic coordination.

Parts of Speech as Isolated Expressions

Some words or phrases are not really grammatically related to a sentence, even though they may communicate a basic idea that comes before or after a sentence. Such words or phrases are called *interjections,* and they are the eighth and final part of speech.

Quite literally, an interjection doesn't fit anywhere in the structure of a sentence:

Darn! I didn't mean to hit my thumb with the hammer!

I would have believed anything in those days. *Ah, youth!*

Hello, my name is Donna Ehrlinger.

Oh, great! I always wanted two tickets to see the ballet.

Shamir has just won the contest! *Outstanding!*

As the above examples show, often interjections are single words; other times they are phrases or clauses; and frequently they are exclamations.

This concludes our discussion of the eight parts of speech in relation to how they function in written English sentences. We emphasize again the most important principle: the part of speech that a word is depends on the way it is used in a sentence.

Verbals

Verbals—classed as *gerunds, participles,* and *infinitives*—are words and phrases formed from verbs but used in sentences as nouns, adjectives, or adverbs. We discuss them here not only because they can be tricky but also because they can be used to add variety to sentence structure, as we will see below.

Gerunds

Gerunds always end in *-ing* and are always nouns because they name activities or ideas. Thus, they can be used in any way that nouns can be used:

Flying is my favorite way to travel. (subject of sentence)

My favorite way to travel is *flying* (predicate nominative)

I learned *skiing* at the resort last winter. (direct object)

I graduated from *skating* to *skiing* in a few months. (objects of prepositions)

Gerunds can also be phrases:

Walking the dog is not my favorite activity. (subject of sentence)

Dudley's major problem is *eating too much.* (predicate nominative)

Participles

There are two kinds of participles: (a) *present,* which end in *-ing,* and (b) *past,* which usually end in *-ed, -en, d,* or *t.* In their usual form they are parts of verbs:

Today I *am flying* to Brownsville, Texas. (present participle *flying* is part of the predicate verb)

Before I knew it, I *had walked* two miles. (past participle *walked* is part of the predicate verb)

But because many verbs not only *convey* but also *describe* action, shifting participles to modifying slots in the sentence can make the participles adjectives:

The smoke *rising* above the cabin told Hawkeye that someone was inside. (present participle, adjective)

The *designated* hitter, some say, has ruined baseball. (past participle, adjective)

John Cohen wrote, *looping* the pen in grand gestures. (present participle, adjective)

Participles can also be phrases:

Bursting through the levee, the river flooded the plain below. (present participle, adjective)

Dejected from his experience in the flood, the farmer gave a deep sigh. (past participle, adjective)

We saw him *coming from what was left of his house.* (present participle, adjective)

Infinitives

Infinitives consist of *to* plus the simple form of the verb: *to win, to fly, to carry, to drive,* and so on. They can be used as nouns, adjectives, or adverbs.

To swim is his great ambition. (noun, subject of sentence)

His great ambition is *to swim.* (noun, predicate nominative)

There is nothing *to eat* in the house. (adjective, modifying the noun *nothing*)

She is certain *to be* ready. (adverb, modifying the adjective *certain*)

Infinitives can also be phrases:

The class voted *to sail to Europe.* (noun, direct object)

He bought the ticket *to please Helen.* (adverb, modifying *bought*)

There were tickets *to sell uptown* and tickets *to sell in the neighborhood.* (adjectives, modifying *tickets*)

Exercise

Identify the *kind* of verbal that is italicized in the following sentences; then explain how it is used in the sentence (that is, as a noun, adjective, or adverb).

1. *Rushing down the staircase,* Trudy forgot that her purse was still on her dresser.
2. Brad was glad *to see her.*
3. The tickets, *forgotten in the abandoned purse,* would not be missed until much later.
4. They went *to eat* and then, *smiling at the ticket taker,* approached the ballroom door.
5. "Don't worry, Trudy," Brad said later; "*forgetting* is something we all do from time to time."
6. "Thanks," Trudy said, *feeling* better, "but not *remembering the tickets* is still a dumb thing *to do.*"

The Four Basic Sentences

Written English has four basic sentence types, classified according to their makeup of clauses. Remember, a clause is a group of words having a subject and a predicate verb. Independent (main) clauses also complete a thought and therefore can stand as sentences. Dependent (subordinate) clauses do not complete a thought and therefore cannot stand as sentences; they must connect in some way, usually as a modifier, with an independent clause. The four basic sentence types are (a) simple, (b) compound, (c) complex, and (d) compound-complex. A good writer uses all four types in his or her writing.

When we say that a good writer uses all four types of sentences in his or her writing, we don't mean to imply that such use is highly conscious. Just as a fluent speaker varies sentence lengths, rhythms, and emphases without forethought, a good, fluent writer also varies these characteristics, so that the "voice" that comes through to the reader is appropriate to the subject matter and "tuned" to the ear of the reader. The more mature and fluent the writer, the more likely that all the types of sentences will be used, quite naturally, in the flow of the finished writing. Of course, there are also times when *any* writer will, during revising, make a conscious effort to change sentence types—for variety, to increase the speed of reading, and so on.

Simple Sentences

A simple sentence consists of one independent (main) clause:

President John F. Kennedy was assassinated in 1963.

Above, we have one subject (*President John F. Kennedy*), one predicate verb (*was assassinated*), and one complete thought. We also have one adverb prepositional phrase (*in 1963*), modifying the predicate verb. As long as we have only one subject, predicate verb, and complete thought, additional nonclause modifiers do not change the sentence's classification; it is still a simple sentence in this form:

The popular President John F. Kennedy was assassinated while on a political trip to Texas in 1963.

The core of the simple sentence remains: President John F. Kennedy [subject] was assassinated [predicate verb, complete thought].

Just because a sentence has simple structure, it is not necessarily simple in its meaning or sophistication. Consider:

> The smiling young president was trying to mend political fences between feuding members of the Texas congressional delegation.

The core is simple here: The president was trying to mend fences. But there is nothing simple about the idea or the language in the sentence.

Compound Sentences

A compound sentence consists of two or more independent (main) clauses, along with the connecting coordinating conjunction(s) or a connecting semicolon. The most common way to create a compound sentence is to join two or more independent clauses with an appropriate coordinating conjunction:

> April's parents bought her a car for graduation, *and* they gave her the keys right after the commencement ceremony.

Above, the two independent clauses are connected by a comma followed by the coordinating conjunction *and*. Similarly:

> "I want you to have fun driving your car," said April's father, "*but* I want you to promise me you will always drive carefully."
>
> April knew she would have to keep her grades up in college, *or* she would lose her driving privileges.

Compound sentences usually unite two independent clauses of approximately equal significance; neither clause is more important than the other. The clauses should be at least roughly parallel in form so as to make reading neither difficult nor unpleasing to the ear.

Complex Sentences

A complex sentence consists of one independent (main) clause and one or more dependent (subordinate) clauses, along with the appropriate subordinating conjunction(s). Complex sentences require the writer to make a rhetorical decision, for whichever clause he or she makes subordinate becomes *less* important than the independent clause. The decision depends on which clause the writer wishes to emphasize. Compare the difference between these two complex sentences; in each, the dependent clause is italicized:

> *Although our main office is in Houston,* our Dallas office is by far our largest.
>
> *Although our Dallas office is by far our largest,* our main office is in Houston.

The first sentence emphasizes that the Dallas office is the largest; the second sentence, that the main office is in Houston. Notice that the essential information in these sentences is the *same;* the difference is emphasis created by *subordination.*

Many times, dependent clauses will actually be modifiers, as is the case here:

> The president *who is credited with building the Panama Canal* is Theodore Roosevelt. (adjective clause, modifying *president*)

Who in the above example is a *pronoun* serving as both the subject of the dependent clause and the subordinating connector of that clause to the independent clause. Also consider this example:

> *While the Great Depression deepened,* President Hoover promised Americans *that "prosperity is just around the corner."*

In the above complex sentence, the first dependent clause is an adverb modifying the verb *promised.* The second dependent clause is not a modifier but a noun clause used as the direct object—what President Hoover promised. (*Americans* is an indirect object.)

Of primary note here is that dependent clauses are necessary components of complex sentences. They make the structure of the sentence more sophisticated than that of compound sentences because they indicate rhetorical decisions of emphasis made by the writer.

Remember, a complex sentence never has more than one independent clause.

Compound-Complex Sentences

A compound-complex sentence consists of at least two independent (main) clauses, at least one dependent (subordinate) clause, and the appropriate conjunction(s). Consider the following sentence:

> When the Sioux annihilated General Custer and his troops, a great victory for Native Americans was won, and the groundwork for a much deeper respect of Native Americans was laid.

The above example contains one dependent clause: *When the Sioux annihilated General Custer and his troops.* It contains two independent clauses: *a great victory for Native Americans was won* and *the groundwork for a much deeper respect of Native Americans was laid.* The dependent clause, which introduces the sentence, is adverbial, modifying the verb phrase *was won.* The independent clauses are joined by a comma with the coordinating conjunction *and.*

The following are also compound-complex sentences. The independent clauses are in all capitals; the dependent clauses are italicized:

> LYNDON B. JOHNSON, *who was formerly a member of Congress and a senator from Texas,* CHOSE HUBERT H. HUMPHREY, *who was a senator from Minnesota,* AS HIS RUNNING MATE IN 1964; and THEY WON THE ELECTION OVERWHELMINGLY.

> THE DEMOCRATIC TICKET OF JOHNSON-HUMPHREY SWAMPED THE REPUBLICAN TICKET OF GOLDWATER-MILLER IN NEARLY EVERY STATE, and 1964's PRESIDENTIAL ELECTION WAS THE MOST ONE-SIDED SINCE 1936, *when President Franklin D. Roosevelt trounced his challenger, Kansas Governor Alf M. Landon.*

Exercise

Identify which of the following sentences are simple, which compound, which complex, and which compound-complex.

1. After Lyndon B. Johnson decided not to run for reelection in 1968, several Democrats, including Johnson's vice-president, Hubert H. Humphrey, declared their candidacy.
2. Soon Democratic Senators Robert F. Kennedy and Eugene McCarthy also declared their candidacy for president in 1968.
3. Ronald Reagan became a principal challenger for the Republican nomination, but that nomination was eventually won by the former vice-president, Richard M. Nixon.
4. The Democratic convention in Chicago proved to be tumultuous, and while demonstrators rioted outside in the streets, Democratic delegates nominated Vice-President Hubert Humphrey as their party's candidate.
5. The great issue in the election of 1968 was the worsening war in Vietnam, but the winner of the election, President Richard M. Nixon, who had vowed to try to end that war, was unable to do so until much later.

As you can see, clausal structures can make sentences powerful conveyers of ideas and information. We will now focus on how manipulation of those structures can enhance your writing style.

Some Sentence Stylistics

Following are eight sentence-manipulation techniques that can help you achieve variety and maturity in your sentence style. Some will prove simpler than others; some will prove more useful than others. No one technique is necessarily better than another, and all are more appropriate in some instances than in others. Judgment, as always, is paramount.

Coordination

Practice in producing sentences following these various stylistic patterns can be enjoyable if you find areas about which students might want to write sentences. Ask students to produce a group of sentences, for example, about their best high school

Essentially, coordination involves combining two or more independent clauses of roughly equal significance, using a comma and an appropriate coordinating conjunction (*and, or, nor, but, for, yet, so*), to create a *compound sentence.* Consider these two sentences:

> The Arkansas River rises on the east side of the Continental Divide in Colorado.

It flows southeastward out of the mountains across the plains of Kansas and Oklahoma.

memory, *former* teachers they've had, or their home towns. Occasional sentence practice in all the patterns suggested here would also make good extra-credit work.

Coordinated, the above sentences might read like this:

The Arkansas River rises on the east side of Colorado's Continental Divide, and it flows southeastward out of the mountains across the plains of Kansas and Oklahoma.

Note: Without the pronoun *it* after the coordinating conjunction, the sentence would not be compound; rather, it would simply have a compound predicate verb.

Sometimes when sentences are closely related they can be coordinated by joining them with a semicolon instead of a comma and coordinating conjunction:

I used to go fishing in the Arkansas River; it flows a short distance from my home town.

The Ohio River begins in Pittsburgh; there the Allegheny and Monongahela rivers join to form the Ohio.

Exercise

Coordinate the following independent clauses (sentences) in each item into a single compound sentence.

1. The Arkansas River gains considerable size in Arkansas. It joins the Mississippi River at the eastern border of Arkansas.
2. The Arkansas River is one of the Mississippi's greatest western tributaries. The greatest western tributary of the Mississippi River is the Missouri River.
3. The greatest western tributary of the Mississippi River is the Missouri River. The greatest eastern tributary of the Mississippi River is the Ohio River.
4. The Continental Divide is the highest elevation above sea level in North America. It runs along the top of the mountains through Montana, Wyoming, Colorado, and New Mexico.
5. Waters drain westward and eastward from the Continental Divide. The Colorado, Snake, and Columbia are major west-running rivers. The Missouri, Arkansas, and Rio Grande are major east-running rivers.

Now write five compound sentences of your own, on any subjects you choose.

Subordination

Subordination involves combining at least one independent clause with at least one dependent clause in order to emphasize the independent clause. We have already seen that making a clause dependent lessens its significance; thus, subordination always requires the writer to make a rhetorical choice. Consider these two independent clauses (sentences):

Dixie Daniels manages the regional office in Phoenix.

Dixie Daniels supervises all sales staff in the Phoenix Region.

Obviously, these two independent clauses could be coordinated. But if the writer wishes to combine them so as to emphasize one of Daniels's responsibilities over the other, the following *subordinating* options would do so:

> Dixie Daniels, *who manages the regional office in Phoenix,* supervises all sales staff in the Phoenix Region. (emphasizes that she supervises sales staff)
>
> Dixie Daniels, *who supervises all sales staff in the Phoenix Region,* manages the regional office in Phoenix. (emphasizes that she manages the regional office)

Exercise

Combine the following two sentences into two different subordinated versions. Make the first version emphasize Michael Stanley's writing ability, and make the second version emphasize his mathematical ability.

1. Michael Stanley is one of our class's best writers.
2. Michael Stanley is one of our class's highest scoring math students.

Subordination creates many possibilities for complex and compound-complex sentences. Here are a few samples:

> I intend to go without shaving *until the Raiders break their losing streak.*
>
> Veronica collects men *who have more intelligence and character than cash.*
>
> Busby would not say *that Pickering was an utter fool,* but he would say *what many had thought: that Pickering was a complete chowderhead.*
>
> One of Emily Dickinson's poems states, "*Because I could not stop for Death* / He kindly stopped for me."

Appositives

Appositives are nouns (or noun phrases or noun clauses) that rename or further identify an immediately preceding noun or pronoun in the sentence. They are sometimes set off by commas. Often you can combine two or more sentences into one by creating appositives. For example:

> My Uncle Benjamin is a driller in the oil field.
>
> He is my favorite uncle.

Combined with an appositive construction, these two sentences might become this:

> Uncle Benjamin, *my favorite uncle,* is an oil-field driller.

Or, depending on what emphasis is wanted, they might become this:

> Uncle Benjamin, *an oil-field driller,* is my favorite uncle.

If the appositive is essential for clear identification, it is not set off with commas:

The novelist *Louise Erdrich* writes of the lives of Native Americans.

Exercise

Combine the following pairs of sentences by creating appositives.

1. Dillard Inglehoff ran the fastest race of the day. Dillard Inglehoff is my first cousin.
2. Ronald W. Reagan was elected president in 1980 and again in 1984. He was the first president to be reelected and serve two full terms since Dwight D. Eisenhower.
3. Jon Bon Jovi enjoyed great popularity as a musician in the late 1980s. He was from New Jersey.

Present and Past Participles

You saw above that present and past participles are single-word adjectives formed from verbs. When expanded into phrases they can be combined with dependent and independent clauses to make effective and interesting sentences. Remember, present participles end in *-ing,* and past participles usually end in *-ed, d, t,* and occasionally *-en.*

Following are examples of each kind of participial phrase combined with clauses for various effects.

Present Participial Phrases

Smiling and speaking, Dan Taylor promised reforms in the company's payroll policy.

Figuring her taxes alone, Dawn insisted she didn't need help from a CPA.

Dallas Turner came into the room, *singing the praises of his CPA* and *rejoicing about getting a refund.*

Frowning at Dallas, Dawn complained because she was not getting a refund.

Past Participial Phrases

The tree bore a message *carved by persons unknown.*

The bat splintered, *broken by the force of the swing,* but the ball fluttered down in fair territory.

Theirs were Broadway dreams *bought and sold by talent scouts.*

He disappeared, *swallowed by the city,* a man *bruised in the business of living*

Exercises

A. Compose three sentences using present participial phrases.
B. Compose three sentences using past participial phrases.

Absolutes

Absolutes are phrases that include a noun followed by an adjective or participle. They can add richness of detail and sentence sophistication. Consider this example:

> In F. Scott Fitzgerald's short story "The Rich Boy," the protagonist, Anson Hunter, finds himself alone in the city, *his arrogance chastened by his own isolation.*

In the above sentence, *arrogance* is the noun in the absolute construction, and it is modified by the past participial phrase *chastened by his own isolation.*
Similarly:

> Once a great and enduring heavyweight boxing champion, Joe Louis suddenly found himself poor, *his problems mounting steadily, his friends disappearing daily.*

In the above example, two absolutes conclude the sentence: in the first, the noun *problems* is modified by the present participial phrase *mounting steadily;* in the second, the noun *friends* is modified by *disappearing daily.* Here is another sentence featuring multiple absolute constructions:

> With a mighty roar, the Delta Tri-Star lifted off the runway, *its engines pulling it skyward in violation of all ordinary logic, its pilot performing a routine aviational miracle.*

Exercise

Compose three sentences, each of which uses at least one absolute construction.

Parallel Series

Combining items in repeated identical or similar structures can create a special and useful stylistic effect. Such combinations should always be in *parallel* structure; that is, each part should be in roughly the same grammatical form. Consider the following example of such combining:

> One problem of this club is that its members prefer parties over worthwhile projects.
>
> Another problem of this club is that its members argue over elections.
>
> Still another problem of this club is that its members fail to make high grades.

The above sentences can be effectively combined into one featuring a parallel series:

> Among the problems of this club are that its members fail to make high grades, that its members argue over elections, and that its members prefer parties over worthwhile projects.

Note that each major series item begins in parallel structure, with *that its members* followed by the predicate verb of the clause.

Single words, phrases, and clauses can all be fruitfully arranged into parallel series:

> Adolf Hitler was one of the most arrogant, deranged, deadly, and hated men in history. (parallel adjectives)
>
> Soaring high above the field, swooping low to investigate slight movement in the furrows, sailing off in a wide arc to return and repeat the procedure, the hungry hawk followed the farmer's plow. (parallel adjective phrases)
>
> Knowing that the notorious Bonnie Parker and Clyde Barrow always returned to the same general area, realizing that the likeliest way to catch them was to wait for such a return, and gambling that eventually someone close to them would betray them, Texas Ranger Captain Frank Hamer plotted the capture of the desperadoes. (parallel participles followed by parallel noun clauses)

Note that items in a series are usually punctuated with commas, with the comma before the last item (if it is preceded by *and*) being optional but recommended. (Placing a comma before the *and* ensures that the last item in the series will be seen as a *separate* item.)

Exercises

A. Compose a sentence in which you employ single-word items in a series.
B. Compose a sentence in which you employ parallel phrases in a series.
C. Compose a sentence in which you employ parallel clauses in a series.

Periodic Sentences

Periodic sentences make use of many of the above techniques (which, you may already have noticed, can overlap) in a fairly long but well-controlled sentence that makes its major point at the *end*; that is, its predicate verb and complete thought come near the period at the end (hence "periodic") rather than near the beginning of the sentence. Here is how a sequence of sentences (the first sentence being the most general) might be combined into one effective periodic sentence:

> The months right after the attack on Pearl Harbor were grim.
>
> The Japanese attacked the Philippines, and General MacArthur was

> ordered from there to Australia so that he could later lead a recovered U.S. effort in the Pacific.
>
> Remaining U.S. forces in the Philippines were eventually forced to surrender and suffer the infamous Bataan "Death March."

Here's the periodic combination, which also makes use of parallel structure:

> Because the Japanese attack on the Philippines forced General MacArthur's retreat to Australia in order to lead our counterattack, and because the remaining U.S. forces in the Philippines eventually had to surrender and suffer the Bataan "Death March," the months right after Pearl Harbor were grim.

The idea of a periodic sentence is to build drama, so that the ending carries significance. To accomplish the dramatic effect, it's important to ensure that length doesn't work against clarity: a sentence that is too long or too complicated defeats the purpose.

Exercise

Compose three periodic sentences.

Cumulative Sentences

Cumulative sentences are the exact opposite of periodic sentences; rather than build to a significant end, they begin with the main point and then add (or accumulate, hence "cumulative") detail that is useful, even elegant, but not really central to the sentence's core meaning. What drama there is comes first; the cumulative sentence doesn't build *toward* something:

> Texas Ranger Captain Frank Hamer and his deputies opened fire on Bonnie Parker and Clyde Barrow, their call for surrender ignored by the notorious couple who tried to escape while their car was raked by a fusillade of powerful bullets.
>
> The fortunes of war irrevocably turned against the Japanese when the United States surprised Japan with a military defeat at Guadalcanal and a naval defeat at the Coral Sea, both engagements coming against greater numbers and odds.
>
> The Japanese Zeroes took off from the aircraft carrier, slowly at first, dipping as they left the edge of the flight deck, then gathering speed and climbing, dim against the early sky over the peaceful waves.

Exercise

Combine the following sentences into first a cumulative and then a periodic sentence:

1. The city of New York has five boroughs, four of which are on islands.

2. Manhattan and Staten Island are both on individual islands.
3. Brooklyn and Queens are on Long Island.
4. Only the Bronx is not on an island.

WRITING ASSIGNMENT

Study the photo on page H-19. The picture is a "still life" that shows a *Farmer's Almanac*, printer's type, and tools. Each of these basic tools helps the user do a job by serving as either a resource (the almanac) or as the implement for creating the product (the type and tools). Now that you've worked through most of the chapters and assignments in this text, have you found that you've developed your own writing "tool collection"? What resources and equipment do you keep by your side as you write? Has your writing equipment changed as you've progressed through the chapters? If you could design an ideal writer's workroom, what would it look like? What tools and resources would it contain?

chapter 30 The Dirty Dozen: Twelve Common Manuscript Problem Areas That Writers Face

A Declaration by the Representatives of the UNITED STATES OF AMERICA, in General Congress assembled.

When in the course of human events it becomes necessary for one people to dissolve the political bands which have connected them with another, and to assume among the powers of the earth the separate and equal station to which the laws of nature & of nature's god entitle them, a decent respect to the opinions of mankind requires that they should declare the causes which impel them to the separation.

We hold these truths to be self-evident; that all men are created equal; that they are endowed by their creator with [inherent & inalienable] rights; that among these are life, liberty, & the pursuit of happiness; that to secure these rights, governments are instituted among men, deriving their just powers from the consent of the governed; that whenever any form of government becomes destructive of these ends, it is the right of the people to alter or to abolish it, & to institute new government, laying it's foundation on such principles & organising it's powers in such form, as to them shall seem most likely to effect their safety & happiness. prudence indeed will dictate that governments long established should not be changed for light & transient causes: and accordingly all experience hath shewn that mankind are more disposed to suffer while evils are sufferable, than to right themselves by abolishing the forms to which they are accustomed. but when a long train of abuses & usurpations [begun at a distinguished period &]pursuing invariably the same object, evinces a design to reduce them under absolute Despotism, it is their right, it is their duty, to throw off such government, & to provide new guards for their future security. such has been the patient sufferance of these colonies; & such is now the necessity which constrains them to [expunge] their former systems of government. the history of the present king of Great Britain is a history of [unremitting] injuries and usurpations, [among which, appears no solitary fact to contradict the uniform tenor of the rest, but all have] in direct object the establishment of an absolute tyranny over these states. to prove this, let facts be submitted to a candid world, [for the truth of which we pledge a faith yet unsullied by falsehood]

Fred Allen (1894–1956) was one of radio's most talented comic personalities. He wrote almost all his own original material and read it over the air in highly entertaining fashion. Still, he was not free from radio script editors, who often went over his writing and made several alterations. Once, when one of his manuscripts was returned to him with extensive revisions, he reportedly confronted his editors: "Where were you fellows when the page was blank?"

"Punctuation, to most people, is a set of arbitrary and silly rules you find in printers' style books, and in the back pages of school grammars. Few people realize that it is the most important single device for making things easier to read."

Rudolf Flesch

While it's true that many of the examples we use here came from our students' papers, we in no way want to imply criticism of our students themselves. The errors shown and discussed here *are* typical, and because they are genuine errors made by genuine students, we think they make our discussion more effective. We take this opportunity again to thank our many students over the years.

This chapter is intended to help you when you revise, edit, and proofread your own or someone else's writing. It is by no means a comprehensive guide, yet we are confident that the overwhelming majority of writers' manuscript problems fall within the twelve problem areas we are about to discuss.

One reason we feel so confident about how common these problem areas are is that we've seen these problems many, many times before, in our nearly fifty years' combined experience as writing teachers. In fact, most of the illustrations in this chapter came from our own students' papers.

Note: The issues treated in this chapter are nothing for you to worry about during *composing;* rather, they pertain to concerns you need to address during revising and especially during final editing.

Because this material is intended to be a guide rather than an item for extensive reading, we present the following skeletal outline of the territory ahead. Feel free to skip to any section that promises to be of help to you.

The Dirty Dozen: Twelve Problem Areas

1. *Sentence Forms (pp. H-56–H-59)*
   a. Fragments—intentional and not, effective and not
   b. Fused, or Run-together, sentences—vital internal punctuation needed
   c. Lack of Parallelism—component structures need to be made similar
2. *Sentence Logic (pp. H-59–H-64)*
   a. Faulty Predication—you can't really say that
   b. Garbles—the sentence clunks and clanks for some reason
   c. How's That Again?—what you're saying isn't clear, or probably isn't what you mean

   d. Overload—you tried to say too much for the reader to process in one sentence

3. *Agreement (pp. H-64–H-66)*
   a. Subject-Verb Agreement—sentence subject and predicate verb do not agree in numbr
   b. Pronoun-Reference Agreement—pronoun does not agree in person or number with its antecedent (the noun it stands for)

4. *Modifier Placement (pp. H-66–H-68)*
   a. Dangling Modifiers—the modifier at the beginning or end of the sentence isn't next to what it modifies, or has no word to modify, creating ambiguous or unclear meaning
   b. Misplaced Modifier—the modifier is not in the right place in the sentence (that is, is not placed as close as possible to the word it modifies), creating ambiguous or unclear meaning
   c. Squinting Modifiers—the modifier is placed between two sentence elements and could modify either one, creating ambiguous or unclear meaning

5. *Shifts (pp. H-68–H-70)*
   a. Verb Tense Shifts—unnecessary changes in the tense (time perspective) in which something is written
   b. Perspective Shifts—change in the point of view from which something is written

6. *Imprecise Diction (pp. H-70–H-77)*
   a. Incorrect Usage—wrong word for the situation; you've confused words that sound alike or are similar in some other way
   b. Inappropriate Word Choice—inappropriate word for the situation, because of connotation, colloquialism, or some similar consideration
   c. Unclear Pronoun Reference—it's not clear what noun the pronoun stands for
   d. Incorrect Pronoun Case—you've used the wrong case (nominative or objective) of the pronoun
   e. Incorrect Idiomatic Preposition—the preposition you've used does not fit the context you've given it; regular usage requires some other preposition

7. *Word and Thought Flab (pp. H-77–H-84)*
   a. Wordiness—you've used more words than you need to get the job done
   b. Redundancy—what you've written is repetitive: it says the same thing twice
   c. Jargon—specialized language particular to a specific group and therefore at least partly obscure to many readers

1. Sentence Forms

The most common problems in sentence form include these:

a. Fragments
b. Fused, or run-together, sentences
c. Lack of parallelism

1.a. Fragments

When a group of words does not have at least one subject, at least one predicate verb, and at least one complete thought, it is a fragment. Although almost every sentence you write should be a complete sentence, most writers, amateur or professional, occasionally write deliberate fragments for stylistic effect. A stylistic fragment catches the reader's eye and momentarily commands special attention, as in this example:

> You'd think that after twenty years my brother would give me some credit and allow me a little discretionary slack. *Wrong*

Note that in the above example—as is the case with most stylistic fragments—the *context* helps create the fragment's effectiveness. Above, the preceding sentence prepares the reader for the reversal the fragment expresses. In fact, a reader can usually tell whether a fragment is intentional by how well it blends with its context. As a writer, you need to remember to use fragments *sparingly;* otherwise, they won't achieve the special effect you seek.

Inexperienced writers occasionally produce fragments without being aware they have done so. Such fragments can create serious problems for readers and often indicate that the writer needs to work on developing a keener sense of sentences—being surer of what constitutes a sentence and of how to detect the subjects, predicate verbs, and complete thoughts that distinguish sentences from fragments. Consider these two examples:

> The smoke rising through the pines on a cold November morning near Ypsilanti, Michigan.
>
> Robert, who was always one of our leaders and who had the most outlandish schemes designed to get other people in trouble.

Both are vivid, and both *seem* to have subjects, predicate verbs, and complete thoughts. But the first has no predicate verb; *rising,* which *looks* like a verb, is actually an adjective modifying the noun (subject) *smoke. Rising* is the present participle form of the verb *to rise,* but without the rest of the necessary verb for predication—such as *was rising* or *is rising*—all we have is an adjective. And thus we have no complete thought expressed about the smoke, either. And the second example has a subject, *Robert,* but no accompanying predicate verb; it has two long adjective clauses modifying Robert (and as clauses they have subjects—*who*—and verbs—*was* and *had*), but no predicate verb completes the thought about Robert.

If the line between grammatical sentences and fragments blurs for you, we suggest you write "fragment intended" in the margin of your paper beside each fragment you *think* you have written. Thus your classmates in workshops or your teacher (or both) can tell you whether

it is indeed a fragment;

it *works well* as a stylistic fragment; or

We especially recommend that you require your students to identify their intentional fragments on their finished papers. The method enables you to respond with particular effectiveness if, as we have often experienced, it becomes obvious that the student writer is uncertain about whether the group of words is or is not a fragment.

it (alas) isn't a fragment (but then they can help you work further on recognizing fragments).

1.b. Fused, or Run-together, Sentences

Fused, or run-together, sentences occur when writers forget to place vital linking punctuation or conjunctions between two independent (main) clauses. Often, what's missing is a semicolon, as in this example:

> California has more people than any other state New York is second in population.

The fusion takes place after the word *state*, which is where the first independent clause ends. A semicolon would solve the problem:

> California has more people than any other state; New York is second in population.

Another remedy is to add a comma and the coordinating conjunction *and*:

> California has more people than any other state, and New York is second in population.

Yet another way to repair the fusion is to create two separate sentences:

> California has more people than any other state. New York is second in population.

The way you fix the problem matters much less than the fact that you recognize the fusion and realize that you should correct it with punctuation or wording.

Note: A comma alone would *not* repair the damage sufficiently; that would substitute a comma splice (see 8.a) for a fused sentence.

1.c. Lack of Parallelism

A frequent problem with sentence form occurs when writers do not present a series in the same grammatical, or parallel, form. Note this example:

> The twenty-minute wait will allow the barbecue coals to get hot, allow the lighter fluid to burn out, and gives you time to prepare the ice cream.

The first two verbs in the series are *will allow,* but the last verb is *gives*—a nonparallel change in tense and form. Compare:

> The twenty-minute wait will allow the barbecue coals to get hot, allow the lighter fluid to burn out, and allow you time to prepare the ice cream.

In the corrected version, all three verbs are *will allow,* and the sentence is much more pleasing to eye and ear. (That's right, we said "ear," too: one of the best ways to make sure your writing is working the way you want it to is to have someone

We think many teachers and students undervalue the strategy of *having someone else read your writing out loud.* When

else read aloud what you've written.) Note that parallelism requires repetition of *form*, not necessarily of words. Consider this sentence:

> I told my mother that I would *watch* out for Dad and *keeping* an eye on my sister.

The first verb, *watch*, is fine, but the second, *keeping*, isn't even a complete verb. The compound verbs aren't parallel. Compare:

> I told my mother that I would *watch* out for Dad and *keep* an eye on my sister.

another reader brings fresh eyes and attitude to a piece you may have been working on for days, something important happens: your first reader engages the text and tries to make sense of what he or she reads. This process quickly reveals problem or potential problem areas, because the reader will typically "stumble" where sentence or sense breaks down. Sometimes such a stumble is correctible without changing the text, but usually it signals an error of some sort, something that can be fixed fairly easily. The key is *hearing* your words as your reader tries to make sense of them.

Exercise

Which of the following are fragments, fused, or nonparallel sentences? How would you fix each one?

1. My favorite activities are reading early American history and fiction, examining early maps of the frontier, and to collect antiques.
2. James Fenimore Cooper's *Leatherstocking Tales* existing as a series of novels about the frontier.
3. Hawkeye is James Fenimore Cooper's most popular fictional character he and Chingachgook are familiar to most students of early American literature.
4. Hawkeye, who could shoot straighter than any previous American fictional hero.
5. In novels like *The Last of the Mohicans*, Cooper gave Hawkeye qualities that legend had given Daniel Boone: a keen sense of justice, an unerring ability to track, and he could appreciate Indian customs.

2. Sentence Logic

Errors in sentence logic cause readers problems in four ways:

a. Faulty predication
b. Garbles
c. How's that again?
d. Overload

Each of these four presents a logical problem for the reader—something just doesn't make sense.

2.a. *Faulty Predication*

Faulty predication occurs when there is a logical discrepancy in the complete thought that is created by the subject and predicate of a sentence. Consider this example:

> The new resort's primary activity is a swimming pool.

Here, though the subject (*activity*) and predicate verb (*is*) do not themselves present a problem, the predicate nominative, *pool,* does not logically rename the subject, *activity,* because swimming pools are not activities but facilities. The sentence as written is saying, illogically, that the resort's primary activity is a pool. The sentence must be recast to eliminate the illogicality:

> The new resort's primary activity is swimming.

Here, *swimming* is a perfectly logical predicate nominative to rename or identify the subject (*activity*). Now consider this sentence written by one of our students:

> The fact that our environment is threatened gained awareness in our nation.

The subject of the sentence is *fact.* The predicate verb is *gained.* The direct object is *awareness.* The writer says that a fact gained awareness—something facts simply cannot do. The student probably meant something more like this:

> The fact that our environment is threatened became known in our nation.

As you can see, faulty predication involves going beyond the logical boundaries of subject and predicate combinations. That's why we often say to our students who have written sentences with faulty predication, "You can't really say that."

2.b. Garbles

Garbles are sentences that seem simultaneously to have two or more different structures, resulting at worst in no clear communication and at best in mild confusion:

> I walked back to my apartment and tried all the keys in which Rachel had given me.

Garbles are one reason we always advise writers to have someone else read their paper back to them *out loud.* A garble will most likely cause the reader to stumble, and the sound itself won't seem right. Compare:

> I walked back to my apartment and tried all the keys Rachel had given me.

That "in which" in the original version seems to come from another pattern or structure, one that isn't needed here. Following is another garble created by "in which," with another preposition, *with,* tossed in:

> Of all the activities I do each day, the one in which I spend the most time with is band.

One of the prepositions must go:

> Of all the activities I do each day, the one in which I spend the most time is band.

or

> Of all the activities I do each day, the one I spend the most time with is band.

Neither of these versions is especially good, but either is better than the original. Our preference would be totally recasting the sentence:

> Of all my activities, band takes the most time.

Not all garbles involve prepositions:

> According to Sam Sava, executive director of the National Association of Elementary School Principals, he believes "to extend the school day to do more of the same ineffective teaching is a mistake."

That "Sam Sava, . . . he believes" creates an unnecessary doubling of the subject, as when someone says, "My brother, he doesn't . . . " Compare:

> According to Sam Sava, executive director of the National Association of Elementary School Principals, "to extend the school day to do more of the same ineffective teaching is a mistake."

Here, once the attribution to Sam Sava is made and Sava is identified, the quotation begins. The "doubling" isn't necessary; it just garbles the sentence.

Some garbles are the result of omissions—leaving out key words—and most omissions are the result of haste. All garbles seem to be caused by the writer's not carefully reading what he or she has written.

2.c *How's That Again?*

This sort of problem is closely related to both faulty predication and garbles. Sometimes a sentence will sound all right at first but then will not withstand thoughtful rereading. The effect such a sentence has on the thoughtful reader is "How's that again?" or "Do you really mean that?" In the following example of what we mean, a student is writing directions on how to find his house:

> You will pass through several red lights.

Sound OK? Well, do you normally drive through red lights? Or do you stop and wait for them to turn green, the way you should? Note, too, that the writer is not being literal; we drive through intersections, not traffic signals. What the student means is this:

> You will pass through several intersections that have traffic signals.

(And, presumably, wait for the signals to turn green if they happen to be showing red at the time!)

Such writing is the result of not thinking closely about what you say. Here is another example:

> A recent study reported an 8 percent decline in hospitalized injuries.

Injuries can cause a person to be hospitalized, but injuries themselves can't be hospitalized. Compare:

> A recent study reported an 8 percent decline in injuries requiring hospitalization of the victim.

Is it picky to insist that such writing be revised? Yes. But it is also necessary. Careless thinking is reflected in careless writing, and careless writing can be costly.

Not all "How's that again?" errors concern illogical wording. Consider this example:

> Although a number of programs are available for adults who want to learn to read, people unable to read are still being passed through our nation's public school systems.

That sentence *sounds* fine. Its *structure* is fine. Yet sounding right and being in a familiar structure are not all that's required for sentences to make sense. In fact, the *structure* of the above sentence leads a reader to expect that the *sense* or *meaning* of the part of the sentence after the comma will offer a counter of some sort to the part before the comma. But that expectation is never fulfilled. What follows the comma is perfectly grammatical but has no *logical* connection with what precedes the comma. In other words, the two parts of the sentence do not fit together in a discernible relationship that makes sense. So why are they combined in the first place? Compare:

> Although a number of programs are available for adults who want to learn to read, *few adults take advantage of such programs.*
>
> *or*
>
> *Although requirements and standards have risen,* people unable to read are still being passed through our nation's public school systems.

In these two revisions, the logical relationship between the first and second parts of the sentence is clear. The way the original sentence was written, there simply *is* no relationship; hence, a reader might well ask, "How's that again?"

Sometimes a writer will unintentionally produce a contradiction, as in this case:

> We scored two quick touchdowns, and each successful drive proved that our inevitable win would soon come. It never did.

The stylistic effect sought by the second, clipped sentence is more or less lost in the confusion—if the win was *inevitable,* how did they lose? Compare:

> We scored two quick touchdowns, and each successful drive seemed to assure us that victory would soon come. It never did.

The only remedy for such problems is to try to write exactly what you mean and to refuse to settle for anything less. Don't be fooled by sounds or structures that seem to be all right; many linguists have proved that some sounds or structures that sound all right alone can fail to carry meaning:

> Colorless green ideas sleep furiously.

Each of those words is a perfectly good word, and there is no problem with the structure of the sentence. But it carries no discernible meaning.

Here's another such sentence, in which only the italicized groups of letters are actual words:

> *The* iddle squoggs frazed dondly *in the* hibbish squidge.

2.d. *Overload*

Overload occurs when a writer tries to cram too much meaning and detail into a sentence for it to be read clearly and smoothly. Long sentences are often the mark of a mature and effective writer. But for a long sentence to work properly, a reader must be able to hold in his or her short-term memory everything that is going into the sentence while the reading occurs. If what the reader must hold in mind gets to be too much, meaning collapses and the sentence fails. Consider this example:

> It was a difficult time for all of us then, what with father losing his job at the plant through no fault of his own, as if all those years of loyal toil meant nothing, and mother's longtime illness worsening, thanks to that quack of a doctor she had prescribing what in fact was the worst possible medicine for her, something that she was allergic to and that was killing her a little more every time she followed the doctor's orders.

That sort of sentence makes a reader want to say, "Whoa, there!" Too much is attempted without keeping the reader in mind. When we read, we need guidance, which can be given in a number of ways, including *ending* sentences before they become too long. Compare:

> Things were difficult for us then, what with father's losing his job at the plant through no fault of his own—as if all those years of loyal work meant nothing—and mother's longtime illness worsening, thanks to that quack of a doctor she had. The doctor prescribed the worst possible medicine for her, something that she was allergic to, something that was killing her gradually as she followed the doctor's orders.

Making two sentences helps the reader without sacrificing the details or effects the writer seeks.

There is an art to writing long sentences. Skillful writers use repetitions (notice the repetition of *something that* in the example above), parallel structures, and similar devices to help readers follow or "track through" long sentences. Sinewy, mature sentences are not the product of stuffing sentences full of haphazard details; rather, they result from carefully controlling the presentation of ideas so that the reader is never lost, never inconvenienced. A good rule of thumb is to avoid sentences that you can't read aloud without stopping to get a breath. Another is to vary the length and complexity of your sentences so that no one type of sentence dominates. Good writing is very much like good talking—versatile, euphonic, engaging.

Exercise

Evaluate each of the following sentences. Decide whether the problem is faulty predication, garble, "How's that again?" or overload. How would you remedy the problem?

1. After sundown throughout the United States and Canada AM radio listeners can often tune in a powerful station broadcasting from the south (Mexican) side of the Rio Grande, a station that over the years has had many different call letters but has featured consistent programming that emphasizes long commercial messages for such extraordinary religious items as genuine pieces of the "actual" cross on which the Savior suffered, and autographed eight-by-ten glossy photos of the Savior (limited supply!); such remarkable medical breakthroughs as a miracle weight-loss pill that "never fails"; and such other amazing offers as a free brochure explaining how to make a million tax-free dollars in less than six (that's right, six) months.
2. With Germany's returning as a possible military power makes many Europeans uneasy.
3. With the growing number of scuba divers all over the world, the need for advances in technology and diver safety must also be improved.
4. I could care less about scuba diving.
5. What characteristics of the diamond make it so applicable to the jewelry industry?

3. Agreement

Agreement problems have to do with number, whether something is singular or plural. Two kinds of agreement errors are frequently made by writers:

a. Subject-verb agreement
b. Pronoun-reference agreement

3.a. *Subject-Verb Agreement*

Put most simply, when the subject of a sentence (or clause) is singular, the verb must also be singular, and when the subject is plural, the verb must also be plural.

Singular The duck flies.

Plural The ducks fly.

Writers rarely have trouble with this sort of agreement in brief sentences like those above, when subjects and verbs are side by side. But when words fall between the subjects and verbs, particularly prepositional phrases (which always end with nouns or pronouns that can be mistaken for subjects), things get trickier:

> Each of the committee members have voted.

This sentence contains an error in subject-verb agreement. The subject of the sentence is *each*, not *members*. *Members* is the object of the preposition *of*, and the object of a preposition can *never* be the subject of a sentence. *Each* is a singular form, meaning "each one." If you ignore the prepositional phrase, the confusion is likely to disappear:

> Each has voted.

The key to avoiding this kind of agreement error is to be proficient at recognizing subjects and predicate verbs, no matter how long or complex the sentence may be. Consider this example:

> Advances in scuba-diving technology and diving medicine is making the sport safer for current and future divers.

The subject above is *Advances;* the predicate verb is *is making*—and is therefore wrong. To agree, the verb must be *are making:*

> Advances in scuba-diving technology and diving medicine are making the sport safer for current and future divers.

Exercise

The following sentences all contain errors in subject-verb agreement. Repair them.

1. Many economists believes this downturn could have serious effects.
2. We must help our young people understand that the using and selling of drugs is not fashionable and "cool."
3. When we checked the baggage conveyer, we noticed that not one of our seven duffel bags were there.
4. Thousands of acres of U.S. farmland has been purchased by foreign investors.

3.b. Pronoun-Reference Agreement

Just as subject nouns and predicate verbs must agree in number, so too must pronouns agree in number with the nouns for which they substitute:

> Marla saved *her* money. (*her* is singular to agree with *Marla*)
>
> The girls saved *their* money. (*their* is plural to agree with *girls*)

Note that singular pronouns must also agree in gender:

> Robert drove *his* car.
>
> Jessica drove *her* car.

Now consider this example:

> When a person chooses their employment they must choose carefully.

The pronouns are *their* and *they;* the noun these refer to is *a person,* which is singular. Therefore, the pronouns do not agree and must be changed:

> When a person chooses his or her employment, he or she must choose carefully.

Because repeating *his or her* and *he or she* grows cumbersome, the simplest solution is to make the referent plural:

> When people choose their employment, they must choose carefully.

(See also section 12, Sexism.)

Exercise

In the following sentences, make sure that the pronouns all agree in number and gender:

1. If a drug dealer is given a stiff sentence, then they will think twice before they sell drugs.
2. You can strike up a conversation with the sushi cook; they are just like bartenders.
3. An abused child is often afraid to go for help on their own.
4. If a candidate is independent, he or she must rely on the voters to write their name on the election ballot.
5. Each of the boys misplaced their cap.

4. Modifier Placement

Modifiers, as we have seen in chapter 29, are words, phrases, or clauses that act as adjectives or adverbs. Adjectives modify nouns or pronouns; adverbs modify verbs, adjectives, or other adverbs. For modifiers to function properly and clearly, they should be placed as close as possible to what they modify. The major kinds of problems involving modifier placement are these:

a. Dangling modifiers
b. Misplaced modifiers
c. Squinting modifiers

4.a. *Dangling Modifiers*

A dangling modifier fails to refer clearly and logically to another word or phrase in the sentence. A dangling modifier is usually a phrase and usually comes at the beginning of the sentence. Because of its placement and its lack of something to modify, it creates an ambiguity—that is, it could mean something not intended by the writer. Consider:

> *After hanging in the closet for five years,* excellent shape was what I found.

Although it seems pretty clear that something else, maybe the *coat,* and not the speaker in the sentence was hanging in the closet, the *placement* of the participial phrase makes it appear that the phrase *After hanging in the closet for five years* modifies *I.* The way to correct the problem is to place the modifying phrase as close as possible to what it modifies; in this case, what the phrase modifies is *coat.* Compare:

> *After hanging in the closet for five years,* the *coat* was in excellent shape, I thought.

Sometimes dangling modifiers appear at the ends of sentences:

> The eyes must be kept on the ball *to be a good golfer.*

In this sentence, the infinitive phrase seems to modify *ball,* but, of course, the ball is not the golfer. Compare:

> *To be a good golfer, you* must keep your eyes on the ball.

4.b. *Misplaced Modifiers*

A misplaced modifier is not placed as close as possible to what it modifies, and thus an ambiguity is created. Consider:

> David baked cookies for his friends *with nuts in them.*

Here, the writer means that David's cookies (not his friends) have nuts in them. The solution, again, is to place the modifying phrase properly:

> David baked cookies *with nuts in them* for his friends.

As you can see, misplaced modifiers are quite similar to dangling modifiers.

4.c. *Squinting Modifiers*

A squinting modifier is a modifier placed between two sentence elements, either one of which it can modify:

> The chef said *on Tuesday* he will prepare lasagna.

In the above example, the phrase *on Tuesday* is placed where it creates ambiguity (at least two possible meanings): does the sentence mean that the chef made his statement on Tuesday, or does it mean that the chef will prepare lasagna on Tuesday? As the sentence is written, it is impossible to know for certain what the writer means. A choice and clarification must be made:

On Tuesday, the chef said he will prepare lasagna.

or

The chef said he will prepare lasagna *on Tuesday.*

The modifier must be moved so that it no longer "squints."

Sometimes a misplaced or squinting modifier can consist of one word. Notice how, for example, the placement of *only* affects the meaning of this sentence:

The boy *only* wanted to get the ballerina's autograph.

The boy wanted *only* to get the ballerina's autograph.

One possible meaning of the first sentence is that the boy—and no one else—wanted the ballerina's autograph; that is, of many people, only the boy wanted the autograph. The second sentence, however, means that the boy wanted nothing else but to get the ballerina's autograph. The writer's meaning, in such cases, determines which placement is correct; notice, however, that placement of *only* at the beginning of the first sentence makes that sentence's meaning clearer:

Only the boy wanted to get the ballerina's autograph.

Exercise

Determine whether the following sentences show a dangling, misplaced, or squinting modifier, and then repair the problem.

1. Since you only have two hands, try to bring just two bags.
2. Turning onto the Pacific Highway, the view opened up.
3. Mr. Green had an apple tree in his backyard with great red apples.
4. We only found a sign that said the market was closed.
5. Cracked from top to bottom, my friend threw away the mirror.

5. Shifts

Shifts create slight reader annoyance mainly because consistency—and therefore a degree of coherence—is lost. Coherence, a vital characteristic of good writing, holds meaning together and thus enhances both meaning and reading. The two major problem areas involving shifts are these:

a. Verb tense shifts

b. Perspective shifts

5.a. Verb Tense Shifts

Everything you write should be consistent in verb tense—that is, if you are writing in the present tense, or time, you should generally remain in that tense; if you are writing in the past tense, you should generally remain in that tense.

Present Luke Skywalker *is* the hero of the *Star Wars* trilogy of films. Luke *is* brave, strong, and resourceful as he *combats* the evil forces of the Empire.

Past Abraham Lincoln *was* the first president of the United States to be assassinated. He *led* the North during the Civil War and *died* on April 14, 1865, a few days after that war's end.

Some *apparent* shifts are occasionally necessary to make meaning or distinction clear, but these should not be confused with actual shifts in verb tense. Consider, for example:

> Earline *began* [past] to play the piano because she *enjoys* [present] music. She *progressed* [past] rapidly.

Though the key events in these sentences are in the past, Earline's enjoyment of music is ongoing; she enjoyed music *before* she began the piano, and she *still* enjoys it. Thus, *enjoys* is not really a verb tense shift; rather, it is the correct verb form to express the intended meaning. Note that such changes in verb tense should always be *logical.*

Now consider this sentence:

> The time had come to say good-bye, but with good-bye a strong suffering tugs at me for us to be together again.

It's a bit confusing, isn't it? The reason for the confusion is that the verb tense changes from past perfect (*had come*) to present (*tugs*). Compare:

> The time had come to say good-bye, but with good-bye a strong suffering tugged at me for us to be together again.

Now both verbs are in past-tense forms—past perfect and simple past. There are three different general tenses—present, past, and future—and variations *within* each of those general tenses to make particular distinctions (past perfect, present progressive, future perfect, and so on). What is important is keeping the *prevailing* general tense consistent.

5.b. Perspective Shifts

Perspective shifts involve not a switch in time focus but a shift in the viewpoint expressed in a sentence. Such shifts can be in voice, person, or number:

Voice Shift After *we* finished cooking the dinner, it was eaten *by us.*

The shift is from active to passive voice and should be corrected this way:

After *we* finished cooking the dinner, *we* ate it.

Person Shift *One* can improve in guitar playing if *you* practice.

The shift is from an unspecific third-person reference, *one*, to a specific second-person reference, *you*. It should be corrected this way:

You can improve in guitar playing if *you* practice.

or

One can improve in guitar playing if *one* practices.

Number Shift *Teachers* are paid considerably less than administrators, even though *a teacher* has primary responsibility for the students' learning.

The shift is in number, from the plural *teachers* to the singular *a teacher*. It can be corrected by making both either singular or plural. For example:

Teachers are paid considerably less than administrators, even though *teachers* have primary responsibility for the students' learning.

Exercise

Determine whether the shifts in the following sentences are in tense (time) or perspective (voice, person, or number), and make corrections as needed.

1. When a person manages a restaurant, you face many challenging situations.
2. The local television news covers national events, but it did not do so in depth.
3. Sometimes local news has no film to use with a national story. A good example was the Berlin Wall story.
4. I think that liver is good, but it is disliked by my children.
5. We stood on the levee, and you could see floodwaters well into the distance.

6. Imprecise Diction

Diction, broadly speaking, means "choice of words." Effective writing always involves choosing words that are appropriate for (a) the meaning the writer intends and (b) the readership the writer has in mind. Imprecision can create vagueness, confusion, misunderstandings—even, in some cases, hard feelings. Among types of imprecise diction that we discuss here are these:

a. Incorrect usage
b. Inappropriate word choice
c. Unclear pronoun reference
d. Incorrect pronoun case
e. Incorrect idiomatic prepositions

6.a. Incorrect Usage

English contains many words that sound alike or are otherwise very similar. Often writers are confused about these words, using one when they mean the other. Here are a few examples, taken from our students' writing, with the incorrect usage italicized and the correct usage bracketed:

> It was all *to* [too] easy to be careless.
> He saw the *flair* [flare] in the night sky.
> Now be *quite* [quiet] and listen to me.
> The nurse began to give the victim first *aide* [aid].

Following is a representative list of words that are similar in sound and/or appearance and are therefore often confused. The list is compiled from student papers at our two schools, but a similar list could be compiled from student papers anywhere. Study the words on this list. Where it is necessary, check their definitions in a dictionary.

accept / except
addition / edition
advice / advise
affect / effect
aid / aide
allude / elude
allusion / illusion
altar / alter
bare / bear
break / brake
breaks / brakes
canvas / canvass
compliment / complement
conscious / conscience
council / counsel
course / coarse
desert / dessert
device / devise
discrete / discreet
eluded / alluded
equivalence / equivalents
excess / access
fair / fare
faze / phase
flare / flair
formerly / formally
hear / here
imminent / eminent
its / it's
loose / lose
patients / patience
perspective / prospective
precede / proceed
principle / principal
rain / reign / rein
respectively / respectfully
role / roll
seam / seem
sight / site / cite
stationary / stationery
then / than
they're / their / there
to / too / two
vary / very
weather / whether
who's / whose

Exercise

Provide the right word for the blank in the following sentences:

1. The miner said he had found a very rich coal ________ . (seem, seam)
2. A thermometer is a ________ for measuring temperature. (device, devise)
3. That necktie will ________ your jacket. (compliment, complement)
4. What ________ will the new policy have on prices? (affect, effect)
5. What is the ________ of the new records building? (cite, site, sight)
6. The bad news didn't ________ Eric. (faze, phase)
7. I think you should obtain legal ________ . (counsel, council)
8. I cannot ________ this gift. (accept, except)
9. Jarrod is the ________ stockholder in the company. (principle, principal)
10. We had pie for ________ . (dessert, desert)

Some Cautions. Some words that are pronounced the same have different meanings signaled by different forms. For example:

any way / anyway

The first is always two words, and *any* modifies *way:*

Is there *any way* we can still win the election?

The second is always one word and is an adverb or interjection:

Anyway, we did the best we could.

We didn't want to win, *anyway.*

You should be sensitive to differences in the following similar pairs:

every day / everyday	He went fishing *every day.* He wore his *everyday* clothes.
may be / maybe	We don't know who the boss *may be.* *Maybe* I will, and *maybe* I won't.
home town / hometown	Although I was born in Batesville, Tyler is my *home town.* The fighter was a *hometown* favorite.

6.b. Inappropriate Word Choice

Words may be inappropriate for a number of reasons—they may have the wrong connotations, for example. As you learned earlier in this book, connotations are the nondictionary, *associated* meanings that can cluster around a given word or expression. Connotations can be positive, negative, or neutral. Consider the connotational differences among these three words, which all mean approximately the same thing:

slender = positive

thin = neutral

skinny = negative

If writers wish to be complimentary, they shouldn't describe a person as *skinny*. *Slender* sounds desirable; *skinny* sounds unhealthy.

Some words are inappropriate because they are too colloquial (informal) for the general tone and purpose of the writing. If formality is the goal, then usually contractions and the first-person point of view are inappropriate, as is slang. Some words aren't words at all but are instead coinages that won't be found in dictionaries. Other words, though they appear in dictionaries, are inappropriate because their denotations (dictionary definitions) will not permit their being used in that particular way.

Consider the following examples:

Her fatigue and weakness caused *collapsion*. (This is a coinage, as far as we can tell.)

I held her until her crying *abased*. (This is a misuse of *abased*. Probably the writer means *abated*.)

The pamphlet gives *suggestive* information for people preparing their own taxes. (The connotations of *suggestive* make it inappropriate here; *suggestive* is an adjective usually used negatively to describe material of a sexual or otherwise-objectionable nature. A clarifying improvement might be this: The pamphlet gives helpful suggestions for people who are preparing their own taxes.)

Using books and other materials *attained* through the university's library, I will produce my report. (The denotation of *attain* won't permit its use here—goals are *attained*; books are *obtained*.)

It so happens that *neither* of the three girls was selected. (*Neither* can be used only to distinguish between two items or choices. *None* or *not one* must be used.)

Racism has been a recurring nightmare for this country from the *get-go*. (Here, the serious and formal level of diction makes the slang expression for "beginning," *get-go*, inappropriate. *Beginning* is consistent with the diction level and tone.)

Another type of poor word choice has to do with trying to be polite, or hoping to avoid hurting someone's feelings. For example, we often employ *euphemisms* (words intended to make things seem better than they are) not only to "dress up" plain situations but also to "soften" the hard realities that other words might make sting. Thus we might say a loved one has "passed away" rather than "died." Though the motive for such usage may be honorable, we must still be careful, for ill-chosen words can sometimes wind up being worse than the frankest words. A humorous illustration used on television a few years ago will help make our point. Trying to think of something complimentary to say to her new acquaintance, a young girl says, "You're very graceful for a fat boy."

Exercise

In the following sentences, some words are inappropriate for one reason or other. Which words are they? How would you revise the word choices?

1. I put the money in the cash registrar.
2. This microphone is very sensual.
3. These statistics infer that our national debt is getting larger.
4. It was Ormsby's studied opinion that Leffingwell was a dweeb.
5. Eating peas with a knife ain't easy.

6.c. *Unclear Pronoun Reference*

As we have noted before, it is essential to use pronouns in a way that makes clear just which nouns they substitute (or "stand") for. Consider, for example, this sentence:

> Debrah asked Karen if *she* could drive.

To whom does the pronoun *she* refer, Debrah or Karen? It's impossible to tell; Debrah may be asking if she, Debrah, can drive, or she may be asking Karen to drive. Such imprecision, as you can readily see, creates confusion. The sentence must be recast, depending on the writer's meaning:

> Debrah asked Karen to drive.
>
> *or*
>
> Debrah asked Karen for permission to drive.

Exercise

Repair the problems caused by unclear pronouns in the following sentences.

1. When he was eighteen years old, Dan's father took him to see a Broadway musical.
2. The interns told the nurses that they would give medicine to the patients.
3. The machinists told the suppliers that their union would be going on strike.
4. Dorothy gave Dianne her keys.
5. When Stan gave James the order, he did not have the requisition slip.

6. The Phillies lost, and then the Padres lost and the Dodgers won. This excited the Pirates.

6.d. *Incorrect Pronoun Case*

As we discussed in chapter 29, pronouns have *case;* that is, they take different forms for different functions. Though pronoun case is usually classified as a matter of grammar, we are discussing it here as a diction problem because it involves choosing the right word, or pronoun, for the particular situation. The *possessive* case gives writers few problems; the forms are distinctive and clearly indicate possession: *my, our, your, his, her, their,* and so forth. Writers have more trouble distinguishing between the *objective* case, called for when the pronoun appears as a direct or indirect object (the object of a preposition, infinitive, or similar construction), and the *nominative* case, called for when the pronoun appears as a subject or predicate nominative. Consider:

> "It's him," the witness said, pointing at the defendant.

Him is the objective case and therefore inappropriate in the above example. *It* is the subject of the sentence, and *is* is the verb, linking *It* to the predicate nominative, which should be *he.*

The way to be certain you have used the correct pronoun case is to decide whether your pronoun appears in an objective or nominative situation. Consider:

> To *whom* do you wish to speak? (object of preposition)
>
> I gave *him* the report. (indirect object)
>
> Karen Feldkamp is the employee *who* won the raffle. (subject of dependent clause)
>
> To tell *her* the truth was Atkins's plan. (indirect object of infinitive)
>
> "May I speak to Elaine Griffin, please?" "This is *she.*" (predicate nominative)

Exercise

Provide the appropriate case for the pronouns used below.

1. It is me with who you must contend.
2. Him and her spent plenty of money on that old car.
3. Us boys have an idea.
4. Between you and I, I don't think Stanley is making a serious effort.
5. Edgar Allan Poe is the poet whom wrote "The Raven."

6.e. *Incorrect Idiomatic Prepositions*

Idioms are words or phrases that are completely governed by usage; they do not necessarily mean what they literally say. Anyone who has studied a foreign language has had to learn that language's idioms—words or phrases for which there is no logical translation. You just have to "know," or memorize, idiomatic usage.

Actually, the concept of "idiom" or "idiomatic" is much broader than we will concern ourselves with here. For example, anyone learning American English might need to learn such metaphoric idioms as "bite the bullet" (make a hard decision and accept the results) or "bought the farm" (died). One learning French might need to learn *c'est la guerre* (that's the way war—or anything else—is). Such idioms, once learned, pose few problems. But one idiomatic area does cause problems for both native and nonnative speakers and writers of English: prepositions. Only certain prepositions will "fit" in certain prepositional situations. And there's no rule—you simply have to know which prepositions will work in those slots. For example, some students write:

> Algebra is different *than* calculus.

Than is not idiomatic in that position. What is called for is *from*. Now consider these:

> Proceed according *with* the plan. (*With* is unidiomatic; *to* is needed.)
>
> I am so bored *of* television. (*Of* must be *by*.)
>
> Comply *to* the rules. (*To* must be *with*.)

Here's a list of typical idiomatic prepositional uses:

accuse *of* murder	disappointed *in* life
happened *by* chance	inferior *to* the other brand
capable *of* anything	apply *for* a position
adhere *to* the rules	infer *from* the speech
acquaint *with* the system	approve *of* the decision

There are many, many more. And some vary, depending on what the object of the preposition is, for example:

> Alcoa is *convenient to* Knoxville. (that is, nearby, easy to travel to)
>
> The lake is *convenient for* swimming. (that is, for the purpose of swimming)
>
> Larrabee and I *disagree on* that issue. (that is, about that particular matter)
>
> I *disagree with* Larrabee. (that is, with that particular person)

A dictionary is the only sure way to check the proper idiomatic usage of a preposition.

Exercise

The following sentences contain unidiomatic prepositions. Correct them.

1. The author intends to criticize the American public from always consulting "experts."

2. A misconception of organ donation is that the donor cannot change his or her mind.
3. As in most college campuses, parking is a problem.
4. An avid listener of heavy-metal music, I admire Led Zeppelin.
5. Warren would not comply by the regulations.

7. Word and Thought Flab

By "flab" here, we mean *excess*—too many words; lazy or imprecise, uneconomical thought; any writing that can and should be reduced to fewer words and sharper reflected thought. Writers create word and thought flab, even when they are trying not to, and no writer ever completely avoids such problems. We certainly don't, as our editors and friends who've read this manuscript assure us. The best we can say about this problem area is that it is persistent and plagues even the ablest of writers. There is always room for improvement, and in that spirit we highlight the following ways word and thought flab creep into writing:

a. Wordiness
b. Redundancy
c. Jargon
d. Polysyllabism
e. Overworked passive
f. Clichés

7.a. Wordiness

Put simply, wordiness is using more words than necessary to make a point. Granted, sometimes style, or what might be called the personality of the writer, demands more words than *could* be used, but such decorative prose should be handled carefully, lest the package be more impressive than the gift. Many young writers, attempting to impress their teachers with either vocabulary or the *pose* of intelligence, often wrap their ideas too gaudily. Here's an example:

> Memory of my grandfather is something that I will treasure for as long as I live.

Now, the idea above is perfectly clear. But the prepositional phrases and the adjective and adverb clauses clutter the sentence with unnecessary nouns and modifiers. Compare:

> I will treasure memory of my grandfather all my life.

In the revision, ten words take the place of sixteen, with no loss of meaning. Moreover, an active verb (*will treasure*) has replaced a linking, state-of-being verb (*is*), giving the sentence more vigor.

Now consider:

> Tuberous begonias are a good example of a plant that will complement any landscape.

Again, a state-of-being verb (*are*) clutters the sentence with an unnecessary noun, in this case *example*, which is truly empty of meaning. After all, a begonia isn't an *example* of a plant—it *is* a plant! The problem with unnecessary state-of-being verbs is that they invariably set up a noun or adjective formation in the predicate (a predicate nominative or predicate adjective), resulting in the use of more words than might be necessary. Compare:

> Tuberous begonias will complement any landscape.

Six words now say the same thing as fourteen words did previously. Notice that often such relative pronouns as *that* and *which* can be dropped at no cost to meaning.

Don't misunderstand us here. Some state-of-being verbs are essential; *to be* is a vitally important verb. But if such verbs can be avoided, they probably should be.

Using unnecessary *to be* verbs isn't the only way unneeded words can creep into your sentences. Consider, for instance, prepositional phrases, which always require nouns or pronouns as objects. Sometimes needless use of such phrases can be remedied by, say, making something possessive or choosing another form:

Wordy Version	The shrill whistle *of the police officer* told us that she was *in hot pursuit of the thief.*
Shortened Version	The police officer's shrill whistle told us she was hotly pursuing the thief.

The original sentence has three prepositional phrases; the revision, none. Eighteen words become thirteen, at no cost to meaning or effectiveness.

Wordiness is a pervasive problem, and we could supply endless examples. The best way to avoid it is to inspect each of your sentences and ask yourself, "Can I make this shorter without sacrificing meaning or effectiveness?" You'll be surprised how often the answer is yes.

Exercise

Each of the following sentences is wordy in some way. Shorten each without sacrificing meaning or effectiveness. (In most cases, your revision will be more effective.)

1. The complexity of the defense problem faced by the British in the year 1940 was enormous.
2. The German air force was a prime example of an efficient machine of war, and it was an air force that was confident that it could bomb Britain into rapid submission.

3. Few doubted that the German soldiers who sang "We are going to England" after the fall of France were, in fact, going to do just that.
4. It is now one of history's brightest moments that the gallant British were able to manage somehow to resist the incessant pounding that the German air force gave them.
5. The miracle of the Battle of Britain is that the leaders of the German army lost confidence that they could make an amphibious invasion of England.

7.b. Redundancy

Redundancy is a special kind of repetition in which different words are used but the meaning is repeated, as in this example:

> Many who were exposed to the severe radiation were *doomed to die.*

If one is *doomed,* death is already certain; thus, there is no need to add *to die.* Likewise:

> The mayor *overexaggerates* the seriousness of the problem.

Exaggerate already means the problem's seriousness has been magnified beyond its actual significance. One cannot *over*exaggerate, for exaggeration *means* overstatement.

Some kinds of redundancy make needlessly explicit that which is already implicit, usually by adding a prepositional phrase:

> The new bus is *blue in color.*

Blue is already known to be a color; to add *in color* is pointless. Likewise:

> Lena is a woman who is *small in size.*
>
> Darryl is twenty-five *years of age.*
>
> From Dallas to Austin is *a distance of* two hundred miles.
>
> Most coins are *round in shape.*

Redundancy is a bad habit to fall into, for it adds nothing to meaning.

Exercise

Repair the redundancy in the following sentences.

1. The sunset turned a glorious orange color.
2. That period of time will always be remembered.
3. "What goes up must come down" is a well-known cliché.
4. Derek ordered pie à la mode with ice cream.
5. It was 3:00 A.M. in the morning.
6. Those are the true facts.

7.c Jargon

Jargon means talk or writing that is nonsensical or meaningless to the listener or reader. Often it is language that is understood only within a special group, and it is technically oriented. Usually jargon has the effect of *excluding* readers who are not members of the special group. Many professionals make liberal use of jargon in writing and speaking to other professionals. The problem is that unless both reader and writer know the jargon, communication can break down.

People who use and enjoy computers, for example, have developed ways of writing and talking about computers that are hard for anyone else to understand. "Initialize the disk," for example, means to prepare ("format") a disk (which might be "hard" or "floppy") for use. "Upward compatible" means that the computer program can be transferred to a more powerful machine; "downward compatible" means the opposite. Sometimes jargon can spill into more general usage. "Interface," for example, in the world of computers means that two different computers can be programmed to work together. Now "interface" is sometimes used to describe a first meeting of two people—whether or not they have anything to do with computers. "User friendly," a phrase first used to describe easy-to-operate computers, is now often used to describe any new equipment that must be operated by people.

Virtually any profession you can name will have its own jargon. What's important to remember is that jargon can be easily misunderstood and should never be used deliberately to obscure facts or impress inexpert people. Unfortunately, some writers resort to jargon to exaggerate their own importance or in some other way deceive readers.

Much jargon is created by adding certain prefixes and suffixes to words, or "pumping up" common, everyday language into lengthy phrases. The result can be such writing as this (translations given in parentheses):

> Plant-operationswise, we are experiencing optimum success factors. (Plant operations are highly successful.)
>
> The young scholars take on their nourishment at the institution's student nutrition center. (The students eat at the school cafeteria.)
>
> It is imperative that we prioritize upward employee-employer interfacing. (We need more office parties.)

Some jargon borrows liberally from the world of sports to make comparisons:

> As computer programmers go, Jack's *a good utility infielder,* but he isn't *a franchise;* he can't *hit the long ball.*

Here, the borrowing is from baseball: a "good utility infielder" is a reasonably good player who can help the team but is far from "franchise," or superstar, status because he can't hit home runs. Jack, in other words, is a good programmer but not a great one.

Exercise

Write everyday translations for the following jargon-riddled sentences.

1. We must maximize the utilization of our hands-on personnel.
2. The maintenance services union insists that its membership responsibilities do not include the washing of windows.
3. After assessing our position vis-à-vis capital outlay and intracompany developmental funding, we determined that it would not be advantageous to declare a dividend now.
4. Dismuke is a driveway sales representative at the Oilco petroleum products dispensary at Eleventh Street and Woodlawn Avenue.
5. When you're in doubt about an option for your company, take the ball to the hoop; a field goal always helps the team.

The jargon is so thick in this exercise that several versions of each could be improvements. Here are our suggestions, but we don't pretend they're the best possible:

1. We need to use our laborers as much as possible.
2. Their union forbids custodians to wash windows.
3. Study of our finances indicates we can't pay stockholders anything now.
4. Dismuke pumps gas at the Oilco station at Eleventh and Woodlawn.
5. Positive action will help your company.

7.d. *Polysyllabism*

Polysyllabism is our coinage (so far as we know) for a kind of word and thought flab that shows a fascination with long, multisyllable words and phrases and a preference for these over shorter, more mundane equivalents. Polysyllabism prefers the word or term on the left:

analyzation—instead of *analysis*
at all times—instead of *always*
at the present time—instead of *now*
at this point in time—instead of *now*
finalize—instead of *finish*
for the purpose of—instead of *for*
in view of the fact that—instead of *because*
in view of the foregoing—instead of *therefore*
occupation—instead of *job*
orientated—instead of *oriented*
pursuant to—instead of *about* or *regarding*
utilize—instead of *use*
visitation—instead of *visit*

And so on. Polysyllabism can be combated by simply asking yourself, "Is this the shortest, clearest word or group of words that will carry my meaning?"

Exercise

Reduce the instances of polysyllabism in the following sentences.

1. In the event that it snows, please dismiss the students.
2. In view of the fact that he had erred in judgment, Middleton terminated his relationship with the company.
3. I prefer not to comment at this point in time.

4. I was struggling in my initial year of higher education because of my disinclination to facilitate fruitful interface of my academic and leisure activities.
5. Please be advised that in the matter of overtime this company will not reflect a flexible posture.

7.e. Overworked Passive

The *active voice* refers to what we have previously called "action" verbs in sentences:

> Paul *drove* his car to work each day.

The active voice provides vigor in sentences and hence is usually preferable to its opposite, called the *passive voice.* In the active voice, the emphasis is on the subject, or actor or agent; in the above sentence, that's Paul. In the passive voice, the emphasis is on the direct object—that which is acted on; in the above sentence, that's Paul's car. Here's the same sentence in the passive voice:

> Paul's car *was driven* by him to work each day.

As you can see, the passive voice calls for more words because it substitutes a "helping" state-of-being verb and a past participle for an action verb, and it often creates a rather clumsily structured sentence. (Moreover, in the above example, we can't be sure that *him* refers to Paul.)

This is not to say that the active voice is *always* preferable to the passive voice; it isn't. But the passive voice can sometimes obscure who or what bears responsibility for an action or decision. In fact, some writers deliberately use the passive voice for just that purpose, to avoid acknowledging responsibility:

> It *was decided* that there would be no free lunch.

The above sentence does not identify who is responsible for the decision. Key to your writing is determining whether the passive voice can profitably be avoided. That is, will the active voice say the same thing, save words, and provide more vivid, forceful language? If so, then prefer the active voice and don't overwork the passive—save the passive voice for the times you really need it.

Exercise

Change the following passive-voice sentences to active-voice ones.

1. The strike was prevented by Mohammad's quick thinking.
2. A trainee vacancy was caused by a resignation.
3. It was determined that the new trainee would be chosen from within the company.
4. Mohammad was suggested for the traineeship by the assistant manager.
5. Mohammad was chosen by the manager to be the new trainee.

7.f. Clichés

Clichés are expressions that were once evocative of a powerful or memorable idea but, because they have been overused, are no longer effective. Clichés are figurative language that no longer seems imaginative, for we hear or see it so often that it no longer prompts the bright mental picture it once did. Still, clichés can be somewhat tricky, for what is a cliché to one person might still be a fairly fresh idea to another.

The point for writers is that lapsing into clichés is lapsing into lazy thought; if you plug in a cliché, you don't have to trouble yourself to think up a new, fresh, vivid way to say something. It's easier—and lazier—to say, for example, "I was as busy as a bee yesterday" than it is to say, "I was as busy as popcorn in a microwave oven yesterday."

Although there's no foolproof way to determine whether an expression is a cliché, there is a reasonably reliable test: if you can begin an expression and a friend can complete it for you, it's probably a cliché. Many people would come up with the same completion for the following expressions; see what you and your classmates come up with:

Pretty as a ____________

Sly as a ____________

Straight as an ____________

Truth is stranger than ____________

When all's said and ____________

Clichés are a dime a ____________

Cosgrove has a lot on the ____________

Don't make a mountain out of a ____________

We keep reinventing the ____________

I heard it through the ____________

In one fell ____________

A good time was had by ____________

How many did you and your classmates agree on? Here are some clichés frequently listed in handbooks. How many have you heard before?

Straighten up and fly right

Ladder of success

Put your nose to the grindstone

Hard as a rock

Hit the nail on the head

Strong as an ox

Needle in a haystack

Gentle as a lamb

Beyond the shadow of a doubt

Just as clichés reflect lazy thought, so too does a related problem, mixed metaphor, reflect careless imagery. (Remember that a metaphor is an implied comparison: "His face was an open book," for example, is a cliché that is also a metaphor.) Consider the logic of combining the metaphors in this sentence:

> The inspiration came in a sudden flash, burying him under a blanket of delight.

Whatever elegance the wording achieves is lost because of the illogic of combining a "sudden flash" (like lightning) with burials and blankets. A mixed metaphor reveals poor thinking, and poor thinking seldom results in good writing.

Exercise

A. Rewrite the following clichés to achieve the same idea expressed in a new, fresh way.

1. Mary Cobb is a track star who runs faster than greased lightning.
2. Dillingworth is a dyed-in-the-wool Republican.
3. Stacy Anne Livingston has climbed the ladder of success.
4. Caught in the act, Zoffke had no choice but to face the music.
5. Maynard resorted to his tried-and-true chili recipe.

B. Sort out the mixed metaphors in the following, and rewrite to create logically consistent metaphors.

1. Third World debt is the snake in the grass that is gnawing the foundations of world peace.
2. Hamlet didn't know whether to take arms against a sea of troubles or just skip it.

8. Punctuation Confusion

Punctuation is a system of visual symbols devised to aid readers. More often than we realize, punctuation helps us to read and understand writing. And most marks of punctuation cause no confusion; periods, for example, clearly mark the ends of declarative sentences, like this one. Question marks unmistakably notify us that a question is being asked—hasn't that always been true? And exclamation points! Their signal lets us know a certain amount of excitement is in order. In fact, all written English sentences end in one of those three marks: a period, a question mark, or an exclamation point.

Unfortunately, other marks of punctuation, marks whose work is more complicated, can cause confusion. Among these are commas—used in myriad situations—semicolons, colons, apostrophes, dashes, and hyphens. We'll concentrate our discussion in this section in five areas:

a. Comma splices

b. Restrictive and nonrestrictive material

c. Semicolons and colons
d. Apostrophes
e. Dashes and hyphens

8.a. Comma Splices

The comma splice is probably the most serious—and seriously overrated—comma error. Many teachers and editors consider the comma splice an error of major proportions, even though it ordinarily creates no significant confusion on the part of the reader. It consists of joining two independent clauses with a comma only, and no conjunction:

> The Lakers are always very competitive, they have consistently been one of the best teams in the National Basketball Association.

The above sentence contains a comma splice. It can be repaired in one of three ways, depending on the writer's choice:

- By making two separate sentences:
  The Lakers are always very competitive. They have consistently been one of the best teams in the National Basketball Association.
- By joining the clauses with a comma and an appropriate coordinating conjunction:
  The Lakers are always very competitive, and they have consistently been one of the best teams in the National Basketball Association.
- By joining the clauses with a semicolon:
  The Lakers are always very competitive; they have consistently been one of the best teams in the National Basketball Association.

Some teachers and editors are tolerant of a comma splice when it joins brief independent clauses that occur in a series:

> I came, I saw, I conquered.

When such conjunctions as *however, moreover, therefore, rather,* and *in fact* are used to connect independent clauses, the semicolon *precedes* the conjunction, and a comma follows:

> Years ago there was a National Basketball Association team in Rochester; however, that team, known as the Royals, later moved to Cincinnati.

Exercise

Repair the following comma splices, using all three methods presented above.

1. In fact, many NBA franchises have moved, for example, the Lakers were once in Minneapolis.
2. Minnesota is proud of its many lakes, that is why the Minneapolis team was called the Lakers.

3. "Lakers" is a rather odd name for a team in Los Angeles, there are very few lakes in the Southern California desert.
4. Probably the most incongruous NBA team nickname is the Utah Jazz, the franchise didn't change the team nickname when it moved from New Orleans to Salt Lake City.
5. One franchise began as the Rochester Royals and moved to Cincinnati, later this franchise moved to Kansas City and changed its nickname to the Kings, now this team is in Sacramento.

8.b. Restrictive and Nonrestrictive Material

Restrictive material is material necessary to the meaning of the sentence in which it appears. *Nonrestrictive* material is just the opposite: material unnecessary to the sentence meaning. Whether material is restrictive or nonrestrictive is sometimes entirely up to the writer; however, distinguishing between the two is important, because restrictive material is *not* set off with commas and nonrestrictive material *is* set off with commas. The significance of this distinction becomes clear when one realizes that two identically worded sentences can have two entirely different meanings, depending on what the writer intends and how that intention is shown by either omitting or including commas:

> My uncle who runs the bakery is an enthusiastic swimmer.
>
> My uncle, who runs the bakery, is an enthusiastic swimmer.

In the first sentence above, the clause *who runs the bakery* is *restrictive;* that is, the clause is necessary in order to identify which uncle the writer is talking about. In this case, the writer has more than one uncle and it is important to identify which one is the enthusiastic swimmer. In the second sentence, the commas setting off the clause *who runs the bakery* indicate that the information is purely incidental; the writer does not need to identify the uncle or indeed do anything else, for the main idea is that the writer's uncle is an enthusiastic swimmer—specifying *which* uncle is unimportant, or perhaps the writer has only one uncle. The nonrestrictive material helps identify the uncle but is not critical to the sentence's meaning.

Such commas suddenly become crucial in understanding what the writer has actually said. Compare:

> Motorists who drink should not be allowed to drive.
>
> Motorists, who drink, should not be allowed to drive.

The first sentence says that only those motorists who drink should be prohibited from driving. The second says—falsely—that *all* motorists drink and should therefore be prohibited from driving.

Some material must always be classified as restrictive or nonrestrictive. In the following sentence, for example, *Wanda Jackson* must be set off with commas because that information is nonessential:

> Sam Jackson's wife, Wanda Jackson, is my aunt.

On the other hand, *Irving Berlin* is essential to the meaning of the following sentence because it identifies the composer; therefore, it is not set off with commas:

> The popular composer Irving Berlin wrote more than a thousand songs.

You can see that a seemingly small thing like placement of commas can be vital to clear meaning. Although the following example has nothing to do with restrictive or nonrestrictive material, it nonetheless proves our point about the importance of commas. Compare:

> Let's eat, Uncle Don, before we go to the movie.
>
> Let's eat Uncle Don before we go to the movie.

The first sentence's commas set off an address to Uncle Don. The second sentence seems to have been written by a cannibalistic moviegoer.

Exercise

What different meanings do the restrictive/nonrestrictive elements make in the following sentence pairs?

1. The young girl who is walking down the street is my sister.
   The young girl, who is walking down the street, is my sister.
2. The old carpenter, standing by the ladder, told the men it was lunchtime.
   The old carpenter standing by the ladder told the men it was lunchtime.
3. My uncle Bert thinks that artists who refuse to accept commissions deserve to be hungry.
   My uncle Bert thinks that artists, who refuse to accept commissions, deserve to be hungry.
4. My brother, who lives in Santa Ana, gave me my first job.
   My brother who lives in Santa Ana gave me my first job.

8.c Semicolons and Colons

Many writers confuse semicolons and colons. These two marks, while similar in appearance, have radically different purposes. Semicolons are used as one way to join closely related independent clauses; they are also used at breaks similar to comma breaks in sentences already containing multiple commas. Colons, on the other hand, usually signal that something is coming: a list, a quotation, a specific statement, or the like. They also have certain other, specific uses, as in time notations, biblical references, parts of bibliographic references, and subtitles.
The following examples illustrate the major uses of the semicolon.

- To join closely related independent clauses:
  > Anne Meyers was one of the greatest players in women's basketball; she played for the UCLA Lady Bruins.

- To separate the second-listed items in a series of double items:

  Newly elected officers of the club are the following: Joe Jeter, president; Alisha Hakimian, vice-president; and Sirhan Sadeghi, treasurer.

- To join clauses with a conjunction (in place of a comma) when multiple commas are already present before and after the conjunction:

  My Aunt Linda, my father's sister, operates retail stores in Wichita, Albuquerque, and Salt Lake City; and she tells us that shoplifting, always a serious problem, is worse than ever before.

  (Some writers and editors do not insist on this particular semicolon usage, but we recommend it because it helps to clarify the major sentence components.)

These examples illustrate the major uses of the colon.

- To signal a list within a sentence:

  The following Texas cities have antipollution ordinances: Fort Worth, Dallas, San Antonio, Waco, and Austin.

- To signal and emphasize a following quotation:

  Ralph Waldo Emerson foretold the age of materialism when he said: "Things are in the saddle, and they ride mankind."

- To set up a long quotation:

  The president said to the National Association of Manufacturers:

  > "I come before you today with a challenge—a challenge that you find within yourselves leadership equal to the tasks of the 1990s as they loom before us like ominous harbingers of doom. Our industrial giant is again asleep, but how much longer can it slumber?"

- To set up a vertical or horizontal list:

  Sampson was told to order the following items:

  A garden rake

  Two garden hoes

  Six cartons of mulch

  A fertilizer spreader

  Two 100-foot hoses

- To express time notations and biblical references:

  The two men met at 6:30 P.M. and read John 3:16 to the group.

- To separate place of publication from publisher's name in bibliographic references:

  Lexington: D. C. Heath and Company

- To separate subtitles from main titles:

  Edward Albee: A Life

Exercise

Provide semicolons and colons where they are called for in the following items.

1. The semicolon is one of the most misunderstood marks of punctuation it is also rather versatile.
2. This is what Solomon said "Meet me at Forbes Field at 1 30 P.M."
3. Robert, who loves backpacking, and Ellen, who loves horseback riding, both came to the same conclusion they could not do both at once.
4. Jerry, who dislikes feeding cattle, said he would do it however, he wanted Marcy to help.
5. The all-star team consists of these players Megan Downy, point guard Rosalinda Martinez, shooting guard DeShondra Hicks, center Rebecca Davignon, power forward Angelina Razo, weak forward.

8.d. Apostrophes

Apostrophes have two primary uses.

First, with an *s* or *es*, they indicate possession on words that otherwise do not show possession:

> the car's brakes, Darrell's car (singular possessive)
>
> the students' lessons, the Smiths' mailbox (plural possession)
>
> the boxes' contents, the Joneses' house (plural possession)

Note that with plural possessives, the apostrophe goes *after* the *s* or *es* unless the word is *already* plural, like *men's* and *children's*.

Second, in contractions apostrophes take the place of the missing letters:

> can't = cannot
>
> wouldn't = would not
>
> Darrell's [*not* possessive] = Darrell is

Apostrophes also have another, minor, highly limited use: to make plural any words referred to as words, letters referred to as letters, and symbols referred to as symbols:

> How many *therefore*'s appear in the Constitution?
>
> How many *l*'s are there in *corollary?*
>
> We will use +'s and -'s in answering the questionnaire.

Note: Words, letters, and symbols referred to as such are italicized (underlined).

The reason we have included apostrophes in our "dirty dozen" is that apostrophes—for reasons we've never understood—are often erroneously used to form plurals of nouns. Here are examples:

Wrong I don't like banana's, but I do like apple's.

Right I don't like bananas, but I do like apples.

Wrong Most gearshift lever's have a diagram of the gears.

Right Most gearshift levers have a diagram of the gears.

Just as unaccountably, writers often forget to add the apostrophe to show possession when it is needed:

Wrong We never know when we might need someones blood.

Right We never know when we might need someone's blood.

Frequently, writers confuse the possessive pronoun *its* with the contraction for *it is:*

Wrong The hurricane was on it's way.

Right The hurricane was on its way. "It's coming," said my father.

Finally, writers often add apostrophes to possessive-case pronouns, which—of course—don't *need* apostrophes:

Wrong Mom was singing in that cheery voice of her's.

Right Mom was singing in that cheery voice of hers.

Wrong The problem is our's, not their's.

Right The problem is ours, not theirs.

Exercise

Correct the erroneously used apostrophes in the following sentences, and add apostrophes where they are needed.

1. Do standardized test's really show a students' ability?
2. Ill see you at the doctors office.
3. Those toy's arent your's.
4. The cat sat on it's tail.
5. Coupon's will save you lot's of money.

8.e. Dashes and Hyphens

Dashes and hyphens can confuse writers because most keyboards lack a dash key. Consequently, such persons think that the hyphen (for which there *is* a key) and the dash are the same. A *dash,* however, is longer than a hyphen and is made by striking the hyphen key twice *without spacing,* like this--.

Typical Dash Uses. Dashes have several uses, none of which should be invoked very frequently, because many teachers and editors consider using dashes to be somewhat pretentious or overly informal. Dashes may be used to mark a sudden break in thought--(like that), or they may set up a list, much as a colon does--

Do the laundry.

Do the shopping.

Write your next chapter.

Get the cards mailed.

Dashes in pairs can be used the same way parentheses can--provided they are not overused this way--but it is important to remember that such cases require their use in pairs. Using dashes instead of parentheses also tends to add emphasis to the material between the dashes. To review, then, dashes are usually used as follows:

- To mark a sudden break in thought--
- To mark a tailing off of an idea--
- To set up a vertical or horizontal list--wash, wax, polish, and service the car
- In pairs to set off parenthetical (incidental) material in sentences--just like this--so that the sentence can proceed

Typical Hyphen Uses. Hyphens, on the other hand, have several more uses than dashes. If you are writing by hand, you make a hyphen shorter than a dash; if you are keyboarding, you make it by one hit of the hyphen key. Hyphen uses include these:

- To combine words into a single unit so that they can be understood as such:
  Those flowers are forget-me-nots.

- To combine compound adjectives:
  I like lemon-meringue pie, but Julia prefers chocolate-covered strawberries.

- To combine spelled-out numbers from twenty-one to ninety-nine (or twenty-first to ninety-ninth).

- To combine nouns or noun and adjective compounds:
  Marsha is my ex-wife, and now she is the mayor-elect.

- To divide words at syllable breaks so that the word can be continued on the next line:
  You are my guar-
  dian angel.
  (*Note:* Always make sure your word-dividing hyphen comes at a syllable break. Never continue a word onto the next page, and avoid carrying just one syllable over onto another line.)

Exercise

Provide dashes or hyphens where they are needed in the following sentences.

1. Rathke is a German American who like many others enjoys polka music.

2. It is a souped up 1956 Chevy with four on the floor, a four barrel carb, chromed wire wheels, baby moon hubcaps, ball fringe pom poms in front and back windows, and a bored and stroked 283 V 8.
3. The following things happened we were strip searched: our car our only possession was torn apart, and all our luggage was ransacked.
4. John is twenty five today.
5. Judy our closest friend in France is a Franco American.

9. Quotation Procedure

We discussed quotation in detail in chapter 23, which we recommend that you review. In addition, we discuss here two frequent quotation problem areas:

a. Short quotations and punctuation
b. A word about attribution

9.a. Short Quotations and Punctuation

Here is a summary that we hope will clarify common problems involving quotation procedures:

- Periods and commas go *inside* closing quotation marks.
- Colons and semicolons go *outside* closing quotation marks.
- Dashes, question marks, and exclamation marks go *inside* the closing quotation marks when they pertain only to what is quoted, and they go *outside* the closing quotation marks when they pertain to the entire sentence.

Thus:

Period The athlete said, "We want to win this one for our coach."

Comma "Don't win it for me," said the coach; "win it for yourselves."

Colon Answer these questions about "Stopping by Woods on a Snowy Evening": Who wrote it? What is its setting? What is its theme?

Semicolon In 1978, a group called Heart had a hit song named "Straight On"; it features strong vocals and excellent electric guitar.

Question Mark *(when the quotation is a question)*
Jennifer asked, "Who sings harmony on this song?"

(when the entire sentence is a question)
Did Roberto sing harmony on "Lemon Tree"?

(when both the quotation and the sentence are questions)
Did Jennifer ask, "Who sings harmony on the song?"

Exclamation Point *(when the quotation is an exclamation)*
Tomas cried, "LaDonna! Look out!"

(when the entire sentence is an exclamation)
I'm sick and tired of singing "Row, Row, Row Your Boat"!

Exercise

Punctuate the following sentences properly in relation to punctuation and closing quotation marks.

1. I like the poem "Dover Beach"
2. "Dover Beach" a poem written by Matthew Arnold, laments the world that Arnold saw changing.
3. Who wrote the song "All Along the Watchtower"
4. Dennis screamed at Nancy, "You leave my sweater alone"
5. The Beatles wrote "Lady Madonna" it was a smash hit in 1968.

9.b. A Word About Attribution

Writers should always make clear to their readers just *whose* words they are using when they quote. Quotations should not appear on the page as if from nowhere; they must be tied logically and clearly to their sources. Attribution is not the same as documentation, which is a technical (and necessary) procedure in reporting research or using sources. Attribution is, rather, a courtesy to readers, so that they will know, as a practical matter, whose words are being used. A good attribution will usually indicate as well *why* the person's words are being used—that, for example, the quoted person is an expert on the subject at hand, has done a pertinent study, or is otherwise qualified to speak on the page.

Here are some typical ways to attribute quotations:

> According to Benjamin T. Russo, author of *Child Care and You,* "Children need to feel responsible, to have something that they are routinely expected to do."
>
> "If parents never expect their children to do household chores, their children indeed won't grow up doing such chores," says Benjamin T. Russo, who has written several books on family life.
>
> Fred T. Williams, recently fired from his job as a White House media aide, characterized the official attitude there as "hostile and unforgiving."

10. Faulty Comparison

Many writers present comparisons incorrectly in their writing. These problems generally fall into three categories:

a. Wrong comparative word

b. Apples and oranges
c. "Better than I" and other bugaboos

10.a. Wrong Comparative Word

This error usually involves using the wrong comparative form of an adjective:

> Of the two girls, Elaine is *tallest.*

Here, *tallest* is the wrong choice, because it is the superlative form of the comparison, to be used when *more than two* items—in this case, girls—are being compared. The adjective in question is *tall;* the comparative form is *taller* (two girls) and the superlative form is *tallest* (three or more girls). Thus the corrected sentence is as follows:

> Of the two girls, Elaine is *taller.*

Writers also need to be careful in using these forms; some words will not take the *-er* and *-est* suffixes and thus require such helpers as *more* and *most.* Others are irregular. For example:

> *bad, worse, worst*

10.b. Apples and Oranges

Not all things can be compared logically. *Unique,* for example, is a word that by definition rules out any comparisons; if something is unique, there is only one thing in the world like it. Hence, it is illogical to say one thing is "more unique" than another, or that something else is the "most unique" thing we've ever seen. Additional words that can't be compared are *perfect, impossible, dead,* and *infinite.*

Other comparisons are problematic because it is not clear exactly what is being compared. Consider:

> The Duckworth Company's medical insurance is better than any other company.

The above sentence seems to compare the Duckworth Company's insurance with other *companies,* not with other companies' *insurance.* The sentence must be rewritten so as to clarify that *insurance* is the basis of the comparison:

> The Duckworth Company's medical insurance is better than that of any other company.

10.c. "Better than I" and Other Bugaboos

Some comparisons are incomplete and therefore problematical, either because writers don't know which pronoun case to use or because they don't know precisely what is being compared. Consider:

> David is taller than [*I* or *me*].

The way to determine which pronoun case to use in such a situation is to *finish* the sentence—and hence the comparison:

> David is taller than *I* am.

In the following example, the incomplete comparison leaves unclear what is being compared:

> Broken glass around a swimming pool is more dangerous than a driveway.

Although this sentence implies driveways are somehow dangerous, that isn't what the writer means to compare broken glass around a swimming pool with. Here's a much clearer version:

> Broken glass around a swimming pool is more dangerous than in a driveway.

Exercise

The following sentences contain faulty comparisons of some kind. Correct them.

1. Of the six alternatives to Wilma's plan, I like the fourth one better.
2. Martha Halloran is the most wealthiest woman in our city.
3. Of all the challenges we've faced, this one is the most impossible.
4. Lately, rain has been as scarce as the Sahara Desert.
5. Leo's income is less than his brother.

11. Spelling

Very few people are excellent spellers, but everyone can improve as a speller. A good writer takes responsibility for being conscientious about spelling. No one should be satisfied with an attitude of "I'm just not a good speller"—that's merely a flimsy excuse to make no effort to improve. Numerous strategies can help you improve your spelling, and you might be surprised at how effective they can be. Among such strategies are the following:

a. Developing a personalized spelling list
b. Learning to use a dictionary for help in your spelling
c. Studying spelling aids
d. Using computerized spellcheckers

11.a. Developing a Personalized Spelling List

Countless handbooks provide lists of commonly misspelled words. But such lists, while helpful to a certain extent, invariably contain several words that you as an individual do not ordinarily use, and thus studying those lists can mean studying several words that you might never need.

If, however, you compile a list of the words that you have *already* misspelled in your *own* writing, then studying *that* list might well prove helpful. After all, such a list would contain no words that you don't use. Quite soon, you would be able to identify those words which are truly part of your vocabulary, words that would be profitable for you to study.

What's the biggest problem involved in making your personalized spelling list? You have to know which words you've misspelled before you can add them—and, of course, you may be unaware that you typically misspell a word. But your teachers and classmates can help you. Start that list! *Any time* anyone tells you that you have misspelled a word, write that word down on your list. Your list will grow, and the more you study it, the more likely you will be to improve your spelling. You can use all the other suggestions below to help, too.

11.b. Learning to Use a Dictionary for Help in Your Spelling

"How can I look up a word in the dictionary if I don't know how to spell it?" is a question commonly asked by bright—and lazy—people who don't really want to improve their spelling. The fact is that many words you may not quite know how to spell can still be found in a dictionary. If you know how the first letter of a word sounds, you stand a good chance of being able to find it in a dictionary, because those first-letter sounds are generally a reliable guide to what the first letter of the spelling is.

Sure, such sounds aren't *always* reliable (one of us once tried to look up *psychology* under *S* in the dictionary), but they *usually* are. So why not give it a try? Try "sounding out" the first syllable; then open your dictionary to the alphabetized letter section your ear suggests. You'll be rewarded more often than not.

11.c. Studying Spelling Aids

Spelling has been a problem for generations (as the spelling of English has become more regularized). Over the years, some educators have developed what they call spelling rules—though usually there are too many exceptions for these to be completely reliable—that in certain cases will help you remember how to spell a given word. Here is a sampling of some of these rules; first, a jingle many generations of students learned:

> *I* before *e*, except after *c*, or when sounded as *ay*, as in *neighbor* and *weigh*.

Such a jingle indeed helps in some instances (one of us thinks of this jingle every time he writes *receive*); unfortunately, however, many exceptions exist, among them *either, neither, forfeit, height, leisure, weird, species,* and *seize*.

Virtually any commercially produced, book-length handbook will provide several of the analytical rules that have been developed. One such rule addresses whether to keep or drop the final *y* in a word when an ending is added:

Change the *y* to *i* if the *y* follows a consonant:
beauty = beauties, worry = worried, deputy = deputize
Keep the *y* if it follows a vowel or ends in *-ing* or a proper name:
day = days, study = studying, Jay = Jays

Such rules invariably are quite complicated and have exceptions; some books list so many rules that it's impossible to believe anyone would be able to remember them all. Still, if you use such rules in conjunction with your personalized spelling list and a dictionary, you can improve your spelling of those words which tend to give you the most trouble.

11.d. Using Computerized Spellcheckers

If you're working with a word processor, its spellchecker can be a great help to you. For example, on the machine with which this book is being written, all we have to do is hit a key called "Spell." That way, we never make spelling mistakes, right? Well, not quite. Spellcheckers are terrific generally, but they have some serious limitations too. For instance, every italicized word in the sentence below is the wrong word choice, but most spellcheckers would not catch the problem:

> The *cite* was *two* full of *draughts too half* the *affect its planers wonted* it *two half.*

Why wouldn't the spellchecker catch those words? Because every one is a perfectly acceptable English word, and that's all the machine knows to check for. The machine isn't smart enough to figure out that *site,* not cite, is needed in that particular context; it can't "know" that *effect,* not *affect,* is needed in this particular sentence. Such is the case with each italicized word.

You *should,* though, use your spellchecker, for it will indeed catch most of your errors. But don't rely on it to catch *all* of them—it won't. There's still no substitute for your own practiced, intelligent, *human* eye during proofreading.

None of the above suggestions is in itself a solution for spelling problems. But each one *can* help. Ultimately, whether or not you are going to become a better speller is up to you.

12. Sexism

In recent years, we have all become more aware that our language reflects certain cultural biases, and one of the most problematic has been sexism. We don't mean that writers are *deliberately* sexist; in fact, much sexist usage is unconscious—in what they write, the writers don't intend to slight, or seem to slight, women or men. But subtle sexism can be found in our language, and we should all try to be more aware of it and seek ways to avoid it.

For example, consider what has been called "the universal masculine"—words like *mankind* and phrases like "*in the history of man.*" Such usage has always meant *all* human beings, male or female, but it has nonetheless discriminated against, by excluding, half of humanity. This universal masculine extended to individual usage, as when a writer, in discussing a single human being, used pronouns like *he*, *him*, and *his*, whether referring to a man or not. It also found its way into a great many nouns: *chairman, congressman, workman, weatherman, mailman,* and so on, even though each of those positions can be, and often is, held by a woman.

Some of the ways you can combat such sexism in your writing follow:

- Substitute, where reasonable, the suffix *-person* where previously you would have used *-man:*

  congressman = congressperson chairman = chairperson

- If substituting *-person* doesn't seem reasonable, use a substitute term that isn't gender-specific:

  mailman = mail carrier workman = worker

  businessman = business owner fireman = fire fighter

- For terms that have traditionally had a gender distinction but in fact are not specific to gender, substitute an equivalent:

  stewardess = flight attendant
  actress/actor = actor

- Whenever *all* human beings are referred to, use genderless terms:

  people, humankind, voters, workers, citizens, and so on

- When pronouns refer to nouns of unspecified gender, make the noun and the pronoun plural:

Sexist A doctor needs to keep *his* license current.

Nonsexist Doctors need to keep *their* licenses current.

Exercise

Eliminate the sexism in the following sentences.

1. Most weathermen are accurate most of the time.
2. An attorney should not get too close to his client.
3. Each athlete must improve his grades if he wants to improve his image.
4. The policemen risk their lives for our safety.
5. A beggar must remember his pride.

Thus we conclude our discussion of the "dirty dozen"—the twelve common problem areas that many writers face in working to improve their manuscripts. We can't treat in a few pages what entire books have been written about, but we do believe that if you can understand and avoid the kinds of problems we have highlighted here, your writing will improve significantly.

WRITING ASSIGNMENT

Consider again the full-page draft of the Declaration of Independence on page H-53. It's comforting and instructive to remember that even the people who write such history-making documents have to work hard at revising in order to make the words come out right. It's probably a natural human tendency for students (and others) to want to make a piece of writing perfect on the first attempt, just as it is a natural tendency for writing teachers to say, "Nothing you ever write will be good enough in its first draft." This chapter has dealt at length with what many people think must be the "rules" for revising—grammatical and mechanical correctness, successful avoidance of such errors as run-together sentences, faulty predication, and dangling modifiers. Yet we have maintained throughout this book that it's the *quality of the content* [the ideas presented and the way(s) they're developed] that first distinguishes a good piece of writing, and that most revising should be in pursuit of that kind of quality. Mechanical and grammatical correctness thus become concerns mostly of the very final stages of the writing process, not really matters of revision at all.

Students hear teachers say such things, yet still come away with the impression that, when grading time comes, *what* you say is definitely less important than *how correctly* you say it. What we'd like you to do, then, is to design a "grading sheet" for classes like the one you're in now. The sheet should give due credit for correct grammar, but should emphasize quality of content. To design this sheet, break down all the different elements that you think should go into a quality piece of student writing, and assign them percentages or point totals. You should be very specific to limit the number of judgment calls the grader has to make; you may want to use examples from your own recent writing. For instance, you can't just have a category like "quality of content = 80 points"; you have to find a way of identifying, for the grader and for the student writers, just what the important components of "quality of content" might be. The same goes for "mechanical and grammatical correctness"—should a dangling modifier be a more or less grievous error than a fused sentence, etc.? Finally, you may want to introduce other qualities into your grading sheet as well—"paper submitted on time," etc.

Review your grading sheet to make sure you think it covers all the important elements, puts them in the right relationship to each other as far as what "counts" most, and defines and exemplifies all the abstract elements ("quality of content," etc.) to minimize misunderstandings and disputes. Then submit the final sheet to your teacher for consideration and feedback. We don't think an assignment such as this could possibly be graded (other than a "satisfactory/unsatisfactory," perhaps), but the dialogue it initiates could well be useful both for students and for teachers.

acknowledgments

Picture Credits

Cover: © Craig Aurness/West Light; **1**: Courtesy of Emily Silver; **5**: © 1989 Robert Koropp, Denver; **15**: Scott Snow (The Image Bank); **35**: UPI/Bettmann; **43**: Photofest; **55**: *The Scream* by Edvard Munch (Scala/Art Resource/N.Y.); **77**: Richard Megna (Fundamental Photographs); **103**: Culver Pictures, Inc.; **135**: Burk Uzzle (Picture Group); **157**: Tribune Media Services, Inc.; **161**: Joe Karius (Picture Group); **171**: Henri Cartier-Bresson (Magnum Photos, Inc.); **199**: Frank Wing (The Image Bank); **217**: Ferranti Electronics/A. Sternberg/Science Photo Library (Photo Researchers, Inc.); **237**: AP/Wide World Photos, Inc.; **271**: Jerzy Kolacz (The Image Bank); **299**: © Mikki Ansin; **303**: Piergiorgio Sclarandis (Black Star); **317**: © Carl Purcell; **339**: © Sheila Beougher; **373**: Michael Fogden (Animals Animals); **413**: Jim Heemstra (Picture Group); **437**: *Relativity.* © 1953 M.C. Escher (Cordon Art—Baarn—Holland); **475**: Antonio Rosario (The Image Bank); **511**: Courtesy of Vivian Baylor; **517**: Photofest; **567**: Ellen Schuster (The Image Bank); **593**: Steve Dunwell (The Image Bank); **631**: Joe Gemignani (Sharpshooters); **659**: Photo by Cliff Haac/Courtesy of Research Triangle Institute, Research Triangle Park, NC; **673**: Richard Pasley (Stock Boston); **697**: THE FAR SIDE COPYRIGHT 1985 UNIVERSAL PRESS SYNDICATE. Reprinted with permission. All rights reserved. **H-5**: Robert Capa (Magnum Photos, Inc.); **H-19**: © Paul Avis; **H-53**: Library of Congress.

Rendered Art: George Barile, Accurate Art, Inc.; **Picture Research**: Connie Komack/Pictures & Words

Text Credits

Robert M. Adams. Reprinted from *The Land and Literature of England, A Historical Account,* by Robert M. Adams, by permission of W. W. Norton & Company, Inc. Copyright © 1983 by Robert M. Adams.

Vivian Baylor. "The Crisis in U.S. Science and Mathematics Education" by Vivian Baylor. *ORNL Review,* Fol. 20, No. 1, Oak Ridge National Laboratory Review.

Peter G. Beidler. From "The Joys Of College Teaching" by Peter G. Beidler. Reprinted from *National Forum—The Phi Kappa Phi Journal,* Winter 1987, Vol. LXVI, Number 1. Permission granted by copyright holder.

Mary Field Belenky et al. Excerpts from *Women's Ways of Knowing* by Mary Field Belenky et al. Copyright © 1986 by Basic Books, Inc. Reprinted by permission of Basic Books, a division of HarperCollins Publishers, Inc.

Bruno Bettelheim. "Why Children Don't Like to Read" from *On Learning to Read* by Bruno Bettelheim and Karen Zelan. Copyright © 1991 by Bruno Bettelheim and Karen Zelan. Reprinted by permission of Alfred A. Knopf, Inc.

Peter Brimelow. "The Untouchables" by Peter Brimelow, excerpted by permission of *Forbes* magazine, November 30, 1987. © Forbes Inc., 1987.

Art Buchwald. "Why We Need Our AK-47s" by Art Buchwald, March 28, 1989. Reprinted with the permission of the author.

Kim Chernin. From *Reinventing Eve* by Kim Chernin. Copyright © 1987 by Kim Chernin. Reprinted by permission of Times Books, a division of Random House, Inc.

Chickasaw Chips, Inc. "The Legend of 'Dirty' Potato Chips." Reprinted by permission of Chickasaw Chips, Inc.

Marcelle Clements. "Ain't Nobody's Business But My Own" by Marcelle Clements, *Cosmopolitan,* March 1989. Reprinted with the permission of the author.

Rowland Evans and Robert Novak. "Congressmen for Life: The Incumbency Scandal" by Rowland Evans and Robert Novak. Reprinted with permission from the June 1989 *Reader's Digest.* Copyright © 1989 by The Reader's Digest Association, Inc.

Robert Frost. "Stopping by Woods on a Snowy Evening" from *The Poetry of Robert Frost* edited by Edward Connery Lathem. Copyright 1923, © 1969 by Holt, Rinehart and Winston. Copyright 1951 by Robert Frost. Reprinted by permission of Henry Holt and Company, Inc.

Robert Fulghum. From *All I Really Need to Know I Learned in Kindergarten* by Robert Fulghum. Copyright © 1986, 1988 by Robert Fulghum. Reprinted by permission of Villard Books, a division of Random House, Inc.

Bob Greene. From "The Man Who Wrote 'Louie Louie'" by Bob Greene, Sept. 1988. Reprinted by permission of Sterling Lord Literistic, Inc. Copyright © 1988 by Bob Greene. From *Cheeseburgers* by Bob Greene. Copyright © 1985 by John Deadline Enterprises, Inc. Reprinted by permission of Ballantine Books, a division of Random House, Inc.

Susan Griffin. "Thoughts on Writing a Diary" by Susan Griffin, reprinted from *The Writer on Her Work,* Edited by Janet Sternburg, by permission of W. W. Norton & Company, Inc. Copyright © 1980 by Janet Sternburg.

Elizabeth Griffith. From *In Her Own Right: The Life of Elizabeth Cady Stanton* by Elizabeth Griffith. Copyright © 1984 by Elizabeth Griffith. Reprinted by permission of Oxford University Press, Inc.

Pete Hamill. "Our Town" by Pete Hamill, Copyright by Pete Hamill. This was originally published in *Esquire.* "Ethics in the 80s: Is There No Longer Right or Wrong?" by Pete Hamill, Copyright © by Pete Hamill. Both are reprinted by permission of Janklow & Nesbit Associates, literary representatives of the author. Pete Hamill is a journalist and novelist.

Ed Henry. "Air Bags vs. Seat Belts: Why You Should Care." Reprinted by permission of *Changing Times,* the Kiplinger Magazine, (March 1988 issue). Copyright 1988 by The Kiplinger Washington Editors, Inc.

William Inge. "A Social Event" from *Summer Brave & Eleven Short Plays* by William Inge. Reprinted by permission of International Creative Management, Inc. Copyright © 1962 by William Inge and renewed in 1990 by Helene Connell.

Garrison Keillor. From *Lake Wobegon Days* by Garrison Keillor. Copyright © 1985 by Garrison Keillor. Used by permission of Viking Penguin, a division of Penguin Books USA, Inc.

Kellogg Company. "Nutrition Information" copyright 1990. Reprinted by permission of The Kellogg Company.

James Kilpatrick. "Homophones Haunt Careless Writers" taken from *A Conservative View* column by James J. Kilpatrick. Copyright 1989. Reprinted with permission of Universal Press Syndicate.

Maxine Hong Kingston. From *The Woman Warrior: Memoirs of a Girlhood Among Ghosts* by Maxine Hong Kingston. Copyright © 1975, 1976 by Maxine Hong Kingston. Reprinted by permission of Alfred A. Knopf, Inc.

Madeleine L'Engle. Excerpts from *A Circle of Quiet* by Madeleine L'Engle. Copyright © 1972 by Crosswicks, Ltd. Reprinted by permission of Farrar, Straus & Giroux, Inc.

Ursula K. Le Guin. "Woman/Wilderness" by Ursula K. Le Guin from *Dancing at the Edge of the World: Thoughts on Words, Women, Places.* Copyright © 1989 by Ursula K. Le Guin. Used by permission of Grove Press, Inc.

Hal May and James G. Lesniak. Excerpts of interviews with Bob Greene, Susan Griffin, and Alice Walker from *Contemporary Authors New Revision Series,* Volume 27, Hal May and James G. Lesniak, editors. Copyright © 1989 by Gale Research, Inc. Reprinted by permission of the publisher.

William Least Heat-Moon. From *Blue Highways* by William Least Heat-Moon. Copyright © 1982 by William Least Heat-Moon. By permission of Little Brown and Company.

Linda Schierse Leonard. Excerpt from *The Wounded Woman* by Linda Schierse Leonard. Reprinted with the permission of The Ohio University Press/Swallow Press, Athens.

Harriet Goldhor Lerner. Excerpt from *The Dance of Anger* by Harriet Goldhor Lerner. Copyright © 1985 by Harriet Goldhor Lerner. Reprinted by permission of HarperCollins Publishers.

Anne Morrow Lindbergh. From *Gift from the Sea* by Anne Morrow Lindbergh. Copyright © 1955 by Anne Morrow Lindbergh. Reprinted by permission of Pantheon Books, a division of Random House, Inc.

Logitech. "Logitech C7 Mouse". Reprinted with permission.

Randi Londer. "Stressed Out: What Puts the Pressure on Families?" by Randi Londer, reprinted from the October 11, 1988 issue of *Family Circle Magazine.* Copyright © 1988 The Family Circle, Inc.

Barry Lopez. Reprinted with permission of Charles Scribner's Sons, an imprint of Macmillan Publishing Company from "Gone Back into the Earth" in *Crossing Open Ground* by Barry Lopez. Copyright © 1981, 1988 Barry Holstun Lopez. (First appeared under a different title in *Notre Dame Magazine,* May 1981).

Bob Lundegaard. From "Be Yourself When Writing College Essays" by Bob Lundegaard. Reprinted with permission of the *Star Tribune,* Minneapolis-St. Paul.

Peter Matthiessen. From *Men's Lives* by Peter Matthiessen. Copyright © 1986 by Peter Matthiessen. Reprinted by permission of Random House, Inc.

Toni Morrison. Two excerpts from *Intimate Things in Place:* A conversation with Toni Morrison by Robert Stepto, Vol. 18, # 3, Fall 1977. Reprinted from *The Massachusetts Review,* © 1977 The Massachusetts Review, Inc.

John Muir. From *The Mountains of California* by John Muir. Reprinted with permission of Sierra Club Books.

Ben F. Nelms. "A Nation at Risk" by Ben F. Nelms, *English Journal,* February 1989. Copyright 1989 by the National Council of Teachers of English. Reprinted with permission.

Wilfred Owen. "Dulce Et Decorum Est" from *Collected Poems.* Copyright © 1963, 1964 by Chatto & Windus, Ltd. Reprinted by permission of New Directions Publishing Corporation.

Eva Pomice. "Madison Avenue's Blind Spot" by Eva Pomice. Copyright 1988, *U.S. News & World Report.*

David Quammen. Excerpts from "Deserts" from *Natural Acts* by David Quammen. Reprinted by permission of David Quammen. All rights reserved. Copyright © 1983 by David Quammen.

William Raspberry. "Majors Don't Matter That Much." © 1990, and "Standardized Tests Are Means, Not Ends" © 1986, Washington Post Writers Group. Reprinted with permission.

Dan Rea. From "Sociology 101 in a Shoe Box" by Dan Rea in *Newsweek,* March 27, 1989. Reprinted with permission of Dan Rea.

The Readers' Guide to Periodical Literature, 1990, page 57. Copyright © 1990 by the H.W. Wilson Company. Material reproduced with permission of the publisher.

Jack Rosenthal. "Dollar Wise, Penny Foolish" by Jack Rosenthal from the *New York Times,* March 9, 1989, p. 22. Copyright © 1989 by The New York Times Company. Reprinted by permission.

Berton Roueche. Text from *Eleven Blue Men* by Berton Roueche. Reprinted by permission of Harold Ober Associates, Inc. Copyright © 1948 by Berton Roueche. Story first appeared in *The New Yorker.*

Carl Sagan. "Can We Know the Universe?" by Carl Sagan in *The World of Science,* ed. Gladys Garner Leithauser and Marilynn Powe Bell. Copyright © 1979 Carl Sagan. All rights reserved. Reprinted by permission of the author.

Jack Schaefer. "Shane" by Jack Schaefer. Copyright 1949 by Jack Schaefer and copyright © renewed 1976 by Jack Schaefer. Reprinted by permission of Houghton Mifflin Company.

Richard Schickel. "In the American Grain" by Richard Schickel. Copyright 1987 by Time Warner, Inc. Reprinted by permission.

Susan Sheehan. Text from *Is There No Place on Earth for Me?* by Susan Sheehan. Copyright © 1982 by Susan Sheehan. Reprinted by permission of Houghton Mifflin Company.

John Steinbeck. "The Chrysanthemums", from *The Long Valley* by John Steinbeck. Copyright 1938, renewed © 1966 by John Steinbeck. Used by permission of Viking Penguin, a division of Penguin Books USA, Inc.

Peter Steinhart. Text from *Audubon* by Peter Steinhart, May 1980, reprinted with permission from *Audubon* Magazine.

Janet Sternburg. Excerpts from "The Writer Herself: An Introduction" by Janet Sternburg, reprinted from *The Writer on Her Work,* Edited by Janet Sternburg, by permission of W. W. Norton & Company, Inc. Copyright © 1980 by Janet Sternburg.

Harry G. Summers, Jr. "A Bankrupt Military Strategy" by Colonel Harry G. Summers, Jr. (*Atlantic Monthly,* June 1989, pp. 34–40). Reprinted with permission.

John Taylor. From *Storming the Magic Kingdom* by John Taylor. Copyright © 1987 by John Taylor. Reprinted by permission of Alfred A. Knopf, Inc.

Lewis Thomas. "The Long Habit" from *The Lives of a Cell* by Lewis Thomas. Copyright © 1974 by Lewis Thomas; Copyright © 1971, 1972, 1973 by The Massachusetts Medical Society. Used by permission of Viking Penguin, a division of Penguin Books USA, Inc.

Calvin Trillin. "Uncivil Liberties" by Calvin Trillin. Appeared in *The Nation.* Copyright © 1989 by Calvin Trillin.

Alice Walker. "The Civil Rights Movement: What Good Was It?" from *In Search of Our Mother's Gardens,* copyright © 1967 by Alice Walker, reprinted by permission of Harcourt Brace Jovanovich, Inc.

John Welter. Text from "The Kansas City Star" by John Welter in the *News-Sentinel,* July 28, 1987. Reprinted by permission of The Knoxville News-Sentinel Co.

George F. Will. "Listen to the Bridges" by George F. Will. From *Newsweek,* April 28, 1988 and copyright © 1988, Newsweek, Inc. All rights reserved. Reprinted by permission.

Clemens P. Work, Steve L. Hawkins, Elaine Carey. "Too Many Planes, Too Little Sky" by Clemens P. Work, Steve L. Hawkins, Elaine Carey. Copyright 1988, *U.S. News & World Report.*

Richard Zoglin. "Putting A Brake on TV 'Sleaze'" by Richard Zoglin, assisted by Mary Cronin and Naushad S. Mehta. Copyright 1989 The Time Inc. Magazine Company. Reprinted by permission.

author/title index

subject index